Educational Psychology

Tenth Edition

Anita Woolfolk
The Ohio State University

PEARSON

Boston | New York | San Francisco
Mexico City | Montreal | Toronto | London | Madrid | Munich | Paris
Hong Kong | Singapore | Tokyo | Cape Town | Sydney

Editor-in-Chief, Education: *Paul A. Smith*
Series Editorial Assistant: *Rachel Lamson*
Senior Marketing Manager: *Tara Kelly*
Developmental Editor: *Alicia Reilly*
Production Editor: *Annette Joseph*
Editorial Production Service: *Kathy Smith*
Composition Buyer: *Linda Cox*
Manufacturing Buyer: *Megan Cochran*
Electronic Composition: *Omegatype Typography, Inc.*
Interior Design: *Carol Somberg*
Photo Researchers: *Kathy Smith and Helane Prottas*
Cover Administrator: *Linda Knowles*
Cover Designer: *Studio Nine*

For related titles and support materials, visit our online catalog at www.ablongman.com.

ISBN: 0-205-45946-3

Between the time website information is gathered and then published, it is not unusual for some sites to have closed. Also, the transcription of URLs can result in typographical errors. The publisher would appreciate notification where these errors occur so that they may be corrected in subsequent editions.

Cataloging-in-Publication Data is on file at the Library of Congress.

Printed in the United States of America

10 9 8 7 6 5 4 3 2 1 RRD-OH 10 09 08 07 06

To my students
For over 35 years you have been my greatest teachers.
You have anchored my writing in your practice.

Brief Contents

CHAPTER 1
Teachers, Teaching, and Educational Psychology 1

PART 1 Students

CHAPTER 2
Cognitive Development and Language 21

CHAPTER 3
Personal, Social, and Emotional Development 63

CHAPTER 4
Learner Differences and Learning Needs 109

CHAPTER 5
Culture and Diversity 161

PART 2 Learning and Motivation

CHAPTER 6
Behavioral Views of Learning 205

CHAPTER 7
Cognitive Views of Learning 247

CHAPTER 8
Complex Cognitive Processes 285

CHAPTER 9
Social Cognitive and Constructivist Views of Learning 329

CHAPTER 10
Motivation in Learning and Teaching 371

CHAPTER 11
Engaged Learning: Cooperation and Community 413

PART 3 Teaching and Assessing

CHAPTER 12
Creating Learning Environments 443

CHAPTER 13
Teaching for Learning 477

CHAPTER 14
Standardized Testing 521

CHAPTER 15
Classroom Assessment and Grading 553

Handbook for Teaching and Lifelong Learning 587

Contents

Preface xix

CHAPTER 1
Teachers, Teaching, and Educational Psychology 1

TEACHERS' CASEBOOK: *What Would You Do?* 1

***Overview* 1**

Teaching After No *Child Left Behind* 2

Do Teachers Make a Difference? 2

Teacher–Student Relationships 3

Teacher Preparation and Quality 3

■ *Stories of Learning/Tributes to Teaching* 3

What Is Good Teaching? 5

Inside Four Classrooms 5

A Bilingual 1st Grade 5

A Suburban 5th Grade 5

An Inclusive Class 6

An Advanced Math Class 6

So What Is Good Teaching? 6

Beware of Either/Or Choices 7

Expert Knowledge 7

The Role of Educational Psychology 8

Some Interesting History 8

Is It Just Common Sense? 9

Taking Turns 9

Helping Students 9

Skipping Grades 10

Obvious Answers? 10

Using Research to Understand and Improve Learning 10

Descriptive Studies 10

Correlation Studies 11

Experimental Studies 12

Single-Subject Experimental Designs 12

Microgenetic Studies 12

The Role of Time in Research 13

Teachers as Researchers 13

What Is Scientifically Based Research? 13

Theories for Teaching 13

■ **Point/Counterpoint:** What Kind of Research Should Guide Education? 14

Becoming a Good Beginning Teacher 15

Concerns 15

Being a Good Beginner 15

Diversity and Convergences in Educational Psychology 16

Diversity 17

Convergences 17

SUMMARY TABLE 17

TEACHERS' CASEBOOK: *Connections to Praxis II™/ What Would They Do?* 19

PART 1 Students

Chapter 2
Cognitive Development and Language 21

TEACHERS' CASEBOOK: *What Would You Do?* 21

***Overview* 21**

A Definition of Development 22

General Principles of Development 22

The Brain and Cognitive Development 22

The Developing Brain: Neurons 23

The Developing Brain: Cerebral Cortex 24

Specialization and Integration 25

Instruction and Brain Development 25

Implications for Teachers 26

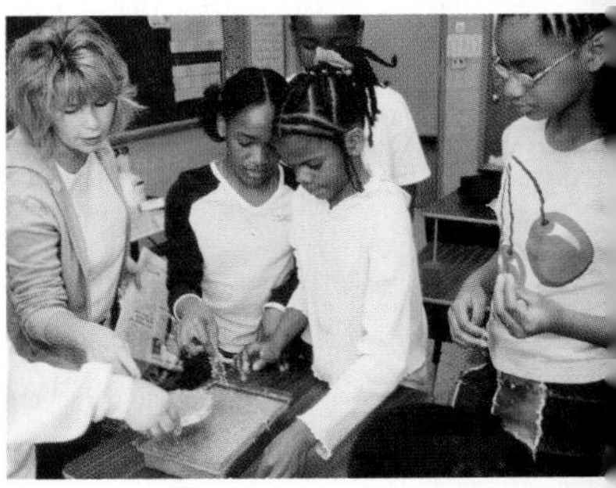

Piaget's Theory of Cognitive Development 26

■ **Point/Counterpoint:** Brain-based Education 27

Influences on Development 27

Basic Tendencies in Thinking 28

Organization 28

Adaptation 29

Equilibration 29

Four Stages of Cognitive Development 29

Infancy: The Sensorimotor Stage 30

Early Childhood to the Early Elementary Years: The Preoperational Stage 30

Later Elementary to the Middle School Years: The Concrete-Operational Stage 32

High School and College: Formal Operations 35

■ ***Stories of Learning/Tributes to Teaching* 35**

Do We All Reach the Fourth Stage? 36

Information-Processing and Neo-Piagetian Views of Cognitive Development 36

Some Limitations of Piaget's Theory 38

The Trouble with Stages 38

Underestimating Children's Abilities 38

Cognitive Development and Culture 38

Vygotsky's Sociocultural Perspective 39

The Social Sources of Individual Thinking 39

Cultural Tools and Cognitive Development 41

The Role of Language and Private Speech 42

Language and Cultural Diversity 42

Private Speech: Vygotsky's and Piaget's Views Compared 42

Self-Talk and Learning 44

The Zone of Proximal Development 44

Private Speech and the Zone 44

The Role of Learning and Development 44

Limitations of Vygotsky's Theory 45

Implications of Piaget's and Vygotsky's Theories for Teachers 46

Piaget: What Can We Learn? 46

Understanding and Building on Students' Thinking 46

Activity and Constructing Knowledge 46

The Value of Play 47

Vygotsky: What Can We Learn? 48

The Role of Adults and Peers 48

Assisted Learning 48

Teaching and the "Magic Middle" 49

Reaching Every Student: Using the Tools of the Culture 50

The Development of Language 51

Diversity in Language: Dual Language Development 52

Language Development in the School Years 54

Pronunciation 54

Grammar 54

Vocabulary and Meaning 54

Pragmatics 55

Metalinguistic Awareness 55

Partnerships with Families 55

■ **Family and Community Partnerships:** Promoting Literacy 56

Diversity and Convergences in Cognitive Development 56

Diversity 56

Convergences 57

SUMMARY TABLE 57

TEACHERS' CASEBOOK: *Connections to Praxis II™/ What Would They Do? 61*

■ **Guidelines**

Teaching the Preoperational Child 32

Teaching the Concrete-Operational Child 34

Helping Students to Use Formal Operations 37

Applying Vygotsky's Ideas in Teaching 50

Chapter 3

Personal, Social, and Emotional Development 63

TEACHERS' CASEBOOK: *What Would You Do? 63*

Overview 63

Physical Development 64

The Preschool Years 64

The Elementary School Years 64

Adolescence 65

The Brain and Adolescent Development 66

Erikson: Stages of Individual Development 67

The Preschool Years: Trust, Autonomy, and Initiative 68

The Elementary and Middle School Years: Industry versus Inferiority 69

Adolescence: The Search for Identity 70

Identity Statuses 71

Beyond the School Years 72

Bronfenbrenner: The Social Context for Development 72
Families 74
Divorce 74
Parenting Styles 74
Culture and Parenting 76
Peers 75
Peer Cultures 76
Who Is Likely to Have Problems with Peers? 77
Peer Aggression 78
Bullies 78
Relational Aggression 79
Victims 79
Social Skills 80
Reaching Every Student: Loneliness and Children with Disabilities 81
Teachers 82
Academic and Personal Caring 82
Teachers and Child Abuse 83
■ ***Stories of Learning/Tributes to Teaching*** 84
Self-Concept: Understanding Ourselves 85
Self-Concept and Self-Esteem 85
The Structure of Self-Concept 85
How Self-Concept Develops 86
Self-Concept and Achievement 86
■ **Point/Counterpoint:** What Should Schools Do to Encourage Students' Self-Esteem? 87
School Life and Self-Esteem 88
Diversity and Identity 88
Diversity and Perception of Self 89
Ethnic and Racial Identity 90
Ethnic Identities: Outcome and Process 91
Racial Identity: Outcome and Process 91
Racial and Ethnic Pride 92
Emotional and Moral Development 92
Emotional Competence 93
Theory of Mind and Intention 93
Moral Development 95
Kohlberg's Theories of Moral Development 95
Criticisms of Kohlberg's Theory 96
Gender Differences: The Morality of Caring 97
Moral Judgments, Social Conventions, and Personal Choices 97
Moral versus Conventional Domains 98
Implications for Teachers 99
Diversity in Reasoning 100
Moral Behavior 101
Cheating 101
Diversity and Convergences in Personal/Social Development 102
Diversity 102
Convergences 103
■ **Family and Community Partnerships:** Building Self-Esteem 103
SUMMARY TABLE 104
TEACHERS' CASEBOOK: *What Would They Do?* 107
■ **Guidelines**
Dealing with Physical Differences in the Classroom 66
Encouraging Initiative in Preschool Children 69
Encouraging Industry 70
Supporting Identity Formation 72
Helping Children of Divorce 75
Dealing with Aggression and Encouraging Cooperation 80
Encouraging Emotional Competence 94
Supporting Personal and Moral Development 100

Chapter 4
Learner Differences and Learning Needs 109

TEACHERS' CASEBOOK: *What Would You Do?* 109
***Overview* 109**
Intelligence 110
Labeling 110
Person-First Language 110
Disorders, Disabilities, and Handicaps 110
What Does Intelligence Mean? 111
Intelligence: One Ability or Many? 112
Multiple Intelligences 113
What Are These Intelligences? 114
Multiple Intelligences Go to School 115
Emotional Intelligence 116
What Is EQ? 116
EQ Goes to School 117
Cautions 117
Intelligence as a Process 117
Measuring Intelligence 119
Binet's Dilemma 119
Group versus Individual IQ Tests 119
What Does an IQ Score Mean? 120
The Flynn Effect: Are We Getting Smarter? 120

Intelligence and Achievement 120
Intelligence: Heredity or Environment? 120

Ability Differences and Teaching 121

Between-Class Grouping 122

Within-Class and Flexible Grouping 122

■ **Point/Counterpoint:** Is Tracking an Effective Strategy? 123

Flexible Grouping 124

Learning Styles 124

Cautions about Learning Preferences 125

Visual/Verbal Distinctions 126

The Value of Considering Learning Styles 126

Individual Differences and the Law 127

Individualized Education Program 127

The Rights of Students and Families 128

Least Restrictive Environment 128

■ **Family and Community Partnerships:** Productive Conferences 129

Section 504 Protections 129

Common Challenges 130

Students with Learning Disabilities 131

Student Characteristics 132
Teaching Students with Learning Disabilities 132

Students with Hyperactivity and Attention Disorders 134

Definitions 134
Treating and Teaching Students with ADHD 135

Reaching Every Student: Higher-Order Thinking 136

Students with Communication Disorders 136

Speech Disorders 137
Language Disorders 138

Students with Intellectual Disabilities 139

Students with Emotional or Behavioral Disorders 140

Suicide 142
Drug Abuse 144

Less Prevalent Problems/More Severe Disabilities 145

Students with Health Impairments 145

Cerebral Palsy and Multiple Disabilities 145
Seizure Disorders (Epilepsy) 146

Students Who Are Deaf 146

Students with Vision Impairments 147

Autism Spectrum Disorders 147

Theory of Mind 148
Interventions 148

Students Who Are Gifted and Talented 148

Who Are These Students? 149

■ ***Stories of Learning/Tributes to Teaching*** 149

What Is the Origin of These Gifts? 150
What Problems Do the Gifted Face? 150

Identifying and Teaching Gifted Students 151

Recognizing Gifts and Talents 151
Teaching Gifted Students 151

Diversity and Convergences in Learning Abilities 153

Diversity 153

Convergences 154

SUMMARY TABLE 154

TEACHERS' CASEBOOK: *What Would They Do? 159*

■ **Guidelines**

Interpreting IQ Scores 120
Grouping by Achievement 125
Teaching Students with Below-Average Intelligence 141
Disciplining Students with Emotional Problems 143

Chapter 5
Culture and Diversity 161

TEACHERS' CASEBOOK: *What Would You Do? 161*

Overview 161

Today's Diverse Classrooms 162

Individuals, Groups, and Society 162

Multicultural Education 163

American Cultural Diversity 164

Culture and Group Membership 164
Cautions in Interpreting Cultural Differences 164

Economic and Social Class Differences 165

Social Class and SES 165

Poverty and School Achievement 166

Health, Environment, and Stress 166
Low Expectations—Low Academic Self-Concept 167
Peer Influences and Resistance Cultures 167
Tracking: Poor Teaching 167
Home Environment and Resources 168

Ethnic and Racial Differences 168

The Changing Demographics: Cultural Differences 168

Cultural Conflicts 169
Cultural Compatibility 170

Ethnic and Racial Differences in School Achievement 170

The Legacy of Discrimination 171

What Is Prejudice? 172
The Development of Prejudice 172
Continuing Discrimination 173

Stereotype Threat 174

Short-Term Effects: Test Performance 174

Long-Term Effects: Disidentification 175
Combating Stereotype Threat 175

Girls and Boys: Differences in the Classroom 176

Sexual Identity 176
Sexual Orientation 176

Gender-Role Identity 177
Gender-Role Stereotyping in the Preschool Years 178
Gender Bias in the Curriculum 179
Sex Discrimination in Classrooms 180

Sex Differences in Mental Abilities 180

Eliminating Gender Bias 181

Language Differences in the Classroom 182

■ **Point/Counterpoint:** Do Boys and Girls Learn Differently? 183

Dialects 183
Dialects and Pronunciation 184
Dialects and Teaching 184

Bilingualism 185
What Does Bilingualism Mean? 185
Becoming Bilingual 185

Reaching Every Student: Recognizing Giftedness in Bilingual Students 186

Bilingual Education 187
Research on Bilingual Programs 188

Creating Culturally Inclusive Classrooms 188

Culturally Relevant Pedagogy 189
Experience Academic Success 190
Develop/Maintain Their Cultural Competence 190
Develop a Critical Consciousness to Challenge the Status Quo 190

Fostering Resilience 191

■ ***Stories of Learning/Tributes to Teaching*** 191
Resilient Students 192
Resilient Classrooms 192
Constructing a Resilient Classroom 193

■ **Family and Community Partnerships:** Building Learning Communities 193

Diversity and Convergences 195

Diversity in Learning 195
Social Organization 195
Cultural Values and Learning Preferences 195
Cautions about Learning Styles Research 196
Sociolinguistics 196
Sources of Misunderstandings 197
The Digital Divide 197

Convergences: Teaching Every Student 198
Know Your Students 198
Respect Your Students 198
Teach Your Students 198

SUMMARY TABLE 200

TEACHERS' CASEBOOK: *What Would They Do? 203*

■ **Guidelines**
Avoiding Sexism in Teaching 182
Culturally Relevant Teaching 199

PART 2 Learning and Motivation

Chapter 6
Behavioral Views of Learning 205

TEACHERS' CASEBOOK: *What Would You Do? 205*

Overview 205

Understanding Learning 206

Learning: A Definition 206

Learning Is Not Always What It Seems 207

Early Explanations of Learning: Contiguity and Classical Conditioning 208

Operant Conditioning: Trying New Responses 210

Types of Consequences 210
Reinforcement 210
Punishment 211

Reinforcement Schedules 212
Extinction 214

Antecedents and Behavior Change 214
Cueing 214
Prompting 214

Applied Behavior Analysis 215

Methods for Encouraging Behaviors 216
Reinforcing with Teacher Attention 216

■ ***Stories of Learning/Tributes to Teaching*** 216
Selecting Reinforcers: The Premack Principle 217
Shaping 218
Positive Practice 219

Coping with Undesirable Behavior 219
Negative Reinforcement 219

Satiation 221
Reprimands 221
Response Cost 222
Social Isolation 222
Some Cautions 222
Reaching Every Student: Functional Behavioral Assessment and Positive Behavior Support 222
Positive Behavioral Supports 223
Doing Functional Behavioral Assessments 224

Behavioral Approaches to Teaching and Management 224
Group Consequences 226
Contingency Contracts 226
Token Reinforcement 227
Reaching Every Student: Severe Behavior Problems 228

Observational Learning and Cognitive Behavior Modification: Thinking about Behavior 229
Observational Learning 229
Elements of Observational Learning 230
Attention 230
Retention 230
Production 231
Motivation and Reinforcement 231
Factors That Influence Observational Learning 232
Observational Learning in Teaching 233
Directing Attention 233
Fine-Tuning Already-Learned Behaviors 233
Strengthening or Weakening Inhibitions 233
Teaching New Behaviors 233
Arousing Emotion 234
Self-Management 234
Goal Setting 235
Monitoring and Evaluating Progress 235
Self-Reinforcement 235
Cognitive Behavior Modification and Self-Instruction 236

■ **Family and Community Partnerships:** Student Self-Management 236

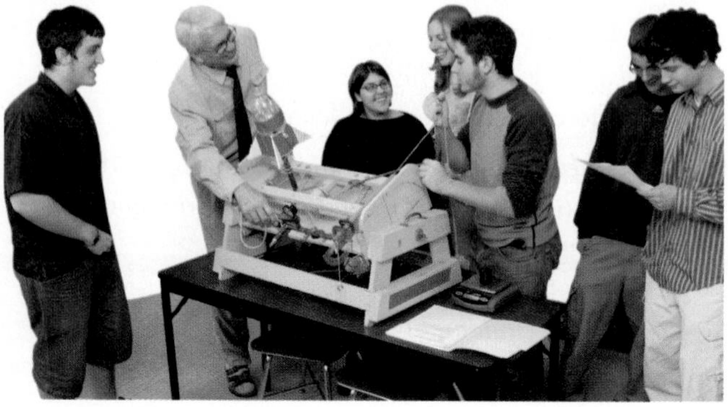

Criticisms of Behavioral Methods 238
Ethical Issues 238

■ **Point/Counterpoint:** Should Students Be Rewarded for Learning? 239
Goals 240
Strategies 240

Diversity and Convergence in Behavioral Learning 240
Diversity 240
Convergences 240

SUMMARY TABLE 241
TEACHERS' CASEBOOK: ***What Would They Do? 245***

■ **Guidelines**
Applying Classical Conditioning 209
Using Praise Appropriately 217
Encouraging Positive Behaviors 220
Using Punishment 223
Using Observational Learning 234

Chapter 7
Cognitive Views of Learning 247

TEACHERS' CASEBOOK: ***What Would You Do? 247***
Overview 247

Elements of the Cognitive Perspective 248
Comparing Cognitive and Behavioral Views 248
The Importance of Knowledge in Learning 249
An Example Study 249
General and Specific Knowledge 249

The Information Processing Model of Memory 250
Sensory Memory 250
Capacity, Duration, and Contents of Sensory Memory 250
Perception 251
The Role of Attention 252
Attention and Teaching 253
Working Memory 253
The Central Executive 254
The Phonological Loop 254
The Visuospatial Sketchpad 255
Duration and Contents of Working Memory 255
Retaining Information from Working Memory 256
Forgetting 257

Long-Term Memory: The Goal of Teaching 257
Capacity, Duration, and Contents of Long-Term Memory 257
Contents of Long-Term Memory: Declarative, Procedural, and Conditional Knowledge 258
Contents of Long-Term Memory: Words and Images 259

Explicit Memories: Semantic and Episodic 259
Propositions and Propositional Networks 259
Images 260
Schemas 260
Episodic Memory 262
Implicit Memories 262
Storing and Retrieving Information in Long-Term Memory 263
Levels of Processing Theory 263
Retrieving Information from Long-Term Memory 264
Spreading Activation 264
Reconstruction 264
Forgetting and Long-Term Memory 265
Metacognition 267
Metacognitive Knowledge and Regulation 267
Reaching Every Student: Metacognitive Strategies for Students with Learning Disabilities 268
Becoming Knowledgeable: Some Basic Principles 269
Development of Declarative Knowledge 269
Making It Meaningful 269
Visual Images and Illustrations 270
■ ***Stories of Learning/Tributes to Teaching*** 270
Mnemonics 271
Rote Memorization 273
■ **Point/Counterpoint:** What's Wrong with Memorizing? 273
Becoming an Expert: Development of Procedural and Conditional Knowledge 274
Automated Basic Skills 275

Domain-Specific Strategies 275
Diversity and Convergences in Cognitive Learning 276
Diversity: Individual Differences and Working Memory 276
Developmental Differences 276
Individual Differences 277
Diversity: Individual Differences and Long-Term Memory 278
Individual Differences in Metacognition 278
Convergences: Connecting with Families 279
■ **Family and Community Partnerships:** Organizing Learning 280
SUMMARY TABLE 280
TEACHERS' CASEBOOK: *What Would They Do? 283*
■ **Guidelines**
Gaining and Maintaining Attention 253
Using Information Processing Ideas in the Classroom 266

Chapter 8
Complex Cognitive Processes 285
TEACHERS' CASEBOOK: *What Would You Do? 285*
Overview 285
Learning and Teaching about Concepts 286
Views of Concept Learning 286
Prototypes and Exemplars 286
Concepts and Schemas 287
Strategies for Teaching Concepts 287
An Example Concept-Attainment Lesson 288
Lesson Components 288
Lesson Structure 289
Extending and Connecting Concepts 289
Teaching Concepts through Discovery 290
Structure and Discovery 290
Discovery in Action 290
Teaching Concepts through Exposition 292
Advance Organizers 292
Steps in an Expository Lesson 293
Reaching Every Student: Learning Disabilities and Concept Teaching 294
Problem Solving 294
Identifying: Problem Finding 295
Defining Goals and Representing the Problem 296
Focusing Attention 296
Understanding the Words 296
Understanding the Whole Problem 296
Translation and Schema Training 298
The Results of Problem Representation 298
Exploring Possible Solution Strategies 298
Algorithms 298
Heuristics 299
Anticipating, Acting, and Looking Back 300

■ **Point/Counterpoint:** Should Students Be Allowed to Use Calculators and Spell-Checkers? 301
Factors That Hinder Problem Solving 302
Fixation 302
Some Problems with Heuristics 302
The Importance of Flexibility 303
Effective Problem Solving: What Do the Experts Do? 303
Expert Knowledge 303
Novice Knowledge 305
Creativity and Creative Problem Solving 305
Defining Creativity 306
What Are the Sources of Creativity? 307
Creativity and Cognition 307
Assessing Creativity 307
Creativity in the Classroom 309
Brainstorming 310
Take Your Time—And Play! 310
The Big C: Revolutionary Innovation 310
Becoming an Expert Student: Learning Strategies and Study Skills 311
Learning Strategies and Tactics 311

Deciding What Is Important 313
Summaries 313
Underlining and Highlighting 313
Taking Notes 313
Visual Tools for Organizing 314
Reading Strategies 314
Applying Learning Strategies 316
Valuing Learning 317
Effort and Efficacy 318
Epistemological Beliefs 318
Teaching for Transfer 319
The Many Views of Transfer 319
Teaching for Positive Transfer 320
What Is Worth Learning? 320
How Can Teachers Help? 321
■ ***Stories of Learning/Tributes to Teaching*** 321
Stages of Transfer for Strategies 322
Diversity and Convergences in Complex Cognitive Processes 322
Diversity 322
■ **Family and Community Partnerships:** Promoting Transfer 323
Creativity and Diversity 323
Convergences 323
SUMMARY TABLE 324
TEACHERS' CASEBOOK: *What Would They Do? 327*
■ **Guidelines**
Applying Bruner's Ideas 292
Applying Ausubel's Ideas 294
Problem Solving 306
Encouraging Creativity 309
Becoming an Expert Student 317

Chapter 9
Social Cognitive and Constructivist Views of Learning 329

TEACHERS' CASEBOOK: *What Would You Do? 329*
Overview 329
Social Cognitive Theory 330
Reciprocal Determinism 330
■ ***Stories of Learning/Tributes to Teaching*** 331
Self-Efficacy 332
Self-Efficacy, Self-Concept, and Self-Esteem 332
Sources of Self-Efficacy 333
Applying Social Cognitive Theory 333
Self-Efficacy and Motivation 333
Teachers' Sense of Efficacy 334
Self-Regulated Learning 335
What Influences Self-Regulation? 335
Models of Self-Regulated Learning and Agency 336
An Individual Example 338
Reaching Every Student: Two Classrooms and the Family 339
Writing 339
Math Problem Solving 339
Families and Self-Regulated Learning 340
Teaching Toward Self-Efficacy and Self-Regulation 340
Complex Tasks 341
Control 342
Self-Evaluation 342
Collaboration 343
Cognitive and Social Constructivism 343
Constructivist Views of Learning 344
Psychological/Individual Constructivism 344

Vygotsky's Social Constructivism 346
Constructionism 346
How Is Knowledge Constructed? 346
Knowledge: Situated or General? 347
Common Elements of Constructivist Perspectives 348
Complex Learning Environments and Authentic Tasks 349
Social Negotiation 349
Multiple Perspectives and Representations of Content 349
Understanding the Knowledge Construction Process 350
Student Ownership of Learning 350
Applying Constructivist Perspectives 350
Inquiry and Problem-Based Learning 351
Examples of Inquiry 351
Problem-Based Learning 352
Research on Inquiry and Problem-Based Learning 354
Dialogue and Instructional Conversations 355
Cognitive Apprenticeships 356

A Cognitive Apprenticeship in Learning Mathematics 358
Apprenticeships in Thinking 359
Developing Thinking in Every Class 359
Critical Thinking 359
■ **Point/Counterpoint:** Should Schools Teach Critical Thinking and Problem Solving? 360
The Language of Thinking 361
An Integrated Constructivist Program: Fostering Communities of Learners 361
Dilemmas of Constructivist Practice 362
Diversity and Convergences in Theories of Learning 362
Diversity 363
■ **Family and Community Partnerships:** Communicating about Innovations 364
Convergences 364
SUMMARY TABLE 366
TEACHERS' CASEBOOK: *What Would They Do? 369*
■ **Guidelines**
Supporting Self-Regulation 340

Chapter 10
Motivation in Learning and Teaching 371

TEACHERS' CASEBOOK: *What Would You Do? 371*
Overview 371
What Is Motivation? 372
Meeting Some Students 372
Intrinsic and Extrinsic Motivation 372
Four General Approaches to Motivation 374
Behavioral Approaches to Motivation 374
Humanistic Approaches to Motivation 374
Maslow's Hierarchy 374
Cognitive and Social Approaches to Motivation 375
Expectancy × Value Theories 375
Sociocultural Conceptions of Motivation 376
■ *Stories of Learning/Tributes to Teaching* 377
Needs: Competence, Autonomy, and Relatedness 377
Self-Determination 377
Self-Determination in the Classroom 378
Information and Control 378
The Need for Relatedness 378
Needs: Lessons for Teachers 379
Goal Orientations and Motivation 380
Types of Goals and Goal Orientations 380
Four Goal Orientations in School 380
Wait—Are Performance Goals Always Bad? 381
Beyond Mastery and Performance 382
Feedback and Goal Acceptance 383
Goals: Lessons for Teachers 383
Interests and Emotions 383
Tapping Interests 383
Catching and Holding Interests 384
Arousal: Excitement and Anxiety in Learning 384
■ **Point/Counterpoint:** Does Making Learning Fun Make for Good Learning? 385
Curiosity: Novelty and Complexity 386
Anxiety in the Classroom 387
How Does Anxiety Interfere with Achievement? 387
Reaching Every Student: Coping with Anxiety 388
Interests and Emotions: Lessons for Teachers 388
Beliefs and Self-Schemas 388
Beliefs about Ability 388
Beliefs about Causes and Control: Attribution Theory 390

Attributions in the Classroom 391
Teacher Actions and Student Attributions 391
Beliefs about Self-Efficacy and Learned Helplessness 392
Beliefs about Self-Worth 393
Beliefs and Self-Schemas: Lessons for Teachers 394

Motivation to Learn in School: On TARGET 395
Tasks for Learning 396
Task Value 396
Authentic Tasks 396
Supporting Autonomy and Recognizing Accomplishment 398
Supporting Choices 398
Recognizing Accomplishment 399
Grouping, Evaluation, and Time 399
Grouping and Goal Structures 399
Evaluation 400
Time 400

Diversity and Convergences in Motivation to Learn 403
Diversity in Motivation 403
Convergences: Strategies to Encourage Motivation 404
Can I Do It? Building Confidence and Positive Expectations 404
Do I Want to Do It? Seeing the Value of Learning 404
Instrumental Value 405

■ **Family and Community Partnerships:** Motivation to Learn 406
What Do I Need to Do to Succeed? Staying Focused on the Task 406
Do I Belong in This Classroom? 407

SUMMARY TABLE 407

TEACHERS' CASEBOOK: *What Would They Do? 411*

■ **Guidelines**
Supporting Self-Determination and Autonomy 379
Building on Students' Interests and Curiosity 386
Coping with Anxiety 389
Encouraging Self-Efficacy and Self-Worth 394

Chapter 11
Engaged Learning: Cooperation and Community 413

TEACHERS' CASEBOOK: *What Would You Do? 413*
Overview 413

Social Processes in Learning 414
Peers 414
Parents and Teachers 415

Collaboration and Cooperation 416
Collaboration, Group Work, and Cooperative Learning 417
Beyond Groups to Cooperation 417
What Can Go Wrong: Misuses of Group Learning 418
Tasks for Cooperative Learning 419
Highly Structured, Review, and Skill-Building Tasks 419
Ill-Structured, Conceptual, and Problem-Solving Tasks 419
Social Skills and Communication Tasks 419
Preparing Students for Cooperative Learning 419
Setting Up Cooperative Groups 420
Giving and Receiving Explanations 420
Assigning Roles 421
Designs for Cooperation 423
Reciprocal Questioning 423
Scripted Cooperation 424
Reaching Every Student: Using Cooperative Learning Wisely 424

■ ***Stories of Learning/Tributes to Teaching* 426**

The Classroom Community 426
Constructive Conflict Resolution 427
Peer Harassment 428
What Can Teachers Do? 428
Peer Mediation and Negotiation 429
Civic Values 429
Character Education 430
Teaching Civic Values through the Curriculum: An Example 430
Getting Started on Community 430

■ **Point/Counterpoint:** Should Schools Teach Character and Compassion? 431
Belonging 432

Violence in Schools 432
Prevention 433
Respect and Protect 434

Community Outside the Classroom: Service Learning 434

Diversity and Convergences in Social Engagement 438

Diversity 438

Convergences 438

SUMMARY TABLE 439

TEACHERS' CASEBOOK: *What Would They Do?* 441

■ **Guidelines**

Using Cooperative Learning 425

Handling Potentially Explosive Situations 434

Using Service Learning 437

PART 3 Teaching and Assessing

Chapter 12
Creating Learning Environments 443

TEACHERS' CASEBOOK: *What Would You Do?* 443

***Overview* 443**

The Need for Organization 444

The Basic Task: Gain Their Cooperation 444

The Goals of Classroom Management 445

More Time for Learning 445

Access to Learning 446

Management for Self-Management 447

Creating a Positive Learning Environment 448

Some Research Results 448

Rules and Procedures Required 448

Procedures 448

Rules 450

Rules for Elementary School 450

Rules for Secondary School 451

Consequences 451

Who Sets the Rules and Consequences? 451

Planning Spaces for Learning 452

Personal Territories 453

Interest Areas 454

Planning for Computer Uses 455

Getting Started: The First Weeks of Class 457

Effective Managers for Elementary Students 457

Effective Managers for Secondary Students 458

Maintaining a Good Environment for Learning 458

Encouraging Engagement 459

Prevention Is the Best Medicine 460

Withitness 460

Overlapping and Group Focus 460

Movement Management 461

Caring Relationships: Connections with School 461

Student Social Skills as Prevention 461

Dealing with Discipline Problems 461

Special Problems with Secondary Students 462

■ ***Stories of Learning/Tributes to Teaching*** 464

■ **Point/Counterpoint:** Is Zero Tolerance a Good Idea? 465

Reaching Every Student: School-wide Positive Behavior Supports 466

The Need for Communication 466

Message Sent—Message Received 466

Diagnosis: Whose Problem Is It? 467

Counseling: The Student's Problem 468

Confrontation and Assertive Discipline 469

"I" Messages 469

Assertive Discipline 469

Confrontations and Negotiations 469

Diversity and Convergences in Learning Environments 470

Diversity: Culturally Responsive Management 470

Convergences: Research on Management Approaches 471

Integrating Ideas 472

Communicating with Families about Classroom Management 472

Family and Community Partnerships: Classroom Management 472

SUMMARY TABLE 473

TEACHERS' CASEBOOK: *What Would They Do?* 475

■ **Guidelines**

Establishing Class Procedures 449

Designing Learning Spaces 454

Using Computers: Management Issues 457

Keeping Students Engaged 459

Imposing Penalties 463

Chapter 13
Teaching for Learning 477

TEACHERS' CASEBOOK: *What Would You Do?* 477

***Overview* 477**

The First Step: Planning 478

Objectives for Learning 479

Mager: Start with the Specific 480

Gronlund: Start with the General 480

Flexible and Creative Plans—Using Taxonomies 481
The Cognitive Domain 481
Bloom 2001 481
The Affective Domain 482
The Psychomotor Domain 482
Another View: Planning from a Constructivist Perspective 483
An Example of Constructivist Planning 484
Integrated and Thematic Plans 485
Teacher-Directed Instruction 485
Characteristics of Effective Teachers 486
Teachers' Knowledge 486
Clarity and Organization 487
Warmth and Enthusiasm 487
Explanation and Direct Instruction 487
Direct Instruction 487
Rosenshine's Six Teaching Functions 488
Why Does Directed Instruction Work? 488
Evaluating Direct Instruction 489
Seatwork and Homework 491
Seatwork 491
Homework 491
■ **Point/Counterpoint:** Is Homework a Valuable Use of Time? 492
Making Seatwork and Homework Valuable 492
Questioning and Recitation 492
■ **Family and Community Partnerships: Homework 493**
Kinds of Questions 494
Fitting the Questions to the Students 495
Responding to Student Answers 495
Group Discussion 496
Teacher Expectations 496
Two Kinds of Expectation Effects 497
Sources of Expectations 498
Do Teachers' Expectations Really Affect Students' Achievement? 498
■ ***Stories of Learning/Tributes to Teaching*** 499
Instructional Strategies 500
Teacher–Student Interactions 500
Student-Centered Teaching: Examples in Reading, Mathematics, and Science 500
Learning and Teaching Reading and Writing 502
Balance in Reading and Writing 502
Comprehension Monitoring and Reading: Reciprocal Teaching 503
Applying Reciprocal Teaching 503
Learning and Teaching Mathematics 505
Learning and Teaching Science 506
Reaching Every Student: Effective Teaching in Inclusive Classrooms 508
Resource Rooms, Collaborative Consultation, and Cooperative Teaching 509
Working with Individual Students 511
Technology and Exceptional Students 511
Diversity and Convergences in Teaching 513
Diversity: Differentiated Instruction 514
Convergences: Beyond the Debates to Outstanding Teaching 515
SUMMARY TABLE 516
TEACHERS' CASEBOOK: *What Would They Do? 519*
■ **Guidelines**
Using Instructional Objectives 483
Teaching Effectively 489
Productive Group Discussions 497
Avoiding the Negative Effects of Teacher Expectations 501
Teaching for Conceptual Change 507

Chapter 14
Standardized Testing 521

TEACHERS' CASEBOOK: *What Would You Do? 521*
Overview 521
Measurement and Assessment 522
Norm-Referenced Test Interpretations 523
Criterion-Referenced Test Interpretations 523
What Do Test Scores Mean? 524
Basic Concepts 524
Frequency Distributions 525
Measurements of Central Tendency and Standard Deviation 525
The Normal Distribution 526
Types of Scores 527
Percentile Rank Scores 527
Grade-Equivalent Scores 528

Standard Scores 529
Interpreting Test Scores 529
Reliability of Test Scores 530
Error in Test Scores 530
Confidence Interval 531
Validity 531
Absence of Bias 532
Types of Standardized Tests 534
Achievement Tests: What Has the Student Learned? 536
Using Information from a Norm-Referenced Achievement Test 536
Diagnostic Tests: What Are the Student's Strengths and Weaknesses? 538
Aptitude Tests: How Well Will the Student Do in the Future? 538
IQ and Scholastic Aptitude 538
■ **Family and Community Partnerships:** Explaining and Using Test Results 539
Discussing Test Results with Families 539
Issues in Standardized Testing 539
Accountability and High-Stakes Testing 540
■ **Point/Counterpoint:** Should Tests Be Used to Hold Teachers Accountable? 541
The Dangers and Possibilities of High-Stakes Testing 541
Documented Problems with High-Stakes Testing 541
Using High-Stakes Testing Well 542
Preparing for Tests 543
Reaching Every Student: Helping Students with Disabilities Prepare for High-Stakes Tests 543
■ ***Stories of Learning/Tributes to Teaching*** 544
New Directions in Assessment 545
Diversity and Convergences in Standardized Testing 546
Diversity 548
Convergences 549
SUMMARY TABLE 549
TEACHERS' CASEBOOK: *What Would They Do?* 551
■ **Guidelines**
Increasing Reliability and Validity 533
Becoming an Expert Test-Taker 535

Chapter 15
Classroom Assessment and Grading 553

TEACHERS' CASEBOOK: *What Would You Do?* 553
***Overview* 553**
Formative and Summative Assessment 554
Getting the Most from Traditional Assessment 555
Planning for Testing 555
When to Test? 555
Judging Textbook Tests 556
Objective Testing 556
Using Multiple-Choice Tests 557
Writing Multiple-Choice Questions 557
Essay Testing 559
Constructing Essay Tests 559
Evaluating Essays: Dangers 559
Evaluating Essays: Methods 559
Alternatives to Traditional Assessments 561
■ **Point/Counterpoint:** Which Is Better—Traditional Tests or Authentic Assessments? 561
Authentic Classroom Assessment 562
Portfolios and Exhibitions 562
Portfolios 563
■ ***Stories of Learning/Tributes to Teaching*** 564
Exhibitions 565
Evaluating Portfolios and Performances 565
Scoring Rubrics 566
Reliability, Validity, Generalizability 567
Diversity and Equity in Performance Assessment 568
Informal Assessments 569
Involving Students in Assessments 570

Effects of Grading on Students 570
Effects of Failure 571
The Value of Failing? 571
Retention in Grade 572
Effects of Feedback 573
Grades and Motivation 573
Grading and Reporting: Nuts and Bolts 574
Criterion-Referenced versus Norm-Referenced Grading 574
The Point System and Percentage Grading 575
The Contract System and Grading Rubrics 577
Other Issues in Grading 578
Grading on Effort and Improvement 578
Cautions: Being Fair 579
Beyond Grading: Communicating with Families 579
■ **Family and Community Partnerships:** Conferences 580
Reaching Every Student: Accommodations in Grading 581

Diversity and Convergences in Classroom Assessment 581
Diversity 582
Convergences 582

SUMMARY TABLE 583
TEACHERS' CASEBOOK: *What Would They Do?* 585

■ **Guidelines**
Writing Multiple-Choice Test Items 558
Creating Portfolios 566
Developing a Rubric 569
Minimizing the Detrimental Effects of Grades 575
Using Any Grading System 578
Standards for Educational and Psychological Testing 583

Handbook for Teaching and Lifelong Learning 587

SECTION 1 ***Creating a Praxis II™/Licensure Examination Study Guide 587***
SECTION 2 ***Standards and Licensure: Praxis II™ and INTASC 590***
SECTION 3 ***Getting a Job: Job Interview Questions That* Educational Psychology *Will Help You Answer 604***
SECTION 4 ***Enhancing Your Expertise: Continuing Your Learning 605***

Glossary 613

References 623

Name Index 665

Subject Index 675

Preface

Many of you reading this book will be enrolled in an educational psychology course as part of your professional preparation for teaching, counseling, speech therapy, or psychology. The material in this text should be of interest to everyone who is concerned about education and learning, from the nursery school volunteer to the instructor in a community program for adults with disabilities. No background in psychology or education is necessary to understand this material. It is as free of jargon and technical language as possible, and many people have worked to make this edition clear, relevant, and interesting.

Since the first edition of *Educational Psychology* appeared, there have been many exciting developments in the field. The tenth edition continues to emphasize the educational implications and applications of research on child development, cognitive science, learning, teaching, and assessment. Theory and practice are not separated, but are considered together; the text shows how information and ideas drawn from research in educational psychology can be applied to solve the everyday problems of teaching. To explore the connections between knowledge and practice, there are many examples, lesson segments, case studies, guidelines, and practical tips from experienced teachers. Throughout the text you will be challenged to think about the value and use of the ideas in each chapter, and you will see principles of educational psychology in action. Professors and students who used the first nine editions found these features very helpful. But what about the new developments?

New Content in the Tenth Edition

New Chapter: In this edition there is a new chapter on "Engaged Learning: Cooperation and Community." Educators are recognizing what parents have known for years—there is more to schooling than academics; the social networks that support learning are critical. This chapter looks at research on cooperative learning, conflict resolution, and classroom communities. The next decade promises to challenge our ability to keep our students behaviorally, cognitively, and emotionally engaged in learning and our schools both safe and compassionate. I hope this chapter will help new teachers meet these challenges.

New Topics: Over 400 new citations have been added to this edition to bring prospective teachers the most current information. Topics include the following:

- History of educational psychology
- Scientifically based research
- No Child Left Behind
- The brain and teaching
- Physical development
- Bronfenbrenner's theory of development
- Neo-Piagetian approaches
- Cultural tools in learning
- The importance of teacher/student relationships
- Theory of mind
- Bullying and relational aggression
- Ethnic, racial, and gender identity
- New perspectives on moral reasoning
- Flynn effect
- Visual/verbal learning styles
- Autism and Asperger syndrome
- Fostering resilience
- Functional behavioral assessment
- Flashbulb memories
- Heuristics
- Concept mapping
- Teaching for self-regulation
- Problem-based learning
- Engagement in learning
- Managing computers in the classroom
- Culture and classroom management
- School-wide positive behavioral supports
- Assistive technology
- Lesson study
- Informal and authentic assessment
- High-stakes testing

The Plan of the Book

The introductory chapter begins with you, the prospective teacher, and the questions you may be asking yourself about a teaching career. What is good teaching, and what does it take to become an excellent teacher? How can educational psychology help you to become such a teacher?

Part 1, "Students" focuses on the learners. How do they develop mentally, physically, emotionally, and socially, and how do all these aspects fit together? Where do individual differences come from, and what do they mean for teachers? What does it mean to create a culturally inclusive classroom, one that makes learning accessible to all students?

Part 2, "Learning and Motivation" looks at learning and motivation from three major perspectives—behavioral, cognitive, and constructivist—with an emphasis on the last two. Learning theories have important implications for instruction at every level. Cognitive research is particularly vital right now and promises to be a wellspring of ideas for teaching in the immediate future. Engaged learning is the goal of all teachers.

Part 3, "Teaching and Assessing" examines how to create learning environments and, then, how to teach and assess. The material in these chapters is based on the most recent research in real classrooms. We examine many teaching strategies and different kinds of testing and grading.

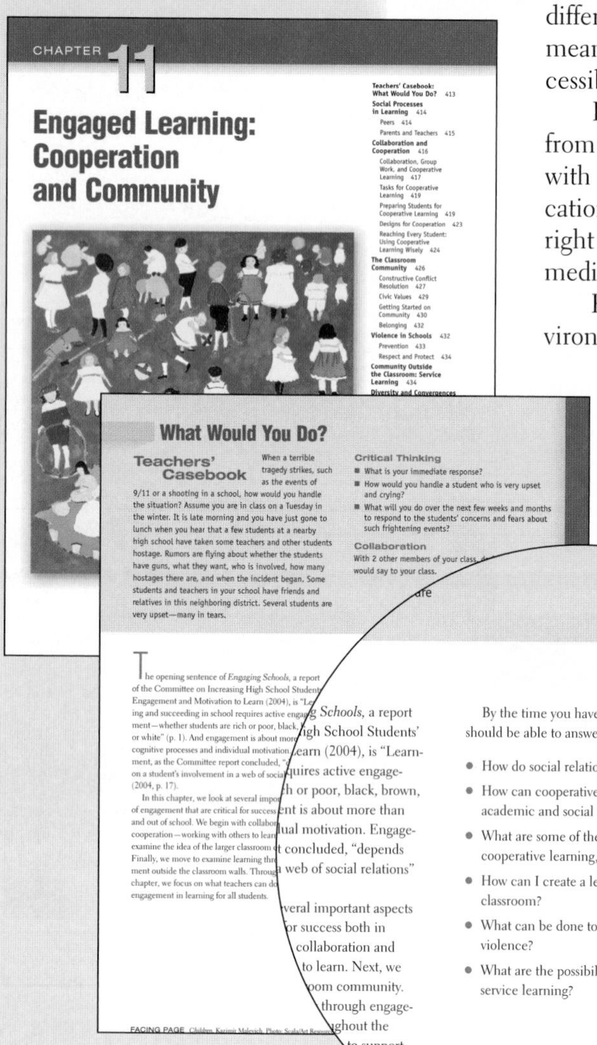

CHAPTER 11
Engaged Learning: Cooperation and Community
What Would You Do?
Teachers' Casebook
Critical Thinking
Collaboration

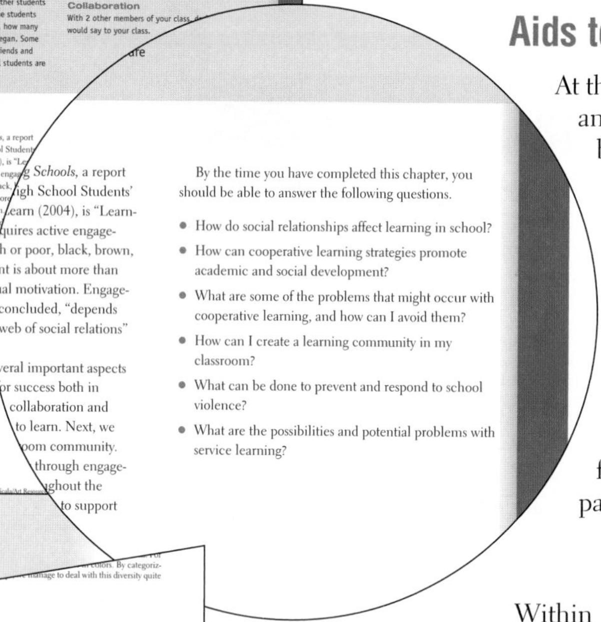

By the time you have completed this chapter, you should be able to answer the following questions.
How do social relationships affect learning in school?
How can cooperative learning strategies promote academic and social development?
What are some of the problems that might occur with cooperative learning, and how can I avoid them?
How can I create a learning community in my classroom?
What can be done to prevent and respond to school violence?
What are the possibilities and potential problems with service learning?

Aids to Understanding

At the beginning of each chapter you will find an **Outline** of the key topics with page numbers for quick reference. Then you are confronted with the question "What would you do?" about a real-life classroom situation related to the information in the chapter. By the time you reach the end of the chapter, you should have even more ideas about how to solve the problem raised, so be alert as you read. The chapter then begins with a quick **Overview** along with a list of Questions to focus your thinking about the upcoming pages.

Within the chapter, headings point out themes, questions, and problems as they arise, so you can look up information easily. These can also serve as a quick review of important points. When a new term or concept is introduced, it appears in boldface type along with a brief margin definition. These **Key Terms** are also defined in a **Summary Table** at the end of each chapter. The Summary Table is an excellent resource for study and review. Throughout the book, graphs, tables, photos, and cartoons have been chosen to clarify and extend the text material—and to add to your enjoyment.

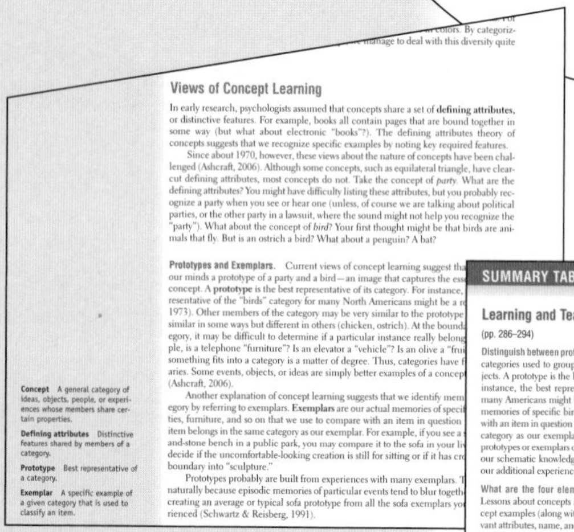

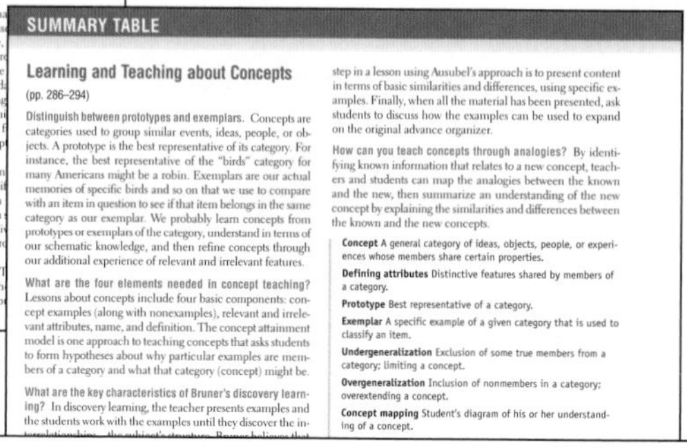

Text Features

As in the previous editions, chapters in the tenth edition include **Guidelines**, the **Teachers' Casebook: Connections to PRAXIS II™**, and **Point/Counterpoints.**

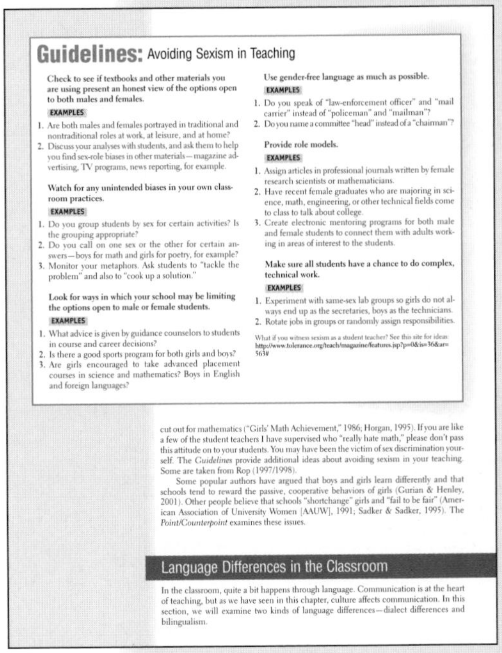

Guidelines

An important reason for studying educational psychology is to gain skills in solving classroom problems. Often, texts give pages of theory and research findings, but little assistance in translating theory into practice. This text is different. Included in every chapter after the first one are several sets of *Guidelines*. These are teaching tips and practical suggestions based on the theory and research discussed in the chapter. Each suggestion is clarified by two or three specific examples. Although the *Guidelines* cannot cover every possible situation, they do provide a needed bridge between knowledge and practice and should help you transfer the text's information to new situations. In addition, every chapter after the first has one set of *Guidelines* that focuses on *Family and Community Partnerships*—an area of growing importance today.

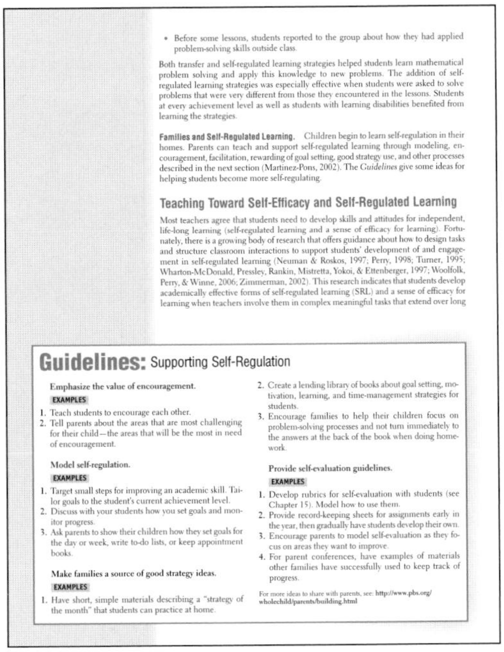

Teaching Toward Self-Efficacy and Self-Regulated Learning
Guidelines: Supporting Self-Regulation

Teachers' Casebook: Connections to PRAXIS II™/ What Would You Do? What Would They Do?

This highly acclaimed and popular feature from the first nine editions is back. At the end of each chapter, master teachers from all over the country offer their own solutions to the problem you encountered at the beginning of each chapter. The case presented and discussed will prepare you for case analyses that are part of licensing exams such as PRAXIS II™—tests you will have to take. This discussion gives you insights into the thinking of expert teachers and allows you to compare their solutions to the ones you came up with. Their ideas truly show educational psychology at work in a range of everyday situations. The *Teachers' Casebook* brings to life the topics and principles discussed in each chapter.

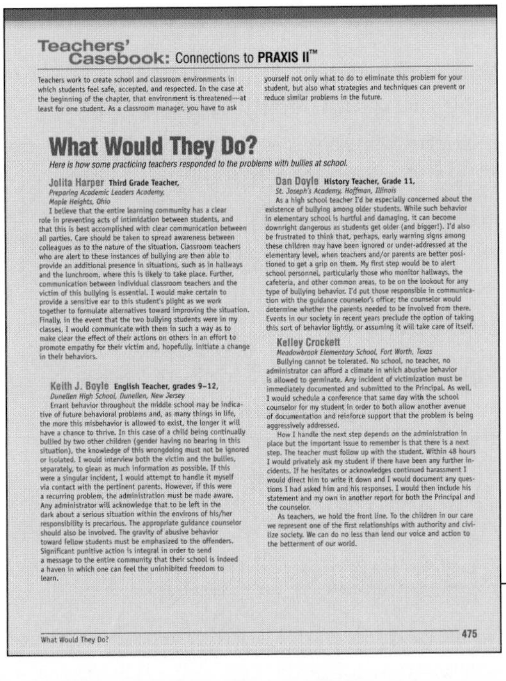

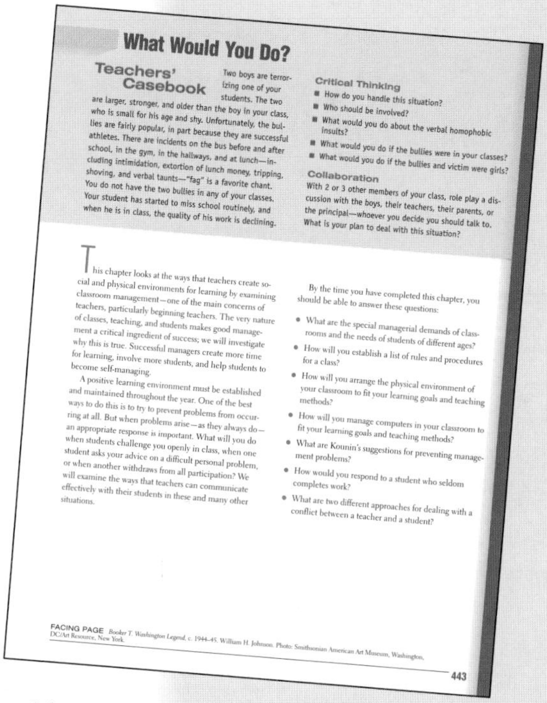

Point/Counterpoint

In every chapter, a debate called *Point/Counterpoint* examines two contrasting perspectives on an important question or controversy related to research or practice in educational psychology; issues such as inclusion, tracking, "paying" kids to learn, zero-tolerance, and character education are examples. Many of the topics considered in these *Point/Counterpoints* have "made the news" recently and are central to the discussions of educational reformers. Helping to drive home these important contrasting perspectives are the video connections between *Point/Counterpoint* topics and the *ABC News/Allyn & Bacon Video: Point/Counterpoint,* which provide news clips from ABC's premier news shows.

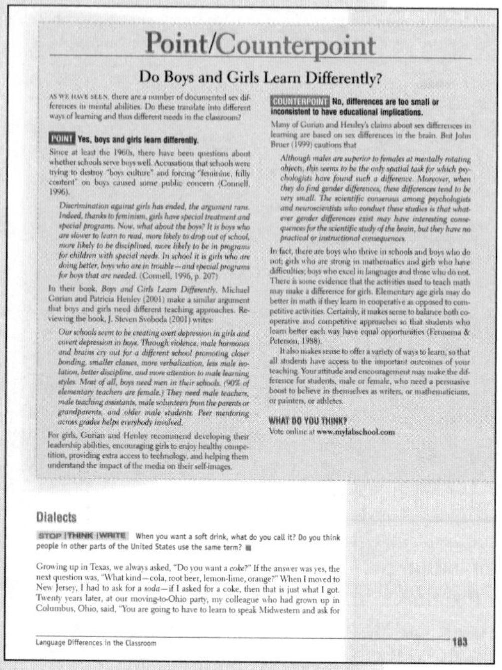

Point/Counterpoint

Do Boys and Girls Learn Differently?

AS WE HAVE SEEN, there are a number of documented sex differences in mental abilities. Do these translate into different ways of learning and thus different needs in the classroom?

POINT Yes, boys and girls learn differently.

Since at least the 1960s, there have been questions about whether schools serve boys well. Accusations that schools were trying to destroy "boys culture" and forcing "feminine, frilly content" on boys caused some public concern (Connell, 1996).

Discrimination against girls has ended, the argument runs. Indeed, thanks to feminism, girls have special treatment and special programs. Now, what about the boys? It is boys who are slower to learn to read, more likely to drop out of school, more likely to be disciplined, more likely to be in programs for children with special needs. In school it is girls who are doing better, boys who are in trouble—and special programs for boys that are needed. (Connell, 1996, p. 207)

In their book, *Boys and Girls Learn Differently,* Michael Gurian and Patricia Henley (2001) make a similar argument that boys and girls need different teaching approaches. Reviewing the book, J. Steven Svoboda (2001) writes:

Our schools seem to be creating overt depression in girls and covert depression in boys. Through violence, male hormones and brains cry out for a different school promoting closer bonding, smaller classes, more verbalization, less male isolation, better discipline, and more attention to male learning styles. Most of all, boys need men in their schools. (90% of elementary teachers are female.) They need male teachers, male teaching assistants, male volunteers from the parents or grandparents, and older male students. Peer mentoring across grades helps everybody involved.

For girls, Gurian and Henley recommend developing their leadership abilities, encouraging girls to enjoy healthy competition, providing extra access to technology, and helping them understand the impact of the media on their self-images.

COUNTERPOINT No, differences are too small or inconsistent to have educational implications.

Many of Gurian and Henley's claims about sex differences in learning are based on sex differences in the brain. But John Bruer (1999) cautions that

Although males are superior to females at mentally rotating objects, this seems to be the only spatial task for which psychologists have found such a difference. Moreover, when they do find gender differences, these differences tend to be very small. The scientific consensus among psychologists and neuroscientists who conduct these studies is that whatever gender differences exist may have interesting consequences for the scientific study of the brain, but they have no practical or instructional consequences.

In fact, there are boys who thrive in schools and boys who do not; girls who are strong in mathematics and girls who have difficulties; boys who excel in languages and those who do not. There is some evidence that the activities used to teach math may make a difference for girls. Elementary age girls may do better in math if they learn in cooperative as opposed to competitive activities. Certainly, it makes sense to balance both cooperative and competitive approaches so that students who learn better each way have equal opportunities (Fennema & Peterson, 1988).

It also makes sense to offer a variety of ways to learn, so that all students have access to the important outcomes of your teaching. Your attitude and encouragement may make the difference for students, male or female, who need a persuasive boost to believe in themselves as writers, or mathematicians, or painters, or athletes.

WHAT DO YOU THINK?
Vote online at **www.mylabschool.com**

Dialects

STOP | THINK | WRITE When you want a soft drink, what do you call it? Do you think people in other parts of the United States use the same term? ■

Growing up in Texas, we always asked, "Do you want a *coke*?" If the answer was yes, the next question was, "What kind—cola, root beer, lemon-lime, orange?" When I moved to New Jersey, I had to ask for a *soda*—if I asked for a coke, then that is just what I got. Twenty years later, at our moving-to-Ohio party, my colleague who had grown up in Columbus, Ohio, said, "You are going to have to learn to speak Midwestern and ask for

Language Differences in the Classroom 183

Chapter 1	What Kind of Research Should Guide Education?
Chapter 2	Brain-based Education
Chapter 3	What Should Schools Do to Encourage Students' Self-Esteem?
Chapter 4	Is Tracking an Effective Strategy?
Chapter 5	Do Boys and Girls Learn Differently?
Chapter 6	Should Students Be Rewarded for Learning?
Chapter 7	What's Wrong with Memorizing?
Chapter 8	Should Students Be Allowed to Use Calculators and Spell-Checkers?
Chapter 9	Should Schools Teach Critical Thinking and Problem Solving?
Chapter 10	Does Making Learning Fun Make for Good Learning?
Chapter 11	Should Schools Teach Character and Compassion?
Chapter 12	Is Zero Tolerance a Good Idea?
Chapter 13	Is Homework a Valuable Use of Time?
Chapter 14	Should Tests Be Used to Hold Teachers Accountable?
Chapter 15	Which Is Better—Traditional Tests or Authentic Assessments?

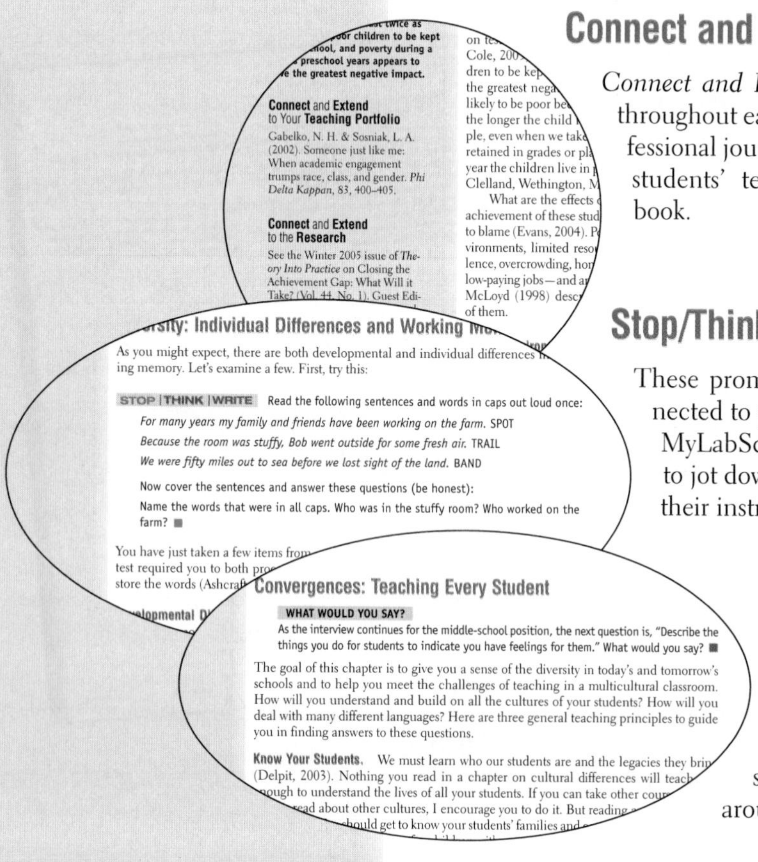

poor children to be kept
school, and poverty during a
preschool years appears to
the greatest negative impact.

Connect and Extend to Your Teaching Portfolio
Gabelko, N. H. & Sosniak, L. A. (2002). Someone just like me: When academic engagement trumps race, class, and gender. *Phi Delta Kappan,* 83, 400–405.

Connect and Extend to the Research
See the Winter 2005 issue of *Theory Into Practice* on Closing the Achievement Gap: What Will it Take? (Vol. 44, No. 1). Guest Edi-

Individual Differences and Working

As you might expect, there are both developmental and individual differences in working memory. Let's examine a few. First, try this:

STOP | THINK | WRITE Read the following sentences and words in caps out loud once:

For many years my family and friends have been working on the farm. SPOT
Because the room was stuffy, Bob went outside for some fresh air. TRAIL
We were fifty miles out to sea before we lost sight of the land. BAND

Now cover the sentences and answer these questions (be honest):

Name the words that were in all caps. Who was in the stuffy room? Who worked on the farm? ■

You have just taken a few items from
test required you to both pr
store the words (Ashcraf

Convergences: Teaching Every Student

WHAT WOULD YOU SAY?
As the interview continues for the middle-school position, the next question is, "Describe the things you do for students to indicate you have feelings for them." What would you say? ■

The goal of this chapter is to give you a sense of the diversity in today's and tomorrow's schools and to help you meet the challenges of teaching in a multicultural classroom. How will you understand and build on all the cultures of your students? How will you deal with many different languages? Here are three general teaching principles to guide you in finding answers to these questions.

Know Your Students. We must learn who our students are and the legacies they bri
(Delpit, 2003). Nothing you read in a chapter on cultural differences will teach
ough to understand the lives of all your students. If you can take other cour
read about other cultures, I encourage you to do it. But reading
should get to know your students' families and

Connect and Extend

Connect and Extend features appear in the margins several times throughout each chapter, linking content to teaching, research, professional journals, the Web, students' thinking and prior knowledge, students' teaching philosophy, and to other chapters in the book.

Stop/Think/Write

These prompts provide "minds-on" experiences. They are connected to possible assignments such as interactive journals. The MyLabSchool website (www.mylabschool.com) allows students to jot down their responses to these prompts and email them to their instructor.

What Would You Say?

Two or three times in every chapter, you are asked how you would answer possible job interview questions based on the text material. These questions were suggested by practicing principals and superintendents around the country.

Stories of Learning/Tributes to Teaching

Every chapter contains a brief story about how a real teacher made a difference in the life of a student. A few years ago, my daughter, a middle school teacher, got a phone call from the parents of a former student. The young girl was not expected to live and had asked for Kelly—one of only two people she wanted to see. The good news is that the girl received a heart transplant and is doing well. The other good news is that her teacher was and is a central part of her life. Each chapter in this book has a story of learning that demonstrates the importance of teachers like Kelly.

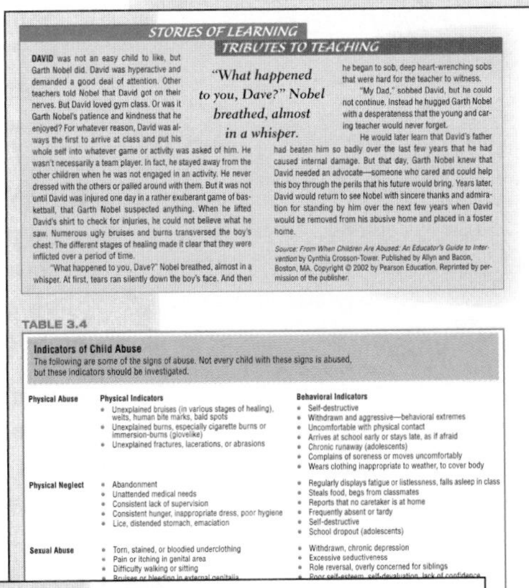

Reaching Every Student

In every chapter after the first, a section called *Reaching Every Student* gives ideas for assessing, teaching, and motivating diverse students and students with learning problems.

Chapter 2	Using the Tools of the Culture
Chapter 3	Loneliness and Children with Disabilities
Chapter 4	Higher-Order Thinking
Chapter 5	Recognizing Giftedness in Bilingual Students
Chapter 6	Functional Behavioral Assessment and Positive Behavior Support
Chapter 7	Metacognitive Strategies for Students with Learning Disabilities
Chapter 8	Learning Disabilities and Concept Teaching
Chapter 9	Two Classrooms and the Family
Chapter 10	Coping with Anxiety
Chapter 11	Using Cooperative Learning Wisely
Chapter 12	School-wide Positive Behavior Supports
Chapter 13	Effective Teaching in Inclusive Classrooms
Chapter 14	Helping Students with Disabilities Prepare for High-Stakes Tests
Chapter 15	Accommodations in Grading

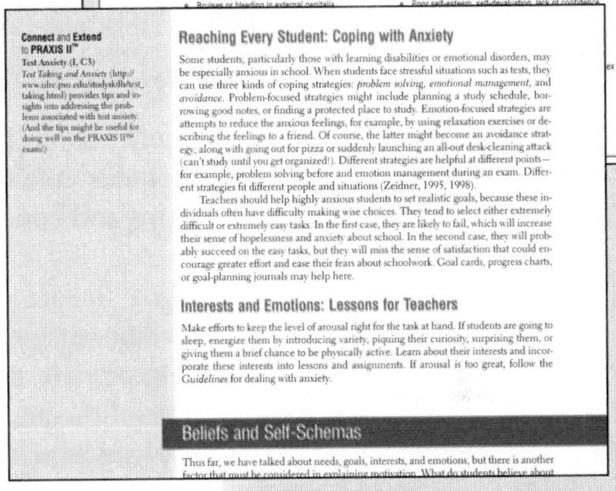

New Features in the Tenth Edition

Diversity and Convergences

Every chapter ends with a section that explores the experiences and characteristics of diverse students in relation to the chapter topics. Then we consider some themes and principles that apply to all students. The goal of this section is to help you understand and value the differences among your students, while also appreciating the great similarities among all of us in development, learning, and motivation.

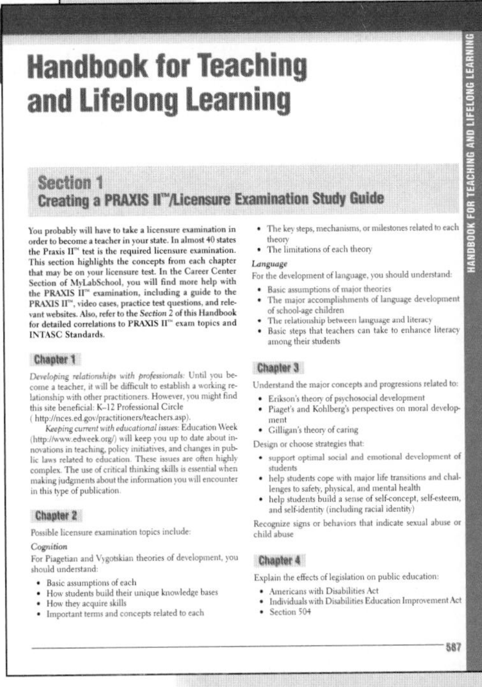

A Handbook for Teaching and Lifelong Learning

At the end of the text is a Handbook with four sections:

1. *Creating a Praxis II™/Licensure Examination Study Guide*: This section is a chapter-by-chapter map for using this text as a personal study guide for licensing tests such as the PRAXIS II™.

2. *Standards and Licensure Appendix: Praxis II™ and INTASC:* Detailed correlations to PRAXIS II™ exam topics addressed in the 10th edition of the text.
3. *Getting a Job: Interview Questions That Educational Psychology Will Help You Answer.* These were suggested by superintendents and principals as questions they like to ask during interviews to select teachers.
4. *Enhancing Your Expertise: Continuing Your Learning:* No matter what your teacher preparation program included or how well you did in that program, you will hear yourself exclaiming, "They never told me about this!" In this section are cases of possible "surprises" taken from the real experiences of teachers I know, along with guidance about how to develop your expertise by exploring the World Wide Web.

The four sections of this Handbook for Teaching and Lifelong Learning should give you even more tools for passing your licensing test, getting a job, and teaching well, no matter what surprises come your way.

Student Supplements

Study Guide. Designed to help students master the material in the text, the Study Guide includes concept maps, case study applications, lists of key points, exercises with key terms and concepts, practice tests, and explanations of why answers are correct.

MyLabSchool. The 10th edition of *Educational Psychology* includes access to a text-specific version of Allyn & Bacon's MyLabSchool, a collection of online tools designed to help prepare students for success in this course as well as in their teaching careers. This state-of-the-art resource is available through an access-code-protected website. Visit www.mylabschool.com to access the following:

- an E-book with integrated pre- and post-tests that generate individualized study plans that identify areas of weakness and strength to help students focus their attention and efforts where they're needed the most
- video footage of real-life classrooms, over 200 different clips showing educational psychology in practice, with opportunities for students to reflect on the videos and offer their own thoughts and suggestions for applying theory to practice
- an extensive archive of text and multimedia cases that provide valuable perspectives on real classrooms and real teaching challenges
- help with research papers using Research Navigator, which provides access to three exclusive databases of credible and reliable source material including EBSCO's ContentSelect Academic Journal Database, *The New York Times* Search by Subject Archive, and "Best of the Web" Link Library
- help with lesson planning and building digital portfolios
- professional resources, including study guides for licensure preparation

CourseCompass™. Powered by Blackboard™ and hosted nationally, Allyn & Bacon's own course management system, CourseCompass™, helps you manage all aspects of teaching your course. For colleges and universities with WebCT™ and Blackboard™ licenses, special course management packages are available in these formats as well.

Instructor Supplements

Instructor's Resource Manual. The Instructor's Resource Manual includes many ideas and activities to help instructors teach the course. For each chapter it provides: teaching outline, learning objectives, learning activities and handouts (including technology activities and activities for field experiences), discussion questions, and video/Internet resources.

Assessment Package. Contains hundreds of challenging questions in multiple-choice, fill-in-the-blank, true/false, short-answer, and case study formats, along with a detailed answer key.

Computerized Test Bank. The printed Test Bank is also available electronically through our computerized testing system: TestGen EQ. Instructors can use TestGen EQ to create exams in just minutes by selecting from the existing database of questions, editing questions, or writing original questions.

PowerPoint™ Presentation. Ideal for lecture presentations or student handouts, the PowerPoint™ presentation created for this text provides dozens of ready-to-use graphic and text images (available on the Woolfolk Web-catalog page at ablongman.com).

ABC News/Allyn & Bacon Video: Point/Counterpoint. Containing fifty minutes of ABC News clips from ABC's premier news shows, the video provides a starting point to discuss the issues raised in the *Point/Counterpoint* feature of the main text. An accompanying instructor's guide outlines teaching strategies and provides discussion questions to use with the clips.

Classroom Insights IV Video. This two-hour video contains classroom footage illustrating key concepts from *Educational Psychology.*

Allyn & Bacon Transparencies for Educational Psychology IV. This updated package includes over 150 full-color acetates.

Digital Media Archive for Education. This CD-ROM contains a variety of media elements that instructors can use to create electronic presentations in the classroom. It includes hundreds of original images, as well as selected art from Allyn & Bacon educational psychology texts, providing instructors with a broad selection of graphs, charts, and tables. For classrooms with full multimedia capability, it also contains video segments and Web links.

Student and Instructor Responses. You are invited to respond to any aspect of this text. We welcome your feedback. You may wish to criticize the solutions in the *Teachers' Casebook*, for example, or suggest topics or materials you think should be added to future editions. We would also like to know what you think of the text features and student supplements. Please send letters to:

Woolfolk/EDUCATIONAL PSYCHOLOGY, 10/E
Allyn & Bacon
75 Arlington Street
Suite 300
Boston, MA 02116

Acknowledgments

During the years I have worked on this book, from initial draft to this most recent revision, many people have supported the project. Without their help, this text simply could not have been written.

Many educators contributed to this project. Carol Weinstein wrote the section in Chapter 12 on spaces for learning. Nancy Perry (University of British Columbia) and Philip Winne (Simon Frasier University) wrote sections of Chapter 9 on self-regulation. Gypsy M. Denzine (Northern Arizona University) is responsible for the *Assessment Package* and the answer feedback material that accompanies each item. The *Instructor's Resource Manual* was created by Robin Rackley (Texas A&M University), the *PowerPoint™ Presentation* was created by Carol Scatena (Lewis University), and the *Study Guide*, by Emilie Wright Johnson (Lindenwood University). The marginal notes and the *Handbook for Teaching and Lifelong Learning* were developed by James O'Kelly (Rutgers

University). Chapters 2 and 3 benefited from the comments of Nancy Knapp (University of Georgia). Several of the *What Would You Say?* questions were suggested by Dr. Michael DiPaola, former Superintendent of Schools, Pitman, New Jersey (College of William and Mary); Dr. Harry Galinsky, former Superintendent of Schools, Paramus, New Jersey; and Andrea Wong, Principal, Hillside Elementary School, Needham, Massachusetts.

As I made decisions about how to revise this edition, I benefited from the ideas of professors around the country who took the time to complete surveys and answer my questions. Thanks to:

Grace M. Burton, *University of North Carolina-Wilmington*
E. J. Caropreso, *University of North Carolina-Wilmington*
Linda Chiang, *Azusa Pacific University*
Annemarie Conley, *University of Michigan*
Carol McDonald Connor, *Florida State University*
Karen Eifler, *University of Portland*
Michael Hardman, *University of Utah*
James Kauffman, *University of Virginia*
Nancy Knapp, *University of Georgia*
Patricia Kopetz, *University of Tennessee–Chattanooga*
William Lan, *Texas Tech University*
John Lloyd, *University of Virginia*
Jim McMillan, *Virginia Commonwealth University*
Avidan Milevsky, *Kutztown University of Pennsylvania*
Susan Avery Mitchell, *Ohio University*
Evan Powell, *The University of Georgia*
Thomas Ratliff, *Central Connecticut State University*
Marla Reese-Weber, *Illinois State University*
Catherine A. Rivoira, *East Carolina University*
Jeff Sandoz, *University of Louisiana–Lafayette*
Sue Schaar, *California State University–Dominguez Hills*
Rosa Hernandez Sheets, *Texas Tech University*
Ken Springer, *Southern Methodist University*
Deborah Switzer, *Clemson University*
Mary Ellen Tillotson, *Rhode Island College*
Sheryl White, *Eastern Michigan University*
Patricia Willems, *Florida Atlantic University*

Many classroom teachers across the country and around the world contributed their experience, creativity, and expertise to the *Teachers' Casebook*. I have thoroughly enjoyed my association with these master teachers, and I am grateful for the perspective they brought to the book.

Jamaal Allan, *J.W. Poynter Middle School, Hillsboro, Oregon*
William Rodney Allen, *Louisiana School for Math, Science, and the Arts, Natchitoches, Louisiana*
Madya Ayala, *Campus Garza Sada, Monterrey, N.L. Mexico*
Suzy L. Boswell, *Pickens County Middle School, Jasper, Georgia*
Karen A. Boyarsky, *Walter C. Black Elementary, Hightstown, New Jersey*
Keith J. Boyle, *Dunellen, New Jersey*
Kimberly D. Bridgers, *Dodson Elementary, Hermitage, Tennessee*
Valerie Chilcoat, *Glenmount School, Baltimore, Maryland*
Katie Churchill, *Oriole Parke Elementary School, Chicago, Illinois*
Kelley Crockett, *Meadowbrook Elementary School, Forth Worth, Texas*
Ashley Dodge, *Los Angeles Unified School District, Los Angeles, California*
Margaret Doolan, *St. Michael's School, Gordonvale, Australia*
Daniel Doyle, *St. Joseph's Academy, Hoffman Estates, Illinois*
Michael J. Ellis, *Quincy High School, Quincy, Massachusetts*
Aimee Fredette, *Fisher Elementary School, Walpole, Massachusetts*
Pam Gaskill, *Riverside Elementary School, Dublin, Ohio*
Sandra Gill, *Hudson Middle School, Hudson, New York*
Linda Glisson, *St. James Episcopal Day School, Baton Rouge, Louisiana*
Jolita Harper, *Weinland Park Elementary, Columbus, Ohio*
Danielle Hartman, *Claymont Elementary, Parkway School District, Ballwin, Missouri*
Jeff D. Horton, *Colton School, Colton, Washington*
W. Sean Kearney, *Galen R. Elolf Elementary School, Converse, Texas*

Mitchell D. Klett, A.C. *New Middle School, Springs, Texas*
Vivian LaColla, *Noxon Road Elementary School, Poughkeepsie, New York*
Kelly McElroy Bonin, *Klein Oak Hill School, Spring, Texas*
Susan Middleton, *St. James Episcopal Day School, Baton Rouge, Louisiana*
Felicia Lowman-Sikes, *Meadowview Elementary, Meadowview, Virginia*
Julie Mohok, *Ponam Primary School, Papua New Guinea*
Thomas Naismith, *Slocum Independent School District, Slocum, Texas*
Thomas W. Newkirk, *Hamilton Heights Middle School, Arcadia, Indiana*
Timothy Norfleet, *Linden McKinley High School, Columbus, OH*
Thomas O'Donnell, *Malden High School, Malden, Massachusetts*
Allan Osborne, *Snug Harbor Community School, Quincy, Massachusetts*
Carey Perkson, *Brown School, Natick, Massachusetts*
Katie Piel, *West Park School, Moscow, Idaho*
Deborah P. Reed, *Darby Woods Elementary School, Galloway, Ohio*
Thomas G. Reed, *Darby Woods Elementary School, Galloway, Ohio*
Randall G. Sampson, *Genoa Middle School, Westerville, Ohio*
Nancy Schaefer, *Cincinnati Hills Christian Academy High School, Cincinnati, Ohio*
Dr. Nancy Sheehan-Melzack, *Snug Harbor Community School, Quincy, Massachusetts*
Mark Smith, *Medford High School, Medford, Massachusetts*
Jennifer Hudson Thomas, *Armidale High School, Armidale, Australia*
Jacalyn Walker, *Treasure Mountain Middle School, Park City, Utah*
Michael Yasis, *L.H. Tanglen Elementary, Minnetonka, Minnesota*
Suzi E. Young, *York Middle School, York, Maine*
Debbie Youngblood, *Hilliard City Schools, Hilliard, Ohio*

In a project of this size so many people make essential contributions. Julie Brown, Permissions Coordinator, worked diligently to obtain permissions for the material reproduced in this text and the supplements. The text designer, Carol Somberg, and cover coordinator, Linda Knowles, made the look of this book the best yet—hard to do after 10 editions. Kathy Smith, Project Manager, routinely performed minor miracles and held all aspects of the project in her wonderfully ordered and intelligent mind. I keep asking her if she would run my whole life, she does so much so well. Annette Joseph, Production Administrator, and Elaine Ober, Production Manager, coordinated all aspects of the project, with amazing skill and grace. Somehow they brought sanity to what could have been chaos and fun to what might have been drudgery. Now the book is in the able hands of Tara Kelly, Senior Marketing Manager, Amy Cronin Jordan, Director of Marketing for Allyn & Bacon Education, Jacqueline McDermott, Senior Advertising Specialist, Kate Conway, Director of Advertising, and their staff. I can't wait to see what they are planning for me now! What a talented and creative group—I am honored to work with them all.

On this edition, I was again privileged to work with an outstanding editorial group, Nancy Forsyth, President of Allyn and Bacon, and Paul A. Smith, Vice President, Editor-in-Chief. Their intelligence, creativity, sound judgment, style, and enduring commitment to quality can be seen on every page of this text. They will always have my deepest respect and enduring friendship. I would keep writing forever just to work with them. Anne Spear, Editorial Assistant, kept everything running smoothly and kept my fax machine and e-mail humming. On this edition I was fortunate again to have the help of Alicia Reilly, an outstanding developmental editor with the perfect combination of knowledge and organizational ability. Once again, she guided this revision in all its many aspects, always staying just ahead of whatever had to happen next, communicating with people around the world—remarkable! The excellent pedagogical supports would not exist without her tireless efforts. The extensive supplements package that accompanies this book was coordinated, with seeming effortlessness, by Adam Whitehurst, Associate Editor.

Finally, I want to thank my family and friends for their kindness and support during the long days and nights that I worked on this book. To my family, Marion, Bob, Eric, Suzie, Elsie, Liz, Wayne K., Marie, Kelly, Tom, Lisa, Lauren and Mike—you are the greatest.

And finally, to Wayne Hoy, my friend, colleague, inspiration, passion, husband—you make every day a gift.

—Anita Woolfolk Hoy

CHAPTER 1

Teachers, Teaching, and Educational Psychology

Teachers' Casebook: What Would You Do? 1

Teaching After *No Child Left Behind* 2

Do Teachers Make a Difference? 2

- Teacher–Student Relationships 3
- Teacher Preparation and Quality 3

What Is Good Teaching? 5

- Inside Four Classrooms 5
- Expert Knowledge 7

The Role of Educational Psychology 8

- Some Interesting History 8
- Is It Just Common Sense? 9
- Using Research to Understand and Improve Learning 10
- What Is Scientifically Based Research? 13
- Theories for Teaching 13
- Becoming a Good Beginning Teacher 15

Diversity and Convergences in Educational Psychology 16

- Diversity 17
- Convergences 17

Summary Table 17

Teachers' Casebook: Connections to PRAXIS II™/What Would They Do? 19

What Would You Do?

Teachers' Casebook

It is your second year as a teacher at the Riverside Combined Campus (Kindergarten–8th grade). The district has just received money from both the state and a private foundation to give three awards in your school for "excellence in teaching." The principal wants the teachers' recommendations for recipients of these awards, so a committee is formed, composed of experienced teachers and one beginner—you. When the principal asked you to serve on the committee, you felt obligated to say yes. All week, the Teachers' Lounge has been buzzing with discussion about the awards. Some teachers are suspicious—they fear the decisions will be purely political. Others are glad to see individuals' efforts in teaching honored. Names are mentioned as "sure winners" and a few teachers who seldom speak to you have become very friendly ever since the committee membership was announced. The first meeting is next week. How will you prepare for it?

Critical Thinking

- What do you need to know about teaching to complete this task?
- What are some indicators of excellent teaching?
- Do different philosophies of teaching provide different answers to this question?
- What are your recommendations, and how would you back them up?

Collaboration

With 3 or 4 other members of your class, draw a concept map or web that graphically depicts "good teaching." For an example of a concept map, see "Figure 8.2: Amy's Molecule" in Chapter 8.

Like many students, you may begin this course with a mixture of anticipation and wariness. Perhaps you are required to take educational psychology as part of a program in teacher education, speech therapy, nursing, or counseling. You may have chosen this class as an elective. Whatever your reason for enrolling, you probably have questions about teaching, schools, students—or even about yourself—that you hope this course may answer. I have written the 10th edition of *Educational Psychology* with questions such as these in mind.

In this first chapter, we begin with education—more specifically, with teaching today and the federal legislation that impacts every teacher. Teachers have been both criticized as ineffective and lauded as the best hope for young people. Do teachers make a difference in students' learning? What characterizes good teaching? Only when you are aware of the challenges and possibilities of teaching and learning today can you appreciate the contributions of educational psychology. After a brief introduction to the world of the teacher, we turn to a discussion of educational psychology itself. How can principles identified by educational psychologists benefit teachers, therapists, parents, and others who are interested in teaching and learning? What exactly is the content of educational psychology, and where does this information come from? By the time you have finished this chapter, you will be in a much better position to answer these questions and many others such as:

- What is the No Child Left Behind Act?
- Does teaching matter?
- What is good teaching?
- What do expert teachers know?
- What are the greatest concerns of beginning teachers?
- Why should I study educational psychology?
- What roles do theory and research play in this field?

FACING PAGE *Lawyers and Clients*, 1993, Jacob Lawrence. Gouache on paper, 20 × 22 inches © 2006 The Jacob and Gwendolyn Lawrence Foundation, Seattle/Artists Rights Society (ARS), New York. Photo: The Jacob and Gwendolyn Lawrence Foundation/Art Resource, New York.

Teaching After *No Child Left Behind*

If you don't know about *No Child Left Behind,* or even if you do, you will hear about it often in this text. On January 8, 2002, President George W. Bush signed into law the *No Child Left Behind (NCLB) Act.* Actually, NCLB was the most recent authorization of the Elementary and Secondary Education Act or ESEA, first passed in 1965. The reauthorization had a new name to reflect the sweeping changes that came with it. In a nutshell, the NCLB Act requires that by the end of the 2005–2006 school year, *all* students in grades 3 through 8 must take standardized achievement tests in reading and mathematics every year; in addition, one more exam will be required in high school. Other subjects will be added later. Based on these test scores, schools are judged to determine if their students are making *Adequate Yearly Progress (AYP)* toward becoming proficient in the subjects tested. States have some say in defining "proficiency" and in setting AYP standards. Regardless of how states define these standards, the NCLB Act requires that all students in the schools must reach proficiency by the end of the 2013–2014 school year. In addition, schools must develop AYP goals and report scores separately for several groups, including racial and ethnic minority students, students with disabilities, students whose first language is not English, and students from low-income homes. The effects on you as a teacher (or parent) will be profound. James Popham, an assessment expert, says:

> Testing—*and teaching*—following the passage of the NCLB Act are certain to be different than testing—*and teaching*—before the law's enactment. Today's public school teachers are now obligated to take part in an educational game whose rules have been dramatically altered because of a significant federal law. The NCLB Act, almost literally, seems likely to trump almost everything it touches. (2005a, p. 4)

I start the first chapter of this text describing the NCLB Act because, as Popham notes, it will affect your teaching life every day. Also, the law addresses what makes a *highly qualified teacher*—the kind that you want to become. By the end of school year 2005–2006, the NCLB Act requires that all teachers of core academic subjects must be "highly qualified" according to the Act's definition. By January 2006, all teachers' assistants must be highly qualified according to the Act's definition for paraprofessionals. What makes a highly qualified teacher?

> To be considered highly qualified under NCLB, new teachers, generally speaking, must be fully certified, have a bachelor's degree, and demonstrate their knowledge and skills in the subjects they are teaching by either having taken sufficient academic coursework in their field or by passing a state test. Veteran teachers who lack the academic coursework required of new teachers can demonstrate competency in the academic subjects they teach through a third means, by meeting the conditions of their state's "high objective uniform state standard of evaluation," or HOUSSE for short. (Center on Education Policy, 2005, p. 148)

By this definition, in 2005, most teachers were considered "highly qualified." But there are some problems. The proportion of "unqualified" teachers is greatest for poor and minority group students, students with special needs, and students in rural schools.

Does being highly qualified guarantee good teaching? In the next pages we look at several answers to the question, "What is good teaching?" But before we consider what defines good teaching, let's examine a more basic question: With all this testing, do teachers make a difference?

Connect and **Extend** to Your **Teaching**

What are the goals of education, real and ideal? What does it mean to be an educated person? What makes a teacher effective? Describe the most effective teacher you ever had. How do you learn best? What do you hope to gain from this course? Your answers will provide the basis for developing a philosophy of teaching.

Do Teachers Make a Difference?

For a while, some researchers reported findings suggesting that wealth and social status, not teaching, were the major factors determining who learned in schools (e.g., Coleman, 1966). In fact, much of the early research on teaching was conducted by educational psychologists who refused to accept these claims that teachers were powerless in the face of poverty and societal problems (Wittrock, 1986).

How could you decide if teaching makes a difference? You could look to your own experience. Were there teachers who had an impact on your life? Perhaps one of your teachers influenced your decision to become an educator. But one of the purposes of educational psychology in general and this text in particular is to go beyond individual experiences and testimonies, powerful as they are, to examine larger groups. Three studies speak to the power of teachers in the lives of students. The first followed 179 children from kindergarten through eighth grade. The second was a large-scale policy study of thousands of students and teachers in all 50 of the United States. The final study examined math achievement for students as they moved through 3rd, 4th, and 5th grades.

Teacher–Student Relationships

Bridgett Harme and Robert Pianta (2001) followed all the children in a small school district who entered kindergarten one year and continued in that district through the 8th grade. The researchers concluded that the quality of the teacher–student relationship in kindergarten (defined in terms of level of conflict with the child, the child's dependency on the teacher, and the teacher's affection for the child) predicted a number of academic and behavioral outcomes through the 8th grade, particularly for students with high levels of behavior problems. Even when the gender, ethnicity, cognitive ability, and behavior ratings of the student were accounted for, the relationship with the teacher still predicted aspects of school success. The researchers concluded that "the association between the quality of early teacher–child relationships and later school performance can be both strong and persistent" (p. 636). Based on the results of this carefully conducted study, it appears that students with significant behavior problems in the early years are less likely to have problems later in school if their teachers are sensitive to their needs and provide frequent, consistent feedback. Read the *Stories of Learning: Tributes to Teaching* feature to put a face on the power of positive teacher-student relationships.

Teacher Preparation and Quality

Using data from a 50-state survey of policies, state case study analyses, the 1993–94 Schools and Staffing Surveys, and the National Assessment of Educational Progress

STORIES OF LEARNING
TRIBUTES TO TEACHING

"You're the only one who gave me a chance."

Maggie pulled her four-year-old son's hand a little harder as she hurried him up the sidewalk. A black pickup truck had slowed alongside them.

"Who's that, Mommy?"

"Let's keep walking," Maggie said. Not recognizing the truck, she picked up the pace.

Just then, her son tripped on a stray branch and pulled on Maggie to wait. As she stopped, the dark glass of the passenger window rolled down and a young man with sunglasses leaned over to get a better look at the sidewalk couple.

"Mrs. Jensen, is that you?" Maggie looked up, responding with caution to the distantly familiar voice. She scooped up her son and took a cautious step back from the street.

The driver stopped the truck, put it in park, and excitedly ran around to meet her. Taking off his sunglasses so Maggie could see him better, he said with a touch of disappointment, "You don't remember me, do you?"

Apprehension turned to delight as Maggie finally recognized her former student. "Of course I do, **JAY.** You're a hard one to forget."

"I never forgot you, Mrs. Jensen. You're the only one who gave me a chance."

Looking at him she could still see the twelve year old who fought the system. As the big, black truck rolled away, Maggie smiled as she read his business card, "Jay Getz, Architect."

Source: Taken from *Apples & Chalkdust* by Vicki Carauna. Copyright © 1998 by Vicki Carauna. Used with permission of Honor Books, an imprint of Cook Communications Ministries.

Connect and **Extend** to the **Research**

For another perspective on teacher quality and teacher preparation, see Borko et al. (2000). Teacher education does matter: A situative view of learning to teach secondary mathematics. *Educational Psychologist*, 35, 193–206.

(NAEP), Linda Darling-Hammond (2000) examined the ways in which teacher qualifications are related to student achievement across states. Her findings indicated that the quality of teachers—as measured by whether the teachers were fully certified and had a major in their teaching field—was related to student performance. In fact, measures of teacher preparation and certification were by far the strongest predictors of student achievement in reading and mathematics, both before and after controlling for student poverty and English language proficiency. For example, look at Table 1.1. All the correlations in the first row of this table are positive and significant. This means that the higher the percentage of teachers with full certification and a major in their teaching field, the higher is their students' achievement in math and in reading. All but one of the correlations in the second row are negative and significant. This indicates that the higher the percentage of teachers who are teaching *outside* of their field, the lower is their students' achievement. (Later in the chapter we will look closely at how to interpret these statistics.) Teacher subject matter knowledge and verbal ability are important in student learning, but teacher preparation and qualifications make a difference too (Darling-Hammond & Youngs, 2002). So being a "highly qualified teacher," as defined by NCLB, is a good first step to becoming a good teacher.

In another study, researchers examined how students are affected by having several effective or ineffective teachers in a row (Sanders & Rivers, 1996). They looked at 5th graders in two large metropolitan school systems in Tennessee. Students who had highly effective teachers for 3rd, 4th, and 5th grades scored an average of 83rd percentile on a standardized mathematics achievement test in one district and 96th percentile in the other (99th percentile is the highest possible score). In contrast, students who had the least effective teachers three years in a row averaged 29th percentile in math achievement in one district and 44th percentile in the other—a difference of over 50 percentile points in both cases! Students who had average teachers or a mixture of teachers with low, average, and high effectiveness for the three years had math scores between these extremes. Sanders and Rivers concluded that the best teachers encouraged good-to-excellent gains in achievement for all students, but lower-achieving students were the first to benefit from good teaching. The effects of teaching were cumulative and residual—that is, better teaching in a later grade could make up *in part* for less-effective teaching in earlier grades, but could not erase all the deficits. In fact, one study found that at least 7% of the differences in test score gains for students could be traced to their teachers (Rivkin, Hanushek, & Kain, 2001).

TABLE 1.1

Correlations between Teacher Quality Variables and Student Achievement on the National Assessment of Educational Progress (controlling for student poverty)

	Grade 4 Math, 1992	Grade 4 Math, 1996	Grade 8 Math, 1996	Grade 4 Reading, 1992	Grade 4 Reading, 1994
Percent of teachers well-qualified (with full certification and a major in their field)	.71**	.61**	.67**	.80**	.75**
Percent of teachers out of field (with less than a minor in the field they teach)	–.48*	–.44*	–.42*	–.56*	–.33*

* $p < .05$

** $p < .01$

Source: From "Teacher Quality and Student Achievement: A Review of State Policy Evidence," by L. Darling-Hammond, 2000, *Educational Policy Analysis Archives, 8*, pp. 1–48. http://epaa.asu.edu/epaa/v8n1/. Copyright © Educational Policy Analysis Archives. Adapted with permission of the EPAA.

Effective teachers who establish positive relationships with their students appear to be a powerful force in those students' lives. Students who have problems seem to benefit the most from good teaching. What makes a teacher effective? What is good teaching?

What Is Good Teaching?

WHAT WOULD YOU SAY?

It is your first interview for a teaching position. The principal takes out a pad of paper and a pen, looks intently into your eyes, and says, "Tell me what you admired about your favorite teacher. What makes a good teacher?" What will you say? ■

Educators, psychologists, philosophers, novelists, journalists, filmmakers, mathematicians, scientists, historians, policymakers, and parents, to name only a few groups, have examined this question; there are hundreds of answers. And good teaching is not confined to classrooms—it occurs in homes and hospitals, museums and sales meetings, therapists' offices, and summer camps. In this book, we are primarily concerned with teaching in classrooms, but much of what you will learn applies to other settings as well.

Connect and **Extend** to **PRAXIS II™**

Teacher Professionalism (IV, A2)
Begin your own development by reading educational publications. One widely read periodical is *Education Week*. You can access it online at **www.edweek.com.**

Inside Four Classrooms

To begin our examination of good teaching, let's step inside the classrooms of four outstanding teachers. All the situations that follow are real. The first two teachers worked with my student teachers in local elementary schools. I have chosen them because one of my former colleagues at Rutgers, Carol Weinstein, has written about them in her book on classroom management (Weinstein & Mignano, 2003). The third teacher became an expert at helping students with severe learning difficulties, with the help of a consultant. The last example is a secondary school teacher who has been studied by other educational psychologists.

A Bilingual 1st Grade. There are 25 students in Viviana's class. Most have recently emigrated from the Dominican Republic; the rest come from Nicaragua, Mexico, Puerto Rico, and Honduras. Even though the children speak little or no English when they begin school, by the time they leave in June, Viviana has helped them master the normal 1st-grade curriculum for their district. She accomplishes this by teaching in Spanish early in the year to aid understanding, then gradually introducing English as the students are ready. Viviana does not want her students segregated or labeled as disadvantaged. She encourages them to take pride in their Spanish-speaking heritage and uses every available opportunity to support their developing English proficiency.

Viviana's expectations for her students are high, and she makes sure the students have the resources they need. She provides materials—pencils, scissors, crayons—so no child lacks the means to learn. And she supplies constant encouragement. "Viviana's commitment to her students is evident. . . . With an energy level that is rare, she motivates, prods, instructs, models, praises, and captivates her students. The pace is brisk and Viviana clearly has a flair for the dramatic; she uses music, props, gestures, facial expressions, and shifts in voice tone to communicate the material" (Weinstein & Mignano, 2003, p. 14). To know more about her students each year, she visits their homes. For Viviana, teaching is not just a job; it is a way of life.

Connect and **Extend** to **Other Chapters**

Ken's process writing, student publishing, and journal writing are examples of a "whole language" approach, discussed in Chapter 13. Ken's "Bill of Rights" is an example of an innovative approach to setting class rules, discussed in Chapter 12.

A Suburban 5th Grade. Ken teaches 5th grade in a suburban elementary school in central New Jersey. Students in the class represent a range of racial, ethnic, family income, and language backgrounds. Ken emphasizes "process writing." His students complete first drafts, discuss them with others in the class, revise, edit, and "publish" their work. The students also keep daily journals and often use them to share personal concerns with Ken. They tell him of problems at home, fights, and fears; he always takes the time to respond in writing. Ken also places the study of science in the context of the real world. Students learn about ocean ecosystems by using a software program called *A Field Trip to the Sea* (Sunburst, 1999). For social studies, the class plays two simulation games that focus on history. One is about coming of age in Native American cultures and the other focuses on the colonization of America.

Throughout the year, Ken is very interested in the social and emotional development of his students; he wants them to learn about responsibility and fairness as well as science and social studies. This concern is evident in the way he develops his class rules at the beginning of the year. Rather than specifying dos and don'ts, Ken and his students devise a "Bill of Rights" for the class, describing the rights of the students. These rights cover most of the situations that might need a "rule."

An Inclusive Class. Eliot was bright and articulate. He easily memorized stories as a child, but he could not read by himself. His problems stemmed from severe learning difficulties with auditory and visual integration and long-term visual memory. When he tried to write, everything got jumbled. Dr. Nancy White worked with Eliot's teacher, Mia Russell, to tailor intensive tutoring that specifically focused on Eliot's individual learning patterns and his errors. With his teachers' help, over the next years, Eliot became an expert on his own learning and an independent learner; he knew which strategies he had to use and when to use them. According to Eliot, "Learning that stuff is not fun, but it works!" (Hallahan & Kauffman, 2006, pp. 184–185).

Connect and Extend to the Research

Robert Moses, founder of the Algebra Project at the Martin Luther King School in Cambridge, Massachusetts, teaches students the concept of number and sign through a physical event: They go for a ride on a subway. Choosing one subway stop as a starting point, students relate inbound and outbound to positive and negative numbers. They translate their subway ride into mathematical language by considering both the number of stops and their direction. By giving students such experiences before introducing the formal language of algebra, Moses has made math more enjoyable and accessible. To read more, see Moses, R. P., & Cobb, C. E. Jr. (2002). *Radical equations: Civil rights from Mississippi to the Algebra Project.* Boston: Beacon Press.

An Advanced Math Class. Hilda Borko and Carol Livingston (1989) describe how Randy, an expert secondary school mathematics teacher, worked with his students' confusion to construct a review lesson about strategies for doing integrals. When one student said that a particular section in the book seemed "haphazard," Randy led the class through a process of organizing the material. He asked the class for general statements about useful strategies for doing integrals. He clarified their suggestions, elaborated on some, and helped students improve others. He asked the students to relate their ideas to passages in the text. Even though he accepted all reasonable suggestions, he listed only the key strategies on the board. By the end of the period, the students had transformed the disorganized material from the book into an ordered and useful outline to guide their learning. They also had a better idea about how to read and understand difficult material.

What do you see in these classrooms? The teachers are committed to their students. They must deal with a wide range of student abilities and challenges: different languages, different home situations, and different abilities and disabilities. They must adapt instruction and assessment to students' needs. They must make the most abstract concepts, such as integrals, real and understandable for their particular students. And then there is the challenge of new technologies and techniques. The teachers must use them appropriately to accomplish important goals, not just to entertain the students. The whole time that these experts are navigating through the academic material, they also are taking care of the emotional needs of their students, propping up sagging self-esteem and encouraging responsibility. If we followed these individuals from the first day of class, we would see that they carefully plan and teach the basic procedures for living and learning in their classes. They can efficiently collect and correct homework, regroup students, give directions, distribute materials, collect lunch money, and deal with disruptions—and do all of this while also making a mental note to find out why one of their students is so tired.

So What Is Good Teaching? Is good teaching science or art, teacher-centered lecture or student-centered discovery, the application of general theories or the invention of situation-specific practices? Is a good teacher a good explainer or a good questioner, a "sage on the stage" or a "guide by the side"? These debates have raged for years. In your other education classes, you probably will encounter criticisms of the scientific, teacher-centered, theory-based, lecturing sages. You will be encouraged to be artistic, inventive, student-centered, questioning guides. Is this the right path? Let's see what the arguments are.

One position is that teaching is a theory-based science. Psychologists have spent decades studying how children think and feel, how learning occurs, what influences motivation, and how teaching affects learning. These general and abstract conceptions apply to a wide range of situations. Why should teachers have to reinvent all this knowledge? Other educators believe that the mark of an excellent teacher is not the ability to apply theories, but the artistry of being **reflective**—thoughtful and inventive—about teaching (Schon, 1983). Educators who adopt this view believe teaching "is specific with respect to task, time, place, participants, and content, and that different subjects vary in those specifics" (Leinhardt, 2001, p. 334). Thus, teaching is so complex, according to this view, that it must be invented anew with every new subject and class.

Beware of Either/Or Choices. Most people agree that teachers must be both theoretically knowledgeable and inventive. They must be able to use a range of strategies, and they must also be able to invent new strategies. They must have some basic research-based routines for managing classes, but they must also be willing and able to break from the routine when the situation calls for change. And teachers need both general theories and situation-specific insights. They need "understandings of students in general—patterns common to particular ages, culture, social class, geography, and gender; patterns in typical student conceptions of the subject matter" (Ball, 1997, p. 773) and they also need to know their own students. "Face to face with actual children who are particular ages and gender, culture and class, teachers must see individuals against a backdrop of sociological and psychological generalizations about groups" (p. 773). The theories you encounter in this text should be used as cognitive tools to help you examine, inspect, and interpret the claims you will hear and read throughout your career (Leinhardt, 2001).

Personally, I hope you all become teachers who are both "sages" about your subject and "on your students' sides" wherever you stand.

Viviana, Ken, Mia, and Randy are examples of expert teachers, the focus of much recent research in education and psychology. For another perspective on the question "What is good teaching?" let's examine this research on what expert teachers know.

Expert Knowledge

Expert teachers have elaborate *systems of knowledge* for understanding problems in teaching. For example, when a beginning teacher is faced with students' wrong answers on math or history tests, all of these answers may seem about the same—wrong. But for an expert teacher, wrong answers are part of a rich system of knowledge that could include how to recognize several types of wrong answers, the misunderstanding or lack of information behind each kind of mistake, the best way to reteach and correct the misunderstanding, materials and activities that have worked in the past, and several ways to test whether the reteaching was successful. In addition, expert teachers have clear goals and take individual differences into account when planning for their students. These teachers are reflective practitioners (Floden & Klinzing, 1990; Hogan, Rabinowitz, & Craven, 2003).

What do expert teachers know that allows them to be so successful? Lee Shulman (1987) has studied this question, and he has identified seven areas of professional knowledge. Expert teachers know:

1. The academic subjects they teach—their content knowledge is deep and interconnected.
2. General teaching strategies that apply in all subjects (such as the principles of classroom management, effective teaching, and evaluation that you will discover in this book).
3. The curriculum materials and programs appropriate for their subject and grade level.
4. Subject-specific knowledge for teaching: special ways of teaching certain students and particular concepts, such as the best ways to explain negative numbers to lower-ability students.
5. The characteristics and cultural backgrounds of learners.
6. The settings in which students learn—pairs, small groups, teams, classes, schools, and the community.
7. The goals and purposes of teaching.

Connect and Extend to Other Chapters

Teacher Professionalism (IV, A1)
Growth as a professional relies on becoming a member of a community of practice, and the national organizations listed here have hundreds of affiliations and chapters across the country with regular conferences, conventions, and meetings to advance instruction in their areas. Take a look at their websites to get a feel for their approaches to issues related to professionalism.

- National Council of Teachers of English **(www.ncte.org)**
- International Reading Association **(www.reading.org)**
- National Science Teachers Association **(www.nsta.org)**
- National Council for the Social Studies **(www.ncss.org)**
- National Council of Teachers of Mathematics **(www.nctm.org)**

Reflective Thoughtful and inventive. Reflective teachers think back over situations to analyze what they did and why and to consider how they might improve learning for their students.

Expert teachers Experienced, effective teachers who have developed solutions for common classroom problems. Their knowledge of teaching process and content is extensive and well organized.

Expert teachers not only know the content of the subjects they teach, they also know how to relate this content to the world outside the classroom and how to keep students involved in learning.

A key factor for expert teachers that may not be clear from the above list is the need to know yourself—your biases, strengths, and blind spots as well as your own cultural identity. Only by having a clear sense of yourself can you understand and respect the cultural identity of your students. Jay Dee and Allan Henkin (2002) note that teachers must be willing to explore beyond their own zone of comfort as members of the majority cultural status quo.

This is quite a list. Obviously, one course cannot give you all the information you need to teach. In fact, a whole program of courses won't make you an expert. That takes time and experience. But studying educational psychology can add to your professional knowledge because at the heart of educational psychology is a concern with learning wherever it occurs. To become a good teacher, you will need to know about your *students* (Part 1 of this book), *learning and motivation* (Part 2), and *teaching and assessing* (Part 3).

The Role of Educational Psychology

For as long as educational psychology has existed—about 100 years—there have been debates about what it really is. Some people believe educational psychology is simply knowledge gained from psychology and applied to the activities of the classroom. Others believe it involves applying the methods of psychology to study classroom and school life (Brophy, 2003; Wittrock, 1992). A look at history shows the close connections between educational psychology and teaching.

Some Interesting History

In one sense, educational psychology is very old. Topics Plato and Aristotle discussed—the role of the teacher, the relationship between teacher and student, methods of teaching, the nature and order of learning, the role of affect in learning—are still studied by educational psychologists today. In the 1500s, Juan Luis Vives had some very contemporary thoughts about the value of practice, the need to tap student interests and adapt instruction to individual differences, and the advantages of using self-comparisons rather than competitive social comparisons in evaluating students' work. In the 1700s, Comenius introduced visual aids in books and teaching and proclaimed that understanding, not memorizing, was the goal of teaching (Berliner, 1993). But let's fast forward to the formal study of psychology.

Connect and **Extend** to the **Research**

The Spring 2001 issue of *Educational Psychologist*, 36(2), is devoted to "Educational Psychology: Yesterday, Today, and Tomorrow" with articles about self-regulated learning, classroom management, teacher expectancy effects, program development, and conceptions of learning.

From the beginning, psychology in the United States was linked to teaching. In 1890, William James at Harvard founded the field of psychology in America and developed a lecture series for teachers entitled *Talks to Teachers about Psychology*. These lectures were given in summer schools for teachers around the country and then published in 1899. James's student, G. Stanley Hall, founded the American Psychological Association. His dissertation was about children's understandings of the world; teachers helped him collect data. Hall encouraged teachers to make detailed observations to study their students' development—as his mother had done when she was a teacher. Hall's student, John Dewey, founded the Laboratory School at the University of Chicago and is considered the father of the progressive education movement (Hilgard, 1996).

Another of William James's students, E. L. Thorndike, wrote the first educational psychology text in 1903 and founded the *Journal of Educational Psychology* in 1910. Thorndike began a shift from the classroom to the laboratory to study learning—a shift decried by both James and Hall. Thorndike's view proved to be too narrow as he sought laws of learning in laboratories that could be applied to teaching without actually evaluating their applications in real classrooms—but it still took 50 years to return to the psychological study of learning in classrooms (Hilgard, 1996).

Developments in teaching continued to be closely tied to psychology in the first half of the 20th century. It was not uncommon for psychologists such as Thorndike, Judd, or their students to be both presidents of the American Psychological Association and authors of materials for teaching or assessing school subjects. During this era, educational psychology was the "guiding science of the school" (Cubberly, 1919, p. 755). In the 1940s and 1950s, the study of educational psychology concentrated on individual differences, assessment, and learning behaviors. In the 1960s and 1970s, the focus of research shifted to the study of cognitive development and learning, with attention to how students learn concepts and remember. Recently, the educational psychologists have investigated how culture and social factors affect learning and development (Pressley & Roehrig, 2003).

What is educational psychology today? The view generally accepted is that **educational psychology** is a distinct discipline with its own theories, research methods, problems, and techniques. Both in the past and today, educational psychologists study learning and teaching and, at the same time, strive to improve educational practice (Pintrich, 2000). But even with this long history of interest in teaching and learning, are the findings of educational psychologists really that helpful for teachers? After all, most teaching is just common sense, isn't it? Let's take a few minutes to examine these questions.

Is It Just Common Sense?

In many cases, the principles set forth by educational psychologists—after spending much thought, time, and money—sound pathetically obvious. People are tempted to say, and usually do say, "Everyone knows that!" Consider these examples.

Taking Turns. What method should a teacher use in selecting students to participate in a primary grade reading class?

Common Sense Answer. Teachers should call on students randomly so that everyone will have to follow the lesson carefully. If a teacher were to use the same order every time, the students would know when their turn was coming up.

Answer Based on Research. Years ago, research by Ogden, Brophy, and Evertson (1977) found that the answer to this question is not so simple. In 1st-grade reading classes, for example, going around the circle in order and giving each child a chance to read led to better overall achievement than calling on students randomly. The critical factor in going around the circle may be that each child gets a chance to participate. Without some system for calling on everyone, students can be overlooked or skipped. Research suggests there are better alternatives for teaching reading than going around the circle, but teachers should make sure that everyone has the chance for practice and feedback whatever approach is used (Tierney, Readence, & Dishner, 1990). See Chapter 13 for more on teaching reading.

Educational psychology The discipline concerned with teaching and learning processes; applies the methods and theories of psychology and has its own as well.

Helping Students. When should teachers provide help for lower-achieving students as they do class work?

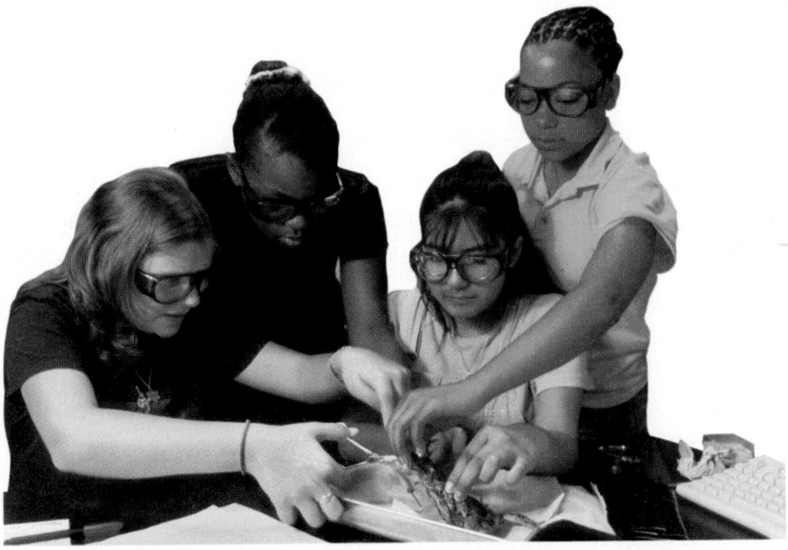

These students are participating in true "hands-on" cooperative learning. Will their knowledge of science improve using this approach? Are there better ways to learn in biology? Educational research should shed light on questions like these.

Common Sense Answer. Teachers should offer help often. After all, these lower-achieving students may not know when they need help or they may be too embarrassed to ask for help.

Answer Based on Research. Sandra Graham (1996) found that when teachers provide help before students ask, the students and others watching are more likely to conclude that the helped student does not have the ability to succeed. The student is more likely to attribute failures to lack of ability instead of lack of effort, so motivation suffers.

Connect and **Extend** to **Other Chapters**

See Chapter 10 for more information on the unintended messages of well-intended teacher actions.

Skipping Grades. Should a school encourage exceptionally bright students to skip grades or to enter college early?

Common Sense Answer. No! Very intelligent students who are a year or two younger than their classmates are likely to be social misfits. They are neither physically nor emotionally ready for dealing with older students and would be miserable in the social situations that are so important in school, especially in the later grades.

Answer Based on Research. Maybe. According to Samuel Kirk and his colleagues (1993), "From early admissions to school to early admissions to college, research studies invariably report that children who have been accelerated have adjusted as well as or better than have children of similar ability who have not been accelerated" (p. 105). Whether acceleration is the best solution for a student depends on many specific individual characteristics, including the intelligence and maturity of the student, and the other available options. For some students, moving quickly through the material and working in advanced courses with older students is a very good idea. See Chapter 4 for more on adapting teaching to students' abilities.

Obvious Answers? Lily Wong (1987) demonstrated that just seeing research results in writing can make them seem obvious. She selected 12 findings from research on teaching; one of them was the "taking turns" result noted above. She presented 6 of the findings in their correct form and 6 in *exactly the opposite form* to both college students and experienced teachers. Both the college students and the teachers rated about half of the *wrong* findings as "obviously" correct. In a follow-up study, another group of subjects was shown the 12 findings and their opposites and was asked to pick which ones were correct. For 8 of the 12 findings, the subjects chose the wrong result more often than the right one.

Connect and **Extend** to the **Research**

Read and discuss the article by Gage, N. L. (1991). The obviousness of social and educational research results. *Educational Researcher, 20*(1), 10–16. *Focus Questions:* What makes findings in educational research seem "obvious"? What is the danger in this kind of thinking?

You may have thought that educational psychologists spend their time discovering the obvious. The preceding examples point out the danger of this kind of thinking. When a principle is stated in simple terms, it can sound simplistic. A similar phenomenon takes place when we see a gifted dancer or athlete perform; the well-trained performer makes it look easy. But we see only the results of the training, not all the work that went into mastering the individual movements. And bear in mind that any research finding—or its opposite—may sound like common sense. The issue is not what *sounds* sensible, but what is demonstrated when the principle is put to the test (Gage, 1991).

Using Research to Understand and Improve Learning

STOP | THINK | WRITE Quickly, list all the different research methods you can name. ■

Conducting research to test possible relationships is one of two major tasks of educational psychology. The other is combining the results of various studies into theories that attempt to present a unified view of such things as teaching, learning, and development.

Descriptive studies Studies that collect detailed information about specific situations, often using observation, surveys, interviews, recordings, or a combination of these methods.

Ethnography A descriptive approach to research that focuses on life within a group and tries to understand the meaning of events to the people involved.

Descriptive Studies. Educational psychologists design and conduct many different kinds of research studies. Some of these are "descriptive," that is, their purpose is simply to describe events in a particular class or several classes. Reports of **descriptive studies** often include survey results, interview responses, samples of actual classroom dialogue, or audio and video records of the class activities.

One descriptive approach, classroom **ethnography**, is borrowed from anthropology. Ethnographic methods involve studying the naturally occurring events in the life of a group and trying to understand the meaning of these events to the people involved. For example, the descriptions of Randy, the expert high school mathematics teacher in the opening pages of this chapter, were taken from an ethnographic study by Borko and Livingston (1989). The researchers made detailed observations in the teachers' classes and analyzed these observations, along with audio recordings and information from interviews with the teachers, in order to describe differences between novice and expert teachers.

In some descriptive studies, the researcher uses **participant observation** and works within the class or school to understand the actions from the perspectives of the teacher and the students. Researchers also employ **case studies.** A case study investigates in depth how a teacher plans courses, for example, or how a student tries to learn specific material.

Correlation Studies. Often, the results of descriptive studies include reports of correlations. We will take a minute to examine this concept, because you need knowledge of correlations to fully understand Table 1.1 and you will encounter many other correlations in the coming chapters. A correlation is a number that indicates both the strength and the direction of a relationship between two events or measurements. **Correlations** range from 1.00 to –1.00. The closer the correlation is to either 1.00 or –1.00, the stronger the relationship. For example, the correlation between height and weight is about .70 (a strong relationship); the correlation between height and number of languages spoken is about .00 (no relationship at all).

The sign of the correlation tells the direction of the relationship. A **positive correlation** indicates that the two factors increase or decrease together. As one gets larger, so does the other. Height and weight are positively correlated because greater height tends to be associated with greater weight. As you saw in Table 1.1, the correlation between the percent of teachers with full teaching credentials and students' math achievement is positive (as the percent of fully credentialed teachers increases, student math achievement increases as well). A **negative correlation** means that increases in one factor are related to decreases in the other. Table 1.1 indicated that as the number of teachers without either a major or a minor in math increases, student math achievement decreases.

It is important to note that correlations do not prove cause and effect (see Figure 1.1). Height and weight are correlated—taller people tend to weigh more than shorter people. But gaining weight obviously does not cause you to grow taller. Knowing a person's weight simply allows you to make a general prediction about that person's height. Educational psychologists identify correlations so they can make predictions about important events in the classroom.

FIGURE 1.1

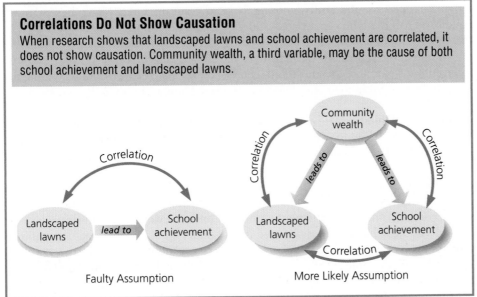

Correlations Do Not Show Causation

When research shows that landscaped lawns and school achievement are correlated, it does not show causation. Community wealth, a third variable, may be the cause of both school achievement and landscaped lawns.

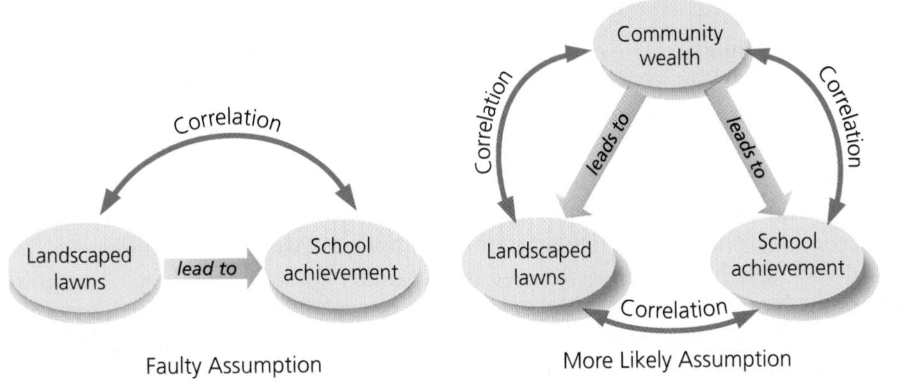

Connect and Extend to Real Life

Perfect positive (1.0) correlation: the radius of a circle and its circumference. Perfect negative (–1.0) correlation: the number of minutes of daylight and the number of minutes of dark each day. Less than perfect positive correlation: the cost of a car and the cost of insuring it. Less than perfect negative correlation: the cost of a theater ticket and the distance from the stage. Zero correlation: the population of India and the winning percentage of the New York Yankees.

Participant observation A method for conducting descriptive research in which the researcher becomes a participant in the situation in order to better understand life in that group.

Case study Intensive study of one person or one situation.

Correlations Statistical descriptions of how closely two variables are related.

Positive correlation A relationship between two variables in which the two increase or decrease together. Example: calorie intake and weight gain.

Negative correlation A relationship between two variables in which a high value on one is associated with a low value on the other. Example: height and distance from top of head to the ceiling.

Experimental Studies. A second type of research—**experimentation**—allows educational psychologists to go beyond predictions and actually study cause and effect. Instead of just observing and describing an existing situation, the investigators introduce changes and note the results. First, a number of comparable groups of participants are created. In psychological research, the term **participants** (also called **subjects**) generally refers to the people being studied—such as teachers or 8th graders. One common way to make sure that groups of participants are essentially the same is to assign each person to a group using a random procedure. **Random** means each participant has an equal chance of being in any group.

In one or more of these groups, the experimenters change some aspect of the situation to see if this change or "treatment" has an expected effect. The results in each group are then compared. Usually, statistical tests are conducted. When differences are described as **statistically significant,** it means that they probably did not happen simply by chance. Look at Table 1.1 again. The $p < .05$ means that these results could happen by chance less than 5 times out of 100, and $p < .01$ means less than 1 time in 100. A number of the studies we will examine attempt to identify cause-and-effect relationships by asking questions such as this: If teachers ignore students who are out of their seats without permission and praise students who are working hard at their desks (cause), will students spend more time working at their desks (effect)?

In many cases, descriptive and experimental research occur together. The study about "taking turns" by Ogden, Brophy, and Evertson (1977) described at the beginning of this section is a good example. In order to answer questions about the relationship between how students are selected to read in a primary-grade class and their achievement in reading, these investigators first observed students and teachers in a number of classrooms and then measured the reading achievement of the students. They found that having students read in a predictable order was associated, or correlated, with gains in reading scores. With a simple correlation such as this, however, the researchers could not be sure that the strategy was actually causing the effect. In the second part of the study, Ogden and her colleagues asked several teachers to call on each student in turn. They then compared reading achievement in these groups with achievement in groups where teachers used other strategies. This second part of the research was thus an experimental study—specifically, a *field experiment* because it took place in a real classroom setting and not a laboratory.

Connect and Extend to What You Know

Are the following studies descriptive (D) or experimental (E)?

1. Researchers observe teachers of classes that have high achievement in order to determine how these teachers are alike.
2. Teachers give three groups of impulsive children different types of training to determine which type of training is most effective in reducing impulsivity.
3. Researchers administer IQ tests to a group of boys and girls to determine if there is a relationship between sex and verbal ability.
4. Teachers instruct two similar groups of math students using two different methods to determine which method leads to higher scores on a math achievement test.

Answers: 1. D 2. E 3. D 4. E

Single-Subject Experimental Designs. The goal of **single-subject experimental studies** is to determine the effects of a therapy or teaching method, or other intervention. One common approach is to observe the individual for a baseline period (A) and assess the behavior of interest; try an intervention (B) and note the results; then remove the intervention and go back to baseline conditions (A); and finally reinstate the intervention (B). This form of single-subject design is called an ABAB experiment. For example, a teacher might record how much students are out of their seats without permission during a week-long baseline (A), and then try ignoring those who are up, but praising those who are seated and recording how many are wandering out of their seats for the week (B). Next, the teacher returns to baseline conditions (A) and records results, then reinstates the praise-and-ignore strategy (B) (Landrum & Kauffman, 2006). Years ago, when this very intervention was tested, the praise-and-ignore strategy proved effective in increasing the time students spent in their seats (Madsen, Becker, Thomas, Koser, & Plager, 1968).

Microgenetic Studies. The goal of **microgenetic** research is to intensively study cognitive processes in the midst of change—as the change is actually happening. For example, researchers might analyze how children learn a particular strategy for adding two-digit numbers over the course of several weeks. The microgenetic approach has three basic characteristics: (a) researchers observe the entire period of the change—from when it starts to the time it is relatively stable; (b) many observations are made, often using videotape recordings, interviews, and transcriptions of the exact words of the individuals being studied; (c) the behavior that is observed is "put under a microscope," that is, examined moment by moment or trial by trial. The goal is to explain the underlying mechanisms of change—for example, what new knowledge or skills are developing to allow change to take place (Siegler & Crowley, 1991). This kind of research is expensive and time-consuming, so often only one or a few children are studied.

Experimentation Research method in which variables are manipulated and the effects recorded.

Participants/Subjects People or animals studied.

Random Without any definite pattern; following no rule.

Statistically significant Not likely to be a chance occurrence.

Single-subject experimental studies Systematic interventions to study effects with one person, often by applying and then withdrawing a treatment.

Microgenetic studies Detailed observation and analysis of changes in a cognitive process as the process unfolds over a several day or week period of time.

The Role of Time in Research. Another distinction is useful in understanding research—a distinction based on time. Many things that psychologists want to study, such as cognitive development, happen over several months or years. Ideally, researchers would study the development by observing their subjects over many years as changes occur. These are called *longitudinal* studies. They are informative, but time-consuming, expensive, and not always practical—keeping up with subjects over years as they grow up and move can be impossible. As a consequence, much research is *cross-sectional*, focusing on groups of children at different ages. For example, to study how children's conceptions of "alive" change from ages 3 to 16, researchers can interview children of several different ages, rather than following the same children for 14 years.

Teachers as Researchers. Research also can be a way to improve teaching in one classroom or one school. The same kind of careful observation, intervention, data gathering, and analysis that occurs in large research projects can be applied in any classroom to answer questions such as "Which writing prompts seem to encourage the best descriptive writing in my class?" "When does Kenyon seem to have the greatest difficulty concentrating on academic tasks?" "Would assigning task roles in science groups lead to more equitable participation of girls and boys in the work?" This kind of problem-solving investigation is called **action research.** By focusing on a specific problem and making careful observations, teachers can learn a great deal about both their teaching and their students.

Connect and Extend to the Research

The Summer 2000 issue of *Educational Psychologist*, 35(3), is devoted to "School Reform and Research in Educational Psychology" with articles about teaching science and mathematics, as well as articles on teacher preparation and professional development.

What Is Scientifically Based Research?

Since 2002, there has been a great debate about the value of research in education. One of the requirements of the landmark No Child Left Behind Act passed in that year was that educational programs and practices receiving federal money had to be consistent with "scientifically based research." The lawmakers believed that scientifically based research produces reliable and valid knowledge because the research is rigorous, systematic, and objective. In fact, the term, "scientifically based research" appeared 110 times in the bill. Specifically, the No Child Left Behind (NCLB) Act stated that scientifically based research:

- Systematically uses observation or experiment to gather valid and reliable data
- Involves rigorous and appropriate procedures for analyzing the data
- Is evaluated using experimental or quasi-experimental designs, preferably with random assignment of participants to conditions
- Makes sure that experimental studies are carefully explained so other researchers can replicate the studies or build systematically on their findings
- Has been through a rigorous, objective, scientific review by a journal or a panel of independent experts

This description of scientifically based research fits the experimental approach described above better than other methods such as ethnographic research or case studies. Because schools are required to base their programs on scientifically based research as defined in the NCLB Act, there is continuing debate about what this means, as you will see in the *Point/Counterpoint* when you turn this page.

Theories for Teaching

The major goal of educational psychology is to understand teaching and learning; research is a primary tool. Reaching this goal is a slow process. There are very few landmark studies that answer a question once and for all. Human beings are too complicated. Instead, research in educational psychology examines limited aspects of a situation—perhaps a few variables at a time or life in one or two classrooms. If enough studies are completed in a certain area and findings repeatedly point to the same conclusions, we eventually arrive at a **principle.** This is the term for an established relationship between two or more factors—between a certain teaching strategy, for example, and student achievement.

Another tool for building a better understanding of the teaching and learning processes is theory. The common sense notion of theory (as in "Oh well, it was only a

Action research Systematic observations or tests of methods conducted by teachers or schools to improve teaching and learning for their students.

Principle Established relationship between factors.

Point/Counterpoint

What Kind of Research Should Guide Education?

POINT Research should be scientific; educational reforms should be based on solid evidence.

According to Robert Slavin, "Education is on the brink of a scientific revolution that has the potential to profoundly transform policy, practice, and research" (Slavin, 2002, p. 15), He goes on to describe several educational reforms from the federal government that will provide money for programs, but only if they are based on scientific research. Included is the No Child Left Behind legislation of 2002. The best example of this kind of research according to Grover Whitehurst, the director or the U.S. Office of Educational Research and Improvement, is randomized experiments. Slavin paints a bright future for educational reform guided by scientifically based research:

> *It is possible that these policy reforms could set in motion a process of research and development on programs and practices affecting children everywhere. This process could create the kind of progressive, systematic improvement over time that has characterized successful parts of our economy and society throughout the 20th century, in fields such as medicine, agriculture, transportation, and technology. In each of these fields, processes of development, rigorous evaluation, and dissemination have produced a pace of innovation and improvement that is unprecedented in history. . . . These innovations have transformed the world. Yet education has failed to embrace this dynamic, and as a result, education moves from fad to fad. Educational practice does change over time, but the change process more resembles the pendulum swings of taste characteristic of art or fashion (think hemlines) rather than the progressive improvements characteristic of science and technology. (p. 16)*

The major reason for extraordinary advances in medicine and agriculture, according to Slavin, is that these fields base their practices on scientific evidence. Randomized clinical trials and replicated experiments are the sources of the evidence.

COUNTERPOINT Experiments are not the only or even the best source of evidence.

David Olson (2004) disagrees strongly with Slavin's position. He claims that we cannot use medicine as an analogy to education. "Treatments" in education are much more complex and unpredictable than administering one drug or another in medicine. And every educational program is changed by classroom conditions and the way it is implemented. Patti Lather, a colleague of mine at Ohio State says, "In improving the quality of practice, complexity and the messiness of practice-in-context cannot be fantasized away. To try to do so yields impoverishment rather than improvement. That loss is being borne by the children, teachers, and administrators in our schools" (2004, p. 30). David Berliner (2002) makes a similar point:

> *Doing science and implementing scientific findings are so difficult in education because humans in schools are embedded in complex and changing networks of social interaction. The participants in those networks have variable power to affect each other from day to day, and the ordinary events of life (a sick child, a messy divorce, a passionate love affair, migraine headaches, hot flashes, a birthday party, alcohol abuse, a new principal, a new child in the classroom, rain that keeps the children from a recess outside the school building) all affect doing science in school settings by limiting the generalizability of educational research findings. Compared to designing bridges and circuits or splitting either atoms or genes, the science to help change schools and classrooms is harder to do because context cannot be controlled.*

Berliner concludes that a complex problem like education needs a whole range of methods for study—"ethnographic research is crucial, as are case studies, survey research, time series, design experiments, action research, and other means to collect reliable evidence for engaging in unfettered argument about education issues. A single method is not what the government should be promoting for educational researchers" (Berliner, 2002, p. 20).

WHAT DO YOU THINK?
Vote online at **www.mylabschool.com**

theory") is "a guess or hunch." But the scientific meaning of theory is quite different. "A **theory** in science is an interrelated set of concepts that is used to explain a body of data and to make predictions about the results of future experiments" (Stanovich, 1992, p. 21). Given a number of established principles, educational psychologists have developed explanations for the relationships among many variables and even whole systems of relationships. There are theories to explain how language develops, how differences in intelligence occur, and, as noted earlier, how people learn.

Theory Integrated statement of principles that attempts to explain a phenomenon and make predictions.

Few theories explain and predict perfectly. In this book, you will see many examples of educational psychologists taking different theoretical positions and disagreeing on the overall explanations of such issues as learning and motivation. Because no one theory offers all the answers, it makes sense to consider what each has to offer.

So why, you may ask, is it necessary to deal with theories? Why not just stick to principles? The answer is that both are useful. Principles of classroom management, for example, will give you help with specific problems. A good *theory* of classroom management, on the other hand, will give you a new way of thinking about discipline problems; it will give you cognitive tools for creating solutions to many different problems and for predicting what might work in new situations. A major goal of this book is to provide you with the best and the most useful theories for teaching—those that have solid evidence behind them. Although you may prefer some theories to others, consider them all as ways of understanding the challenges teachers face.

Becoming a Good Beginning Teacher

STOP | THINK | WRITE Imagine walking into your first day of teaching. List the concerns, fears, and worries you have. What assets do you bring to the job? ■

Concerns. Beginning teachers everywhere share many concerns, including maintaining classroom discipline, motivating students, accommodating differences among students, evaluating student work, dealing with parents, and getting along with other teachers (Conway & Clark, 2003; Veenman, 1984). Many teachers also experience what has been called "reality shock" when they take their first job because they really cannot ease into their responsibilities. On the first day of their first job, beginning teachers face the same tasks as teachers with years of experience. Student teaching, while a critical element, does not really prepare prospective teachers for starting off a school year with a new class. If you listed any of these concerns in the *Stop/Think/Write* box above, you shouldn't be troubled. They come with the job of being a beginning teacher (Borko & Putnam, 1996; Cooke & Pang, 1991). But even with these concerns, you don't have to wait for years to become a good teacher. I have worked with many students who are excellent, even during their practice teaching experiences. Here is what Esme Codell, a gifted 5th-grade teacher in an inner-city Chicago school, remembered about her first year of teaching:

> I feel like we did a lot of interesting things this year. Some of my favorites: When learning about electricity, we made light-up quiz games. When learning about light, we put on shadow-puppet shows. When learning about medieval history, we built an accurate castle, then decorated it with colored marshmallows and put it in our fairy tale book display. When we learned about air, we had a bubble festival. When learning about Asia, we made sushi. We videotaped commercials to promote our favorite books. We had a book character masquerade party. The kids had checking accounts in a classroom economy. We had a cereal box supermarket, and the kids learned to make change. My kids write the best descriptive compositions. They have international pen pals. They illustrated poetry anthologies. They read and wrote treasure maps. They know all the dances from the 60s. (Codell, 2001, pp. 177–178)

With experience, hard work, and good support, most teachers have more time to experiment with new methods or materials. Finally, as confidence grows, seasoned teachers can focus on the *students'* needs. At this advanced stage, teachers judge their success by the successes of their students (Fuller, 1969; Pigge & Marso, 1997). Or as Esme's mentor teacher once told her, "The difference between a beginning teacher and an experienced one is that the beginning teacher asks, 'How am I doing?' and the experienced teacher asks, 'How are the children doing?'" (Codell, 2001, p. 191).

Being a Good Beginner. Becoming an expert teacher takes time and experience, but you can start now by becoming a good beginner. You can develop a repertoire of effective principles and practices for your first years of teaching so that some activities quickly become automatic. You can also develop the habit of questioning and analyzing these accepted practices and your own teaching so you can solve new problems when they arise. You can learn to look behind the effective techniques identified in research to ask: Why

Teaching is one of the few professions in which a new teacher must assume all of the responsibilities of an experienced "pro" during the first week on the job. Veteran teachers can be an excellent source of information and support during these early weeks.

did this approach work with these students? What else might be as good or better? The answers to these questions and your ability to analyze the situations are much more important than the specific techniques themselves. As you ask and answer questions, you will be refining your personal theories of teaching.

My goal in writing this book is to help you become an excellent beginning teacher, one who can both apply and improve many techniques. Even more important, I hope this book will cause you to think about students and teaching in new ways, so you will have the foundation for becoming an expert as you gain experience. Table 1.2 shows some advice a 1st-grade class gave to their student teacher: It looks like the students know about good teaching too.

Diversity and Convergences in Educational Psychology

The last section of every chapter in this book will be "Diversity and Convergences." This section will examine the topic under discussion in relation to student differences in race, ethnicity, family income, disabilities, or gender. Then, we will consider the convergences—the principles or practices that hold well for all students. This first chapter has been about teaching and educational psychology.

TABLE 1.2

Advice for Student Teachers from Their Students

The students in Ms. Amato's elementary school class gave this advice as a gift to their student teacher on her last day.

1. Teach us as much as you can.
2. Give us homework.
3. Help us when we have problems with our work.
4. Help us to do the right thing.
5. Help us make a family in school.
6. Read books to us.
7. Teach us to read.
8. Help us write about faraway places.
9. Give us lots of compliments, like "Oh, that's so beautiful."
10. Smile at us.
11. Take us for walks and on trips.
12. Respect us.
13. Help us get our education.

Source: From *Affirming Diversity: The Sociopolitical Context of Multicultural Education, 4e* by Sonia Neito. Published by Allyn and Bacon, Boston, MA. Copyright © 2004 by Pearson Education. Reprinted by permission of the publishers.

Diversity

Trying to address differences in academic achievement for different groups of students was one of the motivations behind the No Child Left Behind Act. NCLB specifies that Adequate Yearly Progress goals have to be set and tested specifically for racial and ethnic minority students, students with disabilities, students whose first language is not English, and students from low-income homes. In this chapter, we also examined the diversity of research methods in educational psychology—from descriptive studies to experimental studies to teachers' action research.

Convergences

I can see two convergences in this chapter. No matter what educators think of NCLB or what they believe about good teaching, all agree that many children have been left behind in the past and this must stop. I think educational psychology has much to offer teachers who want to see all students achieve. No matter which research methods are used, education and psychology have had a long relationship. Educational psychology stands with a foot in two worlds: scholarship and practice. Merle Wittrock (1992, p. 138) sums it up well, saying that educational psychology focuses on "the psychological study of the everyday problems of education, from which one derives principles, models, theories, teaching procedures, and practical methods of instruction and evaluation, as well as research methods, statistical analyses, and measurement and assessment procedures appropriate for studying the thinking and affective processes of learners and the socially and culturally complex processes of schools." That about covers it.

SUMMARY TABLE

Teaching After *No Child Left Behind* (p. 2)

What is NCLB? The No Child Left Behind Act of 2002 requires standardized achievement testing in reading and mathematics every year for all students in grades 3 through 8 and once more in high school. Based on these test scores, schools are judged to determine if their students are making Adequate Yearly Progress (AYP) toward becoming proficient in the subjects tested. States have some say in defining "proficiency" and in setting AYP standards. Regardless of how states define these standards, the NCLB Act requires that all students in the schools must reach proficiency by the end of the 2013–2014 school year.

What is a highly qualified teacher as defined by NCLB? New teachers must be fully certified, have a bachelor's degree, and demonstrate their knowledge and skills in the subjects they are teaching either by having taken sufficient academic coursework in their field or by passing a state test. Veteran teachers can demonstrate qualifications by taking a test.

Do Teachers Make a Difference? (pp. 2–5)

What evidence is there that teachers make a difference? Three studies speak to the power of teachers in the lives of students. The first found that the quality of the teacher–student relationship in kindergarten predicted several aspects of school success through the 8th grade. The second study of thousands of students and teachers in all 50 of the United States found that teacher quality was the strongest predictor of student achievement in mathematics and reading. The final study examined math achievement for students in two large school districts as they moved through 3rd, 4th, and 5th grades. Again, the quality of the teacher made a difference—students who had three high-quality teachers in a row were way ahead of students who spent one or more years with less competent teachers.

What Is Good Teaching? (pp. 5–8)

What do expert teachers know? It takes time and experience to become an expert teacher. These teachers have a rich store of well-organized knowledge about the many specific situations of teaching. This includes knowledge about the subjects they teach, their students, general teaching strategies, subject-specific ways of teaching, settings for learning, curriculum materials, and the goals of education.

Reflective Thoughtful and inventive. Reflective teachers think back over situations to analyze what they did and why and to consider how they might improve learning for their students.

Expert teachers Experienced, effective teachers who have developed solutions for common classroom problems. Their knowledge of teaching process and content is extensive and well organized.

The Role of Educational Psychology (pp. 8–16)

What is educational psychology? The goals of educational psychology are to understand and to improve the teaching and learning processes. Educational psychologists develop knowledge and methods; they also use the knowledge and methods of psychology and other related disciplines to study learning and teaching in everyday situations.

What are descriptive studies? Reports of descriptive studies often include survey results, interview responses, samples of actual classroom dialogue, or records of the class activities. Ethnographic methods involve studying the naturally occurring events in the life of a group and trying to understand the meaning of these events to the people involved. A case study investigates in depth how a teacher plans courses, for example, or how a student tries to learn specific material.

What are correlations and experimental studies? A correlation is a number that indicates both the strength and the direction of a relationship between two events or measurements. The closer the correlation is to either 1.00 or –1.00, the stronger the relationship. Experimental studies can indicate cause-and-effect relationships and should help teachers implement useful changes. Instead of just observing and describing an existing situation, the investigators introduce changes and note the results.

What are single-subject and microgenetic studies? In single-subject experimental designs, researchers examine the effects of treatments on one person, often by using a baseline/intervention/baseline/intervention or ABAB approach. Microgenetic studies take many detailed observations of subjects to track the progression of change from the very beginning until a process becomes stable.

What is action research? When teachers or schools make systematic observations or test out methods to improve teaching and learning for their students, they are conducting action research.

Distinguish between principles and theories. A principle is an established relationship between two or more factors—between a certain teaching strategy, for example, and student achievement. A theory is an interrelated set of concepts that is used to explain a body of data and to make predictions. The principles from research offer a number of possible answers to specific problems, and the theories offer perspectives for analyzing almost any situation that may arise.

What are the concerns of beginning teachers? Learning to teach is a gradual process. The concerns and problems of teachers change as they progress. During the beginning years, attention tends to be focused on maintaining discipline, motivating students, evaluating students' work, and dealing with parents. Even with these concerns, many beginning teachers bring creativity and energy to their teaching and improve every year. The more experienced teacher can move on to concerns about professional growth and effectiveness with a wide range of students.

Educational psychology The discipline concerned with teaching and learning processes; applies the methods and theories of psychology and has its own as well.

Descriptive studies Studies that collect detailed information about specific situations, often using observation, surveys, interviews, recordings, or a combination of these methods.

Ethnography A descriptive approach to research that focuses on life within a group and tries to understand the meaning of events to the people involved.

Participant observation A method for conducting descriptive research in which the researcher becomes a participant in the situation in order to better understand life in that group.

Case study Intensive study of one person or one situation.

Correlations Statistical descriptions of how closely two variables are related.

Positive correlation A relationship between two variables in which the two increase or decrease together. Example: calorie intake and weight gain.

Negative correlation A relationship between two variables in which a high value on one is associated with a low value on the other. Example: height and distance from top of head to the ceiling.

Experimentation Research method in which variables are manipulated and the effects recorded.

Participants/Subjects People or animals studied.

Random Without any definite pattern; following no rule.

Statistically significant Not likely to be a chance occurrence.

Single-subject experimental studies Systematic interventions to study effects with one person, often by applying and then withdrawing a treatment.

Microgenetic studies Detailed observation and analysis of changes in a cognitive process as the process unfolds over a several day or week period of time.

Action research Systematic observations or tests of methods conducted by teachers or schools to improve teaching and learning for their students.

Principle Established relationship between factors.

Theory Integrated statement of principles that attempts to explain a phenomenon and make predictions.

Teachers' Casebook: Connections to PRAXIS II™

To receive your teaching license, you will have to take some kind of examination, the PRAXIS II™ in almost 40 states or a similar test developed by your state. The bases for all these tests are the professional standards created by the Interstate New Teacher Assessment and Support Consortium (INTASC). Many of these standards are reflected in this book (see the Handbook (p. 590) for all the standards connections).

Case analysis is part of many licensure exams, so this text gives you practice and expert ideas about how to apply educational psychology to analyze cases. The case introducing this chapter asks you to think about excellent teaching. Excellent teachers are reflective—they critically examine every aspect of their teaching experiences, display inventiveness in their practices, and continually work to upgrade their knowledge and skills. As a junior member of the committee to recognize "excellence in teaching," you might find it useful for your work as a committee member and your own professional development to learn how nominees for the "excellence in teaching" award use reflection. Praxis II™ recognizes the role of reflective practice in the development of excellent teachers. Reflective practice includes contact with colleagues, membership in professional associations, and review of professional literature as resources, as well as the ability to understand the current views, significant debates, and research about effective teaching practices.

What Would They Do?

Here is how some practicing teachers responded to the teaching situation presented at the beginning of this chapter about establishing a "Teaching Excellence Award."

Thomas Naismith **Science Teacher, Grades 7–12,**
Slocum Independent School District, Elkhart, Texas

To be fair in selecting recipients of the "Excellence in Teaching" awards, the process must be as objective as possible. Prior to attending the first committee meeting, the beginning teacher should give serious thought to and consult with others concerning items that should be included on a sample evaluation checklist. The items on the checklist might be weighted as to importance, and could include such things as: standardized test scores by the teacher's students, productive participation by the teacher on various school and parent teacher committees, etc. Copies of the checklist should be provided to the other members of the committee for their consideration and input. The other members of the committee should appreciate the preparation of their new colleague and the fact that it is going to save them some time.

Madya Ayala **High School Teacher of Preperatoria Eugenio Garza Lagüera,** *Campus Garza Sada, Monterrey, N.L. Mexico*

The first thing that I would propose is to establish a set of selection criteria. We know that all teachers have strengths and weaknesses and what works the best for each of us. The set of evaluation criteria could change from time to time depending on international, national, and local needs and values. These factors would influence the interpretation of a teacher's psychological, pedagogical, and epistemological strengths as well.

Length of experience should not be a factor, only excellence in performance as a teacher. The main objective should be to make teachers aware of what is expected of them and to set the best examples.

Katie Churchill **Third Grade Teacher,**
Oriole Parke Elementary School, Chicago, Illinois

I would prepare for the meeting by researching how other schools have chosen recipients for similar awards in the past. I would recommend that we select different categories of "excellence" to decide who will be nominated for the awards. I would suggest that we choose recipients fairly, based on their teaching abilities. Finally, I would recommend that we have student input regarding which teachers should receive these awards.

Carey Perkson **Second Grade Teacher,**
Brown School, Natick, Massachusetts

I would have a discussion with the experienced teachers before our committee meeting to pinpoint what qualifications we are looking for in our candidates. Establishing a definition of "excellence in teaching" and constructing a list of recommendations should be a priority of the committee to ensure that all committee members are looking for the same qualifications. By constructing a list of key qualities and accomplishments for each nominee, we would be able to assess who would be the most qualified for the award.

Aimee Fredette **Second Grade Teacher,**
Fisher Elementary School, Walpole, Massachusetts

There are many facets to being an effective teacher, the foremost being that the teacher will reach all children no matter what it takes. Effective teachers will modify curriculum and instruction to allow all ability levels to feel success and to foster a learning environment that builds the self-esteem of their students. This environment and confidence will encourage children to succeed at their own attempts to learn.

Effective teachers, regardless of philosophy, will excite and spark the children's interest. This will help the children to develop their own motivation for learning. I also feel that teachers should fully support the placement of all children into their classroom, regardless of abilities. To be effective, teachers will appropriately modify and implement assignments to meet those levels. A positive learning experience is created with a cooperative relationship among teachers, students, and home.

CHAPTER 2

Cognitive Development and Language

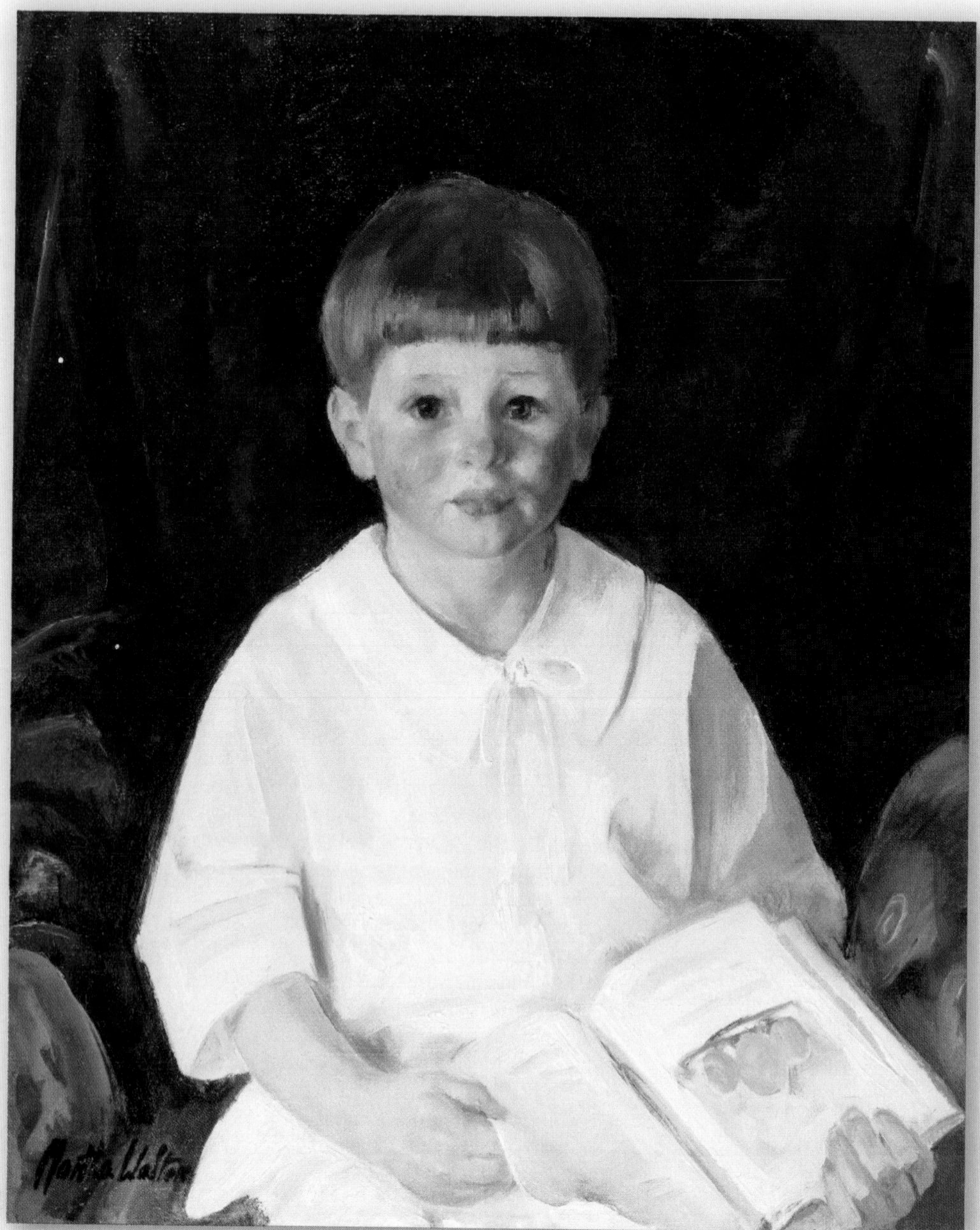

Teachers' Casebook: What Would You Do? 21

A Definition of Development 22

General Principles of Development 22

The Brain and Cognitive Development 22

Piaget's Theory of Cognitive Development 26

Influences on Development 27

Basic Tendencies in Thinking 28

Four Stages of Cognitive Development 29

Information-Processing and Neo-Piagetian Views of Cognitive Development 36

Some Limitations of Piaget's Theory 38

Vygotsky's Sociocultural Perspective 39

The Social Sources of Individual Thinking 39

Cultural Tools and Cognitive Development 41

The Role of Language and Private Speech 42

The Zone of Proximal Development 44

The Role of Learning and Development 44

Limitations of Vygotsky's Theory 45

Implications of Piaget's and Vygotsky's Theories for Teachers 46

Piaget: What Can We Learn? 46

Vygotsky: What Can We Learn? 48

Reaching Every Student: Using the Tools of the Culture 50

The Development of Language 51

Diversity in Language: Dual Language Development 52

Language Development in the School Years 54

Diversity and Convergence in Cognitive Development 56

Diversity 56

Convergences 57

Summary Table 57

Teachers' Casebook: Connections to PRAXIS II™/ What Would They Do? 61

What Would You Do?

Teachers' Casebook

The district curriculum guide calls for a unit on poetry, including lessons on *symbolism* in poems. You are concerned that many of your 4th-grade students may not be ready to understand this abstract concept. To test the waters, you ask a few students what a symbol is.

"It's sorta like a big metal thing that you bang together." Tracy waves her hands like a drum major.

"Yeah," Sean adds, "My sister plays one in the high school band."

You realize they are on the wrong track here, so you try again. "I was thinking of a different kind of symbol, like a ring as a symbol of marriage or a heart as a symbol of love, or . . . "

You are met with blank stares.

Trevor ventures, "You mean like the Olympic torch?"

"And what does that symbolize, Trevor?" you ask.

"Like I said, a torch." Trevor wonders how you could be so dense.

Critical Thinking

- What do these students' reactions tell you about children's thinking?
- How would you approach this unit?
- What more would you do to "listen" to your students' thinking so you could match your teaching to their level of thinking?
- How would you give your students concrete experience with symbolism?
- How will you decide if the students are not developmentally ready for this material?

Collaboration

With 3 or 4 other students in your educational psychology class, plan a lesson about symbolism in poetry that would be appropriate for students in this class. Pair up with another group and teach your lesson.

What is going on with Trevor? In this chapter, you will find out. We begin with a discussion of the general principles of human development and take a brief look at the human brain. Then we will examine the ideas of two of the most influential cognitive developmental theorists, Jean Piaget and Lev Vygotsky. Piaget's ideas have implications for teachers about what their students can learn and when they are ready to learn it. We will consider criticisms of his ideas as well. The work of Lev Vygotsky, a Russian psychologist, is becoming more and more influential. His theory highlights the important role teachers and parents play in the cognitive development of the child. Finally, we will explore language development and discuss the role of the school in developing and enriching language skills.

By the time you have completed this chapter, you should be able to answer these questions:

- What are some general principles of human development?
- How does children's thinking differ at each of the four stages of development Piaget described?
- What are the similarities and differences between Piaget's and Vygotsky's ideas about cognitive development?
- What are the implications of Piaget's and Vygotsky's theories for teaching students of different ages?
- How does language usually develop during the school years, and what happens if children are learning two languages at once?

FACING PAGE *Young Boy in White Reading Book*, 1918, Martha Walter. Oil on canvas. © David David Gallery/SuperStock.

A Definition of Development

The term **development** in its most general psychological sense refers to certain changes that occur in human beings (or animals) between conception and death. The term is not applied to all changes, but rather to those that appear in orderly ways and remain for a reasonably long period of time. A temporary change caused by a brief illness, for example, is not considered a part of development. Psychologists also make a value judgment in determining which changes qualify as development. The changes—at least those that occur early in life—are generally assumed to be for the better and to result in behavior that is more adaptive, more organized, more effective, and more complex (Mussen, Conger, & Kagan, 1984).

Connect and **Extend** to the **Research**

See the Autumn 2004 issue of *Theory Into Practice* on Developmental Psychology: Implications for Teaching (Vol. 43, No. 4). Guest Editor: Chris Andersen.

Human development can be divided into a number of different aspects. **Physical development,** as you might guess, deals with changes in the body. **Personal development** is the term generally used for changes in an individual's personality. **Social development** refers to changes in the way an individual relates to others. And **cognitive development** refers to changes in thinking.

Many changes during development are simply matters of growth and **maturation.** Maturation refers to changes that occur naturally and spontaneously and that are, to a large extent, genetically programmed. Such changes emerge over time and are relatively unaffected by environment, except in cases of malnutrition or severe illness. Much of a person's physical development falls into this category. Other changes are brought about through learning, as individuals interact with their environment. Such changes make up a large part of a person's social development. But what about the development of thinking and personality? Most psychologists agree that in these areas, both maturation and interaction with the environment (or nature and nurture, as they are sometimes called) are important, but they disagree about the amount of emphasis to place on each one.

General Principles of Development

Although there is disagreement about both what is involved in development and the way it takes place, there are a few general principles almost all theorists would support.

1. *People develop at different rates.* In your own classroom, you will have a whole range of examples of different developmental rates. Some students will be larger, better coordinated, or more mature in their thinking and social relationships. Others will be much slower to mature in these areas. Except in rare cases of very rapid or very slow development, such differences are normal and should be expected in any large group of students.
2. *Development is relatively orderly.* People develop abilities in a logical order. In infancy, they sit before they walk, babble before they talk, and see the world through their own eyes before they can begin to imagine how others see it. In school, they will master addition before algebra, Bambi before Shakespeare, and so on. Theorists may disagree on exactly what comes before what, but they all seem to find a relatively logical progression. But "orderly" does not necessarily mean linear or predictable—people might advance, stay the same for a time period, or go backwards.
3. *Development takes place gradually.* Very rarely do changes appear overnight. A student who cannot manipulate a pencil or answer a hypothetical question may well develop this ability, but the change is likely to take time.

Development Orderly, adaptive changes we go through from conception to death.

Physical development Changes in body structure and function over time.

Personal development Changes in personality that take place as one grows.

Social development Changes over time in the ways we relate to others.

Cognitive development Gradual orderly changes by which mental processes become more complex and sophisticated.

Maturation Genetically programmed, naturally occurring changes over time.

The Brain and Cognitive Development

If you have taken an introductory psychology class, you have read about the brain and nervous system. You probably remember that there are several different areas of the brain and that certain areas are involved in particular functions. For example, the feathery looking cerebellum coordinates and orchestrates balance and smooth, skilled movements—from the graceful gestures of the dancer to the everyday action of eating without stabbing yourself in the nose with a fork. The cerebellum may also play a role in higher cognitive functions such as learning. The hippocampus is critical in recalling new information and recent experiences, while the amygdala directs emotions. The thalamus is involved in our ability to learn new information, particularly if it is verbal. The reticular formation plays a role in attention and arousal, blocking some messages and sending others on to higher brain centers for processing, and the corpus callosum moves information from one side of the brain to the other.

Some researchers have described the brain as a jungle of layers and loops, an interconnected and complex organic system (Edelman, 1992). The outer 1/8-inch-thick covering of the cerebrum is the wrinkled-looking cerebral cortex—the largest area of the brain. The cerebral cortex allows the greatest human accomplishments, such as complex problem solving and language. In humans, this area of the brain is much larger than it is in lower animals. The cortex is the last part of the brain to develop, so it is believed to be more susceptible to environmental influences than other areas of the brain (Berk, 2005; Meece, 2002; Wood, Wood, & Boyd, 2005). The cerebral cortex accounts for about 85% of the brain's weight in adulthood and contains the greatest number of **neurons**—the tiny structures that store and transmit information. Let's see how neurons develop.

Connect and Extend to the Research

In the next decade we should see increasing research on the brain, development, learning, and teaching. For example, in 1998, there was a special issue of *Educational Psychology Review* on cognitive neuroscience and education. The authors of this volume emphasized that the brain is a complex collection of systems working together to construct understanding, detect patterns, create rules, and make sense of experience. These systems change over the lifetime as the individual matures and develops.

The Developing Brain: Neurons. About one month after conception, brain development starts. In the tiny tube that is the very beginning of the human brain, neuron cells emerge at the amazing rate of 50,000 to 100,000 per second for the next three months or so. These cells send out long arm- and branch-like fibers to connect with other neuron cells and share information by releasing chemicals that jump across the tiny spaces, called **synapses**, between the fiber ends. By the time we are born, we have all the neurons we will ever have, about 100 to 200 billion, and each neuron has about 2,500 synapses. However, the fibers that reach out from the neurons and the synapses between the fiber ends increase during the first years of life, perhaps into adolescence or longer.

By age 2 to 3, each neuron has around 15,000 synapses; children this age have many more synapses than they will have as adults. In fact, they are *oversupplied* with the neurons and synapses that they will need to adapt to their environments. However, only those neurons that are used will survive, and unused neurons will be "pruned" (Bransford, Brown, & Cocking, 2000). This pruning is necessary and supports cognitive development. In fact, some forms of mental retardation are associated with a gene defect that interferes with pruning (Cook & Cook, 2005).

Two kinds of overproduction and pruning processes take place. One is called *experience-expectant* because synapses are overproduced in certain parts of the brain during certain developmental periods, awaiting (expecting) stimulation. For example, during the first months of life, the brain expects visual and auditory stimulation. If a normal range of sights and sounds occurs, then the visual and auditory areas of the brain develop. But children who are born completely deaf receive no auditory stimulation and, as a result, the auditory processing area of their brains becomes devoted to processing visual information. Similarly, the visual processing area of the brain for children blind from birth becomes devoted to auditory processing (Nelson, 2001; Siegler, 1998).

Experience-expectant overproduction and pruning processes are responsible for general development in large areas of the brain. This may explain why adults have difficulty with pronunciations that are not part of their native language. For example, native Japanese speakers do not distinguish the different sounds of "r" and "l." The capacity to hear these differences was available to the Japanese infants, but the neurons and synapses involved in recognizing these differences may have been "pruned" because they were not used to learn Japanese. Therefore, learning these sounds as an adult requires intense instruction and practice (Bransford et al., 2000).

The second kind of synaptic overproduction and pruning is called *experience-dependent*. Here, synaptic connections are formed based on the individual's experiences. New synapses are formed in response to neural activity in very localized areas of the brain when the individual is not successful in processing information. Again, more synapses are produced than will be kept after "pruning." Experience-dependent processes are involved

Neurons Nerve cells that store and transfer information.

Synapses The tiny space between neurons—chemical messages are sent across these gaps.

in individual learning, such as learning unfamiliar sound pronunciations in a second language you are studying.

Stimulation is important in both development (experience-expectant processes) and learning (experience-dependent processes). In fact, animal studies have shown that rats raised in stimulating environments (with toys, tasks for learning, other rats, and human handling) develop and retain 25% more synapses than rats who are raised with little stimulation. Both social stimulation (interactions with other rats) and physical/sensory stimulation (toys and tasks) are important; some studies showed that toys and tasks alone did not lead to increased brain development (Bransford et al., 2000). And age may matter, too. Stimulating environments may help in the pruning process in early life (experience-expectant period) and support increased synapse development in adulthood (experience-dependent period) (Cook & Cook, 2005).

Early stimulation is important for humans as well. It is clear that extreme deprivation can have negative effects on brain development, but extra stimulation will not necessarily improve development for young children who are getting adequate or typical amounts of stimulation (Byrnes & Fox, 1998; Kolb & Whishaw, 1998). So spending money on expensive toys or baby education programs probably provides more stimulation than is necessary. Pots and pans, blocks and books, sand and water all provide excellent stimulation—especially if accompanied by caring conversations with parents or teachers.

Even though the brain is developing rapidly during early childhood, learning continues over a lifetime. Early severe stimulus deprivation can have lasting effects, but because of brain **plasticity** or adaptability, some compensation can overcome deprivation or damage. Of course, many factors besides stimulus deprivation, such as the mother's intake of drugs (including alcohol and caffeine) during pregnancy, toxins in the infant's environment such as lead paint, or poor nutrition, can have direct and dramatic negative effects on brain development.

Another factor that influences thinking and learning is **myelination,** or the coating of neuron fibers with an insulating fatty covering. This process is something like coating bare electrical wires with rubber or plastic. This myelin coating makes message transmission faster and more efficient. Myelination happens quickly in the early years, but continues gradually into adolescence and is the reason the child's brain grows rapidly in size in the first few years of life.

The Developing Brain: Cerebral Cortex. Let's move from the neuron level to the brain itself. The cerebral cortex develops more slowly than other parts of the brain, and parts of the cortex mature at different rates. The part of the cortex that controls physical motor movement matures first, then the areas that control complex senses such as vision and hearing, and last, the frontal lobe that controls higher-order thinking processes. The temporal lobes of the cortex that play major roles in emotions and language do not develop fully until the high school years and maybe later.

Neuroscientists are just beginning to understand how brain development is related to aspects of childhood and adolescence such as planning, risk-taking, decision making, and managing impulsive behaviors. Getting angry or wanting revenge when we are insulted or hurt are common human emotions. It is the job of the prefrontal cortex to control these impulses through reason, planning, or delay of gratification. But the impulse-inhibiting capacities of the brain are not present at birth (as all new parents quickly discover). An immature prefrontal lobe explains some of the impulsiveness and temper tantrums of 2-year-olds. Emotional regulation is more difficult at this age. Many studies show advances in the prefrontal cortex around 3 to 4 years old (Berger, 2006), but it takes at least two decades for the biological processes of brain development to produce a fully functional prefrontal cortex (Weinberger, 2001). Thus, middle- and high-school students still lack the brain development to balance impulse with reason and planning. Weinberger suggests that parents have to "loan" their children a prefrontal cortex, by helping them set rules and limits and make plans, until the child's own prefrontal cortex can take over. Schools and teachers also can play major roles in cognitive and emotional development if they provide appropriate environments for these developing, but sometimes impulsive, brains (Meece, 2002).

Plasticity The brain's tendency to remain somewhat adaptable or flexible.

Myelination The process by which neural fibers are coated with a fatty sheath called *myelin* that makes message transfer more efficient.

Specialization and Integration. Different areas of the cortex seem to have different functions, as shown in Figure 2.1. Even though different functions are found in different areas of the brain, these specialized functions are quite specific and elementary. To accomplish more complex functions such as speaking or reading, the various areas of the cortex must communicate and work together (Byrnes & Fox, 1998).

Another aspect of brain functioning that has implications for cognitive development is **lateralization,** or the specialization of the two hemispheres of the brain. We know that each half of the brain controls the opposite side of the body. Damage to the right side of the brain will affect movement of the left side of the body and vice versa. In addition, certain areas of the brain affect particular behaviors. For most of us, the left hemisphere of the brain is a major factor in language processing, and the right hemisphere handles much of the spatial-visual information and emotions (nonverbal information). For some left-handed people, the relationship may be reversed, but for most left-handers, and for females on average, there is less hemispheric specialization altogether (Berk, 2005; O'Boyle & Gill, 1998). Before lateralization, damage to one part of the cortex often can be overcome as other parts of the cortex take over the function of the damaged area. But after lateralization, the brain is less able to compensate.

These differences in performance by the brain's hemispheres, however, are more relative than absolute; one hemisphere is just more efficient than the other in performing certain functions. Nearly any task, particularly the complex skills and abilities that concern teachers, requires participation of many different areas of the brain in constant communication with each other. For example, the right side of the brain is better at figuring out the meaning of a story, but the left side is where grammar and syntax are understood, so both sides of the brain have to work together in reading. "The primary implication of these findings is that the practice of teaching to 'different sides of the brain' is not supported by the neuroscientific research" (Byrnes & Fox, 1998, p. 310). Thus, beware of educational approaches based on simplistic views of brain functioning—what Keith Stanovich (1998) has called "the left-brain–right-brain nonsense that has inundated education through workshops, inservices, and the trade publications" (p. 420). Remember, no mental activity is exclusively the work of single part of the brain—so there is no such thing as a "right-brained student" unless that individual has had the left hemisphere removed, a rare and radical treatment for some forms of epilepsy.

FIGURE 2.1

A View of the Cerebral Cortex

This is a simple representation of the left side of the human brain, showing the cerebral cortex. The cortex is divided into different areas, or lobes, each having a variety of regions with different functions. A few of the major functions are indicated here.

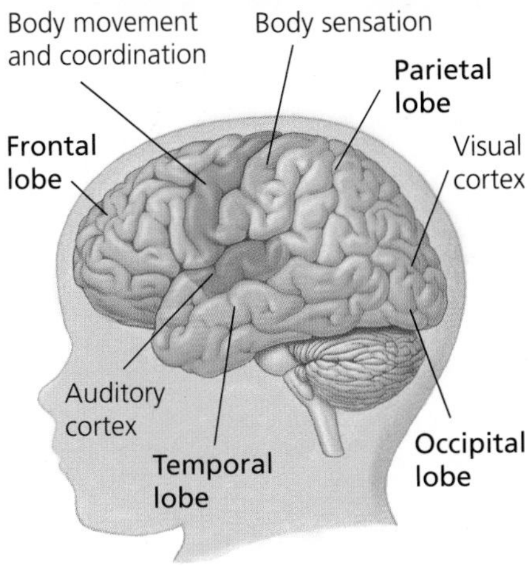

Instruction and Brain Development. Research from animal and human studies shows that both experiences and direct teaching cause changes in the organization and structure of the brain. For example, deaf individuals who use sign language have different patterns of electrical activity in their brains compared to deaf people who do not use sign language. Also, the intensive instruction and practice provided when someone suffers a stroke can help the person regain functioning by forming new connections and using new areas of the brain (Bransford et al., 2000). Bennett Shaywitz and his colleagues (2004) reported a dramatic demonstration of brain changes in children following instruction. The researchers studied 28 children ages 6 to 9 who were good readers and 49 children who were poor readers. A process known as functional magnetic-resonance imaging (MRI) showed differences in the brain activity of the two groups. The poor readers underused parts of their brains' left hemisphere and sometimes overused their right hemispheres. After over 100 hours of intensive instruction in letter–sound combinations, the brains of the poor readers started to function more like those of the good readers and continued this functioning a year later. Poor readers who got the standard school remediation did not show the brain function changes.

In other research, several studies have found that children and adults with ADHD have smaller frontal lobes, basal ganglia, and cerebellums than people without ADHD. These areas are involved with self-regulation of behavior, coordination, and control of motor behavior (Hallahan & Kauffman, 2006).

Connect and **Extend** to the **Web**

See http://www.nih.gov/news/pr/apr2004/nichd-19.htm for a summary of the Shaywitz et al. study.

Connect and **Extend** to the **Web**

See http://www.amenclinic.com/bp/atlas/ch12.php to view brain scans of people with ADHD.

Lateralization The specialization of the two hemispheres (sides) of the brain cortex.

One clear connection between the brain and classroom learning is in the area of emotions and stress. As you will see in Chapter 10, anxiety interferes with learning, whereas challenge, interest, and curiosity can support learning. If students feel unsafe and anxious, they are not likely to be able to focus attention on academics (Sylvester, 2003). But if students are not challenged or interested, learning suffers too. Keeping the level of challenge and support "just right" is a challenge for teachers. And helping students learn to regulate their own emotions and motivation is an important goal for education (see Chapter 3).

WHAT WOULD YOU SAY?

You are interviewing for a job in a great district—it is known for innovation. After a few minutes, the principal asks, "Do you know anything about this brain-based education? I've read a lot about that lately." How would you answer? ■

Implications for Teachers. As you have seen, the brain and learning are intimately related, but what does this mean for teachers? Marcy Driscoll (2005) draws these implications:

1. Many cognitive functions are differentiated—they are associated with different parts of the brain. Thus, learners are likely to have preferred modes of processing (visual, or verbal, for example) as well as different capabilities in these different modes. Using different modalities for instruction and activities that draw on different senses may support learning—for example, using maps and songs to teach geography.
2. The brain is relatively plastic, so enriched active environments and flexible instructional strategies are likely to support cognitive development in young children and learning in adults.
3. Some learning disorders may have a neurological basis, so neurological testing may assist in diagnosing, treating, and evaluating the effects of treatments.

Much has been written lately about brain-based education. Many of these publications for parents and teachers have useful ideas, but beware of suggestions that oversimplify the complexities of the brain. As you can see in the *Point/Counterpoint*, the jury still is out on many of these programs.

We turn next to examine a theory of cognitive development offered by a biologist turned psychologist, Jean Piaget.

Piaget's Theory of Cognitive Development

STOP | THINK | WRITE Can you be in Pittsburgh, Pennsylvania, and the United States all at the same time? Is this a difficult question for you? How long did it take you to answer? ■

Swiss psychologist Jean Piaget devised a model describing how humans go about making sense of their world by gathering and organizing information (Piaget, 1954, 1963, 1970a, 1970b). We will examine Piaget's ideas closely, because they provide an explanation of the development of thinking from infancy to adulthood.

According to Piaget (1954), certain ways of thinking that are quite simple for an adult, such as the question above, are not so simple for a child. For example, Piaget asked a 9-year-old:

> What is your nationality?—*I am Swiss.*—How come?—*Because I live in Switzerland.*—Are you also a Genevan?—*No, that's not possible I'm already Swiss, I can't also be Genevan.* (Piaget, 1965/1995, p. 252)

Imagine teaching this student geography. The student has trouble with classifying one concept (Geneva) as a subset of another (Switzerland). There are other differences between adult and child thinking. Children's concepts of time may be different from your own. They may think, for example, that they will some day catch up to a sibling in age, or they may confuse the past and the future. Let's examine why.

Connect and **Extend** to Your **Teaching**

To experience some of the ways children differ from adults in their thinking, ask children of various ages the following questions:

- What does it mean to be alive?
- Can you name some things that are alive?
- Is the moon alive?
- Where do dreams come from?
- Where do they go?
- Which is farther, to go from the bottom of the hill all the way to the top or go from the top of the hill all the way to the bottom?
- Can a person live in Chicago and in Illinois at the same time?
- Will you be just as old as your big brother some day?
- When is yesterday?
- Where does the sun go at night?

Point/Counterpoint

Brain-based Education

EDUCATORS ARE HEARING more and more about brain-based education, the importance of early stimulation for brain development, the "Mozart effect," and right- and left-brain activities. In fact, based on some research findings that listening to 10 minutes of Mozart can briefly improve spatial reasoning (Rauscher & Shaw, 1998; Steele, Bass, & Crook, 1999), a former governor of Georgia established a program to give a Mozart CD to every newborn (Meece, 2002). Are there clear educational implications from the neuroscience research on the brain?

POINT No, the implications are not clear.

John Bruer, president of the James S. McDonnell Foundation, has written articles that are critical of the brain-based education craze (Bruer, 1999). He notes that many so-called applications of brain research begin with solid science, but then move to unwarranted speculation. He suggests that for each claim, the educator should ask, "Where does the science end and the speculation begin?" For example, one claim that Bruer questions is the notion of right-brain, left-brain learning.

> *"Right brain versus left brain" is one of those popular ideas that will not die. Speculations about the educational significance of brain laterality have been circulating in the education literature for 30 years. Although repeatedly criticized and dismissed by psychologists and brain scientists, the speculation continues. David Sousa devotes a chapter of* How the Brain Learns *to explaining brain laterality and presents classroom strategies that teachers might use to ensure that both hemispheres are involved in learning. . . . Now let's consider the brain sciences and how or whether they offer support for some of the particular teaching strategies Sousa recommends. To involve the right hemisphere in learning, Sousa writes, teachers should encourage students to generate and use mental imagery. . . . What brain scientists currently know about spatial reasoning and mental imagery provides counterexamples to such simplistic claims as these. Such claims arise out of a folk theory about brain laterality, not a neuroscientific one. . . . Different brain areas are specialized for different tasks, but that specialization occurs at a finer level of analysis than "using visual imagery." Using visual imagery may be a useful learning strategy, but if it is useful it is not because it involves an otherwise underutilized right hemisphere in learning.* (Bruer, 1999, pp. 653–654)

COUNTERPOINT Yes, teaching should be brain-based.

If you want to read about programs, strategies, and approaches that have been developed to be consistent with brain research, type "brain-based education" into an Internet search engine. For example, this is the case made on the Jensen Learning Corporation website (http://www.jlcbrain.com/truth.html):

> *Brain-based learning is not a panacea nor magic bullet to solve all of education's problems. Anyone who represents that to others is misleading them. It is not yet a program, a model or package for schools to follow. One critic of brain-based learning, said "It will at least be 25 years before the benefits of brain research reach the classroom." I'll cite just one example to show you why I disagree.*

The reading improvement product *FastForword* was developed by two neuroscientists, Stanford's Dr. Michael Merzenich and Dr. Paula Tallal from Rutgers. That product is already in use today in thousands of classrooms around the country. Many students have been helped by it. It specifically uses discoveries in neural plasticity to change the brain's ability to read the printed word. . . .

Schools should not be run based solely on the biology of the brain. However, to ignore what we do know about the brain would be equally irresponsible. Brain-based learning offers some direction for educators who want more purposeful, informed teaching.

WHAT DO YOU THINK?

Vote online at **www.mylabschool.com**

Influences on Development

Cognitive development is much more than the addition of new facts and ideas to an existing store of information. According to Piaget, our thinking processes change radically, though slowly, from birth to maturity because we constantly strive to make sense of the world. How do we do this? Piaget identified four factors—biological maturation, activity, social experiences, and equilibration—that interact to influence changes in thinking (Piaget, 1970a). Let's briefly examine the first three factors. We'll return to a discussion of equilibration in the next section.

One of the most important influences on the way we make sense of the world is *maturation*, the unfolding of the biological changes that are genetically programmed. Parents

Jean Piaget was a Swiss psychologist whose insightful descriptions of children's thinking changed the way we understand cognitive development.

and teachers have little impact on this aspect of cognitive development, except to be sure that children get the nourishment and care they need to be healthy.

Activity is another influence. With physical maturation comes the increasing ability to act on the environment and learn from it. When a young child's coordination is reasonably developed, for example, the child can discover principles about balance by experimenting with a seesaw. Thus, as we act on the environment—as we explore, test, observe, and eventually organize information—we are likely to alter our thinking processes at the same time.

As we develop, we are also interacting with the people around us. According to Piaget, our cognitive development is influenced by *social transmission,* or learning from others. Without social transmission, we would need to reinvent all the knowledge already offered by our culture. The amount people can learn from social transmission varies according to their stage of cognitive development.

Maturation, activity, and social transmission all work together to influence cognitive development. How do we respond to these influences?

Basic Tendencies in Thinking

As a result of his early research in biology, Piaget concluded that all species inherit two basic tendencies, or "invariant functions." The first of these tendencies is toward **organization**—the combining, arranging, recombining, and rearranging of behaviors and thoughts into coherent systems. The second tendency is toward **adaptation,** or adjusting to the environment.

Organization. People are born with a tendency to organize their thinking processes into psychological structures. These psychological structures are our systems for understanding and interacting with the world. Simple structures are continually combined and coordinated to become more sophisticated and thus more effective. Very young infants, for example, can either look at an object or grasp it when it comes in contact with their hands. They cannot coordinate looking and grasping at the same time. As they develop, however, infants organize these two separate behavioral structures into a coordinated higher-level structure of looking at, reaching for, and grasping the object. They can, of course, still use each structure separately (Flavell, Miller, & Miller, 2002; Miller, 2002).

Piaget gave a special name to these structures: **schemes.** In his theory, schemes are the basic building blocks of thinking. They are organized systems of actions or thought that allow us to mentally represent or "think about" the objects and events in our world. Schemes can be very small and specific, for example, the sucking-through-a-straw scheme or the recognizing-a-rose scheme. Or they can be larger and more general, for example, the drinking scheme or the categorizing-plants scheme. As a person's thinking processes become more organized and new schemes develop, behavior also becomes more sophisticated and better suited to the environment.

Organization Ongoing process of arranging information and experience into mental systems or categories.

Adaptation Adjustment to the environment.

Schemes Mental systems or categories of perception and experience.

Adaptation. In addition to the tendency to organize their psychological structures, people also inherit the tendency to adapt to their environment. Two basic processes are involved in adaptation: assimilation and accommodation.

Assimilation takes place when people use their existing schemes to make sense of events in their world. Assimilation involves trying to understand something new by fitting it into what we already know. At times, we may have to distort the new information to make it fit. For example, the first time many children see a skunk, they call it a "kitty." They try to match the new experience with an existing scheme for identifying animals.

Accommodation occurs when a person must change existing schemes to respond to a new situation. If data cannot be made to fit any existing schemes, then more appropriate structures must be developed. We adjust our thinking to fit the new information, instead of adjusting the information to fit our thinking. Children demonstrate accommodation when they add the scheme for recognizing skunks to their other systems for identifying animals.

People adapt to their increasingly complex environments by using existing schemes whenever these schemes work (assimilation) and by modifying and adding to their schemes when something new is needed (accommodation). In fact, both processes are required most of the time. Even using an established pattern such as sucking through a straw requires some accommodation if the straw is of a different size or length than the type you are used to. If you have tried drinking juice from box packages, you know that you have to add a new skill to your sucking scheme—don't squeeze the box or you will shoot juice through the straw, straight up into the air and into your lap. Whenever new experiences are assimilated into an existing scheme, the scheme is enlarged and changed somewhat, so assimilation involves some accommodation.

There are also times when neither assimilation nor accommodation is used. If people encounter something that is too unfamiliar, they may ignore it. Experience is filtered to fit the kind of thinking a person is doing at a given time. For example, if you overhear a conversation in a foreign language, you probably will not try to make sense of the exchange unless you have some knowledge of the language.

Equilibration. According to Piaget, organizing, assimilating, and accommodating can be viewed as a kind of complex balancing act. In his theory, the actual changes in thinking take place through the process of **equilibration**—the act of searching for a balance. Piaget assumed that people continually test the adequacy of their thinking processes in order to achieve that balance. Briefly, the process of equilibration works like this: If we apply a particular scheme to an event or situation and the scheme works, then equilibrium exists. If the scheme does not produce a satisfying result, then **disequilibrium** exists, and we become uncomfortable. This motivates us to keep searching for a solution through assimilation and accommodation, and thus our thinking changes and moves ahead. Of course, the level of disequilibrium must be just right or optimal—too little and we aren't interested in changing, too much and we may be too anxious to change.

Four Stages of Cognitive Development

WHAT WOULD YOU SAY?

Your interview with the principal seems to be going fairly well. Her next question is, "Students in some of our 11th grade classes are pretty concrete in their thinking but others are quite advanced. How would you differentiate instruction?" ■

Now we turn to the actual differences that Piaget hypothesized for children as they grow. Piaget believed that all people pass through the same four stages (sensorimotor, preoperational, concrete operational, and formal operational) in exactly the same order. These stages are generally associated with specific ages, as shown in Table 2.1 on the next page, but these are only general guidelines, not labels for all children of a certain age. Piaget noted that individuals may go through long periods of transition between stages and that a person may show characteristics of one stage in one situation, but characteristics of a higher or lower stage in other situations. Therefore, knowing a student's age is never a guarantee that you know how the child will think (Orlando & Machado, 1996).

Assimilation Fitting new information into existing schemes.

Accommodation Altering existing schemes or creating new ones in response to new information.

Equilibration Search for mental balance between cognitive schemes and information from the environment.

Disequilibrium In Piaget's theory, the "out-of-balance" state that occurs when a person realizes that his or her current ways of thinking are not working to solve a problem or understand a situation.

TABLE 2.1

Piaget's Stages of Cognitive Development

Stage	Approximate Age	Characteristics
Sensorimotor	0–2 years	Begins to make use of imitation, memory, and thought.
		Begins to recognize that objects do not cease to exist when they are hidden.
		Moves from reflex actions to goal-directed activity.
Preoperational	2–7 years	Gradually develops use of language and ability to think in symbolic form.
		Able to think operations through logically in one direction.
		Has difficulties seeing another person's point of view.
Concrete operational	7–11 years	Able to solve concrete (hands-on) problems in logical fashion.
		Understands laws of conservation and is able to classify and seriate.
		Understands reversibility.
Formal operational	11–adult	Able to solve abstract problems in logical fashion.
		Becomes more scientific in thinking.
		Develops concerns about social issues, identity.

Source: From *Piaget's Theory of Cognitive and Affective Development, 5/e* by B. Wadsworth. Published by Allyn and Bacon, Boston, MA. Copyright © 1996 by Pearson Education. Adapted by permission of the publisher.

Infancy: The Sensorimotor Stage. The earliest period is called the **sensorimotor** stage, because the child's thinking involves seeing, hearing, moving, touching, tasting, and so on. During this period, infants develop **object permanence,** the understanding that objects exist in the environment whether they perceive them or not. This is the beginning of the important ability to construct a mental representation. As most parents discover, before infants develop object permanence, it is relatively easy to take something away from them. The trick is to distract them and remove the object while they are not looking—"out of sight, out of mind." The older infant who searches for the ball that has rolled out of sight is indicating an understanding that objects still exist even when they are not in view (Moore & Meltzoff, 2004). Recent research, however, suggests that infants as young as 3 to 4 months may know that the object still exists, but they do not have the memory skills to "hold on" to the location of the object or the motor skills to coordinate a search (Baillargeon, 1999; Flavell et al., 2002).

A second major accomplishment in the sensorimotor period is the beginning of logical, **goal-directed actions.** Think of the familiar clear plastic container baby toy with a lid and several colorful items inside that can be dumped out and replaced. A 6-month-old baby is likely to become frustrated trying to get to the toys inside. An older child who has mastered the basics of the sensorimotor stage will probably be able to deal with the toy in an orderly fashion by building a "container toy" scheme: (1) get the lid off, (2) turn the container upside down, (3) shake if the items jam, and (4) watch the items fall. Separate lower-level schemes have been organized into a higher-level scheme to achieve a goal.

The child is soon able to reverse this action by refilling the container. Learning to reverse actions is a basic accomplishment of the sensorimotor stage. As we will soon see, however, learning to reverse thinking—that is, learning to imagine the reverse of a sequence of actions—takes much longer.

Early Childhood to the Early Elementary Years: The Preoperational Stage. By the end of the sensorimotor stage, the child can use many action schemes. As long as these schemes remain tied to physical actions, however, they are of no use in recalling the past, keeping track of information, or planning. For this, children need what Piaget called **operations,** or actions that are carried out and reversed mentally rather than physically. At the **preoperational** stage the child has not yet mastered these mental operations, but is moving toward mastery.

Sensorimotor Involving the senses and motor activity.

Object permanence The understanding that objects have a separate, permanent existence.

Goal-directed actions Deliberate actions toward a goal.

Operations Actions a person carries out by thinking them through instead of literally performing the actions.

Preoperational The stage before a child masters logical mental operations.

According to Piaget, the first type of thinking that is separate from action involves making action schemes symbolic. The ability to form and use symbols—words, gestures, signs, images, and so on—is thus a major accomplishment of the preoperational period and moves children closer to mastering the mental operations of the next stage. This ability to work with symbols, such as using the word "horse" or a picture of a horse or even pretending to ride a horse to represent a real horse that is not actually present, is called the **semiotic function.** In fact, the child's earliest use of symbols is in pretending. Children who are not yet able to talk will often use action symbols—pretending to drink from an empty cup or touching a comb to their hair, showing that they know what each object is for. This behavior also shows that their schemes are becoming more general and less tied to specific actions. The eating scheme, for example, can be used in playing house. During the preoperational stage, there is also rapid development of that very important symbol system, language. Between the ages of 2 and 4, most children enlarge their vocabulary from about 200 to 2,000 words.

THE FAMILY CIRCUS
By Bil Keane
HOW OLD ARE YOU NOW, JEFFY?
3-12
©2002 Bil Keane, Inc.
Dist. by King Features Synd.
www.familycircus.com

"I can't tell you 'cause I'm wearin' my mittens."

Family Circus, March 12, 2002. Copyright © 2002 Bill Keane, Inc. Reprinted with special permission of King Features Syndicate.

As the child moves through the preoperational stage, the developing ability to think about objects in symbolic form remains somewhat limited to thinking in one direction only, or using *one-way logic*. It is very difficult for the child to "think backwards," or imagine how to reverse the steps in a task. **Reversible thinking** is involved in many tasks that are difficult for the preoperational child, such as the conservation of matter.

Conservation is the principle that the amount or number of something remains the same even if the arrangement or appearance is changed, as long as nothing is added and nothing is taken away. You know that if you tear a piece of paper into several pieces, you will still have the same amount of paper. To prove this, you know that you can reverse the process by taping the pieces back together. A classic example of difficulty with conservation is found in the preoperational child's response to the following Piagetian task. Leah, a 5-year-old, is shown two identical glasses, both short and wide in shape. Both have exactly the same amount of colored water in them. She agrees that the amounts are "the same." The experimenter then pours the water from one of the glasses into a taller, narrower glass and asks, "Now, does one glass have more water, or are they the same?" Leah responds that the tall glass has more because "It goes up more here" (she points to higher level on taller glass).

Piaget's explanation for Leah's answer is that she is focusing, or centering, attention on the dimension of height. She has difficulty considering more than one aspect of the situation at a time, or **decentering.** The preoperational child cannot understand that decreased diameter compensates for increased height, because this would require taking into account two dimensions at once. Thus, children at the preoperational stage have trouble freeing themselves from their own immediate perceptions of how the world appears.

This brings us to another important characteristic of the preoperational stage. Preoperational children, according to Piaget, have a tendency to be **egocentric,** to see the world and the experiences of others from their own viewpoint. The concept of egocentrism, as Piaget intended it, does not mean selfish; it simply means children often assume that everyone else shares their feelings, reactions, and perspectives. For example, if a little boy at this stage is afraid of dogs, he may assume that all children share this fear. Very young children center on their own perceptions and on the way the situation appears to them. This is one reason it is difficult for these children to understand that your right hand is not on the same side as theirs when you are facing them.

Egocentrism is also evident in the child's language. You may have seen young children happily talking about what they are doing even though no one is listening. This can happen when the child is alone or, even more often, in a group of children—each child talks enthusiastically, without any real interaction or conversation. Piaget called this the **collective monologue.**

Research has shown that young children are not totally egocentric in every situation, however. Children as young as 2 describe more details about a situation to a parent who was not there compared to the descriptions they give to a parent who experienced the situation with them. So young children do seem quite able to take the needs and different perspectives of others into account, at least in certain situations (Flavell et al., 2002). And in fairness to young children, even adults can make assumptions that others feel or think

Semiotic function The ability to use symbols—language, pictures, signs, or gestures—to represent actions or objects mentally.

Reversible thinking Thinking backward, from the end to the beginning.

Conservation Principle that some characteristics of an object remain the same despite changes in appearance.

Decentering Focusing on more than one aspect at a time.

Egocentric Assuming that others experience the world the way you do.

Collective monologue Form of speech in which children in a group talk but do not really interact or communicate.

like they do. For example, have you ever gotten a gift that the giver loved but was clearly inappropriate for you? The *Guidelines* give ideas for working with preoperational thinkers.

Later Elementary to the Middle School Years: The Concrete-Operational Stage. Piaget coined the term **concrete operations** to describe this stage of "hands-on" thinking. The basic characteristics of the stage are the recognition of the logical stability of the physical world, the realization that elements can be changed or transformed and still conserve many of their original characteristics, and the understanding that these changes can be reversed.

Concrete operations Mental tasks tied to concrete objects and situations.

Look at Figure 2.2, which shows examples of the different tasks given to children to assess conservation and the approximate age ranges when most children can solve these problems. According to Piaget, a student's ability to solve conservation problems depends on an understanding of three basic aspects of reasoning: identity, compensation, and re-

Guidelines: Teaching the Preoperational Child

Use concrete props and visual aids whenever possible.

EXAMPLES

1. When you discuss concepts such as "part," "whole," or "one-half," use shapes on a felt board or cardboard "pizzas" to demonstrate.
2. Let children add and subtract with sticks, rocks, or colored chips. This technique also is helpful for early concrete-operational students.

Make instructions relatively short—not too many steps at once. Use actions as well as words.

EXAMPLES

1. When giving instructions about how to enter the room after recess and prepare for social studies, ask a student to demonstrate the procedure for the rest of the class by walking in quietly, going straight to his or her seat, and placing the text, paper, and a pencil on his or her desk.
2. Explain a game by acting out one of the parts.
3. Show students what their finished papers should look like. Use an overhead projector or display examples where students can see them easily.

Help students develop their ability to see the world from someone else's point of view.

EXAMPLES

1. Relate social studies lessons about different people or places back to the children's experiences, pointing out similarities and differences.
2. Be clear about rules for sharing or use of material. Help children understand the value of the rules and develop empathy by asking them to think about how they would like to be treated. Avoid long lectures on "sharing" or being "nice."

Be sensitive to the possibility that students may have different meanings for the same word or different words for the same meaning. Students may also expect everyone to understand words they have invented.

EXAMPLES

1. If a student protests, "I won't take a nap. I'll just rest!" be aware that a nap may mean something such as "changing into pajamas and being in my bed at home."
2. Ask children to explain the meanings of their invented words.

Give children a great deal of hands-on practice with the skills that serve as building blocks for more complex skills such as reading comprehension or collaboration.

EXAMPLES

1. Provide cut-out letters to build words.
2. Supplement paper-and-pencil tasks in arithmetic with activities that require measuring and simple calculations—cooking, building a display area for class work, dividing a batch of popcorn equally.
3. Allow children to clip from used magazines pictures of people collaborating—families, workers, educators, children all helping each other.

Provide a wide range of experiences in order to build a foundation for concept learning and language.

EXAMPLES

1. Take field trips to zoos, gardens, theaters, and concerts; invite storytellers to the class.
2. Give students words to describe what they are doing, hearing, seeing, touching, tasting, and smelling.

For more ideas and connections between Piaget and the Reggio Emilia approach, see **http://www.aquinas.edu/education/ece/reggio.html**

versibility. With a complete mastery of **identity**, the student knows that if nothing is added or taken away, the material remains the same. With an understanding of **compensation**, the student knows that an apparent change in one direction can be compensated for by a change in another direction. That is, if the glass is narrower, the liquid will rise higher in the glass. And with an understanding of reversibility, the student can mentally cancel out the change that has been made. Leah apparently knew it was the same water (identity), but lacked compensation and reversibility, so she was moving toward conservation.

Another important operation mastered at this stage is **classification.** Classification depends on a student's abilities to focus on a single characteristic of objects in a set (for example, color) and group the objects according to that characteristic. More advanced classification at this stage involves recognizing that one class fits into another. A city can be in a particular state or province and also in a particular country, as you probably knew when I asked you earlier about Pittsburgh, Pennsylvania, USA. As children apply this advanced classification to locations, they often become fascinated with "complete" addresses such as Lee Jary, 5116 Forest Hill Drive, Richmond Hill, Ontario, Canada, North America, Northern Hemisphere, Earth, Solar System, Milky Way, Universe.

Classification is also related to **reversibility.** The ability to reverse a process mentally now allows the concrete-operational student to see that there is more than one way to classify a group of objects. The student understands, for example, that buttons can be classified by color, then reclassified by size or by the number of holes.

Seriation is the process of making an orderly arrangement from large to small or vice versa. This understanding of sequential relationships permits a student to construct a logical series in which A < B < C (A is less than B is less than C) and so on. Unlike the preoperational child, the concrete-operational child can grasp the notion that B can be *larger* than A but still *smaller* than C.

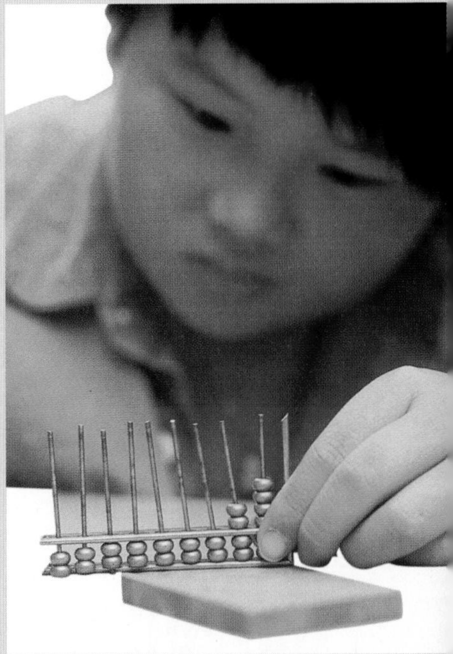

The ability to manipulate concrete objects helps children understand abstract relationships such as the connection between symbols and quantity.

FIGURE 2.2

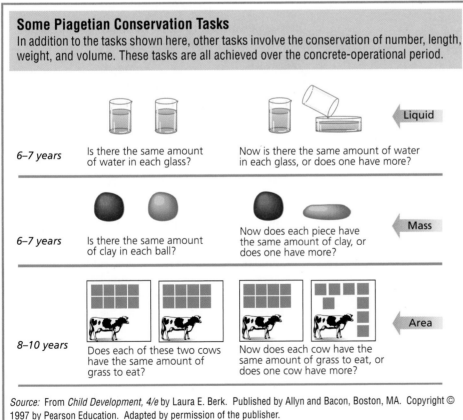

Some Piagetian Conservation Tasks

In addition to the tasks shown here, other tasks involve the conservation of number, length, weight, and volume. These tasks are all achieved over the concrete-operational period.

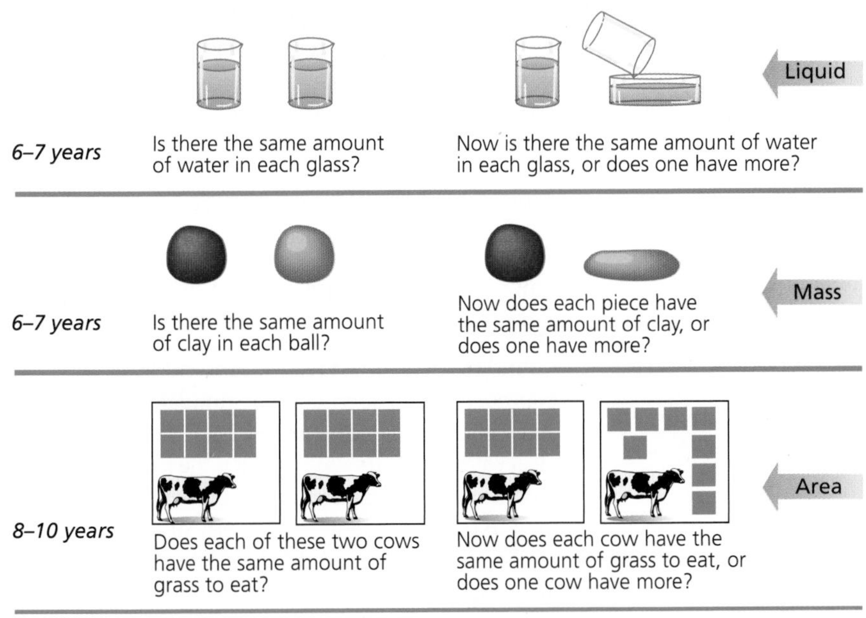
Liquid
6–7 years
Is there the same amount of water in each glass?
Now is there the same amount of water in each glass, or does one have more?
Mass
6–7 years
Is there the same amount of clay in each ball?
Now does each piece have the same amount of clay, or does one have more?
Area
8–10 years
Does each of these two cows have the same amount of grass to eat?
Now does each cow have the same amount of grass to eat, or does one cow have more?

Source: From *Child Development, 4/e* by Laura E. Berk. Published by Allyn and Bacon, Boston, MA. Copyright © 1997 by Pearson Education. Adapted by permission of the publisher.

Identity Principle that a person or object remains the same over time.

Compensation The principle that changes in one dimension can be offset by changes in another.

Classification Grouping objects into categories.

Reversibility A characteristic of Piagetian logical operations—the ability to think through a series of steps, then mentally reverse the steps and return to the starting point; also called *reversible thinking.*

Seriation Arranging objects in sequential order according to one aspect, such as size, weight, or volume.

With the abilities to handle operations such as conservation, classification, and seriation, the student at the concrete-operational stage has finally developed a complete and very logical system of thinking. This system of thinking, however, is still tied to physical reality. The logic is based on concrete situations that can be organized, classified, or manipulated. Thus, children at this stage can imagine several different arrangements for the furniture in their rooms before they move any pieces. They do not have to solve the problem strictly through trial and error by actually making the arrangements. However, the concrete-operational child is not yet able to reason about hypothetical, abstract problems that involve the coordination of many factors at once. This kind of coordination is part of Piaget's next and final stage of cognitive development.

In any grade you teach, knowledge of concrete-operational thinking will be helpful (see the *Guidelines*). In the early grades, the students are moving toward this logical system of thought. In the middle grades, it is in full flower, ready to be applied and extended by your teaching. Students in high school and even adults still commonly use concrete operational thinking, especially in areas that are new or unfamiliar.

Guidelines: Teaching the Concrete-Operational Child

Continue to use concrete props and visual aids, especially when dealing with sophisticated material.

EXAMPLES

1. Use time lines in history and three-dimensional models in science.
2. Use diagrams to illustrate hierarchical relationships such as branches of government and the agencies under each branch.

Continue to give students a chance to manipulate and test objects.

EXAMPLES

1. Set up simple scientific experiments such as the following involving the relationship between fire and oxygen. What happens to a flame when you blow on it from a distance? (If you don't blow it out, the flame gets larger briefly, because it has more oxygen to burn.) What happens when you cover the flame with a jar?
2. Have students make candles by dipping wicks in wax, weave cloth on a simple loom, bake bread, set type by hand, or do other craft work that illustrates the daily occupations of people in the colonial period.

Make sure presentations and readings are brief and well-organized.

EXAMPLES

1. Assign stories or books with short, logical chapters, moving to longer reading assignments only when students are ready.
2. Break up a presentation with a chance to practice the first steps before introducing the next.

Use familiar examples to explain more complex ideas.

EXAMPLES

1. Compare students' lives with those of characters in a story. After reading *Island of the Blue Dolphins* (the true story of a girl who grew up alone on a deserted island), ask "Have you ever had to stay alone for a long time? How did you feel?"
2. Teach the concept of area by having students measure two school rooms that are different sizes.

Give opportunities to classify and group objects and ideas on increasingly complex levels.

EXAMPLES

1. Give students slips of paper with individual sentences written on each paper and ask the students to group the sentences into paragraphs.
2. Compare the systems of the human body to other kinds of systems: the brain to a computer, the heart to a pump. Break down stories into components, from the broad to the specific: author; story; characters, plot, theme; place, time; dialogue, description, actions.

Present problems that require logical, analytical thinking.

EXAMPLES

1. Use mind twisters, brain teasers, and riddles.
2. Discuss open-ended questions that stimulate thinking: "Are the brain and the mind the same thing?" "How should the city deal with stray animals?" "What is the largest number?"
3. Use sports photos or pictures of crisis situations (Red Cross helping in disasters, victims of poverty or war, senior citizens who need assistance) to stimulate problem-solving discussions.

For more ideas see **http://chiron.valdosta.edu/whuitt/col/cogsys/piagtuse.html**

High School and College: Formal Operations. Some students remain at the concrete-operational stage throughout their school years, even throughout life. However, new experiences, usually those that take place in school, eventually present most students with problems that they cannot solve using concrete operations.

STOP | THINK | WRITE You are packing for a long trip, but want to pack light. How many different three-piece outfits (slacks, shirt, jacket) will you have if you include three shirts, three slacks, and three jackets (assuming of course that they all go together in fashion perfection)? Time yourself to see how long it takes to arrive at the answer. ■

What happens when a number of variables interact, as in a laboratory experiment or the question above? Then a mental system for controlling sets of variables and working through a set of possibilities is needed. These are the abilities Piaget called **formal operations.**

At the level of formal operations, the focus of thinking can shift from what *is* to what *might be.* Situations do not have to be experienced to be imagined. Ask a young child how life would be different if people did not sleep, and the child might say, "People do sleep!" In contrast, the adolescent who has mastered formal operations can consider contrary-to-fact questions. In answering, the adolescent demonstrates the hallmark of formal operations—**hypothetico-deductive reasoning.** The formal thinker can consider a hypothetical situation (people do not sleep) and reason *deductively* (from the general assumption to specific implications, such as longer workdays, more money spent on energy and lighting, smaller houses without bedrooms, or new entertainment industries). Formal operations also include *inductive* reasoning, or using specific observations to identify general principles. For example, the economist observes many specific changes in the stock market and attempts to identify general principles about economic cycles. Formal-operational thinkers can form hypotheses, set up mental experiments to test them, and isolate or control variables in order to complete a valid test of the hypotheses. This kind of reasoning is necessary for success in many advanced high school and college courses (Meece, 2002).

After elementary school, the ability to consider abstract possibilities is critical for much of mathematics and science. Most math is concerned with hypothetical situations, assumptions, and givens: "Let $x = 10$," or "Assume $x^2 + y^2 = z^2$," or "Given two sides and an adjacent angle . . . " Work in social studies and literature requires abstract thinking, too: "What did Wilson mean when he called World War I the 'war to end all wars'?" "What are some metaphors for hope and despair in Shakespeare's sonnets?" "What symbols of old age does T. S. Eliot use in *The Waste Land*?" "How do animals symbolize human character traits in Aesop's fables?" Desmond Tutu, a respected reformer and religious leader in South Africa, describes a teacher who understood how to teach abstract mathematical concepts, even in classes as large as 80 in the *Stories of Learning/Tributes to Teaching.*

Formal operations Mental tasks involving abstract thinking and coordination of a number of variables.

Hypothetico-deductive reasoning A formal-operations problem-solving strategy in which an individual begins by identifying all the factors that might affect a problem and then deduces and systematically evaluates specific solutions.

STORIES OF LEARNING
TRIBUTES TO TEACHING

"He made learning his subject so much fun."

Reverend **DESMOND TUTU** attended a school in South Africa that "had most of the characteristics of a ghetto school; hardly any facilities to mention. I went to the laboratory only once in my five or six years at school, there was a wholly inadequate library and very few recreational and games facilities." The overcrowded classes that routinely had over 80 students were held in a poorly furnished church building. Reverend Tutu notes that math was not his favorite subject—he learned math only because it was compulsory—until he met Mr. Ndebele.

However, things changed dramatically after Mr. Nimron Ndebele stood in front of the class. He was a middle-sized man with a fine alto voice. He always had a gentle smile playing around his mouth, a very pleasant image, and he made learning his subject so much fun. He always had objects that he used to illustrate what, up to that point, had been cloaked in mystery and unrelieved gloom. He had an extraordinary knack of making the most complicated and abstruse principle seem so straightforward and obvious. Nobody, just nobody, failed his subject in the public state examinations. In fact, many of his students obtained distinctions.

I thank God for Mr. Ndebele and for what he meant for so many of us.

—The Most Reverend Desmond Mpilo Tutu,
Archbishop of Cape Town, South Africa

Source: From *Mentors, Masters, and Mrs. MacGregor* by J. Bluestein. Published by Health Communications. Copyright © 1995 by Health Communications. Adapted with permission of the publisher.

The organized, scientific thinking of formal operations requires that students systematically generate different possibilities for a given situation. For example, if asked, "How many different shirt/slacks/jacket outfits can you make using three of each kind of clothing?" the child using formal operations can systematically identify the 27 possible combinations (did you get it right?). A concrete thinker might name just a few combinations, using each piece of clothing only once. The underlying system of combinations is not yet available.

Another characteristic of this stage is **adolescent egocentrism.** Unlike egocentric young children, adolescents do not deny that other people may have different perceptions and beliefs; the adolescents just become very focused on their own ideas. They analyze their own beliefs and attitudes. This leads to what Elkind (1981) calls the sense of an *imaginary audience*—the feeling that everyone is watching. Thus, adolescents believe that others are analyzing them: "Everyone noticed that I wore this shirt twice this week." "The whole class thought my answer was dumb!" You can see that social blunders or imperfections in appearance can be devastating if "everybody is watching." Luckily, this feeling of being "on stage" seems to peak in early adolescence by age 14 or 15, although in unfamiliar situations we all may feel our mistakes are being noticed.

Connect and **Extend** to Your **Teaching**

What are the differences (and similarities) between egocentrism in young children and egocentrism in adolescents?

The ability to think hypothetically, consider alternatives, identify all possible combinations, and analyze one's own thinking has some interesting consequences for adolescents. Because they can think about worlds that do not exist, they often become interested in science fiction. Because they can reason from general principles to specific actions, they often are critical of people whose actions seem to contradict their principles. Adolescents can deduce the set of "best" possibilities and imagine ideal worlds (or ideal parents and teachers, for that matter). This explains why many students at this age develop interests in utopias, political causes, and social issues. They want to design better worlds, and their thinking allows them to do so. Adolescents can also imagine many possible futures for themselves and may try to decide which is best. Feelings about any of these ideals may be strong.

Do We All Reach the Fourth Stage? Most psychologists agree that there is a level of thinking more sophisticated than concrete operations. But the question of how universal formal-operational thinking actually is, even among adults, is a matter of debate. The first three stages of Piaget's theory are forced on most people by physical realities. Objects really are permanent. The amount of water doesn't change when it is poured into another glass. Formal operations, however, are not so closely tied to the physical environment. They may be the product of practice in solving hypothetical problems and using formal scientific reasoning—abilities that are valued and taught in literate cultures, particularly in college. Even so, about 50% of undergraduate students fail Piaget's formal operational tasks (Berk, 2005).

Piaget himself (1974) suggested that most adults may be able to use formal-operational thought in only a few areas where they have the greatest experience or interest. Taking a college class fosters formal operational abilities in that subject, but not necessarily in others (Lehman & Nisbett, 1990). So expect many students in your middle-school or high-school class to have trouble thinking hypothetically, especially when they are learning something new. Sometimes, students find shortcuts for dealing with problems that are beyond their grasp; they may memorize formulas or lists of steps. These systems may be helpful for passing tests, but real understanding will take place only if students are able to go beyond this superficial use of memorization. The *Guidelines* may help you support the development of formal operations with your students.

Information-Processing and Neo-Piagetian Views of Cognitive Development

As you will see in Chapter 7, there are explanations for why children have trouble with conservation and other Piagetian tasks. These explanations focus on the child's developing information-processing skills, such as attention, memory capacity, and learning strategies. As children mature and their brains develop, they are better able to focus their attention, process information more quickly, hold more information in memory, and use thinking strategies more easily and flexibly. Siegler (1998, 2000) proposes that as children grow older, they develop progressively better rules and strategies for solving prob-

Adolescent egocentrism
Assumption that everyone else shares one's thoughts, feelings, and concerns.

Guidelines: Helping Students to Use Formal Operations

Continue to use concrete-operational teaching strategies and materials.

EXAMPLES

1. Use visual aids such as charts and illustrations as well as somewhat more sophisticated graphs and diagrams, especially when the material is new.
2. Compare the experiences of characters in stories to students' experiences.

Give students the opportunity to explore many hypothetical questions.

EXAMPLES

1. Have students write position papers, then exchange these papers with the opposing side and debate topical social issues—the environment, the economy, national health insurance.
2. Ask students to write about their personal vision of a utopia; write a description of a universe that has no sex differences; write a description of Earth after humans are extinct.

Give students opportunities to solve problems and reason scientifically.

EXAMPLES

1. Set up group discussions in which students design experiments to answer questions.
2. Ask students to justify two different positions on animal rights, with logical arguments for each position.

Whenever possible, teach broad concepts, not just facts, using materials and ideas relevant to the students' lives (Delpit, 1995).

EXAMPLES

1. When discussing the Civil War, consider racism or other issues that have divided the United States since then.
2. When teaching about poetry, let students find lyrics from popular songs that illustrate poetic devices, and talk about how these devices do or don't work well to communicate the meanings and feelings the songwriters intended.

For more ideas about formal operations, see **http://chiron.valdosta.edu/whuitt/col/cogsys/piagtuse.html**

lems and thinking logically. Teachers can help students develop their capacities for formal thinking by putting the students in situations that challenge their thinking and reveal the shortcomings of their logic. Siegler's approach is called *rule assessment* because it focuses on understanding, challenging, and changing the rules that students use for thinking.

Some developmental psychologists have formulated **neo-Piagetian theories** that retain Piaget's insights about children's construction of knowledge and the general trends in children's thinking, but add findings from information processing about the role of attention, memory, and strategies. For example, Robbie Case (1992, 1998) has devised an explanation of cognitive development suggesting that children develop in stages within specific domains such as numerical concepts, spatial concepts, social tasks, storytelling, reasoning about physical objects, and motor development. As children practice using the schemes in a particular domain (for example, using counting schemes in the number concept area), accomplishing the schemes takes less attention. The schemes become more automatic because the child does not have to "think so hard" about it. This frees up mental resources and memory to do more. The child now can combine simple schemes into more complex ones and invent new schemes when needed (assimilation and accommodation in action).

Within each domain such as numerical concepts or social skills, children move from grasping simple schemes during the early preschool years, to merging two schemes into a unit (between about ages 4 and 6), to coordinating these scheme units into larger combinations, and finally, by about ages 9 to 11, to forming complex relationships that can be applied to many problems (Berk, 2005; Case, 1992, 1998). Children do progress through these qualitatively different stages within each domain, but Case argues that progress in one domain does not automatically affect movement in another. The child must have experience and involvement with the content and the ways of thinking within each domain in order to construct increasingly complex and useful schemes and coordinated conceptual understandings about the domain.

Neo-Piagetian theories More recent theories that integrate findings about attention, memory, and strategy use with Piaget's insights about children's thinking and the construction of knowledge.

Some Limitations of Piaget's Theory

Although most psychologists agree with Piaget's insightful descriptions of *how* children think, many disagree with his explanations of *why* thinking develops as it does.

The Trouble with Stages. Some psychologists have questioned the existence of four separate stages of thinking, even though they agree that children do go through the changes that Piaget described (Miller, 2002). One problem with the stage model is the lack of consistency in children's thinking. For example, children can conserve number (the number of blocks does not change when they are rearranged) a year or two before they can conserve weight (a ball of clay does not change when you flatten it). Why can't they use conservation consistently in every situation? In fairness, we should note that in his later work, even Piaget put less emphasis on *stages* of cognitive development and gave more attention to how thinking *changes* through equilibration (Miller, 2002).

Another problem with the idea of separate stages is that the processes may be more continuous than they seem. For example, rather than appearing all at once, object permanence may progress gradually as children's memories develop. The longer you make the infants wait before searching—the longer you make them remember the object—the older they have to be to succeed. Siegler (1998) notes that change can be both continuous and discontinuous, as described by a branch of mathematics called *catastrophe theory*. Changes that appear suddenly, like the collapse of a bridge, are preceded by many slowly developing changes such as gradual, continuous corrosion of the metal structures. Similarly, gradually developing changes in children can lead to large changes in abilities that appear to be abrupt (Fischer & Pare-Blagoev, 2000).

Underestimating Children's Abilities. It now appears that Piaget underestimated the cognitive abilities of children, particularly younger ones. The problems he gave young children may have been too difficult and the directions too confusing. His subjects may have understood more than they could demonstrate when solving these problems. For example, work by Gelman and her colleagues (Gelman, 2000; Gelman & Cordes, 2001) shows that preschool children know much more about the concept of number than Piaget thought, even if they sometimes make mistakes or get confused. As long as preschoolers work with only 3 or 4 objects at a time, they can tell that the number remains the same, even if the objects are spread far apart or clumped close together. In other words, we may be born with a greater store of cognitive tools than Piaget suggested. Some basic understandings, such as the permanence of objects or the sense of number, may be part of our evolutionary equipment, ready for use in our cognitive development (Geary & Bjorklund, 2000).

Piaget's theory does not explain how even young children can perform at an advanced level in certain areas where they have highly developed knowledge and expertise. An expert 9-year-old chess player may think abstractly about chess moves, while a novice 20-year-old player may have to resort to more concrete strategies to plan and remember moves (Siegler, 1998).

Cognitive Development and Culture. One final criticism of Piaget's theory is that it overlooks the important effects of the child's cultural and social group. Children in Western cultures may master scientific thinking and formal operations because this is the kind of thinking required in Western schools (Berk, 2005; Geary, 1998). Even concrete operations such as classification may develop differently in different cultures. For example, when individuals from the Kpelle people of Africa were asked to sort 20 objects, they created groups that made sense to them—a hoe with a potato, a knife with an orange. The experimenter could not get the Kpelle to change their categories; they said this is how a wise man would do it. Finally, the experimenter asked in desperation, "Well, how would a fool do it?" Then the subjects promptly created the four neat classification piles the experimenter had expected—food, tools, and so on (Rogoff & Morelli, 1989).

There is another increasingly influential view of cognitive development. Proposed years ago by Lev Vygotsky and recently rediscovered, this theory ties cognitive development to culture.

One limitation of Piaget's theory appears to be the underestimation of young children's cognitive abilities. For instance, his theory does not explain how these young girls can play chess at the same level as many adults could.

Vygotsky's Sociocultural Perspective

Psychologists today recognize that culture shapes cognitive development by determining what and how the child will learn about the world. For example, young Zinacanteco Indian girls of southern Mexico learn complicated ways of weaving cloth through informal teachings of adults in their communities. In Brazil, without going to school, children who sell candy on the streets learn sophisticated mathematics in order to buy from wholesalers, sell, barter, and make a profit. Cultures that prize cooperation and sharing teach these abilities early, whereas cultures that encourage competition nurture competitive skills in their children (Bakerman et al., 1990; Ceci & Roazzi, 1994). The stages observed by Piaget are not necessarily "natural" for all children because to some extent they reflect the expectations and activities of Western cultures (Kozulin, 2003; Rogoff, 2003).

A major spokesperson for this **sociocultural theory** (also called *sociohistoric*) was a Russian psychologist who died more than 70 years ago. Lev Semenovich Vygotsky was only 38 when he died of tuberculosis, but during his brief life he produced over 100 books and articles. Some of the translations now available are Vygotsky (1978, 1986, 1987, 1993, 1997). Vygotsky's work began when he was studying learning and development to improve his own teaching. He went on to write about language and thought, the psychology of art, learning and development, and educating students with special needs. His work was banned in Russia for many years because he referenced Western psychologists. But in the past 30 years, with the rediscovery of his work, Vygotsky's ideas have become major influences in psychology and education and have provided alternatives to many of Piaget's theories (Kozulin, 2003; McCaslin & Hickey, 2001; Wink & Putney, 2002).

Connect and **Extend** to the **Research**

See the Spring 1995 issue of the *Educational Psychologist* for a special issue on "Lev S. Vygotsky and Contemporary Educational Psychology."

Vygotsky believed that human activities take place in cultural settings and cannot be understood apart from these settings. One of his key ideas was that our specific mental structures and processes can be traced to our interactions with others. These social interactions are more than simple influences on cognitive development—they actually create our cognitive structures and thinking processes (Palincsar, 1998). In fact, "Vygotsky conceptualized development as the transformation of socially shared activities into internalized processes" (John-Steiner & Mahn, 1996, p. 192). We will examine three themes in Vygotsky's writings that explain how social processes form learning and thinking: the social sources of individual thinking; the role of cultural tools in learning and development, especially the tool of language; and the zone of proximal development (Wertsch & Tulviste, 1992; Driscoll, 2005).

Sociocultural theory Emphasizes role in development of cooperative dialogues between children and more knowledgeable members of society. Children learn the culture of their community (ways of thinking and behaving) through these interactions.

Co-constructed process A social process in which people interact and negotiate (usually verbally) to create an understanding or to solve a problem. The final product is shaped by all participants.

The Social Sources of Individual Thinking

Vygotsky assumed that "every function in a child's cultural development appears twice: first, on the social level and later on the individual level; first between people (interpsychological) and then inside the child (intrapsychological)" (1978, p. 57). In other words, higher mental processes first are **co-constructed** during shared activities between the

Lev Vygotsky, shown here with his daughter, elaborated the sociocultural theory of development. His ideas about language, culture, and cognitive development have become major influences in the fields of psychology and education.

child and another person. Then the processes are internalized by the child and become part of that child's cognitive development. For example, children first use language in activities with others, to regulate the behavior of the others ("No nap!" or "I wanna cookie."). Later, however, the child can regulate her own behavior using private speech ("careful—don't spill"), as you will see in a later section. So, for Vygotsky, social interaction was more than influence, it was the origin of higher mental processes such as problem solving. Consider this example:

> A six-year-old has lost a toy and asks her father for help. The father asks her where she last saw the toy; the child says "I can't remember." He asks a series of questions—did you have it in your room? Outside? Next door? To each question, the child answers, "no." When he says "in the car?" she says "I think so" and goes to retrieve the toy. (Tharp & Gallimore, 1988, p. 14)

Who remembered? The answer is really neither the father nor the daughter, but the two together. The remembering and problem solving were co-constructed—between people—in the interaction. But the child may have internalized strategies to use next time something is lost. At some point, the child will be able to function independently to solve this kind of problem. So, like the strategy for finding the toy, higher functions appear first between a child and a "teacher" before they exist within the individual child (Kozulin, 1990; 2003).

Here is another example of the social sources of individual thinking. Richard Anderson and his colleagues (2001) studied how 4th graders in small-group classroom discussions appropriate (take for themselves and use) argument stratagems that occur in the discussions. An argument stratagem is a particular form such as "I think [POSITION] because [REASON]," where the student fills in the position and the reason. For example, a student might say, "I think that the wolves should be left alone because they are not hurting anyone." Another strategy form is "If [ACTION], then [BAD CONSEQUENCE]," as in "If they don't trap the wolves, then the wolves will eat the cows." Other forms manage participation, for example, "What do you think [NAME]?" or "Let [NAME] talk."

Anderson's research identified 13 forms of talk and argument that helped to manage the discussion, get everyone to participate, present and defend positions, and handle confusion. The researchers found that the use of these different forms of talking and thinking *snowballed*—once a useful argument was employed by one student, it spread to other students and the argument stratagem form appeared more and more in the discussions. Open discussions—students asking and answering each other's questions—were better than teacher-dominated discussion for the development of these argument forms. Over time, these ways of presenting, attacking, and defending positions could be internalized as mental reasoning and decision making for the individual students.

Both Piaget and Vygotsky emphasized the importance of social interactions in cognitive development, but Piaget saw a different role for interaction. He believed that interaction encouraged development by creating disequilibrium—cognitive conflict—that motivated change. Thus, Piaget believed that the most helpful interactions were those between peers because peers are on an equal basis and can challenge each other's thinking. Vygotsky (1978, 1986, 1987, 1993), on the other hand, suggested that children's cognitive development is fostered by interactions with people who are more capable or advanced in their thinking—people such as parents and teachers (Moshman, 1997; Palinscar, 1998). Of course, students can learn from both adults and peers.

Cultural Tools and Cognitive Development

Vygotsky believed that **cultural tools**, including material tools (such as printing presses, plows, rulers, abacus—today, we would add PDAs, computers, the Internet) and psychological tools (signs and symbol systems such as numbers and mathematical systems, Braille and sign language, maps, works of art, codes, and language) play very important roles in cognitive development. For example, as long as the culture provides only Roman numerals for representing quantity, certain ways of thinking mathematically—from long division to calculus—are difficult or impossible. But if a number system has a zero, fractions, positive and negative values, and an infinite quantity of numbers, then much more is possible. The number system is a psychological tool that supports learning and cognitive development—it changes the thinking process. This symbol system is passed from adult to child through formal and informal interactions and teachings.

Vygotsky believed that all higher-order mental processes, such as reasoning and problem solving, are *mediated* by (accomplished through and with the help of) psychological tools, such as language, signs, and symbols. Adults teach these tools to children during day-to-day activities and the children internalize them. Then the psychological tools can help students advance their own development (Karpov & Haywood, 1998). The process is something like this: As children engage in activities with adults or more capable peers, they exchange ideas and ways of thinking about or representing concepts—drawing maps, for example, as a way to represent spaces and places. These co-created ideas are internalized by children. Thus, children's knowledge, ideas, attitudes, and values develop through appropriating or "taking for themselves" the ways of acting and thinking provided by both their culture and other members of their group (Kozulin & Presseisen, 1995).

In this exchange of signs and symbols and explanations, children begin to develop a "cultural tool kit" to make sense of and learn about their world (Wertsch, 1991). The kit is filled with material tools such as pencils or rulers directed toward the external world and psychological tools such as concepts or problem-solving strategies for acting mentally. Children do not just receive the tools, however. They transform the tools as they construct their own representations, symbols, patterns, and understandings. As we learned from Piaget, children's constructions of meaning are not the same as those of adults. In the exchange of signs and symbols such as number systems, children create their own understandings (a

Cultural tools The real tools (computers, scales, etc.) and symbol systems (numbers, language, graphs) that allow people in a society to communicate, think, solve problems, and create knowledge.

Vygotsky emphasized the tools that particular cultures provide to support thinking, and the idea that children use the tools they're given to construct their own understanding of the physical and social worlds.

skunk is a "kitty"). These understandings are gradually changed (a skunk is a skunk) as the children continue to engage in social activities and try to make sense of their world (John-Steiner & Mahn, 1996; Wertsch, 1991). In Vygotsky's theory, language is the most important symbol system in the tool kit, and it is the one that helps to fill the kit with other tools.

The Role of Language and Private Speech

Language is critical for cognitive development because it provides a way to express ideas and ask questions, the categories and concepts for thinking, and the links between the past and the future. Language frees us from the immediate situation to think about what was and what might be (Das, 1995; Driscoll, 2005). Vygotsky thought that:

> the specifically human capacity for language enables children to provide for auxiliary tools in the solution of difficult tasks, to overcome impulsive action, to plan a solution to a problem prior to its execution, and to master their own behavior. (1978, p. 28)

If we study language across cultures, we see that different cultures need and develop different language tools.

Language and Cultural Diversity. In general, cultures develop words for the concepts that are important to them. For example: How many different shades of green can you name? If you have access to a purse, check out the different shades of lipstick inside. In my purse I now have lipsticks called "cozy mauve" and "529A" (well, the 99-cent lipsticks have given up on color names). English-speaking countries have over 3,000 words for colors. Such words are important in our lives for fashion and home design, artistic expression, films and television, and lipstick and eye shadow choices—to name only a few areas (Price & Crapo, 2002). Other cultures care less about color. For example, the Hanunoo people of Midori Island in the Philippines and the Dani in New Guinea each have fewer than 5 words for colors, even though they can recognize many color variations. Eskimos really don't have hundreds of words for snow, but the Ulgunigamiut Eskimo do have more than 160 words for ice, because they have to recognize ice at different stages of freezing in order to hunt and live safely in their environment. My mother grew up on a farm in Wisconsin and she can tell you many different words for horse: mare, foal, stallion, gelding, stud, colt, pony, work horse, jumper. Cultures that care about feelings have many word tools to talk about emotion. Think of the variety of words in English for anger (rage, resentment, disgust, pique, wrath, fury, exasperation, ire, hostility, animosity).

Languages change over time to indicate changing cultural needs and values. The Shoshoni Native Americans have one word that means "to make a crunching sound walking on the sand." This word was valuable in the past to communicate about hunting, but today, new words describing technical tools have been added to the language of the Shoshoni, as their life moves away from nomadic hunting. To hear hundreds of new 21st century tool words, listen to techies talk about computers (Price & Crapo, 2002).

Vygotsky placed more emphasis than Piaget on the role of learning and language in cognitive development. He believed that, "thinking depends on speech, on the means of thinking, and on the child's socio-cultural experience" (Vygotsky, 1987, p. 120). In fact, Vygotsky believed that language in the form of private speech (talking to yourself) guides cognitive development.

Private Speech: Vygotsky's and Piaget's Views Compared. If you have spent much time around young children, you know that they often talk to themselves as they play. Piaget called children's self-directed talk "egocentric speech." He assumed that this egocentric speech is another indication that young children can't see the world through the eyes of others. They talk about what matters to them, without taking into account the needs or interests of their listeners. As they mature, and especially as they have disagreements with peers, Piaget believed, children develop socialized speech. They learn to listen and exchange (or argue) ideas. Vygotsky had very different ideas about young children's **private speech.** Rather than being a sign of cognitive immaturity, Vygotsky suggested that these mutterings play an important role in cognitive development by moving children toward self-regulation: the ability to plan, monitor, and guide one's own thinking and problem solving.

Private speech Children's self-talk, which guides their thinking and action. Eventually, these verbalizations are internalized as silent inner speech.

Vygotsky believed that self-regulation developed in a series of stages. First the child's behavior is regulated by others using language and other signs such as gestures. For example, the parent says, "No!" when the child reaches toward a candle flame. Next, the child learns to regulate the behavior of others using the same language tools. The child says, "No!" to another child who is trying to take away a toy, often even imitating the parent's voice tone. The child also begins to use private speech to regulate her own behavior, saying "no" quietly to herself as she is tempted to touch the flame. Finally, the child learns to regulate her own behavior by using silent inner speech (Karpov & Haywood, 1998). For example, in any preschool room you might hear 4- or 5-year-olds saying, "No, it won't fit. Try it here. Turn. Turn. Maybe this one!" while they do puzzles. As these children mature, their self-directed speech goes underground, changing from spoken to whispered speech and then to silent lip movements. Finally, the children just "think" the guiding words. The use of private speech peaks at around 9 years then decreases, although one study found that some students from ages 11 to 17 still spontaneously muttered to themselves during problem solving (McCafferty, 2004; Winsler, Carlton, & Barry, 2000; Winsler & Naglieri, 2003). In fact, I find myself saying things under my breath like, "Not here—where did I use it last . . . ?" when I can't find a book.

This series of steps from spoken words to silent inner speech is another example of how higher mental functions appear first between people as they communicate and regulate each others' behavior, and then emerge again within the individual as cognitive processes. Through this fundamental process, the child is using language to accomplish important cognitive activities such as directing attention, solving problems, planning, forming concepts, and gaining self-control. Research supports Vygotsky's ideas (Berk & Spuhl, 1995; Emerson & Miyake, 2003). Children and adults tend to use more private speech when they are confused, having difficulties, or making mistakes (Duncan & Cheyne, 1999). Inner speech not only helps us solve problems but also allows us to regulate our behavior. Have you ever thought to yourself something like, "Let's see, the first step is" or "Where did I use my glasses last?" or "If I work to the end of this page, then I can . . . "? You were using inner speech to remind, cue, encourage, or guide yourself. In a really tough situation, such as taking an important test, you might even find that you return to muttering out loud. Table 2.2 contrasts Piaget's and Vygotsky's theories of pri-

Connect and Extend to PRAXIS II™

Distinctions Between Piaget's and Vygotsky's Theories (I, A2)

Consider how two teachers—one based in Vygotskian theory and one based in Piagetian theory—might differ in their concepts of learning and teaching and the instructional techniques that they might prefer.

TABLE 2.2

Differences between Piaget's and Vygotsky's Theories of Egocentric or Private Speech

	Piaget	Vygotsky
Developmental Significance	Represents an inability to take the perspective of another and engage in reciprocal communication.	Represents externalized thought; its function is to communicate with the self for the purpose of self-guidance and self-direction.
Course of Development	Declines with age.	Increases at younger ages and then gradually loses its audible quality to become internal verbal thought.
Relationship to Social Speech	Negative; least socially and cognitively mature children use more egocentric speech.	Positive; private speech develops out of social interaction with others.
Relationship to Environmental Contexts		Increases with task difficulty. Private speech serves a helpful self-guiding function in situations where more cognitive effort is needed to reach a solution.

Source: From "Development of Private Speech among Low-Income Appalachian Children," by L. E. Berk and R. A. Garvin, 1984, *Developmental Psychology, 20,* p. 272. Copyright © 1984 by the American Psychological Association. Adapted with permission.

vate speech. We should note that Piaget accepted many of Vygotsky's arguments and came to agree that language could be used in both egocentric and problem-solving ways (Piaget, 1962).

Self-Talk and Learning. Because private speech helps students to regulate their thinking, it makes sense to allow, and even encourage, students to use private speech in school. Teachers' insisting on total silence when young students are working on difficult problems may make the work even harder for them. Note when muttering increases in your class—this could be a sign that students need help. One approach, called *cognitive self-instruction*, teaches students to use self-talk to guide learning. For example, students learn to give themselves reminders to go slowly and carefully.

The Zone of Proximal Development

According to Vygotsky, at any given point in development, there are certain problems that a child is on the verge of being able to solve. The child just needs some structure, clues, reminders, help with remembering details or steps, encouragement to keep trying, and so on. Some problems, of course, are beyond the child's capabilities, even if every step is explained clearly. The **zone of proximal development (ZPG)** is the area between the child's current development level "as determined by independent problem solving" and the level of development that the child could achieve "through adult guidance or in collaboration with more capable peers" (Vygotsky, 1978, p. 86). This is the area where instruction can succeed, because real learning is possible. Kathleen Berger (2006) called this area the "magic middle"—somewhere between what the student already knows and what the student isn't ready to learn (see Figure 2.3).

Private Speech and the Zone. We can see how Vygotsky's beliefs about the role of private speech in cognitive development fit with the notion of the zone of proximal development. Often, an adult uses verbal prompts and structuring to help a child to solve a problem or accomplish a task. This scaffolding can be gradually reduced as the child takes over the guidance, perhaps first by giving the prompts as private speech and finally as inner speech. Let's move forward to a future day in the life of the girl in the example on page 40 who had lost her toy and listen to her *thoughts* when she realizes that a schoolbook is missing. They might sound something like this:

> "Where's my math book? Used it in class. Thought I put it in my book bag after class. Dropped my bag on the bus. That dope Larry kicked my stuff, so maybe . . ."

The girl can now systematically search for ideas about the lost book without help from anyone else.

The Role of Learning and Development

Piaget defined *development* as the active construction of knowledge and *learning* as the passive formation of associations (Siegler, 2000). He was interested in knowledge construction and believed that cognitive development has to come before learning—the child had to be cognitively "ready" to learn. He said that "learning is subordinated to development and not vice-versa" (Piaget, 1964, p. 17). Students can memorize, for example, that Geneva is in Switzerland, but still insist that they cannot be Genevan and Swiss at the same time. True understanding will take place only when the child has developed the operation of *class inclusion*—one category can be included in another. In contrast, Vygotsky believed that learning was an active process that does not have to wait for readiness. In fact, "properly organized learning results in mental development and sets in motion a variety of developmental processes that would be impossible apart from learning" (Vygotsky, 1978, p. 90). He saw learning as a tool in development—learning pulls development up to higher levels and social interaction is a key in learning (Glassman, 2001; Wink & Putney, 2002). Vygotsky's belief that learning pulls development to higher

Zone of proximal development Phase at which a child can master a task if given appropriate help and support.

FIGURE 2.3

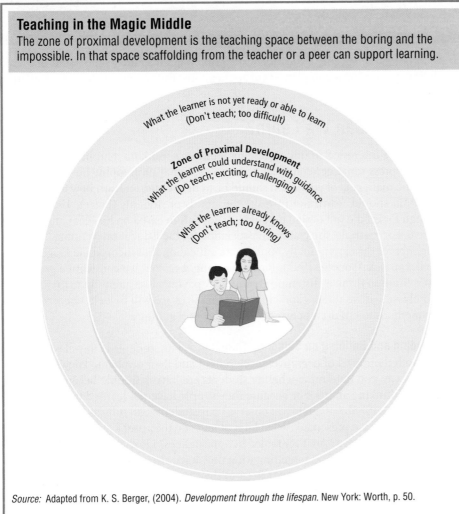

Teaching in the Magic Middle
The zone of proximal development is the teaching space between the boring and the impossible. In that space scaffolding from the teacher or a peer can support learning.

What the learner is not yet ready or able to learn
(Don't teach; too difficult)
Zone of Proximal Development
What the learner could understand with guidance
(Do teach; exciting, challenging)
What the learner already knows
(Don't teach; too boring)

Source: Adapted from K. S. Berger, (2004). *Development through the lifespan.* New York: Worth, p. 50.

levels means that other people, including teachers, play a significant role in cognitive development.

Limitations of Vygotsky's Theory

Vygotsky's theory added important considerations by highlighting the role of culture and social processes in cognitive development, but he may have gone too far. As we have seen in this chapter, we may be born with a greater store of cognitive tools than either Piaget or Vygotsky suggested. Some basic understandings, such as the idea that adding increases quantity, may be part of our biological predispositions, ready for use to guide our cognitive development. Young children appear to figure out much about the world before they have the chance to learn from either their culture or teachers (Schunk, 2004). Also, Vygotsky did not detail the cognitive processes underlying developmental changes—which cognitive processes allow students to engage in more advanced and independent participation in social activities? The major limitation of Vygotsky's theory, however, is that it consists mostly of general ideas; Vygotsky died before he could expand and elaborate on his ideas and pursue his research. His students continued to investigate his ideas, but much of that work was suppressed until the 1950s and 1960s by Stalin's regime (Gredler, 2005; Kozulin, 1990, 2003). A final limitation might be that Vygotsky did not have time to detail the applications of his theories for teaching, even though he was very interested in instruction. So most of the applications described today have been created by others—and we don't even know if Vygotsky would agree with them.

Implications of Piaget's and Vygotsky's Theories for Teachers

Piaget did not make specific educational recommendations and Vygotsky did not have enough time to develop a complete set of applications. But we can glean some guidance from both men.

Piaget: What Can We Learn?

Connect and **Extend** to **PRAXIS II**™

Implications of Piaget's Theory (I, A2)

The music, physical education, and art teachers in a rural, pre-K-to-8 school district work with students who characterize several of Piaget's stages. How should these three teachers adjust their teaching from level to level over the course of a week?

Piaget was more interested in understanding children's thinking than in guiding teachers. He did express some general ideas about educational philosophy, however. He believed that the main goal of education should be to help children learn how to learn, and that education should "form not furnish" the minds of students (Piaget, 1969, p. 70). Even though Piaget did not design programs of education based on his ideas, many other people have. For example, the National Association for the Education of Young Children has guidelines for developmentally appropriate education that incorporate Piaget's findings (Bredekamp & Copple, 1997). Piaget has taught us that we can learn a great deal about how children think by listening carefully, by paying close attention to their ways of solving problems. If we understand children's thinking, we will be better able to match teaching methods to children's current knowledge and abilities.

Understanding and Building on Students' Thinking. The students in any class will vary greatly in both their level of cognitive development and their academic knowledge. As a teacher, how can you determine whether students are having trouble because they lack the necessary thinking abilities or because they simply have not learned the basic facts? To do this, Case (1985b) suggests you observe your students carefully as they try to solve the problems you have presented. What kind of logic do they use? Do they focus on only one aspect of the situation? Are they fooled by appearances? Do they suggest solutions systematically or by guessing and forgetting what they have already tried? Ask your students how they tried to solve the problem. Listen to their strategies. What kind of thinking is behind repeated mistakes or problems? Students are the best sources of information about their own thinking (Confrey, 1990a).

An important implication of Piaget's theory for teaching is what Hunt years ago (1961) called "the problem of the match." Students must be neither bored by work that is too simple nor left behind by teaching they cannot understand. According to Hunt, disequilibrium must be kept "just right" to encourage growth. Setting up situations that lead to unexpected results can help create an appropriate level of disequilibrium. When students experience some conflict between what they think should happen (a piece of wood should sink because it is big) and what actually happens (it floats!), they may rethink the situation, and new knowledge may develop. Capitalizing on the unexpected is a basis for conceptual change teaching in science (see Chapter 13).

Many materials and lessons can be understood at several levels and can be "just right" for a range of cognitive abilities. Classics such as *Alice in Wonderland*, myths, and fairy tales can be enjoyed at both concrete and symbolic levels. It is also possible for a group of students to be introduced to a topic together, then work individually on follow-up activities matched to their learning needs. Tom Good and Jere Brophy (2003) describe a way to use activity cards on three or four different levels to differentiate such follow-up activities. One of the cards should be a good "match" for each student. Often it makes sense to let students choose their own follow-up activities—with encouragement from the teacher to tackle challenges. Using multi-level lessons is called *differentiated instruction* (Tomlinson, 2005b). We look at this approach more closely in Chapter 13.

Activity and Constructing Knowledge. Piaget's fundamental insight was that individuals *construct* their own understanding; learning is a constructive process. At every level of cognitive development, you will also want to see that students are actively engaged in the learning process. In his words:

> Knowledge is not a copy of reality. To know an object, to know an event, is not simply to look at it and make a mental copy or image of it. To know an object is to act on it. To know is to modify, to transform the object, and to understand the process of this transformation, and as a consequence to understand the way the object is constructed. (Piaget, 1964, p. 8)

This active experience, even at the earliest school levels, should not be limited to the physical manipulation of objects. It should also include mental manipulation of ideas that arise out of class projects or experiments (Gredler, 2005). For example, after a social studies lesson on different jobs, a primary-grade teacher might show the students a picture of a woman and ask, "What could this person be?" After answers such as "teacher," "doctor," "secretary," "lawyer," "saleswoman," and so on, the teacher could suggest, "How about a daughter?" Answers such as "sister," "mother," "aunt," and "granddaughter" may follow. This should help the children switch dimensions in their classification and center on another aspect of the situation. Next, the teacher might suggest "American," "jogger," or "blonde." With older children, hierarchical classification might be involved: It is a picture of a woman, who is a human being; a human being is a primate, which is a mammal, which is an animal, which is a life form.

All students need to interact with teachers and peers in order to test their thinking, to be challenged, to receive feedback, and to watch how others work out problems. Disequilibrium is often set in motion quite naturally when the teacher or another student suggests a new way of thinking about something. As a general rule, students should act on, manipulate, observe, and then talk and/or write about (to the teacher and each other) what they have experienced. Concrete experiences provide the raw materials for thinking. Communicating with others makes students use, test, and sometimes change their thinking abilities.

The Value of Play. Maria Montessori once noted, "Play is children's work," and Piaget would agree. We saw that the brain develops with stimulation, and play provides some of that stimulation at every age. Babies in the sensorimotor stage learn by exploring, sucking, pounding, shaking, throwing—acting on their environments. Preoperational preschoolers love pretend play and use pretending to form symbols, use language, and interact with others. They are beginning to play simple games with predictable rules.

Maria Montessori said, "Play is children's work." And in games they learn cooperation, fairness, negotiation, winning, and losing—all important skills for work someday. Without cooperation, there is no game.

Elementary-school-age children also like fantasy, but are beginning to play more complex games and sports, and thus learn cooperation, fairness, negotiation, winning, and losing as well as developing more sophisticated language. As children grow into adolescents, play continues to be part of their physical and social development (Meece, 2002).

Piaget taught us that children do not think like adults. His influence on developmental psychology and education has been enormous, even though recent research has not supported all of his ideas.

Vygotsky: What Can We Learn?

Connect and **Extend** to **PRAXIS II™**

Implications of Vygotsky's Theory (I, A2)

Make a list of scaffolding techniques that would be appropriate with different instructional levels and content areas. Think of scaffolding techniques that others have used when you learned things outside of school (e.g., sports, hobbies).

There are at least three ways that cultural tools can be passed from one individual to another: imitative learning (where one person tries to imitate the other), instructed learning (where learners internalize the instructions of the teacher and use these instructions to self-regulate), and collaborative learning (where a group of peers strives to understand each other and learning occurs in the process) (Tomasello, Kruger, & Ratner, 1993). Vygotsky was most concerned with instructed learning through direct teaching or by structuring experiences that support another's learning, but his theory supports the other forms of cultural learning as well. Thus, Vygotsky's ideas are relevant for educators who teach directly and also create learning environments (Das, 1995; Wink & Putney, 2002). One major aspect of teaching in either situation is assisted learning.

The Role of Adults and Peers. Vygotsky believed that cognitive development occurs through the child's conversations and interactions with more capable members of the culture—adults or more able peers. These people serve as guides and teachers, providing the information and support necessary for the child to grow intellectually. Thus, the child is not alone in the world "discovering" the cognitive operations of conservation or classification. This discovery is assisted or mediated by family members, teachers, and peers. Most of this guidance is communicated through language, at least in Western cultures. In some cultures, observing a skilled performance, not talking about it, guides the child's learning (Rogoff, 1990). Jerome Bruner called this adult assistance **scaffolding** (Wood, Bruner, & Ross, 1976). The term aptly suggests that children use this help for support while they build a firm understanding that will eventually allow them to solve the problems on their own.

Scaffolding Support for learning and problem solving. The support could be clues, reminders, encouragement, breaking the problem down into steps, providing an example, or anything else that allows the student to grow in independence as a learner.

Assisted Learning. Vygotsky's theory suggests that teachers need to do more than just arrange the environment so that students can discover on their own. Children cannot and

According to Vygotsky, much of children's learning is assisted or mediated by teachers and tools in their environment, and most of this guidance is communicated through language.

TABLE 2.3

Assisted Learning: Strategies to Scaffold Complex Learning

- *Procedural facilitators.* These provide a "scaffold" to help students learn implicit skills. For example, a teacher might encourage students to use "signal words" such as *who, what, where, when, why,* and *how* to generate questions after reading a passage.
- *Modeling use of facilitators.* The teacher in the above example might model the generation of questions about the reading.
- *Thinking out loud.* This models the teacher's expert thought processes, showing students the revisions and choices the learner makes in using procedural facilitators to work on problems.
- *Anticipating difficult areas.* During the modeling and presentations phase of instructions, for example, the teacher anticipates and discusses potential student errors.
- *Providing prompt or cue cards.* Procedural facilitators are written on "prompt cards" that students keep for reference as they work. As students practice, the cards gradually become unnecessary. Think of these like the "quick reference cards" that came with your computer or fax machine.
- *Regulating the difficulty.* Tasks involving implicit skills are introduced by beginning with simpler problems, providing for student practice after each stage, and gradually increasing the complexity of the task.
- *Providing half-done examples.* Giving students half-done examples of problems and having them work out the conclusions can be an effective way to teach students how to ultimately solve problems on their own.
- *Reciprocal teaching.* Having the teacher and students rotate the role of teacher. The teacher provides support to students as they learn to lead discussions and ask their own questions.
- *Providing checklists.* Students can be taught self-checking procedures to help them regulate the quality of their responses.

Source: From "Effective Teaching Redux," *ASCD Update, 32*(6), p. 5. The Association for Supervision and Curriculum Development is a worldwide community of educators advocating sound policies and sharing best practices to achieve the success of each learner. To learn more, visit ASCD at www.ascd.org.

should not be expected to reinvent or rediscover knowledge already available in their cultures. Rather, they should be guided and assisted in their learning—so Vygotsky saw teachers, parents, and other adults as central to the child's learning and development (Karpov & Haywood, 1998).

Assisted learning, or guided participation in the classroom, requires the scaffolding described above—giving information, prompts, reminders, and encouragement at the right time and in the right amounts, and then gradually allowing the students to do more and more on their own. Teachers can assist learning by adapting materials or problems to students' current levels; demonstrating skills or thought processes; walking students through the steps of a complicated problem; doing part of the problem (for example, in algebra, the students set up the equation and the teacher does the calculations or vice versa); giving detailed feedback and allowing revisions; or asking questions that refocus students' attention (Rosenshine & Meister, 1992). Cognitive self-instruction is an example of assisted learning. Cognitive apprenticeships and instructional conversations (Chapter 9) are other examples. Look at Table 2.3 for examples of strategies that can be used in any lesson.

Teaching and the "Magic Middle." Both Piaget and Vygotsky probably would agree that students need to be taught in the magic middle (Berger, 2006) or the place of the "match" (Hunt, 1961)—where they are neither bored nor frustrated. Students should be put in situations where they have to reach to understand, but where support from other students or the teacher is also available. Sometimes the best teacher is another student who has just figured out how to solve the problem, because this student is probably operating in the learner's *zone of proximal development.* Students should be guided by explanations, demonstrations, and work with other students—opportunities for cooperative learning. Having a student work with someone who is just a bit better at the activity would also be a good idea—both students benefit in the exchange of explanations, elaborations, and questions. In addition, students should be encouraged to use language to organize their thinking and to talk about what they are trying to accomplish. Dialogue and discussion are important avenues to learning (Karpov & Bransford, 1995; Kozulin & Presseisen, 1995; Wink & Putney, 2002). The *Guidelines* on the next page give more ideas for applying Vygotsky's ideas.

Assisted learning Providing strategic help in the initial stages of learning, gradually diminishing as students gain independence.

Guidelines: Applying Vygotsky's Ideas in Teaching

Tailor scaffolding to the needs of students.

EXAMPLES

1. When students are beginning new tasks or topics, provide models, prompts, sentence starters, coaching, and feedback. As the students grow in competence, give less support and more opportunities for independent work.
2. Give students choices about the level of difficulty or degree of independence in projects; encourage them to challenge themselves, but to seek help when they are really stuck.

Make sure students have access to powerful tools that support thinking.

EXAMPLES

1. Teach students to use learning and organizational strategies, research tools, language tools (dictionaries or computer searches), spreadsheets, and word-processing programs.
2. Model the use of tools; show students how you use an appointment book or electronic notebook to make plans and manage time, for example.

Build on the students' cultural funds of knowledge (Moll et al., 1992).

EXAMPLES

1. Identify family knowledge by having students interview each others' families about their work and home knowledge (agriculture, economics, manufacturing, household management, medicine and illness, religion, child care, cooking, etc.).
2. Tie assignments to these funds of knowledge and use community experts to evaluate assignments.

Capitalize on dialogue and group learning.

EXAMPLES

1. Experiment with peer tutoring; teach students how to ask good questions and give helpful explanations.
2. Experiment with cooperative learning strategies described in Chapter 11.

For more information about Vygotsky and his theories, see **http://tip.psychology.org/vygotsky.html**

Connect and **Extend** to the **Research**

For a full discussion of how to identify students' funds of knowledge, see Moll, L. C., Amanti, C., Neff, D., & Gonzalez, N. (1992). Funds of knowledge: Using a qualitative approach to connect homes and classrooms. *Theory Into Practice, 31,* 132–141 or visit the web at: **http://www.ncrel.org/sdrs/cityschl/city1_1c.htm**

Reaching Every Student: Using the Tools of the Culture

Luis Moll and his colleagues wanted a better way to teach the children of working-class Mexican American families in the barrio schools of Tucson, Arizona (Moll et al., 1992). Rather than adopt a model of remediating the students' deficits, Moll decided to identify and build on the tools and cultural **funds of knowledge** of their families. By interviewing the families, the researchers identified extensive knowledge about the areas in Table 2.4.

When teachers based their assignments on this fund of knowledge, students were more engaged and they learned. Hilda Angiulo is an example of one teacher who worked with Moll who achieved dramatic results with her 6th-grade bilingual class. Hilda's approach of using basal readers supplemented with novels, newspapers, and magazines was not working:

> In response to the research discoveries about her students, Hilda developed an instructional unit around a topic of interest to them: building and construction. She took a big risk since construction was a topic she knew almost nothing about. Hilda did know, however, that her students, their families, and many other people in the community knew quite a bit about construction.
>
> First, Hilda asked students to do library research on building, using books and magazines. She also brought into the classroom a series of books on the subject. Then she directed the students to build model buildings for their homework project. They also wrote short essays in either English or Spanish explaining their research, ideas, and conclusions.
>
> Hilda invited parents and other community members who worked in construction to share their expertise with the children. Some parents talked about their tools and explained how they used numbers and measurements in their work. Others spoke about their work methods and told how they solved problems.
>
> Eventually, the students took the models that they had built and used them as the basis for constructing a model community with streets, parks, and other structures. The follow-up project required additional research, which the students undertook enthusiastically.

Funds of knowledge Knowledge that families and community members have in many areas of work, home, and religious life that can become the basis for teaching.

TABLE 2.4

A Sample of Household Funds of Knowledge

Agriculture

Ranching and farming, horse riding skills, animal management

Soil and irrigation systems, crops

Hunting, tracking, dressing

Mining

Timbering, minerals

Blasting, equipment operation and maintenance

Economics

Business, market values, appraising

Renting and selling

Loans, labor laws, building codes

Consumer knowledge

Accounting, sales

Household Management

Budgets, childcare, cooking

Appliance repairs

Material & Scientific Knowledge

Construction, carpentry, roofing, masonry, painting

Design and architecture

Repair

Airplane, automobile, tractor

House maintenance

Medicine

Contemporary medicine, drugs

First aid procedures, anatomy, midwifery

Folk medicine, herbal knowledge

Folk veterinary cures

Religion

Catechism, baptisms, Bible studies

Moral knowledge and ethics

Source: Adapted from "Funds of knowledge for teaching: Using a qualitative approach to connect homes and classrooms," by L. C. Moll, C. Armanti, D. Neff, & N. Gonzalez. *Theory into Practice,* 31, p. 133.

> Students continued to write up their research and give oral reports to the class. Peer editing groups helped with the process of English and Spanish writing. By the end of the semester, 20 parents and community people had visited Hilda's class and shared their knowledge with her students. By then, the students had successfully completed extensive reading and writing activities.
>
> (http://www.ncrel.org/sdrs/cityschl/city1_1c.htm. Downloaded 1/28/2005)

The students learned, but so did Hilda—she learned about the valuable cognitive resources in the community, and her respect for her students and their families increased.

Piaget and Vygotsky would agree that language plays a major role in learning, both inside and outside the classroom. Let's look at this human capability more closely.

The Development of Language

All children in every culture master the complicated system of their native language, unless severe deprivation or physical problems interfere. This knowledge is remarkable. At the least, sounds, meanings, words and sequences of words, volume, voice tone, inflection, and turn-taking rules must all be coordinated before a child can communicate effectively in conversations.

It is likely that many factors—biological and experiential—play a role in language development. We saw earlier that culture plays a major role by determining what language tools are necessary in the life of the people. The important point is that children develop language as they build on other cognitive abilities by actively trying to make sense of what they hear and by looking for patterns and making up rules to put together the jigsaw puzzle of language. In this process, humans may have built-in biases, rules, and

Connect and **Extend** to **PRAXIS II™**

Language Development
Familiarize yourself with the basic aspects of language development. Focus on actions that teachers can take to maximize students' language and literacy development.

constraints about language that restrict the number of possibilities considered. For example, young children seem to have a constraint specifying that a new label refers to a whole object, not just a part. Another built-in bias leads children to assume that the label refers to a class of similar objects. So the child learning about the rabbit is equipped naturally to assume that *rabbit* refers to the whole animal (not just its ears) and that other similar-looking animals are also rabbits (Markman, 1992). Reward and correction play a role in helping children learn correct language use, but the child's thinking in putting together the parts of this complicated system is very important (Flavell et al., 2002). Table 2.5 shows the milestones of language development, ages 1 to 6, in Western cultures, along with ideas for encouraging development.

Diversity in Language: Dual Language Development

In 2003, about 15% of school-aged children in the United States spoke a language other than English at home. The number grows each year. For example, it is projected that by 2035, about 50% of the kindergarten children in California will speak languages other than English at home (Winsler, Dias, Espinosa, & Rodriquez, 1999).

It is a misconception that young children learn a second language faster than adolescents or adults. In fact, older students go through the stages of language learning faster than young children. Adults have more learning strategies and greater knowledge of language in general to bring to bear in mastering a second language (Diaz-Rico & Weed, 2002). Age is a factor in learning language, but "not because of any critical period that limits the possibility of language learning by adults" (Marinova-Todd, Marshall, & Snow, 2000, p. 28). However, there appears to be a critical period for learning accurate language pronunciation. The earlier people learn a second language, the more their pronunciation is near-native. After adolescence, it is difficult to learn a new language without speaking with an accent (Anderson & Graham, 1994). Kathleen Berger (2006) concludes that the best time to *teach* a second language is during early or middle childhood, but the best time to *learn* on your own through exposure (and to learn native pronunciation) is early childhood.

Luckily, learning a second language does not interfere with understanding in the first language. In fact, the more proficient the speaker is in the first language, the more quickly she or he will master a second language (Cummins, 1984, 1994). For most children who learn two languages simultaneously as toddlers, there is a period between ages 2 and 3 when they progress more slowly because they have not yet figured out that they are learning two different languages. They may mix up the grammar of the two. But

The more proficient speakers are in their first language, the faster they will learn a second language.

TABLE 2.5

Milestones in Language in the First 6 Years and Ways to Encourage Development

Age Range	Milestone	Strategies to Encourage Development
By age 1	Says 1–2 words; recognizes name; imitates familiar sounds; understands simple instructions	• Respond to coos, gurgles, and babbling. • Tell nursery rhymes and sing songs. • Teach the names of everyday items and familiar people. • Play simple games such as "peek-a-boo" and "pat-a-cake."
Between 1 and 2	Uses 5–20 words, including names, says 2-word sentences; vocabulary is growing; waves goodbye; makes "sounds" of familiar animals; uses words (like "more") to make wants known; understands "no"	• Reward and encourage early efforts at saying new words. • Talk about everything you're doing while you're with the child. • Talk simply, clearly, and slowly. • Look at the child when he or she talks to you. • Describe what the child is doing, feeling, hearing. • Let the child listen to children's records and tapes.
Between 2 and 3	Identifies body parts; calls self "me" instead of name; combines nouns and verbs; has a 450-word vocabulary; uses short sentences; matches 3–4 colors, knows "big" and "little"; likes to hear same story repeated; forms some plurals; answers "where" questions	• Help the child listen and follow instructions by playing simple games. • Repeat new words over and over. • Describe what you are doing, planning, thinking. • Have the child deliver simple messages for you. • Show the child you understand what he or she says by answering, smiling, and nodding your head. • Expand what the child says. Child: "more juice," You say, "Chris wants more juice."
Between 3 and 4	Can tell a story; sentence length of 4–5 words; vocabulary about 1000 words; knows last name, name of street, several nursery rhymes	• Talk about how objects are the same or different. • Help the child to tell stories using books and pictures. • Encourage play with other children. • Talk about places you've been or will be going.
Between 4 and 5	Sentence length of 4–5 words; uses past tense; vocabulary of about 1500 words; identifies colors, shapes; asks many questions like "why?" and "who?"	• Help the child sort objects and things (e.g., things to eat, animals). • Teach the child how to use the telephone. • Let the child help you plan activities. • Continue talking about the child's interests. • Let the child tell and make up stories for you.
Between 5 and 6	Sentence length of 5–6 words; average 6-year-old has vocabulary of about 10,000 words; defines objects by their use; knows spatial relations (like "on top" and "far") and opposites; knows address; understands "same" and "different"; uses all types of sentences	• Praise children when they talk about feelings, thoughts, hopes, fears. • Sing songs, rhymes. • Talk with them as you would an adult.
At every age		• Listen and show your pleasure when the child talks to you. • Carry on conversations with the child. • Ask questions to get the child to think and talk. • Read books to the child every day, increasing in length as the child develops.

Source: Adapted from http://www.ldonline.org/ld_indepth/speech-language/lda_milestones.html http://www.med.umich.edu/1libr/yourchild/devmile.htm

researchers believe that by age 4, if they have enough exposure to both languages, they get things straight and speak as well as native *monolinguals*, people who speak only one language (Baker, 1993; Reich, 1986). Also, bilingual children may mix vocabularies of the two languages when they speak, but this is not a sign that they are confused because their bilingual parents often intentionally mix vocabularies as well. It takes from 3 to 5 years to become truly competent in the second language (Berk, 2002; Bhatia & Richie, 1999).

There is no cognitive penalty for students who learn and speak two languages. In fact, there are benefits. Higher degrees of bilingualism are correlated with increased cognitive abilities in such areas as concept formation, creativity, and cognitive flexibility. In addition, these students have more advanced metalinguistic awareness; for example, they are more likely to notice grammar errors. These findings seem to hold as long as there is no stigma attached to being bilingual and as long as students are not expected to abandon their first language to learn the second (Berk, 2005; Bialystok, 1999; Galambos & Goldin-Meadow, 1990; Garcia, 1992; Ricciardelli, 1992). In addition, speaking English plus another language is an asset when graduates enter the business world (Mears, 1998).

Even though the advantages of bilingualism seem clear, as we will see in Chapter 5, many children and adults are losing their **heritage language.** In a large survey of 8th- and 9th-grade first- and second-generation immigrant students in Miami and San Diego, Portes and Hao (1998) found that only 16% had retained the ability to speak their heritage language well. And 72% said they preferred to speak English. The languages of Native Americans are disappearing as well. Only about one-third still exist, and 9 out of 10 of those are no longer spoken by the children (Krauss, 1992).

Language Development in the School Years

By about age 5 or 6, most children have mastered the basics of their native language. What remains for the school-age child to accomplish?

Pronunciation. The majority of 1st graders have mastered most of the sounds of their native language, but a few may remain unconquered. The *j*, *v*, *th*, and *zh* sounds are the last to develop. About 10% of 8-year-olds still have some trouble with *s*, *z*, *v*, *th*, and *zh* (Rathus, 1988). Young children may understand and be able to use many words, but they may prefer to use the words they can pronounce easily.

Grammar. Children master the basics of word order, or **syntax,** in their native language early. But the more complicated forms, such as the passive voice ("The car was hit by the truck"), take longer to master. By early elementary school, many children can understand the meaning of passive sentences, yet they do not use such constructions in their normal conversations, unless the passive construction is common in their culture. Other accomplishments during elementary school include first understanding and then using complex grammatical structures such as extra clauses, qualifiers, and conjunctions. In adolescence, students can understand and use more elaborate grammatical constructions—clauses, connecting words, longer sentences, and so on (Berk, 2005).

Vocabulary and Meaning. The average 6-year-old has a vocabulary of 8,000 to 14,000 words, growing to about 40,000 by age 11. In fact, some researchers estimate that students in the early grades learn up to 20 words a day (Berger, 2003). School-age children enjoy language games and jokes that play on words. In the early elementary years, some children may have trouble with abstract words such as *justice* or *economy*. They also may not understand the subjunctive case ("If I were a butterfly") because they lack the cognitive ability to reason about things that are not true ("But you aren't a butterfly"). They may interpret all statements literally and thus misunderstand sarcasm or metaphor. Fables are understood concretely simply as stories instead of as moral lessons, for example. Many children are in their preadolescent years before they are able to distinguish being kidded from being taunted or before they know that a sarcastic remark is not meant to be taken

Heritage language The language spoken in a student's home or by older members of the family.

Syntax The order of words in phrases or sentences.

literally. But by adolescence, students are able to use their developing cognitive abilities to learn abstract word meanings and to use poetic, figurative language (Berk, 2005; Gerdner, 1982).

Pragmatics. **Pragmatics** involves the appropriate use of language to communicate. For instance, children must learn the rules of turn-taking in conversation. Young children may appear to take turns in conversations, but if you listen in, you realize that they are not exchanging information, only talk time. In later elementary school, children's conversations start to sound like conversations. Contributions are usually on the same topic. Also, by middle childhood, students understand that an observation can be a command, as in "I see too many children at the pencil sharpener." By adolescence, individuals are very adept at varying their language style to fit the situation. Thus, they can talk to their peers in slang that makes little sense to adults, but it marks the adolescent as a member of the group. Yet these same students can speak politely to adults (especially when making requests) and write persuasively about a topic in history. As students grow older, they are more able to judge if their communications are clear to their audience. Interacting with adults, and especially peers who challenge unclear messages, helps develop this skill (Berk, 2005).

Metalinguistic Awareness. Around the age of 5, students begin to develop **metalinguistic awareness.** This means their understanding about language and how it works becomes explicit. They have knowledge about language itself. They are ready to study and extend the rules that have been implicit—understood but not consciously expressed. This process continues throughout life, as we all become better able to use language. One goal of schooling is the development of language and literacy.

Partnerships with Families. Especially in the early years, the students' home experiences are central in the development of language and literacy (Roskos & Neuman, 1993; Whitehurst et al., 1994). In homes that promote literacy, parents and other adults value reading as a source of pleasure, and there are books and other printed materials everywhere. Parents read to their children, take them to bookstores and libraries, limit the amount of television everyone watches, and encourage literacy-related play such as setting up a pretend school or writing "letters" (Pressley, 1996; Roskos & Neuman, 1998; Sulzby & Teale, 1991). Of course, not all homes provide this literacy-rich environment, but teachers can help, as you can see in the *Family and Community Partnerships Guidelines* on the next page.

Pragmatics The rules for when and how to use language to be an effective communicator in a particular culture.

Metalinguistic awareness Understanding about one's own use of language.

Home experiences that emphasize literacy can be central in the development of children's language.

Family and Community Partnerships

Guidelines: Promoting Literacy

Communicate with families about the goals and activities of your program.

EXAMPLES

1. Have someone from the school district, the community, or even an older student translate into the language of the child's family any material you plan to send home.
2. At the beginning of school, send home a description of the goals to be achieved in your class—make sure it is in a clear and readable format.
3. As you start each unit, send home a newsletter describing what students will be studying—give suggestions for home activities that support the learning.

Involve families in decisions about curriculum.

EXAMPLES

1. Have planning workshops at times family members can attend—provide child care for younger siblings, but let children and families work together on projects.
2. Invite parents to come to class to read to students, take dictation of stories, tell stories, record or bind books, and demonstrate skills.

Identify and build on strengths the families already have (Delpit, 2003).

EXAMPLES

1. What are the histories, stories, and skills of family members? Students can draw or write about these.
2. Show respect for the student's language by celebrating poems or songs from the language.

Provide home activities to be shared with family members.

EXAMPLES

1. Encourage family members to work with children to read and follow simple recipes, play language games, keep diaries or journals for the family, and visit the library. Get feedback from families or students about the activities.
2. Give families feedback sheets and ask them to help evaluate the child's school work.
3. Provide lists of good children's literature available locally—work with libraries, clubs, and churches to identify sources.

For more information on Family Literacy Partnerships, see **http://www.famlit.org/**

Source: From *Literacy Development In The Early Years: Helping Children Read and Write, 3/e* (pp. 68–70) by L. M. Morrow. Published by Allyn and Bacon, Boston, MA. Copyright © 1997 by Pearson Education. Adapted by permission of the publisher.

Diversity and Convergences in Cognitive Development

Research across different cultures has confirmed that Piaget was accurate in the sequence of stages he described, but there is diversity in the age ranges for the stages.

Diversity

Western children typically move to the next stage about 2 to 3 years earlier than children in non-Western societies. Careful research has shown that these differences across cultures depend on the subject or domain tested and how much the culture values and teaches knowledge in that domain. For example, children in Brazil who sell candy in the streets instead of attending school appear to fail a certain kind of Piagetian task—class inclusion (Are there more daisies, more tulips, or more flowers in the picture?). But when the tasks are phrased in concepts they understand—selling candy—then these children perform better than Brazilian children the same age who attend school (Ceci & Roazzi, 1994). When a culture or context emphasizes a cognitive ability, children growing up in that culture tend to acquire the ability sooner. In another study that compared Chinese 1st-, 3rd-, and 5th-grade students to American students in the same grades, the Chinese students mastered a Piagetian task that involved distance, time, and speed relationships about 2 years ahead of American students. The Chinese education system puts more emphasis on math and science in the early grades (Zhou, Peverly, Beohm, & Chongde, 2001).

We have also seen that there is diversity in language development. Some children learn two or more languages growing up, others only one. Children in every culture and context learn their native language, but they may learn a different set of rules for language use—pragmatics. For example, Shirley Brice Heath (1989) spent many hours observing White middle-class parents and African American families who were poor. She found that the adults asked different kinds of questions and encouraged different kinds of "talk." White parents asked test-like questions with right answers, such as "How many cars are there?" or "Which car is bigger?" These questions seem odd to African American children whose families don't ask about what they already know. The African American child might wonder "Why would my aunt ask me how many cars? She can see there are 3." Instead, African American families encourage rich storytelling and also teasing that hones their children's quick wit and assertive responses.

Convergences

In spite of these cross cultural differences in cognitive development, there are some convergences. Piaget, Vygotsky, and more recent researchers studying cognitive development and the brain probably would agree with the following big ideas:

1. Cognitive development requires both physical and social stimulation.
2. To develop thinking, children have to be mentally, physically, and linguistically active. They need to experiment, talk, describe, reflect, write, and solve problems. But they also benefit from teaching, guidance, questions, explanations, demonstrations, and challenges to their thinking.
3. Play matters. It is the way children and adolescents try out their thinking and learn to interact with others.
4. Teaching what the student already knows is boring. Trying to teach what the student isn't ready to learn (too difficult, too complex, too little background knowledge) is frustrating and ineffective.
5. Challenge with support will keep students engaged but not fearful.

SUMMARY TABLE

A Definition of Development (pp. 22–26)

What are the different kinds of development? Human development can be divided into physical development (changes in the body), personal development (changes in an individual's personality), social development (changes in the way an individual relates to others), and cognitive development (changes in thinking).

What are three principles of development? Theorists generally agree that people develop at different rates, that development is an orderly process, and that development takes place gradually.

What part of the brain is associated with higher mental functions? The cortex is a crumpled sheet of neurons that serves three major functions: receiving signals from sense organs (such as visual or auditory signals), controlling voluntary movement, and forming associations. The part of the cortex that controls physical motor movement develops or matures first, then the areas that control complex senses such as vision and hearing, and last the frontal lobe, which controls higher-order thinking processes.

What is lateralization and why is it important? Lateralization is the specialization of the two sides, or hemispheres, of the brain. The brain begins to lateralize soon after birth. For most people, the left hemisphere is the major factor in language, and the right hemisphere is prominent in spatial and visual processing. Even though certain functions are associated with certain parts of the brain, the various parts and systems of the brain work together to learn and perform complex activities such as reading and to construct understanding.

Development Orderly, adaptive changes we go through from conception to death.

Physical development Changes in body structure and function over time.

Personal development Changes in personality that take place as one grows.

Social development Changes over time in the ways we relate to others.

Cognitive development Gradual orderly changes by which mental processes become more complex and sophisticated.

Maturation Genetically programmed, naturally occurring changes over time.

Neurons Nerve cells that store and transfer information

Synapses The tiny space between neurons—chemical messages are sent across these gaps.

Plasticity The brain's tendency to remain somewhat adaptable or flexible.

Myelination The process by which neural fibers are coated with a fatty sheath called *myelin* that makes message transfer more efficient.

Lateralization The specialization of the two hemispheres (sides) of the brain cortex.

Piaget's Theory of Cognitive Development (pp. 26–38)

What are the main influences on cognitive development? Piaget's theory of cognitive development is based on the assumption that people try to make sense of the world and actively create knowledge through direct experiences with objects, people, and ideas. Maturation, activity, social transmission, and the need for equilibrium all influence the way thinking processes and knowledge develop. In response to these influences, thinking processes and knowledge develop through changes in the organization of thought (the development of schemes) and through adaptation—including the complementary processes of assimilation (incorporating into existing schemes) and accommodation (changing existing schemes).

What is a scheme? Schemes are the basic building blocks of thinking. They are organized systems of actions or thought that allow us to mentally represent or "think about" the objects and events in our world. Schemes may be very small and specific (grasping, recognizing a square), or they may be larger and more general (using a map in a new city). People adapt to their environment as they increase and organize their schemes.

As children move from sensorimotor to formal-operational thinking, what are the major changes? Piaget believed that young people pass through four stages as they develop: sensorimotor, preoperational, concrete-operational, and formal-operational. In the sensorimotor stage, infants explore the world through their senses and motor activity, and work toward mastering object permanence and performing goal-directed activities. In the preoperational stage, symbolic thinking and logical operations begin. Children in the stage of concrete operations can think logically about tangible situations and can demonstrate conservation, reversibility, classification, and seriation. The ability to perform hypothetico-deductive reasoning, coordinate a set of variables, and imagine other worlds marks the stage of formal operations.

How do neo-Piagetian and information-processing views explain changes in children's thinking over time? Information-processing theories focus on attention, memory capacity, learning strategies, and other processing skills to explain how children develop rules and strategies for making sense of the world and solving problems. Neo-Piagetian approaches also look at attention, memory, and strategies and at how thinking develops in different domains such as numbers or spatial relations.

What are some limitations of Piaget's theory? Piaget's theory has been criticized because children and adults often think in ways that are inconsistent with the notion of invariant stages. It also appears that Piaget underestimated children's cognitive abilities. Alternative explanations place greater emphasis on students' developing information-processing skills and ways teachers can enhance their development. Piaget's work is also criticized for overlooking cultural factors in child development.

Organization Ongoing process of arranging information and experience into mental systems or categories.

Adaptation Adjustment to the environment.

Schemes Mental systems or categories of perception and experience.

Assimilation Fitting new information into existing schemes.

Accommodation Altering existing schemes or creating new ones in response to new information.

Equilibration Search for mental balance between cognitive schemes and information from the environment.

Disequilibrium In Piaget's theory, the "out-of-balance" state that occurs when a person realizes that his or her current ways of thinking are not working to solve a problem or understand a situation.

Sensorimotor Involving the senses and motor activity.

Object permanence The understanding that objects have a separate, permanent existence.

Goal-directed actions Deliberate actions toward a goal.

Operations Actions a person carries out by thinking them through instead of literally performing the actions.

Preoperational The stage before a child masters logical mental operations.

Semiotic function The ability to use symbols—language, pictures, signs, or gestures—to represent actions or objects mentally.

Reversible thinking Thinking backward, from the end to the beginning.

Conservation Principle that some characteristics of an object remain the same despite changes in appearance.

Decentering Focusing on more than one aspect at a time.

Egocentric Assuming that others experience the world the way you do.

Collective monologue Form of speech in which children in a group talk but do not really interact or communicate.

Concrete operations Mental tasks tied to concrete objects and situations.

Identity Principle that a person or object remains the same over time.

Compensation The principle that changes in one dimension can be offset by changes in another.

Classification Grouping objects into categories.

Reversibility A characteristic of Piagetian logical operations—the ability to think through a series of steps, then mentally reverse the steps and return to the starting point; also called *reversible thinking.*

Seriation Arranging objects in sequential order according to one aspect, such as size, weight, or volume.

Formal operations Mental tasks involving abstract thinking and coordination of a number of variables.

Hypothetico-deductive reasoning A formal-operations problem-solving strategy in which an individual begins by identifying all the factors that might affect a problem and then deduces and systematically evaluates specific solutions.

Adolescent egocentrism Assumption that everyone else shares one's thoughts, feelings, and concerns.

Neo-Piagetian theories More recent theories that integrate findings about attention, memory, and strategy use with Piaget's insights about children's thinking and the construction of knowledge.

Vygotsky's Sociocultural Perspective (pp. 39–45)

According to Vygotsky, what are three main influences on cognitive development? Vygotsky believed that human activities must be understood in their cultural settings. He believed that our specific mental structures and processes can be traced to our interactions with others; that the tools of the culture, especially the tool of language, are key factors in development; and the zone of proximal development is the area where learning and development are possible.

What are psychological tools and why are they important? Psychological tools are signs and symbol systems such as numbers and mathematical systems, codes, and language that supports learning and cognitive development—they change the thinking process by enabling and shaping thinking. Many of these tools are passed from adult to child through formal and informal interactions and teachings.

Explain how interpsychological development becomes intrapsychological development. Higher mental processes appear first between people as they are co-constructed during shared activities. As children engage in activities with adults or more capable peers, they exchange ideas and ways of thinking about or representing concepts. These co-created ideas are internalized by children. Thus children's knowledge, ideas, attitudes, and values develop through appropriating, or "taking for themselves," the ways of acting and thinking provided by their culture and by the more capable members of their group.

What are the differences between Piaget's and Vygotsky's perspectives on private speech and its role in development? Vygotsky's sociocultural view asserts that cognitive development hinges on social interaction and the development of language. As an example, Vygotsky describes the role of children's self-directed talk in guiding and monitoring thinking and problem solving, while Piaget suggested that private speech was an indication of the child's egocentrism. Vygotsky, more than Piaget, emphasized the significant role played by adults and more able peers in children's learning. This adult assistance provides early support while students build the understanding necessary to solve problems on their own later.

What is a student's zone of proximal development? At any given point in development, there are certain problems that a child is on the verge of being able to solve and others that are beyond the child's capabilities. The zone of proximal development is the area where the child cannot solve a problem alone, but can be successful under adult guidance or in collaboration with a more advanced peer.

What are two criticisms or limitations of Vygotsky's theory? Vygotsky may have overemphasized the role of social interaction and in cognitive development—children figure out quite a bit on their own. Also, because he died so young, Vygotsky was not able to develop and elaborate on his theories. His students and others since have taken up that work.

Sociocultural theory Emphasizes role in development of cooperative dialogues between children and more knowledgeable members of society. Children learn the culture of their community (ways of thinking and behaving) through these interactions.

Co-constructed process A social process in which people interact and negotiate (usually verbally) to create an understanding or to solve a problem. The final product is shaped by all participants.

Cultural tools The real tools (computers, scales, etc.) and symbol systems (numbers, language, graphs) that allow people in a society to communicate, think, solve problems, and create knowledge.

Private speech Children's self-talk, which guides their thinking and action. Eventually, these verbalizations are internalized as silent inner speech.

Zone of proximal development Phase at which a child can master a task if given appropriate help and support.

Scaffolding Support for learning and problem solving. The support could be clues, reminders, encouragement, breaking the problem down into steps, providing an example, or anything else that allows the student to grow in independence as a learner.

Implications of Piaget's and Vygotsky's Theories for Teachers (pp. 46–51)

What is the "problem of the match" described by Hunt? The "problem of the match" is that students must be neither bored by work that is too simple nor left behind by teaching they cannot understand. According to Hunt, disequilibrium must be carefully balanced to encourage growth. Situations that lead to errors can help create an appropriate level of disequilibrium.

What is active learning? Why is Piaget's theory of cognitive development consistent with active learning? Piaget's fundamental insight was that individuals *construct* their own understanding; learning is a constructive process. At every level of cognitive development, students must be able to incorporate information into their own schemes. To do this, they must act on the information in some way. This active experience, even at the earliest school levels, should include both physical manipulation of objects and mental manipulation of ideas. As a general rule, students should act, manipulate, observe, and then talk and/or write about what they have experienced. Concrete experiences provide the raw materials for thinking. Communicating with others makes students use, test, and sometimes change their thinking abilities.

What is assisted learning, and what role does scaffolding play? Assisted learning, or guided participation in the classroom, requires scaffolding—giving information, prompts, reminders, and encouragement at the right time and in the right amounts, and then gradually allowing the students to do more and more on their own. Teachers can assist learning by adapting materials or problems to students' current levels, demonstrating skills or thought processes, walking students through the steps of a complicated problem, doing part of the problem, giving detailed feedback and allowing revisions, or asking questions that refocus students' attention.

Assisted learning Providing strategic help in the initial stages of learning, gradually diminishing as students gain independence.

Funds of knowledge Knowledge that families and community members have in many areas of work, home, and religious life that can become the basis for teaching.

The Development of Language (pp. 51–56)

How are humans predisposed to develop language? What role does learning play? Children develop language as they build on other cognitive abilities by actively trying to make sense of what they hear, looking for patterns, and making up rules. In this process, built-in biases and rules may limit the search and guide the pattern recognition. Reward and correction play a role in helping children learn correct language use, but the child's thought processes are very important.

What are pragmatics and metalinguistic awareness? Pragmatics is knowledge about how to use language—when, where, how, and to whom to speak. Metalinguistic awareness begins around age 5 or 6 and grows throughout life.

Heritage Language The language spoken in the student's home or by members of the family.

Syntax The order of words in phrases or sentences.

Pragmatics The rules for when and how to use language to be an effective communicator in a particular culture.

Metalinguistic awareness Understanding about one's own use of language.

Teachers' Casebook: Connections to PRAXIS II™

PRAXIS II™ devotes much of its attention to an assessment of your knowledge of human development and its relationship to learning. Below, you can see how practicing teachers responded to the opening scenario of the Teachers' Casebook about teaching abstract concepts such as "symbol." In each case, they either explicitly or implicitly use concepts drawn from theories of cognitive development and language development. Your understanding of these theories will help you design and implement instructional strategies that are appropriate for the developmental levels of your students and will aid you in understanding and interpreting the problems that they might have with learning activities.

What Would They Do?

Here is how some practicing teachers dealt with the Teachers' Casebook challenge of teaching abstract concepts such as "symbol."

Linda Glisson and Sue Middleton **Fifth Grade Team Teachers,**

St. James Episcopal Day School, Baton Rouge, Louisiana

To begin the lesson, I would have the students use a dictionary to define the word *symbolism* (root word—*symbol*) to discover that it means "something that stands for or represents something else." I would then give them a brief "across the curriculum" exercise in ways they incorporate symbols and symbolism into their thinking every day. For example: (social studies, American history): The American flag is just a piece of cloth. Why then do we recite a pledge to it? Stand at attention when it passes in a parade? What does it stand for? (English, literature—fables and fairy tales): What does the wolf usually represent (stand for)? The lion? The lamb? (Art): What color stands for a glorious summer day? Evil? Goodness and purity? I would continue with math symbols, scientific symbols, and music symbols and lead the students toward contributing other examples such as symbols representing holidays. I would then tell them about their own examples of symbolism that I had recorded. The students' participation in and enthusiasm for the exercises would serve to determine whether they were ready for the material.

Dr. Nancy Sheehan-Melzack **Art and Music Teacher,**

Snug Harbor Community School, Quincy, Massachusetts

Even very young children can recognize symbols *if* the symbol is presented first and the explanation required second. A drawing of an octagon on a pole has always elicited the answer, "A stop sign," whenever I have shown it. Children recognize symbols, but the teacher needs to work from their concrete knowledge to the more abstract concept, and there are a great many symbols in their daily life on which one can draw. Children as young as 1st graders can recognize traffic sign shapes, letters of the alphabet, and numbers, and further recognize that they stand for directions, sounds, and how many. When they talk about these very common symbols, they can also realize they all use them for the same meaning.

Valerie A. Chilcoat **Fifth/Sixth Grade Advanced Academics,**

Glenmount School, Baltimore, Maryland

Concrete examples of symbolism must come from the students' own world. Street signs, especially those with pictures and not words, are a great example. These concrete symbols, however, are not exactly the same as symbolism used in poetry. The link has to be made from the concrete to the abstract. Silly poetry is one way to do this. It is motivating to the students to read or listen to, and it can provide many examples of one thing acting as another. This strategy can also be used in lower grades to simply expose children to poetry containing symbolism.

Karen Boyarsky **Fifth Grade Teacher,**

Walter C. Black Elementary School, Hightstown, New Jersey

You can tell a lot about students' thinking simply by interpreting their reactions. Knowing how to interpret students' reactions is just as important as any other assessment tool you might use. In this case, it is clear that the students are confused about the concept of symbolism. This is a difficult concept for many 5th graders to understand and should be approached slowly. One approach to this topic would be to present students with pictures of familiar symbols, such as McDonald's Golden Arches, the Nike Swoosh, or the Target logo. Students could attempt to explain what each of these symbols mean. A discussion about why manufacturers choose to use symbols instead of words would follow. Another approach would be to have the students interpret comparisons that use *like* or *as*. For example, Sue is as pretty as a flower. The teacher would guide the student to see that the author is using a flower to symbolize Sue's looks.

CHAPTER 3

Personal, Social, and Emotional Development

Teachers' Casebook: What Would You Do? 63

Physical Development 64

The Preschool Years 64

The Elementary School Years 64

Adolescence 65

The Brain and Adolescent Development 66

Erikson: Stages of Individual Development 67

The Preschool Years: Trust, Autonomy, and Initiative 68

The Elementary and Middle School Years: Industry versus Inferiority 69

Adolescence: The Search for Identity 70

Bronfenbrenner: The Social Context for Development 72

Families 74

Peers 76

Reaching Every Student: Loneliness and Children with Disabilities 81

Teachers 82

Self-Concept: Understanding Ourselves 85

Self-Concept and Self-Esteem 85

School Life and Self-Esteem 88

Diversity and Identity 88

Diversity and Perception of Self 89

Ethnic and Racial Identity 90

Emotional and Moral Development 92

Emotional Competence 93

Theory of Mind and Intention 93

Moral Development 95

Moral Judgments, Social Conventions, and Personal Choices 97

Diversity in Reasoning 100

Moral Behavior 101

Cheating 101

Diversity and Convergences in Personal/Social Development 102

Diversity 102

Convergences 103

Summary Table 104

Teachers' Casebook Connections to PRAXIS II™/ What Would They Do? 107

What Would You Do?

Teachers' Casebook

You have seen it before, but this year the situation in your middle-school classroom seems especially vicious. A clique of popular girls has made life miserable for several of their former friends—now rejects. The discarded friends have committed the social sins of not fitting in—they wear the wrong clothes or aren't pretty enough or aren't interested in boys yet. To keep the status distinctions clear between themselves and "the others," the popular girls spread gossip about their former friends, often disclosing the intimate secrets revealed when the "out" girls and the "in" girls were *best* friends—only a few months ago. Today, you discover that Stephanie, one of the rejected girls, has written a long, heart-baring e-mail to her former best friend Alison, asking why Alison is "acting so mean." The now-popular Alison forwarded the e-mail to the entire school and Stephanie is humiliated. She has been absent for three days since the incident.

Critical Thinking

- How would you respond to each of the girls?
- What—if anything—would you say to your other students?
- In your teaching, are there ways you can address the issues raised by this situation?
- Reflecting on your years in school, were your experiences more like those of Alison or Stephanie?

Collaboration

With 3 or 4 other students in your class, role play a talk with Stephanie, Alison, or their families. Take turns playing the different roles in your group.

Schooling involves more than cognitive development. As you remember your years in school, what stands out—memories about academic knowledge or memories of feelings, friendships, and fears? In this chapter, we examine personal, social, and emotional development.

We begin with a basic aspect of development that affects all the others—physical changes as students mature. Next, we turn to Erik Erikson and Urie Bronfenbrenner, whose comprehensive theories provide frameworks for studying personal and social development. We then consider the three major influences on children's personal and social development: families, peers, and teachers. Families today have gone through many transitions, and these changes affect the roles of teachers. Next, we explore ideas about how we come to understand ourselves by looking at self-concept and identity, including ethnic and sexual identity. Finally, we look at emotional and moral development. What factors determine our views about morality? What can teachers do to foster such personal qualities as honesty, cooperation, and self-esteem?

By the time you have completed this chapter, you should be able to answer these questions:

- How does physical development affect personal and social development in adolescence?
- What are Erikson's stages of psychosocial development, and what are the implications of his theory for teaching?
- How does Bronfenbrenner's framework describe the social systems that influence development?
- What are the roles of peers, cliques, and friendships in students' lives?
- What can teachers do to deal with aggression and bullying in schools?
- How do relationships with teachers support student development?
- How can teachers foster genuine and appropriate self-esteem in their students?
- How does ethnic identity develop?
- What are Kohlberg's stages of moral reasoning, and what are some of the challenges to his work?
- What encourages cheating in classrooms, and how can teachers respond?

FACING PAGE *Pushball,* Pavel Kusnetsov. Art © Estate of Pavel Kusnetsov/RAO, Moscow/VAGA, New York. Photo: Art Resource/New York.

Connect and **Extend** to **PRAXIS II™**

Human Development (I, A2)
Explain how development in one domain (e.g., physical, emotional) can affect development in other domains.

Physical Development

For most children, at least in the early years, growing up means getting bigger, stronger, more coordinated. It also can be a frightening, disappointing, exciting, and puzzling time.

The Preschool Years

Preschool children are very active. Their gross-motor (large muscle) skills improve greatly over the years from ages 2 to 5 (see Table 3.1). Between ages 2 and about 4 or 5, preschoolers' muscles grow stronger, their balance improves, and their center of gravity moves lower, so they are able to run, jump, climb, and hop. Most of these movements develop naturally if the child has normal physical abilities and the opportunity to play. Children with physical problems, however, may need special training to develop these skills. For young children, as for many adolescents and adults, physical activity can be an end in itself. It is fun just to improve. Because they can't always judge when to stop, preschoolers may need interludes of rest scheduled after periods of physical exertion (Darcey & Travers, 2006).

Fine-motor skills such as tying shoes or fastening buttons, which require the coordination of small movements, also improve greatly during the preschool years (Table 3.1). Children should be given the chance to work with large paintbrushes, fat pencils and crayons, large pieces of drawing paper, large Legos, and soft clay or playdough to accommodate their developing skills. During this time, children will begin to develop a lifelong preference for their right or left hand. By age 5, about 90% of students prefer their right hand for most skilled work, and 10% or so prefer their left hand, with more boys than girls being left-handed (Feldman, 2004). This is a genetically based preference, so don't try to make children switch.

The Elementary School Years

During the elementary-school years, physical development is fairly steady for most children. They become taller, leaner, and stronger, so they are better able to master sports and games. There is tremendous variation, however. A particular child can be much larger or smaller than average and still be perfectly healthy. Because children at this age are very aware of physical differences but are not the most tactful people, you may hear comments such as "You're too little to be in fifth grade. What's wrong with you?" or "How come you're so fat?"

Throughout elementary school, many of the girls are likely to be as large as or larger than the boys in their classes. Between the ages of 11 and 14, girls are, on the average, taller and heavier than boys of the same age (Cook & Cook, 2005). The size discrepancy can give the girls an advantage in physical activities, although some girls may feel conflict over this and, as a result, downplay their physical abilities.

TABLE 3.1

Motor Skills in the Preschool Years
Students' motor skills improve throughout the preschool years.

Approximate Age	Gross-Motor Skills	Fine-Motor Skills
Birth to 3 years	Sits and crawls; begins to run	Picks up, grasps, stacks, and releases objects
3 to 4.5 years	Walks up and down stairs; jumps with both feet; throws ball	Holds crayon; uses utensils; buttons; copies shapes
4.5 to 6 years	Skips; rides two-wheel bicycle; catches ball; plays sports	Uses pencil; makes representational drawing; cuts with scissors, prints letters

Adolescence

Puberty marks the beginning of sexual maturity. It is not a single event, but a series of changes involving almost every part of the body. The sex differences in physical development observed during the later elementary years become even more pronounced at the beginning of puberty. Generally, girls begin puberty between ages 10 and 11, about two years ahead of boys, and reach their final height by age 16 or 17; most boys continue growing until about age 18, but both boys and girls can continue to grow slightly until about 25. Around 80% of American girls have their first menstrual period between the ages of 11 and 14. One tension for adolescents is that they are physically and sexually mature years before they are psychologically or financially ready to shoulder the adult responsibilities of marriage and childrearing.

The physical changes of adolescence have significant effects on the individual's identity. Psychologists have been particularly interested in the academic, social, and emotional differences they have found between adolescents who mature early and those who mature later. Early maturation seems to have certain special advantages for boys. The early maturers' taller, broader-shouldered body type fits the cultural stereotype for the male ideal. Early-maturing boys are more likely to enjoy high social status; they tend to be popular and to be leaders. But they also tend to engage in more delinquent behavior and this is true for White, African American, and Mexican American boys (Cota-Robles, Neiss, & Rowe, 2002). On the other hand, boys who mature late may have a more difficult time. However, some studies show that in adulthood, males who matured later tend to be more creative, tolerant, and perceptive. Perhaps the trials and anxieties of maturing late teach some boys to be better problem solvers (Brooks-Gunn, 1988; Steinberg, 2005).

For girls, these effects are reversed. Maturing way ahead of classmates can be a definite disadvantage. Being larger than everyone else in the class is not a valued characteristic for girls in many cultures (Jones, 2004). A girl who begins to mature early probably will be the first in her peer group to start the changes of puberty. Early maturation is associated with emotional difficulties such as depression, anxiety, and eating disorders, especially in societies that define thin as attractive (Steinberg, 2005). Later-maturing girls seem to have fewer problems, but they may worry that something is wrong with them. All students can benefit from knowing that the "normal" range in rates of maturation is great and that there are advantages for both early and late maturers.

Adolescents going through the changes of puberty are very concerned about their bodies. This has always been true, but today, the emphasis on fitness and appearance makes adolescents even more likely to worry about how their bodies "measure up." Both boys and girls can become dissatisfied with their bodies during adolescence—boys because they do not match the muscular models they see and girls because they don't match the cultural ideals either. For girls, it also appears that conversations with friends about appearance can make dissatisfactions worse (Jones, 2004). For some, the concern becomes excessive. One consequence is eating disorders such as **bulimia** (binge eating) and **anorexia nervosa** (self-starvation), both of which are more common in females than in males. Bulimics often binge, eating an entire gallon of ice cream or a whole cake. Then, to avoid gaining weight, they force themselves to vomit, or they use strong laxatives, to purge themselves of the extra calories. Bulimics tend to maintain a normal weight, but their digestive systems can be permanently damaged.

Anorexia is an even more dangerous disorder, for anorexics either refuse to eat or eat practically nothing while often exercising obsessively. In the process, they may lose 20% to 25% of their body weight, and some (about 20%) literally starve themselves to death. Anorexic students become very thin, and may appear pale, have brittle fingernails, and develop fine dark hairs all over their bodies. They are easily chilled because they have so little fat to insulate their bodies. They often are depressed, insecure, moody, and lonely. Girls may stop having their menstrual period. These eating disorders often begin in adolescence and are becoming more common—about 1% of adolescents (mostly, but not all girls) become anorexic (Rice & Dolgin, 2002). These students usually require professional help—don't ignore the warning signs—less than one-third of people with eating disorders actually receive treatment (Stice & Shaw, 2004). A teacher may be the person

Puberty The physiological changes during adolescence that lead to the ability to reproduce.

Bulimia Eating disorder characterized by overeating, then getting rid of the food by self-induced vomiting or laxatives.

Anorexia nervosa Eating disorder characterized by very limited food intake.

Guidelines: Dealing with Physical Differences in the Classroom

Address students' physical differences in ways that do not call unnecessary attention to the variations.

EXAMPLES

1. Try to seat smaller students so they can see and participate in class activities, but avoid seating arrangements that are obviously based on height.
2. Balance sports and games that rely on size and strength with games that reflect cognitive, artistic, social, or musical abilities, such as charades or drawing games.
3. Don't use or allow students to use nicknames based on physical traits.
4. Make sure there is a good supply of left-handed scissors for preschool classes.

Help students obtain factual information on differences in physical development.

EXAMPLES

1. Set up science projects on sex differences in growth rates.
2. Have readings available that focus on differences between early and late maturers. Make sure that you present the positives and the negatives of each.
3. Find out the school policy on sex education and on informal guidance for students. Some schools, for example, encourage teachers to talk to girls who are upset about their first menstrual period, while other schools expect teachers to send the girls to talk to the school nurse (if your school still has one—budget cuts have eliminated many).
4. Give the students models in literature or in their community of accomplished and caring individuals who do not fit the ideal physical stereotypes.

Accept that concerns about appearance and the opposite sex will occupy much time and energy for adolescents.

EXAMPLES

1. Allow some time at the end of class for socializing.
2. Deal with some of these issues in curriculum-related materials.

For more information about accommodations for physical differences in your classroom, see **http://dos.claremontmckenna.edu/PhysicalLearningDiff.asp**

who begins the chain of help for students with these tragic problems. The *Guidelines* give a few ideas for dealing with physical differences in the classroom.

The Brain and Adolescent Development

Along with all the other changes in puberty come changes in the brain and neurological system that affect personal and social development. Throughout adolescence, changes in the brain increase students' computational skills as well as their ability to control behavior in both low-stress and high-stress situations, to be more purposeful and organized, and to inhibit impulsive behavior. But these abilities are not fully developed until the early 20s, so adolescents may "seem" like adults, at least in low-stress situations, but their brains are not fully developed. They may have trouble controlling emotions and avoiding risky behaviors. In fact, adolescents appear to need more intense emotional stimulation than either children or adults, so these young people are set up for taking risks or seeking thrills. Teachers can take advantage of their adolescent students' intensity by helping them devote their energy to areas such as politics, the environment, or social causes (Price, 2005) or by guiding them to explore emotional connections with characters in history or literature.

Connect and Extend to the Research

See the Autumn 2004 Issue of *Theory Into Practice* on Developmental Psychology: Implications for Teaching (Vol. 43, No. 4). Guest Editor: Chris Andersen.

Other changes in the neurological system during adolescence affect sleep; students need about 9 hours of sleep per night, but many students' biological clocks are reset so it is difficult for them to fall asleep before midnight. Yet in many school districts, high school begins by 7:30, so 9 hours of sleep are impossible and students are continually sleep-deprived. Classes that keep students in their seats, taking notes for the full period may literally "put the students to sleep." With no time for breakfast, and little for lunch, these students' nutrition often is deprived as well (Sprenger, 2005).

We turn now to personal and social development. Two psychologists have proposed broad theories that help us understand development in context: Erik Erikson and Urie Bronfenbrenner.

Erik Erikson proposed a theory of psychosocial development that describes tasks to be accomplished at different stages of life.

Erikson: Stages of Individual Development

Like Piaget, Erik Erikson did not start his career as a psychologist. In fact, Erikson never graduated from high school. He spent his early adult years studying art and traveling around Europe. A meeting with Sigmund Freud in Vienna led to an invitation to study psychoanalysis. Erikson then emigrated to America to practice his profession and to escape the threat of Hitler. In his influential *Childhood and Society* (1963), Erikson offered a basic framework for understanding the needs of young people in relation to the society in which they grow, learn, and later make their contributions. His later books, *Identity, Youth, and Crisis* (1968) and *Identity and the Life Cycle* (1980), expanded on his ideas.

Erikson's **psychosocial** theory emphasized the emergence of the self, the search for identity, the individual's relationships with others, and the role of culture throughout life. Like Piaget, Erikson saw development as a passage through a series of stages, each with its particular goals, concerns, accomplishments, and dangers. The stages are interdependent: Accomplishments at later stages depend on how conflicts are resolved in the earlier years. At each stage, Erikson suggests that the individual faces a **developmental crisis**—a conflict between a positive alternative and a potentially unhealthy alternative. The way in which the individual resolves each crisis will have a lasting effect on that person's self-image and view of society. We will look briefly at all eight stages in Erikson's theory—or, as he called them, the "eight ages of man." Table 3.2 presents the stages in summary form.

Psychosocial Describing the relation of the individual's emotional needs to the social environment.

Developmental crisis A specific conflict whose resolution prepares the way for the next stage.

TABLE 3.2

Erikson's Eight Stages of Psychosocial Development

Stages	Approximate Age	Important Event	Description
1. Basic trust versus basic mistrust	Birth to 12–18 months	Feeding	The infant must form a first loving, trusting relationship with the caregiver or develop a sense of mistrust.
2. Autonomy versus shame/doubt	18 months to 3 years	Toilet training	The child's energies are directed toward the development of physical skills, including walking, grasping, controlling the sphincter. The child learns control but may develop shame and doubt if not handled well.
3. Initiative versus guilt	3 to 6 years	Independence	The child continues to become more assertive and to take more initiative but may be too forceful, which can lead to guilt feelings.
4. Industry versus inferiority	6 to 12 years	School	The child must deal with demands to learn new skills or risk a sense of inferiority, failure, and incompetence.
5. Identity versus role confusion	Adolescence	Peer relationships	The teenager must achieve identity in occupation, gender roles, politics, and religion.
6. Intimacy versus isolation	Young adulthood	Love relationships	The young adult must develop intimate relationships or suffer feelings of isolation.
7. Generativity versus stagnation	Middle adulthood	Parenting/Mentoring	Each adult must find some way to satisfy and support the next generation.
8. Ego integrity versus despair	Late adulthood	Reflection on and acceptance of one's life	The culmination is a sense of acceptance of oneself and a sense of fulfillment.

Source: From *Psychology, 5/e* by Lester A. Lefton. Published by Allyn and Bacon, Boston, MA. Copyright © 1994 by Pearson Education. Reprinted by permission of the publisher.

Connect and **Extend** to **PRAXIS II™**

Erikson's Psychosocial Theory of Development (I, A1, 2)

The school population spans four stages of Erikson's theory. Identify the major crisis of each of these stages. How can teachers support positive resolution of each of these stages? What are implications for negative resolution of these crises?

Children need opportunities to learn things for themselves in order to develop a sense of initiative.

The Preschool Years: Trust, Autonomy, and Initiative

Erikson identifies *trust versus mistrust* as the basic conflict of infancy. According to Erikson, the infant will develop a sense of trust if its needs for food and care are met with comforting regularity and responsiveness from caregivers. In this first year, infants are in Piaget's sensorimotor stage and are just beginning to learn that they are separate from the world around them. This realization is part of what makes trust so important: Infants must trust the aspects of their world that are beyond their control (Isabella & Belsky, 1991; Posada et al., 2002).

Erikson's second stage, ***autonomy*** *versus shame and doubt*, marks the beginning of self-control and self-confidence. Young children begin to assume important responsibilities for self-care such as feeding, toileting, and dressing. During this period, parents must tread a fine line; they must be protective—but not overprotective. If parents do not maintain a reassuring, confident attitude and do not reinforce the child's efforts to master basic motor and cognitive skills, children may begin to feel shame; they may learn to doubt their abilities to manage the world on their own terms. Erikson believes that children who experience too much doubt at this stage will lack confidence in their own abilities throughout life.

For Erikson, the next stage of ***initiative*** *versus guilt* "adds to autonomy the quality of undertaking, planning, and attacking a task for the sake of being active and on the move" (Erikson, 1963, p. 255). The challenge of this period is to maintain a zest for activity and at the same time understand that not every impulse can be acted on. Again, adults must tread a fine line, this time in providing supervision without interference. If children are not allowed to do things on their own, a sense of guilt may develop; they may come to believe that what they want to do is always "wrong." The *Guidelines* suggest ways of encouraging initiative.

Autonomy Independence.

Initiative Willingness to begin new activities and explore new directions.

Guidelines: Encouraging Initiative in Preschool Children

Encourage children to make and to act on choices.

EXAMPLES

1. Have a free-choice time when children can select an activity or game.
2. As much as possible, avoid interrupting children who are very involved in what they are doing.
3. When children suggest an activity, try to follow their suggestions or incorporate their ideas into ongoing activities.
4. Offer positive choices: Instead of saying, "You can't have the cookies now," ask, "Would you like the cookies after lunch or after naptime?"

Make sure that each child has a chance to experience success.

EXAMPLES

1. When introducing a new game or skill, teach it in small steps.
2. Avoid competitive games when the range of abilities in the class is great.

Encourage make-believe with a wide variety of roles.

EXAMPLES

1. Have costumes and props that go along with stories the children enjoy. Encourage the children to act out the stories or make up new adventures for favorite characters.
2. Monitor the children's play to be sure no one monopolizes playing "teacher," "Mommy," "Daddy," or other heroes.

Be tolerant of accidents and mistakes, especially when children are attempting to do something on their own.

EXAMPLES

1. Use cups and pitchers that make it easy to pour and hard to spill.
2. Recognize the attempt, even if the product is unsatisfactory.
3. If mistakes are made, show students how to clean up, repair, or redo.
4. If a student consistently behaves in ways that are highly unusual or unacceptable, seek guidance from the school counselor or psychologist. The best time to help children deal with psychosocial problems is at an early age.

For more ideas, see **http://www.vtaide.com/png/ERIK3.htm**

The Elementary and Middle School Years: Industry versus Inferiority

Let's set the stage for the next phase. Between the ages of 5 and 7, when most children start school, cognitive development is proceeding rapidly. Children can process more information faster and their memory spans are increasing. They are moving from preoperational to concrete operational thinking. As these internal changes progress, the children are spending hours every weekday in the new physical and social world of school. They must now reestablish Erikson's stages of psychosocial development in the unfamiliar school setting. They must learn to *trust* new adults, act *autonomously* in this more complex situation, and *initiate* actions in ways that fit the new rules of school.

The new psychosocial challenge for the school years is what Erikson calls ***industry*** *versus inferiority.* Students are beginning to see the relationship between perseverance and the pleasure of a job completed. In modern societies, children's ability to move between the worlds of home, neighborhood, and school and to cope with academics, group activities, and friends will lead to a growing sense of competence. Difficulty with these challenges can result in feelings of inferiority. Children must master new skills and work toward new goals, at the same time they are being compared to others and risking failure.

The way children cope with these challenges has implications for the rest of their school experience. Two of the best predictors of dropping out of school are low grade point average by the 3rd grade and being held back in one of the primary grades (Paris & Cunningham, 1996). "How well students do in the primary grades matters more for their future success than does their school performance at any other time" (Entwisle & Alexan-

Industry Eagerness to engage in productive work.

Guidelines: Encouraging Industry

Make sure that students have opportunities to set and work toward realistic goals.

EXAMPLES

1. Begin with short assignments, then move on to longer ones. Monitor student progress by setting up progress checkpoints.
2. Teach students to set reasonable goals. Write down goals and have students keep a journal of progress toward these goals.

Give students a chance to show their independence and responsibility.

EXAMPLES

1. Tolerate honest mistakes.
2. Delegate to students tasks such as watering class plants, collecting and distributing materials, monitoring the computer lab, grading homework, keeping records of forms returned, and so on.

Provide support to students who seem discouraged.

EXAMPLES

1. Use individual charts and contracts that show student progress.
2. Keep samples of earlier work so students can see their improvements.
3. Have awards for most improved, most helpful, most hardworking.

For more ideas, see **http://www.vtaide.com/png/ERIK4.htm**

der, 1998, p. 354). Because schools tend to reflect middle-class values and norms, making the transition to school may be especially difficult for children who differ economically or culturally. The achievement test score differences among students from high- and low-socioeconomic groups in 1st grade are relatively small, but by the 6th grade, the differences have tripled. These achievement gaps are discussed more fully in Chapter 5. The *Guidelines* give ideas for encouraging industry.

In the transition to middle school, students confront an increased focus on grades and performance as well as more competition on all fronts—academic, social, and athletic. Just when they are eager to make decisions and assume more independence, these developing minds encounter more rules, required courses, and assignments. They move from a close connection with one teacher all year to more impersonal relations with many teachers in many different subjects across the year, and from being the most mature and highest status students in a small, familiar elementary school to being the "babies" in a large, impersonal middle school (Meece, 2002; Murdock, Hale, & Weber, 2001; Rudolph, Lambert, Clark, & Kurlakowsky, 2001; Wigfield, Eccles, MacIver, Rueman, & Midgley, 1991).

Connect and Extend to Your Teaching

William Glasser talks about self-concept in terms of failure and success identities. Loneliness, apathy, and withdrawal or delinquency characterizes the "failure identity"; the "success identity" is characterized by the ability to give and receive love, and the feeling of doing something that is important to self or others. (Glasser, W. [1969]. *Schools without failure.* New York: Harper and Row.) Given these characteristics, what kind of experiences can a teacher provide to help a student change from a failure identity to a success identity, that is, develop a more positive self-concept?

Adolescence: The Search for Identity

As students move into adolescence, cognitive processes are expanding as the students develop capabilities for abstract thinking and the capacity to understand the perspectives of others. Even greater physical changes are taking place in the students as they approach puberty. So, with developing minds and bodies, young adolescents must confront the central issue of constructing an **identity** that will provide a firm basis for adulthood. The individual has been developing a sense of self since infancy. But adolescence marks the first time that a conscious effort is made to answer the now-pressing question: "Who am I?" The conflict defining this stage is *identity versus role confusion.* Identity refers to the organization of the individual's drives, abilities, beliefs, and history into a consistent image of self. It involves deliberate choices and decisions, particularly about work, values, ideology, and commitments to people and ideas (Marcia, 1987; Penuel & Wertsch, 1995). If adolescents fail to integrate all these aspects and choices, or if they feel unable to choose at all, role confusion threatens.

Identity The complex answer to the question: "Who am I?"

STOP | THINK | WRITE Have you decided on your career? What alternatives did you consider? Who or what was influential in shaping your decision? ■

With developing minds and bodies, young adolescents must confront the central issue of developing an identity that will provide a firm basis for adulthood. With adolescence comes a pressing question: "Who am I?"

Identity Statuses. James Marcia (1991, 1994, 1999) suggests that there are four identity alternatives for adolescents, depending on whether they have *explored* options and made *commitments*. The first, **identity diffusion,** occurs when individuals do not explore any options or commit to any actions. They reach no conclusions about who they are or what they want to do with their lives; they have no firm direction. Adolescents experiencing identity diffusion may be apathetic and withdrawn, with little hope for the future, or they may be openly rebellious. These adolescents often go along with the crowd, so they are more likely to abuse drugs (Archer & Waterman, 1990; Berger & Thompson, 1995; Kroger, 2000).

Identity foreclosure is commitment without exploration. Foreclosed adolescents have not experimented with different identities or explored a range of options, but simply have committed themselves to the goals, values, and lifestyles of others—usually their parents, but sometimes cults or extremist groups. Foreclosed adolescents tend to be rigid, intolerant, dogmatic, and defensive (Frank, Pirsch, & Wright, 1990).

Adolescents in the midst of struggling with choices are experiencing what Erikson called a **moratorium.** Erikson used the term moratorium to describe exploration with a delay in commitment to personal and occupational choices. This delay is very common, and probably healthy, for modern adolescents. Erikson believed that adolescents in complex societies have an *identity crisis* during moratorium. Today, the period is no longer referred to as a crisis because, for most people, the experience is a gradual exploration rather than a traumatic upheaval (Grotevant, 1998).

Identity achievement means that after exploring the realistic options, the individual has made choices and is committed to pursuing them. It appears that few students achieve this status by the end of high school; students who attend college may take a bit longer to decide. Because so many people today go on to college or other continuing education after high school, it is not uncommon for the explorations of moratorium to continue into the early 20s. About 80% of students change their majors at least once (just ask my mom). And some adults may achieve a firm identity at one period in their lives, only to reject that identity and achieve a new one later. So identity, once achieved, may not be unchanging for everyone (Kroger, 2000; Nurmi, 2004).

Both moratorium and identity-achieved statuses are considered healthy. Schools that give adolescents experiences with community service, real-world work, internships, and mentoring help to foster identity formation (Cooper, 1998). Turn the page for *Guidelines* that give other ideas for supporting identity formation.

Connect and Extend to the Research

See the special issue of *Educational Leadership* (April, 2005, Vol. 62, No. 7) on "The Adolescent Learner."

Identity diffusion Uncenteredness; confusion about who one is and what one wants.

Identity foreclosure Acceptance of parental life choices without consideration of options.

Moratorium Identity crisis; suspension of choices because of struggle.

Identity achievement Strong sense of commitment to life choices after free consideration of alternatives.

Guidelines: Supporting Identity Formation

Give students many models for career choices and other adult roles.

EXAMPLES

1. Point out models from literature and history. Have a calendar with the birthdays of eminent women, minority leaders, or people who made a little-known contribution to the subject you are teaching. Briefly discuss the person's accomplishments on his or her birthday.
2. Invite guest speakers to describe how and why they chose their professions. Make sure all kinds of work and workers are represented.

Help students find resources for working out personal problems.

EXAMPLES

1. Encourage them to talk to school counselors.
2. Discuss potential outside services.

Be tolerant of teenage fads as long as they don't offend others or interfere with learning.

EXAMPLES

1. Discuss the fads of earlier eras (neon hair, powdered wigs, love beads).
2. Don't impose strict dress or hair codes.

Give students realistic feedback about their work and support for improving. Adolescents may need many "second chances."

EXAMPLES

1. When students misbehave or perform poorly, make sure they understand the consequences of their behavior—the effects on themselves and others.
2. Give students model answers or show them other students' completed projects so they can compare their work to good examples.
3. Because students are "trying on" roles, keep the roles separate from the person. Criticize the behavior without criticizing the student.

For more ideas about working with adolescents using Erikson's theory, see **http://www.cde.ca.gov/ls/cg/pp/documents/erikson.pdf**

Beyond the School Years. The crises of Erikson's stages of adulthood all involve the quality of human relations. The first of these stages is *intimacy versus isolation.* Intimacy in this sense refers to a willingness to relate to another person on a deep level, to have a relationship based on more than mutual need. Someone who has not achieved a sufficiently strong sense of identity tends to fear being overwhelmed or swallowed up by another person and may retreat into isolation. The next stage is *generativity versus stagnation.* **Generativity** extends the ability to care for another person and involves concern and guidance for both the next generation and future generations. While generativity frequently refers to having and nurturing children, it has a broader meaning. Productivity and creativity are essential features. The last of Erikson's stages is ***integrity*** *versus despair,* coming to terms with death. Achieving integrity means consolidating your sense of self and fully accepting its unique and now unalterable history. Those unable to attain a feeling of integrity and fulfillment sink into despair.

Erikson's work helped start the life-span development approach, and his theories have been especially useful in understanding adolescence. But feminists have criticized his notion that identity precedes intimacy, because their research indicates that for women, identity achievement is fused with achieving intimacy (Miller, 2002). And, as you will see later, recent research has focused on issues not fully explored by Erikson—ethnic and racial identity.

Generativity Sense of concern for future generations.

Integrity Sense of self-acceptance and fulfillment.

Bioecological model Bronfenbrenner's theory describing the nested social and cultural contexts that shape development. Every person develops within a *microsystem,* inside a *mesosystem,* embedded in an *exosystem,* all of which are a part of the *macrosystem* of the culture.

Bronfenbrenner: The Social Context for Development

Erikson highlighted the role of social and cultural context in personal-social development, but Urie Bronfenbrenner went further to map the many interacting social contexts that affect development with his **bioecological model** of development (Bronfenbrenner, 1989; Bronfenbrenner & Evans, 2000). The *bio* aspect of the model recognizes that people bring their biological selves to the developmental process. The *ecological* part recognizes that the social contexts in which we develop are ecosystems because they are in constant interaction and influence each other. Look at Figure 3.1. Every person lives within a *microsystem*, inside a *mesosystem*, embedded in an *exosystem*, all of which are a part of the *macrosystem*—like a set of Russian painted dolls, nested one inside the other.

In the microsystem are the person's immediate relationships and activities. For a child, it might be the immediate family, friends, or teachers and the activities of play and school. Relationships in the microsystem are reciprocal—they flow in both directions. The child affects the parent and the parent influences the child, for example. The mesosystem is the set of interactions and relationships among all the elements of the microsystem—the family members interacting with each other or with the teacher. Again, all relationships are reciprocal—the teacher influences the parents and the parents affect the teacher, and these interactions affect the child. The exosystem includes all the social settings that affect the child, even though the child is not a direct member of the systems. Examples are the teachers' relations with administrators and the school board; parents' jobs; the community resources for health, employment, or recreation; or the family's religious affiliation. The macrosystem is the larger society—its values, laws, conventions, and traditions. For another

FIGURE 3.1

Urie Bronfenbrenner's Bioecological Model of Human Development

Every person develops within a *microsystem* (family, friends, school activities, teacher, etc.) inside a *mesosystem* (the interactions among all the microsystem elements), embedded in an *exosystem* (social settings that affect the child, even though the child is not a direct member—community resources, parents' work place, etc.); all are part of the *macrosystem* (the larger society with its laws, customs, values, etc.).

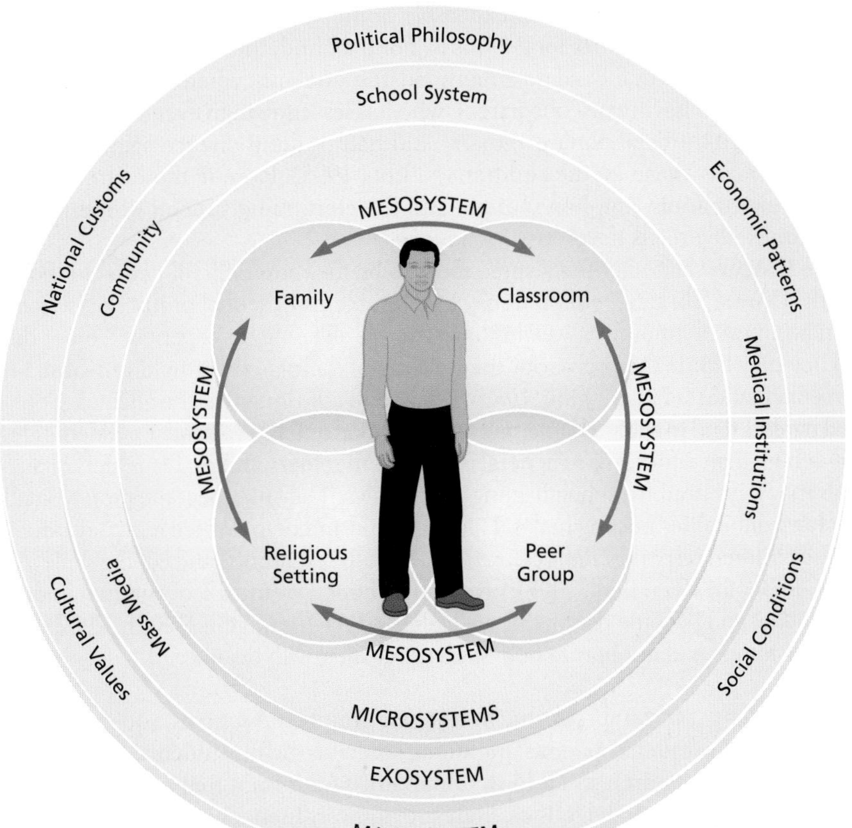

Source: Adapted from K. S. Berger (2004), *The developing person through the lifespan.* New York: Worth, p. 3.

example, think of the teacher's own bioecological system. The teacher is influenced by the microsystem of the principal, colleagues, and students; the mesosystem of the interactions among those people; the exosystem of state and national educational policies, and the macrosystem of cultural norms and values (Woolfolk Hoy, Davis, & Pape, 2007).

Bronfenbrenner's theory has at least two lessons for teachers. First, influences in all social systems are reciprocal. Second, there are many dynamic forces that interact to create the context for individual development. Next, we look at three important social contexts—families, peers, and teachers.

Families

The most appropriate expectation to have about your students' families is no expectation at all. Increasingly, students today have only one or no sibling, or they may be part of **blended families,** with stepbrothers or stepsisters who move in and out of their lives. Some of your students may live with an aunt, with grandparents, with one parent, in foster or adoptive homes, or with an older brother or sister. The best advice is to avoid the phrases "your parents" and "your mother and father" and to speak of "your family" when talking to students. Divorce is one reason why family structures are so varied.

Divorce. The divorce rate in the United States is the highest in the world, over a third higher than the second- and third-ranked nations, New Zealand and Great Britain (Berk, 2005). Some analysts estimate that between 40% and 50% of first-time marriages that took place in the 1990s will end in divorce (Amato, 2001). And as too many of us know from experiences in our own families, separation and divorce are stressful events for all participants, even under the best circumstances. The actual separation of the parents may have been preceded by years of conflict in the home or may come as a shock to all, including friends and children. During the divorce itself, conflict may increase as property and custody rights are being negotiated.

After the divorce, more changes may disrupt the children's lives. The parent who has custody may have to move to a less expensive home, find new sources of income, go to work for the first time, or work longer hours. For the child, this can mean leaving behind important friendships in the old neighborhood or school, just when support is needed the most. It may mean having just one parent, who has less time than ever to be with the children. About two-thirds of parents remarry and half of them divorce again, so there are more adjustments ahead for the children (Nelson, 1993). Even in those rare cases where there are few conflicts, ample resources, and the continuing support of friends and extended family, divorce is never easy for anyone.

The first two years after the divorce seem to be the most difficult period for both boys and girls. During this time, children may have problems in school or just skip school, lose or gain an unusual amount of weight, have trouble sleeping, or experience other difficulties. They may blame themselves for the breakup of their family or hold unrealistic hopes for a reconciliation (Hetherington, 1999). Long-term adjustment is also affected. Sons of divorced parents tend to show a higher rate of behavioral and interpersonal problems at home and in school than either girls in general or boys from intact families. Daughters of divorced parents may have trouble in their dealings with males. They may become more sexually active or have difficulties trusting males. However, adjustment to divorce is an individual matter; some children respond with increased responsibility, maturity, and coping skills (Amato, Loomis, & Booth, 1995; Berk, 2005). Over time, about 75% to 80% of children in divorced families adapt and become reasonably well adjusted (Hetherington & Kelly, 2002). See the *Guidelines* for ideas about how to help students dealing with divorce.

Connect and **Extend** to **PRAXIS II™**
Families (I, B6)
Understand the influence of families, their culture, and values on student learning.

Parenting Styles. If you spend time in teachers' lounges in schools, you may hear quite a bit of talk about students' parents, including some blame for students' problems. Actually, most current research in child development says it's not that simple. As Bronfenbrenner's bioecologial model tells us, there are many influences on children. But parents are still important (Berger, 2006).

One well-known description of **parenting styles** is based on the research of Diane Baumrind (1991). Her early work focused on a careful longitudinal study of 100 (mostly European American, middle-class) preschool children. Through observation of children

Blended families Parents, children, and stepchildren merged into families through remarriages.

Parenting styles The ways of interacting with and disciplining children.

Guidelines: Helping Children of Divorce

Take note of any sudden changes in behavior that might indicate problems at home.

EXAMPLES

1. Be alert to physical symptoms such as repeated headaches or stomach pains, rapid weight gain or loss, fatigue or excess energy.
2. Be aware of signs of emotional distress such as moodiness, temper tantrums, difficulty in paying attention or concentrating.
3. Let parents know about the students' signs of stress.

Talk individually to students about their attitude or behavior changes. This gives you a chance to find out about unusual stress such as divorce.

EXAMPLES

1. Be a good listener. Students may have no other adult willing to hear their concerns.
2. Let students know you are available to talk, and let the student set the agenda.

Watch your language to make sure you avoid stereotypes about "happy" (two-parent) homes.

EXAMPLES

1. Simply say "your families" instead of "your mothers and fathers" when addressing the class.
2. Avoid statements such as "We need volunteers for room mother" or "Your father can help you."

Help students maintain self-esteem.

EXAMPLES

1. Recognize a job well done.
2. Make sure the student understands the assignment and can handle the workload. This is not the time to pile on new and very difficult work.
3. The student may be angry with his or her parents, but may direct the anger at teachers. Don't take the student's anger personally.

Find out what resources are available at your school.

EXAMPLES

1. Talk to the school psychologist, guidance counselor, social worker, or principal about students who seem to need outside help.
2. Consider establishing a discussion group, led by a trained adult, for students whose parents are going through a divorce.

Be sensitive to both parents' rights to information.

EXAMPLES

1. When parents have joint custody, both are entitled to receive information and attend parent–teacher conferences.
2. The noncustodial parent may still be concerned about the child's school progress. Check with your principal about state laws regarding the noncustodial parent's rights.

Be aware of long-term problems for students moving between two households.

EXAMPLES

1. Books, assignments, and gym clothes may be left at one parent's house when the student is currently on visitation with the other parent.
2. Parents may not show up for their turn to pick up their child at school or may miss a parent–teacher conference because the note never got home.

For ideas about helping children understand divorce, see **http://muextension.missouri.edu/xplor/hesguide/humanrel/gh6600.htm**

and parents and interviews with parents, Baumrind and the other researchers who built on her findings identified four styles based on the parents' high or low levels of warmth and control (Berger, 2006):

- *Authoritarian* parents (low warmth, high control) seem cold and controlling in their interactions with their children. The children are expected to be mature and to do what the parent says, "Because I said so!" There is not much talk about emotions. Punishments are strict, but not abusive. The parents love their children, but they are not openly affectionate.
- *Authoritative* parents (high warmth, high control) also set clear limits, enforce rules, and expect mature behavior. But they are warmer with their children. They listen to concerns, give reasons for rules, and allow more democratic decision making. There is less strict punishment and more guidance. Parents help children think through the consequences of their actions (Hoffman, 2001).

- *Permissive* parents (high warmth, low control) are warm and nurturing, but they have few rules or consequences for their children and expect little in the way of mature behavior because "They're just kids."
- *Rejecting/Neglecting* parents (low warmth, low control) don't seem to care at all and can't be bothered with controlling, communicating, or caring for their children.

Culture and Parenting. Authoritarian, authoritative, and permissive parents all love their children and are trying to do their best—they simply have different ideas about the best ways to parent. In broad strokes, there are differences in children associated with these three parenting styles. At least in European American, middle-class families, children of authoritative parents are more likely to be happy with themselves and to relate well to others, whereas children of authoritarian parents are more likely to be guilty or depressed, and children of permissive parents may have trouble interacting with peers—they are used to having their way. Of course, the extreme of permissiveness becomes indulgence. Indulgent parents cater to their children's every whim—perhaps it is easier than being the adult who must make unpopular decisions. Both indulgent and rejecting/neglecting parenting styles are harmful.

Cultures also differ in parenting styles. Research indicates that higher control parenting is linked to better grades for Asian and African American students (Glasgow, Dornbusch, Troyer, Steinberg, & Ritter, 1997). Parenting that is strict and directive, with clear rules and consequences, combined with high levels of warmth and emotional support, is associated with higher academic achievement and greater emotional maturity for inner-city children (Garner & Spears, 2000; Jarrett, 1995). Differences in cultural values and in the danger level of some urban neighborhoods may make tighter parental control appropriate, and even necessary (Smetana, 2000). And it may be a misreading of the parents' actions to perceive their demand for obedience as "authoritarian" in cultures that have a greater respect for elders and a more group-centered rather than individualist philosophy (Nucci, 2001).

Peers

Peers and friendships are central to students' lives. When there has been a falling-out or an argument, when one child is not invited to a sleep-over, when rumors are started and pacts are made to ostracize someone (as with Alison and Stephanie at the beginning of the chapter), the results can be devastating. The immaturity and impulsiveness of the adolescent brain combined with the power of peer cultures can make these problems even more likely.

Peer Cultures. Recently, psychologists have studied the powerful role of peer culture in children's development. Peer cultures are groups of students who have a set of "rules"—how to dress, talk, style their hair. The group determines which activities, music, or other students are in or out of favor. For example, when Jessica, a popular high school student, was asked to explain the rules that her group lives by, she had no trouble:

> OK. No. 1: clothes. You cannot wear jeans any day but Friday, and you cannot wear a ponytail or sneakers more than once a week. Monday is fancy day—like black pants or maybe you bust out with a skirt. You have to remind people how cute you are in case they forgot over the weekend. No. 2: parties. Of course we sit down and discuss which ones we're going to because there is no point in getting all dressed up for a party that's going to be lame. (Talbot, 2002, p. 28)

These peer cultures encourage conformity to the group rules. When another girl in Jessica's group wore jeans on Monday, Jessica confronted her: "Why are you wearing jeans today? Did you forget it was Monday?" (Talbot, 2002, p. 28). Jessica explained that the group had to suspend this "rebel" several times, not allowing her to sit with them at lunch.

To understand the power of peers, we have to look at situations where the values and interests of parents clash with those of peers, and then see whose influence dominates. In these comparisons, peers usually win. But not all aspects of peer cultures are bad or cruel. The norms in some groups are positive and support achievement in school. Peer cultures are more powerful in defining issues of style and socializing. Parents and teachers still are influential in matters of morality, career choice, and religion (Harris, 1998).

Beyond the immediate trauma of being "in" or "out" of the group, peer relationships play significant positive and negative roles in healthy personal and social development. Peer groups influence members' motivation and achievement in school (A. Ryan, 2001). In one study, 6th grade students without friends showed lower levels of academic achievement and positive social behaviors and were more emotionally distressed, even two years later, than students with at least one friend (Wentzel, Barry, & Caldwell, 2004). The characteristics of friends and the quality of the friendships matter, too. Having stable, supportive relationships with friends who are socially competent and mature enhances social development, especially during difficult times such as parents' divorce or transition to new schools (Hartup & Stevens, 1999). Children who are rejected by their peers are less likely to participate in classroom learning activities; they are more likely to drop out of school as adolescents and may even evidence more problems as adults. For example, rejected aggressive students are more likely to commit crimes as they grow older (Coie & Dodge, 1998; Coie et al., 1995; Fredricks, Blumenthal, & Paris, 2004).

Who Is Likely to Have Problems with Peers? Children and adolescents are not always tolerant of differences. New students who are physically, intellectually, ethnically, racially, economically, or linguistically different may be rejected in classes with established peer groups. Students who are aggressive, withdrawn, and inattentive-hyperactive are more likely to be rejected. But classroom context matters too, especially for aggressive or withdrawn students. In classrooms where the general level of aggression is high, being aggressive is less likely to lead to peer rejection. And in classrooms where solitary play and work are more common, being withdrawn is not as likely to lead to rejection. Thus, part of being rejected is being too different from the norm. Also, prosocial behaviors such as sharing, cooperating, and friendly interactions are associated with peer acceptance, no matter what the classroom context. Many aggressive and withdrawn students lack these social skills; inattentive-hyperactive students often misread social cues or have trouble controlling impulses, so their social skills suffer, too (Coplan, Prakash, O'Neil, & Armer, 2004; Stormshak, Bierman, Bruschi, Dodge, & Coie, 1999). A teacher should be aware of how each student gets along with the group. Are there outcasts? Do some students play the bully role? Careful adult intervention can often correct such problems, especially at the late elementary and middle school levels.

Peer relationships in the school years appear to play a significant role in self-esteem, success in school, and success in adult life.

WHAT WOULD YOU SAY?

As part of the interview process for a job in a high school, you are asked the following: "How you could tell if there might be violence among students in our school. What are the warning signs?" ■

Peer Aggression. There are several forms of aggression. The most common form is **instrumental aggression,** which is intended to gain an object or privilege, such as shoving to get in line first or snatching a toy from another child. The intent is to get what you want, not to hurt the other child, but the hurt may happen anyway. A second kind is **hostile aggression**—inflicting intentional harm. Hostile aggression can take the form of either **overt aggression,** such as threats or physical attacks (as in, "I'm gonna beat you up!"), or **relational aggression,** which involves threatening or damaging social relationships (as in, "I'm never going to speak to you again!"). Boys are more likely to use overt aggression and girls, like Alison in the opening case, are more likely to use relational aggression (Berk, 2005). Aggression should not be confused with assertiveness, which means affirming or maintaining a legitimate right. As Helen Bee (1981) explains, "A child who says, 'That's my toy!' is showing assertiveness. If he bashes his playmate over the head to reclaim it, he has shown aggression" (p. 350).

Connect and **Extend** to the **Research**

Galen, B. R., & Underwood, M. K. (1997). A developmental investigation of social aggression among children. *Developmental Psychology, 33,* 589–600.

Modeling plays an important role in the expression of aggression (Bandura, Ross, & Ross, 1963). Children who grow up in homes filled with harsh punishment and family violence are more likely to use aggression to solve their own problems (Patterson, 1997). One very real source of aggressive models is found in almost every home in America—television. In the United States, 82% of TV programs have at least some violence. The rate for children's programs is especially high—an average of 32 violent acts per hour, with cartoons being the worst. And in over 70% of the violent scenes, the violence goes unpunished (Mediascope, 1996; Waters, 1993). Because most children spend more time watching television than they do in any other activity except sleep, the possible influence of television violence is a real concern (Timmer, Eccles, & O'Brien, 1988).

Does watching violent TV increase aggression? Results of a recent longitudinal study indicate a clear, "yes." Rowell Huesmann and colleagues examined the relationship between exposure to violence on television from ages 6 to 10 and aggressive behavior in adulthood 15 years later for over 300 people. Their conclusion? "Childhood exposure to media violence predicts young adult aggressive behavior for both males and females. . . . These relations persist even when the effects of socioeconomic status, intellectual ability, and a variety of parenting factors are controlled" (Huesmann, Moise-Titus, Podolski, & Eron, 2003, p. 201). When the children identified with aggressive TV characters (they said they acted like those characters) and when they thought the violence on TV was like real life, they were more likely to be violent as adults.

You can reduce the negative effects of TV violence by stressing three points with your students: Most people do not behave in the aggressive ways shown on television; the violent acts on TV are not real, but are created by special effects and stunts; and there are better ways to resolve conflicts, and these are the ways most real people use to solve their problems (Huesmann et al., 2003). Also, avoid using TV viewing as a reward or punishment because that makes television even more attractive to children (Slaby et al., 1995). But television is not the only source of violent models. Many popular films and video games are also filled with graphic depictions of violence, often performed by the "hero" who saves the day. Students growing up in the inner cities see gang violence. Newspapers, magazines, and the radio are filled with stories of murders, rapes, and robberies.

Instrumental aggression Strong actions aimed at claiming an object, place, or privilege—not intended to harm, but may lead to harm.

Hostile aggression Bold, direct action that is intended to hurt someone else; unprovoked attack.

Overt aggression A form of hostile aggression that involves physical attack.

Relational aggression A form of hostile aggression that involves verbal attacks and other actions meant to harm social relationships.

Bullies. Aggressive children tend to believe that violence will be rewarded, and they use aggression to get what they want. They are more likely to believe that violent retaliation is acceptable: "It's OK to shove people when you're mad" (Egan, Monson, & Perry, 1998). Seeing violent acts go unpunished probably affirms and encourages these beliefs. In addition to being surrounded by violence and believing that a violent "pay back" is appropriate when you are insulted or harmed, some children, particularly boys, have difficulty reading the intentions of others (Dodge & Pettit, 2003; Zelli, Dodge, Lochman, & Laird, 1999). They assume another child "did it on purpose" when their block tower is

Aggressive children tend to believe that violence will be rewarded, and use aggression to get what they want; one of the best approaches for preventing problems with aggression later in life is to intervene early.

toppled, they are pushed on the bus, or some other mistake is made. Retaliation follows and the cycle of aggression continues.

Helping children handle aggression can make a lasting difference in their lives. For example, one study in Finland asked teachers to rate students' aggression by answering "never," "sometimes," or "often" to statements such as "hurts another child when angry." Teacher-rated aggression when students were age 8 predicted school adjustment problems in early adolescence and long-term unemployment in adulthood (Kokko & Pulkkinen, 2000). Similar results were found in a study conducted in Canada, New Zealand, and the United States. Boys (but not girls) who were often physically aggressive in elementary school were at risk for continuing violent and nonviolent forms of delinquency through adolescence (Broidy et al., 2003).

Connect and **Extend** to the **Research**

Graham, S. (1998). Self-blame and peer victimization in middle school: An attributional analysis. *Developmental Psychology, 34*, 587–599.

One of the best approaches for preventing problems with aggression later in life is to intervene early. For example, one study found that aggressive children whose teachers taught them conflict management strategies were diverted from a life path of aggression and violence (Aber, Brown, & Jones, 2003). Sandra Graham (1996) has successfully experimented with approaches that help aggressive 5th- and 6th-grade boys become better judges of others' intentions. Strategies include engaging in role play, participating in group discussions of personal experiences, interpreting social cues from photographs, playing pantomime games, making videos, and writing endings to unfinished stories. The boys in the 12-session training group showed clear improvement in reading the intentions of others and responding with less aggression. We will look at all these approaches in depth in Chapter 12.

Connect and **Extend** to Your **Teaching/Portfolio**

A good resource for teachers about bullying and peer relations is Keith Sullivan's *The Anti-Bullying Handbook* (Oxford University Press, 2002).

Relational Aggression. Insults, gossip, exclusion, taunts—all are forms of relational aggression, sometimes called *social aggression* because the intent is to harm social connections. Both boys and girls take part in relational aggression, but after 2nd or 3rd grade, girls tend to engage in relational aggression more than boys. This may result because as girls become aware of gender stereotypes, they push their overt aggression underground into verbal, not physical, attacks. This type of aggression can be even more damaging than overt physical aggression—both to the victim and the aggressor. Victims, like Stephanie in the chapter opening, can be devastated. Relational aggressors can be viewed as even more problematic than physical aggressors by teachers and other students (Berger, 2006; Crick, Casas, & Mosher, 1997). As early as preschool, children need to learn how to negotiate social relations without resorting to aggression.

Victims. Some students tend to be bullies; other children are victims. Studies from both Europe and the United States indicate that about 10% of children are chronic victims—the constant targets of physical or verbal attacks. One kind of victim tends to have low self-esteem and to feel anxious, lonely, insecure, and unhappy. These students often are prone to crying and withdrawal; when attacked, generally they won't defend themselves. Recent research suggests that these victims may blame themselves for their situation. They believe that they are rejected because they have character flaws that they cannot change or control—no wonder they are depressed and helpless! There is a second kind of victim—highly emotional and hot-tempered students who seem to provoke aggressive reactions from their peers. Members of this group are rejected by almost all peers and have few friends (Pellegrini, Bartini, & Brooks, 1999).

Garbarino and deLara (2002) estimate that 160,000 children avoid school every day and thousands more drop out of school altogether "because they are always afraid at school" (p. 43). Children who have been chronic victims through elementary and middle school are more depressed and more likely to attempt suicide as young adults (Graham, 1998; Hodges & Perry, 1999)—we will examine suicide in Chapter 4. And students who kill or injure others in schools are more often victims than bullies (Reinke & Herman, 2002a, 2002b). In the past years, we have seen tragic consequences when bullied students turned guns on their tormentors in schools in the United States and in Europe. Interviews with adolescents reveal how much these students count on their teachers and other adults in the school to protect them. Even though they are moving toward independence, these students still want and need your help (Gararino & deLara, 2002). The *Guidelines* may give you ideas for handling aggression and encouraging cooperation.

Social Skills. Different social skills are important at different ages. Table 3.3 gives examples of the Social Development Program sequence from the New Haven Public Schools for grades K–3, 6, and 11 taken from Shriver, Schwab-Stone, and DeFalco

Guidelines: Dealing with Aggression and Encouraging Cooperation

Present yourself as a nonaggressive model.

EXAMPLES

1. Do not use threats of aggression to win obedience.
2. When problems arise, model nonviolent conflict-resolution strategies (see Chapter 11).

Ensure that your classroom has enough space and appropriate materials for every student.

EXAMPLES

1. Prevent overcrowding.
2. Make sure prized toys or resources are plentiful.
3. Remove or confiscate materials that encourage personal aggression, such as toy guns.
4. Avoid highly competitive activities and evaluations.

Make sure students do not profit from aggressive behaviors.

EXAMPLES

1. Comfort the victim of aggression and ignore the aggressor.
2. Use reasonable punishment, especially with older students.

Teach directly about positive social behaviors.

EXAMPLES

1. Incorporate lessons on social ethics/morality through reading selections and discussions.
2. Discuss the effects of antisocial actions such as stealing, bullying, and spreading rumors.
3. Provide models and encouragement—role play appropriate conflict resolution.
4. Build self-esteem by building skills and knowledge.
5. Seek help for students who seem especially isolated and victimized.

Provide opportunities for learning tolerance and cooperation.

EXAMPLES

1. Emphasize the similarities among people rather than the differences.
2. Set up group projects that encourage cooperation.

For more ideas, see the National Youth Violence Prevention Resource Center: **http://www.safeyouth.org/scripts/teens/aggression.asp**

TABLE 3.3

Social Development Programs

Here is the social development program sequence from the New Haven Public Schools for grades K–3, 6, and 11

K–3rd Grade

36–55 lessons taught in each grade 2–3 times a week for the school year

Project Charlie

- Self-awareness
- Relationships
- Decision making
- Chemical use in society
- Violence prevention

Building Blocks: An AIDS Curriculum for Early Elementary Educators (4–6 lessons taught with Project Charlie)

- Germs
- Communicable diseases
- Staying healthy
- Sickness and medicine
- Immune system
- Seeking health information
- Being different
- HIV/AIDS

6th Grade

45 lessons taught 3 times a week for 2 marking periods as a Life Skills Class

Social Problem Solving

- Self-control
- Stress management
- Problem solving
- Decision making
- Communication
- Violence prevention

Substance Use Prevention

- Peer pressure resistance

Human Growth and Development, AIDS Prevention, and Teen Pregnancy Prevention

- Puberty
- Reproduction
- Relationships without sex
- HIV/AIDS

11th Grade

37 lessons integrated in U.S. History II throughout the year and 3 lessons taught in English

A World of Difference (taught in History)

- Beliefs and values
- Prejudice, stereotyping, and discrimination
- Scapegoating and racism
- Violence prevention

Substance Use Prevention (taught in History)

- Effects of drug use in pregnancy and video *Innocent Addicts*

HIV/AIDS Education and Prevention (taught in English)

- Review of basic facts about HIV
- Barriers to prevention
- Living with AIDS

Source: From *Educating Minds and Hearts: Social Emotional Learning and the Passage into Adolescence,* by J. Cohen. Published by Teachers College Press. Copyright © 1991 by Teachers College, Columbia University. Reprinted by permission of the publisher. All rights reserved.

(1999). For example, in the 6th grade, students are taught a six-step problem-solving process keyed to a traffic light poster:

RED	STOP, CALM DOWN, and THINK before you act
YELLOW	Say the PROBLEM and how you FEEL
	Set a POSITIVE GOAL
	Think of lots of SOLUTIONS
	Think ahead of the CONSEQUENCES
GREEN	GO ahead and TRY the BEST PLAN

Connect and Extend to the Research

The entire March 2001 issue of the *Journal of School Psychology* is devoted to schools and mental health.

Connect and Extend to the Research

A new organization, Collaborative for Academic, Social, and Emotional Learning **(www.CASEL.org)**, was established several years ago to gather evidence about high-quality, culturally appropriate social and emotional learning programs.

Reaching Every Student: Loneliness and Children with Disabilities

Jake is a 14-year-old with hearing problems. He has always been shy, but lately he seems more withdrawn. He has stopped hanging out with friends and seems more and more depressed. Maria is a 10-year-old with learning disabilities who is repeating the 4th grade. She feels alone and believes she has nothing in common with other students—she deeply wants friends, but can't seem to connect. Both of these students described by Shireen Pavri

(2003) are lonely. Children with disabilities, especially those with learning disabilities and mental retardation, are especially vulnerable to feelings of loneliness (Pavri & Luftig, 2000). One reason is that students with disabilities may also have trouble reading and understanding cues from others, so they may respond inappropriately to their peers. Also, students with disabilities often are separated from their peers for assessment and teaching, and thus not allowed full participation in all class activities, so they have fewer opportunities to form friendships (Hallahan & Kauffman, 2006). What can be done? First, teachers can detect signs of loneliness. Notice who is rejected and who plays alone. Talk to students about their friends and to parents about their child's experiences with peers. In addition, Pavri (2003) suggests that teachers intervene in these ways:

- Provide social skills training for all students in how to initiate and terminate interactions and manage conflict.
- Create opportunities for interactions through cooperative learning tasks, structured recess and play times, peer tutoring opportunities, and after-school activities such as Boys or Girls Clubs or Special Olympics.
- Capitalize on lonely students' talents and strengths—use these abilities in class work.
- Create an accepting classroom community (see Chapter 11).
- Teach adaptive coping strategies such as engaging in creative activities when alone or initiating contact with others when lonely.
- Enhance students' self-esteem by giving them responsibilities in class and positive reinforcement for jobs well done.

Teachers

The first and most important task of the teacher is to educate, but student learning suffers when there are problems with personal and social development, and teachers are the main adults in students' lives for many hours each week. Teachers have the opportunity to play a significant role in students' personal and social development. For students facing emotional or interpersonal problems, teachers are sometimes the best source of help. When students have chaotic and unpredictable home lives, they need a caring, firm structure in school. They need teachers who set clear limits, are consistent, enforce rules firmly but not punitively, respect students, and show genuine concern. As a teacher, you can be available to talk about personal problems without requiring that your students do so. One of my student teachers gave a boy in her class a journal entitled "Very Hard Thoughts" so that he could write about his parents' divorce. Sometimes he talked to her about the journal entries, but at other times, he just recorded his feelings. The student teacher was very careful to respect the boy's privacy about his writings.

Academic and Personal Caring. When researchers ask students to describe a "good teacher," three qualities are at the center of their descriptions. Good teachers have positive interpersonal relationships—they care about their students. Second, good teachers can keep the classroom organized and maintain authority without being rigid or "mean." Finally, good teachers are good motivators—they can make learning fun by being creative and innovative (Woolfolk Hoy & Weinstein, 2006). Pedro Noguera (2005) said that the students in a "last chance" high school told him they look for three things in a teacher: "They look first for people who care. . . . Second, they respect teachers who are strict and hold students accountable. Third, they like teachers who teach them something" (pp. 17-18). We will look at management in Chapter 12 and at motivation in Chapter 10, so for now let's focus on caring and teaching.

For the past 15 years, research has documented the value and importance of positive relationships with teachers for students at every grade level (Davis, 2003). Tamera Murdock and Angela Miller (2003) found that 8th grade students' perceptions that their teachers cared about them were significantly related to the students' academic motivation, even after taking into account the motivational influences of parents and peers. Students seek respect, affection, trust, a listening ear, patience, and humor in their relationships with teachers (Bosworth, 1995; Phelan et al., 1992; Wentzel, 1997). Frequently, students' decisions about whether to cooperate are based on their liking for the teacher.

As a student in a study by Stinson (1993) commented: "If I don't like 'em . . . I'm not gonna do anything for 'em" (p. 221). Students define caring in two ways. One is academic caring—setting high, but reasonable expectations and helping students reach those goals. The second is personal caring—being patient, respectful, humorous, willing to listen, interested in students' issues and personal problems.

For higher-achieving students, academic caring is especially important, but for students who are placed at risk and often alienated from school, personal caring is critical (Cothran & Ennis, 2000; Woolfolk Hoy & Weinstein, 2006). In fact, in one study in a Texas high school, the Mexican and Mexican American students saw teacher caring as a prerequisite for their own caring about school; in other words, they needed to be *cared for* before they could *care about* school (Valenzuela, 1999). Unfortunately, in the same school, the mostly non-Latino teachers expected the students to care about school before they would invest their caring in the students. And for many teachers, caring about school meant behaving in more "middle-class" ways.

These contrasting student and teacher views can lead to a downward spiral of mistrust. Students withhold their cooperation until teachers "earn it" with their authentic caring. Teachers withhold caring until students "earn it" with respect for authority and cooperation. Marginalized students expect unfair treatment and behave defensively when they sense any unfairness. Teachers get tough and punish. Students feel correct in mistrusting, and become more guarded and defiant. Teachers feel correct in mistrusting and become more controlling and punitive, and so it goes. In fact, this cycle is a classic example of reciprocal determinism, an element of Albert Bandura's social cognitive theory described in Chapter 9.

Of course, students need both academic and personal caring. Katz (1999) interviewed eight Latino immigrant students in a middle school and concluded:

> High expectations without caring can result in setting goals that are impossible for the student to reach without adult support and assistance. On the other hand, caring without high expectations can turn dangerously into paternalism in which teachers feel sorry for "underprivileged" youth but never challenge them academically. High expectations and caring in tandem, however, can make a powerful difference in students' lives. (p. 814)

In short, caring means not giving up on students and their learning as well as demonstrating and teaching kindness in the classroom (Davis, 2003). In Chapter 11, you will learn about strategies and programs for helping students feel a sense of belonging in school.

Teachers and Child Abuse. Certainly, one critical way to care about students is to protect their welfare and intervene in cases of abuse. Accurate information about the number of abused children in the United States is difficult to find; most experts agree that an enormous number of cases go unreported. Every day, an average of 2,455 children are confirmed as abused or neglected (Children's Defense Fund, 2005; National Clearinghouse on Child Abuse and Neglect, 2005). Of course, parents are not the only people who abuse children. Siblings, other relatives, and even teachers have been responsible for the physical and sexual abuse of children.

As a teacher, you must alert your principal, school psychologist, or school social worker if you suspect abuse. In all 50 states, the District of Columbia, and the U.S. territories, the law requires certain professionals, often including teachers, to report suspected cases of child abuse. The legal definition of abuse has been broadened in many states to include neglect and failure to provide proper care and supervision. Most laws also protect teachers who report suspected neglect in good faith (Beezer, 1985). Be sure that you understand the laws in your state or province on this important issue, as well as your own moral responsibility. At least four children die of abuse or neglect each day in the United States, in many cases because no one would "get involved" (Children's Defense Fund, 2005). Turn the page to read a *Story of Learning/Tributes to Teaching* to see how one teacher made a difference. What should you look for as indicators of abuse? Table 3.4 on the next page lists possible indicators.

Connect and **Extend** to Your **Teaching**

Add Table 3.4, *Indicators of Child Abuse*, to your Teaching Resources file.

STORIES OF LEARNING
TRIBUTES TO TEACHING

DAVID was not an easy child to like, but Garth Nobel did. David was hyperactive and demanded a good deal of attention. Other teachers told Nobel that David got on their nerves. But David loved gym class. Or was it Garth Nobel's patience and kindness that he enjoyed? For whatever reason, David was always the first to arrive at class and put his whole self into whatever game or activity was asked of him. He wasn't necessarily a team player. In fact, he stayed away from the other children when he was not engaged in an activity. He never dressed with the others or palled around with them. But it was not until David was injured one day in a rather exuberant game of basketball, that Garth Nobel suspected anything. When he lifted David's shirt to check for injuries, he could not believe what he saw. Numerous ugly bruises and burns transversed the boy's chest. The different stages of healing made it clear that they were inflicted over a period of time.

"What happened to you, Dave?" Nobel breathed, almost in a whisper.

"What happened to you, Dave?" Nobel breathed, almost in a whisper. At first, tears ran silently down the boy's face. And then he began to sob, deep heart-wrenching sobs that were hard for the teacher to witness.

"My Dad," sobbed David, but he could not continue. Instead he hugged Garth Nobel with a desperateness that the young and caring teacher would never forget.

He would later learn that David's father had beaten him so badly over the last few years that he had caused internal damage. But that day, Garth Nobel knew that David needed an advocate—someone who cared and could help this boy through the perils that his future would bring. Years later, David would return to see Nobel with sincere thanks and admiration for standing by him over the next few years when David would be removed from his abusive home and placed in a foster home.

Source: From When Children Are Abused: An Educator's Guide to Intervention by Cynthia Crosson-Tower. Published by Allyn and Bacon, Boston, MA.

TABLE 3.4

Indicators of Child Abuse

The following are some of the signs of abuse. Not every child with these signs is abused, but these indicators should be investigated.

	Physical Indicators	Behavioral Indicators
Physical Abuse	• Unexplained bruises (in various stages of healing), welts, human bite marks, bald spots • Unexplained burns, especially cigarette burns or immersion-burns (glovelike) • Unexplained fractures, lacerations, or abrasions	• Self-destructive • Withdrawn and aggressive—behavioral extremes • Uncomfortable with physical contact • Arrives at school early or stays late, as if afraid • Chronic runaway (adolescents) • Complains of soreness or moves uncomfortably • Wears clothing inappropriate to weather, to cover body
Physical Neglect	• Abandonment • Unattended medical needs • Consistent lack of supervision • Consistent hunger, inappropriate dress, poor hygiene • Lice, distended stomach, emaciation	• Regularly displays fatigue or listlessness, falls asleep in class • Steals food, begs from classmates • Reports that no caretaker is at home • Frequently absent or tardy • Self-destructive • School dropout (adolescents)
Sexual Abuse	• Torn, stained, or bloodied underclothing • Pain or itching in genital area • Difficulty walking or sitting • Bruises or bleeding in external genitalia • Venereal disease • Frequent urinary or yeast infections	• Withdrawn, chronic depression • Excessive seductiveness • Role reversal, overly concerned for siblings • Poor self-esteem, self-devaluation, lack of confidence • Peer problems, lack of involvement • Massive weight change • Suicide attempts (especially adolescents) • Hysteria, lack of emotional control • Sudden school difficulties • Inappropriate sex play or premature understanding of sex • Threatened by physical contact, closeness • Promiscuity

Source: From "Supporting Victims of Child Abuse" by T. Bear, S. Schenk, and L. Buckner, *Educational Leadership, 50*(4). The Association for Curriculum Development is a worldwide community of educators advocating sound policies and sharing best practices to achieve the success of each learner. To learn more, visit ASCD at www.ascd.org.

Self-Concept: Understanding Ourselves

What is self-concept? Is self-concept different from self-esteem or identity? How do we come to understand other people and ourselves? You will see that these areas follow patterns similar to those noted in Chapter 2 for cognitive development. Children's understandings of themselves are concrete at first. Early views of self and friends are based on immediate behaviors and appearances. Children assume that others share their feelings and perceptions. Their thinking about themselves and others is simple, segmented, and rule-bound, not flexible or integrated into organized systems. In time, children are able to think abstractly about internal processes—beliefs, intentions, values, and motivations. With these developments in abstract thinking, then, knowledge of self, others, and situations can incorporate more abstract qualities (Berk, 2005; Harter, 2003).

Self-Concept and Self-Esteem

Psychologists' interests in all aspects of the self have grown steadily. In 1970, about 1 in every 20 publications in psychology was related to the self. By 2000, the ratio was 1 in every 7 (Tesser, Stapel, & Wood, 2002). In educational psychology, much research is focused on self-concept and self-esteem.

The term self-concept is part of our everyday conversation. We talk about people who have a "low" self-concept or individuals whose self-concept is not "strong," as if self-concept were the oil level in a car or your abdominal muscles. These actually are misuses of the term. In psychology, **self-concept** generally refers to individuals' knowledge and beliefs about themselves—their ideas, feelings, attitudes, and expectations (Pajares & Schunk, 2001). We could consider self-concept to be our attempt to explain ourselves to ourselves, to build a scheme (in Piaget's terms) that organizes our impressions, feelings, and beliefs about ourselves. But this model or scheme is not permanent, unified, or unchanging. Our self-perceptions vary from situation to situation and from one phase of our lives to another.

Connect and **Extend** to **PRAXIS II™**

Self-Esteem (I, A2)
Understand the bidirectional effects of school life and self-esteem on each other. What can teachers do to enhance students' self-esteem?

STOP | THINK | WRITE How strongly do you agree or disagree with these statements?

On the whole, I am satisfied with myself.
I feel that I have a number of good qualities.
I wish I could have more respect for myself.
At times, I think that I am no good at all.
I certainly feel useless at times.
I take a positive attitude toward myself.

The questions in the *Stop/Think/Write* box above are taken from a widely used measure of self-esteem (Rosenberg, 1979; Hagborg, 1993). **Self-esteem** is an affective reaction—an evaluative judgment of self-worth—for example, feeling good about your basketball skills. If people evaluate themselves positively—if they "like what they see"—we say that they have high self-esteem (Pintrich & Schunk, 2002). Can you see the evaluative judgments in the *Stop/Think/Write* questions?

Self-concept and self-esteem are often used interchangeably, even though they have distinct meanings. Self-concept is a cognitive structure, a belief about who you are—for example, a belief that you are a good basketball player. Sometimes self-esteem is considered one aspect of self-concept—the evaluative part. Self-esteem is influenced by whether the culture around you values your particular characteristics and capabilities (Bandura, 1997). In research, it has been difficult to find differences between these two concepts, so some writers use self-concept and self-esteem interchangeably. But there is a conceptual difference.

The Structure of Self-Concept. A student's overall self-concept is made up of other, more specific concepts, including nonacademic self-concepts about, for example, social relations or physical appearance, and academic self-concepts in English, mathematics, art, and other subjects. These self-concepts at the second level are themselves made up of more specific, separate conceptions of the self. For example, self-concepts about social relationships might be made up of concepts about relations with peers, teachers, other

Self-concept Individuals' knowledge and beliefs about themselves—their ideas, feelings, attitudes, and expectations.

Self-esteem The value each of us places on our own characteristics, abilities, and behaviors.

adults, and family (particularly parents) (Byrne & Shavelson, 1996; Vispoel, 1995; Yeung, McInerney, Russell-Bowie, Suliman, Chui, & Lau, 2000). These conceptions are based on many experiences and events, such as sports or academic performances, assessment of one's body, friendships, artistic abilities, contributions to community groups, and so on. For older adolescents and adults, the separate, specific self-concepts are not necessarily integrated into an overall self-concept, so self-concept is more situation-specific in adults (Byrne & Worth Gavin, 1996; Marsh & Ayotte, 2003).

The courses selected in high school put students on a path toward the future, so self-concepts about particular academic subjects can be life-changing influences.

How Self-Concept Develops. The self-concept evolves through constant self-evaluation in different situations. Children and adolescents are continually asking themselves, in effect, "How am I doing?" They gauge the verbal and nonverbal reactions of significant people—parents and other family members in the early years and friends, schoolmates, and teachers later—to make judgments (Harter, 1998).

Young children tend to make self-concept appraisals based on their own improvement over time. Researchers followed 60 students in New Zealand from the time they started school until the middle of their third year (Chapman, Tunmer, & Prochnow, 2000). In the first 2 months of school, differences in reading self-concept began to develop, based on the ease or difficulty students had learning to read. Students who entered school with good knowledge about sounds and letters learned to read more easily and developed more positive reading self-concepts. Over time, differences in the reading performance of students with high and low reading self-concepts grew even greater. Thus, the early experiences with the important school task of reading had strong impact on self-concept.

During the middle-school years, students grow more self-conscious (remember, adolescent egocentrism and Elkind's imaginary audience discussed in Chapter 2). At this age, self-concepts are tied to physical appearance and social acceptance as well as school achievement, so these years can be exceedingly difficult for students such as Stephanie, described at the opening of this chapter (Wigfield, Eccles, & Pintrich, 1996). In academics, students compare their performance with their own standards—their performance in math to their performance in English and science, for example—to form self-concepts in these areas. But social comparisons are becoming more influential, too, at least in Western cultures. Students' self-concepts in math are shaped by how their performance compares to that of other students in their math classes and even by comments their classmates make about them (Altermatt, Pomerantz, Ruble, Frey, & Greulich, 2002; Pintrich & Schunk, 2002). Students who are strong in math in an average school feel better about their math skills than do students of equal ability in high-achieving schools. Marsh (1990) calls this the "Big-Fish-Little-Pond Effect (BFLP)." Research that surveyed over 100,000 15-year-olds around the world found the BFLP effect in every one of the 26 participating countries (Marsh & Hau, 2003). Participation in a gifted and talented program seems to have an opposite "Little-Fish-in-a-Big-Pond" effect: Students who participate in gifted programs, compared to similar students who remain in regular classes, tend to show *declines* in academic self-concepts over time, but no changes in nonacademic self-concepts (Marsh & Craven, 2002).

Self-Concept and Achievement. Many psychologists consider self-concept to be the foundation of both social and emotional development. Research has linked self-concept to a wide range of accomplishments—from performance in competitive sports to job satisfaction and achievement in school (Byrne, 2002; Davis-Kean & Sandler, 2001; Marsh & Hau, 2003). One important way self-concept affects learning in school is through course selection. Think back to high school. When you had a chance to choose courses, did you pick your worst subjects—those where you felt least capable? Probably not. Herbert Marsh and Alexander Yeung (1997) examined how 246 boys in early high school in Sydney, Australia, chose their courses. Academic self-concept for a particular subject (mathematics, science, etc.) was the most important predictor of course selection—more important than previous grades in the subject or overall self-concept. In fact, having a positive self-concept in a particular subject was an even bigger factor in selecting courses when self-concept in other subjects was low. The courses selected in high school put students on a path toward the future, so self-concepts about particular academic subjects can be life-changing influences. But the *Point/Counterpoint* shows that educators disagree about the role of the school.

Point/Counterpoint

What Should Schools Do to Encourage Students' Self-Esteem?

MORE THAN 2,000 BOOKS about how to increase self-esteem have been published. Schools and mental-health facilities continue to develop self-esteem programs (Slater, 2002). The attempts to improve students' self-esteem have taken three main forms: personal development activities such as sensitivity training; self-esteem programs where the curriculum focuses directly on improving self-esteem; and structural changes in schools that place greater emphasis on cooperation, student participation, community involvement, and ethnic pride.

POINT The self-esteem movement has problems.

Many of the self-esteem courses are commercial packages—costly for schools but without solid evidence that they make a difference for students (Crisci, 1986; Leming, 1981). As Beane (1991) notes, "Saying 'I like myself and others' in front of a group is not the same as actually feeling that way, especially if I am only doing it because I am supposed to. Being nice has a place in enhancing self-esteem, but it is not enough" (p. 26). Some people have accused schools of developing programs where the main objective is "to dole out a huge heaping of praise, regardless of actual accomplishments" (Slater, 2002, p. 45). But Erik Erikson (1980) warned years ago: "Children cannot be fooled by empty praise and condescending encouragement. They may have to accept artificial bolstering of their self-esteem in lieu of something better. . . ." Erikson went on to explain that a strong and positive identity comes only from "wholehearted and consistent recognition of real accomplishment, that is, achievement that has meaning in their culture" (p. 95).

Frank Pajares and Dale Schunk (2002) point to another problem. "[W]hen what is communicated to children from an early age is that nothing matters quite as much as how they feel or how confident they should be, one can rest assured that the world will sooner or later teach a lesson in humility that may not easily be learned. An obsession with one's sense of self is responsible for an alarming increase in depression and other mental difficulties" (p. 16).

Sensitivity training and self-esteem courses share a common conceptual problem. They assume that we encourage self-esteem by changing the individual's beliefs, making the young person work harder against the odds. But what if the student's environment is truly unsafe, debilitating, and unsupportive? Some people have overcome tremendous problems, but to expect everyone to do so "ignores the fact that having positive self-esteem is almost impossible for many young people, given the deplorable conditions under which they are forced to live by the inequities in our society" (Beane, 1991, p. 27). Worse yet, some psychologists are now contending that low self-esteem is not a problem, whereas high self-esteem may be. For example, they contend, people with high self-esteem are more willing to inflict pain and punishment on others (Slater, 2002). And when people set self-esteem as a main goal, they may pursue that goal in ways that are harmful over the long run. They may, for example, avoid constructive criticisms or challenging tasks (Crocker & Park, 2004).

COUNTERPOINT The self-esteem movement has promise.

Beyond the "feel-good psychology" of some aspects of the self-esteem movement is a basic truth: "Self-esteem is a central feature of human dignity and thus an inalienable human entitlement. As such, schools and other agencies have a moral obligation to help build it and avoid debilitating it" (Beane, 1991, p. 28). If we view self-esteem accurately as a product of our thinking and our actions—our values, ideas, and beliefs as well as our interactions with others—then we see a significant role for the school. Practices that allow authentic participation, cooperation, problem solving, and accomplishment should replace policies that damage self-esteem, such as tracking and competitive grading.

Beane (1991) suggests four principles to guide educators:

> *First, being nice is surely a part of this effort, but it is not enough. Second, there is a place for some direct instruction regarding affective matters, but this is not enough either. Self-esteem and affect are not simply another school subject to be placed in set-aside time slots. Third, the negative affect of "get tough" policies is not a promising route to self-esteem and efficacy. This simply blames young people for problems that are largely not of their own making. Fourth, since self-perceptions are powerfully informed by culture, comparing self-esteem across cultures without clarifying cultural differences is distracting and unproductive. (pp. 29–30)*

Psychologist Lauren Slater (2002) in her article, "The Trouble with Self-Esteem" suggests we rethink self-esteem and move toward honest self-appraisal that will lead to self-control:

> *Maybe self-control should replace self-esteem as a primary peg to reach for. Ultimately, self-control need not be experienced as a constriction; restored to its original meaning, it might be experienced as the kind of practiced prowess an athlete or artist demonstrates, muscles not tamed but trained, so that the leaps are powerful, the spine supple and the energy harnessed and shaped. (p. 47)*

WHAT DO YOU THINK?

Vote online at **www.mylabschool.com**

Source: From "The Trouble with Self-Esteem," by L. Slater, *The New York Times Magazine*, February 3, 2002, pp. 44–47 and "Sorting Out the Self-Esteem Controversy," by J. A. Beane, 1991, *Educational Leadership*, 49(1), pp. 25–30.

School Life and Self-Esteem

We turn now to self-esteem—the students' evaluations and feelings about themselves. For teachers, there are at least two questions to ask about self-esteem: (1) How does self-esteem affect a student's behavior in school? and (2) How does life in school affect a student's self-esteem?

In answer to the first question, it appears that students with higher self-esteem are somewhat more likely to be successful in school, although the strength of the relationship varies greatly, depending on the characteristics of the students and the research methods used (Ma & Kishor, 1997; Marsh & Holmes, 1990). In longitudinal studies, more positive self-beliefs are related to higher academic achievement, especially when the beliefs are specific to the subject studied. But the sizes of the relationships generally are small (Valentine, DuBois, & Cooper, 2004). Of course, as we discussed in Chapter 1, knowing that two variables are related (correlated) does not tell us that one is causing the other. It may be that high achievement and popularity lead to self-esteem, or vice versa. In fact, it probably works both ways (Guay, Larose, & Boivin, 2004; Marsh & Ayotte, 2003).

What about the second question of how school affects self-esteem: Is school important? As you can see from the *Point/Counterpoint*, the school's role in student self-esteem has been hotly debated. A study that followed 322 6th-grade students for two years would say yes. Hoge, Smit, and Hanson (1990) found that students' satisfaction with school, their sense that classes were interesting and teachers cared, and teacher feedback and evaluations influenced students' self-esteem. In physical education, teachers' opinions were especially powerful in shaping students' conceptions of their athletic abilities. Being placed in a low-ability group or being held back in school seems to have a negative impact on students' self-esteem, but learning in collaborative and cooperative settings seems to have a positive effect (Covington, 1992; Deci & Ryan, 1985). Interestingly, special programs such as "Student of the Month" or admission to advanced math classes had little effect on self-esteem. (Relate the latter to the "Big-Fish-Little-Pond Effect.")

Over 100 years ago, William James (1890) suggested that self-esteem is determined by how *successful* we are in accomplishing tasks or reaching goals we *value*. If a skill or accomplishment is *not* important, incompetence in that area doesn't threaten self-esteem. Students must have legitimate success with tasks that matter to them. The way individuals explain their successes or failures also is important. Students must attribute their successes to their own actions, not to luck or to special assistance, in order to build self-esteem.

Teachers' feedback, grading practices, evaluations, and communication of caring for students can make a difference in how students feel about their abilities in particular subjects. But the greatest increases in self-esteem come when students grow more competent in areas they value—including the social areas that become so important in adolescence. *Thus, a teacher's greatest challenge is to help students achieve important understandings and skills.* Given this responsibility, what can teachers do? The recommendations in Table 3.5 on page 89 are a beginning.

Diversity and Identity

WHAT WOULD YOU SAY?

As part of the interview process for a job in a middle school, you are asked the following: "What would you do to help all your students feel good about themselves?" ■

Younger children tend to have positive and optimistic views of themselves. In one study, over 80% of the 1st graders surveyed thought they were the best students in class (Stipek, 1981). As they mature, students become more realistic, but many are not accurate judges of their own abilities (Paris & Cunningham, 1996). In fact, some students suffer from "illusions of incompetence"—they seriously underestimate their own competence (Phillips & Zimmerman, 1990). Gender and ethnic stereotypes can have an impact on these views.

TABLE 3.5

Suggestions for Encouraging Self-Esteem

1. Value and accept all pupils, for their attempts as well as their accomplishments.
2. Create a climate that is physically and psychologically safe for students.
3. Become aware of your own personal biases (everyone has some biases) and expectations.
4. Make sure that your procedures for teaching and grouping students are really necessary, not just a convenient way of handling problem students or avoiding contact with some students.
5. Make standards of evaluation clear; help students learn to evaluate their own accomplishments.
6. Model appropriate methods of self-criticism, perseverance, and self-reward.
7. Avoid destructive comparisons and competition; encourage students to compete with their own prior levels of achievement.
8. Accept a student even when you must reject a particular behavior or outcome. Students should feel confident, for example, that failing a test or being reprimanded in class does not make them "bad" people.
9. Remember that positive self-concept grows from success in operating in the world *and* from being valued by important people in the environment.
10. Encourage students to take responsibility for their reactions to events; show them that they have choices in how to respond.
11. Set up support groups or "study buddies" in school and teach students how to encourage each other.
12. Help students set clear goals and objectives; brainstorm about resources they have for reaching their goals.
13. Highlight the value of different ethnic groups—their cultures and accomplishments.

Sources: Information from "Improving Students' Self-Esteem," by J. Canfield, 1990, *Educational Leadership, 48*(1), pp. 48–50; *Teacher Behavior and Student Self-Concept,* by M. M. Kash and G. Borich, 1978, Menlo Park, CA: Addison-Wesley; "The Development of Self-Concept," by H. H. Marshall, 1989, *Young Children, 44*(5), pp. 44–51.

Connect and **Extend** to Your **Teaching**

Think about your philosophy of teaching, a question you will be asked at most job interviews. How can you support the development of genuine and well-founded self-esteem in your students? (Consult Table 3.5 for ideas.)

Diversity and Perception of Self

A recent study followed 761 middle-class, primarily European American students from 1st grade through high school (Jacobs, Lanza, Osgood, Eccles, & Wigfield, 2002). It is difficult to get longitudinal data, so this is a valuable study. In 1st grade, girls and boys had comparable perceptions of their own abilities in language arts, but boys felt significantly more competent in math and sports. As you can see in Figure 3.2 on the next page, competence beliefs declined for both boys and girls across the grades, but boys fell faster in math so that by high school, math competence beliefs were about the same for boys and girls. In language arts, boys' competence ratings fell more sharply than those of girls after 1st grade, but both leveled off during high school. In sports, competence ratings for both boys and girls dropped, but boys remained significantly more confident in their competence in sports throughout the entire 12 years.

Other studies have also found that girls tend to see themselves as more able than boys in reading and close friendships; boys are more confident about their abilities in math and athletics. Of course, some of these differences in self-confidence may reflect actual differences in achievement—girls tend to be better readers than boys, for example. It is likely that confidence and achievement are reciprocally related—each affects the other (Cole, Martin, Peeke, Seroczynski, & Fier, 1999; Eccles, Wigfield, & Schiefele, 1998; Wilgenbusch & Merrell, 1999). For most ethnic groups (except African Americans), males are more confident about their abilities in math and science. Differences between males and females generally are small, but consistent across studies (Grossman & Grossman, 1994; Kling, Hyde, Showers, & Buswell, 1999). Unfortunately, there are no long-term studies of other ethnic groups, so these patterns may be limited to European Americans.

How do students feel about themselves in general during the school years? Jean Twenge and Keith Campbell (2001) analyzed over 150 samples of students from studies conducted between 1968 and 1994, looking at general self-esteem, not subject-specific competence. They found that self-esteem decreased slightly for both girls and boys in the

FIGURE 3.2

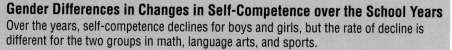

Gender Differences in Changes in Self-Competence over the School Years
Over the years, self-competence declines for boys and girls, but the rate of decline is different for the two groups in math, language arts, and sports.

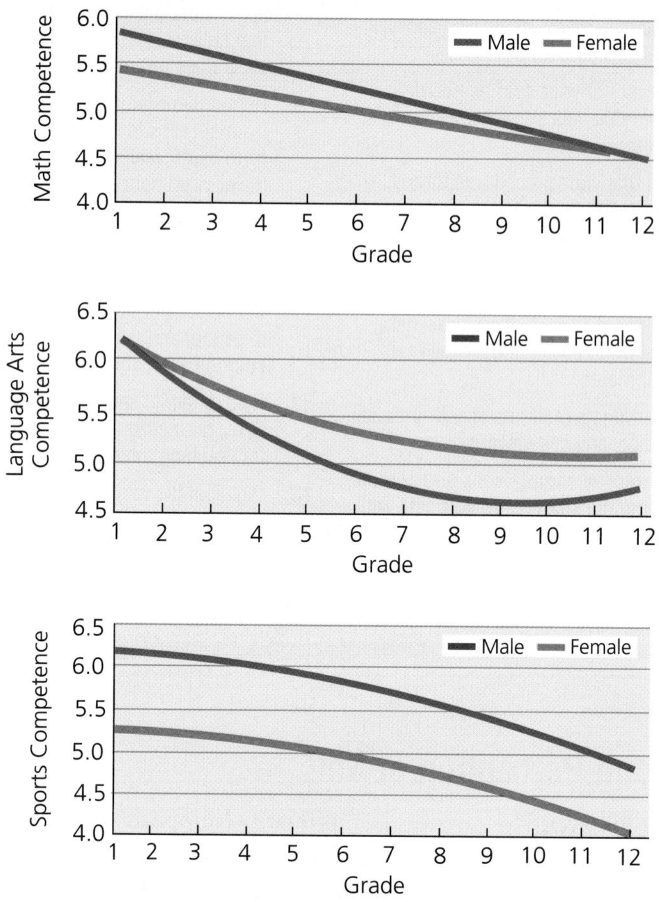

Source: From "Changes in Children's Self-Competence and Values: Gender and Domain Differences across Grades 1 through 12," by J. E. Jacobs, S. Lanza, D. W. Osgood, J. S. Eccles, and A. Wigfield, *Child Development, 73,* p. 516. Copyright © 2002 by the Society for Research in Child Development, University of Michigan Center for Growth & Human Development. Reprinted with permission of the SRCD.

transition to junior high. Then boys' general self-esteem increased dramatically during high school, while girls' self-esteem stayed about the same, leaving girls with significantly lower general self-esteem than boys by the end of high school. When these results are examined together with the findings by Jacobs et al. above that boys and girls differ in their academic self-concepts in various subjects and Marsh and Yeung's (1997) results that academic self-concept influences course selection, it seems that many students make decisions about courses that forever limit their options in life, and often these decisions are not based on ability, but instead on "illusions of incompetence."

Ethnic and Racial Identity

As early as 1903, W. E. B. DuBois wrote about the "double consciousness" of African Americans. In essence, African Americans, like other ethnic or racial groups, are conscious of their ethnic identity as they negotiate being members of the larger culture as well. Because ethnic minority students are members of both majority and minority group cultures, it is complicated for them to establish a clear identity. Values, learning styles, and communication patterns of the students' ethnic culture may be inconsistent with the expectations of the school and the larger society. Embracing the values of mainstream culture may seem to require rejecting ethnic values. Ethnic minority students have to "sift through two sets of cultural values and identity options" to achieve a firm identity, so they may need more time to explore possibilities—a longer *moratorium* in Erikson's terms (Markstrom-Adams, 1992, p. 177). But the exploration is important; some psychologists consider ethnic identity a "master status," one that dominates all other identity concerns when judging the self (Herman, 2004).

Connect and Extend to Other Chapters

Relate this information to concepts you learned in Chapter 2. For example, what aspects of formal-operational thought are helpful (or perhaps necessary) in achieving identity formation? Can you think of people who seem to have established their identity, but who do not seem to have achieved the formal-operational stage? Is identity formation necessarily a conscious process?

Ethnic Identities: Outcome and Process. Jean Phinney (1990; 2003) describes four outcomes for ethnic minority youth in their search for identity. They can try *assimilation*, fully adopting the values and behaviors of the majority culture and rejecting their ethnic culture. At the opposite end, they can be *separated*, associating only with members of their ethnic culture. A third possibility is *marginality*, living in the majority culture, but feeling alienated and uncomfortable in it and disconnected from the minority culture as well. The final alternative is *biculturalism* (sometimes called integration), maintaining ties to both cultures. And there are at least three ways to be bicultural. You could alternate between the two cultures, being fully "majority" in your behavior in one situation and fully "minority" in other situation. Or you could blend the two cultures by finding values and behaviors that are common to both and acting on them. Finally, you could fuse the two cultures by truly merging them into a new and complete whole (Phinney & Devich-Nevarro, 1997). No matter what your identity outcome is, an important factor for good mental health seems to be having strong positive feelings about your own ethnic group (Steinberg, 2005).

Some psychologists have used Marcia's identity statuses to understand the process of forming an ethnic identity. Children may begin with an *unexamined ethnic identity*, either because they have not explored at all (diffusion) or because they have accepted the identity encouraged by others (foreclosure). Many European American adolescents could fit the unexamined category. A period of *ethnic identity exploration* (moratorium) might be followed by a *resolution* of the conflict (identity achieved).

Racial Identity: Outcome and Process. William Cross (1991) devised a framework that specifically addresses African American racial identity. The process he calls **nigrescence** has five stages:

- **Pre-encounter:** At this stage, Cross says that an African American's attitude may range from ignoring race to feeling neutral about race, to actually being anti-Black. African Americans at this stage may adopt certain beliefs of White Americans, including the tendency to see "Whiteness" as superior. Some level of self-hate is a

Nigrescence The process of developing a Black identity.

When majority adolescents are knowledgeable and secure about their own heritage, they are also more respectful of the heritage of others.

possible consequence. At the pre-encounter stage, people do not self-identify with being Black—they may value other aspects of their identity, such as religion, profession, or social status.

- **Encounter:** This stage is often triggered by encounters with overt, covert, or institutional racism. For instance, when an African American is followed around in an upscale store, is assaulted by police, or sees news reports about such assaults, then his or her eyes are opened to the reality that race matters in society. The African American becomes attuned to his or her Blackness.
- **Immersion/Emersion:** Cross sees this as a transition—an in-between state that may cause people to be anxious about "becoming the 'right kind' of Black person" (Cross, 1991, p. 202). In response to encounters with discrimination, the individuals fill their lives with symbols of Blackness; they buy books about Black experiences and socialize mainly with other African Americans, for example. They are eager to understand their racial heritage more deeply.
- **Internalization:** Individuals are firmly connected to and secure in their sense of racial identity. They don't worry about what friends or outsiders think—they are confident in their own standards of Blackness.
- **Internalization-Commitment**: This stage is very closely connected with internalization. The main difference is a person's continued interest in and commitment to Black affairs. Such individuals chart their lives to connect to their Black racial identity; for example, a painter dedicates his life to painting Black images or a researcher dedicates her life to studying African American educational experiences.

Determining a racial identity may be even more complicated for biracial or multiracial adolescents. The parent they live with, the make-up of their neighborhood, their appearance, and experiences of discrimination or support can influence these adolescents' decisions about racial identity. Some psychologists think that these challenges help multiracial youth develop stronger and more complex identities, but other researchers argue that the challenges are an extra burden in an already tough process (Herman, 2004). Perhaps the outcome depends in part on the support adolescents get in facing the challenges.

Connect and **Extend** to the **Research**

See the Summer 2003 issue of *Theory Into Practice* on Teacher Reflection and Race in Cultural Contexts (Vol. 42, No. 3). Guest Editor: H. Richard Milner.

Racial and Ethnic Pride. For all students, pride in family and community is part of the foundation for a stable identity. Special efforts to encourage **racial and ethnic pride** are particularly important, so that students examining their identities do not get the message that differences are deficits (Spencer & Markstrom-Adams, 1990). In one study, African American preschool students whose homes were rich with African American culture had more factual knowledge and better problem-solving skills. Parents who encouraged their children to be proud of their heritage reported fewer behavior problems with their children (Caughy, O'Campo, Randolph, & Nickerson, 2002). In other research, positive racial identity was related to higher self-esteem and fewer emotional problems for both African American and White adolescents (DuBois, Burk-Braxton, Swenson, Tevendale, & Hardesty, 2002).

Each of us has an ethnic heritage. Janet Helms (1995) has written about stages in White identity development. Richard Milner (2003) has pointed to the importance of racial identity development and awareness, especially in teaching. When majority adolescents are knowledgeable and secure about their own heritage, they are also more respectful of the heritage of others. Thus, exploring the racial and ethnic roots of all students should foster both self-esteem and acceptance of others (Rotherham-Borus, 1994).

Emotional and Moral Development

Racial and ethnic pride A positive self-concept about one's racial or ethnic heritage.

As we seek our own identity and form images of ourselves, we are also learning to cope with emotions and trying to understand the "significant others" around us. How do we learn to interpret what others are thinking and feeling?

Emotional Competence

Understanding intentions and taking the perspective of others are elements in the development of emotional competence or the ability to understand and manage emotional situations.

Social and emotional competences are critical for both academic and personal development. In fact, a number of studies that followed students over several years in the United States and in Italy have found that prosocial behaviors and social competence in the early grades are related to academic achievement and popularity with peers as many as five years later (Elias & Schwab, 2006). Table 3.6 describes four skills of emotional competence. How can teachers help students develop emotional competence? The *Guidelines* on the next page give some ideas. In Chapter 9 we look at teaching strategies and programs that encourage self-regulation of emotions.

Connect and **Extend** to Your **Teaching/Portfolio**

For a full description of several programs and strategies that support social emotional learning, see Cohen, J. (Ed.) (1999). *Educating minds and hearts: Social emotional learning and the passage into adolescence.* New York: Teachers College Press.

Theory of Mind and Intention

By 2 or 3 years old, children are beginning to develop a **theory of mind,** an understanding that other people are people too, with their own minds, thoughts, feelings, beliefs, desires, and perceptions (Flavell, Miller, & Miller, 2002). Children need a theory of mind to make sense of other people's behavior. Why is Sarah crying? Does she feel sad because no one will play with her? You will see in Chapter 4 that one explanation for autism is that children with this condition lack a theory of mind to help them understand their own or other people's emotions and behaviors.

Theory of mind An understanding that other people are people too, with their own minds, thoughts, feelings, beliefs, desires, and perceptions.

TABLE 3.6

Essential Social Emotional Skills

Here are examples of four important social/emotional skills and competencies needed for each. The list was developed by the Collaborative for Academic, Social, and Emotional Learning [CASEL] http://www.casel.org/home/index.php

Know Yourself and Others

- *Identify feelings*—Recognize and label feelings in yourself and others.
- *Be responsible*—Understand and act upon obligations to engage in ethical, safe, and legal behaviors.
- *Recognize strengths*—Identify and cultivate positive qualities.

Make Responsible Decisions

- *Manage emotions*—Regulate feelings so that they aid rather than impede the handling of situations.
- *Understand situations*—Accurately understand the circumstances you are in.
- *Set goals and plans*—Establish and work toward the achievement of specific short- and long-term outcomes.
- *Solve problems creatively*—Engage in a creative, disciplined process of exploring alternative possibilities that lead to responsible, goal-directed action, including overcoming obstacles to plans.

Care for Others

- *Show empathy*—Identify and understand the thoughts and feelings of others.
- *Respect others*—Act on the belief that others deserve to be treated with kindness and compassion as part of our shared humanity.
- *Appreciate diversity*—Understand that individual and group differences complement one another and add strength and adaptability to the world around us.

Know How to Act

- *Communicate effectively*—Use verbal and nonverbal skills to express yourself and promote effective exchanges with others.
- *Build relationships*—Establish and maintain healthy and rewarding connections with individuals and groups.
- *Negotiate fairly*—Strive to achieve mutually satisfactory resolutions to conflict by addressing the needs of all concerned.
- *Refuse provocations*—Convey and follow through effectively with decisions not to engage in unwanted, unsafe, and unethical behavior.
- *Seek help*—Identify your need for help and access appropriate assistance and support in pursuit of needs and goals.
- *Act ethically*—Guide decisions and actions by a set of principles or standards derived from recognized legal/professional codes or moral or faith-based systems of conduct.

Source: From "Compliance to responsibility: Social and emotional learning and classroom management," by M. J. Elias & Y. Schwab in *Handbook for classroom management: Research, practice, and contemporary issues,* C. Evertson & C. Weinstein (Eds.), 2006. Reprinted by permission of Lawrence Erlbaum Associates, Inc. and Maurice J. Elias, Ph.D.

Guidelines: Encouraging Emotional Competence

Create a climate of trust in your classroom.

EXAMPLES

1. Avoid listening to "tattle tale" stories about students.
2. Follow through with fair consequences.
3. Avoid unnecessary comparisons and give students opportunities to improve their work.

Help students recognize and express their feelings.

EXAMPLES

1. Provide a vocabulary of emotions and note descriptions of emotions in characters or stories.
2. Be clear and descriptive about your own emotions.
3. Encourage students to write in journals about their own feelings. Protect the privacy of these writings (see trust above).

Help students recognize emotions in others.

EXAMPLES

1. For young children, "Look at Chandra's face. How do you think she feels when you say those things?"
2. For older students, use readings, films, or role reversals to help them identify the emotions of others.

Provide strategies for coping with emotions.

EXAMPLES

1. Discuss or practice alternatives such as stopping to think how the other person feels, seeking help, anger management such as self-talk or leaving the scene.
2. Model strategies for students. Talk about how you handle anger, disappointment, or anxiety.

Help students recognize cultural differences in emotional expression.

EXAMPLES

1. Have students write about or discuss how they show emotions in their family.
2. Teach students to "check it out"—ask the other people how they are feeling.

For ideas about promoting emotional competence, see **http://csefel.uiuc.edu/modules/inventory-of-practices.pdf**

Around the age of 2, children have a sense of *intention,* at least of their own intentions. They will announce, "I wanna peanut butter sandwich." As children develop a theory of mind, they also are able to understand that other people have intentions of their own. Older preschoolers who get along well with their peers are able to separate intentional from unintentional actions and to react accordingly. For example, they will not get angry when another child accidentally knocks over their block tower. But aggressive children have more trouble assessing intention. They are likely to attack anyone who topples their tower, even accidentally (Dodge & Pettit, 2003). As children mature, they are more able to assess and consider the intentions of others.

With a developing theory of mind, children are increasingly able to understand that other people have different feelings and experiences, and therefore may have a different viewpoint or perspective. This **perspective-taking ability** develops over time until it is quite sophisticated in adults. Being able to understand how others might think and feel is important in fostering cooperation and moral development, reducing prejudice, resolving conflicts, and encouraging positive social behaviors in general (Gehlbach, 2004).

Robert Selman (1980) has developed a stage model to describe perspective-taking. As children mature and move toward formal-operational thinking, they take more information into account and realize that different people can react differently to the same situation. At some point between the ages of 10 and 15, most children develop the ability to analyze the perspectives of several people involved in a situation from the viewpoint of an objective bystander. Finally, older adolescents and adults can even imagine how different cultural or social values would influence the perceptions of the bystander. Even though children move through these stages, there can be great variation among children of the same age. Students who have difficulty taking the perspective of others may feel little remorse when they mistreat peers or adults. Some coaching in perspective-taking from the teacher might help if the mistreatment is not part of a deeper emotional or behavioral disorder (Berk, 2005).

Perspective-taking ability Understanding that others have different feelings and experiences.

Moral Development

Along with a more advanced theory of mind and an understanding of intention, children also are developing a sense of right and wrong. In this section we focus on children's **moral reasoning,** their *thinking* about right and wrong and their *active construction* of moral judgments. Some of the earliest moral issues in classrooms involve dividing and sharing materials or **distributive justice** (Damon, 1994). For young children (ages 5 to 6), fair distribution is based on *equality;* thus, teachers often hear, "Keshawn got more than I did—that's not fair!" In the next few years, children come to recognize that some people should get more based on *merit*—they worked harder or performed better. Finally, around age 8, children are able to take need into account and to reason based on *benevolence;* they can understand that some students may get more time or resources from the teacher because those students have special needs.

Another area that involves moral development is an understanding of rules. If you have spent time with young children, you know that there is a period when you can say, "Eating in the living room is not allowed!" and get away with it. For young children, rules simply exist. Piaget (1965) called this the state of **moral realism.** At this stage, the child of 5 or 6 believes that rules about conduct or rules about how to play a game are absolute and can't be changed. If a rule is broken, the child believes that the punishment should be determined by how much damage is done, not by the intention of the child or by other circumstances. So, accidentally breaking three cups is worse than intentionally breaking one, and in the child's eyes, the punishment for the three-cup offense should be greater.

As children interact with others, develop perspective-taking emotional abilities, and see that different people have different rules, there is a gradual shift to a **morality of cooperation.** Children come to understand that people make rules and people can change them. When rules are broken, both the damage done and the intention of the offender are taken into account.

Kohlberg's Theories of Moral Development. Lawrence Kohlberg's (1963, 1975, 1981) theory of moral development is based in part on Piaget's ideas, described earlier.

STOP | THINK | WRITE A man's wife is dying. There is one drug that could save her, but it is very expensive, and the druggist who invented it will not sell it at a price low enough for the man to buy it. Finally, the man becomes desperate and considers stealing the drug for his wife. What should he do, and why? ■

Kohlberg has evaluated the moral reasoning of both children and adults by presenting them with **moral dilemmas,** or hypothetical situations like the one above in which people must make difficult decisions and give their reasons. Based on their reasoning, Kohlberg proposed a detailed sequence of stages of moral reasoning, or judgments about right and wrong. He divided moral development into three levels: (1) preconventional, where judgment is based solely on a person's own needs and perceptions; (2) conven-

Agnes's moral dilemma. How would you rate her reasoning?

From *Agnes*, May 7, 2002. © 2002 Tony Cochran. Reprinted with permission of the Creators Syndicate.

Moral reasoning The thinking process involved in judgments about questions of right and wrong.

Distributive justice Beliefs about how to divide materials or privileges fairly among members of a group; follows a sequence of development from equality to merit to benevolence.

Moral realism Stage of development wherein children see rules as absolute.

Morality of cooperation Stage of development wherein children realize that people make rules and people can change them.

Moral dilemmas Situations in which no choice is clearly and indisputably right.

tional, where the expectations of society and law are taken into account; and (3) post-conventional, where judgments are based on abstract, more personal principles of justice that are not necessarily defined by society's laws. Look at Table 3.7 to see how each of these three levels is then subdivided into stages. Can you find your reasons for your answer to the *Stop/Think/Write* question above in Table 3.7?

Moral reasoning is related to both cognitive and emotional development. As we have seen, abstract thinking becomes increasingly important in the higher stages of moral development, as children move from decisions based on absolute rules to those based on abstract principles such as justice and mercy. The ability to see another's perspective, to judge intentions, and to imagine alternative bases for laws and rules also enters into judgments at the higher stages.

Criticisms of Kohlberg's Theory. Even though there is evidence that the different levels of reasoning identified by Kohlberg do form a hierarchy, with each stage an advancement in reasoning over the one before (Boom, Brugman, & van der Heijden, 2001), his stage theory has been criticized. First, in reality, the stages do not seem to be separate, sequenced, and consistent. People often give reasons for moral choices that reflect several different stages simultaneously. Or a person's choices in one instance may fit one stage and his or her decisions in a different situation may reflect another stage. When asked to reason about helping someone else versus meeting their own needs, both children and

TABLE 3.7

Kohlberg's Theory of Moral Reasoning

Level 1. Preconventional Moral Reasoning

Judgment is based on personal needs and others' rules.

Stage 1	Punishment—Obedience Orientation
	Rules are obeyed to avoid punishment. A good or bad action is determined by its physical consequences.
Stage 2	Personal Reward Orientation
	Personal needs determine right and wrong. Favors are returned along the lines of "You scratch my back, I'll scratch yours."

Level 2. Conventional Moral Reasoning

Judgment is based on others' approval, family expectations, traditional values, the laws of society, and loyalty to country.

Stage 3	Good Boy—Nice Girl Orientation
	Good means "nice." It is determined by what pleases, aids, and is approved by others.
Stage 4	Law and Order Orientation
	Laws are absolute. Authority must be respected and the social order maintained.

Level 3. Postconventional Moral Reasoning

Stage 5	Social Contract Orientation
	Good is determined by socially agreed-upon standards of individual rights. This is a morality similar to that of the U.S. Constitution.
Stage 6*	Universal Ethical Principle Orientation
	Good and right are matters of individual conscience and involve abstract concepts of justice, human dignity, and equality.

*In later work Kohlberg questioned whether Stage 6 exists separately from Stage 5.

Source: From "The Cognitive-Developmental Approach to Moral Education," by L. Kohlberg, 1975, *Phi Delta Kappan, 56,* p. 671. Adapted by permission of the *Journal of Philosophy.*

adolescents reason at higher levels than when they are asked to reason about breaking the law or risking punishment (Arnold, 2000; Eisenberg et al., 1987; Sobesky, 1983).

Second, in everyday life, making moral choices involves more than reasoning. Emotions, competing goals, relationships, and practical considerations all affect choices. People may be able to reason at higher levels, but they may make choices at lower levels based on these other factors (Carpendale, 2000). Kohlberg emphasized cognitive reasoning about morality, but overlooked other aspects of moral maturity, such as character and virtue, that operate to solve moral problems in everyday life (Walker & Pitts, 1998).

Gender Differences: The Morality of Caring. One of the most hotly debated criticisms of Kohlberg's theory is that the stages are biased in favor of Western male values that emphasize individualism. His stages do not represent the way moral reasoning develops either in women or in other cultures, because the stage theory was based on a longitudinal study of American men only (Gilligan, 1982; Gilligan & Attanucci, 1988).

Carol Gilligan (1982) has proposed a different sequence of moral development, an "ethic of care." Gilligan suggests that individuals move from a focus on self-interest to moral reasoning based on commitment to specific individuals and relationships, and then to the highest level of morality based on the principles of responsibility and care for all people (which is a bit like Kohlberg's stage 3). If women never reach what Kohlberg considers the higher stages of justice, are they morally immature?

Actually, recent studies find few significant differences between men and women, or boys and girls, in their level of moral reasoning as measured by Kohlberg's procedures (Eisenberg, Martin, & Fabes, 1996; Turiel, 1998). Walker and his colleagues (Walker, 1991; Walker, Pitts, Hennig, & Matsuba, 1995) asked children, adolescents, and adults to describe a personal moral problem and to analyze a traditional moral dilemma. For both types of problems, males and females revealed both a morality of caring *and* a concern with justice. When they read fables to boys and girls in the 1st and 3rd grades, Andrew Garrod and his colleagues (1990) found no differences in their moral reasoning. However, a few 5th-grade boys (but no girls) suggested solutions involving violence or tricks. So justice and caring seem to be important bases for moral reasoning for both genders. Even though men and women both seem to value caring and justice, there is some evidence that in everyday life, women feel more guilty about violating caring norms (being inconsiderate or untrustworthy) and men feel more guilty when they show violent behaviors (fighting or damaging property) (Williams & Bybee, 1994). Women are somewhat more likely to use a care orientation, but both men and women *can* use both orientations (Skoe, 1998).

Caring for students and helping students learn to care has become a theme for many educators. For example, Nel Noddings (1995) urged that "themes of care" be used to organize the curriculum. Possible themes include "Caring for Self," "Caring for Family and Friends," and "Caring for Strangers and the World." Using the theme of "Caring for Strangers and the World," there could be units on crime, war, poverty, tolerance, ecology, or technology. The events after Hurricane Katrina that left thousands homeless might be a starting point for these units. Table 3.8 on the next page shows how a focus on crime and caring for strangers could be integrated into several high-school classes.

Moral Judgments, Social Conventions, and Personal Choices

STOP | THINK | WRITE

1. If there were no law against it, would it be OK to blind someone?
2. If there were no rule against it, would it be OK to chew gum in class?
3. Who should decide your favorite vegetable or how to style your hair? ■

We probably could agree that it is wrong to blind someone, wrong to break class rules, and wrong to dictate food preferences or hairstyles for other people—but it is a different kind of wrong in each case. The first question is about actions that are inherently immoral. The answer to the question is concerned with conceptions of justice, fairness, human rights, and human welfare. Even young children know that it is not OK to hurt

Connect and **Extend** to Your **Teaching**

Adapt Table 3.8, *Using "Caring for Strangers and the World" as a Teaching Theme*, for the grades and subjects you might teach and add it to your Teaching Resources file.

TABLE 3.8

Using "Caring for Strangers and the World" as a Teaching Theme

As part of a unit on "Caring for Strangers and the World," high school students examine the issue of crime in several classes. In every class, the study of aspects of crime would be continually tied to the theme of caring and to discussions of safety, responsibility, trust in each other and in the community, and commitment to a safer future.

Subject	Elements
Mathematics	Statistics: Gather data on the location and rates of crimes, ages of offenders, and costs of crime to society. Is there a correlation between severity of punishment and incidence of crime? What is the actual cost of a criminal trial?
English and Social Studies	Read *Oliver Twist.* Relate the characters to their social and historical context. What factors contributed to crime in 19th century England?
	Read popular mysteries. Are they literature? Are they accurate depictions of the criminal justice system?
Science	Genetics: Are criminal tendencies heritable? Are there sex differences in aggressive behavior? Are women less competent than men in moral reasoning (and why did some social scientists think so)? How would you test this hypothesis?
Arts	Is graffiti art really art?

Source: From "Teaching Themes of Care," by Nel Noddings, *Phi Delta Kappan, 76,* pp. 675–679. Copyright © 1995 Nel Noddings. Reprinted with permission of the author.

other people or steal from them—law or no law. But some rules, like no gum chewing in question 2, are **social conventions**—agreed-upon rules and ways of doing things in a particular situation. Students (mostly) avoid chewing gum when the class rules (conventions) say so. It is not inherently immoral to chew gum—it is just against the rules. Some classes—in college, for example—work well using different rules. And it is not immoral to dislike lima beans (at least I hope not) or to wear your hair short if you are a female; these are personal choices—individual preferences and private issues.

Other criticisms of Kohlberg's stages are that they mix up moral judgments with decisions about social conventions and also overlook personal choice. Larry Nucci (2001) offers an explanation of moral development that covers all three domains or areas: moral judgments, social conventions, and personal choice. Children's thinking and reasoning develops across all domains, but the pace of development may not be the same in every area.

Moral versus Conventional Domains. For teachers, the most common "right and wrong" situations involve the moral and conventional domains. In the moral domain, beginning with a few basic ideas about right and wrong ("It is wrong to hurt others"), children move through the following stages: a sense that justice means equal treatment for all, an appreciation of equity and special needs, a more abstract integration of equity and equality along with a sense of caring in social relations, and finally, a sense as adults that morality involves beneficence and fairness and that moral principles are independent of the norms of any particular group.

In the conventional domain, children begin by believing that the regularities they see are real and right—men have short hair, women have longer hair, for example, so that is the way it should be. As they mature, children see the exceptions (men with pony tails, women with very short cuts) and realize that conventions are arbitrary. Next, children understand that rules, even though they are arbitrary, are made to maintain order and that people in charge make the rules. But by early adolescence, students begin to question these rules. Because they are arbitrary and made by others, maybe rules are "nothing but" social expectations. As they move through adolescence, there is another swing—from understanding conventions as the appropriate way things have to operate in a social system to again seeing them as nothing but society's standards that have become set because they are used. Finally, adults realize that conventions are useful in coordinating social life, but

Social conventions Agreed-upon rules and ways of doing things in a particular situation.

Educators can create a moral climate in their schools and classrooms by promoting and reinforcing a community of mutual respect.

changeable, too. So, compared to young children, older adolescents and adults generally are more accepting of others who think differently about conventions and customs.

Implications for Teachers. Nucci (2001) offers several suggestions for creating a moral atmosphere in your classroom. First, it is important to establish a community of mutual respect and warmth with a fair and consistent application of the rules. Without that kind of community, all your attempts to create a moral climate will be undermined. Second, teachers' responses to students should be appropriate to the domain of the behavior—moral or conventional. For example, here are some responses to *moral issues* (Nucci, 2001, p. 146):

1. When an act is inherently hurtful or unjust, emphasize the harm done to others: "John, that really hurt Jamal."
2. Encourage perspective-taking: "Chris, how would you feel if someone stole from you?"

Here are two responses to rule or *conventional issues*:

3. Restate the rule: "Lisa, you are not allowed to be out of your seat during announcements."
4. Command: "Howie, stop swearing!"

In all four cases, the teacher's response fits the domain. To create an inappropriate response, just switch responses 1 or 2 with 3 or 4. For example, "Jim, how would you feel if other people got out of their seat during announcements?" Jim might feel just fine. And it is a weak response to a moral transgression to say, "John, it is against the rules to hit." It is more than against the rules—it hurts and it is wrong.

In the third domain, personal, children must sort out what decisions and actions are their personal choices and what decisions are outside personal choice. This process is the foundation for developing moral concepts related to individual rights, fairness, and democracy. Here, different cultures may have very different understandings about individual choice, privacy, and the role of individuality in the larger society. For example, some research has shown that both the parents in cultures that emphasize individualism and the parents in cultures that emphasize group membership believe that children need to be given choices to develop their ability to make good decisions. But middle-class parents tend to encourage making choices earlier, before adolescence. For children living in poverty, making too many choices early may be a bad idea, given the very real dangers they face in their neighborhoods (Nucci, 2001).

Connect and Extend to Your Philosophy

The June 3, 1996 issue of *U.S. News & World Report* had a cover story titled "How to Raise a Moral Child: Let's Hear It for Honesty, Self-Discipline, and Empathy" (pp. 52–59). This is an interesting mix of research and opinion and a good discussion starter.

Guidelines: Supporting Personal and Moral Development

Help students examine the kinds of dilemmas they are currently facing or will face in the near future.

EXAMPLES

1. In elementary school, discuss sibling rivalries, teasing, stealing, prejudice, treatment of new students in the class, and behavior toward classmates with disabilities.
2. In high school, discuss cheating, letting friends drive when they are intoxicated, conforming to be more popular, and protecting a friend who has broken a rule.

Help students see the perspectives of others.

EXAMPLES

1. Ask a student to describe his or her understanding of the views of another; then have the other person confirm or correct the perception.
2. Have students exchange roles and try to "become" the other person in a discussion.

Help students make connections between expressed values and actions.

EXAMPLES

1. Follow a discussion of "What should be done?" with "How would you act? What would be your first step? What problems might arise?"
2. Help students see inconsistencies between their values and their own actions. Ask them to identify inconsistencies, first in others, then in themselves.

Safeguard the privacy of all participants.

EXAMPLES

1. Remind students that in a discussion, they can "pass" and not answer questions.
2. Intervene if peer pressure is forcing a student to say more than he or she wants to.
3. Don't reinforce a pattern of telling "secrets."

Make sure students are really listening to each other.

EXAMPLES

1. Keep groups small.
2. Be a good listener yourself.
3. Recognize students who pay careful attention to each other.

Make sure that as much as possible your class reflects concern for moral issues and values.

EXAMPLES

1. Make clear distinctions between rules based on administrative convenience (keeping the room orderly) and rules based on moral issues.
2. Enforce standards uniformly. Be careful about showing favoritism.

For more information, see The Collaborative for Academic, Social, and Emotional Learning: **http://www.casel.org/home/index.php**

Source: From "What Criteria Should Public School Moral Education Programs Meet?" by J. W. Eiseman, *Oxford Review of Education*, 7, pp. 226–227. Copyright © 1981 by Taylor & Francis, Ltd. Reprinted with permission of Taylor & Francis. **http://www.tandf.co.uk/journals**

Connect and **Extend** to Your **Teaching**

In a classroom discussion about stealing, the teacher finds that many students express the opinion that it is all right to steal if you don't get caught. How should a teacher respond? Would the race, culture, gender, or socioeconomic status of the student influence the teacher's response?

Diversity in Reasoning

There are a number of broad cultural distinctions that might influence moral reasoning. Some cultures can be considered more traditional, with greater emphasis on customs and rituals that change slowly over time. In contrast, traditions and customs tend to change more rapidly in modern cultures. Nucci (2001) suggests that in more traditional cultures, customs may become "moralized." For example, not wearing head coverings in some cultures may seem to be in the conventional domain to outsiders, but is closer to the moral domain for members of the culture, especially when religious beliefs are involved. Consider the findings of one study described by Nucci that asked devout Hindus to rate 35 behaviors that violated community norms. An eldest son eating chicken a day after his father's death was considered the worst violation and beating a disobedient wife was the least offensive. What seems like a convention (eating chicken) is a moral issue because the Hindus believed that the son's behavior would prevent his father from receiving salvation—a terrible and eternal fate. So, to understand what is convention and what is moral, we need to know about the beliefs of the culture.

In cultures that are more family-centered or group-oriented (often called collectivist cultures), the highest moral value might involve putting the opinions of the group before decisions based on individual conscience. Research has found that children's reasoning about moral, conventional, and personal domains is similar across cultures (Berk, 2005). Even in societies such as China that encourage deference to authority, Chinese children agree with Western children that adults have no right to dictate how children spend their free time. And people without authority, including children, should be obeyed when what they want you to do is fair and just, but disobeyed when what they dictate is immoral or unjust (Helwig, Arnold, Tan, & Boyd, 2003; Kim, 1998).

In the last years of his life, Kohlberg was studying moral behavior in schools. We turn to that topic now.

Moral Behavior

As people move toward higher stages of moral reasoning, they also evidence more sharing, helping, and defending of victims of injustice; this relationship between moral reasoning and moral behavior is not very strong, however (Berk, 2005). But many other factors besides reasoning affect behavior. Three important influences on moral behavior are modeling, internalization, and self-concept. First, children who have been consistently exposed to caring, generous adult models will tend to be more concerned for the rights and feelings of others (Cook & Cook, 2005; Eisenberg & Fabes, 1998). Second, most theories of moral behavior assume that young children's moral behavior is first controlled by others through direct instruction, supervision, rewards and punishments, and correction. But in time, children **internalize** the moral rules and principles of the authority figures who have guided them; that is, children adopt the external standards as their own. If children are given reasons they can understand when they are corrected—particularly reasons that highlight the effects of actions on others—then they are more likely to internalize moral principles. They learn to behave morally even when "no one is watching" (Hoffman, 2000).

Finally, we must integrate moral beliefs and values into our total sense of who we are, our self-concept.

> The tendency for a person to behave morally is largely dependent on the extent to which moral beliefs and values are integrated in the personality, and in one's sense of self. The influence our moral beliefs have on our lives, therefore, is contingent on the personal importance that we as individuals attach to them—we must identify and respect them as our own. (Arnold, 2000, p. 372)

The *Guidelines* give ideas for supporting personal and moral development. Let's consider a moral issue that arises in classrooms—cheating.

Cheating

Early research indicates that cheating seems to have more to do with the particular situation than with the general honesty or dishonesty of the individual (Burton, 1963). A student who cheats in math class is probably more likely to cheat in other classes, but may never consider lying to a friend or taking candy from the store. Many students will cheat if the pressure to perform well is great and the chances of being caught are slim. In one study, about 60% of middle-school students and 70% of high-school students believed that cheating was a serious problem in their school (Evans & Craig, 1990). In 1996, Steinberg reported that 66% of the adolescents in his study admitted to cheating on a test in the last year, and figures as high as 90% have been reported for college students (Jensen, Arnett, Feldman, & Cauffman, 2001). But the sad fact is that cheating by all groups has increased over the past 20 years (Jensen, Arnett, Feldman, & Cauffman, 2002; Murdock, Hale, & Weber, 2001).

There are some individual differences in cheating. Most studies of adolescent and college-age students find that males are more likely to cheat than females and lower-achieving students are more likely to cheat than higher achievers. Students focusing on performance goals (making good grades, looking smart) as opposed to learning goals, and students with a low sense of academic self-efficacy (a belief that they probably can't do well in school) are more likely to cheat.

Connect and Extend to PRAXIS II™

Moral Development (I, A2)
Moral issues can have an important impact on the classroom. Identify major issues related to moral development and explain what a teacher can do to appropriately address these issues.

Connect and Extend to Your Own Philosophy

Moral action does not necessarily follow directly from moral judgment. But is it necessary for moral judgment to precede moral action? That is, can a person behave in a moral way even if he or she cannot make a cognitive statement about how one "should" behave?

Internalize Process whereby children adopt external standards as their own.

Cheating is not all about individual differences—the situation plays a role as well. In one study, the level of cheating decreased when students moved from math classes that emphasized competition and grades to classes that emphasized understanding and mastery (Anderman & Midgley, 2004). Students also are particularly likely to cheat when they are behind or "cramming for tests" or when they believe that their teachers do not care about them. For example, Erica had this perspective:

> I am a high school honors student, and I think there are different degrees of cheating. I'm a dedicated student, but when my history teacher bombards me with 50 questions due tomorrow or when a teacher gives me a fill-in-the-blanks worksheet on a night when I have swim practice, church, aerobics—and other homework—I'm going to copy from a friend! . . . Since I only do this when I need to, it isn't a habit. Every kid does this when they're in a pinch. (Jensen et al., 2002, p. 210)

The implications for teachers are straightforward. To prevent cheating, try to avoid putting students in high-pressure situations. Make sure they are well prepared for tests, projects, and assignments so they can do reasonably well without cheating. Focus on learning and not on grades. Encourage collaboration on assignments and experiment with open-book, collaborative, or take-home tests. I often tell my students what concepts will be on the test and encourage them to discuss the concepts and their applications before the test. You might also make extra help available for those who need it. Be clear about your policies in regard to cheating, and enforce them consistently. Help students resist temptation by monitoring them carefully during testing.

Diversity and Convergences in Personal/Social Development

In the areas of physical, personal, and social development, we would expect *diversity* based on differences in social and cultural contexts.

Diversity

- African American girls mature significantly earlier than Mexican American girls, and European American girls mature later still (Chumlea et al., 2003).
- Girls enter puberty earlier than boys.
- Parenting styles in many African American and Asian American homes may be stricter in their expectations for obedience, based on the need to protect their children from unsafe environments or a tradition of respect for elders.
- The good of the family group may be elevated over individualistic concerns.

In their relationships with teachers, high-achieving, middle-class students see caring expressed in help with academic work, whereas students who have been alienated from school value personal caring—teachers who are concerned with the lives and futures of their students. Students may not risk caring about school until the school risks caring about them, and the care should be personal. You will see in Chapter 12 that a teaching style of warmth and caring, coupled with high demands for compliance, characterizes successful classroom managers of African American students. This sounds like the authoritative parenting style discussed earlier.

In terms of self-concept, we saw different patterns for boys and girls across the school years in their sense of competence in math, sports, and language arts. In addition, girls tend to see themselves as more able than boys in reading and close friendships; boys are more confident about their abilities in math and athletics. Unfortunately, there are no long-term studies of other ethnic groups, so these patterns may be limited to European Americans. In terms of self-esteem, the family can play a significant role. A study by John Fantuzzo, Gwendolyn Davis, and Marika Ginsburg (1995) capitalized on the power of families to improve students' self-esteem. The *Family and Community Partnerships Guidelines* list the strategies from their study that proved effective in increasing self-

Family and Community Partnerships

Guidelines: Building Self-Esteem

1. Work with families to co-create methods for family involvement. Offer a range of possible participation methods. Make sure the plans are realistic and fit the lives of the families you are dealing with.
2. Remember that some students' parents have had negative experiences with schools or may fear or mistrust schools and teachers. Find other places to collaborate: before or after ball games, or at a local church or recreation center. Go where families go; don't always expect them to come to school.
3. Maintain regular home–school contact through telephone calls or notes. If a family has no telephone, identify a contact person (relative or friend) who can take messages. If literacy is a problem, use pictures, symbols, and codes for written communication.
4. Make all communications positive, emphasizing growth, progress, and accomplishments.
5. With the families, design family–student celebrations of the student's efforts and successes (a movie, special meal, trip to the park or library, going out for ice cream or pizza).
6. On a regular basis, send home a note in word or picture form that describes the student's progress. Ask families to indicate how they celebrated the success and to return the note.
7. Follow up with a telephone call to discuss progress, answer questions, solicit family suggestions, and express appreciation for the families' contributions.
8. Make sure families feel welcome if they visit the classroom.

For more information on family school partnerships, see **http://www.gse.harvard.edu/hfrp/projects/family.html**

Source: From "Effects of Parent Involvement in Isolation or in Combination with Peer Tutoring on Student Self-Concept and Mathematics Achievement," by J. Fantuzzo, G. Davis, and M. Ginsburg, *Journal of Educational Psychology*, 87, pp. 272–281. Copyright © 1995 by the American Psychological Association. Adapted with permission of the APA.

esteem and mathematics achievement for the 4th- and 5th-grade African American urban-school students who participated.

When we looked at identity, we saw that White students often deny that they have an ethnic identity, whereas ethnic minority groups have to reconcile two identities and may move through stages from not being aware of or denying differences to finally reaching an integration of the two cultures.

When we turned to moral reasoning, we saw that in some cultures, conventions and customs are seen as rules made to make social life smoother, but in other more traditional societies, social conventions may take on a moral meaning. And the range for personal choice also varies by culture, with individualist cultures valuing more personal choice in a wider range of areas.

Connect and Extend to Your Teaching

Add some ideas for parent involvement from this chapter to your Portfolio.

Convergences

In spite of these differences, there are some convergences in many areas of personal and social development. Certainly both Erikson and Bronfenbrenner stress that individuals are influenced by their social and cultural contexts. For example, here are a few big ideas:

1. Students whose parents are divorcing can benefit from authoritative teachers who are both warm and clear about requirements.
2. For all students, self-concepts are increasingly differentiated over time—they may feel competent in one subject, but not in others or very capable as friends or family members, but not good about work in school.
3. For all students, it is a challenge to forge a meaningful identity that integrates their decisions about career, religion, ethnicity, gender roles, and connection to society. Teachers are in a position to support this quest.
4. Being rejected by peers is harmful for all students. Many students need guidance in developing social skills, in more accurately reading the intentions of others, in resolving conflicts, and in coping with aggression. Again, teachers can provide guidance.
5. When working under high pressure, with unreasonable workloads, and with little chance of being caught, many students will cheat. It is up to teachers and schools to avoid these conditions.

Physical Development (pp. 64–66)

Describe the changes in physical development in the preschool, elementary, and secondary grades. During the preschool years, there is rapid development of children's gross- and fine-motor skills. Physical development continues throughout the elementary-school years, with girls often ahead of boys in size. With adolescence comes puberty and emotional struggles to cope with all the related changes.

What are some of the consequences of early and late maturation for boys and girls? Females mature about two years ahead of males. Early-maturing boys are more likely to enjoy high social status; they tend to be popular and to be leaders. But they also tend to engage in more delinquent behavior—this is true for White, African American, and Mexican American boys. Early maturation is not generally beneficial for girls.

What are some of the signs of eating disorders? Anorexic students may appear pale, have brittle fingernails, and have fine dark hairs developing all over their bodies. They are easily chilled because they have so little fat to insulate their bodies. They often are depressed, insecure, moody, and lonely. Girls may stop having their menstrual period.

Puberty The physiological changes during adolescence that lead to the ability to reproduce.

Bulimia Eating disorder characterized by overeating, then getting rid of the food by self-induced vomiting or laxatives.

Anorexia Nervosa Eating disorder characterized by very limited food intake.

Erikson: Stages of Individual Development (pp. 67–72)

Why is Erikson's theory considered a psychosocial perspective? Erikson's emphasis on the relationship between society and the individual is a psychosocial theory of development—a theory that connects personal development (psycho) to the social environment (social).

What are Erikson's stages of psychosocial development? Erikson believed that people go through eight life stages, each of which involves a central crisis. Adequate resolution of each crisis leads to greater personal and social competence and a stronger foundation for solving future crises. In the first two stages, an infant must develop a sense of trust over mistrust and a sense of autonomy over shame and doubt. In early childhood, the focus of the third stage is on developing initiative and avoiding feelings of guilt. In the child's elementary-school years, the fourth stage involves achieving a sense of industry and avoiding feelings of inferiority. In the fifth stage, identity versus role confusion, adolescents consciously attempt to solidify their identity. According to Marcia, these efforts may lead to identity diffusion, foreclosure, moratorium, or achievement. Erikson's three stages of adulthood involve struggles to achieve intimacy, generativity, and integrity.

Psychosocial Describing the relation of the individual's emotional needs to the social environment.

Developmental crisis A specific conflict whose resolution prepares the way for the next stage.

Autonomy Independence.

Initiative Willingness to begin new activities and explore new directions.

Industry Eagerness to engage in productive work.

Identity The complex answer to the question: "Who am I?"

Identity diffusion Uncenteredness; confusion about who one is and what one wants.

Identity foreclosure Acceptance of parental life choices without consideration of options.

Moratorium Identity crisis; suspension of choices because of struggle.

Identity achievement Strong sense of commitment to life choices after free consideration of alternatives.

Generativity Sense of concern for future generations.

Integrity Sense of self-acceptance and fulfillment.

Bronfenbrenner: The Social Context for Development (pp. 72–84)

Describe Bronfenbrenner's bioecological model of development? This model takes into account both the biological aspects internal to the individual and the nested social and cultural contexts that shape development. Every person develops within a *microsystem* (immediate relationships and activities) inside a *mesosystem* (relationships among microsystems), embedded in an *exosystem* (larger social settings such as communities); all of these are part of the *macrosystem* (culture).

What are some aspects of the family that affect students in school? Students probably have experienced different parenting styles and these styles can influence their social adjustment. At least in European American, middle-class families, children of authoritative parents are more likely to be happy with themselves and relate well to others, whereas children of authoritarian parents are more likely to be guilty or depressed, and children of permissive parents may have trouble interacting with peers. But cultures differ in parenting styles. Research indicates that higher-control parenting is linked to better grades for Asian and African American students.

How does divorce affect students? During the divorce itself, conflict may increase as property and custody rights are being decided. After the divorce, the custodial parent may have to move to a less expensive home, go to work for the first time, or work longer hours. For the child, this can mean leaving behind important friendships just when support is needed the most, having only one parent who has less time than ever to be with them, or adjusting to new family structures when parents remarry.

Why are peer relations important? Peer relationships play a significant role in healthy personal and social development. There is strong evidence that adults who had close friends as children have higher self-esteem and are more capable of maintaining intimate relationships than adults who had lonely childhoods. Adults who were rejected as children tend to have more problems, such as dropping out of school or committing crimes.

What are peer cultures and how can aggression develop? Groups of students develop their own norms for appearance and social behavior. Group loyalties can lead to rejection for some students, leaving them upset and unhappy. Peer aggression can be instrumental (intended to gain an object or privilege), or hostile (intended to inflict harm). Hostile aggression can be either overt threats or physical attacks or relational aggression, which involves threatening or damaging social relationships. Boys are more likely to use overt aggression and girls are more likely to use relational aggression.

How can teachers' academic and personal caring affect students? Students value caring in teachers. Caring can be expressed as support for academic learning and as concern for personal problems. For higher-achieving and higher socioeconomic status students, academic caring may be more important, but for students who are alienated from school, personal caring may be more important.

What are some signs of child abuse? Signs of abuse or neglect include unexplained bruises, burns, bites, or other injuries and fatigue, depression, frequent absences, poor hygiene, inappropriate clothing, problems with peers and many others. Teachers must report suspected cases of child abuse and can be instrumental in helping students cope with other risks as well.

Bioecological model Bronfenbrenner's theory describing the nested social and cultural contexts that shape development. Every person develops within a *microsystem,* inside a *mesosystem,* embedded in an *exosystem,* all of which are a part of the *macrosystem* of the culture.

Blended families Parents, children, and stepchildren merged into families through remarriages.

Parenting styles The ways of interacting with and disciplining children.

Instrumental aggression Strong actions aimed at claiming an object, place, or privilege—not intended to harm, but may lead to harm.

Hostile aggression Bold, direct action that is intended to hurt someone else; unprovoked attack.

Overt aggression A form of hostile aggression that involves physical attack.

Relational aggression A form of hostile aggression that involves verbal attacks and other actions meant to harm social relationships.

Self-Concept: Understanding Ourselves
(pp. 85–88)

Distinguish between self-concept and self-esteem. Both self-concept and self-esteem are beliefs about the self. Self-concept is our attempt to build a scheme that organizes our impressions, feelings, and attitudes about ourselves. But this model is not permanent. Self-perceptions vary from situation to situation and from one phase of our lives to another. Self-esteem is an evaluation of who you are. If people evaluate themselves positively, we say that they have high self-esteem. Self-concept and self-esteem are often used interchangeably, even though they have distinct meanings. Self-concept is a cognitive structure and self-esteem is an affective evaluation.

How do self-concept and self-esteem change as children develop? Self-concept (definition of self) and self-esteem (valuing of self) become increasingly complex, differentiated, and abstract as we mature. Self-concept evolves through constant self-reflection, social interaction, and experiences in and out of school. Students develop a self-concept by comparing themselves to personal (internal) standards and social (external) standards. High self-esteem is related to better overall school experience, both academically and socially. Gender and ethnic stereotypes are significant factors as well.

Self-concept Individuals' knowledge and beliefs about themselves—their ideas, feelings, attitudes, and expectations.

Self-esteem The value each of us places on our own characteristics, abilities, and behaviors.

Diversity and Identity (pp. 88–92)

Are there differences in self-concepts for girls and boys? From 1st to 12th grade, competence beliefs decline for both boys and girls in math, language arts, and sports. By high school, boys and girls express about the same competence in math, girls are higher in language arts, and boys are higher in sports. In terms of general self-esteem, both boys and girls report declines in the transition to middle school, but boys' self-esteem goes up in high school while girls' self-esteem stays down.

Describe the formation of ethnic and racial, and sexual identities. Ethnic and racial minority students are confronted with the challenge of forming an identity while living in two worlds—the values, beliefs, and behaviors of their group and of the larger culture. Most explanations for identity development describe stages moving from being unaware of differences between minority group and majority cultures, to different ways of negotiating the differences, finally to an integration of cultures.

Nigrescence The process of developing a Black identity.

Racial and ethnic pride A positive self-concept about one's racial or ethnic heritage.

Emotional and Moral Development
(pp. 92–102)

What are the skills involved in emotional competence? Emotionally competent individuals are aware of their own emotions and the feelings of others—realizing that inner emotions can differ from outward expressions. They can talk about and express emotions in ways that are appropriate for their cultural group, They can feel empathy for others in distress and also cope with their own distressing emotions—they can handle stress. Emotionally competent individuals know that relationships are defined in part by how emotions are communicated within the relationship. All these skills come together to produce a capacity for emotional self-efficacy.

What is a theory of mind and why is it important? A theory of mind is an understanding that other people are people too, with their own minds, thoughts, feelings, beliefs, desires, and perceptions. Children need a theory of mind to make sense of other people's behavior. As children develop a theory of mind, they also are able to understand that other people have intentions of their own.

How do perspective-taking skills change as students mature? An understanding of intentions develops as children mature, but aggressive students often have trouble understanding the intentions of others. Social perspective-taking also changes as we mature. Young children believe that everyone has the same thoughts and feelings they do. Later, they learn that others have separate identities and therefore separate feelings and perspectives on events.

What are the key differences among the preconventional, conventional, and postconventional levels of moral reasoning? Kohlberg's theory of moral development includes three levels: (1) a preconventional level, where judgments are based on self-interest; (2) a conventional level, where judgments are based on traditional family values and social expectations; and (3) a postconventional level, where judgments are based on more abstract and personal ethical principles. Critics suggest that Kohlberg's view does not account for possible cultural differences in moral reasoning or differences between moral reasoning and moral behavior.

Describe Gilligan's levels of moral reasoning. Carol Gilligan has suggested that because Kohlberg's stage theory was based on a longitudinal study of men only, it is very possible that the moral reasoning of women and the stages of women's development were not adequately represented. She has proposed an "ethic of care." Gilligan believes that individuals move from a focus on self-interests to moral reasoning based on commitment to specific individuals and relationships, and then to the highest level of morality based on the principles of responsibility and care for all people. Women are somewhat more likely to use a care orientation, but studies also show that both men and women *can* use both orientations.

How does thinking in the moral and conventional domains change over time? Beliefs about morality move from the young child's sense that justice means equal treatment for all to the adult's understanding that morality involves beneficence and fairness and that moral principles are independent of the norms of any particular group. In thinking about social conventions, children begin by believing that the regularities they see are real and right. After going through several stages, adults realize that conventions are useful in coordinating social life, but changeable too.

What influences moral behavior? Adults first control young children's moral behavior through direct instruction, supervision, rewards and punishments, and correction. A second important influence on the development of moral behavior is modeling. Children who have been consistently exposed to caring, generous adult models will tend to be more concerned for the rights and feelings of others. The world and the media provide many negative models of behavior. In time, children internalize the moral rules and principles of the authority figures who have guided them. If children are given reasons—particularly reasons that highlight the effects of actions on others—they can understand when they are corrected and then they are more likely to internalize moral principles. Some schools have adopted programs to increase students' capacity to care for others. In schools, cheating is a common behavior problems that involves moral issues.

Theory of mind An understanding that other people are people too, with their own minds, thoughts, feelings, beliefs, desires, and perceptions.

Perspective-taking ability Understanding that others have different feelings and experiences.

Moral reasoning The thinking process involved in judgments about questions of right and wrong.

Distributive justice Beliefs about how to divide materials or privileges fairly among members of a group; follows a sequence of development from equality to merit to benevolence.

Moral realism Stage of development wherein children see rules as absolute.

Morality of cooperation Stage of development wherein children realize that people make rules and people can change them.

Moral dilemmas Situations in which no choice is clearly and indisputably right.

Social conventions Agreed-upon rules and ways of doing things in a particular situation.

Internalize Process whereby children adopt external standards as their own.

Teachers' Casebook: Connections to PRAXIS II™

Whether you will be dealing with kindergartners with separation anxieties, work-weary high-school seniors, or—as in this case—cliques in a middle school, you will find that students are far more than mere learners. They bring every personal, social, emotional, and moral triumph, disappointment, and challenge—past and present—into the classroom with themselves, and those factors will influence your teaching and their learning.

Most licensure examinations, including Praxis II™, will require you to be knowledgeable about the personal, emotional, social, moral, and physical development of students. The situation described in the casebook demonstrates why that knowledge is essential. Here, you encountered actions and attitudes that, if managed poorly, could have serious long-term negative consequences both inside and outside the classroom for all the involved students.

What Would They Do?

Here is how some practicing teachers responded to the situation presented at the beginning of this chapter about cliques in middle school, and the difficulties some students face with "fitting in."

Thomas Naismith **Science Teacher,**

Grades 7–12, Slocum Independent School District, Elkhart, Texas

To bring civility to this classroom, I would address the situation in two stages. First, I would meet individually with the two girls involved in the most recent incident. I would make it very clear to Alison that her behavior was totally inappropriate and that such behavior was far beneath her. I would suggest to her that I was sure that it was just a temporary lapse of good judgment on her part and that I was sure that such an incident would not occur again. I would also ask her to play a role in helping to stop some of the other inappropriate behavior that was occurring in my classroom.

I would explain to Stephanie that she did not need to be embarrassed, because her classmates would appreciate the fact that she had made an effort to restore an old "friendship." I would comment on her positive qualities, explain that she should feel good about herself, and suggest that she seek the companionship of students who are open to her friendship.

The second step would be to address the class as a whole. I would be nonspecific in my comments, but I would make it very clear that the gossip and other "ugly" behavior would need to stop. I would explain that our classroom is a mini-society and that every member has the responsibility of treating others appropriately. I would further explain that they did not have to be "friends" with everyone, but should treat everyone with respect and dignity.

Jacalyn D. Walker **8th Grade Science Teacher,**

Treasure Mountain Middle School, Park City, Utah

Never work in a vacuum. This is especially important in a middle school or junior high school. Work with your school counselor, other grade level teachers, and parents. If you are doing this, you will have several options for dealing with this problem. You cannot fake caring about 12-, 13-, and 14-year-olds. They can spot a fake. You must be working with this age group because you truly like them as people. You appreciate their humor and their abilities. With a caring, trusting, and respectful relationship, students will be open to your help and guidance. Parents are often not involved in the classroom at these grade levels, but there are great programs available to get parents involved.

Nancy Schaefer **Grades 9–12,**

Cincinnati Hills Christian Academy High School, Cincinnati, Ohio

I would first make a phone call to Stephanie's home. Under the guise of calling about assignments because of the days she has missed, I would talk to one of her parents or guardians. My first goal would be to find out if the parents are aware of the situation. Sometimes girls like Stephanie are too embarrassed to tell their parents the whole story or even any of the real story. If the parents did not know the entire story, I might try to get Stephanie on the phone and help her tell her parents. Letting the adults around her know what has happened can relieve some of the shame she might be feeling.

I would then work with Stephanie and one or more of her parents, to plan Stephanie's transition back to school. A school counselor might also be involved in this conversation. The adults would help Stephanie come up with a plan for how to handle possible difficult situations: face-to-face encounters with Alison, encounters with other old "friends," mean messages she might receive during the school day, or comments made to her by other students. We would help her think through these situations and practice how she could respond. I would also help facilitate arrangements for a safe place and person to go to at school, which she could access until she was comfortable at school again. This would be a place and a person that Stephanie could go to if the situation becomes too overwhelming and she wants to escape the pressure. If the problem warranted extra measures, I could talk to Stephanie's teachers to work on rearranging groups or seating to move the girls away from each other or to foster other friendships for Stephanie. We could also make arrangements for an older, respected student to talk to Stephanie. Since almost everyone has stories about unfaithful friends, Stephanie might benefit from talking with a freshman or sophomore about that person's experiences and how they made new friends. Finally, I would try to arrange a brief and supervised meeting between Stephanie and Alison. Allowing an encounter to happen in a controlled environment would provide Stephanie an outlet to voice her hurt, without her having to resort to inappropriate actions.

During all of this, I would want to make sure that someone was also working with Alison, to prevent the escalation of events. This may be an administrator responsible for discipline, if school rules were violated, the school counselor, or another teacher with a good relationship with Alison. I would encourage the involvement of Alison's parents, especially if this were not the first vicious episode.

CHAPTER 4

Learner Differences and Learning Needs

Teachers' Casebook: What Would You Do? 109

Intelligence 110
- Labeling 110
- What Does Intelligence Mean? 111
- Multiple Intelligences 113
- Emotional Intelligence 116
- Intelligence as a Process 117
- Measuring Intelligence 119

Ability Differences and Teaching 121
- Between-Class Grouping 122
- Within-Class and Flexible Grouping 122

Learning Styles 124
- Cautions about Learning Preferences 125
- Visual/Verbal Distinctions 126

Individual Differences and the Law 127
- Individualized Education Program 127
- The Rights of Students and Families 128
- Least Restrictive Environment 128
- Section 504 Protections 129

Common Challenges 130
- Students with Learning Disabilities 131
- Students with Hyperactivity and Attention Disorders 134
- Reaching Every Student: Higher-Order Thinking 136
- Students with Communication Disorders 136
- Students with Intellectual Disabilities 139
- Students with Emotional or Behavioral Disorders 140

Less Prevalent Problems/ More Severe Disabilities 145
- Students with Health Impairments 145
- Students Who Are Deaf 146
- Students with Vision Impairment 147
- Autism Spectrum Disorders 147

Students Who Are Gifted and Talented 148
- Who Are These Students? 149
- Identifying and Teaching Gifted Students 151

Diversity and Convergences in Learning Abilities 153
- Diversity 153
- Convergences 154

Summary Table 154

Teachers' Casebook: Connections to PRAXIS II™ What Would They Do? 159

What Would You Do?

Teachers' Casebook

It is a new school year and your district has had a change in policy. Special Education programs have been discontinued and ALL students will now be included in general education classrooms full time. You knew that you were going to have students with a wide range of abilities, social skills, and motivation for learning in your classroom, but now you also have a student who is deaf, two students who speak very little English, and a student with severe learning disabilities. Based on No Child Left Behind, you are accountable for the learning of all of your students so that your school will show that it is making Annual Yearly Progress.

Critical Thinking

- How will you design a standards-based curriculum that will allow all of the students to learn to their fullest potential and demonstrate proficiency toward the standards?
- What can you do to address the specific problems of your students who have been identified with special needs?

Collaboration

With 2 or 3 other students in your class, plan some strategies for teaching and monitoring the progress of all your students.

To answer the questions above, you need an understanding of individual differences. So far, we have talked little about individuals. We have discussed principles of development that apply to everyone—stages, processes, conflicts, and tasks. Our development as human beings is similar in many ways, but not in every way. Even among members of the same family, there are marked contrasts in appearance, interests, abilities, and temperament, and these differences have important implications for teaching. In addition, you probably will have at least one student with special needs in your class, whatever grade you teach. In this chapter, we explore both common and less frequently occurring learning problems that students may have. As we discuss each problem area, we will consider how a teacher might recognize problems, seek help, and plan instruction. By the time you have completed this chapter, you should be able to answer these questions:

- What are the potential problems in categorizing and labeling students?
- What is your personal concept of intelligence?
- What is your stance on ability grouping?
- Should you adapt lessons for students with varying learning styles?
- What are the implications of the Individuals with Disabilities Education Improvement Act (IDEIA) and Section 504 for your teaching?
- In your classroom, how will you identify and teach students with hearing, vision, language, and behavior problems, specific learning disabilities, as well as those who are gifted?

FACING PAGE *School Bus*, Diana Ong, © Diana Ong/SuperStock.

Intelligence

Because the concept of intelligence is so important in education, so controversial, and so often misunderstood, we will spend quite a few pages discussing it. But before we begin, let's examine the practice of labeling people based on differences such as intelligence, ability, or disability.

Labeling

Every child is a distinctive collection of talents, abilities, and limitations. In that sense, all children are "exceptional." But some are called **exceptional students** because their physical, intellectual, or behavioral skills and abilities differ substantially from the norm—either higher or lower. For example, they may have special abilities and talents, learning disabilities, communication disorders, emotional or behavioral disorders, intellectual disabilities, physical disabilities, impaired vision or difficulties hearing, autism, traumatic brain injury, or some combination (Hardman, Drew, & Egan, 2005). Even though we will use terms like these throughout the chapter, a caution is in order: Labeling students is a controversial issue.

A label does not tell which methods to use with individual students. For example, few specific "treatments" automatically follow from a "diagnosis" of intellectual disabilities; many different teaching strategies and materials are appropriate. Further, the labels can become self-fulfilling prophecies. Everyone—teachers, parents, classmates, and even the students themselves—may see a label as a stigma that cannot be changed. Finally, labels are mistaken for explanations, as in, "Santiago gets into fights because he has a behavior disorder." "How do you know he has a behavior disorder?" "Because he gets into fights."

On the other hand, some educators argue that for younger students, at least, being labeled as "special" protects the child. For example, if classmates know a student has intellectual disabilities (sometimes called cognitive disabilities), they will be more willing to accept his or her behaviors. Of course, labels still open doors to some special programs, useful information, special technology and equipment, or financial assistance. Labels probably both stigmatize and help students (Hallahan, Lloyd, Kauffman, Weiss, & Martinez, 2005; Hardman, Drew, & Egan, 2005).

Person-First Language. This caution about labeling also applies to many of the common descriptions heard in schools every day. Today, many people object to labels such as "mentally retarded student" or "at-risk student" because describing a complex person with one or two words implies that the condition labeled is the most important aspect of the person. Actually, the individual has many abilities, and to focus on the disability is to misrepresent the individual. An alternative is "person-first" language or speaking of "students with intellectual disabilities" or "students placed at risk." Here, the emphasis is on the students first, not on the special challenges they face. Other examples suggested by Meece (2002, p. 317) are:

A student with a learning disability	NOT	A learning disabled student
Students receiving special education	NOT	Special education students
A person with epilepsy	NOT	An epileptic
A child with a physical disability	NOT	A crippled child
Children diagnosed with autism	NOT	Autistic children or autistics

Disorders, Disabilities and Handicaps. One more distinction in language is important. A **disorder** is a broad term—a general disturbance in physical or mental functioning, for example, a communications disorder. A **disability** is just what the word implies—an inability to do something specific such as pronounce words or see or walk. A **handicap** is a disadvantage in certain situations. Some disabilities lead to handicaps, but not in all contexts. For example, being blind (a visual disability) is a handicap if you want to drive a car.

Exceptional students Students who have abilities or problems so significant that they require special education or other services to reach their potential.

Disorder A broad term meaning a general disturbance in physical or mental functioning.

Disability The inability to do something specific such as walk or hear.

Handicap A disadvantage in a particular situation, sometimes caused by a disability.

When labels take precedence over individual characteristics, the labels themselves constitute a handicap. Stereotypes about people who use wheelchairs might interfere with recognition of this young girl's other characteristics and her individuality.

But blindness is not a handicap when you are composing music or talking on the telephone. Stephen Hawking, the greatest living physicist, sufferers from Lou Gehrig's disease and no longer can walk or talk. He once said that he is lucky that he became a theoretical physicist "because it is all in the mind. So my disability has not been a serious handicap." It is important that we do not *create* handicaps for people by the way we react to their disabilities. Some educators have suggested that we drop the word "handicap" altogether because the source of the word is demeaning. *Handicap* came from the phrase "cap-in-hand," used to describe people with disabilities who once were forced to beg just to survive (Hardman, Drew, & Egan, 2005).

We can think of all human characteristics as being on a continuum, from very acute hearing to complete deafness for instance. We all fall somewhere on that continuum and we change over our lifetimes. As we age, for example, there are likely to be changes in hearing, vision, even some aspects of intellectual ability, as you will see later in this chapter.

Intelligence is a widely used label in education and life in general. Let us begin with a basic question. . . .

What Does Intelligence Mean?

STOP | THINK | WRITE Who was the most intelligent person in your high school? Write down a name and the first 4 or 5 words that come to mind when you see that person in your mind's eye. What made you pick this individual? ■

The idea that people vary in what we call **intelligence** has been with us for a long time. Plato discussed similar variations over 2,000 years ago. Most early theories about the nature of intelligence involved one or more of the following three themes: (1) the capacity to learn; (2) the total knowledge a person has acquired; and (3) the ability to adapt successfully to new situations and to the environment in general.

During the past century, there was considerable controversy over the meaning of intelligence. Thirteen psychologists in 1921 and 24 psychologists in 1986 met to discuss intelligence. Both times, every psychologist had a different view about the nature of intelligence (Neisser et al., 1996; Sternberg & Detterman, 1986). Both times, about half of the experts mentioned higher-level thinking processes such as abstract reasoning and problem solving as important aspects of intelligence. The 1986 definitions added metacognition and executive processes (monitoring your own thinking), the interaction

Connect and Extend to the Research

Here are a few current ideas about the meaning of intelligence:

- goal-directed adaptive behavior
- ability to solve novel problems
- ability to acquire and think with new conceptual systems
- problem-solving ability
- planning and other metacognitive skills
- memory access speed
- what people think intelligence is
- what IQ tests measure
- the ability to learn from bad teaching

Intelligence Ability or abilities to acquire and use knowledge for solving problems and adapting to the world.

Are these students using both general and specific abilities as they perform?

of knowledge with mental processes, and the cultural context—what is valued by the culture—as elements of intelligence. But in 1921 and again in 1986, the psychologists disagreed about the structure of intelligence—whether it is a single ability or many separate abilities (Gustafsson & Undheim, 1996; Louis, Subotnik, Breland, & Lewis, 2000; Sattler, 2001; Sternberg, 2004).

Intelligence: One Ability or Many? Some theorists believe intelligence is a basic ability that affects performance on all cognitively oriented tasks, from computing mathematical problems to writing poetry or solving riddles. Evidence for this position comes from study after study finding moderate-to-high positive correlations among all the different tests that are designed to measure separate intellectual abilities (Carroll, 1993; McNemar, 1964). What could explain these results? Charles Spearman (1927) suggested there is one mental attribute, which he called *g* or general intelligence, used to perform any mental test, but each test also requires some specific abilities in addition to *g*. For example, memory for a series of numbers probably involves both *g* and some specific ability for immediate recall of what is heard. Spearman assumed that individuals vary in both general intelligence and specific abilities, and that together these factors determine performance on mental tasks.

Another view that has stood the test of time is Raymond Cattell and John Horn's theory of fluid and crystallized intelligence (Cattell, 1963; Horn, 1998). **Fluid intelligence** is mental efficiency that is essentially culture-free and nonverbal. This aspect of intelligence increases until adolescence because it is grounded in brain development, then declines gradually with age. (Every year, it gets harder for me to write that sentence!) Fluid intelligence is sensitive to injuries. In contrast, **crystallized intelligence,** the ability to apply culturally approved problem-solving methods, can increase throughout the life span because it includes the learned skills and knowledge such as vocabulary, facts, and how to hail a cab, make a quilt, or study in college. By *investing fluid intelligence* in solving problems, we *develop our crystallized intelligence,* but many tasks in life such as mathematical reasoning draw on both fluid and crystallized intelligence (Finkel, Reynolds, McArdle, Gatz, & Peterson, 2003; Hunt, 2000).

The most widely accepted view today is that intelligence, like self-concept, has many facets and is a hierarchy of abilities, with general ability at the top and more specific abilities at lower levels of the hierarchy (Sternberg, 2000). Earl Hunt (2000) summarized the current thinking about the structure of intelligence this way:

> After almost a century of such research, that structure is pretty well-established. There is considerable agreement for the bottom two levels of a three-tiered lattice model of intelligence. At the bottom are elementary information-processing actions, and immediately

Fluid intelligence Mental efficiency, nonverbal abilities grounded in brain development.

Crystallized intelligence Ability to apply culturally approved problem-solving methods.

FIGURE 4.1

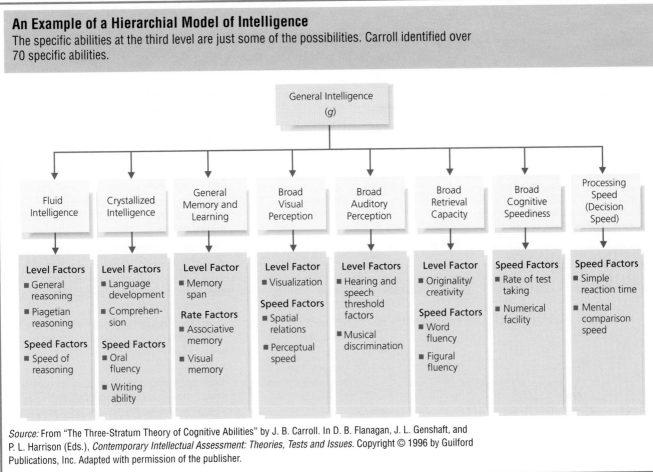

An Example of a Hierarchial Model of Intelligence
The specific abilities at the third level are just some of the possibilities. Carroll identified over 70 specific abilities.

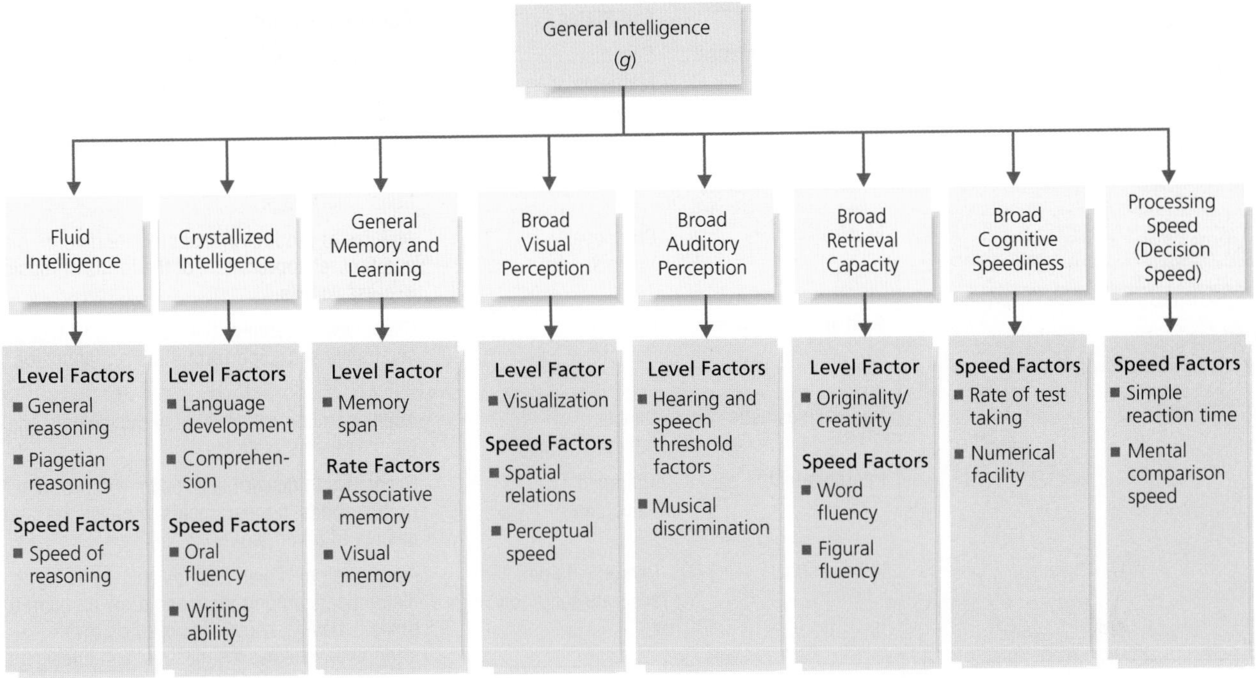

Source: From "The Three-Stratum Theory of Cognitive Abilities" by J. B. Carroll. In D. B. Flanagan, J. L. Genshaft, and P. L. Harrison (Eds.), *Contemporary Intellectual Assessment: Theories, Tests and Issues.* Copyright © 1996 by Guilford Publications, Inc. Adapted with permission of the publisher.

> above them are eight or so secondary abilities. These are more broadly defined capabilities, such as holding and accessing information in short- and long-term memory and, most importantly, the trio of "intellectual" abilities: crystallized intelligence, fluid intelligence, and visual-spatial reasoning ability [which] may be just the most visible of several abilities to manipulate information coded in a particular sensory modality. (p. 123)

Look at Figure 4.1 to see an example of this three-level view of intelligence. John Carroll (1997) identifies one general ability, a few broad abilities (such as fluid and crystallized abilities, learning and memory, visual and auditory perception, processing speed) and at least 70 specific abilities such as language development, memory span, and simple reaction time. General ability may be related to the maturation and functioning of the frontal lobe of the brain, while specific abilities may be connected to other parts of the brain (Byrnes & Fox, 1998).

Multiple Intelligences

In spite of the correlations among the various tests of different abilities, some psychologists insist that there are several separate mental abilities (Gardner, 1983; Guilford, 1988). According to Gardner's (1983, 2003) **theory of multiple intelligences,** there are at least eight separate intelligences: linguistic (verbal), musical, spatial, logical-mathematical, bodily-kinesthetic (movement), interpersonal (understanding others), intrapersonal (understanding self), and naturalist (observing and understanding natural and human-made patterns and systems). Gardner stresses that there may be more kinds of intelligence—eight is not a magic number. Recently, he has speculated that there may be a spiritual intelligence and an existential intelligence—the abilities to contemplate big questions about the meaning of

Theory of multiple intelligences In Gardner's theory of intelligence, a person's eight separate abilities: logical-mathematical, linguistic, musical, spatial, bodily-kinesthetic, interpersonal, intrapersonal, and naturalist.

TABLE 4.1

Eight Intelligences
Howard Gardner's theory of multiple intelligences suggests that there are eight kinds of human abilities. An individual might have strengths or weaknesses in one or several areas.

Intelligence	End States	Core Components
Logical-mathematical	Scientist Mathematician	Sensitivity to, and capacity to discern, logical or numerical patterns; ability to handle long chains of reasoning.
Linguistic	Poet Journalist	Sensitivity to the sounds, rhythms, and meanings of words; sensitivity to the different functions of language.
Musical	Composer Violinist	Abilities to produce and appreciate rhythm, pitch, and timbre; appreciation of the forms of musical expressiveness.
Spatial	Navigator Sculptor	Capacities to perceive the visual-spatial world accurately and to perform transformations on one's initial perceptions.
Bodily-kinesthetic	Dancer Athlete	Abilities to control one's body movements and to handle objects skillfully.
Interpersonal	Therapist Salesman	Capacities to discern and respond appropriately to the moods, temperaments, motivations, and desires of other people.
Intrapersonal	Person with detailed, accurate self-knowledge	Access to one's own feelings and the ability to discriminate among them and draw on them to guide behavior; knowledge of one's own strengths, weaknesses, desires, and intelligence.
Naturalist	Botanist Farmer Hunter	Abilities to recognize plants and animals, to make distinctions in the natural world, to understand systems and define categories (perhaps even categories of intelligence).

Source: From "Multiple Intelligences Go to School," by H. Gardner and T. Hatch, *Educational Researcher, 18*(8), p. 6. Copyright © 1989 by the American Educational Research Association. Reproduced by permission of the publisher. Also *Educational Information and Transformation,* edited by J. Kane. Published by Prentice Hall. Copyright © 2002 by Prentice Hall. Reprinted by permission of Pearson Education, Inc., Upper Saddle River, NJ.

Connect and **Extend** to **PRAXIS II™**

Multiple Intelligences (I, B1)
Many teachers erroneously assume that they must address each of the 8 intelligences in each lesson they design. What are some of the realistic implications of the theory for classroom instructions?

life (Gardner, 2003). Gardner bases his notion of separate abilities on evidence that brain damage (from a stroke, for example) often interferes with functioning in one area, such as language, but does not affect functioning in other areas. Also, individuals may excel in one of these eight areas, but have no remarkable abilities in the other seven. Table 4.1 summarizes these eight intelligences.

What Are These Intelligences? Gardner (1998, 2003) contends that an intelligence is the ability to solve problems and create products or outcomes that are valued by a culture. Varying cultures and eras of history place different values on the eight intelligences. A naturalist intelligence is critical in farming cultures, whereas verbal and mathematical intelligences are important in technological cultures. In addition, Gardner believes that intelligence has a biological base. An intelligence is "a biological and psychological potential; that potential is capable of being realized to a greater or lesser extent as a consequence of the experiential, cultural, and motivational factors that affect a person" (1998, p. 62).

Gardner's multiple intelligences theory has not received wide acceptance in the scientific community, even though it has been embraced by many educators. Some critics suggest that several intelligences are really talents (bodily-kinesthetic skill, musical ability) or personality traits (interpersonal ability). Other "intelligences" are not new at all.

Many researchers have identified verbal and spatial abilities as elements of intelligence. In addition, the eight intelligences are not independent; there are correlations among the abilities. In fact, logical-mathematical and spatial intelligences are highly correlated (Sattler, 2001). So, these "separate abilities" may not be so separate after all. Recent evidence linking musical and spatial abilities has prompted Gardner to consider that there may be connections among the intelligences (Gardner, 1998). Stay tuned for more developments.

Gardner (1998, 2003) has responded to critics by identifying a number of myths and misconceptions about multiple intelligences theory and schooling. One is that intelligences are the same as learning styles. (Gardner doesn't believe that people actually have consistent learning styles.) Another misconception is that multiple intelligences theory disproves the idea of *g*. Gardner does not deny the existence of a general ability, but does question how useful *g* is as an explanation for human achievements.

Multiple Intelligences Go to School. An advantage of Gardner's perspective is that it expands teachers' thinking about abilities and avenues for teaching, but the theory has been misused. Some teachers embrace a simplistic version. They include every "intelligence" in every lesson, no matter how inappropriate. Table 4.2 lists some misuses and positive applications of Gardner's work.

Even though many teachers and schools are enthusiastic about Gardner's ideas, there is not yet strong research evidence that adopting a multiple intelligences approach

TABLE 4.2

Misuses and Applications of Multiple Intelligence Theory

Recently, Howard Gardner described these negative and positive applications of his theory. The quotes are his words on the subject.

Misuses:

1. **Trying to teach all concepts or subjects using all intelligences:** "There is no point in assuming that every subject can be effectively approached in at least seven ways, and it is a waste of effort and time to attempt to do this."
2. **Assuming that it is enough just to apply a certain intelligence, no matter how you use it:** For bodily-kinesthetic intelligence, for example, "random muscle movements have nothing to do with the cultivation of the mind."
3. **Using an intelligence as a background for other activities,** such as playing music while students solve math problems. "The music's function is unlikely to be different from that of a dripping faucet or humming fan."
4. **Mixing intelligences with other desirable qualities:** For example, interpersonal intelligence "is often distorted as a license for cooperative learning," and intrapersonal intelligence "is often distorted as a rationale for self-esteem programs."
5. **Direct evaluation or even grading of intelligences without regard to context:** "I see little point in grading individuals in terms of how 'linguistic' or how 'bodily-kinesthetic' they are."

Good uses:

1. **The cultivation of desired capabilities:** "Schools should cultivate those skills and capabilities that are valued in the community and in the broader society."
2. **Approaching a concept, subject matter, discipline in a variety of ways:** Schools try to cover too much. "It makes far more sense to spend a significant amount of time on key concepts, generative ideas, and essential questions and to allow students to become familiar with these notions and their implications."
3. **The personalization of education:** "At the heart of the MI perspective—in theory and in practice—[is] taking human difference seriously."

Source: "Reflections on Multiple Intelligences: Myths and Messages," by H. Gardner, 1998. In A. Woolfolk (Ed.), *Readings in Educational Psychology* (2nd ed.) (pp. 64–66), Boston: Allyn & Bacon. Copyright © 1998 by Phi Delta Kappan.

will enhance learning. In one of the few carefully designed evaluations, Callahan, Tomlinson, and Plucker (1997) found no significant gains in either achievement or self-concept for students who participated in START, a multiple intelligences approach to identifying and promoting talent in students who were at risk of failing. Learning is still hard work, even if there are multiple paths to knowledge. Perry Klein (2002) argues that the multiple intelligences theory is too broad to tell teachers how to teach. "For instance, the knowledge that basketball relies on 'bodily-kinesthetic intelligence' tells a coach nothing about the skills her players need to learn" (p. 228).

Emotional Intelligence

WHAT WOULD YOU SAY?

As part of the interview process for a job in a middle school, you are asked the following: "What do you think about the idea of emotional intelligence? Would you teach that in your class?" ■

Howard Gardner's theory of multiple intelligences includes intrapersonal and interpersonal intelligences, or intelligence about self and others. Here we look a related perspective—emotional intelligence.

We all know people who are academically or artistically talented, but unsuccessful. They have problems in school, in relationships, and on the job, and can't seem to improve the situations. According to some psychologists, the source of the difficulties may be a lack of emotional intelligence, first defined by Peter Salovey and John Mayer as the ability to process emotional information accurately and efficiently (Mayer & Cobb, 2000; Mayer & Salovey, 1997; Roberts, Zeidner, & Matthews, 2001). Daniel Goleman (1995) popularized the idea of emotional intelligence (E-IQ or EQ) in his best-selling book based on the work of Salovey and Mayer.

What Is EQ? At the center of **emotional intelligence** are four broad abilities: perceiving, integrating, understanding, and managing emotions (Mayer & Cobb, 2000). If you

Success in life requires more than cognitive skills: it is important to be emotionally "smart" as well. Teachers can help students develop emotional as well as cognitive intelligence.

Emotional intelligence (EQ) The ability to process and use emotional information accurately and efficiently.

can't *perceive* what you are feeling, how can you make good choices about jobs, relationships, time management, or even entertainment (Baron, 1998)? Individuals who can *perceive* and *understand* emotions in others (usually by reading the nonverbal cues) and respond appropriately are more successful in working with people and often emerge as leaders (Wood & Wood, 1999). If you can't *integrate* your emotions into your thinking about situations and *understand* your own emotions, how can you communicate your feelings to others accurately? Friends keep asking, "What's wrong?" and you keep saying, "Nothing!"

Finally, you must *manage* your emotions, particularly negative emotions such as anger or depression. The goal is not to suppress feelings, but not to be overwhelmed by them either. Managing emotions includes the ability to focus energy, persist, control impulses, and delay immediate gratification. Emotional management is critical in school. For example, compared to 4-year-old students who act on their impulses immediately, 4-year-old children who can delay instant gratification become much better students in high school (Shoda, Mischel, & Peake, 1990).

Some researchers have criticized the notion of EQ, saying that emotional intelligence is not a cluster of capabilities, but rather a set of personality traits or the application of general intelligence to social situations (Izard, 2001; Nestor-Baker, 1999). Does intelligence inform emotion so we are "smart" about managing our feelings and impulses, or does emotion inform intelligence so we make good decisions and understand other people? Probably both are true. The major point is that success in life requires more than cognitive skills, and teachers are important influences in helping students develop all of these capabilities.

EQ Goes to School. Some research suggests that programs designed to help students build their emotional competencies have beneficial effects, including an increase in cooperative behaviors and a reduction in anti-social activities such as the use of slurs and bullying. For example, Norma Feshbach (1998, 1997) developed a 36-hour program to help elementary students become more empathetic. The program included exercises such as deciding what each person in your family would like most as a birthday present or determining how the world would appear to you if you were a cat. Students also retold stories from the perspective of the different characters in a story, then played the role of each character in videotaped performances of the stories. Students learned to analyze how people looked and sounded as they played each role. Sandra Graham's (1996) program for helping aggressive boys learn to read the intentions of others also included role plays and practice in reading the emotions of others. The educational advantages of decreased student aggression and increased empathy are obvious, but these skills also prepare students for life outside the classroom.

Cautions. One of the problems with innovations in educational psychology is that they are often inadvertently misinterpreted or ill-described in the popular media by writers and reporters who have limited backgrounds in both psychology and education. The concept of emotional intelligence is one innovation that seems to be facing that fate. Make sure the sources you read are based on research.

Intelligence as a Process

As you can see, the theories of Spearman, Cattell and Horn, Carroll, and Gardner tend to describe how individuals differ in the *content* of intelligence—different abilities. Recent work in cognitive psychology has emphasized instead the thinking *processes* that may be common to all people. How do humans gather and use information to solve problems and behave intelligently? New views of intelligence are growing out of this work.

Robert Sternberg's (1985, 2004) **triarchic theory of successful intelligence** is a cognitive process approach to understanding intelligence. Successful intelligence includes "the skills and knowledge needed for success in life, according to one's own definition of success, within one's own sociocultural context" (Sternberg, 2004, p. 326). Sternberg prefers the term successful intelligence to stress that intelligence as more than what is

Triarchic theory of successful intelligence A three-part description of the mental abilities (thinking processes, coping with new experiences, and adapting to context) that lead to more or less intelligent behavior.

TABLE 4.3

Sternberg's Triarchic Theory of Intelligence
Sternberg suggests that intelligent behavior is the product of applying thinking strategies, handling new problems creatively and quickly, and adapting to contexts by selecting and reshaping our environment.

	Analytic *Componential Intelligence*	Creative *Experiential Intelligence*	Practical *Contextual Intelligence*
Definition	Ability to think abstractly, process information; verbal abilities.	Ability to formulate new ideas and combine unrelated facts; creativity—ability to deal with novel situations and make new solutions automatic.	Ability to adapt to a changing environment and shape the environment to make the most of opportunities—problem solving in specific situations.
Examples	Solving analogies or syllogisms, learning vocabulary.	Diagnosing a problem with a car engine; finding resources for a new project.	Taking your telephone off the hook or putting a "do not disturb" sign on the door to limit distractions while studying.

measured by mental abilities tests—intelligence is about success in life. As you might guess from the name, this theory has three parts—analytic, creative, and practical (see Table 4.3).

Analytic/componential intelligence involves the mental processes of the individual that lead to more or less intelligent behavior. These processes are defined in terms of components—elementary information processes that are classified by the functions they serve and by how general they are. *Metacomponents* perform higher-order functions such as planning, strategy selection, and monitoring. Executing the strategies selected is handled by *performance components*. Gaining new knowledge is performed by *knowledge-acquisition components*, such as separating relevant from irrelevant information as you try to understand a new concept (Sternberg, 1985).

Some components are specific; that is, they are necessary for only one kind of task, such as solving analogies. Other components are very general and may be necessary in almost every cognitive task. For example, metacomponents are always operating to select strategies and keep track of progress. This may help to explain the persistent correlations among all types of mental tests. People who are effective in selecting good problem-solving strategies, monitoring progress, and moving to a new approach when the first one fails are more likely to be successful on all types of tests. Metacomponents may be a modern-day version of Spearman's *g*.

The second part of Sternberg's triarchic theory, *creative/experiential intelligence*, involves coping with new experiences. Intelligent behavior is marked by two characteristics: (1) **insight**, or the ability to deal effectively with novel situations, and (2) **automaticity**—the ability to become efficient and automatic in thinking and problem solving. Thus, intelligence involves solving new problems as well as quickly turning new solutions into routine processes that can be applied without much cognitive effort.

The third part of Sternberg's theory, *practical/contextual intelligence*, highlights the importance of choosing to live and work in a context where success is likely, adapting to that context, and reshaping it if necessary. Here, culture is a major factor in defining successful choice, adaptation, and shaping. For example, abilities that make a person successful in a rural farm community may be useless in the inner city or at a country club in the suburbs. People who are successful often seek situations in which their abilities will be valuable, then work hard to capitalize on those abilities and compensate for any weaknesses. Thus, intelligence in this third sense involves practical matters such as career choice or social skills. In a field study in a Russian city, Elena Grigorenko and Robert Sternberg (2001) found that adults with higher practical and analytical intelligence coped better both mentally and physically with the stresses caused by rapid changes in that part of the world.

Practical intelligence is made up mostly of action-oriented **tacit knowledge.** This tacit knowledge is more likely to be learned during everyday life than through formal schooling—it is "knowing how" rather than "knowing that" (Sternberg, Wagner, Williams, &

Insight The ability to deal effectively with novel situations.

Automaticity The result of learning to perform a behavior or thinking process so thoroughly that the performance is automatic and does not require effort.

Tacit knowledge Knowing how rather than knowing that—knowledge that is more likely to be learned during everyday life than through formal schooling.

Horvath, 1995). Recently, however, Sternberg and his colleagues have designed a program for developing practical intelligence for school success by teaching students effective strategies for reading, writing, doing homework, and taking tests (Sternberg, 2002; Williams et al., 1996). As you will see shortly, adaptive skills (similar to practical intelligence) are considered when identifying students with intellectual disabilities (American Association on Mental Retardation [AAMR], 2002; Cuskelly, 2004).

Measuring Intelligence

STOP | THINK | WRITE What is the capital of France? How are an inch and a mile alike? What does *obstreperous* mean? Repeat these numbers backwards: 8 5 7 3 0 2 1 9 7. In what two ways is a lamp better than a candle? If a suit sells for 1/2 of the regular price at $123, what was the original cost of the suit? ■

These items, taken from Sattler (2001, p. 222), are similar to the verbal questions from a common individual intelligence test for children. Another part of the test asks the child to tell what is missing in a picture, put pictures in order to tell a story, copy a design using blocks, assemble part of a puzzle, complete mazes, and copy symbols. Even though psychologists do not agree about what intelligence is, they do agree that intelligence, as measured by standard tests, is related to learning in school. Why is this so? It has to do in part with the way intelligence tests were first developed.

This boy is trying to arrange the red and white blocks so that they match the pattern. His performance is timed. This subtest of the Wechsler Intelligence Scale for children assesses spatial ability.

Binet's Dilemma. In 1904, Alfred Binet was confronted with the following problem by the minister of public instruction in Paris: How can students who will need special instruction and extra help be identified early in their school careers, before they fail in regular classes? Binet was also a political activist, very concerned with the rights of children. He believed that having an objective measure of learning ability could protect students from poor families who might be forced to leave school because they were the victims of discrimination and assumed to be slow learners.

Binet and his collaborator Theodore Simon wanted to measure not merely school achievement, but the intellectual skill students needed to do well in school. After trying many different tests and eliminating items that did not discriminate between successful and unsuccessful students, Binet and Simon finally identified 58 tests, several for each age group from 3 to 13. Binet's tests allowed the examiner to determine a **mental age** for a child. A child who succeeded on the items passed by most 6-year-olds, for example, was considered to have a mental age of 6, whether the child was actually 4, 6, or 8 years old.

Connect and Extend to Other Chapters

The deviation IQ score takes into account variations in performance at different ages by calculating individual deviation from the age-group average. This idea is discussed more fully in Chapter 14.

The concept of **intelligence quotient,** or **IQ,** was added after Binet's test was brought to the United States and revised at Stanford University to give us the Stanford-Binet test. An IQ score was computed by comparing the mental-age score to the person's actual chronological age. The formula was

Intelligence Quotient = Mental Age/Chronological Age × 100

The early Stanford-Binet test has been revised five times, most recently in 2003 (Roid, 2003). The practice of computing a mental age has proven to be problematic because IQ scores calculated on the basis of mental age do not have the same meaning as children get older. To cope with this problem, the concept of deviation IQ was introduced. The **deviation IQ score** is a number that tells exactly how much above or below the average a person scored on the test, compared to others in the same age group, as you will see in the next section.

Mental age In intelligence testing, a performance that represents average abilities for that age group.

Intelligence quotient (IQ) Score comparing mental and chronological ages.

Deviation IQ Score based on statistical comparison of an individual's performance with the average performance of others in that age group.

Group versus Individual IQ Tests. The Stanford-Binet is an individual intelligence test. It has to be administered to one student at a time by a trained psychologist and takes about two hours. Most of the questions are asked orally and do not require reading or writing. A student usually pays closer attention and is more motivated to do well when working directly with an adult.

Psychologists also have developed group tests that can be given to whole classes or schools. Compared to an individual test, a group test is much less likely to yield an accurate picture of any one person's abilities. When students take tests in a group, they may do poorly because they do not understand the instructions, because they have trouble reading, because their pencils break or they lose their place on the answer sheet, because other students distract them, or because the answer format confuses them (Sattler, 2001). As a teacher, you should be very wary of IQ scores based on group tests.

What Does an IQ Score Mean? Most intelligence tests are designed so that they have certain statistical characteristics. For example, the average score is 100; 50% of the people from the general population who take the tests will score 100 or above, and 50% will score below 100. About 68% of the general population will earn IQ scores between 85 and 115. Only about 16% will receive scores below 85, and only 16% will score above 115. Note, however, that these figures hold true for White, native-born Americans whose first language is Standard English. Whether IQ tests should even be used with ethnic minority-group students is hotly debated. The *Guidelines* below will help you interpret IQ scores realistically.

Connect and **Extend** to **PRAXIS II™**

Intelligence Testing (II, C1,4)
The public often misunderstands intelligence testing. Be prepared to respond to questions about the appropriate uses of intelligence tests. What are some inappropriate uses of these tests?

Flynn effect Because of better health, smaller families, increased complexity in the environment, and more and better schooling, IQ test scores are steadily rising.

The Flynn Effect: Are We Getting Smarter? Ever since IQ tests were introduced in the early 1900s, scores in 20 different industrialized countries and in some more traditional cultures have been rising (Daley, Whaley, Sigman, Espinosa, & Neumann, 2003). In fact, in a generation, the average score goes up about 18 points on standardized IQ tests—maybe you really are smarter than your parents! This is called the **Flynn effect** after James Flynn, a political scientist who documented the phenomenon. Some explanations include better nutrition and medical care for children and parents, increasing complexity in the environment that stimulates thinking, smaller families who give more attention to their children, increased literacy of parents, more and better schooling, and better prepa-

Guidelines: Interpreting IQ Scores

Check to see if the score is based on an individual or a group test. Be wary of group test scores.

EXAMPLES

1. Individual tests include the Wechsler Scales (WPPSI, WISC-III, WAIS-III, WAIS Abbreviated), the Stanford-Binet, the McCarthy Scales of Children's Abilities, the Woodcock-Johnson Psycho-Educational Battery, the Kaufman Assessment Battery for Children, the Kaufman Adolescent and Adult Intelligence Test (KAIT), and the Das-Naglieri Cognitive Assessment System.
2. Group tests include the Cognitive Abilities Test (CogAT—formerly the Lorge-Thorndike Intelligence Tests), the Analysis of Learning Potential, the Kuhlman-Anderson Intelligence Tests, the Otis-Lennon School Abilities Test (formerly the Otis-Lennon Intelligence Test), and the School and College Ability Tests (SCAT).

Remember that IQ tests are only estimates of general aptitude for learning.

EXAMPLES

1. Ignore small differences in scores among students.
2. Bear in mind that even an individual student's scores may change over time for many reasons, including measurement error.
3. Be aware that a total score is usually an average of scores on several kinds of questions. A score in the middle or average range may mean that the student performed at the average on every kind of question or that the student did quite well in some areas (for example, on verbal tasks) and rather poorly in other areas (for example, on quantitative tasks).

Remember that IQ scores reflect a student's past experiences and learning.

EXAMPLES

1. Consider these scores to be predictors of school abilities, not measures of innate intellectual abilities.
2. If a student is doing well in your class, do not change your opinion or lower your expectations just because one score seems low.
3. Be wary of IQ scores for minority students and for students whose first language was not English. Even scores on "culture-free" tests are lower for students placed at risk.
4. Remember that both adaptive skills and scores on IQ tests are used to determine intellectual abilities and disabilities.

For more about interpreting IQ scores, see **http://www.wilderdom.com/personality/L2-1UnderstandingIQ.html**

ration for taking tests. One result of the Flynn effect is that the norms used to determine scores (more about norms in Chapter 14) have to be continually revised. In other words, to keep a score of 100 as the average, the test questions have to be made more difficult. This increasing difficulty has implications for any program that uses IQ scores as part of the entrance requirements. For example, some "average" students of the previous generation now might be identified as having intellectual disabilities because the test questions are harder (Kanaya, Scullin, & Ceci, 2003).

Intelligence and Achievement. Intelligence test scores predict achievement in schools quite well, at least for large groups. For example, the correlation is about .4 to .5 between school grades and scores on a popular individual intelligence test, the revised Wechsler Intelligence Scale for Children (WISC-III). Correlations between standardized achievement test and intelligence test scores are higher, around .5 to .7 (Sattler, 2001). This isn't surprising because the tests were designed to predict school achievement. Remember, Binet threw out test items that did not discriminate between good and poor students.

Do people who score high on IQ tests achieve more in life? Here, the answer is less clear. There is evidence that *g*, or general intelligence, correlates with "real-world academic, social, and occupational accomplishments" (Ceci, 1991), but there is great debate about the size and meaning of these correlations (*Current Directions in Psychological Science*, 1993; McClelland, 1993). People with higher intelligence test scores tend to complete more years of school and to have higher-status jobs. However, when the number of years of education is held constant, IQ scores and school achievement are not highly correlated with income and success in later life. Other factors such as motivation, social skills, and luck may make the difference (Goleman, 1995; Neisser et al., 1996; Sternberg & Wagner, 1993).

Intelligence: Heredity or Environment? Nowhere has the nature-versus-nurture debate raged so hard as in the area of intelligence. Should intelligence be seen as a potential, limited by our genetic makeup? Or does intelligence simply refer to an individual's current level of intellectual functioning, as influenced by experience and education? In fact, it is almost impossible to separate intelligence "in the genes" from intelligence "due to experience." Today, most psychologists believe that differences in intelligence are the result of both heredity and environment, probably in about equal proportions for children (Petrill & Wilkerson, 2000). "Genes do not fix behavior. Rather they establish a range of possible reactions to the range of possible experiences that the environment can provide" (Weinberg, 1989, p. 101). And environmental influences include everything from the health of a child's mother during pregnancy to the amount of lead in the child's home to the quality of teaching a child receives.

As a teacher, it is especially important for you to realize that cognitive skills, like any other skills, are always improveable. *Intelligence is a current state of affairs*, affected by past experiences and open to future changes. Even if intelligence is a limited potential, the potential is still quite large, and a challenge to all teachers. For example, Japanese and Chinese students know much more mathematics than American students, but their intelligence test scores are quite similar. This superiority in math probably is related to differences in the way mathematics is taught and studied in the three countries and to the self-motivation skills of many Asian students (Baron, 1998; Stevenson & Stigler, 1992).

Now that you have a sense of what intelligence means, let's consider how to handle cognitive ability differences in teaching.

Ability Differences and Teaching

WHAT WOULD YOU SAY?

You are interviewing for a job in a new middle school, scheduled to open this fall. After about 4 minutes of small talk, the curriculum supervisor says to you, "We have been having some heated debates in this district about ability grouping and tracking. Where do you stand on those issues?" ■

In this section, we consider alternatives for handling differences in academic ability. By the time you finish this section, you should have an answer to the question above. Is ability grouping a solution to the challenge of ability differences?

Between-Class Grouping

When whole classes are formed based on ability, the process is called **between-class ability grouping** or **tracking,** a common practice in secondary schools and some elementary schools as well. Although this seems on the surface to be an efficient way to teach, research has consistently shown that although segregation by ability may benefit high-achieving students, it causes problems for low-achieving students (Castle, Deniz, & Tortora, 2005; Garmon, Nystrand, Berends, & LePore, 1995; Committee on Increasing High School Students' Engagement and Motivation to Learn, 2004; Oakes & Wells, 1998; Robinson & Clinkenbeard, 1998).

Low-ability classes tend to receive lower-quality instruction in general. Teachers emphasize lower-level objectives and routine procedures, with less academic focus. Often, there are more student behavior problems and, along with these problems, increased teacher stress and decreased enthusiasm. These differences in instruction and the teachers' negative attitudes may mean that low expectations are communicated to the students. Attendance may drop along with self-confidence. The lower tracks often have a disproportionate number of minority-group and economically disadvantaged students, so ability grouping, in effect, becomes segregation in school. Possibilities for friendships become limited to students in the same ability range. Assignments to classes are often made on the basis of group IQ tests instead of tests in the subject area itself. However, group IQ tests are not good guides for what someone is ready to learn in a particular subject area (Corno & Snow, 1986; Garmon, Nystrand, Berends, & LePore, 1995; Kulik & Kulik, 1982; Slavin, 1990).

Recently, there has been a movement for **untracking,** or teaching all students in mixed-ability groups, but providing extra help for those who struggle and enrichment for those who learn quickly (Corno, 1995a; Oakes & Wells, 2002). Jeannie Oakes and Amy Wells (2002) described several different ways to teach effectively in secondary schools without tracking.

- Eliminate remedial courses and have one regular and one advanced track.
- Offer honors assignment options or challenge pull-out activities within each course.
- Require all students to take a common core of classes, then allow self-selection into advanced classes after the core.
- Encourage minority-group students to enroll in advanced placement courses.
- Provide additional times during intercessions when struggling students can get extra help.
- Providing tutoring before and after school.
- Staff a homework help center with teachers, parents, and community volunteers.
- Instead of "dumbing down" content, teach students learning strategies for dealing with difficult material.

Not everyone agrees that untracking is a good idea. This movement has been more successful at the elementary level than it has been at the secondary level. The *Point/Counterpoint* looks at both sides.

There are two exceptions to the general finding that between-class ability grouping leads to lower achievement. The first is found in honors or gifted classes, where high-ability students tend to perform better than comparable students in regular classes (Kulik & Kulick, 1997). In the **Joplin Plan,** students stay in their regular, mixed-ability grade-level classes, but are regrouped across grade levels for reading. A reading group might therefore have students from several grades, all working on the same reading level.

Between-class ability grouping/tracking System of grouping in which students are assigned to classes based on their measured ability or their achievements.

Untracking Redesigning schools to teach students in classes that are not grouped by ability.

The Joplin Plan/Nongraded elementary school Arrangement wherein students are grouped by ability in particular subjects, regardless of their ages or grades.

Within-Class and Flexible Grouping

STOP | THINK | WRITE You are preparing a unit on habitats for your students. You decide to do as your old educational psychology professor recommended and give an alternate form of the final unit test as a pretest to find out what the students already know about the subject. After you reassure them that the test won't be graded—you just want an idea about

Point/Counterpoint

Is Tracking an Effective Strategy?

TRACKING STUDENTS INTO different classes or strands (college prep, vocational, remedial, gifted, etc.) has been standard procedure in many schools for a long time, but does it work? Critics say tracking is harmful, while supporters claim it is useful, even though it presents challenges.

POINT Tracking is harmful and should be eliminated.

According to Tom Loveless, writing in the April 1999 issue of *Educational Leadership*, "Prominent researchers and prestigious national reports have argued that tracking stands in the way of equal educational opportunity" (p. 28).

Loveless goes on to cite the work of Braddock and Slavin (1993); Carnegie Council on Adolescent Development (1995); Oakes (1985); and Wheelock (1992)—all of whom make the argument against tracking. What is the basis for these claims? Surprisingly, the evidence is not clear or direct. For example, a few well-done and carefully designed studies found that tracking increases the gap between high and low achievers by depressing the achievement of low-track students and boosting the achievement of high-track students (Gamoran, 1987; Kerckhoff, 1986). And Gamoran also found that the achievement gap between low- and high-track students is greater than the gap between students who drop out of school and students who graduate. Because low-income students and students of color are overrepresented in the lower tracks, they suffer the greatest harm from tracking and should benefit the most from the elimination of tracking (Oakes, 1990b; Oakes & Wells, 2002). Is this likely?

COUNTERPOINT Eliminating tracking will hurt many students.

Researchers who have looked closely at tracking believe that tracking may be harmful for some students some of the time, but not for all students and not all of the time. First, as most people agree, tracking seems to have positive effects for the high-track students. Gifted programs, honors classes, and advanced placement classes seem to work (Fuchs, Fuchs, Hamlett, & Karns, 1998; Robinson & Clinkenbeard, 1998). No one, especially parents, wants to eliminate the positive effects of these programs. And the chance of being assigned to a high track is 10% greater for African American students (Gamoran & Mare, 1989), so detracking could be a special disservice to these students.

What would happen if schools were detracked? Loveless (1999) identifies some possible hidden costs. First, results of a large national study suggest that when low-track 10th graders are assigned to heterogeneous classes rather than low tracks, they gain about 5 percentage points in achievement. So far, so good. But average students lose 2 percentage points when put into heterogeneous classes and high-ability students lose about 5 points.

> *The achievement gap is indeed narrowed, but apparently at the expense of students in regular and high tracks, representing about 70% of 10th graders in the United States. (Loveless, 1999, p. 29)*

Another consequence of detracking is *bright flight*—the withdrawal of the brightest students from the schools. Both African American and White parents distrust mixed-ability classes to meet the needs of their children (Public Agenda Foundation, 1994).

In some classes, using a mixed-ability structure seems to hinder the achievement of all students. For example, students in heterogeneous algebra classes don't learn as much as students in tracked classes—whatever the ability level of the students (Epstein & MacIver, 1992). And a meta-analysis of student self-esteem found that students in low-track classes did *not* have lower self-esteem than students in heterogeneous classes (Kulik & Kulik, 1997).

So what is the answer? As usual, it is more complicated than simply detracking versus tracking. Careful attention to every student's achievement may mean different answers at different times.

WHAT DO YOU THINK?
Vote online at **www.mylabschool.com**

where to go in developing the lesson—the students settle in and seem to take the task seriously. Looking over the papers that night, you are dismayed. A quarter of the students make over 90% on the "final." Quite a few get around half of the questions and problems right, but the rest of the class is clueless. The next day, when you ask Shanequa why she did so well on the test, she explains that in science class last year her group (and several others) chose habitats as the focus of their special project work. You stare at your lesson plans and realize that they fit practically no one in this class. What will you do? ■

Differences like the ones illustrated above are common in most schools and classrooms. It is not unusual to have 3- to 5-year differences in any given classroom (Castle,

Schoolies © 1999 John P. Wood. Reprinted with permission.

Deniz, & Tortora, 2005). But even if you decided to simply forge ahead and teach the same material in the same way to your entire class, you would not be alone. One study found that in 46 different classrooms, 84% of the activities were the same for high-achieving and average-achieving students (Westberg, Archambault, Dobyns, & Slavin, 1993). Differences in student prior knowledge are a major challenge for teachers, especially in subjects that build on previous knowledge and skills such as math and science (Loveless, 1998).

Today, many elementary-school classes are grouped for reading, and some are grouped for math, even though there is no clear evidence that this **within-class ability grouping** is superior to other approaches. Thoughtfully constructed and well-taught ability groups in math and reading can be effective, but other approaches such as cooperative learning are available, too. The point of any grouping strategy should be to provide appropriate challenge and support—that is, to reach children within their "zone of proximal development" (Vygotsky, 1997). Flexible grouping is one possible answer.

Flexible Grouping. In **flexible grouping,** students are grouped and regrouped based on their learning needs. Assessment is continuous so that students are always working within their zone of proximal development. Arrangements might include small groups, partners, individuals, and even the whole class—depending on which grouping best supports each student's learning of the particular academic content. Flexible grouping approaches often include high-level instruction and high expectations for all students, no matter what their group placement. One 5-year longitudinal study of flexible grouping in a high-needs urban elementary school (Castle, Denis, & Tortora, 2005) found 10% to 57% increases in students who reached mastery level, depending on the subject area and grade level. Teachers received training and support in the assessment, grouping, and teaching strategies needed, and by the end of the study, 95% of the teachers were using flexible grouping. The teachers in the study believed that some of the gains came because students were more focused on learning and more confident.

Another way to use flexible grouping is the nongraded elementary school. Students of several ages (for example, 6, 7, and 8) are together in one class, but they are flexibly grouped within the class for instruction based on achievement, motivation, or interest in different subjects. This cross-grade grouping seems to be effective for students of all abilities as long as the grouping allows teachers to give more direct instruction to the groups. *But be sensible about cross-age grouping.* Mixing 3rd, 4th, and 5th graders for math or reading class based on what they are ready to learn makes sense. However, sending a large 4th grader to the 2nd grade, where he is the only older student and stands out like a sore thumb, isn't likely to work well. Also, when cross-age classes are created just because there are too few students for one grade—and not in order to better meet the students' learning needs—the results are not positive (Veenman, 1997). As we will see repeatedly throughout this text, working at a challenging level, but one you can master with effort and support, is more likely to encourage learning and motivation.

If you ever decide to use ability grouping in your class, the *Guidelines* should make the approach more effective (Good & Brophy, 2003).

Within-class ability grouping System of grouping in which students in a class are divided into two or three groups based on ability in an attempt to accommodate student differences.

Flexible grouping. Grouping and regrouping students based on learning needs.

Learning styles Characteristic approaches to learning and studying.

Learning Styles

WHAT WOULD YOU SAY?

During your interview for a teaching job, the department chair says, "We are thinking about having a professional development program on learning styles. What do you know about that idea?" ■

The way a person approaches learning and studying is his or her **learning style.** Although many different learning styles have been described, one theme that unites most of the

Guidelines: Grouping by Achievement

Form and reform groups on the basis of students' *current performance* in the subject being taught.

EXAMPLES

1. Use scores on the most recent reading assessments to establish reading groups, and rely on current math performance to form math groups.
2. Change group placement frequently when students' achievement changes.

Discourage comparisons between groups and encourage students to develop a whole-class spirit.

EXAMPLES

1. Don't seat groups together outside the context of their reading or math group.
2. Avoid naming ability groups—save the names for mixed-ability or whole-class teams.

Group by ability for one or, at the most, two subjects.

EXAMPLES

1. Make sure there are many lessons and projects that mix members from the groups.
2. Experiment with learning strategies in which cooperation is stressed (described in Chapter 11).
3. Keep the number of groups small (two or three at most) so that you can provide as much direct teaching as possible—leaving students alone for too long leads to less learning.

Make sure teachers, methods, and pace are adjusted to fit the needs of the group.

EXAMPLES

1. Organize and teach groups so that low-achieving students get appropriate extra instruction—not just the same material again.
2. Experiment with alternatives to grouping. There are alternatives to within-class grouping that appear more effective for some subjects. DeWayne Mason and Tom Good (1993) found that supplementing whole-class instruction in math with remediation and enrichment for students when they needed it worked better than dividing the class into two ability groups and teaching these groups separately.

For more information about classroom grouping, see these two sites:
http://www.nasponline.org/information/pospaper_ag.html
http://www.nwrel.org/scpd/sirs/1/cu2.html

styles is the differences between deep and surface approaches to processing information in learning situations (Snow, Corno, & Jackson, 1996). Individuals who have a *deep-processing approach* see the learning activities as a means for understanding some underlying concepts or meanings. They tend to learn for the sake of learning and are less concerned about how their performance is evaluated, so motivation plays a role as well. Students who take a *surface-processing* approach focus on memorizing the learning materials, not understanding them. These students tend to be motivated by rewards, grades, external standards, and the desire to be evaluated positively by others. Of course, the situation can encourage deep or surface processing, but there is evidence that individuals have tendencies to approach learning situations in characteristic ways (Biggs, 2001; Coffield, Moseley, Hall, & Eccestone, 2004; Pintrich & Schrauben, 1992; Tait & Entwistle, 1998).

Connect and Extend to PRAXIS II™
Learning/Cognitive Styles (I, B1)
Familiarize yourself with the major issues involved with learning and cognitive styles, and understand their implications for classroom practice.

Cautions about Learning Preferences

Since the late 1970s, a great deal has been written about differences in students' **learning preferences** (Dunn, Dunn, & Price, 2000; Dunn & Griggs, 2003; Gregorc, 1982; Keefe, 1982). Learning preferences are often called *learning styles* in these writings, but I believe preferences is a more accurate label because the "styles" are determined by your preferences for particular learning environments—for example, where, when, with whom, or with what lighting, food, or music you like to study. I like to study and write during large blocks of time—all day if I don't have classes. I usually make some kind of commitment or deadline every week so that I have to work in long stretches to finish the work before that deadline. Then I take a day off. When I plan or think, I have to see my thinking in writing. I have a colleague who draws diagrams of

Learning preferences Preferred ways of studying and learning, such as using pictures instead of text, working with other people versus alone, learning in structured or in unstructured situations, and so on.

relationships when she listens to a speaker or plans a paper. You may be similar or very different, but we all may work effectively. But are these preferences important for learning?

There are a number of instruments for assessing students' learning preferences: The Learning Style Inventory (Dunn, Dunn, & Price, 1989), Learning Styles Inventory (Revised) (Kolb, 1985), and the Learning Style Profile (Keefe & Monk, 1986). But tests of learning style have been strongly criticized for lacking evidence of reliability and validity (Snider, 1990; Wintergerst, DeCapua, & Itzen, 2001). In fact, in an extensive examination of learning styles instruments, researchers at the Learning Skills Research Centre in England concluded, "with regard to Dunn and Dunn (Section 3.2), Gregorc (Section 3.1) and Riding (Section 4.1), our examination of the reliability and validity of their learning style instruments strongly suggests that they should not be used in education or business" (Coffield, et al., 2004, p. 127).

Some proponents of learning styles believe that students learn more when they study in their preferred setting and manner (Dunn, Beaudry, & Klavas, 1989; Lovelace, 2005). And there is evidence that very bright students need less structure and prefer quiet, solitary learning (Torrance, 1986). But most educational psychologists are skeptical about the value of learning preferences. "The reason researchers roll their eyes at learning styles research is the utter failure to find that assessing children's learning styles and matching to instructional methods has any effect on their learning" (Stahl, 2002, p. 99). Why are these ideas so popular? Part of the answer is, "A thriving commercial industry has also been built to offer advice to teachers, tutors and managers on learning styles, and much of it consists of inflated claims and sweeping conclusions which go beyond the current knowledge base and the specific recommendations of particular theorists" (Coffield et al., 2004, p. 127). Some of the teaching ideas may be useful, but not necessarily because they are based on learning styles.

So, before you try to accommodate all your students' learning styles, remember that students, especially younger ones, may not be the best judges of how they should learn. Sometimes, students, particularly those who have difficulty, prefer what is easy and comfortable; real learning can be hard and uncomfortable. Sometimes, students prefer to learn in a certain way because they have no alternatives; it is the only way they know how to approach the task. These students may benefit from developing new—and perhaps more effective—ways to learn. One final consideration: Many of the learning styles advocates imply that the differences in the learner are what matter. But recent research points to the person in context—the entire teaching-learning system as a better way to understand student learning (Coffield et al., 2004). We will examine this again in the next chapter when we consider culture and learning style.

Connect and **Extend** to Your **Teaching Portfolio**

When students fail a grade or a course, they are often "recycled" through the same material on the assumption that repetition will produce learning. Use the concept of cognitive style to argue against this practice.

Visual/Verbal Distinctions

There is one learning styles distinction that has research support. Richard Mayer has been studying the distinction between visual and verbal learners, with a focus on learning from computer-based multimedia. He is finding that there is a visualizer–verbalizer dimension and that it has three facets: *cognitive spatial ability* (low or high), *cognitive style* (visualizer vs. verbalizer), and *learning preference* (verbal learner vs. visual learner), as shown in Table 4.4 (Mayer & Massa, 2003). The picture is more complex than simply categorizing a student as either a visual or a verbal learner. Students might have preferences for learning with pictures, but their low spatial ability could make using pictures to learn less effective. These differences can be reliably measured, but research has not identified the effects of teaching to these styles. Certainly, presenting information in multiple modalities might be useful.

The Value of Considering Learning Styles. Even though much of the work on matching learning styles and preferences to teaching is suspect, with unreliable measures and inflated claims, there is some value in thinking about learning styles. First, by helping students think about how they learn, you can develop thoughtful self-monitoring and self-awareness. In upcoming chapters, we will look at the value of such self-knowledge for

TABLE 4.4

Three Facets of the Visualizer-Verbalizer Dimension

There are three dimensions to visual versus verbal learning: ability, style, and preference. Individuals can be high or low on any or all of these dimensions.

Facet	Types of Learners	Definition
Cognitive Ability	High spatial ability	Good abilities to create, remember, and manipulate images and spatial information
	Low spatial ability	Poor abilities to create, remember, and manipulate images and spatial information
Cognitive Style	Visualizer	Thinks using images and visual information
	Verbalizer	Thinks using words and verbal information
Learning Preference	Visual learner	Prefers instruction using pictures
	Verbal learner	Prefers instruction using words

Source: From R. E. Mayer, & L. J. Massa (2003). "Three facets of visual and verbal learners: Cognitive ability, cognitive style and learning preference." *Journal of Educational Psychology,* 95(4), p. 838.

learning and motivation. Second, looking at individual students' approaches to learning might help teachers appreciate, accept, and accommodate student differences (Coffield, et al., 2004; Rosenfeld & Rosenfeld, 2004).

Thus far, we have focused mostly on the varying abilities and styles of students. For the rest of the chapter, we will consider what can interfere with learning. It is important for all teachers to be aware of these issues because laws and policy changes over the past 30 years have expanded teachers' responsibilities in working with all students.

Connect and **Extend** to the **Research**

The Winter 1996 issue of *Theory Into Practice* is devoted to "The Inclusive School: The Continuing Debate." See **http://www.coe.ohio-state.edu/TIP.** This journal is especially for educators.

Connect and **Extend** to **PRAXIS II™**

Individual Education Programs (IEP) (I, B3)

When you sign an IEP, you are signing an important educational and legal document. Be sure that you can explain the purpose of an IEP, identify its components, and describe the kind of information that can be contained in one.

Individual Differences and the Law

STOP | THINK | WRITE Have you ever had the experience of being the only one in a group who had trouble doing something? How would you feel if every day in school you faced the same kind of difficulty, while everyone else seemed to find the work easier than you? What kind of support and teaching would you need to keep trying? ■

In the United States, beginning in 1975 with PL 94-142 (the Education of the Handicapped Act), a series of laws has led to revolutionary changes in the education of children with disabilities. The legislation, now called the **Individuals with Disabilities Education Improvement Act,** was revised in 1990, 1997, and 2004. You may see this law called IDEA or IDEIA. At the most general level, the law now requires states to provide a free, appropriate public education (FAPE) for all students with disabilities who participate in special education. There are no exceptions—the law requires **zero reject.** This policy also applies to students with communicable diseases such as AIDS. The expenses of meeting the special needs of these students are considered a public responsibility. Let's examine the requirements in these laws. There are three major points of interest to teachers: the individualized education program (IEP), the protection of the rights of students with disabilities and their parents, and the concept of "least restrictive environment."

Individuals with Disabilities Education Improvement Act (IDEIA) Latest amendment of PL 94-142, guarantees a free public education to all children regardless of disability.

Zero reject A basic principle of IDEIA specifying that no student with a disability, no matter what kind or how severe, can be denied a free public education.

Individualized Education Program (IEP) Annually revised program for an exceptional student, detailing present achievement level, goals, and strategies, drawn up by teachers, parents, specialists, and (if possible) the student.

Individualized Education Program

The drafters of the laws recognized that each student is unique and may need a specially tailored program to make progress. The **Individualized Education Program,** or **IEP,** is an agreement between parents and the school about the services that will be provided.

The IEP is written by a team that includes the student's parents or guardians, a general education teacher who works with the student, a special education teacher, a qualified school representative who can interpret the student's evaluation results, and (if appropriate) the student. If the school and parents agree, the team could add other people who have special knowledge of the child (for example, a therapist). The program can be updated each year and must state in writing:

1. The student's present academic achievement and functional performance.
2. Measurable performance goal for the year. Parents must get reports of progress toward goals at least as often as report cards are sent home for all students.
3. A statement of specific special education and related services to be provided to the student and details of when those services will be initiated.
4. A explanation of how much of the student's program WILL NOT be in regular classroom and school settings.
5. A statement about how the student will participate in the state- and district-wide assessments, particularly those required by No Child Left Behind.
6. Beginning at age 14 and by age 16, a statement of needed transitional services to move the student toward further education or work in adult life.

Figure 13.3 on page 512 (Chapter 13) is an excerpt from the IEP of a 15-year-old boy with behavior problems.

The Rights of Students and Families

Several stipulations in these laws protect the rights of parents and students. Schools must have procedures for maintaining the confidentiality of school records. Testing practices must not discriminate against students from different cultural backgrounds. Students must be tested in their native or primary language whenever possible. Parents must consent in writing to the initial evaluation of their child and to the child's special education program. Parents have the right to see all records relating to the testing, placement, and teaching of their child. If they wish, parents may obtain an independent evaluation of their child. Parents may bring an advocate or representative to the meeting at which the IEP is developed. Students whose parents are unavailable must be assigned a surrogate parent to participate in the planning. Parents must receive written notice (in their native language) before any evaluation or change in placement is made. Finally, parents have the right to challenge the program developed for their child, and are protected by due process of law. If you have conferences with your student's family, following the suggestions in the *Family and Community Partnerships Guidelines* can make the meetings more effective.

Least Restrictive Environment

Least restrictive environment (LRE) Educating each child with peers in the regular classroom to the greatest extent possible.

Mainstreaming Teaching children with disabilities in regular classes for part or all of their school day.

Integration Fitting the child with special needs into existing class structures.

Inclusion The integration of all students, including those with severe disabilities, into regular classes.

The laws require states to develop procedures for educating each child in the **least restrictive environment (LRE)**—with their peers in the regular classroom to the greatest extent possible. Therefore, a student's IEP must reflect that the student is being educated in the least restrictive environment appropriate for the student's needs. Over the years, recommended approaches to achieve this have moved from **mainstreaming** (including children with special needs in a few regular education classes as convenient), to **integration** (fitting the child with special needs into existing class structures), to **inclusion** (restructuring educational settings to promote belonging for all students) (Avarmidis, Bayliss, & Burden, 2000; Friend & Bursuck, 2002).

Advocates of inclusion believe that students with disabilities can benefit from involvement with their nondisabled peers and should be educated with them in their regular home-district school, even if doing so means changes in educational requirements, special aids, services, and training or consultation for the regular teaching staff (Haager & Klingner, 2005; Stainback & Stainback, 1992). However, some

Family and Community Partnerships

Guidelines: Productive Conferences

Plan and prepare for a productive conference.

EXAMPLES

1. Have a clear purpose and gather the needed information. If you want to discuss student progress, have work samples available.
2. Send home a list of questions and ask families to bring the information to the conference. **Sample questions from Friend and Bursuck** (2002) are:

- What is your child's favorite class activity?
- Does your child have worries about any class activities? If so, what are they?
- What are your priorities for your child's education this year?
- What questions do you have about your child's education in my class this year?
- How could we at school help make this the most successful year ever for your child?
- Are there any topics you want to discuss at the conference that I might need to prepare for? If so, please let me know.
- Would you like other individuals to participate in the conference? If so, please give me a list of their names.
- Is there particular school information you would like me to have available? If so, please let me know.

During the conference, create and maintain an atmosphere of collaboration and respect.

EXAMPLES

1. Arrange the room for private conversation. Put a sign on your door to avoid interruptions. Meet around a conference table for better collaboration. Have tissues available.
2. Address families as "Mr." and "Ms.," not "Mom" and "Dad" or "Grandma." Use students' names.
3. Listen to families' concerns and build on their suggestions for their children.

After the conference, keep good records and follow up on decisions.

EXAMPLES

1. Make notes to yourself and keep them organized.
2. Summarize any actions or decisions in writing and send a copy to the family and any other teachers or professionals involved.
3. Communicate with families on other occasions, especially when there is good news to share.

For more information about parent conferences, see: **http://teacher.scholastic.com/professional/parentconf/**

researchers caution that inclusion classrooms are not the best placement for every child (Johnson, Duffett, Farkas, & Wilson, 2002). For example, Naomi Zigmond and her colleagues (1995) report in their study of 6 full-inclusion elementary schools that only about half of the students with learning disabilities were able to benefit. A full continuum of services must be available so that students are taught using effective practices in an appropriate setting, which could be anything from full to partial inclusion to special schools.

Section 504 Protections

Not all students who need special accommodations in school are covered by IDEIA or eligible for the services provided by the law. But these students' educational needs may be covered by other legislation. As a consequence of the civil rights movement in the 1960s and 1970s, the federal government passed the Vocational Rehabilitation Act of 1973. **Section 504** of that law prevents discrimination against people with disabilities in any program that receives federal money, such as public schools.

Through Section 504, all school-age children are ensured an equal opportunity to participate in school activities. The definition of "disability" is broad in Section 504. If a student has a condition that substantially limits participation in school, then the school still must develop a plan for giving that student access to education, even though the school gets no extra funds. To get assistance through Section 504, students must be assessed, often by a team, and a plan developed. Unlike IDEIA, however, there are fewer rules about how this must happen, so individual schools design their own procedures

Section 504 A part of civil rights law that prevents discrimination against people with disabilities in programs that receive federal funds, such as public schools.

TABLE 4.5

Examples of Accommodations Under Section 504

The types of accommodations that can be written into a Section 504 plan are almost without limit. Some accommodation may relate to physical changes in the learning environment (for example, air filters are installed to remove allergens). However, many students who have Section 504 plans have functional impairments related to their learning or behavior, and their needs are somewhat similar to those of students with disabilities. The following is a sample of instructional accommodations that could be incorporated into a Section 504 plan:

- Seat the student nearest to where the teacher does most of his/her instruction.
- Have the student sit next to a peer who can help as needed.
- Seat the student away from the distractions of doorways or windows.
- Fold assignments in half so that the student is less overwhelmed by the quantity of work.
- Make directions telegraphic, that is, concise and clear.
- Allow use of a calculator or tape recorder.
- Use voice recognition software on the computer for written assignments.
- Mark right answers instead of wrong answers.
- Send a set of textbooks to be left at home so that the student does not have to remember to bring books from school.
- Provide books on tape so that the student can listen to assignments instead of reading them.

If you review these items, you can see that many of them just make good instructional sense. They are effective instructional practices that help learners with special needs succeed in your classroom.

Source: From *Including Students with Special Needs: A Practical Guide for Classroom Teachers, 3/e* by Marilyn Friend & William D. Bursuck. Published by Allyn and Bacon, Boston, MA. Copyright © 2002 by Pearson Education. Adapted by permission of the publisher.

(Friend & Bursuck, 2002). Look at Table 4.5 to see an example of the kinds of accommodations that might be made for a student. Many of these ideas seem to be "just good teaching." But I have been surprised to see how many teachers won't let students use calculators or tape recorders because "they should learn do it like everyone else!" Two major groups are considered for Section 504 accommodations: students with medical or health needs such as diabetes, drug addiction, severe allergies, communicable diseases, temporary disabilities resulting from accidents, or alcoholism, and students with attention deficit hyperactivity disorder, if they are not already covered by IDEIA.

The **Americans with Disabilities Act of 1990 (ADA)** prohibits discrimination against persons with disabilities in employment, transportation, public access, local government, and telecommunications. This comprehensive legislation extends the protections of Section 504 beyond the school and workplace to libraries, local and state government, restaurants, hotels, theaters, stores, public transportation, and many other settings.

We turn now to the challenges your students may face.

Common Challenges

Look at Table 4.6. You will see that almost 3 million students served under IDEIA have specific learning disabilities and another 1 million have speech and language impairments. If you add children with intellectual disabilities (labeled "mental retardation" in Table 4.6) and students with emotional problems, that totals almost 90% of the students served. With recent changes in the laws and new, more inclusive policies, you are likely to have children from all these categories in your classes.

About one-half of all students receiving some kind of special-education services in the public schools are diagnosed as having learning disabilities—by far the largest category of students with disabilities.

Americans with Disabilities Act of 1990 (ADA) Federal legislation prohibiting discrimination against persons with disabilities in employment, transportation, public access, local government, and telecommunications.

TABLE 4.6

Number of Students Ages 6–21 Served under IDEA

Notice the large increases since 1991 for many of the categories. Reporting in the autism and brain injury categories was optional in 1991–1992, but required beginning in 1992–1993, so the huge percentage increases in those categories are due in part to mandatory reporting.

Disability	1991–1992	2000–2001	Percent Change in Number
Specific learning disabilities	2,247,004	2,887,217	28.5
Speech or language impairments	998,904	1,093,808	9.5
Mental retardation	553,262	612,978	10.8
Emotional disturbance	400,211	473,663	18.4
Multiple disabilities	98,408	122,559	24.5
Hearing impairments	60,727	70,767	16.5
Orthopedic impairments	51,389	73,057	42.2
Other health impairments	58,749	291,850	396.8
Visual impairments	24,083	25,975	7.9
Autism	5,415	78,749	1,354.3
Deaf-blindness	1,427	1,320	–7.5
Traumatic brain injury	245	14,844	5,958.8
Developmental delay	—	28,935	—
All disabilities	4,499,824	5,775,722	28.4

Source: U.S. Department of Education, Office of Special Education Programs, Data Analysis System (DANS), cited in the *Twenty-fourth Annual Report to Congress on the Implementation of the Individuals with Disabilities Education Act* (2002), p. II–21.

Students with Learning Disabilities

How do you explain a student who struggles to read, write, spell, or learn math, even though he or she does not have intellectual disabilities, emotional problems, or educational disadvantages and has normal vision, hearing, and language capabilities? One explanation is that the student has a **learning disability.** This is a relatively new and controversial category of exceptional students. There is no fully agreed-upon definition. A recent text on learning disabilities describes 8 definitions (Hallahan et al., 2005), including the definition used in IDEIA: "a disorder in one or more of the basic psychological processes involved in understanding or using language, spoken or written" (p. 15). Most definitions agree that students with learning disabilities perform significantly below what would be expected, given their other abilities.

In 2001, the U.S. Department of Education Office of Special Education convened a summit meeting on learning disabilities. A definition of specific learning disabilities (SLD) that emerged from that meeting is:

> The central concept of SLD involves disorders of learning and cognition that are intrinsic to the individual. SLD are specific in the sense that these disorders each significantly affect a relatively narrow range of academic and performance outcomes. SLD may occur in combination with other disabling conditions, but they are not due primarily to other conditions, such as mental retardation, behavioral disturbance, lack of opportunities to learn, or primary sensory deficits. (Bradley, Danielson, & Hallahan, 2002, p. 792)

Some educators and psychologists believe the learning disability label is overused and abused. They suggest that many of the students called learning disabled are really slow learners in average schools, average learners in high-achieving schools, students with

Connect and **Extend** to the **Research**

The January 2001 issue of *The Elementary School Journal* is edited by Russell Gersten and Sharon Vaughn and is entirely devoted to "Instructional Interventions for Students with Learning Disabilities." Topics include teaching expressive writing, literacy, self-concept, and higher-order learning.

Learning disability Problem with acquisition and use of language; may show up as difficulty with reading, writing, reasoning, or math.

second-language problems, or students who are behind in their work because they have been absent frequently or have changed schools often (Finlan, 1994).

Student Characteristics. Students with learning disabilities are not all alike. The most common characteristics are specific difficulties in one or more academic areas; poor coordination; problems paying attention; hyperactivity and impulsivity; problems organizing and interpreting visual and auditory information; disorders of thinking, memory, speech, and hearing; and difficulties making and keeping friends (Hallahan & Kauffman, 2006; Hunt & Marshall, 2002). As you can see, many students with other disabilities (such as attention-deficit disorder) and many normal students may have some of the same characteristics. To complicate the situation even more, not all students with learning disabilities will have these problems, and few will have all of the problems. One student may be 3 years behind in reading but above grade level in math, while another student may have the opposite strengths and weaknesses and a third may have problems with organizing and studying that affect almost all subject areas.

Most students with learning disabilities have difficulties reading. Table 4.7 lists some of the most common problems, although these problems are not always signs of learning disabilities. These difficulties appear to be caused by problems with relating sounds to letters that make up words, making spelling hard as well (Stanovich, 1994; Willcutt et al., 2001).

Math, both computation and problem solving, is the second most common problem area for students with learning disabilities. The writing of some of these students is virtually unreadable, and their spoken language can be halting and disorganized. Students

TABLE 4.7

Reading Habits and Errors of Students with Learning Disabilities

Do any of your students show these signs? They could be indications of learning disabilities.

Poor Reading Habits

- Frequently loses his or her place
- Jerks head from side to side
- Expresses insecurity by crying or refusing to read
- Prefers to read with the book held within inches from face
- Shows tension while reading, such as reading in a high-pitched voice, biting lips, and fidgeting

Word Recognition Errors

- Omitting a word (e.g., "He came to the park," is read, "He came to park")
- Inserting a word (e.g., "He came to the [beautiful] park")
- Substituting a word for another (e.g., "He came to the *pond*")
- Reversing letters or words (e.g., *was* is read *saw*)
- Mispronouncing words (e.g., *park* is read *pork*)
- Transposing letters or words (e.g., "The dog ate fast," is read, "The dog fast ate")
- Not attempting to read an unknown word by breaking it into familiar units
- Slow, laborious reading, less than 20 to 30 words per minute

Comprehension Errors

- Recalling basic facts (e.g., cannot answer questions directly from a passage)
- Recalling sequence (e.g., cannot explain the order of events in a story)
- Recalling main theme (e.g., cannot give the main idea of a story)

Source: From *Child and Adolescent Development for Educators,* by J. L. Meece. Published by McGraw-Hill. Copyright © 1997 McGraw-Hill. Reprinted with permission from The McGraw-Hill Companies.

Difficulties with social relationships are often present in students with LD, ADHD, and other disabilities.

with learning disabilities often lack effective ways of approaching academic tasks. They don't know how to focus on the relevant information, get organized, apply learning strategies and study skills, change strategies when one isn't working, or evaluate their learning. They tend to be passive learners, in part because they don't know *how* to learn. Working independently is especially trying, so homework and seatwork are often left incomplete (Hallahan et al., 2005).

Early diagnosis is important so that students with learning disabilities do not become terribly frustrated and discouraged. The students themselves do not understand why they are having such trouble, and they may become victims of **learned helplessness.** This condition was first identified in learning experiments with animals. The animals were put in situations where they received punishment (electric shocks) that they could not control. Later, when the situation was changed and they could have escaped the shocks or turned them off, the animals didn't even bother trying (Seligman, 1975). They had learned to be helpless victims. Students with learning disabilities may also come to believe that they cannot control or improve their own learning. This is a powerful belief. The students never exert the effort to discover that they can make a difference in their own learning, so they remain passive and helpless.

Connect and Extend to Other Chapters

The concept of learned helplessness will be discussed again in Chapter 5 as one explanation for the lower achievement of children of poverty and again in Chapter 10 as a factor influencing motivation.

Students with learning disabilities may also try to compensate for their problems and develop bad learning habits in the process, or they may begin avoiding certain subjects out of fear of not being able to handle the work. To prevent these things from happening, the teacher should refer the students to the appropriate professionals in the school as early as possible.

Teaching Students with Learning Disabilities. There is also controversy over how best to help these students. A promising approach seems to be to emphasize study skills and methods for processing information in a given subject such as reading or math. Many of the principles of cognitive learning from Chapters 7 and 8 can be applied to help all students improve their attention, memory, and problem-solving abilities (Sawyer, Graham, & Harris, 1992). Here are some general strategies taken from Hardman, Drew, and Egan (2005):

Preschool years

Keep verbal instructions short and simple.
Match the level of content carefully to the child's developmental level.
Give multiple examples to clarify meaning.
Allow more practice than usual, especially when material is new.

Learned helplessness The expectation, based on previous experiences with a lack of control, that all one's efforts will lead to failure.

Elementary School Years

Keep verbal instructions short and simple; have students repeat directions back to you to be sure they understand.

Use mnemonics (memory strategies) in instruction to teach students how to remember.

Repeat main points several times.

Provide additional time for learning and practice—reteach when necessary.

Secondary School and Transition Years

Directly teach self-monitoring strategies, such as cueing students to ask, "Was I paying attention?"

Connect new material to knowledge students already have.

Teach students to use external memory strategies and devices (tape-recording, note-taking, to-do lists,etc.).

You may be thinking that these are good ideas for many students who need more support and direct teaching of study skills. You are right.

In teaching reading, a combination of teaching letter–sound (phonological) knowledge and word identification strategies appears to be effective. For example, Maureen Lovett and her colleagues (Lovett et al., 2000) in Canada taught students with severe reading disabilities to use the four different word identification strategies: (1) identifying words by analogy, (2) seeking the part of the word that you know, (3) attempting different vowel pronunciations, and (4) "peeling off" prefixes and suffixes in a multisyllabic word. Teachers worked one-to-one with the students to learn and practice these four strategies, along with analysis of word sounds and blending sounds into words (phonological knowledge). Direct teaching of skills and strategies is especially important for students with reading disabilities.

Students with Hyperactivity and Attention Disorders

STOP | THINK | WRITE If a student is struggling with time management and organization issues, what kind of accommodations would you provide? ■

You probably have heard and may even have used the term "hyperactivity." The notion is a modern one; there were no hyperactive children 50 to 60 years ago. Such children, like Mark Twain's Huckleberry Finn, were seen as rebellious, lazy, or "fidgety" (Nylund, 2000). Today, if anything, the term is applied too often and too widely. Many student teachers in my program have classes that include 5 or 6 students diagnosed as "hyperactive," and in one class, there are 10 students with that diagnosis. Actually, hyperactivity is not one particular condition, but two kinds of problems that may or may not occur together—attention disorders and impulsive-hyperactivity problems.

Connect and Extend to PRAXIS II™

ADHD (I, B2)

A new student's parent calls you to tell you that a neurologist has diagnosed her child with ADHD. What typical behaviors can you expect from the student? What can you do to support that student's development?

Definitions. Today, most psychologists agree that the main problem for children labeled hyperactive is directing and maintaining attention, not simply controlling their physical activity. The American Psychiatric Association has established a diagnostic category called **attention-deficit hyperactivity disorder (ADHD)** to identify children with this problem. Table 4.8 lists some indicators of ADHD used by this group.

Children with ADHD are not only more physically active and inattentive than other children, they also have difficulty responding appropriately and working steadily toward goals (even their own goals). In addition, they may not be able to control their behavior on command, even for a brief period. The problem behaviors are generally evident in all situations and with every teacher. It is difficult to know how many children should be classified as hyperactive. The most common estimate is 3% to 5% of the elementary school population, with over half of these students having the combined attention and hyperactivity conditions (Hardman et al., 2005; Sagvolden, 1999). About 3 to 4 times more boys than girls are identified as hyperactive, but the gap appears to be narrowing (Hallahan et al., 2005). Just a few years ago, most psychologists thought that ADHD diminished as children entered adolescence, but now there are some researchers who believe that the problems can persist into adulthood (Hallowell & Ratey, 1994). Adolescence—with the increased stresses of puberty, transition to middle or high school, more demanding aca-

Attention-deficit hyperactivity disorder (ADHD) Current term for disruptive behavior disorders marked by overactivity, excessive difficulty sustaining attention, or impulsiveness.

TABLE 4.8

Indicators of ADHD: Attention-Deficit Hyperactivity Disorder
Do any of your students show these signs? They could be indications of ADHD.

Problems with *Inattention*

- Often does not give close attention to details or makes careless mistakes
- Has trouble keeping attention in tasks or play activities
- Does not seem to listen when spoken to directly
- Does not follow through on instructions and fails to finish schoolwork (not due to oppositional behavior or failure to understand instructions)
- Has difficulty organizing tasks or activities
- Avoids, dislikes, or is reluctant to engage in tasks that require sustained mental effort (such as schoolwork or homework)
- Loses things necessary for tasks or activities
- Is easily distracted by extraneous stimuli
- Is forgetful in daily activities

Problems with *Impulse Control*

- Often blurts out answers before questions have been completed
- Has trouble awaiting his/her turn
- Often interrupts or intrudes on others in conversations or games

Hyperactivity

- Often fidgets with hands or feet or squirms in seat
- Often gets up from seat when remaining seated is expected
- Often runs about or climbs excessively in situations in which it is inappropriate (in adolescents may be limited to subjective feelings of restlessness)
- Often has difficulty playing or engaging in leisure activities quietly
- Often talks excessively
- Often acts as if "driven by a motor" and cannot remain still

Source: Reprinted with permission from *Diagnostic and Statistical Manual of Mental Disorders,* Fourth Edition, Text Revision. (Copyright 2000). American Psychiatric Association.

demic work, and more engrossing social relationships—can be an especially difficult time for students with ADHD (Taylor, 1998).

Treating and Teaching Students with ADHD. Today, there is an increasing reliance on drug therapy for ADHD. In fact, from 1990 to 1998, there was a 700% increase in the production of Ritalin in the United States (Diller, 1998). Ritalin and other prescribed drugs such as Adderall and Cylert are stimulants, but in particular dosages, they tend to have paradoxical effects on many children with ADHD: Short-term effects include possible improvements in social behaviors such as cooperation, attention, and compliance. Research suggests that about 70% to 80% of children with ADHD are more manageable when on medication. But for many there are negative side effects such as increased heart rate and blood pressure, interference with growth rate, insomnia, weight loss, and nausea (Friend & Bursuck, 2002; Hallahan et al., 2005; Panksepp, 1998). In addition, little is known about the long-term effects of drug therapy, so be cautious. Many studies have concluded that the improvements in behavior from the drugs *seldom* lead to improvements in academic learning or peer relationships, two areas where children with ADHD have great problems. Because students appear to improve dramatically in their behavior, parents and teachers, relieved to see change, may assume the problem has been cured. It hasn't. The students still need special help in learning (Doggett, 2004; Purdie, Hattie, & Carroll, 2002). One large study in Australia concluded:

> Multimodal approaches to intervention have been found to be most effective in terms of lasting change. For most, but not all children and adolescents, treatment with psychostimulants has beneficial effects, provided that it is accompanied by remedial tuition, counselling, and behaviour management by parents/teachers, as required. Thus, advice from several different professions may be necessary. (van Kraayenoord, Rice, Carroll, Fritz, Dillon, & Hill, 2001, p. 7)

What can teachers do? Long assignments may overwhelm students with attention deficits, so give them a few problems or paragraphs at a time with clear consequences for completion. Another promising approach combines instruction in learning and memory strategies with motivational training. The goal is to help students develop the "skill and will" to improve their achievement (Paris, 1988). They are also taught to monitor their own behavior and encouraged to be persistent and to see themselves as "in control" (Reid & Borkowski, 1987).

The notion of being in control is part of a new therapy strategy for dealing with ADHD, one that stresses personal agency. Rather than treating the problem child, David Nylund's (2000) idea is to enlist the child's strengths to conquer the child's problems—put the child in control. New metaphors for the situation are developed. Rather than seeing the problems as inside the child, Nylund helps everyone see ADHD, Trouble, Boredom, and other enemies of learning as outside the child—demons to be conquered or unruly spirits to be enlisted in the service of what *the child* wants to accomplish. The focus is on solutions. The steps of the SMART approach are:

> **S**eparating the problem of ADHD from the child
> **M**apping the influence of ADHD on the child and family
> **At**tending to the exceptions to the ADHD story
> **R**eclaiming special abilities of children diagnosed with ADHD
> **T**elling and celebrating the new story. (Nylund, 2000, p. xix)

As a teacher, you can look for times when the student is engaged—even short times. What is different about these times? Discover the student's strengths and allow yourself to be amazed by them. Make changes in your teaching that support the changes the student is trying to make. Nylund gives the following example: Chris (age 9) and his teacher, Ms. Baker, became partners in putting Chris in control of his concentration in school. Ms. Baker moved Chris's seat to the front of the room. The two designed a subtle signal to get Chris back on track, and Chris organized his messy desk. These sound like some of the Section 504 accommodations in Table 4.5. When Chris's concentration improved, Chris received an award at a party given in his honor. Chris described how he was learning to listen in class: "You just have to have a strong mind and tell ADHD and Boredom not to bother you" (Nylund, 2000, p. 166).

The above methods should be thoroughly tested with the student before drugs are used. Even if students in your class are on medication, it is critical that they also learn the academic and social skills they will need to survive. Again, this will not happen by itself, even if behavior improves with medication (Purdie et al., 2002).

Connect and **Extend** to Your **Teaching**

Students with ADHD make these recommendations for their teachers (Nylund, 2000):

- Use lots of pictures (visual clues) to help me learn.
- Recognize cultural and racial identity.
- Know when to bend the rules.
- Notice when I am doing well.
- Don't tell the other kids that I am taking Ritalin.
- Offer us choices.
- Don't just lecture—it's boring!
- Realize that I am intelligent.
- Let me walk around the classroom.
- Don't give tons of homework.
- More recess!
- Be patient.

Reaching Every Student: Higher-Order Thinking

Reading instruction for students with learning disabilities does not have to focus on low-level skills. Joanna Williams (2002) developed the *Theme Identification Program* to help middle-school students with severe learning disabilities understand and use the abstract idea of themes in literature as briefly described in Table 4.9.

Students with learning disabilities sometimes also have another challenge, attention disorders. In fact, some researchers estimate that there is a 25% to 70% overlap between learning disabilities and attention-deficit hyperactivity disorder (Hardman et al., 2005). And students who are gifted as well as students with other conditions such as behavior disorders, depression, lead poisoning, seizure disorders, or fetal alcohol syndrome may have ADHD symptoms as well (Doggett, 2004). We turn to this disorder next.

Students with Communication Disorders

For the ages of 6 to 21, students with communication disorders are the second largest group served by special education. They make up about 19% of students receiving services. Language disorders can arise from many sources, because so many different aspects of the individual are involved in learning language. A child with a hearing impairment

TABLE 4.9

Higher-Order Comprehension and Severe Learning Disabilities

In the *Theme Identification Program* (Williams, 2002), middle-school students with severe learning disabilities learned to understand and use the abstract idea of themes in literature. Teachers taught 12 different lessons using 12 stories. Briefly (see the article for more detail) the process for each lesson was:

Prereading: The teacher defines a theme and discusses the value of themes, drawing on students' personal experiences.

Reading: The teacher reads the story and inserts questions while reading to help students connect what they know to the story. At the end of the reading, the class discusses the main point in the story and the teacher reads a summary highlighting the points.

Discussing Using the Theme Scheme: The teacher and students discuss the important information using six organizing questions. The first four questions focused on the story content:

- Who was the main character?
- What was her/his problem?
- What did she/he do?
- What happened at the end of the story?

The last two questions encouraged students to make judgments in order to identify a theme:

- Was what happened good or bad?
- Why was it good or bad?

Identifying the Theme: Students then state the theme in a standard format:

[The main character] learned that she (he) should (not) ___________.

We should (not) ___________.

The theme of the story is ___________.

Application of Theme: The students learn to ask three questions to generalize the theme:

- Can you name someone who should (not) ___________?
- When is it important for (that person) to do (or not do) ___________?
- In what situation will this help?

Multimodal Activity: Every lesson after the first one included a role-play of the story theme where the students acted out the characters in the story, an art activity to show the theme, or a music activity such as writing a rap song that communicated the theme.

Review: A recap of the Theme Scheme and a preview of the next lesson.

Source: For a summary of research about teaching higher-order skills to students with learning disabilities, see "Research on Interventions for Adolescents with Learning Disabilities: A Meta-analysis of Outcomes Related to Higher-order Processing," by H. L. Swanson, 2001, *The Elementary School Journal, 101,* 332–348. Copyright © 2001 by The University of Chicago Press. Adapted with permission.

will not learn to speak normally. Injuries can cause neurological problems that interfere with speech or language. Children who are not listened to, or whose perception of the world is distorted by emotional problems, will reflect these problems in their language development. Because speaking involves movements, any impairment of the motor functions involved with speech can cause language disorders. And because language development and thinking are so interwoven, any problems in cognitive functioning can affect ability to use language.

Speech Disorders. Students who cannot produce sounds effectively for speaking are considered to have a **speech disorder.** About 5% of school-age children have some form of speech impairment. Articulation problems and stuttering are the two most common problems.

Speech disorder Inability to produce sounds effectively for speaking.

Articulation disorders include substituting one sound for another (*thunthine* for *sunshine*), distorting a sound (*shoup* for *soup*), adding a sound (*ideer* for *idea*), or omitting sounds (*po-y* for *pony*) (Smith, 1998). Keep in mind, however, that most children are 6 to 8 years old before they can successfully pronounce all English sounds in normal conversation. The sounds of the consonants *l*, *r*, *y*, *s*, and *z* and the consonant blends *sh*, *ch*, *zh*, and *th* are the last to be mastered. Also, there are dialect differences based on geography that do not represent articulation problems. A child in your class from New England might say "ideer" for "idea," but have no speech impairment.

Stuttering generally appears between the ages of 3 and 4. Causes of stuttering are unclear, but might include emotional or neurological problems or learned behavior. Whatever the cause, stuttering can lead to embarrassment and anxiety for the sufferer. If stuttering continues more than a year or so, the child should be referred to a speech therapist. Early intervention can make a big difference (Hardman et al., 2005).

Voicing problems, a third type of speech impairment, include speaking with an inappropriate pitch, quality, or loudness, or in a monotone (Hallahan & Kauffman, 2006). A student with any of these problems should be referred to a speech therapist. Recognizing the problem is the first step. Be alert for students whose pronunciation, loudness, voice quality, speech fluency, expressive range, or rate is very different from that of their peers. Pay attention also to students who seldom speak. Are they simply shy, or do they have difficulties with language?

Language Disorders. Language differences are not necessarily language disorders. Students with language disorders are those who are markedly deficient in their ability to understand or express language, compared with other students of their own age and cultural group (Owens, 1999). Students who seldom speak, who use few words or very short sentences, or who rely only on gestures to communicate should be referred to a qualified school professional for observation or testing. Table 4.10 gives ideas for promoting language development for all students.

Communication skills are an important component of a student's IEP. Adaptations such as assistive communication devices can help students with communication disorders participate in general education activities.

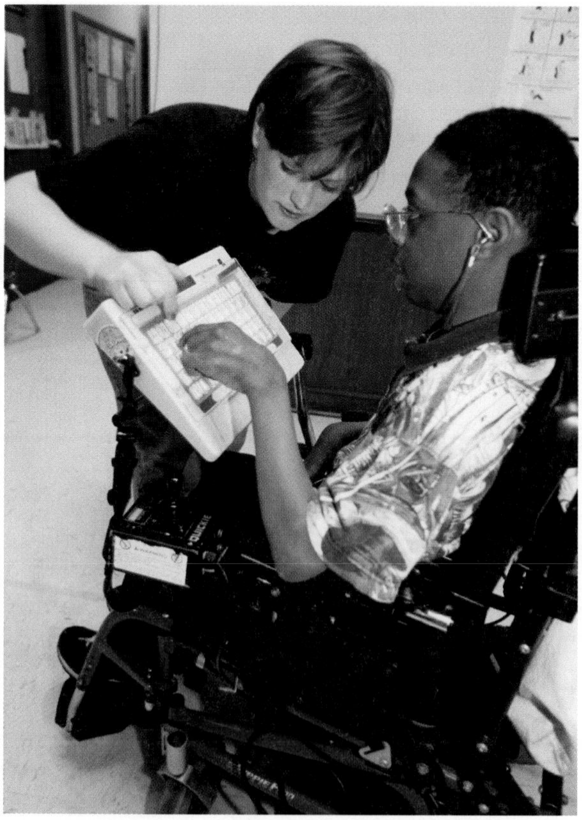

Articulation disorders Any of a variety of pronunciation difficulties, such as the substitution, distortion, or omission of sounds.

Voicing problems Inappropriate pitch, quality, loudness, or intonation.

TABLE 4.10

Encouraging Language Development

- Talk about things that interest children.
- Follow the children's lead. Reply to their initiations and comments. Share their excitement.
- Don't ask too many questions. If you must, use questions such as *how did/do . . . , why did/do . . .* , and *what happened . . .* that result in longer explanatory answers.
- Encourage children to ask questions. Respond openly and honestly. If you don't want to answer a question, say so and explain why. (*I don't think I want to answer that question; it's very personal.*)
- Use a pleasant tone of voice. You need not be a comedian, but you can be light and humorous. Children love it when adults are a little silly.
- Don't be judgmental or make fun of children's language. If you are overly critical of children's language or try to catch and correct all errors, they will stop talking to you.
- Allow enough time for children to respond.
- Treat children with courtesy by not interrupting when they are talking.
- Include children in family and classroom discussions. Encourage participation and listen to their ideas.
- Be accepting of children and of their language. Hugs and acceptance can go a long way.
- Provide opportunities for children to use language and to have that language work for them to accomplish their goals.

Source: From *Language Disorders, 3/e* by Robert E. Owens, Jr. Published by Allyn and Bacon, Boston, MA. Copyright © 1999 by Pearson Education. Reprinted by permission of the publisher.

Students with Intellectual Disabilities

Intellectual disability is a more current name for **mental retardation.** As defined by the American Association on Mental Retardation (AAMR) (2002, p.1), "mental retardation is a disability characterized by significant limitations in both intellectual functioning and adaptive behavior as expressed in conceptual, social, and practical adaptive skills. This disability originates before age 18."

Intellectual function is usually measured by IQ tests with a cutoff score of 70 as one indicator of retardation. But an IQ score below the 70 range is *not* enough to diagnose a child as having intellectual disabilities. There must also be problems with adaptive behavior, day-to-day independent living, and social functioning. This caution is especially important when interpreting the scores of students from different cultures. Defining retardation based on test scores alone can create what some critics call "the 6-hour retarded"—students who are seen as retarded only for the part of the day they attend school.

Only about 1% of the population fit the AAMR's definition of having retardation in both intellectual functioning and adaptive behavior. For years, retardation was further divided into mild (IQ 50–69), moderate (IQ 35–49), severe (IQ 20–34), and profound levels (IQ below 20). Many school districts still use this system, and so does the World Health Organization. However, the IQ ranges are not perfect predictors of individuals' abilities to function, so the AAMR now recommends a classification scheme based on the amount of support that a person requires to function at his or her highest level (Taylor, Richards, & Brady, 2005). Table 4.11 on the next page summarizes this newer classification system.

Intellectual disabilities/Mental retardation Significantly below-average intellectual and adaptive social behavior, evident before age 18.

As a regular teacher, you may not have contact with children needing extensive or pervasive support unless your school is participating in a full inclusion program for exceptional students (described earlier in this chapter), but you probably will work with

TABLE 4.11

AAMR Classification Scheme for Mental Retardation

This new scheme for classification is based on the level of support a student would need to function as completely as possible.

Intermittent	Supports on an "as needed basis." Characterized by episodic nature, person not always needing the support(s), or short-term supports needed during life-span transitions (e.g., job loss or an acute medical crisis). Intermittent supports may be high or low intensity when provided.
Limited	An intensity of supports characterized by consistency over time and time-limited but not of an intermittent nature, may require fewer staff members and less cost than more intense levels of support (e.g., time-limited employment training or transitional supports during the school-to-adult period).
Extensive	Supports characterized by regular involvement (e.g., daily) in at least some environments (such as work or home) and not time-limited (e.g., long-term home living support).
Pervasive	Supports characterized by their constancy, high intensity, provided across environments; potential life-sustaining nature. Pervasive supports typically involve more staff members and intrusiveness than do extensive or time-limited supports.

Source: From *Mental Retardation: Definition, Classification, and Systems of Support* (10th ed., p. 152), by AAMR Ad Hoc Committee on Terminology and Classification, 2002. Copyright © 2002 by the American Association of Mental Retardation. Reprinted with permission from the AAMR.

children with mild retardation. In the early grades, these students may simply learn more slowly than their peers. They need more time and more practice to learn and have difficulty transferring learning from one setting to another or putting small skills together to accomplish a more complex task. The *Guidelines* list suggestions for teaching students with below-average general intelligence.

Learning goals for many students with intellectual disabilities between the ages of 9 and 13 include basic reading, writing, arithmetic, learning about the local environment, social behavior, and personal interests. In junior and senior high school, the emphasis is on vocational and domestic skills, literacy for living (using the telephone book; reading signs, labels, and newspaper ads; completing a job application), job-related behaviors such as courtesy and punctuality; health self-care; and citizenship skills. Today, there is a growing emphasis on **transition programming**—preparing the student to live and work in the community. As you saw earlier in the chapter, the law requires that schools design an IEP, or individualized educational program, for every child with disabilities. An ITP, or individualized transition plan, may be part of the IEP for students with retardation (Friend, 2005).

Students with Emotional or Behavioral Disorders

Students with **emotional and behavioral disorders** can be among the most difficult to teach in a regular class, and are a source of concern for many prospective teachers (Avramidis, Bayliss, & Burden, 2000). Professionals in education state that behavioral disorders are behaviors that deviate so much from the norm that they interfere with the child's own growth and development and/or the lives of others. Clearly, deviation implies a difference from some standard, and standards of behavior differ from one situation, age group, culture, ethnic group, and historical period to another. What passes for team spirit in the football bleachers might be seen as disturbed behavior in a bank or restaurant. In addition, the deviation must be more than a temporary response to stressful events; it must be consistent across time and in different situations and the student must not have responded to direct interventions in general education (Forness & Knitzer, 1992).

There are other definitions. The language in IDEIA describes *emotional disturbances (ED)* that involve inappropriate behaviors, unhappiness or depression, fears and anxi-

Transition programming Gradual preparation of exceptional students to move from high school into further education or training, employment, or community involvement.

Emotional and behavioral disorders Behaviors or emotions that deviate so much from the norm that they interfere with the child's own growth and development and/or the lives of others—inappropriate behaviors, unhappiness or depression, fears and anxieties, and trouble with relationships.

Guidelines: Teaching Students with Below-Average Intelligence

1. Determine readiness: However little a child may know, he or she is ready to learn the next step.
2. State and present objectives simply.
3. Base specific learning objectives on an analysis of the child's learning strengths and weaknesses.
4. Present material in small, logical steps. Practice extensively before going on to the next step.
5. Work on practical skills and concepts based on the demands of adult life.
6. Do not skip steps. Students with average intelligence can form conceptual bridges from one step to the next, but children with below-average intelligence need every step and bridge made explicit. Make connections for the student. Do not expect him or her to "see" the connections.
7. Be prepared to present the same idea in many different ways.
8. Go back to a simpler level if you see the student is not following.
9. Be especially careful to motivate the student and maintain attention.
10. Find materials that do not insult the student. A junior high boy may need the low vocabulary of "See Spot run," but will be insulted by the age of the characters and the content of the story.
11. Focus on a few target behaviors or skills so you and the student have a chance to experience success. Everyone needs positive reinforcement.
12. Be aware that students with below-average intelligence must overlearn, repeat, and practice more than children of average intelligence. They must be taught how to study, and they must frequently review and practice their newly acquired skills in different settings.
13. Pay close attention to social relations. Simply including students with below-average intelligence in a regular class will not guarantee that they will be accepted or that they will make and keep friends.

For more information, see:
http://www.aamr.org/Policies/mental_retardation.shtml
http://www.ed.wright.edu/~prenick/karen.htm

eties, and trouble with relationships. The American Psychological Association and the medical community refer to *mental disorders* (Friend, 2006). Table 4.12 on the next page describes a few of the specific disorders covered by the *Diagnostic and Statistical Manual of Mental Disorders* (4th edition, revised), also called the *DSM-IV-TR*.

However they are defined, in the school year 2000–2001, there were almost 475,000 students with emotional disturbances identified making this the 4th largest group receiving services. This number has increased 18% since 1991–1992. As with learning disabilities and ADHD, there are more boys than girls diagnosed with these disorders. For behavioral disorders, the numbers are about 6 to 9 times as many boys as girls. One troubling fact is that African American students are overrepresented in this category. They make up about 15% of the population, but about 27% of the students identified with emotional and behavioral disorders.

The range of possible emotional and behavioral disorders is wide. And students with other disabilities—learning disabilities, intellectual disabilities, or ADHD, for example—may have emotional or behavioral problems also as they struggle in school. Methods from applied behavioral analysis (Chapter 6) and direct teaching of social skills (Chapter 3) are two useful approaches. Another possibility that has proved helpful for these students is to provide structure, organizational tools, and choices. Here are some ideas from Terri Swanson (2005):

Structure the environment by minimizing visual and auditory stimulation, establishing clear visual boundaries between areas where different behaviors are expected, or organizing supplies in easy-to-use holders.

Structure schedules by posting monthly and daily schedules, having clear starting and ending signals and clear procedures for turning in work.

Structure activities by color-coding subject folders (blue for math, etc.), posting verbal instructions with visual prompts, or putting all materials needed for an activity in a "Science box."

Connect and **Extend** to **Other Chapters**

In Chapter 12, you will find ideas for dealing with mild-to-moderate behavior problems.

TABLE 4.12

Examples of Emotional and Behavioral Disorders from the *Diagnostic and Statistical Manual of Mental Disorders*

The definition of emotional and behavior disorders in IDEA is general: It does not list particular conditions. However, in the medical community many specific disorders have been identified, and these are included in the *Diagnostic and Statistical Manual of Mental Disorders* (fourth edition, text revision) (*DSM-IV-TR*). Instead of being called emotional and behavior disorders, they are referred to as mental disorders. The following list, although not complete, includes examples of mental disorders listed in that publication that educators would consider emotional and behavior disorders:

- **Anxiety disorders.** Anxiety disorders occur when students experience an overwhelming sense of fear or dread. One example is obsessive-compulsive disorder (OCD) in which students cannot stop themselves from worrying excessively about a specific concern, for example, germs. Other examples include phobias (fear of specific items, such as spiders, or fear of certain activities, such as going to school) and postraumatic stress disorder (PTSD) in which students re-live in nightmares or flashbacks a traumatic event that they witnessed.
- **Disruptive behavior disorders.** This category includes three types of disorders:
  - *Attention deficit-hyperactivity disorder* . . . is characterized by inattention, a high level of activity and impulsivity, or a combination of these. Note, though, that it often is not considered a disability.
  - *Oppositional defiant disorder* (ODD) is diagnosed when students are defiant with adults and vindictive or blaming with peers to an excessive degree over a long period of time.
  - *Conduct disorders* are diagnosed when students fight, bully, display cruelty to animals or people, or otherwise repeatedly break serious rules.
- **Eating disorders.** The most common eating disorder is anorexia nervosa in which students believe they are overweight and refuse to eat, even when they are near starvation.
- **Mood disorders.** Also called affective disorders, this group includes depression . . . and bipolar disorder, also called manic depression, in which students' moods swing from extreme highs (manic) to extreme lows (depression).
- **Tic disorders.** Tics are involuntary, rapid, stereotyped movements of specific muscle groups. Students with tics may blink their eyes or repeatedly sniff. The most well known tic disorder is Tourette syndrome, a disorder that ranges from mild to severe and includes both facial or other physical tics as well as vocal tics, often "barking" or profanity.

Source: From "Diagnostic and Statistical Manual of Mental Health" in *Special Education: Contemporary Perspectives for School Professionals* by M. Friend. Published by Allyn and Bacon, Boston, MA. Copyright © 2006 by Pearson Education. Reprinted by permission of the publisher.

Structure rules and routines, for example, giving students a script to use in asking other students to play a game with them, writing rules out in a positive way, or preparing students for changes in routines such as spring break by reviewing pictures of what will be happening over the break.

Offer choices by providing a short list of alternatives to complete assignments or projects.

Because students with emotional and behavioral disorders frequently break rules and push the limits, teachers often find themselves disciplining the students. Be aware that there have been court rulings on disciplining students with serious emotional problems (Yell, 1990). The *Guidelines* may help when you are faced with these situations.

Let's consider an area where teachers may be able to detect problems and make a difference—suicide.

Suicide. Of course, not every student with emotional or behavioral problems will consider suicide, and many people without such problems will. But depression often is associated with suicide. Up to 10% of adolescents have attempted suicide at some point, but even more have considered it. Native Americans and students living in rural communities are more likely to commit suicide. There are four general risk factors, and they seem to apply to both male and female African American, Latino, and White adolescents: de-

Guidelines: Disciplining Students with Emotional Problems

Be careful not to violate due process rights of students—students and parents must know the behaviors expected and the consequences for misbehavior.

EXAMPLES

1. Communicate expectations clearly and in writing.
2. Ask parents and students to sign a copy of the classroom rules.
3. Post rules and consequences in class and on a class Web page.

Be very careful with severe punishments that remove students from class for a long time. These constitute a change in the child's educational program (IEP) and require due process.

EXAMPLES

1. Suspensions of more than 10 days require due process.
2. Prolonged periods of time-out (in-school suspension) may require due process.

Punishments for students with severe emotional problems must serve a clear educational purpose.

EXAMPLES

1. Give a rationale for punishment or correction that ties an action to student's learning or the learning of others in the class.
2. Use written behavior contracts that include a rationale.

Make sure the rule and the punishment are reasonable.

EXAMPLES

1. Consider the student's age and physical condition.
2. Does the punishment match the offense and the way others in the class are treated?
3. Do other teachers handle similar situations in the same way?
4. Try less intrusive punishments first. Be patient. Move to more severe actions only when less severe procedures fail.

Keep good records and work collaboratively so all involved are informed.

EXAMPLES

1. Document the punishment of all students in a journal or log. List what precipitated the punishment, what procedures were used, how long the punishment lasted, the results, modifications to the punishment, and new results.
2. Note meetings with families, special education teachers, and the principal.
3. Make any changes involving management plans with families and other teachers.

Always use positive consequences in conjunction with negative ones.

EXAMPLES

1. If students lose points for breaking rules, give them ways to regain points through positive behavior.
2. Recognize genuine accomplishment and small steps—DON'T say, "Well it's about time you . . ."

For more information on disciplining students with disabilities, see:
http://www.nasponline.org/publications/cq262discipline.html
http://wrightslaw.com/
http://www.schwablearning.org/

pression and substance abuse, history of suicide in the family, being under stress, and family rejection or conflict. Having more than one of these risk factors is especially dangerous (Steinberg, 2005). In addition, there is concern today that some drugs prescribed for depression may increase the risk of suicide in adolescents.

Suicide often comes as a response to life problems—problems that parents and teachers sometimes dismiss. There are many warning signs that trouble is brewing. Watch for changes in eating or sleeping habits, weight, grades, disposition, activity level, or interest in friends or activities that were once fun. Students at risk sometimes suddenly give away prized possessions such as stereos, CDs, clothing, or pets. They may seem depressed or hyperactive and may say things like "Nothing matters anymore," "You won't have to worry about me anymore," or "I wonder what dying is like." They may start missing school or quit doing work. It is especially dangerous if the student not only talks about suicide, but also has a plan for carrying it out.

If you suspect that there is a problem, talk to the student directly. One feeling shared by many people who attempt suicide is that no one really takes them seriously. "A question about suicide does not provoke suicide. Indeed, teens (and adults) often experience relief when someone finally cares enough to ask" (Range, 1993, p. 145). Be realistic, not poetic,

TABLE 4.13

Myths and Facts about Suicide

Myth:	People who talk about suicide don't kill themselves.
Fact:	Eight out of ten people who commit suicide tell someone that they're thinking about hurting themselves before they actually do it.
Myth:	Only certain types of people commit suicide.
Fact:	All types of people commit suicide—male and female, young and old, rich and poor, country people and city people. It happens in every racial, ethnic, and religious group.
Myth:	When a person talks about suicide, you should change the subject to get his or her mind off it.
Fact:	You should take them seriously. Listen carefully to what they are saying. Give them a chance to express their feelings. Let them know you are concerned. And help them get help.
Myth:	Most people who kill themselves really want to die.
Fact:	Most people who kill themselves are confused about whether they want to die. Suicide is often intended as a cry for help.

Source: From *Changing Bodies, Changing Lives: A Book for Teens on Sex and Relationships* (p. 142), by R. Bell, 1980, New York: Random House.

about suicide. Ask about specifics, and take the student seriously. Also, be aware that teenage suicides often occur in clusters. After one student acts or when stories about a suicide are reported in the media, other teens are more likely to copy the suicide (Lewinsohn, Rohde, & Seeley, 1994; Rice & Dolgin, 2002). Table 4.13 lists common myths and facts about suicide.

Drug Abuse. Although drug abuse is not always associated with emotional or behavioral problems and people without these challenges may abuse drugs, many adolescents with emotional problems also abuse drugs. Modern society makes growing up a very confusing process. Notice the messages from films and billboards. "Beautiful," popular people drink alcohol and smoke cigarettes with little concern for their health. We have over-the-counter drugs for almost every common ailment. Coffee wakes us up, and a pill helps us sleep. And then we tell students to "say no!" to drugs.

For many reasons, not just because of these contradictory messages, drug use has become a problem for students. Accurate statistics are hard to find, but estimates from the *Monitoring the Future* survey conducted by the University of Michigan indicate that 15% of 8th graders, 31% of 10th graders, and 39% of 12th graders had used an illicit drug in the past year, with marijuana being the most popular drug. Drug use among secondary-school students has been gradually declining or holding steady since about 2001, with the exception of inhalants. Inhalants (glues, paint thinners, nail polish remover, aerosol sprays, etc.) are inexpensive and available. Also, students don't realize that they are risking injury or death when they use inhalants. The proportion of 8th and 10th graders who believe that inhalants are dangerous is actually declining (Johnston, O'Malley, Bachman, & Schulenberg, 2004).

We should distinguish between experimentation and abuse. Many students try something at a party, but do not become regular users. The best way to help students who have trouble saying no appears to be through peer programs that teach them how to say no assertively. Also, the older students are when they experiment with drugs, the more likely they are to make responsible choices, so helping younger students say no is a clear benefit.

Prevention. Providing information or "scare" tactics such as the DARE drug prevention program seem to have little positive effect and may even encourage curiosity and experimentation (Dusenbury & Falco, 1995; Tobler & Stratton, 1997). The most effective prevention programs include developmentally appropriate language and concepts; teach students to resist social pressure; provide accurate information about rates of behavior (*not* everyone is doing it); use interactive teaching methods such as role-playing or small groups; provide training in skills that help in many situations such as the 6-step problem-solving strategy described in Chapter 12; give thorough coverage of the topic with follow-up; and practice cultural sensitivity.

Debra Stipek and her colleagues (1999) describe many ways that teachers embed life lessons into school subjects and informal discussions. For example, class rules emphasize respect ("there are no stupid questions"); students learn to give "put ups" not "put downs"; the lives of historical figures provide opportunities to discuss choices and how to deal with stresses; and student conflicts become life lessons in relationships. In addition, students are given a "Toolbox of Coping Skills" that contains concrete objects to be used to address problems. The Toolbox includes Post-it® notes to record student concerns and troubling situations, so that the incidents can be dealt with at an appropriate time. Exit and U-turn signs remind students that the best strategy may be to "exit" the situation. "Exiting to a safe place, without explanation, is taught as one appropriate face-saving, and possibly life-saving, response" (Stipek et al., 1999, p. 443). Early indicators are that students do learn to use these skills.

Less Prevalent Problems/ More Severe Disabilities

In this section, we meet students with more severe disabilities. In your first years of teaching, you may encounter only a few of these students, but you still can make a difference in their lives.

Students with Health Impairments

Some students must use special devices such as braces, special shoes, crutches, or wheelchairs to participate in a normal school program. If the school has the necessary architectural features, such as ramps, elevators, and accessible rest rooms, and if teachers allow for the physical limitations of students, little needs to be done to alter the usual educational program. Two other health impairments you may encounter are cerebral palsy and seizure disorders.

Cerebral Palsy and Multiple Disabilities. Damage to the brain before or during birth or during infancy can cause a child to have difficulty moving and coordinating his or her body. The problem may be very mild, so the child simply appears a bit clumsy, or so

Physical and instructional accommodations can enable students with many kinds of disabilities to participate in general education classrooms. A specially designed desk enables this young girl with disabilities due to cerebral palsy to work independently in class.

severe that voluntary movement is practically impossible. The most common form of **cerebral palsy** is characterized by **spasticity** (overly tight or tense muscles). Many children with cerebral palsy also have secondary handicaps (Kirk, Gallagher, & Anastasiow, 1993). In the classroom, these secondary handicaps are the greatest concern—and these are generally what the regular teacher can help with most. For example, many children with cerebral palsy also have visual impairments, speech problems, or mild intellectual disabilities. The strategies described in this chapter should prove helpful in such situations.

Seizure Disorders (Epilepsy). A seizure is a cluster of behaviors that occurs in response to abnormal neurochemical activities in the brain (Hardman, Drew, & Egan, 2005). People with **epilepsy** have recurrent seizures, but not all seizures are the result of epilepsy; temporary conditions such as high fevers or infections can also trigger seizures. Seizures take many forms and differ with regard to the length, frequency, and movements involved. A partial or absence seizure involves only a small part of the brain, whereas a **generalized** or **tonic-clonic seizure** includes much more of the brain.

Most generalized seizures (once called *grand mal*) are accompanied by uncontrolled jerking movements that ordinarily last two to five minutes, possible loss of bowel or bladder control, and irregular breathing, followed by a deep sleep or coma. On regaining consciousness, the student may be very weary, confused, and in need of extra sleep. Most seizures can be controlled by medication. If a student has a seizure accompanied by convulsions in class, the teacher must take action so the student will not be injured. The major danger to a student having such a seizure is getting hurt by striking a hard surface during the violent jerking.

Connect and **Extend** to the **Web**

For more ideas and information, see the Epilepsy Foundation of America website at http://www.epilepsyfoundation.org/answerplace/.

If a student has a seizure, stay calm and reassure the rest of the class. Do not try to restrain the child's movements; you can't stop the seizure once it starts. Lower the child gently to the floor, away from furniture or walls. Move hard objects away. Loosen scarves, ties, or anything that might make breathing difficult. Turn the child's head gently to the side, put a soft coat or blanket under the student's head. Never put anything in the student's mouth—it is NOT true that people having seizures can swallow their tongues. Don't attempt artificial respiration unless the student does not start breathing again after the seizure stops. Find out from the student's parents how they deal with seizures. If one seizure follows another and the student does not regain consciousness in between, if the student is pregnant or has a medical ID that does not say "epilepsy, seizure disorder," if there are signs of injury, or if the seizure goes on for more than 5 minutes, get medical help right away (Friend, 2005).

Not all seizures are dramatic. Sometimes the student just loses contact briefly. The student may stare, fail to respond to questions, drop objects, and miss what has been happening for 1 to 30 seconds. These were once called *petit mal*, but they are now referred to as **absence seizures** and can easily go undetected. If a child in your class appears to daydream frequently, does not seem to know what is going on at times, or cannot remember what has just happened when you ask, you should consult the school psychologist or nurse. The major problem for students with absence seizures is that they miss the continuity of the class interaction—these seizures can occur as often as 100 times a day. If their seizures are frequent, students will find the lessons confusing. Question these students to be sure they are understanding and following the lesson. Be prepared to repeat yourself periodically.

Cerebral palsy Condition involving a range of motor or coordination difficulties due to brain damage.

Spasticity Overly tight or tense muscles, characteristic of some forms of cerebral palsy.

Epilepsy Disorder marked by seizures and caused by abnormal electrical discharges in the brain.

Generalized seizure A seizure involving a large portion of the brain.

Absence seizure A seizure involving only a small part of the brain that causes a child to lose contact briefly.

Students Who Are Deaf

You will hear the term, "hearing impaired," to describe these students, but the deaf community and researchers object to this term, so I will use their preferred terms, deaf and hard of hearing. The number of deaf students has been declining over the past three decades, but when the problem does occur, the consequences for learning are serious (Hunt & Marshall, 2002). Signs of hearing problems are turning one ear toward the speaker, favoring one ear in conversation, or misunderstanding conversation when the speaker's face cannot be seen. Other indications include not following directions, seeming distracted or confused at times, frequently asking people to repeat what they have said, mispronouncing new words or names, and being reluctant to participate in class discussions. Take note particularly of students who have frequent earaches, sinus infections, or allergies.

In the past, educators have debated whether oral or manual approaches are better for children who are deaf or hard of hearing. Oral approaches involve speech reading (also called lip reading) and training students to use whatever limited hearing they may have. Manual approaches include sign language and finger spelling. Research indicates that children who learn some manual method of communicating perform better in academic subjects and are more socially mature than students who are exposed only to oral methods. Today, the trend is to combine both approaches (Hallahan & Kauffman, 2006).

Another perspective suggests that people who are deaf are part of a different culture with a different language, values, social institutions, and literature. Hunt and Marshall (2002) quote one deaf professional: "How would women like to be referred to as male-impaired, or whites like to be called black-impaired? I'm not impaired; I'm deaf!" (p. 348). From this perspective, a goal is to help deaf children become bilingual and bicultural, to enable them to function effectively in both cultures. Technological innovations such as teletypewriters in homes and public phones and the many avenues of communication through e-mail and the Internet have expanded communication possibilities for all people, including those with hearing problems.

Students with Vision Impairments

In the United States, only about 1 child in 1,000 has visual impairments so serious that special educational services are needed. Most members of this group needing special services are classified as having **low vision.** This means they can read with the aid of a magnifying glass or large-print books. A small group of students, about 1 in every 2,500, is **educationally blind.** These students must use hearing and touch as their predominant learning channels (Kirk, Gallagher, & Anastasiow, 1993).

Students who have difficulty seeing often hold books either very close to or very far from their eyes. They may squint, rub their eyes frequently, or complain that their eyes burn or itch. The eyes may actually be swollen, red, or encrusted. Students with vision problems may misread material on the chalkboard, describe their vision as being blurred, be very sensitive to light, or hold their heads at an odd angle. They may become irritable when they have to do deskwork or lose interest if they have to follow an activity taking place across the room (Hunt & Marshall, 2002). Any of these signs should be reported to a qualified school professional.

Special materials and equipment that help these students to function in regular classrooms include large-print books; software that converts printed material to speech or to braille; personal organizers (like a Palm) that have talking appointment books or address books; variable-speed tape recorders (allowing teachers to make time-compressed tape recordings, which speed up the rate of speech without changing the voice pitch); special calculators; an abacus; three-dimensional maps, charts, and models; and special measuring devices. For students with visual problems, the quality of the print is often more important than the size, so watch out for hard-to-read handouts and blurry copies.

The arrangement of the room is also an issue. Students with visual problems need to know where things are, so consistency matters—a place for everything and everything in its place. Leave plenty of space for moving around the room and make sure to monitor possible obstacles and safety hazards such as trash cans in aisles and open cabinet doors. If you rearrange the room, give students with visual problems a chance to learn the new layout. Make sure the students have a buddy for fire drills or other emergencies (Friend & Bursuck, 2002).

Autism Spectrum Disorders

You may be familiar with the term "autism." In 1990, **autism** was added to the IDEA list of disabilities qualifying for special services. It is defined as "a developmental disability significantly affecting verbal and nonverbal communication and social interaction, generally evident before age three, that adversely affects the child's educational performance"

Connect and **Extend** to the **Web**

The Instructional Materials Reference Center of the American Printing House for the Blind (http://www.aph.org/) has catalogs of instructional materials for students with visual impairments.

Low vision Vision limited to close objects.

Educationally blind Needing Braille materials in order to learn.

Autism/Autism Spectrum Disorders Developmental disability significantly affecting verbal and nonverbal communication and social interaction, generally evident before age 3 and ranging from mild to major.

(34 Federal Code of Regulations § 300.7). I have used the term preferred by professionals in the field, "**autism spectrum disorders,**" to emphasize that autism includes a range of disorders from mild to major. From an early age, children with autism spectrum disorders may have difficulties in social relations. They do not form connections with others, avoid eye contact, or don't share feelings such as enjoyment or interest with others. Communication is impaired. About half of these students are nonverbal; they have very few or no language skills. Others make up their own language. They may obsessively insist on regularity and sameness in their environments—change is very disturbing. They may repeat behaviors and have restricted interests, watching the same DVD over and over, for example. They may be very sensitive to light, sound, touch, or other sensory information—sounds may be painful, for example. They may be able to memorize words or steps in problem solving, but not use them appropriately or be very confused when the situation changes or questions are asked in a different way (Friend, 2006).

Asperger syndrome is one of the disabilities included in the autistic spectrum. These children have many of the characteristics described above, but their greatest trouble is with social relations. Language is less affected. Their speech may be fluent, but unusual, mixing up pronouns of "I" and "you," for example (Friend, 2006). Many students with autism also have moderate-to-severe intellectual disabilities, but those with Asperger syndrome usually have average-to-above average-intelligence.

Theory of Mind. One current explanation for autism and Asperger syndrome is that children with these disorders lack a theory of mind—an understanding that they and other people have minds, thoughts, and emotions. They have difficulty explaining their own behaviors, appreciating that other people might have different feelings, and predicting how behaviors might affect emotions. So, for example, a student may not understand why classmates are bored by his constant repetition of stories or obscure facts about topics he finds fascinating. Or the student may stand too close or too far away when interacting, not realizing that she is making other people uncomfortable (Friend, 2006).

Interventions. Early and intense interventions that focus on communication and social relations are particularly important for children with autism spectrum disorders. As they move into elementary school, some of these students will be in inclusive settings, others in specialized classes, and many in some combination of these two. Collaboration among teachers and the family is particularly important. Supports such as smaller classes, structured environments, providing a safe "home base" for times of stress, consistency in instruction, assistive technologies, and the use of visual supports may be part of a collaborative plan (Friend, 2006). Through adolescence and the transition to adulthood, life, work, and social skills are important educational goals.

We end the chapter with another group that has special needs, but is not covered by IDEIA or Section 504—highly intelligent or talented students.

Students Who Are Gifted and Talented

Consider this situation, a true story.

> Latoya was already an advanced reader when she entered 1st grade in a large urban school district. Her teacher noticed the challenging chapter books Latoya brought to school and read with little effort. After administering a reading assessment, the school's reading consultant confirmed that Latoya was reading at the 5th grade level. Latoya's parents reported with pride that she had started to read independently when she was 3 years old and "had read every book she could get her hands on." (Reis et al., 2002)

In her struggling urban school, Latoya received no particular accommodations, and by 5th grade, she was still reading at just above the 5th grade level. Her 5th grade teacher had no idea that Latoya had ever been an advanced reader.

Latoya is not alone. There is a group with special needs that is often overlooked by the schools: **gifted and talented students.** In the past, providing an enriched education

Gifted student A very bright, creative, and talented student.

for extremely bright or talented students was seen as undemocratic and elitist. Now, there is a growing recognition that gifted students are being poorly served by most public schools. A national survey found that more than one-half of all gifted students do not achieve in school at a level equal to their ability (Tomlinson-Keasey, 1990). In 1988, the federal government passed the Gifted and Talented Students Education Act that recognized that these students need special services, but the law did not require states to provide services that would enable students like Latoya to get an appropriate education.

Who Are These Students?

There are many definitions of gifted because individuals can have many different gifts. Remember that Gardner (2003) identified eight separate "intelligences" and Sternberg (1997) suggests a triarchic model. Renzulli and Reis (2003) have a different three-part conception of giftedness: above-average general ability, a high level of creativity, and a high level of task commitment or motivation to achieve. One of the most inclusive definitions comes from the U.S. Department of Education (1993):

> Children and youth with outstanding talent perform or show the potential for performing at remarkably high levels of accomplishment when compared with others of their age, experience, or environment. These children and youth exhibit high capability in intellectual, creative, and/or artistic areas, possess an unusual leadership capacity, or excel in specific academic fields. They require services or activities not ordinarily provided by the schools. Outstanding talents are present in children and youth from all cultural groups, across all economic strata, and in all areas of human endeavor. (p. 26)

Truly gifted children are not the students who simply learn quickly with little effort. The work of gifted students is original, extremely advanced for their age, and potentially of lasting importance. These children may read fluently with little instruction by age 3 or 4. They may play a musical instrument like a skillful adult, turn a visit to the grocery store into a mathematical puzzle, and become fascinated with algebra when their friends are having trouble carrying in addition (Winner, 2000). Recent conceptions widen the view of giftedness to include attention to the children's culture, language, and exceptionalities (Association for the Gifted, 2001). These newer conceptions are more likely to identify children like Charelle in the *Stories of Learning/Tributes to Teaching* feature.

Connect and **Extend** to the **Research**

A follow-up of Terman subjects 60 years later found that Terman's subjects who were popular and outgoing as children were less likely to maintain serious intellectual interests as adults. The authors of the study speculate that an active social life may divert interest away from intellectual pursuits (Tomlinson-Keasey & Little, 1990). In fact, gifted children tend to be introverted—they don't mind being alone and may even need solitude to develop their talents (Winner, 2000). Every path has its benefits and its liabilities for the individual.

STORIES OF LEARNING
TRIBUTES TO TEACHING

"Charelle seems to be hungry, not so much for food as for knowledge."

CHARELLE is an African American student in the third grade, on free lunch, homeless for much of the year, and much loved and supported by both parents. Her mother is a housekeeper in a local hospital. Her father "flips burgers" (her words) at a fast-food restaurant. Now in housing in a different school zone, Charelle still attends the school in which she began, because her mother makes the long bus ride with Charelle, continuing on to her own job via public transportation. Charelle is often as much as an hour late for class because of the extended bus ride, but when she arrives in her classroom, she becomes immediately absorbed in her schoolwork. Charelle's teacher feels the long ride seems worthwhile to Charelle's parents because the school has been nurturing to the family, and that Project START "may have been the icing on the cake (that kept them coming)."

Charelle seems to be hungry, not so much for food as for knowledge. She often asks for extra schoolwork to do at home. Her current teacher calls her "a joy. I feel lucky to have her in my class. There are few children intrinsically motivated like Charelle. She's a real big ham. She would act out anything. She's just kind of bright and bubbly and effervescent and gregarious. She writes. She loves to tell stories. She's a good leader in a group. Not as a forceful leader, but she coaches, like, 'Well, maybe we should do this.' She's blown the doors off math in here. I have her well into fourth-grade math." Charelle's second-grade teacher echoes, "She's very talented in writing and reading. She is very creative, good in art, good in all subjects." The teacher points out a piece of Charelle's artwork, which is permanently displayed in the school corridor.

For resources on gifted students, see the Johns Hopkins University Center for Talented Youth: http://www.jhu.edu/~gifted/

Source: From "Challenging Expectations: Case Studies of High Potential, Culturally Diverse Young Children," by C. Tomlinson, C. Callahan, and K. Lelli, *Gifted Child Quarterly, 41*(2), pp. 5–17. Reprinted by permission of the National Association of Gifted Children.

What do we know about these remarkable individuals? A classic study of the characteristics of the academically and intellectually gifted was started decades ago by Lewis Terman and colleagues (1925, 1947, 1959; Holahan & Sears, 1995). This huge project is following the lives of 1,528 gifted males and females and will continue until the year 2010. The subjects all have IQ scores in the top 1% of the population (140 or above on the Stanford-Binet individual test of intelligence). They were identified on the basis of these test scores and teacher recommendations.

Terman and colleagues found that these gifted children were larger, stronger, and healthier than the norm. They often walked sooner and were more athletic. They were more emotionally stable than their peers and became better-adjusted adults than the average individual. They had lower rates of delinquency, emotional difficulty, divorce, drug problems, and so on. Of course, the teachers in Terman's study who made the nominations may have selected students who were better adjusted initially. And remember, Terman's study just tells about academically gifted students. There are many other kinds of gifts.

What Is the Origin of These Gifts? For years, researchers have debated the nature/nurture question about people with extraordinary abilities and talents. As usual, there is evidence that it takes both. Studies of prodigies and geniuses in many fields document that deep and prolonged practice is necessary to achieve at the highest levels. For example, it took Newton 20 years to move from his first ideas to his ultimate contribution (Howe, Davidson, & Sloboda, 1998; Winner, 2000).

I remember listening to the early reports of Bloom's study of talent (1982). His research team had interviewed, among others, the top tennis players in the world, their coaches, parents, siblings, and friends. One coach said that he would make a suggestion, and a few days later the young athlete would have mastered the move. Then the parents told how the child had practiced that move for hours on end after getting the coach's tip. So, focused, intense practice plays a role. Also, the families of prodigies tend to be child-centered and to devote hours to supporting the development of their child's gifts. Bloom's research team described tremendous sacrifices made by families: rising before dawn to drive their child to a coach in another city, working two jobs, or even moving the whole family to another part of the country to find the best teachers or coaches. The children responded to the family's sacrifices by working harder and the families responded to the child's hard work by sacrificing more—an upward spiral of investment and achievement.

But hard work will never make me a world-class tennis player or a Newton. There is a role for nature as well. The children studied by Bloom showed early and clear talent in the areas they later developed. As children, great sculptors were constantly drawing and mathematicians were fascinated with dials, gears, and gauges. Parents' investments in their children came after the children showed early high-level achievement (Winner, 2000; 2003). Recent research suggests that gifted children, at least those with extraordinary abilities in mathematics, music, and visual arts, may have unusual brain organization—which can have both advantages and disadvantages. Giftedness in mathematics, music, and visual arts appears to be associated with superior visual-spatial abilities and enhanced development of the right side of the brain. Children with these gifts are also more likely not to have right-hand dominance and to have language related-problems. These brain differences are evidence that "gifted children, child prodigies, and savants are not made from scratch but are born with unusual brains that enable rapid learning in a particular domain" (Winner, 2000, p. 160).

What Problems Do the Gifted Face? In spite of Bloom's and Terman's findings, it would be incorrect to say that every gifted student is superior in adjustment and emotional health. In fact, gifted adolescents, especially girls, are more likely to be depressed and to report social and emotional problems (Berk, 2005). Many difficulties confront a gifted child, including boredom and frustration in school as well as isolation (sometimes even ridicule) from peers. Schoolmates may be consumed with baseball or worried about failing math, while the gifted child is fascinated with Mozart, focused on a social issue, or totally absorbed in computers, drama, or geology. Gifted children may be impatient with friends, parents, and even teachers who do not share their interests or abilities. Because their language is well developed, they may be seen as show-offs when they are simply expressing themselves. They are sensitive to the expectations and feelings of others, so these students may be very vulnerable to criticisms and taunts. Because they are goal-directed and focused, they may seem stubborn and uncooperative. Their keen sense of humor can be used as a weapon against teachers and other students. Adjustment problems seem to be greatest for the most gifted, those in the highest range of academic ability (e.g., above 180 IQ) (Hardman, Drew, & Egan, 2005; Robinson & Clinkenbeard, 1998).

Identifying and Teaching Gifted Students

WHAT WOULD YOU SAY?

Another job interview question: Describe a learning activity that you have planned for a class and ways that you have accommodated individual learning needs. ■

Identifying gifted children is not always easy, and teaching them well may be even more challenging. Many parents provide early educational experiences for their children. Even very advanced reading ability in the early grades does not guarantee that students will still be outstanding readers years later (Mills & Jackson, 1990). In junior high and high school, some very able students deliberately earn lower grades, making their abilities even harder to recognize. Girls are especially likely to hide their abilities (Berk, 2005).

Recognizing Gifts and Talents. Teachers are successful only about 10% to 50% of the time in picking out the gifted children in their classes (Fox, 1981). Here are a few questions to guide identification, suggested by Marilyn Friend (2005). Who can easily manipulate abstract symbol systems such as mathematics? Who can concentrate for long periods of time on personal interests? Who remembers easily? Who developed language and reading early, like Latoya described at the beginning of this section? Who is curious and has many interests? Whose work is original and creative? These students may also prefer to work alone, have a keen sense of justice and fairness, be energetic and intense, form strong commitments to friends—often older students, and struggle with perfectionism.

Group achievement and intelligence test tend to underestimate the IQs of very bright children. Group tests may be appropriate for screening, but they are not appropriate for making placement decisions. Many psychologists recommend a case study approach to identifying gifted students. This means gathering many kinds of information about the student in different contexts: test scores, grades, examples of work, projects and portfolios, letters or ratings from community or church members, self-ratings, nominations from teachers or peers, and so on (Renzulli & Reis, 2003; Sisk, 1988). Especially for recognizing artistic talent, experts in the field can be called in to judge the merits of a child's creations. Science projects, exhibitions, performances, auditions and interviews are all possibilities. Creativity tests may identify some children not picked up by other measures, particularly minority students who may be at a disadvantage on the other types of tests (Maker, 1987). Remember, students with remarkable abilities in one area may have much less impressive abilities in others. In fact, there may be up to 180,000 students in American schools who are gifted and learning disabled (Davis & Rimm, 1985).

Teaching Gifted Students. Some educators believe that gifted students should be accelerated—moved quickly through the grades or through particular subjects. Other educators prefer enrichment—giving the students additional, more sophisticated, and more thought-provoking work, but keeping them with their age-mates in school. Actually, both may be appropriate (Torrance, 1986). One way of doing this is through *curriculum compacting*—assessing students' knowledge of the material in the instructional unit, then

Connect and **Extend** to the **Research**

The September 2001 issue of *Psychology in the Schools* has several articles on identifying and teaching underrepresented gifted students.

Connect and **Extend** to the **Research**

There are three groups of students who are underrepresented in gifted education programs: women, students with learning disabilities, and students living in poverty (Stormont, Stebbins, & Holliday, 2001).

Girls and Giftedness

As young girls develop their identities in adolescence, they often reject being labeled as gifted—being accepted and popular—"fitting in" may become more important than achievement (Basow & Rubin, 1999; Stormont et al., 2001). How can teachers reach girls with gifts? Here are some ideas:

- Notice when girls' test scores seem to decline in middle or high school.
- Encourage assertiveness, achievement, high goals, and demanding work from all students.
- Provide models of achievement through speakers, internships, or readings.
- Look for and support gifts in arenas other than academic achievement.

Gifted Students with Learning Disabilities: Twice-Exceptional

Here are some ideas for supporting twice-exceptional students (McCoach, Kehle, Bray, & Siegle, 2001):

- Identify these students by looking longitudinally at achievement.
- Remediate skill deficits, but also identify and develop talents and strengths.
- Provide emotional support; it is important for all students, but especially for this group.
- Help students learn to compensate directly for their learning problems, and assist them in "tuning in" to their own strengths and difficulties.

TABLE 4.14

Examples of How to Modify Content for Students with Gifts and Talents

	Subject			
Modification	***Math***	***Science***	***Language Arts***	***Social Studies***
Acceleration	Algebra in fifth grade	Early chemistry and physics	Learning grammatical structure early	Early introduction to world history
Enrichment	Changing bases in number systems	Experimentation and data collecting	Short story and poetry writing	Reading biographies for historical insight
Sophistication	Mastering the laws of arithmetic	Learning the laws of physics	Mastering the structural properties of plays, sonnets, and so on	Learning and applying the principles of economics
Novelty	Probability and statistics	Science and its impact on society	Rewriting Shakespeare's tragedies with happy endings	Creating future societies and telling how they are governed

Gifted Students who Live in Poverty

Health problems, lack of resources, homelessness, fears about safety and survival, frequent moves, and responsibilities for the care of other family members all make achievement in school more difficult. To identify student with gifts:

- Use alternative assessment, teacher nomination, and creativity tests.
- Be sensitive to cultural differences in values about cooperative or solitary achievement (Ford, 2000).
- Use multicultural strategies to encourage both achievement and the development of racial identities.

teaching only for those goals not yet reached. The time saved can be used for learning goals that include enrichment, sophistication, and novelty (Reis & Renzulli, 2004). Look at Table 4.14 to see examples of how content can be modified through acceleration, enrichment, sophistication, and novelty.

Many people object to acceleration, but most careful studies indicate that truly gifted students who begin primary, elementary, middle, high school, college, or even graduate school early do as well as, and usually better than, nongifted students who are progressing at the normal pace. Social and emotional adjustment does not appear to be impaired. Gifted students tend to prefer the company of older playmates and may be miserably bored if kept with children of their own age. Skipping grades may not be the best solution for a particular student, but it does not deserve the bad reputation it has received (Jones & Southern, 1991; Kulik & Kulik, 1984; Richardson & Benbow, 1990). An alternative to skipping grades is to accelerate students in one or two particular subjects or allow concurrent enrollment in advanced placement courses, but keep them with peers for most classes (Robinson & Clinkenbeard, 1998). For students who are extremely advanced intellectually (for example, those scoring 160 or higher on an individual intelligence test), the only practical solution may be to accelerate their education (Hardman, Drew, & Egan, 2005; Hunt & Marshall, 2002).

Teaching methods for gifted students should encourage abstract thinking (formal-operational thought), creativity, reading of high-level and original texts, and independence, not just the learning of greater quantities of facts. One approach that does *not* seem promising with gifted students is cooperative learning in mixed-ability groups. Gifted students tend to learn more when they work in groups with other high-ability peers (Fuchs, Fuchs, Hamlett, & Karns, 1998; Robinson & Clinkenbeard, 1998). In working with gifted and talented students, a teacher must be imaginative, flexible, tolerant, and unthreatened by the capabilities of these students. The teacher must ask: What do these children need most? What are they ready to learn? Who can help me to challenge them? Challenge and support are critical for all students. But challenging students who know more than anyone else in the school about history or music or science or math can be a challenge! Answers might come from faculty members at nearby colleges, retired professionals, books, museums, or older students. Strategies might be as simple as letting the child do math with the next grade. Other options are summer institutes; courses at nearby colleges; classes with local artists, musicians, or dancers; independent research projects; selected classes in high school for younger students; honors classes; and special-interest clubs (Mitchell, 1984).

TABLE 4.15

Making a Referral

1. Contact the student's parents. It is very important that you discuss the student's problems with the parents *before* you refer.
2. Before making a referral, check *all* the student's school records. Has the student ever:
   - had a psychological evaluation?
   - qualified for special services?
   - been included in other special programs (e.g., for disadvantaged children; speech or language therapy)?
   - scored far below average on standardized tests?
   - been retained?

   Do the records indicate:
   - good progress in some areas, poor progress in others?
   - any physical or medical problem?
   - that the student is taking medication?
3. Talk to the student's other teachers and professional support personnel about your concern for the student. Have other teachers also had difficulty with the student? Have they found ways of dealing successfully with the student? Document the strategies that you have used in your class to meet the student's educational needs. Your documentation will be useful as evidence that will be helpful to or be required by the committee of professionals who will evaluate the student. Demonstrate your concern by keeping written records. Your notes should include items such as:
   - exactly what you are concerned about
   - why you are concerned about it
   - dates, places, and times you have observed the problem
   - precisely what you have done to try to resolve the problem
   - who, if anyone, helped you devise the plans or strategies you have used
   - evidence that the strategies have been successful or unsuccessful

Remember that you should refer a student only if you can make a convincing case that the student may have a handicapping condition and probably cannot be served appropriately without special education. Referral for special education begins a time-consuming, costly, and stressful process that is potentially damaging to the student and has many legal ramifications.

Source: From *What Should I Know about Special Education? Answers for Classroom Teachers,* by P. L. Pullen & J. M. Kauffman, 1987. Copyright © 1987 PRO-ED, Austin, Texas. Reprinted by permission.

In the midst of providing challenge, don't forget the support. We all have seen the ugly sights of parents, coaches, or teachers forcing the joy out of their talented students by demanding practice and perfection beyond the child's interest. Just as we should not force children to stop investing in their talent ("Oh, Michaelangelo, quit fooling with those sketches and go outside and play"), we also should avoid destroying intrinsic motivation with heavy doses of pressure and external rewards.

This has been a brief, selective look at the needs of children. If you decide that students in your class might benefit from special services of any kind, the first step is making a referral. How would you begin? Table 4.15 guides you through the referral process. In Chapter 12, when we discuss effective teaching, we will look at more ways to reach all your students.

Diversity and Convergences in Learning Abilities

Diversity

Even though there are many good tests and careful procedures for making special education placement decisions, racial and ethnic minority students are overrepresented in the disability categories and underrepresented in gifted programs. For example, almost 20% of all students defined as having disabilities under IDEIA are African American, but only 15% of all students are African American. The overrepresentation is worse when we look at specific categories: 34% of all students identified as having intellectual disabilities/mental retardation and 27% of students identified as having emotional disturbance are African American—twice as many as we would expect based on the percentage of African American students in the United States. And these students are more likely than White or Asian students to be placed outside of the general education system for most of their school day. In contrast, African American and Latina/o students make up only about 8% each of the students served in gifted and talented programs (Friend, 2006).

For almost four decades, educators have struggled to understand the causes of these over- and underrepresentations. Explanations include the higher poverty rates among African American and Latina/o families, which lead to poorer prenatal care, nutrition, and health care; systematic biases in teachers' attitudes, curriculum, instruction, and the referral process itself; and lack of preparation for teachers to work effectively with ethnic minority students (Friend, 2006). To deal with the referral problem, educators have recommended gathering more information about a student before a formal referral is made. How long has the student been in the United States? What about proficiency with English? Are there unusual stressors such as being homeless? Does the curriculum build on the student's funds of cultural knowledge (Chapter 3)? Is the classroom culturally compatible (Chapter 5) and engaging (Chapter 11)? Is the teacher knowledgeable about and respectful of the student's culture? Can the student's abilities be assessed through alternative approaches such as creativity tests and portfolios or performances (Chapter 15)? Having more knowledge about the student and his or her circumstances outside of school should help teachers make better decisions about what programs are appropriate (Friend, 2006; Gonzales, Brusca-Vega, & Yawkey, 1997; National Alliance of Black School Educators, 2002). In fact, instruction should be differentiated to better match the needs of all students, as we will see in Chapter 13.

Convergences

This chapter is about diversity—the many differences among individuals in abilities and disabilities, learning styles and preferences, strengths and challenges. But even with this diversity, differences among individuals are very small compared to all the characteristics we share. Take race for example. For any two humans chosen at random, an average of only .012% (about one-hundredth of one percent) of the alphabetic sequence of their genetic codes is different due to race (Myers, 2005).

Another convergence should be in the uses of testing. We saw that intelligence tests originally were developed, in part, to protect the rights of children from poorer families who might be denied an education on the false grounds that they weren't able to learn. We also saw that intelligence tests predict school success similarly for students of different races and income levels. Even so, these tests can never be free of cultural content, so they always will have some biases built in. Keep this in mind when you see your students' scores on any test. Finally, remember that the results of every assessment for every student should be used to support that student's learning and development and to identify effective practices, not to deny the student resources or appropriate teaching.

Connect and **Extend** to Your **Teaching Portfolio**

Students with AIDS can have many of the problems discussed in this chapter: intellectual disabilities, attention-deficit hyperactivity disorder, seizures, neurological impairments similar to cerebral palsy, behavior disorders, and so on. Most states have policies that emphasize the education of children with AIDS in the regular classroom.

SUMMARY TABLE

Intelligence (pp. 110–121)

What are the advantages of and problems with labels? Labels and diagnostic classifications of exceptional students can easily become both stigmas and self-fulfilling prophecies, but they can also open doors to special programs and help teachers develop appropriate instructional strategies.

What is person-first language? "Person-first" language ("students with intellectual disabilities," "students placed at risk," etc.) is an alternative to labels that describe a complex person with one or two words, implying that the condition labeled is the most important aspect of the person. With person-first language, the emphasis is on the students first, not on the special challenges they face.

Distinguish between a disability and a handicap. A disability is an inability to do something specific such as see or walk. A handicap is a disadvantage in certain situations. Some disabilities lead to handicaps, but not in all contexts. Teachers must avoid imposing handicaps on disabled learners.

What is *g*? Spearman suggested there is one mental attribute, which he called g or general intelligence, that is used to perform any mental test, but that each test also requires some specific abilities in addition to g. A current version of the general plus specific abilities theory is Carroll's work identifying a few broad abilities (such as learning and memory, visual perception, verbal fluency) and at least 70 specific abilities. Fluid and crystallized intelligence are two of the broad abilities identified in most research.

What is Gardner's view of intelligence and his position on *g*? Gardner contends that an intelligence is a biological and psychological potential to solve problems and create outcomes that are valued by a culture. These intelligences are realized to a greater or lesser extent as a consequence of the experiential, cultural, and motivational factors in a person's environment. The intelligences are: linguistic, musical, spatial, logical-mathematical, bodily-kinesthetic, interpersonal, intrapersonal, naturalist, and perhaps existential. Gardner does not deny the existence of g, but questions how useful g is as an explanation for human achievements. The concept of emotional intelligence, or EQ, is similar to Gardner's intrapersonal and interpersonal intelligences.

What are the elements in Sternberg's theory of intelligence? Sternberg's triarchic theory of intelligence is a cognitive process approach to understanding intelligence: Analytic/componential intelligence involves mental processes that are defined in terms of components: metacomponents, performance components, and knowledge-acquisition components. Creative/experiential intelligence involves coping with new experiences through insight and automaticity. Practical/contextual intelligence involves choosing to live and work in a context where success is likely, adapting to that context, and reshaping it if necessary. Practical intelligence is made up mostly of action-oriented tacit knowledge learned during everyday life.

How is intelligence measured, and what does an IQ score mean? Intelligence is measured through individual tests (Stanford-Binet, Wechsler, etc.) and group tests (Cognitive Abilities Test, Analysis of Learning Potential, School and College Ability Tests, etc.). Compared to an individual test, a group test is much less likely to yield an accurate picture of any one person's abilities. The average score is 100. About 68% of the general population will earn IQ scores between 85 and 115. Only about 16% of the population will receive scores below 85 or above 115. These figures hold true for White, native-born Americans whose first language is Standard English. Intelligence predicts success in school, but is less predictive of success in life when level of education is taken into account.

What is the Flynn effect and what are its implications? Since the early 1900s, IQ scores have been rising. To keep 100 as the average for IQ test scores, questions have to be made more difficult. This increasing difficulty has implications for any program that uses IQ scores as part of the entrance requirements. For example, students who were not identified as having intellectual disabilities a generation ago might be identified as disabled now because the test questions are harder.

Exceptional students Students who have abilities or problems so significant that they require special education or other services to reach their potential.

Disorder A broad term meaning a general disturbance in physical or mental functioning,

Disability The inability to do something specific such as walk or hear.

Handicap A disadvantage in a particular situation, sometimes caused by a disability.

Intelligence Ability or abilities to acquire and use knowledge for solving problems and adapting to the world.

Fluid intelligence Mental efficiency, nonverbal abilities grounded in brain development.

Crystallized intelligence Ability to apply culturally approved problem-solving methods.

Theory of multiple intelligences In Gardner's theory of intelligence, a person's eight separate abilities: logical-mathematical, linguistic, musical, spatial, bodily-kinesthetic, interpersonal, intrapersonal, and naturalist.

Emotional intelligence (EQ) The ability to process and use emotional information accurately and efficiently.

Triarchic theory of successful intelligence A three-part description of the mental abilities (thinking processes, coping with new experiences, and adapting to context) that lead to more or less intelligent behavior.

Insight The ability to deal effectively with novel situations.

Automaticity The result of learning to perform a behavior or thinking process so thoroughly that the performance is automatic and does not require effort.

Tacit knowledge Knowing how rather than knowing that—knowledge that is more likely to be learned during everyday life than through formal schooling.

Mental age In intelligence testing, a performance that represents average abilities for that age group.

Intelligence quotient (IQ) Score comparing mental and chronological ages.

Deviation IQ Score based on statistical comparison of an individual's performance with the average performance of others in that age group.

Flynn effect Because of better health, smaller families, increased complexity in the environment, and more and better schooling, IQ test scores are steadily rising.

Ability Differences and Teaching (pp. 121–124)

What are the problems with between-class ability grouping? Academic ability groupings can have both disadvantages and advantages for students and teachers. For low-ability students, however, between-class ability grouping generally has a negative effect on achievement, social adjustment, and self-esteem. Teachers of low-achievement classes tend to emphasize lower-level objectives and routine procedures, with less academic focus. Often, there are more student behavior problems, increased teacher stress, lowered expectations, and decreased enthusiasm. Ability grouping can promote segregation within schools.

What are the alternatives available for grouping in classes, including flexible grouping? Cross-age grouping by subject can be an effective way to deal with ability differences in a school. Within-class ability grouping, if handled sensitively and flexibly, can have positive effects, but alternatives such as cooperative learning may be better.

Between-class ability grouping/tracking System of grouping in which students are assigned to classes based on their measured ability or their achievements.

Untracking Redesigning schools to teach students in classes that are not grouped by ability.

The Joplin Plan/nongraded elementary school Arrangement wherein students are grouped by ability in particular subjects, regardless of their ages or grades.

Within-class ability grouping System of grouping in which students in a class are divided into two or three groups based on ability in an attempt to accommodate student differences.

Flexible grouping Grouping and regrouping students based on learning needs.

Learning Styles and Preferences (pp. 124–127)

Distinguish between learning styles and learning preferences. Learning styles are the characteristic ways a person approaches learning and studying. Learning preferences are individual preferences for particular learning modes and environments. Even though learning styles and learning preferences are not related to intelligence or effort, they can affect school performance.

Should teachers match instruction to individual learning styles? Results of some research indicate that students learn more when they study in their preferred setting and manner, but most research does not show a benefit. Many students would do better to develop new—and perhaps more effective—ways to learn.

What learning style distinctions are the most well-supported by research? One distinction that is repeatedly found in research is deep versus surface processing. Individuals who have a *deep-processing approach* see the learning activities as a means for understanding some underlying concepts or meanings. Students who take a *surface-processing* approach focus on memorizing the learning materials, not understanding them. A second is Mayer's visualizer–verbalizer dimension that it has three facets: *cognitive spatial ability* (low or high), *cognitive style* (a visualizer vs. a verbalizer), and *learning preference* (a verbal learner vs. a visual learner).

Learning styles Characteristic approaches to learning and studying.

Learning preferences Preferred ways of studying and learning, such as using pictures instead of text, working with other people versus alone, learning in structured or in unstructured situations, and so on.

Individual Differences and the Law (pp. 127–130)

Describe the main legal requirements that pertain to students with disabilities. Beginning with Public Law 94-142 (1975) and continuing with many reauthorizations including the Individuals with Disabilities Education Improvement Act (2004), the requirements for teaching students with disabilities are spelled out. Each exceptional learner or student with special needs (zero reject) should be educated in the least restrictive environment according to an individualized education program (IEP). The laws also protect the rights of students with special needs and their parents. In addition, Section 504 of the Vocational Rehabilitation Act of 1973 prevents discrimination against people with disabilities in any program that receives federal money, such as public schools. Through Section 504, all school-age children are ensured an equal opportunity to participate in school activities. The definition of "disability" is broad in Section 504 and in the Americans with Disabilities Act.

Individuals with Disabilities Education Improvement Act (IDEIA) Latest amendment of PL 94-142, guarantees a free public education to all children regardless of disability.

Zero reject A basic principle of IDEIA specifying that no student with a disability, no matter what kind or how severe, can be denied a free public education.

Individualized Education Program (IEP) Annually revised program for an exceptional student, detailing present achievement level, goals, and strategies, drawn up by teachers, parents, specialists, and (if possible) the student.

Least Restrictive Environment (LRE) Educating each child with peers in the regular classroom to the greatest extent possible.

Mainstreaming Teaching children with disabilities in regular classes for part or all of their school day.

Integration Fitting the child with special needs into existing class structures.

Inclusion The integration of all students, including those with severe disabilities, into regular classes.

Section 504 A part of civil rights law that prevents discrimination against people with disabilities in programs that receive federal funds, such as public schools.

Americans with Disabilities Act of 1900 (ADA) Federal legislation prohibiting discrimination against persons with disabilities in employment, transportation, public access, local government, and telecommunications.

The Most Common Challenges (pp. 130–145)

What is a learning disability? Specific learning disabilities are disorders in one or more of the basic psychological processes involved in understanding or using spoken or written language. Listening, speaking, reading, writing, reasoning, or mathematical abilities might be affect-ed. These disorders are intrinsic to the individual, presumed to be the result of central nervous system dysfunction, and may occur across the life span. Students with learning disabilities may become victims of learned helplessness when they come to believe that they cannot control or improve their own learning and therefore cannot succeed. A focus on learning strategies often helps students with learning disabilities.

What is ADHD and how is it handled in school? Attention-deficit hyperactivity disorder (ADHD) is the term used to describe individuals of any age with hyperactivity and attention difficulties. Use of medication to address ADHD is controversial, but currently on the rise. For many students there are negative side effects. In addition, little is known about the long-term effects of drug therapy. There also is no evidence that the drugs lead to improvement in academic learning or peer relationships. Two promising approaches are behavior modification and techniques that combine motivational training with instruction in learning and memory strategies. The SMART approach that focuses on the abilities of children is another possibility.

What are the most common communication disorders? Common communication disorders include speech impairments (articulation disorders, stuttering, and voicing problems) and oral language disorders. If these problems are addressed early, great progress is possible.

What defines intellectual disabilities? Before age 18, students must score below about 70 on a standard measure of intelligence and must have problems with adaptive behavior, day-to-day independent living, and social functioning.

What are the best approaches for students with emotional and behavorial disorders? Methods from applied behavioral analysis and direct teaching of social skills are two useful approaches. Students also may respond to structure and organization in the environment, schedules, activities, and rules.

What are some warning signs of potential suicide? Students at risk of suicide may show changes in eating or sleeping habits, weight, grades, disposition, activity level, or interest in friends. They sometimes suddenly give away prized possessions such as stereos, CDs, clothing, or pets. They may seem depressed or hyperactive and may start missing school or quit doing work. It is especially dangerous if the student not only talks about suicide, but also has a plan for carrying it out.

Learning disability Problem with acquisition and use of language; may show up as difficulty with reading, writing, reasoning, and math.

Learned helplessness The expectation, based on previous experiences with a lack of control, that all one's efforts will lead to failure.

Attention-deficit hyperactivity disorder Current term for disruptive behavior disorders marked by overactivity, excessive difficulty sustaining attention, or impulsiveness.

Speech disorder Inability to produce sounds effectively for speaking.

Articulation disorders Any of a variety of pronunciation difficulties, such as the substitution, distortion, or omission of sounds.

Voicing problems Inappropriate pitch, quality, loudness, and intonation.

Intellectual disabilities/mental retardation Significantly below-average intellectual and adaptive social behavior, evident before age 18.

Transition programming Gradual preparation of exceptional students to move from high school into further education or training, employment, or community involvement.

Emotional and behavioral disorders Behaviors or emotions that deviate so much from the norm that they interfere with the child's own growth and development and/or the lives of others—inappropriate behaviors, unhappiness or depression, fears and anxieties, and trouble with relationships.

Less Prevalent Problems/More Severe Disabilities (pp. 145–148)

How can schools accommodate the needs of students with physical disabilities? If the school has the necessary architectural features, such as ramps, elevators, and accessible rest rooms, and if teachers allow for the physical limitations of students, little needs to be done to alter the usual educational program. Identifying a peer to help with movements and transitions can be useful.

How would you handle a seizure in class? Do not restrain the child's movements. Lower the child gently to the floor, away from furniture or walls. Move hard objects away. Turn the child's head gently to the side, put a soft coat or blanket under the student's head, and loosen any tight clothing. Never put anything in the student's mouth. Find out from the student's parents how they deal with seizures. If one seizure follows another and the student does not regain consciousness in between, if the student is pregnant, or if the seizure goes on for more than 5 minutes, get medical help right away.

What are some signs of hearing and visual impairment? Signs of hearing problems are turning one ear toward the speaker, favoring one ear in conversation, or misunderstanding conversation when the speaker's face cannot be seen. Other indications include not following directions, seeming distracted or confused at times, frequently asking people to repeat what they have said, mispronouncing new words or names, and being reluctant to participate in class discussions.

Take note particularly of students who have frequent earaches, sinus infections, or allergies. Holding books very close or far away, squinting, rubbing eyes, misreading the chalkboard, and holding the head at an odd angle are possible signs of visual problems.

How does autism differ from Asperger syndrome? Asperger syndrome is one of the autism spectrum disorders. Many students with autism also have moderate-to-severe intellectual disabilities, but those with Asperger syndrome usually have average-to-above-average intelligence and better language abilities than other children with autism.

Cerebral Palsy Condition involving a range of motor or coordination difficulties due to brain damage.

Spasticity Overly tight or tense muscles, characteristic of some forms of cerebral palsy.

Epilepsy Disorder marked by seizures and caused by abnormal electrical discharges in the brain.

Generalized seizure/tonic-clonic seizure A seizure involving a large portion of the brain.

Absence seizure A seizure involving only a small part of the brain that causes a child to lose contact briefly.

Low vision: Vision limited to close objects.

Educationally blind Needing Braille materials in order to learn.

Autism/Autism Spectrum Disorders Developmental disability significantly affecting verbal and nonverbal communication and social interaction, generally evident before age 3 and ranging from mild to major.

Students Who Are Gifted and Talented

(pp. 148–153)

What are the characteristics of gifted students? Gifted students learn easily and rapidly and retain what they have learned; use common sense and practical knowledge; know about many things that the other children don't; use a large number of words easily and accurately; recognize relations and comprehend meaning; are alert and keenly observant and respond quickly; are persistent and highly motivated on some tasks; and are creative or make interesting connections. Teachers should make special efforts to support underrepresented gifted students—girls, students who also have learning disabilities, and children living in poverty.

Is acceleration a useful approach with gifted students? Many people object to acceleration, but most careful studies indicate that truly gifted students who are accelerated do as well as, and usually better than, nongifted students who are progressing at the normal pace. Gifted students tend to prefer the company of older playmates and may be bored if kept with children their own age. Skipping grades may not be the best solution for a particular student, but for students who are extremely advanced intellectually (with a score of 160 or higher on an individual intelligence test), the only practical solution may be to accelerate their education.

Gifted student A very bright, creative, and talented student.

Teachers' Casebook: Connections to PRAXIS II™

Over the school year, teachers make thousands of decisions based on knowledge of intelligence, academic ability, grouping practices, learning disabilities, giftedness, physical disabilities, and state and federal legislation. In fact, most licensure exams, including PRAXIS II™, will require you to be knowledgeable about intelligence, ability grouping practices, learning styles, inclusion, and the legal requirements of IDEIA.

This chapter opens with a situation that would challenge even the most seasoned teacher. Your first class may well pose similar challenges.

What Would They Do?

Here is how some practicing teachers responded to the wide range of abilities and disabilities in the class described at the beginning of the chapter.

Deborah P. Reed

Darby Woods Elementary School, Galloway, OH

Thomas G. Reed

Beechcroft High School Columbus, OH

Structuring a standards-based program for diverse learners and learners with special needs begins with carefully designed pre-assessment activities that accurately determine existing levels of student achievement and mirror assessment techniques commonly used on state-adopted achievement tests.

Daily instruction should be designed so that all students participate in all facets of learning activities and use short-cycle formative assessments such as running records and writing samples scored on rubrics that serve as ongoing indicators of student growth in reading and math, subject areas specifically targeted by No Child Left Behind and measured as annual yearly progress.

When necessary, use multiple grouping schemes to target instruction toward clusters of students with similar learning needs and utilize instructional aides and trusted volunteers to work with individuals and small groups. When other adults are not available, establish collaborative groupings that foster peer-to-peer intervention, allowing students to learn from other students who have demonstrated mastery of specific standards.

Debbie Youngblood **Sixth Grade Wellness and Physical Education Teacher,**

Hilliard City Schools, Hilliard, Ohio

To design a standards-based curriculum that will allow each of the students to learn to their fullest potential and to demonstrate proficiency toward the standards I would begin by acquiring a copy of the current state standards for the core content areas for the grade I am teaching and for one grade above and below, allowing for curriculum mapping of key concepts for the diverse learning needs of all of my students. I would then review achievement test scores for my students to determine areas of strength and deficiency. Next, I would determine whether any of my students had an Individualized Education Plan or a 504 plan. Having determined any accommodations for each student that are necessary by law, I would match the special needs of my students to the appropriate curricular levels and would design teaching methods for each of their abilities. I would enlist the support and recommendations of the English Language Learners' prior teachers to determine best practices and starting places, as well as locating native language interpreters for key communications between school and home. I would determine the extent of the disability for my hearing impaired student, and if possible would continue to provide the accommodations utilized in the past to allow this student to be successful.

Randall G. Sampson **Assistant-Principal,**

Genoa Middle School, Westerville, Ohio

The educational leader (principal/academic coach) must provide an academic assessment for a learning matrix. The matrix provides teachers with a list of individual needs as prescribed by standardized test performance. The matrix can instantly provide teachers with the necessary academic performance data, in order to better and more efficiently meet the academic needs of the students. With such a matrix, teachers would be able to provide a more personalized learning experience while seeking to differentiate instruction for all students. Such practices are essential for identifying and providing for the needs of all students, as mandated by the 2001 No Child Left Behind Act, and meeting the criteria for Annual Yearly Progress.

W. Sean Kearney **Former Assistant Principal,**

Galen R. Elolf Elementary School, Converse, Texas

Know the law, and seek additional training if necessary. Students with special education needs have an individualized education plan that still needs to be followed, even if all services cannot be provided in the classroom. Once you understand the specific needs of your students, seek out training from your district. If not offered by your district, seek out training or resources outside of your district. Pertinent training will improve the quality of the education you will be able to deliver to your students. Finally, work with your colleagues. If this is a new district wide-policy, then the other teachers on your grade level/subject area are in the same boat. Work together throughout the year to prepare lessons and hone strategies that work.

Felicia Lowman-Sikes **Kindergarten Teacher,**

Meadowview Elementary School, Meadowview, VA

I use classroom space to carry out lessons in different ways. This addresses the different learning styles of students while allowing them to participate in the lesson together. I have four different centers in my room that students rotate through, spending fifteen minutes at each center. In my library center, the books are shelved by reading level, which allows those students with special needs to easily find a book that is not too hard to read or focuses on pre-reading skills. In the phonics center, children are given a hands-on activity to help learn letter sounds, such as sorting pictures based on beginning sounds using animal cards. When students go to the vocabulary center, they use new words. Those with special needs may illustrate a picture describing the word of the day, instead of writing and using those words in sentences. They may also spend time making picture dictionaries. Finally, students join me and we work on any concepts that have yet to be mastered. I assign each small group a color, and then place that group's individual work in a corresponding folder. Children with similar needs are grouped together, which allows them to work at their instructional level. This format can easily be changed to fit the needs of math, science, and social studies lessons as well.

CHAPTER 5

Culture and Diversity

Teachers' Casebook: What Would You Do? 161

Today's Diverse Classrooms 162

Individuals, Groups, and Society 162

Multicultural Education 163

American Cultural Diversity 164

Economic and Social Class Differences 165

Social Class and SES 165

Poverty and School Achievement 166

Ethnic and Racial Differences 168

The Changing Demographics: Cultural Differences 168

Ethnic and Racial Differences in School Achievement 170

The Legacy of Discrimination 171

Stereotype Threat 174

Girls and Boys: Differences in the Classroom 176

Sexual Identity 176

Gender-Role Identity 177

Sex Differences in Mental Abilities 180

Eliminating Gender Bias 181

Language Differences in the Classroom 182

Dialects 183

Bilingualism 185

Reaching Every Student: Recognizing Giftedness in Bilingual Students 186

Bilingual Education 187

Creating Culturally Inclusive Classrooms 188

Culturally Relevant Pedagogy 189

Fostering Resilience 191

Diversity and Convergences 195

Diversity in Learning 195

Convergences: Teaching Every Student 198

Summary Table 200

Teachers' Casebook: Connections to PRAXIS II™/What Would They Do? 202

What Would You Do?

Teachers' Casebook

Your high-school classes this year are about equally divided among three groups—African Americans, Asians, and Latinos/as. Students from each of the three groups seem to stick together, rarely making friends with students from "outside." When you ask people to select partners for projects, the divisions are usually on ethnic lines. At times, there are insults exchanged between the groups and the atmosphere of the class is getting tense. Often the Asian or Latino students communicate in their native language—one you don't understand—and you assume that the joke is on you because of the looks and laughs directed your way.

Critical Thinking

- What is the real problem here?
- How would you handle the situation?
- How would you teach the class to help the students feel more comfortable with each other?
- What are your first goals in working on this problem?
- How will these issues affect the grade levels you will teach?

Collaboration

With 4 or 5 other members of your class, brainstorm as many reasonable ways as you can to address this situation. Come to a consensus on the two best solutions and present them to the class, with your rationale for why these are good choices.

The cultural composition of American classrooms is changing. The same can be said for many countries today. In a talk to the American Educational Research Association, Frank Pajares, one of the wisest educational psychologists I know, said, "The critical questions in education involve matters that cannot be settled by universal prescription. They demand attention to the cultural forces that shape our lives" (Pajares, 2000, p. 5). I believe he is right. In this chapter, we examine the many cultures that form the fabric of our society. We begin by tracing the schools' responses to different ethnic and cultural groups and consider the concept of multicultural education. With a broad conception of culture as a basis, we then examine three important dimensions of every student's identity: social class, ethnicity, and gender. Then, we turn to a consideration of language and bilingual education. The last section of the chapter presents three general principles for teaching every student.

By the time you have completed this chapter, you should be able to answer these questions:

- What is the difference between the melting pot and multicultural education?
- What is *culture* and what groups make up your own cultural identity?
- Why does the school achievement of low-income students often fall below that of middle- and upper-income students?
- What are some examples of conflicts and compatibilities between home and school cultures?
- What is the school's role in the development of gender differences?
- What is effective teaching in bilingual classrooms?
- What are examples of culturally relevant pedagogy that fit the grades and subjects you will teach?
- How can you create a resilient classroom?

FACING PAGE *The Storyteller*, 1995, Christian Pierre. Acrylic on canvas.

Today's Diverse Classrooms

Connect and **Extend** to **PRAXIS II™**
Multicultural Education (III, B)
Know the major dimensions of multicultural education. Describe how these dimensions influence each other.

Who are the students in American classrooms today? Here are a few statistics (taken from Banks, 2002; Children's Defense Fund, 2005; Duncan & Brooks-Gunn, 2000; Grant & Sleeter, 1989; Halford, 1999; McLoyd, 1998; Meece & Kurtz-Costes, 2001; Payne & Biddle, 1999):

- 1 in 6 American children lives in poverty and 1 in 14 lives in extreme poverty. Nearly 50% of all African American children are poor.
- The number of children in poverty in the United States is almost 50% higher than in *any other developed Western nation* and 5 to 8 times higher than in many prominent industrialized nations.
- Children growing up in poverty are twice as likely to be retained in a grade, drop out of school, or experience a violent crime.
- 1 child in 3 is born to unmarried parents. 1 in 5 is born to a mother who did not graduate from high school. 1 child in 3 lives with a single parent, usually a working mother.
- 1 in 83 children will be in state or federal prison before age 20. 1 in 1,339 will be killed by guns before age 20.
- 18% of the United States population speaks a language other than English at home—half of these families speak Spanish.
- By the year 2020, over 66% of all school-age children in the United States will be African American, Asian, Hispanic, or Native American, and many will be the children of new immigrants.
- By 2050, there will be no majority race or ethnicity in the United States; every American will be a member of a minority group.

Even though students in classrooms are increasingly diverse in race, ethnicity, language, and economic level, teachers are less diverse—the percentage of White teachers is increasing (now about 91%), while the percentage of Black teachers is falling, down to about 7%. Clearly, it is important for all teachers to better understand and work effectively with all their students.

Individuals, Groups, and Society

Connect and **Extend** to the **Research**
See Banks, J. et al. (2001). Diversity within unity: Essential principles for teaching and learning within a multicultural society. *Phi Delta Kappan, 83*, 196–212, for a synthesis of research on diversity and education.

Since the beginning of the 20th century, a flow of immigrants has entered the United Kingdom, Western Europe, Canada, Australia, the United States, and many other developed countries. These new (mostly European) immigrants were expected to assimilate—that is, to enter the cultural **melting pot** and become like those who had arrived earlier. For years, the goal of American schools was to be the fire under the melting pot. Immigrant children who spoke different languages and had diverse religious and cultural heritages were expected to come to the schools, master English, and learn to become mainstream Americans. Of course, most schools were designed to serve European American middle-class children, so the immigrant children rather than the schools were expected to do the adapting and changing. Involuntary immigrants, descendants of the slaves forced to the United States, often were not welcome in the cultural melting pot.

In the 1960s and 1970s, some educators suggested that students of color and poor students had problems in school because they were "culturally disadvantaged" or "culturally handicapped." The assumption of this **cultural deficit model** was that the students' home culture was inferior because it had not prepared them to fit into the schools. Today, educational psychologists reject the idea of cultural deficits. They believe that no culture is deficient, but rather that there may be incompatibilities between the student's home culture and the expectations of the school (Gallimore & Goldenberg, 2001).

Melting pot A metaphor for the absorption and assimilation of immigrants into the mainstream of society so that ethnic differences vanish.

Cultural deficit model A model that explains the school achievement problems of ethnic minority students by assuming that their culture is inadequate and does not prepare them to succeed in school.

Also during the 1960s and 1970s, there was growing concern for civil and human rights and an increasing sense among many ethnic groups that they did not want to assimilate completely into mainstream American society. Rather, they wanted to maintain their culture and identity while still being a respected part of the larger society. Multiculturalism was the goal.

FIGURE 5.1

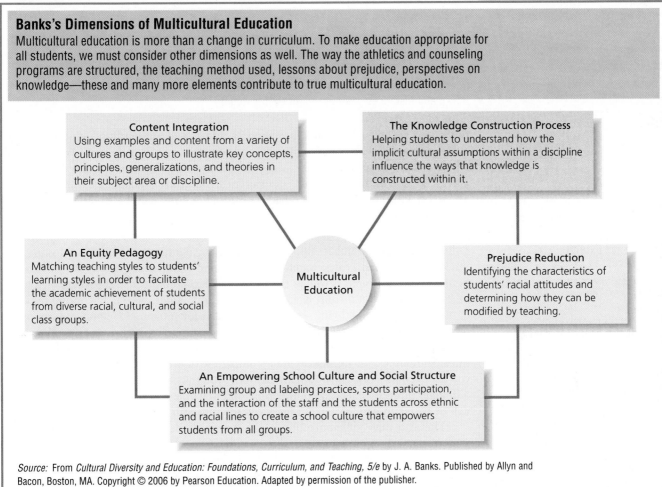

Banks's Dimensions of Multicultural Education
Multicultural education is more than a change in curriculum. To make education appropriate for all students, we must consider other dimensions as well. The way the athletics and counseling programs are structured, the teaching method used, lessons about prejudice, perspectives on knowledge—these and many more elements contribute to true multicultural education.

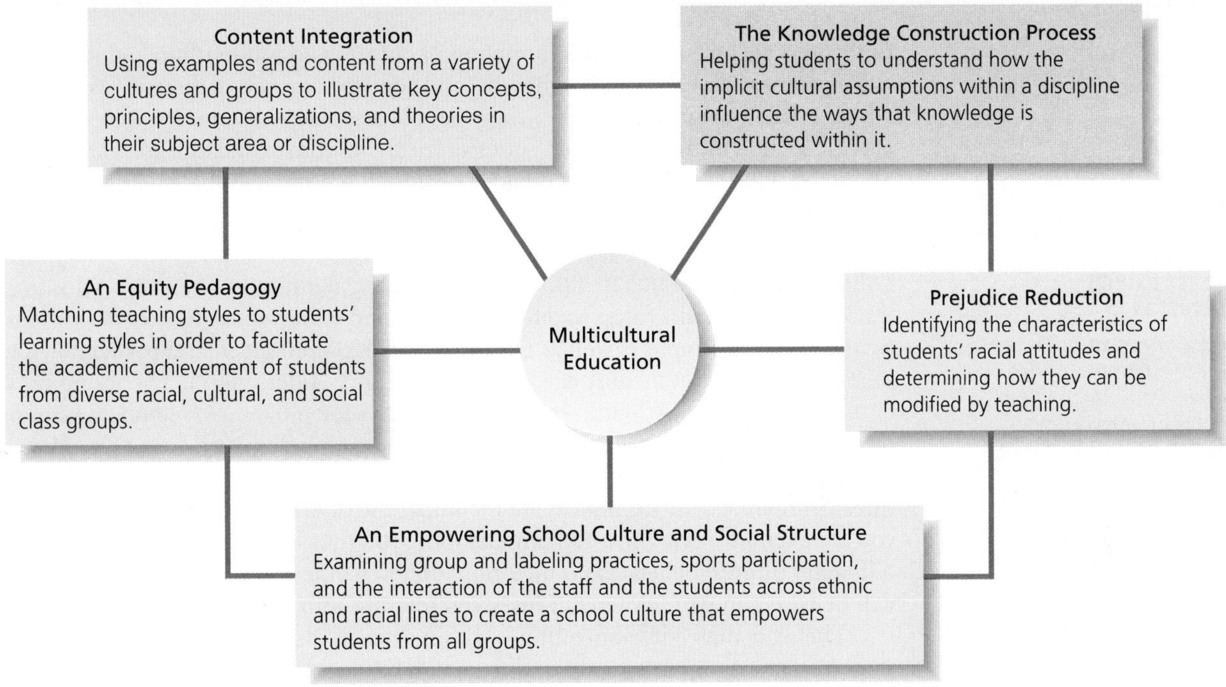

Content Integration
Using examples and content from a variety of cultures and groups to illustrate key concepts, principles, generalizations, and theories in their subject area or discipline.
The Knowledge Construction Process
Helping students to understand how the implicit cultural assumptions within a discipline influence the ways that knowledge is constructed within it.
An Equity Pedagogy
Matching teaching styles to students' learning styles in order to facilitate the academic achievement of students from diverse racial, cultural, and social class groups.
Multicultural Education
Prejudice Reduction
Identifying the characteristics of students' racial attitudes and determining how they can be modified by teaching.
An Empowering School Culture and Social Structure
Examining group and labeling practices, sports participation, and the interaction of the staff and the students across ethnic and racial lines to create a school culture that empowers students from all groups.

Source: From *Cultural Diversity and Education: Foundations, Curriculum, and Teaching, 5/e* by J. A. Banks. Published by Allyn and Bacon, Boston, MA. Copyright © 2006 by Pearson Education. Adapted by permission of the publisher.

Multicultural Education

Multicultural education is "a field of study designed to increase educational equity for all students" (Banks & Banks, 1995, p. xii). Multicultural education is one response to the increasing diversity of the school population as well as to the growing demand for equity for all groups. An examination of the alternative approaches to multicultural education is beyond the scope of an educational psychology text, but be aware that there is no general agreement about the "best" approach.

James Banks (2006) suggests that multicultural education has five dimensions, as shown in Figure 5.1. Many people are familiar only with the dimension of *content integration*, using examples and content from a variety of cultures when teaching a subject. Because they believe that multicultural education is simply a change in curriculum, some teachers assume that it is irrelevant for subjects such as science and mathematics. But if you consider the other four dimensions—helping students understand how knowledge is influenced by beliefs, reducing prejudice, creating social structures in schools that support learning and development for all students, and using teaching methods that reach all students—then you will see that this view of multicultural education is relevant to all subjects and all students.

Multicultural education rejects the idea of the melting pot and supports a society that values diversity—more a salad bowl of many contributions (Banks, 1997, 2006; Sleeter, 1995). Let's take a closer look at the differences that make up the mosaic of cultural diversity.

Multicultural education Education that promotes equity in the schooling of all students.

American Cultural Diversity

STOP | THINK | WRITE Take a quick break from reading and turn on the television. (Don't do this if you won't come back to reading until next Tuesday!). Find a channel with commercials (I know, it is harder to find one without). Listen to about 15 commercials. For each one, is the voice or the character in the ad a male or a female? Old or young? Economically privileged or poor? What is the character's ethnicity or race? Do a quick tally of how many instances you observe in each category. ■

In this text we take a broad interpretation of culture and multicultural education, so we will examine social class, race, ethnicity, and gender as aspects of diversity. We begin with a look at the meaning of culture. Many people associate this concept with the "cultural events" section of the newspaper—art galleries, museums, Shakespeare, classical music, and so on. Culture has a much broader meaning; it embraces the whole way of life of a group of people.

Connect and Extend to the Research

The Spring 1998 issue of *Theory Into Practice* is devoted to "Preparing Teachers for Cultural Diversity." See **http://www.coe.ohio-state.edu/TIP.** This journal is especially for educators.

See the *Review of Educational Research*, Spring 2000, for a whole issue on cultural competence and teaching.

See *Educational Leadership*, Vol. 60, Number 4 (2003), for an entire issue on "Equity and Opportunity."

Culture and Group Membership. There are many definitions of **culture**. Most include the knowledge, skills, rules, traditions, beliefs, and values that guide behavior in a particular group of people as well as the art and artifacts produced and passed down to the next generation (Betancourt & Lopez, 1993; Pai & Alder, 2001). The group creates a culture—a program for living—and communicates the program to members. Groups can be defined along regional, ethnic, religious, racial, gender, social class, or other lines. Each of us is a member of many groups, so we all are influenced by many different cultures. Sometimes, the influences are incompatible or even contradictory. For example, if you are a feminist but also a Roman Catholic, you may have trouble reconciling the two different cultures' beliefs about the ordination of women as priests. Your personal belief will be based, in part, on how strongly you identify with each group (Banks, 1994).

There are many different cultures within every modern country. In the United States, students growing up in a small rural town in the Great Plains are part of a cultural group that is very different from that of students in a large urban center or students in a Florida suburb. In Canada, students living in the suburbs of Toronto certainly differ in a number of ways from students growing up in a Vancouver high-rise apartment or on a farm in Quebec. Within those small towns in the Great Plains or Quebec, the son or daughter of a convenience store clerk grows up in a different culture from the child of the town doctor or dentist. Individuals of African, Asian, Hispanic, Native American, or European descent have distinctive histories and traditions. The experiences of males and females are different in most ethnic and economic groups. Everyone living within a particular country shares many common experiences and values, especially because of the influence of the mass media. But other aspects of their lives are shaped by differing cultural backgrounds.

Cautions in Interpreting Cultural Differences. Before we examine the bases for cultural differences, two cautions are necessary. First, we will consider social class, ethnicity, and gender separately, because much of the available research focuses on only one of these variables. Of course, real children are not just African American, or middle class, or female; they are complex beings and members of many groups.

The second caution comes from James Banks (1993), who has written several books on multicultural education:

> Although membership in a gender, racial, ethnic, social-class, or religious group can provide us with important clues about an individual's behavior, it cannot enable us to predict behavior. *Membership in a particular group does not determine behavior but makes certain types of behavior more probable.* (pp. 13–14)

Keep this in mind as you read about characteristics of economically disadvantaged students or Asian Americans or males. The information we will examine reflects tendencies and probabilities. It does not tell you about the specific students you will teach. For example, if a minority group student in your class consistently arrives late, it may be

Culture The knowledge, values, attitudes, and traditions that guide the behavior of a group of people and allow them to solve the problems of living in their environment.

that the student has a job before school, must walk a long distance, is responsible for getting younger siblings to school, or even that he or she dreads school.

Economic and Social Class Differences

Even though most researchers would agree that social class is one of the most meaningful cultural dimensions in people's lives, those same researchers have great difficulty defining social class (Liu et al., 2004). Different terms are used—social class, socioeconomic status (SES), economic background, wealth, poverty, or privilege. Some people consider only economic differences; others add considerations of power, influence, mobility, control over resources, and prestige.

Social Class and SES

In modern societies, levels of wealth, power, and prestige are not always consistent. Some people—for instance, university professors—are members of professions that are reasonably high in terms of social status, but provide little wealth or power (believe me). Other people have political power even though they are not wealthy, or they may be members of the social register in a town, even though their family money is long gone. Most people are generally aware of their social class—that is, they perceive that some groups are above them in social class and some are below. They may even show a kind of "classism" (like racism or sexism), believing that they are "better" than members of lower social classes and avoiding association with them.

There is another way of thinking about class differences that is commonly used in research. Sociologists and psychologists combine variations in wealth, power, control over resources, and prestige into an index called **socioeconomic status**, or **SES**. In contrast to social class, most people are not conscious of their SES designation. SES is usually ascribed to people by researchers; different formulas for determining SES might lead to different assignments (Liu et al., 2004). No single variable, not even income, is an effective measure of SES. Most researchers identify four general levels of SES: upper, middle, working, and lower classes. The main characteristics of these four levels are summarized in Table 5.1. As you watched the commercials (*Stop/Think/Write* on page 164), how many people did you see who appeared to be lower SES?

Connect and Extend to PRAXIS II™
Economic Conditions/ Socioeconomic Status (SES) (IV, B2)
Be aware of the possible effects of socioeconomic status on student achievement. Consider what steps teachers can take to minimize those effects.

Connect and Extend to the Research
Children's Defense Fund: Where America Stands *August 2004*
Among industrialized countries, the United States ranks:

1st in military technology
1st in military exports
1st in Gross Domestic Product
1st in the number of millionaires and billionaires
1st in health technology
1st in defense expenditures
12th in living standards among our poorest one-fifth
13th in the gap between rich and poor
14th in efforts to lift children out of poverty
16th in low-birth weight rates
18th in the percent of children in poverty
23rd in infant mortality
Last in protecting our children against gun violence

Socioeconomic status (SES) Relative standing in the society based on income, power, background, and prestige.

TABLE 5.1

Selected Characteristics of Different Social Classes

	Upper Class	Middle Class	Working Class	Lower Class
Income	$160,000+	$80,000–$160,000 (1/2) $40,000–$80,000 (1/2)	$25,000–$40,000	Below $25,000
Occupation	Corporate, professional, family money	White-collar, skilled blue-collar	Blue-collar	Minimum-wage unskilled labor
Education	Prestigious colleges and professional schools	High school, college, or professional school	High school	High school or less
Home ownership	At least one home	Usually own home	About half own a home	No
Health coverage	Full	Usually	Limited	No
Neighborhoods	Exclusive or comfortable	Comfortable	Modest	Deteriorating
Afford children's college	Easily	Usually	Seldom	No
Political power	National, state, or local	State or local	Limited	No

Source: Information from *Sociology* (9th ed.) (pp. 276–280), by J. J. Macionis, 2003, Saddle River, NJ: Prentice-Hall.

Poverty and School Achievement

About one in six Americans under the age of 18 lives in poverty, defined in 2005 by the United States Department of Health and Human Services as an income of $19,350 for a family of four ($24,190 in Alaska and $22,260 in Hawaii). That means about 13 million children. The United States has the highest rate of poverty for children of all developed nations, as much as five to eight times higher than other industrialized countries. And almost half of these children can be classified as living in deep poverty—in families with incomes 50% below the poverty threshold. For a while, there were improvements. In 2000, the number of families in poverty was the lowest in 21 years—about 6.2 million (U.S. Census Bureau, September 25, 2001), but rates have been rising again since then.

In 2003, the absolute number of children living in poverty was about the same for non-Hispanic White children (4.2 million), Latina/o children (4.1 million), and Black children (3.9 million). But the rate of poverty is higher for Black and Latino children—34% of Black and 30% of Latino children lived in poverty in 2003, while 12.5% of Asian and 9.8% of non-Hispanic White children were poor. Contrary to many stereotypes, more poor children live in suburban and rural areas than in central cities, and poor families have only 2.2 children on average (Children's Defense Fund, 2005).

Poor children are at least twice as likely as non-poor children to be kept back in school, and poverty during a child's preschool years appears to have the greatest negative impact.

Connect and **Extend** to Your **Teaching Portfolio**

Gabelko, N. H. & Sosniak, L. A. (2002). Someone just like me: When academic engagement trumps race, class, and gender. *Phi Delta Kappan*, 83, 400–405.

Connect and **Extend** to the **Research**

See the Winter 2005 issue of *Theory Into Practice* on Closing the Achievement Gap: What Will it Take? (Vol. 44, No. 1). Guest Editors: Cynthia L. Uline and Joseph F. Johnson, Jr.

High-SES students of all ethnic groups show higher average levels of achievement on test scores and stay in school longer than low-SES students (Gutman, Sameroff, & Cole, 2003; McLoyd, 1998). Poor children are at least twice as likely as non-poor children to be kept back in school. Poverty during a child's preschool years appears to have the greatest negative impact. Unfortunately, families with young children are the most likely to be poor because young parents have the lowest paying jobs or no jobs at all. And the longer the child is in poverty, the stronger the impact is on achievement. For example, even when we take into account parents' education, the chance that children will be retained in grades or placed in special education classes increases by 2% to 3% for every year the children live in poverty (Ackerman, Brown, & Izard, 2004; Bronfenbrenner, McClelland, Wethington, Moen, & Ceci, 1996; Sherman, 1994).

What are the effects of low socioeconomic status that might explain the lower school achievement of these students? Many factors maintain a cycle of poverty—no one cause is to blame (Evans, 2004). Poor health care for mother and child, dangerous or unhealthy environments, limited resources, family stress, interruptions in schooling, exposure to violence, overcrowding, homelessness, discrimination, and other factors lead to school failures, low-paying jobs—and another generation born in poverty. Garcia (1991), Evans (2004), and McLoyd (1998) describe other possible explanations. Let's take a closer look at each of them.

Health, Environment, and Stress. Poor children breathe more polluted air and drink more contaminated water (Evans, 2004). Children who live in older houses with lead paint and lead-soldered pipes, which exist in many inner city areas, have greater concentrations of lead in their blood. Poor children are at least twice as likely as non-poor children to suffer lead poisoning, which is associated with lower school achievement and long-term neurological impairment (McLoyd, 1998). Pedro Noguera (2005) believes "If we focused on removing lead from the environment, we could boost achievement ten points on the Stanford 9," a commonly used standardized test (p. 13). About 55% of poor Americans experience serious deprivations and stress during the year—lack of food, utility shutoffs, crowded or substandard housing, or lack of a stove or refrigerator. Poor children are more than 15 times as likely to experience hunger (Children's Defense Fund, 2005). Families in poverty have less access to good prenatal and infant health care and nutrition. Over half of all adolescent mothers receive no prenatal care at all. Poor mothers and adolescent mothers are more likely to have premature babies, and prematurity is associated with many cognitive and learning problems. Children in poverty are more likely to be exposed to both legal drugs (nicotine, alcohol) and illegal drugs (cocaine, heroin) before birth. Children whose mothers take drugs during pregnancy can have problems with organization, attention, and language skills.

Low Expectations—Low Academic Self-Concept. Because poor students may wear old clothes, speak in a dialect, or be less familiar with books and school activities, teachers and other students may assume that these students are not bright. The teacher may avoid calling on them to protect them from the embarrassment of giving wrong answers or because they make the teacher uncomfortable. Thus, low expectations become institutionalized and the educational resources provided are inadequate (Borman & Overman, 2004). Ultimately, the children come to believe that they aren't very good at schoolwork (Elrich, 1994). The following true story shows how powerful this effect on academic self-concept can be. Terrence Quinn, principal of an elementary school in New York, spends his mornings serving coffee and doughnuts in a welfare hotel six blocks from his school, trying to convince parents to send their children to school.

> Last spring, Jacqueline, a 6th-grader who had lived at the hotel, was selected as the school's valedictorian. One month before the official announcement, she entered Quinn's office and asked to speak to him in private. "Can someone on welfare actually be the valedictorian?" she asked. (Reed & Sautter, 1990, p. K2)

Low expectations, along with a lower-quality educational experience, can lead to a sense of helplessness, described in the previous chapter. That is, economically disadvantaged students (or any students who fail continually) may come to believe that doing well in school is impossible. In fact, about one-fourth of children from poor families drop out of school (Bennett, 1995). Without a high-school diploma, these students find few rewards awaiting them in the work world. Many available jobs barely pay a living wage. If the head of a family of three works full time at the minimum wage, the family's income will still be below the poverty line. Low-SES children, particularly those who also encounter racial discrimination, "become convinced that it is difficult if not impossible for them to advance in the mainstream by doing well in school" (Goleman, 1988).

Peer Influences and Resistance Cultures. Some researchers have suggested that low-SES students may become part of a **resistance culture**. To members of this culture, making it in school means selling out and trying to act "middle class." In order to maintain their identity and their status within the group, low-SES students must reject the behaviors that would make them successful in school—studying, cooperating with teachers, even coming to class (Bennett, 1995; Ogbu, 1987, 1997). John Ogbu linked identification in a resistance culture to poor Latino American, Native American, and African American groups, but similar reactions have been noted for poor White students both in the United States and in England (Willis, 1977) and high-school students in Papua New Guinea (Woolfolk Hoy, Demerath, & Pape, 2002). This is not to say that all low-SES students resist achievement. Adolescents whose parents value academic achievement tend to select friends who also share those values (Berndt & Keefe, 1995). Many young people, like Jacqueline described above, are high achievers in spite of either their economic situation or negative peer influences (O'Connor, 1997). And we should not forget that some aspects of schooling—competitive grading, public reprimands, stressful testing and assignments, and repetitive work that is too hard or too easy—can encourage resistance in all students (Okagaki, 2001).

Tracking: Poor Teaching. Another explanation for the lower achievement of many low-SES students is that these students experience **tracking** and therefore have a different academic socialization; that is, they are actually taught differently (Oakes, 1990b). If they are tracked into "low-ability" or "general" classes, they may be taught to memorize and be passive. Middle-class students are more likely to be encouraged to think and be creative in their classes (Anyon, 1980). When low-SES students receive an inferior education, their academic skills are inferior and their life chances are limited. Adam Gamoran (1987) found that the achievement differences between low-track and high-track students were greater than the differences between high-school dropouts and graduates. In an interview with Marge Scherer (1993), Jonathan Kozol described the cruel predictive side of tracking:

> [T]racking is so utterly predictive. The little girl who gets shoved into the low reading group in 2nd grade is very likely to be the child who is urged to take cosmetology instead

Connect and **Extend** to **Other Chapters**

The concepts of teacher expectation effects and self-fulfilling prophecies are very important in a consideration of cultural differences in the classroom. These concepts are discussed fully in Chapter 13.

Connect and **Extend** to **Other Chapters**

The concept of learned helplessness was discussed in Chapter 4 as one explanation for the lower achievement of students with learning disabilities and will be discussed again in Chapter 10 as a factor influencing motivation.

Connect and **Extend** to Your **Teaching Portfolio**

What is your stance on multicultural education? On tracking? Add these ideas to your philosophy of teaching statement. Include ideas for the integration of multicultural material.

Resistance culture Group values and beliefs about refusing to adopt the behaviors and attitudes of the majority culture.

Tracking Assignment to different classes and academic experiences based on achievement.

Connect and **Extend** to **Other Chapters**

Related information on the effects of ability grouping and tracking appears in Chapter 4.

of algebra in the 8th grade, and most likely to be in vocational courses, not college courses, in the 10th grade, if she hasn't dropped out by then. (p. 8)

Even if they are not tracked, low-income students are more likely to attend schools with inadequate resources and less-effective teachers (Evans, 2004).

Home Environment and Resources. Families in poverty seldom have access to high-quality preschool care for their young children. Research has shown that such high-quality care enhances cognitive and social development (Duncan & Brooks-Gunn, 2000). Poor children read less and spend more time watching television; they have less access to books, computers, libraries, trips, and museums (Evans, 2004). These home and neighborhood resources seem to have the greatest impact on children's achievement when school is not in session—during the summer or before students enter school. For example, Entwisle, Alexander, and Olson (1997) found that low-SES and high-SES students made comparable gains in reading and math when schools were open, but the low-SES students lost ground during summer while the high-SES students continued to improve academically. Another study found that lack of cognitive stimulation in the home accounted for one-third to one-half of the disadvantages in verbal, reading, and math skills of poor children in a national study (Korenman, Miller, & Sjaastad, 1995).

Again, not all low-income families lack resources. Many of these families provide rich learning environments for their children. When parents of any SES level support and encourage their children—by reading to them, providing books and educational toys, taking the children to the library, making time and space for learning—the children tend to become better, more enthusiastic readers (Morrow, 1983; Peng & Lee, 1992; Shields, Gordon, & Dupree, 1983).

Ethnic and Racial Differences

Connect and **Extend** to the **Research**

See *Educational Psychologist*, Winter 2001. This entire issue is devoted to "Schooling of Ethnic Minority Children and Youth." The guest editors are Judith Meece and Beth Kurtz-Costes.

Ethnicity is used to refer to "groups that are characterized in terms of a common nationality, culture, or language" (Betancourt & Lopez, 1993, p. 631). We all have some ethnic heritage, whether our background is Italian, Jewish, Ukrainian, Hmong, Chinese, Japanese, Navajo, Hawaiian, Puerto Rican, Cuban, Hungarian, German, African, or Irish—to name only a few. **Race**, on the other hand, is defined as "a category composed of men and women who share biologically transmitted traits that are defined as socially significant," such as skin color or hair texture (Macionis, 2003, p. 354). Depending on the traits you measure and the theory you follow, there are between 3 and 300 races. In effect, race is a label people apply to themselves and to others based on appearances. There are no biologically pure races (Betancourt & Lopez, 1993). In fact, as you saw in Chapter 4, for any two humans chosen at random, an average of only .012% (about one-hundredth of one percent) of the alphabetic sequence of their genetic codes is different due to race (Myers, 2005). Still, race is a powerful construct. At the individual level, race is part of our identity—how we understand ourselves and interact with others. At the group level, race is involved with economic and political structures (Omi & Winant, 1994).

Sociologists sometimes use the term **minority group** to label a group of people that receives unequal or discriminatory treatment. Strictly speaking, however, the term refers to a numerical minority compared to the total population. Referring to particular racial or ethnic groups as "minorities" is technically incorrect in some situations, because in certain places, such as Chicago or Mississippi, the "minority" group—African Americans—is actually the majority. This practice of referring to people as "minorities" because of their racial or ethnic heritage has been criticized because it is misleading.

Ethnicity A cultural heritage shared by a group of people.

Race A group of people who share common biological traits that are seen as self-defining by the people of the group.

Minority group A group of people who have been socially disadvantaged—not always a minority in actual numbers.

The Changing Demographics: Cultural Differences

Between 1981 and 1990, the number of immigrants entering the United States was the largest ever. By the year 2020, almost two-thirds of the school-age population will be from

Many cultures, races, and ethnicities are represented in the United States, and demographic changes are predicted to continue for many years to come.

African American, Asian, Latina/Latino, or other ethnic groups (Meece & Kurtz-Costes, 2001). So many different cultures are represented in the United States.

Ricardo Garcia (1991) compares culture to an iceberg. One-third of the iceberg is visible; the rest is hidden and unknown. The visible signs of culture, such as costumes and marriage traditions, reflect only a small portion of the differences among cultures. Many of the differences are "below the surface." They are implicit, unstated, even unconscious biases and beliefs (Casanova, 1987; Sheets, 2005). Cultures differ in rules for conducting interpersonal relationships, for example. In some groups, listeners give a slight affirmative nod of the head and perhaps an occasional "uh huh" to indicate they are listening carefully. But members of other cultures listen without giving acknowledgment, or with eyes downcast, as a sign of respect. In some cultures, high-status individuals initiate conversations and ask the questions, and low-status individuals only respond. In other cultures, the pattern is reversed.

Cultural influences are widespread and pervasive. Some psychologists even suggest that culture defines intelligence. For example, physical grace is essential in Balinese social life, so the ability to master physical movements is a mark of intelligence in that culture. Manipulating words and numbers is important in Western societies, so in these cultures such skills are indicators of intelligence (Gardner, 1983). But it would be wrong to assume that every member of a cultural group is identical in beliefs, actions, or values. Eugene Garcia (2002) suggests that culture is "attributes that are made available to members of a group, but may not be shared by all members" (p. 93).

Connect and **Extend** to **PRAXIS II™**

The Larger Community (IV, B1,3)

Familiarize yourself with the predicted changes in the U.S. population over the next several decades. How are those changes likely to affect education? What can schools and teachers do to adjust positively to those changes?

Cultural Conflicts. The differences between cultures may be very obvious, such as holiday customs, or they may be very subtle, such as how to get your turn in conversations. The more subtle and unconscious the difference, the more difficult it is to change or even recognize (Casanova, 1987). Cultural conflicts are usually about below-the-surface differences, because when subtle cultural differences meet, misunderstandings are common. These conflicts can happen when the values and competencies of the dominant, mainstream culture are used to determine what is considered "normal" or appropriate behavior in schools. In these cases, children who have been socialized in a different culture may be perceived as acting inappropriately, not following the rules, or being rude and disrespectful.

Rosa Hernandez Sheets (2005) describes a 5-year-old Mexican American girl who tried to bring a bread roll, part of her school cafeteria lunch, home to give to her little brother every day. Her parents were proud of her for sharing, but the school officials made her throw the roll away, because it was against school rules to take food from the cafeteria. The girl was conflicted about following school rules versus honoring her family's cultural values. The teacher in this case solved the problem by talking to the cafeteria cook, getting the roll in a baggie, and putting the baggie in the girl's backpack to be taken home after school.

Cultural Compatibility. Not all cultural differences lead to clashes in school, however. A study comparing mothers in the People's Republic of China, Chinese American mothers, and Caucasian American mothers found dramatic differences in beliefs about motivation and the value of education (Hess, Chih-Mei, & McDevitt, 1987). For example, the mothers from the Republic of China attributed school failure to lack of effort more often than the Caucasian American mothers. The Chinese American mothers were in the middle, attributing failure to lack of effort more often than the Caucasian American mothers, but less often than the Republic of China mothers.

This does not mean that all Chinese American children are perfectly equipped for the American school, however. Children may perform well on tests and assignments, but feel uncomfortable in social situations, where subtle rules for interacting are not second nature to them (Casanova, 1987; Yee, 1992). Later in this chapter, we will explore other ways to make classrooms compatible with the home cultures of students. First, however, we need to examine some of the effects of cultural conflicts and discrimination on student achievement.

Ethnic and Racial Differences in School Achievement

A major concern in schools is that some ethnic groups consistently achieve below the average for all students (Byrnes, 2003; Uline & Johnson, 2005). This pattern of results tends to hold for all standardized achievement tests, but the gaps have been narrowing over the past two to three decades. Level of educational attainment is improving too, as you can see in Figure 5.2. In 2000, 94% of White, 87% of African American, and 63% of Hispanic adults between ages 25 and 29 had graduated from high school.

FIGURE 5.2

Educational Attainment

This figure compares the educational attainment levels of 25- to 29-year-old Whites, African Americans, and Latinos in March 1971 and March 2000.

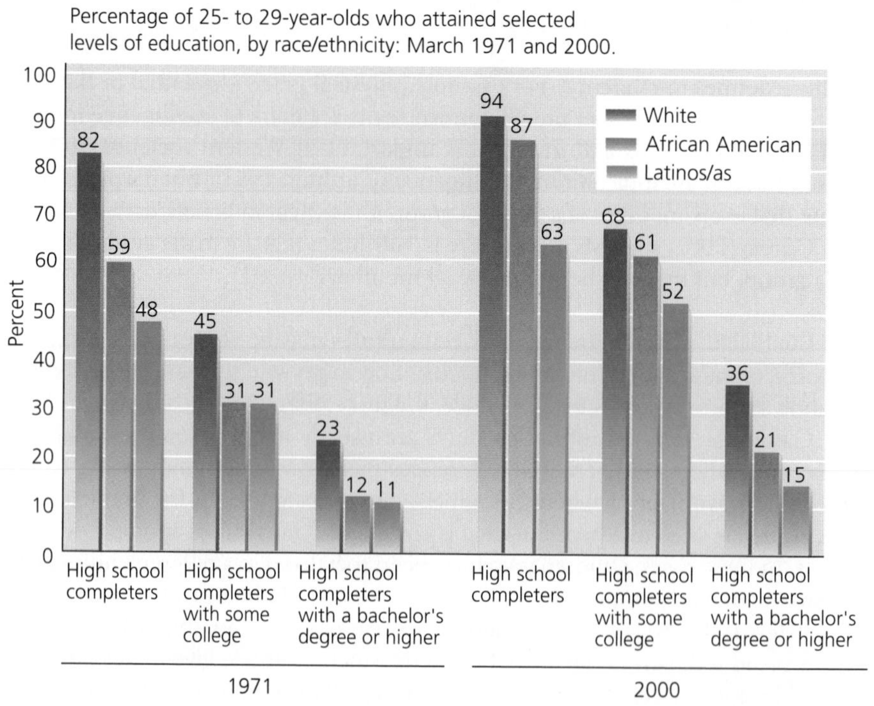

Source: From the National Center for Education Statistics, US Department of Education, retrieved 5/14/02 from http://nces.ed.gov/programs/coe/2001/section3/indicator31.html#info

Although there are consistent differences among ethnic groups on tests of cognitive abilities, most researchers agree that these differences are mainly the legacy of discrimination, the product of cultural mismatches, or a result of growing up in a low-SES environment. Because many students from minority groups are also economically disadvantaged, it is important to separate the effects of these two sets of influences on school achievement. When we compare students from different ethnic and racial groups who are all at the same SES level, then their achievement differences diminish (Gleitman, Fridlund, & Reisberg, 1999). For example, in an analysis of National Assessment of Educational Progress (NAEP) mathematics test results, James Byrnes (2003) found that less than 5% of the variance in math test scores was associated with race, but about 50% of the variance came from differences in SES, motivation, and exposure to learning opportunities (course work, calculator use, homework, etc.).

Nine-year-old Linda Brown, the plaintiff in *Brown* v. *Board of Education of Topeka*.

The Legacy of Discrimination

WHAT WOULD YOU SAY?

As part of your interview for a job in a very diverse middle school, the lead teacher for one of the home-based sections asks: "Describe how your life experiences will contribute to our goal to create an active anti-racist school system." ■

When we considered explanations for why low-SES students have trouble in school, we listed the low expectations and biases of teachers and fellow students. This has been the experience of many ethnic minority students as well. Imagine that the child described below is your own. What would you do?

> [In] the city of Topeka, Kansas, a minister walked hand in hand with his seven-year-old daughter to an elementary school four blocks from their home. Linda Brown wanted to enroll in the 2nd grade, but the school refused to admit her. Instead, public school officials required her to attend another school two miles away. This meant that she had to walk six blocks to a bus stop, where she sometimes waited half an hour for the bus. In bad weather, Linda Brown would be soaking wet by the time the bus came; one day she became so cold at the bus stop that she walked back home. Why, she asked her parents, could she not attend the school only four blocks away? (Macionis, 2003, p. 353)

Her parents' answer to this question, with the help of other concerned families, was to file a suit challenging the school policy. You know the outcome of the 1954 *Brown* v. *the Board of Education of Topeka* ruling. "Separate but equal" schools for Black children were declared inherently unequal. Even though segregation in schools became illegal over 50 years ago, about two-thirds of all African American students still attend schools where members of minority groups make up at least 50% of the student body. Segregation in housing and neighborhoods persists and some areas have drawn school boundary lines deliberately to separate school enrollments along racial lines (Kantor & Lowe, 1995; Ladson-Billings, 2004; Schofield, 1991).

Years of research on the effects of desegregation have mostly shown that legally mandated integration is not a quick solution to the detrimental effects of centuries of racial inequality. In part because White students left integrated schools as the number of students of color increased, many urban schools today are more segregated than they were before the Supreme Court ordered busing and other desegregation measures. The schools in Los Angeles, Miami, Baltimore, Chicago, Dallas, Memphis, Houston, and Detroit have fewer than 11% non-Hispanic White students. And in almost 90% of the schools that have mostly African American and Latina/o students, at least half of the students live in poverty, so racial segregation becomes economic segregation as well (Ladson-Billings, 2004; Orfield & Frankenberg, 2005).

Too often, even in integrated schools, minority-group students are resegregated in low-ability tracks. Simply putting people in the same building does not mean that they will come to respect each other or even that they will experience the same quality of education (Ladson-Billings, 2004; Pettigrew, 1998).

Doonesbury. Copyright © 1988 Garry B. Trudeau. Reprinted with permission from Universal Press Syndicate. All rights reserved.

What Is Prejudice? The word *prejudice* is closely related to the word *prejudge*. **Prejudice** is a rigid and irrational generalization—a prejudgment—about an entire category of people. Prejudice is made up of beliefs, emotions, and tendencies toward particular actions. For example, you are prejudiced against people who are overweight if you believe they are lazy (belief), feel disgusted (emotion), and refuse to date them (action) (Myers, 2005). Prejudice can be positive or negative; that is, you can have positive as well as negative irrational beliefs about a group, but the word usually refers to negative attitudes. Targets of prejudice can be based on race, ethnicity, religion, politics, geographic location, language, sexual orientation, gender, or appearance.

Racial prejudice is pervasive. The United States is a racist society, and this racism is not confined to one group (Clark, Anderson, Clark, & Williams, 1999). Blatant prejudice has decreased in the past 30 years. For example, in 1970, over 50% of Americans agreed that it was all right to keep minorities out of their neighborhoods. By 1995, the number had dropped to about 10% (Myers, 2005). But subtle, below-the-surface racism continues. After several police shootings of unarmed Black men, researchers created a videogame that showed a series of White or Black men holding either a gun or a nonweapon such as a flashlight or wallet. Participants in the research were told to "shoot" whenever the person in the videogame held a weapon. Race was not mentioned. Nevertheless, participants shot armed targets more quickly and more frequently when those targets were Black, rather than White, but decided not to shoot unarmed targets more quickly and more frequently when they were White (Greenwald, Oakes, & Hoffman, 2003). When the participants in another study were actual police officers, they were more likely to mistakenly shoot unarmed Black suspects compared with unarmed White suspects (Plant & Peruche, 2005).

The Development of Prejudice. Prejudice starts early. By about age 6, over half the White children in a United States sample and 85% of students in a Canadian sample had significant pro-White, anti-Black biases. Two popular beliefs are that young children are innocently color-blind and that they will not develop biases unless their parents teach them to be prejudiced. Although these beliefs are appealing, they are not supported by research. Even without direct coaching from their parents, many young children develop racial prejudice. Current explanations of the development of prejudice combine personal and social factors (Katz, 2003).

One source of prejudice is the human tendency to divide the social world into two categories—*us* and *them,* or the *in-group* and the *out-group*. These divisions may be made on the basis of race, religion, sex, age, ethnicity, or even athletic team membership. We tend to see members of the out-group as inferior and different from us, but similar to each other—"they all look alike" (Aboud, 2003; Lambert, 1995). Also, those who have more (more money, more social status, more prestige) may justify their privilege by assuming that they deserve to "have" because they are superior to the "have-nots." This can lead to blaming the victims: People who live in poverty or women who are raped are seen as causing their problems by their behavior—"they got what they deserved." Emotions play a part

Prejudice Prejudgment or irrational generalization about an entire category of people.

as well. When things go wrong, we look for someone or some whole group to blame. For example, after the tragic events of 9/11, some people vented their anger by attacking innocent Arab Americans (Myers, 2005).

But prejudice is more than a tendency to form in-groups, a self-justification, or an emotional reaction—it is also a set of cultural values. Children learn about valued traits and characteristics from their families, friends, teachers, and the world around them. Think back to your analysis of commercials—did you observe many women or people of color? For years, most of the models presented in books, films, television, and advertising were middle- and upper-class European Americans. People of different ethnic and racial backgrounds were seldom the "heroes" (Ward, 2004). This is changing. In 2002, the Oscar awards for best actress and best actor went to African Americans, but Denzel Washington won for his portrayal of a villain. In 2005, Jamie Fox won for his remarkable portrayal of Ray Charles—a hero.

STOP | THINK | WRITE List 3 traits most characteristic of:

College freshmen ______________________

Politicians ______________________

Athletes ______________________

Buddhists ______________________

Members of the National Rifle Association ______________________

Prejudice is difficult to combat because it can be part of our thinking processes. You saw in Chapter 2 that children develop *schemas*—organized bodies of knowledge—about objects, events, and actions. We have schemas that organize our knowledge about people we know, the meaning of words, how to drink from a straw, and all our daily activities. We can also form schemas about groups of people. When I asked you to list the traits most characteristic of college freshmen, politicians, athletes, Buddhists, and members of the National Rifle Association, you probably could generate a list. That list would show that you have a **stereotype**—a schema—that organizes what you know (and believe) about the group (Wyler, 1988).

As with any schema, we use our stereotypes to make sense of the world. You will see in Chapter 7 that having a schema allows you to process information more quickly and efficiently, but it also allows you to distort information to make it fit your schema better (Macrae, Milne, & Bodenhausen, 1994). This is the danger in racial and ethnic stereotypes. We notice information that confirms or agrees with our stereotype—our schema—and miss or dismiss information that does not fit. For example, if a juror has a negative stereotype of Asian Americans and is listening to evidence in the trial of an Asian American, the juror may interpret the evidence more negatively. The juror may actually forget testimony in favor of the defendant, and remember more damaging testimony instead. Information that fits the stereotype is even processed more quickly (Anderson, Klatzky, & Murray, 1990; Baron, 1998).

Continuing Discrimination. Prejudice consists of beliefs and feelings (usually negative) about an entire category of people. The third element of prejudice is a tendency to act, called discrimination. **Discrimination** is unequal treatment of particular categories of people. Clearly, many Americans face prejudice and discrimination in subtle or blatant ways every day. One of the most discouraging findings I encountered while writing this chapter is that only .6% of the senior managers in Fortune 500 industrial and service companies are African American. In the 2001–2002 school year, 465 U.S. citizens and permanent residents got a doctorate in mathematics. Six percent were Latino, Black, or Native American (Herzig, 2004). Less than 10% of the scientists, engineers, and mathematicians in the United States are either African American or Hispanic American, whereas more than 25% of the total population is from one of these groups. Even though their attitudes toward science and math are more favorable than those of White students, Black and Hispanic students begin to lose out in science and math as early as elementary

Connect and **Extend** to **PRAXIS II™**

Racial Bias (IV, B4)
Describe the possible effects of racial discrimination and bias on minority students. What can teachers and schools do to address the lingering effects of this discrimination?

Stereotype Schema that organizes knowledge or perceptions about a category.

Discrimination Treating or acting unfairly toward particular categories of people.

school. They are chosen less often for gifted classes and acceleration or enrichment programs. They are more likely to be tracked into "basic skills" classes. As they progress through junior high, high school, and college, their paths take them farther and farther out of the pipeline that produces our scientists. If they do persist and become scientists or engineers, they, along with women, will still be paid less than White employees for the same work (National Science Foundation, 1996).

There is another problem caused by stereotypes and prejudice that can undermine academic achievement—stereotype threat.

Stereotype Threat

Stereotype threat is an "apprehensiveness about confirming a stereotype" (Aronson, 2002, p. 282). The basic idea is that when individuals are in situations in which a stereotype applies, they bear an extra emotional and cognitive burden. The burden is the possibility of confirming the stereotype, either in the eyes of others or in their own eyes. Thus, when girls are asked to solve complicated mathematics problems, for example, they are at risk of confirming widely held stereotypes that girls are inferior to boys in mathematics. It is not necessary that the individual even believe the stereotype. All that matters is that the person is *aware* of the stereotype and *cares about performing* well enough to disprove its unflattering implications (Aronson, Lustina, Good, Keough, Steele, & Brown, 1999). What are the results of stereotype threat? Recent research provides answers that should interest all teachers.

Short-Term Effects: Test Performance. In the short run, the fear that you might confirm a negative stereotype can induce test anxiety and undermine performance. In a series of experiments, Joshua Aronson, Claude Steele, and their colleagues have demonstrated that when African American or Latino college students are put in situations that induce stereotype threat, their performance suffers (Aronson, 2002; Aronson & Salinas, 1998; Aronson & Steele, 2005; Aronson, Steele, Salinas, & Lustina, 1999). For example, African American and White undergraduate subjects in an experiment at Stanford University were told that the test they were about to take would precisely measure their verbal ability. A similar group of subjects was told that the purpose of the test was to understand the psychology of verbal problem solving and not to assess individual ability. As shown in Figure 5.3, when the test was presented as diagnostic of verbal ability, the African American students solved about half as many problems as the White students. In the non-threat situation, the two groups solved about the same number of problems.

All groups, not just minority-group students, can be susceptible to stereotype threat. In another study, the subjects were White male college students who were very strong in mathematics. One group was told that the test they were taking would help experimenters determine why Asian students performed so much better than Whites on that particular test. Another group just took the test. The group that faced the stereotype threat of confirming that "Asians are better in math" scored significantly lower on the test (Aronson et al., 1999).

Being vulnerable to stereotype threat varies among individuals. In one study, Aronson and Inzlicht (2004) found that African American college students who were more vulnerable to stereotype threat were less accurate in assessing their performance on a test. In addition, their sense of academic competence varied more widely from day to day. And who is most vulnerable? Those who care the most and who are most deeply invested in high performance. The pressures of *No Child Left Behind* testing are likely to increase vulnerability.

Why does stereotype threat affect test performance? One link is anxiety. Jason Osborne (2001) studied a large, representative national sample of White, African American, and Latino high school seniors who took achievement tests and tests of anxiety at the same time. The White students scored significantly higher, but anxiety played a role in those differences. Even after controlling for prior achievement in school, anxiety explained almost one-third of the racial differences in the scores. Anxiety and distraction appeared to be the main problems in the studies of college students, too. The African American stu-

Stereotype threat The extra emotional and cognitive burden that your performance in an academic situation might confirm a stereotype that others hold about you.

FIGURE 5.3

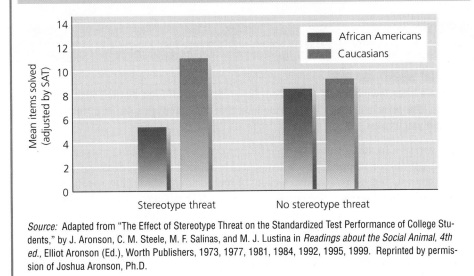

The Impact of Stereotype Threat on College Students' Standardized Test Performance

When African American college students were told that they were taking a test that would diagnose their verbal ability (stereotype threat), they solved about one-half as many problems as another group of African American students who were not told the test would assess ability. The performance of Caucasian students was not affected by the threat conditions.

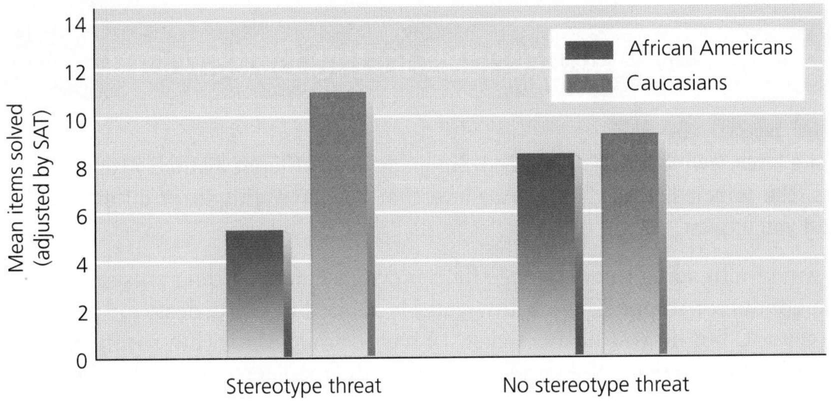

Source: Adapted from "The Effect of Stereotype Threat on the Standardized Test Performance of College Students," by J. Aronson, C. M. Steele, M. F. Salinas, and M. J. Lustina in *Readings about the Social Animal, 4th ed.*, Elliot Aronson (Ed.), Worth Publishers, 1973, 1977, 1981, 1984, 1992, 1995, 1999. Reprinted by permission of Joshua Aronson, Ph.D.

dents were more likely to be thinking about the stereotypes as they tried to work (Spencer, Steele, & Quinn, 1999).

Long-Term Effects: Disidentification. As we will see in Chapter 10, students often develop self-defeating strategies to protect their self-esteem about academics. They withdraw, claim to not care, exert little effort, or even drop out of school—they psychologically disengage from success in the domain and claim "math is for nerds" or "school is for losers." Once students define academics as "uncool," it is unlikely they will exert the effort needed for real learning. There is some evidence that Black male students are more likely than Black female students and White students to *disidentify* with academics—that is, to separate their sense of self-esteem from their academic achievement (Cokley, 2002; Major & Schmader, 1998; Steele, 1992). Other studies have questioned this connection, however. Historically, education has been valued among African American communities (Walker, 1996). One study found that African American adolescents who had strong Afrocentric beliefs also had higher achievement goals and self-esteem than adolescents who identified with the larger White culture (Spencer, Noll, Stoltzfus, & Harpalani, 2001). The message for teachers is to help all students see academic achievement as part of their ethnic, racial, and gender identity.

Combating Stereotype Threat. Stereotypes are pervasive and difficult to change. Rather than wait for changes, it may be better to acknowledge that these images exist, at least in the eyes of many, and give students ways of coping with the stereotypes. In Chapter 10, we will discuss test anxiety and how to overcome the negative effects of anxiety. Many of those strategies are also appropriate for helping students resist stereotype threat.

Aronson (2002) demonstrated the powerful effects of changing beliefs about intelligence. African American and White undergraduates were asked to write letters to "at-risk" middle-school students to encourage them to persist in school. Some of the undergraduates were given evidence that intelligence is *improvable* and encouraged to communicate this information to their pen pals. Others were given information about multiple intelligences, but not told that these multiple abilities can be improved. The middle-school students were not real, but the process of writing persuasive letters about improving intelligence proved powerful. The African American college students, and the White students to a lesser extent, who were encouraged to believe that intelligence can be improved had higher grade-point averages and reported greater enjoyment of and engagement in school when contacted at the end of the next school quarter. Thus, believing that intelligence can be improved might inoculate students against stereotype threat.

Girls and Boys: Differences in the Classroom

WHAT WOULD YOU SAY?

You are interviewing for a job in a 2nd/3rd grade in an affluent district. After a few questions, the principal asks, "Do you believe that boys and girls learn differently?" How would you answer? ■

While I was proofreading this very page for a previous edition, riding cross-country on a train, the conductor stopped beside my seat. He said, "I'm sorry, dear, for interrupting your homework, but do you have a ticket?" I had to smile at his (I'm sure unintended) sexism. I doubt that he made the same comment to the man across the aisle who was writing on his legal pad. Like racial discrimination, messages of sexism can be subtle.

In this section, we examine the development of two related identities that can be the basis for discrimination—sexual identity and gender-role identity. We particularly focus on how men and women are socialized and the role of teachers in providing an equitable education for both sexes.

Sexual Identity

Connect and **Extend** to the **Research**

See the Spring 2004 issue of *Theory Into Practice* on "Sexual Identities and Schooling" (Vol. 43, No. 2). Guest Editors: Mollie V. Blackburn and Randal Donelson.

The word *gender* usually refers to traits and behaviors that a particular culture judges to be appropriate for men and for women. In contrast, *sex* refers to biological differences (Brannon, 2002; Deaux, 1993). **Sexual identity** includes gender identity, gender-role behaviors, and sexual orientation (Patterson, 1995). *Gender identity* is a person's self-identification as male or female. Gender-role behaviors are those behaviors and characteristics that the culture associates with each gender, and *sexual orientation* involves the person's choice of a sexual partner. Relations among these three elements are complex. For example, a woman may identify herself as a female (gender-identity), but behave in ways that are not consistent with the gender role (play football), and may be heterosexual, bisexual, or homosexual in her orientation. So sexual identity is a complicated construction of beliefs, attitudes, and behaviors.

Sexual Orientation. During adolescence, about 8% of boys and 6% of girls report engaging is some same-sex activity or feeling strong attractions to same-sex individuals. Males are more likely than females to experiment with same-sex partners as adolescents, but females are more likely to experiment later, often in college. Fewer adolescents actually have a homosexual or bisexual orientation—about 4% of adolescents identify themselves as gay (males who chose male partners), lesbian (females who chose female partners), or bisexual (people who have partners of both sexes). This number increases to about 8% for adults (Savin-Williams & Diamond, 2004; Steinberg, 2005).

Scientists debate the origins of homosexuality. Most of the research has been with men, so less is known about women. Evidence so far suggests that both biological and social factors are involved. For example, sexual orientation is more similar for identical twins than for fraternal twins, but not all identical twins have the same sexual orientation (Berk, 2005). There are quite a few models describing the development of sexual orientation. Most focus on how adolescents develop an identity as gay, lesbian, or bisexual. Generally, the models include the following or similar stages (Berk, 2005; Yarhouse, 2001):

Sexual identity A complex combination of beliefs and orientations about gender roles and sexual orientation.

TABLE 5.2

Reaching Out to Help Students Struggling with Sexual Identity

These ideas come from the *Attic Speakers Bureau*, a program of The Attic Youth Center, where trained peer educators reach out to youth and youth-service providers in schools, organizations, and health-care facilities.

Reaching Out

If a lesbian, gay, bisexual, or transgender youth or a youth questioning his or her own sexual orientation should come to you directly for assistance, remember the following simple, 5-point plan:

LISTEN It seems obvious, but the best thing that you can do in the beginning is allow that individual to vent and express what is going on in his or her life.

AFFIRM Tell them, "You are not alone."—this is crucial. A lot of l/g/b/t/q youth feel isolated and lack peers with whom they can discuss issues around sexual orientation. Letting them know that there are others dealing with the same issues is invaluable. This statement is also important because it does not involve a judgment call on your part.

REFER You do not have to be the expert. A referral to someone who is trained to deal with these issues is a gift you are giving to that student, not a dismissal of responsibility.

ADDRESS Deal with harassers—do not overlook issues of verbal or physical harassment around sexual orientation. It is important to create and maintain an environment where all youth feel comfortable and welcome.

FOLLOW-UP Be sure to check in with the individual to see if the situation has improved and if there is anything further you may be able to do.

There are also some things that you as an individual can do to better serve l/g/b/t/q youth and youth dealing with issues around sexual orientation:

- Work on your own comfortability around issues of sexual orientation and sexuality.
- Get training on how to present information on sexual orientation effectively.
- Dispel myths around sexual orientation by knowing facts and sharing that information.
- Work on setting aside your own personal biases to better serve students dealing with issues around sexual orientation and sexuality.

Source: From Figure 3. Copyright © The Attic Speakers Bureau and Carrie E. Jacobs, Ph.D. Reprinted with permission.

- *Feeling different*—Beginning around age 6, the child may be less interested in the activities of other children who are the same sex. Some children may find this difference troubling and fear being "found out." Others do not experience these anxieties.
- *Feeling confused*—In adolescence, as they feel attractions for the same sex, students may be confused, upset, lonely, unsure of what to do. They may lack role models and try to change to activities and dating patterns that fit heterosexual stereotypes.
- *Acceptance*—As young adults, many of these youth sort through sexual orientation issues and identify themselves as gay, lesbian, or bisexual. They may or may not make their sexual orientation public, but might share the information with a few friends.

The problem with phase models of identity development is that the identity achieved is assumed to be final. Actually, newer models emphasize that sexual orientation can be flexible, complex, and multifaceted; it can change over the lifetime. For example, people may have dated or married opposite-sex partners at one point in their lives, but have same-sex attractions or partners later in their lives, or vice versa (Garnets, 2002).

Parent and teachers are seldom the first people to hear about the adolescent's sexual identity concerns. But if a student does seek your counsel, Table 5.2 has some ideas for reaching out.

Gender-Role Identity

Gender-role identity is the image each individual has of himself or herself as masculine or feminine in characteristics—a part of self-concept. Erikson and many other earlier

Gender-role identity Beliefs about characteristics and behaviors associated with one sex as opposed to the other.

Recognizing gender schemas as potential barriers to success may allow children's choices to become less gender driven. The 2002 film, *Bend It Like Beckham,* in which a teenaged girl from a traditional Indian family aspires to succeed as a professional soccer player, explores how society and different cultures define appropriate activities for girls and boys.

Connect and **Extend** to the **Research**

For a lively debate on the terminology of gender and sex, see the March 1993 issue of *Psychological Science*.

psychologists thought that identifying your gender and accepting gender roles were straightforward; you simply realized that you were male or female and acted accordingly. But today, we know that some people experience conflicts about their gender identity. For example, transsexuals often report feeling trapped in the wrong body; they experience themselves as female, but their biological sex is male or vice versa (Berk, 2005; Yarhouse, 2001).

How do gender-role identities develop? As early as age 2, children are aware of gender differences—they know whether they are girls or boys and that mommies are girls and daddies are boys. It is likely that biology plays a role. Very early, hormones affect activity level and aggression, with boys tending to prefer active, rough, noisy play. By age 4, children have a beginning sense of gender roles—they believe that some toys are for boys (trucks, for example) and some are for girls (dolls) and that some jobs are for girls (nurse) and others are for boys (police officer) (Berk, 2005). Play styles lead young children to prefer same-sex play partners with similar styles, so by age 4, children spend three times as much play time with same-sex playmates as with opposite-sex playmates; by age 6, the ratio is 11 to 1 (Benenson, 1993; Maccoby, 1998). Of course, these are averages and individuals do not always fit the average. In addition, many other factors—social and cognitive—affect gender-role identity.

Parents are more likely to react positively to assertive behavior on the part of their sons and emotional sensitivity in their daughters (Brody, 1999; Fagot & Hagan, 1991). Through their interactions with family, peers, teachers, and the environment in general, children begin to form **gender schemas**, or organized networks of knowledge about what it means to be male or female. Gender schemas help children make sense of the world and guide their behavior (see Figure 5.4). So a young girl whose schema for "girls" includes "girls play with dolls and not with trucks" or "girls can't be scientists" will pay attention to, remember, and interact more with dolls than trucks, and she may avoid science activities (Berk, 2005; Leaper, 2002; Liben & Signorella, 1993).

Gender schemas Organized networks of knowledge about what it means to be male or female.

Gender-Role Stereotyping in the Preschool Years. Different treatment of the sexes and gender-role stereotyping continue in early childhood. Researchers have found that boys

FIGURE 5.4

Gender Schema Theory

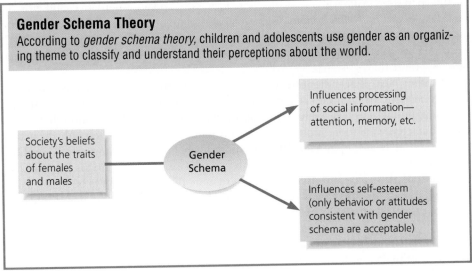

According to *gender schema theory,* children and adolescents use gender as an organizing theme to classify and understand their perceptions about the world.

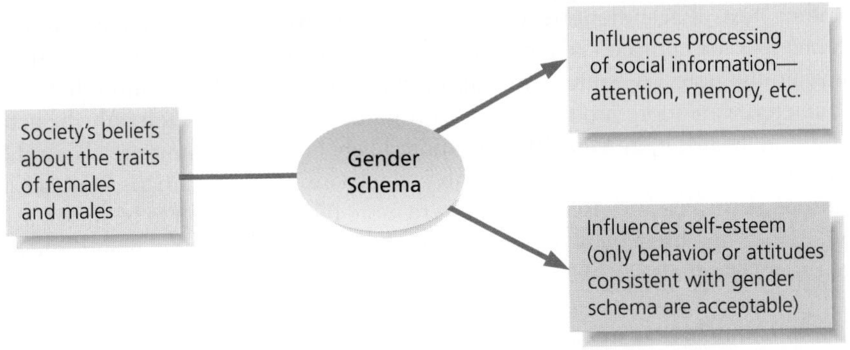
Society's beliefs about the traits of females and males
Gender Schema
Influences processing of social information—attention, memory, etc.
Influences self-esteem (only behavior or attitudes consistent with gender schema are acceptable)

are given more freedom to roam the neighborhood, and they are not protected for as long a time as girls from potentially dangerous activities such as playing with sharp scissors or crossing the street alone. Parents quickly come to the aid of their daughters, but are more likely to insist that their sons handle problems themselves. Thus, independence and initiative seem to be encouraged more in boys than in girls (Brannon, 2002; Fagot, Hagan, Leinbach, & Kronsberg, 1985).

And then there are the toys! Walk through any store's toy section and see what is offered to girls and boys. Dolls and kitchen sets for girls and toy weapons for boys have been with us for decades, but what about even more subtle messages? Margot Mifflin went shopping for a toy for her 4-year-old that was not gender-typed and found a Wee Waffle farm set. Then she discovered that "the farmer plugged into a round hole in the driver's seat of the tractor, but the mother—literally a square peg in a round hole—didn't" (Mifflin, 1999, p. 1). But we cannot blame the toy makers alone. Adults buying for children favor gender-typed toys and fathers tend to discourage young sons from playing with "girl's" toys (Brannon, 2002).

By age 4 or 5, children have developed a gender schema that describes what clothes, games, toys, behaviors, and careers are "right" for boys and girls—and these ideas can be quite rigid (Brannon, 2002). Many of my student teachers are surprised when they hear young children talk about gender roles. Even in this era of great progress toward equal opportunity, a preschool girl is more likely to tell you she wants to become a nurse than to say she wants to be an engineer. After she had given a lecture on the dangers of sex stereotyping in schools, a colleague of mine brought her young daughter to her college class. The students asked the little girl, "What do you want to be when you grow up?" The child immediately replied, "A doctor," and her professor/mother beamed with pride. Then the girl whispered to the students in the front row, "I really want to be a nurse, but my Mommy won't let me." Actually, this is a common reaction for young children. Preschoolers tend to have more stereotyped notions of sex roles than older children, and all ages seem to have more rigid and traditional ideas about male occupations than about what females do (Berk, 2005).

Gender Bias in the Curriculum. During the elementary school years, children continue to learn about what it means to be male or female. Unfortunately, schools often foster these **gender biases** in a number of ways. Most of the textbooks produced for the early grades before 1970 portrayed both males and females in stereotyped roles. Publishers have established guidelines to prevent these problems, but it still makes sense to check your teaching materials for stereotypes. For example, even though children's books now have an equal number of males and females as central characters, there still are more

Gender biases Different views of males and females, often favoring one gender over the other.

Connect and **Extend** to **PRAXIS II™**

Gender Bias (IV, B4)

There has been much debate in the news media over possible gender bias in schools. What can you as a teacher do to reduce or eliminate gender bias and its effects?

males in the titles and the illustrations, and the characters (especially the boys) continue to behave in stereotypic ways. Boys are more aggressive and argumentative, and girls are more expressive and affectionate. Girl characters sometimes cross gender roles to be more active, but boy characters seldom show "feminine" expressive traits (Brannon, 2002; Evans & Davies, 2000). Videos, computer programs, and testing materials also often feature boys more than girls (Meece, 2002).

Another "text" that students read long before they arrive in your classroom is television. Remember the commercial count break I asked you to take earlier? (No—you can't take another one here.) A content analysis of television commercials found that White male characters were more prominent than any other group. Even when only the actor's voice could be heard, men were 10 times more likely to narrate commercials. And the same pattern of men as the "voice of authority" on television occurred in the United Kingdom, Europe, Australia, and Asia. Women were more likely than men to be shown as dependent on men and often were depicted at home (Brannon, 2002). So, before and after going to school, students are likely to encounter texts that overrepresent males.

Sex Discrimination in Classrooms. There has been quite a bit of research on teachers' treatment of male and female students. You should know, however, that most of these studies have focused on White students, so the results reported in this section hold mostly for White male and female students. One of the best-documented findings of the past 25 years is that teachers have more overall interactions and more negative interactions, but not more positive interactions, with boys than with girls (Jones & Dindia, 2004). This is true from preschool to college. Teachers ask more questions of males, give males more feedback (praise, criticism, and correction), and give more specific and valuable comments to boys. As girls move through the grades, they have less and less to say. By the time students reach college, men are twice as likely to initiate comments as women (Bailey, 1993; Sadker & Sadker, 1994). The effect of these differences is that from preschool through college, girls, on the average, receive 1,800 fewer hours of attention and instruction than boys (Sadker, Sadker, & Klein, 1991). Of course, these differences are not evenly distributed. Some boys, generally high-achieving White students, receive more than their share, whereas high-achieving girls receive the least teacher attention.

The imbalances of teacher attention given to boys and girls are particularly dramatic in math and science classes. In one study, boys were questioned in science class 80% more often than girls (Baker, 1986). Teachers wait longer for boys to answer and give more detailed feedback to the boys (Meece, 2002; Sadker & Sadker, 1994). Boys also dominate the use of equipment in science labs, often dismantling the apparatus before the girls in the class have a chance to perform the experiments (Rennie & Parker, 1987).

Stereotypes are perpetuated in many ways, some obvious, some subtle. Boys with high scores on standardized math tests are more likely to be put in the high-ability math group than girls with the same scores. Guidance counselors, parents, and teachers often do not protest at all when a bright girl says she doesn't want to take any more math or science courses, but when a boy of the same ability wants to forget about math or science, they will object. More women than men are teachers, but men tend to be the administrators, coaches, and advanced math and science teachers. In these subtle ways, students' stereotyped expectations for themselves are reinforced (Sadker & Sadker, 1994).

Sex Differences in Mental Abilities

Connect and **Extend** to the **Research**

See Latham, A. S. (1998). Gender differences on assessments. *Educational Leadership*, 55(4), 88–89.

Only 23% of the scientists and engineers and just 10% of the physicists in the United States are women, even though women earn about half of the bachelor's degrees in chemistry, biology, and mathematics and about 20% of the bachelor's degrees in physics and engineering (Angier & Chang, 2005; Bleeker & Jacobs, 2004). But let's not overlook the boys. There are areas when boys lag behind girls. For example, women earn 30% more bachelor's degrees overall than men and 50% more master's degrees. And African American women now earn twice as many college degrees as African American men (Hulbert, 2005). The International Comparisons in Fourth-Grade Reading Literacy: Findings from the Progress in International Reading Literacy Study (Mullis, Martin,

Gonzalez, & Kennedy, 2003) revealed that in 34 countries, 4th grade boys scored below girls in reading literacy. Are these differences due to ability, interest, culture, social pressure, discrimination . . . ? Let's see if we can make sense of this issue.

From infancy through the preschool years, most studies find few differences between boys and girls in overall mental and motor development or in specific abilities. During the school years and beyond, psychologists find no differences in general intelligence on the standard measures—these tests have been designed and standardized to minimize sex differences. However, scores on some tests of specific abilities show sex differences. For example, from elementary through high school, girls score higher than boys on tests of reading and writing, and fewer girls require remediation in reading (Berk, 2005; Halpern, 2000). But academically gifted boys in the United States perform better than girls on advanced mathematics tests. In 2001, twice as many boys as girls scored over 700 on the math SATs, but boys also were more likely than girls to get all the answers wrong (Angier & Chang, 2005). In fact, the scores of males tend to be more variable in general, so there are more males than females with very high *and* very low scores on tests (Berk, 2005; Willingham & Cole, 1997). There also are more boys diagnosed with learning disabilities, ADHD, and autism. Diane Halpern (2004) summarized the research:

> Females and males show different average patterns of academic achievement and scores on cognitive ability tests. Females obtain higher grades in school, score much higher on tests of writing and content-area tests on which the questions are similar to material that was learned in school, attain a majority of college degrees, and are closing the gap in many careers that were traditionally male. By contrast, males score higher on standardized tests of mathematics and science that are not directly tied to their school curriculum, show a large advantage on visuospatial tests (especially those that involve judgments of velocity and navigation through three-dimensional space), and are much more knowledgeable about geography and politics. (p. 135)

There is a caution, however. In most studies of sex differences, race and socioeconomic status are not taken into account. When racial groups are studied separately, African American females outperform African American males in high school mathematics; there is little or no difference in the performance of Asian American girls and boys in math or science (Grossman & Grossman, 1994; Yee, 1992). And girls in general tend to get higher grades than boys in mathematics classes (Halpern, 2004). Also, international studies of 15-year-olds in 41 countries show no sex differences in mathematics for half of the countries tested. In fact, in Iceland, girls significantly outperformed boys on all the math tests, just as they usually do on their national math exams (Angier & Chang, 2005).

What is the basis for the differences? The answers are complex. For example, males on average are better on tests that require mental rotation of a figure in space, prediction of the trajectories of moving objects, and navigating. Some researchers argue that evolution has favored these skills in males (Buss, 1995; Geary, 1995, 1999), but others relate these skills to males' more active play styles and to their participation in athletics (Linn & Hyde, 1989; Newcombe & Baenninger, 1990; Stumpf, 1995). The cross-cultural comparisons suggest that much of the difference in mathematics scores comes from learning, not biology. And studies showing that adults rated a math paper attributed to "John T. McKay" a full point higher on a 5-point scale than the same paper attributed to "Joan T. McKay" suggests that discrimination plays a role as well (Angier & Chang, 2005).

Eliminating Gender Bias

There is some evidence that teachers treat girls and boys differently in mathematics classes. For example, some elementary school teachers spend more academic time with boys in math and with girls in reading. In one study, high-school geometry teachers directed most of their questions to boys, even though the girls asked questions and volunteered answers more often. Several researchers have found that some teachers tend to accept wrong answers from girls, saying, in effect, "Well, at least you tried." But when boys give the wrong answer, the teachers are more likely to say, "Try harder! You can figure this out." These messages, repeated time and again, can convince girls that they just aren't

Bonnie Bessler, an associate professor of molecular biology at Princeton University investigating the chemical signaling mechanisms that bacteria use to communicate with each other, defies stereotypes about women's ability to succeed in scientific fields.

Connect and **Extend** to **PRAXIS II™**

Cultural and Gender Differences in the Classroom (III, B)

What are the sources of possible miscommunication between students and teachers in the classroom because of cultural or gender differences? Identify steps a teacher can take to minimize such problems.

Connect and **Extend** to Your **Teaching Portfolio**

Sadker, D. (1998). Gender equity: Still knocking at the classroom door. *Educational Leadership*, 56(7), 22–27. Special section on Gender Equity, *Phi Delta Kappan*, Vol. 84, No. 3, 2002, pp. 235–245.

Guidelines: Avoiding Sexism in Teaching

Check to see if textbooks and other materials you are using present an honest view of the options open to both males and females.

EXAMPLES

1. Are both males and females portrayed in traditional and nontraditional roles at work, at leisure, and at home?
2. Discuss your analyses with students, and ask them to help you find sex-role biases in other materials—magazine advertising, TV programs, news reporting, for example.

Watch for any unintended biases in your own classroom practices.

EXAMPLES

1. Do you group students by sex for certain activities? Is the grouping appropriate?
2. Do you call on one sex or the other for certain answers—boys for math and girls for poetry, for example?
3. Monitor your metaphors. Ask students to "tackle the problem" and also to "cook up a solution."

Look for ways in which your school may be limiting the options open to male or female students.

EXAMPLES

1. What advice is given by guidance counselors to students in course and career decisions?
2. Is there a good sports program for both girls and boys?
3. Are girls encouraged to take advanced placement courses in science and mathematics? Boys in English and foreign languages?

Use gender-free language as much as possible.

EXAMPLES

1. Do you speak of "law-enforcement officer" and "mail carrier" instead of "policeman" and "mailman"?
2. Do you name a committee "head" instead of a "chairman"?

Provide role models.

EXAMPLES

1. Assign articles in professional journals written by female research scientists or mathematicians.
2. Have recent female graduates who are majoring in science, math, engineering, or other technical fields come to class to talk about college.
3. Create electronic mentoring programs for both male and female students to connect them with adults working in areas of interest to the students.

Make sure all students have a chance to do complex, technical work.

EXAMPLES

1. Experiment with same-sex lab groups so girls do not always end up as the secretaries, boys as the technicians.
2. Rotate jobs in groups or randomly assign responsibilities.

What if you witness sexism as a student teacher? See this site for ideas: **http://www.tolerance.org/teach/magazine/features.jsp?p=0&is=36&ar=563#**

cut out for mathematics ("Girls' Math Achievement," 1986; Horgan, 1995). If you are like a few of the student teachers I have supervised who "really hate math," please don't pass this attitude on to your students. You may have been the victim of sex discrimination yourself. The *Guidelines* provide additional ideas about avoiding sexism in your teaching. Some are taken from Rop (1997/1998).

Some popular authors have argued that boys and girls learn differently and that schools tend to reward the passive, cooperative behaviors of girls (Gurian & Henley, 2001). Other people believe that schools "shortchange" girls and "fail to be fair" (American Association of University Women [AAUW], 1991; Sadker & Sadker, 1995). The *Point/Counterpoint* examines these issues.

Language Differences in the Classroom

In the classroom, quite a bit happens through language. Communication is at the heart of teaching, but as we have seen in this chapter, culture affects communication. In this section, we will examine two kinds of language differences—dialect differences and bilingualism.

Point/Counterpoint

Do Boys and Girls Learn Differently?

AS WE HAVE SEEN, there are a number of documented sex differences in mental abilities. Do these translate into different ways of learning and thus different needs in the classroom?

POINT Yes, boys and girls learn differently.

Since at least the 1960s, there have been questions about whether schools serve boys well. Accusations that schools were trying to destroy "boys culture" and forcing "feminine, frilly content" on boys caused some public concern (Connell, 1996).

> *Discrimination against girls has ended, the argument runs. Indeed, thanks to feminism, girls have special treatment and special programs. Now, what about the boys? It is boys who are slower to learn to read, more likely to drop out of school, more likely to be disciplined, more likely to be in programs for children with special needs. In school it is girls who are doing better, boys who are in trouble—and special programs for boys that are needed.* (Connell, 1996, p. 207)

In their book, *Boys and Girls Learn Differently*, Michael Gurian and Patricia Henley (2001) make a similar argument that boys and girls need different teaching approaches. Reviewing the book, J. Steven Svoboda (2001) writes:

> *Our schools seem to be creating overt depression in girls and covert depression in boys. Through violence, male hormones and brains cry out for a different school promoting closer bonding, smaller classes, more verbalization, less male isolation, better discipline, and more attention to male learning styles. Most of all, boys need men in their schools. (90% of elementary teachers are female.) They need male teachers, male teaching assistants, male volunteers from the parents or grandparents, and older male students. Peer mentoring across grades helps everybody involved.*

For girls, Gurian and Henley recommend developing their leadership abilities, encouraging girls to enjoy healthy competition, providing extra access to technology, and helping them understand the impact of the media on their self-images.

COUNTERPOINT No, differences are too small or inconsistent to have educational implications.

Many of Gurian and Henley's claims about sex differences in learning are based on sex differences in the brain. But John Bruer (1999) cautions that

> *Although males are superior to females at mentally rotating objects, this seems to be the only spatial task for which psychologists have found such a difference. Moreover, when they do find gender differences, these differences tend to be very small. The scientific consensus among psychologists and neuroscientists who conduct these studies is that whatever gender differences exist may have interesting consequences for the scientific study of the brain, but they have no practical or instructional consequences.*

In fact, there are boys who thrive in schools and boys who do not; girls who are strong in mathematics and girls who have difficulties; boys who excel in languages and those who do not. There is some evidence that the activities used to teach math may make a difference for girls. Elementary age girls may do better in math if they learn in cooperative as opposed to competitive activities. Certainly, it makes sense to balance both cooperative and competitive approaches so that students who learn better each way have equal opportunities (Fennema & Peterson, 1988).

It also makes sense to offer a variety of ways to learn, so that all students have access to the important outcomes of your teaching. Your attitude and encouragement may make the difference for students, male or female, who need a persuasive boost to believe in themselves as writers, or mathematicians, or painters, or athletes.

WHAT DO YOU THINK?
Vote online at **www.mylabschool.com**

Dialects

STOP | THINK | WRITE When you want a soft drink, what do you call it? Do you think people in other parts of the United States use the same term? ■

Growing up in Texas, we always asked, "Do you want a *coke*?" If the answer was yes, the next question was, "What kind—cola, root beer, lemon-lime, orange?" When I moved to New Jersey, I had to ask for a *soda*—if I asked for a coke, then that is just what I got. Twenty years later, at our moving-to-Ohio party, my colleague who had grown up in Columbus, Ohio, said, "You are going to have to learn to speak Midwestern and ask for a *'bottlapop.'*" Different regions have different ways of speaking—both in their accents and in their word usage.

A **dialect** is any variety of a language spoken by a particular group. Eugene Garcia (2002) defines a dialect as "a regional variation of language characterized by distinct grammar, vocabulary, and pronunciation" (p. 218). The dialect is part of the group's collective identity. Actually, every person reading this book speaks at least one dialect, maybe more, because there is no one absolute standard English. The English language has several dialects, for example, Australian, Canadian, British, and American. Within each of these dialects are variations. A few examples for American English are Southern, Bostonian, Cajun, and African American Vernacular (Garcia, 2002).

Dialects differ in their rules about pronunciation, grammar, and vocabulary, but it is important to remember that these differences are not errors. Each dialect is logical, complex, and rule-governed. An example of this is the use of the double negative. In many versions of American English, the double negative construction, such as "I don't have no more," is incorrect. But in many dialects such as some varieties of African American Vernacular English, and in other languages (for instance, Russian, French, Spanish, and Hungarian), the double negative is part of the grammatical rules. To say "I don't want anything" in Spanish, you must literally say, "I don't want nothing," or "No quiero nada."

Dialects and Pronunciation. Another area in which dialects differ is pronunciation, which can lead to spelling problems. In some varieties of African American Vernacular English and in Southern dialects, for instance, there is less attention paid to pronouncing the ends of words. A lack of attention to final consonants, such as *s*, can lead to failure to indicate possession, third-person singular verbs, and plurals in the standard way. So *John's book* might be *John book*, and the singular and plural will sound the same for words such as *thinks*, *wasps*, and *lists*. When endings are not pronounced, there are more *homonyms* (words that sound alike but have different meanings) in the student's speech than the unknowing teacher may expect; *spent* and *spend* might sound alike, for example. Even without the confusions caused by dialect differences, there are many homonyms in English. Usually, special attention is given to words such as these when they come up in spelling lessons. If teachers are aware of the special homonyms in student dialects, they can teach these differences directly.

Dialects and Teaching. What does all of this mean for teachers? How can they cope with linguistic diversity in the classroom? First, they can be sensitive to their own possible negative stereotypes about children who speak a different dialect. Second, teachers can ensure comprehension by repeating instructions using different words and by asking students to paraphrase instructions or give examples.

But what about the use of home language in the classroom? The best teaching approach seems to be to focus on understanding the children and to accept their language as a valid and correct system, but to teach the alternative forms of English (or whatever the dominant language is in your country) that are used in more formal work settings and writing so that the students will have access to a range of opportunities. For example, Lisa Delpit (1995) describes Martha Demientieff, a Native Alaskan teacher of Athabaskan children in a small village. The teacher's goal is for her students to become fluent in both their dialect, which she calls "Heritage English," and the "Formal English" of employers and others outside the village. She explains to her students that people outside the village will judge them by the way they talk and write. She goes on to explain:

> We have to feel sorry for them because they have only one way to talk. We're going to learn two ways to say things. One will be our Heritage way. The other will be Formal English. Then when we go to get jobs, we'll be able to talk like those people who only know and can only listen to one way. Maybe after we get the jobs we can help them to learn how it feels to have another language, like ours, that feels so good. We'll talk like them when we have to, but we'll always know our way is best. (p. 41)

Moving between two speech forms is called **code-switching**—something we all have learned to do. Sometimes, the code is formal speech for educational or professional communication. Sometimes, the code is informal for talk among friends and family. And

Connect and **Extend** to the **Research**

See the Autumn 2000 issue of *Theory Into Practice* on "Children and Languages in School." See **http://www.coe.ohio-state.edu/TIP.** This journal is especially for educators.

Dialect Rule-governed variation of a language spoken by a particular group.

Code-switching Successful switching between cultures in language, dialect, or nonverbal behaviors to fit the situation.

sometimes, the codes are different dialects. Even young children recognize variations in codes. Delpit (1995) describes the reaction of one of her 1st grade students to her very first reading lesson. After she carefully recited the memorized introduction from the teacher's manual, a student raised his hand and asked, "Teacher, how come you talkin' like a white person? You talkin' just like my momma talk when she get on the phone."

Learning the alternative versions of a language is easy for most children, as long as they have good models, clear instruction, and opportunities for authentic practice.

Bilingualism

Bilingualism is a topic that sparks heated debates and touches many emotions. One reason is the changing demographics discussed earlier in this chapter. About 18% of the United States population speaks a language other than English at home—half of these families speak Spanish. In the past 10 years, there has been a 65% increase in the number of Spanish-speaking students and almost a 100% increase in the number of students who speak Asian languages. In some states, almost one-fourth of all students speak a first language other than English—usually Spanish (Gersten, 1996a). By 2050, about one-fourth of the entire United States population is expected to be Latina/o (Yetman, 1999). Right now, there is one qualified teacher for every 100 English language learners (Hawkins, 2004).

Two terms that you will see associated with bilingualism are English language learners (ELL), describing students whose primary or heritage language is not English, and English as a Second Language (ESL) classrooms, where these students learn English.

Connect and Extend to the Research

Research-Based Principles for Educating English Language Learners
The English Language Learners Knowledge Base compiled by the Education Alliance at Brown University describes nine researched-based principles for supporting English Language Learners. The principles are available online at **http://www.helpforschools.com/ELLKBase/guidelines/PrinciplesELL.shtml**

What Does Bilingualism Mean? There are disagreements about the meaning of *bilingualism*. Some definitions focus exclusively on a language-based meaning: Bilingual people, or bilinguals, speak two languages. But this limited definition minimizes the significant problems that bilingual students face. Consider the words of these two students:

> A 9th-grade boy, who recently arrived in California from Mexico: "There is so much discrimination and hate. Even from other kids from Mexico who have been here longer. They don't treat us like brothers. They hate even more. It makes them feel more like natives. They want to be American. They don't want to speak Spanish to us; they already know English and how to act. If they are with us, other people will treat them more like wetbacks, so they try to avoid us." (Olsen, 1988, p. 36)

> A 10th-grade Chinese-American girl who had been in America for several years: "I don't know who I am. Am I the good Chinese daughter? Am I an American teenager? I always feel I am letting my parents down when I am with my friends because I act so American, but I also feel that I will never really be an American. I never feel really comfortable with myself anymore." (Olsen, 1988, p. 30)

The experiences of these two students show that there is more to being bilingual than just speaking two languages. You must also be able to move back and forth between two cultures while still maintaining a sense of your own identity (Hakuta & Garcia, 1989). Being bilingual and bicultural means mastering the knowledge necessary to communicate in two cultures as well as dealing with potential discrimination. As a teacher, you will have to help your students learn all these skills.

Connect and Extend to Your Teaching Portfolio

Add Table 5.4 "Ideas for Promoting Learning and Language Acquisition" to your Teaching Resources file.

Becoming Bilingual. Proficiency in a second language has two separate aspects: face-to-face communication (known as basic or contextualized language skills) and academic uses of language such as reading and writing about school subjects (known as academic English) (Fillmore & Snow, 2000; Garcia, 2002). It takes students about two to three years in a good-quality program to be able to communicate face-to-face in a second language, but mastering academic language skills in the new language takes five to seven years. So students who seem in conversation to "know" a second language may still have great difficulty with complex schoolwork in that language (Cummins, 1994; Ovando, 1989). Here is how one Spanish-speaking international student, who went on to earn a doctoral degree and teach at a university, described her struggles with texts in college:

> I could not understand why I was doing so poorly. After all, my grammar and spelling were excellent. It took me a long time to realize that the way text is organized in English

Bilingualism Speaking two languages fluently.

TABLE 5.3

Myths about Bilingual Students
In the following table, L1 means the original language and L2 means the second language.

Myth	Truth
Learning a second language (L2) takes little time and effort.	Learning English as a second language takes 2–3 years for oral and 5–7 years for academic language use.
All language skills (listening, speaking, reading, writing) transfer from L1 to L2.	Reading is the skill that transfers most readily.
Code-switching is an indication of a language disorder.	Code-switching indicates high-level language skills in both L1 and L2.
All bilinguals easily maintain both languages.	It takes great effort and attention to maintain high-level skills in both languages.
Children do not lose their first language.	Loss of L1 and underdevelopment of L2 are problems for second language learners (**semilingual** in L1 and L2).
Exposure to English is sufficient for L2 learning.	To learn L2, students need to have a reason to communicate, access to English speakers, interaction, support, feedback, and time.
To learn English, students' parents need to speak only English at home.	Children need to use both languages in many contexts.
Reading in L1 is detrimental to learning English.	Literacy-rich environments in either L1 or L2 support development of necessary prereading skills.
Language disorders must be identified by tests in English.	Children must be tested in both L1 and L2 to determine language disorders.

Source: From *The Hispanic Child: Speech, Language, Culture and Education* by Alejandro E. Brice. Published by Allyn and Bacon, Boston, MA. Copyright © 2002 by Pearson Education. Adapted by permission of the publisher.

is considerably different from the way text is organized in a romance language, Spanish. The process involved a different set of rhetorical rules which were grounded in cultural ways of being. I had never heard of the thesis statement, organizational rules, cohesion, coherence, or other features of discourse. (Sotillo, 2002, p. 280)

There are a number of misconceptions about becoming bilingual. Table 5.3 summarizes a few of these taken from Brice (2002). Because they may be struggling with academic English, even though they are very knowledgeable, bilingual students may be overlooked for gifted and talented programs. The next section tells you how to avoid this situation.

Reaching Every Student: Recognizing Giftedness in Bilingual Students

To identify gifted bilingual students, you can use a case study or portfolio approach in order to collect a variety of evidence, including interviews with parents and peers, formal and informal assessments, samples of student work and performances, and student self-assessments. This checklist from Castellano and Diaz (2002) is a useful guide. Watch for students who:

_____ Learn English quickly
_____ Take risks in trying to communicate in English
_____ Practice English skills by themselves
_____ Initiate conversations with native English speakers
_____ Do not frustrate easily
_____ Are curious about new words or phrases and practice them

Semilingual Not proficient in any language; speaking one or more languages inadequately.

_____ Question word meanings; for example, "How can a bat be an animal and also something you use to hit a ball?"
_____ Look for similarities between words in their native language and English
_____ Are able to modify their language for less capable English speakers
_____ Use English to demonstrate leadership skills; for example, use English to resolve disagreements and to facilitate cooperative learning groups
_____ Prefer to work independently or with students whose level of English proficiency is higher than theirs
_____ Are able to express abstract verbal concepts with a limited English vocabulary
_____ Are able to use English in a creative way; for example, can make puns, poems, jokes, or original stories in English
_____ Become easily bored with routine tasks or drill work
_____ Have a great deal of curiosity
_____ Are persistent; stick to a task
_____ Are independent and self-sufficient
_____ Have a long attention span
_____ Become absorbed with self-selected problems, topics, and issues
_____ Retain, easily recall, and use new information
_____ Demonstrate social maturity, especially in the home or community

Bilingual Education

Virtually everyone agrees that all citizens should learn the official language of their country. But when and how should instruction in that language begin? Here, the debate is bitter at times, but it is clear the United States has not solved the problem. For example, "Spanish-speaking students—even when taught and tested in Spanish—still score at the [bottom] 32nd percentile in relation to a national comparison group (taught and tested in English)" (Goldenberg, 1996, p. 353).

Is it better to teach **English Language learners (ELL)** to read first in their native language or should they begin reading instruction in English? Do these children need some oral lessons in English before reading instruction can be effective? Should other subjects, such as mathematics and social studies, be taught in the primary (home) language until the children are fluent in English? On these questions there are two basic positions, which have given rise to two contrasting teaching approaches, one that focuses on making the *transition* to English as quickly as possible and the other that attempts to *maintain* or improve the native language and use the native language as the primary teaching language until English skills are more fully developed.

Connect and **Extend** to Your **Teaching Portfolio**

Is the increasing cultural plurality of the United States making the learning of foreign languages (namely, Spanish) more important in U.S. schools than was the case in the past?

Proponents of the *transition* approach believe that English ought to be introduced as early as possible; they argue that valuable learning time is lost if students are taught in their native language. Most bilingual programs today follow this line of thinking. Proponents of *native-language maintenance instruction*, however, raise four important issues (Gersten, 1996b; Goldenberg, 1996; Hakuta & Garcia, 1989). First, children who are forced to try to learn math or science in an unfamiliar language are bound to have trouble. What if you had been forced to learn fractions or biology in a second language that you had studied for only a semester? Some psychologists believe students taught by this approach may become *semilingual*; that is, they are not proficient in either language. Being semilingual may be one reason the dropout rate is so high for low-SES Latino students (Ovando & Collier, 1998).

Second, students may get the message that their home languages (and therefore, their families and cultures) are second class. You saw the seeds of these feelings in the stories of the two students at the beginning of this section. Third, the academic content (math, science, history, etc.) that students are taught in their native language is learned—they do not forget the knowledge and skills when they are able to speak English.

Fourth is what Kenji Hakuta (1986) calls a "paradoxical attitude of admiration and pride for school-attained bilingualism on the one hand and scorn and shame for home-brewed immigrant bilingualism on the other" (p. 229). Ironically, by the time students have mastered academic English and let their home language deteriorate, they reach

English Language Learners (ELL) Students whose primary or heritage language is not English.

Even though most people agree that all citizens should learn the official language of their country, how this should be accomplished in school remains a very controversial question.

secondary school and are encouraged to learn a second language. Hakuta (1986) suggests that the goals of the educational system could be the development of *all students* as functional bilinguals. The United States is "one of the few countries in the world that takes pride in the fact that we speak only one language" (Noguera, 2005, p. 13).

One approach to reaching this goal is to create classes that mix students who are learning a second language with students who are native speakers. The objective is for both groups to become fluent in both languages (Sheets, 2005). My daughter spent a summer in such a program in Quebec and was ahead in every French class after that. For truly effective bilingual education, we will need many bilingual teachers. If you have a competence in another language, you might want to develop it fully for your teaching.

Research on Bilingual Programs. It is difficult to separate politics from practice in the debate about bilingual education. It is clear that high-quality bilingual education programs can have positive results. Students improve in the subjects that were taught in their native language, in their mastery of English, and in self-esteem as well (Crawford, 1997; Hakuta & Gould, 1987; Wright & Taylor, 1995). **English as a second language (ESL)** programs seem to have positive effects on reading comprehension (Fitzgerald, 1995). But attention today is shifting from debate about general approaches to a focus on effective teaching strategies. As you will see many times in this book, a combination of clarity of learning goals and direct instruction in needed skills—including learning strategies and tactics, teacher- or peer-guided practice leading to independent practice, authentic and engaging tasks, opportunities for interaction and conversation that are academically focused, and warm encouragement from the teacher—seems to be effective (Chamot & O'Malley, 1996; Gersten, 1996b; Goldenberg, 1996). Table 5.4 provides a set of constructs for promoting learning and language acquisition that capture many of these methods for effective instruction.

We have dealt with a wide range of differences in this chapter. How can teachers provide an appropriate education for all their students? One answer is culturally inclusive classrooms.

Connect and Extend to Professional Journals

Thomas, W. P., & Collier, V. P. (1998). Two languages are better than one. *Educational Leadership*, 55(4), 23–27. This article makes the case that native and non-native speakers of English benefit greatly from learning together in two languages.

Connect and Extend to PRAXIS II™

Bilingual Issues (IV, B4)

Identify the major issues related to the debate over bilingual education. Explain the major approaches to bilingual education, and describe steps that a teacher can take to promote the learning and language acquisition of non–English-speaking students.

English as a second language (ESL) Designation for programs and classes to teach English to students who are not native speakers of English.

Culturally inclusive classrooms Classrooms that provide culturally diverse students equitable access to the teaching-learning process.

Creating Culturally Inclusive Classrooms

Sheets (2005) uses the term "culturally inclusive" to describe classrooms that provide culturally diverse students with equitable access to the teaching-learning process. The goal of creating **culturally inclusive classrooms** is to eliminate racism, sexism, classism, and

TABLE 5.4

Ideas for Promoting Learning and Language Acquisition

Effective teaching for students in bilingual and ESL classrooms combines many strategies—direct instruction, mediation, coaching, feedback, modeling, encouragement, challenge, and authentic activities.

1. Structures, frameworks, scaffolds, and strategies
   - Provide support to students by "thinking aloud," building on and clarifying input of students
   - Use visual organizers, story maps, or other aids to help students organize and relate information
2. Relevant background knowledge and key vocabulary concepts
   - Provide adequate background knowledge to students and informally assess whether students have background knowledge
   - Focus on key vocabulary words and use consistent language
   - Incorporate students' primary language meaningfully
3. Mediation/feedback
   - Give feedback that focuses on meaning, not grammar, syntax, or pronunciation
   - Give frequent and comprehensible feedback
   - Provide students with prompts or strategies
   - Ask questions that press students to clarify or expand on initial statements
   - Provide activities and tasks that students can complete
   - Indicate to students when they are successful
   - Assign activities that are reasonable, avoiding undue frustration
   - Allow use of native language responses (when context is appropriate)
   - Be sensitive to common problems in second language acquisition
4. Involvement
   - Ensure active involvement of all students, including low-performing students
   - Foster extended discourse
5. Challenge
   - Implicit (cognitive challenge, use of higher-order questions)
   - Explicit (high but reasonable expectations)
6. Respect for—and responsiveness to—cultural and personal diversity
   - Show respect for students as individuals, respond to things students say, show respect for culture and family, and possess knowledge of cultural diversity
   - Incorporate students' experiences into writing and language arts activities
   - Link content to students' lives and experiences to enhance understanding
   - View diversity as an asset, reject cultural deficit notions

Source: From "Literacy Instruction for Language-Minority Students: The Transition Years," by R. Gersten, 1996, *The Elementary School Journal, 96,* pp. 241–242. Copyright © 1996 by the University of Chicago Press. Adapted with permission.

prejudice while adapting the content and methods of instruction to meet the needs of all students. In the past, discussions of teaching low-income students from racial, ethnic, or language minority groups have focused on remediating problems or overcoming perceived deficits. But thinking today emphasizes teaching to the strengths and the resilience of these students. In this section, we look at two positive approaches—culturally relevant pedagogy and fostering resilience.

Connect and Extend to the Research

See the Summer 2003 issue of *Theory Into Practice* on Teacher Reflection and Race in Cultural Contexts (Vol. 42, No. 3). Guest Editor: H. Richard Milner.

Culturally Relevant Pedagogy

Several researchers have focused on teachers who are especially successful with students of color and students in poverty (Delpit, 1995; Ladson-Billings, 1994, 1995; Moll, Amanti, Neff, & Gonzalez, 1992; Siddle Walker, 2001). The work of Gloria Ladson-Billings (1990, 1992, 1995) is a good example. For three years, she studied excellent teachers in a California school district that served an African American community. In order to select the teachers, she asked parents and principals for nominations. Parents nominated teachers who respected them, created enthusiasm for learning in their children, and understood their children's need to operate successfully in two different worlds—the home community and the White world beyond. Principals nominated teachers who had few discipline referrals, high attendance rates, and high standardized test scores. Ladson-Billings was able to examine in depth 8 of the 9 teachers who were nominated by *both parents and principals.*

Based on her research, Ladson-Billings developed a conception of teaching excellence. She uses the term **culturally relevant pedagogy** to describe teaching that rests on three propositions. Students must:

Connect and Extend to Your Teaching Portfolio

Menkart, D. J. (1999). Deepening the meaning of heritage months. *Educational Leadership, 56*(7), 19–21. This article discusses how to get past foods and festivals to increase students' understandings of heritage.

Culturally relevant pedagogy Excellent teaching for students of color that includes academic success, developing/maintaining cultural competence, and developing a critical consciousness to challenge the status quo.

Experience Academic Success. "Despite the current social inequities and hostile classroom environments, students must develop their academic skills. The ways those skills are developed may vary, but all students need literacy, numeracy, technological, social, and political skills in order to be active participants in a democracy" (Ladson-Billings, 1995, p. 160).

Develop/Maintain Their Cultural Competence. As they become more academically skilled, students still retain their cultural competence. "Culturally relevant teachers utilize students' culture as a vehicle for learning" (Ladson-Billings, 1995, p. 161). For example, one teacher used rap music to teach about literal and figurative meaning, rhyme, alliteration, and onomatopoeia in poetry. Another brought in a community expert known for her sweet potato pies to work with students. Follow-up lessons included investigations of George Washington Carver's sweet potato research, numerical analyses of taste tests, marketing plans for selling pies, and research on the educational preparation needed to become a chef.

Connect and **Extend** to Your **Teaching Portfolio**

Midobuche, E. (1999). Respect in the classroom: Reflections of a Mexican-American educator. *Educational Leadership*, 56(7), 80–83. The story of the early school experiences of a Spanish-speaking child in an all-English world.

Develop a Critical Consciousness to Challenge the Status Quo. In addition to developing academic skills while retaining cultural competence, excellent teachers help students "develop a broader sociopolitical consciousness that allows them to critique the social norms, values, mores, and institutions that produce and maintain social inequities" (Ladson-Billings, 1995, p. 162). For example, in one school, students were upset that their textbooks were out of date. They mobilized to investigate the funding formulas that allowed middle-class students to have newer books, wrote letters to the newspaper editor to challenge these inequities, and updated their texts with current information from other sources.

Ladson-Billings (1995) noted that many people have said her three principles "are just good teaching." She agrees that she is describing good teaching, but questions "why so little of it seems to be occurring in classrooms populated by African American students" (p. 159). Geneva Gay (2000) uses the term *culturally responsive teaching* to describe a similar approach that uses the "cultural knowledge, prior experiences, frames of reference, and performance styles of ethnically diverse students to make learning encounters more relevant to and effective for them. It *teaches to and through* the strengths of these students. It is culturally *validating and affirming*" (p. 29).

Lisa Delpit (2003) describes three steps for teaching students of color that are consistent with culturally relevant pedagogy: (1) Teachers must be convinced of the inherent intellectual capability, humanity, and spiritual character of their students—they must believe in the children. There are many examples around the country of schools where

Culturally competent teachers believe in children, connect with their lives and cultures, and learn who they really are.

low-income African American students are reading well above grade level and doing advanced math. When scores are low, the fault is not in the students but in their education. (2) Teachers must fight the foolishness that high test scores or scripted lessons are evidence of good learning and good teaching. Delpit says that successful instruction is "constant, rigorous, integrated across disciplines, connected to students' lived cultures, connected to their intellectual legacies, engaging, and designed for critical thinking and problem solving that is useful beyond the classroom" (p. 18). (3) Teachers must learn who their students are and the legacies they bring. Then, students can explore their own intellectual legacies and understand the important reasons for academic, social, physical, and moral excellence—not just to "get a job" but also "for our community, for your ancestors, for your descendents" (p. 19).

The qualities of good teachers and the descriptions of best practices described by Ladson-Billings and Gay are evident in the characteristics of schools that were valued by African American families during the time of segregation in the South (Siddle Walker, 2001). Exemplary African American teachers are described repeatedly by their students as having high expectations and a demanding teaching style. They insisted that students learn and refused to lower their standards, even if it meant working extra hours with students after school. Consistent with the research on teacher quality described in Chapter 1, these exemplary teachers often had more education than White teachers in the same states. The teachers also were respected members of the community who cared deeply about the children in their classes, as you can see in the story of Vivian Gunn Morris, now a professor of education, in the *Stories of Learning/Tributes to Teaching* feature.

Fostering Resilience

In any given week, the 12% to 15% of school-age children who have urgent needs for social and emotional support are not getting help. Community and mental health services often don't reach the students who are at the highest risk. But many children at risk for academic failure not only survive—they thrive. They are resilient students. What can we learn from these students? What can teachers and schools do to encourage **resilience**?

Resilience The ability to adapt successfully in spite of difficult circumstances and threats to development.

STORIES OF LEARNING / TRIBUTES TO TEACHING

"School broadened my horizons about different ways of doing things."

For me, caring was personified by **MRS. WILLIE MAE THOMPSON,** my home economics teacher. Mrs. Thompson was like a third mother to me—third only to my biological mother and favorite aunt (Earline). As with my friends, we lived in the same neighborhood (as did most of our teachers and principals). Most families attended one of the four Black churches in the community. Hence, many of the teachers also taught us in Sunday school as well. We were welcome to Mrs. Thompson's anytime and could visit without calling. So it is no surprise that home economics was probably my favorite subject (if I had to choose a favorite). I liked being able to immediately apply what I learned. Because of home economics, my family enjoyed (or suffered) my preparation of foods in new and different ways. School broadened my horizons about different ways of doing things. Thanks to Mrs. Thompson, I made most of my own clothes after taking home economics in seventh grade. But I was also fortunate to have many other outstanding and caring teachers as well.

At the risk of painting an overly idyllic portrait of my school experience, let me point out that children were pretty much the same as they are today. Bullying seems to be a common school experience and is part of my memories as well. In first grade, some of my classmates decided to bully me and threw rocks at me on my way home from school. I reported the incident to Mrs. Magnolia Watkins, my first-grade teacher. Mrs. Watkins intervened and it never happened again.

Source: From "No More Cotton Picking: African American Voices from a Small Southern Town," by Vivian Gunn Morris and C. L. Morris. In Gloria Swindler Boutte (Ed.), *Resounding Voices: School Experiences of People from Diverse Ethnic Backgrounds.* Published by Allyn and Bacon, Boston, MA.

Resilient Students. People vary in their capacity to be resilient. Students who seem able to thrive in spite of serious challenges are actively engaged in school. They have good interpersonal skills, confidence in their own ability to learn, positive attitudes toward school, pride in their ethnicity, and high expectations (Borman & Overman, 2004; Lee, 2005). Also, students who have high intelligence or valued talents are more protected from risks. Being easy-going and optimistic is associated with resilience as well. Factors outside the student—interpersonal relationships and social support—matter, too. It helps to have a warm relationship with a parent who has high expectations and supports learning by organizing space and time at home for study. But even without such a parent, a strong bond with someone competent—a grandparent, aunt, uncle, teacher, mentor, or other caring adult—can serve the same supportive function. Involvement in school, community, or religious activities can provide more connections to concerned adults and also teach lessons in social skills and leadership (Berk, 2005).

Resilient Classrooms. You can't choose personalities or parents for your students. Even if you could, stresses can build up for even the most resilient students. Beth Doll and her colleagues (2005) suggest that we have to change classrooms instead of kids because "alternative strategies will be more enduring and most successful when they are integrated into naturally occurring systems of support [like schools] that surround children" (p. 3). In addition, there is some evidence that changes in classrooms—such as reducing class size and forming supportive relationships with teachers—have a greater impact on the academic achievement of African American students compared to Latino and White students (Borman & Overman, 2004). So how can you create a classroom that supports resilience?

Borman and Overman (2004) identified two characteristics of schools associated with academic resilience: a safe, orderly environment, and positive teacher–student relationships. In their book on resilient classrooms, Doll and her colleagues (2005) draw on research in education and psychology on best practices for children in poverty and children with disabilities to describe the characteristics of resilient classrooms. There are two strands of elements that bind students to their classroom community. One strand emphasizes the self-agency of students—their capacity to set and pursue goals; the second strand emphasizes caring and connected relationships in the classroom and the school.

Self-Agency Strand

- ***Academic self-efficacy***, a belief in your own ability to learn, is one of the most consistent predictors of academic achievement. As you will see in Chapters 9 and 10, self-efficacy emerges when students tackle challenging, meaningful tasks with the support needed to be successful and observe other students doing the same thing. Accurate and encouraging feedback from teachers also helps.
- ***Behavioral self-control***, or student self-regulation, is essential for a safe and orderly learning environment. Chapters 6, 9, and 12 will give you ideas for helping students develop self-regulation knowledge and skills.
- ***Academic self-determination***, making choices, setting goals, and following through, is the third element in the self-agency strand. As you will see in Chapter 10, students who are self-determined are more motivated and committed to learning.

Relationship Strand

- ***Caring teacher–student relationships*** are consistently associated with better school performance, especially for students who face serious challenges. We saw the power of caring teachers in Chapter 3 and will return to this theme in Chapter 11.
- ***Effective peer relations***, as we saw in Chapter 3, also are critical in connecting students to school.
- ***Effective home–school relationships*** are the final element in building a caring, connected network for students. In the School Development program, James Comer has

Family and Community Partnerships

Guidelines: Building Learning Communities

Joyce Epstein (1995) describes six types of family/school/community partnerships. The following guidelines are based on her six categories:

Parenting partnerships: Help all families establish home environments to support children as students.

EXAMPLES

1. Offer workshops, videos, courses, family literacy fairs, and other informational programs to help parents cope with parenting situations that they identify as important.
2. Establish family support programs to assist with nutrition, health, and social services.
3. Find ways to help families share information with the school about the child's cultural background, talents, and needs—learn from the families.

Communication: Design effective forms for school-to-home and home-to-school communication.

EXAMPLES

1. Make sure communications fit the needs of families. Provide translations, visual support, large print—whatever is needed to make communication effective.
2. Visit families in their territory after gaining their permission. Don't expect family members to come to school until a trusting relationship is established.
3. Balance messages about problems with communications of accomplishments and positive information.

Volunteering: Recruit and organize parent help and support.

EXAMPLES

1. Do an annual postcard survey to identify family talents, interests, times available, and suggestions for improvements.
2. Establish a structure (telephone tree, etc.) to keep all families informed. Make sure families without telephones are included.
3. If possible, set aside a room for volunteer meetings and projects.

Learning at home: Provide information and ideas for families about how to help children with schoolwork and learning activities.

EXAMPLES

1. Provide assignment schedules, homework policies, and tips on how to help with schoolwork without doing the work.
2. Get family input into curriculum planning—have idea and activity exchanges.
3. Send home learning packets and enjoyable learning activities, especially over holidays and summers.

Decision-making partnerships: Include families in school decisions, developing family and community leaders and representatives.

EXAMPLES

1. Create family advisory committees for the school with parent representatives.
2. Make sure all families are in a network with their representative.

Community partnerships: Identify and integrate resources and services from the community to strengthen school programs, family practices, and student learning and development.

EXAMPLES

1. Have students and parents research existing resources—build a database.
2. Identify service projects for students—explore service learning.
3. Identify community members who are school alumni and get them involved in school programs.

For more ideas on partnerships with parents, see **http://www.ssta.sk.ca/EducationServices/EduationalIssues/ParentSchoolPartnership/Types.htm**

Source: Excerpt from pp. 704–705, "School/Family/Community Partnerships: Caring for Children We Share," by J. L. Epstein, *Phi Delta Kappan, 76*, pp. 701–712. Copyright © 1995 by Phi Delta Kappan. Reprinted with permission of Phi Delta Kappan and the author.

found that when parents stay involved, their children's grades and test scores improve (Comer, Haynes, & Joyner, 1996). The *Family and Community Partnerships Guidelines* give some ideas for connecting with families.

Connect and Extend to Your Teaching Portfolio

Use the Family and Community Partnerships Guidelines to brainstorm ideas for family involvement in helping your students "take their learning home."

Constructing a Resilient Classroom. In order to build student self-agency and relationships, the two strands of resilience, Doll and her colleagues (2005) provide student questionnaires for gathering data about your classroom. Figure 5.5 on the next page is an example of the "teacher relationship" part of the student questionnaire. One teacher

FIGURE 5.5

Creating a Resilient Classroom

Here is an example of a student questionnaire about perceptions of relationships with the teacher. Using results from this questionnaire, one teacher, Ellie, made plans to improve her relationships with her students using teh Plan Record Worksheet below.

QUESTIONNAIRE

Ellie's students circled YES, SOMETIMES, or NEVER in answer to these questions:

1. My teacher listens carefully to me when I talk.	YES	SOMETIMES	NEVER
2. My teacher helps me when I need help.	YES	SOMETIMES	NEVER
3. My teacher respects me.	YES	SOMETIMES	NEVER
4. My teacher believes that I am an important member of this class.	YES	SOMETIMES	NEVER
5. My teacher makes it fun to be in class.	YES	SOMETIMES	NEVER
6. My teacher is fair to me.	YES	SOMETIMES	NEVER

PLAN RECORD WORKSHEET

Classroom: *Ellie's third grade* Record for week of: ____________

	Did this happen?
Activity 1 What will be done? *Take turns giving "special time" at lunch to the three kids that are struggling most: Matthew, Lisette, Arnie.* Who will do it? *Ellie.* When? *Every Tuesday and Thursday at lunch period.* Where? *In the classroom.*	YES PARTLY NO
Activity 2 What will be done? *Plan a fun learning game for the mid-morning break.* Who will do it? *Ellie and the class.* When? *Every day from 10 to 10:20 a.m.* Where? *In the classroom.*	YES PARTLY NO
Activity 3 What will be done? *Make friendship bracelets to remind us to be kind to classmates.* Who will do it? *Classroom students.* When? *Week 1.* Where? *In the classroom.*	YES PARTLY NO

Source: From *Resilient classrooms: Creating healthy environments for learning* by B. Doll, S. Zucker, & K. Brehm.

used this questionnaire and found that almost half of her students did not listen carefully or have any fun in class. They said the teacher was not fair and did not help, respect, or believe in them. Figure 5.5 also shows the plan the teacher developed based on the results of the questionnaire.

Diversity and Convergences

This entire chapter has been about diversity, so here I want to focus on four areas where diversity among students can affect their learning in classrooms: social organization, cultural values and learning preferences, sociolinguistics, and the digital divide. The chapter will conclude with ideas that apply to all students.

Diversity in Learning

Roland Tharp (1989) outlines several dimensions of classrooms that reflect the diversity of the students. The dimensions—social organization, cultural values and learning styles, and sociolinguistics—can be tailored to better fit the background of students.

Connect and **Extend** to the **Research**

For an entire volume devoted to educating students who face challenges, see Stringfield, S., & Land, D. (2002). *Educating at-risk students: Yearbook of the National Society for the Study of Education* (NSSE) (Vol. 2). Chicago, IL: University of Chicago Press.

Social Organization. Tharp (1989) states that "a central task of educational design is to make the organization of teaching, learning, and performance compatible with the social structures in which students are most productive, engaged, and likely to learn" (p. 350). Social structure or social organization in this context means the ways people interact to accomplish a particular goal. For example, the social organization of Hawaiian society depends heavily on collaboration and cooperation. Children play together in groups of friends and siblings, with older children often caring for the younger ones. When cooperative work groups of four or five boys and girls were established in Hawaiian classrooms, student learning and participation improved (Okagaki, 2001). The teacher worked intensively with one group while the children in the remaining groups helped each other. But when the same structure was tried in a Navajo classroom, students would not work together. These students are socialized to be more solitary and not to play with the opposite sex. By setting up same-sex working groups of only two or three Navajo students, teachers encouraged them to help each other. If you have students from several cultures, you may need to provide choices and variety in grouping structures.

Connect and **Extend** to **Professional Journals**

O'Neil, J. (1990). Link between style, culture proves divisive. *Educational Leadership*, 48(2), 8.

Focus Question: Why do some educators argue against linking learning styles to cultural differences?

Cultural Values and Learning Preferences. Rosa Hernandez Sheets (2005) describes three characteristics of teachers who design culturally inclusive classrooms. The teachers (1) recognize the various ways all their students display their capabilities; (2) respond to students' preferred ways of learning; and (3) understand that a particular group's cultural practices, values, and learning preferences may not apply to everyone in that group.

Results of some research suggest that Hispanic American students are more oriented toward family and group loyalty. This may mean that these students prefer cooperative activities and dislike being made to compete with fellow students (Garcia, 1992; Vasquez, 1990). Four values shared by many Latina/o students (not all—remember Sheets's 3rd characteristic cited above) are:

Familismo—tightly knit families. Discussing family problems or business may be seen as disloyal.

Simpatia—value of interpersonal harmony. Assertively voicing personal opinions or arguing may be seen as inappropriate.

Respecto—respect for people in authority, for example, teachers and government officials.

Personalismo—valuing of close interpersonal relationships; discomfort with distant, cold, professional relationships. (Dingfelder, 2005)

The learning styles of African Americans may be inconsistent with teaching approaches in most schools. Some of the characteristics of this learning style are a visual/global approach rather than a verbal/analytic approach; a preference for reasoning by inference rather than by formal logic; a focus on people and relationships; a preference for energetic involvement in several activities simultaneously rather than routine, step-by-step learning; a tendency to approximate numbers, space and time; and a greater dependence on nonverbal communication. Students of color who identify with their traditional cultures tend to respond better to open-ended questions with more than one answer, as opposed to single, right-answer questions. Questions that focus on meaning or the "big picture" may be more productive than questions that focus on details (Bennett, 1999; Gay, 2000; Sheets, 2005).

Native Americans also appear to have a more global, visual style of learning. For example, Navajo students prefer hearing a story all the way through to the end before discussing the parts of the story. Teachers who stop to ask questions seem odd to these students and interrupt the learning process (Tharp, 1989). Also, these students sometimes show strong preferences for learning privately, through trial and error, rather than having their mistakes made public (Vasquez, 1990).

There has been little research on the learning styles of Asian Americans, perhaps because they are seen as "successful minorities." Some educators suggest that Asian children tend to value teacher approval and to work well in structured, quiet learning environments where there are clear goals and social support (Manning & Baruth, 1996). But there are dangers in stereotyping both Asian and Asian American students as quiet, hardworking, and passive. Suzuki (1983) suggests that this practice "tends to reinforce conformity and stifle creativity. Asian and Pacific American students, therefore, frequently do not develop the ability to assert and express themselves verbally and are channeled in disproportionate numbers into the technical/scientific fields. As a result, many Asian and Pacific American students are overly conforming, and have their academic and social development narrowly circumscribed" (p. 9).

Suzuki's cautions are echoed by many critics of the research on ethnic differences in learning styles (Yee, 1992).

Cautions about Learning Styles Research. In considering this research on learning styles, you should keep two points in mind. First, the validity of some of the learning styles research has been strongly questioned, as we saw in the previous chapter. Second, there is a heated debate today about whether identifying ethnic group differences in learning styles and preferences is a dangerous, racist, sexist exercise. In our society, we are quick to move from the notion of "difference" to the idea of "deficits" and stereotypes (Gordon, 1991; O'Neil, 1990). I have included the information about learning style differences because I believe that, used sensibly, this information can help you better understand your students.

It is dangerous and incorrect, however, to assume that every individual in a group shares the same learning style. The best advice for teachers is to be sensitive to individual differences in all your students and to make available alternative paths to learning. Never prejudge how a student will learn best on the basis of assumptions about the student's ethnicity or race. Get to know the individual.

Sociolinguistics. **Sociolinguistics** is the study of "the courtesies and conventions of conversation across cultures" (Tharp, 1989, p. 351). A knowledge of sociolinguistics will help you understand why communication sometimes breaks down in classrooms. The classroom is a special setting for communicating; it has its own set of rules for when, how, to whom, about what subject, and in what manner to use language. Sometimes, the sociolinguistic skills of students do not fit the expectations of teachers or counselors, as we saw earlier.

In order to be successful, students must know the communication rules; that is, they must understand the **pragmatics** of the classroom—when, where, and how to communicate. This is not such an easy task. As class activities change, rules change. Sometimes you have to raise your hand (during the teacher's presentation), but sometimes you don't (during story time on the rug). Sometimes it is good to ask a question (during discussion), but other times it isn't so good (when the teacher is reprimanding you). These differing activity rules are called **participation structures,** and they define appropriate participation for each class activity. Most classrooms have many different participation structures. To be competent communicators in the classroom, students sometimes have to read very subtle, nonverbal cues telling them which participation structures are currently in effect. For example, in one classroom, when the teacher stood in a particular area of the room,

Sociolinguistics The study of the formal and informal rules for how, when, about what, to whom, and how long to speak in conversations within cultural groups.

Pragmatics The rules for when and how to use language to be an effective communicator in a particular culture.

Participation structures The formal and informal rules for how to take part in a given activity.

put her hands on her hips, and leaned forward at the waist, the children in the class were signaled to "stop and freeze," look at the teacher, and anticipate an announcement (Shultz & Florio, 1979).

Sources of Misunderstandings. Some children are simply better than others at reading the classroom situation because the participation structures of the school match the structures they have learned at home. The communication rules for most school situations are similar to those in middle-class homes, so children from these homes often appear to be more competent communicators. They know the unwritten rules. Students from different cultural backgrounds may have learned participation structures that conflict with the behaviors expected in school. For example, one study found that the home conversation style of Hawaiian children is to chime in with contributions to a story. In school, however, this overlapping style is viewed as "interrupting." When the teachers in one school learned about these differences and made their reading groups more like their students' home conversation groups, the young Hawaiian children in their classes improved in reading (Au, 1980; Tharp, 1989).

The source of misunderstanding can be a subtle sociolinguistic difference, such as how long the teacher waits to react to a student's response. White and Tharp (1988) found that when Navajo students in one class paused in giving a response, their Anglo teacher seemed to think that they were finished speaking. As a result, the teacher often unintentionally interrupted students. In another study, researchers found that Pueblo Indian students participated twice as much in classes where teachers waited longer to react. Waiting longer also helps girls to participate more freely in math and science classes (Grossman & Grossman, 1994).

It seems that even students who speak the same language as their teachers may still have trouble communicating, and thus learning school subjects, if their knowledge of pragmatics does not fit the school situation. What can teachers do? Especially in the early grades, you should make communication rules for activities clear and explicit. Do not assume students know what to do. Use cues to signal students when changes occur. Explain and demonstrate appropriate behavior. I have seen teachers show young children how to use their "inside voice," "six-inch voice," or "whisper voice." One teacher said and then demonstrated, "If you have to interrupt me while I'm working with other children, stand quietly beside me until I can help you." Be consistent in responding to students. If students are supposed to raise their hands, don't call on those who break the rules. In these ways you teach students how to learn in school.

Sources of misunderstanding can be very subtle. The families of racial and ethnic minority students often have to be vigilant about discrimination to protect their children. They may teach their children to notice and resist possible discrimination. Teachers may unintentionally offend these families if they are not sensitive to possible messages of discrimination. Carol Orange (2005) described a teacher who sent home a holiday worksheet that featured an alphabetical list of all the students in the class. Three students' names were not in the typed list, but were handwritten, out of order, and on the side of the sheet. Two of these students were Latino and one was African American. The mother of the African American student was very upset that her son was truly "marginalized" (written in the margins) on the list. These three students were added to the class (and hence, the list) later in the year, after the list was set up, but the teacher could have avoided this insult (unintended on her part) by redoing the list to give every student a place—a small but important symbol that she valued each one of them.

The Digital Divide. One area of teaching that often places students at risk is the use of technology. Many students have limited access to technology at home or in their communities. For example, in 2003, almost 26% of White individuals ages 3 and older lived in a household with broadband access, compared to about 14% for African Americans, 34% for Asian Americans and Pacific Islanders, and 13% for Latino Americans. When the family income was $24,000 a year or less, the number was under 10%, whereas a household income of greater than $150,000 had 58% with broadband in their homes (National Telecommunications and Information Administration, 2004). This split in access to technology has been called the **digital divide.**

Connect and Extend to the Research

See the Autumn 2003 issue of *Theory Into Practice* on "Classroom Management in a Diverse Society" (Vol. 42, No. 4). Guest Editor: Carol Weinstein.

Connect and Extend to Your Teaching Portfolio

For a concise discussion of cultural styles and the possible clashes of styles in classrooms, see Hilliard, A. G., III (1989). Teachers and cultural styles in a pluralistic society. *NEA Today*, 7(6), 65–69. Hilliard notes: "[T]he misunderstanding of behavioral styles leads teachers to mistake achievement in academic areas such as creative expression. Many teachers from Eurocentric cultures have a linear storytelling style. Many African-American children, on the other hand, exhibit a spiraling storytelling style with many departures from an initial point, but a return to make a story whole. Many teachers of these children are unable to follow the children's coherent stories. Some teachers even believe that the children's stories have no coherence at all. Some lose patience with the children and indicate that they are doing badly." (p. 69)

Digital divide The disparaties in access to technology between poor and more affluent students and families.

Convergences: Teaching Every Student

WHAT WOULD YOU SAY?

As the interview continues for the middle-school position, the next question is, "Describe the things you do for students to indicate you have feelings for them." What would you say? ■

The goal of this chapter is to give you a sense of the diversity in today's and tomorrow's schools and to help you meet the challenges of teaching in a multicultural classroom. How will you understand and build on all the cultures of your students? How will you deal with many different languages? Here are three general teaching principles to guide you in finding answers to these questions.

Know Your Students. We must learn who our students are and the legacies they bring (Delpit, 2003). Nothing you read in a chapter on cultural differences will teach you enough to understand the lives of all your students. If you can take other courses in college or read about other cultures, I encourage you to do it. But reading and studying are not enough. You should get to know your students' families and communities. Elba Reyes, a successful bilingual teacher for children with special needs, describes her approach:

> Usually I find that if you really want to know a parent, you get to know them on their own turf. This is key to developing trust and understanding the parents' perspective. First, get to know the community. Learn where the local grocery store is and what the children do after school. Then schedule a home visit at a time that is convenient for the parents. The home environment is not usually as ladened with failure. I sometimes observed the child being successful in the home, for example, riding a bicycle or helping with dinner. (Bos & Reyes, 1996, p. 349)

Try to spend time with students and parents on projects outside school. Ask parents to help in class or to speak to your students about their jobs, their hobbies, or the history and heritage of their ethnic group. In the elementary grades, don't wait until a student is in trouble to have the first meeting with a family member. Watch and listen to the ways that your students interact in large and small groups. Have students write to you, and write back to them. Eat lunch with one or two students. Spend some nonteaching time with them.

Respect Your Students. From knowledge ought to come respect for your students' learning strengths—for the struggles they face and the obstacles they have overcome. We must believe in our students (Delpit, 2003). For a child, genuine acceptance is a necessary condition for developing self-esteem. Sometimes the self-image and occupational aspirations of minority children actually decline in their early years in public school, probably because of the emphasis on majority culture values, accomplishments, and history. By presenting the accomplishments of particular members of an ethnic group or by bringing that group's culture into the classroom (in the form of literature, art, music, or any cultural knowledge), teachers can help students maintain a sense of pride in their cultural group. This integration of culture must be more than the "tokenism" of sampling ethnic foods or wearing costumes. Students should learn about the socially and intellectually important contributions of the various groups. There are many excellent references that provide background information, history, and teaching strategies for different groups of students (e.g., Banks, 2002; Gay, 2000; Irvine & Armento, 2001; Ladson-Billings, 1995).

Connect and Extend to the Research

The Summer 1995 issue of *Theory Into Practice* is devoted to "Culturally Relevant Teaching." See **http://www.coe.ohio-state.edu/TIP.** This journal is especially for educators.

Teach Your Students. The most important thing you can do for your students is teach them to read, write, speak, compute, think, and create—through constant, rigorous, culturally connected instruction (Delpit, 2003). Too often, goals for low-SES or minority group students have focused exclusively on basic skills. Students are taught words and sounds, but the meaning of the story is supposed to come later. Knapp, Turnbull, and Shields (1990, p. 5) make these suggestions:

- Focus on meaning and understanding from beginning to end—for example, by orienting instruction toward comprehending reading passages, communicating important ideas in written text, or understanding the concepts underlying number facts.
- Balance routine skill learning with novel and complex tasks from the earliest stages of learning.

- Provide context for skill learning that establishes clear reasons for needing to learn the skills.
- Influence attitudes and beliefs about the academic content areas as well as skills and knowledge.
- Eliminate unnecessary redundancy in the curriculum (e.g., repeating instruction in the same mathematics skills year after year).

And finally, teach students directly about how to be students. In the early grades, this could mean directly teaching the courtesies and conventions of the classroom: how to get a turn to speak, how and when to interrupt the teacher, how to whisper, how to get help in a small group, how to give an explanation that is helpful. In the later grades, it may mean teaching the study skills that fit your subject. You can ask students to learn "how we do it in school" without violating principle number two above—respect your students. Ways of asking questions around the kitchen table at home may be different from ways of asking questions in school, but students can learn both ways, without deciding that either way is superior. And you can expand ways of doing it in school to include more possibilities. The *Guidelines* give more ideas.

Guidelines: Culturally Relevant Teaching

Experiment with different grouping arrangements to encourage social harmony and cooperation.

EXAMPLES

1. Try "study buddies" and pairs.
2. Organize heterogeneous groups of four or five.
3. Establish larger teams for older students.

Provide a range of ways to learn material to accommodate a range of learning styles.

EXAMPLES

1. Give students verbal materials at different reading levels.
2. Offer visual materials—charts, diagrams, models.
3. Provide tapes for listening and viewing.
4. Set up activities and projects.

Teach classroom procedures directly, even ways of doing things that you thought everyone would know.

EXAMPLES

1. Tell students how to get the teacher's attention.
2. Explain when and how to interrupt the teacher if students need help.
3. Show which materials students can take and which require permission.
4. Demonstrate acceptable ways to disagree with or challenge another student.

Learn the meaning of different behaviors for your students.

EXAMPLES

1. Ask students how they feel when you correct or praise them. What gives them this message?
2. Talk to family and community members and other teachers to discover the meaning of expressions, gestures, or other responses that are unfamiliar to you.

Emphasize meaning in teaching.

EXAMPLES

1. Make sure students understand what they read.
2. Try storytelling and other modes that don't require written materials.
3. Use examples that relate abstract concepts to everyday experiences; for instance, relate negative numbers to being overdrawn in your checkbook.

Get to know the customs, traditions, and values of your students.

EXAMPLES

1. Use holidays as a chance to discuss the origins and meaning of traditions.
2. Analyze different traditions for common themes.
3. Attend community fairs and festivals.

Help students detect racist and sexist messages.

EXAMPLES

1. Analyze curriculum materials for biases.
2. Make students "bias detectives," reporting comments from the media.
3. Discuss the ways that students communicate biased messages about each other and what should be done when this happens.
4. Discuss expressions of prejudice such as anti-Semitism.

For ways to use technology for culturally relevant teaching, see: **http://preservicetech.edreform.net/techindicator/culturallyrelevantpedagogy**

Today's Diverse Classrooms (pp. 162–165)

Distinguish between the "melting pot" and multiculturalism. Statistics point to increasing cultural diversity in American society. Old views—that minority group members and immigrants should lose their cultural distinctiveness and assimilate completely in the American "melting pot" or be regarded as culturally deficient—are being replaced by new emphases on multiculturalism, equal educational opportunity, and the celebration of cultural diversity.

What is multicultural education? Multicultural education is a field of study designed to increase educational equity for all students. According to the multicultural ideal, America should be transformed into a society that values diversity. James Banks suggests that multicultural education has five dimensions: integrating content, helping students understand how knowledge is influenced by beliefs, reducing prejudice, creating social structures in schools that support learning and development for all students, and using teaching methods that reach all students.

What is culture? There are many conceptions of culture, but most include the knowledge, skills, rules, traditions, beliefs, and values that guide behavior in a particular group of people: Culture is a program for living. Everyone is a member of many cultural groups, defined in terms of geographic region, nationality, ethnicity, race, gender, social class, and religion. Membership in a particular group does not determine behavior or values, but makes certain values and kinds of behavior more likely. Wide variations exist within each group.

Melting pot A metaphor for the absorption and assimilation of immigrants into the mainstream of society so that ethnic differences vanish.

Cultural deficit model A model that explains the school achievement problems of ethnic minority students by assuming that their culture is inadequate and does not prepare them to succeed in school.

Multicultural education Education that promotes equity in the schooling of all students.

Culture The knowledge, values, attitudes, and traditions that guide the behavior of a group of people and allow them to solve the problems of living in their environment.

Economic and Social Class Differences (pp. 165–168)

What is SES, and how does it differ from social class? Social class reflects a group's prestige and power in a society. Most people are aware of the social class that they share with similar peers. Socioeconomic status (SES) is a term used by sociologists for variations in wealth, power, control over resources, and prestige. Socioeconomic status is determined by several factors—not just income—and often overpowers other cultural differences. No single variable is an effective measure of SES, but most researchers identify four general levels of SES: upper, middle, working, and lower classes. The main characteristics of these four levels are summarized in Table 5.1.

What is the relationship between SES and school achievement? Socioeconomic status and academic achievement are closely related. High-SES students of all ethnic groups show higher average levels of achievement on test scores and stay in school longer than low-SES students. Poverty during a child's preschool years appears to have the greatest negative impact. And the longer the child is in poverty, the stronger the impact is on achievement. Why is there a correlation between SES and school achievement? Low-SES students may suffer from inadequate health care, teachers' lowered expectations of them, low self-esteem, learned helplessness, participation in resistance cultures, school tracking, and understimulating home environments. A striking finding is that low-SES children lose academic ground outside school over the summer, while higher-SES children continue to advance.

Socioeconomic status (SES) Relative standing in the society based on income, power, background, and prestige.

Resistance culture Group values and beliefs about refusing to adopt the behaviors and attitudes of the majority culture.

Tracking Assignment to different classes and academic experiences based on achievement.

Ethnic and Racial Differences (pp. 168–176)

Distinguish between ethnicity and race. Ethnicity (culturally transmitted behavior) and race (biologically transmitted physical traits) are socially significant categories people use to describe themselves and others. Minority groups (either numerically or historically unempowered) are rapidly increasing in population.

How can differences in ethnicity of teachers and students affect school performance? Conflicts can arise from differences between teachers and students in culture-based beliefs, values, and expectations. Cultural conflicts are usually about below-the-surface differences, because when subtle cultural differences meet, misunderstandings are common. Students in some cultures learn attitudes and behaviors that are more consistent with school expectations. Differences among ethnic groups in cognitive and academic abilities are largely the legacy of racial segregation and continuing prejudice and discrimination.

Distinguish among prejudice, discrimination, and stereotype threat. Prejudice is a rigid and irrational generalization—a prejudgment or attitude—about an entire category of people. Prejudice may target people in particular racial, ethnic, religious, political, geographic, or language groups, or it may be directed toward the gender or sexual orientation of the individual. Discrimination is unequal treatment of or actions toward particular categories of people. Stereotype threat is the extra emotional and cognitive burden that your performance in an academic situation might confirm a stereotype that others hold about you. It is not necessary that the individual even believe the stereotype. All that matters is that the person is *aware* of the stereotype and *cares about performing* well enough to disprove its unflattering implications. In the short run, the fear that you might confirm a negative stereotype can induce test anxiety and undermine performance. Over time, experiencing stereotype threat may lead to disidentification with schooling and academic achievement.

Ethnicity A cultural heritage shared by a group of people.

Race A group of people who share common biological traits that are seen as self-defining by the people of the group.

Minority group A group of people who have been socially disadvantaged—not always a minority in actual numbers.

Prejudice Prejudgment or irrational generalization about an entire category of people.

Stereotype Schema that organizes knowledge or perceptions about a category.

Discrimination Treating or acting unfairly toward particular categories of people.

Stereotype threat The extra emotional and cognitive burden that your performance in an academic situation might confirm a stereotype that others hold about you.

Girls and Boys: Differences in the Classroom (pp. 176–182)

What are the stages for achieving a sexual orientation for gay and lesbian youth? Stages of achieving a sexual orientation for gay and lesbian students can also follow a pattern from discomfort to confusion to acceptance. Some researchers contend that sexual identity is not always permanent and can change over the years.

What is gender-role identity and how do gender-role identities develop? Gender-role identity is the image each individual has of himself or herself as masculine or feminine in characteristics—a part of self-concept. Biology (hormones) plays a role, as does the differential behavior of parents and teachers toward male and female children. Through their interactions with family, peers, teachers, and the environment in general, children begin to form gender schemas, or organized networks of knowledge about what it means to be male or female. Research shows that gender-role stereotyping begins in the preschool years and continues through gender bias in the school curriculum and sex discrimination in the classroom. Teachers often unintentionally perpetuate these problems.

Are there sex differences in cognitive abilities? Some measures of achievement and SAT tests have shown sex-linked differences, especially in verbal and spatial abilities and mathematics. Males seem to be superior on tasks that require mental rotation of objects and females are better on tasks that require acquisition and use of verbal information. Research on the causes of these differences has been inconclusive, except to indicate that academic socialization and teachers' treatment of male and female students in mathematics classes do play a role. Teachers can use many strategies for reducing gender bias.

Sexual identity A complex combination of beliefs and orientations about gender roles and sexual orientation.

Gender-role identity Beliefs about characteristics and behaviors associated with one sex as opposed to the other.

Gender schemas Organized networks of knowledge about what it means to be male or female.

Gender biases Different views of males and females, often favoring one gender over the other.

Language Differences in the Classroom

(pp. 182–188)

What are the origins of language differences in the classroom? Language differences among students include dialects, bilingualism, and culture-based communication styles. Dialects are not inferior languages and should be respected, but Formal English should be taught for academic contexts. Dialects often affect the pronunciation of words, so teachers have to be able to distinguish a mistake from a dialect difference in oral language. Students who speak in dialect and students who are bilingual often use code-switching to communicate in different groups.

What is bilingual education? Bilingual students speak a first language other than English, learn English as a second language, may have some degree of limitation in English proficiency, and also must often struggle with social adjustment problems relating to biculturalism. Although there is much debate about the best way to help bilingual students master English, studies show it is best if they are not forced to abandon their first language. The more proficient students are in their first language, the faster they will master the second. Mastering academic language skills in any new language takes five to seven years.

Dialect Rule-governed variation of a language spoken by a particular group.

Code-switching Successful switching between cultures in language, dialect, or nonverbal behaviors to fit the situation.

Bilingualism Speaking two languages fluently.

English Language Learners (ELL) Students whose primary or heritage language is not English.

English as a Second Language (ESL) Designation for programs and classes to teach English to students who are not native speakers of English.

Semilingual Not proficient in any language; speaking one or more languages inadequately.

Creating Culturally Inclusive Classrooms
(pp. 188–194)

What is culturally relevant pedagogy? "Culturally relevant pedagogy is an approach to teaching that uses the cultural knowledge, prior experiences, frames of references, and learning styles of ethnically diverse students to make learning encounters more relevant and effective for them. It teaches *to and through* the strengths of these students" (Gay, 2000). Gloria Ladson-Billings describes culturally relevant teaching that rests on three propositions: Students must experience academic success, develop/maintain their cultural competence, and develop a critical consciousness to challenge the status quo.

What are the elements of a resilient classroom? There are two strands of elements that bind students to their classroom community. One strand emphasizes the self-agency of students—their capacity to set and pursue goals. This includes academic self-efficacy, self-control, and self-determination. The second strand emphasizes caring and connected relationships with the teacher, peers, and the home.

Culturally Inclusive Classrooms: Classrooms that provide culturally diverse students equitable access to the teaching-learning process.

Resilience: The ability to adapt successfully in spite of difficult circumstances and threats to development.

Diversity and Convergences (pp. 195–199)

Sociolinguistics The study of the formal and informal rules for how, when, about what, to whom, and how long to speak in conversations within cultural groups.

Pragmatics The rules for when and how to use language to be an effective communicator in a particular culture.

Participation structures The formal and informal rules for how to take part in a given activity.

Culturally relevant pedagogy Excellent teaching for students of color that includes academic success, developing/maintaining cultural competence, and developing a critical consciousness to challenge the status quo.

Digital divide The disparities in access to technology between poor and more affluent students and families.

Teachers' Casebook: Connections to PRAXIS II™

A classroom should be a community of learners, and the community described in the Teachers' Casebook is fractured along several lines. Divisions and attitudes that undermine the goal of that community—learning—must be addressed fairly, firmly, and tactfully. As the leader of that community, your practices and attitudes will be major factors that determine whether that community moves toward your goal.

In PRAXIS II™, you will be presented with scenarios and questions that will test your knowledge of the increasingly complex learning communities that teachers and students inhabit. You will be challenged to implement strategies and practices that foster learning for each of the varied students who are in that community with you.

What Would They Do?

Here is how some practicing teachers responded to the teaching situation presented at the beginning of this chapter about bringing together a class that was divided along ethnic lines.

Jamaal Allan **Language Arts Teacher, Seventh Grade,**
J. W. Poynter Middle School, Hillsboro, Oregon

Working in a middle school, social issues are often deemed more important than academics. The biggest issue is that each student has an identity within his or her group, but fears that identity is lost when communicating cross-culturally. Teaching Language Arts, there are numerous activities in cultural awareness that would assist team and community building within this diverse classroom. Students at this age must be taught to celebrate differences, not shun them. Rather than ignoring the problem, or placating it, it must be attacked head-on and a dialogue opened between students to discuss these cultural issues. Each student needs to understand that his or her identity and cultural background will be preserved when they become a member of a larger, more diverse community. (To "force" integration in seating and groups, write each student's name on a Popsicle stick and draw lots to randomly assign groups.)

Deborah P. Reed
Darby Woods Elementary School, Galloway, Ohio

Thomas G. Reed
Beechcroft High School, Columbus, OH

Cultural differences, whether rooted in ethnicity, social class, or geography, can lead to feelings of alienation and student disengagement. Although such feelings my be symptomatic of a larger school or community-wide problem, you can minimize cultural tension and promote greater understanding of individual and cultural differences.

For example, early in the school year carefully assign all pairings or groupings of students, and require them to work collaboratively in short activities for no longer than 10 or 15 minutes. During these activities, use team-building exercises that allow students to learn about each other as individuals rather than as a members of a larger cultural group. Invite adults from the community to come into the classroom to model teamwork and demonstrate ways they gain cultural understanding.

As the class breaks through the cultural barriers and biases, begin to allow groupings of students from the same cultures to work collaboratively on standards-based classroom projects and present their work in ways specific to their culture. Further, as you conference with different groups about their projects, ask them to teach you common words and phrases from their native languages that show respect. This builds rapport with students and shows them that you value their contributions to the classroom.

Debbie Youngblood **Sixth Grade Wellness and Physical Education Teacher,**
Hillard City Schools, Hilliard, Ohio

My first goal is to establish a safe classroom environment that is nurturing, supportive, free from bullying and that honors and applauds differences. I would begin by modeling the behavior that I am expecting from my students and would talk with them about what kinds of behaviors they believe would help create a supportive classroom environment. Together we would write a classroom code of conduct pledge that each student would be asked to sign as a way of honoring their commitment to be part of our new learning community. After posting the classroom pledge, I would assign a class project of creating individual collages (posters) from magazines, family photos, hand drawn pictures, words and phrases that answers the question: "Who would you say you are?" By getting to know as much as possible about each other, we would begin to break down the walls of misunderstanding and cultural bias. I would consider it vitally important to invest the necessary time to change the climate to one supportive of all students so that academic achievement can take place.

Randall G. Sampson **Assistant-Principal,**
Genoa Middle School, Westerville, Ohio

The collaboration of educational leader and teacher is essential. As educational leader, I would suggest that the teacher provide multiple ways for students to personalize the content standards/academic indicators with the students' culture, providing personal relevance for the students. The teacher should attempt to help the students create a personal comfort and pride about their individual cultures through implementation of writing, research and various mediums of presentation. The teacher is providing an opportunity for students to respect their own cultures, thereby simultaneously establishing the foundation of academic efficacy and mastery of academic content. With such a foundation students will be more likely to understand the experiences of their classmates, leading to a more respectful peer culture.

W. Sean Kearney **Former Assistant Principal**
Galen R. Elolf Elementary School, Converse, Texas

What an asset this is to have a variety of language and cultures in one classroom! People are comfortable with the familiar. Consider changing the way students are grouped to mix up the peer groups, or providing opportunities for students to present different aspects of their cultures with their classmates. These could include music, food, clothing, or customs. Many schools will dedicate one day out of the year to various cultures. Consider broadening this approach to incorporate various cultures throughout the year. If there are multiple languages spoken in your classroom, consider asking bilingual students to teach the class some basic words. Use these "experts" to increase the knowledge base of all your students.

CHAPTER 6

Behavioral Views of Learning

Teachers' Casebook: What Would You Do? 205

Understanding Learning 206

Learning: A Definition 206

Learning Is Not Always What It Seems 207

Early Explanations of Learning: Contiguity and Classical Conditioning 208

Operant Conditioning: Trying New Responses 210

Types of Consequences 210

Reinforcement Schedules 212

Antecedents and Behavior Change 214

Applied Behavior Analysis 215

Methods for Encouraging Behaviors 216

Coping with Undesirable Behavior 219

Reaching Every Student: Functional Behavioral Assessment and Positive Behavior Support 222

Behavioral Approaches to Teaching and Management 224

Group Consequences 226

Contingency Contracts 226

Token Reinforcement 227

Reaching Every Student: Severe Behavior Problems 228

Observational Learning and Cognitive Behavior Modification: Thinking about Behavior 229

Observational Learning 229

Elements of Observational Learning 230

Observational Learning in Teaching 233

Self-Management 234

Cognitive Behavior Modification and Self-Instruction 236

Problems and Issues 238

Criticisms of Behavioral Methods 238

Ethical Issues 238

Diversity and Convergences in Behavioral Learning 240

Diversity 240

Convergences 240

Summary Table 241

Teachers' Casebook: Connections to PRAXIS II™/What Would They Do? 245

What Would You Do?

Teachers' Casebook

You were hired in January to take over the classes of a teacher who moved away. This is a great district and a terrific school. If you do well, you might be in line for a full-time opening next fall. As you are introduced around the school, you get a number of sympathetic looks and many—too many—offers of help: "Let me know if I can do anything for you."

After the first hour, you begin to understand why so many teachers volunteered their help. Evidently the previous teacher had no management system—no order. Several students walk around the room while you are talking to the class, interrupt you when you are working with a group, torment each other, and open their lunches (or those of other students) for a self-determined snack. There is one very charismatic leader who causes regular disruptions, resists your authority, and destroys your efforts to develop a community of learners. Simply taking roll and introducing the first activity lasts 10 minutes. You end the first day exhausted and discouraged, having lost both your voice and your patience. You wonder how you can possibly establish a workable management system and still teach students what they will need to know for the spring proficiency tests.

Critical Thinking

- How would you approach the situation?
- Which problem behaviors would you tackle first?
- Would giving rewards or administering punishments be useful in this situation?
- Why or why not?

Collaboration

With 2 other members of your class, role play an orientation meeting between this new teacher and the mentor teacher assigned to help. How should the mentor prepare the new teacher for the assignment? What plans could be made to handle the situation?

We begin this chapter with a general definition of learning that takes into account the opposing views of different theoretical groups. We will highlight one group, the behavioral theorists, in this chapter; another major group, the cognitive theorists, in Chapters 7 and 8; and then look at current social cognitive views and constructivism in Chapter 9.

Our discussion in this chapter will focus on four behavioral learning processes: contiguity, classical conditioning, operant conditioning, and observational learning, with the greatest emphasis on the last two processes. After examining the implications of applied behavior analysis for teaching, we look at two recent directions in behavioral approaches to learning—self-management and cognitive behavior modification.

By the time you have completed this chapter, you should be able to answer these questions:

- What is learning?
- What are the similarities and differences among contiguity, classical conditioning, and operant conditioning?
- What are examples of four different kinds of consequences that can follow any behavior, and what effect is each likely to have on future behavior?
- How could you use applied behavior analysis (group consequences, contingency contracts, token economies or functional behavioral analysis) to solve common academic or behavior problems?
- What and how can students learn through observation?
- What is cognitive behavior modification, and how does it apply to teaching?

FACING PAGE *Playing Ball*, 1999, Christian Pierre. Acrylic on canvas.

Understanding Learning

When we hear the word *learning,* most of us think of studying and school. We think about subjects or skills we intend to master, such as algebra, Spanish, chemistry, or karate. But learning is not limited to school. We learn every day of our lives. Babies learn to kick their legs to make the mobile above their cribs move, teenagers learn the lyrics to all their favorite songs, middle-aged people like me learn to change their diet and exercise patterns, and every few years we all learn to find a new style of dress attractive when the old styles (the styles we once loved) go out of fashion. This last example shows that learning is not always intentional. We don't try to like new styles and dislike old ones; it just seems to happen that way. We don't intend to become nervous when we hear the sound of a dentist's drill or when we step onto a stage, yet many of us do. So what is this powerful phenomenon called learning?

Learning: A Definition

In the broadest sense, **learning** occurs when experience causes a relatively permanent change in an individual's knowledge or behavior. The change may be deliberate or unintentional, for better or for worse, correct or incorrect, and conscious or unconscious (Hill, 2002). To qualify as learning, this change must be brought about by experience—by the interaction of a person with his or her environment. Changes simply caused by maturation, such as growing taller or turning gray, do not qualify as learning. Temporary changes resulting from illness, fatigue, or hunger are also excluded from a general definition of learning. A person who has gone without food for two days does not learn to be hungry, and a person who is ill does not learn to run more slowly. Of course, learning plays a part in how we respond to hunger or illness.

Our definition specifies that the changes resulting from learning are in the individual's knowledge or behavior. Most psychologists would agree with this statement, but some tend to emphasize the change in knowledge, others the change in behavior. Cognitive psychologists, who focus on changes in knowledge, believe learning is an internal mental activity that cannot be observed directly. As you will see in the next chapter, cognitive psychologists studying learning are interested in unobservable mental activities such as thinking, remembering, and solving problems (Schwartz, Wasserman, & Robbins, 2002).

The psychologists discussed in this chapter, on the other hand, favor **behavioral learning theories**. The behavioral view generally assumes that the outcome of learning is change in behavior, and it emphasizes the effects of external events on the individual. Some early behaviorists such as J. B. Watson took the radical position that because think-

What is learning? Behavioral theorists emphasize the role of outside stimuli, focusing on behavior and observable responses.

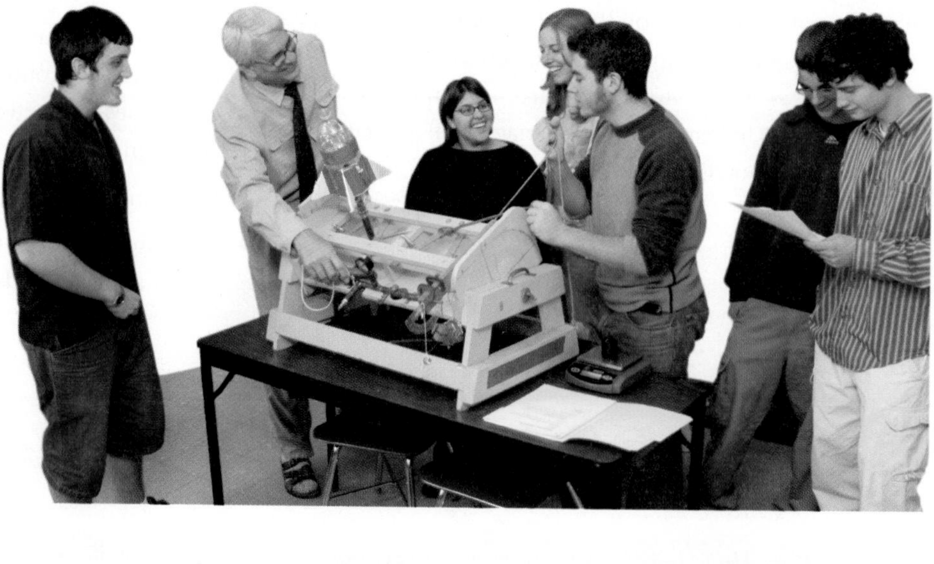

Learning Process through which experience causes permanent change in knowledge or behavior.

Behavioral learning theories Explanations of learning that focus on external events as the cause of changes in observable behaviors.

ing, intentions, and other internal mental events could not be seen or studied rigorously and scientifically, these "mentalisms," as he called them, should not even be included in an explanation of learning. Before we look in depth at behavioral explanations of learning, let's step into an actual classroom and note the possible results of learning.

Learning Is Not Always What It Seems

After weeks of working with her cooperating teacher in an 8th-grade social studies class, Elizabeth was ready to take over on her own. As she moved to the front of the room, she saw another adult approach the classroom door. It was Mr. Ross, her supervisor from college. Elizabeth's neck and facial muscles suddenly became very tense and her hands trembled.

"I've stopped by to observe your teaching," Mr. Ross said. "This will be my first of six visits. I couldn't reach you last night to tell you."

Elizabeth tried to hide her reaction, but her hands trembled as she gathered the notes for the lesson.

"Let's start today with a kind of game. I will say some words, then I want you to tell me the first words you can think of. Don't bother to raise your hands. Just say the words out loud, and I will write them on the board. Don't all speak at once, though. Wait until someone else has finished to say your word. Okay, here is the first word: Slavery."

"Civil War." "Lincoln." "Freedom." "Emancipation Proclamation." The answers came quickly, and Elizabeth was relieved to see that the students understood the game.

"All right, very good," she said. "Now try another one: South."

"South Carolina." "South Dakota." "South Street Seaport," "No, the Confederacy, you dummy." "*Cold Mountain.*" "Jude Law." With this last answer, a ripple of laughter moved across the room.

"Jude Law!" Elizabeth sighed dreamily. "*Cold Mountain* was on television last week." Then she laughed too. Soon all the students were laughing. "Okay, settle down," Elizabeth said. "Here is another word: North."

"Bluebellies." The students continued to laugh. "Jelly Bellies." "Belly-dancers." More laughter and a few appropriate gestures.

"Just a minute," Elizabeth pleaded. "These ideas are getting a little off base!"

"Off base? Baseball," shouted the boy who had first mentioned Jude Law. He stood up and started throwing balls of paper to a friend in the back of the room, simulating the style of Roger Clemens.

"The New York Mets." "No, the Astros." "Ball games." "Hot dogs." "Popcorn." "Movies." "DVDs." "*Cold Mountain.*" "Jude Law." The responses now came too fast for Elizabeth to stop them. For some reason, the Jude Law line got an even bigger laugh the second time around, and Elizabeth suddenly realized she had lost the class.

"Okay, because you know so much about the Civil War, close your books and take out a pen," Elizabeth said, obviously angry. She passed out the worksheet that she had planned as a cooperative, open-book project. "You have 20 minutes to finish this test!"

"You didn't tell us we were having a test!" "This isn't fair!" "We haven't even covered this stuff yet!" "I didn't do anything wrong!" There were moans and disgusted looks, even from the most mellow students. "I'm reporting you to the principal; it's a violation of students' rights!"

This last comment hit hard. The class had just finished discussing human rights as preparation for this unit on the Civil War. As she listened to the protests, Elizabeth felt terrible. How was she going to grade these "tests"? The first section of the worksheet involved facts about events during the Civil War, and the second section asked students to create a news-style program interviewing ordinary people touched by the war.

"All right, all right, it won't be a test. But you do have to complete this worksheet for a grade. I was going to let you work together, but your behavior this morning tells me that you are not ready for group work. If you can complete the first section of the sheet working quietly and seriously, you may work together on the second section." Elizabeth knew that her students would like to work together on writing the script for the news interview program.

Elizabeth was afraid to look back at her supervisor. What was he writing on his observation form?

It appears, on the surface at least, that very little learning of any sort was taking place in Elizabeth's classroom. In fact, Elizabeth had some good ideas, but she also made some mistakes in her application of learning principles. We will return to this episode several times in the chapter to analyze various aspects of what took place. To get us started, four events can be singled out, each possibly related to a different learning process.

First, the students were able to associate the words *Carolina* and *Dakota* with the word *South*. Second, Elizabeth's hands trembled when her college supervisor entered the room. Third, one student continued to disrupt the class with inappropriate responses. And fourth, after Elizabeth laughed at a student comment, the class joined in her laughter. The four learning processes represented are contiguity, classical conditioning, operant conditioning, and observational learning. In the following pages we will examine these four kinds of learning, starting with contiguity.

Early Explanations of Learning: Contiguity and Classical Conditioning

Connect and Extend to PRAXIS II™

Learning by Association (I, A1) Quite a bit of classroom learning can be attributed to contiguity (i.e., learning by association). What are some things that you might have learned because your teacher paired certain stimuli (e.g., names of the letters of the alphabet)?

One of the earliest explanations of learning came from Aristotle (384–322 B.C.). He said that we remember things together (1) when they are similar, (2) when they contrast, and (3) when they are *contiguous*. This last principle is the most important, because it is included in all explanations of *learning by association*. The principle of **contiguity** states that whenever two or more sensations occur together often enough, they will become associated. Later, when only one of these sensations (a **stimulus**) occurs, the other will be remembered too (a **response**) (Rachlin, 1991; Wasserman & Miller, 1997). For example, when Elizabeth said "South," students associated the words "Carolina" and "Dakota." They had heard these words together many times. Other learning processes may also be involved when students learn these phrases, but contiguity is a factor. Contiguity also plays a major role in another learning process best known as *classical conditioning*.

STOP | THINK | WRITE Close your eyes and focus on a vivid image of the following: The smell of French fries cooking. A time you were really embarrassed in school. The taste of chocolate fudge. The sound of a dentist's drill. What did you notice as you formed these images? ■

If you are like me, imagining the sound of the dentist's drill tightens your neck muscles. I can actually salivate when I imagine salty fries or smooth rich chocolate (especially because it is 1:01 PM and I haven't had lunch yet). The first embarrassing school incident I remembered was falling flat as I did a cartwheel in front of the whole high school. A small cringe still accompanies the memory. **Classical conditioning** focuses on the learning of *involuntary* emotional or physiological responses such as fear, increased muscle tension, salivation, or sweating. These sometimes are called **respondents** because they are automatic responses to stimuli. Through the process of classical conditioning, humans and animals can be trained to react involuntarily to a stimulus that previously had no effect—or a very different effect—on them. The stimulus comes to *elicit*, or bring forth, the response automatically.

Classical conditioning was discovered in the 1920s by Ivan Pavlov, a Russian physiologist trying to determine how long it took a dog to secrete digestive juices after it had been fed. But the intervals of time kept changing. At first, the dogs salivated as expected while they were being fed. Then the dogs began to salivate as soon as they saw the food and then as soon as they heard the scientists walking toward the lab. Pavlov decided to make a detour from his original experiments and examine these unexpected interferences.

In one of his first experiments, Pavlov began by sounding a tuning fork and recording a dog's response. As expected, there was no salivation. At this point, the sound of the tuning fork was a **neutral stimulus** because it brought forth no salivation. Then Pavlov fed the dog. The response was salivation. The food was an **unconditioned stimulus (US)** because no prior training or "conditioning" was needed to establish the natural connection between food and salivation. The salivation was an **unconditioned response (UR)**, again because it was elicited automatically—no conditioning required.

Using these three elements—the food, the salivation, and the tuning fork—Pavlov demonstrated that a dog could be conditioned to salivate after hearing the tuning fork. He

Contiguity Association of two events because of repeated pairing.

Stimulus Event that activates behavior.

Response Observable reaction to a stimulus.

Classical conditioning Association of automatic responses with new stimuli.

Respondents Responses (generally automatic or involuntary) elicited by specific stimuli.

Neutral stimulus Stimulus not connected to a response.

Unconditioned stimulus (US) Stimulus that automatically produces an emotional or physiological response.

Unconditioned response (UR) Naturally occurring emotional or physiological response.

did this by contiguous pairing of the sound with food. He sounded the fork and then quickly fed the dog. After Pavlov repeated this several times, the dog began to salivate after hearing the sound, but before receiving the food. Now the sound had become a **conditioned stimulus (CS)** that could bring forth salivation by itself. The response of salivating after the tone was now a **conditioned response (CR).**

If you think that Pavlovian conditioning is of historical interest only, consider this excerpt from *USA Today* describing an advertising campaign for products aimed at "Gen Y," those people born between 1977 and 1994:

> Mountain Dew executives have their own term for this [advertising strategy]: the Pavlovian connection. By handing out samples of the brand at surfing, skateboard and snowboard tournaments, "There's a Pavlovian connection between the brand and the exhilarating experience," says Dave Burwich, a top marketing executive at Pepsi, which makes Mountain Dew. (Horovitz, April 22, 2002, p. B2)

Maybe they could hand out math homework too!

It is possible that many of our emotional reactions to various situations are learned in part through classical conditioning. Physicians have a term, "white coat syndrome," that describes people whose blood pressure (an involuntary response) goes up when tested in the doctor's office, usually by someone in a white coat. Another example, Elizabeth's trembling hands when she saw her college supervisor, might be traced to previous unpleasant experiences during past evaluations of her performance. Now just the thought of being observed elicits a pounding heart and sweaty palms. Classical conditioning has implications for teachers as well as marketing managers. Remember that emotions and attitudes as well as facts and ideas are learned in classrooms. This emotional learning can sometimes interfere with academic learning. Procedures based on classical conditioning also can be used to help people learn more adaptive emotional responses, as the *Guidelines* suggest.

Conditioned stimulus (CS) Stimulus that evokes an emotional or physiological response after conditioning.

Conditioned response (CR) Learned response to a previously neutral stimulus.

Guidelines: Applying Classical Conditioning

Associate positive, pleasant events with learning tasks.

EXAMPLES

1. Emphasize group competition and cooperation over individual competition. Many students have negative emotional responses to individual competition that may generalize to other learning.
2. Make division drills fun by having students decide how to divide refreshments equally, then letting them eat the results.
3. Make voluntary reading appealing by creating a comfortable reading corner with pillows, colorful displays of books, and reading props such as puppets (see Morrow & Weinstein, 1986, for more ideas).

Help students to risk anxiety-producing situations voluntarily and successfully.

EXAMPLES

1. Assign a shy student the responsibility of teaching two other students how to distribute materials for map study.
2. Devise small steps toward a larger goal. For example, give ungraded practice tests daily, and then weekly, to students who tend to "freeze" in test situations.
3. If a student is afraid of speaking in front of the class, let the student read a report to a small group while seated, then read it while standing, then give the report from notes instead of reading it verbatim. Next, move in stages toward having the student give a report to the whole class.

Help students recognize differences and similarities among situations so they can discriminate and generalize appropriately.

EXAMPLES

1. Explain that it is appropriate to avoid strangers who offer gifts or rides, but safe to accept favors from adults when parents are present.
2. Assure students who are anxious about taking college entrance exams that this test is like all the other achievement tests they have taken.

If you would like to learn more about classical conditioning, see these sites: **http://www.class.uidaho.edu/psyc390/lessons/lesson02/lesson2.htm** **http://www.dushkin.com/connectext/psy/ch06/ccapps.mhtml**

Operant Conditioning: Trying New Responses

So far, we have concentrated on the automatic conditioning of involuntary responses such as salivation and fear. Clearly, not all human learning is so automatic and unintentional. Most behaviors are not involuntary responses. People actively "operate" on their environment to produce different kinds of consequences. These deliberate actions are called **operants**. The learning process involved in operant behavior is called **operant conditioning** because we learn to behave in certain ways as we operate on the environment.

The person generally thought to be responsible for developing the concept of operant conditioning is B. F. Skinner (1953). Skinner began with the belief that the principles of classical conditioning account for only a small portion of learned behaviors. Many human behaviors are operants, not respondents. Classical conditioning describes only how existing behaviors might be paired with new stimuli; it does not explain how new operant behaviors are acquired.

Connect and **Extend** to **PRAXIS II™**

Basics of Operant Conditioning (I, A1)

Be able to explain learning from the behavioral perspective. Incorporate concepts of *reward* and *punishment* into your explanation. Have a firm grasp of the effects of reinforcement schedules on learning.

Behavior, like response or action, is simply a word for what a person does in a particular situation. Conceptually, we may think of a behavior as sandwiched between two sets of environmental influences: those that precede it (its **antecedents**) and those that follow it (its **consequences**) (Skinner, 1950). This relationship can be shown very simply as antecedent–behavior–consequence, or A–B–C. As behavior is ongoing, a given consequence becomes an antecedent for the next ABC sequence. Research in operant conditioning shows that operant behavior can be altered by changes in the antecedents, the consequences, or both. Early work focused on consequences, often using rats or pigeons as subjects.

Types of Consequences

STOP | THINK | WRITE Think back over teachers you have had who used rewards or punishments. *Try to remember different types of rewards:*

Concrete rewards (stickers, food, prizes, certificates) ____________

Activity rewards (free time, puzzles, free reading) ____________

"Exemption" rewards (no homework, no weekly test) ____________

Social rewards (praise, recognition) ____________

What about punishments?

Loss of privileges (cannot sit where you want, cannot work with friends)

____

Fines (lost points, grades, money) ____________

Extra work (homework, laps, push-ups) ____________ ■

According to the behavioral view, consequences determine to a great extent whether a person will repeat the behavior that led to the consequences. The type and timing of consequences can strengthen or weaken behaviors. We will look first at consequences that strengthen behavior.

Reinforcement. Although **reinforcement** is commonly understood to mean "reward," this term has a particular meaning in psychology. A **reinforcer** is any consequence that strengthens the behavior it follows. So, by definition, *reinforced behaviors increase in frequency or duration.* Whenever you see a behavior persisting or increasing over time, you can assume the consequences of that behavior are reinforcers for the individual involved (Landrum & Kauffman, 2006). The reinforcement process can be diagrammed as follows:

		CONSEQUENCE		EFFECT
Behavior	→	Reinforcer	→	Strengthened or repeated behavior

Operants Voluntary (and generally goal-directed) behaviors emitted by a person or an animal.

Operant conditioning Learning in which voluntary behavior is strengthened or weakened by consequences or antecedents.

Antecedents Events that precede an action.

Consequences Events that follow an action.

Reinforcement Use of consequences to strengthen behavior.

Reinforcer Any event that follows a behavior and increases the chances that the behavior will occur again.

We can be fairly certain that food will be a reinforcer for a hungry animal, but what about people? It is not clear why an event acts as a reinforcer for an individual, but there are many theories about why reinforcement works. For example, some psychologists suggest that reinforcers satisfy needs, while other psychologists believe that reinforcers reduce tension or stimulate a part of the brain (Rachlin, 1991). Whether the consequences of any action are reinforcing probably depends on the individual's perception of the event and the meaning it holds for her or him. For example, students who repeatedly get themselves sent to the principal's office for misbehaving may be indicating that something about this consequence is reinforcing for them, even if it doesn't seem desirable to you. By the way, Skinner did not speculate about why reinforcers increase behavior. He believed that it was useless to talk about "imaginary constructs" such as meaning, expectations, needs, or tensions. Skinner simply described the tendency for a given operant to increase after certain consequences (Hill, 2002; Skinner, 1953, 1989).

There are two types of reinforcement. The first, called **positive reinforcement**, occurs when the behavior produces a new stimulus. Examples include pecking on the red key producing food for a pigeon, wearing a new outfit producing many compliments, or falling out of your chair producing cheers and laughter from classmates.

Notice that positive reinforcement can occur even when the behavior being reinforced (falling out of a chair) is not "positive" from the teacher's point of view. In fact, positive reinforcement of inappropriate behaviors occurs unintentionally in many classrooms. Teachers help maintain problem behaviors by inadvertently reinforcing them. For example, Elizabeth may have unintentionally reinforced problem behavior in her class by laughing the first time the boy answered, "Jude Law." The problem behavior may have persisted for other reasons, but the consequence of Elizabeth's laughter could have played a role.

When the consequence that strengthens a behavior is the *appearance* (*addition*) of a new stimulus, the situation is defined as *positive* reinforcement. In contrast, when the consequence that strengthens a behavior is the *disappearance* (*subtraction*) of a stimulus, the process is called ***negative* reinforcement**. If a particular action leads to avoiding or escaping an **aversive** situation, the action is likely to be repeated in a similar situation. A common example is the car seatbelt buzzer. As soon as you put on your seatbelt, the irritating buzzer stops. You are likely to repeat this behavior (putting on the seatbelt) in the future because the action made an aversive stimulus (buzzer) disappear. Consider students who continually "get sick" right before a test and are sent to the nurse's office. The behavior allows the students to escape aversive situations—tests—so getting "sick" is being maintained, in part, through negative reinforcement. It is negative because the stimulus (the test) disappears; it is reinforcement because the behavior that caused the stimulus to disappear (getting "sick") increases or repeats. It is also possible that classical conditioning plays a role. The students may have been conditioned to experience unpleasant physiological reactions to tests.

The "negative" in negative reinforcement does not imply that the behavior being reinforced is necessarily negative or bad. The meaning is closer to that of "negative" numbers—something is subtracted. Associate *positive* and *negative* reinforcement with *adding* or *subtracting* something following a behavior that strengthens (reinforces) the behavior.

Punishment. Negative reinforcement is often confused with punishment. The process of reinforcement (positive or negative) always involves strengthening behavior. **Punishment**, on the other hand, involves *decreasing or suppressing behavior.* A behavior followed by a punisher is *less* likely to be repeated in similar situations in the future. Again, it is the effect that defines a consequence as punishment, and different people have different perceptions of what is punishing. One student may find suspension from school punishing, while another student wouldn't mind at all. The process of punishment is diagrammed as follows:

		CONSEQUENCE		EFFECT
Behavior	→	Punisher	→	Weakened or decreased behavior

Connect and Extend to Your Teaching

To become aware of the prevalence of reinforcement in daily life, keep a log, noting every time you give or receive reinforcement. Look for positive and negative reinforcement and also record the kind of schedule operating. Another possibility is to note reinforcement and schedules in a field placement classroom or even in college classes. What examples of reinforcement are present in your education classes?

Connect and Extend to Your Teaching

Positive reinforcement: Praise for good grades, bonus points on tests, a class pizza party when everyone makes above 85 on the weekly spelling test. *Negative reinforcement:* Removing a stone from your shoe; calling on a child who is madly waving his hand and shouting, "I know, I know!"(you are negatively reinforced because the noise stops); wearing a certain pair of shoes on trips to avoid aching feet; saying "I'm really sorry" to your spouse to avoid his or her anger. *Presentation punishment:* Running extra laps; reprimands; bad grades; corporal punishment. *Removal punishment:* Fines; being grounded; missing recess; not being allowed to go on the field trip; getting fired.

Positive reinforcement Strengthening behavior by presenting a desired stimulus after the behavior.

Negative reinforcement Strengthening behavior by removing an aversive stimulus when the behavior occurs.

Aversive Irritating or unpleasant.

Punishment Process that weakens or suppresses behavior.

Like reinforcement, punishment may take one of two forms. The first type has been called Type I punishment, but this name isn't very informative, so I use the term **presentation punishment.** It occurs when the appearance of a stimulus following the behavior suppresses or decreases the behavior. When teachers assign demerits, extra work, running laps, and so on, they are using presentation punishment. I call the other type of punishment (Type II punishment) **removal punishment** because it involves removing a stimulus. When teachers or parents take away privileges after a young person has behaved inappropriately, they are applying removal punishment. With both types, the effect is to decrease the behavior that led to the punishment. Figure 6.1 summarizes the processes of reinforcement and punishment.

Reinforcement Schedules

When people are learning a new behavior, they will learn it faster if they are reinforced for every correct response. This is a **continuous reinforcement schedule**. Then, when the new behavior has been mastered, they will maintain it best if they are reinforced intermittently rather than every time. An **intermittent reinforcement schedule** helps students to maintain skills without expecting constant reinforcement.

There are two basic types of intermittent reinforcement schedules. One—called an **interval schedule**—is based on the amount of time that passes between reinforcers. The other—a **ratio schedule**—is based on the number of responses learners give between reinforcers. Interval and ratio schedules may be either *fixed* (predictable) or *variable* (unpredictable). Table 6.1 summarizes the five possible reinforcement schedules (the continuous schedule and the four kinds of intermittent schedules).

FIGURE 6.1

Kinds of Reinforcement and Punishment

Negative reinforcement and punishment are often confused. It may help you to remember that reinforcement is always associated with increases in behaviors, and punishment always involves decreasing or suppressing behavior.

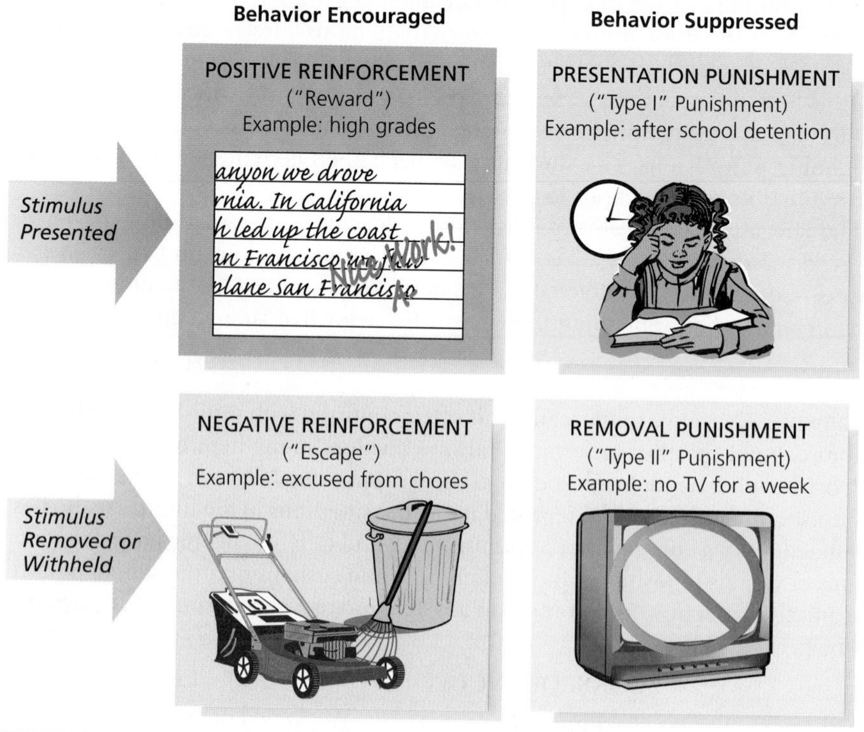

Behavior Encouraged
Behavior Suppressed
POSITIVE REINFORCEMENT
("Reward")
Example: high grades
PRESENTATION PUNISHMENT
("Type I" Punishment)
Example: after school detention
Stimulus Presented
NEGATIVE REINFORCEMENT
("Escape")
Example: excused from chores
REMOVAL PUNISHMENT
("Type II" Punishment)
Example: no TV for a week
Stimulus Removed or Withheld

Connect and **Extend** to Your **Teaching**

Recall an instance of punishment that you have experienced at some time during your life. What were your feelings when you were being punished? List the feelings. (Negative feelings, such as embarrassment, resentment, hurt, anger, etc., probably will account for 90% of the responses.) Does the punishment work? What are some other negative effects of punishment? If punishment is ineffective and also produces negative side effects, why do so many teachers rely on it so much?

Connect and **Extend** to Your **Teaching Portfolio**

When a teacher decides to begin ignoring a behavior that he or she wants to extinguish, there is frequently an increase in the behavior for a short time before it decreases. How do you explain this phenomenon?

Presentation punishment Decreasing the chances that a behavior will occur again by presenting an aversive stimulus following the behavior; also called Type I punishment.

Removal punishment Decreasing the chances that a behavior will occur again by removing a pleasant stimulus following the behavior; also called Type II punishment.

Continuous reinforcement schedule Presenting a reinforcer after every appropriate response.

Intermittent reinforcement schedule Presenting a reinforcer after some but not all responses.

Interval schedule Length of time between reinforcers.

Ratio schedule Reinforcement based on the number of responses between reinforcers.

TABLE 6.1

Reinforcement Schedules

Schedule	Definition	Example	Response Pattern	Reaction When Reinforcement Stops
Continuous	Reinforcement after every response	Turning on the television	Rapid learning of response	Very little persistence; rapid disappearance of response
Fixed-interval	Reinforcement after a set period of time	Weekly quiz	Response rate increases as time for reinforcement approaches, then drops after reinforcement	Little persistence; rapid drop in response rate when time for reinforcement passes and no reinforcer appears
Variable-interval	Reinforcement after varying lengths of time	Pop quizzes	Slow, steady rate of responding; very little pause after reinforcement	Greater persistence; slow decline in response rate
Fixed-ratio	Reinforcement after a set number of responses	Piece work Bake sale	Rapid response rate; pause after reinforcement	Little persistence; rapid drop in response rate when expected number of responses are given and no reinforcer appears
Variable-ratio	Reinforcement after a varying number of responses	Slot machines	Very high response rate; little pause after reinforcement	Greatest persistence; response rate stays high and gradually drops off

What are the effects of different schedules? Speed of performance depends on control. If reinforcement is based on the number of responses you give, then you have more control over the reinforcement: The faster you accumulate the correct number of responses, the faster the reinforcement will come. A teacher who says, "As soon as you complete these 10 problems correctly, you may go to the student lounge," can expect higher rates of performance than a teacher who says, "Work on these ten problems for the next 20 minutes. Then I will check your papers and those with 10 correct may go to the lounge."

Persistence in performance depends on unpredictability. Continuous reinforcement and both kinds of fixed reinforcement (ratio and interval) are quite predictable. We come to expect reinforcement at certain points and are generally quick to give up when the reinforcement does not meet our expectations. To encourage persistence of response, variable schedules are most appropriate. In fact, if the schedule is gradually changed until it becomes very "lean"—meaning that reinforcement occurs only after many responses or a long time interval—then people can learn to work for extended periods without any reinforcement at all. Just watch gamblers playing slot machines to see how powerful a lean reinforcement schedule can be.

Casino slot machines are a good example of the effectiveness of intermittent reinforcement: People "learn" to persist in losing their money, because they might be rewarded with a jackpot, albeit infrequently and unpredictably.

Reinforcement schedules influence how persistently we will respond when reinforcement is withheld. What happens when reinforcement is completely withdrawn?

Extinction. In classical conditioning, the conditioned response is extinguished (disappears) when the conditioned stimulus appeared, but the unconditioned stimulus did not follow (tone, but no food). In operant conditioning, a person or an animal will not persist in a certain behavior if the usual reinforcer is withheld long enough. The behavior will eventually be extinguished (stop). For example, if you repeatedly e-mail a professor but never get a reply, you may give up. Removal of reinforcement altogether leads to **extinction.** The process may take a while, however, as you know if you have tried to extinguish a child's tantrums by withholding your attention. Often the child wins—you give up ignoring and instead of extinction, intermittent reinforcement occurs. This, of course, may encourage even more persistent tantrums in the future.

Connect and Extend to Your Teaching

Examples of stimulus control: I found myself (more than once) about to turn into my old office parking lot, even after my department had been moved to a new building across town. The old cues kept me heading automatically to the old office. Another example is the supposedly true story of a getaway car driver in a bank robbery who sped through town, only to be caught by the police when she dutifully stopped at a red light. The stimulus of the red light had come to have automatic control.

Antecedents and Behavior Change

In operant conditioning, antecedents—the events preceding behaviors—provide information about which behaviors will lead to positive consequences and which will lead to unpleasant ones. Skinner's pigeons learned to peck for food when a light was on, but not to bother when the light was off, because no food followed pecking when the light was off. In other words, they learned to use the antecedent light as a cue to discriminate the likely consequence of pecking. The pigeons' pecking was under **stimulus control**, controlled by the discriminative stimulus of the light.

We all learn to discriminate—to read situations. When should you ask to borrow your roommate's car—after a major disagreement or after you both have had a great time at a party? The antecedent cue of a school principal standing in the hall helps students discriminate the probable consequences of running or attempting to break into a locker. We often respond to such antecedent cues without fully realizing that they are influencing our behavior. But teachers can use cues deliberately in the classroom.

Connect and Extend to Your Teaching Portfolio

Suggest the cues or prompts you would use to elicit the following behaviors: (1) the class looks at you to hear your directions; (2) the students open their books to the assigned page when the bell rings; (3) the students give you their full attention when you are making an important point; and (4) a student walks instead of running to the door when the dismissal bell rings.

Cueing. By definition, **cueing** is the act of providing an antecedent stimulus just before a particular behavior is supposed to take place. Cueing is particularly useful in setting the stage for behaviors that must occur at a specific time, but are easily forgotten. In working with young people, teachers often find themselves correcting behaviors after the fact. For example, they may ask students, "When are you going to start remembering to . . . ?" Such reminders often lead to irritation. The mistake is already made, and the young person is left with only two choices: to promise to try harder or to say, "Why don't you leave me alone?" Neither response is very satisfying. Presenting a nonjudgmental cue can help prevent these negative confrontations. When a student performs the appropriate behavior after a cue, the teacher can reinforce the student's accomplishment instead of punishing the student's failure.

Connect and Extend to PRAXIS II™

Antecedents (I, A1)

Understand how antecedents can affect learning. Be particularly familiar with the effective uses of prompting and cueing.

Prompting. Sometimes students need help learning to respond to a cue in an appropriate way so the cue becomes a discriminative stimulus. One approach is to provide an additional cue, called a **prompt,** following the first cue. There are two principles for using a cue and a prompt to teach a new behavior. First, make sure the environmental stimulus that you want to become a cue occurs immediately before the prompt you are using, so students will learn to respond to the cue and not rely only on the prompt. Second, fade the prompt as soon as possible so students do not become dependent on it (Alberto & Troutman, 2006).

An example of cueing and prompting is providing students with a checklist or reminder sheet. Figure 6.2 is a checklist for the steps in peer tutoring. Working in pairs is the cue; the checklist is the prompt. As students learn the procedures, the teacher may stop using the checklist, but may remind the students of the steps. When no written or oral prompts are necessary, the students have learned to respond appropriately to the environmental cue of working in pairs—they have learned how to behave in tutoring situations. However, the teacher should continue to monitor the process, recognize good work, and correct mistakes. Before a tutoring session, the teacher might ask students to close their eyes

Extinction The disappearance of a learned response.

Stimulus control Capacity for the presence or absence of antecedents to cause behaviors.

Cueing Providing a stimulus that "sets up" a desired behavior.

Prompt A reminder that follows a cue to make sure the person reacts to the cue.

FIGURE 6.2

Written Prompts: A Peer-Tutoring Checklist

By using this checklist, students are reminded how to be effective tutors. As they become more proficient, the checklist may be less necessary.

Remember to…

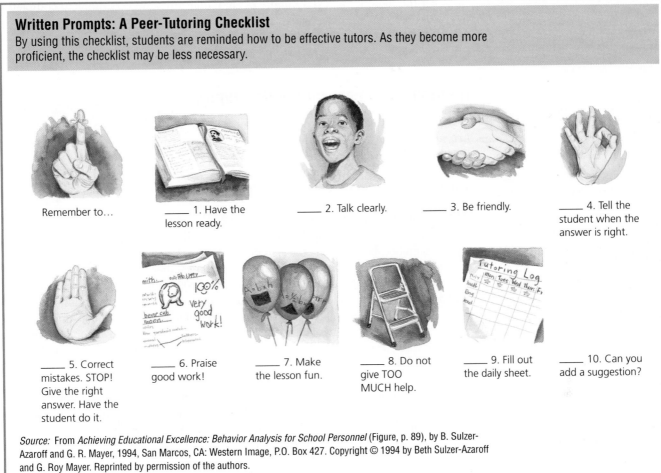

____ 1. Have the lesson ready.

____ 2. Talk clearly.

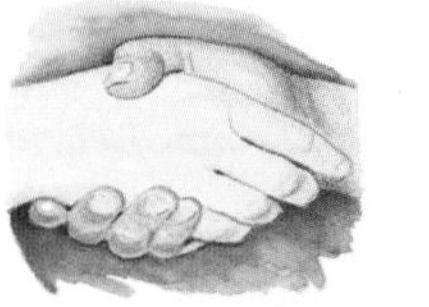

____ 3. Be friendly.

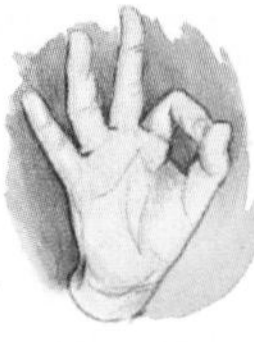

____ 4. Tell the student when the answer is right.

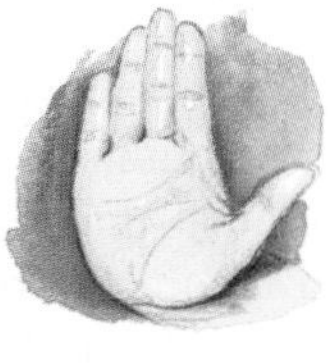

____ 5. Correct mistakes. STOP! Give the right answer. Have the student do it.

____ 6. Praise good work!

____ 7. Make the lesson fun.

____ 8. Do not give TOO MUCH help.

____ 9. Fill out the daily sheet.

____ 10. Can you add a suggestion?

Source: From *Achieving Educational Excellence: Behavior Analysis for School Personnel* (Figure, p. 89), by B. Sulzer-Azaroff and G. R. Mayer, 1994, San Marcos, CA: Western Image, P.O. Box 427. Copyright © 1994 by Beth Sulzer-Azaroff and G. Roy Mayer. Reprinted by permission of the authors.

and "see" the checklist, focusing on each step. As students work, the teacher could listen to their interactions and continue to coach students as they improve their tutoring skills.

Applied Behavior Analysis

Applied behavior analysis is the application of behavioral learning principles to change behavior. The method is sometimes called **behavior modification**, but this term has negative connotations for many people and is often misunderstood (Alberto & Troutman, 2006; Kazdin, 2001).

Ideally, applied behavior analysis requires clear specification of the behavior to be changed, careful measurement of the behavior, analysis of the antecedents and reinforcers that might be maintaining inappropriate or undesirable behavior, interventions based on behavioral principles to change the behavior, and careful measurement of changes. In research on applied behavior analysis, an ABAB design (described in Chapter 1) is common. That is, researchers take a baseline measurement of the behavior (A), then apply the intervention (B), then stop the intervention to see if the behavior goes back to the baseline level (A), and then reintroduce the intervention (B).

In classrooms, teachers usually cannot follow all the ABAB steps, but they can do the following:

1. Clearly specify the behavior to be changed and note the current level. For example, if a student is "careless," does this mean 2, 3, 4, or more computation errors for every 10 problems?

Connect and Extend to PRAXIS II™

Applied Behavior Analysis (I, C4)
When teachers need to change inappropriate or ineffective classroom behaviors that have not changed in response to standard behavioral techniques (e.g., response cost), they often employ applied behavior analysis. Familiarize yourself with the steps in developing and implementing an intervention based on that technique.

Applied behavior analysis The application of behavioral learning principles to understand and change behavior.

Behavior modification Systematic application of antecedents and consequences to change behavior.

2. Plan a specific intervention using antecedents, consequences, or both. For example, offer the student one extra minute of computer time for every problem completed with no errors.
3. Keep track of the results, and modify the plan if necessary.

Let's consider some specific methods for accomplishing step 2—the *intervention.*

Methods for Encouraging Behaviors

Connect and **Extend** to the **Research**

For an up-to-date look at applied behavior analysis, see: Kazdin, A. E. (2001). *Behavior modification in applied settings* (6th ed.). Belmont, CA: Wadsworth and Alberto, P. A., & Troutman, A. C. (2006). *Applied behavior analysis for teachers* (6th ed.). Saddle River, NJ: Prentice-Hall.

As we discussed earlier, to encourage behavior is to reinforce it. See the *Stories of Learning/Tributes to Teaching* feature to read how one educator remembers the positive practices of her teacher over a half-century ago.

There are several specific ways to encourage existing behaviors or teach new ones. These include praise, the Premack principle, shaping, and positive practice.

Reinforcing with Teacher Attention. Many psychologists advise teachers to "accentuate the positive"—praise students for good behavior, while ignoring misbehavior. In fact, some researchers believe that "the systematic application of praise and attention may be the most powerful motivational and classroom management tool available to teachers" (Alber & Heward, 1997, p. 277; Alber & Heward, 2000). A related strategy is *differential reinforcement,* or ignoring inappropriate behaviors, while being sure to reinforce appropriate behaviors as soon as they occur. For example, if a student is prone to making irrelevant comments ("When is the game this Friday?"), you should ignore the off-task comment, but recognize a task-related contribution as soon as it occurs (Landrum & Kauffman, 2006).

This *praise-and-ignore approach* can be helpful, but don't expect it to solve all classroom management problems. Several studies have shown that disruptive behaviors persist when teachers use positive consequences (mostly praise) as their only classroom management strategy (McGoey & DuPaul, 2000; Pfiffner & O'Leary, 1987; Sullivan & O'Leary, 1990). Also, if peer attention is maintaining the problem behaviors, the teacher's ignoring them won't help much.

STORIES OF LEARNING
TRIBUTES TO TEACHING

MY THIRD-GRADE TEACHER taught a really comprehensive program. She was a good model. She brought in home economics, she read stories, she did all kinds of things that made you know that you could do anything in the world.

I can remember hearing about New York City from her reading a book, and I got the idea back then: "One of these days, I'm going to go to New York City."

She talked about the high-rise apartments and the elevators, and I could just feel myself going up the elevators and coming down, and I'd never seen an elevator before, growing up in rural Mississippi!

She was the kind who always gave you incentives for doing something. She would take two people from the class, either weekly or monthly, to go to her house for a meal. She had all kinds of ways you could earn that privilege—maybe by coming to school every day, by doing your work every day, or by being a good citizen; all kinds of things. It was possible for everybody to earn that nice gift. You didn't have to be an A student, you could always do other things. I am sure that she had it set up so that every student got a chance to go to her house during the school year. The way she had it fixed, everybody was a winner; nobody would lose. When we went to her house, we would help her to prepare the meal. She would teach us how to set the table because we didn't have the silver at home to do it. She taught us that you put the fork on the left and the knife and the spoon on the right.

"The way she had it fixed, everybody was a winner; nobody would lose."

—Virgie Binford, Educational Consultant, Richmond, Virginia

Source: From *Mentors, Masters, and Mrs. MacGregor* (pp. 229–230) by J. Bluestein. Copyright © 1995 by Health Communications. Adapted by permission of the publisher.

There is a second consideration in using praise. The positive results found in research occur when teachers carefully and systematically praise their students (Landrum & Kauffman, 2006). Merely "handing out compliments" will not improve behavior. To be effective, praise must (1) be contingent on the behavior to be reinforced, (2) specify clearly the behavior being reinforced, and (3) be believable (O'Leary & O'Leary, 1977). In other words, the praise should be sincere recognition of a well-defined behavior so students understand what they did to warrant the recognition. Teachers who have not received special training often violate these conditions (Brophy, 1981). Ideas for using praise effectively, based on Brophy's extensive review of the subject, are presented in the *Guidelines*.

Some psychologists have suggested that teachers' use of praise tends to focus students on learning to win approval rather than on learning for its own sake. Perhaps the best advice is to be aware of the potential dangers of the overuse or misuse of praise and to navigate accordingly.

Selecting Reinforcers: The Premack Principle. In most classrooms, there are many readily available reinforcers other than teacher attention, such as the chance to talk to other students or feed the class animals. However, teachers tend to offer these opportunities in a rather haphazard way. Just as with praise, by making privileges and rewards directly contingent on learning and positive behavior, the teacher can greatly increase both learning and desired behavior.

Guidelines: Using Praise Appropriately

Be clear and systematic in giving praise.

EXAMPLES

1. Make sure praise is tied directly to appropriate behavior.
2. Make sure the student understands the specific action or accomplishment that is being praised. Say, "You returned this poster on time and in good condition," not, "You were very responsible."

Recognize genuine accomplishments.

EXAMPLES

1. Reward the attainment of specified goals, not just participation.
2. Do not reward uninvolved students just for being quiet and not disrupting the class.
3. Tie praise to students' improving competence or to the value of their accomplishment. Say, "I noticed that you double-checked all your problems. Your score reflects your careful work."

Set standards for praise based on individual abilities and limitations.

EXAMPLES

1. Praise progress or accomplishment in relation to the individual student's past efforts.
2. Focus the student's attention on his or her own progress, not on comparisons with others.

Attribute the student's success to effort and ability so the student will gain confidence that success is possible again.

EXAMPLES

1. Don't imply that the success may be based on luck, extra help, or easy material.
2. Ask students to describe the problems they encountered and how they solved them.

Make praise really reinforcing.

EXAMPLES

1. Don't attempt to influence the rest of the class by singling out some students for praise. This tactic frequently backfires, because students know what's really going on. In addition, you risk embarrassing the student you have chosen to praise.
2. Don't give undeserved praise to students simply to balance failures. It is seldom consoling and calls attention to the student's inability to earn genuine recognition.

For more information on teacher praise, see: **http://moodle.ed.uiuc.edu/wiked/index.php/Praise**

To assess your students' preferences for praise, see: **http://www.csu.edu.au/research/staff/burnett/PraisePercScale.htm**

"Hey wait a minute! You're cleaning erasers as a punishment? I'm cleaning erasers as a reward!"

A helpful guide for choosing the most effective reinforcers is the **Premack principle**, named for David Premack (1965). According to the Premack principle, a high-frequency behavior (a preferred activity) can be an effective reinforcer for a low-frequency behavior (a less-preferred activity). This is sometimes referred to as "Grandma's rule": First, do what I want you to do, then you may do what you want to do. Elizabeth used this principle in her class when she told them they could work together on their Civil War news program after they quietly completed the first section of the worksheet on their own.

If students didn't have to study, what would they do? The answers to this question may suggest many possible reinforcers. For most students, talking, moving around the room, sitting near a friend, being exempt from assignments or tests, reading magazines, using the computer, or playing games are preferred activities. The best way to determine appropriate reinforcers for your students may be to watch what they do in their free time.

For the Premack principle to be effective, the low-frequency (less preferred) behavior must happen first. In the following dialogue, notice how the teacher loses a perfect opportunity to use the Premack principle:

Students: Oh, no! Do we have to work on grammar again today? The other classes got to discuss the film we saw in the auditorium this morning.

Teacher: But the other classes finished the lesson on sentences yesterday. We're almost finished too. If we don't finish the lesson, I'm afraid you'll forget the rules we reviewed yesterday.

Students: Why don't we finish the sentences at the end of the period and talk about the film now?

Teacher: Okay, if you promise to complete the sentences later.

Discussing the film could have served as a reinforcer for completing the lesson. As it is, the class may well spend the entire period discussing the film. Just as the discussion becomes fascinating, the teacher will have to end it and insist that the class return to the grammar lesson.

Shaping. What happens when students continually fail to gain reinforcement because they simply cannot perform a skill in the first place? Consider these examples:

- A 4th-grade student looks at the results of the latest mathematics test. "No credit on almost half of the problems again because I made one dumb mistake in each problem. I hate math!"
- A 10th-grade student tries each day to find some excuse for avoiding the softball game in gym class. The student cannot catch a ball and now refuses to try.

In both situations, the students are receiving no reinforcement for their work because the end product of their efforts is not good enough. A safe prediction is that the students will soon learn to dislike the class, the subject, and perhaps the teacher and school in general. One way to prevent this problem is the strategy of **shaping**, also called **successive approximations.** Shaping involves reinforcing progress instead of waiting for perfection.

In order to use shaping, the teacher must take the final complex behavior the student is expected to master and break it down into a number of small steps. One approach that identifies the small steps is **task analysis**, originally developed by R. B. Miller (1962) to help the armed services train personnel. Miller's system begins with a definition of the final performance requirement, what the trainee (or student) must be able to do at the end of the program or unit. Then, the steps that will lead to the final goal are specified. The procedure simply breaks skills and processes down into subskills and subprocesses.

Consider an example of task analysis in which students must write a position paper based on library research. If the teacher assigned the position paper without analyzing the task in this way, what could happen? Some of the students might not know how to do computer research. They might search through one or two encyclopedias, then write a

Connect and **Extend** to **PRAXIS II™**

Encouraging/Discouraging Behaviors (I, B2)

Understand the appropriate uses of techniques to encourage or discourage various classroom behaviors. Know the limitations and problems associated with these types of interventions.

Premack principle Principle stating that a more-preferred activity can serve as a reinforcer for a less-preferred activity.

Shaping Reinforcing each small step of progress toward a desired goal or behavior.

Successive approximations Small components that make up a complex behavior.

Task analysis System for breaking down a task hierarchically into basic skills and subskills.

summary of the issues based only on the encyclopedia articles. Another group of students might know how to use computers, tables of contents, and indexes, but have difficulty reaching conclusions. They might hand in lengthy papers listing summaries of different ideas. Another group of students might be able to draw conclusions, but their written presentations might be so confusing and grammatically incorrect that the teacher could not understand what they were trying to say. Each of the groups would have failed in fulfilling the assignment, but for different reasons.

A task analysis gives a picture of the logical sequence of steps leading toward the final goal. An awareness of this sequence can help teachers make sure that students have the necessary skills before they move to the next step. In addition, when students have difficulty, the teacher can pinpoint problem areas. Many behaviors can be improved through shaping, especially skills that involve persistence, endurance, increased accuracy, greater speed, or extensive practice to master. Because shaping is a time-consuming process, however, it should not be used if success can be attained through simpler methods such as cueing.

Positive Practice. In **positive practice**, students replace one behavior with another. This approach is especially appropriate for dealing with academic errors. When students make a mistake, they must correct it as soon as possible and practice the correct response (Gibbs & Luyben, 1985; Kazdin, 1984). The same principle can be applied when students break classroom rules. Instead of being punished, the student might be required to practice the correct alternative action.

The *Guidelines* on the next page summarize approaches encouraging positive behavior.

Coping with Undesirable Behavior

No matter how successful you are at accentuating the positive, there are times when you must cope with undesirable behavior, either because other methods fail or because the behavior itself is dangerous and calls for direct action. For this purpose, negative reinforcement, satiation, reprimands, response cost, and social isolation all offer possible solutions.

Connect and **Extend** to Your **Teaching Portfolio**

Examples of negative reinforcement: A 10th-grade teacher tells her class that those students who turn in sloppy, careless work will have to use their free-choice time to redo it. A 1st-grade teacher tells an angry boy that he must sit by the tree until he feels able to rejoin the kickball game without arguing.

Negative Reinforcement. Recall the basic principle of negative reinforcement: If an action stops or avoids something unpleasant, then the action is likely to occur again in similar situations. Negative reinforcement was operating in Elizabeth's classroom. When they moaned and complained, her students escaped the test, so they may have learned to complain more in the future through negative reinforcement.

Negative reinforcement can also be used to enhance learning. To do this, you place students in mildly unpleasant situations so they can "escape" when their behavior improves. Consider these examples:

Teacher to a 3rd-grade class: "When the supplies are put back in the cabinet and each of you is sitting quietly, we will go outside. Until then, we will miss our recess."

High-school teacher to a student who seldom finishes in-class assignments: "As soon as you complete the assignment, you may join the class in the auditorium. But until you finish, you must work in the study hall."

Actually, a true behaviorist might object to identifying these situations as examples of negative reinforcement because too much student thinking and understanding is required to make them work. Teachers cannot treat students like lab animals, delivering a mild shock to their feet until they give a right answer, then turning off the shock briefly. But teachers can make sure that unpleasant situations improve when student behavior improves.

You may wonder why the negative reinforcement examples above are not considered punishment. Surely staying in during recess or not accompanying the class to a special program is punishing. But the focus in each case is on strengthening specific behaviors

Positive practice Practicing correct responses immediately after errors.

Guidelines: Encouraging Positive Behaviors

Make sure you recognize positive behavior in ways that students value.

EXAMPLES

1. When presenting class rules, set up positive consequences for following rules as well as negative consequences for breaking rules.
2. Recognize honest admissions of mistakes by giving a second chance: "Because you admitted that you copied your paper from a book, I'm giving you a chance to rewrite it."
3. Offer desired rewards for academic efforts, such as extra recess time, exemptions from homework or tests, or extra credit on major projects.

When students are tackling new material or trying new skills, give plenty of reinforcement.

EXAMPLES

1. Find and comment on something right in every student's first life drawing.
2. Reinforce students for encouraging each other. "French pronunciation is difficult and awkward at first. Let's help each other by eliminating all giggles when someone is brave enough to attempt a new word."

After new behaviors are established, give reinforcement on an unpredictable schedule to encourage persistence.

EXAMPLES

1. Offer surprise rewards for good participation in class.
2. Start classes with a short, written extra-credit question. Students don't have to answer, but a good answer will add points to their total for the semester.
3. Make sure the good students get compliments for their work from time to time. Don't take them for granted.

Use the Premack principle to identify effective reinforcers.

EXAMPLES

1. Watch what students do with their free time.
2. Notice which students like to work together. The chance to work with friends is often a good reinforcer.

Use cueing to help establish new behaviors.

EXAMPLES

1. Put up humorous signs in the classroom to remind students of rules.
2. At the beginning of the year, as students enter class, call their attention to a list on the board of the materials they should have with them when they come to class.

Make sure all students, even those who often cause problems, receive some praise, privileges, or other rewards when they do something well.

EXAMPLES

1. Review your class list occasionally to make sure all students are receiving some reinforcement.
2. Set standards for reinforcement so that all students will have a chance to be rewarded.
3. Check your biases. Are boys getting more opportunities for reinforcement than girls, or vice versa? How about students of different races?

Establish a variety of reinforcers.

EXAMPLES

1. Let students suggest their own reinforcers or choose from a "menu" of reinforcers with "weekly specials."
2. Talk to other teachers or parents about ideas for reinforcers.

For more ideas about building positive behaviors, see these sites:
http://www.afcec.org/tipsforteachers/tips_c4.html

(putting away supplies or finishing in-class assignments). The teacher strengthens (reinforces) the behaviors by removing something aversive *as soon as the desired behaviors occur.* Because the consequence involves removing or "subtracting" a stimulus, the reinforcement is negative.

Negative reinforcement also gives students a chance to exercise control. Missing recess and staying behind in study hall are unpleasant situations, but in each case, the students retain control. As soon as they perform the appropriate behavior, the unpleasant situation ends. In contrast, punishment occurs after the fact, and a student cannot so easily control or terminate it.

There are several rules for negative reinforcement: Describe the desired change in a positive way. Don't bluff. Make sure you can enforce your unpleasant situation. Follow through despite complaints. Insist on action, not promises. If the unpleasant situation terminates when students promise to be better next time, you have reinforced making promises, not making changes (Alberto & Troutman, 2006; O'Leary, 1995).

Satiation. Another way to stop problem behavior is to insist that students continue the behavior until they are tired of doing it. This procedure, called **satiation**, should be applied with care. Forcing students to continue some behaviors may be physically or emotionally harmful, or even dangerous.

An example of an appropriate use of satiation is related by Krumboltz and Krumboltz (1972). In the middle of a 9th-grade algebra class, the teacher suddenly noticed four students making all sorts of unusual motions. In response to persistent teacher questioning, the students finally admitted they were bouncing imaginary balls. The teacher pretended to greet this idea with enthusiasm and suggested the whole class do it. At first, there was a great deal of laughing and joking. After a minute, this stopped, and one student even quit. The teacher, however, insisted that all the students continue. After 5 minutes and a number of exhausted sighs, the teacher allowed the students to stop. No one bounced an imaginary ball in that class again.

Teachers also can allow students to continue some action until they stop by themselves, if the behavior is not interfering with the rest of the class. A teacher can do this by simply ignoring the behavior. Remember that responding to an ignorable behavior may actually reinforce it.

In using satiation, a teacher must take care not to give in before the students do. It is also important that the repeated behavior be the one you are trying to end. If the algebra teacher above had insisted that the students write, "I will never bounce imaginary balls in class again" 500 times, the students would have become satiated with writing rather than with bouncing balls.

Reprimands. In the *Junction Journal*, my daughter's elementary-school newspaper, I read the following lines in a story called "Why I Like School," written by a 4th grader: "I also like my teacher. She helps me understand and learn. She is nice to everyone I like it when she gets mad at somebody, but she doesn't yell at them in front of the class, but speaks to them privately."

Soft, calm, private **reprimands** are more effective than loud, public reprimands in decreasing disruptive behavior (Landrum & Kauffman, 2006). Research has shown that when reprimands are loud enough for the entire class to hear, disruptions increase or continue at a constant level. Some students enjoy public recognition for misbehavior, or they don't want classmates to see them "lose" to the teacher. If they are not used

Research has shown that scolding a student in front of the entire class may actually reinforce his or her disruptive behavior by drawing more attention to it; thus, calm, private reprimands may be more effective.

Connect and **Extend** to Your **Teaching Portfolio**

Satiation: A 6th-grade teacher discovered one of his students making paper airplanes during an independent work time. He gave that student a stack of paper and told her to continue making airplanes until the stack of paper was gone. The student thought it was great fun for the first 10 minutes, but then she got weary and wanted to stop. After this experience, this student made better use of her independent work times.

Connect and **Extend** to Your **Teaching Portfolio**

Soft reprimands: During reading in Miss McCormick's 1st-grade class, she noticed that Kenny wasn't concentrating on his book. She was working with a group at the time and could have called out, "Kenny, you'd better get back to work. You're not concentrating," but she decided this would embarrass him as well as disturb the concentration of others. Instead, Miss McCormick walked over to him, asked him a couple of questions about the story, and asked him to let her know how the story ended. She achieved her goal without causing embarrassment, and she provided Kenny with an impetus and motive to concentrate on his story again.

Satiation Requiring a person to repeat a problem behavior past the point of interest or motivation.

Reprimands Criticisms for misbehavior; rebukes.

too often, and if the classroom is generally a positive, warm environment, then students usually respond quickly to private reprimands (Kaplan, 1991; Van Houten & Doleys, 1983).

Response Cost. The concept of **response cost** is familiar to anyone who has ever paid a fine. For certain infractions of the rules, people must lose some reinforcer—money, time, privileges (Walker, Shea, & Bauer, 2004). In a class, the concept of response cost can be applied in a number of ways. The first time a student breaks a class rule, the teacher gives a warning. The second time, the teacher makes a mark beside the student's name in the grade book. The student loses 2 minutes of recess for each mark accumulated. For older students, a certain number of marks might mean losing the privilege of working in a group or going on a class trip.

Social Isolation. One of the most controversial behavioral methods for decreasing undesirable behavior is the strategy of **social isolation**, often called **time out** from reinforcement. The process involves removing a highly disruptive student from the classroom for 5 to 10 minutes. The student is placed in an empty, uninteresting room alone—the punishment is brief isolation from other people. A trip to the principal's office or confinement to a chair in the corner of the regular classroom does not have the same effect as sitting alone in an empty room.

Some Cautions. Punishment in and of itself does not lead to any positive behavior. Harsh punishment communicates to students that "might makes right" and may encourage retaliation (Alberto & Troutman, 2006; Walker et al., 2004). Thus, whenever you consider the use of punishment, you should make it part of a two-pronged attack. The first goal is to carry out the punishment and suppress the undesirable behavior. The second goal is to make clear what the student should be doing instead and to provide reinforcement for those desirable actions. Thus, while the problem behaviors are being suppressed, positive alternative responses are being strengthened. As you will see next, recent approaches really emphasize supporting positive behaviors. The *Guidelines* give ideas for using punishment for positive purposes.

Connect and **Extend** to Your **Teaching Portfolio**

What is your stance on using extrinsic reinforcement and punishment in teaching? Be prepared to answer questions about these issues in your interviews.

Reaching Every Student: Functional Behavioral Assessment and Positive Behavior Support

Teachers in both regular and special education classes have had success with a new approach that begins by asking, "What are students getting out of their problem behaviors—what functions do these behaviors serve?" The focus is on the *why* of the behavior, not on the *what* (Lane, Falk, & Wehby, 2006). The reasons for problem behaviors generally fall into four categories (Barnhill, 2005; Maag & Kemp, 2003). Students act out to:

1. receive attention from others—teachers, parent, or peers.
2. escape from some unpleasant situation—an academic or social demand.
3. get a desired item or activity.
4. meet sensory needs, such as stimulation from rocking or flapping arms for some children with autism.

If the reason for the behavior is known, then the teacher can devise ways of supporting positive behaviors that will serve the same "why" function. For example, I once worked with a middle-school principal who was concerned about a boy who had lost his father a few years earlier and was having trouble in a number of subjects, especially math. The student disrupted the math at least twice a week and ended up in the principal's office. When he arrived, the boy got the principal's undivided attention. After a scolding, they talked about sports because the principal liked the student and was concerned that he had no male role models. It is easy to spot the function of the classroom disruptions—

Response cost Punishment by loss of reinforcers.

Social isolation Removal of a disruptive student for 5 to 10 minutes.

Time out Technically, the removal of all reinforcement. In practice, isolation of a student from the rest of the class for a brief time.

Guidelines: Using Punishment

Try to structure the situation so you can use negative reinforcement rather than punishment.

EXAMPLES

1. Allow students to escape unpleasant situations (completing additional workbook assignments, weekly tests of math facts) when they reach a level of competence.
2. Insist on actions, not promises. Don't let students convince you to change the terms of the agreement.

Be consistent in your application of punishment.

EXAMPLES

1. Avoid inadvertently reinforcing the behavior you are trying to punish. Keep confrontations private, so that students don't become heroes for standing up to the teacher in a public showdown.
2. Let students know in advance the consequences of breaking the rules by posting major class rules for younger students or outlining rules and consequences in a course syllabus for older students.
3. Tell students they will receive only one warning before punishment is given. Give the warning in a calm way, then follow through.
4. Make punishment as unavoidable and immediate as is reasonably possible.

Focus on the students' actions, not on the students' personal qualities.

EXAMPLES

1. Reprimand in a calm but firm voice.
2. Avoid vindictive or sarcastic words or tones of voice. You might hear your own angry words later when students imitate your sarcasm.
3. Stress the need to end the problem behavior instead of expressing any dislike you might feel for the student.
4. Be aware that students of color are disproportionately punished, sent to detention, and expelled from school—are your policies fair?

Adapt the punishment to the infraction.

EXAMPLE

1. Ignore minor misbehaviors that do not disrupt the class, or stop these misbehaviors with a disapproving glance or a move toward the student.
2. Make sure the punishment fits the crime—don't take away all the free time a student has earned for one infraction of the rules, for example (Landrum & Kauffman, 2006).
3. Don't use homework as a punishment for misbehaviors such as talking in class.
4. When a student misbehaves to gain peer acceptance, removal from the group of friends can be effective, because this is really time out from a reinforcing situation.
5. If the problem behaviors continue, analyze the situation and try a new approach. Your punishment may not be very punishing, or you may be inadvertently reinforcing the misbehavior.

For more information on punishment, see **http://www.ext.vt.edu/pubs/family/350-111/350-111.html**

they always led to (1) escape from math class (negative reinforcement) and (2) one-on-one time with the principal (positive reinforcement after a little bit of reprimanding). The principal, teacher, and I developed a way to support the students positive behaviors in math by getting him some extra tutoring and by giving him time with the principal when he completed math problems instead of when he acted up in class. The new positive behaviors served many of the same functions as the old problem behaviors.

Positive Behavioral Supports. The Individuals with Disabilities Education Improvement Act (IDEIA, 2004) discussed in Chapter 4 requires positive behavioral supports (PBS) for students with disabilities and those at-risk for special education placement. **Positive behavioral supports** are interventions designed to replace problem behaviors with new actions that serve the same purpose for the student. The process of understanding the problem behavior is known as a **functional behavioral assessment (FBA)**—"a collection of methods or procedures used to obtain information about antecedents, behaviors, and consequences to determine the reason or function of the behavior" (Barnhill, 2005, p. 132). With information from this assessment, teachers can develop an intervention package, as we did above with the math student.

Positive behavior supports based on functional behavioral assessments can help students with disabilities succeed in inclusion classrooms. For example, the disruptive behavior of a five-year-old boy with mental retardation was nearly eliminated in a relatively

Positive Behavioral Supports (PBS) Interventions designed to replace problem behaviors with new actions that serve the same purpose for the student.

Functional Behavioral Assessment (FBA) Procedures used to obtain information about antecedents, behaviors, and consequences to determine the reason or function of the behavior short time through a PBS intervention that was based on a functional assessment conducted by the regular teaching staff and the special education teacher. The intervention included making sure tasks assigned were at the right difficulty level, providing assistance with these tasks, teaching the student how to request assistance, and teaching the student how to request a break from assigned work (Soodak & McCarthy, 2006; Umbreit, 1995). But these approaches are not only for students with special needs. Research shows that disciplinary referrals decrease when the whole school uses these approaches for all students (Lewis, Sugai, & Colvin, 1998). Because about 5% of students account for half of the discipline referrals, it makes sense to develop interventions for those students. Positive behavior interventions based on functional assessments can reduce these behavior problems by 80% (Crone & Horner, 2003).

Doing Functional Behavioral Assessments. Many different procedures might help you determine the functions of a behavior. You can simply interview students about their behaviors. In one study, students were asked to describe what they did that got them in trouble in school, what happened just before, and what happened right after they acted out. Even though the students were not always sure why they acted out, they seemed to benefit from talking to a concerned adult who was trying to understand their situation, not just reprimand them (Murdock, O'Neill, & Cunningham, 2005). Teachers also can observe students with these questions in mind: When and where does the problem behavior occur? What people or activities are involved? What happens right before—what do others do or say and what did the target student do or say? What happens right after the behavior—what did you, other students, or the target student do or say? What does the target student gain or escape from—what changes after the student acts out? A more structured approach is shown in Figure 6.3—an observation and planning worksheet for functional behavioral assessment.

Behavioral Approaches to Teaching and Management

Connect and **Extend** to **PRAXIS II™**

Teaching and Management (I, A1; II, A3; I, C4)

Identify major approaches to teaching and classroom management that are based on behavioral principles. Understand the advantages and disadvantages of each.

The behavioral approach to learning has made several important contributions to instruction, including systems for specifying learning objectives, mastery learning, and direct instruction (we will look at these topics in Chapter 13 when we discuss teaching) and class management systems such as group consequences, contingency contracts and token economies (Landrum & Kauffman, 2006). These approaches are useful when the goal is to learn *explicit information* or change *behaviors* and when the material is *sequential* and *factual.*

First, let's consider one element that is part of every behavioral learning program—specific practice of correct behaviors. Contrary to popular wisdom, practice does not make *perfect.* Instead, practice makes *permanent* the behaviors practiced, so practicing

Rules, consequences, and rewards are posted in this elementary school classroom to serve as reminders about appropriate behavior.

FIGURE 6.3

A Structured Observation Guide for Functional Behavioral Analysis

Student Name: ______________________________ **Date:** ______________

Target Behavior: Operationally define the behavior that most interferes with the student's functioning in the classroom. Include intensity (high, medium, or low), frequency, and duration.

____

____

When, where, with whom, and in what condition is the target behavior *least* likely to occur?

____

Setting Events or Context Variables (i.e., hunger, lack of sleep, medications, problems on bus):

____

Immediate Antecedents & Consequences

Antecedents	*Problematic Settings*	*Consequences*
___ Demand/Request	___ Unstructured setting	___ Behavior ignored
___ Difficult task	___ Unstructured activity	___ Reprimanded
___ Time of day	___ Individual seat work	___ Verbal redirection
___ Interruption in routine	___ Group work	___ Time-out (duration: ___)
___ Peer tease/provoked	___ Specials	___ Loss of incentives
___ No materials/activities	___ Specific subject/task	___ Physical redirection
___ Could not get desired item	___ Crowded setting	___ Physical restraint
___ People ____________	___ Noisy setting	___ Sent to office
___ Alone	___ Other ____________	___ Suspension
___ Other ____________	___ Other ____________	___ Other ____________

What function(s) does the target behavior seem to serve for the student?

___ Escape from:	___ demand/request	___ person	___ activity/task	___ school	___ other ____________
___ Attention from:	___ adult	___ peer	___ other ____________		
___ Gain desired:	___ item	___ activity	___ area	___ other ____________	

___ Automatic sensory stimulation: ______________________________

Hypothesis:

When ____________ (antecedent) occurs in the context of ____________ (problematic setting)

the student exhibits ____________ (target behavior) in order to ____________ (perceived function).

This behavior is more likely to occur when ____________ (setting event/context variables).

Replacement or competing behavior that could still serve the same function for the student:

____

Is the replacement behavior in the student's repertoire, or will it need to be taught directly? ____________

If so, how will it be taught? ____________

List some potential motivators for student: ____________

____

Source: From "Functional behavior assessment in schools" by G. P. Barnhill, *Intervention in School and Clinic,* 40, p. 138. Copyright 2005 by PRO-ED, Inc. Reprinted with permission.

accurate behaviors is important. Describing Tiger Woods in a *Newsweek* article, Devin Gordon (2001) said,

> Tiger's habit of pounding golf ball after golf ball long into the twilight—often during tournament play—has already become part of his legend. During his so-called slump earlier this year, Woods claimed he was simply working on shots he would need for the Masters in April. People rolled their eyes. Until he won the Masters. (p. 45)

No doubt Tiger has continued specific practice of the shots he needs for each tournament.

As an example of a behavioral approach, consider group consequences.

Group Consequences

A teacher can base reinforcement for the class on the cumulative behavior of all members of the class, usually by adding each student's points to a class or a team total. The **good behavior game** is an example of this approach. Teachers and students discuss what would make the classroom a better place. Then, they identify behaviors that get in the way of learning. Based on this discussion, class rules are developed and the class is divided into two teams. Each time a student breaks one of the rules, that student's team is given a mark. The team with the fewest marks at the end of the period receives a special reward or privilege (longer recess, first to lunch, and so on). If both teams earn fewer than a preestablished number of marks, both teams receive the reward. Most studies indicate that even though the game generates only small improvements in academic achievement, it can produce definite improvements in the behaviors listed in the good behavior rules and it can prevent many behavior problems (Embry, 2002).

You can also use **group consequences** without dividing the class into teams; that is, you can base reinforcement on the behavior of the whole class. Wilson and Hopkins (1973) conducted a study using group consequences to reduce classroom noise levels. Radio music served effectively as the reinforcer for students in a family and consumer science class. Whenever noise in the class was below a predetermined level, students could listen to the radio; when the noise exceeded the level, the radio was turned off. Given the success of this simple method, such a procedure might be considered in any class where music does not interfere with the task at hand.

However, caution is needed using group approaches. The whole group should not suffer for the misbehavior or mistakes of one individual if the group has no real influence over that person (Epanchin, Townsend, & Stoddard, 1994). I saw an entire class break into cheers when the teacher announced that one boy was transferring to another school. The chant "No more points! No more points!" filled the room. The "points" referred to the teacher's system of giving one point to the whole class each time anyone broke a rule. Every point meant 5 minutes of recess lost. The boy who was transferring had been responsible for many losses. He was not very popular to begin with, and the point system, though quite effective in maintaining order, had made the boy an outcast in his own class.

Peer pressure in the form of support and encouragement, however, can be a positive influence. Group consequences are recommended for situations in which students care about the approval of their peers (Theodore, Bray, Kehle, & Jenson, 2001). If the misbehavior of several students seems to be encouraged by the attention and laughter of other students, then group consequences could be helpful. Teachers might show students how to give support and constructive feedback to classmates. If a few students seem to enjoy sabotaging the system, those students may need separate arrangements.

Contingency Contracts

In a **contingency contract** program, the teacher draws up an individual contract with each student, describing exactly what the student must do to earn a particular privilege or reward. In some programs, students suggest behaviors to be reinforced and the rewards that can be gained. The negotiating process itself can be an educational experience, as students learn to set reasonable goals and abide by the terms of a contract. And, if students participate in setting the goals, they often are more committed to reaching them (Locke & Latham, 2002; Pintrich & Schunk, 2002).

An example of a contract for completing assignments that is appropriate for intermediate and upper-grade students is presented in Figure 6.4. This chart serves as a contract, assignment sheet, and progress record. Information about progress can support student motivation (Schunk, 2004). Something like this might even help you keep track of assignments and due dates in your college classes.

The few pages devoted here to token reinforcement and contingency contracts can offer only an introduction to these programs. If you want to set up a large-scale reward program in your classroom, you should probably seek professional advice. Often, the school psychologist, counselor, or principal can help.

Good behavior game Arrangement where a class is divided into teams and each team receives demerit points for breaking agreed-upon rules of good behavior.

Group consequences Rewards or punishments given to a class as a whole for adhering to or violating rules of conduct.

Contingency contract A contract between the teacher and a student specifying what the student must do to earn a particular reward or privilege.

FIGURE 6.4

A Contingency Contract for Completing Assignments

The teacher and student agree on the due dates for each assignment, marking them in blue on the chart. Each time an assignment is turned in, the date of completion is marked in black on the chart. As long as the actual completion line is above the planned completion line, the student earns free time or other contracted rewards.

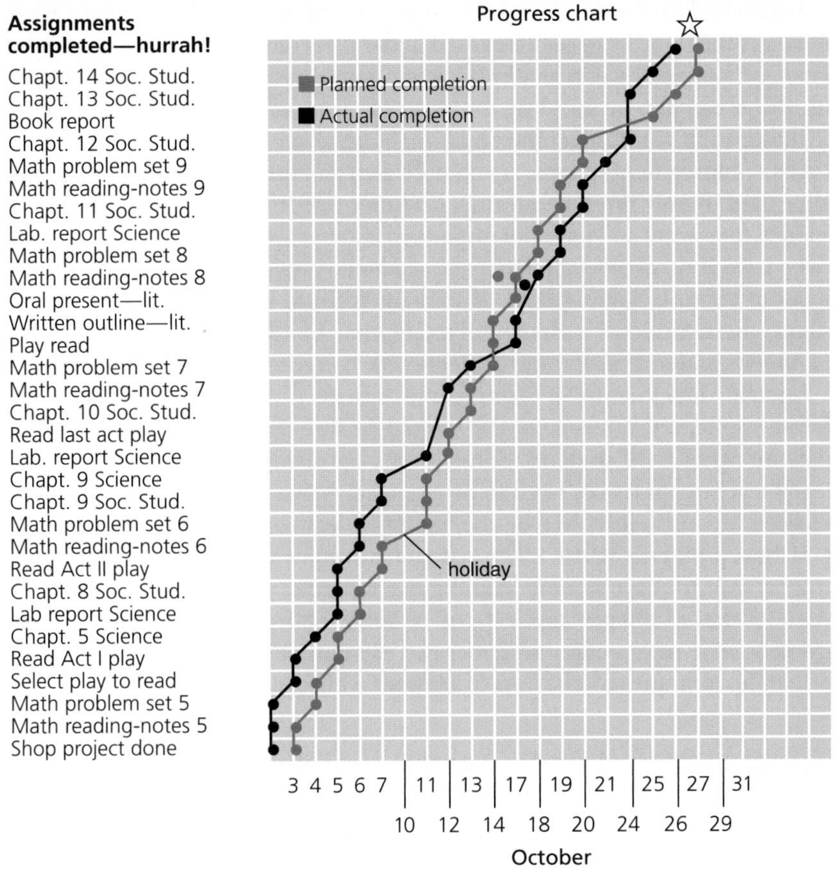

Source: From *Achieving Educational Excellence: Behavior Analysis for School Personnel* (Figure, p. 89), by B. Sulzer-Azaroff and G. R. Mayer, 1994, San Marcos, CA: Western Image, P.O. Box 427. Copyright © 1994 by Beth Sulzer-Azaroff and G. Roy Mayer. Reprinted with permission.

Connect and Extend to Your Teaching Portfolio

Add Figure 6.2 "Written Prompts: A Peer-Tutoring Checklist," Figure 6.3, "A Structured Observation Guide for Functional Behavioral Analysis," Figure 6.4, "A Contingency Contract for Completing Assignments," and Figure 6.6, "Posters to Remind Students to 'Talk Themselves Through' Listening, Planning, Working, and Checking in School" to your Teaching Resources file.

Token Reinforcement

STOP | THINK | WRITE Have you ever participated in a program where you earned points or credits that you could exchange for a reward? Are you a member of a frequent flyer club, or do you get points on your credit card? Do you collect Subway Club stamps? (My husband has hundreds right now.) Do you get one free movie for every 10 rentals? Does being a part of such a program affect your buying habits? How? Go to http://www.bookitprogram.com and see a reading incentive club for pizza eaters. ■

Often, it is difficult to provide positive consequences for all the students who deserve them. A **token reinforcement system** can help solve this problem by allowing all students to earn tokens for both academic work and positive classroom behavior. The tokens may be points, checks, holes punched in a card, chips, play money, or anything else that is easily identified as the student's property. Periodically, the students exchange the tokens they have earned for some desired reward (Kazdin, 2001; Alberto &Troutman, 2006).

Token reinforcement system System in which tokens earned for academic work and positive classroom behavior can be exchanged for some desired reward.

Depending on the age of the student, the rewards could be small toys, school supplies, free time, special class jobs, or other privileges. When a "token economy," as this kind of system is called, is first established, the tokens should be given out on a fairly continuous schedule, with chances to exchange the tokens for rewards often available. Once the system is working well, however, tokens should be distributed on an intermittent schedule and saved for longer periods of time before they are exchanged for rewards.

Another variation is to allow students to earn tokens in the classroom and then exchange them for rewards at home. These plans are very successful when parents are willing to cooperate. Usually a note or report form is sent home daily or twice a week. The note indicates the number of points earned in the preceding time period. The points may be exchanged for minutes of television viewing, access to special toys, or private time with parents. Points can also be saved up for larger rewards such as trips. Do not use this procedure, however, if you suspect the child might be severely punished for poor reports.

Token reinforcement systems are complicated and time-consuming. Generally, they should be used in only three situations: (1) to motivate students who are completely uninterested in their work and have not responded to other approaches; (2) to encourage students who have consistently failed to make academic progress; and (3) to deal with a class that is out of control. Some groups of students seem to benefit from token economies more than others. Students with mental retardation, children who have failed often, students with few academic skills, and students with behavior problems all seem to respond to the concrete, direct nature of token reinforcement.

Before you try a token system, you should be sure that your teaching methods and materials are right for the students. Sometimes, class disruptions or lack of motivation indicate that teaching practices need to be changed. Maybe the class rules are unclear or are enforced inconsistently. Maybe the text is too easy or too hard. Maybe the pace is wrong. If these problems exist, a token system may improve the situation temporarily, but the students will still have trouble learning the academic material.

Many of the systematic applications of behavioral principles focus on classroom management. The next section describes two examples that successfully applied behavioral principles to improve behaviors of students with special needs.

Reaching Every Student: Severe Behavior Problems

Students with severe behavior problems provide some of the most difficult challenges for teachers. Two studies show how behavioral principles can be useful in helping these students.

Lea Theodore and her colleagues (2001) worked with the teacher of five adolescent males who were diagnosed as having severe emotional disorders. A short list of clear rules was established (e.g., no obscene words, comply with teacher's requests within five seconds, no verbal putdowns). The rules were written on index cards taped to each student's desk. The teacher had a checklist on his desk with each student's name to note any rule-breaking. This checklist was easily observable, so students could monitor their own and each others' performance. At the end of the 45-minute period, a student chose a "criterion" from a jar. The possible criteria were: performance of the whole group, student with the highest score, student with the lowest score, the average of all students, or a random single student. If the student or students selected to be the criterion had five checks or fewer for rule-breaking, then the whole class got a reward, also chosen randomly from a jar. The possible rewards were things like a soda, a bag of chips, a candy bar, or a late-to-class pass. An ABAB design was used—baseline, two-week intervention, two-week withdrawal of intervention, and two-week return to group consequences. All students showed clear improvement in following the rules when the reward system was in place, as you can see in Figure 6.5, a chart for one of the students. Students liked the approach and the teacher found it easy to implement.

In the second study, Kara McGoey and George DuPaul (2000) worked with teachers in three preschool classrooms to address problem behaviors of four students diagnosed as having Attention-Deficit Hyperactive Disorder. The teachers tried both a token reinforcement program (students earned small and large buttons on a chart for following class

FIGURE 6.5

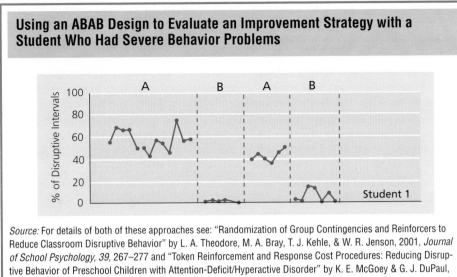

Using an ABAB Design to Evaluate an Improvement Strategy with a Student Who Had Severe Behavior Problems

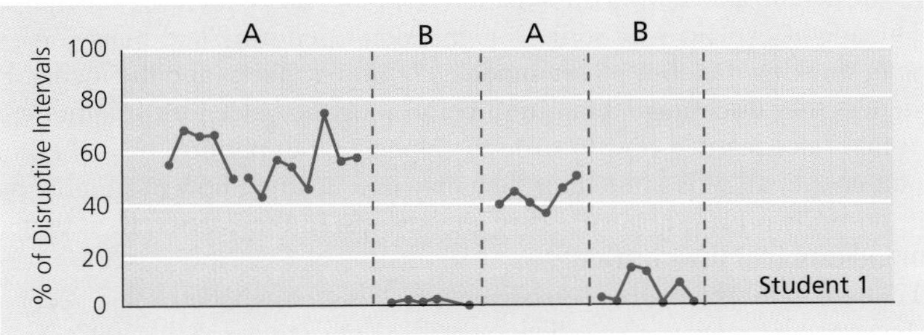

Source: For details of both of these approaches see: "Randomization of Group Contingencies and Reinforcers to Reduce Classroom Disruptive Behavior" by L. A. Theodore, M. A. Bray, T. J. Kehle, & W. R. Jenson, 2001, *Journal of School Psychology, 39,* 267–277 and "Token Reinforcement and Response Cost Procedures: Reducing Disruptive Behavior of Preschool Children with Attention-Deficit/Hyperactive Disorder" by K. E. McGoey & G. J. DuPaul, 2000, *School Psychology Quarterly, 15,* 330–343.

rules), and a response cost system (students began with five small buttons and one large button per activity each day and lost buttons for not following rules). Both procedures were effective in lowering rule-breaking, but the teachers found the response cost system easier to implement.

As behavioral approaches to learning developed, some researchers added a new element—thinking about behavior.

Observational Learning and Cognitive Behavior Modification: Thinking about Behavior

In recent years, most behavioral psychologists have found that operant conditioning offers too limited an explanation of learning. Many have expanded their view of learning to include the study of cognitive processes that cannot be directly observed, such as expectations, thoughts, mental maps, and beliefs. Three examples of this expanded view are observational learning, self-management, and cognitive behavior modification.

Connect and **Extend** to **PRAXIS II™**

Observational Learning (II, B2)
Identify situations in which observational learning may be a wise approach, and describe the essential elements of effective observational learning.

Observational Learning

Over 30 years ago, Albert Bandura noted that the traditional behavioral views of learning were accurate—but incomplete—because they gave only a partial explanation of learning and overlooked important elements, particularly social influences. His early work on learning was grounded in the behavioral principles of reinforcement and punishment, but he added a focus on *learning from observing others.* This expanded view was labeled **social learning theory;** it was considered a *neobehavioral* approach (Bandura, 1977; Hill, 2002, Zimmerman & Schunk, 2003).

To explain some limitations of the behavioral model, Bandura distinguished between the *acquisition of knowledge* (learning) and the *observable performance based on that knowledge* (behavior). In other words, Bandura suggested that we all may know more than we show. An example is found in one of Bandura's early studies (1965). Preschool children saw a film of a model kicking and punching an inflatable "Bobo" doll. One group saw the model rewarded for the aggression, another group saw the model punished, and a third group saw no consequences. When they were moved to a room with the Bobo

Social learning theory Theory that emphasizes learning through observation of others.

Albert Bandura expanded on behavioral theories to emphasize observational learning.

doll, the children who had seen the punching and kicking reinforced on the film were the most aggressive toward the doll. Those who had seen the attacks punished were the least aggressive. But when the children were promised rewards for imitating the model's aggression, all of them demonstrated that they had learned the behavior.

Thus, incentives can affect performance. Even though learning may have occurred, it may not be demonstrated until the situation is appropriate or there are incentives to perform. This might explain why some students don't perform "bad behaviors" such as swearing or smoking that they all see modeled by adults, peers, and the media. Personal consequences may discourage them from performing the behaviors. In other examples, children may have learned how to write the alphabet, but perform badly because their fine motor coordination is limited, or they may have learned how to simplify fractions, but perform badly on a test because they are anxious. In these cases, their performance is not an indication of their learning.

Recently, Bandura has focused on cognitive factors such as beliefs, self-perceptions, and expectations, so his theory is now called a social cognitive theory (Hill, 2002). **Social cognitive theory** (discussed more thoroughly in Chapters 9 and 10) distinguishes between enactive and vicarious learning. *Enactive learning* is learning by doing and experiencing the consequences of your actions. This may sound like operant conditioning all over again, but it is not, and the difference has to do with the role of consequences. Proponents of operant conditioning believe that consequences strengthen or weaken behavior. In enactive learning, however, consequences are seen as providing information. Our interpretations of the consequences create expectations, influence motivation, and shape beliefs (Schunk, 2004). We will see many examples of enactive learning—learning by doing—throughout this book.

Connect and **Extend** to the **Research**

For a look at social cognitive theory and school achievement, see Schunk, D. H. (1999). Social-self interaction and achievement behavior. *Educational Psychologist, 34*, 219–227.

Vicarious learning is learning by observing others. People and animals can learn merely by observing another person or animal learn, and this fact challenges the behaviorist idea that cognitive factors are unnecessary in an explanation of learning. If people can learn by watching, they must be focusing their attention, constructing images, remembering, analyzing, and making decisions that affect learning. Thus, much is going on mentally before performance and reinforcement can even take place. Cognitive apprenticeships, discussed in Chapter 9, are examples of vicarious learning—learning by observing others.

Elements of Observational Learning

STOP | THINK | WRITE Your interview for a position in the middle school is going well. The next question is: "Who are your models as teachers? Do you hear yourself saying or see yourself doing things that other teachers have done? Are there teachers from films or books that you would like to be like?" ■

Through **observational learning,** we learn not only how to perform a behavior but also what will happen to us in specific situations if we do perform it. Observation can be a very efficient learning process. The first time children hold hairbrushes, cups, or tennis rackets, they usually brush, drink, or swing as well as they can, given their current muscle development and coordination. Let's take a closer look at how observational learning occurs. Bandura (1986) notes that observational learning includes four elements: *paying attention, retaining information or impressions, producing behaviors,* and *being motivated* to repeat the behaviors.

Attention. In order to learn through observation, we have to pay attention. In teaching, you will have to ensure students' attention to the critical features of the lesson by making clear presentations and highlighting important points. In demonstrating a skill (for example, threading a sewing machine or operating a lathe), you may need to have students look over your shoulder as you work. Seeing your hands from the same perspective as they see their own directs their attention to the right features of the situation and makes observational learning easier.

Social cognitive theory Theory that adds concern with cognitive factors such as beliefs, self-perceptions, and expectations to social learning theory.

Observational learning Learning by observation and imitation of others.

Retention. In order to imitate the behavior of a model, you have to remember it. This involves mentally representing the model's actions in some way, probably as verbal steps

("Hwa-Rang, the eighth form in Tae Kwan Do karate, is a palm-heel block, then a middle riding stance punch, then . . ."), or as visual images, or both. Retention can be improved by mental rehearsal (imagining imitating the behavior) or by actual practice. In the retention phase of observational learning, practice helps us remember the elements of the desired behavior, such as the sequence of steps.

Production. Once we "know" how a behavior should look and remember the elements or steps, we still may not perform it smoothly. Sometimes, we need a great deal of practice, feedback, and coaching about subtle points before we can reproduce the behavior of the model. In the production phase, practice makes the behavior smoother and more expert.

Motivation and Reinforcement. As mentioned earlier, social learning theory distinguishes between acquisition and performance. We may acquire a new skill or behavior through observation, but we may not perform that behavior until there is some motivation or incentive to do so. Reinforcement can play several roles in observational learning. If we anticipate being reinforced for imitating the actions of a model, we may be more motivated to pay attention, remember, and reproduce the behaviors. In addition, reinforcement is important in maintaining learning. A person who tries a new behavior is unlikely to persist without reinforcement (Ollendick, Dailey, & Shapiro, 1983; Schunk, 2004). For example, if an unpopular student adopted the dress of the "in" group, but was ignored or ridiculed, it is unlikely that the imitation would continue.

Bandura identifies three forms of reinforcement that can encourage observational learning. First, of course, the observer may reproduce the behaviors of the model and receive direct reinforcement, as when a gymnast successfully executes a front flip/round-off combination and the coach/model says, "Excellent!"

But the reinforcement need not be direct—it may be **vicarious reinforcement.** The observer may simply see others reinforced for a particular behavior and then increase his or her production of that behavior. For example, if you compliment two students on the attractive illustrations in their lab reports, several other students who observe your compliments may turn in illustrated lab reports next time. Most TV ads hope for this kind of effect. People in commercials become deliriously happy when they drive a particular car or drink a specific juice, and the viewer is supposed to do the same; the viewer's behavior is reinforced vicariously by the actors' obvious pleasure. Punishment can also be vicarious: You may slow down on a stretch of highway after seeing several people get speeding tickets there.

Observational theories of learning consider the importance of learning by doing and learning by observing others.

Vicarious reinforcement Increasing the chances that we will repeat a behavior by observing another person being reinforced for that behavior.

The final form of reinforcement is **self-reinforcement**, or controlling your own reinforcers. This sort of reinforcement is important for both students and teachers. We want our students to improve not because it leads to external rewards, but because the students value and enjoy their growing competence. And as a teacher, sometimes self-reinforcement is all that keeps you going.

Factors That Influence Observational Learning. What causes an individual to learn and perform modeled behaviors and skills? Several factors play a role, as shown in Table 6.2. The developmental level of the observer makes a difference in learning. As children grow older, they are able to focus attention for longer periods of time, use memory strategies to retain information, and motivate themselves to practice. A second influence is the status of the model. Children are more likely to imitate the actions of others who seem competent, powerful, prestigious, and enthusiastic, so parents, teachers, older siblings, athletes, action heroes, rock stars, or film personalities may serve as models, depending on the age and interests of the child. Third, by watching others, we learn about what behaviors are appropriate for people like ourselves, so models who are seen as similar are more readily imitated (Pintrich & Schunk, 2002). All students need to see successful, capable models who look and sound like them, no matter what their ethnicity, socioeconomic status, or gender.

Connect and Extend to Other Chapters

Sense of self-efficacy is discussed more fully in Chapter 9, as is the related concept of teacher efficacy. Background: Two books by Bandura about self-efficacy: Bandura, A. (1997). *Self-efficacy: The exercise of control.* New York: Freeman. Bandura, A. (Ed.). (1995). *Self-efficacy in changing societies.* New York: Cambridge University Press.

Look at Table 6.2. The last three influences involve goals and expectations. If observers expect that certain actions of models will lead to particular outcomes (such as particular practice regimens leading to improved athletic performance) and the observers value those outcomes or goals, then the observers are more likely to pay attention to the models and try to reproduce their behaviors. Finally, observers are more likely to learn from models if the observers have a high level of **self-efficacy**—that is, if they believe they are capable of doing the actions needed to reach the goals, or at least of learning how to do so (Bandura, 1997; Pintrich & Schunk, 2002). We will discuss goals, expectations, and self-efficacy in greater depth in Chapter 10 on motivation.

TABLE 6.2

Factors That Affect Observational Learning

Characteristic	Effects of Modeling
Developmental Status	Improvements with development include longer attention and increased capacity to process information, use strategies, compare performances with memorial representations, and adopt intrinsic motivators.
Model Prestige and Competence	Observers pay greater attention to competent, high-status models. Consequences of modeled behaviors convey information about functional value. Observers attempt to learn actions they believe they will need to perform.
Vicarious Consequences	Consequences to models convey information about behavioral appropriateness and likely outcomes of actions. Valued consequences motivate observers. Similarity in attributes or competence signals appropriateness and heightens motivation.
Outcome Expectations	Observers are more likely to perform modeled actions they believe are appropriate and will result in rewarding outcomes.
Goal Setting	Observers are likely to attend to models who demonstrate behaviors that help observers attain goals.
Self-efficacy	Observers attend to models when they believe they are capable of learning or performing the modeled behavior. Observation of similar models affects self-efficacy ("If they can do it, I can too").

Source: From *Learning Theories: An Education Perspective* (4th ed.), by D. H. Schunk. Published by Prentice Hall. Copyright © 2004 by Prentice Hall. Reprinted by permission of Pearson Education, Inc., Upper Saddle River, NJ.

Self-Reinforcement Controlling your own reinforcers.

Self-efficacy A person's sense of being able to deal effectively with a particular task.

Observational Learning in Teaching

STOP | THINK | WRITE How would you incorporate observational learning into your teaching? What are the skills, attitudes, and strategies that can be modeled in teaching your subject? ■

"Dad, can you read?"

What is this son learning by observing his father?

There are five possible outcomes of observational learning: directing attention, encouraging existing behaviors, changing inhibitions, teaching new behaviors and attitudes, and arousing emotions. Let's look at each of these as they occur in classrooms.

Directing Attention. By observing others, we not only learn about actions but also notice the objects involved in the actions. For example, in a preschool class, when one child plays enthusiastically with a toy that has been ignored for days, many other children may want to have the toy, even if they play with it in different ways or simply carry it around. This happens, in part, because the children's attention has been drawn to that particular toy.

Fine-Tuning Already-Learned Behaviors. All of us have had the experience of looking for cues from other people when we find ourselves in unfamiliar situations. Observing the behavior of others tells us which of our already-learned behaviors to use: the proper fork for eating the salad, when to leave a gathering, what kind of language is appropriate, and so on. Adopting the dress and grooming styles of TV or music idols is another example of this kind of effect.

Strengthening or Weakening Inhibitions. If class members witness one student breaking a class rule and getting away with it, they may learn that undesirable consequences do not always follow rule breaking. If the rule breaker is a well-liked, high-status class leader, the effect of the modeling may be even more pronounced, as we saw in the case at the beginning of this chapter. This **"ripple effect"** (Kounin, 1970) can work for the teacher's benefit. When the teacher deals effectively with a rule breaker, especially a class leader, the idea of breaking this rule may be inhibited for the other students viewing the interaction. This does not mean that teachers must reprimand each student who breaks a rule, but once a teacher has called for a particular action, following through is an important part of capitalizing on the ripple effect.

Teaching New Behaviors. **Modeling** has long been used, of course, to teach dance, sports, and crafts, as well as skills in subjects such as food science, chemistry, and welding. Modeling can also be applied deliberately in the classroom to teach mental skills and to broaden horizons—to teach new ways of thinking. Teachers serve as models for a vast range of behaviors, from pronouncing vocabulary words, to reacting to the seizure of a student with epilepsy, to being enthusiastic about learning. For example, a teacher might model sound critical thinking skills by thinking "out loud" about a student's question. Or a high-school teacher concerned about girls who seem to have stereotyped ideas about careers might invite women with nontraditional jobs to speak to the class. Studies indicate that modeling can be most effective when the teacher makes use of all the elements of observational learning described in the previous section, especially reinforcement and practice.

Models who are the same age as the students may be particularly effective. For example, Schunk and Hanson (1985) compared two methods for teaching subtraction to 2nd graders who had difficulties learning this skill. One group of students observed other 2nd graders learning the procedures, while another group watched a teacher's demonstration. Then both groups participated in the same instructional program. The students who observed peer models learning not only scored higher on tests of subtraction after instruction but also gained more confidence in their own ability to learn. For students who doubt their own abilities, a good model is a low-achieving student who keeps trying and finally masters the material (Schunk, 2004).

Connect and **Extend** to **PRAXIS II™**

Modeling (II, B2)

Teachers often utilize modeling to teach students new behaviors. Identify the characteristics that tend to make models effective in instructional context.

Ripple effect "Contagious" spreading of behaviors through imitation.

Modeling Changes in behavior, thinking, or emotions that occur through observing another person—a model.

Guidelines: Using Observational Learning

Model behaviors and attitudes you want your students to learn.

EXAMPLES

1. Show enthusiasm for the subject you teach.
2. Be willing to demonstrate both the mental and the physical tasks you expect the students to perform. I once saw a teacher sit down in the sandbox while her 4-year-old students watched her demonstrate the difference between "playing with sand" and "throwing sand."
3. When reading to students, model good problem solving. Stop and say, "Now let me see if I remember what happened so far," or "That was a hard sentence. I'm going to read it again."
4. Model good problem solving—think out loud as you work through a difficult problem.

Use peers, especially class leaders, as models.

EXAMPLES

1. In group work, pair students who do well with those who are having difficulties.
2. Ask students to demonstrate the difference between "whispering" and "silence—no talking."

Make sure students see that positive behaviors lead to reinforcement for others.

EXAMPLES

1. Point out the connections between positive behavior and positive consequences in stories.
2. Be fair in giving reinforcement. The same rules for rewards should apply to the problem students as to the good students.

Enlist the help of class leaders in modeling behaviors or the entire class.

EXAMPLES

1. Ask a well-liked student to be friendly to an isolated, fearful student.
2. Let high-status students lead an activity when you need class cooperation or when students are likely to be reluctant at first. Popular students can model dialogues in foreign-language classes or be the first to tackle dissection procedures in biology.

For more information on observational learning, see:
http://mentalhelp.net/psyhelp/chap4/chap4g.htm

Arousing Emotion. Finally, through observational learning, people may develop emotional reactions to situations they have never experienced personally, such as flying or driving. A child who watches a friend fall from a swing and break an arm may become fearful of swings. After the terrible events of September 11, 2001, children may be anxious when they see airplanes flying close to the ground. News reports of shark attacks have many of us anxious about swimming in the ocean. Note that hearing and reading about a situation are also forms of observation. Some terrible examples of modeling occur with "copy cat killings" in schools. When frightening things happen to people who are similar in age or circumstances to your students, they may need to talk about their emotions.

The *Guidelines* will give you some ideas about using observational learning in the classroom.

Connect and **Extend** to Your **Teaching Portfolio**

Concern with self-management is not restricted to any one group or theory. Psychologists who study Vygotsky's ideas about cognitive development (Chapter 2) are involved, as are cognitive psychologists interested in learning strategies (Chapters 7 and 8) and motivational psychologists pointing to self-regulation as a critical factor in motivation (Chapters 10 and 11).

Self-management Use of behavioral learning principles to change your own behavior.

Self-Management

WHAT WOULD YOU SAY?

The Physical Therapy unit where you are interviewing is a state-of-the-art facility. You feel as though the interview for a patient-educator position is going well. The next question asked of you is: "One of our biggest problems here, and in most rehabilitation centers for that matter, is getting our clients to stick to an exercise program. What ideas do you have for helping these clients maintain their prescribed regimens?" ■

If one goal of education is to produce people who are capable of educating themselves, then students must learn to manage their own lives, set their own goals, and provide their own reinforcement. In adult life, rewards are sometimes vague and goals often take a long time to reach. Think about how many small steps are required to complete an education and find your first job. Life is filled with tasks that call for this sort of **self-management** (Rachlin, 2000).

Students may be involved in any or all of the steps in implementing a basic behavior change program. They may help set goals, observe their own work, keep records of it, and evaluate their own performance. Finally, they can select and deliver reinforcement.

Goal Setting. It appears that the goal-setting phase is very important in self-management (Pintrich & Schunk, 2002; Reeve, 1996). In fact, some research suggests that setting specific goals and making them public may be the critical elements of self-management programs. For example, S. C. Hayes and his colleagues identified college students who had serious problems with studying and taught them how to set specific study goals. Students who set goals and announced them to the experimenters performed significantly better on tests covering the material they were studying than students who set goals privately and never revealed them to anyone (Hayes, Rosenfarb, Wulfert, Munt, Korn, & Zettle, 1985).

Higher standards tend to lead to higher performance (Locke & Latham, 2002). Unfortunately, student-set goals have a tendency to reflect lower and lower expectations. Teachers can help students maintain high standards by monitoring the goals set and reinforcing high standards.

Monitoring and Evaluating Progress. Students may also participate in the monitoring and evaluation phases of a behavior change program (Mace, Belfiore, & Hutchinson, 2001). Some examples of behaviors that are appropriate for self-monitoring are the number of assignments completed, time spent practicing a skill, number of books read, number of problems correct, and time taken to run a mile. Tasks that must be accomplished without teacher supervision, such as homework or private study, are also good candidates for self-monitoring. Students keep a chart, diary, or checklist that records the frequency or duration of the behaviors in question. A progress record card can help older students break down assignments into small steps, determine the best sequence for completing the steps, and keep track of daily progress by setting goals for each day. The record card itself serves as a prompt that can be faded out.

Self-evaluation is somewhat more difficult than simple self-recording because it involves making a judgment about quality. Students can evaluate their behavior with reasonable accuracy, especially if they learn standards for judging a good performance or product. For example, Sweeney, Salva, Cooper, and Talbert-Johnson (1993) taught secondary students how to evaluate their handwriting for size, slant, shape, and spacing. One key to accurate self-evaluation seems to be for the teacher to periodically check students' assessments and give reinforcement for accurate judgments. Older students may learn accurate self-evaluation more readily than younger students. Again, bonus points can be awarded when the teachers' and students' evaluations match (Kaplan, 1991). Self-correction can accompany self-evaluation. Students first evaluate, then alter and improve their work, and finally, compare the improvements to the standards again (Mace, Belfiore, & Hutchinson, 2001).

Self-Reinforcement. The last step in self-management is self-reinforcement. There is some disagreement, however, as to whether this step is actually necessary. Some psychologists believe that setting goals and monitoring progress alone are sufficient and that self-reinforcement adds nothing to the effects (Hayes et al., 1985). Others believe that rewarding yourself for a job well done can lead to higher levels of performance than simply setting goals and keeping track of progress (Bandura, 1986). If you are willing to be tough and really deny yourself something you want until your goals are reached, then perhaps the promise of the reward can provide extra incentive for work. With that in mind, you may want to think of some way to reinforce yourself when you finish reading this chapter. A similar approach helped me write the chapter in the first place.

At times, families can be enlisted to help their children develop self-management abilities. Working together, teachers and parents can focus on a few goals and, at the same time, support the growing independence of the students. The *Family and Community Partnerships Guidelines* on the next page give some ideas.

Connect and **Extend** to the **Research**

Here is a checklist, taken from Belfiore & Hornyak (1998) to help students manage their homework:

1. *Did I turn in yesterday's homework?*
2. *Did I write all homework assignments in my notebook?*
3. *Is all the homework in the homework folder?*
4. *Are all my materials to complete my homework with me?*
5. *Begin homework.*
6. *Are all homework papers completed?*
7. *Did someone check homework to make sure it was completed?*
8. *After checking, did I put all homework back in folder?*
9. *Did I give this paper to teacher?* (*p. 190*).

Family and Community Partnerships

Guidelines: Student Self-Management

Introduce the system to parents and students in a positive way.

EXAMPLES

1. Invite family participation and stress possible benefits to all family members.
2. Consider starting the program just with volunteers.
3. Describe how you use self-management programs yourself.

Help families and students establish reachable goals.

EXAMPLES

1. Have examples of possible self-management goals for students such as starting homework early in the evening, or keeping track of books read.
2. Show families how to post goals and keep track of progress. Encourage everyone in the family to work on a goal.

Give families ways to record and evaluate their child's progress (or their own).

EXAMPLES

1. Divide the work into easily measured steps.
2. Provide models of good work where judgments are more difficult, such as in creative writing.
3. Give families a record form or checklist to keep track of progress.

Encourage families to check the accuracy of student records from time to time, and help their children to develop forms of self-reinforcement.

EXAMPLES

1. Have many checkups when students are first learning, and fewer later.
2. Have siblings check one another's records.
3. Where appropriate, test the skills that students are supposed to be developing at home and reward students whose self-evaluations match their test performances.
4. Have students brainstorm ideas with their families for rewarding themselves for jobs well done.

For a self-management checklist, see: **http://www.coun.uvic.ca/learn/program/hndouts/slfman.html**

Sometimes, teaching students self-management can solve a problem for teachers and provide fringe benefits as well. For example, the coaches of a competitive swim team with members aged 9 to 16 were having difficulty persuading swimmers to maintain high work rates. Then the coaches drew up four charts indicating the training program to be followed by each member and posted the charts near the pool. The swimmers were given the responsibility of recording both their numbers of laps and their completion of each training unit. Because the recording was public, swimmers could see their own and their teammates progress and keep accurate track of the work units completed. Work output increased by 27%. The coaches also liked the system because swimmers could begin to work immediately without waiting for instructions (McKenzie & Rushall, 1974).

Cognitive Behavior Modification and Self-Instruction

Self-management generally means getting students involved in the basic steps of a behavior change program. **Cognitive behavior modification** adds an emphasis on thinking and self-talk. For this reason, many psychologists consider cognitive behavior modification more a cognitive approach than a behavioral one. I present it here because it serves as a bridge to Chapters 7 and 8 on cognitive learning.

As noted in Chapter 2, there is a stage in cognitive development when young children seem to guide themselves through a task using private speech. They talk to themselves, often repeating the words of a parent or teacher. In cognitive behavior modification, students are taught directly how to use **self-instruction.** Meichenbaum (1977) outlined the steps:

Cognitive behavior modification Procedures based on both behavioral and cognitive learning principles for changing your own behavior by using self-talk and self-instruction.

Self-instruction Talking oneself through the steps of a task.

1. An adult model performs a task while talking to him- or herself out loud (cognitive modeling).
2. The child performs the same task under the direction of the model's instructions (overt, external guidance).

3. The child performs the task while instructing him- or herself aloud (overt, self-guidance).
4. The child whispers the instructions to him- or herself as he/she goes through the task (faded, overt self-guidance).
5. The child performs the task while guiding his/her performance via private speech (covert self-instruction). (p. 32)

Brenda Manning and Beverly Payne (1996) list four skills that can increase student learning: *listening, planning, working,* and *checking.* How might cognitive self-instruction help students develop these skills? One possibility is to use personal booklets or class posters that prompt students to "talk to themselves" about these skills. For example, one 5th-grade class designed a set of prompts for each of the four skills and posted the prompts around the classroom. The prompts for listening included "Does this make sense?" "Am I getting this?" "I need to ask a question now before I forget." "Pay attention!" "Can I do what he's saying to do?" Planning prompts were "Do I have everything together?" "Do I have my friends tuned out for right now?" "Let me get organized first." "What order will I do this in?" "I know this stuff!" Posters for these and the other two skills, working and checking, are shown in Figure 6.6. Part of the power of this process is in getting students involved in thinking about and creating their own guides and prompts. Having the discussion and posting the ideas makes students more self-aware and in control of their own learning.

Actually, cognitive behavior modification as it is practiced by Meichenbaum and others has many more components than just teaching students to use self-instruction.

FIGURE 6.6

Posters to Remind Students to "Talk Themselves Through" Listening, Planning, Working, and Checking in School

These four posters were designed by a 5th-grade class to help them remember to use self-instruction. Some of the reminders reflect the special world of these preadolescents.

Poster 1

While Listening:

1. Does this make sense?
2. Am I getting this?
3. I need to ask a question now before I forget.
4. Pay attention.
5. Can I do what he's saying to do?

Poster 2

While Planning:

1. Do I have everything together?
2. Do I have my friends tuned out for right now?
3. Let me get organized first.
4. What order will I do this in?
5. I know this stuff!

Poster 3

While Working:

1. Am I working fast enough?
2. Stop staring at my girlfriend and get back to work.
3. How much time is left?
4. Do I need to stop and start over?
5. This is hard for me, but I can manage.

Poster 4

While Checking:

1. Did I finish everything?
2. What do I need to recheck?
3. Am I proud of this work?
4. Did I write all the words? Count them.
5. I think I finished. I organized myself. Did I daydream too much?

Source: From *Self-Talk for Teachers and Students: Metacognitive Strategies for Personal and Classroom Use* by Brenda H. Manning, Beverly D. Payne. Published by Allyn and Bacon, Boston, MA. Copyright © 1996 by Pearson Education. Adapted by permission of the publisher.

Meichenbaum's methods also include dialogue and interaction between teacher and student, modeling, guided discovery, motivational strategies, feedback, careful matching of the task with the student's developmental level, and other principles of good teaching. The student is even involved in designing the program (Harris, 1990; Harris & Pressley, 1991). Given all this, it is no surprise that students seem to be able to generalize the skills developed with cognitive behavior modification to new learning situations (Harris, Graham, & Pressley, 1992).

Problems and Issues

The preceding sections provide an overview of several strategies for changing classroom behavior. However, you should be aware that these strategies are tools that can be used both responsibly or irresponsibly. What, then, are some issues you should keep in mind?

Criticisms of Behavioral Methods

WHAT WOULD YOU SAY?

During your job interview, the principal asks, "A teacher last year got in trouble for bribing his students with homework exemptions to get them to behave in class. What do you think about using rewards and punishments in teaching?" What do you say? ■

While you think about your answer to this question, look at the *Point/Counterpoint* on "Should Students Be Rewarded for Learning?" to see two different perspectives. Properly used, the strategies in this chapter can be effective tools to help students learn academically and grow in self-sufficiency. Effective tools, however, do not automatically produce excellent work, and behavioral strategies are often implemented haphazardly, inconsistently, incorrectly, or superficially (Landrum & Kauffman, 2006). The indiscriminate use of even the best tools can lead to difficulties.

Some psychologists fear that rewarding students for all learning will cause them to lose interest in learning for its own sake (Deci, 1975; Deci & Ryan, 1985; Kohn, 1993, 1996; Lepper & Greene, 1978; Lepper, Keavney, & Drake, 1996; Ryan & Deci, 1996). Studies have suggested that using reward programs with students who are already interested in the subject matter may, in fact, cause students to be less interested in the subject when the reward program ends, as you can see in the *Point/Counterpoint.* In addition, there is some evidence that praising students for being intelligent when they succeed can undermine their motivation if they do not perform as well the next time. After they fail, students who had been praised for being smart may be less persistent and enjoy the task less compared to students who had been praised earlier for working hard (Mueller & Dweck, 1998).

Just as you must take into account the effects of a reward system on the individual, you must also consider its impact on other students. Using a reward program or giving one student increased attention may have a detrimental effect on the other students in the classroom. Is it possible that other students will learn to be "bad" in order to be included in the reward program? Most of the evidence on this question suggests that using individual adaptations such as reward programs does not have any adverse effects on students who are not participating if the teacher believes in the program and explains the reasons for using it to the nonparticipating students. After interviewing 98 students in grades 1 through 6, Cindy Fulk and Paula Smith (1995) concluded that "Teachers may be more concerned about equal treatment of students than students are" (p. 416). If the conduct of some students does seem to deteriorate when their peers are involved in special programs, many of the same procedures discussed in this chapter should help them return to previous levels of appropriate behavior (Chance, 1992, 1993).

Ethical Issues

The ethical questions related to the use of the strategies described in this chapter are similar to those raised by any process that seeks to influence people. What are the goals? How

Point/Counterpoint

Should Students Be Rewarded for Learning?

FOR YEARS, EDUCATORS and psychologists have debated whether students should be rewarded for school work and academic accomplishments. In the early 1990s, Paul Chance and Alfie Kohn exchanged opinions in several issues of *Phi Delta Kappan* (March 1991; November 1992; June 1993). Then, Judy Cameron and W. David Pierce (1996) published an article on reinforcement in the *Review of Educational Research* that precipitated extensive criticisms and rebuttals in the same journal from Mark Lepper, Mark Keavney, Michael Drake, Alfie Kohn, Richard Ryan, and Edward Deci. Many of the same people exchanged opinions in the November 1999 issue of *Psychological Bulletin*. What are the arguments?

POINT Students are punished by rewards.

Alfie Kohn (1993) argues that "Applied behaviorism, which amounts to saying, 'do this and you'll get that,' is essentially a technique for controlling people. In the classroom it is a way of doing things *to* children rather than working *with* them" (p. 784). He contends that rewards are ineffective because when the praise and prizes stop, the behaviors stop too. After analyzing 128 studies of extrinsic rewards, Edward Deci, Richard Koestner, and Richard Ryan (1999) concluded that "tangible rewards tend to have a substantial effect on intrinsic motivation, with the limiting conditions we have specified. Even when tangible rewards are offered as indicators of good performance, they typically decrease intrinsic motivation for interesting activities" (pp. 658–659).

The problem with rewards does not stop here. According to Kohn, rewarding students for learning actually makes them less interested in the material:

> *All of this means that getting children to think about learning as a way to receive a sticker, a gold star, or a grade—or even worse, to get money or a toy* for *a grade, which amounts to an extrinsic motivator for an extrinsic motivator—is likely to turn learning from an end into a means. Learning becomes something that must be gotten through in order to receive the reward. Take the depressingly pervasive program by which children receive certificates for pizzas when they have read a certain number of books. John Nicholls of the University of Illinois comments, only half in jest, that the likely consequence of this program is "a lot of fat kids who don't like to read." (p. 785)*

COUNTERPOINT Learning should be rewarding.

According to Paul Chance (1993):

> *Behavioral psychologists in particular emphasize that we learn by* acting on *our environment. As B. F. Skinner put it: "[People] act on the world, and change it, and are changed in turn by the consequences of their actions." Skinner, unlike Kohn, understood that people learn best in a responsive environment. Teachers who praise or otherwise reward student performance provide such an environment. . . . If it is immoral to let students know they have answered questions correctly, to pat students on the back for a good effort, to show joy at a student's understanding of a concept, or to recognize the achievement of a goal by providing a gold star or a certificate—if this is immoral, then count me a sinner. (p. 788)*

Do rewards undermine interest? In their review of research, Cameron and Pierce (1994) concluded, "When tangible rewards (e.g., gold star, money) are offered contingent on performance on a task [not just on participation] or are delivered unexpectedly, intrinsic motivation is maintained" (p. 49). In a later review of research, Eisenberg, Pierce, and Cameron (1999) added that "Reward procedures requiring specific high task performance convey a task's personal or social significance, increasing intrinsic motivation" (p. 677). Even psychologists such as Edward Deci and Mark Lepper who suggest that rewards might undermine intrinsic motivation agree that rewards can also be used positively. When rewards provide students with information about their growing mastery of a subject or when the rewards show appreciation for a job well done, then the rewards bolster confidence and make the task more interesting to the students, especially students who lacked ability or interest in the task initially. Nothing succeeds like success. As Chance points out, if students master reading or mathematics with the support of rewards, they will not forget what they have learned when the praise stops. Would they have learned without the rewards? Some would, but some might not. Would you continue working for a company that didn't pay you, even though you liked the work? Will freelance writer Alfie Kohn, for that matter, lose interest in writing because he gets paid fees and royalties?

WHAT DO YOU THINK?

Vote online at **www.mylabschool.com**

Source: From "Sticking Up for Rewards," by P. Chance, June 1993, *Phi Delta Kappan*, pp. 787–790. Copyright © 1993 by *Phi Delta Kappan*. Reprinted with permission of Phi Delta Kappan and the author. From "Rewards versus Learning: A Response to Paul Chance," by A. Kohn, June 1993, *Phi Delta Kappan*, p. 783 and 785. Copyright © 1993 by Alfie Kohn. Reprinted from *Phi Delta Kappan* with the author's permission.

do these goals fit with those of the school as a whole? What effect will a strategy have on the individuals involved? Is too much control being given to the teacher, or to a majority?

Goals. The strategies described in this chapter could be applied exclusively to teaching students to sit still, raise their hands before speaking, and remain silent at all other times (Winett & Winkler, 1972). This certainly would be an unethical use of the techniques. It is true that a teacher may need to establish some organization and order, but stopping with improvements in conduct will not ensure academic learning. On the other hand, in some situations, reinforcing academic skills may lead to improvements in conduct. Whenever possible, emphasis should be placed on academic learning. Academic improvements generalize to other situations more successfully than do changes in classroom conduct.

Strategies. Punishment can have negative side effects: It can serve as a model for aggressive responses, and it can encourage negative emotional reactions. Punishment is unnecessary and even unethical when positive approaches, which have fewer potential dangers, might work as well. When simpler, less-restrictive procedures fail, then more complicated procedures should be tried.

A second consideration in the selection of a strategy is the impact of the strategy on the individual student. For example, some teachers arrange for students to be rewarded at home with a gift or special activities based on good work in school. But if a student has a history of being severely punished at home for bad reports from school, a home-based reinforcement program might be very harmful to that student. Reports of unsatisfactory progress at school could lead to increased abuse at home.

Diversity and Convergences in Behavioral Learning

Diversity

There is great *diversity* in the learning histories of students. Every person in your class will come to you with different fears and anxieties. Some students may be terrified of speaking in public or of failing in competitive sports. Others will be anxious around various animals. Different activities or objects will serve as reinforcers for some students, but not others. Some students will work for the promise of good grades—others could care less. All of your students will have learned from different models in their homes, neighborhoods, churches, or communities.

The research and theories presented in this chapter should help you understand how the learning histories of your students might have taught them to respond automatically to tests with sweaty palms and racing hearts—possible classical conditioning at work. Their learning histories might have included being reinforced for persistence or for whining—operant conditioning at work. The chance to work in a group may be a reinforcer for some students and a punisher for others. Some teachers use questionnaires such as the one in Table 6.3 to identify effective reinforcers for their students. Remember, what works for one student may not be right for another. And students can get "too much of a good thing"; reinforcers can lose their potency if they are overused.

Connect and **Extend** to the **Web**

Theories of Learning
http://tip.psychology.org/

In addition to providing a diversity of reinforcers, teachers, classrooms, and schools should provide a diversity of models because students learn through observation. Do students see themselves in the social studies and science texts? Are there characters and authors in literature that reflect the background and values of the students and the community? Whose work is posted in the room? Who gets the privileges and responsibilities?

Connect and **Extend** to Your **Teaching Portfolio**

Use Table 6.3, "What Do You Like? Reinforcement Ideas from Students" to generate ideas for appropriate reinforcers for students you will teach and include these ideas in your Portfolio.

Convergences

Even though your classroom will be filled with many different learning histories, there are some convergences—principles that apply to all people:

TABLE 6.3

What Do You Like? Reinforcement Ideas from Students

Name ______________________ **Grade** _____ **Date** _______

Please answer all the questions as completely as you can.

1. The school subjects I like best are:
2. Three things I like most to do in school are:
3. If I had 30 minutes' free time at school each day to do what I really liked, it would be:
4. My two favorite snacks are:
5. At recess I like most to (three things):
6. If I had $1 to spend on anything, I would buy:
7. Three jobs I would enjoy in the class are:
8. The two people I most like to work with in school are:
9. At home I really enjoy (three things):

Source: From *Modification of Child and Adolescent Behavior* (3rd ed.), by G. Blackman and A. Silberman. Published by Wadsworth, Belmont, CA. Copyright © 1979 by Wadsworth Publishing Co. Reprinted with permission of the publisher.

1. No one eagerly repeats behaviors that have been punished or ignored. Without some sense of progress, it is difficult to persist.
2. When actions lead to consequences that are positive for the person involved, those actions are likely to be repeated.
3. Teachers often fail to use reinforcement to recognize appropriate behavior; they respond instead to inappropriate behaviors, sometimes providing reinforcing attention in the process.
4. To be effective, praise must be a sincere recognition of a real accomplishment.
5. Whatever their current level of functioning, students can learn to be more self-managing.

SUMMARY TABLE

Understanding Learning (pp. 206–208)

What is learning? Although theorists disagree about the definition of learning, most would agree that learning occurs when experience causes a change in a person's knowledge or behavior. Changes simply caused by maturation, illness, fatigue, or hunger are excluded from a general definition of learning. Behavioral theorists emphasize the role of environmental stimuli in learning and focus on behavior—observable responses. Behavioral learning processes include contiguity learning, classical conditioning, operant conditioning, and observational learning.

Learning Process through which experience causes permanent change in knowledge or behavior.

Behavioral learning theories Explanations of learning that focus on external events as the cause of changes in observable behaviors.

Early Explanations of Learning: Contiguity and Classical Conditioning (pp. 208–209)

How does a neutral stimulus become a conditioned stimulus? In classical conditioning, which was discovered by Pavlov, a previously neutral stimulus is repeatedly paired with a stimulus that evokes an emotional or physiological response. Later, the previously neutral stimulus alone evokes the response—that is, the neutral stimulus is conditioned to bring forth a conditioned response. The neutral stimulus has become a conditioned stimulus.

What are some everyday examples of classical conditioning? Here are a few; add your own. Salivating when you smell your favorite foods, tension when you hear a dentist's drill, nervousness when you step on stage, ...

Contiguity Association of two events because of repeated pairing.

Stimulus Event that activates behavior.

Response Observable reaction to a stimulus.

Classical conditioning Association of automatic responses with new stimuli.

Respondents Responses (generally automatic or involuntary) elicited by specific stimuli.

Neutral stimulus Stimulus not connected to a response.

Unconditioned stimulus (US) Stimulus that automatically produces an emotional or physiological response.

Unconditioned response (UR) Naturally occurring emotional or physiological response.

Conditioned stimulus (CS) Stimulus that evokes an emotional or physiological response after conditioning.

Conditioned response (CR) Learned response to a previously neutral stimulus.

Operant Conditioning: Trying New Responses (pp. 210–215)

What defines a consequence as a reinforcer? As a punisher? According to Skinner's concept of operant conditioning, people learn through the effects of their deliberate responses. For an individual, the effects of consequences following an action may serve as either reinforcers or punishers. A consequence is defined as a reinforcer if it strengthens or maintains the response that brought it about, whereas a consequence is defined as a punishment if it decreases or suppresses the response that brought it about.

Negative reinforcement is often confused with punishment. How are they different? The process of reinforcement (positive or negative) always involves strengthening behavior. The teacher strengthens (reinforces) desired behaviors by removing something aversive *as soon as the desired behaviors occur.* Because the consequence involves removing or "subtracting" a stimulus, the reinforcement is negative. Punishment, on the other hand, involves *decreasing or suppressing behavior.* A behavior followed by a "punisher" is *less* likely to be repeated in similar situations in the future.

How can you encourage persistence in a behavior? Ratio schedules (based on the number of responses) encourage higher rates of response, and variable schedules (based on varying numbers of responses or varying time intervals) encourage persistence of responses.

What is the difference between a prompt and a cue? A cue is an antecedent stimulus just before a particular behavior is to take place. A prompt is an additional cue following the first cue. Make sure the environmental stimulus that you want to become a cue occurs immediately before the prompt you are using, so students will learn to respond to the cue and not rely only on the prompt. Then, fade the prompt as soon as possible so students do not become dependent on it.

Operants Voluntary (and generally goal-directed) behaviors emitted by a person or an animal.

Operant conditioning Learning in which voluntary behavior is strengthened or weakened by consequences or antecedents.

Antecedents Events that precede an action.

Consequences Events that follow an action.

Reinforcement Use of consequences to strengthen behavior.

Reinforcer Any event that follows a behavior and increases the chances that the behavior will occur again.

Positive reinforcement Strengthening behavior by presenting a desired stimulus after the behavior.

Negative reinforcement Strengthening behavior by removing an aversive stimulus when the behavior occurs.

Aversive Irritating or unpleasant.

Punishment Process that weakens or suppresses behavior.

Presentation punishment Decreasing the chances that a behavior will occur again by presenting an aversive stimulus following the behavior; also called Type I punishment.

Removal punishment Decreasing the chances that a behavior will occur again by removing a pleasant stimulus following the behavior; also called Type II punishment.

Continuous reinforcement schedule Presenting a reinforcer after every appropriate response.

Intermittent reinforcement schedule Presenting a reinforcer after some but not all responses.

Interval schedule Length of time between reinforcers.

Ratio schedule Reinforcement based on the number of responses between reinforcers.

Extinction The disappearance of a learned response.

Stimulus control Capacity for the presence or absence of antecedents to cause behaviors.

Cueing Providing a stimulus that "sets up" a desired behavior.

Prompt A reminder that follows a cue to make sure the person reacts to the cue.

Applied Behavior Analysis (pp. 215–224)

What are the steps in applied behavior analysis? The steps are: (1) Clearly specify the behavior to be changed and note the current level. (2) Plan a specific intervention using antecedents, consequences, or both. (3) Keep track of the results, and modify the plan if necessary.

How can the Premack principle help you identify reinforcers? The Premack principle states that a high-frequency behavior (a preferred activity) can be an effective reinforcer for a low-frequency behavior (a less-preferred activity). The best way to determine appropriate reinforcers for your students may be to watch what they do in their free time. For most students, talking, moving around the room, sitting near a friend, being exempt from assignments or tests, reading magazines, or playing games are preferred activities.

When is shaping an appropriate approach? Shaping helps students develop new responses a little at a time, so it is useful for building complex skills, working toward difficult goals, and increasing persistence, endurance, accuracy, or speed. Because shaping is a time-consuming process, however, it should not be used if success can be attained through simpler methods such as cueing.

What are some cautions in using punishment? Punishment in and of itself does not lead to any positive behavior. Thus, whenever you consider the use of punishment, you should make it part of a two-pronged attack. First, carry out the punishment and suppress the undesirable behavior. Second, make clear what the student should be doing instead and provide reinforcement for those desirable actions. Thus, while the problem behaviors are being suppressed, positive alternative responses are being strengthened.

How can functional behavioral assessment and positive behavioral supports be used to improve student behaviors? In doing a functional behavioral assessment, a teacher studies the antecedents and consequences of problem behaviors to determine the reason or function of the behavior. Then, positive behavioral supports are designed to replace problem behaviors with new actions that serve the same purpose for the student, but do not have the same problems.

Applied behavior analysis The application of behavioral learning principles to understand and change behavior.

Behavior modification Systematic application of antecedents and consequences to change behavior.

Premack principle Principle stating that a more-preferred activity can serve as a reinforcer for a less-preferred activity.

Shaping Reinforcing each small step of progress toward a desired goal or behavior.

Successive approximations Small components that make up a complex behavior.

Task analysis System for breaking down a task hierarchically into basic skills and subskills.

Positive practice Practicing correct responses immediately after errors.

Satiation Requiring a person to repeat a problem behavior past the point of interest or motivation.

Reprimands Criticisms for misbehavior; rebukes.

Response cost Punishment by loss of reinforcers.

Social isolation Removal of a disruptive student for 5 to 10 minutes.

Time out Technically, the removal of all reinforcement. In practice, isolation of a student from the rest of the class for a brief time.

Positive behavioral supports (PBS) Interventions designed to replace problem behaviors with new actions that serve the same purpose for the student.

Functional behavioral assessment (FBA) Procedures used to obtain information about antecedents, behaviors, and consequences to determine the reason or function of the behavior.

Behavioral Approaches to Teaching and Management (pp. 224–229)

Describe the managerial strategies of group consequences, contracts, and token programs. Using group consequences involves basing reinforcement for the whole class on the behavior of the whole class. In a contingency contract program, the teacher draws up an individual contract with each student, describing exactly what the student must do to earn a particular privilege or reward. In token programs, students earn tokens (points, checks, holes punched in a card, chips, etc.) for both academic work and positive classroom behavior. Periodically, the students exchange the tokens they have earned for some desired reward. A teacher must use these programs with caution, emphasizing learning and not just "good" behavior.

Good behavior game Arrangement where a class is divided into teams and each team receives demerit points for breaking agreed-upon rules of good behavior.

Group consequences Rewards or punishments given to a class as a whole for adhering to or violating rules of conduct.

Token reinforcement system System in which tokens earned for academic work and positive classroom behavior can be exchanged for some desired reward.

Contingency contract A contract between the teacher and a student specifying what the student must do to earn a particular reward or privilege.

Observational Learning and Cognitive Behavior Modification: Thinking about Behavior (pp. 229–238)

Distinguish between social learning and social cognitive theories. Social learning theory was an early neobehavioral theory that expanded behavioral views of reinforcement and punishment. In behavioral views, reinforcement and punishment directly affect behavior. In social learning theory, seeing another person, a model, reinforced or punished can have similar effects on the observer's behavior. Social cognitive theory expands social learning theory to include cognitive factors such as beliefs, expectations, and perceptions of self.

Distinguish between enactive and vicarious learning. *Enactive learning* is learning by doing and experiencing the consequences of your actions. *Vicarious learning* is learning by observing, which challenges the behaviorist idea that cognitive factors are unnecessary in an explanation of learning. Much is going on mentally before performance and reinforcement can even take place.

What are the elements of observational learning? In order to learn through observation, we have to pay attention to aspects of the situation that will help us learn. In order to imitate the behavior of a model, you have to retain the information.

This involves mentally representing the model's actions in some way, probably as verbal steps. In the production phase, practice makes the behavior smoother and more expert. Sometimes, we need a great deal of practice, feedback, and coaching about subtle points before we can reproduce the behavior of the model. Finally, motivation shapes observational learning through incentives and reinforcement. We may not perform a learned behavior until there is some motivation or incentive to do so. Reinforcement can focus attention, encourage reproduction or practice, and maintain the new learning.

What are the steps in self-management? Students can apply behavior analysis on their own to manage their own behavior. Teachers can encourage the development of self-management skills by allowing students to participate in setting goals, keeping track of progress, evaluating accomplishments, and selecting and giving their own reinforcers. Teachers can also use cognitive behavior modification, a behavior change program described by Meichenbaum in which students are directly taught how to use self-instruction.

Social learning theory Theory that emphasizes learning through observation of others.

Social cognitive theory Theory that adds concern with cognitive factors such as beliefs, self-perceptions, and expectations to social learning theory.

Observational learning Learning by observation and imitation of others.

Vicarious reinforcement Increasing the chances that we will repeat a behavior by observing another person being reinforced for that behavior.

Self-reinforcement Controlling your own reinforcers.

Self-efficacy A person's sense of being able to deal effectively with a particular task.

Ripple effect "Contagious" spreading of behaviors through imitation.

Modeling Changes in behavior, thinking, or emotions that occur through observing another person—a model.

Self-management Use of behavioral learning principles to change your own behavior.

Cognitive behavior modification Procedures based on both behavioral and cognitive learning principles for changing your own behavior by using self-talk and self-instruction.

Self-instruction Talking oneself through the steps of a task.

Problems and Issues (pp. 238–240)

What are the main criticisms of behavioral approaches? The misuse or abuse of behavioral learning methods is unethical. Critics of behavioral methods also point out the danger that reinforcement could decrease interest in learning by overemphasizing rewards and could have a negative impact on other students. Teachers can use behavioral learning principles appropriately and ethically.

Teachers' Casebook: Connections to PRAXIS II™

Whether you begin your teaching career on the first day of the school year in your own classroom or as a mid-year substitute, the earliest public indicators of your teaching competence often will be the conduct of your students and your classroom management skills. As you read and discuss this chapter, you will encounter many principles of behaviorism that you can employ to foster appropriate classroom conduct and to establish effective routines and procedures. These principles also may be used to explain some of the learning that occurs in classrooms, and they are useful in understanding the complex factors that motivate students to learn. (Do you remember how the daily calendar review in kindergarten helped you learn to recognize numerals and the names of days and months? Did any of your elementary-school teachers participate in book-reading reward programs that were sponsored by corporations?) Look for PRAXIS II™ to test your knowledge of behaviorism to address many common classroom situations.

What Would They Do?

Here is how some practicing teachers responded to the teaching situation presented at the beginning of this chapter about an out-of-control class.

Timothy Norfleet **High School Teacher, Grades 9–12,**
Linden McKinley High School, Columbus, Ohio

One of the first steps in establishing order in the classroom is to set up daily routines that students are expected to follow. Having the warm-up activity, objective, and assignment posted daily on the board encourages the students to begin working right away. The next goal should be to establish class rules, rewards, and consequences with student input. Students respond well to a fair governance structure in which they have had input. They are more likely to adhere to the rules and their peers will help regulate inappropriate behavior. I use class managers for this purpose. Students are responsible for specific classroom management functions such as taking attendance, answering the door, and collecting homework. Allowing students to have roles in the management of the classroom provides an outlet for those who show leadership, and the jobs can be rotated to give several students opportunities to develop positive leadership skills.

Jolita Harper **Third Grade Teacher,**
Preparing Academic Leaders Academy, Maple Heights, Ohio

As I began day two with my new class, I would work with the students to establish an agreed-upon set of classroom rules. I feel it is important to include students in this process because they are aware of the disruptions and problems that exist within the classroom. My next goal would be to establish a relationship of mutual respect with the charismatic classroom leader; once we establish a respectful rapport, other students will be inclined to imitate behaviors conducive to learning exhibited by this individual. Finally, I would periodically remind my students of the classroom rules by verbally praising those students who are on-task. Drawing attention to appropriate behavior is far more effective than frequent yelling and public reprimands, which may inadvertently draw attention to and reinforce misbehavior.

Jamaal Allan **Language Arts Teacher, Seventh Grade,**
J. W. Poynter Middle School, Hillsboro, Oregon

The ambiguity, or absence, of structure has told these students that they are free to create their own behavioral guidelines. New to this classroom, I would have the advantage of a fresh start. To create a structure conducive to learning, I would start by introducing myself, my learning goals, and my classroom expectations. The expectations must be simple and understandable. An expectation of "treating the classroom and everyone in it with respect" serves as a blanket covering any "rule." We would follow up by discussing different theoretical situations and deciding which types of behavior are permitted within our expectations. Because the students have been involved in the process of creating the behavioral guidelines, they will be more apt to follow them. Once the behavioral expectations are understood, a learning environment will have been created and learning will be able to take place.

Danielle Hartman **Second Grade Teacher,**
Claymont Elementary School, Ballwin, Missouri

Walking into a situation like this is never easy. Try to stay positive. Remember that these are not bad kids. They just may not know what is expected of them. Therefore, you need to start by setting aside time to build community and establish your expectations. Be prepared, this will take a lot of time. Don't worry about not getting to every lesson plan for a few weeks. Taking this time now will pay off greatly in the end. Set up a schedule and routines. Students need and want structure in their classroom. I would really work on getting to know the one student who is causing a lot of the disruptions in class. Try to find out the reason he is behaving this way. Maybe he just needs some extra attention. Show him that you care about him and his success in school.

One way to build community is by having morning meetings to discuss any concerns the students may be having and work on ways to solve these problems. Don't forget to also share compliments and positive things that are happening. These meetings give the students ownership of their classroom. Let them know you value their ideas and opinions. Once you have built a positive climate, there will be a greater amount of time for you and the students to focus on their learning.

Felicia Lowman-Sikes **Kindergarten Teacher,**
Meadowview Elementary School, Meadowview, Virginia

Teachers beginning a placement mid-year need to be patient and firm. Changes in student behavior will not happen immediately. Students must become accustomed to new classroom rules and consequences. If the teacher follows through with a clearly delineated discipline plan . . . rules and consequences for breaking the rules . . . the students will learn which behaviors are acceptable and which are not, leading to a calmer classroom environment. Both teacher and students can develop a mutual respect and all involved in the reshaping of the classroom may feel a new sense of pride.

CHAPTER 7

Cognitive Views of Learning

Teachers' Casebook: What Would You Do? 247

Elements of the Cognitive Perspective 248

Comparing Cognitive and Behavioral Views 248

The Importance of Knowledge in Learning 249

The Information Processing Model of Memory 250

Sensory Memory 250

Working Memory 253

Long-Term Memory: The Goal of Teaching 257

Capacity, Duration, and Contents of Long-Term Memory 257

Explicit Memories: Semantic and Episodic 259

Implicit Memories 262

Storing and Retrieving Information in Long-Term Memory 263

Metacognition 267

Metacognitive Knowledge and Regulation 267

Reaching Every Student: Metacognitive Strategies for Students with Learning Disabilities 268

Becoming Knowledgeable: Some Basic Principles 269

Development of Declarative Knowledge 269

Becoming an Expert: Development of Procedural and Conditional Knowledge 274

Diversity and Convergences in Cognitive Learning 276

Diversity: Individual Differences and Working Memory 276

Diversity: Individual Differences and Long-Term Memory 278

Individual Differences in Metacognition 278

Convergences: Connecting with Families 279

Summary Table 280

Teachers' Casebook: Connections to PRAXIS II™/ What Would They Do? 283

What Would You Do?

Teachers' Casebook

The students in your senior history classes seem to equate understanding with memorizing. They prepare for each unit test by memorizing the exact words of the textbook. Even the best students seem to think that flash cards are the only learning strategy possible. In fact, when you try to get them to think about history by reading some original sources, debating issues in class, or examining art and music from the time period you are studying, they rebel. "Will this be on the test?" "Why are we looking at these pictures—will we have to know who painted them and when?" "What's this got to do with history?" Even the students who participate in the debates seem to use words and phrases straight from the textbook without knowing what they are saying.

Critical Thinking

- What are these students' beliefs and expectations, and how do these affect their learning?
- Why do you think they insist on using the rote memory approach?
- How would you use what the students already know to help them learn in better, more meaningful ways?
- How will these issues affect the grade levels you will teach?

Collaboration

With 2 or 3 other people in your class, talk about teachers you've had who helped you develop deep knowledge about a topic. How did they guide your thinking to move past memorizing to a more complete understanding?

We turn from behavioral theories of learning to the cognitive perspective in this chapter. This means a shift from "viewing the learners and their behaviors as products of incoming environmental stimuli" to seeing the learners as "sources of plans, intentions, goals, ideas, memories, and emotions actively used to attend to, select, and construct meaning from stimuli and knowledge from experience" (Wittrock, 1982, pp. 1–2). We will begin with a discussion of the general cognitive approach to learning and memory and the importance of knowledge in learning. To understand memory, we will consider a widely accepted cognitive model, information processing, which suggests that information is manipulated in different storage systems. Next, we will explore metacognition, a field of study that may provide insights into individual and developmental differences in learning. Then, we turn to ideas about how teachers can help their students become more knowledgeable. By the time you have completed this chapter, you should be able to answer these questions:

- What is the role of knowledge in learning?
- What is the human information processing model of memory?
- How do perception, attention, schemas, and scripts influence learning and remembering?
- What are declarative, procedural, and conditional knowledge?
- Why do students forget what they have learned?
- What is the role of metacognition in learning and remembering?
- What are the stages in the development of cognitive skills?

FACING PAGE *Looking at a Star*, 1999, © Christian Pierre/SuperStock.

Elements of the Cognitive Perspective

Connect and **Extend** to **Other Chapters**

Two different models of instruction based on principles of cognitive learning—Bruner's discovery learning and Ausubel's expository teaching—are described in Chapter 8.

The cognitive perspective is both the oldest and one of the youngest members of the psychological community. It is old because discussions of the nature of knowledge, the value of reason, and the contents of the mind date back at least to the ancient Greek philosophers (Hernshaw, 1987). From the late 1800s until several decades ago, however, cognitive studies fell from favor and behaviorism thrived. Then, research during World War II on the development of complex human skills, the computer revolution, and breakthroughs in understanding language development all stimulated a resurgence in cognitive research. Evidence accumulated indicating that people plan their responses, use strategies to help themselves remember, and organize the material they are learning in their own unique ways (Miller, Galanter, & Pribram, 1960; Shuell, 1986). Educational psychologists became interested in how people think, learn concepts, and solve problems (e.g., Ausubel, 1963; Bruner, Goodnow, & Austin, 1956).

Interest in concept learning and problem solving soon gave way, however, to interest in how knowledge is represented in the mind and particularly how it is remembered. Remembering and forgetting became major topics for investigation in cognitive psychology in the 1970s and 1980s, and the information processing model of memory dominated research.

Today, there is renewed interest in learning, thinking, and problem solving. The **cognitive view of learning** can be described as a generally agreed-upon philosophical orientation. This means that cognitive theorists share basic notions about learning and memory. Most importantly, cognitive psychologists assume that mental processes exist, that they can be studied scientifically, and that humans are active participants in their own acts of cognition (Ashcraft, 2006).

Comparing Cognitive and Behavioral Views

Connect and **Extend** to Your **Teaching/Portfolio**

Use the section on the differences between behavioral and cognitive approaches to learning to refine your teaching philosophy. How will you answer the job interview question, "What is your theory of learning and why?"

The cognitive and behavioral views differ in their assumptions about what is learned. According to the cognitive view, knowledge is learned, and changes in knowledge make changes in behavior possible. In the behavioral view, the new behaviors themselves are learned (Shuell, 1986). Both behavioral and cognitive theorists believe reinforcement is important in learning, but for different reasons. The strict behaviorist maintains that reinforcement strengthens responses; cognitive theorists see reinforcement as a source of information that provides feedback about what is likely to happen if behaviors are repeated or changed.

The cognitive view sees learning as extending and transforming the understanding we already have, not simply writing associations on the blank slates of our brains (Greeno,

The cognitive view sees learning as an active process in which learners, rather than simply "receiving" knowledge, seek new information to solve problems and reorganize what they already know to achieve new insights.

Cognitive view of learning A general approach that views learning as an active mental process of acquiring, remembering, and using knowledge.

Collins, & Resnick, 1996). Instead of being passively influenced by environmental events, people actively choose, practice, pay attention, ignore, reflect, and make many other decisions as they pursue goals. Older cognitive views emphasized the *acquisition* of knowledge, but newer approaches stress its *construction* (Anderson, Reder, & Simon, 1996; Greeno, Collins, & Resnick, 1996; Mayer, 1996).

The methods of cognitive and behavioral researchers also differ. Much of the work on behavioral learning principles has been with animals in controlled laboratory settings. The goal is to identify a few general laws of learning that apply to all higher organisms—including humans, regardless of age, intelligence, or other individual differences. Cognitive psychologists, on the other hand, study a wide range of learning situations. Because of their focus on individual and developmental differences in cognition, they have not been as concerned with general laws of learning. This is one of the reasons that there is no single cognitive model or theory of learning that is representative of the entire field.

The Importance of Knowledge in Learning

STOP | THINK | WRITE Quickly, list 10 terms that pertain to educational psychology. Now list 10 terms that relate to ceramic engineering. ■

Unless you are studying ceramic engineering, it probably took you longer to list 10 terms from that field than from educational psychology. Some of you may still be asking, "What is ceramic engineering anyway?" Your answers depend on your knowledge of ceramic engineering. (*Hint:* Think fiber optics, ceramic teeth and bones, ceramic semi-conductors for computers, heat-shielding tiles for space shuttles.)

Knowledge and knowing are the outcomes of learning. When we learn the history of cognitive psychology, the products of ceramic engineering, or the rules of tennis, we know something new. However, knowing is more than the end product of previous learning; it also guides new learning. The cognitive approach suggests that one of the most important elements in the learning process is what the individual brings to new learning situations. What we already know is the foundation and frame for constructing all future learning. Knowledge determines to a great extent what we will pay attention to, perceive, learn, remember, and forget (Alexander, 1996; Bransford, Brown, & Cocking, 2000).

An Example Study. A study by Recht and Leslie (1988) shows the importance of knowledge in understanding and remembering new information. These psychologists identified junior-high-school students who were either very good or very poor readers. They tested the students on their knowledge of baseball and found that knowledge of baseball was not related to reading ability. So the researchers were able to identify four groups of students: *good readers/high baseball knowledge, good readers/low baseball knowledge, poor readers/high baseball knowledge,* and *poor readers/low baseball knowledge.* Then, students in all four groups read a passage describing a baseball game and were tested in a number of ways to see if they understood and remembered what they had read.

The results demonstrated the power of knowledge. Poor readers who knew baseball remembered more than good readers with little baseball knowledge and almost as much as good readers who knew baseball. Poor readers who knew little about baseball remembered the least of what they had read. Thus, a good basis of knowledge can be more important than good reading skills in understanding and remembering—but extensive knowledge plus good reading skills are even better.

General and Specific Knowledge. Knowledge in the cognitive perspective includes both subject-specific understandings (math, history, soccer, etc.) and general cognitive abilities, such as planning, solving problems, and comprehending language (Greeno, Collins, & Resnick, 1996). So, there are different kinds of knowledge. Some is **domain-specific knowledge** that pertains to a particular task or subject. For example, knowing that the shortstop plays between second and third base is specific to the domain of baseball. Some knowledge, on the other hand, is general—it applies to many different situations. For example, **general knowledge** about how to read or write or use a computer is

Domain-specific knowledge Information that is useful in a particular situation or that applies mainly to one specific topic.

General knowledge Information that is useful in many different kinds of tasks; information that applies to many situations.

useful both in and out of school. Of course, there is no absolute line between general and domain-specific knowledge. When you were first learning to read, you may have studied specific facts about the sounds of letters. At that time, knowledge about letter sounds was specific to the domain of reading. But now you can use both knowledge about sounds and the ability to read in more general ways (Alexander, 1992; Schunk, 2004).

What we know exists in our memory. To know something is to remember it over time and be able to find it when you need it. Psychologists have studied memory extensively. Let's see what they have learned.

The Information Processing Model of Memory

Connect and **Extend** to Your **Teaching/Portfolio**

Consider these proverbs about memory taken from Klatzky, R. L. (1984). *Memory and awareness: An information processing perspective.* New York: Freeman, p. 122.

On Learning

Learning teacheth more in one year than experience in twenty. (Roger Ascham)

What we have to learn to do, we learn by doing. (Aristotle)

On Memory

The true art of memory is the art of attention. (Samuel Johnson)

A man's memory may almost become the art of continually varying and misrepresenting his past, according to his interests in the present. (George Santayana)

On Forgetting

The mind is slow in unlearning what it has been long in learning. (Seneca)

Soon learnt, soon forgotten. (Proverb)

Out of sight, out of mind. (Proverb)

An injury is much sooner forgotten than an insult. (Lord Chesterfield)

There are a number of theories of memory, but the most common are the information processing explanations (Ashcraft, 2006; Hunt & Ellis, 1999; Sternberg, 1999). We will use this well-researched framework for examining learning and memory.

Early **information processing** views of memory used the computer as a model. Like the computer, the human mind takes in information, performs operations on it to change its form and content, stores the information, retrieves it when needed, and generates responses to it. Thus, processing involves gathering information and organizing it in relation to what you already know, or *encoding;* holding information, or *storage;* and getting at the information when needed, or *retrieval.* The whole system is guided by *control processes* that determine how and when information will flow through the system.

For most cognitive psychologists, the computer model is only a metaphor for human mental activity. But other cognitive scientists, particularly those studying artificial intelligence, try to design and program computers to "think" and solve problems like human beings (Anderson, 2005; Schunk, 2000). Some theorists suggest that the operation of the brain resembles a large number of very slow computers, all operating in parallel (at the same time), with each computer dedicated to a different, specific task (Ashcraft, 2006).

Figure 7.1 is a schematic representation of a typical information processing model of memory, derived from the ideas of several theorists (Atkinson & Shiffrin, 1968; R. Gagné, 1985; Neisser, 1976). In order to understand this model, let's examine each element.

Sensory Memory

Stimuli from the environment (sights, sounds, smells, etc.) constantly bombard our body's mechanisms for seeing, hearing, tasting, smelling, and feeling. **Sensory memory** is the initial processing that transforms these incoming stimuli into information so we can make sense of them. Even though sights and sounds may last only fractions of a second, the transformations (information) that represent these sensations are briefly held in the *sensory register* or *sensory information store* so that this initial processing can take place (Driscoll, 2005; Sperling, 1960).

Capacity, Duration, and Contents of Sensory Memory. The *capacity* of sensory memory is very large, and can take in more information than we can possibly handle at once. But this vast amount of sensory information is fragile in *duration.* It lasts between one and three seconds.

STOP | THINK | WRITE Wave a pencil (or your finger) back and forth before your eyes while you stare straight ahead. What exactly do you see? Pinch your arm and let go. What do you feel just after you let go? ■

You just experienced this brief holding of sensory information in your own sensory register. You could see a trace of the pencil after the actual stimulus has been removed and feel the pinch after you let go. The sensory register held information about the stimuli very briefly after the actual stimulus had left (Lindsay & Norman, 1977).

Information processing The human mind's activity of taking in, storing, and using information.

Sensory memory System that holds sensory information very briefly.

FIGURE 7.1

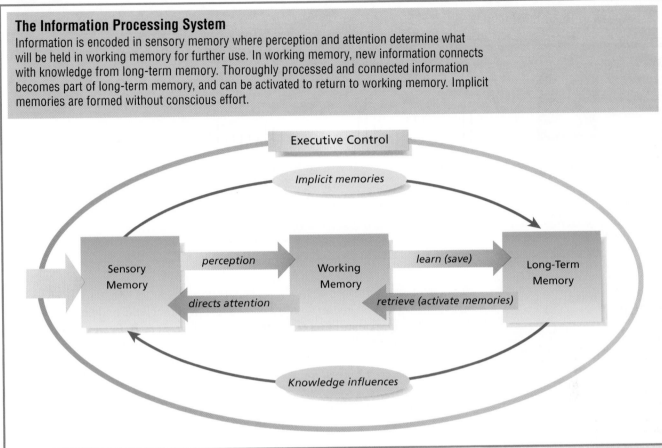

The Information Processing System

Information is encoded in sensory memory where perception and attention determine what will be held in working memory for further use. In working memory, new information connects with knowledge from long-term memory. Thoroughly processed and connected information becomes part of long-term memory, and can be activated to return to working memory. Implicit memories are formed without conscious effort.

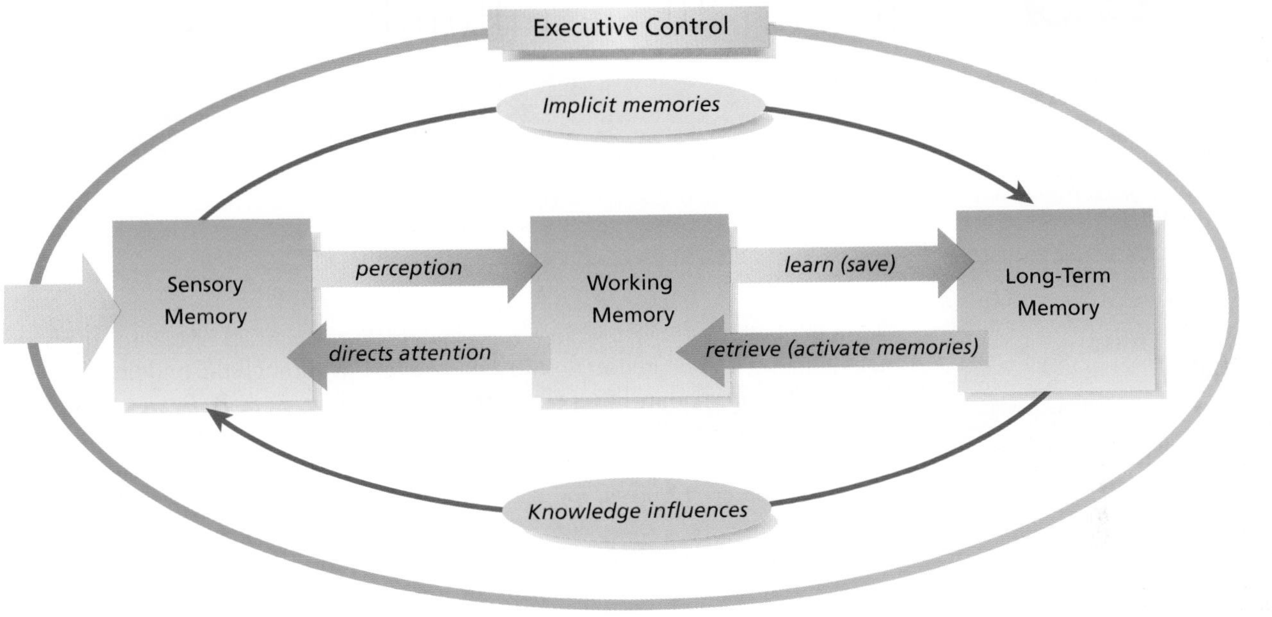

The information *content* of sensory memory resembles the sensations from the original stimulus. Visual sensations are coded briefly by the sensory register as images, almost like photographs. Auditory sensations are coded as sound patterns, similar to echoes. It may be that the other senses also have their own codes. Thus, for a second or so, a wealth of data from sensory experience remains intact. In these moments, we have a chance to select and organize information for further processing. Perception and attention are critical at this stage.

Perception. The process of detecting a stimulus and assigning meaning to it is called **perception**. This meaning is constructed based on both physical representations from the world and our existing knowledge. For example, consider these marks: **I3**. If asked what the letter is, you would say "B." If asked what the number is, you would say "13." The actual marks remain the same; their meaning changes in keeping with your expectation to recognize a letter or a number. To a child without appropriate knowledge to perceive either a letter or a number, the marks would probably be meaningless (F. Smith, 1975).

Some of our present-day understanding of perception is based on studies conducted in Germany early in this century (and later in the United States) by psychologists called *Gestalt theorists.* **Gestalt**, which means "pattern" or "configuration" in German, refers to people's tendency to organize sensory information into patterns or relationships. Instead of perceiving bits and pieces of unrelated information, we usually perceive organized, meaningful wholes. Figure 7.2 on page 252 presents a few Gestalt principles.

The Gestalt principles are reasonable explanations of certain aspects of perception, but they do not provide the whole story. There are two other kinds of explanations in information processing theory for how we recognize patterns and give meaning to sensory events. The first is called *feature analysis*, or **bottom-up processing** because the stimulus must be analyzed into features or components and assembled into a meaningful pattern

Perception Interpretation of sensory information.

Gestalt German for *pattern* or *whole.* Gestalt theorists hold that people organize their perceptions into coherent wholes.

Bottom-up processing Perceiving based on noticing separate defining features and assembling them into a recognizable pattern.

FIGURE 7.2

Examples of Gestalt Principles

Gestalt principles of perception explain how we "see" patterns in the world around us.

a. Figure-ground What do you see? Faces or a vase? Make one figure—the other ground.

b. Proximity You see these lines as 3 groups because of the proximity of the lines.

c. Similarity You see these lines as an alternating pattern because of the similarity in height of lines.

d. Closure You perceive a circle instead of dotted curved lines.

Source: From *Learning Theories: An Educational Perspective* (4th ed.), by D. H. Schunk. Published by Prentice Hall. Copyright © 2004 by Prentice Hall. Reprinted by permission of Pearson Education, Inc., Upper Saddle River, NJ.

"from the bottom up." For example, a capital letter A consists of two relatively straight lines joined at a 45-degree angle and a horizontal line through the middle. Whenever we see these features, or anything close enough, including, A, *A*, **A**, A, 𝒜, and A, we recognize an A (Anderson, 2005). This explains how we are able to read words written in other people's handwriting. We also have a **prototype** (a best example or classic case) of an A stored in memory to use along with features to help us detect the letter A (Driscoll, 2005).

If all perception relied only on feature analysis and prototypes, learning would be very slow. Luckily, humans are capable of another type of perception based on knowledge and expectation often called **top-down processing**. To recognize patterns rapidly, in addition to noting features, we use what we already know about the situation—what we know about words or pictures or the way the world generally operates. For example, you would not have seen the marks above as the letter A if you had no knowledge of the Roman alphabet. So, what you know also affects what you are able to perceive. The role of knowledge in perception is represented by the arrows pointing left in Figure 7.1 from long-term memory (stored knowledge) to working memory and then to sensory memory.

The Role of Attention. If every variation in color, movement, sound, smell, temperature, and so on ended up in working memory, life would be impossible. But attention is selective. By paying **attention** to selected stimuli and ignoring others, we limit the possibilities that we will perceive and process. What we pay attention to is guided to a certain extent by what we already know and what we need to know, so attention is involved in and influenced by all three memory processes in Figure 7.1. Attention is also affected by what else is happening at the time, by the complexity of the task, and by your ability to control or focus your attention (Driscoll, 2005). Some students with attention-deficit disorder have great difficulty focusing attention or ignoring competing stimuli.

But attention takes effort and is a limited resource. I imagine you have to work a bit to pay attention to these words about attention! We can pay attention to only one cognitively demanding task at time (Anderson, 2005). For example, when I was learning to drive, I couldn't listen to the radio and drive at the same time. After some practice, I could listen, but I had to turn the radio off when traffic was heavy. After years of practice, I can plan a class, listen to the radio, and carry on a conversation as I drive. This is possible because many processes that initially require attention and concentration become automatic with practice. Actually, **automaticity** probably is a matter of degree; we are not completely automatic, but rather more or less automatic in our performances depending on how much practice we have had and the situation. For example, even experienced drivers might become very attentive and focused during a blinding blizzard (Anderson, 2005).

Connect and Extend to PRAXIS II™

Attention has an important place in instructional activities. What steps can a teacher take to gain and maintain student attention during instruction?
Memory and Recall (I, A1)

Connect and Extend to the Research

Over 20 years ago, Flavell (1985) described four aspects of attention in developing children:

1. *Controlled:* Develop longer attention spans and ability to focus on important details, ignoring minor ones.
2. *Tailored to task:* Older children focus attention on most difficult material being learned (Berk, 2002).
3. *Directive:* They develop a feel for cues (teacher's voice, gestures) telling them when/how to direct their attention.
4. *Self-monitoring:* They learn to decide if they are using the right strategy, and to change if it's not working.

Prototype A best example or best representative of a category.

Top-down processing Perceiving based on the context and the patterns you expect to occur in that situation.

Attention Focus on a stimulus.

Automaticity The ability to perform thoroughly learned tasks without much mental effort.

Attention and Teaching. The first step in learning is paying attention. Students cannot process information that they do not recognize or perceive (Lachter, Forster, & Ruthruff, 2004). Many factors in the classroom influence student attention. Eye-catching or startling displays or actions can draw attention at the beginning of a lesson. A teacher might begin a science lesson on air pressure by blowing up a balloon until it pops. Bright colors, underlining, highlighting of written or spoken words, calling students by name, surprise events, intriguing questions, variety in tasks and teaching methods, and changes in voice level, lighting, or pacing can all be used to gain attention. And students have to maintain attention—they have to stay focused on the important features of the learning situation. The *Guidelines* offer additional ideas for capturing and maintaining students' attention.

Working Memory

The information in sensory memory is available for further processing as soon as it is noticed and transformed into patterns of images or sounds (or perhaps other types of sensory codes). **Working memory** is the "workbench" of the memory system, the interface where new information is held temporarily and combined with knowledge from long-term memory, to solve problems or comprehend a lecture, for example. Working memory "contains"

Working memory The information that you are focusing on at a given moment.

Guidelines: Gaining and Maintaining Attention

Use signals.

EXAMPLES

1. Develop a signal that tells students to stop what they are doing and focus on you. Some teachers move to a particular spot in the room, flick the lights, tap the table, or play a chord on the class piano. Mix visual and auditory signals.
2. Avoid distracting behaviors, such as tapping a pencil while talking, that interfere with both signals and attention to learning.
3. Give short, clear directions before, not during, transitions.
4. Be playful with younger children: Use a dramatic voice, sensational hat, or clapping game (Miller, 2005).

Reach out rather than call out (Miller, 2005).

EXAMPLES

1. Walk to the child, look into his or her eyes.
2. Speak in a firm but nonthreatening voice.
3. Use child's name.

Make sure the purpose of the lesson or assignment is clear to students.

EXAMPLES

1. Write the goals or objectives on the board and discuss them with students before starting. Ask students to summarize or restate the goals.
2. Explain the reasons for learning, and ask students for examples of how they will apply their understanding of the material.
3. Tie the new material to previous lessons—show an outline or map of how the new topic fits with previous and upcoming material.

Incorporate variety, curiosity, and surprise.

EXAMPLES

1. Arouse curiosity with questions such as "What would happen if?"
2. Create shock by staging an unexpected event such as a loud argument just before a lesson on communication.
3. Alter the physical environment by changing the arrangement of the room or moving to a different setting.
4. Shift sensory channels by giving a lesson that requires students to touch, smell, or taste.
5. Use movements, gestures, and voice inflection—walk around the room, point, and speak softly and then more emphatically. (My husband has been known to jump up on his desk to make an important point in his college classes!)

Ask questions and provide frames for answering.

EXAMPLES

1. Ask students why the material is important, how they intend to study, and what strategies they will use.
2. Give students self-checking or self-editing guides that focus on common mistakes or have them work in pairs to improve each other's work—sometimes it is difficult to pay attention to your own errors.

For more ideas about gaining student attention, see **http://www.inspiringteachers.com/tips/management/attention.html**

what you are thinking about at the moment. For this reason, some psychologists consider the working memory to be synonymous with "consciousness" (Sweller, van Merrienboer, & Paas, 1998). Unlike sensory memory or long-term memory, working memory capacity is very limited—something many of your professors seem to forget as they race through a lecture while you work to hold and process the information.

You may have heard the term **short-term memory**. This was an earlier name for the brief memory component of the information processing system. Short-term memory is not exactly the same as working memory. Working memory includes both temporary storage and active processing—the workbench of memory—where active mental effort is applied to both new and old information. But short-term memory usually means just storage, the immediate memory for new information that can be held about 15 to 20 seconds (Baddeley, 2001). Early experiments suggested that the capacity of short-term memory was only about 5 to 9 separate new items at once (Miller, 1956). Later, we will see that this limitation can be overcome using strategies such as chunking or grouping, but the 5 to 9 limit generally holds true in everyday life. It is quite common to remember a new phone number after looking it up, as you walk across the room to make the call. But what if you have two phone calls to make in succession? Two new phone numbers (14 digits) probably cannot be stored simultaneously.

A current view of working memory is that it is composed of at least three elements: the central executive that controls attention and other mental resources (the "worker" of working memory), the phonological loop that holds verbal and acoustical (sound) information, and the visuospatial sketchpad for visual and spatial information (Gathercole, Pickering, Ambridge, & Wearing, 2004).

STOP | THINK | WRITE Solve this problem from Ashcraft (2006, p. 190) and pay attention to how you go about the process:

$$\frac{(4 + 5) \times 2}{3 + (12/4)}$$

The Central Executive. As you solved the problem above, the central executive of your working memory focused your attention on the facts that you needed (what is 4 + 5? 9 × 2?), retrieved rules for which operations to do first, and recalled how to divide. The **central executive** supervises attention, makes plans, retrieves, and integrates information. Language comprehension, reasoning, rehearsing information to transfer to long-term memory—all these activities and more are handled by the central executive, as you can see in Figure 7.3. Two systems help out and support the central executive—the phonological loop and the visuospatial sketchpad.

The Phonological Loop. The **phonological loop** is a system for rehearsing words and sounds for short-term memory. It is the place you put the "18" (4 + 5 = 9 × 2 = 18) from the top line of the problem above while you calculated the 3 + (12/4) on the bottom of the problem. Baddeley (1986, 2001) suggests that we can hold as much in the phonological loop as we can rehearse (say to ourselves) in 1.5 to 2 seconds. The 7-digit telephone number fits this limitation. But what if you tried to hold these 7 words in mind: *disentangle appropriation gossamer anti-intellectual preventative foreclosure documentation* (Gray, 2002)? Besides being a mouthful, these words take longer than 2 seconds to rehearse and are more difficult to hold in working memory than 7 single digits or 7 short words.

Remember—put in your working memory—that we are discussing temporarily holding *new information*. In daily life we certainly can hold more than 5 to 9 bits or 1.5 seconds of information at once. While you are dialing that 7-digit phone number you just looked up, you are bound to have other things "on your mind"—in your memory—such as how to use a telephone, whom you are calling, and why. You don't have to pay attention to these things; they are not new knowledge. Some of the processes, such as dialing the phone, have become automatic. However, because of the working memory's limitations, if you were in a foreign country and were attempting to use an unfamiliar telephone

Short-term memory Component of memory system that holds information for about 20 seconds.

Central executive The part of working memory that is responsible for monitoring and directing attention and other mental resources.

Phonological loop Part of working memory. A memory rehearsal system for verbal and sound information of about 1.5 to 2 seconds.

FIGURE 7.3

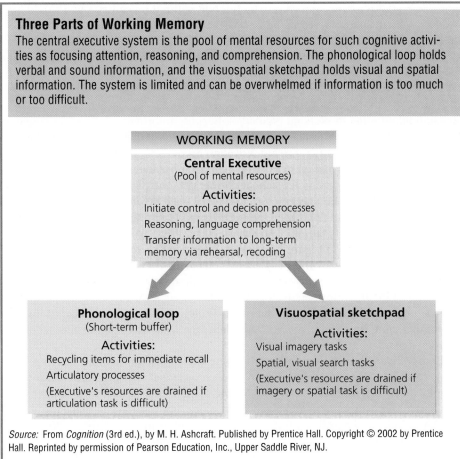

Three Parts of Working Memory

The central executive system is the pool of mental resources for such cognitive activities as focusing attention, reasoning, and comprehension. The phonological loop holds verbal and sound information, and the visuospatial sketchpad holds visual and spatial information. The system is limited and can be overwhelmed if information is too much or too difficult.

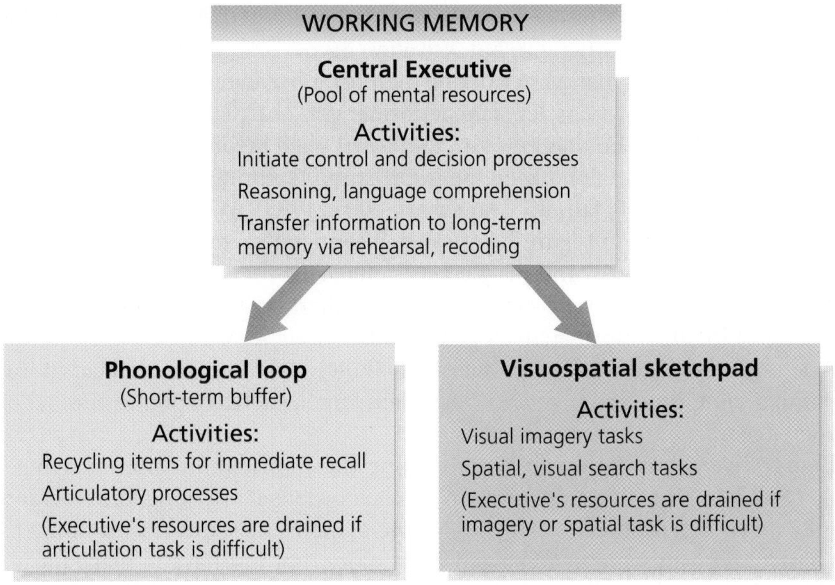

Source: From *Cognition* (3rd ed.), by M. H. Ashcraft. Published by Prentice Hall. Copyright © 2002 by Prentice Hall. Reprinted by permission of Pearson Education, Inc., Upper Saddle River, NJ.

system, you might very well have trouble remembering the phone number because your central executive was trying to figure out the phone system at the same time. Even a few bits of new information can be too much to remember if the new information is very complex or unfamiliar or if you have to integrate several elements to make sense of a situation (Sweller, van Merrienboer, & Paas, 1998).

The Visuospatial Sketchpad. Now try this problem from Gray (2002).

STOP | THINK | WRITE If you rotate a *p* 180 degrees, do you get a *b* or a *d*?

Most people answer the question above by creating a visual image of a "p" and rotating it. The **visuospatial sketchpad** is the place where you manipulated the image (after your central executive retrieved the meaning of "180 degrees," of course). Working in the visuospatial sketchpad has some of the same aspects as actually looking at a picture or object. If you have to solve the "p" problem and also pay attention to an image on a screen, you will be slowed down just like you would be if you had to look back and forth between two different objects. But if you had to solve the "p" problem while repeating digits, there is little slow down. You can use your phonological loop and your visuospatial sketchpad at the same time, but each is quickly filled and easily overburdened. In fact, each kind of task—verbal and visual—appears to happen in different areas of the brain. As we will see later, there are some individual differences in the capacities of these systems, too (Ashcraft, 2006; Gray, 2002).

Duration and Contents of Working Memory. It is clear that the *duration* of information in the working memory system is short, about 5 to 20 seconds, unless you keep rehearsing

Visuospatial sketchpad Part of working memory. A holding system for visual and spatial information.

the information or process it some other way. It may seem to you that a memory system with a 20-second time limit is not very useful, but, without this system, you would have already forgotten what you read in the first part of this sentence before you came to these last few words. This would clearly make understanding sentences difficult.

The *contents* of information in working memory may be in the form of sounds and images that resemble the representations in sensory memory, or the information may be structured more abstractly, based on meaning.

Connect and **Extend** to **PRAXIS II™**

Memory and Instruction (II, A1) To maximize the learning derived from instructional activities, a teacher should be aware of the characteristics of working memory. Consider the techniques or tactics a teacher can employ that complement those characteristics.

Retaining Information in Working Memory. Because information in working memory is fragile and easily lost, it must be kept activated to be retained. Activation is high as long as you are focusing on information, but activation decays or fades quickly when attention shifts away. Holding information in working memory is like keeping a series of plates spinning on top of poles in a circus act. The performer gets one plate spinning, moves to the next plate, and the next, but has to return to the first plate before it slows down too much and falls off its pole. If we don't keep the information "spinning" in working memory—keep it activated—it will "fall off" (Anderson, 2005, 1995). When activation fades, forgetting follows, as shown in Figure 7.4. To keep information activated in working memory for longer than 20 seconds, most people keep rehearsing the information mentally.

There are two types of rehearsal (Craik & Lockhart, 1972). **Maintenance rehearsal** involves repeating the information in your mind. As long as you repeat the information, it can be maintained in working memory indefinitely. Maintenance rehearsal is useful for retaining something you plan to use and then forget, such as a phone number or a location on a map.

Elaborative rehearsal involves connecting the information you are trying to remember with something you already know, with knowledge from long-term memory. For example, if you meet someone at a party whose name is the same as your brother's, you don't have to repeat the name to keep it in memory; you just have to make the association. This kind of rehearsal not only retains information in working memory but also helps move information to long-term memory. Rehearsal is a process the central executive controls to manage the flow of information through the information processing system.

The limited capacity of working memory can also be somewhat circumvented by the process of **chunking**. Because the number of bits of information, not the size of each bit, is a limitation for working memory, you can retain more information if you can group individual bits of information. For example, if you have to remember the six digits 3, 5, 4, 8, 7, and 0, it is easier to put them together into three chunks of two digits each (35, 48,

Maintenance rehearsal Keeping information in working memory by repeating it to yourself.

Elaborative rehearsal Keeping information in working memory by associating it with something else you already know.

Chunking Grouping individual bits of data into meaningful larger units.

FIGURE 7.4

Working Memory

Information in working memory can be kept activated through maintenance rehearsal or transferred into long-term memory by being connected with information in long-term memory (elaborative rehearsal).

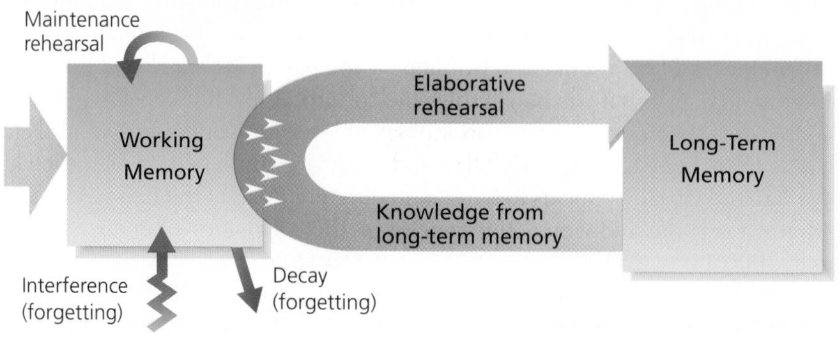

70) or two chunks of three digits each (354, 870). With these changes, there are only two or three bits of information rather than six to hold at one time. Chunking helps you remember a telephone number or a social security number (Driscoll, 2005).

Forgetting. Information may be lost from working memory through interference or decay (see Figure 7.4). Interference is fairly straightforward: Processing new information interferes or gets confused with old information. As new thoughts accumulate, old information is lost from working memory. Information is also lost by time **decay**. If you don't continue to pay attention to information, the activation level decays (weakens) and finally drops so low that the information cannot be reactivated—it disappears altogether.

Actually, forgetting is very useful. Without forgetting, people would quickly overload their working memories and learning would cease. Also, it would be a problem if you remembered permanently every sentence you ever read, every sound you ever heard, every picture you ever saw . . . you get the idea. Finding a particular bit of information in all that sea of knowledge would be impossible. It is helpful to have a system that provides temporary storage and that "weeds out" some information from everything you experience.

We turn next to long-term memory. Because this is such an important topic for teachers, we will spend quite a bit of time on it.

Long-Term Memory: The Goal of Teaching

Working memory holds the information that is currently activated, such as a telephone number you have just found and are about to dial. **Long-term memory** holds the information that is well learned, such as all the other telephone numbers you know.

Capacity, Duration, and Contents of Long-Term Memory

There are a number of differences between working and long-term memory, as you can see in Table 7.1. Information enters working memory very quickly. To move information into long-term storage requires more time and a bit of effort. Whereas the capacity of working memory is limited, the capacity of long-term memory appears to be, for all practical purposes, unlimited. In addition, once information is securely stored in long-term memory, it can remain there permanently. Our access to information in working memory is immediate because we are thinking about the information at that very moment. But access to information in long-term memory requires time and effort. Recently, some psychologists have suggested that there are not two separate memory stores (working and long-term). Rather, working memory is the part of long-term memory that works on

Decay The weakening and fading of memories with the passage of time.

Long-term memory Permanent store of knowledge.

TABLE 7.1

Working and Long-Term Memory

Type of Memory	Input	Capacity	Duration	Contents	Retrieval
Working	Very fast	Limited	Very brief: 5–20 sec.	Words, images, ideas, sentences	Immediate
Long-Term	Relatively slow	Practically unlimited	Practically unlimited	Propositional networks, schemata, productions, episodes, perhaps images	Depends on representation and organization

Source: From *Comprehension and Learning: A Conceptual Framework for Teachers,* by F. Smith, 1975, New York: Holt, Rinehart, and Winston. Copyright © Holt, Rinehart, and Winston. Adapted with permission of the author.

(processes) currently activated information—so working memory is more about processing than storage (Wilson, 2001). Another take on the information processing model is the notion of long-term working memory (Kintsch, 1998). **Long-term working memory** holds the retrieval structures and strategies that pull from long-term memory the information needed at the moment. As you develop knowledge and expertise in an area, you create efficient long-term working memory structures for solving problems in that area. So long-term working memory involves a set of domain-specific access tools that improve as you gain expertise in that domain.

Contents of Long-Term-Memory: Declarative, Procedural, and Conditional Knowledge. What we know is stored in long-term memory. Earlier, we talked about general and specific knowledge. Another way to categorize knowledge is as declarative, procedural, or conditional (Paris & Cunningham, 1996; Paris, Lipson, & Wixson, 1983). **Declarative knowledge** is knowledge that can be declared, through words and symbol systems of all kinds—Braille, sign language, dance or musical notation, mathematical symbols, and so on (Farnham-Diggory, 1994). Declarative knowledge is "knowing that" something is the case. The history students in the opening "What Would You Do?" situation were focusing exclusively on declarative knowledge about history. The range of declarative knowledge is tremendous. You can know very specific facts (the atomic weight of gold is 196.967), or generalities (leaves of some trees change color in autumn), or personal preferences (I don't like lima beans), or rules (to divide fractions, invert the divisor and multiply). Small units of declarative knowledge can be organized into larger units; for example, principles of reinforcement and punishment can be organized in your thinking into a theory of behavioral learning (Gagné, Yekovich, & Yekovich, 1993).

Procedural knowledge is "knowing how" to do something such as divide fractions or clean a carburetor—it is knowledge in action. Procedural knowledge must be demonstrated. Notice that repeating the rule "to divide fractions, invert the divisor and multiply" shows *declarative* knowledge—the student can state the rule. But to show *procedural* knowledge, the student must act. When faced with a fraction to divide, the student must divide correctly. Students demonstrate procedural knowledge when they translate a passage into Spanish, correctly categorize a geometric shape, or craft a coherent paragraph.

Conditional knowledge is "knowing when and why" to apply your declarative and procedural knowledge. Given the many kinds of math problems, it takes conditional knowledge to know when to apply one procedure and when to apply another to solve each problem. It takes conditional knowledge to know when to read every word in a text and when to skim. For many students, conditional knowledge is a stumbling block. They have the facts and can do the procedures, but they don't seem to understand how to apply what they know at the appropriate time.

Table 7.2 illustrates how declarative, procedural, and conditional knowledge can be either general or domain-specific.

Long-term working memory Holds the strategies for pulling information from long-term memory into working memory.

Declarative knowledge Verbal information; facts; "knowing that" something is the case.

Procedural knowledge Knowledge that is demonstrated when we perform a task; "knowing how."

Conditional knowledge "Knowing when and why" to use declarative and procedural knowledge.

TABLE 7.2

Kinds of Knowledge

	General Knowledge	Domain-Specific Knowledge
Declarative	Hours the library is open	The definition of "hypotenuse"
	Rules of grammar	The lines of the poem "The Raven"
Procedural	How to use your word processor	How to solve an oxidation-reduction equation
	How to drive	How to throw a pot on a potter's wheel
Conditional	When to give up and try another approach	When to use the formula for calculating volume
	When to skim and when to read carefully	When to rush the net in tennis

Contents of Long-Term-Memory: Words and Images. Allan Paivio (1971, 1986; Clark & Paivio, 1991) suggests that information is stored in long-term memory as either visual images or verbal units, or both. Psychologists who agree with this point of view believe that information coded both visually and verbally is easiest to learn (Mayer & Sims, 1994). This may be one reason why explaining an idea with words and representing it visually in a figure, as we do in textbooks, has proved helpful to students. For example, Richard Mayer and his colleagues (Mayer, 1999a, 2001; Mautone & Mayer, 2001) have found that illustrations like the one in Figure 7.8 on page 271 are helpful in improving students' understanding of science concepts. Paivio's ideas have support, but critics contend that many images are actually stored as verbal codes and then translated into visual information when an image is needed (Driscoll, 2005).

Most cognitive psychologists distinguish two categories of long-term memory, explicit and implicit, with subdivisions under each category, as shown in Figure 7.5. **Explicit memory** is knowledge from long-term memory that can be recalled and consciously considered. We are aware of these memories—we know we have remembered them. **Implicit memory,** on the other hand, is knowledge that we are not conscious of recalling, but that influences behavior or thought without our awareness. These different kinds of memory are associated with different parts of the brain (Ashcraft, 2006).

Explicit Memories: Semantic and Episodic

In Figure 7.5, you will see that explicit memories can be either semantic or episodic. **Semantic memory**, very important in schools, is memory for meaning, including words, facts, theories, and concepts—declarative knowledge. These memories are not tied to particular experiences and are stored as *propositions*, *images*, and *schemas*.

Propositions and Propositional Networks. A *proposition* is the smallest unit of knowledge that can be judged true or false. The statement, "Ida borrowed the antique tablecloth" has two propositions:

1. Ida borrowed the tablecloth.
2. The tablecloth is an antique.

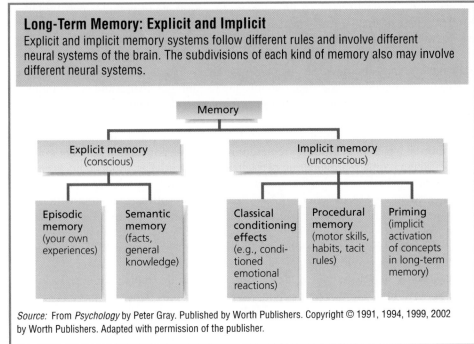

FIGURE 7.5

Long-Term Memory: Explicit and Implicit
Explicit and implicit memory systems follow different rules and involve different neural systems of the brain. The subdivisions of each kind of memory also may involve different neural systems.

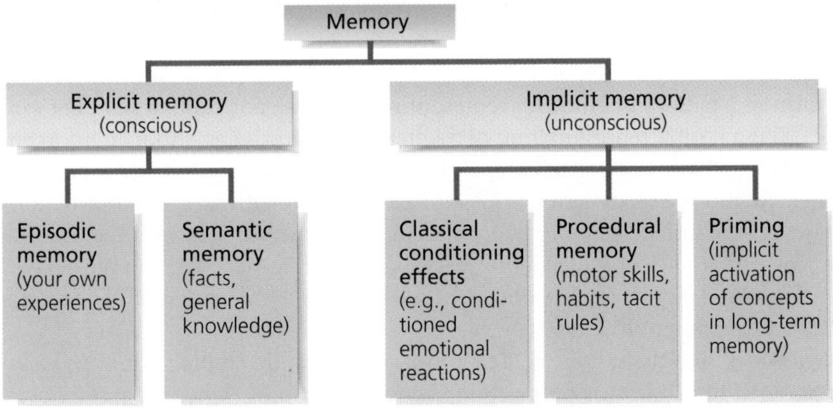

Source: From *Psychology* by Peter Gray. Published by Worth Publishers. Copyright © 1991, 1994, 1999, 2002 by Worth Publishers. Adapted with permission of the publisher.

Explicit memory Long-term memories that involve deliberate or conscious recall.

Implicit memory Knowledge that we are not conscious of recalling, but influences behavior or thought without our awareness.

Semantic memory Memory for meaning.

Propositions that share information, such as the two above that share information about the tablecloth (Ida borrowed the tablecloth and the tablecloth is an antique), are linked in what cognitive psychologists call **propositional networks**. It is the meaning, not the exact words or word order, that is stored in the network. The same propositional network would apply to the sentence: "The antique tablecloth was borrowed by Ida." The meaning is the same, and it is this *meaning* that is stored in memory as a set of relationships.

It is possible that most information is stored and represented in propositional networks. When we want to recall a bit of information, we can translate its meaning (as represented in the propositional network) into familiar phrases and sentences, or mental pictures. Also, because propositions are networked, recall of one bit of information can trigger or *activate* recall of another. We are not aware of these networks, for they are not part of our conscious memory (Anderson, 1995a). In much the same way, we are not aware of underlying grammatical structure when we form a sentence in our own language; we don't have to diagram a sentence in order to say it.

Images. **Images** are representations based on the structure or appearance of the information (Anderson, 1995a). As we form images (like you did in the "p" problem), we try to remember or recreate the physical attributes and spatial structure of information. For example, when asked how many windowpanes are in their living room, most people call up an image of the windows "in their mind's eye" and count the panes—the more panes, the longer it takes to respond. If the information were represented only in a proposition such as "my living room has seven window panes," then everyone would take about the same time to answer, whether the number was 1 or 24 (Mendell, 1971). However, as we saw earlier, researchers don't agree on exactly how images are stored in memory. Some psychologists believe that images are stored as pictures; others believe we store propositions in long-term memory and convert to pictures in working memory when necessary.

There probably are features of each process involved—some memory for images and some verbal or propositional descriptions of the image. Seeing images "in your mind's eye" is not exactly the same as seeing the actual image. It is more difficult to perform complicated transformations on mental images than on real images (Driscoll, 2005; Matlin & Foley, 1997). For example, if you had a plastic "p," you could very quickly rotate it. Rotating mentally takes more time for most people. Nevertheless, images are useful in making many practical decisions such as how a sofa might look in your living room or how to line up a golf shot. Images may also be helpful in abstract reasoning. Physicists, such as Faraday and Einstein, report creating images to reason about complex new problems. Einstein claimed that he was visualizing chasing a beam of light and catching up to it when the concept of relativity came to him (Kosslyn & Koenig, 1992).

Schemas. Propositions and single images are fine for representing single ideas and relationships, but often our knowledge about a topic combines images and propositions. To explain this kind of complex knowledge, psychologists developed the idea of a schema (Gagné, Yekovich, & Yekovich, 1993). **Schemas** (sometimes called ***schemata***) are abstract knowledge structures that organize vast amounts of information. A schema (the singular form) is a pattern or guide for representing an event, concept, or skill. For example, Figure 7.6 is a partial representation of a schema for knowledge about "reinforcement."

The schema tells you what features are typical of a category, what to expect about an object or situation. The pattern has "slots" that are filled with specific information as we apply the schema in a particular situation. And schemas are personal. For example, my schema of reinforcement is less richly developed than Skinner's schema must have been. You encountered a very similar concept of scheme in the discussion of Piaget's theory of cognitive development in Chapter 2.

When you hear the sentence, "Ida borrowed the antique tablecloth," you know even more about it than the two propositions because you have schemas about borrowing, tablecloths, antiques, and maybe even Ida herself. You know without being told, for example, that the lender does not have the tablecloth now, because it is in Ida's possession, and that Ida has an obligation to return the tablecloth to the lender (Gentner, 1975).

Connect and **Extend** to **PRAXIS II™**

Prior Knowledge (I, A1)
Prior knowledge strongly influences how we build and reorganize new knowledge. Be familiar with the role of schemas and propositional networks in the construction of knowledge and how they affect learning.
Memory Strategies (II, A1)

Propositional network Set of interconnected concepts and relationships in which long-term knowledge is held.

Images Representations based on the physical attributes—the appearance—of information.

Schemas (singular, **Schema**) Basic structures for organizing information; concepts.

FIGURE 7.6

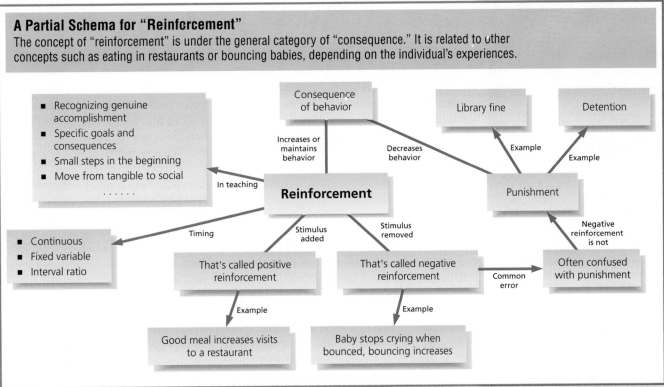

A Partial Schema for "Reinforcement"

The concept of "reinforcement" is under the general category of "consequence." It is related to other concepts such as eating in restaurants or bouncing babies, depending on the individual's experiences.

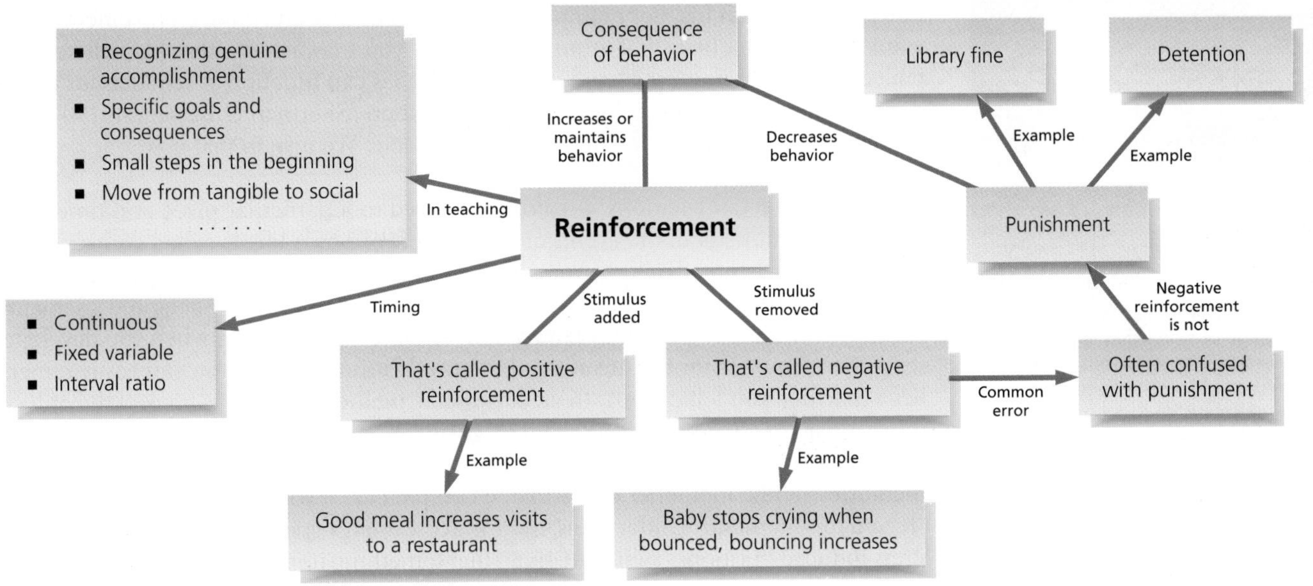

None of this information is explicitly stated, but it is part of our schema for the meaning of "borrow." Other schemas allow you to infer that the cloth is not plastic (if it is a real antique) and that Ida has probably invited guests for a meal. If you actually knew Ida, your schema about her may even allow you to predict how promptly the cloth will be returned and in what condition.

Another type of schema, a **story grammar** (sometimes called a schema for text or story structure) helps students to understand and remember stories (Gagné, Yekovich, & Yekovich, 1993; Rumelhart & Ortony, 1977). A story grammar could be something like this: murder discovered, search for clues, murderer's fatal mistake identified, trap set to trick suspect into confessing, murderer takes bait . . . mystery solved! In other words, a story grammar is a typical general structure that could fit many specific stories. To comprehend a story, we select a schema that seems appropriate. Then, we use this framework to decide which details are important, what information to seek, and what to remember. It is as though the schema is a theory about what should occur in the story. The schema guides us in "interrogating" the text, pointing to the specific information we expect to find so that the story makes sense. If we activate our "murder mystery schema," we may be alert for clues or a murderer's fatal mistake. Without an appropriate schema, trying to understand a story, textbook, or classroom lesson is a very slow, difficult process, something like finding your way through a new town without a map. A schema representing the typical sequence of events in an everyday situation is called a **script** or an *event schema*. Children as young as age 3 have basic scripts for the familiar events in their lives (Nelson, 1986).

WHAT WOULD YOU SAY?

During your interview, the supervisor for the primary grades asks you, "What is your script for a typical day? Tell me how a good day should go in terms of what you would plan and how much time you would give to each segment of your day." ■

Storing knowledge of the world in schemas and scripts has both advantages and disadvantages. A schema can be applied in many contexts, depending on what part of the

Connect and Extend to Your Teaching/Portfolio

How can schemas about differences among individuals, groups, and social contexts determine how new information about people and situations is interpreted?

Story grammar Typical structure or organization for a category of stories.

Script Schema or expected plan for the sequence of steps in a common event such as buying groceries or ordering take-out pizza.

Implicit memory includes the knowledge of skills that may have taken a while to learn, but once learned, tend to be remembered for a long time, and performed without intense concentration.

schema is relevant. You can use what you know about reinforcement, for example, to take a test in educational psychology, to analyze why a student continues to be sent to the principal's office, or to design an incentive program for your employees. Having a well-developed schema about Ida lets you recognize her (even as her appearance changes), remember many of her characteristics, and make predictions about her behavior. But it also allows you to be wrong. You may have incorporated incorrect or biased information into your schema of Ida. For example, if Ida is a member of an ethnic group different from yours and if you believe that group is dishonest, you may assume that Ida will keep the tablecloth. In this way, racial and ethnic stereotypes can function as schemas for misunderstanding individuals and for racial discrimination (Sherman & Bessenoff, 1999).

The second kind of explicit memory is episodic. We turn to that now.

Episodic Memory. Memory for information tied to a particular place and time, especially information about the events or episodes of your own life, is called episodic memory. **Episodic memory** is about events we have experienced, so we often can explain *when* the event happened. In contrast, we usually can't describe when we acquired a semantic memory. For example, you may have a difficult time remembering when you developed semantic memories for the meaning of the word "injustice," but you can easily remember a time that you felt unjustly treated. Episodic memory also keeps track of the order of things, so it is a good place to store jokes, gossip, or plots from films.

Memories for dramatic or emotional moments in your life are called **flashbulb memories**. These memories are vivid and complete, as if your brain demanded that you "record this moment." Under stress, more glucose energy goes to fuel brain activity, while stress-induced hormones signal the brain that something important is happening (Myers, 2005). So when we have strong emotional reactions, memories are stronger and more lasting. Many people have vivid memories of very positive or very negative events in school, winning a prize or being humiliated, for example. You probably know just where you were and what you were doing on 9/11. People over 50 have vivid memories of the day John Kennedy was assassinated. My whole school had walked to the main street of our suburb of Ft. Worth, Texas, to applaud as his motorcade drove by en route to the airport for the flight to Dallas. By the time I got back to geometry class, we heard the announcement that he had been shot in Dallas. My friend who had been at breakfast with him that very day was devastated.

Implicit Memories

Look back at Figure 7.5 on page 259. You see that there are three kinds of implicit or out-of-awareness memories: classical conditioning, procedural memory, and priming effects. In classical conditioning, as we saw in Chapter 6, some out-of-awareness memories may cause you to feel anxious as you take a test or make your heart rate increase when you hear a dentist's drill.

The second type of implicit memory is **procedural memory** for skills, habits, and how to do things—in other words, memory for procedural knowledge. It may take a while to learn a procedure—such as how to ski, serve a tennis ball, or factor an equation, but once learned, this knowledge tends to be remembered for a long time. Procedural memories are represented as *condition-action rules*, sometimes called productions. **Productions** specify what to do under certain conditions: If A occurs, then do B. A production might be something like, "If you want to snow ski faster, lean back slightly," or "If your goal is to increase student attention and a student has been paying attention a bit longer than usual, then praise the student." People can't necessarily state all their condition-action rules, and don't even know that they are following these rules, but they act on them nevertheless. The more practiced the procedure, the more automatic the action and the more implicit the memory (Anderson, 1995a).

STOP | THINK | WRITE Fill in these blanks: ME _ _ _ _

The final type of implicit memory involves **priming**, or activating information that already is in long-term memory through some out-of-awareness process. You might have

Episodic memory Long-term memory for information tied to a particular time and place, especially memory of the events in a person's life.

Flashbulb memories Clear, vivid memories of emotionally important events in your life.

Procedural memory Long-term memory for how to do things.

Productions The contents of procedural memory; rules about what actions to take, given certain conditions.

Priming Activating a concept in memory or the spread of activation from one concept to another.

seen an example of priming in the fill-in-the-blank question above. If you wrote MEMORY instead of MENTOR or MEMBER, or METEOR or other ME words, then priming may have played a role because the word "memory" has occurred many times in this chapter. Priming may be the fundamental process for retrieval as associations are activated and spread through the memory system (Ashcraft, 2005).

Storing and Retrieving Information in Long-Term Memory

Just what is done to "save" information permanently—to create explicit and implicit memories? How can we make the most effective use of our practically unlimited capacity to learn and remember? *The way you learn information in the first place*—the way you process it in working memory at the outset—strongly affects its recall later. One important requirement is that you integrate new information with knowledge already stored in long-term memory as you construct an understanding. Here, *elaboration, organization*, and *context* play a role.

Connect and **Extend** to Your **Teaching/Portfolio**

See the Teachers' Casebook for practicing teachers' ideas about how to help students retain and retrieve information.

Elaboration is adding meaning to new information by connecting with already existing knowledge. In other words, we apply our schemas and draw on already existing knowledge to construct an understanding. Frequently, we change our existing knowledge in the process. We often elaborate automatically. For example, a paragraph about an historic figure in ancient Rome tends to activate our existing knowledge about that period; we use the old knowledge to understand the new.

Material that is elaborated when first learned will be easier to recall later. First, as we saw earlier, elaboration is a form of rehearsal. It keeps the information activated in working memory long enough to have a chance for the new information to be linked with knowledge in long-term memory. Second, elaboration builds extra links to existing knowledge. The more one bit of information or knowledge is associated with other bits, the more routes there are to follow to get to the original bit. To put it another way, you have several "handles" or priming/retrieval cues to "pick up" or recognize the information you might be seeking (Schunk, 2004).

The more students elaborate new ideas, the more they "make them their own," the deeper their understanding and the better their memory for the knowledge will be. We help students to elaborate when we ask them to translate information into their own words, create examples, explain to a peer, draw or act out the relationships, or apply the information to solve new problems. Of course, if students elaborate new information by developing misguided explanations, these misconceptions will be remembered too.

Organization is a second element of processing that improves learning. Material that is well organized is easier to learn and to remember than bits and pieces of information, especially if the information is complex or extensive. Placing a concept in a structure will help you learn and remember both general definitions and specific examples. The structure serves as a guide back to the information when you need it. For example, Table 7.1 gives an organized view of the capacity, duration, contents, and retrieval of information from working and long-term memory; Table 7.2 organizes information about types of knowledge; and Figure 7.6 organizes my knowledge about reinforcement.

Connect and **Extend** to **PRAXIS II™**

Cognitivists emphasize the role that elaboration, organization, and context have in effective encoding of information into long-term memory. Be aware of techniques that make use of those processes.

Context is a third element of processing that influences learning. Aspects of physical and emotional context—places, rooms, moods, who is with us—are learned along with other information. Later, if you try to remember the information, it will be easier if the current context is similar to the original one. Context is a kind of priming that activates the information. This has been demonstrated in the laboratory. Students who learned material in one type of room performed better on tests taken in a similar room than they did on comparable tests taken in a very different-looking room (Smith, Glenberg, & Bjork, 1978). So, studying for a test under "test-like" conditions may result in improved performance. Of course, you can't always go back to the same place or a similar one in order to recall something. But if you can picture the setting, the time of day, and your companions, you may eventually reach the information you seek.

Elaboration Adding and extending meaning by connecting new information to existing knowledge.

Organization Ordered and logical network of relations.

Context The physical or emotional backdrop associated with an event.

Levels of processing theory Theory that recall of information is based on how deeply it is processed.

Levels of Processing Theory. Craik and Lockhart (1972) first proposed their **levels of processing theory** as an alternative to short-/long-term memory models, but levels of processing theory is particularly related to the notion of elaboration described earlier. Craik and Lockhart suggested that what determines how long information is remembered is *how extensively* the information is analyzed and connected with other information. The more completely information is processed, the better are our chances of remembering it. For example, according to the levels of processing theory, if I ask you to sort pictures of dogs based on the color of their coats, you might not remember many of the pictures later. But if I ask you to rate each dog on how likely it is to chase you as you jog, you probably would remember more of the pictures. To rate the dogs, you must pay attention to details in the pictures, relate features of the dogs to characteristics associated with danger, and so on. This rating procedure requires "deeper" processing and more focus on the *meaning* of the features in the photos.

Retrieving Information from Long-Term Memory. When we need to use information from long-term memory, we search for it. Sometimes, the search is conscious, as when you see a friend approaching and search for her name. At other times, locating and using information from long-term memory is automatic, as when you dial a telephone or solve a math problem without having to search for each step, or the word "memory" pops to mind when you see ME _ _ _ _. Think of long-term memory as a huge shelf full of tools (skills, procedures) and supplies (knowledge, schemas) ready to be brought to the workbench of working memory to accomplish a task. The shelf (long-term memory) stores an incredible amount, but it may be hard to find what you are looking for quickly. The workbench (working memory) is small, but anything on it is immediately available. Because it is small, however, supplies (bits of information) sometimes are lost when the workbench overflows or when one bit of information covers (interferes with) another (E. Gagné, 1985).

Spreading Activation. The size of the network in long-term memory is huge, but only small parts from it are activated at any one time. Only the information we are currently thinking about is in working memory. Information is retrieved in this network through **spreading activation**. When a particular proposition or image is active—when we are thinking about it—other closely associated knowledge can be *primed* or triggered as well, and activation can spread through the network (Anderson, 2005; Gagné, Yekovich, & Yekovich, 1993). Thus, as I focus on the propositions, "I'd like to go for a drive to see the fall leaves," related ideas such as, "I should rake leaves," and "The car needs an oil change," come to mind. As activation spreads from the "car trip" to the "oil change," the original thought, or active memory, disappears from working memory because of the limited space. Thus, **retrieval** from long-term memory occurs partly through the spreading of activation from one bit of knowledge to related ideas in the network. We often use this spreading in reverse to retrace our steps in a conversation, as in, "Before we got onto the topic of where to get the oil changed, what were we talking about? Oh yes, seeing the leaves." The learning and retrieving processes of long-term memory are diagrammed in Figure 7.7.

Reconstruction. In long-term memory, the information is still available, even when it is not activated, even when you are not thinking about it at the moment. If spreading activation does not "find" the information we seek, then we might still come up with an answer through **reconstruction**, a cognitive tool or problem-solving process that makes use of logic, cues, and other knowledge to *construct* a reasonable answer by filling in any missing parts (Koriat, Goldsmith, & Pansky, 2000). Sometimes reconstructed recollections are incorrect. For example, in 1932, F. C. Bartlett conducted a series of famous studies on remembering stories. He read a complex, unfamiliar Native American tale to students at England's Cambridge University and, after various lengths of time, asked the students to recall the story. Stories the students recalled were generally shorter than the original and were translated into the concepts and language of the Cambridge student culture. The story told of a seal hunt, for instance, but many students remembered (reconstructed) a "fishing trip," an activity closer to their experiences and more consistent with their schemas.

Spreading activation Retrieval of pieces of information based on their relatedness to one another. Remembering one bit of information activates (stimulates) recall of associated information.

Retrieval Process of searching for and finding information in long-term memory.

Reconstruction Recreating information by using memories, expectations, logic, and existing knowledge.

FIGURE 7.7

Long-Term Memory

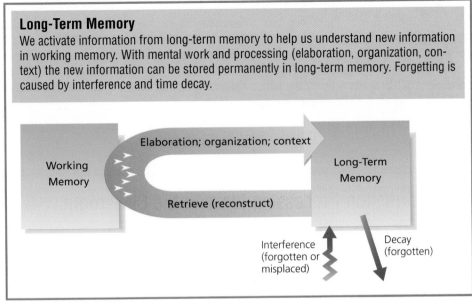

We activate information from long-term memory to help us understand new information in working memory. With mental work and processing (elaboration, organization, context) the new information can be stored permanently in long-term memory. Forgetting is caused by interference and time decay.

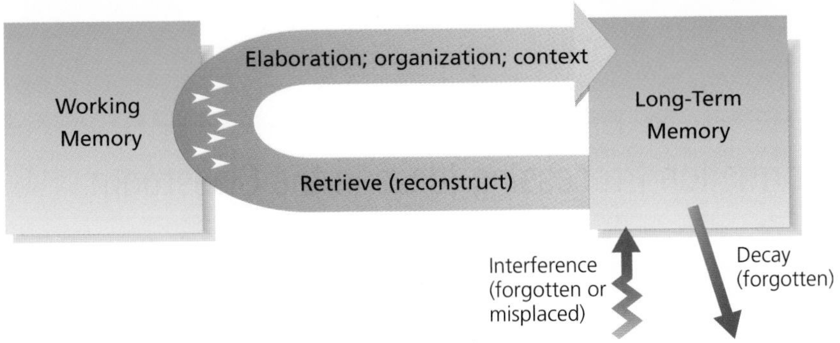

One area where reconstructed memory can play a major role is eyewitness testimony. Elizabeth Loftus and her colleagues have conducted a number of studies showing that misleading questions or other information during questioning can affect memory. For example, in a classic study, Loftus and Palmer (1974) showed subjects slides of a car wreck. Later, the experimenters asked some subjects, "How fast were the cars going when they *hit* each other?" while other subjects who saw the same slides were asked, "How fast were the cars going when they *smashed* into each other?" The difference in verbs was enough to bias the subjects' memories—the "hit" subjects estimated the cars were traveling an average of 34 miles per hour, but the "smashed" subjects estimated almost 41 miles per hour. And one week later, 32% of the "smashed" subjects remembered seeing broken glass at the scene of the wreck, while only 14% of the "hit" subjects remembered glass. (There was no broken glass visible in any of the slides.)

Forgetting and Long-Term Memory. Information in working memory that is lost before it has a chance to integrate into the network of long-term memory truly disappears. No amount of effort or searching will bring it back. But information stored in long-term memory may be available, given the right cues. Some people believe that nothing is ever lost from long-term memory; however, research casts doubts on this assertion (Schwartz, Wasserman, & Robbins, 2002).

WHAT WOULD YOU SAY?

As part of your interview, the principal says, "We have to cover so much material to get our students ready for the state assessments. What would you do to help your students remember what they have learned in your classes?" ■

Information appears to be lost from long-term memory through time decay and **interference**. For example, memory for Spanish–English vocabulary decreases for about 3 years after a person's last course in Spanish, then stays level for about 25 years, then drops again for the next 25 years. One explanation for this decline is that neural connections, like muscles, grow weak without use. After 25 years, it may be that the memories are still somewhere in the brain, but they are too weak to be reactivated (Anderson, 2005, 1995). And some neurons simply die. Finally, newer memories may interfere with or obscure older memories, and older memories may interfere with memory for new material.

Interference The process that occurs when remembering certain information is hampered by the presence of other information.

Even with decay and interference, long-term memory is remarkable. In a review of almost 100 studies of memory for knowledge taught in school, George Semb and John Ellis (1994) concluded that, "contrary to popular belief, students retain much of the knowledge taught in the classroom" (p. 279). It appears that teaching strategies that encourage student engagement and lead to higher levels of *initial* learning (such as frequent reviews and tests, elaborated feedback, high standards, mastery learning, and active involvement in learning projects) are associated with longer retention. The *Guidelines* give applications of information processing for teaching.

Guidelines: Using Information Processing Ideas in the Classroom

Make sure you have the students' attention.

EXAMPLES

1. Develop a signal that tells students to stop what they are doing and focus on you. Make sure students respond to the signal—don't let them ignore it. Practice using the signal.
2. Move around the room, use gestures, and avoid speaking in a monotone.
3. Begin a lesson by asking a question that stimulates interest in the topic.
4. Regain the attention of individual students by walking closer to them, using their names, or asking them a question.

Help students separate essential from nonessential details and focus on the most important information.

EXAMPLES

1. Summarize instructional objectives to indicate what students should be learning. Relate the material you are presenting to the objectives as you teach: "Now I'm going to explain exactly how you can find the information you need to meet Objective One on the board—determining the tone of the story."
2. When you make an important point, pause, repeat, ask a student to paraphrase, note the information on the board in colored chalk, or tell students to highlight the point in their notes or readings.

Help students make connections between new information and what they already know.

EXAMPLES

1. Review prerequisites to help students bring to mind the information they will need to understand new material: "Who can tell us the definition of a quadrilateral? Now, what is a rhombus? Is a square a quadrilateral? Is a square a rhombus? What did we say yesterday about how you can tell? Today we are going to look at some other quadrilaterals."
2. Use an outline or diagram to show how new information fits with the framework you have been developing. For example, "Now that you know the duties of the FBI, where would you expect to find it in this diagram of the branches of the U.S. government?"
3. Give an assignment that specifically calls for the use of new information along with information already learned.

Provide for repetition and review of information.

EXAMPLES

1. Begin the class with a quick review of the homework assignment.
2. Give frequent, short tests.
3. Build practice and repetition into games, or have students work with partners to quiz each other.

Present material in a clear, organized way.

EXAMPLES

1. Make the purpose of the lesson very clear.
2. Give students a brief outline to follow. Put the same outline on an overhead transparency so you can keep yourself on track. When students ask questions or make comments, relate these to the appropriate section of the outline.
3. Use summaries in the middle and at the end of the lesson.

Focus on meaning, not memorization.

EXAMPLES

1. In teaching new words, help students associate the new word to a related word they already understand: "*Enmity* is from the same base as *enemy.*"
2. In teaching about remainders, have students group 12 objects into sets of 2, 3, 4, 5, 6, and ask them to count the "leftovers" in each case.

For more information on information processing, see: **http://chiron.valdosta.edu/whuitt/col/cogsys/infoproc.html**

One question that intrigues many cognitive psychologists is why some people learn and remember more than others. For those who hold an information processing view, part of the answer lies in the concept of metacognition.

Metacognition

The **executive control processes** shown in Figure 7.1 guide the flow of information through the information processing system. We have already discussed a number of control processes, including attention, maintenance rehearsal, elaborative rehearsal, organization, and elaboration. These executive control processes are sometimes called *metacognitive skills*, because they can be intentionally used to regulate cognition.

Metacognitive Knowledge and Regulation

Donald Meichenbaum and his colleagues described **metacognition** as people's "awareness of their own cognitive machinery and how the machinery works" (Meichenbaum, Burland, Gruson, & Cameron, 1985, p. 5). Metacognition literally means cognition about cognition—or knowledge about knowing and learning. This metacognitive knowledge is higher-order cognition used to monitor and regulate cognitive processes such as reasoning, comprehension, problem solving, learning, and so on (Metcalfe & Shimamura, 1994). Because people differ in their metacognitive knowledge and skills, they differ in how well and how quickly they learn (Brown, Bransford, Ferrara, & Campione, 1983; Morris, 1990).

Metacognition involves the three kinds of knowledge we discussed earlier: (1) *declarative knowledge* about yourself as a learner, the factors that influence your learning and memory, and the skills, strategies, and resources needed to perform a task—knowing *what* to do; (2) *procedural knowledge* or knowing *how* to use the strategies; and (3) *conditional knowledge* to ensure the completion of the task—knowing *when* and *why* to apply the procedures and strategies (Bruning, Schraw, Norby, & Ronning, 2004). Metacognition is the strategic application of this declarative, procedural, and conditional knowledge to accomplish goals and solve problems (Schunk, 2004).

Metacognitive knowledge is used to regulate thinking and learning (Brown, 1987; Nelson, 1996). There are three essential skills that allow us to do this: planning, monitoring, and evaluating. *Planning* involves deciding how much time to give to a task, which strategies to use, how to start, what resources to gather, what order to follow, what to skim and what to give intense attention to, and so on. *Monitoring* is the real-time awareness of "how I'm doing." Monitoring entails asking, "Is this making sense? Am I trying to

Metacognition involves *choosing* the best way to approach a learning task. Students with good metacognitive skills set goals, organize their activities, select among various approaches to learning, and change strategies if needed.

Connect and **Extend** to the **Research**

See the entire issue of *Learning and Individual Differences* (1996, #4) on individual differences in metacognition.

Connect and **Extend** to **PRAXIS II™**

Metacognition (I, A1)

Often the difference between two students—one a successful learner, and the other a struggling learner—is the effective use of metacognitive processes. Identify strategies that teachers can use to enhance the role of metacognition in instruction.

Executive control processes Processes such as selective attention, rehearsal, elaboration, and organization that influence encoding, storage, and retrieval of information in memory.

Metacognition Knowledge about our own thinking processes.

go too fast? Have I studied enough?" *Evaluating* involves making judgments about the processes and outcomes of thinking and learning. "Should I change strategies? Get help? Give up for now? Is this paper (painting, model, poem, plan, etc.) finished?"

Of course, we don't have to be metacognitive all the time. Some actions become routine. Metacognition is most useful when tasks are challenging, but not too difficult. Then planning, monitoring, and evaluating can be helpful. And even when we are planning, monitoring, and evaluating, these processes are not necessarily conscious, especially in adults. We may use them automatically without being aware of our efforts (Perner, 2000). Experts in a field plan, monitor, and evaluate as second nature; they have difficulty describing their metacognitive knowledge and skills (Bargh & Chartrand, 1999; Reder, 1996).

Reaching Every Student: Metacognitive Strategies for Students with Learning Disabilities

For students with learning disabilities, executive control processes (that is, metacognitive strategies) such as planning, organizing, monitoring progress, and making adaptations are especially important, but often underdeveloped (Kirk, Gallagher, Anastasiow, & Colemen, 2006). It makes sense to teach these strategies directly. Some approaches make use of mnemonics to remember the steps. For example, teachers can help older students use a writing strategy called DEFENDS (Deshler, Ellis, & Lenz, 1996):

- **D**ecide on audience, goals, and position.
- **E**stimate main ideas and details.
- **F**igure best order of main ideas and details.
- **E**xpress your position in the opening.
- **N**ote each main idea and supporting points.
- **D**rive home the message in the last sentence.
- **S**earch for errors and correct.

Of course, you have to do more than just tell students about the strategy—you have to teach it. Michael Pressley and his colleagues (1995) developed the *Cognitive Strategies Model* as a guide for teaching students to improve their metacognitive strategies. Table 7.3 describes the steps in teaching these strategies.

TABLE 7.3

Teaching Strategies for Improving Students' Metacognitive Knowledge and Skills

These eight guidelines taken from Pressley and Woloshyn (1995) should help you in teaching any metacognitive strategy.

- Teach a few strategies at a time, intensively and extensively as part of the ongoing curriculum.
- Model and explain new strategies.
- If parts of the strategy were not understood, model again and re-explain strategies in ways that are sensitive to those confusing or misunderstood aspects of strategy use.
- Explain to students where and when to use the strategy.
- Provide plenty of practice, using strategies for as many appropriate tasks as possible.
- Encourage students to monitor how they are doing when they are using strategies.
- Increase students' motivation to use strategies by heightening their awareness that they are acquiring valuable skills—skills that are at the heart of competent functioning.
- Emphasize reflective processing rather than speedy processing; do all possible to eliminate high anxiety in students; encourage students to shield themselves from distractions so they can attend to academic tasks.

For a list of strategies and how to teach them see: http://www.unl.edu/csi/bank.html

Source: Adapted from Pressley, M., & Woloshyn, V. (1995). *Cognitive strategy instruction that really improves children's academic performance.* Cambridge, MA: Brookline Books, p. 18.

Now that we have examined the information processing explanation of how knowledge is represented and remembered, let's turn to the really important question: How can teachers support the development of knowledge?

Becoming Knowledgeable: Some Basic Principles

Understanding a concept such as "reinforcement" involves *declarative knowledge* about characteristics and images as well as *procedural knowledge* about how to apply rules to categorize specific consequences. We will discuss the development of declarative and procedural knowledge separately, but keep in mind that real learning is a combination and integration of these elements.

Development of Declarative Knowledge

Within the information processing perspective, to learn declarative knowledge is really to integrate new ideas with existing knowledge and construct an understanding. As you have seen, people learn best when they have a good base of knowledge in the area they are studying. With many well-elaborated schemas and scripts to guide them, new material makes more sense, and there are many possible spots in the long-term memory network for connecting new information with old. But students don't always have a good base of knowledge. In the early phases of learning, students of any age must grope around the landscape a bit, searching for landmarks and direction. Even experts in an area must use some learning strategies when they encounter unfamiliar material or new problems (Alexander, 1996, 1997; Garner, 1990; Perkins & Salomon, 1989; Shuell, 1990).

What are some possible strategies? Perhaps the best single method for helping students learn is to make each lesson as meaningful as possible.

Making It Meaningful. Meaningful lessons are presented in vocabulary that makes sense to the students. New terms are clarified through ties with more familiar words and ideas. Meaningful lessons are well organized, with clear connections between the different elements of the lesson. Finally, meaningful lessons make natural use of old information to help students understand new information through examples or analogies.

The importance of meaningful lessons is emphasized below in an example presented by Smith (1975).

STOP | THINK | WRITE Look at the three lines below. Begin by covering all but the first line. Look at it for a second, close the book, and write down all the letters you remember. Then repeat this procedure with the second and third lines.

1. KBVODUWGPJMSQTXNOGMCTRSO
2. READ JUMP WHEAT POOR BUT SEEK
3. KNIGHTS RODE HORSES INTO WAR ■

Each line has the same number of letters, but the chances are great that you remembered all the letters in the third line, a good number of letters in the second line, and very few in the first line. The first line makes no sense. There is no way to organize it in a brief glance. Working memory is simply not able to hold and process all that information quickly. The second line is more meaningful. You do not have to see each letter because your long-term memory brings prior knowledge of spelling rules and vocabulary to the task. The third line is the most meaningful. Just a glance and you can probably remember all of it because you bring to this task prior knowledge not only of spelling and vocabulary but also of rules about syntax and probably some historical information about knights (they didn't ride in tanks). This sentence is meaningful because you have existing schemas for assimilating it. It is relatively easy to associate the words and meaning with other information already in long-term memory (Sweller, van Merrienboer, & Paas, 1998).

The challenge for teachers is to make lessons less like learning the first line and more like learning the third line. Although this may seem obvious, think about the times when *you* have read a sentence in a text or heard an explanation from a professor that might just as well have been KBVODUWGPJMSQTXNOGMCTRSO. But remember, attempts to change the ways that students are used to learning—moving from memorizing to meaningful activities as in the opening "What Would You Do?" situation—are not always greeted with student enthusiasm. Students may be concerned about their grades; at least when memorization gains an A, they know what is expected. Meaningful learning can be riskier and more challenging. In Chapters 8, 9, 11, and 13 we will examine a variety of ways in which teachers can support meaningful learning and understanding. For now, see how one teacher made learning meaningful for her new students in *Stories of Learning/Tributes to Teaching*.

Visual Images and Illustrations. Is a picture worth 1000 words in teaching? Richard Mayer (1999a, 2001) has studied this question for several years and found that the right combination of pictures and words can make a significant difference in students' learning. Mayer's cognitive theory of multimedia learning includes three ideas:

Dual Coding: Visual and verbal materials are processed in different systems (Clark & Paivio, 1991).
Limited Capacity: Working memory for verbal and visual material is severely limited (Baddeley, 2001).
Generative Learning: Meaningful learning happens when students focus on relevant information and generate or build connections (Mayer, 1999a).

The problem: How to build complex understandings that integrate information from visual (pictures, diagrams, graphs, films) and verbal (text, lecture) sources, given the limitations of working memory. The answer: Make sure the information is available at the same time or in focused small bites. Mayer and Gallini (1990) provide an example. They used three kinds of texts to explain how a bicycle pump works. One text used only words,

STORIES OF LEARNING
TRIBUTES TO TEACHING

> **"I began to get excited about learning."**

SUSAN lived in what seemed to be a normal upper middle-class home, but her abusive father caused problems for the entire family. It was difficult for her to devote attention to school work. Susan thought she was just dumb, but she enjoyed art and dance and had the strong support of many family members. When her mother divorced and moved the family to another state, Susan encountered some wonderful teachers who captured her imagination and capitalized on her talents. Susan went on to earn a PhD in early childhood education and counseling—using her experiences as a resilient child to help others. She describes her senior English teacher.

The most exciting thing about my move was starting over academically. I was placed in a superior English class that year and I was also in pretty good classes across the board.

I'll never forget the first time I heard my English teacher, Mr. Borders, teach. I was sitting in class, and, for the first time in my life, I was able to really listen, pay attention, and focus on what the teacher was saying. It was an overwhelming experience and a wonderful feeling. I felt like the top of my head was off and everything that had previously clouded my brain and life was being lifted. I could use my brain like it was supposed to be used. There was a sense of quiet where I was free to think and process information without worrying about what was happening at home or how my mom was doing.

I began getting excited about learning. In fact, I liked learning because Mr. Borders, my "Superior English" teacher, made it exciting. He also introduced me to project work. I was able to make a Shakespearean character for one of my projects. I loved doing this project. I remember the great detail I took to make this character look authentic. I also saw myself excelling academically even though I thought I wasn't supposed to be smart. I was also drawing my cousin's lab pictures for her college biology class. Of course, art was one of my gifts and it didn't take brains to do this, I thought, but, nevertheless, I felt proud. So, I began to surprise my mom as well as myself.

Source: From "Hidden Lives: Examining the Lives of Resilient European American Children," by S. G. Hendley. In Gloria Swindler Boutte (Ed.), *Resounding Voices: School Experiences of People from Diverse Ethnic Backgrounds.* Published by Allyn & Bacon, Boston, MA.

FIGURE 7.8

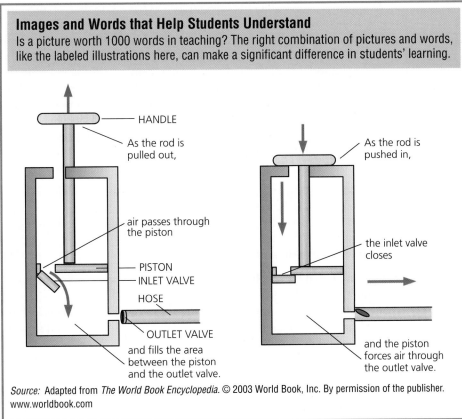

Images and Words that Help Students Understand

Is a picture worth 1000 words in teaching? The right combination of pictures and words, like the labeled illustrations here, can make a significant difference in students' learning.

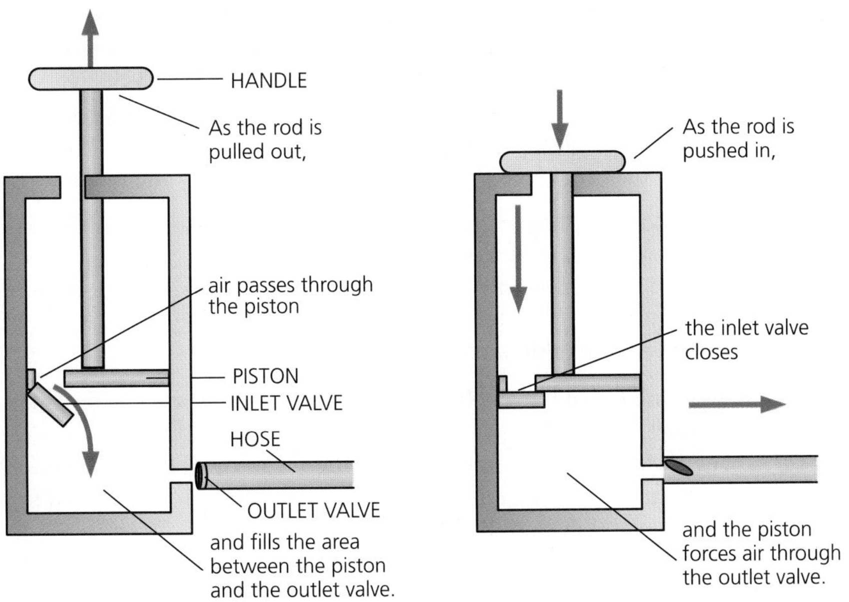

HANDLE
As the rod is pulled out,
air passes through the piston
PISTON
INLET VALVE
HOSE
OUTLET VALVE
and fills the area between the piston and the outlet valve.
As the rod is pushed in,
the inlet valve closes
and the piston forces air through the outlet valve.

Source: Adapted from *The World Book Encyclopedia.* © 2003 World Book, Inc. By permission of the publisher. www.worldbook.com

the second had pictures that just showed the parts of the brake system and the steps, and the third (this one improved student learning and recall) showed both the "on" and the "off" states of the pumps with labels for each step, as in Figure 7.8.

The moral of the story? Give students multiple ways to understand—pictures *and* explanations. But don't overload working memory—"package" the visual and verbal information together in bite-size (or memory-size) pieces.

Another memory strategy that often makes use of images is mnemonics.

Mnemonics. **Mnemonics** are systematic procedures for improving memory (Atkinson et al., 1999; Levin, 1994; Rummel, Levin, & Woodward, 2003). When information has little inherent meaning, mnemonic strategies build in meaning by connecting what is to be learned with established words or images.

The **loci method** derives its name from the plural of the Latin word *locus,* meaning "place." To use loci, you must first imagine a very familiar place, such as your own house or apartment, and pick out particular locations. Every time you have a list to remember, the same locations serve as "pegs" to "hang" memories. Simply place each item from your list in one of these locations. For instance, let's say you want to remember to buy milk, bread, butter, and cereal at the store. Imagine a giant bottle of milk blocking the entry hall, a lazy loaf of bread sleeping on the living room couch, a stick of butter melting all over the dining room table, and cereal covering the kitchen floor. When you want to remember the items, all you have to do is take an imaginary walk through your house. Other **peg-type mnemonics** use a standard list of words (one is bun, two is shoe) as pegs. Then, the items to be remembered are linked to the pegs through images or stories. The rhyming primes the list of pegs.

If you need to remember information for long periods of time, an acronym may be the answer. An **acronym** is a form of abbreviation—a word formed from the first letter of each word in a phrase, for example, HOMES to remember the Great Lakes (Huron, Ontario, Michigan, Erie, Superior). Another method forms phrases or sentences out of

Connect and Extend to PRAXIS II™

Medical students often use mnemonics to remember the vast amounts of information they encounter in their studies. Be familiar with the major mnemonic methods and the kinds of information that they are most suitable for. **Attention (I, A1)**

Connect and Extend to Your Teaching/Portfolio

Use the section on mnemonics to generate ideas for helping your students learn key vocabulary in science or social studies subjects and include these ideas in your **Teaching Resources** file.

Mnemonics Techniques for remembering; also, the art of memory.

Loci method Technique of associating items with specific places.

Peg-type mnemonics Systems of associating items with cue words.

Acronym Technique for remembering names, phrases, or steps by using the first letter of each word to form a new, memorable word.

"How many times must I tell you—it's 'cat' before 'temple' except after 'slave.'"

Source: By permission of Bo Brown, From *Phi Delta Kappan.*

the first letter of each word or item in a list, for example, Every Good Boy Does Fine to remember the lines on the G clef—E, G, B, D, F. Because the words must make sense as a sentence, this approach also has some characteristics of **chain mnemonics**, methods that connect the first item to be memorized with the second, the second item with the third, and so on. In one type of chain method, each item on a list is linked to the next through some visual association or story. Another chain-method approach is to incorporate all the items to be memorized into a jingle such as "i before e except after c."

The mnemonic system that has been most extensively researched in teaching is the **keyword method**. Joel Levin and his colleagues use a mnemonic (the 3 *Rs*) to teach the keyword mnemonic method:

- *Recode* the to-be-learned vocabulary item as a more familiar, concrete keyword—this is the keyword.
- *Relate* the keyword clue to the vocabulary item's definition through a sentence.
- *Retrieve* the desired definition.

For example, to remember that the English word *carlin* means *old woman*, you might recode *carlin* as the more familiar keyword *car*. Then, make up a sentence such as *The old woman was driving a car.* When you are asked for the meaning of the word *carlin*, you think of the keyword *car*, which triggers the sentence about the car and the *old woman*, the meaning (Jones, Levin, Levin, & Beitzel, 2000).

The keyword method has been used extensively in foreign language learning. For example, the Spanish word *carta* (meaning "letter") sounds like the English word "cart." *Cart* becomes the keyword: You imagine a shopping cart filled with letters on its way to the post office, or you make up a sentence such as "The cart full of letters tipped over" (Pressley, Levin, & Delaney, 1982). A similar approach has been used to help students connect artists with particular aspects of their paintings. For example, students are told to imagine that the heavy dark lines of paintings by Rouault are made with a *ruler* (Rouault) dipped in black paint (Carney & Levin, 2000). Figure 7.9 is an example of using mnemonic pictures as aids in learning complicated science concepts (Carney & Levin, 2002).

FIGURE 7.9

Using Mnemonics to Promote Learning Complex Concepts

The illustration tells a story that provides a frame for remembering and pegs for hanging the concept names in the biological subdivision of angiosperms.

To remember that the subdivision **angiosperms** includes the class **dicotyledons**, which in turn includes the three orders **rubales**, **sapindales**, and **rosales**, study the picture of the angel with the pet **dinosaur** that is walking up the **Rubik's cubes** so that he can lick the sweet **sap** that drips down from the **rose** tree.

Source: From "Pictorial Illustrations Still Improve Students' Learning From Text," by R. N. Carney and J. R. Levin, *Educational Psychology Review, 14.* Copyright © 2002 by Kluwer Academic Publishers. Reprinted with permission of the publisher and authors.

The keyword method does not work well if it is difficult to identify a keyword for a particular item. Many words and ideas that students need to remember are quite a challenge to associate with keywords (Hall, 1991; Pressley, 1991). Also, vocabulary learned with keywords can be easily forgotten if students are given keywords and images instead of being asked to supply words and images that are relevant to them. When the teacher provides the memory links, these associations may not fit the students' existing knowledge and may be forgotten or confused later; as a result, remembering suffers (Wang & Thomas, 1995; Wang, Thomas, & Ouelette, 1992). Younger students have some difficulty forming

Connect and **Extend** to Your **Teaching/Portfolio**

What is the memory strategy used in each of the following examples?

a. To remember that Bismarck is the capital of North Dakota, a student imagines N.D. on a biscuit.
b. To help students remember how to spell "separate," the teacher says, "There is a rat in separate."
c. A student lists the products of Alabama so that the first letters spell CAPS—for cotton, apples, paper products, and soybeans.
d. Columbus sailed the ocean blue in fourteen hundred and ninety-two.
e. To remember a grocery list, Mrs. Tarent imagines cheese on her TV, limes on the sofa, milk on the table, beans in the wicker basket, and tomatoes on the stove.
f. The teacher uses a time line to show the major events before, during, and after the Vietnam War.
g. Students are asked to compare their present home chores with chores they might have if they lived during Civil War times.

Chain mnemonics Memory strategies that associate one element in a series with the next element.

Keyword method System of associating new words or concepts with similar-sounding cue words and images.

their own images. For them, memory aids that rely on auditory cues—rhymes such as "Thirty days hath September" seem to work better (Willoughby, Porter, Belsito, & Yearsley, 1999).

Many teachers use a mnemonic system to quickly learn their students' names. Until we have some knowledge to guide learning, it may help to use some mnemonic approaches to build vocabulary and facts. Not all educators agree, however, as you will see in the *Point/Counterpoint.*

Rote Memorization. *Very few things need to be learned by rote.* The greatest challenge teachers face is to help students think and understand, not just memorize. Unfortunately,

Point/Counterpoint

What's Wrong with Memorizing?

FOR YEARS, STUDENTS have relied on memorization to learn vocabulary, procedures, steps, names, and facts. Is this a bad idea?

POINT Rote memorization creates inert knowledge.

Years ago William James (1912) described the limitations of rote learning by telling a story about what can happen when students memorize but do not understand:

> *A friend of mine, visiting a school, was asked to examine a young class in geography. Glancing at the book, she said: "Suppose you should dig a hole in the ground, hundreds of feet deep, how should you find it at the bottom—warmer or colder than on top?" None of the class replying, the teacher said: "I'm sure they know, but I think you don't ask the question quite rightly. Let me try." So, taking the book, she asked: "In what condition is the interior of the globe?" And received the immediate answer from half the class at once. "The interior of the globe is in a condition of igneous fusion."* (p. 150)

The students had memorized the answer, but they had no idea what it meant. Perhaps they didn't understand the meaning of "interior," "globe," or "igneous fusion." At any rate, the knowledge was useful to them only when they were answering test questions, and only then when the questions were phrased exactly as they had been memorized. Students often resort to memorizing the exact words of definitions when they have no hope for actually understanding the terms or when teachers count off for definitions that are not exact.

Howard Gardner has been a vocal critic of rote memorization and a champion of "teaching for understanding." In an interview in *Phi Delta Kappan* (Siegel & Shaughnessy, 1994), Gardner says:

> *My biggest concern about American education is that even our better students in our better schools are just going through the motions of education. In* The Unschooled Mind, *I review ample evidence that suggests an absence of understanding—the inability of students to take knowledge, skills, and other apparent attainments and apply them successfully in new situations. In the absence of such flexibility and adaptability, the education that the students receive is worth little.* (pp. 563–564)

COUNTERPOINT Rote memorization can be effective.

Memorization may not be such a bad way to learn new information that has little inherent meaning, such as foreign language vocabulary. Alvin Wang, Margaret Thomas, and Judith Ouellette (1992) compared learning Tagalog (the national language of the Philippines) using either rote memorization or the keyword approach. The keyword method is a way of creating connections and meaning for associating new words with existing words and images. In their study, even though the keyword method led to faster and better learning initially, long-term forgetting was *greater* for students who had used the keyword method than for students who had learned by rote memorization.

There are times when students must memorize and we do them a disservice if we don't teach them how. Every discipline has its own terms, names, facts, and rules. As adults, we want to work with physicians who have memorized the correct names for the bones and organs of the body or the drugs needed to combat particular infections. Of course, they can look up some information or research certain conditions, but they have to know where to start. We want to work with accountants who give us accurate information about the new tax codes, information they probably had to memorize because it changes from year to year in ways that are not necessarily rational or meaningful. We want to deal with computer salespeople who have memorized their stock and know exactly which printers will work with our computer. Just because something was learned through memorization does not mean it is inert knowledge. The real question, as Gardner points out above, is whether you can *use* the information flexibly and effectively to solve new problems.

WHAT DO YOU THINK?

Vote online at **www.mylabschool.com**

many students, including those in the scenario opening this chapter, see **rote memorizing** and learning as the same thing (Iran-Nejad, 1990).

However, on rare occasions we have to memorize something word-for-word, such as lines in a song, poem, or play. How would you do it? If you have tried to memorize a list of items that are all similar to one another, you may have found that you tended to remember items at the beginning and at the end of the list, but forgot those in the middle. This is called the **serial-position effect**. **Part learning**, breaking the list into smaller segments, can help prevent this effect, because breaking a list into several shorter lists means there will be fewer middle items to forget.

Another strategy for memorizing a long selection or list is the use of **distributed practice**. A student who studies Hamlet's soliloquy intermittently throughout the weekend will probably do much better than a student who tries to memorize the entire speech on Sunday night. Studying for an extended period is called massed practice. **Massed practice** leads to fatigue and lagging motivation. Distributed practice gives time for deeper processing and the chance to move information into long-term memory (Mumford, Costanza, Baughman, Threlfall, & Fleishman, 1994). What is forgotten after one session can be relearned in the next with distributed practice.

Becoming an Expert: Development of Procedural and Conditional Knowledge

Experts in a particular field have a wealth of domain-specific knowledge, that is, knowledge that applies specifically to their area or domain. This includes *declarative knowledge* (facts and verbal information), *procedural knowledge* (how to perform various cognitive activities), and *conditional knowledge* (knowing when and why to apply what they know). In addition, it appears that experts have developed their *long-term working memories* in the domain and can quickly access relevant knowledge and strategies for solving problems in that domain.

Another characteristic distinguishes experts from novices. Much of the expert's declarative knowledge has become "proceduralized," that is, incorporated into routines they can apply automatically without making many demands on working memory. Explicit memories have become implicit and the expert is no longer aware of them. Skills that are applied without conscious thought are called **automated basic skills**. An example is shifting gears in a standard transmission car. At first you had to think about every

Driving a car employs both automated basic skills and domain-specific strategies.

Rote memorization Remembering information by repetition without necessarily understanding the meaning of the information.

Serial-position effect The tendency to remember the beginning and the end but not the middle of a list.

Part learning Breaking a list of rote learning items into shorter lists.

Distributed practice Practice in brief periods with rest intervals.

Massed practice Practice for a single extended period.

Automated basic skills Skills that are applied without conscious thought.

step, but as you became more expert (if you did), the procedure became automatic. But not all procedures can be automatic, even for experts in a particular domain. For example, no matter how expert you are in driving, you still have to consciously watch the traffic around you. This kind of conscious procedure is called a *domain-specific strategy*. Automated basic skills and domain-specific strategies are learned in different ways (Gagné, Yekovich, & Yekovich, 1993).

WHAT WOULD YOU SAY?

As part of your interview, the department chair asks, "What are the basic skills for your students—the foundations of their more advanced learning—and how would you teach them?" ■

Connect and Extend to PRAXIS II™

Developing Basic Skills (II, A3)
Efficient and effective performance as a learner requires the automatic use of basic skills. Describe what teachers can do to help students develop automatic basic skills.

Automated Basic Skills. Most psychologists identify three stages in the development of an automated skill: *cognitive, associative,* and *autonomous* (Anderson, 1995b; Fitts & Posner, 1967). At the *cognitive stage*, when we are first learning, we rely on declarative knowledge and general problem-solving strategies to accomplish our goal. For example, to learn to assemble a bookshelf, we might try to follow steps in the instruction manual, putting a check beside each step as we complete it to keep track of progress. At this stage, we have to "think about" every step and perhaps refer back to the pictures of parts to see what a "4-inch metal bolt with lock nut" looks like. The load on working memory is heavy. There can be quite a bit of trial-and-error learning at this stage when, for example, the bolt we chose doesn't fit.

At the *associative stage*, individual steps of a procedure are combined or "chunked" into larger units. We reach for the right bolt and put it into the right hole. One step smoothly cues the next. With practice, the associative stage moves to the *autonomous stage*, where the whole procedure can be accomplished without much attention. So if you assemble enough bookshelves, you can have a lively conversation as you do, paying little attention to the assembly task. This movement from the cognitive to the associative to the autonomous stage holds for the development of basic cognitive skills in any area, but science, medicine, chess, and mathematics have been most heavily researched.

What can teachers do to help their students pass through these three stages and become more expert learners? In general, it appears that two factors are critical: *prerequisite knowledge* and *practice with feedback*. First, if students don't have the essential prior knowledge (schemas, skills, etc.), the load on working memory will be too great. In order to compose a poem in a foreign language, for example, you must know some of the vocabulary and grammar of that language, and you must have some understanding of poetry forms. To learn the vocabulary, grammar, *and* forms as you also try to compose the poem would be too much.

Second, practice with feedback allows you to form associations, recognize cues automatically, and combine small steps into larger condition-action rules or *productions*. Even from the earliest stage, some of this practice should include a simplified version of the whole process in a real context. Practice in real contexts helps students learn not only *how* to do a skill but also *why* and *when* (Collins, Brown, & Newman, 1989; Gagné, Yekovich, & Yekovich, 1993). Of course, as every athletic coach knows, if a particular step, component, or process is causing trouble, that element might be practiced alone until it is more automatic, and then put back into the whole sequence, to lower the demands on working memory (Anderson, Reder, & Simon, 1996).

Domain-Specific Strategies. As we saw earlier, some procedural knowledge, such as monitoring the traffic while you drive, is not automatic because conditions are constantly changing. Once you decide to change lanes, the maneuver may be fairly automatic, but the decision to change lanes was conscious, based on the traffic conditions around you. **Domain-specific strategies** are consciously applied skills that organize thoughts and actions to reach a goal. To support this kind of learning, teachers need to provide opportunities for practice in many different situations—for example, practice reading with newspapers, package labels, magazines, books, letters, operating manuals, and so on. In the next chapter's discussion of problem-solving and study strategies, we will examine

Domain-specific strategies Consciously applied skills to reach goals in a particular subject or problem area.

other ways to help students develop domain-specific strategies. For now, let's turn to a consideration of diversity and convergence in cognitive learning.

Diversity and Convergences in Cognitive Learning

Many of the concepts and processes discussed in this chapter—the importance of knowledge in learning; the sensory, working, and long-term memory; metacognition—apply to all students. But there are developmental and individual differences in what students know and how their memory processes are used.

Diversity: Individual Differences and Working Memory

As you might expect, there are both developmental and individual differences in working memory. Let's examine a few. First, try this:

STOP | THINK | WRITE Read the following sentences and words in caps out loud once:

For many years my family and friends have been working on the farm. SPOT

Because the room was stuffy, Bob went outside for some fresh air. TRAIL

We were fifty miles out to sea before we lost sight of the land. BAND

Now cover the sentences and answer these questions (be honest):

Name the words that were in all caps. Who was in the stuffy room? Who worked on the farm? ■

You have just taken a few items from a test of working memory span (Engle, 2001). The test required you to both process and store—process the meaning of the sentences and store the words (Ashcraft, 2006). How did you do?

Developmental Differences. Research indicates that young children have very limited working memories, but their memory span improves with age. Recent research shows that the three components of working memory—the central executive, phonological loop, and visuospatial sketch pad—all increase in capacity from ages 4 through adolescence (Gathercole, Pickering, Ambridge, & Wearing, 2004). It is not clear whether these differences are the result of changes in memory *capacity* or improvements in *strategy* use. Case (1998) suggests that the total amount of "space" available for processing information is the same at each age, but young children must use quite a bit of this space to remember how to execute basic operations, such as reaching for a toy, finding the right word for an object, or counting. Using a new operation takes up a large portion of the child's working memory. Once an operation is mastered, however, there is more working memory available for short-term storage of new information. For very young children, biology may play a role, too. As the brain and neurological system of the child mature, processing may become more efficient so that more working-memory space is available (Bransford, Brown, & Cocking, 2000).

As children grow older, they develop more effective strategies for remembering information. At about age 4, children begin to understand that "remembering" means recalling something from the past. Before age 4, children think remembering means what they see or know now and forgetting means not knowing (Perner, 2000). Most children spontaneously discover rehearsal around age 5 or 6. Siegler (1998) describes a 9-year-old boy who witnessed a robbery, then mentally repeated the license number of the getaway car until he could give the number to the police. Younger children can be taught to rehearse, and will use the strategy effectively as long as they are reminded, but they will not apply the strategy spontaneously. Children are 10 to 11 years old before they have adult-like working memories.

According to Case (1998), young children often use reasonable, but incorrect strategies to solve problems because of their limited memories. They try to simplify the task by

There are several developmental differences in how students use process information in working and long-term memory.

ignoring important information or skipping steps to reach a correct solution. This puts less strain on memory. For example, when comparing quantities, young children may consider only the height of the water in a glass, not the diameter of the glass, because this approach demands less of their memory. According to Case, this explains young children's inability to solve the classic Piagetian conservation problem. (See Figure 2.2 on page 33.)

There are several developmental differences in how students use organization, elaboration, and knowledge to process information in working memory. Around age 6, most children discover the value of using *organizational strategies* and by 9 or 10, they use these strategies spontaneously. So, given the following words to learn:

couch, orange, rat, lamp, pear, sheep, banana, rug, pineapple, horse, table, dog

an older child or an adult might organize the words into three short lists of furniture, fruit, and animals. Younger children can be taught to use organization to improve memory, but they probably won't apply the strategy unless they are reminded. Children also become more able to use elaboration as they mature, but this strategy is developed late in childhood. Creating images or stories to remember ideas is more likely for older elementary school students and adolescents (Siegler, 1998).

Individual Differences. Besides developmental differences, there are other individual variations in working memory, and these differences have implications for learning. For example, the correlation between scores on a test of working memory span (like the one you just took in the *Stop/Think/Write* exercise) and the verbal portion of the Scholastic Assessment Test (SAT) are about .59. But there is no correlation between the SAT and simple short-term memory span (repeating digits). Working-memory span is also related to scores on intelligence tests. If a task requires controlled attention or higher-level thinking, then working-memory span probably is a factor in performing that task (Ashcraft, 2006; Hambrick, Kane, & Engle, 2005; Ackerman, Beier, & Boyle, 2005; Unsworth & Engle, 2005).

Some people seem to have more efficient working memories than others (Cariglia-Bull & Pressley, 1990; DiVesta & Di Cintio, 1997; Jurden, 1995), and differences in working memory may be associated with giftedness in math and verbal areas. For example, subjects in one research study were asked to remember lists of numbers, the locations of marks on a page, letters, and words (Dark & Benbow, 1991). Subjects who excelled in mathematics remembered numbers and locations significantly better than subjects talented in verbal areas. The verbally talented subjects, on the other hand, had better memories for words. Based on these results, Dark and Benbow believe that basic differences in information processing abilities play a role in the development of mathematical and verbal talent.

Diversity: Individual Differences and Long-Term Memory

The major individual difference that affects long-term memory is knowledge. When students have more *domain-specific declarative* and *procedural knowledge*, they are better at learning and remembering material in that domain (Alexander, 1997). Think about what it is like to read a very technical textbook in an area you know little about. Every line is difficult. You have to stop and look up words or turn back to read about concepts you don't understand. It is hard to remember what you are reading because you are trying to understand and remember at the same time. But with a good basis of knowledge, learning and remembering become easier; the more you know, the easier it is to know more. This is true in part because having knowledge improves strategy use. Another factor is related to developing domain knowledge and remembering it: interest. To develop expert understanding and recall in a domain requires the "continuous interplay of skill (i.e., knowledge) and thrill (i.e., interest)" (Alexander, Kulikowich, & Schulze, 1994, p. 334).

People also differ in their abilities to use images in remembering. There are both developmental and individual differences. Children are more likely than adults to use images. As they mature cognitively, children may replace using images with using verbal propositions. As adults, some people are better than others at using imagery, but most people could improve their imagery abilities with practice (Schunk, 2004).

As we have seen throughout this book, because people grow up in different cultural contexts, they have different funds of knowledge (Moll, 1994; Nieto, 2004). Table 2.4 on page 51 lists possible knowledge areas for the Latino families in Luis Moll's studies of cultural knowledge. Remember the baseball study earlier in this chapter—attention, learning, and memory are supported when teaching builds on the prior knowledge of students.

Individual Differences in Metacognition

Some differences in metacognitive abilities are the result of development. Younger children, for example, may not be aware of the purpose of a lesson—they may think the point is simply to finish. They also may not be good at gauging the difficulty of a task—they may think that reading for fun and reading a science book are the same (Gredler, 2005). As children grow older, they are more able to exercise executive control over strategies. For example, they are more able to determine if they have understood instructions (Markman, 1977, 1979) or if they have studied enough to remember a set of items (Flavell, Friedrichs, & Hoyt, 1970). Metacognitive abilities begin to develop around ages 5 to 7 and improve throughout school (Flavell, Green, & Flavell, 1995; Garner, 1990). In her work with 1st and 2nd graders, Nancy Perry found that asking students two questions helped them become more metacognitive. The questions were "What did you learn about yourself as a reader/writer today?" and "What did you learn that you can do again and again and again?" When teachers asked these questions regularly during class, even young students demonstrated fairly sophisticated levels of metacognitive understanding and action (Perry et al., 2000).

Not all differences in metacognitive abilities have to do with age or maturation. There is great variability even among students of the same developmental level, but these differences do not appear to be related to intellectual abilities. In fact, superior metacognitive skills can compensate for lower levels of ability, so these metacognitive skills can be especially important for students who often have trouble in school (Schunk, 2004; Swanson, 1990).

Some individual differences in metacognitive abilities are probably caused by biological differences or by variations in learning experiences. Students can vary greatly in their ability to attend selectively to information in their environment. In fact, many students diagnosed as having learning disabilities actually have attention disorders (Hallahan & Kauffman, 2006), particularly with long tasks (Pelham, 1981). Other attention and behavior difficulties associated with attention disorders may stem from sociocultural, emotional, developmental, cognitive, or educational sources, as indicated in Table 7.4.

Convergences: Connecting with Families

The last several sections of this chapter have described many ideas for helping students become knowledgeable—memory strategies, mnemonics, metacognitive skills such as planning or monitoring comprehension, and cognitive skills. Some students have an advantage in school because they learn these strategies and skills at home. One way to capitalize on this diversity is to connect with the family in support of the child's learning. The *Family and Community Partnerships Guidelines* on the next page give ideas for working with families to give all your students more support and practice developing these skills.

TABLE 7.4

Questioning the Sources of Difficulties with Attention

If we take a holistic perspective on students, we can understand and capitalize on their differences. In working with students diagnosed with ADHD, ask these questions:

Paradigm or Perspective	Key Question	Key Experts	Examples of Potential Assessments	Examples of Potential Interventions
Sociocultural	How much of the child's attention and behavior difficulties results from cultural differences?	Culturally sensitive social worker, psychologist, teacher	Home visits; classroom observations	Provision of culturally sensitive curriculum; celebration of cultural diversity
Psychoaffective	How much of the child's attention and behavior difficulties results from emotional trauma, anxiety/depression, or temperamental differences?	Clinical psychologist; psychiatrist; licensed counselor	Assessments for depression, anxiety; temperament assessments	Psychotherapy; family therapy; provision of emotionally supportive classroom environment
Developmental	How much of the child's attention and behavior difficulties results from a different pace of development?	Developmental pediatrician; child development specialist	Child development indexes; observation in natural settings	Provision of developmentally appropriate curriculum; readjustment of behavioral expectations
Cognitive	How much of the child's attention and behavior difficulties results from creative behavior or other positive cognitive differences?	Gifted and talented specialist; cognitive psychologist	Creativity instruments; cognitive style assessments	Use of expressive arts, creative curriculum, gifted and talented curriculum, and other creative approaches
Biological	How much of the child's attention and behavior difficulties results from biological problems or neurobiological differences?	Family physician; medical specialist (e.g., neurologist, psychiatrist)	Medical examination; specialized medical tests	Medications (e.g., Ritalin); treatment for underlying physical problems
Educational	How much of the child's attention and behavior difficulties results from learning differences?	Learning specialist; classroom teacher	Learning style inventories; multiple intelligences assessments, authentic assessments, portfolios of the child's work	Teaching strategies tailored to the child's individual learning style/multiple intelligences

Source: Adapted from *ADD/ADHD alternatives in the classroom* (p. 54) by T. Armstrong. The Association for Supervision and Curriculum Development is a worldwide community of educators advocating sound policies and sharing best practices to achieve the success of each learner. To learn more, visit ASCD at www.ascd.org.

Family and Community Partnerships

Guidelines: Organizing Learning

Give families specific strategies to help their children practice and remember.

EXAMPLES

1. Develop "super learner" homework assignments that include material to be learned and a "parent coaching card" with a description of a simple memory strategy—appropriate for the material—that parents can teach their child.
2. Provide a few comprehension check questions so a family member can review reading assignments and check the child's understanding.
3. Describe the value of distributed practice and give family members ideas for how and when to work skills practice into home conversations and projects.

Ask family members to share their strategies for organizing and remembering.

EXAMPLES

1. Create a family calendar.
2. Encourage planning discussions in which family members help students break large tasks into smaller jobs, identify goals, and find resources.

Discuss the importance of attention in learning.

EXAMPLES

1. Encourage families to create study spaces that are away from distractions.
2. Make sure parents know the purpose of homework assignments.

For a website directed to high-school study skills that might help parents, see **http://www.mtsu.edu/~studskl/hsindex.html**

For help with parent involvement, see **http://www.nea.org/parents/schoolinvolve.html**

SUMMARY TABLE

Elements of the Cognitive Perspective
(pp. 248–250)

Contrast cognitive and behavioral views of learning in terms of what is learned and the role of reinforcement. In the cognitive view, knowledge is learned, and changes in knowledge make changes in behavior possible. In the behavioral view, the new behaviors themselves are learned. Both behavioral and cognitive theorists believe reinforcement is important in learning, but for different reasons. The strict behaviorist maintains that reinforcement strengthens responses; cognitive theorists see reinforcement as a source of feedback about what is likely to happen if behaviors are repeated or changed—as a source of information.

How does knowledge affect learning? The cognitive approach suggests that one of the most important elements in the learning process is knowledge the individual brings to the learning situation. What we already know determines to a great extent what we will pay attention to, perceive, learn, remember, and forget.

Cognitive view of learning A general approach that views learning as an active mental process of acquiring, remembering, and using knowledge.

Domain-specific knowledge Information that is useful in a particular situation or that applies mainly to one specific topic.

General Knowledge: Information that is useful in many different kinds of tasks; information that applies to many situations.

The Information Processing Model of Memory (pp. 250–257)

Give two explanations for perception. The Gestalt principles are valid explanations of certain aspects of perception, but there are two other kinds of explanations in information processing theory for how we recognize patterns and give meaning to sensory events. The first is called *feature analysis*, or *bottom-up processing*, because the stimulus must be analyzed into features or components and assembled into a meaningful pattern. The second type of perception, *top-down processing*, is based on knowledge and expectation. To recognize patterns rapidly, in addition to noting features, we use what we already know about the situation.

What is working memory? Working memory is both short-term storage in the phonological loop and visuospatial sketchpad and processing guided by the central executive—it is the workbench of conscious thought. To keep information activated in working memory for longer than 20 seconds, people use maintenance rehearsal (mentally repeating) and elaborative rehearsal (making connections with knowledge from long-term memory). Elaboration rehearsal also helps move new information to long-term memory. The limited capacity of working memory can also be somewhat circumvented by the control process of chunking.

Information processing The human mind's activity of taking in, storing, and using information.

Sensory memory System that holds sensory information very briefly.

Perception Interpretation of sensory information.

Gestalt German for *pattern* or *whole*. Gestalt theorists hold that people organize their perceptions into coherent wholes.

Bottom-up processing Perceiving based on noticing separate defining features and assembling them into a recognizable pattern.

Prototype A best example or best representative of a category.

Top-down processing Perceiving based on the context and the patterns you expect to occur in that situation.

Attention Focus on a stimulus.

Automaticity The ability to perform thoroughly learned tasks without much mental effort.

Working memory The information that you are focusing on at a given moment.

Short-Term memory Component of memory system that holds information for about 20 seconds.

Central executive The part of working memory that is responsible for monitoring and directing attention and other mental resources.

Phonological loop Part of working memory. A memory rehearsal system for verbal and sound information of about 1.5 to 2 seconds.

Visuospatial sketchpad Part of working memory. A holding system for visual and spatial information.

Maintenance rehearsal Keeping information in working memory by repeating it to yourself.

Elaborative rehearsal Keeping information in working memory by associating it with something else you already know.

Chunking Grouping individual bits of data into meaningful larger units.

Decay The weakening and fading of memories with the passage of time.

Long-Term Memory: The Goal of Teaching (pp. 257–267)

Compare declarative, procedural, and conditional knowledge. Declarative knowledge is knowledge that can be declared, usually in words or other symbols. Declarative knowledge is "knowing that" something is the case. Procedural knowledge is "knowing how" to do something; it must be demonstrated. Conditional knowledge is "knowing when and why" to apply your declarative and procedural knowledge.

How is information represented in long-term memory, and what role do schemas play? Memories may be explicit (semantic or episodic) or implicit (procedural, classical conditioning, or priming). In long-term memory, bits of information may be stored and interrelated in terms of propositional networks or images and in schemas that are data structures that allow us to represent large amounts of complex information, make inferences, and understand new information.

What learning processes improve long-term memory? The way you learn information in the first place affects its recall later. One important requirement is to integrate new material with knowledge already stored in long-term memory using elaboration, organization, and context. Another view of memory is the levels of processing theory, in which recall of information is determined by how completely it is processed.

Why do we forget? Information lost from working memory truly disappears, but information in long-term memory may be available, given the right cues. Information appears to be lost from long-term memory through time decay (neural connections, like muscles, grow weak without use) and interference (newer memories may obscure older memories, and older memories may interfere with memory for new material).

Long-term memory Permanent store of knowledge.

Long-term working memory Holds the strategies for pulling information from long-term memory into working memory.

Declarative knowledge Verbal information; facts; "knowing that" something is the case.

Procedural knowledge Knowledge that is demonstrated when we perform a task; "knowing how."

Conditional knowledge "Knowing when and why" to use declarative and procedural knowledge.

Explicit memory Long-term memories that involve deliberate or conscious recall.

Implicit memory Knowledge that we are not conscious of recalling, but influences behavior or thought without our awareness.

Semantic memory Memory for meaning.

Propositional network Set of interconnected concepts and relationships in which long-term knowledge is held.

Images Representations based on the physical attributes—the appearance—of information.

Schemas (singular, **schema**) Basic structures for organizing information; concepts.

Story grammar Typical structure or organization for a category of stories.

Script Schema or expected plan for the sequence of steps in a common event such as buying groceries or ordering pizza.

Episodic memory Long-term memory for information tied to a particular time and place, especially memory of the events in a person's life.

Flashbulb memories Clear, vivid memories of emotionally important events in your life.

Procedural memory Long-term memory for how to do things.

Productions The contents of procedural memory; rules about what actions to take, given certain conditions.

Priming Activating a concept in memory or the spread of activation from one concept to another.

Elaboration Adding and extending meaning by connecting new information to existing knowledge.

Organization Ordered and logical network of relations.

Context The physical or emotional backdrop associated with an event.

Levels of processing theory Theory that recall of information is based on how deeply it is processed.

Spreading activation Retrieval of pieces of information based on their relatedness to one another. Remembering one bit of information activates (stimulates) recall of associated information.

Retrieval Process of searching for and finding information in long-term memory.

Reconstruction Recreating information by using memories, expectations, logic, and existing knowledge.

Interference The process that occurs when remembering certain information is hampered by the presence of other information.

Metacognition (pp. 267–269)

What are the three metacognitive skills? The three metacognitive skills used to regulate thinking and learning are planning, monitoring, and evaluating. Planning involves deciding how much time to give to a task, which strategies to use, how to start, and so on. Monitoring is the awareness of "how I'm doing." Evaluating involves making judgments about the processes and outcomes of thinking and learning and acting on those judgments.

How can using better metacognitive strategies improve children's working and long-term memories? Younger children can be taught to use organization to improve memory, but they probably won't apply the strategy unless they are reminded. Children also become more able to use elaboration as they mature, but this strategy is developed late in childhood. Creating images or stories to remember ideas is more likely for older elementary school students and adolescents.

Executive control processes Processes such as selective attention, rehearsal, elaboration, and organization that influence encoding, storage, and retrieval of information in memory.

Metacognition Knowledge about our own thinking processes.

Becoming Knowledgeable: Some Basic Principles (pp. 269–276)

Describe three ways to develop declarative knowledge. Declarative knowledge develops as we integrate new information with our existing understanding. The most useful and effective way to learn and remember is to understand and use new information. Making the information to be remembered meaningful is important and often is the greatest challenge for teachers. Mnemonics are memorization aids: They include peg-type approaches such as the loci method, acronyms, chain mnemonics, and the keyword method. A powerful but limiting way to accomplish this is rote memorization, which can best be supported by part learning and distributed practice.

Describe some methods for developing procedural knowledge. Automated basic skills and domain-specific strategies—two types of procedural knowledge—are learned in different ways. There are three stages in the development of an automated skill: cognitive (following steps or directions guided by declarative knowledge), associative (combining individual steps into larger units), and autonomous (where the whole procedure can be accomplished without much attention). Prerequisite knowledge and practice with feedback help students move through these stages. Domain-specific strategies are consciously applied skills of organizing thoughts and actions to reach a goal. To support this kind of learning, teachers need to provide opportunities for practice and application in many different situations.

Mnemonics Techniques for remembering; the art of memory.

Loci method Technique of associating items with specific places.

Peg-type mnemonics Systems of associating items with cue words.

Acronym Technique for remembering by using the first letter of each word to form a new, memorable word.

Chain mnemonics Memory strategies that associate one element in a series with the next element.

Keyword method System of associating new words or concepts with similar-sounding cue words and images.

Rote memorization Remembering information by repetition without necessarily understanding the meaning of the information.

Serial-position effect The tendency to remember the beginning and the end but not the middle of a list.

Part learning Breaking a list of items into shorter lists.

Distributed practice Practice in brief periods with rest intervals.

Massed practice Practice for a single extended period.

Automated basic skills Skills that are applied without conscious thought.

Domain-specific strategies Consciously applied skills to reach goals in a particular subject or problem area.

Teachers' Casebook: Connections to PRAXIS II™

The predicament that you face in the Teachers' Casebook demonstrates the interconnected nature of the topics of educational psychology. Ask yourself these questions: Am I able to call these students self-regulated learners? What do they understand about the value and demands of the learning tasks that I have presented to them? How extensive is their set of sophisticated learning strategies? Research based on the cognitive perspective addresses these topics and many more.

Knowledge of human memory and learning has influenced nearly every aspect of classroom practice from the design of curricula and tests to the design of textbooks and instructional software. PRAXIS II™ will assess your knowledge of the contributions of the cognitive perspective.

What Would They Do?

Here is how some practicing teachers responded to the teaching situation presented at the beginning of this chapter about history students intent on memorizing.

Mark Smith Ninth–Twelfth Grade Teacher,
Medford High School, Medford, Massachusetts

The students in this class have always used memorization, and although they have probably been somewhat successful in the past, there comes a point where learners must get into higher-level thinking. Because this is a senior history class and many of these students will be heading off to college, they must be taught different ways of learning and thinking.

A critical piece of learning is being able to debate a topic and do so with a convincing argument. If I were the teacher in this class and the students were so worried about tests and grades, I would add more oral presentations and writing assignments that make the students think about the facts and try to analyze the information. Knowing facts and details in history is not as important as understanding how they affected the present and why the past is important for today and tomorrow.

Ashley Dodge Ninth and Tenth Grade Teacher,
Los Angeles Unified School District, Los Angeles, California

These students are obviously using strategies that have worked for them in the past (memorization and regurgitation of facts and dates), but they have not developed any critical thinking skills. Many students are very successful with these techniques up to a certain point. They become obsessed with learning only what is necessary to pass the class.

In order to give these students the opportunity to see history as something more than a time line, I would announce to the class that for the next unit, there would be no test. Instead, we would create projects reflective of the era. Perhaps we would produce a play, a fashion show with period clothing, or a festival. Some students may wish to construct a city at the time being studied, focusing on the differences in the city as it was then compared to now. The students would need to use the information in the text to incorporate their ideas into their projects, but it would not need to be memorized. They would be graded on both the originality and the quality of their work, and the project grade would count as two unit grades.

Mitchell D. Klett Twelfth Grade Teacher,
A.C. New Middle School, Springs, Texas

Students need to understand that the events of the past have a profound influence on the world today. The adage, "those who don't know history are doomed to repeat it," rings true. As their teacher, I would emphasize cause-and-effect relationships throughout history and compare them with one another. By focusing on the causes of specific events, such as revolutions caused by economic rifts, students can better understand the cyclic nature of these types of revolutions. Events such as the French Revolution and the Russian Revolution could be examined through inquiry learning, group discussion, or role playing. Students could be given the opportunity to explore the nature of revolutions and apply what they have learned to new situations.

Madya Ayala High School Teacher of Preperatoria Eugenio Garza Lagüera,
Campus Garza Sada, Monterrey, N.L. Mexico

I observe that there are two existing conflicts. First, the students' available cognitive strategies (memorizing) don't fit the assigned task (higher-level thinking). Second, the students can't see connections between current situations and past events. For the first conflict I would use cognitive strategies such as mind mapping, schemas, comparative tables, and other advanced organizers that would enable students to learn the material. For the second, I'd recommend establishing a relationship between past and present realities by focusing students' attention on an important event from the past and asking them to link it to a present-day international, national, local, or even a social problem, perhaps one that is happening in their school.

Kimberly D. Bridgers Kindergarten Teacher,
Dodson Elementary, Hermitage, Tennessee

Get out of the textbook! Make history relevant by "updating" the issues to hook students before ever talking about dates. I always lay out the situation first before going into what period we're talking about. For example, the American Revolution is essentially about some folks trying hard just to get by when the "big rich man" starts taking what little money they have so that he gets richer. Put into these terms, my inner city students immediately understood and sympathized with the colonists. Suddenly, they wanted to know how the colonists stopped the king because it just might help them. Then, we'll do some role playing and reenactments, which they really get into! Once the historical situation has become personal for them, then they're ready to read the text for all of the "juicy details."

CHAPTER 8

Complex Cognitive Processes

Teachers' Casebook: What Would You Do? 285

Learning and Teaching about Concepts 286

Views of Concept Learning 286

Strategies for Teaching Concepts 287

Teaching Concepts through Discovery 290

Teaching Concepts through Exposition 292

Reaching Every Student: Learning Disabilities and Concept Teaching 294

Problem Solving 294

Identifying: Problem Finding 295

Defining Goals and Representing the Problem 296

Exploring Possible Solution Strategies 298

Anticipating, Acting, and Looking Back 300

Factors That Hinder Problem Solving 302

Effective Problem Solving: What Do the Experts Do? 303

Creativity and Creative Problem Solving 305

Defining Creativity 306

What Are the Sources of Creativity? 307

Assessing Creativity 307

Creativity in the Classroom 309

The Big C: Revolutionary Innovation 310

Becoming an Expert Student: Learning Strategies and Study Skills 311

Learning Strategies and Tactics 311

Visual Tools for Organizing 314

Reading Strategies 314

Applying Learning Strategies 316

Teaching for Transfer 319

The Many Views of Transfer 319

Teaching for Positive Transfer 320

Diversity and Convergences in Complex Cognitive Processes 322

Diversity 322

Convergences 323

Summary Table 324

Teachers' Casebook: Connections to PRAXIS II™/ What Would They Do? 327

What Would You Do?

Teachers' Casebook

You know that your students need good study skills to do well in both their current and future classes. But many of the students just don't seem to know how to study. They can't read a longer assignment, understand it, and remember what they read. They have trouble completing larger projects—many wait until the last minute. They can't organize their work or decide what is most important. You are concerned because they will need all of these skills and strategies as they progress through their education. You have so much material to cover to meet district guidelines, but many of your students are just drowning in the amount of work.

Critical Thinking

- What study skills do students need for your subject or class?
- What could you do to teach these skills, while still covering the material that will be on the proficiency or achievement tests the students will have to take in the spring?

Collaboration

With 3 or 4 members of your class, identify the learning skills and study strategies that students will need in a grade you might teach. Then analyze the study skills necessary for your class using this text.

We focused on the development of knowledge—how people make sense of and remember information and ideas—in the previous chapter. In this chapter, we consider complex cognitive processes that lead to understanding. Understanding is more than memorizing. It is more than retelling in your own words. Understanding involves appropriately *transforming* and *using* knowledge, skills, and ideas. These understandings are considered "higher-level cognitive objectives" in a commonly used system of educational objectives (Anderson & Krathwohl, 2001; Bloom, Engelhart, Frost, Hill, & Krathwohl, 1956). We will focus on the implications of cognitive theories for the day-to-day practice of teaching.

Because the cognitive perspective is a philosophical orientation and not a unified theoretical model, teaching methods derived from it are varied. In this chapter, we will first examine four important areas in which cognitive theorists have made suggestions for learning and teaching: concept learning, problem solving, creativity, and learning strategies and tactics. Finally, we will explore the question of how to encourage the transfer of learning from one situation to another to make learning more useful.

By the time you have completed this chapter, you should be able to answer these questions:

- What are the characteristics of a good lesson for teaching a key concept in your subject area?
- What are the steps in solving complex problems?
- What are the roles of problem representation, algorithms, and heuristics in problem solving?
- How can teachers encourage creativity in their students?
- How could you apply new learning strategies and tactics to prepare for tests and assignments in your current courses?
- What are three ways a teacher might encourage positive transfer of learning?

FACING PAGE *Claude & Paloma*, 1954. Pablo Picasso.

Learning and Teaching about Concepts

STOP | THINK | WRITE What makes a cup a cup? List the characteristics of *cupness.* What is a fruit? Is a banana a fruit? Is a tomato a fruit? How about a squash? A watermelon? A sweet potato? An olive? How did you learn what makes a fruit a fruit? ■

Connect and **Extend** to Your **Teaching/Portfolio**

According to Piaget, a person cannot think in abstract terms until the stage of formal operations is reached. How then can a child learn abstract concepts such as "yesterday" and "happy"? Can abstract concepts be taught through the use of prototypes?

Most of what we know about cups and fruits and the world involves concepts and relations among concepts (Ashcraft, 2006). But what exactly is a concept? A **concept** is a category used to group similar events, ideas, objects, or people. When we talk about a particular concept such as *student,* we refer to a category of people who are similar to one another—they all study a subject. The people may be old or young, in school or not; they may be studying baseball or Bach, but they all can be categorized as students. Concepts are abstractions. They do not exist in the real world. Only individual examples of concepts exist. Concepts help us organize vast amounts of information into manageable units. For instance, there are about 7.5 million distinguishable differences in colors. By categorizing these colors into some dozen or so groups, we manage to deal with this diversity quite well (Bruner, 1973).

Views of Concept Learning

In early research, psychologists assumed that concepts share a set of **defining attributes,** or distinctive features. For example, books all contain pages that are bound together in some way (but what about electronic "books"?). The defining attributes theory of concepts suggests that we recognize specific examples by noting key required features.

Since about 1970, however, these views about the nature of concepts have been challenged (Ashcraft, 2006). Although some concepts, such as equilateral triangle, have clear-cut defining attributes, most concepts do not. Take the concept of *party.* What are the defining attributes? You might have difficulty listing these attributes, but you probably recognize a party when you see or hear one (unless, of course we are talking about political parties, or the other party in a lawsuit, where the sound might not help you recognize the "party"). What about the concept of *bird*? Your first thought might be that birds are animals that fly. But is an ostrich a bird? What about a penguin? A bat?

Prototypes and Exemplars. Current views of concept learning suggest that we have in our minds a prototype of a party and a bird—an image that captures the essence of each concept. A **prototype** is the best representative of its category. For instance, the best representative of the "birds" category for many North Americans might be a robin (Rosch, 1973). Other members of the category may be very similar to the prototype (sparrow) or similar in some ways but different in others (chicken, ostrich). At the boundaries of a category, it may be difficult to determine if a particular instance really belongs. For example, is a telephone "furniture"? Is an elevator a "vehicle"? Is an olive a "fruit"? Whether something fits into a category is a matter of degree. Thus, categories have fuzzy boundaries. Some events, objects, or ideas are simply better examples of a concept than others (Ashcraft, 2006).

Another explanation of concept learning suggests that we identify members of a category by referring to exemplars. **Exemplars** are our actual memories of specific birds, parties, furniture, and so on that we use to compare with an item in question to see if that item belongs in the same category as our exemplar. For example, if you see a strange steel-and-stone bench in a public park, you may compare it to the sofa in your living room to decide if the uncomfortable-looking creation is still for sitting or if it has crossed a fuzzy boundary into "sculpture."

Prototypes probably are built from experiences with many exemplars. This happens naturally because episodic memories of particular events tend to blur together over time, creating an average or typical sofa prototype from all the sofa exemplars you have experienced (Schwartz & Reisberg, 1991).

Concept A general category of ideas, objects, people, or experiences whose members share certain properties.

Defining attributes Distinctive features shared by members of a category.

Prototype Best representative of a category.

Exemplar A specific example of a given category that is used to classify an item.

Concepts and Schemas. In addition to prototypes and exemplars, there is a third element involved when we recognize a concept—our schematic knowledge related to the concept. How do we know that counterfeit money is not "real" money, even though it perfectly fits our "money" prototype and exemplars? We know because of its history. The "wrong" people printed the money. So our understanding of the concept of money is connected with concepts of crime, forgery, the federal treasury, and many others.

Jacob Feldman (2003) suggests a final aspect of concept learning—the simplicity principle. Feldman says that when humans are confronted with examples, they induce the simplest category or rule that would cover all the examples. Sometimes it is easy to come up with a simple rule (triangles) and sometimes it is more difficult (fruit), but humans seek a simple hypothesis for collecting all the examples under one concept. Feldman suggests that this simplicity principle is one of the oldest ideas in cognitive psychology: "organisms seek to understand their environment by reducing incoming information to a simpler, more coherent, and more useful form" (p. 231). Does this remind you of the Gestalt principles of perception in Chapter 7?

Connect and Extend to PRAXIS II™

Teaching Concepts (II, A2)
Teachers devote much effort to the development of concepts that are vital in learning subject matter and skills. Understand the major approaches to teaching concepts and be able to describe their strengths and limitations.

Strategies for Teaching Concepts

WHAT WOULD YOU SAY?

You are interviewing for a job in a school that serves many immigrant families. The principal asks, "How would you teach abstract concepts to a student who just arrived from Somalia and can't even read in her native language, much less English?" ■

Both prototypes and defining attributes are important in learning. Children first learn many concepts in the real world from the best examples or prototypes, pointed out by adults (Tennyson, 1981). But when examples are ambiguous (is an olive a fruit?), we may consult the defining attributes to make a decision. Olives are foods with seeds in the edible parts, which matches the defining attributes for fruits, so they must be fruits, even though they are not typical or prototypic fruits (Schunk, 2004).

Like the learning of concepts, the teaching of concepts can combine both defining attributes and prototypes. One approach to teaching about concepts is called *concept attainment*—a way of helping students construct an understanding of specific concepts and practice thinking skills such as hypothesis testing (Joyce, Weil, & Calhoun, 2006; Klausmeier, 1992).

Concepts have many attributes and may not remain constant, for example recent technological applications such as instant messaging may have changed the concept of "conversation."

"City children have trouble with the concept of harvest."

© Martha Campbell—From *Phi Delta Kappan*. Reprinted by permission.

An Example Concept-Attainment Lesson. Here is how a 5th-grade teacher helped his students learn about a familiar concept and practice thinking skills at the same time (Eggen & Kauchak, 2001, pp. 148–151). The teacher began a lesson by saying that he had an idea in mind and wanted students to "figure out what it is." He placed two signs on a table—"Examples" and "Nonexamples." Then he placed an apple in front of the "Examples" sign and a rock in front of the "Nonexamples" sign. He asked his students, "What do you think the idea might be?" "Things we eat" was the first suggestion. The teacher wrote "HYPOTHESES" on the board and, after a brief discussion of the meaning of "hypotheses," listed "things we eat" under this heading. Next he asked for other hypotheses—"living things" and "things that grow on plants" came next. After some discussion about plants and living things, the teacher brought out a tomato for the "Examples" side and a carrot for the "Nonexamples." Animated reconsideration of all the hypotheses followed these additions and a new hypothesis—"red things"—was suggested. Through discussion of more examples (peach, squash, orange) and nonexamples (lettuce, artichoke, potato), the students narrowed their hypothesis to "things with seeds in the parts you eat." The students had "constructed" the concept of "fruit"—foods with seeds in the edible parts (or, a more advanced definition, any engorged ovary, such as a pea pod, nut, tomato, pineapple, or the edible part of the plant developed from a flower).

Lesson Components. Whatever strategy you use for teaching concepts, you will need four components in any lesson: examples and nonexamples, relevant and irrelevant attributes, the name of the concept, and a definition (Joyce, Weil, & Calhoun, 2006). In addition, visual aids such as pictures, diagrams, or maps can improve learning of many concepts (Anderson & Smith, 1987; Mayer, 2001).

Examples. More examples are needed in teaching complicated concepts and in working with younger or less knowledgeable students. Both examples and nonexamples (sometimes called positive and negative instances) are necessary to make the boundaries of the category clear. A discussion of why a bat is not a bird (nonexample) will help students define the boundaries of the bird concept.

Relevant and Irrelevant Attributes. The ability to fly, as we've seen, is not a relevant attribute for classifying animals as birds. Even though many birds fly, some birds do not (ostrich, penguin), and some nonbirds do (bats, flying squirrels). The ability to fly would have to be included in a discussion of the bird concept, but students should understand that flying alone does not define an animal as a bird.

Name. Simply learning a label does not mean the person understands the concept, although the label is necessary for the understanding. In the example above, students probably already used the "fruit" name, but may not have understood that tomatoes, squash, and avocados are fruits.

Definition. A good definition has two elements: a reference to any more general category for the new concept, and a statement of the new concept's defining attributes (Klausmeier, 1976). For example, a fruit is food (general category) with seeds in the edible parts (defining attributes). An equilateral triangle is a plane, a simple, closed figure (general category), with three equal sides and three equal angles (defining attributes). This kind of definition helps place the concept in a schema of related knowledge.

In teaching some concepts, "a picture is worth a thousand words"—or at least a few hundred, as we saw in Chapter 7. Handling specific examples, or pictures of examples, helps young children learn concepts. For students of all ages, the complex concepts in history, science, and mathematics can often be illustrated in diagrams or graphs. For example, Anderson and Smith (1983) found that when their students just read about the

FIGURE 8.1

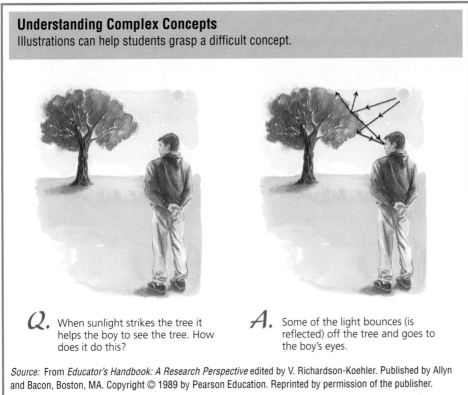

Understanding Complex Concepts
Illustrations can help students grasp a difficult concept.

Q. When sunlight strikes the tree it helps the boy to see the tree. How does it do this?

A. Some of the light bounces (is reflected) off the tree and goes to the boy's eyes.

Source: From *Educator's Handbook: A Research Perspective* edited by V. Richardson-Koehler. Published by Allyn and Bacon, Boston, MA. Copyright © 1989 by Pearson Education. Reprinted by permission of the publisher.

concept of light, only 20% could understand the role of reflected light in our ability to see objects. But when the students worked with diagrams such as the one in Figure 8.1, almost 80% understood the concept.

Lesson Structure. The fruit lesson above is an example of good concept teaching for several reasons. First, it is more effective to examine examples and nonexamples before discussing attributes or definitions (Joyce, Weil, & Calhoun, 2000). Start your concept lesson with prototypes, or best examples, to help the students establish the category. In the fruit lesson, the teacher began with the classic fruit example, an apple, then moved to less typical examples such as tomatoes and squash. These examples show the wide range of possibilities the category includes and the variety of irrelevant attributes within a category. Including fruits that have one seed or many, have a sweet taste or not, are different colors, and have thick or thin skin, will prevent **undergeneralization,** or the exclusion of some foods, such as squash, from their rightful place in the category fruit.

Nonexamples should be very close to the concept, but miss by one or just a few critical attributes. For instance, sweet potatoes and rhubarb are *not* fruits, even though sweet potatoes are sweet and rhubarb is used to make pies. Including nonexamples will prevent **overgeneralization,** or the inclusion of substances that are not fruits.

After the students seem to have grasped the concept under consideration, it is useful to ask them to think about the ways that they formed and tested their hypotheses. Thinking back helps students develop their metacognitive skills and shows them that different people approach problems in different ways (Joyce, Weil, & Calhoun, 2006).

Extending and Connecting Concepts. Once students have a good sense of a concept, they should use it. This might mean doing exercises, solving problems, writing, reading, explaining, or any other activity that requires them to apply their new understanding. This will connect the concept into the students' web of related schematic knowledge. One approach that you may see in some texts and workbooks for students above the primary

Undergeneralization Exclusion of some true members from a category; limiting a concept.

Overgeneralization Inclusion of nonmembers in a category; overextending a concept.

TABLE 8.1

Phases of the Concept Attainment Model
There are three main phases in concept attainment teaching. First the teacher presents examples/nonexamples and students identify the concept, then the teacher checks for understanding, and finally students analyze their thinking strategies.

Phase One: Presentation of Data and Identification of Concept	Phase Two: Testing Attainment of the Concept	Phase Three: Analysis of Thinking Strategies
Teacher presents labeled examples.	Students identify additional unlabeled examples as yes or no.	Students describe thoughts.
Students compare attributes in positive and negative examples.	Teacher confirms hypotheses, names concept, and restates definitions according to essential attributes.	Students discuss role of hypotheses and attributes.
Students generate and test hypotheses.	Students generate examples.	Students discuss type and number of hypotheses.
Students state a definition according to the essential attributes.		

Source: From *Models of Teaching, 6/e* by Bruce Joyce and Marsha Weil. Published by Allyn and Bacon, Boston, MA.

grades is **concept mapping** (Novak & Musonda, 1991). Students "diagram" their understanding of the concept, as Amy has in Figure 8.2. Amy's map shows a reasonable understanding of the concept of "molecule," but also indicates that Amy holds one misconception. She thinks that there is no space between the molecules in solids.

Table 8.1 summarizes the phases of the concept attainment model.

Connect and **Extend** to **PRAXIS II**™
Concept Mapping (II, A2)
For advice and additional information about the creation and use of concept maps, go to the website *Graphic Organizers* (http://www.graphic.org/concept.html).

Connect and **Extend** to **PRAXIS II**™
Reasoning (II, A1)
Be able to distinguish between inductive and deductive reasoning. Explain the role that each plays in the learning of concepts.

Teaching Concepts through Discovery

Jerome Bruner's early research on thinking (Bruner, Goodnow, & Austin, 1956) inspired his interest in educational approaches that encourage concept learning and the development of thinking. Bruner's work emphasized the importance of understanding the structure of a subject being studied, the need for active learning as the basis for true understanding, and the value of inductive reasoning in learning.

Structure and Discovery. Subject structure refers to the fundamental ideas, relationships, or patterns of the field—the essential information. Because structure does not include specific facts or details, the essential structure of an idea can be represented simply as a diagram, a set of principles, or a formula. According to Bruner, learning will be more meaningful, useful, and memorable for students if they focus on understanding the structure of the subject being studied.

In order to grasp the structure of information, Bruner believes, students must be active—they must identify key principles for themselves rather than simply accepting teachers' explanations. This process has been called **discovery learning.** In discovery learning, the teacher presents examples and the students work with the examples until they discover the interrelationships—the subject's structure. Thus, Bruner believes that classroom learning should take place through **inductive reasoning,** that is, by using specific examples to formulate a general principle. The concept attainment lesson on fruit above used this approach.

Discovery in Action. An inductive approach requires **intuitive thinking** on the part of students. Bruner suggests that teachers can nurture this intuitive thinking by encouraging students to make guesses based on incomplete evidence and then to confirm or disprove the guesses systematically (Bruner, 1960). After learning about ocean currents and the shipping industry, for example, students might be shown old maps of three harbors and asked to guess which one became a major port. Then, they could check their guesses through systematic research. Unfortunately, educational practices often discourage intuitive thinking by punishing wrong guesses and rewarding safe, but uncreative answers.

Concept mapping Student's diagram of his or her understanding of a concept.

Discovery learning Bruner's approach, in which students work on their own to discover basic principles.

Inductive reasoning Formulating general principles based on knowledge of examples and details.

Intuitive thinking Making imaginative leaps to correct perceptions or workable solutions.

FIGURE 8.2

Amy's Molecule

Amy, an 8th grader, has drawn a map to represent her understanding of the concept of "molecule." Her concept includes one misconception—that there is no space between molecules in solids.

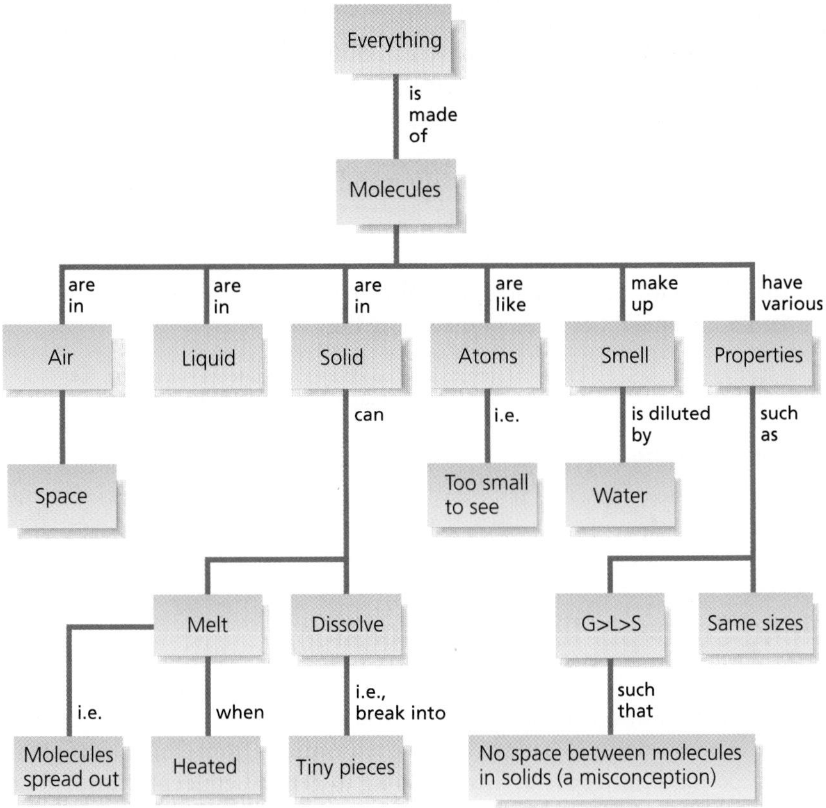

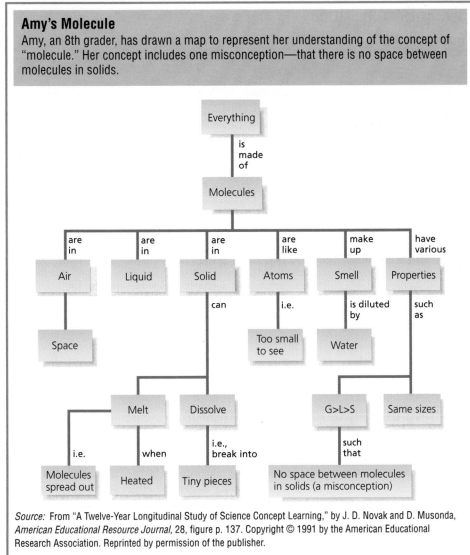

Source: From "A Twelve-Year Longitudinal Study of Science Concept Learning," by J. D. Novak and D. Musonda, *American Educational Resource Journal,* 28, figure p. 137. Copyright © 1991 by the American Educational Research Association. Reprinted by permission of the publisher.

A distinction is usually made between pure discovery learning, in which the students work on their own to a very great extent, and **guided discovery,** in which the teacher provides some direction. Reviewing 30 years of research on pure discovery learning, Richard Mayer (2004) concludes:

> Like some zombie that keeps returning from its grave, pure discovery continues to have its advocates. However, anyone who takes an evidence-based approach to educational practice must ask the same question: Where is the evidence that it works? In spite of calls for free discovery in every decade, the supporting evidence is hard to find. (p. 17)

Unguided or pure discovery may be appropriate for preschool children, but in a typical elementary or secondary classroom, unguided activities usually prove unmanageable and unproductive. For these situations, guided discovery is preferable. Students are presented with intriguing questions, baffling situations, or interesting problems: Why does the flame go out when we cover it with a jar? Why does this pencil seem to bend when you put it in water? What is the rule for grouping these words together? Instead of explaining how to solve the problem, the teacher provides the appropriate materials and encourages students to make observations, form hypotheses, and test solutions. Turn the page for more *Guidelines* to help you apply Bruner's suggestions.

Connect and **Extend** to **PRAXIS II™**

Discovery Learning (I, A1)
Many teachers, especially in mathematics and science, believe that meaningful learning in their areas is best supported by discovery learning. Be prepared to answer questions about the assumptions, techniques, strengths, and limitations of this instructional strategy.

Guided discovery An adaptation of discovery learning, in which the teacher provides some direction.

Guidelines: Applying Bruner's Ideas

Present both examples and nonexamples of the concepts you are teaching.

EXAMPLES

1. In teaching about mammals, include people, kangaroos, whales, cats, dolphins, and camels as examples, and chickens, fish, alligators, frogs, and penguins as nonexamples.
2. Ask students for additional examples and nonexamples.

Encourage students to make intuitive guesses.

EXAMPLES

1. Instead of giving a word's definition, say, "Let's guess what it might mean by looking at the words around it."
2. Give students a map of ancient Greece and ask where they think the major cities were.
3. Don't comment after the first few guesses. Wait for several ideas before giving the answer.
4. Use guiding questions to focus students when their discovery has led them too far astray.

Help students see connections among concepts.

EXAMPLES

1. Ask questions such as these: What else could you call this apple? (Fruit.) What do we do with fruit? (Eat.) What do we call things we eat? (Food.)
2. Use diagrams, outlines, and summaries to point out connections.

Pose a question and let students try to find the answer.

EXAMPLES

1. How could the human hand be improved?
2. What is the relation between the area of one tile and the area of the whole floor?

For more information on Bruner and discovery learning, see: **http://evolution.massey.ac.nz/assign2/HB/jbruner.html**

Teaching Concepts through Exposition

In contrast to Bruner, David Ausubel (1963, 1977, 1982) believed that people acquire knowledge primarily through reception, not discovery. Concepts, principles, and ideas are presented and understood using **deductive reasoning**—from general ideas to specific cases, not discovered from specific cases leading to general concepts. Ausubel's **expository teaching** model stresses what is known as **meaningful verbal learning**—verbal information, ideas, and relationships among ideas, taken together. Rote memorization is not meaningful learning, because material learned by rote is not *connected* with existing knowledge.

Connect and Extend to PRAXIS II™

Advance Organizers (II, A3)

The advance organizer is an important element in many teacher-centered/expository approaches to instruction. Be able to explain the role of the advance organizer in these approaches, and identify the basic types of organizers.

Advance Organizers. Ausubel's strategy always begins with an **advance organizer.** This is an introductory statement broad enough to encompass all the information that will follow. The organizers can serve three purposes: They direct your attention to what is important in the coming material, they highlight relationships among ideas that will be presented, and they remind you of relevant information you already have.

In general, advance organizers fall into one of two categories, *comparative* and *expository* (Mayer, 1984). Comparative organizers *activate* (bring into working memory) already existing schemas. They remind you of what you already know, but may not realize is relevant. A comparative advance organizer for a history lesson on revolutions might be a statement that contrasts military uprisings with the physical and social changes involved in the Industrial Revolution; you could also compare the common aspects of the French, English, Mexican, Russian, Iranian, and American revolutions (Salomon & Perkins, 1989).

In contrast, *expository organizers* provide *new* knowledge that students will need to understand the upcoming information. In an English class, you might begin a large thematic unit on rites of passage in literature with a very broad statement of the theme and why it has been so central in literature—something like, "A central character coming of age must learn to know himself or herself, often makes some kind of journey of self-discovery, and must decide what in the society is to be accepted and what rejected."

Deductive reasoning Drawing conclusions by applying rules or principles; logically moving from a general rule or principle to a specific solution.

Expository teaching Ausubel's method—teachers present material in complete, organized form, moving from broadest to more specific concepts.

Meaningful verbal learning Focused and organized relationships among ideas and verbal information.

Advance organizer Statement of inclusive concepts to introduce and sum up material that follows.

Expository teaching methods present information to learners in an organized, "finished" form, rather than having them discover it themselves.

The general conclusion of research on advance organizers (Corkill, 1992; Langan-Fox, Waycott, & Albert, 2000; Morin & Miller, 1998) is that they do help students learn, especially when the material to be learned is quite unfamiliar, complex, or difficult—if two conditions are met. First, to be effective, the organizer must be understood by the students. This was demonstrated dramatically in a study by Dinnel and Glover (1985). They found that instructing students to paraphrase an advance organizer—which, of course, requires them to understand its meaning—increased the effectiveness of the organizer. Second, the organizer must really be an organizer: It must indicate relations among the basic concepts and terms that will be used. Concrete models, diagrams, or analogies seem to be especially good organizers (Robinson, 1998; Robinson & Kiewra, 1995).

Connect and **Extend** to the **Research**

Explanatory analogies can help children acquire information from expository text. For example, "an infection is like a war," "a stomach is like a blender" (Vosniadou & Schommer, 1988).

Steps in an Expository Lesson. After the advance organizer, the next step is to present content in terms of similarities and differences using specific examples, perhaps provided by the students themselves. Assume you are teaching the coming-of-age theme in literature, using *The Diary of Anne Frank* and *The Adventures of Huckleberry Finn.* As the students read, you might ask them to compare the central character's growth, state of mind, and position in society with characters from other novels, plays, and films (connect to students' prior knowledge). Then students can compare Anne Frank's inner journey with Huck Finn's trip down the Mississippi. As comparisons are made, you should underscore the goal of the lesson and elaborate the advance organizer.

The best way to point out similarities and differences is with examples. Huck Finn's and Anne Frank's dilemmas must be clear. Finally, when all the material has been presented, ask students to discuss how the examples can be used to expand on the original advance organizer. The phases of expository teaching are summarized in Figure 8.3.

Expository teaching is more developmentally appropriate for students at or above later elementary school, that is, around the 5th or 6th grade (Luiten, Ames, & Ackerson, 1980). The *Guidelines* on the next page should help you follow the main steps in expository teaching.

FIGURE 8.3

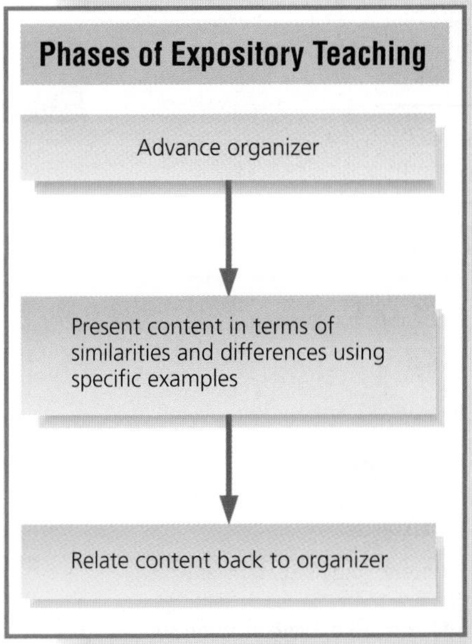
Phases of Expository Teaching
Advance organizer
Present content in terms of similarities and differences using specific examples
Relate content back to organizer

Guidelines: Applying Ausubel's Ideas

Use advance organizers.

EXAMPLES

1. *English:* Shakespeare used the social ideas of his time as a framework for his plays—*Julius Caesar, Hamlet,* and *Macbeth* dealt with concepts of natural order, a nation as the human body, etc.
2. *Social studies:* Geography dictates economy in preindustrialized regions or nations.
3. *History:* Important concepts during the Renaissance were symmetry, admiration of the classical world, the centrality of the human mind.

Use a number of examples.

EXAMPLES

1. In mathematics class, ask students to point out all the examples of right angles that they can find in the room.
2. In teaching about islands and peninsulas, use maps, slides, models, postcards.

Focus on both similarities and differences.

EXAMPLES

1. In a history class, ask students to list the ways in which the North and South were alike and different before the Civil War.
2. In a biology class, ask students how they would transform spiders into insects or an amphibian into a reptile.

For more information on advance organizers, see: **http://moodle.ed.uiuc.edu/wiked/index.php/Advance_organizers**

Reaching Every Student: Learning Disabilities and Concept Teaching

A recent approach to teaching concepts that also emphasizes connections with prior knowledge is called **analogical instruction** (Bulgren, Deshler, Schumaker, & Lenz, 2000). This approach has proved helpful for teaching scientific or cultural knowledge in heterogeneous secondary classes that include students who are less academically prepared and students with learning disabilities. In secondary classrooms, as the amount and complexity of content increases, these students are especially at risk for failure. The goal of analogical instruction is to identify knowledge that these students already have in memory that can be used as a starting point for learning the new, complex material. Analogies have long been used in problem solving, as you will see in the next section, but until recently, studies of analogies in teaching content have been rare.

Problem Solving

WHAT WOULD YOU SAY?

You're interviewing with the district superintendent for a position as a school psychologist. The man is known for his unorthodox interview questions. He hands you a pad of paper and a ruler and says, "Tell me, what is the exact thickness of a single sheet of paper?" ■

This is a true story—I was asked the paper thickness question in an interview years ago. The answer was to measure the thickness of the entire pad and divide by the number of pages in the pad. I got the answer and the job, but what a tense moment that was. I suppose the superintendent was interested in my ability to solve problems—under pressure!

A **problem** has an initial state (the current situation), a goal (the desired outcome), and a path for reaching the goal (including operations or activities that move you toward the goal). Problem solvers often have to set and reach subgoals as they move toward the final solution. For example, if your goal is to drive to the beach, but at the first

Analogical instruction Teaching new concepts by making connections (analogies) with information that the student already understands.

Problem Any situation in which you are trying to reach some goal and must find a means to do so.

stop sign you skid through the intersection, you may have to reach a subgoal of fixing your brakes before you can continue toward the original goal (Schunk, 2004). Also, problems can range from *well-structured* to *ill-structured*, depending on how clear-cut the goal is and how much structure is provided for solving the problem. Most arithmetic problems are well-structured, but finding the right college major is ill-structured—many different solutions and paths to solutions are possible. Life presents many ill-structured problems.

Problem solving is usually defined as formulating new answers, going beyond the simple application of previously learned rules to achieve a goal. Problem solving is what happens when no solution is obvious—when, for example, you can't afford new brakes for the car that skidded on the way to the beach (Mayer & Wittrock, 1996). Some psychologists suggest that most human learning involves problem solving (Anderson, 1993).

Connect and Extend to the Research

You might want to note that, although interest in problem solving is great today, many of the early ideas of John Dewey are consistent with the recent emphasis on teaching students to be effective problem solvers.

There is a debate about problem solving. Some psychologists believe that effective problem-solving strategies are specific to the problem area. That is, the problem-solving strategies in mathematics are unique to math; the strategies in art are unique to art, and so on. The other side of the debate claims that there are some general problem-solving strategies that can be useful in many areas. Actually, there is evidence for both sides of the argument. In their research with 8- to 12-year-olds, Robert Kail and Lynda Hall (1999) found that both domain-specific and general factors affected performance on arithmetic word problems. The influences were *arithmetic knowledge*—assessed by the time needed and errors produced in solving simple addition and subtraction problems—and *general information-processing skills*, including reading and information processing time and, to a lesser extent, memory span.

It appears that people move between general and specific approaches, depending on the situation and their level of expertise. Early on, when we know little about a problem area or domain, we can rely on general learning and problem-solving strategies to make sense of the situation. As we gain more domain-specific knowledge (particularly procedural knowledge about how to do things in the domain), we consciously apply the general strategies less and less; our problem solving becomes more automatic. But if we encounter a problem outside our current knowledge, we may return to relying on general strategies to attack the problem (Alexander, 1992, 1996; Shuell, 1990).

Let's consider general problem-solving strategies first. Think of a general problem-solving strategy as a beginning point, a broad outline. Such strategies usually have five stages (Derry, 1991; Gallini, 1991; Gick, 1986). John Bransford and Barry Stein (1993) use the acronym IDEAL to identify the five steps:

Connect and Extend to PRAXIS II™

Problem Solving (II, A1)

Be prepared to identify the steps in the general problem-solving process. Describe the techniques that students can employ to build useful representations of problems.

I *Identify* problems and opportunities.
D *Define* goals and represent the problem.
E *Explore* possible strategies.
A *Anticipate* outcomes and *Act*.
L *Look* back and *Learn*.

We will examine each of these steps because they are found in many approaches to problem solving.

Identifying: Problem Finding

The first step, identifying that a problem exists and treating the problem as an opportunity, begins the process. This is not always straightforward. There is a story about tenants who were angry because the elevators in their building were slow. Consultants hired to "fix the problem" reported that the elevators were no worse than average and that improvements would be very expensive. One day, as the building supervisor watched people waiting impatiently for an elevator, he realized that the problem was not slow elevators, but the fact that people were bored; they had nothing to do while they waited. When the boredom problem was identified and seen as an opportunity to improve the "waiting experience," the simple solution of installing a mirror by the elevator on each floor eliminated complaints.

Problem solving Creating new solutions for problems.

Identifying the problem is a critical first step. Research indicates that people often hurry through this important step and "leap" to naming the first problem that comes to mind ("the elevators are too slow!"). Experts in a field are more likely to spend time carefully considering the nature of the problem (Bruning, Schraw, Norby, & Ronning, 2004). Finding a solvable problem and turning it into an opportunity is the process behind many successful inventions, such as the ballpoint pen, garbage disposal, appliance timer, alarm clock, self-cleaning oven, and thousands of others.

Once a *solvable* problem is identified, what next?

Defining Goals and Representing the Problem

Let's take a real problem: The machines designed to pick tomatoes are damaging the tomatoes. What should we do? If we represent the problem as a faulty machine design, then the goal is to improve the machine. But if we represent the problem as a faulty design of the tomatoes, then the goal is to develop a tougher tomato. The problem-solving process follows two entirely different paths, depending on which representation and goal are chosen (Bransford & Stein, 1993). To represent the problem and set a goal, you have to *focus attention* on relevant information, *understand* the words of the problem, and *activate the right schema* to understand the whole problem.

STOP | THINK | WRITE If you have black socks and white socks in your drawer, mixed in the ratio of four to five, how many socks will you have to take out to make sure you have a pair the same color (adapted from Sternberg & Davidson, 1982)? ■

Focusing Attention. Representing the problem often requires finding the relevant information and ignoring the irrelevant details. For example, what information was relevant in solving the above sock problem? Did you realize that the information about the four-to-five ratio of black socks to white socks is irrelevant? As long as you have only two different colors of socks in the drawer, you will have to remove only three socks before two of them have to match.

Connect and **Extend** to **Other Chapters**

Piaget (Chapter 2) identified children's difficulties with part–whole relations years ago when he asked questions such as, "There are six daisies and two daffodils; are there more daisies or flowers?" Young children usually answer, "Daisies!"

Understanding the Words. The second task in representing a story problem is understanding the meaning of the words and sentences (Mayer, 1992). For example, the main stumbling block in representing many word problems is the students' understanding of *part-whole relations* (Cummins, 1991). Students have trouble figuring out what is part of what, as is evident in this dialogue between a teacher and a 1st grader:

Teacher: Pete has three apples. Ann also has some apples. Pete and Ann have nine apples altogether. How many apples does Ann have?
Student: Nine.
Teacher: Why?
Student: Because you just said so.
Teacher: Can you retell the story?
Student: Pete had three apples. Ann also had some apples. Ann had nine apples. Pete also has nine apples. (Adapted from De Corte & Verschaffel, 1985, p. 19)

The student interprets "altogether" (the whole) as "each" (the parts). Sometimes, students are taught to search for key words (more, less, greater, etc.), pick a strategy or formula based on the key words (more means "add"), and apply the formula. Actually, this gets in the way of forming a conceptual understanding of the whole problem.

Understanding the Whole Problem. The third task in representing a problem is to assemble all the relevant information and sentences into an accurate understanding or translation of the total problem. This means that students need to form a conceptual model of the problem—they have to understand what the problem is really asking (Jonassen, 2003). Consider this example.

STOP | THINK | WRITE Two train stations are 50 miles apart. At 2 P.M. one Saturday afternoon, two trains start toward each other, one from each station. Just as the trains pull

FIGURE 8.4

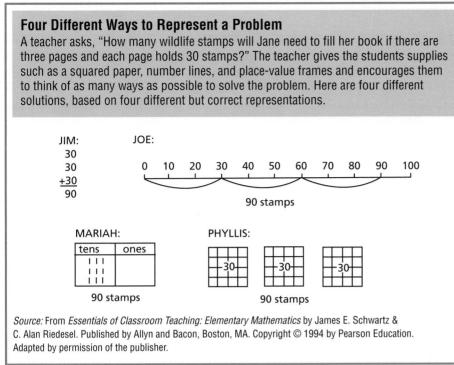

Four Different Ways to Represent a Problem

A teacher asks, "How many wildlife stamps will Jane need to fill her book if there are three pages and each page holds 30 stamps?" The teacher gives the students supplies such as a squared paper, number lines, and place-value frames and encourages them to think of as many ways as possible to solve the problem. Here are four different solutions, based on four different but correct representations.

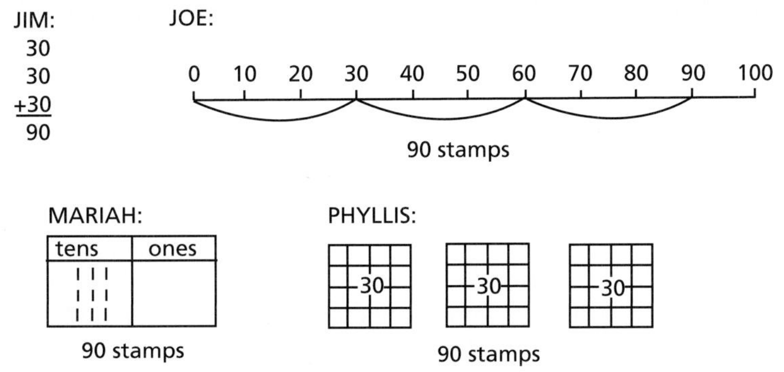

Source: From *Essentials of Classroom Teaching: Elementary Mathematics* by James E. Schwartz & C. Alan Riedesel. Published by Allyn and Bacon, Boston, MA. Copyright © 1994 by Pearson Education. Adapted by permission of the publisher.

out of the stations, a bird springs into the air in front of the first train and flies ahead to the front of the second train. When the bird reaches the second train it turns back and flies toward the first train. The bird continues to do this until the trains meet. If both trains travel at the rate of 25 miles per hour and the bird flies at 100 miles per hour, how many miles will the bird have flown before the trains meet? (Posner, 1973) ■

Your interpretation of the problem is called a *translation* because you translate the problem into a schema that you understand. If you translate this as a *distance* problem and set a goal ("I have to figure out how far the bird travels before it meets the oncoming train and turns around, then how far it travels before it has to turn again, and finally add up all the trips back and forth"), then you have a very difficult task on your hands. But there is a better way to structure the problem. You can represent it as a question of *time* and focus on the time the bird is in the air. The solution could be stated like this:

> The trains are going the same speed so they will meet in the middle, 25 miles from each station. This will take *one hour* because they are traveling 25 mph. In an hour, the bird will cover 100 miles because it is flying at 100 miles per hour. Easy!

Research shows that students can be too quick to decide what a problem is asking. Once a problem is categorized—"Aha, it's a distance problem!"—a particular schema is activated. The schema directs attention to relevant information and sets up expectations for what the right answer should look like (Kalyuga, Chandler, Tuovinen, & Sweller, 2001; Reimann & Chi, 1989).

When students lack the necessary schemas to represent problems, they often rely on surface features of the situation and represent the problem incorrectly, like the student who wrote "15 + 24 = 39" as the answer to, "Joan has 15 bonus points and Louise has 24. How many more does Louise have?" This student saw two numbers and the word "more," so he applied the *add to get more* procedure. When students use the wrong schema, they overlook critical information, use irrelevant information, and may even misread or misremember critical information so that it fits the schema. But when students use the proper schema to represent a problem, they are less likely to be confused by irrelevant information or tricky wording, such as *more* in a problem that really requires *subtraction* (Resnick, 1981). Figure 8.4 gives examples of different ways students might represent a simple mathematics problem.

Translation and Schema Training. How can students improve translation and schema selection? To answer this question, we often have to move from general to area-specific problem-solving strategies because schemas are specific to content areas. In mathematics, for example, it appears that students benefit from seeing many different kinds of example problems worked out correctly for them. The common practice of showing students a few examples, then having students work many problems on their own, is less effective. Worked-out examples are helpful especially when problems are unfamiliar or difficult and when students have less knowledge (Cooper & Sweller, 1987). When students are learning, worked-out examples should deal with one source of information at a time (Marcus, Cooper, & Sweller, 1996). Ask students to compare examples. What is the same about each solution? What is different? Why?

The same procedures may be effective in areas other than mathematics. Adrienne Lee and Laura Hutchinson (1998) found that undergraduate students learned more when they had examples of chemistry problem solutions that were annotated to show an expert problem solver's thinking at critical steps. In Australia, Slava Kalyuga and colleagues (2001) found that worked-out examples helped apprentices to learn about electrical circuits when the apprentices had less experience in the area. Asking students to reflect on the examples helped too; thus, both explanation and reflection can make worked-out examples more effective. Some of the benefit from worked-out examples comes when students use the examples to explain to themselves what is happening at each step or to check their understanding by anticipating the next step; in this way, students have to be mentally engaged in making sense of the examples (Atkinson, Renkl, & Merrill, 2003).

Familiar examples can serve as analogies or models for solving new problems. But beware. Novices are likely to remember the surface features of an example or case instead of the deeper meaning or the structure. It is the meaning or structure, not the surface similarities, that help in solving new, analogous problems (Gentner, Lowenstein, & Thompson, 2003). I have heard students complain that the test preparation problems in their math classes were about river currents, but the test asked about wind speed. They protested, "There were no problems about boats on the test!" In fact, the problems on the test about wind were solved in exactly the same way as the "boat" problems, but the students were focusing only on the surface features. One way to overcome this tendency is to have students compare examples or cases so they can develop a general problem-solving schema that captures the common structure, not the surface features, of the cases (Gentner et al., 2003).

How else might students develop the schemas they will need to represent problems in a particular subject area? Mayer (1983b) has recommended giving students practice in the following: (1) recognizing and categorizing a variety of problem types; (2) representing problems—either concretely in pictures, symbols, or graphs, or in words; and (3) selecting relevant and irrelevant information in problems.

The Results of Problem Representation. There are two main outcomes of the problem representation stage of problem solving, as shown in Figure 8.5. If your representation of the problem suggests an immediate solution, your task is done. In one sense, you haven't really solved a new problem; you have simply recognized the new problem as a "disguised" version of an old problem that you already know how to solve. This has been called **schema-driven problem solving.** In terms of Figure 8.5, you have taken the *schema-activated route* and have proceeded directly to a solution. But what if you have no existing way of solving the problem or if your activated schema fails? Time to search for a solution!

Exploring Possible Solution Strategies

Schema-driven problem solving Recognizing a problem as a "disguised" version of an old problem for which one already has a solution.

Algorithm Step-by-step procedure for solving a problem; prescription for solutions.

If you do not have existing schemas that suggest an immediate solution, then you must take the *search-based route* indicated in Figure 8.5. Obviously, this path is not as efficient as activating the right schema, but sometimes it is the only way. In conducting your search for a solution, you have available two general kinds of procedures: algorithmic and heuristic.

Algorithms. An **algorithm** is a step-by-step prescription for achieving a goal. It usually is domain-specific; that is, it is tied to a particular subject area. In solving a problem, if

FIGURE 8.5

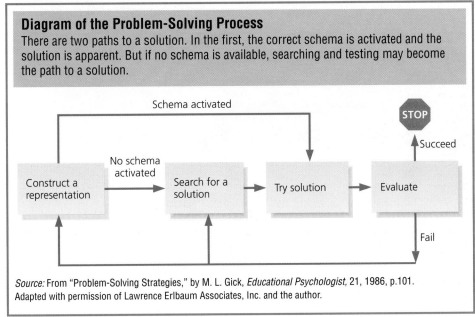

Diagram of the Problem-Solving Process

There are two paths to a solution. In the first, the correct schema is activated and the solution is apparent. But if no schema is available, searching and testing may become the path to a solution.

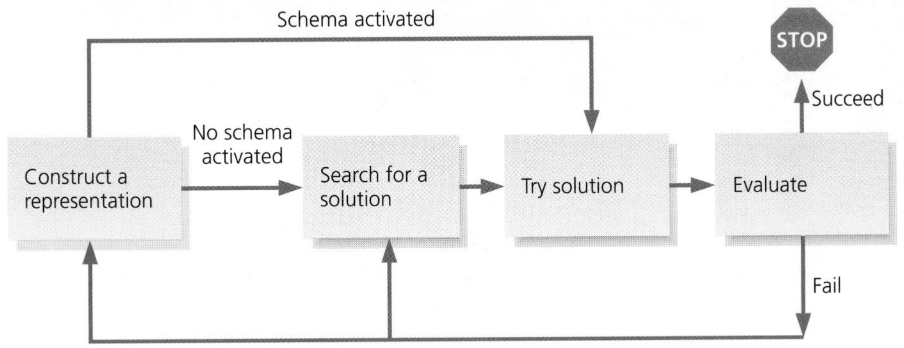

Source: From "Problem-Solving Strategies," by M. L. Gick, *Educational Psychologist,* 21, 1986, p.101. Adapted with permission of Lawrence Erlbaum Associates, Inc. and the author.

you choose an appropriate algorithm and implement it properly, a right answer is guaranteed. Unfortunately, students often apply algorithms unsystematically. They try first this, then that. They may even happen on the right answer, but not understand how they found it. For some students, applying algorithms haphazardly could be an indication that formal operational thinking and the ability to work through a set of possibilities systematically, as described by Piaget, is not yet developed.

Many problems cannot be solved by algorithms. What then?

Heuristics. A **heuristic** is a general strategy that might lead to the right answer. Because many of life's problems (careers, relationships, etc.) are not straightforward and have ill-defined problem statements and no apparent algorithms, the discovery or development of effective heuristics is important (Korf, 1999). Let's examine a few.

In **means-ends analysis,** the problem is divided into a number of intermediate goals or subgoals, and then a means of solving each intermediate subgoal is figured out. For example, writing a 20-page term paper can loom as an insurmountable problem for some students. They would be better off breaking this task into several intermediate goals, such as selecting a topic, locating sources of information, reading and organizing the information, making an outline, and so on. As they attack a particular intermediate goal, they may find that other goals arise. For example, locating information may require that they find someone to refresh their memory about using the library computer search system. Keep in mind that psychologists have yet to discover an effective heuristic for students who are just starting their term paper the night before it is due.

A second aspect of means-ends analysis is *distance reduction,* or pursuing a path that moves directly toward the final goal. People tend to look for the biggest difference between the current state of affairs and the goal and then search for a strategy that reduces the difference. We resist taking detours or making moves that are indirect as we search for the quickest way to reach the goal. So when you realize that reaching the goal of completing a term paper may require a detour of relearning the library computer search system, you may resist at first because you are not moving directly and quickly toward your final objective (Anderson, 1993).

Some problems lend themselves to a **working-backward strategy,** in which you begin at the goal and move back to the unsolved initial problem. Working backward is sometimes an effective heuristic for solving geometry proofs. It can also be a good way to set intermediate deadlines ("Let's see, if I have to submit this chapter in three weeks,

Connect and **Extend** to Your **Teaching/Portfolio**

The following five heuristics that might help students solve college math problems are from Schoenfeld (1979):

1. Draw a diagram, if possible.
2. If the problem has an "N" that takes on integer values, try substituting numbers such as 1, then 2, then 3, then 4 for the "N," and look for a pattern in the results.
3. If you are trying to prove a statement, for example, "If X is true, then Y is true," try proving the contrapositive, "If X is false, then Y is false," or try assuming the statement you want to prove is false and look for a contradiction.
4. Try solving a similar problem with fewer variables.
5. Try to set up subgoals.

Heuristic General strategy used in attempting to solve problems.

Means-ends analysis Heuristic in which a goal is divided into subgoals.

Working-backward strategy Heuristic in which one starts with the goal and moves backward to solve the problem.

One of the advantages of having students work in groups in problem-solving situations is that they will be called on to explain their proposed solutions to one another. Putting solutions into words usually improves problem solving.

Connect and **Extend** to Your **Teaching/Portfolio**

Guidelines for encouraging problem solving in children:

1. Provide problems, not just solutions.
2. Encourage viewing problems from different angles.
3. Make sure students have necessary background information.
4. Make sure students understand the problem.
   - Make accurate and useful representation.
   - Understand through associations and analogies.
5. Help students tackle the problem systematically.
   - Verbalize.
   - Describe and compare.
6. Practice with worked-out examples.

Analogical thinking Heuristic in which one limits the search for solutions to situations that are similar to the one at hand.

Verbalization Putting your problem-solving plan and its logic into words.

then it has to be in the mail by the 28th, so I should have a first draft finished by the 11th").

Another useful heuristic is **analogical thinking** (Copi, 1961; Genter et al., 2003), which limits your search for solutions to situations that have something in common with the one you currently face. When submarines were first designed, for example, engineers had to figure out how battleships could determine the presence and location of vessels hidden in the depths of the sea. Studying how bats solve an analogous problem of navigating in the dark led to the invention of sonar.

Analogical reasoning can lead to faulty problem solving, too. When word processors first came out, some people used the analogy of the typewriter and failed to take advantage of the computer's features. They were focusing on the surface similarities. It seems that people need knowledge in both the problem domain and the analogy domain in order to use an analogy effectively (Gagné, Yekovich, & Yekovich, 1993). In addition, they must focus on meaning, and not surface similarities when forming the analogies.

Putting your problem-solving plan into words and giving reasons for selecting it can lead to successful problem solving (Lee & Hutchinson, 1998). You may have discovered the effectiveness of this **verbalization** process accidentally, when a solution popped into your head as you were explaining a problem to someone else.

Anticipating, Acting, and Looking Back

WHAT WOULD YOU SAY?

You are interviewing with chair of the department. She asks, "What do you think about letting students use calculators and spell checkers? Do you think this is making learning too easy?" ■

After representing the problem and exploring possible solutions, the next step is to select a solution and *anticipate the consequences*. For example, if you decide to solve the damaged tomato problem by developing a tougher tomato, how will consumers react? If you take time to learn a new graphics program to enhance your term paper (and your grade), will you still have enough time to finish the paper?

After you choose a solution strategy and implement it, evaluate the results by checking for evidence that confirms or contradicts your solution. Many people tend to stop working before reaching the best solution and simply accept an answer that works in some cases. In mathematical problems, evaluating the answer might mean applying a checking routine, such as adding to check the result of a subtraction problem or, in a long addition problem, adding the column from bottom to top instead of top to bottom. Another possibility is estimating the answer. For example, if the computation was 11×21, the answer should be around 200, because 10×20 is 200. A student who reaches an answer of 2,311 or 23 or 562 should quickly realize these answers cannot be correct. Estimating an answer is particularly important when students rely on calculators or computers, because they cannot go back and spot an error in the figures. See the *Point/Counterpoint* for opinions on the use of technology in checking answers.

Point/Counterpoint

Should Students Be Allowed to Use Calculators and Spell Checkers?

NOT ALL EDUCATORS believe that teachers should allow students to use calculators and other technical tools for performing operations and proofing work.

POINT Calculators and spell checkers are crutches that harm learning.

When I polled my graduate class[1] of experienced teachers and principals, I got various opinions, such as: "When students are given calculators to do math in the early grades, most of them never learn rudimentary mathematical concepts; they only learn to use the calculator" and "To learn math, students need repetition and practice on the concepts to remember the operations—calculators get in the way." In a summary of the issue online, Nancy Ayres (http://www.math.twsu.edu/history/topics/calculators.html#calc) noted, "David Gelernter, professor of computer science at Yale University, believes calculators should be totally eliminated from the classroom. He feels that allowing children to use calculators produces adults who can't do basic arithmetic, doomed to wander through life in a numeric haze. In 1997, California legislation would prohibit the use of calculators in schools prior to the sixth grade. Whereas, the state of Virginia purchased 200,000 graphing calculators to be used by all middle school and high school math students." In terms of word processing, results of the National Assessment of Educational Progress (1997) indicated that even though the use of word processors by 11th graders increased from 19% in 1984 to 96% in 1997, the average writing scores of 11th graders declined during those years.

COUNTERPOINT Calculators and spell checkers support learning.

Just because students learned mathematics in the past with paper-and-pencil procedures and practice does not mean that this is the best way to learn. Today, we have to consider each teaching situation on a case-by-case basis to determine if paper-and-pencil procedures or technology or some combination provides the best way to learn (Waits & Demana, 2000). For example, in the Third International Mathematics and Science Study (TIMSS, 1998), on every test at the advanced level, students who said that they used calculators in their daily math coursework performed much better than students who rarely or never used calculators. In fact, rather than eroding basic skills, the research on calculators over the past decade has found that using calculators has positive effects on students' problem-solving skills and attitudes toward math (Waits & Demana, 2000).

What about word processors and spelling checkers? Pricilla Norton and Debra Sprague (2001) suggest that "no other technology resource has had as great an impact on education as word processing" (p. 78). They list the following effects: Word processing enhances learners' perceptions of themselves as "real" writers, lets students reflect on the thinking that goes on behind the writing, facilitates collaborative writing, and helps students be more critical and creative in their writing. In my class, an advisor working with undergraduate engineering students pointed out another plus for technology: "We have many international students who have an average-to-good command of English. In my opinion, they need Spellcheck to catch the errors as well as to 'teach' them the corrected form. Spellcheck is at times a nuisance to us by questioning everything, but I think it's very helpful to ESL students and for general proofreading purposes."

WHAT DO YOU THINK?
Vote online at **www.mylabschool.com**

[1]Thanks to Ohio State students Debbie Lanam and Charles Page for sharing their ideas.

Connect and **Extend** to Your **Teaching/Portfolio**

A student was given the problem "Find the value of x and y that solves both equations":

$8x + 4y = 28 \qquad 4x + 2y = 10$

The student quickly responded $x = 2, y = 3$, correctly addressing the first problem, but neglecting to check the solution on the second. How could you help the student be more reflective?

Functional fixedness Inability to use objects or tools in a new way.

Response set Rigidity; tendency to respond in the most familiar way.

Representativeness heuristic Judging the likelihood of an event based on how well the events match your prototypes—what you think is representative of the category.

Factors That Hinder Problem Solving

STOP | THINK | WRITE You enter a room. There are two ropes suspended from the ceiling. You are asked by the experimenter to tie the two ends of the ropes together and are assured that the task is possible. On a nearby table are a few tools, including a hammer and pliers. You grab the end of one of the ropes and walk toward the other rope. You immediately realize that you cannot possibly reach the end of the other rope. You try to extend your reach using the pliers but still cannot grasp the other rope. What can you do? (Maier, 1933) ■

Fixation. Problem solving requires seeing things in new ways. The rope problem can be solved if you tie the hammer or the pliers to the end of one rope and start swinging it like a pendulum. Then you will be able to catch it while you are standing across the room holding the other rope. You can use the weight of the tool to make the rope come to you instead of trying to stretch the rope. People often fail to solve this problem, because they fixate on conventional uses for materials. This difficulty is called **functional fixedness** (Duncker, 1945). In your everyday life, you may often exhibit functional fixedness. Suppose a screw on a dresser-drawer handle is loose. Will you spend 10 minutes searching for a screwdriver or will you fix it with a ruler edge or a dime?

Another kind of fixation that blocks effective problem solving is **response set,** getting stuck on one way of representing a problem. Try this:

STOP | THINK | WRITE In each of the four matchstick arrangements below, move only one stick to change the equation so that it represents a true equality such as V = V.

V = VII   VI = XI   XII = VII   VI = II

You probably figured out how to solve the first example quite quickly. You simply move one matchstick from the right side over to the left to make VI = VI. Examples two and three can also be solved without too much difficulty by moving one stick to change the V to an X or vice versa. But the fourth example (taken from Raudsepp & Haugh, 1977) probably has you stumped. To solve this problem, you must change your response set or switch schemas, because what has worked for the first three problems will not work this time. The answer here lies in changing from Roman numerals to Arabic numbers and using the concept of square root. By overcoming response set, you can move one matchstick from the right to the left to form the symbol for square root; the solution reads $\sqrt{1} = 1$, which is simply the symbolic way of saying that the square root of 1 equals 1. Recently, a creative reader of this text e-mailed some other solutions. Jamaal Allan, then a masters' student at Pacific University, pointed out that you could use any of the matchsticks to change the = sign to ≠. Then, the last example would be V ≠ II or 5 does not equal 2, an accurate statement. He suggested that you also might move one matchstick to change = to < or >, and the statements would still be true (but not equalities as specified in the problem above). Can you come up with any other solutions?

Some Problems with Heuristics. We often apply heuristics automatically to make quick judgments; that saves us time in everyday problem solving. The mind can react automatically and instantaneously, but the price we often pay for this efficiency may be bad problem solving, which can be costly. Making judgments by invoking your stereotypes leads even smart people to make dumb decisions. For example, we might use **representativeness heuristics** to make judgments about possibilities based on our prototypes—what we think is representative of a category. Consider this:

STOP | THINK | WRITE If I ask you whether a slim, short stranger who enjoys poetry is more likely to be a truck driver or an Ivy League classics professor, what would you say? ■

You might be tempted to answer based on your prototypes of truck drivers or professors. But consider the odds. With about 10 Ivy League schools and 4 or so classics professors per school, we have 40 professors. Say 10 are both short and slim, and half of those like poetry—we are left with 5. But there are at least 400,000 truck drivers in the United

States. If only 1 in every 800 of those truck drivers were short, slim, poetry lovers, we have 500 truck drivers who fit the description. With 500 truck drivers versus 5 professors, it is 100 times more likely that our stranger is a truck driver (Myers, 2005).

Teachers and students are busy people, and they often base their decisions on what they have in their minds at the time. When judgments are based on the availability of information in our memories, we are using the **availability heuristic.** If instances of events come to mind easily, we think they are common occurrences, but that is not necessarily the case; in fact, it is often wrong. People remember vivid stories and quickly come to believe that such events are the norm, but often they are wrong. For example, you may have been surprised to read in Chapter 5 that the average family in poverty has only 2.2 children if you have vivid memories of hearing that "people on welfare just keep having children" or if you saw a powerful film about a large, poor family. Again, data do not support that judgment. But **belief perseverance,** or the tendency to hold on to our beliefs, even in the face of contradictory evidence, may make us resist change.

The **confirmation bias** is the tendency to search for information that confirms our ideas and beliefs: this arises from our eagerness to get a good solution. You have often heard the saying "Don't confuse me with the facts." This aphorism captures the essence of the confirmation bias. Most people seek evidence that supports their ideas more readily than they search for facts that might refute them (Myers, 2005). For example, once you decide to buy a certain car, you are likely to notice reports about the good features of the car you chose, not the good news about the cars you rejected. Our automatic use of heuristics to make judgments, our eagerness to confirm what we like to believe, and our tendency to explain away failure combine to generate *overconfidence.* Students usually are overconfident about how fast they can get their papers written; it typically takes twice as long as they estimate (Buehler, Griffith, & Ross, 1994). In spite of their underestimation of their completion time, they remain overly confident of their next prediction.

The Importance of Flexibility. Functional fixedness, response set, the confirmation bias, and belief perseverance point to the importance of flexibility in understanding problems. If you get started with an inaccurate or inefficient representation of the true problem, it will be difficult—or at least very time-consuming—to reach a solution. Sometimes, it is helpful to "play" with the problem. Ask yourself: "What do I know? What do I need to know to answer this question? Can I look at this problem in other ways?" Try to think conditionally rather than rigidly, and divergently rather than convergently. Ask "What could this be?" instead of "What is it?" (Benjafield, 1992).

If you open your mind to multiple possibilities, you may have what the Gestalt psychologists called an insight. **Insight** is the sudden reorganization or reconceptualization of a problem that clarifies the problem and suggests a feasible solution. The supervisor described earlier, who suddenly realized that the problem in his building was not slow elevators but impatient, bored tenants, had an insight that allowed him to reach the solution of installing mirrors by the elevators.

Effective Problem Solving: What Do the Experts Do?

Most psychologists agree that effective problem solving is based on an ample store of knowledge about the problem area. In order to solve the matchstick problem, for example, you had to understand Roman and Arabic numbers as well as the concept of square root. You also had to know that the square root of 1 is 1. Let's take a moment to examine this expert knowledge.

Expert Knowledge. The modern study of expertise began with investigations of chess masters (Simon & Chase, 1973). Results indicated that masters can quickly recognize about 50,000 different arrangements of chess pieces. They can look at one of these patterns for a few seconds and remember where every piece on the board was placed. It is as though they have a "vocabulary" of 50,000 patterns. Michelene Chi (1978) demonstrated that 3rd- through 8th-grade chess experts had a similar ability to remember chess piece arrangements. For all the masters, patterns of pieces are like words. If you were shown any

Availability heuristic Judging the likelihood of an event based on what is available in your memory, assuming those easily remembered events are common.

Belief perseverance The tendency to hold onto beliefs, even in the face of contradictory evidence.

Confirmation bias Seeking information that confirms our choices and beliefs, while disconfirming evidence.

Insight Sudden realization of a solution.

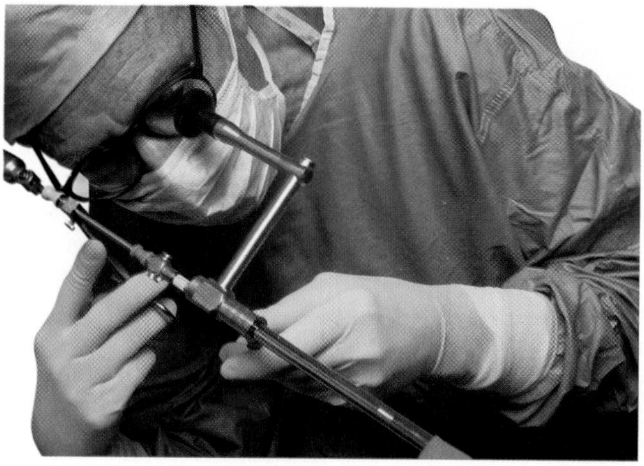

Experts have a rich store of declarative, procedural, and conditional knowledge. While basic intelligence is certainly a factor, hard work and practice are also required to become an expert in any given field.

word from your vocabulary store for just a few seconds, you would be able to remember every letter in the word in the right order (assuming you could spell the word).

But a series of letters arranged randomly is hard to remember, as you saw in Chapter 7. An analogous situation holds for chess masters. When chess pieces are placed on a board randomly, masters are no better than average players at remembering the positions of the pieces. The master's memory is for patterns that make sense or could occur in a game.

A similar phenomenon occurs in other fields. There may be an intuition about how to solve a problem based on recognizing patterns and knowing the "right moves" for those patterns. Experts in physics, for example, organize their knowledge around central principles, whereas beginners organize their smaller amounts of physics knowledge around the specific details stated in the problems (Ericsson, 1999). For instance, when asked to sort physics problems from a textbook in any way they wanted, novices sorted based on superficial features such as the kind of apparatus mentioned—a lever or a pulley—whereas the experts grouped problems according to the underlying physics principle needed to solve the problem, such as Boyle's or Newton's laws (Hardiman, Dufresne, & Mestre, 1989).

In addition to representing a problem very quickly, experts know what to do next. They have a large store of productions or *condition-action schemas* about what action to take in various situations. Thus, the steps of understanding the problem and choosing a solution happen simultaneously and fairly automatically (Ericsson & Charness, 1999). Of course, this means that they must have many, many schemas available. A large part of becoming an expert is simply acquiring a great store of *domain knowledge* or knowledge that is particular to a field (Alexander, 1992). To do this, you must encounter many different kinds of problems in that field, see problems solved by others, and practice solving many yourself. Some estimates are that it takes 10 years or 10,000 hours of study to become an expert in most fields (Simon, 1995).

Experts' rich store of knowledge is *elaborated* and *well practiced,* so that it is easy to retrieve from long-term memory when needed (Anderson, 1993). Experts can use their extensive knowledge to *organize* information for easier learning and retrieval. Compared to 4th-graders with little knowledge of soccer, 4th-graders who were soccer experts learned and remembered far more new soccer terms, even though the abilities of the two groups to learn and remember nonsoccer terms were the same. The soccer experts organized and clustered the soccer terms to aid in recall (Schneider & Bjorklund, 1992). Even very young children who are experts on a topic can use strategies to organize their knowledge. To get an example of the use of category knowledge about dinosaurs, I called my nephews, Lucas and Geoffrey (4 and 3 years old at the time). They promptly ran down the list of large and small plant- and meat-eating dinosaurs (their organizing categories), from the well-known stegosaurus (large, plant eater) to the less familiar ceolophysis (small, meat eater).

With organization comes planning and monitoring. Experts spend more time analyzing problems, drawing diagrams, breaking large problems down into subproblems, and making plans. Whereas a novice might begin immediately—writing equations for a physics problem or drafting the first paragraph of a paper, experts plan out the whole solution and often make the task simpler in the process. As they work, experts monitor progress, so time is not lost pursuing dead ends or weak ideas (Schunk, 2004).

Chi, Glaser, and Farr (1988) summarize the superior capabilities of experts. Experts (1) perceive large, meaningful patterns in given information, (2) perform tasks quickly and with few errors, (3) deal with problems at a deeper level, (4) hold more information in working and long-term memories, (5) take a great deal of time to analyze a given problem, and (6) are better at monitoring their performance. When the area of problem solving is fairly well defined, such as chess or physics or computer programming, then these skills of expert problem solvers hold fairly consistently. But when the problem-solving area is less well defined and has fewer clear underlying principles, such as problem solving in economics or psychology, then the differences between experts and novices are not as clear-cut (Alexander, 1992).

Novice Knowledge. Studies of the differences between experts and novices in particular areas have revealed some surprising things about how novices understand and misunderstand a subject. Physics again provides many examples. Most beginners approach physics with a great deal of misinformation, partly because many of their intuitive ideas about the physical world are wrong. Most elementary school children believe that light helps us see by brightening the area around objects. They do not realize that we see an object because the light is reflected by the object to our eyes. This concept does not fit with the everyday experience of turning on a light and "brightening" the dark area. Researchers from the Elementary Science Project at Michigan State University found that even after completing a unit on light in which materials explicitly stated the idea of reflected light and vision, most 5th-grade students—about 78%—continued to cling to their intuitive notions. But when new materials were designed that directly confronted the students' misconceptions, only about 20% of the students failed to understand (Eaton, Anderson, & Smith, 1984).

It seems quite important for science teachers to understand their students' intuitive models of basic concepts. If the students' intuitive model includes misconceptions and inaccuracies, then the students are likely to develop inadequate or misleading representations of a problem. (You should note that some researchers don't use the term "misconception," but refer to *naïve* or *intuitive conceptions* to describe students' beginning knowledge in an area.) In order to learn new information and solve problems, students must sometimes "unlearn" common-sense ideas. Changing your intuitive ideas about concepts involves motivation, too. Pintrich, Marx, and Boyle (1993) suggest that four conditions are necessary for people to change basic concepts: (1) Students have to be dissatisfied with the current concept; that is, their existing concept must be seen as inaccurate, incomplete, or not useful. (2) Students must understand the new concept. (3) The new concept must be plausible—it must fit in with what the students already know. (4) The new concept must be fruitful—it must be seen as useful in solving problems or answering questions.

The *Guidelines* on the next page give some ideas for helping students become expert problem solvers.

Creativity and Creative Problem Solving

STOP | THINK | WRITE Consider this student. He had severe dyslexia—a learning disability that made reading and writing exceedingly difficult. He described himself as an "underdog." In school, he knew that if the reading assignment would take others an hour, he had to allow two or three hours. He knew that he had to keep a list of all his most frequently misspelled words in order to be able to write at all. He spent hours alone in his room. Would you expect his writing to be creative? Why or why not? ■

The person in the box above is John Irving, celebrated author of what one critic called "wildly inventive" novels such as *The World According to Garp*, *The Cider House Rules*, and *A Prayer for Owen Meany* (Amabile, 2001). How do we explain his amazing creativity? What is creativity?

Guidelines: Problem Solving

Ask students if they are sure they understand the problem.

EXAMPLES

1. Can they separate relevant from irrelevant information?
2. Are they aware of the assumptions they are making?
3. Encourage them to visualize the problem by diagramming or drawing it.
4. Ask them to explain the problem to someone else. What would a good solution look like?

Encourage attempts to see the problem from different angles.

EXAMPLES

1. Suggest several different possibilities yourself, and then ask students to offer some.
2. Give students practice in taking and defending different points of view on an issue.

Let students do the thinking; don't just hand them solutions.

EXAMPLES

1. Offer individual problems as well as group problems, so that each student has the chance to practice.
2. Give partial credit if students have good reasons for "wrong" solutions to problems.
3. If students are stuck, resist the temptation to give too many clues. Let them think about the problem overnight.

Help students develop systematic ways of considering alternatives.

EXAMPLES

1. Think out loud as you solve problems.
2. Ask, "What would happen if?"
3. Keep a list of suggestions.

Teach heuristics.

EXAMPLES

1. Use analogies to solve the problem of limited parking in the downtown area. How are other "storage" problems solved?
2. Use the working backward strategy to plan a party.

For more resources on problem solving, see **http://www.hawaii.edu/suremath/home.html**

Defining Creativity

Let's start with what creativity is not. Here are four myths about creativity (Plucker, Beghetto, & Dow, 2004):

1. **People are born creative.** Actually, years of research show that creativity can be developed, enhanced, and supported by the individual's or groups' environment.
2. **Creativity is intertwined with negative qualities.** It is true that some creative people are nonconforming or some may have mental or emotional problems, but many noncreative people do, too. The danger with this myth is that teachers may expect creative students to be troublemakers and treat these students in a biased way (Scott, 1999).
3. **Creativity is a fuzzy, soft construct.** In contrast to seeing a creative person as mentally unbalanced, some people think creative individuals are New Age hippies. Actually, even though creative people may be open to new experiences and be generally nonconforming, they also may be focused, organized, and flexible.
4. **Creativity is enhanced within a group.** It is true that brainstorming in a group can lead to creative ideas, but these group efforts tend to be more creative if individuals brainstorm on their own first.

So what is creativity? **Creativity** is the ability to produce work that is original, but still appropriate and useful (Berk, 2005). Most psychologists agree that there is no such thing as "all-purpose creativity"; people are creative *in a particular area*, as John Irving was in writing fiction. But to be creative, the "invention" must be intended. An accidental spilling of paint that produces a novel design is not creative unless the artist recognizes the potential of the "accident" or uses the spilling technique intentionally to create new works (Weisberg, 1993). Although we frequently associate the arts with creativity, any subject can be approached in a creative manner.

Creativity Imaginative, original thinking or problem solving.

A definition that combines many aspects of creativity (Plucker et al., 2004) highlights that creativity:

- often involves more than one person,
- happens when people apply their abilities as part of a helpful process in a supportive environment, and
- results in an identifiable product that is new and useful in a particular culture or situation.

Creativity requires knowledge, flexibility, motivation, and persistence; social support plays an important role as well.

What Are the Sources of Creativity?

Researchers have studied cognitive processes, personality factors, motivational patterns, and background experiences to explain creativity (Simonton, 2000). But to truly understand creativity, we must look at the social environment too. Both intrapersonal (cognition, personality) and social factors support creativity (Amabile, 1996; 2001; Simonton, 2000). Teresa Amabile (1996) proposes a three-component model of creativity. Individuals or groups must have:

1. *Domain-relevant skills* including talents and competencies that are valuable for working in the domain. An example would be Michelangelo's skills in shaping stone, developed when he lived with a stonecutter's family as a child.
2. *Creativity-relevant processes* including work habits and personality traits such as a John Irving's habit of working 10-hour days to write and rewrite and rewrite until he perfected his stories.
3. *Intrinsic task motivation* or a deep curiosity and fascination with the task. This aspect of creativity can be greatly influenced by the social environment (as we will see in Chapter 10), and by supporting autonomy, stimulating curiosity, encouraging fantasy, and providing challenge.

Another social factor that influences creativity is whether the field is ready and willing to acknowledge the creative contribution (Nakamura & Csikszentmihalyi, 2001). History is filled with examples of creative breakthroughs rejected at the time (for example, Galileo's theory of the sun at the center of the solar system) and of rivalries between creators that led each to push the edges of creativity (the friendly and productive rivalry between Picasso and Matisse).

Creativity and Cognition. Having a rich store of knowledge in an area is the basis for creativity, but something more is needed. For many problems, that "something more" is the ability to break set—**restructuring** the problem to see things in a new way, which leads to a sudden insight. Often this happens when a person has struggled with a problem or project, then sets it aside for a while. Some psychologists believe that time away from the problem allows for *incubation*, a kind of unconscious working through the problem. It is more likely that leaving the problem for a time interrupts rigid ways of thinking so you can restructure your view of the situation (Gleitman, Fridlund, & Reisberg, 1999). So it seems that creativity requires extensive knowledge, flexibility, and the continual reorganizing of ideas. And we saw that motivation, persistence, and social support play important roles in the creative process as well.

Assessing Creativity

STOP | THINK | WRITE How many uses can you list for a brick? Take a moment and brainstorm—write down as many as you can. ■

Like the author John Irving, Paul Torrance also had a learning disability; he became interested in educational psychology when he was a high school English teacher (Neumeister & Cramond, 2004). Torrance was known as the "Father of Creativity." He developed two types of creativity tests: verbal and graphic (Torrance, 1972; Torrance & Hall, 1980). In the verbal test, you might be instructed to think up as many uses as possible for a brick (as you did above) or asked how a particular toy might be changed to

Restructuring Conceiving of a problem in a new or different way.

FIGURE 8.6

A Graphic Assessment of the Creativity of an Eight-Year-Old

The titles she gave her drawings, from left to right, are as follows: "Dracula," "one-eyed monster," "pumpkin," "Hula-Hoop," "poster," "wheelchair," "earth," "moon," "planet," "movie camera," "sad face," "picture," "stoplight," "beach ball," "the letter O," "car," "glasses."

Source: "A Graphic Assessment of the Creativity of an Eight-Year-Old," from *The Torrance Test of Creative Thinking* by E.P. Torrance, 1986, 2000. Reprinted with permission of Scholastic Testing Service, Inc., Bensonville, IL 60106 USA.

make it more fun. On the graphic test, you might be given 30 circles and asked to create 30 different drawings, with each drawing including at least one circle. Figure 8.6 shows the creativity of an 8-year-old girl in completing this task.

These tests require **divergent thinking,** an important component of many conceptions of creativity. Divergent thinking is the ability to propose many different ideas or answers. **Convergent thinking** is the more common ability to identify only one answer. Responses to all these creativity tasks are scored for originality, fluency, and flexibility, three aspects of divergent thinking. *Originality* is usually determined statistically. To be original, a response must be given by fewer than 5 or 10 people out of every 100 who take the test. *Fluency* is the number of different responses. *Flexibility* is generally measured by the number of different categories of responses. For instance, if you listed 20 uses of a

Agnes is able to think divergently.

Agnes, May 24, 2002. © Tony Cochran. Reprinted with permission of the Creators Syndicate.

Divergent thinking Coming up with many possible solutions.

Convergent thinking Narrowing possibilities to a single answer.

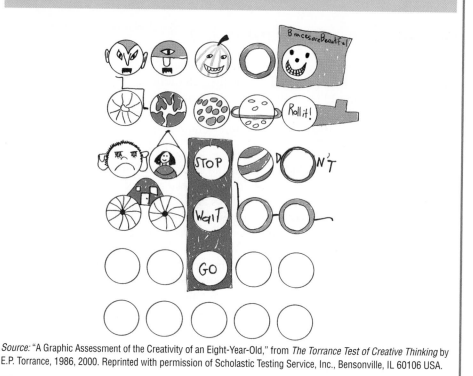

brick, but each was to build something, your fluency score might be high, but your flexibility score would be low. Of the three measures, fluency—the number of responses—is the best predictor of divergent thinking, but there is more to real-life creativity than divergent thinking (Plucker et al., 2004).

Teachers are not always the best judges of creativity. In fact, Torrance (1972) reports data from a 12-year follow-up study indicating no relationship between teachers' judgments of their students' creative abilities and the actual creativity these students revealed in their adult lives. A few possible indicators of creativity in your students are curiosity, concentration, adaptability, high energy, humor (sometimes bizarre), independence, playfulness, nonconformity, risk taking, attraction to the complex and mysterious, willingness to fantasize and daydream, intolerance for boredom, and inventiveness (Sattler, 1992).

Creativity in the Classroom

Today's and tomorrow's complex problems require creative solutions. And creativity is important for an individual's psychological, physical, social, and career success (Plucker et al., 2004). How can teachers promote creative thinking? All too often, in the crush of day-to-day classroom life, teachers stifle creative ideas without realizing what they are doing. Teachers are in an excellent position to encourage or discourage creativity through their acceptance or rejection of the unusual and imaginative. The *Guidelines*, adapted from Fleith (2000) and Sattler (1992), describe other possibilities for encouraging creativity.

Connect and Extend to Your Teaching/Portfolio

For a wonderful story of a first-year teacher with truly creative ideas, see Codell, E. R. (2001). *Educating Esme: Diary of a teacher's first year.* Chapel Hill, NC: Algonquin Books.

Guidelines: Encouraging Creativity

Accept and encourage divergent thinking.

EXAMPLES

1. During class discussion, ask: "Can anyone suggest a different way of looking at this question?"
2. Reinforce attempts at unusual solutions to problems, even if the final product is not perfect.
3. Offer choices in topics for projects or modes of presentation (written, oral, visual or graphic, using technology).

Tolerate dissent.

EXAMPLES

1. Ask students to support dissenting opinions.
2. Make sure nonconforming students receive an equal share of classroom privileges and rewards.

Encourage students to trust their own judgment.

EXAMPLES

1. When students ask questions you think they can answer, rephrase or clarify the questions and direct them back to the students.
2. Give ungraded assignments from time to time.

Emphasize that everyone is capable of creativity in some form.

EXAMPLES

1. Avoid describing the feats of great artists or inventors as if they were superhuman accomplishments.
2. Recognize creative efforts in each student's work. Have a separate grade for originality on some assignments.

Provide time, space, and materials to support creative projects.

EXAMPLES

1. Collect "found" materials for collages and creations—buttons, stones, shells, paper, fabric, beads, seeds, drawing tools, clay—try flea markets and friends for donations. Have mirrors and pictures for drawing faces.
2. Make a well-lighted space available where children can work on projects, leave them, and come back to finish them.
3. Follow up on memorable occasions (field trips, news events, holidays) with opportunities to draw, write, or make music.

Be a stimulus for creative thinking.

EXAMPLES

1. Use a class brainstorming session whenever possible.
2. Model creative problem solving by suggesting unusual solutions for class problems.
3. Encourage students to delay judging a particular suggestion for solving a problem until all the possibilities have been considered.

See **http://ceep.crc.uiuc.edu/eecearchive/digests/1995/edward95.html** for more ideas.

Dilbert leads his coworkers in brainstorming.

Dilbert, February 21, 2002. Copyright © 2002 Scott Adams. Reprinted with permission of United Features Syndicate, Inc.

Brainstorming. In addition to encouraging creativity through everyday interactions with students, teachers can try brainstorming. The basic tenet of **brainstorming** is to separate the process of creating ideas from the process of evaluating them because evaluation often inhibits creativity (Osborn, 1963). Evaluation, discussion, and criticism are postponed until all possible suggestions have been made. In this way, one idea inspires others; people do not withhold potentially creative solutions out of fear of criticism. John Baer (1997, p. 43) gives these rules for brainstorming:

Connect and Extend to the Research

For recent research on brainstorming, see: Brown, V. R., & Paulus, P. B. (2002). Making group brainstorming more effective: Recommendations from an associative memory perspective. *Current Directions in Psychological Science, 11*, 208–212.

1. Defer judgment.
2. Avoid ownership of ideas. When people feel that an idea is "theirs," egos sometimes get in the way of creative thinking. They are likely to be more defensive later when ideas are critiqued, and they are less willing to allow their ideas to be modified.
3. Feel free to "hitchhike" on other ideas. This means that it's okay to borrow elements from ideas already on the table, or to make slight modifications of ideas already suggested.
4. Encourage wild ideas. Impossible, totally unworkable ideas may lead someone to think of other, more possible, more workable ideas. It's easier to take a wildly imaginative bad idea and tone it down to fit the constraints of reality than to take a boring bad idea and make it interesting enough to be worth thinking about.

Individuals as well as groups may benefit from brainstorming. In writing this book, for example, I have sometimes found it helpful to list all the different topics that could be covered in a chapter, then leave the list and return to it later to evaluate the ideas.

Take Your Time—and Play! Years ago, Sigmund Freud (1959) linked creativity and play: "Might we not say that every child at play behaves like a creative writer, in that he creates a world of his own, or, rather, rearranges the things of his world in a new way which pleases him? The creative writer does the same as the child at play. He creates a world of phantasy which he takes very seriously—that is, which he invests with large amounts of emotion" (pp. 143–144). There is some evidence that preschool children who spend more time in fantasy and pretend play are more creative. In fact, playing before taking a creativity test resulted in higher scores on the test for the young students in one study (Berk, 2001; Bjorklund, 1989). Teachers can encourage students of all ages to be more reflective—to take time for ideas to grow, develop, and be restructured.

The Big C: Revolutionary Innovation

Ellen Winner (2000) describes the "big-C creativity" or innovation that establishes a new field or revolutionizes an old one. Even child prodigies do not necessarily become adult innovators. Prodigies have mastered well-established domains very early, but innovators change the entire domain. "Individuals who ultimately make creative breakthroughs

Brainstorming Generating ideas without stopping to evaluate them.

tend from their earliest days to be explorers, innovators, and tinkerers. Often this adventurousness is interpreted as insubordination, though more fortunate tinkerers receive from teachers or peers some form of encouragement for their experimentation" (Gardner, 1993a, pp. 32–33). What can parents and teachers do to encourage these potential creators? Winner (2000) lists four dangers to avoid:

1. Avoid pushing so hard that the child's intrinsic passion to master a field becomes a craving for extrinsic rewards.
2. Avoid pushing so hard that the child later looks back on a missed childhood.
3. Avoid freezing the child into a safe, technically perfect way of performing that has led to lavish rewards.
4. Be aware of the psychological wounds that can follow when the child who can perform perfectly becomes the forgotten adult who can do nothing more than continue to perform perfectly—without ever creating something new.

Finally, teachers and parents can encourage students with outstanding abilities and creative talents to give back to the society that has provided the extra support and resources that they needed. Service learning, discussed in Chapter 11, is one opportunity.

We may not all be revolutionary in our creativity, but we all can be experts in one area—learning.

Becoming an Expert Student: Learning Strategies and Study Skills

WHAT WOULD YOU SAY?

As part of your interview, the department chair asks, "Many of our students go on to high-pressure colleges and don't seem to know how to study when they don't have daily homework deadlines. How would you help them prepare to handle the heavy work load in those institutions?" ■

Most teachers will tell you that they want their students to "learn how to learn." Years of research indicate that using good learning strategies helps students learn and that these strategies can be taught (Hamman, Berthelot, Saia, & Crowley, 2000). But were you taught "how to learn"? Powerful and sophisticated learning strategies and study skills are seldom taught directly until high school or even college, so students have little practice with these powerful strategies. In contrast, early on, students usually discover repetition and rote learning on their own, so they have extensive practice with these strategies. And, unfortunately, some teachers think that memorizing is learning (Hofer & Pintrich, 1997; Woolfolk Hoy & Murphy, 2001). This may explain why many students cling to flash cards and memorizing—they don't know what else to do (Willoughby, Porter, Belsito, & Yearsley, 1999).

As we saw in Chapter 7, the way something is learned in the first place greatly influences how readily we remember and how appropriately we can apply the knowledge later. First, students must be *cognitively engaged* in order to learn—they have to focus attention on the relevant or important aspects of the material. Second, they have to *invest effort*, make connections, elaborate, translate, organize, and reorganize in order to *think and process deeply*—the greater the practice and processing, the stronger the learning. Finally, students must *regulate and monitor* their own learning—keep track of what is making sense and notice when a new approach is needed. The emphasis today is on helping students develop effective learning strategies and tactics that *focus attention and effort*, *process information deeply*, and *monitor understanding*.

Connect and **Extend** to the **Research**

Willoughby, T., Porter, L., Belsito, L., & Yearsley, T. (1999). Use of elaboration strategies by grades two, four, and six. *Elementary School Journal, 99*, 221–231.

This study tested the effectiveness of verbal elaboration (answer why each fact is true), imagery (create a mental picture), and keyword (create a mental picture using the keywords provided) in helping 2nd, 4th, and 6th grade Canadian students remember information from stories. Verbal elaboration worked for all three grades, especially when the students had some prior knowledge related to the stories. Imagery was more helpful than elaborations for older students when the students lacked prior knowledge about the story content, but 2nd graders needed support to use imagery.

Learning Strategies and Tactics

Learning strategies are ideas for accomplishing learning goals, a kind of overall plan of attack. **Learning tactics** are the specific techniques that make up the plan (Derry, 1989).

Learning strategies General plans for approaching learning tasks.

Learning tactics Specific techniques for learning, such as using mnemonics or outlining a passage.

Connect and **Extend** to **PRAXIS II™**

Learning Strategies (I, A1)
For suggestions about their effective use, take a look at the study skills site developed by the Virginia Polytechnic Institute (http://www.ucc.vt.edu/stdysk/stdyhlp.html), and also see http://www.studygs.net/ for more ideas.

Connect and **Extend** to Your **Teaching/Portfolio**

Use Table 8.2 plus the section titled Learning Strategies and Tactics to generate ideas for appropriate learning strategies and tactics for the students you will teach.

Your strategy for learning the material in this chapter might include the tactics of using mnemonics to remember key terms, skimming the chapter to identify the organization, and then writing answers to possible essay questions. Your use of strategies and tactics reflects metacognitive knowledge. Using learning strategies and study skills is related to higher GPAs in high school and staying in school in college (Robbins et al., 2004). Researchers have identified several important principles:

1. Students must be exposed to a number of *different strategies,* not only general learning strategies but also very specific tactics, such as the graphic strategies described later in this section.
2. Students should be taught *conditional knowledge* about when, where, and why to use various strategies. Although this may seem obvious, teachers often neglect this step. A strategy is more likely to be maintained and employed if students know when, where, and why to use it.
3. Students may know when and how to use a strategy, but unless they also *develop the desire to employ these skills,* general learning ability will not improve. Several learning strategy programs include a motivational training component. In Chapter 10 we look more closely at this important issue of motivation.
4. Students should receive *direct instruction in schematic knowledge;* this is often an important component of strategy training. In order to identify main ideas—a critical skill for a number of learning strategies—you must have an appropriate schema for making sense of the material. It will be difficult to summarize a paragraph about ichthyology, for example, if you don't know much about fish. Table 8.2 summarizes several tactics for learning declarative (verbal) knowledge and procedural skills (Derry, 1989).

TABLE 8.2

Examples of Learning Tactics

	Examples	Use When?
Tactics for Learning Verbal Information	1. Attention Focusing	
	• Making outlines, underlining	With easy, structured materials; for good readers
	• Looking for headings and topic sentences	For poorer readers; with more difficult materials
	2. Schema Building	
	• Story grammars	With poor text structure, goal is to encourage active comprehension
	• Theory schemas	
	• Networking and mapping	
	3. Idea Elaboration	
	• Self-questioning	To understand and remember specific ideas
	• Imagery	
Tactics for Learning Procedural Information	1. Pattern Learning	
	• Hypothesizing	To learn attributes of concepts
	• Identifying reasons for actions	To match procedures to situations
	2. Self-instruction	
	• Comparing own performance to expert model	To tune, improve complex skills
	3. Practice	
	• Part practice	When few specific aspects of a performance need attention
	• Whole practice	To maintain and improve skill

Source: Based on "Putting Learning Strategies to Work," by S. Derry, 1989, *Educational Leadership, 47*(5), pp. 5–6.

Deciding What Is Important. You can see from the first entry in Table 8.2, that learning begins with focusing attention—deciding what is important. But distinguishing the main idea from less important information is not always easy. Often students focus on the "seductive details" or the concrete examples, perhaps because they are more interesting (Gardner, Brown, Sanders, & Menke, 1992). You may have had the experience of remembering a joke or an intriguing example from a lecture, but not being clear about the larger point the professor was trying to make. Finding the central idea is especially difficult if you lack prior knowledge in an area and the amount of new information provided is extensive. Teachers can give students practice using signals in texts such as headings, bold words, outlines, or other indicators to identify key concepts and main ideas. Teaching students to summarize material can be helpful, too (Lorch, Lorch, Ritchey, McGovern, & Coleman, 2001).

Summaries. Creating summaries can help students learn, but students have to be taught how to summarize (Byrnes, 1996; Palincsar & Brown, 1984). Jeanne Ormrod (2004) summarizes these suggestions for helping students create summaries. For each summary, ask students to:

- find or write a *topic sentence* for each paragraph or section,
- identify *big ideas* that cover several specific points,
- find some *supporting information* for each big idea, and
- delete any *redundant information* or unnecessary details.

Begin doing summaries of short, easy, well-organized readings. Introduce longer, less organized, and more difficult passages gradually. Ask students to compare their summaries and discuss what ideas they thought were important and why—what's their evidence?

Two other study strategies that are based on identifying key ideas are *underlining* texts and *taking notes.*

STOP | THINK | WRITE How do you make notes as you read? Look back over the past several pages of this chapter. Are my words highlighted yellow or pink? Are there marks or drawings in the margins and if so, do the notes pertain to the chapter or are they grocery lists and e-mail addresses? ■

Underlining and Highlighting. Do you underline or highlight key phrases in textbooks? Underlining and note taking are probably two of the most commonly but ineffectively used strategies among college students. One common problem is that students underline or highlight too much. It is far better to be selective. In studies that limit how much students can underline—for example, only one sentence per paragraph—learning has improved (Snowman, 1984). In addition to being selective, you also should actively transform the information into your own words as you underline or take notes. Don't rely on the words of the book. Note connections between what you are reading and other things you already know. Draw diagrams to illustrate relationships. Finally, look for organizational patterns in the material and use them to guide your underlining or note taking (Irwin, 1991; Kiewra, 1988).

Taking Notes. As you sit in class, filling your notebook with words or furiously trying to keep up with a lecturer, you may wonder if taking notes makes a difference. It does, if used well:

- Taking notes focuses attention during class and helps encode information so it has a chance of making it to long-term memory. In order to record key ideas in your own words, you have to translate, connect, elaborate, and organize. Even if students don't review notes before a test, taking them in the first place appears to aid learning, especially for those who lack prior knowledge in an area. Of course, if taking notes distracts you from actually listening to and making sense of the lecture, then note taking may not be effective (Kiewra, 1989; Van Meter, Yokoi, & Pressley, 1994).
- Notes provide extended external storage that allows you to return and review. Students who use their notes to study tend to perform better on tests, especially if they

Connect and **Extend** to Your **Teaching/Portfolio**

Examples of elaboration strategies from Weinstein, Ridley, Dahl, & Weber (1988/1989).

What is the main idea of this story?
If this principle were not true, what would that imply?
What does this remind me of?
How could I use this information in the project I am working on?
How could I represent this in a diagram?
How do I feel about the author's opinion?
How could I put this in my own words?
What might be an example of this?
If I were going to interview the author, what would I ask her?
How does this apply to my life?

Connect and **Extend** to **Other Chapters**

Direct instruction in learning strategies is especially important for students with learning disabilities, as described in Chapter 4.

Connect and **Extend** to Your **Teaching/Portfolio**

READS is similar to a well-known strategy you might have encountered in school, called **PQ4R** (Thomas & Robinson, 1972):

Preview. Survey the major topics and sections and set a purpose for reading.

Question. For each major section, write questions that are related to your reading purposes. One way is to turn the headings and subheadings into questions.

Read. At last! The questions you have formulated can be answered through reading.

Reflect. While you are reading, try to think of examples or create images of the material. Elaborate and try to make connections between what you are reading and what you already know.

Recite. After reading each section, sit back and think about your initial purposes and questions. Can you answer the questions without looking at the book?

Review. Effective review incorporates new material more thoroughly into your long-term memory. As study progresses, review should be cumulative, including the sections and chapters you read previously.

take many high-quality notes—more is better as long as you are capturing key ideas, concepts, and relationships, not just intriguing details (Kiewra, 1985, 1989; Peverly, Brobst, Graham, & Shaw, 2003).

- Expert students match notes to their anticipated use and modify strategies after tests or assignments; use personal codes to flag material that is unfamiliar or difficult; fill in holes by consulting relevant sources (including other students in the class); record information verbatim only when a verbatim response will be required. In other words, they are *strategic* about taking and using notes (Van Meter, Yokoi, & Pressley, 1994).
- To help students organize their note taking, some teachers provide matrices or maps. When students are first learning to use these maps, you might fill in some of the spaces for them. If you use maps and matrices with your students, encourage them to exchange their filled-in maps and explain their thinking to each other.

Visual Tools for Organizing

To use underlining and note taking effectively, you must identify main ideas. In addition, you must understand the *organization* of the text or lecture—the connections and relationships among ideas. Some visual strategies have been developed to help students with this key element (Van Meter, 2001). There is some evidence that creating graphic organizers such as maps or charts is more effective than outlining in learning from texts (Robinson, 1998; Robinson & Kiewra, 1995). "Mapping" relationships by noting causal connections, comparison/contrast connections, and examples improved recall. Students should compare "maps" and discuss the differences. Amy's molecule (Figure 8.2, p. 291) is a hierarchical graphic depiction of the relationships among concepts. There are other ways to visualize organization, such as *Venn diagrams*, which show how ideas or concepts overlap and *tree diagrams*, which show how ideas branch off each other. Time lines organize information in sequence and are useful in classes such as history or geology.

An exciting possibility is **Cmaps**, developed by researchers at the Institute for Human Machine Cognition (IHMC). Joseph Novak, a senior researcher at the institute, developed concept mapping in the 1970s at Cornell University (Amy's Molecule came from his work). Now, Novak and the IHMC have developed tools to create concept maps that are available for downloading at no cost. My students at Ohio State use these tools—one even planned his dissertation and organized all the reading for his doctoral examinations using the them. Computer Cmaps can be linked to the Internet and students in different classrooms and schools all over the world can collaborate on them. The home page of the Cmap tools is shown in Figure 8.7.

Reading Strategies

As we saw above, effective learning strategies and tactics should help students focus attention, invest effort (elaborate, organize, summarize, connect, translate) so they process information deeply, and monitor their understanding. There are a number of strategies that support these processes in reading. Many use mnemonics to help students remember the steps involved. For example, one strategy for any grade above later elementary is **READS:**

R *Review* headings and subheadings.
E *Examine* boldface words.
A *Ask*, "What do I expect to learn?"
D *Do* it—Read!
S *Summarize* in your own words. (Friend & Bursuck, 1996)

A strategy that can be used in reading literature is **CAPS:**

C Who are the *characters*?
A What is the *aim* of the story?
P What *problem* happens?
S How is the problem *solved*?

Cmaps Tools for concept mapping developed by the Institute for Human Machine Cognition that are connected to many knowledge maps and other resources on the Internet.

READS A five-step reading strategy: *Review* headings; *Examine* boldface words; *Ask*, "What do I expect to learn?"; *Do* it—Read; *Summarize* in your own words.

CAPS A strategy that can be used in reading literature: *Characters*, *Aim* of story, *Problem*, *Solution*.

FIGURE 8.7

The Website for the Institute for Human Machine Cognition Cmap Tools at http://cmap.ihmc.us/

At this site, you can download concept mapping tools to construct, share, and criticize knowledge on any subject.

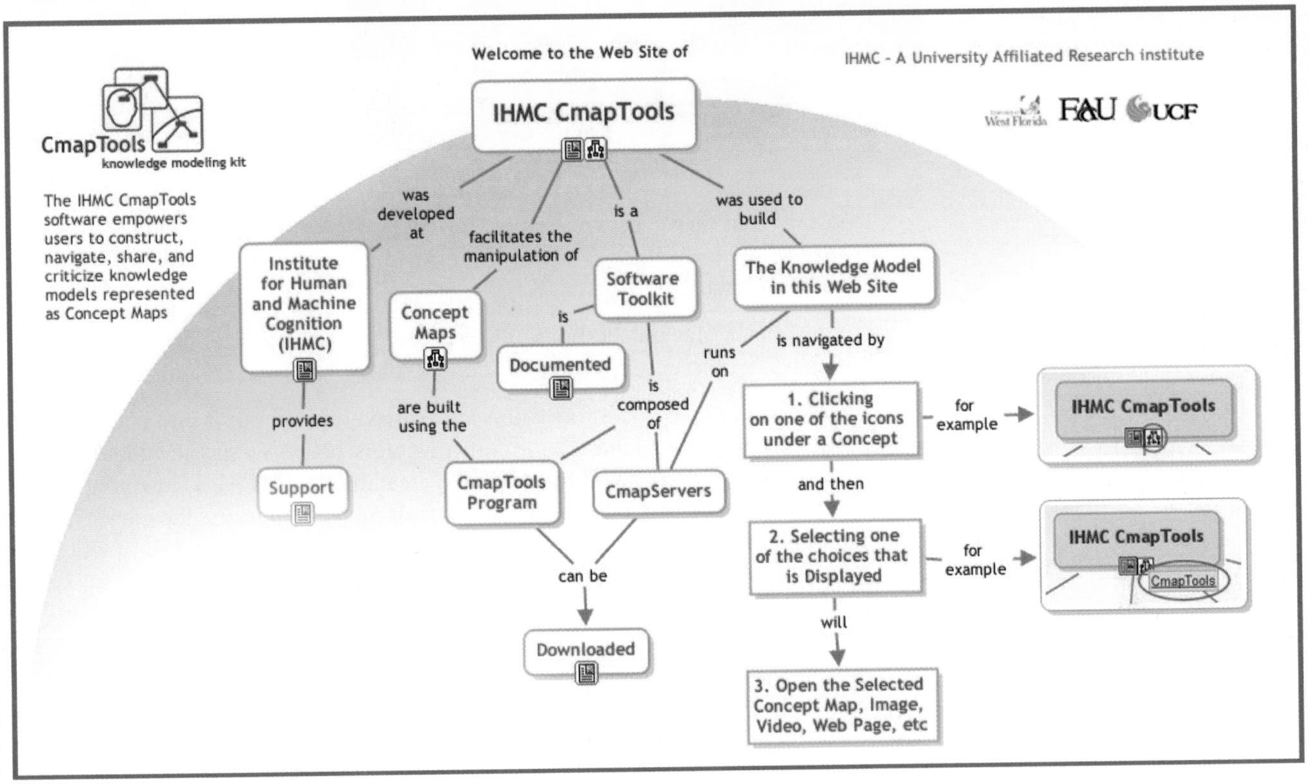

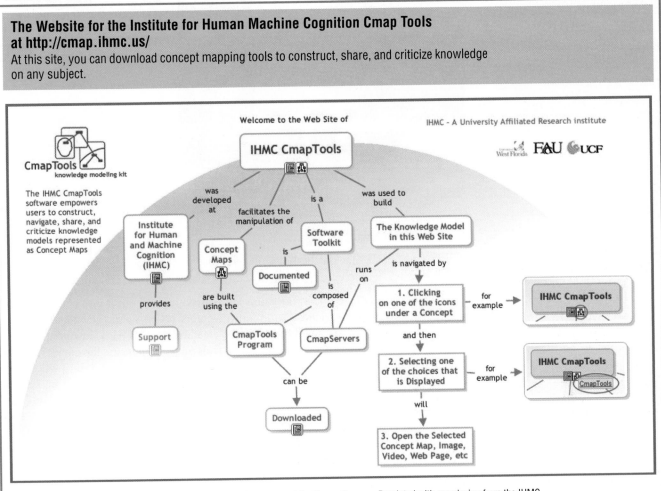

Source: Institute for Human Machine Cognition Cmap Tools home page. http://cmap.ihmc.us. Reprinted with permission from the IHMC.

Anderson (1995a) suggests several reasons why strategies such as CAPS or READS are effective. First, following the steps makes students more aware of the organization of a given chapter. How often have you skipped reading headings entirely and thus missed major clues about the way the information was organized? Next, these steps require students to study the chapter in sections instead of trying to learn all the information at once. This makes use of distributed practice. Creating and answering questions about the material forces students to process the information more deeply and with greater elaboration (Doctorow, Wittrock, & Marks, 1978; Hamilton, 1985).

Many of the cooperating teachers I work with use a strategy called **KWL** to guide reading and inquiry in general. This general frame can be used with most grade levels. The steps are:

K What do I already *know* about this subject?
W What do I *want* to know?
L At the end of the reading or inquiry, what have I *learned*?

No matter what strategies you use, students have to be taught how to use them. Direct teaching, explanation, modeling, and practice with feedback are necessary. Direct teaching of learning and reading strategies is especially important for students with learning challenges and students whose first language is not English. Marilyn Friend and William Bursuck (2002) describe how one teacher used modeling and discussion to teach the KWL strategy. After reviewing the steps, the teacher models an example and a nonexample of using KWL to learn about "crayons."

Connect and **Extend** to Your **Teaching/Portfolio**

Add Figure 8.7, "Cmaps," to your file of Teaching Resources.

Connect and **Extend** to the **Research**

See Peterson, D., & Van Der Wege, C. (2002). Guiding children to be strategic readers. *Phi Delta Kappan*, 83, 437–440.

KWL A strategy to guide reading and inquiry: Before—What do I already *know?* What do I *want* to know? After—What have I *learned?*

One cooperative learning strategy used by many teachers to guide reading and inquiry is called KWL: What do I know? What do I want to know? What have I learned?

Teacher: What do we do now that we have a passage assigned to read? First, I brainstorm, which means I try to think of anything I already know about the topic and write it down.

The teacher writes on the board or overhead known qualities of crayons, such as "made of wax," "come in many colors," "can be sharpened," "several different brands."

Teacher: I then take this information I already know and put it into categories, like "what crayons are made of" and "crayon colors." Next, I write down any questions I would like to have answered during my reading, such as "Who invented crayons? When were they invented? How are crayons made? Where are they made?" At this point, I'm ready to read, so I read the passage on crayons. Now I must write down what I learned from this passage. I must include any information that answers the questions I wrote down before I read and any additional information. For example, I learned that colored crayons were first made in the United States in 1903 by Edwin Binney and E. Harold Smith. I also learned that the Crayola Company owns the company that made the original magic markers. Last, I must organize this information into a map so I can see the different main points and any supporting points.

At this point, the teacher draws a map on the chalkboard or overhead.

Teacher: Let's talk about the steps I used and what I did before and after I read the passage.

A class discussion follows.

Teacher: Now I'm going to read the passage again, and I want you to evaluate my textbook reading skills based on the KWL Plus strategy we've learned.

The teacher then proceeds to demonstrate the strategy *incorrectly*.

Teacher: The passage is about crayons. Well, how much can there really be to know about crayons besides there are hundreds of colors and they always seem to break in the middle? Crayons are for little kids, and I'm in junior high so I don't need to know that much about them. I'll just skim the passage and go ahead and answer the question. Okay, how well did I use the strategy steps?

The class discusses the teacher's inappropriate use of the strategy. Notice how the teacher provides both an example and a nonexample—good concept teaching.

The *Guidelines* provide a summary of ideas about studying.

Applying Learning Strategies

Assuming students have a repertoire of powerful learning strategies, will they use them? Several conditions must be met (Ormrod, 2004). First, of course, the learning task must be appropriate. Why would students use more complex learning strategies when the task set by the teacher is to "learn and return" the exact words of the text or lecture? With these

Guidelines: Becoming an Expert Student

Make sure you have the necessary declarative knowledge (facts, concepts, ideas) to understand new information.

EXAMPLES

1. Keep definitions of key vocabulary available as you study.
2. Review required facts and concepts before attempting new material.

Find out what type of test the teacher will give (essay, short answer), and study the material with that in mind.

EXAMPLES

1. For a test with detailed questions, practice writing answers to possible questions.
2. For a multiple-choice test, use mnemonics to remember definitions of key terms.

Make sure you are familiar with the organization of the materials to be learned.

EXAMPLES

1. Preview the headings, introductions, topic sentences, and summaries of the text.
2. Be alert for words and phrases that signal relationships, such as *on the other hand, because, first, second, however, since.*

Know your own cognitive skills and use them deliberately.

EXAMPLES

1. Use examples and analogies to relate new material to something you care about and understand well, such as sports, hobbies, or films.
2. If one study technique is not working, try another—the goal is to stay involved, not to use any particular strategy.

Study the right information in the right way.

EXAMPLES

1. Be sure you know exactly what topics and readings the test will cover.
2. Spend your time on the important, difficult, and unfamiliar material that will be required for the test or assignment.
3. Keep a list of the parts of the text that give you trouble and spend more time on those pages.
4. Process the important information thoroughly by using mnemonics, forming images, creating examples, answering questions, making notes in your own words, and elaborating on the text. Do not try to memorize the author's words—use your own.

Monitor your own comprehension.

EXAMPLES

1. Use questioning to check your understanding.
2. When reading speed slows down, decide if the information in the passage is important. If it is, note the problem so you can reread or get help to understand. If it is not important, ignore it.
3. Check your understanding by working with a friend and quizzing one another.

For more resources on studying, see:
http://www.ucc.vt.edu/stdysk/stdyhlp.html or
http://www.d.umn.edu/student/loon/acad/strat/

Source: From "Research Synthesis on Study Skills" by B. B. Armbruster and T. H. Anderson. *Educational Leadership*, 39. The Association for Supervision and Curriculum Development is a worldwide community of educators advocating sound policies and sharing best practices to achieve the success of each learner. To learn more, visit ASCD at www.ascd.org.

tasks, memorizing will be rewarded and the best strategies involve distributed practice and perhaps mnemonics (described in Chapter 7). But we hope that there are few of these kinds of tasks in contemporary teaching, so if the task is understanding, not memorizing, what else is necessary?

Valuing Learning. The second condition for using sophisticated strategies is that students must care about learning and understanding. They must have goals that can be reached using effective strategies (Zimmerman & Schunk, 2001). I was reminded of this one semester when I enthusiastically shared with my educational psychology class an article from the newspaper, *USA Today*, about study skills. The gist of the article was that students should continually revise and rewrite their notes from a course, so that by the end, all their understanding could be captured in one or two pages. Of course, the majority of the knowledge at that point would be reorganized and connected well with other knowledge. "See," I told the class, "these ideas are real—not just trapped in texts. They can help you study smarter

Connect and Extend to Other Chapters

The guidelines for study skills apply to everyone who wishes to become an expert learner and involve the metacognitive abilities and executive control processes discussed in Chapter 7. See Chapter 7 for a discussion of declarative, procedural, and conditional knowledge.

in college." After a heated discussion, one of the best students said in exasperation, "I'm carrying 18 hours—I don't have time to *learn* this stuff!" She did not believe that her goal—to survive the 18 hours—could be reached by using time-consuming study strategies.

Effort and Efficacy. The student above also was concerned about effort. The third condition for applying learning strategies is that students must believe the effort and investment required to apply the strategies are *reasonable*, given the likely return (Winne, 2001). And of course, students must believe that they are capable of using the strategies; that is, they must have self-efficacy for using the strategies to learn the material in question (Schunk, 2004). This is related to another condition. Students must have a base of knowledge and/or experience in the area. No learning strategies will help students accomplish tasks that are completely beyond their current understandings.

Connect and Extend to the Research

See the Winter 2004 special issue of the *Educational Psychologist* on "Personal Epistemology: Paradigmatic Approaches to Understanding Students' Beliefs about Knowledge and Knowing" (Vol. 39, No. 1). Guest Editor: Barbara K. Hofer.

Epistemological Beliefs. Finally, what students believe about knowledge and learning (their epistemological beliefs) will influence the kinds of strategies that they use.

STOP | THINK | WRITE How would you answer these questions taken from Chan & Sachs (2001)?

1. The most important thing in learning math is to: (a) remember what the teacher has taught you, (b) practice lots of problems, (c) understand the problems you work on.
2. The most important thing you can do when trying to do science is (a) faithfully do the work the teacher tells you, (b) try to see how the explanation makes sense, (c) try to remember everything you are supposed to know.
3. If you wanted to know everything there is about something, say animals, how long would you have to study it? (a) less than a year if you study hard, (b) about one or two years, (c) forever.
4. As you learn more and more about something (a) the questions get more and more complex, (b) the questions get easier and easier, (c) the questions all get answered. ■

Using questions like those above, researchers have identified several dimensions of **epistemological beliefs** (Chan & Sachs, 2001; Schommer, 1997; Schommer-Aikins, 2002; Schraw & Olafson, 2002). For example:

- **Structure of Knowledge:** Is knowledge in a field a simple set of facts or a complex structure of concepts and relationships?
- **Stability/Certainty of Knowledge:** Is knowledge fixed or evolving over time?
- **Ability to Learn:** Is the ability to learn fixed (based on innate ability) or changeable?
- **Speed of Learning:** Can we gain knowledge quickly or does it take time to develop knowledge?
- **Nature of Learning:** Does learning mean memorizing facts passed down from authorities and keeping the facts isolated, or developing your own integrated understandings?

Students' beliefs about knowing and learning affect their use of learning strategies. For example, if you believe that knowledge should be gained quickly, you are likely to try one or two quick strategies (read the text once, spend 2 minutes trying to solve the word problem) and then stop. If you believe that learning means developing integrated understandings, you will process the material more deeply, connect to existing knowledge, create your own examples, or draw diagrams, and generally elaborate the information to make it your own (Hofer & Pintrich, 1997; Kardash & Howell, 2000). In one study, elementary school students (grades 4 and 6), who believed that learning is understanding, processed science texts more deeply than students who believed that learning is reproducing facts (Chan & Sachs, 2001). The questions about learning in the *Stop/Think/Write* box above were used in that study to assess the students' beliefs. The answers associated with a belief in complex, evolving, knowledge that takes time to understand and grows from active learning are 1c, 2b, 3c, and 4a.

Here is an important question: What is the purpose of all that studying if you never use the knowledge—if you never transfer it to new situations?

Epistemological beliefs Beliefs about the structure, stability, and certainty of knowledge and how knowledge is best learned.

Teaching for Transfer

STOP | THINK | WRITE Think back for a moment to a class in one of your high-school subjects that you have not studied in college. Imagine the teacher, the room, the textbook. Now remember what you actually learned in class. If it was a science class, what were some of the formulas you learned? Oxidation reduction? Boyle's law? ■

If you are like most of us, you may remember that you learned these things, but you will not be quite sure exactly what you learned. Were those hours wasted? These questions are about the transfer of learning. We turn to that important topic next. Let's begin with a definition of transfer.

Whenever something previously learned influences current learning or when solving an earlier problem affects how you solve a new problem, **transfer** has occurred (Mayer & Wittrock, 1996). Erik De Corte (2003) calls transfer "the productive use of cognitive tools and motivations" (p. 142). This meaning of transfer emphasizes doing something new (productive), not just reproducing a previous application of the tools. If students learn a mathematical principle in one class and use it to solve a physics problem days or weeks later in another class, then transfer has taken place. However, the effect of past learning on present learning is not always positive. *Functional fixedness* and *response set* (described earlier in this chapter) are examples of negative transfer because they are attempts to apply familiar but *inappropriate* strategies to a new situation.

Connect and Extend to PRAXIS II™
Transfer of Learning
Successful transfer of learning from the school to other contexts is evidence of superior instruction. What can teachers do to optimize transfer of knowledge and skills to the broader world?

The Many Views of Transfer

Transfer has been a focus of research in educational psychology for over 100 years. After all, the productive use of knowledge, skills, and motivations across a lifetime is a fundamental goal of education (De Corte, 2003). Early work focused on specific transfer of skills and the general transfer of mental discipline gained from studying rigorous subjects such as Latin or mathematics. But in 1924, E. L. Thorndike demonstrated that there was no mental discipline benefit from learning Latin. Learning Latin just helped you learn more Latin. So, thanks to Thorndike, you were not required to take Latin in high school. Other researchers looked at positive and negative transfer, such as the appropriate and inappropriate uses of heuristics in solving problems.

More recently, researchers distinguish between the automatic, direct use of skills such as reading or writing in everyday applications versus the extraordinary transfer of knowledge and strategies to arrive at creative solutions to problems (Bereiter, 1995; Bransford & Schwartz, 1999; Salomon & Perkins, 1989). Gabriel Salomon and David Perkins (1989) describe these two kinds of transfer, termed low-road and high-road transfer. **Low-road transfer** "involves the spontaneous, automatic transfer of highly practiced skills, with little need for reflective thinking" (p. 118). The key to low-road transfer is practicing a skill often, in a variety of situations, until your performance becomes automatic. So if you worked one summer for a temporary secretarial service and were sent to many different offices to work on all kinds of computers, by the end of the summer you probably would be able to handle most machines easily. Your practice with many machines would let you transfer your skill automatically to a new situation. Bransford and Schwartz (1999) refer to this kind of transfer as *direct-application transfer.*

High-road transfer, on the other hand, involves consciously applying abstract knowledge or strategies learned in one situation to a different situation. This can happen in one of two ways. First, you may learn a principle or a strategy, intending to use it in the future—*forward-reaching* transfer. For example, if you plan to apply what you learn in anatomy class this semester to work in a life-drawing course you will take next semester, you may search for principles about human proportions, muscle definition, and so on. Second, when you are faced with a problem, you may look back on what you have learned in other situations to help you in this new one—*backward-reaching* transfer. Analogical thinking is an example of this kind of transfer. You search for other, related situations that might provide clues to the current problem. Bransford and Schwartz (1999) consider this kind of high-road transfer to be *preparation for future learning.*

Transfer Influence of previously learned material on new material.

Low-road transfer Spontaneous and automatic transfer of highly practiced skills.

High-road transfer Application of abstract knowledge learned in one situation to a different situation.

TABLE 8.3

Kinds of Transfer

	Low-Road Transfer (Direct-Application)	High-Road Transfer (Preparation for Future Learning)
Definition	Automatic transfer of highly practiced skill	Conscious application of abstract knowledge to a new situation Productive use of cognitive tools and motivations
Key Conditions	Extensive practice Variety of settings and conditions Overlearning to automaticity	Mindful focus on abstracting a principle, main idea, or procedure that can be used in many situations Learning in powerful teaching-learning environments
Examples	Driving many different cars Finding your gate in an airport	Applying KWL or READS strategies Applying procedures from math in designing a page layout for the school newspaper

The key to high-road transfer is *mindful abstraction*, or the deliberate identification of a principle, main idea, strategy, or procedure that is not tied to one specific problem or situation, but could apply to many. Such an abstraction becomes part of your metacognitive knowledge, available to guide future learning and problem solving. Bransford and Schwartz (1999) add another key—a resource-rich environment that supports productive, appropriate transfer. Table 8.3 summarizes the types of transfer.

Teaching for Positive Transfer

Years of research and experience show that students will master new knowledge, problem-solving procedures, and learning strategies, but usually they will not use them unless prompted or guided. For example, studies of real-world mathematics show that people do not always apply math procedures learned in school to solve practical problems in their homes or grocery stores (Lave, 1988; Lave & Wenger, 1991). This happens because learning is *situated;* that is, learning happens in specific situations. We learn solutions to particular problems, not general, all-purpose solutions that can fit any problem. Because knowledge is learned as a tool to solve particular problems, we may not realize that the knowledge is relevant when we encounter a problem that seems different, at least on the surface (Driscoll, 2005; Singley & Anderson, 1989). How can you make sure your students will use what they learn, even when situations change?

What Is Worth Learning? First, you must answer the question "What is worth learning?" The learning of basic skills such as reading, writing, computing, cooperating, and speaking will definitely transfer to other situations, because these skills are necessary for later work both in and out of school—writing job applications, reading novels, paying bills, working on a team, locating and evaluating health care services, among others. All later learning depends on positive transfer of these basics to new situations.

Teachers must also be aware of what the future is likely to hold for their students, both as a group and as individuals. What will society require of them as adults? As a child growing up in Texas in the 1950s and 1960s, I studied nothing about computers, even though my father was a computer systems analyst; yet now I spend hours at my Mac. Computer programming and word processing were not part of my high-school curriculum, but I learned to use a slide rule. Now, calculators and computers have made this skill obsolete. My mom encouraged me to take advanced math and physics instead of typing in high school. Those were great classes, but I struggle with typing every day at my computer—who knew? Undoubtedly, changes as extreme and unpredictable as these await the students you will teach. For this reason, the general transfer of principles, attitudes, learning strategies, motivations, and problem solving will be just as important for your students as the specific transfer of basic skills.

How Can Teachers Help? For basic skills, greater transfer can also be ensured by **overlearning**, practicing a skill past the point of mastery. Many of the basic facts students learn in elementary school, such as the multiplication tables, are traditionally overlearned. Overlearning helps students retrieve the information quickly and automatically when it is needed. See the *Stories of Learning/Tributes to Teaching* feature for an example of active engagement and overlearning.

For higher-level transfer, students must first learn and understand. Students will be more likely to transfer knowledge to new situations if they have been actively involved in the learning process. They must be encouraged to form abstractions that they will apply later. Erik De Corte (2003) believes that teachers support transfer, the productive use of cognitive tools and motivations, when they create powerful teaching-learning environments using these design principles:

- The environments should support constructive learning processes in all students.
- The environments should encourage the development of student self-regulation, so that teachers gradually give over more and more responsibilities to the students.
- Learning should involve interaction and collaboration.
- Learners should deal with problems that have personal meaning for them, problems like they will face in the future.
- The classroom culture should encourage students to become aware of and develop their cognitive and motivational processes. In order to be productive users of these tools, students must know about and value them.

The next three chapters delve in depth about how to support constructive learning, motivation, self-regulation, collaboration, and self-awareness in all students.

There is one last kind of transfer that is especially important for students—the transfer of the learning strategies we encountered in the previous section. Learning strategies and tactics are meant to be applied across a wide range of situations, but this often does not happen, as you will see below.

Connect and **Extend** to Your **Teaching/Portfolio**

"The greatest enemy of understanding is coverage. As long as you are determined to cover everything, you actually ensure that most kids are not going to understand." Howard Gardner in Brandt, R. (1993). On teaching for understanding: A Conversation with Howard Gardner. *Educational Leadership, 50*(7), 7.

Overlearning Practicing a skill past the point of mastery.

STORIES OF LEARNING / TRIBUTES TO TEACHING

ESME CODELL, a first-year teacher in an urban school, describes how she helped her students learn and succeed in a real-world task that was especially difficult for them—public speaking.

"I know in the face of the wide world these are small victories . . ."

May 12

Storyteller's Workshop is going well. I got a small grant. After school a couple of times a week, I train about a dozen children to give dramatic performances of folktales. I specifically picked children who are particularly shy or challenged in reading or speaking. We went on a field trip to see a professional storyteller, and they all own copies of the books they are going to perform. For the past six weeks I've been training them, modeling for them, and—to some extent—pressuring them. I had them go "on tour" to other classes during school hours to help them gain confidence and to get feedback. We are hosting a school-wide storytelling festival in less than two weeks.

Maurissa didn't want to perform for the fourth grade. Her dark skin paled to the color of ash, she was so afraid. I sent her with Ruben and Latoya, to watch and support her. She begged me not to make her go. Secretly, I wondered if she would throw up. But I literally pushed her out the door anyway and told her not to return until the mission was accomplished, that I knew she could do it. She came back fifteen minutes later—I should say leapt in—smiling broadly, her color back to normal.

"I did it! I did a beautiful job." She burst out laughing and crying at the same time, and we embraced.

Rochelle, another shy girl I sent out, returned breathing heavily. "You were right! The kids did join in on the repeated lines." I'm so proud of their successes. I know in the face of the wide world these are small victories, but sometimes a little song is sweet to hear, even if an orchestra is more accomplished.

Source: From Codell, 2001, pp. 156–158.

Concept learning, problem solving, and strategy learning are likely affected by prior knowledge, beliefs, and skills that are based on individual experience and culture.

Stages of Transfer for Strategies. Sometimes students simply don't understand that a particular strategy applies in new situations or they don't know how to adapt it to fit. As we saw above, they may think the strategy takes too much time (Schunk, 2004).

Gary Phye (1992, 2001; Phye & Sanders, 1994) suggests we think of the transfer of learning strategies as a tool to be used in a "mindful" way to solve academic problems. He describes three stages in developing strategic transfer. In the *acquisition phase*, students should not only receive instruction about a strategy and how to use it, but they should also rehearse the strategy and practice being aware of when and how they are using it. In the *retention phase*, more practice with feedback helps students hone their strategy use. In the *transfer phase*, the teacher should provide new problems that can be solved with the same strategy, even though the problems appear different on the surface. To enhance motivation, point out to students how using the strategy will help them solve many problems and accomplish different tasks. These steps help build both procedural and conditional knowledge—how to use the strategy as well as when and why.

Diversity and Convergences in Complex Cognitive Processes

This chapter has covered quite a bit of territory, partly because the cognitive perspective has so many implications for instruction. Although they are varied, you can see that most of the cognitive ideas for teaching concepts, creative problem-solving skills, and learning strategies emphasize the role of the student's prior knowledge and the need for active, mindful learning.

Diversity

Concept learning, problem solving, and strategy-learning processes may be similar for all students, but the prior knowledge, beliefs, and skills they bring to the classroom are bound to vary, based on their experience and culture. For example, Zhe Chen and his colleagues (2004) wondered if college students might use familiar folk tales—one kind of cultural knowledge—as analogies to solve problems. That is just what happened. Chinese students were better at solving a problem of weighing a statue because the problem was similar to their folk tale about how to weigh an elephant (by water displacement). American students were better at solving a problem of finding the way out of a cave (leaving a trail), by using an analogy to Hansel and Gretel, a common American folk tale. In another study in Australia, Volet (1999) found that some culturally based knowledge and motivation of Asian students—such as high achievement motivation, a deep processing and effortful approach to learning, and a recognition of the benefits of collaboration—

Family and Community Partnerships

Guidelines: Promoting Transfer

Keep families informed about their child's curriculum so they can support learning.

EXAMPLES

1. At the beginning of units or major projects, send a letter summarizing the key goals, a few of the major assignments, and some common problems students have in learning the material for that unit.
2. Ask parents for suggestions about how their child's interests could be connected to the curriculum topics.
3. Invite parents to school for an evening of "strategy learning." Have the students teach their family members one of the strategies they have learned in school.

Give families ideas for how they might encourage their children to practice, extend, or apply learning from school.

EXAMPLES

1. To extend writing, ask parents to encourage their children to write letters or e-mail to companies or civic organizations asking for information or free products. Provide a shell letter form for structure and ideas and include addresses of companies that provide free samples or information.
2. Ask family members to include their children in some projects that require measurement, halfing or doubling recipes, or estimating costs.
3. Suggest that students work with grandparents to do a family memory book. Combine historical research and writing.

Show connections between learning in school and life outside school.

EXAMPLES

1. Ask families to talk about and show how they use the skills their children are learning in their jobs, hobbies, or community involvement projects.
2. Ask family members to come to class to demonstrate how they use reading, writing, science, math, or other knowledge in their work.

Make families partners in practicing learning strategies.

EXAMPLES

1. Focus on one learning tactic at a time—ask families to simply remind their children to use a particular tactic with homework that week.
2. Develop a lending library of books and videotapes to teach families about learning strategies.
3. Give parents a copy of the Becoming an Expert Student Guidelines on page 317, rewritten for your grade level.

For more information on promoting transfer see:
http://www.kidsource.com/education/motivation.lang.learn.html#2

transferred well to Western-oriented schools. Other culturally based beliefs, such as valuing rote memorization or solitary learning might cause conflicts with the expectations of some schools. For example, we saw in Chapter 5 that the native Hawaiian style of interacting was seen as interrupting by non-Hawaiian teachers until the teachers learned more about the family communication styles of their students.

Creativity and Diversity. Even though creativity has been studied for centuries, as Dean Simonton said, "Psychologists still have a long way to go before they come anywhere close to understanding creativity in women and minorities" (2000, p. 156). The focus of creativity research and writing over the years has been white males. Patterns of creativity in other groups are complex—sometimes matching and sometimes diverging from patterns found in traditional research. The *Family and Community Partnerships Guidelines* give ideas for enlisting the support of families in encouraging transfer.

In another connection between creativity and culture, research suggests that being on the outside of mainstream society, being bilingual, or being exposed to other cultures might encourage creativity (Simonton, 1999, 2000). In fact, true innovators often break rules. "Creators have a desire to shake things up. They are restless, rebellious, and dissatisfied with the status quo" (Winner, 2000, p. 167).

Convergences

As you have seen throughout this chapter, in the beginning, as students learn problem solving or try to transfer cognitive tools to new situations, there is a tendency to focus on surface features. For all novices, their challenge is to grasp the abstractions: underlying principles, structures, strategies, or big ideas. It is those larger ideas that lead to understanding and serve as a foundation for future learning (Chen & Mo, 2004).

A second convergence: For all students, there is a positive relationship between using learning strategies and academic gains such as high-school GPA and retention in college (Robbins, Le, & Lauver, 2005). Some students will learn productive strategies on their own, but all students can benefit from direct teaching, modeling, and practice of learning strategies and study skills. This is one important way to prepare all your students for their futures. Newly mastered concepts, principles, and strategies must be applied in a wide variety of situations and problems (Chen & Mo, 2004). Positive transfer is encouraged when skills are practiced under authentic conditions, similar to those that will exist when the skills are needed later. Students can learn to write by corresponding with e-mail pen pals in other countries. They can learn historical research methods by researching their own families. Some of these applications should involve complex, ill-defined, unstructured problems, because many of the problems to be faced in later life, both in school and out, will not come to students complete with instructions.

Connect and **Extend** to Your **Teaching/Portfolio**

Use the Family and Community Partnerships Guidelines to brainstorm ideas for family involvement in helping your students "take their learning home."

SUMMARY TABLE

Learning and Teaching about Concepts

(pp. 286–294)

Distinguish between prototypes and exemplars. Concepts are categories used to group similar events, ideas, people, or objects. A prototype is the best representative of its category. For instance, the best representative of the "birds" category for many Americans might be a robin. Exemplars are our actual memories of specific birds and so on that we use to compare with an item in question to see if that item belongs in the same category as our exemplar. We probably learn concepts from prototypes or exemplars of the category, understand in terms of our schematic knowledge, and then refine concepts through our additional experience of relevant and irrelevant features.

What are the four elements needed in concept teaching? Lessons about concepts include four basic components: concept examples (along with nonexamples), relevant and irrelevant attributes, name, and definition. The concept attainment model is one approach to teaching concepts that asks students to form hypotheses about why particular examples are members of a category and what that category (concept) might be.

What are the key characteristics of Bruner's discovery learning? In discovery learning, the teacher presents examples and the students work with the examples until they discover the interrelationships—the subject's structure. Bruner believes that classroom learning should take place through inductive reasoning, that is, by using specific examples to formulate a general principle.

What are the stages of Ausubel's expository teaching? Ausubel believes that learning should progress deductively: from the general to the specific, or from the rule or principle to examples. After presenting an advance organizer, the next step in a lesson using Ausubel's approach is to present content in terms of basic similarities and differences, using specific examples. Finally, when all the material has been presented, ask students to discuss how the examples can be used to expand on the original advance organizer.

How can you teach concepts through analogies? By identifying known information that relates to a new concept, teachers and students can map the analogies between the known and the new, then summarize an understanding of the new concept by explaining the similarities and differences between the known and the new concepts.

Concept A general category of ideas, objects, people, or experiences whose members share certain properties.

Defining attributes Distinctive features shared by members of a category.

Prototype Best representative of a category.

Exemplar A specific example of a given category that is used to classify an item.

Undergeneralization Exclusion of some true members from a category; limiting a concept.

Overgeneralization Inclusion of nonmembers in a category; overextending a concept.

Concept mapping Student's diagram of his or her understanding of a concept.

Discovery learning Bruner's approach, in which students work on their own to discover basic principles.

Inductive reasoning Formulating general principles based on knowledge of examples and details.

Intuitive thinking Making imaginative leaps to correct perceptions or workable solutions.

Guided discovery An adaptation of discovery learning, in which the teacher provides some direction.

Expository teaching Ausubel's method—teachers present material in complete, organized form, moving from broadest to more specific concepts.

Deductive reasoning Drawing conclusions by applying rules or principles; logically moving from a general rule or principle to a specific solution.

Meaningful verbal learning Focused and organized relationships among ideas and verbal information.

Advance organizer Statement of inclusive concepts to introduce and sum up material that follows.

Analogical instruction Teaching new concepts by making connections (analogies) with information that the student already understands.

Problem Solving (pp. 294–305)

What are the steps in the general problem-solving process? Problem solving is both general and domain-specific. The five stages of problem solving are contained in the acronym IDEAL: *I*dentify problems and opportunities; *D*efine goals and represent the problem; *E*xplore possible strategies; *A*nticipate outcomes and Act; *L*ook back and *L*earn.

Why is the representation stage of problem solving so important? To represent the problem accurately, you must understand both the whole problem and its discrete elements. Schema training may improve this ability. The problem-solving process follows entirely different paths, depending on what representation and goal are chosen. If your representation of the problem suggests an immediate solution, the task is done; the new problem is recognized as a "disguised" version of an old problem with a clear solution. But if there is no existing way of solving the problem or if the activated schema fails, then students must search for a solution. The application of algorithms and heuristics—such as means-ends analysis, analogical thinking, working backward, and verbalization—may help students solve problems.

Describe factors that can interfere with problem solving. Factors that hinder problem solving include functional fixedness or rigidity (response set). These disallow the flexibility needed to represent problems accurately and to have insight into solutions. Also, as we make decisions and judgments, we may overlook important information because we base judgments on what seems representative of a category (representativeness heuristic) or what is available in memory (availability heuristic), then pay attention only to information that confirms our choices (confirmation bias) so that we hold onto beliefs, even in the face of contradictory evidence (belief perseverance).

What are the differences between expert and novice knowledge in a given area? Expert problem solvers have a rich store of declarative, procedural, and conditional knowledge. They organize this knowledge around general principles or patterns that apply to large classes of problems. They work faster, remember relevant information, and monitor their progress better than novices.

How do misconceptions interfere with learning? If the students' intuitive model includes misconceptions and inaccuracies, then the students are likely to develop inadequate or misleading representations of a problem. In order to learn new information and solve problems, students must sometimes "unlearn" common-sense ideas.

Problem Any situation in which you are trying to reach some goal and must find a means to do so.

Problem solving Creating new solutions for problems.

Schema-driven problem solving Recognizing a problem as a "disguised" version of an old problem for which one already has a solution.

Algorithm Step-by-step procedure for solving a problem; prescription for solutions.

Heuristic General strategy used in attempting to solve problems.

Means-ends analysis Heuristic in which a goal is divided into subgoals.

Working-backward strategy Heuristic in which one starts with the goal and moves backward to solve the problem.

Analogical thinking Heuristic in which one limits the search for solutions to situations that are similar to the one at hand.

Verbalization Putting your problem-solving plan and its logic into words.

Functional fixedness Inability to use objects or tools in a new way.

Response set Rigidity; tendency to respond in the most familiar way.

Representativeness heuristic Judging the likelihood of an event based on how well the events match your prototypes—what you think is representative of a category.

Availability heuristic Judging the likelihood of an event based on what is available in your memory, assuming those easily remembered events are common.

Belief perseverance The tendency to hold onto beliefs, even in the face of contradictory evidence.

Confirmation bias Seeking information that confirms our choices and beliefs, while disconfirming evidence.

Insight Sudden realization of a solution.

Creativity and Creative Problem Solving (pp. 305–311)

What are some myths about creativity? These four statements are completely or partly wrong. Creativity is determined at birth. Creativity comes with negative personality traits. Creative people are disorganized hippie types. Working in a group enhances creativity. The facts are: Creativity can be developed. A few but not all creative people are nonconforming or have emotional problems. Many creative people are focused, organized, and part of the mainstream. Finally, groups can limit as well as enhance creativity.

What is creativity and how is it assessed? Creativity is a process that involves independently restructuring problems to see things in new, imaginative ways. Creativity is difficult to measure, but tests of divergent thinking can assess originality, fluency, and flexibility. Originality is usually determined statistically. To be original, a response must be given by fewer than 5 or 10 people out of every 100 who take the test. Fluency is the number of different responses. The number of different categories of responses measures flexibility. Teachers can encourage creativity by providing opportunities for play, using brainstorming techniques, and accepting divergent ideas.

What can teachers do to support creativity in the classroom? Teachers can encourage creativity in their interactions with students by accepting unusual, imaginative answers, modeling divergent thinking, using brainstorming, and tolerating dissent.

Creativity Imaginative, original thinking or problem solving.

Restructuring Conceiving of a problem in a new or different way.

Divergent thinking Coming up with many possible solutions.

Convergent thinking Narrowing possibilities to a single answer.

Brainstorming Generating ideas without stopping to evaluate them.

Becoming an Expert Student: Learning Strategies and Study Skills (pp. 311–318)

Distinguish between learning strategies and tactics. Learning strategies are ideas for accomplishing learning goals, a kind of overall plan of attack. Learning tactics are the specific techniques that make up the plan. A strategy for learning might include several tactics such as mnemonics to remember key terms, skimming to identify the organization, and then writing answers to possible essay questions. Use of strategies and tactics reflects metacognitive knowledge.

What key functions do learning strategies play? Learning strategies help students *become cognitively engaged*—focus attention on the relevant or important aspects of the material. Second, they encourage students to *invest effort*, make connections, elaborate, translate, organize, and reorganize in order to *think and process deeply*—the greater the practice and processing, the stronger the learning. Finally, strategies help students *regulate and monitor* their own learning—keep track of what is making sense and notice when a new approach is needed.

Describe some procedures for developing learning strategies. Expose students to a number of different strategies, not only general learning strategies but also very specific tactics, such as the graphic strategies. Teach conditional knowledge about when, where, and why to use various strategies. Develop motivation to use the strategies and tactics by showing students how their learning and performance can be improved. Provide direct instruction in content knowledge needed to use the strategies.

When will students apply learning strategies? If they have appropriate strategies, students will apply them if they are faced with a task that requires good strategies, value doing well on that task, think the effort to apply the strategies will be worthwhile, and believe that they can succeed using the strategies. Also, to apply deep processing strategies, students must assume that knowledge is complex and takes time to learn and that learning requires their own active efforts.

Learning strategies General plans for approaching learning tasks.

Learning tactics Specific techniques for learning, such as using mnemonics or outlining a passage.

Cmaps Tools for concept mapping developed by the Institute for Human Machine Cognition that are connected to many knowledge maps and other resources on the Internet.

READS A five-step reading strategy: *Review* headings; *Examine* boldface words; *Ask*, "What do I expect to learn?"; *Do* it—Read; *Summarize* in your own words.

CAPS A strategy that can be used in reading literature: *Characters, Aim* of story, *Problem, Solution*.

KWL A strategy to guide reading and inquiry: Before—What do I already *know*? What do I *want* to know? After—What have I *learned*?

Epistemological beliefs Beliefs about the structure, stability, and certainty of knowledge and how knowledge is best learned.

Teaching for Transfer (pp. 319–322)

What is transfer? Transfer occurs when a rule, fact, or skill learned in one situation is applied in another situation; for example, applying rules of punctuation to write a job application letter. Transfer also involves applying to new problems the principles learned in other, often dissimilar situations.

Distinguish between low-road and high-road transfer. Transfer involving spontaneity and automaticity in familiar situations has been called *low-road transfer. High-road transfer* involves reflection and conscious application of abstract knowledge to new situations. Learning environments should support active constructive learning, self-regulation, collaboration, and awareness of cognitive tools and motivational processes. In addition, students should deal with problems that have meaning in their lives. In addition, teachers can help students transfer learning strategies by teaching strategies directly, providing practice with feedback, and then expanding the application of the strategies to new and unfamiliar situations.

Transfer Influence of previously learned material on new material; the productive (not reproductive) uses of cognitive tools and motivations.

Low-road transfer Spontaneous and automatic transfer of highly practiced skills.

High-road transfer Application of abstract knowledge learned in one situation to a different situation.

Overlearning Practicing a skill past the point of mastery.

Teachers' Casebook: Connections to PRAXIS II™

In this chapter's Teachers' Casebook you recognized that your students need good study skills to do well in their classes now and those in the future. But how can you help them develop these skills and still learn all the material demanded by your district curriculum guides? Here is how some practicing teachers responded to the challenge. PRAXIS II™ often includes questions on learning strategies and study skills.

What Would They Do?

Here is how some practicing teachers would help their students develop study skills as they teach content.

Vivian M. LaColla **Special Education Teacher,**

Noxon Road Elementary School, Poughkeepsie, New York

The majority of children need to be taught "how to study." Teaching skills to help them study and manage time should be started with smaller reading assignments and spelling tests that begin as early as first grade. Incorporating strategies taken from SQRW (Survey, Question, Ready, Write) and REDW (Read, Examine, Decide, Write) with shorter passages can help students develop these skills toward reading, understanding, and remembering longer assignments. Note taking, outlining, use of index cards, acronyms, and mnemonics are essential skills that are applied during proficiency or achievement tests. To help students manage time with larger projects, it is important to teach students how to break down each assignment into smaller tasks and apply reasonable due dates. This can be done as a whole group while prioritizing and creating checklists for each task. Developing organizational skills using calendars, schedules, and checklists at the early grades is essential.

Deborah P. Reed

Darby Woods Elementary School, Galloway, OH

Thomas J. Reed

Beechcroft High School, Columbus, OH

In order to help students develop effective study strategies and organizational skills, model exemplary processes and provide multiple opportunities for practice. To model exemplary processes, show long passages of text on an overhead and articulate the processes that identify the main idea, the ways to organize information, and the connections to one's own experiences. As students gain competencies in their own study skills, allow them to model their processes, choices, and connections to the rest of the class. To provide opportunities for practice, establish checkpoints for students assigned to large projects. Breaking the project down into short intervals of three to seven days, require students to complete specific tasks related to the project, and provide timely, content-specific feedback on everything students submit. If at any time a student is falling behind, employ a variety of interventions to help the student get back on track.

Debbie Youngblood **Sixth Grade Wellness and Physical Education Teacher,** *Hillard City Schools, Hillard, Ohio*

I would begin by modeling the necessary organizational skills. State standards, benchmarks, and indicators for each content area would be posted in the classroom, and daily learning objectives for each subject would be written on the chalkboard, allowing students to focus on what is most important. Students would be provided with a list of required organizational school supplies, including an age-appropriate daily planner divided into core content areas, ring binders, dividers, pencils, pens, and highlighters. Class time would be utilized during the first week of school to walk the students through the organization of their binders with a section for each subject. Assignments would be recorded daily in their planners and on assignment logs for each subject. By working backwards from the due dates for each assignment, we would map out and record timelines for successful completion of each one. I would divide larger projects into smaller assignments with frequent completion checkpoints along the way.

Randall G. Sampson **Assistant-Principal,**

Genoa Middle School, Westerville, Ohio

Students' demonstration of their ability to synthesize and evaluate newly aquired knowledge should be a pinnacle of the assessment for learning process. Teachers should encourage and require all students to utilize their writing skills in order to synthesize information. I would recommend that teachers provide students with short cycle goals, a comprehensive rubric, and efficacy focused on mastery orientation.

W. Sean Kearney **Former Assistant Principal,**

Galen R. Elolf Elementary School, Converse, Texas

Consider how material is being delivered in the classroom setting. Are the various learning styles of students being addressed (kinesthetic, auditory, visual)? If not, then look at your lesson plans to see how you can alter them to make them more memorable for students. Most local colleges offer courses in study skills. Consider asking someone from the local community college or university to visit your class and present information on study skills. If they are not able to come, ask for relevant information so that you can present it to the class yourself. Don't forget to use the parents as a resource. Phone calls or conferences with parents will provide the at-home follow-up to ensure individual success.

CHAPTER 9

Social Cognitive and Constructivist Views of Learning

Teachers' Casebook: What Would You Do? 329

Social Cognitive Theory 330

Reciprocal Determinism 330

Self-Efficacy 332

Applying Social Cognitive Theory 333

Self-Efficacy and Motivation 333

Teachers' Sense of Efficacy 334

Self-Regulated Learning 335

An Individual Example 338

Reaching Every Student: Two Classrooms and the Family 339

Teaching Toward Self-Efficacy and Self-Regulated Learning 340

Cognitive and Social Constructivism 343

Constructivist Views of Learning 344

How Is Knowledge Constructed? 346

Knowledge: Situated or General? 347

Common Elements of Constructivist Perspectives 348

Applying Constructivist Perspectives 350

Inquiry and Problem-Based Learning 351

Dialogue and Instructional Conversations 355

Cognitive Apprenticeships 356

Apprenticeships in Thinking 359

An Integrated Constructivist Program: Fostering Communities of Learners 361

Dilemmas of Constructivist Practice 362

Diversity and Convergences in Theories of Learning 362

Diversity 363

Convergences 364

Summary Table 366

Teachers' Casebook: Connections to PRAXIS II™/ What Would They Do? 369

What Would You Do?

Teachers' Casebook

You have finally landed a job teaching English and writing in a high school. The first day of class, you discover that a number of students appear to be just learning English. You make a mental note to meet with them to determine how much and what kind of reading they can handle. To get a sense of the class's interest, you ask them to write a "review" of the last book they read, as if they were on TV doing a "Book Beat" program. There is a bit of grumbling, but the students seem to be writing, so you take a few minutes to try to talk with one of the students who seems to have trouble with English.

That night you look over the "book reviews." Either the students are giving you a hard time, or no one has read anything lately. Several students mention a text from another class, but their reviews are one-sentence evaluations—usually containing the words "lame" or "useless" (often misspelled). In stark contrast are the papers of three students—they are a pleasure to read, worthy of publication in the school literary magazine (if there were one), and they reflect a fairly sophisticated understanding of some good literature.

Critical Thinking

- How would you adapt your plans for this group?
- What will you do tomorrow?
- What teaching approaches do you think will work with this class?
- How will you work with the three students who are more advanced and the students who are just learning English?

Collaboration

With 2 or 3 other students in your class, redesign the assignment to get students more engaged. How could you prepare them to use what they know to succeed on this assignment?

For the past three chapters, we have analyzed different aspects of learning. We considered behavioral and information processing explanations of what and how people learn. We have examined complex cognitive processes such as concept learning and problem solving. These explanations of learning focus on the individual and what is happening in his or her "head." Recent perspectives have called attention to two other aspects of learning that are critical—social and cultural factors. In this chapter, we look at the role of other people and the cultural context in learning.

Two general theoretical frames include social and cultural factors as major elements. The first, social cognitive theory, has its roots in Bandura's early social learning theories of observational learning and vicarious reinforcement. You read about these early versions in Chapter 6. The second, sociocultural constructivist theories, have roots in cognitive perspectives, but have moved well beyond these early explanations. Rather than debating the merits of each approach, we will consider the contributions of these different models of instruction, grounded in different theories of learning. Don't feel that you must choose the "best" approach—there is no such thing. Even though theorists argue about which model is best, excellent teachers apply all the approaches as appropriate.

By the time you have completed this chapter, you should be able to answer these questions:

- What is reciprocal determinism and what role does it play in social cognitive theory?
- What is self-efficacy, and how does it affect learning in school?
- What is teachers' sense of efficacy?
- How can teachers support the development of self-efficacy and self-regulated learning?
- What are three constructivist perspectives on learning?
- How could you incorporate inquiry, problem-based learning, instructional conversations, and cognitive apprenticeships in your teaching?
- What dilemmas do constructivist teachers face?

FACING PAGE *Brighton Beach,* Edward Henry Potthast. Oil on wood panel © Christie's Images/SuperStock.

Social Cognitive Theory

As we saw in Chapter 6, in the early 1960s, Albert Bandura demonstrated that people can learn by observing the actions and consequences of others. Bandura's **social learning theory** emphasized observation, modeling, and vicarious reinforcement. Over time, Bandura's explanations of learning included more attention to cognitive factors such as expectations and beliefs in addition to the social influences of models. His current perspective is called **social cognitive theory**.

Reciprocal Determinism

In social cognitive theory, both internal and external factors are important. Environmental events, personal factors, and behaviors are seen as interacting in the process of learning. Personal factors (beliefs, expectations, attitudes, and knowledge), the physical and social environment (resources, consequences of actions, other people, and physical settings), and behavior (individual actions, choices, and verbal statements) all influence and are influenced by each other. Bandura calls this interaction of forces **reciprocal determinism.**

Figure 9.1 shows the interaction of person, environment, and behaviors in learning settings (Schunk, 2004). Social factors such as models, instructional strategies, or feedback (elements of the *environment* for students) can affect student *personal* factors such as goals, sense of efficacy for the task (described in the next section), attributions (beliefs about causes for success and failure), and processes of self-regulation such as planning, monitoring, and controlling distractions. For example, teacher feedback can lead students to set higher goals. Social influences in the environment and personal factors encourage the *behaviors* that lead to achievement such as persistence and effort (motivation) and learning. But these behaviors also reciprocally impact personal factors. As students achieve, their confidence and interest increase, for example. And behaviors also affect the social environment. For example, if students do not persist or if they seem to misunderstand, teachers may change instructional strategies or feedback.

FIGURE 9.1

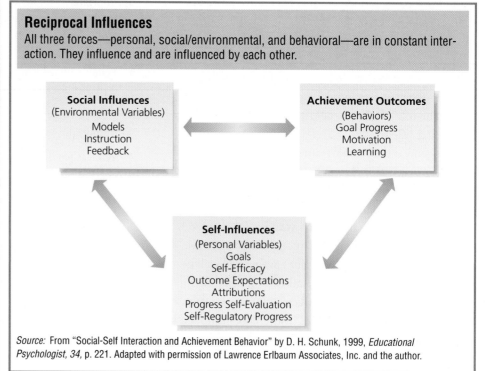

Reciprocal Influences

All three forces—personal, social/environmental, and behavioral—are in constant interaction. They influence and are influenced by each other.

Source: From "Social-Self Interaction and Achievement Behavior" by D. H. Schunk, 1999, *Educational Psychologist, 34,* p. 221. Adapted with permission of Lawrence Erlbaum Associates, Inc. and the author.

Social learning theory Theory that emphasizes learning through observation of others.

Social cognitive theory Theory that adds concern with cognitive factors such as beliefs, self-perceptions, and expectations to social learning theory.

Reciprocal determinism An explanation of behavior that emphasizes the mutual effects of the individual and the environment on each other.

Think for a minute about the power of reciprocal determinism in classrooms. If personal factors, behaviors, and the environment are in constant interaction, then cycles of events are progressive and self-perpetuating. Suppose a student who is new to the school walks into class late because he got lost in the unfamiliar building. The student has a tattoo and several visible pierced body parts. The student actually is anxious about his first day and hopes to do better at this new school, but the teacher's initial reaction to the late entry and dramatic appearance is a bit hostile. The student feels insulted and responds in kind, so the teacher begins to form expectations about the student and acts more vigilant, less trusting. The student senses the distrust. He decides that this school will be just as worthless as his previous one—and wonders why he should bother to try. The teacher sees the student's disengagement, invests less effort in teaching him, and the cycle continues.

For a positive example of the complex interplay of forces that can affect students' experiences in school and their lives, see the *Stories of Learning/Tributes to Teaching*.

STORIES OF LEARNING
TRIBUTES TO TEACHING

The impact of teachers has been captured powerfully in works of fiction. The following story shows both the impact of teachers and the dangers of acting on negative expectations (discussed in Chapter 13). It is adapted from a longer version of this story, available at http://www.saintjohnonline.com/centennialschool/cs_inspirations.html. The teacher, **Miss Thompson,** encountered **Teddy** in her second year of teaching fifth grade. He was dirty and had a strange smell. He fell farther and farther behind. She remembered:

While I did not actually ridicule the boy, my attitude was obviously quite apparent to the class, for he quickly became the class "goat," the outcast: the unlovable and the unloved. He knew I didn't like him, but he didn't know why. All I know is that he was a little boy no one cared about, and I made no effort on his behalf. I knew that Teddy would never catch up in time to be promoted to the sixth grade level. To justify myself, I went to his cumulative folder. First grade: Teddy shows promise by work and attitude, but has poor home situation. Second grade: Teddy could do better. Mother terminally ill. He receives little help at home. Third grade: Teddy is a pleasant boy. Helpful, but too serious. Slow learner. Mother passed away end of the year. Fourth grade: Very slow, but well behaved. Father shows no interest. Well, they had passed him four times, but he will certainly repeat fifth grade! Do him good! I said to myself.

And then the last day before the holiday arrived. Many gifts were heaped underneath our little tree, waiting for the big moment. As I removed the last bit of masking tape from the brown paper on Teddy's gift, two items fell to my desk: a gaudy rhinestone bracelet with several stones missing and a small bottle of dime-store cologne—half empty.

I could hear the snickers and whispers as I placed the bracelet on my wrist. "Teddy, would you help me fasten it?" He smiled shyly as he fixed the clasp, and I held up my wrist for all of them to admire. There were a few hesitant ooh's and ahh's, but as I dabbed the cologne behind my ears, all the little girls lined up for a dab behind their ears.

"I locked the door, sat down at my desk, and wept . . ."

When all the students had left, Teddy walked up to me. "You smell just like my mom," he said softly. "Her bracelet looks real pretty on you too. I'm glad you liked it." He left quickly. I locked the door, sat down at my desk, and wept, resolving to make up to Teddy what I had deliberately deprived him of—a teacher who cared. I stayed every afternoon with Teddy from the end of holidays until the last day of school. Sometimes we worked together. Sometimes he worked alone while I drew up lesson plans or graded papers. Slowly but surely he caught up with the rest of the class. In fact, his final averages were among the highest in the class.

I did not hear from Teddy until seven years later, when his first letter appeared in my mailbox.

"Dear Miss Thompson, I just wanted you to be the first to know, I will be graduating second in my class next month.

Very Truly Yours, Teddy Stallard"

Four years later, Teddy's second letter came.

"Dear Miss Thompson, I wanted you to be the first to know. I was just informed that I will be graduating first in my class. The university has not been easy, but I liked it.

Very Truly Yours, Teddy Stallard"

And now today, Teddy's third letter.

"Dear Miss Thompson, I wanted you to be the first to know. As of today I am Theodore Stallard, M.D. How about that!!?? I'm going to be married in July, the 27th, to be exact. I wanted to ask if you could come and sit where Mom would sit if she were here. I'll have no family there as Dad died last year.

Very Truly Yours, Teddy Stallard"

Source:

Self-Efficacy

Connect and Extend to Other Chapters

Sense of self-efficacy is discussed again in Chapter 10. Background: Two books by Bandura about self-efficacy: Bandura, A. (1997). *Self-efficacy: The exercise of control.* New York: Freeman. Bandura, A. (Ed.). (1995). *Self-efficacy in changing societies.* New York: Cambridge University Press.

WHAT WOULD YOU SAY?

The last question in your interview for the 8th grade position is, "We have some pretty discouraged students and parents because our scores were so low last year. What would you do to help students believe in their ability to learn?" ■

Albert Bandura (1986, 1997) suggests that predictions about possible outcomes of behavior are critical for learning because they affect motivation. "Will I succeed or fail? Will I be liked or laughed at?" "Will I be more accepted by teachers in this new school?" These predictions are affected by **self-efficacy**—our beliefs about our personal competence or effectiveness *in a given area.* Bandura (1997) defines self-efficacy as "beliefs in one's capabilities to organize and execute the courses of action required to produce given attainments" (p. 3).

Self-Efficacy, Self-Concept, and Self-Esteem. Most people assume self-efficacy is the same as self-concept or self-esteem, but it isn't. Self-efficacy is future-oriented, "a context-specific assessment of competence to perform a specific task" (Pajares, 1997, p. 15). Self-concept is a more global construct that contains many perceptions about the self, including self-efficacy. Self-concept is developed as a result of external and internal comparisons, using other people or other aspects of the self as frames of reference. But self-efficacy focuses on *your* ability to successfully accomplish a particular task with no need for comparisons—the question is whether *you* can do it, not whether others would be successful. Also, self-efficacy beliefs are strong predictors of behavior, but self-concept has weaker predictive power (Bandura, 1997).

Compared to self-esteem, self-efficacy is concerned with judgments of personal capabilities; self-esteem is concerned with judgments of self-worth. There is no direct relationship between self-esteem and self-efficacy. It is possible to feel highly efficacious in one area and still not have a high level of self-esteem, or vice versa (Valentine, DuBois, & Cooper, 2004). For example, I have very low self-efficacy for singing, but my self-esteem is not affected, probably because my life does not require singing. But if my

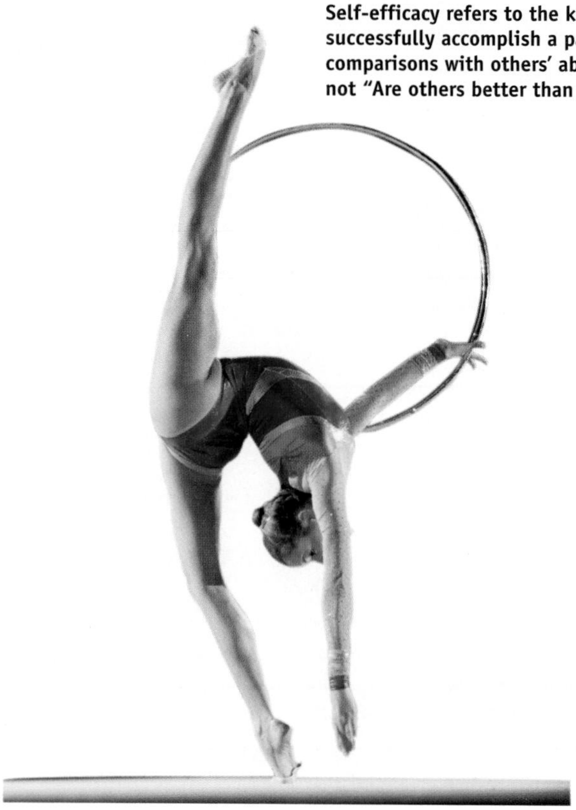

Self-efficacy refers to the knowledge of one's own ability to successfully accomplish a particular task with no need for comparisons with others' ability—the question is "Can I do it?" not "Are others better than I am?"

Self-efficacy A person's sense of being able to deal effectively with a particular task.

self-efficacy for teaching a particular class started dropping after several bad experiences, I know my self-esteem would suffer.

Sources of Self-Efficacy. Bandura identified four sources of self-efficacy expectations: mastery experiences, physiological and emotional arousal, vicarious experiences, and social persuasion. **Mastery experiences** are our own direct experiences—the most powerful source of efficacy information. Successes raise efficacy beliefs, while failures lower efficacy. Level of **arousal** affects self-efficacy, depending on how the arousal is interpreted. As you face the task, are you anxious and worried (lowers efficacy) or excited and "psyched" (raises efficacy) (Bandura, 1997; Pintrich & Schunk, 2002)?

In **vicarious experiences**, someone else models accomplishments. The more closely the student identifies with the model, the greater the impact on self-efficacy will be. When the model performs well, the student's efficacy is enhanced, but when the model performs poorly, efficacy expectations decrease. Although mastery experiences generally are acknowledged as the most influential source of efficacy beliefs in adults, Keyser and Barling (1981) found that children (6th graders in this study) rely more on **modeling** as a source of self-efficacy information.

Social persuasion can be a "pep talk" or specific performance feedback. Social persuasion alone can't create enduring increases in self-efficacy, but a persuasive boost in self-efficacy can lead a student to make an effort, attempt new strategies, or try hard enough to succeed (Bandura, 1982). Social persuasion can counter occasional setbacks that might have instilled self-doubt and interrupted persistence. The potency of persuasion depends on the credibility, trustworthiness, and expertise of the persuader (Bandura, 1997).

Applying Social Cognitive Theory

Self-efficacy and self-regulated learning are two key elements of social cognitive theory that are especially important in learning and teaching.

STOP | THINK | WRITE On a scale from 1 to 100, how confident are you that you will finish reading this chapter today? ■

Self-Efficacy and Motivation

Let's assume your sense of efficacy is around 90 for completing this chapter. Greater efficacy leads to greater effort and persistence in the face of setbacks, so even if you are interrupted in your reading, you are likely to return to the task. I believe I can finish writing this section tonight, so I have returned to working on it after stopping to visit a friend in the hospital. Of course, that could make for a late night, because I have to teach two classes tomorrow as well. Self-efficacy also influences motivation through goal setting. If we have a high sense of efficacy in a given area, we will set higher goals, be less afraid of failure, and find new strategies when old ones fail. If your sense of efficacy for reading this chapter is high, you are likely to set high goals for completing the chapter—maybe you will take some notes, too. If your sense of efficacy is low, however, you may avoid the reading altogether or give up easily when problems arise (Bandura, 1993, 1997; Zimmerman, 1995).

What is the most motivating level of efficacy? Should students be accurate, optimistic, or pessimistic in their predictions? There is evidence that a higher sense of self-efficacy supports motivation, even when the efficacy is an overestimation. Children and adults who are optimistic about the future are more mentally and physically healthy, less depressed, and more motivated to achieve (Flammer, 1995). After examining almost 140 studies of motivation, Sandra Graham concluded that these qualities characterize many African Americans. She found that the African Americans studied had strong self-concepts and high expectations, even in the face of difficulties (Graham, 1994, 1995).

Mastery experiences Our own direct experiences—the most powerful source of efficacy information.

Arousal Physical and psychological reactions causing a person to feel alert, excited, or tense.

Vicarious experiences Accomplishments that are modeled by someone else.

Modeling Changes in behavior, thinking, or emotions that happen through observing another person—a model.

Social persuasion A "pep talk" or specific performance feedback—one source of self-efficacy.

As you might expect, there are dangers in underestimating abilities because then students are more likely to put out a weak effort and give up easily. But there are dangers in continually overestimating performance as well. Students who think that they are better readers than they actually are may not be motivated to go back and repair misunderstandings as they read. They don't discover that they did not really understand the material until it is too late (Pintrich & Zusho, 2002).

Research indicates that performance in school is improved and self-efficacy is increased when students (a) adopt short-term goals so it is easier to judge progress; (b) are taught to use specific learning strategies such as outlining or summarizing that help them focus attention; and (c) receive rewards based on achievement, not just engagement, because achievement rewards signal increasing competence (Graham & Weiner, 1996).

Teachers' Sense of Efficacy

Much of my own research has focused on a particular kind of self-efficacy—teachers' sense of efficacy (Hoy & Woolfolk, 1990, 1993; Tschannen-Moran & Woolfolk Hoy, 2001; Tschannen-Moran, Woolfolk Hoy, & Hoy, 1998; Woolfolk & Hoy, 1990; Woolfolk Hoy & Burke-Spero, 2005). **Teachers' sense of efficacy**, a teacher's belief that he or she can reach even difficult students to help them learn, appears to be one of the few personal characteristics of teachers that is correlated with student achievement. Self-efficacy theory predicts that teachers with a high sense of efficacy work harder and persist longer even when students are difficult to teach, in part because these teachers believe in themselves and in their students. Also, they are less likely to experience burn-out (Fives, Hamman, & Olivarez, 2005).

We have found that prospective teachers tend to increase in their personal sense of efficacy as a consequence of completing student teaching. But sense of efficacy may go down after the first year as a teacher, perhaps because the support that was there for you in student teaching is gone (Woolfolk Hoy & Burke-Spero, 2005). Teachers' sense of efficacy is higher in schools where the other teachers and administrators have high expectations for students and where teachers receive help from their principals in solving instructional and management problems (Capa, 2005; Hoy & Woolfolk, 1993). Another important conclusion from our research is that efficacy grows from real success with students, not just from the moral support or cheerleading of professors and colleagues. Any experience or training that helps you succeed in the day-to-day tasks of teaching will give you a foundation for developing a sense of efficacy in your career.

As with any kind of efficacy, there may be both benefits and dangers in overestimating abilities. Optimistic teachers probably set higher goals, work harder, reteach when necessary, and persist in the face of problems. But some benefits might follow from having doubts about your efficacy. Doubts might foster reflection, motivation to learn, greater

Research shows that teachers' sense of efficacy grows from real success with students. Experience or training that helps teachers succeed in the day-to-day tasks of teaching will contribute to their sense of efficacy.

Teachers' sense of efficacy A teacher's belief that he or she can reach even the most difficult students and help them learn.

responsiveness to diversity, productive collaboration, and the kind of disequilibrium described by Piaget that motivates change (Wheatley, 2002). I believe that a sense of efficacy for learning to teach would be necessary to respond to doubts in these positive ways, but it is true that persistent high efficacy perceptions in the face of poor performance can produce avoidance rather than action.

Self-Regulated Learning

STOP | THINK | WRITE How are you studying right now? What goals have you set for your reading today? What is your plan for learning, and what strategies are you using right now to learn? How did you learn those strategies? ■

Barry Zimmerman (2002) defines **self-regulation** as the process we use to activate and sustain our thoughts, behaviors, and emotions in order to reach our goals. When the goals involve learning, we talk about self-regulated learning.

Today, people change jobs an average of seven times before they retire. Many of these career changes require new learning that must be self-initiated and self-directed (Martinez-Pons, 2002; Weinstein, 1994). Thus, one goal of teaching should be to free students from the need for teachers, so the students can continue to learn independently throughout their lives. To continue learning independently throughout life, you must be a self-regulated learner. Self-regulated learners have a combination of academic learning skills and self-control that makes learning easier, so they are more motivated; in other words, they have the *skill* and the *will* to learn (McCombs & Marzano, 1990; Murphy & Alexander, 2000). Self-regulated learners transform their mental abilities, whatever they are, into academic skills and strategies (Zimmerman, 2002). Many studies link strategy use to different measures of academic achievement, especially for middle-school and high-school students (Fredricks et al., 2004).

What Influences Self-Regulation? The concept of self-regulated learning integrates much of what is known about effective learning and motivation. As you can see from the processes described above, three factors influence skill and will: knowledge, motivation, and self-discipline or volition.

To be self-regulated learners, students need *knowledge* about themselves, the subject, the task, strategies for learning, and the contexts in which they will apply their learning. "Expert" students know about *themselves* and how they learn best. For example, they know their preferred learning styles; what is easy and what is hard for them; how to cope with the difficult parts; what their interests and talents are; and how to use their strengths (see Chapter 4 of this book). These experts also know quite a bit about the *subject* being studied—and the more they know, the easier it is to learn more (Alexander, 2006). They probably understand that different *learning tasks* require different approaches on their part. A simple memory task, for example, might require a mnemonic strategy (see Chapter 7), whereas a complex comprehension task might be approached by means of concept maps of the key ideas (see Chapter 8). Also, these self-regulated learners know that learning is often difficult and knowledge is seldom absolute; there usually are different ways of looking at problems as well as different solutions (Pressley, 1995; Winne, 1995).

These expert students not only know what each task requires but they also can apply the *strategy* needed. They can skim or read carefully. They can use memory strategies or reorganize the material. As they become more knowledgeable in a field, they apply many of these strategies automatically. In short, they have mastered a large, flexible repertoire of learning strategies and tactics (see Chapter 8).

Finally, expert learners think about the *contexts* in which they will apply their knowledge—when and where they will use their learning—so they can set motivating goals and connect present work to future accomplishments (Wang & Palincsar, 1989; Weinstein, 1994; Winne, 1995).

Self-regulated learners are *motivated* to learn (see Chapter 10). They find many tasks in school interesting because they value learning, not just performing well in the eyes of others. But even if they are not intrinsically motivated by a particular task, they are serious

Connect and Extend to PRAXIS II™

Self-Regulation (II, A1)

Take a look at *The Learning Base* (http://www.allkindsofminds.org/library/challenges/GTPSelfregulatingLearning.htm) for tips to help students develop the goals, metacognitive skills, and self-regulatory practices that can support a lifelong devotion to learning.

Self-regulation Process of activating and sustaining thoughts, behaviors, and emotions in order to reach goals.

Self-regulated learners have a combination of academic learning skills and self-control that makes learning easier; they have the *skill* and the *will* to learn.

about getting the intended benefit from it. They know *why* they are studying, so their actions and choices are self-determined and not controlled by others. However, knowledge and motivation are not always enough. Self-regulated learners need volition or self-discipline. "Where motivation denotes commitment, volition denotes follow-through" (Corno, 1992, p. 72).

It is late Thursday morning, the last day of March. I am in Florida, but I have been writing almost all day every day since last weekend. My right arm is aching from a fall last week, but I want to keep writing because the deadline for this chapter is very near. I have knowledge and motivation, but to keep going I need a good dose of *volition*. **Volition** is an old-fashioned word for will-power. The technical definition for volition is *protecting opportunities to reach goals by applying self-regulated learning.* Self-regulated learners know how to protect themselves from distractions—where to study, for example, so they are not interrupted. They know how to cope when they feel anxious, drowsy, or lazy (Corno, 1992, 1995b; Snow, Corno, & Jackson, 1996). And they know what to do when tempted to stop working and have (another) cup of coffee—the temptation I'm facing now—that, and a beautiful sunny day that beckons me to the beach.

Obviously, not all of your students will be expert self-regulated learners when it comes to academics. In fact, some psychologists suggest that you think of this capacity as one of many characteristics that distinguish individuals (Snow, Corno, & Jackson, 1996). Some students are much better at it than others. How can you help more students become self-regulated learners in school? What is involved in being self-regulated?

Models of Self-Regulated Learning and Agency. Models of **self-regulated learning** describe how learners—like you!—make choices among the skills they use to learn and how they manage factors that affect learning. There are several models (Puustinen & Pulkkinen, 2001). Let's look at one developed by Phil Winne and Allyson Hadwin (1998), depicted in Figure 9.2. It has many facets, as it should when the topic at hand is how you manage your academic life.

The model of self-regulated learning in Figure 9.2 is based on a position that learners are agents. **Agency** is the capacity to coordinate learning skills, motivation, and emotions to reach your goals. Agents are not puppets on strings held by teachers, textbook authors, or web page designers. Instead, agents control many factors that influence how they learn. Self-regulating learners exercise agency as they engage in a cycle of four main stages: analyzing the task, setting goals and designing plans, engaging in learning, and adjusting their approach to learning.

1. Analyzing the learning task. You are familiar with this stage of self-regulated learning. What do you do when a professor announces there will be a test? You ask about con-

Volition Will power; self-discipline; work styles that protect opportunities to reach goals by applying self-regulated learning.

Self-regulated learning A view of learning as skills and will applied to analyzing learning tasks, setting goals, and planning how to do the task, applying skills, and especially making adjustments about how learning is carried out.

Agency The capacity to coordinate learning skills, motivation, and emotions to reach your goals.

FIGURE 9.2

The Cycle of Self-Regulated Learning

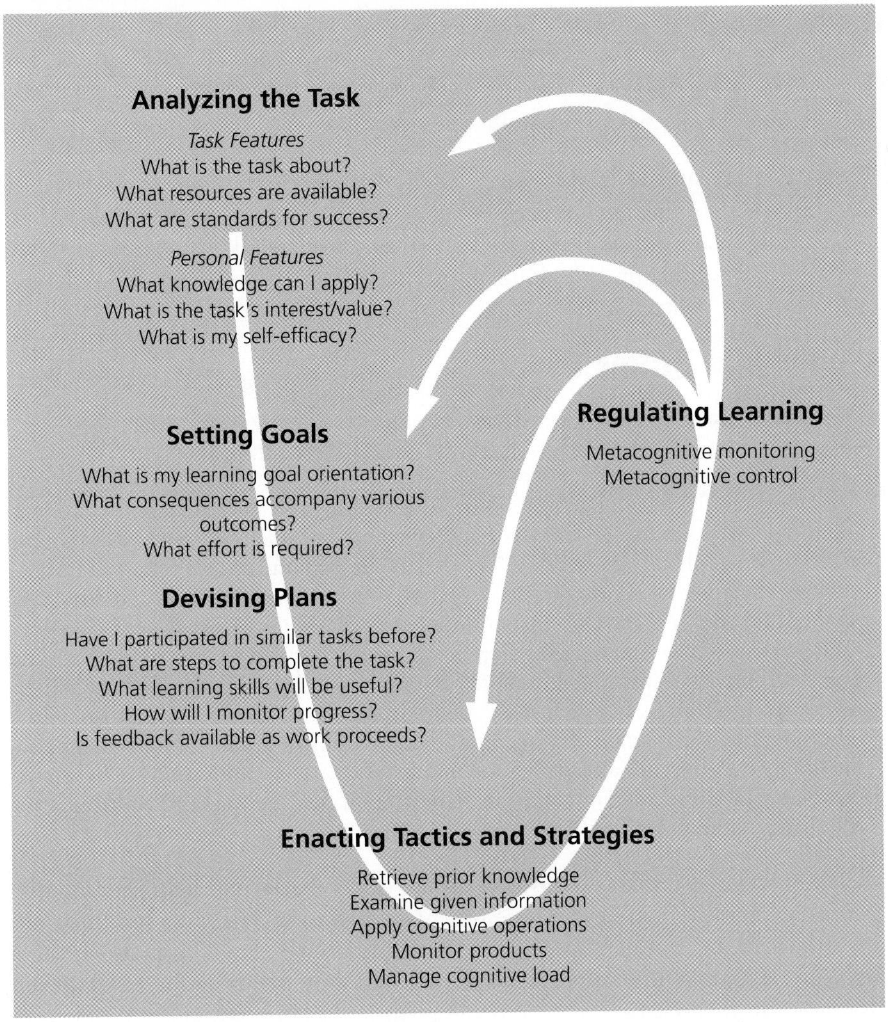
Analyzing the Task
Task Features
What is the task about?
What resources are available?
What are standards for success?
Personal Features
What knowledge can I apply?
What is the task's interest/value?
What is my self-efficacy?
Setting Goals
What is my learning goal orientation?
What consequences accompany various outcomes?
What effort is required?
Devising Plans
Have I participated in similar tasks before?
What are steps to complete the task?
What learning skills will be useful?
How will I monitor progress?
Is feedback available as work proceeds?
Regulating Learning
Metacognitive monitoring
Metacognitive control
Enacting Tactics and Strategies
Retrieve prior knowledge
Examine given information
Apply cognitive operations
Monitor products
Manage cognitive load

Source: "The Cycle of Self-Regulated Learning" from *Educational Psychology* (3rd Canadian ed.) by A. E. Woolfolk, P. H. Winne, and N. E. Perry. Toronto: Pearson, 2006, p. 307, Fig 8.9. Adapted with permission of Pearson Education Canada and Philip Winne.

ditions you believe will influence how you'll study. Is it essay or multiple-choice? Is my best friend more up-to-date than I? In general, learners examine whatever information they think is relevant in order to construct a sense of what the task is about, what resources to bring to bear, and how they feel about the work to be done.

2. Setting goals and devising plans. Knowing conditions that influence work on tasks provides information that learners use to create goals for learning. Then, plans can be developed about how to reach those goals. What goals for studying might you set for a quiz covering only one chapter that counts just 3% toward your course grade? Would your goals change if the test covered the last six chapters and counted 30% toward your course grade? What targets are identified in these goals—repeating definitions, being able to discuss how a teacher could apply findings from key research studies described in the textbook, or critiquing theoretical positions? Choosing goals affects the shape of a learner's plans for how to study. Is cramming (massed practice) the best approach? Is a better plan to study a half-hour each day, overlapping content a bit from one day to the next (distributed practice)?

3. Enacting tactics and strategies to accomplish the task. Self-regulated learners are especially alert during this stage as they monitor how well the plan is working. This is metacognitive monitoring (see Chapter 7). Are you reaching your goals? Is the approach you take to learning too effortful for the results you are achieving? Is your progress rate fast enough to be prepared for the test?

4. Regulating learning. In this stage of self-regulated learning, learners make decisions about whether changes are needed in any of the three preceding stages. For example, if learning is slow: Should you study with your best friend? Do you need to review some prior material that provides foundations for the content you are now studying?

An Individual Example

Students today are faced with constant distractions. Barry Zimmerman (2002, p. 64) describes Tracy, a high-school student who is devoted to MTV:

> An important mid-term math exam is two weeks away, and she had begun to study while listening to popular music "to relax her." Tracy has not set any study goals for herself—instead she simply tells herself to do as well as she can on the test. She uses no specific learning strategies for condensing and memorizing important material and does not plan out her study time, so she ends up cramming for a few hours before the test. She has only vague self-evaluative standards and cannot gauge her academic preparation accurately. Tracy attributes her learning difficulties to an inherent lack of mathematical ability and is very defensive about her poor study methods. However, she does not ask for help from others because she is afraid of "looking stupid," or seek out supplementary materials from the library because she "already has too much to learn." She finds studying to be anxiety-provoking, has little self-confidence in achieving success, and sees little intrinsic value in acquiring mathematical skill.

Clearly, Tracy is unlikely to do well on the test. What would help? For an answer, let's consider Zimmerman's cycle of self-regulated learning. His cycle has three phases and is similar to the Winne and Hadwin model described above. In phase 1, the *forethought phase* (like Winne & Hadwin's steps 1 and 2 of analyzing the task and setting goals), Tracy needs to set clear, reasonable goals and plan a few strategies for accomplishing those goals. And Tracy's beliefs about motivation make a difference at this point too. If Tracy had a sense of self-efficacy for applying the strategies that she planned, if she believed that using those strategies would lead to math learning and success on the test, if she saw some connections between her own interests and the math learning, and if she were trying to master the material—not just look good or avoid looking bad—then she would be on the road to self-regulated learning.

Moving to phase 2, from the forethought to the *performance phase* (similar to Winne and Hadwin's step 3 of enacting the strategies) brings new challenges. Now Tracy must have a repertoire of self-control (volitional) and learning strategies, including using imagery, mnemonics, attention focusing, and other techniques such as those described in Chapters 7 and 8 (Kiewra, 2002). She also will need to self-observe, that is, monitor how things are going so she can change strategies if needed. Actual recording of time spent, problems solved, or pages written may provide clues about when or how to make the best use of study time. Turning off the music would help, too.

Finally, Tracy needs to move to phase 3, similar to Winne and Hadwin's step 4 of regulating learning, by looking back on her performance and *reflecting* on what happened. It will help her develop a sense of efficacy if she attributes successes to effort and good strategy use and avoids self-defeating actions and beliefs such as making weak efforts, pretending not to care, or assuming she is "no good at math."

Both Zimmerman's and Winne and Hadwin's models emphasize the cyclical nature of self-regulated learning: Each phase flows into the next, and the cycle continues as students encounter new learning challenges. Both models begin with being informed about the task so you can set good goals. Having a repertoire of learning strategies and tactics also is necessary in both models. And self-monitoring of progress followed by modifying plans if needed are critical to both. Notice also that the way students think about the task and their ability to do it—their sense of efficacy for self-regulation—is key as well.

Reaching Every Student: Two Classrooms and the Family

Students differ in their self-regulation knowledge and skills. But teachers must work with an entire classroom, and still "reach every student." Here are two examples of real situations where teachers did just that. The first involves writing, the second math problem solving—both complex tasks.

Writing. Carol is a 2nd grade student described by Nancy Perry and Lynn Drummond (2003). Lynn was Carol's teacher; she characterizes Carol as "a very weak writer." Carol has difficulty finding facts, and then transforming those facts into meaningful prose for a research report. Also, she has difficulty with the mechanics of writing, which, according to Lynn, "holds her back."

Over the course of the year, Lynn involved her grade 2 and 3 students in three projects about animals. Through this writing, she wanted students to learn how to: (a) do research, (b) write expository text, (c) edit and revise their writing, and (d) use the computer as a tool for researching and writing. For the first report, the class worked on one topic together (Chipmunks). They did the fact-finding and writing together, because Lynn needed to show them how to do research and write a report. Also, the class developed frameworks for working collaboratively as a community of learners. When they wrote the second report (on Penguins), Lynn offered students many more choices and encouraged them to depend more on themselves and one another. Finally, for the third report, students chose an animal, conducted a self-regulated research project, and wrote a report. Now that they knew how to do research and write a report, they could work alone or together and be successful at this complex task.

Carol worked with a student in grade 3 (Carol was in grade 2) who was doing research on a related topic. He showed Carol how to use a table of contents, and offered advice about how to phrase ideas in her report. Also, Carol underlined words she thought were misspelled so she could check them later when she met with Lynn to edit her report. Unlike many low-achieving students who have not learned strategies for self-regulating learning, Carol was not afraid to attempt challenging tasks, and she was confident about her ability to develop as a writer. Reflecting on her progress across the school year, Carol said, "I learned a lot from when I was in grade 1 because I had a lot of trouble then."

Math Problem Solving. Lynn Fuchs and her colleagues (2003) assessed the value of incorporating self-regulated learning strategies into math problem-solving lessons in real classrooms. The researchers worked with 24 teachers. All of the teachers taught the same content in their 3rd grade classes. Some of these teachers (randomly chosen) taught in their usual way. Another randomly chosen group incorporated strategies to encourage problem-solving *transfer*—using skills and knowledge learned in the lessons to solve problems in other situations and classes. The third group of teachers added transfers and self-regulated learning strategies to their units on math problem solving. Here are a few of the transfer and self-regulated learning strategies taught:

- Using a key, students scored their homework and gave it to a homework collector (a peer).
- Students graphed their completion of homework on a class report.
- Students used individual thermometer graphs that were kept in folders to chart their daily scores on individual problems.
- At the beginning of each session, students inspected their previous charts and set goals to beat their previous scores.
- Students discussed with partners how they might apply problem-solving strategies outside class.

- Before some lessons, students reported to the group about how they had applied problem-solving skills outside class.

Both transfer and self-regulated learning strategies helped students learn mathematical problem solving and apply this knowledge to new problems. The addition of self-regulated learning strategies was especially effective when students were asked to solve problems that were very different from those they encountered in the lessons. Students at every achievement level as well as students with learning disabilities benefited from learning the strategies.

Families and Self-Regulated Learning. Children begin to learn self-regulation in their homes. Parents can teach and support self-regulated learning through modeling, encouragement, facilitation, rewarding of goal setting, good strategy use, and other processes described in the next section (Martinez-Pons, 2002). The *Guidelines* give some ideas for helping students become more self-regulating.

Teaching Toward Self-Efficacy and Self-Regulated Learning

Most teachers agree that students need to develop skills and attitudes for independent, life-long learning (self-regulated learning and a sense of efficacy for learning). Fortunately, there is a growing body of research that offers guidance about how to design tasks and structure classroom interactions to support students' development of and engagement in self-regulated learning (Neuman & Roskos, 1997; Perry, 1998; Turner, 1995; Wharton-McDonald, Pressley, Rankin, Mistretta, Yokoi, & Ettenberger, 1997; Woolfolk, Perry, & Winne, 2006; Zimmerman, 2002). This research indicates that students develop academically effective forms of self-regulated learning (SRL) and a sense of efficacy for learning when teachers involve them in complex meaningful tasks that extend over long

Guidelines: Supporting Self-Regulation

Emphasize the value of encouragement.

EXAMPLES

1. Teach students to encourage each other.
2. Tell parents about the areas that are most challenging for their child—the areas that will be the most in need of encouragement.

Model self-regulation.

EXAMPLES

1. Target small steps for improving an academic skill. Tailor goals to the student's current achievement level.
2. Discuss with your students how you set goals and monitor progress.
3. Ask parents to show their children how they set goals for the day or week, write to-do lists, or keep appointment books.

Make families a source of good strategy ideas.

EXAMPLES

1. Have short, simple materials describing a "strategy of the month" that students can practice at home.
2. Create a lending library of books about goal setting, motivation, learning, and time-management strategies for students.
3. Encourage families to help their children focus on problem-solving processes and not turn immediately to the answers at the back of the book when doing homework.

Provide self-evaluation guidelines.

EXAMPLES

1. Develop rubrics for self-evaluation with students (see Chapter 15). Model how to use them.
2. Provide record-keeping sheets for assignments early in the year, then gradually have students develop their own.
3. Encourage parents to model self-evaluation as they focus on areas they want to improve.
4. For parent conferences, have examples of materials other families have successfully used to keep track of progress.

For more ideas to share with parents, see: **http://www.pbs.org/wholechild/parents/building.html**

periods of time, much like the constructivist activities described later in this chapter. Also, to develop self-regulated learning and self-efficacy for learning, students need to have some control over their learning processes and products—they need to make choices. And because self-monitoring and self-evaluation are key to effective SRL and a sense of efficacy, teachers can help students develop SRL by involving them in setting criteria for evaluating their learning processes and products, then giving them opportunities to make judgments about their progress using those standards. Finally, it helps to work collaboratively with peers and seek feedback from them. Let's examine each of these more closely.

Complex Tasks. Teachers don't want to assign students tasks that are too difficult and that lead to frustration. This is especially true when students have learning difficulties or disabilities. In fact, research indicates that the most motivating and academically beneficial tasks for students are those that challenge, but don't overwhelm them (Rohrkemper & Corno, 1988; Turner, 1997); complex tasks need not be overly difficult for students.

The term *complex* refers to the design of tasks, not their level of difficulty. From a design point of view, tasks are complex when they address multiple goals and involve large chunks of meaning, such as projects and thematic units. Furthermore, complex tasks extend over long periods of time, engage students in a variety of cognitive and metacognitive processes, and allow for the production of a wide range of products (Perry, VandeKamp, Mercer, & Nordby, 2002; Wharton-McDonald et al., 1997). For example, a study of Egyptian pyramids might result in the production of written reports, maps, diagrams, and models.

Even more important, complex tasks provide students with information about their learning progress. These tasks require them to engage in deep, elaborative thinking and problem solving. In the process, students develop and refine their cognitive and metacognitive strategies. Furthermore, succeeding at such tasks increases students' self-efficacy and intrinsic motivation (McCaslin & Good, 1996; Turner, 1997). Rohrkemper and Corno (1988) advised teachers to design complex tasks that provide opportunities for students to modify the learning conditions in order to cope with challenging problems.

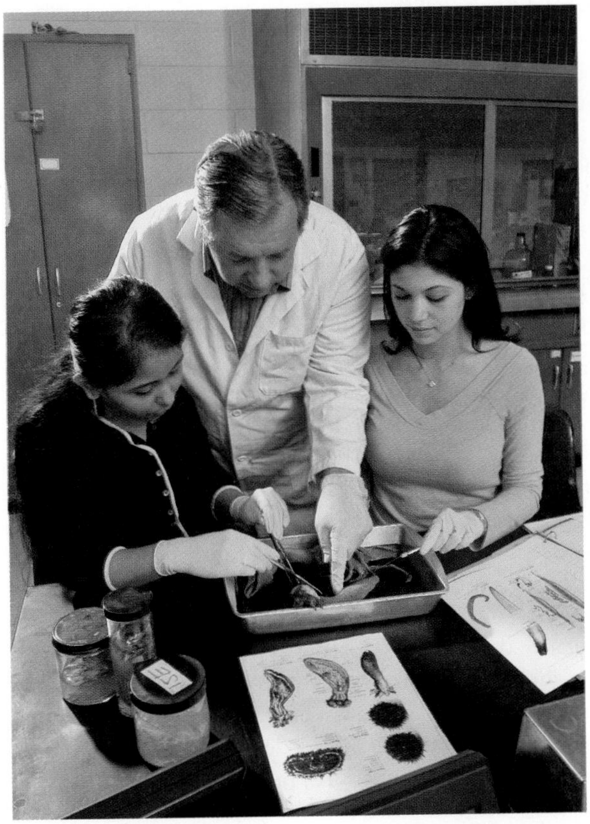

In order to develop self-regulated learning and self-efficacy for learning, students need to have some control over their learning processes and products; teachers can help by involving students in evaluating their learning processes, products, and progress.

Learning to cope with stressful situations and make adaptations is an important educational goal. Remember from Chapter 4, that according to Sternberg, one aspect of intelligence is choosing or adapting environments so that you can succeed.

Control. Teachers can share control with students by giving them choices. When students have choices (e.g., about what to produce, how to produce it, where to work, who to work with), they are more likely to anticipate a successful outcome (increased self-efficacy) and consequently increase effort and persist when difficulty arises (Turner & Paris, 1995). Also, by involving students in making decisions, teachers invite them to take responsibility for learning by planning, setting goals, monitoring progress, and evaluating outcomes (Turner, 1997). These are qualities of highly effective, self-regulating learners.

Giving students choices creates opportunities for them to adjust the level of challenge particular tasks present (e.g., they can choose easy or more challenging reading materials, determine the nature and amount of writing in a report, supplement writing with other expressions of learning). But what if students make poor academic choices? Highly effective, high-SRL teachers carefully consider the choices they give to students. They make sure students have the knowledge and skills they need to operate independently and make good decisions (Perry & Drummond, 2002). For example, when students are learning new skills or routines, teachers can offer choices with constraints (e.g., students must write a minimum of four sentences/paragraphs/pages, but they can choose to write more; they must demonstrate their understanding of an animal's habitat, food, and babies, but they can write, draw, or speak their knowledge).

Highly effective teachers also teach and model good decision making. For example, when students are choosing partners, they ask them to consider what they need from their partner (e.g., shared interest and commitment, perhaps knowledge or skills that they need to develop). When students are making choices about how best to use their time, these teachers ask, "What can you do when you're finished? What can you do if you are waiting for my help?" Often, lists are generated and posted, so students can refer to them while they work. Finally, highly effective teachers give students feedback about the choices they make and tailor the choices they give to suit the unique characteristics of particular learners. For example, they might encourage some students to select research topics for which resources are readily available and written at a level that is accessible to the learner. Alternatively, they might encourage some students to work collaboratively versus independently to ensure they have the support they need to be successful.

Self-Evaluation. Evaluation practices that support SRL are nonthreatening. They are embedded in ongoing activities, emphasize process as well as products, focus on personal progress, and help students to interpret errors as opportunities for learning to occur. In these contexts, students enjoy and actually seek challenging tasks because the cost of participation is low (Paris & Ayres, 1994). Involving students in generating evaluation criteria and evaluating their own work also reduces the anxiety that often accompanies assessment by giving students a sense of control over the outcome. Students can judge their work in relation to a set of qualities both they and their teachers identify as "good" work. They can consider the effectiveness of their approaches to learning and alter their behaviors in ways that enhance it (Winne & Perry, 2000).

In high-SRL classrooms, there are both formal and informal opportunities for students to evaluate their learning. For example, one student teacher asked 4th- and 5th-grade students to submit reflections journals describing the games they designed with a partner or small group of collaborators in a probability and statistics unit (Perry, Phillips, & Dowler, 2004). Their journals explained their contribution to the group's process and product, and described what they learned from participating. The student teacher took these reflections into account when she evaluated the games. More informally, teachers ask students "What have you learned about yourself as a writer today?" "What do good researchers and writers do?" "What can we do that we couldn't do before?" Questions like these, posed to individuals or embedded in class discussions, prompt students' metacognition, motivation, and strategic action—the components of SRL.

Collaboration. The *Committee on Increasing High School Students' Motivation to Learn* (2004) concluded that when students can put their heads together, they are more receptive to challenging assignments—the very kind of complex task that develops self-regulation. The Committee added:

> Collaborative work also can help students develop skills in cooperation. Furthermore, it helps create a community of learners who have responsibility for each other's learning, rather than a competitive environment, which is alienating to many students, particularly those who do not perform as well as their classmates. (p. 51)

The most effective uses of cooperative/collaborative relationships to support SRL are those that reflect a climate of community and shared problem solving (Perry & Drummond, 2002; Perry, VandeKamp, Mercer, & Nordby, 2002). In these contexts, teachers and students actually co-regulate one another's learning (McCaslin & Good, 1996), offering support, whether working alone, in pairs, or small groups. This support is instrumental to individuals' development and use of metacognition, intrinsic motivation, and strategic action (e.g., sharing ideas, comparing strategies for solving problems, identifying *everyone's* area of expertise). High-SRL teachers spend time at the start of each school year teaching routines and establishing norms of participation (e.g., how to give constructive feedback and how to interpret and respond to peers' suggestions). As you will see in Chapter 12, developing useful management and learning procedures and routines takes time in the beginning of the year, but it is time well spent. Once routines and patterns of interaction are established, students can focus on learning and teachers can attend to teaching academic skills and the curriculum.

The last element of teaching for self-regulation, collaboration, is an important ingredient in constructivist learning. We will spend the rest of the chapter exploring more closely this important and very current perspective.

Cognitive and Social Constructivism

Consider this situation:

> A young child who has never been to the hospital is in her bed in the pediatric wing. The nurse at the station down the hall calls over the intercom above the bed, "Hi Chelsea, how are you doing? Do you need anything?" The girl looks puzzled and does not answer. The nurse repeats the question with the same result. Finally, the nurse says emphatically, "Chelsea, are you there? Say something!" The little girl responds tentatively, "Hello wall—I'm here."

Connect and **Extend** to the **Research**

The 2000 Yearbook of the National Society for the Study of Education (NSSE) is devoted to the examination of constructivism. Phillips, D. C. (Ed.) (2000). *Constructivism in education: Opinions and second opinions on controversial issues.* Chicago, IL: University of Chicago Press.

Chelsea encountered a new situation—a talking wall. The wall is persistent. It sounds like a grown-up wall. She shouldn't talk to strangers, but she is not sure about walls. She uses what she knows and what the situation provides to *construct* meaning and to act.

Here is another example of constructing meaning taken from Berk (2001, p. 31). This time, a father and his 4-year-old son co-construct understandings as they walk along a California beach, collecting litter after a busy day:

Ben: (running ahead and calling out) Some bottles and cans. I'll get them.
Mel: If the bottles are broken, you could cut yourself, so let me get them. *(Catches up and holds out the bag as Ben drops items in)*
Ben: Dad, look at this shell. It's a whole one, really big. Colors all inside!
Mel: Hmmm, might be an abalone shell.
Ben: What's abalone?
Mel: Do you remember what I had in my sandwich on the wharf yesterday? That's abalone.
Ben: You eat it?
Mel: Well, you can. You eat a meaty part that the abalone uses to stick to rocks.

Ben: Ewww. I don't want to eat it. Can I keep the shell?
Mel: I think so. Maybe you can find some things in your room to put in it. *(Points to the shell's colors)* Sometimes people make jewelry out of these shells.
Ben: Like mom's necklace?
Mel: That's right. Mom's necklace is made out of a kind of abalone with a very colorful shell—pinks, purples, blues. It's called Paua. When you turn it, the colors change.
Ben: Wow! Let's look for Paua shells!
Mel: You can't find them here, only in New Zealand.
Ben: Where's that? Have you been there?
Mel: No, someone brought Mom the necklace as a gift. But I'll show you New Zealand on the globe. It's far away, halfway around the world.

Look at the knowledge being co-constructed about sea creatures and their uses for food or decoration; safety; environmental responsibility; and even geography. Constructivist theories of learning focus on how people make meaning, both on their own like Chelsea and in interaction with others like Ben.

Constructivist Views of Learning

Constructivism is a broad term used by philosophers, curriculum designers, psychologists, educators, and others. Ernst Von Glasersfeld calls it "a vast and woolly area in contemporary psychology, epistemology, and education" (1997, p. 204). Constructivist perspectives are grounded in the research of Piaget, Vygotsky, the Gestalt psychologists, Bartlett, and Bruner as well as the philosophy of John Dewey, to mention just a few intellectual roots.

There is no one constructivist theory of learning, but "most constructivists share two main ideas: that learners are active in constructing their own knowledge and that social interactions are important to knowledge construction" (Bruning, Schraw, Norby, & Ronning, 2004, p. 195). Constructivism views learning as more than receiving and processing information transmitted by teachers or texts. Rather, learning is the active and personal construction of knowledge (de Kock, Sleegers, and Voeten, 2004). Thus, many theories in cognitive science include some kind of constructivism because these theories assume that individuals construct their own cognitive structures as they interpret their experiences in particular situations (Palincsar, 1998). There are constructivist approaches in science and mathematics education, in educational psychology and anthropology, and in computer-based education. Even though many psychologists and educators use

Constructivist theories are based on the ideas that learners actively develop their knowledge, rather than passively receive it, in package form, from teachers or outside sources.

Constructivism View that emphasizes the active role of the learner in building understanding and making sense of information.

the term *constructivism*, they often mean very different things (Driscoll, 2005; McCaslin & Hickey, 2001; Phillips, 1997).

One way to organize constructivist views is to talk about two forms of constructivism: psychological and social construction (Palincsar, 1998; Phillips, 1997). We could oversimplify a bit and say that psychological constructivists focus on how individuals use information, resources, and even help from others to build and improve their mental models and problem-solving strategies. In contrast, social constructivists see learning as increasing our abilities to participate with others in activities that are meaningful in the culture (Windschitl, 2002). Let's look a bit closer at each type of constructivism.

Psychological/Individual Constructivism. Psychological constructivists "are concerned with how *individuals* build up certain elements of their cognitive or emotional apparatus" (Phillips, 1997, p. 153). These constructivists are interested in individual knowledge, beliefs, self-concept, or identity, so they are sometimes called *individual* constructivists or *cognitive* constructivists; they all focus on the inner psychological life of people. When Chelsea talked to the wall in the previous section, she was making meaning using her own individual knowledge and beliefs about how to respond when someone (or something) talks to you. She was using what she knew to impose intellectual structure on her world (Piaget, 1971; Windschitl, 2002).

Using these standards, the most recent information processing theories are constructivist (Mayer, 1996). Information processing approaches to learning regard the human mind as a symbol processing system. This system converts sensory input into symbol structures (propositions, images, or schemas), and then processes (rehearses or elaborates) those symbol structures so knowledge can be held in memory and retrieved. The outside world is seen as a source of input, but once the sensations are perceived and enter working memory, the important work is assumed to be happening "inside the head" of the individual (Schunk, 2000; Vera & Simon, 1993). Some psychologists, however, believe that information processing is "trivial" or "weak" constructivism because the individual's only constructive contribution is to build accurate representations of the outside world (Derry, 1992; Garrison, 1995; Marshall, 1996; Windschitl, 2002).

In contrast, Piaget's psychological (cognitive) constructivist perspective is less concerned with "correct" representations and more interested in meaning as constructed by the individual. As we saw in Chapter 2, Piaget proposed a sequence of cognitive stages that all humans pass through. Thinking at each stage builds on and incorporates previous stages as it becomes more organized and adaptive and less tied to concrete events. Piaget's special concern was with logic and the construction of universal knowledge that cannot be learned directly from the environment—knowledge such as conservation or reversibility (Miller, 2002). Such knowledge comes from reflecting on and coordinating our own cognitions or thoughts, not from mapping external reality. Piaget saw the social environment as an important factor in development, but did not believe that social interaction was the main mechanism for changing thinking (Moshman, 1997). Some educational and developmental psychologists have referred to Piaget's kind of constructivism as **"first wave constructivism"** or "solo" constructivism, with its emphasis on individual meaning-making (De Corte, Greer, and Verschaffel, 1996; Paris, Byrnes, & Paris, 2001).

"Maybe it's not a wrong answer—maybe it's just a different answer."

At the extreme end of individual constructivism is the notion of **radical constructivism.** This perspective holds that there is no reality or truth in the world, only the individual's perceptions and beliefs. Each of us constructs meaning from our own experiences, but we have no way of understanding or "knowing" the reality of others (Woods & Murphy, 2002). A difficulty with this position is that, when pushed to the extreme of relativism, all knowledge and all beliefs are equal because they are all valid individual perceptions. There are problems with this thinking for educators. First, teachers have a professional responsibility to emphasize some values, such as honesty or justice, over others such as bigotry and deception. All perceptions and beliefs are not equal. As teachers, we ask students to work hard to learn. If learning cannot advance understanding

First wave constructivism A focus on the individual and psychological sources of knowing, as in Piaget's theory.

Radical constructivism Knowledge is assumed to be the individual's construction; it cannot be judged right or wrong.

because all understandings are equally good, then, as David Moshman (1997) notes, "we might just as well let students continue to believe whatever they believe" (p. 230). Also, it appears that some knowledge, such as counting and one-to-one correspondence, is not constructed, but universal. Knowing one-to-one correspondence is part of being human (Geary, 1995; Schunk, 2000).

Vygotsky's Social Constructivism. As you also saw in Chapter 2, Vygotsky believed that social interaction, cultural tools, and activity shape individual development and learning, just as Ben's interactions on the beach with his father shaped Ben's learning about sea creatures, safety, environmental responsibility, and geography. By participating in a broad range of activities with others, learners **appropriate** (internalize or take for themselves) the outcomes produced by working together; these outcomes could include both new strategies and knowledge. Putting learning in social and cultural context is **"second wave" constructivism** (Paris, Byrnes, & Paris, 2001).

Because his theory relies heavily on social interactions and the cultural context to explain learning, most psychologists classify Vygotsky as a social constructivist (Palincsar, 1998; Prawat, 1996). However, some theorists categorize him as a psychological constructivist because he was primarily interested in development within the individual (Moshman, 1997; Phillips, 1997). In a sense, Vygotsky was both. One advantage of his theory of learning is that it gives us a way to consider both the psychological and the social: He bridges both camps. For example, Vygotsky's concept of the zone of proximal development—the area where a child can solve a problem with the help (scaffolding) of an adult or more able peer—has been called a place where culture and cognition create each other (Cole, 1985). Culture creates cognition when the adult uses tools and practices from the culture (language, maps, computers, looms, or music) to steer the child toward goals the culture values (reading, writing, weaving, dance). Cognition creates culture as the adult and child together generate new practices and problem solutions to add to the cultural group's repertoire (Serpell, 1993). One way of integrating individual and social constructivism is to think of knowledge as individually constructed and socially mediated (Windschitl, 2002).

The term constructionism is sometimes used to talk about how public knowledge is created. Although this is not our main concern in educational psychology, it is worth a quick look.

Constructionism. Social construc*tionists* do not focus on individual learning. Their concern is how public knowledge in disciplines such as science, math, economics, or history is constructed. Beyond this kind of academic knowledge, constructionists also are interested in how common-sense ideas, everyday beliefs, and commonly held understandings about people and the world are communicated to new members of a sociocultural group (Gergen, 1997; Phillips, 1997). Questions raised might include who determines what constitutes history, what is the proper way to behave in public, or how to get elected class president. All knowledge is socially constructed, and, more important, some people have more power than others to define what constitutes such knowledge. Relationships between and among teachers, students, families, and the community are the central issues. Collaboration to understand diverse viewpoints is encouraged, and traditional bodies of knowledge often are challenged (Gergen, 1997). The philosophies of Jacques Dierrida and Michel Foucault are important sources for constructionists. Vygotsky's theory, with its attention to how cognition creates culture, has some elements in common with constructionism.

These different perspectives on constructivism raise some general questions, and disagree on the answers. These questions can never be fully resolved, but different theories tend to favor different positions. Let's consider the questions.

Appropriate Internalize or take for yourself knowledge and skills developed in interaction with others or with cultural tools.

Second wave constructivism A focus on the social and cultural sources of knowing, as in Vygotsky's theory.

How Is Knowledge Constructed?

One tension among different approaches to constructivism is based on *how* knowledge is constructed. Moshman (1982) describes three explanations.

1. *The realities and truths of the external world direct knowledge construction.* Individuals *reconstruct* outside reality by building accurate mental representations such as propositional networks, concepts, cause-and-effect patterns, and condition-action production rules that reflect "the way things really are." The more the person learns, the deeper and broader his or her experience is, the closer that person's knowledge will reflect objective reality. Information processing holds this view of knowledge (Cobb & Bowers, 1999).
2. *Internal processes such as Piaget's organization, assimilation, and accommodation direct knowledge construction.* New knowledge is abstracted from old knowledge. Knowledge is not a mirror of reality, but rather an abstraction that grows and develops with cognitive activity. Knowledge is not true or false; it just grows more internally consistent and organized with development.
3. *Both external and internal factors direct knowledge construction.* Knowledge grows through the *interactions* of internal (cognitive) and external (environmental and social) factors. Vygotsky's description of cognitive development through the appropriation and use of cultural tools such as language is consistent with this view (Bruning, Schraw, Norby, & Ronning, 2004). Another example is Bandura's theory of reciprocal interactions among people, behaviors, and environments (Schunk, 2000). Table 9.1 summarizes the three general explanations about how knowledge is constructed.

Knowledge: Situated or General?

A second question that cuts across many constructivist perspectives is whether knowledge is internal, general, and transferable or bound to the time and place in which it is constructed. Psychologists who emphasize the social construction of knowledge and situated learning affirm Vygotsky's notion that learning is inherently social and embedded in a particular cultural setting (Cobb & Bowers, 1999). What is true in one time and place—such as the "fact" before Columbus's time that the earth was flat—becomes false in another time and place. Particular ideas may be useful within a specific **community of practice,** such as 15-century navigation, but useless outside that community. What counts as new knowledge is determined in part by how well the new idea fits with current accepted practice. Over time, the current practice may be questioned and even overthrown, but until such major shifts occur, current practice will shape what is considered valuable.

Situated learning emphasizes that learning in the real world is not like studying in school. It is more like an apprenticeship where novices, with the support of an expert guide and model, take on more and more responsibility until they are able to function independently. Proponents of this view believe situated learning explains learning in

Community of practice Social situation or context in which ideas are judged useful or true.

Situated learning The idea that skills and knowledge are tied to the situation in which they were learned and difficult to apply in new settings.

TABLE 9.1

How Knowledge Is Constructed

Type	Assumptions about Learning and Knowledge	Example Theories
External Direction	Knowledge is acquired by constructing a representation of the outside world. Direct teaching, feedback, and explanation affect learning. Knowledge is accurate to the extent that it reflects the "way things really are" in the outside world.	Information processing
Internal Direction	Knowledge is constructed by transforming, organizing, and reorganizing previous knowledge. Knowledge is not a mirror of the external world, even though experience influences thinking and thinking influences knowledge. Exploration and discovery are more important than teaching.	Piaget
Both External and Internal Direction	Knowledge is constructed based on social interactions and experience. Knowledge reflects the outside world a filtered through and influenced by culture, language, beliefs, interactions with others, direct teaching, and modeling. Guided discovery, teaching, models, and coaching as well as the individual's prior knowledge, beliefs, and thinking affect learning.	Vygotsky

factories, around the dinner table, in high school halls, in street gangs, in the business office, and on the playground.

Situated learning is often described as "enculturation," or adopting the norms, behaviors, skills, beliefs, language, and attitudes of a particular community. The community might be mathematicians or gang members or writers or students in your 8th-grade class or soccer players—any group that has particular ways of thinking and doing. Knowledge is seen *not* as individual cognitive structures but as a creation of the community over time. The practices of the community—the ways of interacting and getting things done, as well as the tools the community has created—constitute the knowledge of that community. Learning means becoming more able to participate in those practices, use the tools, and take on the identity of a member of the community (Derry, 1992; Garrison, 1995; Greeno, Collins, & Resnick, 1996; Rogoff, 1998).

At the most basic level, "situated learning emphasizes the idea that much of what is learned is specific to the situation in which it is learned" (Anderson, Reder, & Simon, 1996, p. 5). Thus, some would argue, learning to do calculations in school may help students do more school calculations, but it may not help them balance a checkbook, because the skills can be applied only in the context in which they were learned, namely school (Lave, 1997; Lave & Wenger, 1991). But it also appears that knowledge and skills can be applied across contexts that were not part of the initial learning situation, as when you use your ability to read and calculate to do your income taxes, even though income tax forms were not part of your high school curriculum (Anderson, Reder, & Simon, 1996).

Learning that is situated in school does not have to be doomed or irrelevant (Bereiter, 1997). As you saw in Chapter 8, a major question in educational psychology and education in general concerns the *transfer* of knowledge from one situation to another. How can you encourage this transfer? Help is on the way in the next section.

Common Elements of Constructivist Perspectives

Connect and **Extend** to the **Research**

For more on constructivism and education, see Marshall, H. H. (Ed.) (1992). *Redefining student learning: Roots of educational change.* Norwood, NJ: Ablex.

STOP | THINK | WRITE What makes a lesson student-centered? List the characteristics and features that put the student in the center of learning. ■

We have looked at some areas of disagreement among the constructivist perspectives, but what about areas of agreement? All constructivist theories assume that knowing develops as learners, like Chelsea and Ben, try to make sense of their experiences. "Learners, therefore, are not empty vessels waiting to be filled, but rather active organisms seeking meaning" (Driscoll, 2005, p. 487). These learners construct mental models or schemas and continue to revise them to make better sense of their experiences. Their constructions do not necessarily resemble external reality; rather, they are the unique interpretations of the learner, like Chelsea's friendly, persistent wall. This doesn't mean that all constructions are equally useful or viable. Learners test their understandings against experience and the understandings of other people—they negotiate and co-construct meanings like Ben did with his father.

Constructivists share similar goals for learning. They emphasize knowledge in use rather than the storing of inert facts, concepts, and skills. Learning goals include developing abilities to find and solve ill-structured problems, critical thinking, inquiry, self-determination, and openness to multiple perspectives (Driscoll, 2005).

Even though there is no single constructivist theory, many constructivist approaches recommend five conditions for learning:

1. Embed learning in complex, realistic, and relevant learning environments.
2. Provide for social negotiation and shared responsibility as a part of learning.
3. Support multiple perspectives and use multiple representations of content.
4. Nurture self-awareness and an understanding that knowledge is constructed.
5. Encourage ownership in learning. (Driscoll, 2005; Marshall, 1992)

Before we discuss particular teaching approaches, let's look more closely at these dimensions of constructivist teaching.

Constructivist approaches recommend that educators emphasize complex, realistic, and relevant learning environments, as well as the importance of social interactions in the learning process. For example, the students here are collaborating to create a household budget.

Complex Learning Environments and Authentic Tasks. Constructivists believe that students should not be given stripped-down, simplified problems and basic skills drills, but instead should encounter **complex learning environments** that deal with "fuzzy," ill-structured problems. The world beyond school presents few simple problems or step-by-step directions, so schools should be sure that *every* student has experience solving complex problems. Complex problems are not simply difficult ones; they have many parts. There are multiple, interacting elements in complex problems and multiple solutions are possible. There is no one right way to reach a conclusion, and each solution may bring a new set of problems. These complex problems should be embedded in authentic tasks and activities, the kinds of situations that students will face as they apply what they are learning to the real world (Needles & Knapp, 1994). Students may need support as they work on these complex problems, with teachers helping them find resources, keeping track of their progress, breaking larger problems down into smaller ones, and so on. This aspect of constructivist approaches is consistent with self-regulation and situated learning in emphasizing learning in *situations* where the learning will be applied.

Social Negotiation. Many constructivists share Vygotsky's belief that higher mental processes develop through **social negotiation** and interaction, so collaboration in learning is valued. The Language Development and Hypermedia Group (1992) suggests that a major goal of teaching is to develop students' abilities to establish and defend their own positions while respecting the positions of others and working together to negotiate or co-construct meaning. To accomplish this exchange, students must talk and listen to each other. It is a challenge for children in cultures that are individualistic and competitive, such as the United States, to adopt what has been called an **intersubjective attitude**—a commitment to build shared meaning by finding common ground and exchanging interpretations.

Multiple Perspectives and Representations of Content. When students encounter only one model, one analogy, one way of understanding complex content, they often oversimplify as they try to apply that one approach to every situation. I saw this happen in my educational psychology class when six students were presenting an example of guided discovery learning. The students' presentation was a near copy of a guided discovery demonstration I had given earlier in the semester, but with some major misconceptions. My students knew only one way to represent discovery learning. Resources for the class

Complex learning environments Problems and learning situations that mimic the ill-structured nature of real life.

Social negotiation Aspect of learning process that relies on collaboration with others and respect for different perspectives.

Intersubjective attitude A commitment to build shared meaning with others by finding common ground and exchanging interpretations.

should have provided **multiple representations of content** using different analogies, examples, and metaphors.

Rand Spiro and his colleagues (1991) suggest that "revisiting the same material, at different times, in rearranged contexts, for different purposes, and from different conceptual perspectives is essential for attaining the goals of advanced knowledge acquisition" (p. 28). This idea is consistent with Jerome Bruner's (1966) **spiral curriculum**, a structure for teaching that introduces the fundamental structure of all subjects—the "big ideas"—early in the school years, then revisits the subjects in more and more complex forms over time.

Understanding the Knowledge Construction Process. Constructivist approaches emphasize making students aware of their own role in constructing knowledge (Cunningham, 1992). The assumptions we make, our beliefs, and our experiences shape what each of us comes to "know" about the world. Different assumptions and different experiences lead to different knowledge. If students are aware of the influences that shape their thinking, they will be more able to choose, develop, and defend positions in a self-critical way while respecting the positions of others.

Student Ownership of Learning. "While there are several interpretations of what [constructivist] theory means, most agree that it involves a dramatic change in the focus of teaching, putting the students' own efforts to understand at the center of the educational enterprise" (Prawat, 1992, p. 357). Student ownership does not mean that the teacher abandons responsibility for instruction. Because the design of teaching is a central issue in this book, we will spend the rest of this chapter discussing examples of ownership of learning and student-centered instruction.

Connect and Extend to PRAXIS II™
Student-Centered Learning (II, A3)
Many of the major initiatives to reform content-area curricula (e.g., science, mathematics) emphasize student-centered/constructivist approaches to learning. Describe the major principles of these approaches and explain how they differ from teacher-centered approaches.

Connect and Extend to the Research
Confrey, J. (1990). What constructivism implies for teaching. In R. Davis, C. Maher, & N. Noddings (Eds.), *Constructivist views on the teaching and learning of mathematics* (pp. 107–122). Monograph 4 of the National Council of Teachers of Mathematics, Reston, VA.

Applying Constructivist Perspectives

Even though there are many applications of constructivist views of learning, we can recognize constructivist approaches by the activities of the teacher and the students. Mark Windschitl (2002) suggests that the following activities encourage meaningful learning:

- Teachers elicit students' ideas and experiences in relation to key topics, then fashion learning situations that help students elaborate on or restructure their current knowledge.
- Students are given frequent opportunities to engage in complex, meaningful, problem-based activities.
- Teachers provide students with a variety of information resources as well as the tools (technological and conceptual) necessary to mediate learning.
- Students work collaboratively and are given support to engage in task-oriented dialogue with one another.
- Teachers make their own thinking processes explicit to learners and encourage students to do the same through dialogue, writing, drawings, or other representations.
- Students are routinely asked to apply knowledge in diverse and authentic contexts, to explain ideas, interpret texts, predict phenomena, and construct arguments based on evidence, rather than to focus exclusively on the acquisition of predetermined "right answers."
- Teachers encourage students' reflective and autonomous thinking in conjunction with the conditions listed above.
- Teachers employ a variety of assessment strategies to understand how students' ideas are evolving and to give feedback on the processes as well as the products of their thinking. (p. 137)

In this section, we will examine three specific teaching approaches that put the student at the center: inquiry and problem-based learning, dialogue and instructional conversations, and cognitive apprenticeships. Two other approaches consistent with construc-

Multiple representations of content Considering problems using various analogies, examples, and metaphors.

Spiral curriculum Bruner's design for teaching that introduces the fundamental structure of all subjects early in the school years, then revisits the subjects in more and more complex forms over time.

tivism are cooperative learning, discussed in Chapter 11, and conceptual change, discussed in Chapter 13.

Inquiry and Problem-Based Learning

John Dewey described the basic **inquiry learning** format in 1910. There have been many adaptations of this strategy, but the form usually includes the following elements (Echevarria, 2003; Lashley, Matczynski, & Rowley, 2002). The teacher presents a puzzling event, question, or problem. The students:

- formulate hypotheses to explain the event or solve the problem,
- collect data to test the hypotheses,
- draw conclusions, and
- reflect on the original problem and the thinking processes needed to solve it.

Connect and **Extend** to **PRAXIS II™**

Inquiry Learning (II, A2, 3)
Inquiry learning is a student-centered approach to learning that pre-dates many "traditional" forms of instruction. Describe the basic structure of this approach to learning. What are its strengths and limitations? What roles does the teacher have?

Examples of Inquiry. In one kind of inquiry, teachers present a problem and students ask yes/no questions to gather data and test hypotheses. This allows the teacher to monitor students' thinking and guide the process. Here is an example:

1. *Teacher presents discrepant event* (after clarifying ground rules). The teacher blows softly across the top of an 8½" × 11" sheet of paper, and the paper rises. She tells students to figure out why it rises.
2. *Students ask questions* to gather more information and to isolate relevant variables. Teacher answers only "yes" or "no." Students ask if temperature is important (no). They ask if the paper is of a special kind (no). They ask if air pressure has anything to do with the paper rising (yes). Questions continue.
3. *Students test causal relationships.* In this case, they ask if the nature of the air on top causes the paper to rise (yes). They ask if the fast movement of the air results in less pressure on the top (yes). Then they test out the rule with other materials—for example, thin plastic.
4. *Students form a generalization* (principle): "If the air on the top moves faster than the air on the bottom of a surface, then the air pressure on top is lessened, and the object rises." Later lessons expand students' understanding of the principles and physical laws through further experiments.
5. *The teacher leads students in a discussion of their thinking processes.* What were the important variables? How did you put the causes and effects together? and so on. (Pasch et al., 1991, pp. 188–189)

Shirley Magnusson and Annemarie Palincsar have developed a teachers' guide for planning, implementing, and assessing different phases of inquiry science units (Palincsar, Magnusson, Marano, Ford, & Brown, 1998). The model, called *Guided Inquiry Supporting Multiple Literacies* or GIsML, is shown in Figure 9.3 on the next page.

The teacher first identifies a curriculum area and some general guiding questions, puzzles, or problems. For example, an elementary teacher chooses communication as the area and asks this general question: "How and why do humans and animals communicate?" Next, several specific focus questions are posed. "How do whales communicate?" "How do gorillas communicate?" The focus questions have to be carefully chosen to guide students toward important understandings. One key idea in understanding animal communication is the relationship among the animal's structures, survival functions, and habitat. Animals have specific *structures* such as large ears or echo-locators, which *function* to find food or attract mates or identify predators, and these structures and functions are related to the animals' *habitats*. Thus, focus questions must ask about animals with different structures for communication, different functional needs for survival, and different habitats. Questions about animals with the same kinds of structures or the same habitats would not be good focus points for inquiry (Magnusson & Palincsar, 1995).

Inquiry learning Approach in which the teacher presents a puzzling situation and students solve the problem by gathering data and testing their conclusions.

The next phase is to engage students in the inquiry, perhaps by playing different animal sounds, having students make guesses and claims about communication, and asking the students questions about their guesses and claims. Then, the students conduct

FIGURE 9.3

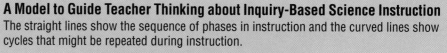

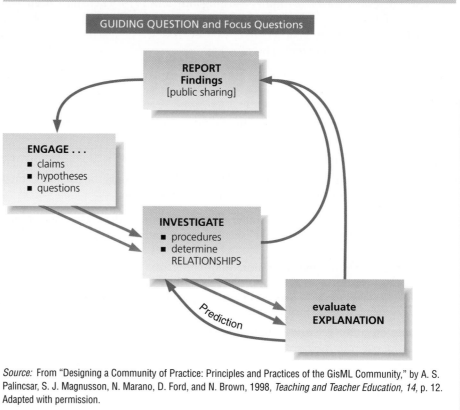

A Model to Guide Teacher Thinking about Inquiry-Based Science Instruction
The straight lines show the sequence of phases in instruction and the curved lines show cycles that might be repeated during instruction.

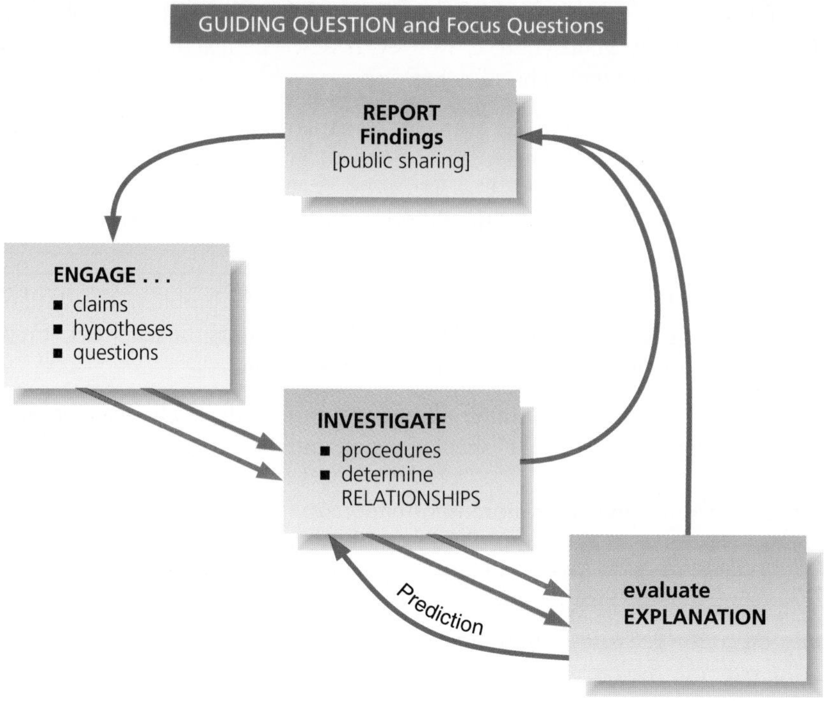

Source: From "Designing a Community of Practice: Principles and Practices of the GisML Community," by A. S. Palincsar, S. J. Magnusson, N. Marano, D. Ford, and N. Brown, 1998, *Teaching and Teacher Education, 14,* p. 12. Adapted with permission.

both first-hand and second-hand investigations. *First-hand investigations* are direct experiences and experiments, for example, measuring the size of bats' eyes and ears in relation to their bodies (using pictures or videos—not real bats!). In *second-hand investigations,* students consult books, the Internet, interviews with experts, and other resources to find specific information or get new ideas. As part of their investigating, the students begin to identify patterns. The curved line in Figure 9.3 shows that cycles can be repeated. In fact, students might go through several cycles of investigating, identifying patterns, and reporting results before moving on to constructing explanations and making final reports. Another possible cycle is to evaluate explanations before reporting by making and then checking predictions, applying the explanation to new situations.

Inquiry teaching allows students to learn content and process at the same time. In the examples above, students learned about the effects of air pressure, how airplanes fly, how animals communicate, and how structures are related to habitats. In addition, they learned the inquiry process itself—how to solve problems, evaluate solutions, and think critically.

Problem-Based Learning. The goals of **problem-based learning** are to help students develop flexible knowledge that can be applied in many situations, in contrast to inert knowledge. Inert knowledge is information that is memorized but seldom applied (Cognition and Technology Group at Vanderbilt [CTGV], 1996; Whitehead, 1929). Other goals of problem-based learning are to enhance intrinsic motivation and skills in problem solving, collaboration, and self-directed lifelong learning. In problem-based learning, students are confronted with a problem that launches their inquiry as they collaborate to find solutions. The process of problem-based learning is similar to the GIsML, shown in

Problem-based learning Methods that provide students with realistic problems that don't necessarily have "right" answers.

Figure 9.3. The students are confronted with a problem scenario; they identify and analyze the problem based on the facts from the scenario; and then they begin to generate hypotheses about solutions. As they suggest hypotheses, they identify missing information—what do they need to know to test their solutions? This launches a phase of self-directed learning and research. Then, students apply their new knowledge, evaluate their problem solutions, recycle to research again if necessary, and finally reflect on the knowledge and skills they have gained (Hmelo-Silver, 2004).

In true problem-based learning, the problem is real and the students' actions matter. In one example, a teacher capitalized on current affairs to encourage student reading, writing, and social studies problem solving:

> Cathie's elementary class learned about the Alaskan oil spill. She brought a newspaper article to class that sequenced in logbook fashion the events of the oil spill in Prince William Sound. To prepare her students to understand the article, she had her students participate in several background-building experiences. First, they used a world map, an encyclopedia, and library books to gather and share relevant information. Next, she simulated an oil spill by coating an object with oil. By then, the class was eager to read the article. (Espe, Worner, & Hotkevich, 1990, p. 45)

After they read and discussed the newspaper article, the teacher asked the class to imagine how the problem might have been prevented. Students had to explain and support their proposed solutions. The next week, the students read another newspaper article about how people in their state were helping with the cleanup efforts in Alaska. The teacher asked if the students wanted to help, and they replied with an enthusiastic "Yes!" The students designed posters and made speeches requesting donations of clean towels to be used to clean the oil-soaked animals in Prince William Sound. The class sent four large bags of towels to Alaska to help in the cleanup. The teacher's and the students' reading, writing, research, and speaking were directed toward solving a real-life problem (Espe, Worner, & Hotkevich, 1990). Other authentic problems that might be the focus for student projects are reducing pollution in local rivers, resolving student conflicts in school, raising money for tsunami or hurricane relief, or building a playground for young children. The teacher's role in problem-based learning is summarized in Table 9.2.

Some problems are not authentic in the sense that they affect the students' lives, but they are engaging. For example, the Cognition and Technology Group at Vanderbilt

TABLE 9.2

The Teacher's Role in Problem-Based Learning

Phase	Teacher Behavior
Phase 1 Orient students to the problem	Teacher goes over the objectives of the lesson, describes important logistical requirements, and motivates students to engage in self-selected problem-solving activity.
Phase 2 Organize students for study	Teacher helps students define and organize study tasks related to the problem.
Phase 3 Assist independent and group investigation	Teacher encourages students to gather appropriate information, conduct experiments, and search for explanations and solutions.
Phase 4 Develop and present artifacts and exhibits	Teacher assists students in planning and preparing appropriate artifacts such as reports, videos, and models and helps them share their work with others.
Phase 5 Analyze and evaluate the problem-solving process	Teacher helps students to reflect on their investigations and the processes they used.

Source: From *Classroom Instruction and Management* (p. 161), by R. I. Arends. Published by McGraw-Hill. Copyright © 1997 by McGraw-Hill. Reprinted with permission of The McGraw-Hill Companies.

University (1990, 1993) has developed a videodisc-based learning environment that focuses on mathematics instruction for the 5th and 6th grades. The series, called *The Adventures of Jasper Woodbury*, presents students with complex situations that require problem finding; subgoal setting; and the application of mathematics, science, history, and literature concepts to solve problems. Even though the situations are complex and lifelike, the problems can be solved using data embedded in the stories presented. Often the adventures have real-life follow-up problems that build on the knowledge developed. For example, after designing a playground for a hypothetical group of children in one Jasper adventure, students can tackle building a real playhouse for a preschool class.

The Vanderbilt group calls its problem-solving approach **anchored instruction.** The *anchor* is the rich, interesting situation. This anchor provides a focus—a reason for setting goals, planning, and using mathematical tools to solve problems. The intended outcome is to develop knowledge that is useful and flexible, not inert. Project-based science is another approach similar to problem-based learning. Table 9.3 compares these three approaches to learning that are situated in problem-solving experiences.

Research on Inquiry and Problem-Based Learning. Inquiry methods are similar to discovery learning and share some of the same problems, so inquiry must be carefully planned and organized, especially for less-prepared students who may lack the background knowledge and problem-solving skills needed to benefit. Some research has shown that discovery methods are ineffective and even detrimental for lower-ability students (Corno & Snow, 1986; Mayer, 2004). When Ted Bredderman (1983) analyzed the results of 57 comparisons of activity-based learning and more traditional approaches for teaching science, he concluded that activity-based methods were superior to content-based traditional approaches in terms of students' understanding of the scientific method and creativity, but about the same for learning science content.

Anchored instruction A type of problem-based learning that uses a complex interesting situation as an anchor for learning.

TABLE 9.3

Three Approaches to Learning Situated in Problem-Solving Experiences

Problem-based learning (PBL), anchored instruction, and project-based science all begin with problems to be solved.

	PBL	Anchored instruction	Project-based science
Problem	Realistic ill-structured problem	Video-based narrative ending with complex problem	Driving question
Role of problem	Focus for learning information and reasoning strategies	Provide shared experience so students can understand how knowledge can support problem solving Video supports problem comprehension	Focus for scientific inquiry process leading to artifact production
Process	Identify facts, generate ideas and learning issues, SDL, revisit, and reflect	Guided planning and subgoal generation	Prediction, observation, explanation cycles
Role of teacher	Facilitate learning process and model reasoning	Engage students' prior knowledge, model problem-solving strategies, provide content instruction when needed by students	Introduce relevant content before and during inquiry
Collaboration	Negotiation of ideas Individual students bring new knowledge to group for application to problem	Negotiation of ideas and strategies within small groups and whole class	Guides inquiry process Negotiation of ideas with peers and local community members
Tools	Structured whiteboard Student-identified learning resources	Video controller Problem-specific tools (e.g., maps, compasses)	Computer-based tools that support planning, data collection and analysis, modeling, and information-gathering

Source: From C. E. Hmelo-Silver, "Problem-based learning: What and how do students learn?" *Educational Psychology Review,* 16, p. 238. Plenum Publishing Corporation, 2004.

In 1993, a similar comparison was made of problem-based instruction in medical school. Students learning through problem-based instruction were better at clinical skills such as problem formation and reasoning, but they were worse in their basic knowledge of science and felt less prepared in science (Albanese & Mitchell, 1993). In another study, MBA students who learned a concept using problem-based methods were better at explaining the concept than students who had learned the concept from lecture and discussion (Capon & Kuhn, 2004). Students who are better at self-regulation may benefit more from problem-based methods (Evensen, Salisbury-Glennon, & Glenn, 2001), but using problem-based methods over time can help students to develop self-directed learning skills.

In terms of the goals of problem-based learning listed earlier, Cindy Hmelo-Silver (2004) reviewed the research and found good evidence that problem-based learning supports the construction of flexible knowledge and the development of problem-solving and self-directed learning skills, but there is less evidence that participating in problem-based learning is intrinsically motivating or that it teaches students to collaborate. In addition, most of the research has been done in higher education, especially medical schools.

The best approach in elementary and secondary schools may be a balance of content-focused and inquiry or problem-based methods (Arends, 2004). For example, Eva Toth, David Klahr, and Zhe Chen (2000) tested a balanced approach for teaching 4th graders how to use the controlled variable strategy in science to design good experiments. The method had three phases: (1) in small groups, students conducted exploratory experiments to identify variables that made a ball roll farther down a ramp; (2) the teacher led a discussion, explained the controlled variable strategy, and modeled good thinking about experiment design; and (3) the students designed and conducted application experiments to isolate which variables caused the ball to roll farther. The combination of inquiry, discussion, explanation, and modeling was successful in helping the students understand the concepts.

Another constructivist approach that relies heavily on interaction is instructional conversations.

Dialogue and Instructional Conversations

One implication of Vygotsky's theory of cognitive development is that important learning and understanding require interaction and conversation. Students need to grapple with problems in their zone of proximal development, and they need the scaffolding provided by interaction with a teacher or other students. Here is a good definition of scaffolding that emphasizes the knowledge that both teacher and student bring—both are experts on something: "Scaffolding is a powerful conception of teaching and learning in which teachers and students create meaningful connections between teachers' cultural knowledge and the everyday experience and knowledge of the student" (McCaslin & Hickey, 2001, p. 137). Look back at the beach conversation between Ben and his father at the beginning of the previous section. Notice how the father used the abalone sandwich and the necklace—connections to Ben's experience and knowledge—to scaffold Ben's understanding.

Connect and Extend to PRAXIS II™

Dialogue and Conversation (II, A2)

Engaging discussions and instructional conversations are often students' most memorable and valuable learning experiences. Understand the principles involved in utilizing conversations and dialogue as an instructional strategy.

Instructional conversations are *instructional* because they are designed to promote learning, but they are *conversations,* not lectures or traditional discussions. Here is a segment of conversation from a literature group in a bilingual 3rd-grade classroom (Moll & Whitmore, 1993). The conversation shows how the participants mediate each other's learning through dialogue about the shared experience.

T: Sylvester and the Magic Pebble. What did you think about this story?
Rita: I think they cared a lot for him.
T: What do you mean? You mean his parents?
Rita: Yes.
T: What made you think that when you read the story?
Rita: Because they really worried about him.
T: Who else wants to share something? I'd like to hear everybody's ideas. Then we can decide what we want to talk about. Sarah?

Instructional conversation Situation in which students learn through interactions with teachers and/or other students.

Sarah: I think he got the idea of it when he was little, or maybe one of his friends got lost or something?
T: What do you mean, he got the idea?
Sarah: He got the idea for his parents to think that Sylvester got lost.
T: You're talking about where William Steig might have gotten his ideas.
Sarah: Yes.
T: That maybe something like this happened to him or someone he knew. A lot of times authors get their ideas from real life things, don't they? Jon, what did you think about this story?
Jon: It was like a moral story. It's like you can't wish for everything. But, in a sense, everything happened to him when he was panicking.
T: When did you think he panicked?
Jon: Well, when he saw the lion, he started to panic.
Richard: And he turned himself into a rock.
Jon: Yeah. He said, "I wish I were a rock."
T: Right. And it happened, didn't it?
Richard: It was stupid of him.
T: So maybe he wasn't thinking far enough ahead? What would you have wished instead of a rock? (pp. 24–25)

Connect and **Extend** to Your **Teaching/Portfolio**

For more information on instructional conversations, including examples of class transcripts and instruments to assess instructional conversations, contact: Dissemination Center, National Center for Research on Cultural Diversity and Second Language Learning, Center for Applied Linguistics, 1118 22nd Street NW, Washington, DC 20037.

The conversation continues as the students contribute different levels of interpretation of the story. The teacher notes these interpretations in her summary: "Look at all the different kinds of things you had to say. Rita talked about the characters in the story and what they must be feeling. Sarah took the author's point of view. And you saw it as a particular kind of story, Jon, a moral story."

In instructional conversations, the teacher's goal is to keep everyone cognitively engaged in a substantive discussion. In the above conversation, the teacher takes almost every other turn. As the students become more familiar with this learning approach, we would expect them to talk more among themselves with less teacher talk. These conversations do not have to be long. Even taking up lunch money can be an opportunity for an instructional conversation:

> During the first few minutes of the day, Ms. White asked how many children wanted hot lunches that day. Eighteen children raised their hands. Six children were going to eat cold lunches. Ms. White asked, "How many children are going to eat lunch here today?"
>
> By starting with 18 and counting on, several children got to the answer of 24. One child got out counters and counted out a set of 18 and another set of 6. He then counted all of them and said "24."
>
> Ms. White then asked, "How many more children are eating hot lunch than are eating cold lunch?"
>
> Several children counted back from 18 to 12. The child with the blocks matched 18 blocks with 6 blocks and counted the blocks left over.
>
> Ms. White asked the children who volunteered to tell the rest of the class how they got the answer. Ms. White continued asking for different solutions until no one could think of a new way to solve the problem. (Peterson, Fennema, & Carpenter, 1989, p. 45)

Ms. White created an environment in which students can make sense of mathematics and use mathematics to make sense of the world. To accomplish these goals, teaching begins with the student's current understanding. Teachers can capitalize on the natural use of counting strategies to see how many different ways students can solve a problem. The emphasis is on mathematical thinking, not on math "facts" or on learning the one best (teacher's) way to solve the problem. The teacher is a guide, helping students construct their own understandings through dialogue (Putnam & Borko, 1997).

Table 9.4 summarizes the elements of productive instructional conversations.

Cognitive Apprenticeships

Over the centuries, apprenticeships have proved to be an effective form of education. By working alongside a master and perhaps other apprentices, young people have learned

TABLE 9.4

Elements of the Instructional Conversation

Good instructional conversations must have elements of both instruction and conversation.

Instruction	Conversation
1. *Thematic focus.* Teacher selects a theme on which to focus the discussion and has a general plan for how the theme will unfold, including how to "chunk" the text to permit optimal exploration of the theme.	**6.** *Fewer "known-answer" questions.* Much of the discussion centers on questions for which there might be more than one correct answer.
2. *Activation and use of background knowledge.* Teacher either "hooks into" or provides students with pertinent background knowledge necessary for understanding a text, weaving the information into the discussion.	**7.** *Responsiveness to student contributions.* While having an initial plan and maintaining the focus and coherence of the discussion, teacher is also responsive to students' statements and the opportunities they provide.
3. *Direct teaching.* When necessary, teacher provides direct teaching of a skill or concept.	**8.** *Connected discourse.* The discussion is characterized by multiple, interactive, connected turns; succeeding utterances build on and extend previous ones.
4. *Promotion of more complex language and expression.* Teacher elicits more extended student contributions by using a variety of elicitation techniques: invitation to expand, questions, restatements, and pauses.	**9.** *Challenging, but non-threatening, atmosphere.* Teacher creates a challenging atmosphere that is balanced by a positive affective climate. Teacher is more collaborator than evaluator and students are challenged to negotiate and construct the meaning of the text.
5. *Promotion of bases for statements or positions.* Teacher promotes students' use of text, pictures, and reasoning to support an argument or position, by gently probing: "What makes you think that?" or "Show us where it says ____."	**10.** *General participation, including self-selected turns.* Teacher does not hold exclusive right to determine who talks; students are encouraged to volunteer or otherwise influence the selection of speaking turns.

Source: From *Instructional Conversations and Their Classroom Application* (p. 7), by Claude Goldenberg, 1991, Santa Cruz, CA and Washington, DC: National Center for Research on Cultural Diversity and Second Language Learning. Copyright © 1991 by National Center for Research on Cultural Diversity and Second Language Learning. Reprinted with permission.

many skills, trades, and crafts. Knowledgeable guides provide models, demonstrations, and corrections, as well as a personal bond that is motivating. The performances required of the learner are real and important and grow more complex as the learner becomes more competent (Collins, Brown, & Holum, 1991; Collins, Brown, & Newman, 1989; Hung, 1999). With *guided participation* in real tasks comes *participatory appropriation*—students appropriate the knowledge, skills, and values involved in doing the tasks (Rogoff, 1995, 1998). In addition, both the newcomers to learning and the old-timers contribute to the community of practice by mastering and remastering skills—and sometimes improving these skills in the process (Lave & Wenger, 1991).

Connect and **Extend** to Your **Teaching/Portfolio**

Add Table 9.4, "Elements of the Instructional Conversation" to your Teaching Resources file.

Allan Collins and his colleagues (1989) suggest that knowledge and skills learned in school have become too separated from their use in the world beyond school. To correct this imbalance, some educators recommend that schools adopt many of the features of apprenticeships. But rather than learning to sculpt or dance or build a cabinet, apprenticeships in school would focus on cognitive objectives such as reading comprehension, writing, or mathematical problem solving. There are many **cognitive apprenticeship** models, but most share six features:

- Students observe an expert (usually the teacher) *model* the performance.
- Students get external support through *coaching* or tutoring (including hints, feedback, models, and reminders).
- Students receive conceptual *scaffolding,* which is then gradually faded as the student becomes more competent and proficient.
- Students continually *articulate* their knowledge—putting into words their understanding of the processes and content being learned.
- Students *reflect* on their progress, comparing their problem solving to an expert's performance and to their own earlier performances.
- Students are required to *explore* new ways to apply what they are learning—ways that they have not practiced at the master's side.

Cognitive apprenticeship A relationship in which a less experienced learner acquires knowledge and skills under the guidance of an expert.

Cognitive apprenticeship approaches may use knowledgeable guides or "masters" to provide models, demonstrations, and corrections in learning tasks, as well as a personal bond that is motivating to younger or less experienced "apprentices" as they perform and perfect the tasks.

As students learn, they are challenged to master more complex concepts and skills and to perform them in many different settings (Roth & Bowen, 1995; Shuell, 1996).

How can teaching provide cognitive apprenticeships? Mentoring in teaching is one example. Another is cross-age grouping. In the Key School, an inner-city public elementary school in Indianapolis, Indiana, students of different ages work side-by-side for part of every day on a "pod" designed to have many of the qualities of an apprenticeship. The pods might focus on a craft or a discipline. Examples include gardening, architecture, and "making money." Many levels of expertise are evident in the students of different ages, so students can move at a comfortable pace, but still have the model of a master available. Community volunteers, including many parents, visit to demonstrate a skill that is related to the pod topic.

Another successful example of cognitive apprenticeships, the reciprocal teaching approach for reading comprehension, is discussed in Chapter 13.

Connect and Extend to PRAXIS II™

Thinking Skills (II, A1)

A nearly universal goal of educational programs across the country is the development of thinking skills. Describe what a teacher can do to cultivate these skills in the classroom. Read *Teaching Thinking Skills* (http://www.nwrel.org/scpd/sirs/6/cu11.html) for a concise overview of research, issues, and key factors related to this topic.

A Cognitive Apprenticeship in Learning Mathematics. Schoenfeld's (1989, 1994) teaching of mathematical problem solving is another example of the cognitive apprenticeship instructional model. Schoenfeld found that novice problem solvers began ineffective solution paths and continued on these paths even though they were not leading toward a solution. In comparison, expert problem solvers moved toward solutions using various cognitive processes such as planning, implementing, and verifying, altering their behavior based on judgments of the validity of their solution processes.

To help students become more expert problem solvers, Schoenfeld asks students three important questions: What are you doing? Why are you doing it? and How will success in what you are doing help you find a solution to the problem? These questions help students control the processes they use and build their metacognitive awareness. Here is an example:

> Problem sessions begin when I hand out a list of questions. . . . Often one student has an "inspiration.". . . My task is not to say yes or no, or even to evaluate the suggestion. Rather it is to raise the issue for discussion. . . . Typically a number of students respond [that they haven't made sense of the problem]. When we have made sense of the problem, the suggestion [X] simply doesn't make sense. . . . When this happens, I step out of my role as moderator to make the point to the whole class: If you make sure you understand the problem before you jump into a solution, you are less likely to go off on a wild goose chase. (Schoenfeld, 1987, p. 201)

Connect and Extend to the Research

Perkins, D., Jay, E., & Tishman, S. (1993). New conceptions of thinking: From ontology to education. *Educational Psychologist, 28,* 67–85; see also Tishman, S., Perkins, D., and Jay, E. (1995). *The thinking classroom: Learning and teaching in a culture of thinking.* Boston: Allyn and Bacon.

This monitoring of the understanding of a problem and the problem-solving process help students begin to think and act as mathematicians. Throughout this process, Schoenfeld repeats his three questions (What are you doing? Why? How will this help?). Each of these components is essential in helping students to be aware of and to regulate their behaviors.

Apprenticeships in Thinking

Many educational psychologists believe that good thinking can and should be developed in school. But clearly, teaching thinking entails much more than the standard classroom practices of answering "thought" questions at the end of the chapter or participating in teacher-led discussions. What else is needed? One approach has been to focus on the development of *thinking skills,* either through stand-alone programs that teach skills directly, or through indirect methods that embed development of thinking in the regular curriculum. The advantage of **stand-alone thinking skills programs** is that students do not need extensive subject matter knowledge to master the skills. Students who have had trouble with the traditional curriculum may achieve success—and perhaps an enhanced sense of self-efficacy—through these programs. The disadvantage is that the general skills often are not used outside the program unless teachers make a concerted effort to show students how to apply the skills in specific subjects (Mayer & Wittrock, 1996; Prawat, 1991).

"We did that last year—how come we have to do it again this year?"

© W.A. Vanslow—From *Phi Delta Kappan.* Reprinted by permission.

Developing Thinking in Every Class. Another way to develop students' thinking is to provide cognitive apprenticeships in analysis, problem solving, and reasoning through the regular lessons of the curriculum. David Perkins and his colleagues (Perkins, Jay, & Tishman, 1993) propose that teachers do this by creating a culture of thinking in their classrooms. This means that there is a spirit of inquisitiveness and critical thinking, a respect for reasoning and creativity, and an expectation that students will learn and understand. In such a classroom, education is seen as *enculturation,* a broad and complex process of acquiring knowledge and understanding consistent with Vygotsky's theory of mediated learning. Just as our home culture taught us lessons about the use of language, the culture of a classroom can teach lessons about thinking by giving us models of good thinking; providing direct instruction in thinking processes; and encouraging practice of those thinking processes through interactions with others.

Stand-alone thinking skills programs Programs that teach thinking skills directly without need for extensive subject matter knowledge.

Critical thinking Evaluating conclusions by logically and systematically examining the problem, the evidence, and the solution.

Critical Thinking. **Critical thinking** skills are useful in almost every life situation—even in evaluating the media ads that constantly bombard us. When you see a group of gorgeous people extolling the virtues of a particular brand of orange juice as they frolic in skimpy bathing suits, you must decide if sex appeal is a relevant factor in choosing a fruit drink

Many educational psychologists believe that good thinking can and should be developed in school and that thinking skills can be taught through stand-alone programs that teach thinking skills directly.

Point/Counterpoint

Should Schools Teach Critical Thinking and Problem Solving?

The question of whether schools should focus on process or content, problem-solving skills or core knowledge, higher-order thinking skills or academic information has been debated for years. Some educators suggest that students must be taught how to think and solve problems, while other educators assert that students cannot learn to "think" in the abstract. They must be thinking about something—some content. Should teachers focus on knowledge or thinking?

POINT Problem solving and higher-order thinking can and should be taught.

An article in the April, 28, 1995, issue of the *Chronicle of Higher Education* makes this claim:

> *Critical thinking is at the heart of effective reading, writing, speaking, and listening. It enables us to link together mastery of content with such diverse goals as self-esteem, self-discipline, multicultural education, effective cooperative learning, and problem solving. It enables all instructors and administrators to raise the level of their own teaching and thinking. (p. A-71)*

How can students learn to think critically? Some educators recommend teaching thinking skills directly with widely used techniques such as the Productive Thinking Program or CoRT (Cognitive Research Trust). Other researchers argue that learning computer programming languages such as LOGO will improve students' minds and teach them how to think logically. For example, Papert (1980) believes that when children learn through discovery how to give instructions to computers in LOGO, "powerful intellectual skills are developed in the process" (p. 60). Finally, because expert readers automatically apply certain metacognitive strategies, many educators and psychologists recommend directly teaching novice or poor readers how to apply these strategies. Michael Pressley's Good Strategy User model and Palincsar and Brown's (1984) reciprocal teaching approach are successful examples of direct teaching of metacognitive skills. Research on these approaches generally shows improvements in achievement and comprehension for students of all ages who participate (Pressley, Barkowski, & Schneider, 1987; Rosenshine & Meister, 1994).

COUNTERPOINT Thinking and problem-solving skills do not transfer.

According to E. D. Hirsch, a vocal critic of critical thinking programs:

> *But whether such direct instruction of critical thinking or self-monitoring does in fact improve performance is a subject of debate in the research community. For instance, the research regarding critical thinking is not reassuring. Instruction in critical thinking has been going on in several countries for over a hundred years. Yet researchers found that students from nations as varied as Israel, Germany, Australia, the Philippines, and the United States, including those who have been taught critical thinking continue to fall into logical fallacies. (1996, p. 136)*

The CoRT program has been used in over 5,000 classrooms in 10 nations. But Polson and Jeffries (1985) report that "after 10 years of widespread use we have no adequate evidence concerning the effectiveness of the program" (p. 445). In addition, Mayer and Wittrock (1996) note that field studies of problem solving in real situations show that people often fail to apply the mathematical problem-solving approaches they learn in school to actual problems encountered in the grocery store or home.

Even though educators have been more successful in teaching metacognitive skills, critics still caution that there are times when such teaching hinders rather than helps learning. Robert Siegler (1993) suggests that teaching self-monitoring strategies to low-achieving students can interfere with the students' development of adaptive strategies. Forcing students to use the strategies of experts may put too much burden on working memory as the students struggle to use an unfamiliar strategy and miss the meaning or content of the lesson. For example, rather than teach students strategies for figuring out words from context, it may be helpful for students to focus on learning more vocabulary words.

WHAT DO YOU THINK?

Vote online at **www.mylabschool.com**

(remember Pavlovian advertising from Chapter 6). As you can see in the *Point/Counterpoint*, educators don't agree about the best way to foster creative thinking in schools.

No matter what approach you use to develop critical thinking, it is important to follow up with additional practice. One lesson is not enough. For example, if your class examined a particular historical document to determine if it reflected bias or propaganda, you should follow up by analyzing other written historical documents, contemporary advertisements, or news stories. Until thinking skills become overlearned and relatively

TABLE 9.5

Examples of Critical Thinking Skills

Defining and Clarifying the Problem

1. Identify central issues or problems.
2. Compare similarities and differences.
3. Determine which information is relevant.
4. Formulate appropriate questions.

Judging Information Related to the Problem

5. Distinguish among fact, opinion, and reasoned judgment.
6. Check consistency.
7. Identify unstated assumptions.
8. Recognize stereotypes and clichés.
9. Recognize bias, emotional factors, propaganda, and semantic slanting.
10. Recognize different value systems and ideologies.

Solving Problems/Drawing Conclusions

11. Recognize the adequacy of data.
12. Predict probable consequences.

Source: From "California Assesses Critical Thinking," by P. Kneedler. In A. Costa (Ed.), *Developing Minds: A Resource Book for Teaching Thinking,* p. 277.

automatic, they are not likely to be transferred to new situations. Instead, students will use these skills only to complete the lesson in social studies, not to evaluate the claims made by friends, politicians, toy manufacturers, or diet plans. Table 9.5 provides a representative list of critical thinking skills.

STOP | THINK | WRITE How many different words can you list that describe aspects of thinking? Try to "think" of at least 20. ■

The Language of Thinking. My computer's thesaurus just found over 100 more words when I highlighted "thinking." The language of thinking consists of natural language terms that refer to mental processes and mental products—"words like think, believe, guess, conjecture, hypothesis, evidence, reasons, estimate, calculate, suspect, doubt, and theorize—to name just a few" (Tishman, Perkins, & Jay, 1995, p. 8). The classroom should be filled with a clear, precise, and rich vocabulary of thinking. Rather than saying, "What do you think about Jamie's answer?" the teacher might ask questions that expand thinking such as, "What evidence can you give to refute or support Jamie's answer?" "What assumptions is Jamie making?" "What are some alternative explanations?" Students surrounded by a rich language of thinking are more likely to think deeply about thinking. Students learn more when they engage in talk that is interpretive and that analyzes and gives explanations. Talk that just describes is less helpful in learning than talk that explains, give reasons, identifies parts, makes a case, defends a position, or evaluates evidence (Palincsar, 1998).

Connect and **Extend** to Your **Teaching/Portfolio**

List all the different words related to thinking that you hear during one of your college classes. You might contrast the "thinking language" in a class that seems to challenge you to think with that of a class that focuses on skills and facts.

An Integrated Constructivist Program: Fostering Communities of Learners

Fostering Communities of Learners (FCL) is "a system of interacting activities that results in a self-consciously active and reflective learning environment" (Brown & Campione, 1996, p. 292). This is an entire instructional program grounded in constructivist learning theories.

It is tempting to reduce the complex processes and understandings of FCL into a simple set of steps or procedures. But the inventors, Ann Brown and Joseph Campione, caution that in considering FCL, our emphasis should be on philosophy and principles, not procedures and steps. At the heart of FCL is a three-part process: Students engage in

Fostering communities of learners (FCL) A system of interacting activities that results in a self-consciously active and reflective learning environment, and uses a research, share, perform learning cycle.

independent and group research on one aspect of the class inquiry topic—for example, animal adaptation and survival. The goal is for the entire class to develop a deep understanding of the topic. Because the material is complex, class mastery requires that students become experts on different aspects of the larger topic and share their expertise. The sharing is motivated by a consequential task—a performance that matters. The task may be a traditional test or it may be a public performance, service project, or competition. Thus, the heart of FCL is *research,* in order to *share* information, in order to *perform* a consequential task (Brown, 1997; Brown & Campione, 1996).

This inquiry cycle may not seem that new, but what sets FCL apart, among other things, is having a variety of research-based ways of accomplishing each phase and paying careful attention to teaching students how benefit intellectually and socially from each step. *Research* can take many forms, such as reading, studying, research seminars, guided writing, consulting with experts face-to-face or electronically, or peer and cross-age tutoring. In order to do research, students are taught and coached in powerful comprehension-monitoring and comprehension-extending strategies such as summarizing and predicting for younger students, and for older students, forming analogies, giving causal explanations, providing evidence, and making sound arguments and predictions. Students are taught explicitly how to *share* information by asking for and giving help, majoring (developing special interest and expertise in an area), learning from each others' exhibitions, participating in cooperative groups, and joining in whole-class cross-talk sessions to check the progress of the research groups. *Performing* consequential tasks includes publishing; designing; creating solutions to real problems; setting up exhibitions; staging performances; and taking tests, quizzes, and authentic assessments that can hardly be distinguished from ongoing teaching.

Thoughtful reflection and deep disciplinary content surround and support the *research, share, perform* cycle. FCL teachers create a culture of thinking—self-conscious reflection about important and complex disciplinary units. As Brown and Campione (1996) point out, we "cannot expect students to invest intellectual curiosity and disciplined inquiry on trivia" (p. 306). In FCL classrooms, the teachers' main ploy is to "trap students into thinking deeply" about complex content (Brown & Campione, 1996, p. 302).

Connect and **Extend** to Your **Teaching/Portfolio**

John Cronin lists these four common misconceptions about authentic learning:

Misconception #1: If you can't take 'em to Spain, they might as well not learn Spanish at all. The fact that living with native speakers is the best way to learn Spanish does not make using the language in classroom conversations a poor alternative. Look for the small and obvious ways to make learning more authentic—especially if you can't take 'em to Spain.

Misconception #2: If you don't have your chef's license, then you'll have to starve. You don't need special training or materials to create authentic instruction. Good teachers have been doing it for years.

Misconception #3: If it isn't real fun, then it isn't real. Important learning and valuable life skills are not always fun to learn or fun to use. Self-discipline is part of growing up authentically.

Misconception #4: If you want to learn to play the piano, you must start with mastering Chopin. Not all learning has to be complicated; some important life skills are simple. From Cronin, J. F. (1993). Four misconceptions about authentic learning. *Educational Leadership, 50*(7), 78–80.

Dilemmas of Constructivist Practice

Years ago, Larry Cremin (1961) observed that progressive, innovative pedagogies require infinitely skilled teachers. Today, the same could be said about constructivist teaching. We have already seen that there are many varieties of constructivism and many practices that flow from these different conceptions. We also know that all teaching today happens in a context of high-stakes testing and accountability. In these situations, constructivist teachers face many challenges. Mark Windschitl (2002) identified four teacher dilemmas of constructivism in practice, summarized in Table 9.6. The first is conceptual: How do I make sense of cognitive versus social conceptions of constructivism and reconcile these different perspectives with my practice? The second dilemma is pedagogical: How do I teach in truly constructivist ways that both honor my students' attempts to think for themselves, but still insure that they learn the academic material? Third are cultural dilemmas: What activities, cultural knowledge, and ways of talking will build a community in a diverse classroom? Finally, there are political dilemmas: How can I teach for deep understanding and critical thinking, but still satisfy the accountability demands of parents and the requirements of *No Child Left Behind*?

Connect and **Extend** to Your **Teaching/Portfolio**

Use the *Guidelines* to brainstorm ideas for how you would explain your teaching innovations to families. Experiment by drafting a "Newsletter."

Diversity and Convergences in Theories of Learning

WHAT WOULD YOU SAY?

As part of your interview for a job in a large district, the superintendent asks, "What is your conception of learning? How do students learn?" ■

TABLE 9.6

Teachers' Dilemmas of Constructivism in Practice

Teachers face conceptual, pedagogical, cultural, and political dilemmas as they implement constructivist practices. Here are explanations of these dilemmas and some representative questions that teachers face as they confront them.

Teachers' Dilemma category	Representative Questions of Concern
I. *Conceptual dilemmas:* Grasping the underpinnings of cognitive and social constructivism; reconciling current beliefs about pedagogy with the beliefs necessary to support a constructivist learning environment.	Which version of constructivism is suitable as a basis for my teaching? Is my classroom supposed to be a collection of individuals working toward conceptual change or a community of learners whose development is measured by participation in authentic disciplinary practices? If certain ideas are considered correct by experts, should students internalize those ideas instead of constructing their own?
II. *Pedagogical dilemmas:* Honoring students' attempts to think for themselves while remaining faithful to accepted disciplinary ideas; developing deeper knowledge of subject matter; mastering the art of facilitation; managing new kinds of discourse and collaborative work in the classroom.	Do I base my teaching on students' existing ideas rather than on learning objectives? What skills and strategies are necessary for me to become a facilitator? How do I manage a classroom where students are talking to one another rather than to me? Should I place limits on students' construction of their own ideas? What types of assessments will capture the learning I want to foster?
III. *Cultural dilemmas:* Becoming conscious of the culture of your classroom; questioning assumptions about what kinds of activities should be valued; taking advantage of experiences, discourse patterns, and local knowledge of students with varied cultural backgrounds.	How can we contradict traditional, efficient classroom routines and generate new agreements with students about what is valued and rewarded? How do my own past images of what is proper and possible in a classroom prevent me from seeing the potential for a different kind of learning environment? How can I accommodate the worldviews of students from diverse backgrounds while at the same time transforming my own classroom culture? Can I trust students to accept responsibility for their own learning?
IV. *Political dilemmas:* Confronting issues of accountability with various stakeholders in the school community; negotiating with key others the authority and support to teach for understanding.	How can I gain the support of administrators and parents for teaching in such a radically different and unfamiliar way? Should I make use of approved curriculums that are not sensitive enough to my students' needs, or should I create my own? How can diverse problem-based experiences help students meet specific state and local standards? Will constructivist approaches adequately prepare my students for high-stakes testing for college admissions?

Source: M. Windschitl (2002). Framing constructivism in practice as the negotiation of dilemmas: An analysis of the conceptual, pedagogical, cultural, and political challenges facing teachers. *Review of Educational Research, 72,* p. 133. Copyright © 2002 by the American Educational Research Association. Reproduced with permission of the publisher.

Diversity

The power and value of diversity is part of the theoretical frameworks of social cognitive and constructivist theories of learning. Social cognitive theory describes the unique reciprocal interactions among personal, environmental, and behavioral factors that shape the individual's learning and motivation. Culture, social context, personal history, ethnicity, language, and racial identity—to name only a few factors—all shape personal characteristics such as knowledge and beliefs, environmental features such as resources and challenges, and behavioral actions and choices. And a major tenet of constructivist theories is that knowing is socially constructed—shaped by the culture and the families in which the knowers learn, develop, and create their identities.

One of the political dilemmas for teachers indicated in Table 9.6 is that families often question and criticize educational reforms. Many teachers using nontraditional approaches to learning find that they must explain these approaches to students' families.

Family and Community Partnerships

Guidelines: Communicating about Innovations

Be confident and honest.

EXAMPLES

1. Write out your rationale for the methods you are using—consider likely objections and craft your responses.
2. Admit mistakes or oversights—explain what you have learned from them.

Treat parents as equal partners.

EXAMPLES

1. Listen carefully to parents' objections, take notes, and follow up on requests or suggestions—remember, you both want the best for the child.
2. Give parents the telephone number of an administrator who will answer their questions about a new program or initiative.
3. Invite families to visit your room or assist in the project in some way.

Communicate effectively.

EXAMPLES

1. Use plain language and avoid jargon. If you must use a technical term, define it in accessible ways. Use your best teaching skills to educate parents about the new approach.
2. Encourage local newspapers or television stations to feature stories about the "great learning" going on in your classroom or school.
3. Create a lending library of articles and references about the new strategies.

Have examples of projects and assignments available for parents when they visit your class.

EXAMPLES

1. Encourage parents to try math activities. If they have trouble, show them how your students (and their child) are successful with the activities and highlight the strategies the students have learned.
2. Keep a library of students' favorite activities to demonstrate for parents.

Develop family involvement packages.

EXAMPLES

1. Once a month, send families, via their children, descriptions and examples of the math, science, or language skills to be learned in the upcoming unit. Include activities children can do with their parents.
2. Make the family project count, for example, as a homework grade.

Source: From "Addressing Parents' Concerns over Curriculum Reform," by M. Meyer, M. Delgardelle, and J. Middleton. *Educational Leadership*, 53(7). Copyright © 1996 by the American Association for Supervision and Curriculum Development. Reprinted with permission from ASCD. All rights reserved. The Association for Supervision and Curriculum Development is a worldwide community of educators advocating sound policies and sharing best practices to achieve the success of each learner. To learn more, visit ASCD at www.ascd.org.

Connect and **Extend** to Your **Teaching/Portfolio**

Can different formats, such as lecture or seatwork, be used in the service of different models, such as direct instruction or constructivist approaches?

The *Guidelines* give ideas for communicating with parents about innovative constructivist teaching and learning.

For the past four chapters, we have examined different aspects of learning. We considered behavioral, information processing, social cognitive, constructivist, and situated learning explanations of what people learn and how they learn it. Table 9.7 presents a summary of several of these perspectives on learning.

Convergences

Rather than debating the merits of each approach, consider their contributions to understanding learning and improving teaching. Don't feel that you must choose the "best" approach—there is no such thing. Chemists, biologists, and nutritionists rely on different theories to explain and improve health. Different views of learning can be used together to create productive learning environments for the diverse students you will teach. Behavioral theory helps us understand the role of cues in setting the stage for behaviors and the role of consequences and practice in encouraging or discouraging behaviors. But much of humans' lives and learning is more than behaviors. Language and higher-order thinking require complex information processing and memory—something the cognitive models of the thinker-as-computer have helped us understand. And what about the person as a creator and constructor of knowledge, not just a processor of information? Here, constructivist perspectives have much to offer.

I like to think of the three main learning theories in Table 9.7 as three pillars for teaching. Students must first understand and make sense of the material (constructivist); then they must remember what they have understood (cognitive—information processing); and then they must practice and apply (behavioral) their new skills and understanding to make them more fluid and automatic—a permanent part of their repertoire. Failure to attend to any part of the process means lower-quality learning.

Connect and Extend to Your Teaching/Portfolio

Use Table 9.7, "Four Views of Learning," to think about your own philosophy of learning. Would you incorporate elements from different theoretical approaches into your personal conception of learning?

TABLE 9.7

Four Views of Learning

There are variations within each of these views of learning that differ in emphasis. There is also an overlap in constructivist views.

		Cognitive	Constructivist	
	Behavioral	***Information Processing***	***Psychological/Individual***	***Social/Situated***
	Skinner	*J. Anderson*	*Piaget*	*Vygotsky*
Knowledge	Fixed body of knowledge to acquire Stimulated from outside	Fixed body of knowledge to acquire Stimulated from outside Prior knowledge influences how information is processed	Changing body of knowledge, individually constructed in social world Built on what learner brings	Socially constructed knowledge Built on what participants contribute, construct together
Learning	Acquisition of facts, skills, concepts Occurs through drill, guided practice	Acquisition of facts, skills, concepts, and strategies Occurs through the effective application of strategies	Active construction, restructuring prior knowledge Occurs through multiple opportunities and diverse processes to connect to what is already known	Collaborative construction of socially defined knowledge and values Occurs through socially constructed opportunities
Teaching	Transmission Presentation (Telling)	Transmission Guide students toward more "accurate" and complete knowledge	Challenge, guide thinking toward more complete understanding	Co-construct knowledge with students
Role of Teacher	Manager, supervisor Correct wrong answers	Teach and model effective strategies Correct misconceptions	Facilitator, guide Listen for student's current conceptions, ideas, thinking	Facilitator, guide Co-participant Co-construct different interpretation of knowledge; listen to socially constructed conceptions
Role of Peers	Not usually considered	Not necessary but can influence information processing	Not necessary but can stimulate thinking, raise questions	Ordinary part of process of knowledge construction
Role of Student	Passive reception of information Active listener, direction-follower	Active processor of information, strategy user Organizer and reorganizer of information Rememberer	Active construction (within mind) Active thinker, explainer, interpreter, questioner	Active co-construction with others and self Active thinker, explainer, interpreter, questioner Active social participator

Source: From *Reconceptualizing Learning for Restructured Schools* by H. H. Marshall. Paper presented at the Annual Meeting of the American Educational Research Association, April 1992. Copyright © Hermine H. Marshall. Adapted with permission.

Social Cognitive Theory

(pp. 330–333)

Distinguish between social learning and social cognitive theories. Social learning theory expanded behavioral views of reinforcement and punishment. In behavioral views, reinforcement and punishment directly affect behavior. In social learning theory, seeing another person, a model, reinforced or punished can have similar effects on the observer's behavior. Social cognitive theory expands social learning theory to include cognitive factors such as beliefs, expectations, and perceptions of self.

What is reciprocal determinism? Personal factors (beliefs, expectations, attitudes, and knowledge), the physical and social environment (resources, consequences of actions, other people, and physical settings), and behavior (individual actions, choices, and verbal statements) all influence and are influenced by each other.

What is self-efficacy, and how is it different from other self-schemas? Self-efficacy is distinct from other self-schemas in that it involves judgments of capabilities *specific to a particular task.* Self-concept is a more global construct that contains many perceptions about the self, including self-efficacy. Compared to self-esteem, self-efficacy is concerned with judgments of personal capabilities; self-esteem is concerned with judgments of self-worth.

What are the sources of self-efficacy? Four sources are mastery experiences (direct experiences), level of arousal as you face the task, vicarious experiences (accomplishments are modeled by someone else), and social persuasion (a "pep talk" or specific performance feedback).

Social learning theory Theory that emphasizes learning through observation of others.

Social cognitive theory Theory that adds concern with cognitive factors such as beliefs, self-perceptions, and expectations to social learning theory.

Reciprocal determinism An explanation of behavior that emphasizes the mutual effects of the individual and the environment on each other.

Self-efficacy A person's sense of being able to deal effectively with a particular task.

Mastery experiences Our own direct experiences—the most powerful source of efficacy information.

Arousal Physical and psychological reactions causing a person to feel alert, excited, or tense.

Vicarious experiences Accomplishments that are modeled by someone else.

Modeling Changes in behavior, thinking, or emotions that happen through observing another person—a model.

Social persuasion A "pep talk" or specific performance feedback—one source of self-efficacy.

Applying Social Cognitive Theory (pp. 333–343)

How does efficacy affect motivation? Greater efficacy leads to greater effort, persistence in the face of setbacks, higher goals, and finding new strategies when old ones fail. If sense of efficacy is low, however, people may avoid a task altogether or give up easily when problems arise.

What is teacher's sense of efficacy? One of the few personal characteristics of teachers related to student achievement is a teacher's efficacy belief that he or she can reach even difficult students to help them learn. Teachers with a high sense of efficacy work harder, persist longer, and are less likely to experience burn-out. Teachers' sense of efficacy is higher in schools where the other teachers and administrators have high expectations for students and where teachers receive help from their principals in solving instructional and management problems. Efficacy grows from real success with students, so any experience or training that helps you succeed in the day-to-day tasks of teaching will give you a foundation for developing a sense of efficacy in your career.

What factors are involved in self-regulated learning? One important goal of teaching is to prepare students for lifelong learning. To reach this goal, students must be self-regulated learners; that is, they must have a combination of the knowledge, motivation to learn, and volition that provides the skill and will to learn independently and effectively. Knowledge includes an understanding of self, subject, task, learning strategy, and contexts for application. Motivation to learn provides the commitment, and volition is the follow-through that combats distraction and protects persistence.

What is the self-regulated learning cycle? There are several models of self-regulated learning. Winne and Hadwin describe a 4-phase model: analyzing the task, setting goals and designing plans, enacting tactics to accomplish the task, and regulating learning. Zimmerman notes three similar phases: forethought (which includes setting goals, making plans, self-efficacy, and motivation); performance (which involves self-control and self-monitoring); and reflection (which includes self-evaluation and adaptations, leading to the forethought/planning phase again).

How can teachers support the development of self-efficacy and self-regulated learning? Teachers should involve students in complex meaningful tasks that extend over long periods of time; provide them control over their learning processes and products—they need to make choices. Involve students in setting criteria for evaluating their learning processes and products, then give them opportunities to make judgments about their progress using those standards. Finally, encourage students work collaboratively with and seek feedback from peers.

Teachers' sense of efficacy A teacher's belief that he or she can reach even the most difficult students and help them learn.

Self-regulation Process of activating and sustaining thoughts, behaviors, and emotions in order to reach goals.

Volition Will power; self-discipline; work styles that protect opportunities to reach goals by applying self-regulated learning.

Self-regulated learning A view of learning as skills and will applied to analyzing learning tasks, setting goals and planning how to do the task, applying skills, and especially making adjustments about how learning is carried out.

Agency The capacity to coordinate learning skills, motivation and emotions to reach your goals.

Cognitive and Social Constructivism

(pp. 343–350)

Describe two kinds of constructivism. And distinguish these from constructionism. *Psychological* constructivists such as Piaget are concerned with how *individuals* make sense of their world, based on individual knowledge, beliefs, self-concept, or identity—also called *first wave constructivism. Social* constructivists such as Vygotsky believe that social interaction, cultural tools, and activity shape individual development and learning—also called *second wave constructivism.* By participating in a broad range of activities with others, learners appropriate the outcomes produced by working together; they acquire new strategies and knowledge of their world. Finally, constructionists are interested in how public knowledge in academic disciplines is constructed as well as how everyday beliefs about the world are communicated to new members of a sociocultural group.

In what ways do constructivist views differ about knowledge sources, accuracy, and generality? Constructivists debate whether knowledge is constructed by mapping external reality, by adapting and changing internal understandings, or by an interaction of external forces and internal understandings. Most psychologists posit a role for both internal and external factors, but differ in how much they emphasize one or the other. Also, there is discussion about whether knowledge can be constructed in one situation and applied to another or whether knowledge is situated, that is, specific and tied to the context in which it was learned.

What are some common elements in most constructivist views of learning? Even though there is no single constructivist theory, many constructivist approaches recommend complex, challenging learning environments and authentic tasks; social negotiation and co-construction; multiple representations of content; understanding that knowledge is constructed; and student ownership of learning.

Constructivism View that emphasizes the active role of the learner in building understanding and making sense of information.

First wave constructivism A focus on the individual and psychological sources of knowing, as in Piaget's theory.

Radical constructivism Knowledge is assumed to be the individual's construction; it cannot be judged right or wrong.

Appropriate Internalize or take for yourself knowledge and skills developed in interaction with others or with cultural tools.

Second wave constructivism A focus on the social and cultural sources of knowing, as in Vygotsky's theory.

Community of practice Social situation or context in which ideas are judged useful or true.

Situated learning The idea that skills and knowledge are tied to the situation in which they were learned and difficult to apply in new settings.

Complex learning environments Problems and learning situations that mimic the ill-structured nature of real life.

Social negotiation Aspect of learning process that relies on collaboration with others and respect for different perspectives.

Intersubjective attitude A commitment to build shared meaning with others by finding common ground and exchanging interpretations.

Multiple representations of content Considering problems using various analogies, examples, and metaphors.

Spiral curriculum Bruner's design for teaching that introduces the fundamental structure of all subjects early in the school years, then revisits the subjects in more and more complex forms over time.

Applying Constructivist Perspectives

(pp. 350–362)

Distinguish between inquiry methods and problem-based learning. The inquiry strategy begins when the teacher presents a puzzling event, question, or problem. The students ask questions (only yes-no questions in some kinds of inquiry) and then formulate hypotheses to explain the event or solve the problem; collect data to test the hypotheses about casual relationships; form conclusions and generalizations; and reflect on the original problem and the thinking processes needed to solve it. Problem-based learning may follow a similar path, but the learning begins with an authentic problem—one that matters to the students. The goal is to learn math or science or history or some other important subject while seeking a real solution to a real problem.

What are instructional conversations? Instructional conversations are *instructional* because they are designed to promote learning, but they are *conversations*, not lectures or traditional discussions. They are responsive to students' contributions, challenging but not threatening, connected, and interactive—involving all the students. The teacher's goal is to keep everyone cognitively engaged in a substantive discussion.

Describe six features that most cognitive apprenticeship approaches share. Students observe an expert (usually the teacher) *model* the performance; get external support through *coaching* or tutoring; and receive conceptual *scaffolding*, which is then gradually faded as the student becomes more competent and proficient. Students continually *articulate* their knowledge—putting into words their understanding of the processes and content being learned. They *reflect* on their progress, comparing their problem solving to an expert's performance and to their own earlier performances. Finally, students *explore* new ways to apply what they are learning—ways that they have not practiced at the master's side.

What is meant by thinking as enculturation? *Enculturation* is a broad and complex process of acquiring knowledge and understanding consistent with Vygotsky's theory of mediated learning. Just as our home culture taught us lessons about the use of language, the culture of a classroom can teach lessons about thinking by giving us *models* of good thinking; providing *direct instruction* in thinking processes; and encouraging *practice* of those thinking processes through *interactions* with others.

What is critical thinking? Critical thinking skills include defining and clarifying the problem, making judgments about the consistency and adequacy of the information related to a problem, and drawing conclusions. No matter what approach you use to develop critical thinking, it is important to follow up activities with additional practice. One lesson is not enough.

What is FCL? Fostering Communities of Learners is an approach to organizing classrooms and schools. The heart of FCL is *research*, in order to *share* information, in order to *perform* a consequential task that involves deep disciplinary content. Students engage in independent and group research so the entire class can develop an understanding of the topic. Because the material is complex, class mastery requires that students become experts on different aspects of the larger topic and share their expertise. The sharing is motivated by a consequential task—a performance that matters.

Inquiry learning Approach in which the teacher presents a puzzling situation and students solve the problem by gathering data and testing their conclusions.

Problem-based learning Methods that provide students with realistic problems that don't necessarily have "right" answers.

Anchored instruction A type of problem-based learning that uses a complex interesting situation as an anchor for learning.

Instructional conversation Situation in which students learn through interactions with teachers and/or other students.

Cognitive apprenticeship A relationship in which a less experienced learner acquires knowledge and skills under the guidance of an expert.

Stand-alone thinking skills programs Programs that teach thinking skills directly without need for extensive subject matter knowledge.

Critical thinking Evaluating conclusions by logically and systematically examining the problem, the evidence, and the solution.

Fostering communities of learners (FCL) A system of interacting activities that results in a self-consciously active and reflective learning environment and uses a research, share, perform learning cycle.

Teachers' Casebook: Connections to PRAXIS II™

One influential idea from the constructivist perspective on learning is that visiting materials in different contexts for different purposes can enhance the acquisition of knowledge. In a sense, the teacher and students "crisscross" a learning landscape. This chapter's Teachers' Casebook is a landscape especially well suited for several visits. Thoughtful learning activities about such topics as motivation, learning environments, evaluation, and instructional strategies could well be explored through the instructional challenges here.

For a first excursion through this landscape, let's examine student-centered models of instruction, one of the major topics of this chapter. A problem you seem to face in this scenario is a mismatch between the students and the curriculum that exists for them. Most of the students appear unmotivated. Perhaps they see your activities as unconnected to their lives or they feel that they have no responsibility for their own learning. Knowledge of student-centered models of instruction can help you address those concerns and draw your students into active, meaningful learning in your classroom.

What Would They Do?

Here is how some practicing teachers responded to the awful "book reviews."

Mark H. Smith **Teacher, Grades Nine–Twelve,**
Medford High School, Medford, Massachusetts

Experience is the best teacher. In an ideal world you can plan your course with what you think would be great material and be ready with a curriculum to meet the level you expect. But reality sets in when you see the true level of the class. High standards and expectations are great goals but they must be reasonable for the students in your class. The education profession is one that needs constant flexibility and adjustment to situations. Students learn in different ways and teachers who can adapt to classes and curricula have a better chance of succeeding.

Because this class has many different levels it will be important to find some common ground that will interest them as well as get them involved in learning. It will probably be a good idea to do different activities and even let the three top students help teach some of the others. It will not be easy to get everybody on the same page and you will probably have to spend lots of time planning, but with patience and effort you can find the level that fits and get the students to respond.

Thomas W. Newkirk **Eighth Grade Teacher,**
Hamilton Heights Middle School, Arcadia, Indiana

It would be wonderful from the outset to have a class enthralled with world literature, but you are more likely to have a class frustrated with the prospect of reading another "lame" book. Therefore, it is important to find books with themes relevant to my students. Fortunately, on the reading list there are already some selections related to recent films, and probably there are some selections related to music, television, or even commercials. The more connections I can make between the literature and my students' lives, the more likely I am to motivate them.

Jeff D. Horton **Seventh–Tenth Grade Teacher,**
Colton School, Colton, Washington

One problem may be the materials that the teacher planned to use. I do believe that students need to be introduced to the "classics" in literature. However, teachers are self-motivated to read and study these writings. We must remember that most students do not feel the same way. The teacher in this scenario must present the "classics" in a way that will hold the students' interest. Instead of reading a whole book, pick out parts that reflect the writing style or message of the author. Then present other parts of the book using other teaching tools. There are movies available that are presented in a more current style that will appeal to students. Whatever the teaching tool used, there must always be a learning activity connected to it.

While three students in the class demonstrate a sophisticated understanding of literature, every student in the class can bring a fresh insight into a discussion and be recognized for his or her contribution. In addition to class discussion, individual and group projects can be designed to encourage students to respond to the material. Considering the diversity of the class, I would evaluate student achievement with grading contracts that challenge students performing at different levels.

Michael J. Ellis **Tenth and Eleventh Grade English Teacher,** *Quincy High School, Quincy, Massachusetts*

It seems the purpose behind the curriculum for this class is to expose the students to a wide array of great literature. That is a noble goal. In teaching, however, nobility must frequently give way to practicality. A teacher's first duty is to guide his students in the acquisition of necessary skills. Sometimes having them read Dickens isn't the best way to do that. The curriculum worked up over the summer will probably work well with the three standouts in the class. I'd try splintering them off from the rest. This can be a logistical nightmare and it effectively doubles your prep time for the class, but it's the best way to be sure that the students of a particular ability level don't stagnate while you cater to another group.

With the rest of the class, it's time to shift on the fly and ditch the original reading list. Emphasizing longer novels in a class dominated by poor readers is nothing less than a suicide attempt spread over 40 weeks. If you rely instead on shorter selections and young adult fiction titles with catchy plot lines, then you've at least given yourself a fighting chance at a class that actually finishes the books. It's also never a bad idea to throw video material into the mix.

CHAPTER 10

Motivation in Learning and Teaching

Teachers' Casebook: What Would You Do? 371

What Is Motivation? 372

Meeting Some Students 372

Intrinsic and Extrinsic Motivation 372

Four General Approaches to Motivation 374

Needs: Competence, Autonomy, and Relatedness 377

Self-Determination 377

Needs: Lessons for Teachers 379

Goal Orientations and Motivation 380

Types of Goals and Goal Orientations 380

Feedback and Goal Acceptance 383

Goals: Lessons for Teachers 383

Interests and Emotions 383

Tapping Interests 383

Arousal: Excitement and Anxiety in Learning 384

Reaching Every Student: Coping with Anxiety 388

Interests and Emotions: Lessons for Teachers 388

Beliefs and Self-Schemas 388

Beliefs about Ability 388

Beliefs about Causes and Control: Attribution Theory 390

Beliefs about Self-Efficacy and Learned Helplessness 392

Beliefs about Self-Worth 393

Beliefs and Self-Schemas: Lessons for Teachers 394

Motivation to Learn in School: On TARGET 395

Tasks for Learning 396

Supporting Autonomy and Recognizing Accomplishment 398

Grouping, Evaluation, and Time 399

Diversity and Convergences in Motivation to Learn 403

Diversity in Motivation 403

Convergences: Strategies to Encourage Motivation 404

Summary Table 407

Teachers' Casebook: Connections to PRAXIS II™/ What Would They Do? 411

What Would You Do?

Teachers' Casebook

It is July and you have finally gotten a teaching position. The district wasn't your first choice, but job openings were really tight, so you're pleased to have a job in your field. You are discovering that the teaching resources in your school are slim to none; the only resources are some aging texts and the workbooks that go with them. Every idea you have suggested for software, simulation games, visual aids, or other more active teaching materials has been met with the same response, "There's no money in the budget for that." As you look over the texts and workbooks, you wonder how the students could be anything but bored by them. To make matters worse, the texts look pretty high-level for your students. But the objectives in the workbooks are important. Besides, the district curriculum requires these units. Students will be tested on them in district-wide assessments next spring required by *No Child Left Behind*.

Critical Thinking

- How would you arouse student curiosity and interest about the topics and tasks in the workbooks?
- How would you establish the value of learning this material?
- How would you handle the difficulty level of the texts?
- What do you need to know about motivation to solve these problems?
- What do you need to know about your students in order to motivate them?

Collaboration

With 2 or 3 other members of your class, brainstorm what you could do to motivate your students.

Most educators agree that motivating students is one of the critical tasks of teaching. In order to learn, students must be cognitively, emotionally, and behaviorally engaged in productive class activities. We begin with the question "What is motivation?" and examine many of the answers that have been proposed, including a discussion of intrinsic and extrinsic motivation and four general theories of motivation: behavioral, humanistic, cognitive, and sociocultural.

Next, we consider more closely several personal factors that frequently appear in discussions of motivation: needs, goal orientations; interests and emotions; and beliefs, including the important concept of self-efficacy.

How do we put all this information together in teaching? How do we create environments, situations, and relationships that encourage motivation and engagement in learning? First, we consider how the personal influences on motivation come together to support motivation to learn. Then, we examine how motivation is influenced by the academic work of the class, the value of the work, and the setting in which the work must be done. Finally, we discuss a number of strategies for developing motivation as a constant state in your classroom and as a permanent trait in your students.

By the time you have completed this chapter, you should be able to answer these questions:

- What are intrinsic and extrinsic motivation and motivation to learn?
- How is motivation conceptualized in the behavioral, humanistic, cognitive, and sociocultural perspectives?
- What are the possible motivational effects of success and failure, and how do these effects relate to beliefs about ability?
- What are the roles of goals, interests, emotions, and beliefs about the self in motivation?
- What external factors can teachers influence that will encourage students' motivation to learn?
- What is your strategy for teaching your subject to an uninterested student?

FACING PAGE *Two Girls at the Piano*, 1892. Auguste Renoir. Photo: Erich Lessing/Art Resource, New York.

What Is Motivation?

Motivation is usually defined as *an internal state that arouses, directs, and maintains behavior.* Psychologists studying motivation have focused on five basic questions:

1. *What choices do people make about their behavior?* Why do some students, for example, focus on their homework and others watch television?
2. *How long does it take to get started?* Why do some students start their homework right away, while others procrastinate?
3. *What is the intensity or level of involvement in the chosen activity?* Once the backpack is opened, is the student absorbed and focused or just going through the motions?
4. *What causes a person to persist or to give up?* Will a student read the entire Shakespeare assignment or just a few pages?
5. *What is the individual thinking and feeling while engaged in the activity?* Is the student enjoying Shakespeare, feeling competent, or worrying about an upcoming test (Graham & Weiner, 1996; Pintrich, Marx, & Boyle, 1993)?

Connect and **Extend** to the **Research**

For a thorough discussion of the many terms and concepts related to motivation, see Murphy, P. K., & Alexander, P. A. (2000). A motivated exploration of motivation terminology. *Contemporary Educational Psychology, 25,* 3–53.

Connect and **Extend** to Your **Teaching/Portfolio**

Hopeless Geraldo is an example of a student experiencing *learned helplessness,* discussed later in the chapter.

Safe Sumey is an example of a student who is motivated by *extrinsic* factors, sets *performance goals,* fears *failure,* and views *ability as fixed.* She is also a (successful) *failure-avoiding student*—discussed later in the chapter.

Satisfied Spenser is an example of a student motivated by *intrinsic* factors. He set *learning goals* in his areas of interest, but just wants to perform "OK" in other areas. These concepts are discussed later in the chapter.

Defensive Daleesha is an example of a student who is motivated by extrinsic factors, sets *performance goals, fears failure,* and views *ability as fixed.* She is also a *failure-avoiding student.* Because she avoids work, she may soon become a *failure-accepting student*—discussed later in the chapter.

Anxious Amee is an example of a student experiencing debilitating *anxiety,* discussed later in the chapter.

Meeting Some Students

As you will see in this chapter and the next, there are many factors that influence motivation and engaged learning. To get a sense of the complexity, let's step into a middle-school general-science classroom just after the teacher has given directions for a class activity. The student profiles are adapted from Stipek (2002).

Hopeless Geraldo won't even start the assignment—as usual. He just keeps saying, "I don't understand," or "This is too hard." When he answers your questions correctly, he "guessed" and he "doesn't really know." Geraldo spends most of his time staring into space; he is falling farther and farther behind.

Safe Sumey checks with you about every step—she wants to be perfect. You once gave her bonus points for doing an excellent color drawing of the apparatus, and now she produces a work of art for lab every time. But Sumey won't risk getting a B. If it isn't required or on the test, Sumey isn't interested.

Satisfied Spenser on the other hand, is interested in this project. In fact, he knows more than you do about it. Evidently he spends hours reading about chemistry and performing experiments. But his overall grade in your class is between B^- and C^+ because when you were studying biology, Spenser was satisfied with the C he could get on tests without even trying.

Defensive Daleesha doesn't have her lab manual—again, so she has to share with another student. Then she pretends to be working, but spends most of her time making fun of the assignment or trying to get answers from other students when your back is turned. She is afraid to try because if she makes an effort and fails, she fears that everyone will know she is "dumb."

Anxious Amee is a good student in most subjects, but she freezes on science tests and "forgets" everything she knows when she has to answer questions in class. Her parents are scientists and expect her to become one too, but her prospects for this future look dim.

STOP | THINK | WRITE Each student above has problems with at least one of the five areas of motivation: choices, getting started, intensity, persistence, or thoughts and feelings. Can you diagnose the problems? The answers are on page 374. ■

Each student presents a different motivational challenge, yet you have to teach the entire class. In the next few pages, we will look more closely at the meaning of motivation so we can better understand these students.

Intrinsic and Extrinsic Motivation

We all know how it feels to be motivated, to move energetically toward a goal or to work hard, even if we are bored by the task. What energizes and directs our behavior? The

Motivation An internal state that arouses, directs, and maintains behavior.

explanation could be drives, needs, incentives, fears, goals, social pressure, self-confidence, interests, curiosity, beliefs, values, expectations, and more. Some psychologists have explained motivation in terms of personal *traits* or individual characteristics. Certain people, so the theory goes, have a strong *need* to achieve, a *fear* of tests, or an enduring *interest* in art, so they work hard to achieve, avoid tests, or spend hours in art galleries. Other psychologists see motivation more as a *state*, a temporary situation. If, for example, you are reading this paragraph because you have a test tomorrow, you are motivated (at least for now) by the situation. Of course, the motivation we experience at any given time usually is a combination of trait and state. You may be studying because you value learning *and* because you are preparing for a test.

As you can see, some explanations of motivation rely on internal, personal factors such as needs, interests, and curiosity. Other explanations point to external, environmental factors—rewards, social pressure, punishment, and so on. A classic distinction in motivation is between intrinsic and extrinsic. **Intrinsic motivation** is the natural tendency to seek out and conquer challenges as we pursue personal interests and exercise capabilities (Deci & Ryan, 1985, 2002; Reeve, 1996). When we are intrinsically motivated, we do not need incentives or punishments, because *the activity itself is rewarding.* Satisfied Spenser studies chemistry outside school simply because he loves the activity; no one makes him do it.

In contrast, when we do something in order to earn a grade, avoid punishment, please the teacher, or for some other reason that has very little to do with the task itself, we experience **extrinsic motivation.** We are not really interested in the activity for its own sake; we care only about what it will gain us. Safe Sumey works for the grade; she has little interest in the subject itself.

According to psychologists who adopt the intrinsic/extrinsic concept of motivation, it is impossible to tell just by looking if a behavior is intrinsically or extrinsically motivated. The essential difference between the two types of motivation is the student's reason for acting, that is, whether the **locus of causality** for the action (the location of the cause) is internal or external—inside or outside the person. Students who read or practice their backstroke or paint may be reading, swimming, or painting because they freely chose the activity based on personal interests (*internal locus* of causality/intrinsic motivation), or because someone or something else outside is influencing them (*external locus* of causality/extrinsic motivation) (Reeve, 1996).

As you think about your own motivation, you probably realize that the dichotomy between intrinsic and extrinsic motivation is too simple—too all-or-nothing. One explanation is that our activities fall along a continuum from fully *self-determined* (intrinsic motivation) to fully *determined by others* (extrinsic motivation). For example, students may freely choose to work hard on activities that they don't find particularly enjoyable because they know the activities are important in reaching a valued goal—such as spending hours studying educational psychology in order to become a good teacher. Is this intrinsic or extrinsic motivation? Actually, it is in between—the person is freely choosing to accept outside causes such as licensure requirements and then is trying to get the most benefit from the requirements. The person has *internalized an external cause.*

Recently, the notion of intrinsic and extrinsic motivation as two ends of a continuum has been challenged. An alternative explanation is that just as motivation can include both trait and state factors, it also can include both intrinsic and extrinsic factors. Intrinsic and extrinsic tendencies are two independent possibilities, and, at any given time, we can be motivated by some of each (Covington & Mueller, 2001). Teaching can create intrinsic motivation by connecting to students' interests and supporting growing competence. But you know this won't work all the time. Did you find long division inherently interesting? Was your curiosity piqued by irregular verbs? If teachers count on intrinsic motivation to energize all their students all of the time, they will be disappointed. There are situations where incentives and external supports are necessary. Teachers must encourage and nurture intrinsic motivation, while making sure that extrinsic motivation supports learning (Brophy, 1988, 2003; Deci, Koestner, & Ryan, 1999; Ryan & Deci, 1996). To do this, they need to know about the factors that influence motivation.

Intrinsic motivation Motivation associated with activities that are their own reward.

Extrinsic motivation Motivation created by external factors such as rewards and punishments.

Locus of causality The location—internal or external—of the cause of behavior.

STOP | THINK | WRITE **ANSWERS**

> **Hopeless Geraldo** has trouble with question 2 (getting started) and with question 5; during the activity he feels defeated and helpless. **Safe Sumey** (1) makes good choices, (2) gets started right away, and (3) persists. But she is not really engaged and takes little pleasure in the work (4 and 5). As long as he is following his own choices, **Satisfied Spenser** is prompt in getting started, engaged, persistent, and enjoys the task. **Defensive Daleesha** makes poor choices, procrastinates, avoids engagement, and gives up easily because she is so concerned about how others will judge her. **Anxious Amee's** problems have to do with question 5—what she thinks and how she feels as she works. Her worry and anxiety may lead her to make poor choices and procrastinate, which only makes her more anxious at test time.

Four General Approaches to Motivation

STOP | THINK | WRITE Why are you reading this chapter? Are you curious about motivation and interested in the topic? Or is there a test in your near future? Do you need this course to earn a teaching license or to graduate? Maybe you believe that you will do well in this class, and that belief keeps you working. Perhaps it is some combination of these reasons. What motivates you to study motivation? ■

Connect and Extend to the Research

See the entire issue of *Educational Leadership*, September 2002 (Vol. 60, No. 1) for 14 articles on "Do Students Care About Learning?" These articles discuss how to create enthusiasm, excitement, and investment in learning.

Motivation is a vast and complicated subject encompassing many theories. Some theories were developed through work with animals in laboratories. Others are based on research with humans in situations that used games or puzzles. Some theories grew out of the work done in clinical or industrial psychology. Our examination of the field will be selective; otherwise we would never finish the topic.

Behavioral Approaches to Motivation. According to the behavioral view, an understanding of student motivation begins with a careful analysis of the incentives and rewards present in the classroom. A **reward** is an attractive object or event supplied as a consequence of a particular behavior. For example, Safe Sumey was rewarded with bonus points when she drew an excellent diagram. An **incentive** is an object or event that encourages or discourages behavior. The promise of an A+ was an incentive to Sumey. Actually receiving the grade was a reward.

Connect and Extend to PRAXIS II™

Maslow (I, C1)

Consider how problems with satisfying Maslow's needs can affect student learning. Link these ideas to direct or vicarious experiences you might have had in school.

If we are consistently reinforced for certain behaviors, we may develop habits or tendencies to act in certain ways. For example, if a student is repeatedly rewarded with affection, money, praise, or privileges for earning letters in baseball, but receives little recognition for studying, the student will probably work longer and harder on perfecting her fastball than on understanding geometry. Providing grades, stars, stickers, and other reinforcers for learning—or demerits for misbehavior—is an attempt to motivate students by extrinsic means of incentives, rewards, and punishments.

Reward An attractive object or event supplied as a consequence of a behavior.

Incentive An object or event that encourages or discourages behavior.

Humanistic interpretation Approach to motivation that emphasizes personal freedom, choice, self-determination, and striving for personal growth.

Hierarchy of needs Maslow's model of seven levels of human needs, from basic physiological requirements to the need for self-actualization.

Self-actualization Fulfilling one's potential.

Humanistic Approaches to Motivation. In the 1940s, proponents of humanistic psychology such as Carl Rogers argued that neither of the dominant schools of psychology, behavioral or Freudian, adequately explained why people act as they do. **Humanistic interpretations** of motivation emphasize such intrinsic sources of motivation as a person's needs for "self-actualization" (Maslow, 1968, 1970), the inborn "actualizing tendency" (Rogers & Freiberg, 1994), or the need for "self-determination" (Deci, Vallerand, Pelletier, & Ryan, 1991). So, from the humanistic perspective, to motivate means to encourage people's inner resources—their sense of competence, self-esteem, autonomy, and self-actualization. Maslow's theory has been an influential humanistic explanation of motivation.

Maslow's Hierarchy. Abraham Maslow (1970) suggested that humans have a **hierarchy of needs** ranging from lower-level needs for survival and safety to higher-level needs for intellectual achievement and finally self-actualization. **Self-actualization** is Maslow's

According to Maslow's hierarchy, when the needs for love and belongingness are met, individuals can then address the so-called higher level needs of intellectual achievement and self-actualization.

term for self-fulfillment, the realization of personal potential. Each of the lower needs must be met before the next higher need can be addressed.

Maslow (1968) called the four lower-level needs—for survival, then safety, followed by belonging, and then self-esteem—**deficiency needs.** When these needs are satisfied, the motivation for fulfilling them decreases. He labeled the three higher-level needs—intellectual achievement, then aesthetic appreciation, and finally self-actualization—**being needs.** When they are met, a person's motivation does not cease; instead, it increases to seek further fulfillment. Unlike the deficiency needs, these being needs can never be completely filled. For example, the more successful you are in your efforts to develop as a teacher, the harder you are likely to strive for even greater improvement.

Maslow's theory has been criticized for the very obvious reason that people do not always appear to behave as the theory would predict. Most of us move back and forth among different types of needs and may even be motivated by many different needs at the same time. Some people deny themselves safety or friendship in order to achieve knowledge, understanding, or greater self-esteem.

Criticisms aside, Maslow's theory does give us a way of looking at the whole student, whose physical, emotional, and intellectual needs are all interrelated. A child whose feelings of safety and sense of belonging are threatened by divorce may have little interest in learning how to divide fractions. If school is a fearful, unpredictable place where neither teachers nor students know where they stand, they are likely to be more concerned with security and less with learning or teaching. Belonging to a social group and maintaining self-esteem within that group, for example, are important to students. If doing what the teacher says conflicts with group rules, students may choose to ignore the teacher's wishes or even defy the teacher.

A more recent approach to motivation that focuses on human needs is self-determination theory (Deci & Ryan, 2002), discussed later in this chapter.

Cognitive and Social Cognitive Approaches to Motivation. In cognitive theories, people are viewed as active and curious, searching for information to solve personally relevant problems. Thus, cognitive theorists emphasize intrinsic motivation. In many ways, cognitive theories of motivation also developed as a reaction to the behavioral views. Cognitive theorists believe that behavior is determined by our thinking, not simply by whether we have been rewarded or punished for the behavior in the past (Stipek, 2002). Behavior is initiated and regulated by plans (Miller, Galanter, & Pribram, 1960), goals (Locke & Latham, 2002), schemas (Ortony, Clore, & Collins, 1988), expectations (Vroom, 1964), and attributions (Weiner, 2000). We will look at goals and attributions later in this chapter.

Expectancy × Value Theories. Theories that take into account both the behaviorists' concern with the effects or outcomes of behavior and the cognitivists' interest in the

Deficiency needs Maslow's four lower-level needs, which must be satisfied first.

Being needs Maslow's three higher-level needs, sometimes called growth needs.

impact of individual thinking can be characterized as **expectancy × value theories.** This means that motivation is seen as the product of two main forces: the individual's expectation of reaching a goal and the value of that goal to him or her. In other words, the important questions are, "If I try hard, can I succeed?" and "If I succeed, will the outcome be valuable or rewarding to me?" Motivation is a product of these two forces, because if either factor is zero, there is no motivation to work toward the goal. For example, if I believe I have a good chance of making the basketball team (high expectation), and if making the team is very important to me (high value), then my motivation should be strong. But if either factor is zero (I believe I haven't a prayer of making the team, or I couldn't care less about playing basketball), then my motivation will be zero, too (Tollefson, 2000).

Jacqueline Eccles and Allan Wigfield add the element of *cost* to the expectancy × value equation. Values have to be considered in relation to the cost of pursuing them. How much energy will be required? What could I be doing instead? What are the risks if I fail? Will I look stupid (Eccles & Wigfield, 2001; Wigfield & Eccles, 1992)? Bandura's theory of self-efficacy, discussed later in this chapter, is a social cognitive expectancy × value approach to motivation (Feather, 1982; Pintrich & Schunk, 2002).

Sociocultural Conceptions of Motivation. Finish this sentence: I am a/an ____________. What is your identity? With what groups do you identify most strongly? **Sociocultural views of motivation** emphasize participation in communities of practice. People engage in activities to maintain their identities and their interpersonal relations within the community. Thus, students are motivated to learn if they are members of a classroom or school community that values learning. Just as we learn through socialization to speak or dress or order food in restaurants—by watching and learning from more capable members of the culture—we also learn to be students by watching and learning from members of our school community. In other words, we learn by the company we keep (Hickey, 2003; Rogoff, Turkanis, & Bartlett, 2001).

The concept of identity is central in sociocultural views of motivation. When we see ourselves as soccer players, or sculptors, or engineers, or teachers, or psychologists, we have an identity within a group. Part of our socialization is moving from legitimate peripheral participation to central participation in that group. **Legitimate peripheral participation** means that beginners are genuinely involved in the work of the group, even if their abilities are undeveloped and their contributions are small. The novice weaver learns to dye wool before spinning and weaving, and the novice teacher learns to tutor one child before working with the whole group. Each task is a piece of the real work of the expert. The identities of both the novice and the expert are bound up in their participation in the community. They are motivated to learn the values and practices of the community to keep their identity as community members (Lave & Wenger, 1991; Wenger, 1998). *The Stories of Learning/Tributes to Teaching* feature describes how instructors and friends supported a Korean student in her efforts to learn.

Some classrooms are intentionally structured as learning communities. For example, Brown and Campione (1996) developed learning communities for middle-school students around research projects in science, as we saw in Chapter 9. Scardamalia and Bereiter (1996) designed a learning community using a computer system called CSILE—Computer-Supported Intentional Learning Environment—that encourages collaboration among students about questions, hypotheses, and findings. The challenge in these approaches is to be sure that all students are fully participating members of the community, because motivation comes from both identity and legitimate participation. Daniel Hickey (2003) says it this way. Engagement is "meaningful participation in a context where to-be-learned knowledge is valued and used" (p. 411).

The behavioral, humanistic, cognitive, and sociocultural approaches to motivation are summarized in Table 10.1. These theories differ in their answers to the question, "What is motivation?" but each contributes in its own way toward a comprehensive understanding.

To organize the many ideas about motivation in a way that is useful for teaching, let's examine four broad areas. Most contemporary explanations of motivation include a discussion of needs, goals, interests and emotions, and self-perceptions (Murphy & Alexander, 2000).

Expectancy × value theories Explanations of motivation that emphasize individuals' expectations for success combined with their valuing of the goal.

Sociocultural views of motivation Perspectives that emphasize participation, identities, and interpersonal relations within communities of practice.

Legitimate peripheral participation Genuine involvement in the work of the group, even if your abilities are undeveloped and contributions are small.

STORIES OF LEARNING
TRIBUTES TO TEACHING

These are the words of **LEA LEE,** a Korean woman who came to the United States to become a professor and scholar. She had to be far from her family and her culture to pursue her dream, but she was supported in her efforts by instructors and friends who shared their culture and embraced hers.

"Without my friends and instructors . . . I would not be who I am today."

All of the school experiences were difficult for me. From taking lecture notes in class and taking exams to writing term papers, I struggled with the language barrier. I really wanted to understand the entire lecture. I understood only 30 to 40 percent of the information received during lectures during my first semester. I needed a guide who could show me how to study and how to be an outstanding student. Often, instructors don't consider that international students have special needs and require some adaptations during lectures and exams. It would have been a great help if the instructor had assigned a buddy who would have allowed me to copy lecture notes. No matter what type of problems I faced, however, I never gave up. I searched for solutions to problems so that I could achieve my goal. For example, when I could not understand a subject, I read textbooks repeatedly. I even memorized the text so that I would be able to pass the course with a good grade.

After tolerating many painful years, I finally became a professor and scholar in America. My ceaseless efforts were necessary, but not sufficient to achieve my goal. Without my friends and instructors, who were encouraging and willing to give support, I know that I would not be who I am today. Many of my true friends embraced the Korean culture and encouraged me to be proud of my culture. Those friends' names and faces will live deep in my heart for a long, long time.

Source: From "Six Buckets of Tears: Korean Americans' School Experiences," by Lea Lee. In Gloria Swindler-Boutte (Ed.), *Resounding Voices: School Experiences of People from Diverse Ethnic Backgrounds.* Published by Allyn and Bacon, Boston, MA. Copyright © 2002 by Pearson Education. Adapted by permission of the publisher.

Needs: Competence, Autonomy, and Relatedness

We have already seen one motivation theory that focused on needs—Maslow's hierarchy of needs. Other early research in psychology conceived of motivation in terms of trait-like needs or consistent personal characteristics. Three of the main needs studied extensively were the needs for achievement, power, and affiliation (Pintrich, 2003). We will look at one recent theory that emphasizes similar needs through a focus on self-determination.

Self-Determination

Self-determination theory suggests that we all need to feel competent and capable in our interactions in the world, to have some choices and a sense of control over our lives, and to be connected to others—to belong to a social group. Notice that these are similar to

TABLE 10.1

Four Views of Motivation

	Behavioral	Humanistic	Cognitive	Sociocultural
Source of Motivation	Extrinsic	Intrinsic	Intrinsic	Intrinsic
Important Influences	Reinforcers, rewards, incentives, and punishers	Need for self-esteem, self-fulfillment, and self-determination	Beliefs, attributions for success and failure, expectations	Engaged participation in learning communities; maintaining identity through participation in activities of group
Key Theorists	Skinner	Maslow Deci	Weiner Graham	Lave Wenger

earlier conceptions of basic needs: competence (achievement), autonomy and control (power), and relatedness (affiliation).

Need for autonomy is central to self-determination because it is the desire to have our own wishes, rather than external rewards or pressures, determine our actions (Deci & Ryan, 2002; Reeve, Deci, & Ryan, 2004; Ryan & Deci, 2000). People strive to be in charge of their own behavior. They constantly struggle against pressure from external controls such as the rules, schedules, deadlines, orders, and limits imposed by others. Sometimes, even help is rejected so that the individual can remain in command (deCharms, 1983).

Connect and Extend to PRAXIS II™

Self-Determination (I, C3)
Understand how this sense can boost or diminish motivation and describe practical steps that teachers can take to establish a sense of self-determination in students.

Self-Determination in the Classroom. Classroom environments that support student self-determination and autonomy are associated with greater student interest, sense of competence, creativity, conceptual learning, and preference for challenge. These relationships appear to hold from 1st grade through graduate school (Deci & Ryan, 2002; Williams, Wiener, Markakis, Reeve, & Deci, 1993). When students can make choices, they are more likely to believe that the work is important, even if it is not "fun." Thus, they tend to internalize educational goals and take them as their own.

In contrast to autonomy-supporting classrooms, controlling environments tend to improve performance only on rote recall tasks. When students are pressured to perform, they often seek the quickest, easiest solution. One discomforting finding, however, is that both students and parents seem to prefer more controlling teachers, even though the students learn more when their teachers support autonomy (Flink, Boggiano, & Barrett, 1990). Assuming you are willing to risk going against popular images, how can you support student autonomy? One answer is to focus on *information*, not *control*, in your interactions with students.

Connect and Extend to the Research

To capture the difference between self- and other-determination, Richard deCharms (1976, 1983) used the metaphor of people as "origins" and "pawns." Origins perceive themselves as the origin or source of their intention to act in a certain way. As pawns, people see themselves as powerless participants in a game controlled by others. When people feel like pawns, play becomes work, leisure feels like obligation, and intrinsic motivation becomes extrinsic motivation. For example, you may have had the experience of deciding to wash the car or clean your room, only to have your motivation dampened by a parent who insists that you tackle the chore. Your chance to be an origin seems spoiled by outside attempts at control. You don't want to wash the car anymore because your sense of self-determination is taken away. DeCharms observed that students are too little governed by their own intrinsic motivation and too powerless over external controls. To deal with the issue, he developed programs to help teachers support student self-determination. The programs emphasized setting realistic goals, personal planning of activities to reach the goals, personal responsibility for actions, and feelings of self-confidence.

Information and Control. Many things happen to students throughout the school day. They are praised or criticized, reminded of deadlines, assigned grades, given choices, lectured about rules, and on and on. **Cognitive evaluation theory** (Deci & Ryan, 2002; Ryan & Deci, 2000) explains how these events can influence the students' intrinsic motivation by affecting their sense of self-determination and competence. According to this theory, all events have two aspects, controlling and informational. If an event is highly controlling, that is, if it pressures students to act or feel a certain way, then students will experience less control and their *intrinsic motivation* will be diminished. If, on the other hand, the event provides information that increases the students' sense of competence, then intrinsic motivation will increase. Of course, if the information provided makes students feel less competent, it is likely that motivation will decrease (Pintrich, 2003).

For example, a teacher might praise a student by saying, "Good for you! You got an A because you finally followed my instructions correctly." This is a highly controlling statement, giving the credit to the teacher and thus undermining the student's sense of self-determination and intrinsic motivation. The teacher could praise the same work by saying, "Good for you! Your understanding of the author's use of metaphors has improved tremendously. You earned an A." This statement provides information about the student's growing competence and should increase intrinsic motivation.

What can teachers do to support student needs for autonomy and competence? An obvious first step is to limit their controlling messages to their students and make sure the information they provide highlights students' growing competence. The *Guidelines* give ideas.

Need for autonomy The desire to have our own wishes, rather than external rewards or pressures, determine our actions.

Cognitive evaluation theory Suggests that events affect motivation through the individual's perception of the events as controlling behavior or providing information.

The Need for Relatedness. The need for relatedness is the desire to establish close emotional bonds and attachments with others. When teachers and parents are responsive and demonstrate that they care about the children's interests and well-being, the children show high intrinsic motivation. But, when children are denied the interpersonal involvement they seek from adults—when adults, for example, are unresponsive to their needs—the children lose intrinsic motivation (Solomon, Battistich, Watson, Schaps, & Lewis, 2000). Students who feel a sense of relatedness to teachers, parents, and peers are

Guidelines: Supporting Self-Determination and Autonomy

Allow and encourage students to make choices.

EXAMPLES

1. Design several different ways to meet a learning objective (e.g., a paper, a compilation of interviews, a test, a news broadcast) and let students choose one. Encourage them to explain the reasons for their choice.
2. Appoint student committees to make suggestions about streamlining procedures such as caring for class pets or distributing equipment.
3. Provide time for independent and extended projects.

Help students plan actions to accomplish self-selected goals.

EXAMPLES

1. Experiment with goal cards. Students list their short- and long-term goals and then record 3 or 4 specific actions that will move them toward the goals. Goal cards are personal—like credit cards.
2. Encourage middle- and high-school students to set goals in each subject area, record them in a goal book or on a floppy disk, and check progress toward the goals on a regular basis.

Hold students accountable for the consequences of their choices.

EXAMPLES

1. If students choose to work with friends and do not finish a project because too much time was spent socializing, grade the project as it deserves and help the students see the connection between lost time and poor performance.
2. When students choose a topic that captures their imagination, discuss the connections between their investment in the work and the quality of the products that follow.

Provide rationales for limits, rules, and constraints.

EXAMPLES

1. Explain reasons for rules.
2. Respect rules and constraints in your own behavior.

Acknowledge that negative emotions are valid reactions to teacher control.

EXAMPLES

1. Communicate that it is okay (and normal) to feel bored waiting for a turn, for example.
2. Communicate that sometimes important learning involves frustration, confusion, weariness.

Use noncontrolling, positive feedback.

EXAMPLES

1. See poor performance or behavior as a problem to be solved, not a target of criticism.
2. Avoid controlling language, "should," "must," "have to."

For more information on self-determination theory see: **http://www.psych.rochester.edu/SDT/**

Source: From *150 Ways to Increase Intrinsic Motivation in the Classroom*, by James P. Raffini. Published by Allyn and Bacon, Boston, MA. Copyright © 1996 by Pearson Education and from *Motivating Others: Nurturing Inner Motivational Resources* by Johnmarshall Reeve. Published by Allyn and Bacon, Boston, MA. Copyright © 1996 by Pearson Education. Adapted by permission of the publisher.

more emotionally engaged in school (Furrer & Skinner, 2003). In addition, emotional and physical problems—ranging from eating disorders to suicide—are more common among people who lack social relationships (Baumeister & Leary, 1995). Relatedness is similar to a sense of belonging, discussed in Chapter 3. We will explore belonging and engaged learning in the next chapter (Osterman, 2000).

Needs: Lessons for Teachers

From infancy to old age, people want to be both competent and connected. Students are more likely to participate in activities that help them grow more competent and less likely to engage in activities that cause them to fail. This means that the students need appropriately challenging tasks—not too easy, but not impossible either. They also benefit from ways of watching their competence grow, perhaps through self-monitoring systems or portfolios. To be connected, students need to feel that people in school care about them and can be trusted to help them learn.

What else matters in motivation? Many theories include goals as key elements.

Goal Orientations and Motivation

STOP | THINK | WRITE On a scale from 1 (Strongly Agree) to 5 (Strongly Disagree), how would you answer these questions:

I feel really pleased in school when

___ I solve problems by working hard
___ I know more than the others
___ I don't have to work hard
___ I keep busy
___ I finish first
___ All the work is easy
___ I learn something new
___ I am the only one who gets an A
___ I am with my friends

Connect and **Extend** to the **Research**

For a synthesis of the research on goals from two founders of the theory, see: Locke, E. A., & Latham, G. P. (2002). Building a practically useful theory of goal setting and task motivation: A 35-year odyssey. *American Psychologist, 57,* 705–717.

A **goal** is an outcome or attainment an individual is striving to accomplish (Locke & Latham, 2002). When students strive to read a chapter or make a 4.0 GPA, they are involved in *goal-directed behavior.* In pursuing goals, students are generally aware of some current condition (I haven't even opened my book), some ideal condition (I have understood every page), and the discrepancy between the current and ideal situations. Goals motivate people to act in order to reduce the discrepancy between "where they are" and "where they want to be." Goal setting is usually effective for me. In addition to the routine tasks, such as eating lunch, which will happen without much attention, I often set goals for each day. For example, today I intend to finish this section, walk four miles, and wash another load of clothes (I know—not too exciting). Having decided to do these things, I will feel uncomfortable if I don't complete the list.

According to Locke and Latham (2002), there are four main reasons why goal setting improves performance. Goals:

1. *Direct our attention* to the task at hand and away from distractions. Every time my mind wanders from this chapter, my goal of finishing the section helps direct my attention back to the writing.
2. *Energize effort.* The more challenging the goal, to a point, the greater the effort.
3. *Increase persistence.* When we have a clear goal, we are less likely to give up until we reach the goal: Hard goals demand effort and tight deadlines lead to faster work.
4. *Promote the development of new knowledge and strategies* when old strategies fall short. For example, if your goal is making an A and you don't reach that goal on your first quiz, you might try a new study approach for the next quiz, such as explaining the key points to a friend.

Types of Goals and Goal Orientations

The types of goals we set influence the amount of motivation we have to reach them. Goals that are specific, moderately difficult, and likely to be reached in the near future tend to enhance motivation and persistence (Pintrich & Schunk, 2002; Stipek, 2002). Specific goals provide clear standards for judging performance. If performance falls short, we keep going. For example, I have decided to "finish this section" instead of deciding to "work on the book." Anything short of having the section ready to mail means "keep working" (looks like another late night!). Moderate difficulty provides a challenge, but not an unreasonable one. I can finish this section if I stay with it. Finally, goals that can be reached fairly soon are not likely to be pushed aside by more immediate concerns. Groups such as Alcoholics Anonymous show they are aware of the motivating value of short-term goals when they encourage their members to stop drinking "one day at a time."

Goal What an individual strives to accomplish.

Goal orientations Patterns of beliefs about goals related to achievement in school.

Four Goal Orientations in School. Goals are specific targets. **Goal orientations** are patterns of beliefs about goals related to achievement in school. Goal orientations include the reasons we pursue goals and the standards we use to evaluate progress toward those goals. For example, your target might be to make an A in this course. Are you doing so in

Goal orientations refer to the reasons individuals pursue goals and the standards by which progress toward them is measured. This contestant may have as her main goal to master spelling, outperform others, or perhaps she simply enjoys puzzling through the words.

order to master educational psychology—to learn all about it, or to perform—to look good in the eyes of your friends and family? There are four main goal orientations—mastery (learning), performance (looking good), work-avoidance, and social (Murphy & Alexander, 2000; Pintrich & Schunk, 2002). In the *Stop/Think/Write* exercise on the preceding page, can you tell which goal orientations are reflected in the different answers? Most of the questions were adapted from a study on students' theories about learning mathematics (Nicholls, Cobb, Wood, Yackel, Patashnick, 1990).

The most common distinction in research on students' goals is between mastery goals (also called *task goals* or *learning goals*) and performance goals (also called *ability goals* or *ego goals*) (Midgley, 2001). The point of a **mastery goal** is to improve, to learn, no matter how awkward you appear. Students who set mastery goals tend to seek challenges and persist when they encounter difficulties. Because they focus on the task at hand and are not worried about how their performance "measures up" compared to others in the class, these students have been called **task-involved learners** (Nicholls & Miller, 1984). We often say that these people "get lost in their work." In addition, they are more likely to seek appropriate help, use deeper cognitive processing strategies, apply better study strategies, and generally approach academic tasks with confidence (Butler & Neuman, 1995; Midgley, 2001; Young, 1997).

The second kind of goal is a performance goal. Students with **performance goals** care about demonstrating their ability to others. They may be focused on getting good test scores and grades, or they may be more concerned with winning and beating other students (Wolters, Yu, & Pintrich, 1996). Students whose goal is outperforming others may do things to look smart, such as reading easy books in order to "read the most books" (Young, 1997). The evaluation of their performance by others, not what they learn, is what matters. These students have been called **ego-involved learners** because they are preoccupied with themselves. Students with performance goals may act in ways that actually interfere with learning. For example, they may cheat or use short-cuts to get finished, work hard only on graded assignments, be upset and hide papers with low grades, choose tasks that are easy, and be very uncomfortable with assignments that have unclear evaluation criteria (Stipek, 2002).

Wait—Are Performance Goals Always Bad? Performance goals sound pretty dysfunctional, don't they? Earlier research indicated that performance goals generally were detrimental to learning, but like extrinsic motivation, a performance goal orientation may not be all bad all of the time. In fact, some research indicates that both mastery and performance goals are associated with using active learning strategies and high self-efficacy (Midgley, Kaplan, & Middleton, 2001; Stipek, 2002). And, like intrinsic and extrinsic motivation, students can, and often do pursue mastery and performance goals at the same time.

To account for these recent findings, educational psychologists have added the distinction of approach/avoidance to the mastery/performance distinction. In other words,

Mastery goal A personal intention to improve abilities and learn, no matter how performance suffers.

Task-involved learners Students who focus on mastering the task or solving the problem.

Performance goal A personal intention to seem competent or perform well in the eyes of others.

Ego-involved learners Students who focus on how well they are performing and how they are judged by others.

TABLE 10.2

Goal Orientations

Students may have either an approach or an avoidance focus for mastery and performance goal orientations.

Goal Orientation	Approach Focus	Avoidance Focus
Mastery	*Focus:* Mastering the task, learning, understanding	*Focus:* Avoiding misunderstanding or not mastering the task
	Standards Used: Self-improvement, progress, deep understanding (task-involved)	*Standards Used:* Just don't be wrong; perfectionists don't make mistakes
Performance	*Focus:* Being superior, winning, being the best	*Focus:* Avoiding looking stupid, avoid losing
	Standards Used: Normative—getting the highest grade, winning the competition (ego-involved goal)	*Standards Used:* Normative—don't be the worst, get the lowest grade, or be the slowest (ego-involved goal)

Source: From *Motivation in Education: Theory, Research, and Applications* (2nd ed.), by P. Pintrich and D. Schunk. Published by Prentice Hall.

students may be motivated to either approach mastery or avoid misunderstanding. They may approach performance or avoid looking dumb. Table 10.2 shows examples and the effects of each kind of goal orientation. Where do you see the most problems? Do you agree that the real problems are with avoidance? Students who fear misunderstanding (mastery avoid) may be perfectionist—focused on getting it exactly right. Students who avoid looking dumb (performance avoid) may adopt defensive, failure-avoiding strategies like Defensive Daleesha described earlier—they pretend not to care, make a show of "not really trying," or cheat (Harackiewiz, Barron, Pintrich, Elliot, & Thrash, 2002).

Beyond Mastery and Performance. Some students don't want to learn or to look smart; they just want to avoid work. These students try to complete assignments and activities as quickly as possible without exerting much effort (Pintrich & Schunk, 2002). John Nicholls (1984) called these students **work-avoidant learners**—they feel successful when they don't have to try hard, when the work is easy, or when they can "goof off."

A final category of goals becomes more important as students get older—**social goals.** As students move into adolescence, their social networks change to include more peers. Nonacademic activities such as athletics, dating, and "hanging out" compete with schoolwork (Urdan & Maehr, 1995). Social goals include a wide variety of needs and motives that have different relationships to learning—some help, but some hinder learning. For example, adolescents' goal of maintaining friendly relations can get in the way of learning when cooperative learning group members don't challenge wrong answers or misconceptions because they are afraid to hurt each other's feelings (Anderson, Holland, & Palincsar, 1997). Certainly, pursuing goals such as having fun with friends or avoiding being labeled a "nerd" can get in the way of learning. But the goal of bringing honor to your family or team by working hard can also support learning (Urdan & Maehr, 1995). Social goals that include being a part of peer groups that value academics certainly can support learning (Pintrich, 2003; A. Ryan, 2001).

We talk about goals in separate categories, but students have to coordinate their goals so they can make decisions about what to do and how to act. As noted above, sometimes social and academic goals are incompatible. For example, if students do not see a connection between achievement in school and success in life, particularly because discrimination prevents them from succeeding, then those students are not likely to set academic achievement as a goal. Such anti-academic peer groups probably exist in every high school (Committee on Increasing High School Students' Engagement and Motivation to Learn, 2004; Wentzel, 1999). Sometimes, succeeding in the peer group means not succeeding in school—and succeeding in the peer group is important. The need for social relationships is basic and strong for most people.

Work-avoidant learners Students who don't want to learn or to look smart, but just want to avoid work.

Social goals A wide variety of needs and motives to be connected to others or part of a group.

Feedback and Goal Acceptance

"What do I get for just neatness?"

(© Glenn Bernhardt) Reprinted by Permission.

Besides having specific goals and creating supportive social relationships, there are two additional factors that make goal-setting in the classroom effective. The first is *feedback.* In order to be motivated by a discrepancy between "where you are" and "where you want to be," you must have an accurate sense of both your current status and how far you have to go. There is evidence that feedback emphasizing progress is the most effective. In one study, feedback to adults emphasized either that they had accomplished 75% of the standards set or that they had fallen short of the standards by 25%. When the feedback highlighted accomplishment, the subjects' self-confidence, analytic thinking, and performance were all enhanced (Bandura, 1997).

The second factor affecting motivation to pursue a goal is *goal acceptance.* If students reject goals set by others or refuse to set their own goals, then motivation will suffer. Generally, students are more willing to commit to the goals of others if the goals seem realistic, reasonably difficult, and meaningful—and if good reasons are given for the value of the goals (Grolnick, Gurland, Jacob, & Decourcey, 2002). Commitment matters—the relationship between higher goals and better performance is strongest when people are committed to the goals (Locke & Latham, 2002).

Goals: Lessons for Teachers

Students are more likely to work toward goals that are clear, specific, reasonable, moderately challenging, and attainable within a relatively short period of time. If teachers focus on student performance, high grades, and competition, they may encourage students to set performance goals. This could undermine the students' ability to learn and become task-involved (Anderman & Maehr, 1994). Students may not yet be expert at setting their own goals or keeping these goals in mind, so encouragement and accurate feedback are necessary. If you use any reward or incentive systems, be sure the goal you set is to *learn and improve* in some area, not just to perform well or look smart. And be sure the goal is not too difficult. Students, like adults, are unlikely to stick with tasks or respond well to teachers who make them feel insecure or incompetent.

What else do we know about motivation? Feelings matter.

Interests and Emotions

How do you feel about learning? Excited, bored, curious, fearful? Today, researchers emphasize that learning is not just about the *cold cognition* of reasoning and problem solving. Learning and information processing also are influenced by emotion, so *hot cognition* plays a role in learning as well (Miller, 2002; Pintrich, 2003). Students are more likely to pay attention to, learn about, and remember events, images, and readings that provoke emotional responses (Alexander & Murphy, 1998; Cowley & Underwood, 1998; Reisberg & Heuer, 1992) or that are related to their interests (Renninger, Hidi, & Krapp, 1992). Sometimes, emotions interfere with learning by taking up attention or working memory space that could be used for learning (Pekrun, Goetz, Titz, & Perry, 2002). How can we use these findings to support learning in school?

Tapping Interests

WHAT WOULD YOU SAY?

As part of your interview for a job in a large high school, the principal asks, "How would you get students interested in learning? Could you tap their interests in your teaching?" ■

When Walter Vispoel and James Austin (1995) surveyed over 200 middle-school students, "lack of interest in the topic" received the highest rating as the reason for school failures. Interest was second only to effort as a choice for explaining successes.

Connect and **Extend** to the **Research**

Vispoel, W. P., & Austing, J. R. (1995). Success and failure in junior high school: A critical incident approach to understanding students' attributional beliefs. *American Educational Research Journal*, 32, 377–412.

Students' interest in and excitement about what they're learning is one of the most important factors in education.

There are two kinds of interests—personal (individual) and situational—the trait and state distinction again. *Personal* or *individual interests* are more enduring aspects of the person, such as an enduring tendency to be attracted to or to enjoy subjects such as languages, history, or mathematics, or activities such as sports, music, or films. Students with individual interests in learning in general seek new information and have more positive attitudes toward schooling. *Situational interests* are more short-lived aspects of the activity, text, or materials that catch and keep the student's attention. Both personal and situational interests are related to learning from texts—greater interest leads to more positive emotional responses to the material, then to greater persistence, deeper processing, better remembering of the material, and higher achievement (Ainley, Hidi, & Berndorf, 2002; Pintrich, 2003; Schraw & Lehman, 2001). And interests increase when students feel competent, so even if students are not initially interested in a subject or activity, they may develop interests as they experience success (Stipek, 2002).

Catching and Holding Interests. Whenever possible, it helps to connect academic content to students' enduring personal interests. But given that the content you will teach is determined by standards in most classrooms today, it will be difficult to tailor lessons to each student's personal interests. You will have to rely more on situational interest. Here, the challenge is to not only *catch* but also *hold* students' interest (Pintrich, 2003). For example, Mathew Mitchell (1993) found that using computers, groups, and puzzles caught students' interest in secondary mathematics classes, but the interests did not hold. Lessons that held interests over time included math activities that were related to real-life problems and active participation in laboratory activities and projects. However, there are cautions in responding to students' interests, as you can see in the *Point/Counterpoint*.

Another source of interest is fantasy. For example, Cordova and Lepper (1996) found that students learned more math facts during a computer exercise when they were challenged, as captains of star ships, to navigate through space by solving math problems. The students got to name their ships, stock the (imaginary) galley with their favorite snacks, and name all the crew members after their friends.

Arousal: Excitement and Anxiety in Learning

Arousal Physical and psychological reactions causing a person to be alert, attentive, wide awake.

Just as we all know how it feels to be motivated, we all know what it is like to be aroused. **Arousal** involves both psychological and physical reactions—changes in brain wave patterns, blood pressure, heart rate, and breathing rate. We feel alert, wide awake, even

Point/Counterpoint

Does Making Learning Fun Make for Good Learning?

WHEN MANY BEGINNING teachers are asked about how to motivate students, they often mention making learning fun. But is it necessary for learning to be fun?

POINT Teachers should make learning fun.

When I searched "making learning fun" on Google.com, I found 10 pages of resources and references. Clearly, there is interest in making learning fun. Research shows that passages in texts that are more interesting are remembered better (Pintrich & Schunk, 2002). For example, students who read books that interested them spent more time reading, read more words in the books, and felt more positively about reading (Guthrie & Alao, 1997). Games and simulations can make learning more fun, too.

For example, when my daughter was in the 8th grade, all the students in her grade spent three days playing a game her teachers had designed called ULTRA. Students were divided into groups and formed their own "countries." Each country had to choose a name, symbol, national flower, and bird. They wrote and sang a national anthem and elected government officials. The teachers allocated different resources to the countries. To get all the materials needed for the completion of assigned projects, the countries had to establish trade with one another. There was a monetary system and a stock market. Students had to work with their fellow citizens to complete cooperative learning assignments. Some countries "cheated" in their trades with other nations, and this allowed debate about international relations, trust, and war. Liz says she had fun—but she also learned how to work in a group without the teacher's supervision and gained a deeper understanding of world economics and international conflicts.

A highly motivating 3rd-grade teacher in another study had her class set up a post office for the whole school. Each classroom in the school had an address and zip code. Students had jobs in the post office, and everyone in the school used the post office to deliver letters to students and teachers. Students designed their own stamps and set postal rates. The teacher said that the system "improves their creative writing without them knowing it" (Dolezal, Welsh, Pressley, & Vincent, 2003, p. 254).

COUNTERPOINT Fun can get in the way of learning.

As far back as the early 1900s, educators warned about the dangers of focusing on fun in learning. None other than John Dewey, who wrote extensively about the role of interest in learning, cautioned that you can't make boring lessons interesting by mixing in fun like you can make bad chili good by adding some spicy hot sauce. Dewey wrote, "When things have to be made interesting, it is because interest itself is wanting. Moreover, the phrase itself is a misnomer. The thing, the object, is no more interesting than it was before" (Dewey, 1913, pp. 11–12).

There is a good deal of research now indicating that adding interest by adding fascinating but irrelevant details actually gets in the way of learning the important information. These "seductive details," as they have been called, divert the readers' attention from the less interesting main ideas (Harp & Mayer, 1998). For example, students who read biographies of historical figures remembered more very interesting but unimportant information compared to interesting main ideas (Wade, Schraw, Buxton, & Hayes, 1993).

Shannon Harp and Richard Mayer (1997) found similar results with high-school science texts. These texts added emotional interest and seductive details about swimmers and golfers who are injured by lightning to a lesson on the process of lightning. They concluded that, "in the case of emotional interest versus cognitive interest, the verdict is clear. Adjuncts aimed at increasing emotional interest failed to improve understanding of scientific explanations" (p. 100). The seductive details may have disrupted students' attempts to follow the logic of the explanations and thus interfered with comprehending the text. Harp and Mayer conclude that "the best way to help students enjoy a passage is to help them understand it" (p. 100).

WHAT DO YOU THINK?
Vote online at **www.mylabschool.com**

excited. To understand the effects of arousal on motivation, think of two extremes. The first is late at night. You are trying for the third time to understand a required reading, but you are so sleepy. Your attention drifts as your eyes droop. You decide to go to bed and get up early to study (a plan that you know seldom works). At the other extreme, imagine that you have a critical test tomorrow—one that determines whether you will get into the school you want. You feel tremendous pressure from everyone to do well. You know that you need a good night's sleep, but you are wide awake. In the first case, arousal is too low and in the second, too high.

Guidelines: Building on Students' Interests and Curiosity

Relate content objectives to student experiences.

EXAMPLES

1. With a teacher in another school, establish pen pals across the classes. Through writing letters, students exchange personal experiences, photos, drawings, written work, and ask and answer questions ("Have you learned cursive writing yet?" "What are you doing in math now?" "What are you reading?"). Letters can be mailed in one large mailer to save stamps.
2. Identify classroom experts for different assignments or tasks. Who knows how to use the computer for graphics? How to search the Net? How to cook? How to use an index?
3. Have a "Switch Day" when students exchange roles with a school staff or support person. Students must research the role by interviewing their staff member, prepare for the job, dress the part for the day they take over, and then evaluate their success after the switch.

Identify student interests, hobbies, and extracurricular activities that can be incorporated into class lessons and discussions.

EXAMPLES

1. Have students design and conduct interviews and surveys to learn about each other's interests.
2. Keep the class library stocked with books that connect to students' interests and hobbies.
3. Allow choices (stories in language arts or projects in science) based on students' interests.

Support instruction with humor, personal experiences, and anecdotes that show the human side of the content.

EXAMPLES

1. Share your own hobbies, interests, and favorites.
2. Tell students there will be a surprise visitor; then dress up as the author of a story and tell about "yourself" and your writing.

Use original source material with interesting content or details.

EXAMPLES

1. Letters and diaries in history.
2. Darwin's notes in biology.

Create surprise and curiosity.

EXAMPLES

1. Have students predict what will happen in an experiment, then show them that they are wrong.
2. Provide quotes from history and ask students to guess who said it.

For more information on students' interests and motivation, see:
http://mathforum.org/~sarah/Discussion.Sessions/biblio.motivation.html

Source: From *150 Ways to Increase Intrinsic Motivation in the Classroom*, by James P. Raffini. Published by Allyn and Bacon, Boston, MA. Copyright © 1996 by Pearson Education. Adapted by permission of the publisher. Also *Motivation in Education (2nd ed.)* by P. Pintrich and D. Schunk, 2002, Merrill/Prentice-Hall, pp. 298–299.

Psychologists have known for years that there is an optimum level of arousal for most activities (Yerkes & Dodson, 1908). Generally speaking, higher levels of arousal are helpful on simple tasks such as sorting laundry, but lower levels of arousal are better for complex tasks such as taking the GRE. Let's look for a moment at how to increase arousal by arousing curiosity.

Connect and Extend to the Research

Lowenstein, G. (1994). The psychology of curiosity: A review and reinterpretation. *Psychological Bulletin*, *117*, 75–98. This article connects curiosity to perceived gaps in information.

Curiosity: Novelty and Complexity. Interest and curiosity are related. Curiosity could be defined as a tendency to be interested in a wide range of areas (Pintrich, 2003). Almost 40 years ago, psychologists suggested that individuals are naturally motivated to seek novelty, surprise, and complexity (Berlyne, 1966). Research on teaching has found that variety in teaching approaches and tasks can support learning (Brophy & Good, 1986; Stipek, 2002). For younger students, the chance to manipulate and explore objects relevant to what is being studied may be the most effective way to keep curiosity stimulated. For older students, well-constructed questions, logical puzzles, and paradoxes can have the same effect. But remember that you have to do more than catch students' interest, you have to hold it, so the questions and puzzles should be related to meaningful learning.

George Lowenstein (1994) suggests that curiosity arises when attention is focused on a gap in knowledge. "Such information gaps produce the feeling of deprivation labeled *curiosity*. The curious person is motivated to obtain the missing information to reduce or eliminate the feeling of deprivation" (p. 87). This idea is similar to Piaget's concept of disequilibrium, discussed in Chapter 2, and has a number of implications for teaching. First, students need some base of knowledge before they can experience gaps in knowledge leading to curiosity. Second, students must be aware of the gaps in order for curiosity to result. Asking students to make guesses and then providing feedback can be helpful. Also, mistakes, properly handled, can stimulate curiosity by pointing to missing knowledge. Finally, the more we learn about a topic, the more curious we may become about that subject. As Maslow (1970) predicted, fulfilling the need to know increases, not decreases, the need to know more. See the *Guidelines* for more about building interest and curiosity in the classroom.

As we discussed earlier, sometimes arousal is too high, not too low. Because classrooms are places where students are tested and graded, anxiety can become a factor in classroom motivation.

Anxiety in the Classroom. At one time or another, everyone has experienced **anxiety**, or a general uneasiness, a feeling of self-doubt, and sense of tension. The effects of anxiety on school achievement are clear. "From the time of the earliest work on this problem, starting with the pioneering work of Yerkes and Dodson (1908), to the present day, researchers have consistently reported a negative correlation between virtually every aspect of school achievement and a wide range of anxiety measures" (Covington & Omelich, 1987, p. 393). Anxiety can be both a cause and an effect of school failure—students do poorly because they are anxious, and their poor performance increases their anxiety. Anxiety probably is both a trait and a state. Some students tend to be anxious in many situations (trait anxiety), but some situations are especially anxiety provoking (state anxiety) (Covington, 1992; Zeidner, 1998).

Anxiety seems to have both cognitive and affective components. The cognitive side includes worry and negative thoughts—thinking about how bad it would be to fail and worrying that you will, for example. The affective side involves physiological and emotional reactions such as sweaty palms, upset stomach, racing heartbeat, or fear (Pintrich & Schunk, 2002; Zeidner, 1995, 1998). Whenever there are pressures to perform, severe consequences for failure, and competitive comparisons among students, anxiety may be encouraged (Wigfield & Eccles, 1989). Also, research with school-age children shows a relationship between the quality of sleep (how quickly and how well you sleep) and anxiety. Better-quality sleep is associated with positive arousal or an "eagerness" to learn. Poor-quality sleep, on the other hand, was related to debilitating anxiety and decreased school performance. You may have discovered these relationships for yourself in your own school career (Meijer & van den Wittenboer, 2004).

How Does Anxiety Interfere with Achievement? Anxiety interferes with learning and test performance at three points: focusing attention, learning, and testing. When students are learning new material, they must pay attention to it. Highly anxious students evidently divide their attention between the new material and their preoccupation with how worried and nervous they are feeling. Instead of concentrating, they keep noticing the tight feelings in their chest, thinking, "I'm so tense, I'll never understand this stuff!" From the beginning, anxious students may miss much of the information they are supposed to learn because their thoughts are focused on their own worries (Cassady & Johnson, 2002; Paulman & Kennelly, 1984).

But the problems do not end here. Even if they are paying attention, many anxious students have trouble learning material that is somewhat disorganized and difficult—material that requires them to rely on their memory. Unfortunately, much material in school could be described this way. In addition, many highly anxious students have poor study habits. Simply learning to be more relaxed will not automatically improve these students' performance; their learning strategies and study skills must be improved as well (Naveh-Benjamin, 1991).

Finally, anxious students often know more than they can demonstrate on a test. They may lack critical test-taking skills, or they may have learned the materials but "freeze and forget" on tests (Naveh-Benjamin, McKeachie, & Lin, 1987).

Anxiety General uneasiness, a feeling of tension.

Connect and **Extend to PRAXIS II™**

Test Anxiety (I, C3)

Test Taking and Anxiety (http://www.ulrc.psu.edu/studyskills/test_taking.html) provides tips and insights into addressing the problems associated with test anxiety. (And the tips might be useful for doing well on the PRAXIS II™ exam!)

Reaching Every Student: Coping with Anxiety

Some students, particularly those with learning disabilities or emotional disorders, may be especially anxious in school. When students face stressful situations such as tests, they can use three kinds of coping strategies: *problem solving, emotional management*, and *avoidance*. Problem-focused strategies might include planning a study schedule, borrowing good notes, or finding a protected place to study. Emotion-focused strategies are attempts to reduce the anxious feelings, for example, by using relaxation exercises or describing the feelings to a friend. Of course, the latter might become an avoidance strategy, along with going out for pizza or suddenly launching an all-out desk-cleaning attack (can't study until you get organized!). Different strategies are helpful at different points—for example, problem solving before and emotion management during an exam. Different strategies fit different people and situations (Zeidner, 1995, 1998).

Teachers should help highly anxious students to set realistic goals, because these individuals often have difficulty making wise choices. They tend to select either extremely difficult or extremely easy tasks. In the first case, they are likely to fail, which will increase their sense of hopelessness and anxiety about school. In the second case, they will probably succeed on the easy tasks, but they will miss the sense of satisfaction that could encourage greater effort and ease their fears about schoolwork. Goal cards, progress charts, or goal-planning journals may help here.

Interests and Emotions: Lessons for Teachers

Make efforts to keep the level of arousal right for the task at hand. If students are going to sleep, energize them by introducing variety, piquing their curiosity, surprising them, or giving them a brief chance to be physically active. Learn about their interests and incorporate these interests into lessons and assignments. If arousal is too great, follow the *Guidelines* for dealing with anxiety.

Beliefs and Self-Schemas

Thus far, we have talked about needs, goals, interests, and emotions, but there is another factor that must be considered in explaining motivation. What do students believe about themselves—their competence and the causes for success or failure? Let's start with a basic question—What do they believe about ability?

Beliefs about Ability

STOP | THINK | WRITE Rate these statements taken from Dweck (2000) on a scale from 1 (Strongly Agree) to 6 (Strongly Disagree).

___ You have a certain amount of intelligence and you really can't do much to change it.

___ You can learn new things, but you can't really change your basic intelligence.

___ No matter who you are, you can change your intelligence a lot.

___ No matter how much intelligence you have, you can always change it quite a bit.

Some of the most powerful beliefs affecting motivation in school are about *ability*. By examining these beliefs and how they affect motivation, we will understand why some people set inappropriate, unmotivating goals; why some students adopt self-defeating strategies; and why some students seem to give up altogether.

Entity view of ability Belief that ability is a fixed characteristic that cannot be changed.

Incremental view of ability Belief that ability is a set of skills that can be changed.

Adults use two basic concepts of ability (Dweck, 1999, 2002). An **entity view of ability** assumes that ability is a *stable, uncontrollable* trait—a characteristic of the individual that cannot be changed. According to this view, some people have more ability than others, but the amount each person has is set. An **incremental view of ability**, on the other

Guidelines: Coping with Anxiety

Use competition carefully.

EXAMPLES

1. Monitor activities to make sure no students are being put under undue pressure.
2. During competitive games, make sure all students involved have a reasonable chance of succeeding.
3. Experiment with cooperative learning activities.

Avoid situations in which highly anxious students will have to perform in front of large groups.

EXAMPLES

1. Ask anxious students questions that can be answered with a simple yes or no, or some other brief reply.
2. Give anxious students practice in speaking before smaller groups.

Make sure all instructions are clear. Uncertainty can lead to anxiety.

EXAMPLES

1. Write test instructions on the board or on the test itself instead of giving them orally.
2. Check with students to make sure they understand. Ask several students how they would do the first question, exercise, or sample question on a test. Correct any misconceptions.
3. If you are using a new format or starting a new type of task, give students examples or models to show how it is done.

Avoid unnecessary time pressures.

EXAMPLES

1. Give occasional take-home tests.
2. Make sure all students can complete classroom tests within the period given.

Remove some of the pressures from major tests and exams.

EXAMPLES

1. Teach test-taking skills; give practice tests; provide study guides.
2. Avoid basing most of a report-card grade on one test.
3. Make extra-credit work available to add points to course grades.
4. Use different types of items in testing because some students have difficulty with particular formats.

Develop alternatives to written tests.

EXAMPLES

1. Try oral, open-book, or group tests.
2. Have students do projects, organize portfolios of their work, make oral presentations, or create a finished product.

Teach students self-regulation strategies (Schutz & Davis, 2000).

EXAMPLES

1. Before the test: Encourage students to see the test as an important and challenging task that they have the capabilities to prepare for. Help students stay focused on the task of getting as much information as possible about the test.
2. During the test: Remind students that the test is important (but not overly important). Encourage task focus—pick out the main idea in the question, slow down, stay relaxed.
3. After the test: Think back on what went well and what could be improved. Focus on controllable attributions—study strategies, effort, careful reading of questions, relaxation strategies.

For more information about test anxiety, see:
http://www.couns.uiuc.edu/Brochures/testanx.htm

hand, suggests that ability is unstable and controllable—"an ever-expanding repertoire of skills and knowledge" (Dweck & Bempechat, 1983, p. 144). By hard work, study, or practice, knowledge can be increased and thus ability can be improved. What is your view of ability? Look back at your answers in the *Stop/Think/Write* box to see.

Young children tend to hold an exclusively incremental view of ability. Through the early elementary grades, most students believe that effort is the same as intelligence. Smart people try hard, and trying hard makes you smart. If you fail, you aren't smart and you didn't try hard (Dweck, 2000; Stipek, 2002). Children are age 11 or 12 before they can differentiate among effort, ability, and performance. About this time, they come to believe that someone who succeeds without working at all must be *really* smart. This is when beliefs about ability begin to influence motivation (Anderman & Maehr, 1994).

Students who hold an entity (unchangeable) view of intelligence tend to set performance goals to avoid looking bad in the eyes of others. They seek situations where they can look smart and protect their self-esteem. Like Safe Sumey, they keep doing what they can do well without expending too much effort or risking failure, because either one—working hard or failing—indicates (to them) low ability. To work hard but still fail would be devastating. Students with learning disabilities are more likely to hold an entity view.

Teachers who hold entity views are quicker to form judgments about students and slower to modify their opinions when confronted with contradictory evidence (Stipek, 2002). Teachers who hold incremental views, in contrast, tend to set mastery goals and seek situations in which students can improve their skills, because improvement means getting smarter. Failure is not devastating; it simply indicates more work is needed. Ability is not threatened. Incremental theorists tend to set moderately difficult goals, the kind we have seen are the most motivating.

Beliefs about ability are related to other beliefs about what you can and cannot control in learning.

Beliefs about Causes and Control: Attribution Theory

Connect and **Extend** to **PRAXIS II™**

Attribution Theory (I, C1)
Go to the *Encyclopedia of Psychology* (http://www.psychology.org/links/Environment_Behavior_Relationships/Motivation/) and follow its link for Attribution Theory to learn more about using principles derived from this theory to boost intrinsic motivation to learn.

One well-known explanation of motivation begins with the assumption that we try to make sense of our own behavior and the behavior of others by searching for explanations and causes. To understand our own successes and failures, particularly unexpected ones, we all ask "Why?" Students ask themselves, "Why did I flunk my midterm?" or "Why did I do so well this grading period?" They may attribute their successes and failures to ability, effort, mood, knowledge, luck, help, interest, clarity of instructions, the interference of others, unfair policies, and so on. To understand the successes and failures of others, we also make attributions—that the others are smart or lucky or work hard, for example. **Attribution theories** of motivation describe how the individual's explanations, justifications, and excuses about self or others influence motivation.

Bernard Weiner is one of the main educational psychologists responsible for relating attribution theory to school learning (Weiner, 1979, 1986, 1992, 1994a, 1994b, 2000; Weiner & Graham, 1989). According to Weiner, most of the attributed causes for successes or failures can be characterized in terms of three dimensions:

1. *locus* (location of the cause—internal or external to the person),
2. *stability* (whether the cause is likely to stay the same in the near future or can change), and
3. *controllability* (whether the person can control the cause).

Every cause for success or failure can be categorized on these three dimensions. For example, luck is external (locus), unstable (stability), and uncontrollable (controllability). Table 10.3 shows some common attributions for success or failure on a test. Notice that ability is usually considered stable and uncontrollable, but incremental theorists (described above) would argue that ability is unstable and controllable. Weiner's locus and controllability dimensions are closely related to Deci's concept of *locus of causality*.

Weiner believes that these three dimensions have important implications for motivation because they affect expectancy and value. The *stability* dimension, for example, seems to be closely related to expectations about the future. If students attribute their failure to stable factors such as the difficulty of the subject, they will expect to fail in that subject in the future. But if they attribute the outcome to unstable factors such as mood or luck, they can hope for better outcomes next time. The *internal/external locus* seems to be closely related to feelings of self-esteem (Weiner, 2000). If success or failure is attributed to internal factors, success will lead to pride and increased motivation, whereas failure will diminish self-esteem. The *controllability* dimension is related to emotions such as anger, pity, gratitude, or shame. If we feel responsible for our failures, we may feel guilt; if we feel responsible for successes, we may feel proud. Failing at a task we cannot control can lead to shame or anger.

Also, feeling in control of your own learning seems to be related to choosing more difficult academic tasks, putting out more effort, using better strategies, and persisting longer in school work (Schunk, 2000; Weiner, 1994a, 1994b). Factors such as continuing discrimination against women, people of color, and individuals with special needs can affect these individuals' perceptions of their ability to control their lives (Beane, 1991; van Laar, 2000).

Attribution theories Descriptions of how individuals' explanations, justifications, and excuses influence their motivation and behavior.

TABLE 10.3

Weiner's Theory of Causal Attribution

There are many explanations students can give for why they fail a test. Below are eight reasons representing the eight combinations of locus, stability, and responsibility in Weiner's model of attributions.

Dimension Classification	Reason for Failure
Internal-stable-uncontrollable	Low aptitude
Internal-stable-controllable	Never studies
Internal-unstable-uncontrollable	Sick the day of the exam
Internal-unstable-controllable	Did not study for this particular test
External-stable-uncontrollable	School has hard requirements
External-stable-controllable	Instructor is biased
External-unstable-uncontrollable	Bad luck
External-unstable-controllable	Friends failed to help

Source: From *Human Motivation: Metaphors, Theories and Research,* by B. Weiner. Published by Sage Publications, Newbury Park, CA. Copyright © 1992 by Sage Publications. Adapted with permission of the publisher.

Attributions in the Classroom. When usually successful students fail, they often make internal, controllable attributions: They misunderstood the directions, lacked the necessary knowledge, or simply did not study hard enough, for example. As a consequence, they usually focus on strategies for succeeding next time. This response often leads to achievement, pride, and a greater feeling of control (Ames, 1992; Stipek, 2002).

The greatest motivational problems arise when students attribute failures to stable, uncontrollable causes. Such students may seem resigned to failure, depressed, helpless—what we generally call "unmotivated" (Weiner, 2000). These students respond to failure by focusing even more on their own inadequacy; their attitudes toward schoolwork may deteriorate even further (Ames, 1992). Apathy is a logical reaction to failure if students believe the causes are stable, unlikely to change, and beyond their control. In addition, students who view their failures in this light are less likely to seek help; they believe nothing and no one can help (Ames & Lau, 1982).

Connect and Extend to Your Teaching/Portfolio

Read Clifford, M. M. (1990). Students need challenge, not easy success. *Educational Leadership,* 48(1), 22–26. Evaluate Clifford's claim that students need some experience with failure. For whom is this experience most needed?

Teacher Actions and Student Attributions. How do students determine the causes of their successes and failures? Remember, we also make attributions about the causes of other people's successes and failures. When teachers assume that student failure is attributable to forces beyond the students' control, the teachers tend to respond with sympathy and avoid giving punishments. If, however, the failures are attributed to a controllable factor such as lack of effort, the teacher's response is more likely to be irritation or anger, and reprimands may follow. These tendencies seem to be consistent across time and cultures (Weiner, 1986, 2000).

What do students make of these reactions from their teachers? Sandra Graham (1991, 1996) gives some surprising answers. There is evidence that when teachers respond to students' mistakes with pity, praise for a "good try," or unsolicited help, the students are more likely to attribute their failure to an uncontrollable cause—usually lack of ability. For example, Graham and Barker (1990) asked subjects of various ages to rate the effort and ability of two boys viewed on a videotape. On the tape, a teacher circulated around the class while students worked. The teacher stopped to look at the two boys' papers, did not make any comments to the first boy, but said to the second, "Let me give you a hint. Don't forget to carry your tens." The second boy had not asked for help and did not appear to be stumped by the problem. All the age groups watching the tapes, even the youngest, perceived the boy who received help as being lower in ability than the boy who did not get help. It is as if the subjects read the teacher's behavior as saying, "You poor child, you just don't have the ability to do this hard work, so I will help."

Connect and Extend to the Research

Graham, S. (1991). A review of attribution theory in achievement contexts. *Educational Psychology Review,* 3, 5–39. This article reviews several major principles of attribution theory as they relate to achievement strivings, including the antecedents to particular self-ascriptions, the emotional consequences of causal attributions for success and failure, help-seeking and help-giving, peer acceptance and rejection, achievement evaluation, and attributional process in African American populations.

Does this mean that teachers should be critical and withhold help? Of course not! But it is a reminder that "praise as a consolation prize" for failing (Brophy, 1985) or oversolicitous help can give unintended messages. Graham (1991) suggests that many minority-group students could be the victims of well-meaning pity from teachers. Seeing the very real problems that the students face, teachers may "ease up" on requirements so the students will "experience success." But a subtle communication may accompany the pity, praise, and extra help: "You don't have the ability to do this, so I will overlook your failure." Graham says, "The pertinent question for blacks is whether their own history of academic failure makes them more likely to be the targets of sympathetic feedback from teachers and thus the recipients of low-ability cues" (1991, p. 28). This kind of benevolent feedback, even if well-intended, can be a subtle form of racism.

Beliefs about Self-Efficacy and Learned Helplessness

We have already examined one of the most important self beliefs affecting motivation: self-efficacy. **Self-efficacy** is our belief about our personal competence or effectiveness *in a given area.* Bandura (1997) defines self-efficacy as "beliefs in one's capabilities to organize and execute the courses of action required to produce given attainments" (p. 3). In schools, we are particularly interested in self-efficacy for learning mathematics, writing, history, science, sports, and other subjects, as well as for using learning strategies and for the many other challenges that classrooms present. Because it is a key concept in social cognitive theory, we discussed self-efficacy in depth in Chapter 9.

Self-efficacy and attributions affect each other. If success is attributed to internal or controllable causes such as ability or effort, then self-efficacy is enhanced. But if success is attributed to luck or to the intervention of others, then self-efficacy may not be strengthened. And efficacy affects attributions, too. People with a strong sense of self-efficacy for a given task ("I'm good at math") tend to attribute their failures to lack of effort ("I should have double-checked my work"). But people with a low sense of self-efficacy ("I'm terrible at math") tend to attribute their failures to lack of ability ("I'm just dumb"). So having a strong sense of self-efficacy for a certain task encourages controllable attributions, and controllable attributions increase self-efficacy. You can see that if a student held an entity view (ability cannot be changed) and a low sense of self-efficacy, motivation would be destroyed when failures were attributed to lack of ability ("I just can't do this and I'll never be able to learn") (Bandura, 1997; Pintrich & Schunk, 2002).

Connect and **Extend** to the **Research**

A recent study found that anxiety played a significant role in judging self-efficacy for middle-school students. See Klassen, R. M. (2002). *Motivational beliefs for Indo-Canadian and Anglo-Canadian early adolescents: A cross-cultural investigation of self and collective efficacy.* Dissertation. Simon Fraser University. Burnaby, B. C., Canada.

Whatever the label, most theorists agree that a sense of efficacy, control, or self-determination is critical if people are to feel intrinsically motivated. When people come to believe that the events and outcomes in their lives are mostly uncontrollable, they have developed **learned helplessness** (Seligman, 1975). To understand the power of learned helplessness, consider this experiment (Hiroto & Seligman, 1975): Subjects receive either solvable or unsolvable puzzles. In the next phase of the experiment, all subjects are given a series of solvable puzzles. The subjects who struggled with unsolvable problems in the first phase of the experiment usually solve significantly fewer puzzles in the second phase. They have learned that they cannot control the outcome, so why even try?

Self-efficacy is a factor in motivation. This student likely attributes at least part of her success to internal factors such as her own ability and effort.

Self-efficacy Beliefs about personal competence in a particular situation.

Learned helplessness The expectation, based on previous experiences with a lack of control, that all one's efforts will lead to failure.

Learned helplessness appears to cause three types of deficits: motivational, cognitive, and affective. Students who feel hopeless will be unmotivated and reluctant to attempt work. Like Hopeless Geraldo described earlier, they expect to fail, so why should they even try—thus motivation suffers. Because they are pessimistic about learning, these students miss opportunities to practice and improve skills and abilities, so they develop cognitive deficits. Finally, they often suffer from affective problems such as depression, anxiety, and listlessness (Alloy & Seligman, 1979). Once established, it is very difficult to reverse the effects of learned helplessness.

Connect and Extend to Other Chapters
The concept of learned helplessness was first introduced in Chapter 4 during the discussion of learning disabilities. Learned helplessness is also an issue for students at risk of failing, as described in Chapter 5. Consider the many factors in a classroom that might lead to learned helplessness, including physical or cognitive disabilities, racial prejudice, sex-role stereotyping, poverty, and so on.

Beliefs about Self-Worth

What are the connections between attributions and beliefs about ability, self-efficacy, and self-worth? Covington and his colleagues suggest that these factors come together in three kinds of motivational sets: *mastery-oriented, failure-avoiding*, and *failure-accepting*, as shown in Table 10.4 (Covington, 1992; Covington & Mueller, 2001).

Mastery-oriented students tend to value achievement and see ability as improvable (an incremental view), so they focus on mastery goals in order to increase their skills and abilities. They are not fearful of failure, because failing does not threaten their sense of competence and self-worth. This allows them to set moderately difficult goals, take risks, and cope with failure constructively. They generally attribute success to their own effort, and thus they assume responsibility for learning and have a strong sense of self-efficacy. They perform best in competitive situations, learn fast, have more self-confidence and energy, are more aroused, welcome concrete feedback (it does not threaten them), and are eager to learn "the rules of the game" so that they can succeed. All of these factors make for persistent, successful learning (Covington & Mueller, 2001; McClelland, 1985).

Failure-avoiding students tend to hold an entity view of ability, so they set performance goals. They lack a strong sense of their own competence and self-worth separate from their performance. In other words, they feel only as smart as their last test grade, so they never develop a solid sense of self-efficacy. In order to feel competent, they must protect themselves (and their self-images) from failure. If they have been generally successful, they may avoid failure like Safe Sumey, simply by taking few risks and "sticking with what they know." If, on the other hand, they have experienced a good bit of failure, then they, like Defensive Daleesha, may adopt self-defeating strategies such as feeble efforts, setting very low or ridiculously high goals, or claiming not to care. Just before a test, a student might say, "I didn't study at all!" or "All I want to do is pass." Then, any grade above passing is a success. Procrastination is another self-protective strategy. Low grades do not imply low ability if the student can claim, "I did okay considering I didn't start the term paper until last night." Some evidence suggests that blaming anxiety for poor test performance can also be a self-protective strategy (Covington & Omelich, 1987). Very little learning is going on.

Mastery-oriented students Students who focus on learning goals because they value achievement and see ability as improvable.

Failure-avoiding students Students who avoid failure by sticking to what they know, by not taking risks, or by claiming not to care about their performance.

TABLE 10.4

Mastery-Oriented, Failure-Avoiding, and Failure-Accepting Students

	Attitude toward Failure	Goals Set	Attributions	View of Ability	Strategies
Mastery-Oriented	Low fear of failure	Learning goals: moderately difficult and challenging	Effort, use of right strategy, sufficient knowledge is cause of success	Incremental; improvable	Adaptive strategies; e.g., try another way, seek help, practice/study more
Failure-Avoiding	High fear of failure	Performance goals; very hard or very easy	Lack of ability is cause of failure	Entity; set	Self-defeating strategies; e.g., make a feeble effort, pretend not to care
Failure-Accepting	Expectation of failure; depression	Performance goals or no goals	Lack of ability is cause of failure	Entity; set	Learned helplessness; likely to give up

Unfortunately, failure-avoiding strategies generally lead to the very failure the students were trying to avoid. If failures continue and excuses wear thin, the students may finally decide that they are incompetent. Their sense of self-worth and self-efficacy deteriorate. They give up and thus become **failure-accepting students.** They are convinced that their problems are due to low ability. As we saw earlier, those students who attribute failure to low ability and believe ability is fixed are likely to become depressed, apathetic, and helpless. Like Hopeless Geraldo, they have little hope for change.

Teachers may be able to prevent some failure-avoiding students from becoming failure-accepting by helping them to find new and more realistic goals. Also, some students may need support in aspiring to higher levels in the face of sexual or ethnic stereotypes about what they "should" want or what they "should not" be able to do well. This kind of support could make all the difference. Instead of pitying or excusing these students, teachers can teach them how to learn and then hold them accountable. This will help the students develop a sense of self-efficacy for learning and avoid learned helplessness.

Connect and **Extend** to Your **Teaching/Portfolio**

Think about your philosophy of teaching, a question you will be asked at most job interviews. What do you believe about motivating hard-to-reach students? How can you support the development of genuine and well-founded self-efficacy in your students? (Consult the *Guidelines* for ideas.)

Beliefs and Self-Schemas: Lessons for Teachers

If students believe they lack the ability to deal with higher mathematics, they will probably act on this belief even if their actual abilities are well above average. These students are likely to have little motivation to tackle trigonometry or calculus, because they expect to do poorly in these areas. If students believe that failing means they are stupid, they are likely to adopt many self-protective, but also self-defeating, strategies. Just telling students to "try harder" is not particularly effective. Students need real evidence that effort will pay off, that setting a higher goal will not lead to failure, that they can improve, and that abilities can be changed. They need authentic mastery experiences. The *Guidelines* provide ideas for encouraging self-efficacy and self-worth.

How can we put together all this information about motivation? How can teachers create environments, situations, and relationships that encourage motivation? We address these questions next.

Failure-accepting students Students who believe their failures are due to low ability and there is little they can do about it.

Guidelines: Encouraging Self-Efficacy and Self-Worth

Emphasize students' progress in a particular area.

EXAMPLES

1. Return to earlier material in reviews and show how "easy" it is now.
2. Encourage students to improve projects when they have learned more.
3. Keep examples of particularly good work in portfolios.

Set learning goals for your students, and model a mastery orientation for them.

EXAMPLES

1. Recognize progress and improvement.
2. Share examples of how you have developed your abilities in a given area and provide other models ofachievement who are similar to your students—no supermen or superwomen whose accomplishments seem unattainable.
3. Read stories about students who overcame physical, mental, or economic challenges.
4. Don't excuse failure because a student has problems outside school. Help the student succeed inside school.

Make specific suggestions for improvement, and revise grades when improvements are made.

EXAMPLES

1. Return work with comments noting what the students did right, what they did wrong, and why they might have made the mistakes.
2. Experiment with peer editing.
3. Show students how their revised, higher grade reflects greater competence and raises their class average.

Stress connections between past efforts and past accomplishments.

EXAMPLES

1. Have individual goal-setting and goal-review conferences with students, in which you ask students to reflect on how they solved difficult problems.
2. Confront self-defeating, failure-avoiding strategies directly.

For more information on self-efficacy, see: **http://www.emory.edu/EDUCATION/mfp/self-efficacy.html**

Motivation to Learn in School: On TARGET

Teachers are concerned about developing a particular kind of motivation in their students—the motivation to learn. Jere Brophy (1988) describes student **motivation to learn** as "a student tendency to find academic activities meaningful and worthwhile and to try to derive the intended academic benefits from them. Motivation to learn can be construed as both a general trait and a situation-specific state" (pp. 205–206). Motivation to learn involves more than wanting or intending to learn. It includes the quality of the student's mental efforts. For example, reading the text 10 times may indicate persistence, but motivation to learn implies more thoughtful, active study strategies, such as summarizing, elaborating the basic ideas, outlining in your own words, drawing graphs of the key relationships, and so on (Brophy, 1988).

What makes student motivation to learn a challenge in classrooms? In an interview, Jere Brophy listed five obstacles:

> First, school attendance is compulsory and curriculum content and learning activities are selected primarily on the basis of what society believes students need to learn, not on the basis of what students would choose to do if given the opportunity. . . . Second, teachers usually work with classes of 20 or more students and therefore cannot always meet each individual's needs, so some students are often bored and others are often confused or frustrated. Third, classrooms are social settings in which much that occurs is public, so that failures often produce not only personal disappointment but public embarrassment. Fourth, students are graded, and periodic reports are sent home to their parents. Finally, teachers and students often settle into familiar routines that become the "daily grind." School reduces to covering content (for the teachers) and completing assignments (for the students). (Gaedke & Shaughnessy, 2003, pp. 206–207)

In this challenging context, it would be wonderful if all our students came to us filled with the motivation to learn, but they don't. As teachers, we have three major goals. The first is to get students productively involved with the work of the class; in other words, to create a *state* of motivation to learn. The second and longer-term goal is to develop in our students the *trait* of being motivated to learn so they will be able "to educate themselves throughout their lifetime" (Bandura, 1993, p. 136). And finally, we want our students to be cognitively engaged—to think deeply about what they study. In other words, we want them to be *thoughtful* (Blumenfeld, Puro, & Mergendoller, 1992).

In this chapter we examined the roles of intrinsic and extrinsic motivation, attributions, goals, interests, emotions, and self-schemas in motivation. Table 10.5 shows how each of these factors contributes to motivation to learn.

Connect and **Extend** to Your **Teaching/Portfolio**

Relate the information in Chapter 5 to the discussion in this chapter of the challenges teachers face in helping to motivate all students.

Motivation to learn The tendency to find academic activities meaningful and worthwhile and to try to benefit from them.

TABLE 10.5

Building a Concept of Motivation to Learn

Motivation to learn is encouraged when the following six elements come together:

	Optimum Characteristics of Motivation to Learn	Characteristics That Diminish Motivation to Learn
Source of Motivation	INTRINSIC: Personal factors such as needs, interests, curiosity, enjoyment	EXTRINSIC: Environmental factors such as rewards, social pressure, punishment
Type of Goal Set	LEARNING GOAL: Personal satisfaction in meeting challenges and improving; tendency to choose moderately difficult and challenging goals	PERFORMANCE GOAL: Desire for approval for performance in others' eyes; tendency to choose very easy or very difficult goals
Type of Involvement	TASK-INVOLVED: Concerned with mastering the task	EGO-INVOLVED: Concerned with self in others' eyes.
Achievement Motivation	Motivation to ACHIEVE: Mastery orientation	Motivation to AVOID FAILURE: Prone to anxiety
Likely Attributions	Successes and failures attributed to CONTROLLABLE effort and ability	Success and failures attributed to UNCONTROLLABLE causes
Beliefs about Ability	INCREMENTAL VIEW: Belief that ability can be improved through hard work and added knowledge and skills	ENTITY VIEW: Belief that ability is a stable, uncontrollable trait

Connect and **Extend** to **PRAXIS II™**

TARGET (I, C1,2,3)
Describe the major features of the TARGET model and identify related strategies that are likely to boost motivation.

Connect and **Extend** to Your **Teaching/Portfolio**

Use the TARGET model (Table 10.6) to generate motivational strategies for the grade you will teach.

The central questions for the remainder of the chapter are: What can teachers do to encourage and support motivation to learn? How can teachers use knowledge about attributions, goals, interests, beliefs, and self-schemas to increase motivation to learn? To organize our discussion, we will use the TARGET model.

Carol Ames (1990, 1992) has identified six areas where teachers make decisions that can influence student motivation to learn: the nature of the *task* that students are asked to do, the *autonomy* students are allowed in working, how students are *recognized* for their accomplishments, *grouping* practices, *evaluation* procedures, and the scheduling of *time* in the classroom. Epstein (1989) coined the acronym TARGET to organize these areas of possible teacher influence, as shown in Table 10.6.

Tasks for Learning

To understand how an **academic task** can affect students' motivation, we need to analyze the task. Tasks can be interesting or boring for students. And tasks have different values for students.

Task Value. As you probably recall, many theories suggest that the strength of our motivation in a particular situation is determined by both our *expectation* that we can succeed and the *value* of that success to us. Students' beliefs about the value of a task seem to predict the choices they make, such as whether to enroll in advanced science classes or join a team. Efficacy expectations predict achievement in doing the task—how well the students actually perform in the advance science class or on the team (Wigfield & Eccles, 2002b).

We can think of a task value as having four components: importance, interest, utility, and cost (Eccles & Wigfield, 2001; Eccles, Wigfield, & Schiefele, 1998). **Importance** or **attainment value** is the significance of doing well on the task; this is closely tied to the needs of the individual (for example, the need to be well-liked, athletic, etc.). For instance, if someone has a strong need to appear smart and believes that a high grade on a test shows you are smart, then the test has high attainment value for that person. A second component is **interest** or **intrinsic value.** This is simply the enjoyment one gets from the activity itself. Some people like the experience of learning. Others enjoy the feeling of hard physical effort or the challenge of solving puzzles. Tasks also can have **utility value;** that is, they help us achieve a short-term or long-term goal such as earning a degree. Finally, tasks have costs—negative consequences that might follow from doing the task such as not having time to do other things or looking awkward as you perform the task.

You see from our discussion of task value that personal and environmental influences on motivation interact constantly. The task we ask students to accomplish is an aspect of the environment; it is external to the student. But the value of accomplishing the task is bound up with the internal needs, beliefs, and goals of the individual.

Connect and **Extend** to the **Research**

See the special issue on "authentic learning" in the April 1993 issue of *Educational Leadership.*

Academic tasks The work the student must accomplish, including the content covered and the mental operations required.

Importance/Attainment value The importance of doing well on a task; how success on the task meets personal needs.

Intrinsic or interest value The enjoyment a person gets from a task.

Utility value The contribution of a task to meeting one's goals.

Authentic task Tasks that have some connection to real-life problems the students will face outside the classroom.

Problem-based learning Methods that provide students with realistic problems that don't necessarily have right answers.

Authentic Tasks. Recently, there has been a great deal written about the use of authentic tasks in teaching. An **authentic task** is one that has some connection to the real-life problems and situations that students will face outside the classroom, both now and in the future. If you ask students to memorize definitions they will never use, to learn the material only because it is on the test, or to repeat work they already understand, then there can be little motivation to learn. But if the tasks are authentic, students are more likely to see the genuine utility value of the work and are also more likely to find the tasks meaningful and interesting. **Problem-based learning** is one example of the use of authentic tasks in teaching.

An example problem presented to one group of 7th and 8th graders in Illinois was, "What should be done about a nuclear waste dump site in our area?" The students soon learned that this real problem was not a simple one. Scientists disagreed about the dangers. Environmental activists demanded that the materials be removed, even if this bankrupted the company involved—one that employed many local residents. Some members of the state assembly wanted the material taken out of state, even though no place in the country was licensed to receive the toxic materials. The company believed the safest so-

TABLE 10.6

The TARGET Model for Supporting Student Motivation to Learn

Teachers make decisions in many areas that can influence motivation to learn. The TARGET acronym highlights task, autonomy, recognition, grouping, evaluation, and time.

TARGET Area	Focus	Objectives	Examples of Possible Strategies
Task	How learning tasks are structured—what the student is asked to do	Enhance intrinsic attractiveness of learning tasks Make learning meaningful	Encourage instruction that relates to students' backgrounds and experience Avoid payment (monetary and other) for attendance, grades, or achievement Foster goal setting and self-regulation
Autonomy/Responsibility	Student participation in learning/school decisions	Provide optimal freedom for students to make choices and take responsibility	Give alternatives in making assignments Ask for student comments on school life—and take them seriously Encourage students to take initiatives and evaluate their own learning Establish leadership opportunities for *all* students
Recognition	The nature and use of recognition and reward in the school setting	Provide opportunities for *all* students to be recognized for learning Recognize *progress* in goal attainment Recognize challenge seeking and innovation	Foster "personal best" awards Reduce emphasis on "honor rolls" Recognize and publicize a wide range of school-related activities of students
Grouping	The organization of school learning and experiences	Build an environment of acceptance and appreciation of all students Broaden the range of social interaction, particularly of at-risk students Enhance social skills development	Provide opportunities for cooperative learning, problem solving, and decision making Encourage multiple group membership to increase range of peer interaction Eliminate ability-grouped classes
Evaluation	The nature and use of evaluation and assessment procedures	Grading and reporting processes Practices associated with use of standardized tests Definition of goals and standards	Reduce emphasis on social comparisons of achievement Give students opportunities to improve their performance (e.g., study skills, classes) Establish grading/reporting practices that portray student progress in learning Encourage student participation in the evaluation process
Time	The scheduling of the school day	Provide opportunities for extended and significant student involvement in learning tasks Allow the learning task and student needs to dictate scheduling	Allow students to *progress at their own rate* whenever possible Encourage flexibility in the scheduling of learning experiences Give teachers greater control over time usage through, for example, block scheduling

Source: From "Reinventing Schools for Early Adolescents: Emphasizing Task Goals," by M. L. Maehr and E. M. Anderman, *The Elementary School Journal, 93.5,* pp. 604–605. Copyright © 1993 by The University of Chicago Press. Adapted with permission.

lution was to leave the materials buried. The students had to research the situation, interview parties involved, and develop recommendations to be presented to state experts and community groups. "In problem-based learning students assume the roles of scientists, historians, doctors, or others who have a real stake in the proposed problem. Motivation soars because students realize it's their problem" (Stepien & Gallagher, 1993, p. 26).

Connect and **Extend** to **Other Chapters**

See Chapter 9 for a complete discussion of problem-based learning.

Supporting Autonomy and Recognizing Accomplishment

The second area in the TARGET model involves how much choice and autonomy students are allowed. Choice in schools is not the norm. Children and adolescents spend literally thousands of hours in schools where other people decide what will happen. Yet we know that self-determination and a sense of internal locus of causality are critical to maintaining intrinsic motivation (Reeve, Nix, & Hamm, 2003). What can teachers do to support choice without creating chaos?

Connect and **Extend** to the **Research**

The June 1998 issue of *Educational Psychology Review,* edited by Karen Harris and Pat Alexander, has a series of articles describing models of integrated teaching that include student choice. One article by Ruth Garner (pp. 227–238) describes the power of bounded choices.

Supporting Choices. Like totally unguided discovery or aimless discussions, unstructured or unguided choices can be counterproductive for learning (Garner, 1998). For example, Dyson (1997) found that children become anxious and upset when directed by teachers to draw or write about anything they want in any way they want. Dyson says that students see this *unbounded choice* as a "scary void." I know that graduate students in my classes also find it disconcerting if I ask them to design a final project that will determine their grade, just as I panic when I am asked to give a talk on "whatever you want."

The alternative is *bounded choice*—giving students a range of options that set valuable tasks for them, but also allow them to follow personal interests. The balance must be just right: "too much autonomy is bewildering and too little is boring" (Guthrie et al., 1998, p. 185). Guthrie describes how a student in a 5th-grade class exercised her choices about researching and writing. The class was studying the life cycle of the Monarch butterfly. Each child worked in a heterogeneous team and each team had a chrysalis to observe as it grew. The class had organized a library of multilevel expository books, trade books, literary books, reference books, maps, electronic data bases, and other resources. The teacher had taught specific skills that would be needed—using an index and table of contents, setting goals, and writing summaries—but the students were able to choose topics and appropriate resources for crafting their own chapter.

Students also can exercise autonomy about how they receive feedback from the teacher or from classmates. Figure 10.1 describes a strategy called "Check It Out," in

FIGURE 10.1

Student Autonomy: Check It Out

Using this technique to support student autonomy, the teacher decides on a set of skills that will be developed over a unit, but the student decides which skill(s) will be evaluated on any given assignment. Over the course of the unit, all the skills have to be "checked out." This student has indicated that she wants the teacher to "check out" her creativity and verb tense.

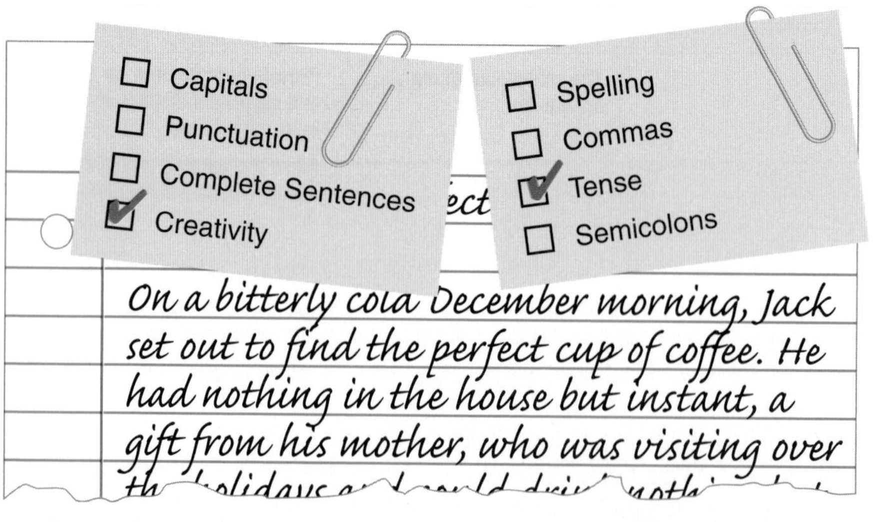
Capitals
Punctuation
Complete Sentences
Creativity
Spelling
Commas
Tense
Semicolons
set out to find the perfect cup of coffee. He
had nothing in the house but instant, a
gift from his mother, who was visiting over

Source: From *150 Ways to Increase Intrinsic Motivation in the Classroom,* by James P. Raffini. Published by Allyn and Bacon, Boston, MA. Copyright © 1996 by Pearson Education. Adapted by permission of the publisher.

which students specify the skills that they want to have evaluated in a particular assignment. Over the course of a unit, all the skills have to be "checked out," but students choose when each one is evaluated.

Recognizing Accomplishment. The third TARGET area is *recognition* for accomplishments. Students should be recognized for improving on their own personal best, for tackling difficult tasks, for persistence, and for creativity—not just for performing better than others. In Chapter 6 we noted that giving students rewards for activities that they already enjoy can undermine intrinsic motivation. But nothing in teaching is simple. At times, praise can have paradoxical effects. For example, if two students succeed and the teacher praises only one of them, the message, to other children at least, may be that the praised student had less ability and had to work harder to succeed, thus earning praise. So students may use the teacher's praise or criticism as cues about capabilities—praise means I'm not very smart, so when I succeed, I deserve recognition. Criticism means my teacher thinks I'm smart and could do better (Stipek, 2002).

What sort of recognition leads to engagement? One answer comes from a study by Ruth Butler (1987). Students in the 5th and 6th grades were given interesting divergent thinking tasks followed by either individual personalized comments, standardized praise ("very good"), grades, or no feedback. Interest, performance, attributions to effort, and task involvement were higher after personalized comments. Ego-involved motivation (the desire to look good or do better than others) was greater after grades and standard praise.

Grouping, Evaluation, and Time

You may remember a teacher who made you want to work hard—someone who made a subject come alive. Or you may remember how many hours you spent practicing as a member of a team, orchestra, choir, or theater troupe. If you do, then you know the motivational power of relationships with other people.

Grouping and Goal Structures. Motivation can be greatly influenced by the ways we relate to the other people who are also involved in accomplishing a particular goal. Johnson and Johnson (1999) have labeled this interpersonal factor the **goal structure** of the task. There are three such structures: cooperative, competitive, and individualistic, as shown in Table 10.7 on the next page.

When the task involves complex learning and problem-solving skills, cooperation leads to higher achievement than competition, especially for students with lower abilities. Students learn to set attainable goals and negotiate. They become more altruistic. The interaction with peers that students enjoy so much becomes a part of the learning process. The result? The need for belonging described by Maslow is more likely to be met and motivation is increased (Stipek, 2002; Webb & Palincsar, 1996). There are many approaches to peer learning or group learning. We will examine these approaches in depth in Chapter 11.

Goal structure The way students relate to others who are also working toward a particular goal.

TABLE 10.7

Different Goal Structures

Each goal structure is associated with a different relationship between the individual and the group. This relationship influences motivation to reach the goal.

	Cooperative	Competitive	Individualistic
Definition	Students believe their goal is attainable only if other students will also reach the goal.	Students believe they will reach their goal if and only if other students do not reach the goal.	Students believe that their own attempt to reach a goal is not related to other students' attempts to reach the goal.
Examples	Team victories—each player wins only if all the team members win: a relay race, a quilting bee, a barn raising, a symphony, a play.	Golf tournament, singles tennis match, a 100-yard dash, valedictorian, Miss America pageant.	Lowering your handicap in golf, jogging, learning a new language, enjoying a museum, losing or gaining weight, stopping smoking.

Source: From *Learning Together and Alone: Cooperation, Competition, and Individualization,* (5th ed.), by D. Johnson & R. Johnson. Published by Allyn and Bacon, Boston, MA. Copyright © 1999 by Pearson Education. Adapted by permission of the publisher.

Evaluation. The greater the emphasis on competitive evaluation and grading, the more students will focus on performance goals rather than mastery. And low-achieving students who have little hope of either performing well or mastering the task may simply want to get it over with. One study of 1st graders found that low-achieving students made up answers, filled in the page with patterns, or copied from other students, just to get through their seatwork. As one student said when she finished a word/definition matching exercise, "I don't know what it means, but I did it" (Anderson, Brubaker, Alleman-Brooks, & Duffy, 1985, p. 132). On closer examination, the researchers found that the work was much too hard for these students, so they connected words and definitions at random.

How can teachers prevent students from simply focusing on the grade or doing the work "just to get finished"? The most obvious answer is to de-emphasize grades and emphasize learning in the class. Students need to understand the value of the work. Instead of saying, "You will need to know this for the test," tell students how the information will be useful in solving problems they want to solve. Suggest that the lesson will answer some interesting questions. Communicate that understanding is more important than finishing. Unfortunately, many teachers do not follow this advice. Jere Brophy (1988) reports that when he and several colleagues spent about 100 hours observing how six teachers introduced their lessons, they found that most introductions were routine, apologetic, or unenthusiastic. The introductions described procedures, made threats, emphasized finishing, or promised tests on the material.

One way to emphasize learning rather than grades is to use self-evaluation. This strategy also supports autonomy. The self-evaluation and goal planning sheet in Figure 10.2 could be adapted for almost any grade.

Time. Most experienced teachers know that there is too much work and not enough time in the school day. Even if they become engrossed in a project, students must stop and turn their attention to another class when the bell rings or when the teacher's schedule indicates it's time to move on to a new subject. Furthermore, students must progress as a group. If particular individuals can move faster or if they need more time, they may still have to follow the pace of the whole group. So scheduling often interferes with motivation by making students move faster or slower than would be appropriate or by interrupting their involvement. It is difficult to develop persistence and a sense of self-efficacy when students are not allowed to stick with a challenging activity. As a teacher, will you be able to make time for engaged and persistent learning? Some elementary classrooms have *DEAR* time—Drop Everything And Read—to give extended periods when everyone, even the teacher, reads. Some middle and high schools have block scheduling in which teachers work in teams to plan larger blocks of class time.

Connect and Extend to the Research

For a thorough review of research on different forms of cooperative learning, see O'Donnell, A. M., & O'Kelly, J. (1994). Learning from peers: Beyond the rhetoric of positive results. *Educational Psychology Review, 6,* 321–350.

Connect and Extend to the Research

Brophy (1988) reports these examples of lesson introductions that focus on procedures and threats:

"You don't expect me to give you baby work to do every day, do you?"

"My talkers are going to get a third page to do during lunch."

"If you are done by 10 o'clock, you can go outside." (p. 204)

Connect and Extend to Other Chapters

Chapter 12 discusses how to make more time for learning by decreasing disruptions, smoothing transitions, and avoiding discipline problems.

We can see how these motivational elements come together in real classrooms. Sara Dolezal and her colleagues observed and interviewed 3rd-grade teachers in eight Catholic schools and determined if their students were low, moderate, or high in their level of motivation (Dolezal, Welsh, Pressley, & Vincent, 2003). Table 10.8 on the next page summarizes the dramatic differences in these classrooms between strategies that support motivation and those that undermine it. Students in the low-engagement classes were restless and chatty as they faced their easy, undemanding seatwork. The classrooms were bare, unattractive, and filled with management problems. Instruction was disorganized. The class atmosphere was generally negative. The moderately engaged classrooms were organized to be "student friendly," with reading areas, group work area, posters, and student artwork. The teachers were warm and caring, and they connected lessons to students' background knowledge. Management routines were smooth and organized, and the class atmosphere was positive. The teachers were good at catching student attention and encouraging students to become more self-regulating, but they had trouble holding attention, probably because the tasks were too easy. Highly engaging teachers had all the positive qualities of student-friendly classrooms—positive atmosphere, smooth management routines, support for student self-regulation, and effective instruction—but they added more challenging tasks along with the support to succeed. These excellent motivators did not rely on one or two approaches to motivate their students; they applied a large repertoire of strategies from Table 10.8.

FIGURE 10.2

Self-Evaluation and Goals Planning

By completing this form, students evaluate their own work in relation to their own goals and set new goals for the future.

Name ____________________ Advisor ____________________

Subject ____________________ Quarter ____________________

1. Self-Evaluation:

a. How am I doing in this course? ____________________

b. What difficulties have I been having? ____________________

c. How much time and effort have I been spending in this course?

____

d. Do I need more help in this course? __________ If yes, how have I tried to get it?

2. Academic Goal

a. My goal to achieve before the end of the quarter is ____________________

b. I want to work on this goal because ____________________

c. I will achieve this goal by ____________________

3. Behavior or Social Goal

a. My goal to achieve before the end of the quarter is ____________________

b. I want to work on this goal because ____________________

c. I will achieve this goal by ____________________

Variations

Advisors may choose to use this activity at the beginning of each quarter and adapt self-evaluation and goal planning sheets to specific grade levels. Follow-up conferences are also useful for helping students evaluate their plans.

Source: From *150 Ways to Increase Intrinsic Motivation in the Classroom,* by James P. Raffini. Published by Allyn & Bacon, Boston, MA. Copyright © 1996 by Pearson Education. Adapted by permission of the publisher.

TABLE 10.8

Strategies That Support and Undermine Motivation in the Classroom

A Few Strategies That Support Motivation

Strategy	Example
Messages of accountability and high expectations	The teacher asks students to have parents review and sign some assignments.
Teacher communicates importance of work	"We need to check it for at least 1 minute, which means looking over it carefully."
Clear goals/directions	The teacher explains exactly how the students are to separate into groups and complete their nominations for their favorite book.
Connections across the curriculum	The teacher relates the concept of ratios in math to compare/contrast skills in reading.
Opportunities to learn about and practice dramatic arts	After studying about historical figures, students write and produce their own plays.
Attributions to effort	During a word game, the teacher says to a student, "Did you study last night?" The student nods. "See how it helps?"
Encouraging risk-taking	"I need a new shining face. Someone I haven't called on yet. I need a risk-taker."
Uses games and play to reinforce concept or review material	During a math lesson using balance, students spend 5 minutes weighing the favorite toy they were asked to bring in that day.
Home–school connections	As part of math science unit, a recycling activity asks families to keep a chart of everything they recycle in a week.
Multiple representations of a task	The teacher uses 4 ways to teach multiplication: "magic multipliers," sing-along multiplication facts, whole-class flash card review, "Around-the-World" game.
Positive classroom management, praise, private reprimands	"Thumbs up when you are ready to work. Table 7 has thumbs up, table 7. I like the way table 7 is waiting patiently."
Stimulating creative thought	"We are going to use our imaginations today. We are going to take a trip to an imaginary theater in our heads."
Opportunities for choice	Students can choose to use prompts for their journal writing or pick their own topic.
Teacher communicates to students that they can handle challenging tasks	"This is hard stuff and you are doing great. I know adults who have trouble with this."
Value students—communicate caring	The teacher allows a new student to sit with a buddy for the day.

A Few Strategies That Undermine Motivation

Strategy	Example
Attributions to intellect rather than effort	When students remark during a lesson, "I'm stupid" or "I'm a dork," the teacher says nothing, then replies, "Let's have someone who is smart."
Teacher emphasizes competition rather than working together	The teacher conducts a poetry contest where students read poems to class and the class members hold up cards with scores rating how well each student performed.
Few displays of student work	Public bulletin boards are used for posting grades.
No scaffolding for learning a new skill	The teacher is loud and critical when students have trouble: "Just look back in the glossary and don't miss it because you are too lazy to look it up."
Ineffective/negative feedback	"Does everyone understand?" A few students say yes and the teacher moves on.
Lack of connections	On Martin Luther King Day, the teacher leads a brief discussion of King, then the remainder of the activities are about Columbus.
Easy tasks	The teacher provides easy work and "fun" activities that teach little.
Negative class atmosphere	"Excuse me, I said page number. If you follow and listen, you would know."
Punitive classroom management	The teacher threatens bad grades if students do not look up words in the glossary.
Work that is much too difficult	The teacher assigns independent math work that only one or two students can do.
Slow pacing	The pace is set for the slowest students—others finish and have nothing to do.
Emphasis on finishing, not learning	The teacher communicates the purpose is to finish, not learn or use the vocabulary.
Sparse, unattractive classroom	There are no decorated bulletin boards, maps, charts, or displays of student work.
Poor planning	Missing handouts force the teacher to have large instead of smaller work groups.
Public punishment	All students stand, and the teacher reads a list of those who finished the assignment and they sit down. The teacher gives public lecture on responsibility to those left standing.

Source: Adapted from "How do nine third-grade teachers motivate their students?" by S. E. Dolezal, L. M. Welsh, M. Pressley, & M. Vincent. *Elementary School Journal,* 2003, 103, pp. 247–248.

Diversity and Convergences in Motivation to Learn

We have seen that motivation to learn grows from the individual's needs, goals, interests, emotions, beliefs, and attributions in interaction with the tasks set, autonomy and recognition provided, grouping structures, evaluation procedures, and time allowed.

Diversity in Motivation

Because students differ in terms of language, culture, economic privilege, personality, knowledge, and experience, they will also differ in their needs, goals, interests, and beliefs. For example, self-efficacy is a central concept in motivation because it is strong predictor of academic performance. But there are cultural differences as well. Males and African American students are more likely to be overconfident in their academic abilities, so their predictions of future achievement are less accurate than the predictions of Asian American students and female students who are much less likely to express overconfidence in their abilities. Gifted male students are less likely to be overconfident, and gifted female students are likely to underestimate their abilities, whereas students with disabilities tend to be overconfident in their sense of efficacy (Pajares, 2000).

Taking this diversity into account when designing tasks, supporting autonomy, recognizing accomplishments, grouping, making evaluations, and managing time can encourage motivation to learn. Take interest, for example. Embedding student writing tasks in cultural contexts is one way to *catch* and *hold* situational interest (Alderman, 2004; Bergin, 1999). When Latina/o immigrant students in junior-high classes moved from writing using work sheets and standard assignments to writing about such topics as immigration, bilingualism, and gang life—factors that were important to them and to their families—their papers got longer and the writing quality was better (Rueda & Moll, 1994).

Language is a central factor in students' connections with the school. When bilingual students are encouraged to draw on both English and their heritage language, motivation and participation can increase. Robert Jimenez (2000) found in his study of bilingual Latino/a students that successful readers saw reading as a process of making sense; they used both of their languages to understand the material. For instance, they might look for Spanish word parts in English words to help them translate. Less-successful students had a different goal. They believed that reading just meant saying the words correctly in English. It is likely their interest and sense of efficacy for reading in English would be less, too.

Encouraging students to capitalize on their cultural knowledge can increase motivation and meaning in school. But this doesn't happen often enough. "The lack of congruence between students' life experiences and instruction in most schools has been well documented, especially for low income students, students of color, and English language learners" (Committee on Increasing High School Students' Engagement and Motivation to Learn, 2004, p. 66).

Taking cultural diversity into account when designing tasks capitalizes on students' cultural knowledge and can increase motivation and meaning in school.

Convergences: Strategies to Encourage Motivation

Connect and **Extend** to Your **Teaching/Portfolio**

Adapt all the *Guidelines* from the chapter for the age group you plan to teach.

Until four basic conditions are met for every student and in every classroom, no motivational strategies will succeed. First, the classroom must be relatively organized and free from constant interruptions and disruptions. (Chapter 12 will give you the information you need to make sure this requirement is met.) Second, the teacher must be a patient, supportive person who never embarrasses students for mistakes. Everyone in the class should see mistakes as opportunities for learning (Clifford, 1990, 1991). Third, the work must be challenging, but reasonable. If work is too easy or too difficult, students will have little motivation to learn. They will focus on finishing, not on learning. Finally, the learning tasks must be authentic, and what makes a task authentic is influenced by culture, as we have seen (Bergin, 1999; Brophy & Kher, 1986; Stipek, 1993).

Once these four basic conditions are met, the influences on students' motivation to learn in a particular situation can be summarized in four questions: Can I succeed at this task? Do I want to succeed? What do I need to do to succeed? Do I belong? (Committee on Increasing High School Students' Engagement and Motivation to Learn, 2004; Eccles & Wigfield, 1985). We want students to have confidence in their ability so they will approach learning with energy and enthusiasm. We want them to see the value of the tasks involved and work to learn, not just try to get the grade or get finished. We want students to believe that success will come when they apply good learning strategies instead of believing that their only option is to use self-defeating, failure-avoiding, face-saving strategies. When things get difficult, we want students to stay focused on the task, and not get so worried about failure that they "freeze." And we want students to feel as though they belong in school—that their teachers and classmates care about them and can be trusted.

Can I Do It? Building Confidence and Positive Expectations No amount of encouragement or "cheerleading" will substitute for real accomplishment. To ensure genuine progress:

1. *Begin work at the students' level and move in small steps.* The pace should be brisk, but not so fast that students have to move to the next step before they understand the one they are working on. This may require assigning different tasks to different students. One possibility is to have very easy and very difficult questions on every test and assignment, so all students are both successful and challenged. When grades are required, make sure all the students in class have a chance to make at least a C if they work hard.
2. *Make sure learning goals are clear, specific, and possible to reach in the near future.* When long-term projects are planned, break the work into subgoals and help students feel a sense of progress toward the long-term goal. If possible, give students a range of goals at different levels of difficulty and let them choose.
3. *Stress self-comparison, not comparison with others.* Help students see the progress they are making by showing them how to use self-management strategies such as those described in Chapter 6. Give specific feedback and corrections. Tell students what they are doing right as well as what is wrong and *why* it is wrong. Periodically, give students a question or problem that was once hard for them but now seems easy. Point out how much they have improved.
4. *Communicate to students that academic ability is improvable* and specific to the task at hand. In other words, the fact that a student has trouble in algebra doesn't necessarily mean that geometry will be difficult or that he or she is a bad English student. Don't undermine your efforts to stress improvement by displaying only the 100% papers on the bulletin board.
5. *Model good problem solving,* especially when *you* have to try several approaches. Students need to see that learning is not smooth and error-free, even for the teacher.

Do I Want to Do It? Seeing the Value of Learning Teachers can use intrinsic and extrinsic motivation strategies to help students see the value of the learning task.

Attainment and Intrinsic Value. To establish attainment value, we must connect the learning task with the needs of the students. First, it must be possible for students to meet their needs for safety, belonging, and achievement in our classes. The classroom should not be a frightening or lonely place. Second, we must be sure that sexual or ethnic stereotypes do not interfere with motivation. For example, we must make it clear that both women and men can be high achievers in all subjects and that no subjects are the territory of only one sex. It is not "unfeminine" to be strong in mathematics, science, car mechanics, or sports. It is not "unmasculine" to be good in literature, art, music, or French.

There are many strategies for encouraging *intrinsic* (interest) motivation. Several of the following are taken from Brophy (1988).

1. *Tie class activities to student interests* in sports, music, current events, pets, common problems or conflicts with family and friends, fads, television and cinema personalities, or other significant features of their lives (Schiefele, 1991). But be sure you know what you are talking about. For example, if you use a verse from a Mariah Carey song to make a point, you had better have some knowledge of the music and the performer. When possible, give students choices of research paper or reading topics so they can follow their own interests.
2. *Arouse curiosity.* Point out puzzling discrepancies between students' beliefs and the facts. For example, Stipek (1993) describes a teacher who asked her 5th-grade class if there were "people" on some of the other planets. When the students said yes, the teacher asked if people needed oxygen to breathe. Since the students had just learned this fact, they responded yes to this question also. Then the teacher told them that there is no oxygen in the atmosphere of the other planets. This surprising discrepancy between what the children knew about oxygen and what they believed about life on other planets led to a rousing discussion of the atmospheres of other planets, the kinds of beings that could survive in these atmospheres, and so on. A straight lecture on the atmosphere of the planets might have put the students to sleep, but this discussion led to real interest in the subject.
3. *Make the learning task fun.* Many lessons can be taught through simulations or games, as you saw in the *Point/Counterpoint* on making learning fun. Used appropriately so that the activity connects with learning, these experiences can be very worthwhile and fun, too.
4. *Make use of novelty and familiarity.* Don't overuse a few teaching approaches or motivational strategies. We all need some variety. Varying the goal structures of tasks (cooperative, competitive, individualistic) can help, as can using different teaching media. When the material being covered in class is abstract or unfamiliar to students, try to connect it to something they know and understand. For example, talk about the size of a large area, such as the Acropolis in Athens, in terms of football fields. Brophy (1988) describes one teacher who read a brief passage from *Spartacus* to personalize the unit on slavery in the ancient world.

Instrumental Value. Sometimes it is difficult to encourage intrinsic motivation, and so teachers must rely on the utility or "instrumental" value of tasks. It is important to learn many skills because they will be needed in more advanced classes or for life outside school.

1. When these connections are not obvious, you should *explain the connections to your students.* Jeanette Abi-Nader (1991) describes one project, the PLAN program, that makes these connections come alive for Hispanic high-school students. The three major strategies used in the program to focus students' attention on their future are: (1) working with mentors and models—often PLAN graduates—who give advice about how to choose courses, budget time, take notes, and deal with cultural differences in college; (2) storytelling about the achievements of former students—sometimes the college term papers of former students are posted on PLAN bulletin boards; and (3) filling the classroom with future-oriented talk such as "When you go to college, you will encounter these situations" or, "You're at a parents' meeting—you want a good education for your children—and you are the ones who must speak up; that's why it is important to learn public speaking skills" (p. 548).
2. In some situations, teachers can *provide incentives and rewards for learning* (see Chapter 6). Remember, though, that giving rewards when students are already interested in the activity may undermine intrinsic motivation.
3. Use *ill-structured problems and authentic tasks* in teaching. Connect problems in school to real problems outside.

Connect and **Extend** to **PRAXIS II™**

Promoting Intrinsic Motivation to Learn (I, C2, 3)

For a set of practical tips, guidelines, and suggestions for boosting and maintaining motivation to learn, go to *Increasing Student Engagement and Motivation: From Time-on-Task to Homework* (http://www.nwrel.org/request/oct00/textonly.html).

Connect and **Extend** to the **Research**

Abi-Nader, J. (1991). Creating a vision of the future: Strategies for motivating minority students. *Phi Delta Kappan*, 72, 546–549. *Focus Questions:* Why do minority-group students sometimes find schooling unmotivating? What can be done?

Family and Community Partnerships

Guidelines: Motivation to Learn

Understand family goals for children.

EXAMPLES

1. In an informal setting, around coffee or snacks, meet with families individually or in small groups to listen to what they want for their children.
2. Mail out questionnaires or send response cards home with students, asking what skills the families believe their children most need to work on. Pick one goal for each child and develop a plan for working toward the goal both inside and outside school. Share the plan with the families and ask for feedback.

Identify student and family interests that can be related to goals.

EXAMPLES

1. Ask a member of the family to share a skill or hobby.
2. Identify "family favorites"—favorite foods, music, vacations, sports, colors, activities, hymns, movies, games, snacks, recipes, memories. Tie class lessons to interests.

Give families a way to track progress toward goals.

EXAMPLES

1. Provide simple "progress charts" or goal cards that can be posted on the refrigerator.
2. Ask for parents' feedback (and mean it) about your effectiveness in helping their children.

Work with families to build confidence and positive expectations.

EXAMPLES

1. Avoid comparing one child in a family to another during conferences and discussions with family members.
2. Ask family members to highlight strong points of homework assignments. They might attach a note to assignments describing the three best aspects of the work and one element that could be improved.

Make families partners in showing the value of learning.

EXAMPLES

1. Invite family members to the class to demonstrate how they use mathematics or writing in their work.
2. Involve parents in identifying skills and knowledge that could be applied at home and prove helpful to the family right now, for example, keeping records on service agencies, writing letters of complaint to department stores or landlords, or researching vacation destinations.

Provide resources that build skill and will for families.

EXAMPLES

1. Give family members simple strategies for helping their children improve study skills.
2. Involve older students in a "homework hotline" telephone network for helping younger students.

Have frequent celebrations of learning.

EXAMPLES

1. Invite families to a "museum" at the end of a unit on dinosaurs. Students create the museum in the auditorium, library, or cafeteria. After visiting the museum, families go to the classroom to examine their child's portfolio for the unit.
2. Place mini-exhibits of student work at local grocery stores, libraries, or community centers.

For more information on family partnerships and motivation, see: **http://www.naesp.org/ContentLoad.do?contentId=896**

What Do I Need to Do to Succeed? Staying Focused on the Task When students encounter difficulties, as they must if they are working at a challenging level, they need to keep their attention on the task. If the focus shifts to worries about performance, fear of failure, or concern with looking smart, then motivation to learn is lost.

1. *Give students frequent opportunities to respond* through questions and answers, short assignments, or demonstrations of skills. Make sure you check the students' answers so you can correct problems quickly. You don't want students to practice errors too long. Computer learning programs give students the immediate feedback they need to correct errors before they become habits.
2. When possible, *have students create a finished product*. They will be more persistent and focused on the task when the end is in sight. We all have experienced the power

of the need for closure. For example, I often begin a house-painting project thinking I will work for just an hour and then find myself still painting hours later because I want to see the finished product.

3. *Avoid heavy emphasis on grades and competition.* An emphasis on grades forces students to be ego-involved rather than task-involved. Anxious students are especially hard hit by highly competitive evaluation.
4. *Reduce the task risk without oversimplifying the task.* When tasks are risky (failure is likely and the consequences of failing are grave), student motivation suffers. For difficult, complex, or ambiguous tasks, provide students with plenty of time, support, resources, help, and the chance to revise or improve work.
5. *Model motivation to learn for your students.* Talk about your interest in the subject and how you deal with difficult learning problems.
6. *Teach the particular learning tactics* that students will need to master the material being studied. Show students how to learn and remember so they won't be forced to fall back on self-defeating strategies or rote memory.

Do I Belong in This Classroom? This last question will take more than a page or two to address, so I have devoted a large part of the next chapter (Chapter 11) to the notion of engagement and belonging. We will look at cooperative learning and at creating learning communities. The support of families can be helpful as you design strategies for your students. The *Family and Community Partnerships Guidelines* on page 406 give ideas for working with families.

Connect and **Extend** to Your **Teaching/Portfolio**

Add some ideas for parent involvement from this chapter to your Portfolio.

SUMMARY TABLE

What Is Motivation? (pp. 372–377)

Define motivation. Motivation is an internal state that arouses, directs, and maintains behavior. The study of motivation focuses on how and why people initiate actions directed toward specific goals, how long it takes them to get started in the activity, how intensively they are involved in the activity, how persistent they are in their attempts to reach these goals, and what they are thinking and feeling along the way.

What is the difference between intrinsic and extrinsic motivation? Intrinsic motivation is the natural tendency to seek out and conquer challenges as we pursue personal interests and exercise capabilities—it is motivation to do something when we don't have to. Extrinsic motivation is based on factors not related to the activity itself. We are not really interested in the activity for its own sake; we care only about what it will gain us.

How does locus of causality apply to motivation? The essential difference between intrinsic and extrinsic motivation is the person's reason for acting, that is, whether the locus of causality for the action is inside or outside the person. If the locus is internal, the motivation is intrinsic; if the locus is external, the motivation is extrinsic. Most motivation has elements of both. In fact, intrinsic and extrinsic motivation may be two separate tendencies—both can operate at the same time in a given situation.

What are the key factors in motivation according to a behavioral viewpoint? A humanistic viewpoint? A cognitive viewpoint? A sociocultural viewpoint? Behaviorists tend to emphasize extrinsic motivation caused by incentives, rewards, and punishment. Humanistic views stress the intrinsic motivation created by the need for personal growth, fulfillment, and self-determination. Cognitive views stress a person's active search for meaning, understanding, and competence, and the power of the individual's attributions and interpretations. Sociocultural views emphasize legitimate engaged participation and identity within a community.

Distinguish between deficiency needs and being needs in Maslow's theory. Maslow called four lower-level needs—survival, safety, belonging, and self-esteem—deficiency needs. When these needs are satisfied, the motivation for fulfilling them decreases. He labeled the three higher-level needs—intellectual achievement, aesthetic appreciation, and self-actualization—being needs. When they are met, a person's motivation increases to seek further fulfillment.

What are expectancy × value theories? Expectancy × value theories suggest that motivation to reach a goal is the product of our expectations for success and the value of the goal to us. If either is zero, our motivation is zero also.

What is legitimate peripheral participation? Legitimate peripheral participation means that beginners are genuinely involved in the work of the group, even if their abilities are undeveloped and their contributions are small. The identities of the novice and the expert are bound up in their participation in the community. They are motivated to learn the values and practices of the community to keep their identity as community members.

Motivation An internal state that arouses, directs, and maintains behavior.

Intrinsic motivation Motivation associated with activities that are their own reward.

Extrinsic motivation Motivation created by external factors such as rewards and punishments.

Locus of causality The location—internal or external—of the cause of behavior.

Reward An attractive object or event supplied as a consequence of a behavior.

Incentive An object or event that encourages or discourages behavior.

Humanistic interpretation Approach to motivation that emphasizes personal freedom, choice, self-determination, and striving for personal growth.

Hierarchy of needs Maslow's model of seven levels of human needs, from basic physiological requirements to the need for self-actualization.

Self-actualization Fulfilling one's potential.

Deficiency needs Maslow's four lower-level needs, which must be satisfied first.

Being needs Maslow's three higher-level needs, sometimes called growth needs.

Expectancy × value theories Explanations of motivation that emphasize individuals' expectations for success combined with their valuing of the goal.

Sociocultural views of motivation Perspectives that emphasize participation, identities, and interpersonal relations within communities of practice.

Legitimate peripheral participation Genuine involvement in the work of the group, even if your abilities are undeveloped and contributions are small.

Needs: Competence, Autonomy, and Relatedness (pp. 377–379)

What are the basic needs that affect motivation and how does self-determination affect motivation? Self-determination theory suggests that motivation is affected by the need for competence, autonomy and control, and relatedness. When students experience self-determination, they are intrinsically motivated—they are more interested in their work, have a greater sense of self-esteem, and learn more. Whether students experience self-determination depends in part on if the teacher's communications with students provide information or seek to control them. In addition, teachers must acknowledge the students' perspective, offer choices, provide rationales for limits, and treat poor performance as a problem to be solved rather than a target for criticism.

Need for autonomy The desire to have our own wishes, rather than external rewards or pressures, determine our actions.

Cognitive evaluation theory Suggests that events affect motivation through the individual's perception of the events as controlling behavior or providing information.

Goal Orientations and Motivation

(pp. 380–383)

What kinds of goals are the most motivating? Goals increase motivation if they are specific, moderately difficult, and able to be reached in the near future.

Describe mastery, performance, work-avoidant, and social goals. A mastery goal is the intention to gain knowledge and master skills, leading students to seek challenges and persist when they encounter difficulties. A performance goal is the intention to get good grades or to appear smarter or more capable than others, leading students to be preoccupied with themselves and how they appear (ego-involved learners). Students can approach or avoid these two kinds of goals—the problems are greatest with avoidance. Another kind of avoidance is evident with work-avoidant learners, who simply want to find the easiest way to handle the situation. Students with social goals can be supported or hindered in their learning, depending on the specific goal (i.e., have fun with friends or bring honor to the family).

What makes goal-setting effective in the classroom? In order for goal-setting to be effective in the classroom, students need accurate feedback about their progress toward goals and they must accept the goals set. Generally, students are more willing to adopt goals that seem realistic, reasonably difficult, and meaningful, and for which good reasons are given for the value of the goals.

Goal What an individual strives to accomplish.

Goal orientations Patterns of beliefs about goals related to achievement in school.

Mastery goal A personal intention to improve abilities and learn, no matter how performance suffers.

Task-involved learners Students who focus on mastering the task or solving the problem.

Performance goal A personal intention to seem competent or perform well in the eyes of others.

Ego-involved learners Students who focus on how well they are performing and how they are judged by others.

Work-avoidant learners Students who don't want to learn or to look smart, but just want to avoid work.

Social goals A wide variety of needs and motives to be connected to others or part of a group.

Interests and Emotions (pp. 383–388)

How do interests and emotions affect learning? Learning and information processing are influenced by emotion. Students are more likely to pay attention to, learn, and remember events, images, and readings that provoke emotional responses or that are related to their personal interests. However, there are cautions in responding to students' interests. "Seductive details," interesting bits of information that are not central to the learning, can hinder learning.

What is the role of arousal in learning? There appears to be an optimum level of arousal for most activities. Generally speaking, a higher level of arousal is helpful on simple tasks, but lower levels of arousal are better for complex tasks. When arousal is too low, teachers can stimulate curiosity by pointing out gaps in knowledge or using variety in activities. Severe anxiety is an example of arousal that is too high for optimal learning.

How does anxiety interfere with learning? Anxiety can be the cause or the result of poor performance; it can interfere with attention to, learning of, and retrieval of information. Many anxious students need help in developing effective test-taking and study skills.

Arousal Physical and psychological reactions causing a person to be alert, attentive, wide awake.

Anxiety General uneasiness, a feeling of tension.

Beliefs and Self-Schemas (pp. 388–394)

How do beliefs about ability affect motivation? When people hold an entity theory of ability—that is, they believe that ability is fixed—they tend to set performance goals and strive to protect themselves from failure. When they believe ability is improvable (an incremental theory), however, they tend to set mastery goals and handle failure constructively.

What are the three dimensions of attributions in Weiner's theory? According to Weiner, most of the attributed causes for successes or failures can be characterized in terms of three dimensions: *locus* (location of the cause internal or external to the person), *stability* (whether the cause stays the same or can change), and *responsibility* (whether the person can control the cause). The greatest motivational problems arise when students attribute failures to stable, uncontrollable causes. These students may seem resigned to failure, depressed, helpless—what we generally call "unmotivated."

What is self-efficacy, and how does it relate to learned helplessness? Self-efficacy is a belief about personal competence in a particular situation such as learning or teaching fractions. A sense of efficacy, control, or self-determination is critical if people are to feel intrinsically motivated. When people come to believe that the events and outcomes in their lives are mostly uncontrollable, they have developed learned helplessness, which is associated with three types of deficits: motivational, cognitive, and affective. Students who feel hopeless will be unmotivated and reluctant to attempt work. They miss opportunities to practice and improve skills and abilities, so they develop cognitive deficits and they often suffer from affective problems such as depression, anxiety, and listlessness.

How does self-worth influence motivation? Mastery-oriented students tend to value achievement and see ability as improvable, so they focus on mastery goals, take risks, and cope with failure constructively. A low sense of self-worth seems to be linked with the failure-avoiding and failure-accepting strategies intended to protect the individual from the consequences of failure. These strategies may seem to help in the short term, but are damaging to motivation and self-esteem in the long run.

Entity view of ability Belief that ability is a fixed characteristic that cannot be changed.

Incremental view of ability Belief that ability is a set of skills that can be changed.

Attribution theories Descriptions of how individuals' explanations, justifications, and excuses influence their motivation and behavior.

Self-efficacy Beliefs about personal competence in a particular situation.

Learned helplessness The expectation, based on previous experiences with a lack of control, that all one's efforts will lead to failure.

Mastery-oriented students Students who focus on learning goals because they value achievement and see ability as improvable.

Failure-avoiding students Students who avoid failure by sticking to what they know, by not taking risks, or by claiming not to care about their performance.

Failure-accepting students Students who believe their failures are due to low ability and there is little they can do about it.

Motivation to Learn in School: On TARGET (pp. 395–402)

Define motivation to learn. Teachers are interested in a particular kind of motivation—student motivation to learn. Student motivation to learn is both a trait and a state. It involves taking academic work seriously, trying to get the most from it, and applying appropriate learning strategies in the process.

What does TARGET stand for? TARGET is an acronym for the six areas where teachers make decisions that can influence student motivation to learn: the nature of the *task* that students are asked to do, the *autonomy* students are allowed in working, how students are *recognized* for their accomplishments, *grouping* practices, *evaluation* procedures, and the scheduling of *time* in the classroom.

How do tasks affect motivation? The tasks that teachers set affect motivation. When students encounter tasks that are related to their interests, stimulate their curiosity, or are connected to real-life situations, the students are more likely to be motivated to learn. Tasks can have attainment, intrinsic, or utility value for students. Attainment value is the importance to the student of succeeding. Intrinsic value is the enjoyment the student gets from the task. Utility value is determined by how much the task contributes to reaching short-term or long-term goals.

Distinguish between bounded and unbounded choices. Like totally unguided discovery or aimless discussions, unstructured or unbounded choices can be counterproductive for learning. The alternative is bounded choice—giving students a range of options that set out valuable tasks for them, but also allow them to follow personal interests. The balance must be just right so that students are not bewildered by too much choice or bored by too little room to explore.

How can recognition undermine motivation and a sense of self-efficacy? Recognition and reward in the classroom will support motivation to learn if the recognition is for personal progress rather than competitive victories. Praise and rewards should focus on students' growing competence. At times, praise can have paradoxical effects when students use the teacher's praise or criticism as cues about capabilities.

List three goal structures and distinguish among them. How students relate to their peers in the classroom is influenced by the goal structure of the activities. Goal structures can be competitive, individualistic, or cooperative. Cooperative goal structures can encourage motivation and increase learning, especially for low-achieving students.

How does evaluative climate affect goal-setting? The more competitive the grading, the more students set performance goals and focus on "looking competent," that is, the more they are ego-involved. When the focus is on performing rather than learning, students often see the goal of classroom tasks as simply finishing, especially if the work is difficult.

What are some effects of time on motivation? In order to foster motivation to learn, teachers should be flexible in their use of time in the classroom. Students who are forced to move faster or slower than they should or who are interrupted as they become involved in a project are not likely to develop persistence for learning.

Motivation to learn The tendency to find academic activities meaningful and worthwhile and to try to benefit from them.

Academic tasks The work the student must accomplish, including the content covered and the mental operations required.

Importance/attainment value The importance of doing well on a task; how success on the task meets personal needs.

Intrinsic or interest value The enjoyment a person gets from a task.

Utility value The contribution of a task to meeting one's goals.

Authentic task Tasks that have some connection to real-life problems the students will face outside the classroom.

Problem-based learning Methods that provide students with realistic problems that don't necessarily have right answers.

Goal structure The way students relate to others who are also working toward a particular goal.

mylabschool™
Where the classroom comes to life!

MyLabSchool is a collection of online tools for your success in this course, your licensure exams, and your teaching career. Visit **www.mylabschool.com** to access the following:

- On-line Study Guide
- Video Cases from real classrooms
- Help with your research papers using Research Navigator
- Career Center with resources for:
  - Praxis and Licensure Preparation
  - Professional Portfolio Development
  - Job Search and Interview Techniques
  - Lesson Planning

Teachers' Casebook: Connections to PRAXIS II™

Consider these questions as you reflect on the case at the beginning of the chapter: How much *self-determination* did you have in choosing to work in this school district and in taking this assignment? What kinds of *expectations* are being communicated to you when you request resources? Are the curriculum and the district-wide assessments causing you to establish *goals* for yourself and your students?

What Would They Do?

Here is how some practicing teachers responded to motivate students when resources are slim.

Aimee Fredette **Second Grade Teacher,**
Fisher Elementary School, Walpole, Massachusetts

A very effective way that I use to get the children curious and interested is to pose a question to the class before the start of a lesson. This gives the children a focus for the lesson. As the year progresses, the children begin coming up with questions of their own. Another very successful way to spark interest and curiosity is the use of three-column activators, a brainstorming activity that the teacher and students do together. The students brainstorm WHAT WE THINK WE KNOW about the topic. The teacher records *all* responses, writing them on chart paper. Then the children brainstorm WHAT WE WANT TO KNOW about the topic. Again the teacher would record their responses. The third column, titled WHAT WE HAVE LEARNED, is added to as the theme progresses. The first two columns are referred to as the children learn about the theme.

Danielle Hartman **Second Grade Teacher,**
Claymont Elementary School, Ballwin, Missouri

First of all, don't get discouraged. You don't need a textbook in order to be a successful teacher. Look over the district's curriculum guides and see what the objectives are for each unit you will be teaching. Once you know the objectives, get creative. Keeping the students motivated and interested in learning is essential. By giving them choice and using a variety of teaching methods you will allow them to stay actively engaged in their learning. You will be amazed at what the students will come up with when they are given choices.

Michael Yasis
L.H. Tanglen Elementary School, Minnetonka, Minnesota

Most learning is acquired through active learning and participation. Therefore, the workbooks that focus on drill and practice, if given as the primary source of learning, most likely would bore the students. I would approach this situation by first engaging the students in a discussion to assess their prior knowledge. I would then challenge and extend their understanding of the concepts through guided discovery, building on similar examples from the "boring" workbooks. While they work on the concepts independently in their workbooks, their confidence and self-esteem will increase.

Kelly McElroy Bonin **High School Counselor,**
Klein Oak High School, Spring, Texas

Simply being excited to be working with the 3rd graders and showing interest and enthusiasm for the subject matter should arouse the students' interest and encourage them to learn. How many times have you heard it said, "Mrs. Energy was the best teacher I ever had. She took the most boring, difficult subject and made it fun and interesting." I have heard this so many times both as a student and as a teacher, and it proves my point. Just the fact that the teacher is excited about the material shows the students that this is important information that they need, plus they are curious about the material when they respect and like their teacher. If I felt like the difficulty level of the text books was too great, I would have to break the lessons down into smaller increments and use different techniques—discussion, re-teaching, group projects, etc.—to enrich the students and adapt to their level of learning. When your students are motivated, they can accomplish anything—it doesn't matter what materials are available to them, what the difficulty level of the textbook is, and so on. Kids will be motivated when their teacher truly cares about them, is passionate about the material, and makes school interesting.

Pam Gaskill **Second Grade Teacher,**
Riverside Elementary School, Dublin, Ohio

Teaching is inherently creative. Use your time and creativity this summer to acquaint yourself with the required objectives and think about ways in which you can make them meaningful and relevant to your students. Explore other available resources in the community, such as libraries, speakers' bureaus, and resource centers. Plan to incorporate a variety of activities such as videos, group work, field trips, projects, and speakers so that your students will remain interested and involved. Utilize materials that your students have access to from home—books, videos, artifacts, Internet printouts. It is amazing how cooperative parents can be when asked to help in specified ways. You might even make use of the old workbook pages, not in the traditional way, but for cooperative work. You can facilitate student success by pairing weaker readers with more competent readers to discuss and complete the worksheets. Stress that everyone needs to work together to learn the material. Active participation and engagement with the materials will help your students to construct their own meanings more effectively.

CHAPTER 11

Engaged Learning: Cooperation and Community

Teachers' Casebook: What Would You Do? 413

Social Processes in Learning 414

Peers 414

Parents and Teachers 415

Collaboration and Cooperation 416

Collaboration, Group Work, and Cooperative Learning 417

Tasks for Cooperative Learning 419

Preparing Students for Cooperative Learning 419

Designs for Cooperation 423

Reaching Every Student: Using Cooperative Learning Wisely 424

The Classroom Community 426

Constructive Conflict Resolution 427

Civic Values 429

Getting Started on Community 430

Belonging 432

Violence in Schools 432

Prevention 433

Respect and Protect 434

Community Outside the Classroom: Service Learning 434

Diversity and Convergences in Social Engagement 438

Diversity 438

Convergences 438

Summary Table 439

Teachers' Casebook: Connections to PRAXIS II™/What Would They Do? 441

What Would You Do?

Teachers' Casebook

When a terrible tragedy strikes, such as the events of 9/11 or a shooting in a school, how would you handle the situation? Assume you are in class on a Tuesday in the winter. It is late morning and you have just gone to lunch when you hear that a few students at a nearby high school have taken some teachers and other students hostage. Rumors are flying about whether the students have guns, what they want, who is involved, how many hostages there are, and when the incident began. Some students and teachers in your school have friends and relatives in this neighboring district. Several students are very upset—many in tears.

Critical Thinking

- What is your immediate response?
- How would you handle a student who is very upset and crying?
- What will you do over the next few weeks and months to respond to the students' concerns and fears about such frightening events?

Collaboration

With 2 other members of your class, draft what you would say to your class.

The opening sentence of *Engaging Schools*, a report of the Committee on Increasing High School Students' Engagement and Motivation to Learn (2004), is "Learning and succeeding in school requires active engagement—whether students are rich or poor, black, brown, or white" (p. 1). And engagement is about more than cognitive processes and individual motivation. Engagement, as the Committee report concluded, "depends on a student's involvement in a web of social relations" (2004, p. 17).

In this chapter, we look at several important aspects of engagement that are critical for success both in and out of school. We begin with collaboration and cooperation—working with others to learn. Next, we examine the idea of the larger classroom community. Finally, we move to examine learning through engagement outside the classroom walls. Throughout the chapter, we focus on what teachers can do to support engagement in learning for all students.

By the time you have completed this chapter, you should be able to answer the following questions.

- How do social relationships affect learning in school?
- How can cooperative learning strategies promote academic and social development?
- What are some of the problems that might occur with cooperative learning, and how can I avoid them?
- How can I create a learning community in my classroom?
- What can be done to prevent and respond to school violence?
- What are the possibilities and potential problems with service learning?

FACING PAGE *Children*, Kazimir Malevich. Photo: Scala/Art Resource, New York.

This girl is clearly engaged in learning. What web of social relations might support her engagement?

The focus of this chapter is engaged learning. In some ways, the chapter is a culmination of what we have learned so far about individual differences, learning, and motivation. Engagement includes *behaviors* such as attention, effort, persistence, and resistance to distractions as well as *emotions* such as enthusiasm, pride, interest, and enjoyment. Students can be engaged with their schools through friendships with peers and teachers, participation in team sports, and involvement in extra-curricular activities, so engagement may incorporate *social connections.* Finally, engagement is *cognitive* because engaged students are investing their mental abilities in learning. They are using cognitive and metacognitive strategies, processing information, remembering, and forming beliefs about themselves as learners.

Engaged learning is important for all students and schools because engaged students tend to be higher-achieving students; disengaged students are more likely to skip classes or drop out of school altogether (Fredricks, Blumenfeld, & Paris, 2004). The consequences of disengagement are serious, especially for students placed at risk by poverty or discrimination. Students from privileged families can recover from dropping out of school, whether the dropping out is psychological or actual. But students without advantages pay dearly in terms of life choices if they are disengaged. Without educational credentials and skills, these students are at risk of poverty, unemployment, poor health, and involvement in the criminal justice system. Yet many schools serving these students fail to engage them cognitively, emotionally, or behaviorally (Committee on Increasing High School Students' Engagement and Motivation to Learn, 2004). What is needed? Attention to social processes is critical.

Social Processes in Learning

Connect and Extend to the Research

The May 1999 and the May 2000 issues of *The Elementary School Journal* are entirely devoted to the non-subject-matter outcomes of school such as social-emotional development, self-regulation, physical activity, and service learning.

Connect and Extend to the Research

See the entire issue of *Educational Leadership*, September 2002 (Vol. 60, No. 1) for 14 articles on "Do Students Care About Learning?" These articles discuss how to create enthusiasm, excitement, and investment in learning.

When you think about engagement in school, do you think about social and cultural influences on the students' learning? For example, do reading and books have different meanings for various students in your classes. Have your students seen different models of reading in their lives outside school. In the following pages, we will discuss how people learn through interactions with others and how social interaction, dialogue, and culture affect learning—all are increasingly important topics in educational psychology. Two decades ago, Jerome Bruner, who pioneered the study of individual concept learning, said, "I have come increasingly to recognize that learning in most settings is a communal activity, a sharing of culture" (1986, p. 27).

Let's consider three social influences on students—peers, parents, and teachers.

Peers

STOP | THINK | WRITE Think back to high school—did you have friends in any of these groups: normals, populars, brains, jocks, partyers, druggies, others? What were the main "crowds" at your school? How did your friends influence you? ■

Laurence Steinberg and his colleagues have studied the role of parents, peers, and community contexts in school achievement (Durbin, Darling, Steinberg, & Brown, 1993; Steinberg, 1996, 1998). Based on a three-year study that surveyed 20,000 students in nine high schools in Wisconsin and California, Steinberg concluded that about 40% of these students were just going through the motions of learning. When they were in class, they were not really paying attention or trying very hard to learn. About 90% had copied someone else's homework and 66% had cheated on a test within the last year. Steinberg claims that this lack of investment is due in part to peer pressure. "For a large number of adolescents, peers—not parents—are the chief determinants of how intensely they are invested in school and how much effort they devote to their education" (1998, p. 331). Results of his research indicate that peers provide incentives for certain activities and ridicule others, which creates a school culture that affects the way the teachers behave.

One in every five students said that their friends make fun of people who tried to do well in school. When asked what crowd they would most like to belong to:

> [F]ive times as many students say the "populars" or "jocks" as say the "brains." Three times as many say they would rather be "partyers" or "druggies" than "brains." And of all the crowds, the "brains" were least happy with who they are—nearly half wished they were in a different crowd. (Steinberg, 1998, p. 332)

Children are not randomly assigned to friendship groups, cliques, and crowds. In elementary school, children tend to select friends who share their orientation toward school (Wentzel, 1999). A study by Jill Hamm (2000) comparing friendship patterns of African American, Asian American, and European American adolescents found that members of all three groups chose friends who were similar (but not identical) in substance use and somewhat similar in academic orientation. African Americans were more likely than the other two groups to select friends who were similar in terms of ethnic identity, however.

There also is some evidence that academic achievement is less valued in African American peer groups than in Asian American or European American groups (Steinberg, Dornbusch, & Brown, 1992; Wentzel & Battle, 2001). But we have to be careful about research that overlooks possible individual and group differences. For example, when European American, Hispanic American, and African American adolescents were asked to nominate peers they most admired, respected, and wanted to be like, girls in all three groups and European American boys nominated high-achieving peers. In contrast, African American and Hispanic American boys nominated low-achieving boys as their most admired peers (Graham, Taylor, & Hudley, 1998).

Parents and Teachers

Parents and teachers play a role, too. When 3,407 9th- through 12th-grade European American students described their parents' styles and their peer-group orientation, adolescents who characterized their parents as authoritative (demanding but responsive, rational, and democratic) were more likely to favor well-rounded crowds that rewarded both adult- and peer-supported norms such as "normals" and "brains." Students, especially girls, who characterized their parents as uninvolved were more likely to be oriented toward "partyers" and "druggies" who did not endorse adult values. Finally, boys with indulgent parents were more likely to be oriented toward fun-cultures such as "partyers" (Durbin, Darling, Steinberg, & Brown, 1993). In fact, adolescents with authoritative parents are more likely to respond to peer pressure to do well in school and less likely to be swayed by peer pressure to use drugs or alcohol, especially when their friends also have authoritative parents (Collins, Maccoby, Steinberg, Hetherington, & Bornstein, 2000).

Connect and **Extend** to **Other Chapters**

We saw in Chapter 3 that caring teachers are especially important for students who are placed at risk in schools.

When children do not have friends or have few friends, parents and teachers can play an important role in supporting school achievement. Kathryn Wentzel and her colleagues have found that perceived support from teachers is related to positive motivation for learning and adjustment in school for students (Wentzel & Battle, 2001). In addition, being liked by teachers can offset the negative effects of peer rejection in middle school. And students who have few friends, but are not rejected—simply ignored by other students—can remain well-adjusted academically and socially when they are liked and supported by teachers.

We can sum up the importance of social processes in supporting engaged learning by listening to the report of the Committee on Increasing High School Students' Engagement and Motivation to Learn (2004):

> Although learning involves cognitive processes that take place within each individual, motivation to learn also depends on the student's involvement in a web of social relationships that supports learning. The likelihood that students will be motivated and engaged is increased to the extent that their teachers, family, and friends effectively support their purposeful involvement in learning in school. Thus a focus on engagement calls attention to the connection between a learner and the social context in which learning takes place. Engaging schools promote a sense of belonging by personalizing instruction, showing an interest in students' lives, and creating a supportive, caring social environment. (p. 3)

In order to explore how to create a supportive, caring social environment, we begin by examining collaboration and cooperation.

Collaboration and Cooperation

Even with all the concern about academic standards, performance on proficiency tests, and international comparisons of student achievement, schooling has always been about more than academic learning. Of course, academics are the prime directive, "but schools have major responsibilities for other aspects of students' development as well, such as helping students develop the attitudes, skills, and orientations needed to lead humane lives and act effectively as citizens to sustain democratic institutions" (Battistich, Watson, Solomon, Lewis, & Schaps, 1999). In addition, an education that prepares students to live humane lives has value in the corporate marketplace:

> Most corporations are looking for employees who are not only good at the mastery of a particular set of academic skills but who also have the ability to work harmoniously with a wide variety of coworkers as a cooperative team, to demonstrate initiative and responsibility, and to communicate effectively. (Aronson, 2000, p. 91)

Connect and **Extend** to the **Research**

The Winter 2002 issue of *Theory Into Practice* is devoted to "Promoting Thinking Through Peer Learning." The editor for this volume was Angela O'Donnell, one of the top researchers in the area of cooperative learning. There are articles by Noreen Webb, Alison King, Annemarie Palincsar, and others.

For the past three decades, researchers have examined collaboration and cooperation in schools. Although there are some inconsistencies, the majority of the studies indicate that truly cooperative groups have positive effects on students' empathy, tolerance for differences, feelings of acceptance, friendships, self-confidence, and even school attendance (Solomon, Watson, & Battistich, 2001). It is even argued that cooperative learning experiences are crucial in preventing many of the social problems that plague children and adolescents (Gillies, 2003, 2004).

Effectively used cooperative learning strategies enhance collaborative skills, positive interdependence, and individual accountability.

Collaboration, Group Work, and Cooperative Learning

The terms *collaboration, group work,* and *cooperative learning* often are used as if they meant the same thing. Certainly there is some overlap, but there are differences as well. The distinctions between collaboration and cooperation are not always clear. Ted Panitz (1996) suggests the following differences. **Collaboration** is a philosophy about how to relate to others—how to learn and work. Collaboration is a way of dealing with people that respects differences, shares authority, and builds on the knowledge that is distributed among other people. **Cooperation,** on the other hand, is a way of working with others to attain a shared goal (Gillies, 2003). Collaborative learning has roots in the work of British teachers who wanted their students to respond to literature in more active ways as they learned. Cooperative learning has American roots in the work of psychologists John Dewey and Kurt Lewin. You could say that cooperative learning is one way to collaborate.

Group work, on the other hand, is simply several students working together—they may or may not be cooperating. Many activities can be completed in groups. For example, students can work together to conduct a local survey. How do people feel about the plan to build a new mall that will bring more shopping and more traffic? Would the community support or oppose the building of a nuclear power plant? If students must learn 10 new definitions in a biology class, why not let students divide up the terms and definitions and teach one another? Be sure, however, that everyone in the group can handle the task. Sometimes, one or two students end up doing the work of the entire group.

Group work can be useful, but true cooperative learning requires much more than simply putting students in groups. Angela O'Donnell and Jim O'Kelly, colleagues of mine at Rutgers University, describe a teacher who claimed to be using "cooperative learning" by asking students to work in pairs on a paper, each writing one part. Unfortunately, the teacher allowed no time to work together and provided no guidance or preparation in cooperative social skills. Students got a grade for their individual part and a group grade for the whole project. One student received an A for his part, but a C for the group project because his partner earned an F—he never turned in any work. So one student was punished with a C for a situation he could not control while the other was rewarded with a C for doing no work at all. This was not cooperative learning—it wasn't even group work (O'Donnell & O'Kelly, 1994).

Connect and Extend to Other Chapters

The need for belonging is the third level of Maslow's hierarchy, discussed in Chapter 10. The need to maintain relationships is strong. I was reminded of this when my daughter was reprimanded by her 4th-grade teacher for passing notes during class. Liz's explanation was that there had been a fight during lunch, "and we had to work it out!"

Beyond Groups to Cooperation. **Cooperative learning** has a long history in American education. In the early 1900s, John Dewey criticized the use of competition in education and encouraged educators to structure schools as democratic learning communities. These ideas fell from favor in the 1940s and 1950s, and were replaced by a resurgence of competition. In the 1960s, there was a swing back to individualized and cooperative learning structures, stimulated in part by concern for civil rights and interracial relations (Webb & Palincsar, 1996). Today, evolving constructivist perspectives on learning fuel interest in collaboration and cooperative learning and "there is a heightened interest in situations where elaboration, interpretation, explanation, and argumentation are integral to the activity of the group and where learning is supported by other individuals" (Webb & Palincsar, 1996, p. 844).

Different learning theory approaches favor cooperative learning for different reasons (O'Donnell, 2002; O'Donnell & O'Kelly, 1994). Information processing theorists point to the value of group discussion in helping participants rehearse, elaborate, and expand their knowledge. As group members question and explain, they have to organize their knowledge, make connections, and review—all processes that support information processing and memory. Advocates of a Piagetian perspective suggest that the interactions in groups can create the cognitive conflict and disequilibrium that lead an individual to question his or her understanding and try out new ideas—or, as Piaget (1985) said, "to go beyond his current state and strike out in new directions" (p. 10). Those who favor Vygotsky's theory suggest that social interaction is important for learning because higher mental functions such as reasoning, comprehension, and critical thinking originate in social interactions

Collaboration A philosophy about how to deal with people that respects differences, shares authority, and builds on the knowledge of others.

Cooperation Working together with others to reach a shared goal.

Cooperative learning Arrangement in which students work in mixed-ability groups and are rewarded on the basis of the success of the group.

TABLE 11.1

Different Forms of Cooperative Learning for Different Purposes

Different forms of cooperative learning (Elaboration, Piagetian, and Vygotskian) fit different purposes, need different structures, and have their own potential problems and possible solutions.

Considerations	Elaboration	Piagetian	Vygotskian
Group size	Small (2–4)	Small	Dyads
Group composition	Heterogeneous/homogeneous	Homogeneous	Heterogeneous
Tasks	Rehearsal/integrative	Exploratory	Skills
Teacher role	Facilitator	Facilitator	Model/guide
Potential problems	Poor help-giving Unequal participation	Inactive No cognitive conflict	Poor help-giving Providing adequate time/dialogue
Averting problems	Direct instruction in help-giving Modeling help-giving Scripting interaction	Structuring controversy	Direct instruction in help-giving Modeling help-giving

Source: From *Educational Psychology Review, 6,* p. 327, "Learning from Peers: Beyond the Rhetoric of Positive Results," by A. M. O'Donnell and J. O'Kelly. Copyright © 1994 by Plenum Publishing Corporation. Reprinted with kind permission from Springer Science and Business Media.

and are then internalized by individuals. Children can accomplish mental tasks with social support before they can do them alone. Thus, cooperative learning provides the social support and scaffolding that students need to move learning forward.

Table 11.1 summarizes the functions of cooperative learning from different theoretical perspectives, and describes some of the elements of each kind of group. To benefit from these dimensions of cooperative learning, groups must *be cooperative*—all members must participate. But, as any teacher or parent knows, cooperation is not automatic when students are put into groups.

What Can Go Wrong: Misuses of Group Learning. Without careful planning and monitoring by the teacher, group interactions can hinder learning and reduce rather than improve social relations in classes. For example, if there is pressure in a group for conformity—perhaps because rewards are being misused or one student dominates the others—interactions can be unproductive and unreflective. Misconceptions might be reinforced or the worst, not the best, ideas may be combined to construct a superficial understanding (Battistich, Solomon, & Delucci, 1993). Students who work in groups but arrive at wrong answers may be more confident that they are right—a case of "two heads are worse than one" (Puncochar & Fox, 2004). Also, the ideas of low-status students may be ignored or even ridiculed while the contributions of high-status students are accepted and reinforced, regardless of the merit of either set of ideas (Anderson, Holland, & Palincsar, 1997; Cohen, 1986). Mary McCaslin and Tom Good (1996) list several other disadvantages of group learning:

- Students often value the process or procedures over the learning. Speed and finishing early take precedence over thoughtfulness and learning.
- Rather than challenging and correcting misconceptions, students support and reinforce misunderstandings.
- Socializing and interpersonal relationships may take precedence over learning.
- Students may simply shift dependency from the teacher to the "expert" in the group—learning is still passive and what is learned can be wrong.
- Status differences may be increased rather than decreased. Some students learn to "loaf" because the group progresses with or without their contributions. Others become even more convinced that they are unable to understand without the support of the group.

The next sections examine how teachers can avoid these problems and encourage true cooperation.

Tasks for Cooperative Learning

Like so many other decisions in teaching, plans for using cooperative groups begin with a goal. What are students supposed to accomplish? What is the task? Tasks for cooperative groups may be more or less structured. Highly structured tasks include work that has right answers—drill and practice, applying routines or procedures, answering questions from readings, computations in mathematics, and so on. Ill-structured complex tasks have multiple answers and unclear procedures, requiring problem finding and higher-order thinking. These ill-structured problems are true group tasks; that is, they are likely to require the resources (knowledge, skills, problem-solving strategies, creativity) of all the group members to accomplish, whereas highly structured tasks often can be accomplished just as effectively by individuals. These distinctions are important because ill-structured, complex, true group tasks appear to require more and higher-quality interactions than routine tasks, if learning and problem solving are to occur (Cohen, 1994; Gillies, 2004).

Highly Structured, Review, and Skill-Building Tasks. A relatively structured task such as reviewing previously learned material for an exam might be well served by a structured technique such as STAD (Student Teams Achievement Divisions), in which teams of four students compete to determine which team's members can amass the greatest improvement over previous achievement levels (Slavin, 1995). Praise, recognition, or extrinsic rewards can enhance motivation, effort, and persistence under these conditions, and thus increase learning. Focusing the dialogue by assigning narrow roles also may help students stay engaged when the tasks are routine, practice, or review.

Ill-Structured, Conceptual, and Problem-Solving Tasks. If the task is ill-structured and more cognitive in nature, then an open exchange and elaborated discussion will be more helpful (Cohen, 1994; Ross & Raphael, 1990). Thus, strategies that encourage extended and productive interactions are appropriate when the goal is to develop higher-order thinking and problem solving. In these situations, a tightly structured process, competition among groups for rewards, and rigid assignment of roles is likely to inhibit the richness of the students' interactions and interfere with progress toward the goal. Open-ended techniques such as reciprocal questioning (King, 1994), reciprocal teaching (Palincsar & Brown, 1984; Rosenshine & Meister, 1994), pair-share (Kagan, 1994), or jigsaw should be more productive because, when used appropriately, they encourage more extensive interaction and elaborate thought in situations where students are being exposed to complex materials. In these instances, the use of rewards may well divert the group away from the goal of in-depth cognitive processing. When rewards are offered, the goal often becomes achieving the reward as efficiently as possible (Webb & Palincsar, 1996).

Social Skills and Communication Tasks. When the goal of peer learning is enhanced social skills or increased intergroup understanding and appreciation of diversity, the assignment of specific roles and functions within the group might support communication (Cohen, 1994; Kagan, 1994). In these situations, it can be helpful to rotate leadership roles so that minority group students and females have the opportunity to demonstrate and develop leadership skills; in addition, all group members can experience the leadership capabilities of each individual (Miller & Harrington, 1993). Rewards probably are not necessary, and they may actually get in the way because the goal is to build community, a sense of respect, and responsibility for all team members.

Preparing Students for Cooperative Learning

WHAT WOULD YOU SAY?

As part of the interview process for a job in an elementary school, you are asked the following: "Do you use group work in your teaching? Why or why not? How would you use it in this school?" ■

David and Roger Johnson (1999) list five elements that define true cooperative learning groups:

Face-to-face interaction	Positive interdependence	Individual accountability
Collaborative skills	Group processing	

Connect and **Extend** to **PRAXIS II™**

Characteristics of Cooperative Learning (II, A2)

Many instructional strategies labeled as "cooperative learning" lack one or more qualities that are essential components of such techniques. List those essential qualities and explain the role of each.

Students *interact face-to-face* and close together, not across the room. Group members experience *positive interdependence*—they need each other for support, explanations, and guidance. Even though they work together and help each other, members of the group must ultimately demonstrate learning on their own; they are held *individually accountable* for learning, often through individual tests or other assessments. *Collaborative skills* are necessary for effective group functioning. Often, these skills, such as giving constructive feedback, reaching consensus, and involving every member, must be taught and practiced before the groups tackle a learning task. Finally, members monitor *group processes* and relationships to make sure the group is working effectively and to learn about the dynamics of groups. They take time to ask, "How are we doing as a group? Is everyone working together?"

Research in grades 8 through 12 in Australia found that students in cooperative groups structured to require positive interdependence and mutual helping learned more in math, science, and English than students in unstructured learning groups (Gillies, 2003). In addition, compared to students in the unstructured groups, students in the structured groups also said learning was more fun.

Setting Up Cooperative Groups. How large should a cooperative group be? Again, the answer depends on your learning goals. If the purpose is for the group members to review, rehearse information, or practice, 4 to 5 or 6 students is about the right size. But if the goal is to encourage each student to participate in discussions, problem solving, or computer learning, then groups of 2 to 4 members work best. Also, when setting up cooperative groups, it often makes sense to balance the number of boys and girls. Some research indicates that when there are just a few girls in a group, they tend to be left out of the discussions unless they are the most able or assertive members. By contrast, when there are only one or two boys in the group, they tend to dominate and be "interviewed" by the girls unless these boys are less able than the girls or are very shy. In general, for very shy and introverted students, individual learning may be a better approach (O'Donnell & O'Kelly, 1994; Webb, 1985; Webb & Palincsar, 1996). Whatever the case, teachers must monitor groups to make sure everyone is contributing and learning.

Giving and Receiving Explanations. In practice, the effects of learning in a group vary, depending on what actually happens in the group and who is in it. If only a few people take responsibility for the work, these people will learn, but the nonparticipating members probably will not. Students who ask questions, get answers, and attempt explanations are more likely to learn than students whose questions go unasked or unanswered. In fact, there is evidence that the more a student provides elaborated, thoughtful explanations to other students in a group, the more the *explainer* learns. Giving good explanations appears to be even more important for learning than receiving explanations (Webb, Farivar, & Mastergeorge, 2002; Webb & Palincsar, 1996). In order to explain, you have to organize the information, put it into your own words, think of examples and analogies (which connect the information to things you already know), and test your understanding by answering questions. These are excellent learning strategies (King, 1990, 2002; O'Donnell & O'Kelly, 1994).

Good explanations are relevant, timely, correct, and elaborated enough to help the listener correct misunderstandings; the best explanations tell why (Webb et al., 2002; Webb & Mastergeorge, 2003). For example, in a middle-school mathematics class, students worked in groups on the following problem:

> Find the cost of a 30-minute telephone call to the prefix 717 where the first minute costs \$0.22 and each additional minute costs \$0.13.

The level of explanation and help students received was significantly related to learning; the higher the level, the more learning. Table 11.2 shows the different levels of help. Of

TABLE 11.2

Levels of Help in Cooperative Groups
Students are more likely to learn if they give and get higher level help.

Level	Description and Example
Highest	
6	Verbally labeled explanation of how to solve part or all of the problem ("Multiply 13 cents by 29, because 29 minutes are left after the first minute.")
5	Numerical rule with no verbal labels for the numbers ("This is 30, so you minus 1.")
4	Numerical expression or equation ("13 times 29.")
3	Numbers to write or copy ("Put 13 on top, 29 on the bottom. Then you times it.")
2	Answer to part or all of the problem ("I got $3.77.")
1	Non-content or non-informational response ("Just do it the way she said.")
0	No response
Lowest	

Source: From "Productive helping in cooperative groups," by N. M. Webb, S. H. Farviar, & A. M. Mastergeorge. *Theory in Practice,* 41(1), p. 14.

course, the students must pay attention to and use the help to learn. And the help-receiver also has responsibilities if learning is to go well. For example, if a helper says, "13 times 29" then the receiver should say, "Why is it 29?" Asking good questions and giving clear explanations are critical, and usually these skills must be taught.

Assigning Roles. Some teachers assign roles to students to encourage cooperation and full participation. Several roles are described in Table 11.3. If you use roles, be sure that

TABLE 11.3

Possible Student Roles in Cooperative Learning Groups
Depending on the purpose of the group and the age of the participants, having these assigned roles might help students cooperate and learn. Of course, students may have to be taught how to enact each role effectively, and roles should be rotated so students can participate in different aspects of group learning.

Role	Description
Encourager	Encourages reluctant or shy students to participate
Praiser/Cheerleader	Shows appreciation of other's contributions and recognizes accomplishments
Gate Keeper	Equalizes participation and makes sure no one dominates
Coach	Helps with the academic content, explains concepts
Question Commander	Makes sure all students' questions are asked and answered
Checker	Checks the group's understanding
Taskmaster	Keeps the group on task
Recorder	Writes down ideas, decisions, and plans
Reflector	Keeps group aware of progress (or lack of progress)
Quiet Captain	Monitors noise level
Materials Monitor	Picks up and returns materials

Source: From *Cooperative Learning* by S. Kagan. Published by Kagan Publishing, San Clemente, CA. 1-800-WEE CO-OP.

Connect and **Extend** to Your **Teaching/Portfolio**

Add Table 11.3, "Possible Student Roles in Cooperative Learning Groups" and Table 11.5, "Question Stems to Encourage Dialogue in Reciprocal Questioning,"

the roles support learning. In groups that focus on social skills, roles should support listening, encouragement, and respect for differences. In groups that focus on practice, review, or mastery of basic skills, roles should support persistence, encouragement, and participation. In groups that focus on higher-order problem solving or complex learning, roles should encourage thoughtful discussion, sharing of explanations and insights, probing, brainstorming, and creativity. Make sure that you don't communicate to students that the major purpose of the groups is simply to do the procedures—the roles. Roles are supports for learning, not ends in themselves (Woolfolk Hoy & Tschannen-Moran, 1999).

Often, cooperative learning strategies include group reports to the entire class. If you have been on the receiving end of these class reports, you know that they can be deadly dull. To make the process more useful for the audience as well as the reporters, Annemarie Palincsar and Leslie Herrenkohl (2002) taught the class members to use intellectual roles as they listened to reports. These roles were based on the scientific strategies of predicting and theorizing, summarizing results, and relating predictions and theories to results. Some audience members were assigned the role of checking the reports for clear relationships between predictions and theories. Other students in the audience listened for clarity in the findings. And the rest of the students were responsible for evaluating how well the group reports linked prediction, theories, and findings. Research shows that using these roles promotes class dialogue, thinking and problem solving, and conceptual understanding (Palincsar & Herrenkohl, 2002). Table 11.4 summarizes the considerations in designing cooperative learning, based on the goals of the group.

TABLE 11.4

What Should You Consider in Planning and Doing Cooperative Learning?

Considerations	Social Skills Tasks: Team Building, Cooperation Skills	Structured Tasks: Review, Practice Facts, and Skills	Unstructured Tasks Conceptual, Problem Solving, Thinking and Reasoning
Group Size and Composition	groups of 2–5, common interest groups, mixed groups, random groups	groups of 2–4, mixed ability, high medium/medium-low or high low/medium-medium	groups of 2–4, select members to encourage interaction
Why Assign Roles?	to monitor participation and conflict, rotate leadership	to monitor engagement and ensure low-status students have resources to offer, i.e. Jigsaw	only to encourage interaction, divergent thinking, and extended, connected discourse, i.e. debate sides, group facilitator
Extrinsic Rewards/Incentives	not necessary, may be helpful	to support motivation, effort, persistence	not necessary
Teacher's Role	model, encourager	model, director, coach	model facilitator
Student Skills Needed	listening, turn-taking, encouraging, managing conflict	questioning, explaining, encouraging, content knowledge, learning strategies	questioning, explaining, elaborating, probing, divergent thinking, providing rationales, synthesizing
What Supports Learning? Watch and listen for . . .	modeling and practice	giving multiple, elaborated explanations, attention and practice	quantity and quality of interactions, using and connecting knowledge resources, probing, and elaboration
Potential Problems	unproductive conflict, nonparticipation	poor help-giving skills, disengaged or excluded students,	disengaged or excluded students cognitive loafing, superficial thinking, avoiding controversy
Averting Problems	simpler task, direct teaching of social skills, team building, conflict resolution skills, discuss group process	structure interdependence and individual accountability, teach helping and explaining	structure controversy, assign "thinking roles," allow adequate time
Small Start	one or two skills, i.e., listening and paraphrasing	pairs of students quizzing each other	numbered heads together

Source: From "Implications of cognitive approaches to peer learning for teacher education," by A. Woolfolk Hoy & M. Tschannen-Moran in *Cognitive perspectives on peer learning,* A. O'Donnell and A. King (Eds.), 1999, p. 278. Adapted with permission of Lawrence Erlbaum Associates, Inc. and Anita Woolfolk Hoy.

Designs for Cooperation

We now turn to different strategies that build in structures to support both social and cognitive learning.

Reciprocal Questioning. **Reciprocal questioning** requires no special materials or testing procedures and can be used with a wide range of ages. After a lesson or presentation by the teacher, students work in pairs or triads to ask and answer questions about the material (King, 1990, 1994, 2002). The teacher provides question stems (see Table 11.5), then students are taught how to develop specific questions on the lesson material using the generic question stems. The students create questions, then take turns asking and answering. This process has proved more effective than traditional discussion groups because it seems to encourage deeper thinking about the material. Questions such as those in Table 11.5, which encourage students to make connections between the lesson and previous knowledge or experience, seem to be the most helpful. For example, using the question stems in Table 11.5, a small group in Mr. Garcia's 9th-grade world cultures class had the following discussion about the concept of "culture":

Sally: In your own words, what does *culture* mean?

Jim: Well, Mr. Garcia said in the lesson that a culture is the knowledge and understandings shared by the members of a society. I guess it's all the things and beliefs and activities that people in a society have in common. It includes things like religion, laws, music, medical practices, stuff like that.

Sally: And dance, art, family roles.

Barry: Knowledge includes language. So, I guess cultures includes language, too.

Jim: I guess so. Actually, I have a question about that: How does a culture influence the language of a society?

Barry: Well, for one thing, the language is made up of words that are important to the people of that culture. Like, the words name things that the people care about, or need, or use. And so, different cultures would have different vocabularies. Some cultures may not even have a word for *telephone*, because they don't have any. But, phones are important in our culture, so we have lots of different words for phones, like *cell phone, digital phone, desk phone, cordless phone, phone machine*, and . . .

Jim (laughing): I'll bet desert cultures don't have any words for *snow* or *skiing*.

Connect and Extend to the Research

King, A. (1990). Enhancing peer interaction and learning in the classroom through reciprocal questioning. *American Educational Research Journal, 27*, 664–687.

TABLE 11.5

Question Stems to Encourage Dialogue in Reciprocal Questioning
After studying materials or participating in a lesson, students use these stems to develop questions and share answers.

What is a new example of . . . ?	How are . . . and . . . similar? How are . . . and . . . different?
How would you use . . . to . . . ?	What is the best . . . and why?
What would happen if . . . ?	Compare . . . and . . . with regard to . . .
What are the strengths and weaknesses of . . . ?	What do you think causes . . . ?
How does . . . tie in with what we learned before?	What conclusions can you draw about . . . ?
Explain why . . . Explain how . . .	Do you agree or disagree with this statement . . . ? Support your answer.
How does . . . affect . . . ?	
What is the meaning of . . . ?	
Why is . . . important?	

Source: From "Structuring peer interaction to promote high-level cognitive processing," by A. King. *Theory in Practice*, 41(1), p. 34–35.

Reciprocal questioning Approach where groups of two or three students ask and answer each other's questions after a lesson or presentation.

Sally (turning to Barry): What's your question?

Barry: I've got a great question! You'll never be able to answer it. What would happen if there was a group somewhere without any spoken language? Maybe they were all born not being able to speak, or something like that. How would that affect their culture, or could there even *be* a culture?

Sally: Well, it would mean they couldn't communicate with each other.

Jim: And they wouldn't have any music! Because they wouldn't be able to sing.

Barry: But wait! Why couldn't they communicate? Maybe they would develop a nonverbal language system, you know, the way people use hand signals, or the way deaf people use sign language. (King, 2002, pp. 34–35)

Connect and **Extend** to **PRAXIS II™**

Forms of Cooperative Learning (II, A2)

STAD and Jigsaw are just two of many cooperative learning techniques, each designed for certain instructional purposes. Go to *Cooperative Learning* (http://www.utc.edu/Teaching-Resource-Center/CoopLear.html), sponsored by the University of Tennessee at Chattanooga, to learn about techniques and uses for cooperative learning.

Scripted Cooperation. Donald Dansereau and his colleagues have developed a method for learning in pairs called **scripted cooperation.** Students work together on almost any task, including reading a selection of text, solving math problems, or editing writing drafts. In reading, for example, both partners read a passage, then one student gives an oral summary. The other partner comments on the summary, noting omissions or errors. Next, the partners work together to elaborate on the information—create associations, images, mnemonics, ties to previous work, examples, analogies, and so on. The partners switch roles of summarizer and listener for the next section of the reading, and then continue to take turns until they finish the assignment (Dansereau, 1985; O'Donnell & O'Kelly, 1994).

In addition to these approaches, Spencer Kagan (1994) has developed many cooperative learning structures designed to accomplish different kinds of academic and social tasks. The *Guidelines* give you ideas for incorporating cooperative learning in to your classes.

Reaching Every Student: Using Cooperative Learning Wisely

Connect and **Extend** to Your **Teaching/Portfolio**

Add examples of how you would use cooperative learning structures to your Portfolio.

Cooperative learning always benefits from careful planning, but sometimes including students with special needs requires extra attention to planning and preparation. For example, cooperative structures such as scripted questioning and peer tutoring depend on a balanced interaction between the person taking the role of questioner or explainer and the student who is answering or being taught. In these interactions, you want to see and hear explaining and teaching, not just telling or giving right answers. But many students with learning disabilities have difficulties understanding new concepts, so both the explainer and the student can get frustrated, and social rejection for the student with learning disabilities might follow. Because students with learning disabilities often have problems with social relations, it is not a good idea to put them in situations where more rejection is likely. So when students are learning new or difficult-to-grasp concepts, cooperative learning might not be the best choice for students with learning disabilities (Kirk et al., 2006). In fact, research has found that cooperative learning in general is not always effective for students with learning disabilities (Smith, 2006).

Gifted students also may not benefit from cooperative learning when groups are mixed in ability. The pace often is too slow, the tasks too simple, and there is too much repetition. Also, gifted students often fall into the role of teacher or end up just doing the work quickly for the whole group. The challenges, if you use mixed-ability groups and include gifted students, are to use complex tasks that allow work at different levels and to keep gifted students engaged without losing the rest of the class (Smith, 2006).

Cooperative learning may be an excellent choice, however, for English language learners (ELL). In many classrooms today, there are 4, 5, 6, or more languages represented. Teachers can't be expected to master every heritage language spoken by all their students every year. In these classrooms, cooperative groups can help as students work together on academic tasks. Students who speak 2 languages can help translate and explain lessons to others in the group. Speaking in a smaller group may be less anxiety-provoking for students who are learning another language; thus, ELL students may get more language practice with feedback in these groups (Smith, 2006).

Scripted cooperation A learning strategy in which two students take turns summarizing material and critiquing the summaries.

Guidelines: Using Cooperative Learning

Fit group size and composition to your learning goals.

EXAMPLES

1. For social skills and team-building goals, use groups of 2–5, common interest groups, mixed groups, or random groups.
2. For structured fact and skill-based practice and review tasks, use groups of 2–4, mixed ability such as high-middle and middle-low or high-low and middle-middle group compositions.
3. For higher-level conceptual and thinking tasks, use groups of 2–4; select members to encourage interaction.

Assign appropriate roles.

EXAMPLES

1. For social skills and team-building goals, assign roles to monitor participation and conflict; rotate leadership of the group.
2. For structured fact and skill-based practice and review tasks, assign roles to monitor engagement and insure low-status students have resources to offer, as in Jigsaw.
3. For higher-level conceptual and thinking tasks, assign roles only to encourage interaction, divergent thinking, and extended, connected discourse, as in debate teams, group facilitator. Don't let roles get in the way of learning.

Make sure you assume a supporting role as the teacher.

EXAMPLES

1. For social skills and team-building goals, be a model and encourager.
2. For structured fact and skill-based practice and review tasks, be a model, director, or coach.
3. For higher-level conceptual and thinking tasks, be a model and facilitator.

Move around the room and monitor the groups.

EXAMPLES

1. For social skills and team-building goals, watch for listening, turn-taking, encouraging, and managing conflict.
2. For structured fact and skill-based practice and review tasks, watch for questioning, giving multiple elaborated explanations, attention, and practice.
3. For higher-level conceptual and thinking tasks, watch for questioning, explaining, elaborating, probing, divergent thinking, providing rationales, synthesizing, using and connecting knowledge sources.

Start small and simple until you and the students know how to use cooperative methods.

EXAMPLES

1. For social skills and team-building goals, try one or two skills, such as listening and paraphrasing.
2. For structured fact and skill-based practice and review tasks, try pairs of students quizzing each other.
3. For higher-level conceptual and thinking tasks, try reciprocal questioning using pairs and just a few question stems.

For more information on cooperative learning, see:
http://www.ncsu.edu/felder-public/Cooperative_Learning.html
http://www.co-operation.org/
http://edtech.kennesaw.edu/intech/cooperativelearning.htm

Source: Adapted from "Implications of Cognitive Approaches to Peer Learning for Teacher Education," by A. Woolfolk Hoy and M. Tschannen-Moran, 1999. In A. O'Donnell and A. King (Eds.), *Cognitive Perspectives on Peer Learning* (pp. 257–284). Mahwah, NJ: Lawrence Erlbaum.

The jigsaw cooperative structure is especially helpful for ELL students because these students have information that the group needs, so they also must talk, explain, and interact. In fact, the jigsaw approach was developed in response to needs for creating high interdependence in diverse groups. Elliot Aronson and his graduate students invented the Jigsaw Classroom when he was a professor of social psychology (and I was a student) at the University of Texas at Austin. Some of my friends worked on his research team. Aronson developed the approach: "as a matter of absolute necessity to help defuse a highly explosive situation" (Aronson, 2000, p. 137). The Austin schools had just been desegregated by court order. White, African American, and Hispanic students were together in classrooms for the first time. Hostility and turmoil ensued with fistfights in corridors and classrooms. Aronson's answer was the Jigsaw classroom.

In **Jigsaw,** each group member is given part of the material to be learned by the whole group and becomes an "expert" on his or her piece. Students have to teach each other, so everyone's contribution is important. A more recent version, Jigsaw II, adds expert groups in which the students who have the same material from each learning group confer to

Jigsaw A cooperative structure in which each member of a group is responsible for teaching other members one section of the material.

STORIES OF LEARNING
TRIBUTES TO TEACHING

Years after inventing the Jigsaw strategy, Elliot Aronson received the following letter:

Dear Professor Aronson:

I am a senior at _____ University. Today I got a letter admitting me to the Harvard Law School. This may not seem odd to you but, let me tell you something. I am the sixth of seven children my parents had—and I am the only one who ever went to college, let alone graduate, or go to law school.

By now, you are probably wondering why this stranger is writing to you and bragging to you about his achievements. Actually, I'm not a stranger although we never met. You see, last year I was taking a course in social psychology and we were using a book you wrote called The Social Animal, *and when I read about prejudice and jigsaw it all sounded very familiar—and then, I realized that I was in that very first class you ever did jigsaw in—when I was in the 5th grade in Austin. And as I read on, it dawned on me that I was the boy that you called* **CARLOS**. *And then I remembered you when you first came to our classroom and how I was scared and how I hated school and how I was so stupid and didn't know anything. And you came in—it all came back to me when I read your book—you were very tall—about 6 feet—and you had a big black beard and you were funny and made us all laugh.*

And, most important, when we started to do work in jigsaw groups, I began to realize that I wasn't really that stupid. And the kids I thought were cruel and hostile became my friends and the teacher acted friendly and nice to me and I actually began to love school, and I began to love to learn things and now I'm about to go to Harvard Law School.

You must get a lot of letters like this but I decided to write anyway because let me tell you something. My mother tells me that when I was born I almost died. I was born at home and the cord was wrapped around my neck and the midwife gave me mouth to mouth and saved my life. If she were still alive, I would write to her too, to tell her that I grew up smart and good and I'm going to law school. But she died a few years ago. I'm writing to you because, no less than her, you saved my life too.

"I began to realize that I wasn't really that stupid."

Source: From *Nobody Left to Hate: Teaching Compassion after Columbine*, by E. Aronson. Published by Worth Publishers. Copyright © 2001 by Worth Publishers. Reprinted with permission from Henry Holt and Company, LLC.

make sure they understand their assigned part and then plan ways to teach the information to their learning group members. Next, students return to their learning groups, bringing their expertise to the sessions. In the end, students take an individual test covering all the material and earn points for their learning team score. Teams can work for rewards or simply for recognition (Aronson, 2000; Slavin, 1995). But in Aronson's eyes, an even greater lesson is learned about respect and compassion. The *Stories of Learning/Tributes to Teaching* feature tells about an ELL student who was in one of those early Jigsaw classes in Austin.

Judy Pitts (1992) describes a lesson about how to do library research that has a jigsaw format. The overall project for each group is to educate the class about a different country. Groups have to decide what information to present and how to make it interesting for their classmates. In the library, each group member is responsible for mastering a particular resource (Readers' Guide, NewsBank, reference sets, almanacs, etc.) and teaching other group members how to use it, if the need arises. Students learning about each resource meet first in expert groups to be sure all the "teachers" know how to use the resource.

In this class, students confront complex, real-life problems, and not simplified worksheets. They learn by doing and by teaching others. The students must take positions and argue for them—how should our group educate the class about Turkey, for example—while being open to the ideas of others. They may encounter different representations of the same information—graphs, databases, maps, interviews, or encyclopedia articles—and have to integrate information from different sources. This lesson exemplifies many of the characteristics of constructivist approaches described in Chapter 9. The students have a good chance of learning how to do library research by actually doing it.

The Classroom Community

David and Roger Johnson (1999) describe three Cs for safe and productive schools: cooperative community, constructive conflict resolution, and civic values. At the heart of

Handling conflict can be difficult for young people. Studies have shown that many conflicts among middle- and high-school students are resolved in destructive ways or never at all.

the community is the idea of positive interdependence—individuals working together to achieve mutual goals. We have spent several pages talking about cooperation in learning. Now let's consider the other two Cs—constructive conflict resolution and civic values.

Constructive Conflict Resolution

Constructive conflict resolution is essential in the community because conflicts are inevitable and even necessary for learning. Piaget's theory of development and the research on conceptual change teaching tell us that true learning requires cognitive conflict. And individuals trying to exist in groups will have interpersonal conflicts, which also can lead to learning. Table 11.6 shows how academic and interpersonal conflicts can be positive forces in a learning community. One study of 10th graders found that students who were wrong, but for different reasons, were sometimes able to correct their misunderstandings if they argued together about their conflicting wrong answers (Schwarz, Neuman, & Biezuner, 2000).

TABLE 11.6

Academic and Interpersonal Conflict and Learning

Conflict, if handled well, can support learning. Academic conflicts can lead to critical thinking and conceptual change. Conflicts of interest are unavoidable, but can be handled so no one is the loser.

Academic Controversy	Conflicts of Interest
One person's ideas, information, theories, conclusions, and opinions are incompatible with those of another, and the two seek to reach an agreement.	The actions of one person attempting to maximize benefits prevents, blocks or interferes with another person maximizing her or his benefits.
Controversy Procedure	*Integrative (Problem-Solving) Negotiations*
Research and prepare positions	Describe wants
Present and advocate positions	Describe feelings
Refute opposing position and refute attacks on own position	Describe reasons for wants and feelings
Reverse perspectives	Take other's perspective
Synthesize and integrate best evidence and reasoning from all sides	Invent three optional agreements that maximize joint outcomes
	Choose one and formalize agreement

Source: From "The Three Cs of School and Classroom Management," by D. Johnson and R. Johnson. In H. J. Freiberg (Ed.), *Beyond Behaviorism: Changing the Classroom Management Paradigm.* Boston: Allyn and Bacon. Copyright © 1999 by Allyn & Bacon. Adapted with permission.

Connect and **Extend** to Your **Teaching/Portfolio**

Add Table 11.6, "Academic and Interpersonal Conflict and Learning" to your file of Teaching Resources.

Connect and **Extend** to **PRAXIS II™**

Conflict Resolution (II, A2)

For guidelines and concrete actions for achieving cooperation in classrooms, read *Cooperation, Conflict, Resolution, and School Violence: A Systems Approach* (http://iume.tc.columbia.edu/choices/briefs/choices05.html).

Peer Harassment. One common form of conflict in schools involves teasing and harassment, often called bullying. Teachers tend to underestimate the amount of bullying that takes place in schools. For example, in one survey of 8th graders, 60% of the students said that they had been harassed by a bully, but teachers in their schools estimated the number would be about 16% (Barone, 1997). A national survey found that about 33% of 6th through 10th graders had been involved in moderate or frequent bullying (Nansel et al., 2001). The line between good-natured exchanges and hostile teasing may seem thin, but a rule of thumb is that teasing someone who is less powerful or less popular or using any racial, ethnic, or religious slur should not be tolerated.

What Can Teachers Do? In every community there are conflicts. Learning to resolve them is an important life skill. In fact, one longitudinal study that followed a representative sample of 1st- through 6th-grade students for two years found that aggressive children whose teachers taught them conflict management strategies were moved away from a life path of aggression and violence (Aber, Brown, & Jones, 2003). But when teachers are silent about aggression and teasing, students may "hear" agreement with the insult (Weinstein, 2003). Table 11.7 presents a list of dos and don'ts about teasing in schools.

Handling conflict is difficult for most of us—and for young people it can be even harder. Given the public's concern about violence in schools, it is surprising how little we know about conflicts among students (Johnson, Johnson, Dudley, Ward, & Magnuson, 1995; Rose & Gallup, 2001). There is some evidence that in elementary schools, conflicts most often center on disputes over resources (school supplies, computers, athletic equipment, or toys) and over preferences (which activity to do first or what game to play). Over 30 years ago, a large study of more than 8,000 junior- and senior-high students and 500 faculty from three major cities concluded that 90% of the conflicts among students are resolved in destructive ways or are never resolved at all (DeCecco & Richards, 1974). The few studies conducted since that time have reached similar conclusions.

TABLE 11.7

Dos and Don'ts about Teasing

Teasing has led to some tragic situations. Talk about what to do in your class.

Do:	Don't:
1. Be careful of others' feelings.	1. Tease someone you don't know well.
2. Use humor gently and carefully.	2. [If you are a boy] tease girls about sex.
3. Ask whether teasing about a certain topic hurts someone's feelings.	3. Tease about a person's body.
4. Accept teasing from others if you tease.	4. Tease about a person's family members.
5. Tell others if teasing about a certain topic hurts your feelings.	5. Tease about a topic when a student has asked you not to.
6. Know the difference between friendly gentle teasing and hurtful ridicule or harassment.	6. Tease someone who seems agitated or whom you know is having a bad day.
7. Try to read others' "body language" to see if their feelings are hurt—even when they don't tell you.	7. Be thin-skinned about teasing that is meant in a friendly way.
8. Help a weaker student when he or she is being ridiculed.	8. Swallow your feelings about teasing—tell someone in a direct and clear way what is bothering you.

Source: From *Secondary Classroom Management: Lessons from Research and Practice* (3rd ed.), by C. S. Weinstein. Published by McGraw-Hill. Copyright © 2003 by McGraw-Hill. Adapted with permission from The McGraw-Hill Companies.

Avoidance, force, and threats seem to be the major strategies for dealing with conflict (Johnson et al., 1995). But there are better ways—peer mediation and negotiation strategies that teach lifelong lessons.

Peer Mediation and Negotiation. David Johnson and his colleagues (1995) provided conflict resolution training to 227 students in 2nd through 5th grade. Students learned a five-step negotiating strategy:

1. *Jointly define the conflict.* Separate the person from the problem and the actions involved, avoid win–lose thinking, and get both parties' goals clear.
2. *Exchange positions and interests.* Present a tentative proposal and make a case for it; listen to the other person's proposal and feelings; and stay flexible and cooperative.
3. *Reverse perspectives.* See the situation from the other person's point of view and reverse roles and argue for that perspective.
4. *Invent at least three agreements that allow mutual gain.* Brainstorm, focus on goals, think creatively, and make sure everyone has power to invent solutions.
5. *Reach an integrative agreement.* Make sure both sets of goals are met. If all else fails, flip a coin, take turns, or call in a third party—a mediator.

In addition to learning conflict resolution, all students in Johnson and Johnson's study were trained in mediation strategies. The role of the mediator was rotated—every day the teacher chose two students to be the class mediators and to wear the mediators' T-shirts. Johnson and his colleagues found that students learned the conflict resolution and mediation strategies and used them successfully, both in school and at home, to handle conflicts in a more productive way.

Connect and **Extend** to the **Research**

For details of the strategies, see the *Theory into Practice* issue on "Conflict Resolution and Peer Mediation" edited by David and Roger Johnson (2004).

Peer mediation has also been successful with older students and those with serious problems (Sanchez & Anderson, 1990). In one program, selected gang members were given mediation training, then all members were invited to participate voluntarily in the mediation process, supervised by school counselors. Strict rules governed the process leading to written agreements signed by gang representatives. Sanchez and Anderson (1990) found that gang violence in the school was reduced to a bare minimum—"The magic of the mediation process was communication" (p. 56).

Even if you do not have formal peer mediation training in your school, you can help your students handle conflict more productively. For example, Esme Codell, the excellent first-year teacher we met in Chapter 1, taught her 5th graders a simple four-step process and posted the steps on a bulletin board: "1. Tell person what you didn't like. 2. Tell person how it made you feel. 3. Tell person what you want in the future. 4. Person responds with what they can do. Congratulations! You are a Confident Conflict Conqueror!" (Codell, 2001, p. 23).

Civic Values

The last C is civic values—the understandings and beliefs that hold the community together. Values are learned through direct teaching, modeling, reading literature, engaging in group discussions, and sharing concerns. Some teachers have a "Concerns Box" where students can put written concerns and comments. The box is opened once a week at a class meeting and the concerns are discussed. Johnson and Johnson (1999) give the example of a class meeting about respect. One student tells her classmates that she felt hurt during recess the day before because no one listened when she was trying to teach them the rules to a new game. The students discussed what it means to be respectful and why respect is important. Then the students shared personal experiences of times when they felt respected versus not respected.

STOP | THINK | WRITE Consider this situation, described by Aronson (2000, p. 171). You are a high-school social studies teacher. Just as you are opening a topic for discussion, Dave, a struggling student, says, "I've decided one thing anyway. I don't want to be an American. As soon as I get the chance, I'm leaving!" What would you do? ■

Respect begins with the teacher. In response to Dave's statement above about not wanting to be an American, his teacher Ms. Santos, modeled respect:*

> "Do you have another country in mind, Dave?"
>
> It turns out that Dave does have two or three countries in mind, but when he mentions them, some of the other students respond by bringing up specific problems in those countries. A lively and vigorous discussion ensues. Dave holds his own, but, as the discussion continues, he appears increasingly willing to listen to and to think about the views being expressed by some of the other students. Throughout most of this discussion, Ms. Santos does not take an active part, but sits still, leans forward, and listens attentively.
>
> After a while, Ms. Santos asks, "Do you want to live in a country without problems?" Her tone is calm, but the question is provocative. She has directed her question to Dave, in the context of the discussion, but the question embraces all of the students. Several of them begin to address the implications of that question. The teacher then helps the students think through the potential value of living in a country that can be considered "a work in progress"; that is, a country where there is still important and worthwhile work to be done. The students are inspired. They begin to come up with examples of people who have taken up that challenge—the challenge of working to make the country a better place for all of its citizens: Eleanor Roosevelt, Martin Luther King, Jr., Cesar Chavez, and the like. After a while, Dave comes up with an example himself. His voice has taken on a tone of interest and excitement. He seems less anguished, less disillusioned, more hopeful.

Connect and **Extend** to the **Research**

For a complete discussion of the debate about character education, see Abbeduto, L. (Ed.) (2002). *Taking sides: Clashing on controversial issues in educational psychology* (pp. 128–155). Guilford, CT: McGraw-Hill/Duskin.

Character Education. Some educators believe that civic values are best taught through character education. Not everyone agrees that character should be taught in schools, as you can see in the *Point/Counterpoint.*

Teaching Civic Values through the Curriculum: An Example. Esme Codell (2001, p. 34) describes how she used literature to teach about the pain of being teased. Esme's 5th-grade class had read *The Hundred Dresses*, a story about a poor immigrant girl who was teased mercilessly by other girls in her class. After reading the story, one student, Ashworth, whispered in Esme's ear that he had something he wanted to tell the class:

> I faced him toward the class and put my hands on his shoulders. He was trembling terribly. "Ashworth has something personal to share with you. I hope you will keep in mind *The Hundred Dresses* when he tells you."
>
> "I only have nine and a half fingers," he choked. "Please don't tease me about it." He held up his hands.
>
> The class hummed, impressed, then was silent as Ashworth shifted on his feet. Finally, Billy called out, "I'll kick the ass of anyone who makes fun of you!"
>
> "Yeah, me too!" said Kirk.
>
> "Yeah, Ash! You just tell us if anyone from another class messes with you, we'll beat their ass up and down!"
>
> Yeah, yeah, yeah! The class became united in the spirit of ass-kicking. Ashworth sighed and smiled at me. The power of literature!

Connect and **Extend** to the **Research**

See the March 2003 issue of *Educational Leadership* for several articles on "Creating Caring Schools." There are articles on bullying, trust in schools, service learning, creating community, and others.

See the September 2003 issue of *Educational Leadership* for several articles on "Building Classroom Relationships." There are articles on listening to students, empathy, and motivation.

See Johnson, D. W., & Johnson, R. (2005). Special Issue: Peace education. *Theory Into Practice*, 44(4).

Getting Started on Community

You may wonder what are the first steps in setting up a community. Here is how a 7th-grade teacher described her experiences working with one English class to establish rules and procedures together (Freiberg, 1999, p. 171):

> I began with my first-period class. We started slowly, with my asking them about what it would take for the class to work for them. I then told them what it would take for the class to work for me. I was amazed at the overlap. They wanted to know up front what I expected in terms of tests, quantity and quality of work, late assignments, talking in class, and amount and how often they would have homework, where they could sit, grading and whether classroom participation counted. We talked about the best classes and the worst classes. We talked about respect and the need to respect ideas and each other, to listen to and be willing to be an active participant without [verbally] running over other people

**Source:* Adapted from *Nobody left to hate: Teaching compassion after Columbine* by E. Aronson, 2000, New York: Worth, pp. 171–173.

Point/Counterpoint

Should Schools Teach Character and Compassion?

NOT ALL EDUCATORS believe that schools should teach compassion, tolerance, or other aspects of character and morality. Here are the two contrasting opinions.

POINT Schooling should include character education.

Proponents of character education point to violence in the schools, teenage pregnancy, and drug use among young people as evidence that educators need to address issues of morality and virtue. They argue that families are no longer doing a good job in this area, so schools must assume the burden. Thomas Lickona (2002) describes character education as the deliberate effort to cultivate personal qualities such as wisdom, honesty, kindness, and self-discipline. The goals of character education are to produce good people (who can work and love), good schools (that are caring and conducive to learning), and a good society (that deals effectively with problems such as violence and poverty). To accomplish these goals, Lickona believes that students need knowledge and moral reasoning capabilities, emotional qualities such as self-respect and empathy, and skills such as cooperation and communication. Character education strategies include modeling kindness and cooperation, creating a classroom community that is democratic and supportive, using cooperative learning strategies, including reflection on moral issues in the curriculum, and teaching conflict resolution.

COUNTERPOINT Character education is ineffective and dangerous.

Alfie Kohn (2002) cautions that the term "character education" has two meanings. The first is the general concern shared by most parents and educators that students grow into good, caring, honest people. The second is a narrow set of programs and strategies for teaching a particular set of values. Few people disagree with the general concern, but there is disagreement about the narrower programs. For example, Kohn (2002) says:

> *What goes by the name of character education nowadays is, for the most part, a collection of exhortations and extrinsic inducements designed to make children work harder and do what they're told. Even when other values are also promoted—caring or fairness, say—the preferred method of instruction is tantamount to indoctrination. The point is to drill students in specific behaviors rather than engage them in deep, critical reflection about certain ways of being. (p. 138)*

Kohn suggests that rather than try to "fix" students' character, we should fix the structure of schools to make them more just and caring.

WHAT DO YOU THINK?
Vote online at **www.mylabschool.com**

> in the class or being run over. I talked about "my teacher time" and their "student time." Well, this was five months ago and I am amazed at the level of cooperation. I am well ahead of last year in the curriculum; we have class meetings once a week to see how things are going and adjust as needed. We created a classroom constitution and had a constitutional convention when we felt it needed to be changed. I didn't believe it would make a difference, the students really surprised me with their level of maturity and responsibility and I surprised myself with my own willingness to change. This has been a great year and I am sorry to see it end and my students leave to another grade level. I am considering asking my principal to move me to eighth grade so I could have the same students again. I have been teaching for fourteen years and this has been my best year. I feel supported by my students and my students told me they feel supported by me.

Another example of respect for students and their lives comes from Esme Codell. "Madame Esme" (the name she preferred) had a morning ritual:

> In the morning, three things happen religiously. I say good morning, real chipper, to every single child and make sure they say good morning back. Then I collect "troubles" in a "Trouble Basket," a big green basket into which the children pantomime unburdening their home worries so they can concentrate on school. Sometimes a kid has no troubles. Sometimes a kid piles it in, and I in turn pantomime bearing the burden. This way, too, I can see what disposition the child is in when he or she enters. Finally, before they can come in, they must give me a word, which I print on a piece of tag board and keep in an envelope. It can be any word, but preferably one that they heard and don't really know or one that is personally meaningful. We go over the words when we do our private reading conferences. (Codell, 2001, p. 30)

Students are more likely to have a sense of belonging in school when they believe their teachers care about them academically and personally.

Belonging

When students perceive their schools are competitive places where they are treated differently based on race, gender, or ethnicity, then they are more likely to act out or withdraw altogether. But when they feel that they have choices, that the emphasis is on personal improvement and not comparisons, and when they feel respected and supported by teachers, students are more likely to bond with schools (Osterman, 2000). We have talked in other chapters about encouraging student engagement and promoting positive attitudes toward education. We saw that culturally responsive teaching can provide access to learning for more students. We looked at authentic tasks and problem-based learning as ways to connect with students' lives and interests. We examined the TARGET model for ideas about building motivation to learn. Here we consider research that specifically examines what helps students, particularly adolescents, feel connected to school.

Students are more likely to have a sense of belonging in school when they believe their teachers care about them. We saw in Chapter 3 that caring can be both academic and personal. When Kathryn Wentzel (1998, 2002) asked students how they knew that their teachers cared about them, they talked about teachers who tried to make classes interesting, who were fair and honest with them, who made sure they understood the materials, and who asked if something was wrong when they seemed upset. In other research, students describe teachers who notice when they are absent and ask why. Students believe teachers care when disciplinary procedures are fair and respectful and when the teachers use humor to connect with their students. In other words, the teachers trust and respect their students and care about them as learners and as people (Committee on Increasing High School Students' Engagement and Motivation to Learn, 2004).

Connect and **Extend** to the **Research**

To read how school-based interventions can make a difference for children on the path to violence, see Aber, J. L., Brown, J. L., & Jones, S. M. (2003). Developmental trajectories toward violence in middle childhood: Course, demographic differences, and response to school-based intervention. *Developmental Psychology, 39,* 324–348.

Violence in Schools

STOP | THINK | WRITE What did your high school do in reaction to the series of shootings that occurred in the late 1990s and early 2000s? Do you remember your thoughts and feelings? ■

In the weeks and months after the killings at Columbine High School, educators, parents, psychologists, politicians, and journalists struggled to explain what happened—and to understand how to prevent recurrences. How could two above-average students from stable families commit such heinous crimes? In 2005, another shooting at Red Lake High

School in Minnesota reminded us that the problems continue. The book, *No One Left to Hate: Teaching Compassion After Columbine*, by Elliot Aronson (2000), is the best explanation I have found for what happened that day and what can be done now. In the book and in the research described are some fundamental lessons for all educators.

As Aronson recounts, the tragic events of Columbine have been blamed on the emotional pathology of the shooters, easy access to guns in the United States, the absence of good security and surveillance in the school, and violence in both the media and video games. The solutions suggested have included early identification of potential troublemakers through student informants or searches of student property and web postings, metal detectors in schools, better gun control, and censorship of violence in the media. Clearly these issues deserve attention.

Each of these "solutions" might improve the situation in some schools, but each has problems. Eric Harris and Dylan Klebold, the shooters at Columbine, stood out in their appearance in school, but they functioned reasonably well, did their homework, and had decent grades. There are literally thousands of students like them in schools across the country. Metal detectors might be useful, but in some schools the atmosphere created could undermine the learning community teachers are trying to establish. And some school shooters have waited outside the schools to attack. Metal detectors would not detect those guns. Gun control has been difficult to accomplish politically and may never solve the problem of children's easy access to guns. Censorship brings with it threats to individual rights. None of these approaches gets at the true causes of the tragedy at Columbine. Aronson (2000, p. 88) points out that:

> Looking for root causes in individual pathology is an approach that seems sensible on the surface, but it does not get to the root of the problem. What is it about the atmosphere in the schools themselves that makes these young people so desperate, diabolical, and callous? Why do they seek revenge, or a twisted notion of glory, by shooting their classmates? In what ways have they felt rejected, ignored, humiliated, or treated unfairly at school? Are the schools doing the best they can to develop students' characters as well as their intellects? Can schools do better at creating inclusive, caring communities with positive role models for students?

Even though violence in high schools is actually decreasing, interpersonal violence among youth is a concern for both parents and teachers (Lowry, Sleet, Duncan, Powell, & Kolbe, 1995). Every day in America, 8 children or youth under age 20 are killed by firearms (Children's Defense Fund, 2005). Young people ages 12 to 24 are the most likely victims of nonfatal violence in American society, and many of these attacks take place on school property. About one-third of all injury-related deaths are the result of interpersonal violence—and young people are often the victims or the attackers in these violent acts (Peterson & Newman, 2000). This problem has many causes; it is a challenge for every element of society.

Connect and Extend to the Research

See Petit, G. S. & Dodge, K. A. (2003). Violent Children: Special Issue. *Developmental Psychology*, 39 (2).

Prevention

The best answer to school violence is prevention. As a teacher, you may have little to say about violence on television, metal detectors, or gun control—but you have much to say about the way students treat each other and the sense of community created in your classes. You can teach acceptance and compassion through direct and indirect means. And you can create a culture of belonging for all your students.

Some Chicano gang members in Chicago reported that they turned to gang activities when their teachers insulted them, called them names, humiliated them publicly, belittled their culture, ignored them in class, or blamed all negative incidents on particular students. The students reported joining gangs for security and to escape teachers who treated them badly or expected little of them because they were Latino (Padilla, 1992; Parks, 1995). Another two-year study in Ohio found that gang members respected teachers who insisted in a caring way that they focus on academic performance (Huff, 1989). I once asked a gifted educator in an urban New Jersey high school which teachers were most effective with the really tough students. He said there are two kinds, teachers who can't be intimidated or fooled and expect their students to learn, and teachers who really care about the students. When I asked, "Which kind are you?" he answered "Both!" He is an example of a "warm demander," as you will see in the next section.

Guidelines: Handling Potentially Explosive Situations

Move slowly and deliberately toward the problem situation.

EXAMPLES

1. Walk slowly, then be as still as possible.
2. Establish eye-level position.

Be respectful.

EXAMPLES

1. Keep a reasonable distance.
2. Do not crowd the student. Do not get "in the student's face."
3. Speak respectfully. Use the student's name.
4. Avoid pointing or gesturing.

Be brief.

EXAMPLES

1. Avoid long-winded statements or nagging.
2. Stay with the agenda. Stay focused on the problem at hand. Do not get sidetracked.
3. Deal with less severe problems later.

Avoid power struggles.

EXAMPLES

1. Speak privately if possible.
2. Do not get drawn into "I won't, you will" arguments.
3. Don't make threats or raise your voice.

Inform the student of the expected behavior and the negative consequence as a choice or decision for the student to make. Then withdraw from the student and allow some time for the student to decide.

EXAMPLES

1. "Michael, you need to return to your desk, or I will have to send for the principal. You have a few seconds to decide." The teacher then moves away, perhaps attending to other students.
2. If Michael does not choose the appropriate behavior, deliver the negative consequences. ("You are choosing to have me call the principal.") Follow through with the consequence.

For more ideas, see: **http://www.njcap.org/templated/Programs.html**

Source: Adapted from *Secondary Classroom Management: Lessons from Research and Practice*, 3rd ed., by C. S. Weinstein. Copyright © 2003 by McGraw-Hill. Adapted with permission from The McGraw-Hill Companies.

Connect and **Extend** to the **Research**

Parks, C. P. (1995). Gang behavior in the schools: Myth or reality? *Educational Psychology Review, 7*, 41–68.

Abstract
The purpose of this review is to explore the nature of gang behavior in U.S. schools, with a particular focus on the extent to which such behavior affects or exacerbates the larger issue of school violence. An unanticipated finding was the absence of strong empirical support for school gang violence. The evidence does show youth gangs have changed dramatically over the last several decades and have become more violent, largely due to drugs and weapons-carrying. One major impact of this violence on schools has been the dissolving of the school as the "neutral zone," where gang activity ceased. Thus, it appears that the similar "turf" issues of the street gangs have infiltrated the schools. The review explores problems related to school gang violence definitions and literature, trends in school-related gang activity, reasons for gang membership, at-risk youth, and proposed strategies for ameliorating the problem.

Teachers and students need to know the warning signs of potential dangers. Table 11.8 describes two kinds of signs—immediate warning and potential problems. What can schools do? The *Guidelines* for handling potentially explosive situations are taken from Weinstein (2003).

Respect and Protect

One system that has been developed to combat violence in the schools is *Respect and Protect* from the Johnson Institute, Minneapolis, Minnesota. The program is founded on five ideas: First, everyone is obliged to respect and protect the rights of others. Second, violence is not acceptable. Third, the program targets the violence-enabling behaviors of staff, students, and parents such as denying, rationalizing, justifying, or blaming others for violence. Fourth, there is a clear definition of what constitutes violence that distinguishes two kinds of violence—bully/victim violence and violence that arises from normal conflicts. Finally, the program has both adult-centered prevention that improves the school climate and student-centered interventions that give students choices and clear consequences (Rembolt, 1998). Table 11.9 on page 436 gives an overview of the levels of choices and consequences.

Another approach that builds respect and acceptance moves outside the classroom—service learning.

Community Outside the Classroom: Service Learning

Service learning is another approach to combining academic learning with personal and social development for secondary and college students (Fredricks, 2003; Woolfolk Hoy,

TABLE 11.8

Recognizing the Warning Signs of Violence

The following lists were developed by the American Psychological Association. Other resources are available at: http://helping.apa.org/warningsigns/

If you see these immediate warning signs, violence is a serious possibility:

- loss of temper on a daily basis
- frequent physical fighting
- significant vandalism or property damage
- increase in use of drugs or alcohol
- increase in risk-taking behavior
- detailed plans to commit acts of violence
- announcing threats or plans for hurting others
- enjoying hurting animals
- carrying a weapon

If you notice the following signs over a period of time, the potential for violence exists:

- a history of violent or aggressive behavior
- serious drug or alcohol use
- gang membership or strong desire to be in a gang
- access to or fascination with weapons, especially guns
- threatening others regularly
- trouble controlling feelings like anger
- withdrawal from friends and usual activities
- feeling rejected or alone
- having been a victim of bullying
- poor school performance
- history of discipline problems or frequent run-ins with authority
- feeling constantly disrespected
- failing to acknowledge the feelings or rights of others

Source: From "Warning Signs." Copyright © 1999 by the American Psychological Association. Adapted with permission of the APA. For more information, consult the website—*http://apahelpcenter.org/featuredtopics/feature.php?id=38.*

Demerath, & Pape, 2002). The Alliance for Service Learning in Education Reform (1993) lists several characteristics of service learning. The activities:

- Are organized and meet actual community needs.
- Are integrated into the student's curriculum.
- Provide time to reflect and write about the service experience.
- Provide opportunities to apply newly learned academic skills and knowledge.
- Enhance both academic learning and a sense of caring for others.

Service learning activities may involve direct service (tutoring, serving meals at homeless shelters), indirect service (collecting food for shelters, raising money), or advocacy (design and distribute posters about a food drive, write newspaper articles) (Johnson & Notah, 1999). Service learning also could be a form of problem-based learning, described

Connect and Extend to Your Teaching/Portfolio

Add Table 11.8, "Recognizing the-Warning Signs of Violence" and Table 11.9, "Respect and Protect" to your file of Teaching Resources.

Service learning An approach to combining academic learning with personal and social development.

Community service projects can promote adolescents' moral development, feelings of competence and agency, and tolerance of differences, and encourage them to reflect critically on their roles in society.

TABLE 11.9

Respect and Protect

This overview of choices, consequences, and contracts shows measured responses to each level of violence.

Violence Level*	Level One	Level Two	Level Three	Level Four	Level Five
Violation	Rule Violation (Minor infraction)	Misuse of Power (Repeat violation)	Abuse of Power (Serious)	Continued Abuse (Severe)	Pathology (Intractable)
Staff Action	Confront behavior Stop violence Deal with problem File intervention report Review No Violence rule Suggest anger management, conflict resolution, peer mediation, or class meeting	Confront behavior Stop violence Refer to office File intervention report Try to assess type of conflict Evaluate for talk with parent	Confront behavior Stop violence Refer to office File intervention report Try to assess type of conflict Parent conference Suggest parenting program	Confront behavior Stop violence Refer to office File intervention report Assess type of conflict Do psychosocial evaluation Hold parent conference Mandate parenting program Suggest family counseling	Confront behavior Stop violence Refer to office File intervention report Follow psychosocial recommendations Hold parent conference Mandate parenting program Suggest intensive therapy or treatment for student
Student Consequences	Review of activity for violence Parent notified (optional) Restitution Legal action	Office referral Life Skills worksheet Parent notified Restricted until worksheet finished Restitution Legal action	Office referral Parent notified Minimum time-out Violence Group Anger management Connections Empowerment Restitution Legal action	Office referral Parent notified Maximum time-out Violence Group Reconnections Restitution Legal action	Office referral Parent notified Maximum time-out Placement into an alternative setting Restitution Legal action
Contracts**	Verbal Promise	Simple Contract	Turf Contract I	Turf Contract II	Bottom-Line Contract

*Students are placed at Levels 1–5 depending on the frequency and severity of their violent behavior. Any violent act that is racial, sexual, involves physical fighting, or is committed against staff results in the student being placed immediately at Level 3 or higher. The program manual provides lists of behaviors that correlate with each level of violence.

**See source for a complete description of the different contracts.

Source: From "Making Violence Unacceptable," by C. Rembolt, *Educational Leadership, 56*(1), p. 36. The Association for Supervision and Curriculum Development is a worldwide community of educators advocating sound policies and sharing best practices to achieve the success of each learner. To learn more visit ASCD at *www.ascd.org.*

in Chapter 9, where the problem involves how to serve an identified need in the community.

Participation in community service learning can promote political and moral development for adolescents. Through service learning projects, adolescents experience their own competence and agency by working with others in need. Students see themselves as political and moral agents, rather than as merely good citizens (Youniss & Yates, 1997). In addition, community service learning can help adolescents think in new ways about their relationships with people who are unlike them, and thus can lead them to become more tolerant of difference (Tierney, 1993). Finally, service learning experiences foster an "ethic of care" that can result in a growing commitment to confront difficult social problems (Rhodes, 1997). In this sense, student involvement in community service learning can motivate and empower adolescents to critically reflect on their role in society (Woolfolk Hoy, Demerath, & Pape, 2002; Claus & Ogden, 1999).

Guidelines: Using Service Learning

The service should be ongoing, not just a brief project.

EXAMPLES

1. Instead of having a two-week food drive with a party for the class that collected the most, involve students in a longer commitment to cook or serve food at shelters for homeless families.
2. Contact local agencies to identify real needs that your students could address or search online by zip code: http://www.volunteermatch.org/ or http://www.usafreedomcorps.gov/

Consider virtual volunteering. See http://www.serviceleader.org/new/virtual/

EXAMPLES

1. Translate a document into another language.
2. Provide multimedia expertise, such as preparing a PowerPoint™, Hypercard™, QuickTime™ or other computer-based presentation.
3. Design an agency's newsletter or brochure, or copyedit an agency's publication or proposal.
4. Proofread drafts of paper and online publications.
5. Research and write articles for brochures, newsletters, web sites.
6. Design a logo for an agency or program, or fill other illustration needs.

Make sure learning is at the center of service learning.

EXAMPLES

1. Have clear learning objectives for the projects.
2. Examine grade-level standards in science, history, health, literature, and so on to see how some might be met through service projects—for example, how might concepts in biology be learned through designing a nutrition education project for senior citizens or preschool students?
3. Have students reflect over time about their experiences, keep journals, write or draw what they have learned, and include these reflections in class discussions.

Make sure the service draws on the students' talents and skills so that it is actually valuable to the recipients and the students gain a sense of accomplishment and usefulness from applying their skills to help others.

EXAMPLES

1. Students who have artistic talents might help redecorate a game room at a senior citizens' center.
2. Students who are good storytellers could work with children a day care center or in a children's clinic.
3. Students who are bilingual might help teachers translate school newsletters into parents; languages or serve as translators at local clinics.

For more ideas, see: **http://www.service-learningpartnership.org/site/PageServer** or **http://www.fiu.edu/~time4chg/Library/bigdummy.html**

A number of schools now have participation in service learning as a graduation requirement, but some educators question if "required" service is fair or appropriate. At least three of the school requirements have been challenged in court, but so far, the requirements have been upheld (Johnson & Notah, 1999).

Studies of service learning have produced mixed results. Some studies have found modest gains on measures of social responsibility, tolerance for others, empathy, attitude toward adults, and self-esteem (Solomon et al., 2001). A case study at an urban parochial high school describes a successful service-learning experience (Youniss & Yates, 1999). This program was required for juniors at the school and was part of a year-long course on social justice. In the class, students examined the moral implications of current events such as homelessness, poverty, exploitation of immigrant laborers, and urban violence. Students also were required to serve four times (approximately 20 hours) at an inner-city soup kitchen. The researchers concluded that students emerged from the course with "a deeper awareness of social injustice, a greater sense of commitment to confront these injustices, and heightened confidence in their abilities overall" (Yates & Youniss, 1999, p. 64).

If you decide to use service learning, consider the *Guidelines*, many of which are taken from Richard Sagor (2003) and Elias and Schwab (2006).

Diversity and Convergences in Social Engagement

Diversity

Understanding and appreciation of diversity is a central consideration in supporting engaged learning. In setting up cooperative groups, for example, be aware that assigning group members by "categories" such as race or language background may encourage the students to continue to think of one another as members of a category rather than as individuals. Make sure that everyone in cooperative learning groups has something to add to the group. This has implications for the group tasks you design, group membership, and roles. Tasks can be designed that draw upon the cultural knowledge of the members. Who has experience raising animals or fixing machines? Who has cared for younger children? Who speaks a second language? Who draws, organizes, sings, or prints well? This knowledge can be built into the tasks, and members with this expertise can be distributed across the groups.

To increase engagement and belonging for every student, Richard Sagor (2003) recommends that you conduct a Cultural Audit in your class. Table 11.10 will show you how.

Connect and **Extend** to Your **Teaching/Portfolio**

Add Table 11.10, "Conducting a Cultural Audit of Your Classroom" to your file of Teaching Resources.

Convergences

What are the convergences about behavioral, emotional, social, and cognitive engagement in schools? The research on school-based youth development and problem prevention programs points to three factors for success. Successful programs focus on enhancing students' social and emotional competence, connections to others, and contributions to their communities (Greenberg et al., 2003). These three factors parallel the major sections of this chapter—cooperation in classroom groups, creating classroom communities, and connection to communities outside the school.

A recent conference brought together key researchers, educators, and policy makers to discuss what is known—the convergences—about the role of school connections in learning. The group developed *The Wingspread Declaration on School Connections* (Blum, 2005), presented in Table 11.11. This declaration is a good summary of the convergences related to engaged learning.

TABLE 11.10

Conducting a Cultural Audit of Your Classroom

Richard Sagor suggests that you conduct a cultural audit to help determine whether your classroom is a place where students from different cultures will feel a sense of belonging. You can do this 4-step activity by yourself or with other faculty members.

____**Step 1. Record and Collect**

On a typical day, tape record your lessons and collect all of the instructional materials you used.

____**Step 2. Review**

Review all your lectures, explanations, and discussions and the materials and handouts you used for examples or illustrations drawn from nonmajority cultures.

____**Step 3. Share Your Findings (Optional)**

Share your findings with colleagues to see if there is a pattern of multicultural or monocultural perspectives in the school or classroom.

____**Step 4. Seek Outside Review and Collaboration**

If you are not satisfied with the inclusiveness of your instruction and your materials, invite some culturally different parents or school patrons to review your data and to provide suggestions for you on incorporating multiple perspectives in to your program

Source: From *Motivating students and teachers in an era of standards* by R. Sagor, pp. 78–79. Copyright © 2003 by the Association for Supervision and Curriculum Development. Reprinted with permission from ASCD. All rights reserved. The Association for Supervision and Curriculum Development is a worldwide community of educators advocating sound policies and sharing best practices to achieve the success of each learner. To learn more, visit ASCD at *www.ascd.org.*

TABLE 11.11

The Wingspread Declaration on School Connections

A recent conference brought together key researchers, educators, and policy makers to discuss what is known about the role of school connections in learning. The group developed this declaration.

Wingspread Declaration on School Connections

Students are more likely to succeed when they feel connected to school. School connection is the belief by students that adults in the school care about their learning as well as about them as individuals. The critical requirements for feeling connected include students' experiencing

- High academic expectations and rigor coupled with support for learning.
- Positive adult/student relationships.
- Physical and emotional safety.

Increasing the number of students connected to school is likely to influence critical accountability measures, such as

- Academic performance.
- Incidents of fighting, bullying, or vandalism.
- Absenteeism.
- School completion rates.

Strong scientific evidence demonstrates that increased student connection to school promotes

- Motivation.
- Classroom engagement.
- Improved school attendance.

These factors in turn increase academic achievement. These findings apply across racial, ethnic, and income groups.

Likewise, there is strong evidence that a student who feels connected to school is less likely to exhibit

- Disruptive behavior.
- School violence.
- Substance and tobacco use.
- Emotional distress.
- Early age of first sex.

The most effective strategies for increasing the likelihood that students will be connected to school include

- Implementing high standards and expectations and providing academic support to all students.
- Applying fair and consistent disciplinary policies that are collectively agreed upon and fairly enforced.
- Creating trusting relationships among students, teachers, staff, administrators, and families.
- Hiring and supporting capable teachers skilled in content, teaching techniques, and classroom management to meet each learner's needs.
- Fostering high parent/family expectations for school performance and school completion.
- Ensuring that every student feels close to at least one supportive adult at school.

Source: From "A case for school connectedness." by R. W. Blum. *Educational Leadership,* 62(7), p. 20. Copyright © 2005 by the Association for Supervision and Curriculum Development. Reprinted with permission from ASCD. All rights reserved. The Association for Supervision and Curriculum Development is a worldwide community of educators advocating sound policies and sharing best practices to achieve the success of each learner. To learn more, visit ASCD at *www.ascd.org.*

SUMMARY TABLE

Social Processes in Learning (pp. 414–416)

What are some of the social factors that influence learning in school? Peers, parents, and teachers influence norms and values about school achievement. Children tend to select friends that share their orientations and interests, and these peer groups, in turn, influence children's academic motivation. But parents and teachers play a role, too. Students with authoritative parents are more likely to choose positive peer groups and to resist peer pressure for antisocial behaviors such as drug use. If students have few or no friends, being liked by the teacher can be especially important.

Collaboration and Cooperation (pp. 416–426)

What are the differences between collaboration and cooperation? One view is that collaboration is a philosophy about how to relate to others—how to learn and work. Collaboration is a way of dealing with people that respects differences, shares authority, and builds on the knowledge that is distributed among other people. Cooperation, on the other hand, is a way of working together with others to attain a shared goal.

What are the learning theory underpinnings of cooperative learning? Learning can be enhanced in cooperative groups through rehearsal and elaboration (information processing theories), creation and resolution of disequilibrium (Piaget's theory), or scaffolding of higher mental processes (Vygotsky's theory).

Describe five elements that define true cooperative learning. Students *interact face-to-face* and close together, not across the room. Group members experience *positive interdependence*—they need each other for support, explanations, and guidance. Even though they work together and help each other, members of the group must ultimately demonstrate learning on their own—they are held *individually accountable* for learning, often through individual tests or other assessments. If necessary, the *collaborative skills* important for effective group functioning, such as giving constructive feedback, reaching consensus, and involving every member, are taught and practiced before the groups tackle a learning task. Finally, members monitor *group* *processes* and relationships to make sure the group is working effectively and to learn about the dynamics of groups.

How should tasks match design in cooperative learning? A relatively structured task works well with a structured technique; extrinsic rewards can enhance motivation, effort, and persistence under these conditions; roles, especially roles that focus attention on the work to be accomplished, also may be productive. On the other hand, strategies that encourage extended and productive interactions are appropriate when the goal is to develop higher-order thinking and problem solving. The use of rewards may well divert the group away from the goal of in-depth cognitive processing. When the goal of peer learning is enhanced social skills or increased intergroup understanding and appreciation of diversity, the assignment of specific roles and functions within the group might support communication. Rewards probably are not necessary and may actually get in the way because the goal is to build community, a sense of respect, and responsibility for team members.

What are some possible strategies for cooperative learning? Strategies include reciprocal questioning, scripted cooperation, Jigsaw, and many others described by Spencer Kagan.

Collaboration A philosophy about how to deal with people that respects differences, shares authority, and builds on the knowledge of others.

Cooperation Working together with others to reach a shared goal.

Cooperative learning Arrangement in which students work in mixed-ability groups and are rewarded on the basis of the success of the group.

Reciprocal questioning Approach where groups of two or three students ask and answer each other's questions after a lesson or presentation.

Scripted cooperation A learning strategy in which two students take turns summarizing material and critiquing the summaries.

Jigsaw A cooperative structure in which each member of a group is responsible for teaching other members one section of the material.

The Classroom Community (pp. 426–432)

What are Johnson and Johnson's three Cs of establishing a classroom community? The three Cs are cooperative community, constructive conflict resolution, and civic values. Classroom management begins by establishing a community based on cooperative learning. At the heart of the community is the idea of positive interdependence—individuals working together to achieve mutual goals. Constructive conflict resolution is essential in the community because conflicts are inevitable and even necessary for learning. But, teachers often underestimate the amount of peer conflict and bullying that happens in schools. Peer mediation is one good possibility for dealing with peer harassment. The steps for peer mediation are: (1) Jointly define the conflict. (2) Exchange positions and interests. (3) Reverse perspectives. (4) Invent at least three agreements that allow mutual gain. (5) Reach an integrative agreement. The last C is civic values—the understandings and beliefs that hold the community together. Values are learned through direct teaching, modeling, reading literature, engaging in group discussions, and sharing concerns.

How do teachers get started on a caring community? To get started on building community, teachers should make expectations for both academic work and student behaviors clear. Respect for students' needs and rights should be at the center of class procedures. Students know that their teachers care about them when teachers try to make classes interesting, are fair and honest with them, make sure they understand the materials, and have ways to cope with students' concerns and troubles.

Violence in Schools (pp. 432–434)

What can be done about violence in schools? Violence is actually decreasing in the schools, but incidents such as school shootings bring attention from the media. But young people ages 12 to 24 are the most likely group to be victims of nonfatal violence—often on school property. Possibilities to deal with violence include preventing violence by creating compassionate, respectful classrooms. It is especially important to respect the cultural heritages of the students while also maintaining high expectations for learning, School-wide programs such as *Respect and Protect* may provide the support teachers need to deal with violence..

Community Outside the Classroom: Service Learning (pp. 434–437)

What is service learning? Service learning activities are organized and meet actual community needs. They are integrated into the student's curriculum, and provide time for the student to reflect about the service experience and to apply newly learned academic skills and knowledge. It is critical that both aspects of service learning are accomplished—both giving a valuable service and supporting the learning of students.

Service learning An approach to combining academic learning with personal and social development.

Teachers' Casebook: Connections to PRAXIS II™

Your generation of teachers may influence the profession more than any generation before it. The folk wisdom, institutional memory, and history of teaching in this country provide little guidance for working with millions of students who have the shared experiences—vicarious or actual—of school shootings, terrorist bombings, and sniper attacks. An earlier generation of teachers conducted air raid drills to protect students from dangers from afar; the next generation of teachers will conduct "lock-downs" to protect students from dangers from within our country.

These events will affect students' emotions and how they interact with you and each other, the ways in which educators manage classrooms and schools, and the values that teachers emphasize in their classrooms and curricula. You and your colleagues will have significant roles in shaping the responses that schools and communities make to the realities of modern life.

What Would They Do?

Here is how some practicing teachers responded to help students deal with traumatic situations.

William Rodney Allen **Eleventh and twelfth grades,**
Louisiana School for Math, Science, and the Arts, Natchitoches, Louisiana

I had a class on the morning of September 11, and I made the decision to take my students to our auditorium, where we saw on our large-screen TV the World Trade Center Towers collapse. In the days ahead, we talked both about the terrorism itself and our reactions to it. Some students seemed deeply troubled by September 11, while others seemed to take it in stride. I found that my discussions of tragic events in America's past—slavery, the horrors in the trenches of World War I, the pandemic of AIDS in Africa—seemed to be more affecting to students who had just lived through a great national tragedy of their own.

I would encourage students, both in class and during my office hours, to express any concerns they had about the event. We also have three counselors who are available to help students deal with emotional problems. As the parent of two daughters, I know that teenagers sometimes like to act as though nothing can bother them too much—even when that's far from the case. It helps teens a great deal just to have a sympathetic adult listen to their problems.

Suzi E. Young **Fifth Grade Teacher,**
York Middle School, York, Maine

If a tragedy were to strike where teachers and students were being held hostage, I am sure that the principal of our school would have the school make some sort of statement about whatever had happened. I would have to wait for direction from her to see what I am allowed to say or not say for that day.

After that initial response from the school, I would try to gather all of the facts that I could about the incident. Then, if my 5th grade students were to ask me questions directly or wish to discuss the matter, I would make sure that they understood the event. I have found in the past that my 5th graders just usually want clarification because they just don't understand what happened. I tell them everything that I know and point out anything that may be an opinion. Because we study facts and opinions, I point out facts versus opinions in news reporting and others telling the events as they see them. I tell them my opinion when they want it. Fifth graders want truth, honesty, and they also want to move on. I feel that when I have shared my fears with them, they tend to be grateful because they may be feeling the same way, or they have heard their parents say some of the same things. They are not as scared when they know that others may be having the same feelings that they are.

Students don't like to belabor the situation, no matter how tragic it may be. They like normalcy. I have found that if I make any conversation safe to talk about, we talk about anything they need to discuss for as long as they need to discuss it, and then move on.

Keith J. Boyle **English Teacher, grades 9–12,**
Dunellen, New Jersey

Such a situation warrants a firm voice of reason amid what would likely be an extremely intense atmosphere. I would attempt to quell any dissemination of further rumors and find out the facts as quickly as possible. In the aftermath of the event, communication is paramount. The best way to try to gain some understanding of the event and its emotional or psychological impact upon one's students is simply to talk things out. Also, allow students to take any path of vocalizing their concerns, be that through written exercises or just allowing students to vent. Everyone needs an outlet; allow the students a level of freedom to exercise their outlets.

Karen Boyarsky **Fifth Grade Teacher,**
Walter C. Black Elementary School, Hightstown, New Jersey

One way to help ease students' concerns would be to help them see the difference between worrying about things we have control over and worrying about things we do not have control over. Begin by having students list the things they worry about. Some of their worries may include keeping their room clean, getting good grades or terrorist attacks. Discuss the difference between the worries they can control and the worries they cannot control. For example, worrying about getting homework done is a controlled fate,whereas worrying about getting in a car accident is not. Ease fears and concerns by encouraging students to focus on the things they can control rather than the things they cannot.

Kimberly D. Bridgers **Kindergarten Teacher,**
Dodson Elementary, Hermitage, Tennessee

Terrible tragedies are memories that stay with you forever. You remember where you were and what you were doing on 9/11. Likewise, the children you teach will always remember days like that, but the memories of how they felt relies a lot on how you handled the situation. When a tragedy or major news event occurs, I turn the TV on (low volume), but continue with the day as originally planned. This way, children can feel like they're a part of history, but continue with their normal day so that it doesn't become overly traumatic or depressing. As the days and weeks go by, follow your children's cues. Let them bring up the subject and discuss it for as long as they are interested in it. Answer their questions as best you can and encourage open discussion of thoughts and feelings.

CHAPTER 12

Creating Learning Environments

Teachers' Casebook: What Would You Do? 443

The Need for Organization 444

- The Basic Task: Gain Their Cooperation 444
- The Goals of Classroom Management 445

Creating a Positive Learning Environment 448

- Some Research Results 448
- Rules and Procedures Required 448
- Planning Spaces for Learning 452
- Planning for Computer Uses 455
- Getting Started: The First Weeks of Class 457

Maintaining a Good Environment for Learning 458

- Encouraging Engagement 459
- Prevention Is the Best Medicine 460
- Dealing with Discipline Problems 461
- Special Problems with Secondary Students 462
- Reaching Every Student: School-wide Positive Behavior Supports 466

The Need for Communication 466

- Message Sent—Message Received 466
- Diagnosis: Whose Problem Is It? 467
- Counseling: The Student's Problem 468
- Confrontation and Assertive Discipline 469

Diversity and Convergences in Learning Environments 470

- Diversity: Culturally Responsive Management 470
- Convergences: Research on Management Approaches 471

Summary Table 473

Teachers' Casebook: Connections to PRAXIS II™/ What Would They Do? 475

What Would You Do?

Teachers' Casebook

Two boys are terrorizing one of your students. The two are larger, stronger, and older than the boy in your class, who is small for his age and shy. Unfortunately, the bullies are fairly popular, in part because they are successful athletes. There are incidents on the bus before and after school, in the gym, in the hallways, and at lunch—including intimidation, extortion of lunch money, tripping, shoving, and verbal taunts—"fag" is a favorite chant. You do not have the two bullies in any of your classes. Your student has started to miss school routinely, and when he is in class, the quality of his work is declining.

Critical Thinking

- How do you handle this situation?
- Who should be involved?
- What would you do about the verbal homophobic insults?
- What would you do if the bullies were in your classes?
- What would you do if the bullies and victim were girls?

Collaboration

With 2 or 3 other members of your class, role play a discussion with the boys, their teachers, their parents, or the principal—whoever you decide you should talk to. What is your plan to deal with this situation?

This chapter looks at the ways that teachers create social and physical environments for learning by examining classroom management—one of the main concerns of teachers, particularly beginning teachers. The very nature of classes, teaching, and students makes good management a critical ingredient of success; we will investigate why this is true. Successful managers create more time for learning, involve more students, and help students to become self-managing.

A positive learning environment must be established and maintained throughout the year. One of the best ways to do this is to try to prevent problems from occurring at all. But when problems arise—as they always do—an appropriate response is important. What will you do when students challenge you openly in class, when one student asks your advice on a difficult personal problem, or when another withdraws from all participation? We will examine the ways that teachers can communicate effectively with their students in these and many other situations.

By the time you have completed this chapter, you should be able to answer these questions:

- What are the special managerial demands of classrooms and the needs of students of different ages?
- How will you establish a list of rules and procedures for a class?
- How will you arrange the physical environment of your classroom to fit your learning goals and teaching methods?
- How will you manage computers in your classroom to fit your learning goals and teaching methods?
- What are Kounin's suggestions for preventing management problems?
- How would you respond to a student who seldom completes work?
- What are two different approaches for dealing with a conflict between a teacher and a student?

FACING PAGE *Booker T. Washington Legend*, c. 1944–45. William H. Johnson. Photo: Smithsonian American Art Museum, Washington, DC/Art Resource, New York.

The Need for Organization

Connect and **Extend** to Your **Teaching/Portfolio**

Some educators object to the metaphor of teacher as manager. These critics suggest that the image brings with it notions of manipulation and detachment. Is the metaphor of manager an appropriate choice? What other metaphors can you suggest for teachers acting to maintain order and discipline? My research in this area suggests that images of group leaders (coaches, guides, etc.), problem solvers (physicians, chess players), and nurturers (mother, father, gardeners) are common for beginning teachers.

In study after study of the factors related to student achievement, classroom management stands out as the variable with the largest impact (Marzano & Marzano, 2003). Knowledge and expertise in classroom management are marks of expertise in teaching; stress and exhaustion from managerial difficulties are precursors of burn-out in teaching (Emmer & Stough, 2001). What is it about classrooms that makes management so critical?

Classes are particular kinds of environments. They have distinctive features that influence their inhabitants no matter how the students or the desks are organized or what the teacher believes about education (Doyle, 1986; 2006). Classrooms are *multidimensional.* They are crowded with people, tasks, and time pressures. Many individuals, all with differing goals, preferences, and abilities, must share resources, accomplish various tasks, use and reuse materials without losing them, move in and out of the room, and so on. In addition, actions can have multiple effects. Calling on low-ability students may encourage their participation and thinking, but may slow the discussion and lead to management problems if the students cannot answer. And events occur *simultaneously*—everything happens at once and the *pace is fast.* Teachers have literally hundreds of exchanges with students during a single day.

In this rapid-fire existence, events are *unpredictable.* Even when plans are carefully made, the overhead projector is in place, and the demonstration is ready, the lesson can still be interrupted by a burned-out bulb in the projector or a loud, angry discussion right outside the classroom. Because classrooms are *public,* the way the teacher handles these unexpected intrusions is seen and judged by all. Students are always noticing if the teacher is being "fair." Is there favoritism? What happens when a rule is broken? Finally, classrooms have *histories.* The meaning of a particular teacher's or student's actions depends in part on what has happened before. The fifteenth time a student arrives late requires a different response from the teacher than the first late arrival. In addition, the history of the first few weeks of school affects life in the class all year.

The Basic Task: Gain Their Cooperation

Connect and **Extend** to **Other Chapters**

Motivation and classroom management are closely related. The motivational strategies described in Chapter 10 are good first steps in effective class management.

No productive activity can take place in a group without the cooperation of all members. This obviously applies to classrooms. Even if some students don't participate, they must allow others to do so. (We all have seen one or two students bring an entire class to a halt.) So the basic management task for teachers is to achieve order and harmony by gaining and maintaining student cooperation in class activities (Doyle, 2006). Given the multidimensional, simultaneous, fast-paced, unpredictable, public, and historical nature of classrooms, this is quite a challenge.

Gaining student cooperation means much more than dealing effectively with misbehavior. It means planning activities, having materials ready, making appropriate behavioral and academic demands on students, giving clear signals, accomplishing transitions smoothly, foreseeing problems and stopping them before they start, selecting and sequencing activities so that flow and interest are maintained—and much more. Also, different activities require different managerial skills. For example, a new or complicated activity may be a greater threat to classroom management than a familiar or simple activity. And appropriate student participation varies across different activities. For example, loud student comments during a hip-hop reading of *Green Eggs and Ham* in an urban classroom are indications of engagement and cooperation, not disorderly call-outs (Doyle, 2006).

Obviously, gaining the cooperation of kindergartners is not the same task as gaining the cooperation of high-school seniors. Jere Brophy and Carolyn Evertson (1978) identified four general stages of classroom management, defined by age-related needs. During kindergarten and the first few years of elementary school, direct teaching of classroom rules and procedures is important. For children in the middle-elementary years, many classroom routines have become relatively automatic, but new procedures for a particular activity may have to be taught directly, and the entire system still needs monitoring and maintenance.

While the stereotypical classroom consists of students seated quietly in rows, their hands folded neatly on their desks, the reality is that teachers are often called on to keep track of many different activities at one time.

Toward the end of elementary school, some students begin to test and defy authority. The management challenges at this stage are to deal productively with these disruptions and to motivate students who are becoming less concerned with teachers' opinions and more interested in their social lives. By the end of high school, the challenges are to manage the curriculum, fit academic material to students' interests and abilities, and help students become more self-managing. The first few classes each semester may be devoted to teaching particular procedures for using materials and equipment, or for keeping track of and submitting assignments. But most students know what is expected of them.

The Goals of Classroom Management

STOP | THINK | WRITE You are interviewing for a job in a great district—it is known for innovation. The assistant principal looks at you for a moment and then asks, "What is classroom management?" How would you answer? ■

The aim of **classroom management** is to maintain a positive, productive learning environment. But order for its own sake is an empty goal. As we discussed in Chapter 6, it is unethical to use classroom management techniques just to keep students docile and quiet. What, then, is the point of working so hard to manage classrooms? There are at least three reasons.

Connect and **Extend** to Your **Teaching/Portfolio**

Think about your philosophy of teaching, a question you will be asked at most job interviews. What is your philosophy of classroom management? What rules will you set and how will you establish them? (Consult the *Guidelines* for ideas.)

More Time for Learning. I once used a stopwatch to time the commercials during a TV quiz show. I was amazed to find that half of the program was devoted to commercials. Actually, very little quizzing took place. If you used a similar approach in classrooms, timing all the different activities throughout the day, you might be surprised by how little actual teaching takes place. Many minutes each day are lost through interruptions, disruptions, late starts, and rough transitions (Karweit, 1989; Karweit & Slavin, 1981).

Obviously, students can only learn what they encounter. Almost every study examining time and learning has found a significant relationship between time spent on content and student learning (Berliner, 1988). In fact, the correlations between content studied and student learning are usually larger than the correlations between specific teacher behaviors and student learning (Rosenshine, 1979). Thus, one important goal of classroom management is to expand the sheer number of minutes available for learning. This is sometimes called **allocated time.**

Classroom management Techniques used to maintain a healthy learning environment, relatively free of behavior problems.

Allocated time Time set aside for learning.

Simply making more time for learning will not automatically lead to achievement. To be valuable, time must be used effectively. As you saw in the chapters on cognitive learning, the way students process information is a central factor in what they learn and remember. Basically, students will learn what they practice and think about (Doyle, 1983). Time spent actively involved in specific learning tasks often is called **engaged time,** or sometimes **time on task.**

Again, however, engaged time doesn't guarantee learning. Students may be struggling with material that is too difficult or using the wrong learning strategies. When students are working with a high rate of success—really learning and understanding—we call the time spent **academic learning time.** Another goal of class management is to increase academic learning time by keeping students *actively engaged in worthwhile, appropriate learning activities.* Figure 12.1 shows how the 1,000+ hours of time mandated for school in most states can become only about 333 hours of quality academic learning time for a typical student.

Getting students engaged in learning early in their school careers can make a big difference. Several studies have shown that teachers' rating of students' on-task, persistent engagement in 1st grade predicts achievement test score gains and grades through 4th grade, as well as the decision to drop out of high school (Fredricks, Blumenfeld, & Paris, 2004).

Access to Learning. Each classroom activity has its own rules for participation. Sometimes these rules are clearly stated by the teacher, but often they are implicit and unstated. Teacher and students may not even be aware that they are following different rules for different activities (Berliner, 1983). For example, in a reading group, students may

FIGURE 12.1

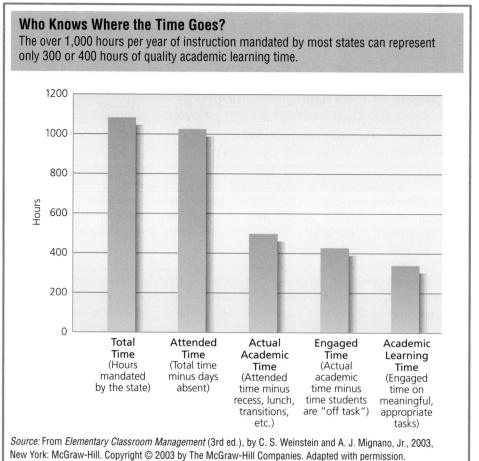

Who Knows Where the Time Goes?

The over 1,000 hours per year of instruction mandated by most states can represent only 300 or 400 hours of quality academic learning time.

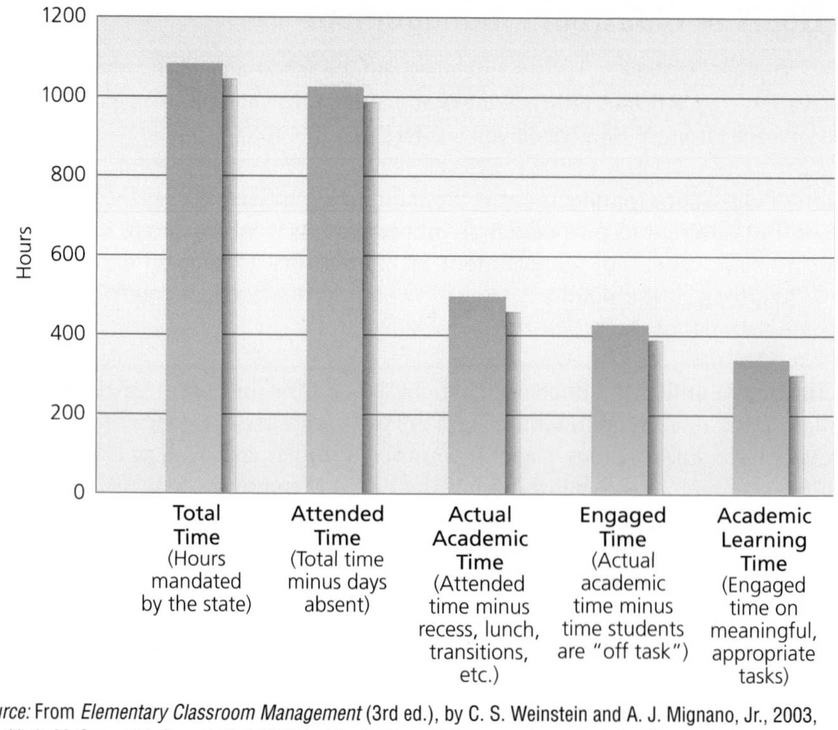

Source: From *Elementary Classroom Management* (3rd ed.), by C. S. Weinstein and A. J. Mignano, Jr., 2003, New York: McGraw-Hill. Copyright © 2003 by The McGraw-Hill Companies. Adapted with permission.

Engaged time/Time on task Time spent actively engaged in the learning task at hand.

Academic learning time Time when students are actually succeeding at the learning task.

have to raise their hands to make a comment, but in a show-and-tell circle in the same class, they may simply have to catch the teacher's eye.

As we saw in Chapter 5, the rules defining who can talk, what they can talk about, and when, to whom, and how long they can talk are often called **participation structures.** In order to participate successfully in a given activity, students must understand the participation structure. Some students, however, seem to come to school less able to participate than others. The participation structures they learn at home in interactions with siblings, parents, and other adults do not match the participation structures of school activities (Tharp, 1989). But teachers are not necessarily aware of this conflict. Instead, the teachers see that a child doesn't quite fit in, always seems to say the wrong thing at the wrong time, or is very reluctant to participate, and they are not sure why.

What can we conclude? To reach the second goal of good classroom management—giving all students access to learning—you must make sure everyone knows *how to participate* in class activities. The key is awareness. What are your rules and expectations? Are they understandable, given your students' cultural backgrounds and home experiences? What unspoken rules or values may be operating? Are you clearly signaling appropriate ways to participate? For some students, particularly those with behavioral and emotional challenges, direct teaching and practicing of the important behaviors may be required (Emmer & Stough, 2001).

An example of being sensitive to participation structures was documented by Adrienne Alton-Lee and her colleagues in a classroom in New Zealand (2001). As a critical part of a unit on children in hospitals, the teacher, Ms. Nikora, planned to have one of her students, a Maori girl named Huhana, describe a recent visit to the hospital. Huhana agreed. But when the time came and the teacher asked her to come to the front of the class and share her experiences, Huhana looked down and shook her head. Rather than confront or scold Huhana, the teacher simply said, "All right. If we sit in a circle . . . Huhana might be able to tell us about what happened." When students were in a circle, the teacher said, "All right, Huhana, after Ms. Nikora called your mum and she . . . Where did she take you to?" As Huhana began to share her experience, the teacher scaffolded her participation by asking questions, providing reminders of details the teacher had learned in previous conversations with Huhana, and waiting patiently for the student's responses. Rather than perceiving the *child* as lacking competence, the teacher saw the *situation* as hindering competent expression.

Connect and Extend to Your Teaching/Portfolio

Are there cultural differences in the verbal and nonverbal ways that students show respect, pay attention, and bid for a turn in conversation? How can cultural differences in interaction styles and expectations make classroom management more challenging?

Management for Self-Management. The third goal of any management system is to help students become better able to manage themselves. If teachers focus on student compliance, they will spend much of the teaching/learning time monitoring and correcting. Students come to see the purpose of school as just following rules, not constructing deep understanding of academic knowledge. And complex learning structures such as cooperative or problem-based learning require student self-management. Compliance with rules is not enough to make these learning structures work (McCaslin & Good, 1998).

The movement from demanding obedience to teaching self-regulation and self-control is a fundamental shift in discussions of classroom management today (Weinstein, 1999). Tom Savage (1999) says simply, "the most fundamental purpose of discipline is the development of self-control. Academic knowledge and technological skill will be of little consequence if those who possess them lack self-control" (p. 11). Through self-control, students demonstrate *responsibility*—the ability to fulfill their own needs without interfering with the rights and needs of others (Glasser, 1990). Students learn self-control by making choices and dealing with the consequences, setting goals and priorities, managing time, collaborating to learn, mediating disputes and making peace, and developing trusting relations with trustworthy teachers and classmates (Bear, 2005; Rogers & Frieberg, 1994).

Encouraging **self-management** requires extra time, but teaching students how to take responsibility is an investment well worth the effort. When elementary and secondary teachers have very effective class management systems but neglect to set student self-management as a goal, their students often find that they have trouble working independently after they graduate from these "well-managed" classes.

Connect and Extend to Your Teaching/Portfolio

Many computer programs exist to help teachers manage their own activities both inside and outside the classroom. Typical activities include online standard forms, IEPs, student home and school databases, student reports, letters to parents, archiving and locating information, electronic mail, financial planning, and scheduling.

Participation structures Rules defining how to participate in different activities.

Self-management Management of your own behavior and acceptance of responsibility for your own actions.

Creating a Positive Learning Environment

Connect and **Extend** to **Other Chapters**

In Chapter 13 you will learn about the importance of careful planning and clear objectives. Good planning is an important aspect of classroom management.

In making plans for your class, much of what you have already learned in this book should prove helpful. You know, for example, that problems are prevented when individual variations, such as those discussed in Chapters 2, 3, 4, and 5, are taken into account in instructional planning. Sometimes students become disruptive because the work assigned is too difficult. And students who are bored by lessons well below their ability levels may be interested in finding more exciting activities to fill their time.

In one sense, teachers prevent discipline problems whenever they make an effort to motivate students. A student engaged in learning is usually not involved in a clash with the teacher or other students at the same time. All plans for motivating students are steps toward preventing problems.

Some Research Results

Connect and **Extend** to the **Research**

For a description of a study that tested the Emmer/Evertson management principles along with other approaches, such as reinforcement strategies with adolescents in several schools, see Gottfredson, D. C., Gottfredson, G. D., & Hybl, L. G. (1993). Managing adolescent behavior: A multiyear, multischool study. *American Educational Research Journal, 30*, 179–217. Generally, the application of these principles improved behavior.

What else can teachers do? For several years, educational psychologists at the University of Texas at Austin studied classroom management quite thoroughly (Emmer & Stough, 2001; Emmer, Evertson, & Anderson, 1980; Emmer & Gerwels, 2006). Their general approach was to study a large number of classrooms, making frequent observations the first weeks of school and less frequent visits later in the year. After several months, there were dramatic differences among the classes. Some had very few management problems, while others had many. The most and least effective teachers were identified on the basis of the quality of classroom management and student achievement later in the year.

Next, the researchers looked at their observation records of the first weeks of class to see how the effective teachers got started. Other comparisons were made between the teachers who ultimately had harmonious, high-achieving classes and those whose classes were fraught with problems. On the basis of these comparisons, the researchers developed management principles. They then taught these principles to a new group of teachers, and the results were quite positive. Teachers who applied the principles had fewer problems; their students spent more time learning and less time disrupting; and achievement was higher. The findings of these studies formed the basis for two books on classroom management (Emmer, Evertson, & Worsham, 2006; Evertson, Emmer, & Worsham, 2006). Many of the ideas in the following pages are from these books.

Rules and Procedures Required

STOP | THINK | WRITE What are the three or four most important rules you will have for your classroom? ■

At the elementary-school level, teachers must lead 20 to 30 students of varying abilities through many different activities each day. Without efficient rules and procedures, a great deal of time is wasted answering the same question over and over. "My pencil broke. How can I do my math?" "I'm finished with my story. What should I do now?" "Carlos tripped me!" "I left my homework in my locker."

At the secondary-school level, teachers must deal daily with over 100 students who use dozens of materials and often change rooms. Secondary-school students are also more likely to challenge teachers' authority. The effective managers studied by Emmer, Evertson, and their colleagues had planned procedures and rules for coping with these situations.

Procedures Prescribed steps for an activity.

Procedures. How will materials and assignments be distributed and collected? Under what conditions can students leave the room? How will grades be determined? What are the special routines for handling equipment and supplies in science, art, or vocational classes? **Procedures** (often called routines) describe how activities are accomplished in classrooms, but they are seldom written down; they are simply the ways of getting things done in class. Carol Weinstein and Andy Mignano (Weinstein, 2003; Weinstein and Mignano, 2003) suggest that teachers establish routines to cover the following areas:

1. *Administrative routines,* such as taking attendance.
2. *Student movement,* such as entering and leaving or going to the bathroom.
3. *Housekeeping,* such as watering plants or storing personal items.
4. *Routines for accomplishing lessons,* such as how to collect assignments or return homework.
5. *Interactions between teacher and student,* such as how to get the teacher's attention when help is needed.
6. *Talk among students,* such as giving help or socializing.

You might use these six areas as a framework for planning your class procedures and routines. The *Guidelines* should help you as you plan.

Connect and Extend to PRAXIS II™

Procedures and Routines (I, C4)
Efficient procedures and routines reduce confusion and opportunities for misbehavior and they save time that can be devoted to learning tasks. Identify frequent activities or classroom events that would benefit from well-structured procedures or routines. Explain principles for establishing procedures and routines so that students are likely to observe them.

Guidelines: Establishing Class Procedures

Determine procedures for student upkeep of desks, classroom equipment, and other facilities.

EXAMPLES

1. Set aside a cleanup time each day or once a week in self-contained classes.
2. Demonstrate and have students practice how to push chairs under the desk, take and return materials stored on shelves, sharpen pencils, use the sink or water fountain, assemble lab equipment, and so on.
3. Put a rotating monitor in charge of equipment or materials.

Decide how students will be expected to enter and leave the room.

EXAMPLES

1. Have a procedure for students to follow as soon as they enter the room. Some teachers have a standard assignment ("Have your homework out and be checking it over").
2. Inform students under what conditions they can leave the room, and make sure they understand when they need to ask for permission to do so.
3. Tell students how they should gain admission to the room if they are late.
4. Set up a policy about class dismissal. Many teachers require students to be in their seats and quiet before they can leave at the end of class. The teacher, not the bell, dismisses class.

Establish a signal and teach it to your students.

EXAMPLES

1. In the classroom, flick the lights on and off, sound a chord on a piano or recorder, sound a bell like the "ring bell for service" at a sales counter, move to the podium and stare silently at the class, use a phrase like "Eyes, please," take out your grade book, or move to the front of the class.
2. In the halls, raise a hand, clap once, or use some other signal to indicate "Stop."
3. On the playground, raise a hand or whistle to indicate "Line up."

Set procedures for student participation in class.

EXAMPLES

1. Decide whether you will have students raise their hands for permission to speak or simply require that they wait until the speaker has finished.
2. Determine a signal to indicate that you want everyone to respond at once. Some teachers raise a cupped hand to their ear. Others preface the question with "Everyone."
3. Make sure you are clear about differences in procedures for different activities: reading group, learning center, discussion, teacher presentation, seatwork, film, peer learning group, library, and so forth.
4. Establish how many students at a time can be at the pencil sharpener, teacher's desk, learning center, sink, bookshelves, reading corner, or bathroom.

Determine how you will communicate, collect, and return assignments.

EXAMPLES

1. Establish a place for listing assignments. Some teachers reserve a particular corner of the board for listing assignments. Others write assignments in colored chalk. For younger students, it may be better to prepare assignment sheets or folders, color-coding them for math workbook, reading packet, and science kit.
2. Be clear about how and where assignments should be collected. Some teachers collect assignments in a box or bin; others have a student collect work while they introduce the next activity.

For ideas about involving students in developing rules and procedures, see **http://www.educationworld.com/a_lesson/lesson/lesson274.shtml**

Classroom rules that are clearly understood by all students can help maintain a classroom environment that is respectful and more conducive to effective learning.

Connect and **Extend** to **PRAXIS II™**

Rules (I, C4)

Fair, consistently enforced rules can have a positive effect on motivation to learn by promoting a safe and warm classroom environment. Describe how to establish and maintain effective rules. Keep in mind age-related concerns.

Connect and **Extend** to Your **Teaching/Portfolio**

Visit elementary school classes and note the rules posted by different teachers at the same grade level. Identify rules that are common to all or most classes, as well as those that are unusual.

Connect and **Extend** to **PRAXIS II™**

Rules (I, C4)

Fair, consistently enforced rules can have a positive effect on motivation to learn by promoting a safe and warm classroom environment. Describe how to establish and maintain effective rules. Keep in mind age-related concerns.

Rules. **Rules** specify expected and forbidden actions in the class. They are the dos and don'ts of classroom life. Unlike procedures, rules are often written down and posted. In establishing rules, you should consider what kind of atmosphere you want to create. What student behaviors will help you teach effectively? What limits do the students need to guide their behavior? The rules you set should be consistent with school rules, and also in keeping with principles of learning. For example, we know from the research on small-group learning that students benefit when they explain work to peers. They learn as they teach. A rule that forbids students to help each other may be inconsistent with good learning principles. Or a rule that says, "No erasures when writing" may make students focus more on preventing mistakes than on communicating clearly in their writing (Burden, 1995; Emmer & Stough, 2001; Weinstein & Mignano, 2003).

Rules should be positive and observable (raise your hand to be recognized). Having a few general rules that cover many specifics is better than listing all the dos and don'ts. But, if specific actions are forbidden, such as leaving the campus or smoking in the bathrooms, then a rule should make this clear (Emmer & Gerwels, 2006).

Rules for Elementary School. Evertson and her colleagues (2006) give four examples of general rules for elementary-school classes:

1. *Respect and be polite to all people.* Give clear explanations of what you mean by "polite," including not hitting, fighting, or teasing. Examples of polite behavior include waiting your turn, saying "please" and "thank you," and not calling names. This applies to behavior toward adults (including substitute teachers) and children.
2. *Be prompt and prepared.* This rule highlights the importance of the academic work in the class. Being prompt includes the beginning of the day and transitions between activities.
3. *Listen quietly while others are speaking.* This applies to the teacher and other students, in both large-class lessons or small-group discussions.
4. *Obey all school rules.* This reminds students that all school rules apply in your classroom. Then students cannot claim, for example, that they thought it was okay to chew gum or listen to a radio in your class, even though these are against school rules, "because you never made a rule against it for us."

Whatever the rule, students need to be taught the behaviors that the rule includes and excludes. Examples, practice, and discussion will be needed before learning is complete.

Rules Statements specifying expected and forbidden behaviors; dos and don'ts.

As you've seen, different activities often require different rules. This can be confusing for elementary students until they have thoroughly learned all the rules. To prevent confusion, you might consider making signs that list the rules for each activity. Then, before the activity, you can post the appropriate sign as a reminder. This provides clear and consistent cues about participation structures so all students, not just the "well-behaved," know what is expected. Of course, these rules must be explained and discussed before the signs can have their full effect.

Connect and Extend to Your Teaching/Portfolio

Adapt these rules for the students you will teach.

Rules for Secondary School. Emmer and colleagues (2006) suggest six examples of rules for secondary students:

1. *Bring all needed materials to class.* The teacher must specify the type of pen, pencil, paper, notebook, texts, and so on.
2. *Be in your seat and ready to work when the bell rings.* Many teachers combine this rule with a standard beginning procedure for the class, such as a warm-up exercise on the board or a requirement that students have paper with a proper heading ready when the bell rings.
3. *Respect and be polite to all people.* This covers fighting, verbal abuse, and general troublemaking. All people includes the teacher.
4. *Respect other people's property.* This means property belonging to the school, the teacher, or other students.
5. *Listen and stay seated while someone else is speaking.* This applies when the teacher or other students are talking.
6. *Obey all school rules.* As with the elementary class rules, this covers many behaviors and situations, so you do not have to repeat every school rule for your class. It also reminds the students that you will be monitoring them inside and outside your class. Make sure you know all the school rules. Some secondary students are very adept at convincing teachers that their misbehavior "really isn't against the rules."

Connect and Extend to Your Teaching/Portfolio

Here are some tips for using consequences from Richard Curwin:

- Always implement a consequence when a rule is broken.
- Select the most appropriate consequence from the list of alternatives, taking into account the offense, situation, student involved, and the best means of helping that student.
- State the rule and consequence to the offending student. Nothing more need be said.
- Be private. Only the student(s) involved should hear.
- Do not embarrass the student.
- Do not think of the situation as win–lose. This is not a contest. Do not get involved in a power struggle.
- Control your anger. Be calm and speak quietly, but accept no excuses from the student.
- Sometimes it is best to let the student choose the consequence.
- The professional always looks for ways to help the client.

Source: From Richard Curwin. *Rediscovering Hope: Our Greatest Teaching Strategy*, Copyright 1992, pp. 79–80. Permission to excerpt granted by the National Education Service, Bloomington, IN. To obtain a copy, contact the NES at 1-800-733-6786 or FAX 812-336-7790 or email NES@Bluemarble.net. All rights reserved by NES.

Consequences. As soon as you decide on your rules and procedures, you must consider what you will do when a student breaks a rule or does not follow a procedure. It is too late to make this decision after the rule has been broken. For many infractions, the logical consequence going back to "do it right." Students who run in the hall may have to return to where they started and walk properly. Incomplete papers can be redone. Materials left out should be put back (Charles, 2002b). You can use **natural or logical consequences** to support social/emotional development by doing the following (Elias & Schwab, 2006):

- Your response should separate the deed from the doer—the problem is the behavior, not the student.
- Emphasize to students that they have the power to choose their actions and thus avoid losing control.
- Encourage student reflection, self-evaluation, and problem solving—avoid teacher lecturing.
- Help students identify and give a rationale for what they could do differently next time in a similar situation.

The main point here is that decisions about penalties (and rewards) must be made early on, so students know before they break a rule or use the wrong procedure what this will mean for them. I encourage my student teachers to get a copy of the school rules and their cooperating teacher's rules, and then plan their own. Sometimes, consequences are more complicated. In their case studies of four expert elementary-school teachers, Weinstein and Mignano (2003) found that the teachers' negative consequences fell into seven categories, as shown in Table 12.1 on the next page.

Natural/logical consequences Instead of punishing, have students redo, repair, or in some way face the consequences that naturally flow from their actions.

Who Sets the Rules and Consequences? In the first chapter, I described Ken, an expert teacher who worked with his students to establish a students' "Bill of Rights" instead of defining rules. These "rights" cover most situations that might require a "rule" and help

TABLE 12.1

Seven Categories of Penalties for Students

1. *Expressions of disappointment.* If students like and respect their teacher, then a serious, sorrowful expression of disappointment may cause students to stop and think about their behavior.
2. *Loss of privileges.* Students can lose free time. If they have not completed homework, for example, they can be required to do it during a free period or recess.
3. *Exclusion from the group.* Students who distract their peers or fail to cooperate can be separated from the group until they are ready to cooperate. Some teachers give a student a pass for 10 to 15 minutes. The student must go to another class or study hall, where the other students and teachers ignore the offending student for that time.
4. *Written reflections on the problem.* Students can write in journals, write essays about what they did and how it affected others, or write letters of apology—if this is appropriate. Another possibility is to ask students to describe objectively what they did; then the teacher and the student can sign and date this statement. These records are available if parents or administrators need evidence of the students' behavior.
5. *Detentions.* Detentions can be very brief meetings after school, during a free period, or at lunch. The main purpose is to talk about what has happened. (In high school, detentions are often used as punishments; suspensions and expulsions are available as more extreme measures.)
6. *Visits to the principal's office.* Expert teachers tend to use this penalty rarely, but they do use it when the situation warrants. Some schools require students to be sent to the office for certain offenses, such as fighting. If you tell a student to go to the office and the student refuses, you might call the office saying the student has been sent. Then the student has the choice of either going to the office or facing the principal's penalty for "disappearing" on the way.
7. *Contact with parents.* If problems become a repeated pattern, most teachers contact the student's family. This is done to seek support for helping the student, not to blame the parents or punish the student.

Source: From *Elementary Classroom Management* (3rd ed.), by C. S. Weinstein and A. J. Mignano, Jr., New York: McGraw-Hill. Copyright © 2003 by The McGraw-Hill Companies. Adapted with permission.

the students move toward the goal of becoming self-managing. The rights for one recent class are in Table 12.2. Developing rights and responsibilities rather than rules makes an important point to students. "Teaching children that something is wrong *because there is a rule against it* is not the same as teaching them that there is a rule against it *because it is wrong*, and helping them to understand why this is so" (Weinstein, 1999, p. 154). Students should understand that the rules are developed so that everyone can work and learn together. I might add that when Ken has had some very difficult classes, he and his students have had to establish some "laws" that protect students' rights.

If you are going to involve students in setting rules or creating a constitution, you may need to wait until you have established a sense of community in your classroom. Before students can contribute meaningfully to the class rules, they need to trust the teacher and the situation (Elias & Schwab, 2006).

Another kind of planning that affects the learning environment is designing the physical arrangement of the class furniture, materials, and learning tools.

Connect and Extend to PRAXIS II™

Classroom Space (I, C4)
The physical organization of a class has an effect on student behavior and learning. Describe how the physical layout of classrooms can affect the learning environment. Apply principles of classroom organization to enhance learning and minimize disruption.

Planning Spaces for Learning

STOP | THINK | WRITE Think back over all the rooms in all the schools you have attended. Which ones stand out as inviting or exciting? Which ones were cold and empty? Did one teacher have a design that let different students do different things at once? ■

Spaces for learning should invite and support the activities you plan in your classroom, and they should respect the inhabitants of the space. This respect begins at the classroom door for young children by helping them identify their class. One school that has won awards for its architecture paints each classroom door a different bright color, so young

TABLE 12.2

A Bill of Rights for Students and Teachers

Students' Bill of Rights

Students in this class have the following rights:

- To whisper when the teacher isn't talking or asking for silence.
- To celebrate authorship or other work at least once a month.
- To exercise outside on days there is no physical education class.
- To have 2-minute breaks.
- To have healthy snacks during snack time.
- To participate in choosing a table.
- To have privacy. Get permission to touch anyone else's possessions.
- To be comfortable.
- To chew gum without blowing bubbles or making a mess.
- To make choices about the day's schedule.
- To have free work time.
- To work with partners.
- To talk to the class without anyone else talking.
- To work without being disturbed.

Source: From *Elementary Classroom Management* (3rd ed.), by C. S. Weinstein and A. J. Mignano, Jr., New York: McGraw-Hill. Copyright © 2003 by The McGraw-Hill Companies. Adapted with permission.

children can find their "home" (Herbert, 1998). Once inside, spaces can be created that invite quiet reading, group collaboration, or independent research. If students are to use materials, they should be able to reach them. In an interview with Marge Scherer (1999), Herb Kohl describes how he creates a positive environment in his classes.

> What I do is put up the most beautiful things I know—posters, games, puzzles, challenges—and let the children know these are provocations. These are ways of provoking them into using their minds. You have to create an environment that makes kids walk in and say, "I really want to see what's here. I would really like to look at this." (p. 9)

In terms of classroom arrangement, there are two basic ways of organizing space: personal territories and interest areas.

Personal Territories. Can the physical setting influence teaching and learning in classrooms organized by territories? Front-seat location does seem to increase participation for students who are predisposed to speak in class, whereas a seat in the back will make it more difficult to participate and easier to sit back and daydream (Woolfolk & Brooks, 1983). But the **action zone** where participation is greatest may be in other areas such as on one side, or near a particular learning center (Good, 1983a; Lambert, 1994). To "spread the action around," Weinstein and Mignano (2003) suggest that teachers move around the room when possible, establish eye contact with and direct questions to students seated far away, and vary the seating so the same students are not always consigned to the back.

Connect and **Extend** to Your **Teaching/Portfolio**

Add the floor plan from Figure 12.2 to your Teaching Resources file.

Horizontal rows share many of the advantages of the traditional row and column arrangements. Both are useful for independent seatwork and teacher, student, or media presentations; they encourage students to focus on the presenter and simplify housekeeping. Horizontal rows also permit students to work more easily in pairs. However, this is a poor arrangement for large-group discussion.

Clusters of four or circle arrangements are best for student interaction. Circles are especially useful for discussions but still allow for independent seatwork. Clusters permit

Action zone Area of a classroom where the greatest amount of interaction takes place.

Guidelines: Designing Learning Spaces

Note the fixed features and plan accordingly.

EXAMPLES

1. Remember that the audiovisual center and computers need an electrical outlet.
2. Keep art supplies near the sink, small-group work by a blackboard.

Create easy access to materials and a well-organized place to store them.

EXAMPLES

1. Make sure materials are easy to reach and visible to students.
2. Have enough shelves so that materials need not be stacked.

Provide students with clean, convenient surfaces for studying.

EXAMPLES

1. Put bookshelves next to the reading area, games by the game table.
2. Prevent fights by avoiding crowded work spaces.

Avoid dead spaces and "racetracks."

EXAMPLES

1. Don't have all the interest areas around the outside of the room, leaving a large dead space in the middle.
2. Avoid placing a few items of furniture right in the middle of this large space, creating a "racetrack" around the furniture.

Arrange things so you can see your students and they can see all instructional presentations.

EXAMPLES

1. Make sure you can see over partitions.
2. Design seating so that students can see instruction without moving their chairs or desks.

Make sure work areas are private and quiet.

EXAMPLES

1. Make sure there are no tables or work areas in the middle of traffic lanes; a person should not have to pass through one area to get to another.
2. Keep noisy activities as far as possible from quiet ones. Increase the feeling of privacy by placing partitions, such as bookcases or pegboards, between areas or within large areas.

Provide choices and flexibility.

EXAMPLES

1. Establish private cubicles for individual work, open tables for group work, and cushions on the floor for whole-class meetings.
2. Give students a place to keep their personal belongings. This is especially important if students don't have personal desks.

Try new arrangements, then evaluate and improve.

EXAMPLES

1. Have a "two-week arrangement," then evaluate.
2. Enlist the aid of your students. They have to live in the room, too, and designing a classroom can be a very challenging educational experience.

For more ideas on classroom design, see
http://www.edfacilities.org/rl/classroom_design.cfm

students to talk, help one another, share materials, and work on group tasks. Both arrangements, however, are poor for whole-group presentations and may make class management more difficult.

The fishbowl or stack special formation, where students sit close together near the focus of attention (the back row may even be standing), should be used only for short periods of time, because it is not comfortable and can lead to discipline problems. On the other hand, the fishbowl can create a feeling of group cohesion and is helpful when the teacher wants students to watch a demonstration, brainstorm on a class problem, or see a small visual aid.

Connect and Extend to the Research

To read three case studies describing how teachers planned the physical environments in their rooms, see Pointon, P. & Kershner, R. (2000). Making decisions about organizing the primary classroom as a context for learning: The views of three experienced teachers and their pupils. *Teaching and Teacher Education, 16,* 117–127.

Interest Areas. The design of interest areas can influence the way the areas are used by students. For example, working with a classroom teacher, Carol Weinstein (1977) was able to make changes in interest areas that helped the teacher meet her objectives of hav-

FIGURE 12.2

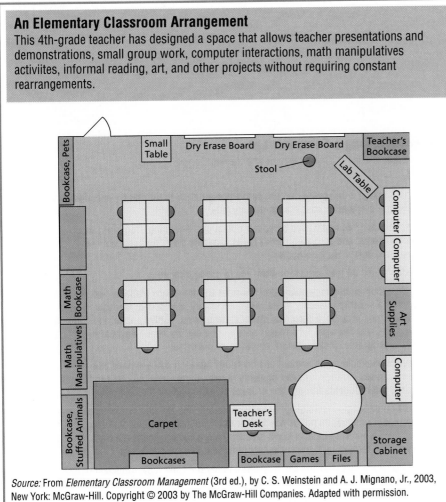

An Elementary Classroom Arrangement

This 4th-grade teacher has designed a space that allows teacher presentations and demonstrations, small group work, computer interactions, math manipulatives activiites, informal reading, art, and other projects without requiring constant rearrangements.

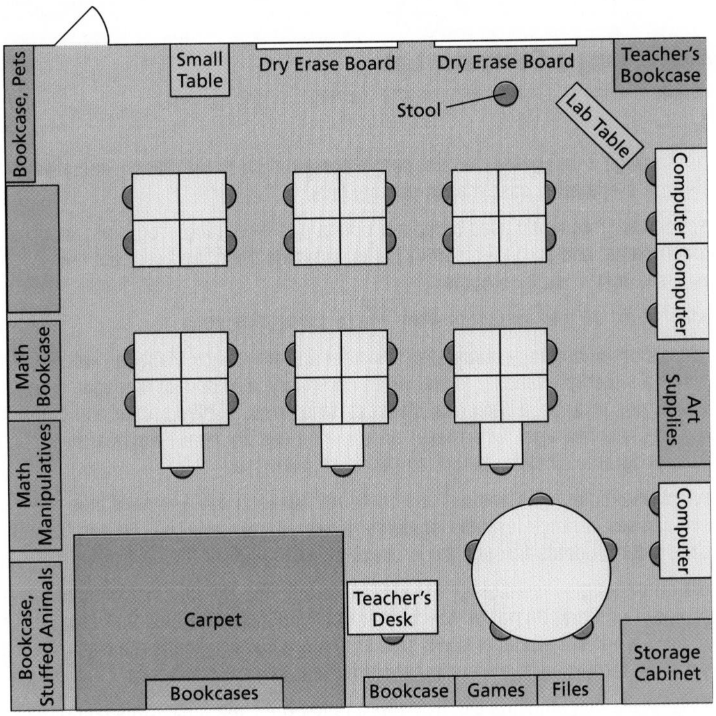

Source: From *Elementary Classroom Management* (3rd ed.), by C. S. Weinstein and A. J. Mignano, Jr., 2003, New York: McGraw-Hill. Copyright © 2003 by The McGraw-Hill Companies. Adapted with permission.

ing more girls involved in the science center and having all students experiment more with a variety of manipulative materials. In a second study, changes in a library corner led to more involvement in literature activities throughout the class (Morrow & Weinstein, 1986). If you design interest areas for your class, keep the *Guidelines* in mind.

Personal territories and interest areas are not mutually exclusive; many teachers use a design that combines these types of organizations. Individual students' desks—their territories—are placed in the center, with interest areas in the back or around the periphery of the room. This allows the flexibility needed for both large- and small-group activities. Figure 12.2 shows an elementary classroom that combines interest area and personal territory arrangements

Planning for Computer Uses

Many classrooms today have computers. Some classes have only one, others have several, and some classes are labs with a computer for every student. Using computers productively brings with it management challenges. Computers can be used to connect to powerful knowledge bases around the world; to act as tools for writing, drawing, calculating, and designing; to simulate scientific experiments or life in other times and places; to collaborate and communicate with people across the hall or across the ocean; to publish work or make presentations; and to keep track of appointments, assignments, or grades.

To get the greatest benefits from computers in your classroom, teachers must have good management systems. Table 12.3 summarizes strategies for managing computer labs.

Most classrooms will not have a computer for every student. In fact, many have only one computer or none at all. The *Guidelines* discuss using computers in regular classrooms.

TABLE 12.3

Tips for Managing a Computer Lab

All these ideas are from Cheryl Bolick and James Cooper (2006).

- Always run through a technology lesson *before* presenting it to the class—and always have a back-up lesson prepared in case the technology fails.
- Type directions for frequently used computer operations—opening programs, inserting clip art, printing documents, and so on—on index cards, laminate them, and connect them with a circle ring. Keep a set next to each computer.
- Have students turn *off* their monitors when you're giving directions.
- Appoint classroom technology managers. Consider an Attendance Manager, who takes attendance and serves as a substitute teacher helper when necessary; a Materials Manager, who passes out materials and runs errands; a Technical Manager, who helps resolve printer and computer issues; and an End-of-Class Manager, who makes sure work areas are neat—keyboards pushed in, mice straight, and programs closed—before students are dismissed.
- If you have classes filtering in and out of a computer lab each day and have little or no time to set up between classes, arrange for older students to help. Simply end your lesson five minutes early and walk the older students through the process of setting up for the next class.
- When working on lengthy technology projects, print out step-by-step instructions. Include some that say "Save your work; do not go any further until you help your neighbors reach this point." This helps less-proficient students solve problems more quickly, keeps the class at roughly the same point in the project, and fosters collaborative learning.
- Make it a class rule that students can help one another but cannot ever touch another student's computer. That way, you can be sure that learning occurs even when students help one another.
- Keep a red plastic cup at each computer. When students need help, have them place the highly visible cups on top of their monitors.
- Before students leave class, have them turn their mice upside down so the trackballs are showing. You'll lose fewer trackballs that way.
- Place different colored sticker dots on the left and the right bottom corners of each monitor. Use these to indicate which side of the screen you are talking about—very helpful when using certain programs, such as the new Kid Pix—and to determine whose turn it is if students share a computer.
- Plug all speakers into a main power bar. Turn the bar off when you're teaching and turn it on when students are working. If the room becomes too noisy, turn off the power bar to get students' attention.
- Use a Video Out card to project a monitor display onto a television screen.
- Type PLEASE WAIT FOR INSTRUCTIONS on 8 by 11 papers, laminate them, and tape one sheet to the top of every monitor. Students flip the signs to the back of the monitor *after* you've given directions.
- Create a folder in the Start menu and place any programs you use with students in that folder. Students never have to click Programs—everything they use is in one folder.
- When working in a computer lab, assign each student a computer. Students can line up in "computer lab order" in their classrooms. Seating goes very quickly when they get to the lab.
- If you're working on a network, ask your technology coordinator to set up a shared folder for Internet resources. Then, when you're planning an Internet lesson, simply save a shortcut to the Web site in that folder. During lab time, students can go to the shared folder, double click the link, and go right to the site without typing the URL. This saves time and stress for both students and teachers.

Source: "Tips for Managing a Computer Lab" from C. M. Bolick & J. M. Cooper (2006). "Classroom management and technology," in C. Evertson & C. Weinstein (Eds.), *Handbook for classroom management: Research, practice, and contemporary issues.* Reprinted by permission of Lawrence Erlbaum Associates, Inc. and Cheryl Mason Bolick, Ph.D.

Guidelines: Using Computers: Management Issues

If you have only one computer in your classroom:
Provide convenient access.

EXAMPLES

1. Find a central location if the computer is used to display material for the class.
2. Find a spot on the side of the room that allows seating and view of the screen, but does not crowd or disturb other students if the computer is used as a workstation for individuals or small groups.

Be prepared.

EXAMPLES

1. Check to be sure software needed for a lesson or assignment is installed and working.
2. Make sure instructions for using the software or doing the assignment are in an obvious place and clear.
3. Provide a checklist for completing assignments.

Create "trained experts" to help with computers.

EXAMPLES

1. Train student experts, and rotate experts.
2. Use adult volunteers—parents, grandparents, or older siblings.

Develop systems for using the computer.

EXAMPLES

1. Make up a schedule to insure that all students have access to the computer and no students monopolize the time.
2. Create standard ways of saving student work.

If you have more than one computer in your classroom:
Plan the arrangement of the computers to fit your instructional goals.

EXAMPLES

1. For cooperative groups, arrange so students can cluster around their group's computer.
2. For different projects at different computer stations, allow for easy rotation from station to station.

Experiment with other models for using computers.

EXAMPLES

1. *Navigator Model*—4 students per computer: One student is the (mouse and keyboard) driver, another is the "navigator." "Back-seat driver 1" manages the group's progress and "back-seat driver 2" serves as the timekeeper. The navigator attends a 10-minute to 20-minute training session in which the facilitator provides an overview of the basics of particular software. Navigators cannot touch the mouse. Driver roles are rotated.
2. *Facilitator Model*—6 students per computer: the facilitator has more experience, expertise, or training—serves as the guide or teacher.
3. *Collaborative Group Model*—7 students per computer: Each small group is responsible for creating some component of the whole group's final product. For example, one part of the group writes a report, another creates a map, and a third uses the computer to gather and graph census data.

For more ideas, see
http://www.internet4classrooms.com/one_computer.htm

Getting Started: The First Weeks of Class

Determining a room design, rules, and procedures are the first steps toward having a well-managed class, but how do effective teachers gain students' cooperation in those early critical days and weeks? One study carefully analyzed the first weeks' activities of effective and ineffective elementary teachers, and found striking differences (Emmer, Evertson, & Anderson, 1980). By the second or third week of school, students in the ineffective teachers' classrooms were more and more disruptive, less and less on task.

Effective Managers for Elementary Students. In the effective teachers' classrooms, the very first day was well organized. Name tags were ready. There was something interesting for each child to do right away. Materials were set up. The teachers had planned carefully to avoid any last-minute tasks that might take them away from their students. These teachers dealt with the children's pressing concerns first. "Where do I put my things?" "How do I pronounce my teacher's name?" "Can I whisper to my neighbor?" "Where is the bathroom?" The effective teachers were explicit about their expectations. They had a workable, easily understood set of rules and taught the students the most important rules

Connect and **Extend** to Your **Teaching/Portfolio**

Five excellent and very practical discussions of classroom management are:

Evertson, C. M., Emmer, E. T., & Worsham, M. E. (2006). *Classroom management for elementary teachers* (7th ed.). Boston: Allyn & Bacon.

Emmer, E. T., Evertson, C. M., & Worsham, M. E. (2006). *Classroom management for secondary teachers* (7th ed.). Boston: Allyn & Bacon.

Freiberg, H. J. (Ed.). (1999). *Beyond behaviorism: Changing the classroom management paradigm*. Boston: Allyn & Bacon.

Weinstein, C. S., & Mignano, A. J., Jr. (2003). *Elementary classroom management: Lessons from research and practice* (2nd ed.). New York: McGraw-Hill.

Weinstein, C. S. (2003). *Secondary classroom management: Lessons from research and practice* (2nd ed.). New York: McGraw-Hill.

right away. They taught the rules like any other subject—with lots of explanation, examples, and practice.

Throughout the first weeks, the effective managers continued to spend quite a bit of time teaching rules and procedures. Some used guided practice to teach procedures; others used rewards to shape behavior. Most taught students to respond to a bell or some other signal to gain their attention. These teachers worked with the class as a whole on enjoyable academic activities. They did not rush to get students into small groups or to get them started in readers. This whole-class work gave the teachers a better opportunity to continue monitoring all students' learning of the rules and procedures. Misbehavior was stopped quickly and firmly, but not harshly.

In the poorly managed classrooms, the first weeks were quite different. Rules were not workable; they were either too vague or very complicated. For example, one teacher made a rule that students should "be in the right place at the right time." Students were not told what this meant, so their behavior could not be guided by the rule. Neither positive nor negative behaviors had clear, consistent consequences. After students broke a rule, ineffective managers might give a vague criticism, such as "Some of my children are too noisy," or issue a warning, but not follow through with the threatened consequence.

In the poorly managed classes, procedures for accomplishing routine tasks varied from day to day and were never taught or practiced. Instead of dealing with these obvious needs, ineffective managers spent time on procedures that could have waited. For example, one teacher had the class practice for a fire drill the first day, but left unexplained other procedures that would be needed every day. Students wandered around the classroom aimlessly and had to ask each other what they should be doing. Often the students talked to one another because they had nothing productive to do. Ineffective teachers frequently left the room. Many became absorbed in paperwork or in helping just one student. They had not made plans for how to deal with late-arriving students or interruptions. One ineffective manager tried to teach students to respond to a bell as a signal for attention, but later let the students ignore it. All in all, the first weeks in these classrooms were disorganized and filled with surprises for teachers and students alike.

Effective Managers for Secondary Students. What about getting started in a secondary school class? It appears that many of the differences between effective and ineffective elementary school teachers hold at the secondary level as well. Again, effective managers focus on establishing rules, procedures, and expectations on the first day of class. These standards for academic work and class behavior are clearly communicated to students and consistently enforced during the first weeks of class. Student behavior is closely monitored, and infractions of the rules are dealt with quickly. In classes with lower-ability students, work cycles are shorter; students are not required to spend long, unbroken periods on one type of activity. Instead, during each period, they are moved smoothly through several different tasks. In general, effective teachers carefully follow each student's progress, so students cannot avoid work without facing consequences (Emmer & Evertson, 1982).

With all this close monitoring and consistent enforcement of the rules, you may wonder if effective secondary teachers have to be grim and humorless. Not necessarily. The effective managers in one study also smiled and joked more with their students (Moskowitz & Hayman, 1976). As any experienced teacher can tell you, there is much more to smile about when the class is cooperative.

Maintaining a Good Environment for Learning

A good start is just that—a beginning. Effective teachers build on this beginning. They maintain their management system by preventing problems and keeping students engaged in productive learning activities. We have discussed several ways to keep students engaged. In the chapter on motivation, for example, we considered stimulating curiosity, relating lessons to student interests, establishing learning goals instead of performance goals, and having positive expectations. What else can teachers do?

Encouraging Engagement

STOP | THINK | WRITE What activities keep you completely engaged—the time just seems to disappear? What is it about those activities that keeps you focused? ■

The format of a lesson affects student involvement. In general, as teacher supervision increases, students' engaged time also increases (Emmer & Evertson, 1981). One study, for example, found that elementary students working directly with a teacher were on task 97% of the time, whereas students working on their own were on task only 57% of the time (Frick, 1990). This does not mean that teachers should eliminate independent work for students. It simply means that this type of activity usually requires careful planning and monitoring.

When the task provides continuous cues for the student about what to do next, involvement will be greater. Activities with clear steps are likely to be more absorbing, because one step leads naturally to the next. When students have all the materials they need to complete a task, they tend to stay involved. If their curiosity is piqued, students will be motivated to continue seeking an answer. And, as you now know, students will be more engaged if they are involved in authentic tasks—activities that have connections to real life. Also, activities are more engaging when the level of challenge is higher and when students' interests are incorporated into the tasks (Emmer & Gerwels, 2006).

Of course, teachers can't supervise every student all the time, or rely on curiosity. Something else must keep students working on their own. In their study of elementary and secondary teachers, Evertson, Emmer, and their colleagues found that effective class managers at both levels had well-planned systems for encouraging students to manage their own work (Emmer, Evertson, & Worsham, 2006; Evertson, Emmer, & Worsham, 2006). The *Guidelines* are based on their findings.

Connect and Extend to PRAXIS II™

Promoting Student Engagement (I, C4)

A principle of educational psychology is that the more students are cognitively engaged in an activity, the more they are likely to learn. What tactics can teachers employ to maximize their students' cognitive engagement during learning tasks?

Guidelines: Keeping Students Engaged

Make basic work requirements clear.

EXAMPLES

1. Specify and post the routine work requirements for headings, paper size, pen or pencil use, and neatness.
2. Establish and explain rules about late or incomplete work and absences. If a pattern of incomplete work begins to develop, deal with it early; speak with parents if necessary.
3. Make due dates reasonable, and stick to them unless the student has a very good excuse for lateness.

Communicate the specifics of assignments.

EXAMPLES

1. With younger students, have a routine procedure for giving assignments, such as writing them on the board in the same place each day. With older students, assignments may be dictated, posted, or given in a syllabus.
2. Remind students of upcoming assignments.
3. With complicated assignments, give students a sheet describing what to do, what resources are available, due dates, and so on. Older students should also be told your grading criteria.
4. Demonstrate how to do the assignment, do the first few questions together, or provide a sample worksheet.

Monitor work in progress.

EXAMPLES

1. When you make an assignment in class, make sure each student gets started correctly. If you check only students who raise their hands for help, you will miss those who think they know what to do but don't really understand, those who are too shy to ask for help, and those who don't plan to do the work at all.
2. Check progress periodically. In discussions, make sure everyone has a chance to respond.

Give frequent academic feedback.

EXAMPLES

1. Elementary students should get papers back the day after they are handed in.
2. Good work can be displayed in class and graded papers sent home to parents each week.
3. Students of all ages can keep records of grades, projects completed, and extra credits earned.
4. For older students, break up long-term assignments into several phases, giving feedback at each point.

For more ideas, see **http://www.cat.ilstu.edu/teaching_tips/handouts/engage.shtml** or **http://trc.virginia.edu/Publications/Teaching_Concerns/TC_Topic/Engaging_Students.htm**
These citations are for college students, but have many good ideas.

Movement management refers to keeping lessons and students moving at an appropriate pace with smooth transitions as activities and the locations for those activities change throughout the day.

Prevention Is the Best Medicine

The ideal way to manage problems, of course, is to prevent them in the first place. In a classic study, Jacob Kounin (1970) examined classroom management by comparing effective teachers, whose classes were relatively free of problems, with ineffective teachers, whose classes were continually plagued by chaos and disruption. Observing both groups in action, Kounin found that they were not very different in the way they handled discipline once problems arose. The difference was that the successful managers were much better at preventing problems. Kounin concluded that effective classroom managers were especially skilled in four areas: *"withitness," overlapping activities, group focusing,* and *movement management* (Doyle, 1977). More recent research confirms the importance of these factors (Emmer & Stough, 2001; Evertson, 1988).

Withitness. **Withitness** means communicating to students that you are aware of everything that is happening in the classroom—that you aren't missing anything. "With-it" teachers seem to have eyes in the back of their heads. They avoid becoming absorbed or interacting with only a few students, because this encourages the rest of the class to wander. They are always scanning the room, making eye contact with individual students, so the students know they are being monitored (Charles, 2002a; Brooks, 1985).

These teachers prevent minor disruptions from becoming major. They also know who instigated the problem, and they make sure they deal with the right people. In other words, they do not make what Kounin called *timing errors* (waiting too long before intervening) or *target errors* (blaming the wrong student and letting the real perpetrators escape responsibility for their behavior).

If two problems occur at the same time, effective managers deal with the more serious one first. For example, a teacher who tells two students to stop whispering, but ignores even a brief shoving match at the pencil sharpener communicates a lack of awareness. Students begin to believe they can get away with almost anything if they are clever (Charles, 2002b).

Overlapping and Group Focus. **Overlapping** means keeping track of and supervising several activities at the same time. For example, a teacher may have to check the work of an individual and at the same time keep a small group working by saying, "Right, go on," and stop an incident in another group with a quick "look" or reminder (Burden, 1995; Charles, 2002b).

Maintaining a **group focus** means keeping as many students as possible involved in appropriate class activities and avoiding narrowing in on just one or two students. All students should have something to do during a lesson. For example, the teacher might ask everyone to write the answer to a question, then call on individuals to respond while the other students compare their answers. Choral responses might be required while the

Withitness According to Kounin, awareness of everything happening in a classroom.

Overlapping Supervising several activities at once.

Group focus The ability to keep as many students as possible involved in activities.

teacher moves around the room to make sure everyone is participating (Charles, 2002b). For example, during a grammar lesson the teacher might say, "Everyone who thinks the answer is *have run*, hold up the red side of your card. If you think the answer is *has run*, hold up the green side" (Hunter, 1982). This is one way teachers can ensure that all students are involved and that everyone understands the material.

Movement Management. **Movement management** means keeping lessons and the group moving at an appropriate (and flexible) pace, with smooth transitions and variety. The effective teacher avoids abrupt transitions, such as announcing a new activity before gaining the students' attention or starting a new activity in the middle of something else. In these situations, one-third of the class will be doing the new activity, many will be working on the old lesson, several will be asking other students what to do, some will be taking the opportunity to have a little fun, and most will be confused. Another transition problem Kounin noted is the *slowdown*, or taking too much time to start a new activity. Sometimes teachers give too many directions. Problems also arise when teachers have students work one at a time while the rest of the class waits and watches.

Caring Relationships: Connections with School. When students and teachers have positive, trusting relationships, many management problems never develop. Students respect teachers who maintain their authority without being rigid, harsh, or unfair and who use creative instructional practices to "make learning fun." Students also value teachers who show academic and personal caring by acting like real people (not just as teachers), sharing responsibility, minimizing the use of external controls, including everyone, searching for students' strengths, communicating effectively, and showing an interest in their students' lives and pursuits (Elias & Schwab, 2006; Woolfolk Hoy & Weinstein, 2006). All efforts at building positive relationships and classroom community are steps toward preventing management problems. Students who feel connected with school are happier, more self-disciplined, and less likely to engage in dangerous behaviors such as substance abuse, violence, and early sexual activity (Freiberg, 2006; McNeely, Nonnemaker, & Blum, 2002).

Student Social Skills as Prevention. But what about the students? What can they do? When students lack social and emotional skills such as being able to share materials, read the intentions of others, or handle frustration, classroom management problems often follow. So all efforts to teach social and emotional self-regulation are steps for preventing management problems. Over the short term, educators can teach and model these skills, then give students feedback and practice using them in a variety of settings. Over the long term, teachers can help to change attitudes that value aggression over cooperation and compromise (Elias & Schwab, 2006). Chapters 3 and 11 gave ideas for teaching social and emotional skills and competencies.

Dealing with Discipline Problems

WHAT WOULD YOU SAY?

You are interviewing for a job to take over a class in the middle of the school year. The lead principal asks, "In your experience with students in any capacity, what was your most challenging discipline problem so far and how did you handle it?" ■

In 2005, Phi Delta Kappa published the 37th annual Gallup Poll of the public's attitude toward public schools. From 1969 until 1999, "lack of discipline" was named as the number one problem facing the schools almost every year (Rose & Gallup, 1999). Beginning in 2000, lack of financial support took over the number one place, but lack of discipline remained a close second or third every year. Clearly, the public sees discipline as an important challenge for teachers.

Being an effective manager does not mean publicly correcting every minor infraction of the rules. This kind of public attention may actually reinforce the misbehavior, as we saw in Chapter 6. Teachers who frequently correct students do not necessarily have

Connect and **Extend** to the **Research**

Every year, the September issue of *Phi Delta Kappan* contains the "*Annual Phi Delta Kappa/Gallup Poll of the Public's Attitudes Toward the Public Schools.*" Questions usually ask respondents to "grade" the schools, identify the problems facing the schools, rate strategies for improvement, and give opinions about current issues such as school choice, home schooling, vouchers, and values.

Movement management Keeping lessons and the group moving at an appropriate (and flexible) pace, with smooth transitions and variety.

the best behaved classes (Irving & Martin, 1982). The key is being aware of what is happening and knowing what is important so you can prevent problems.

Most students comply quickly when the teacher gives a desist order (a "stop doing that") or redirects behavior. But some students are the targets of more than their share of desists. One study found that these disruptive students seldom complied with the first teacher request to stop. Often, the disruptive students responded negatively, leading to an average of 4 to 5 cycles of teacher desists and student responses before the student complied (Nelson & Roberts, 2000). Emmer and colleagues (2006) and Levin and Nolan (2000) suggest seven simple ways to stop misbehavior quickly, moving from least to most intrusive:

Connect and **Extend** to the **Research**

For a description of an extensive research project examining how teachers cope with problem behaviors, see Brophy, J., & McCaslin, M. (1992). Teachers' reports of how they perceive and cope with problem students. *Elementary School Journal*, 93, 3–68.

- *Make eye contact* with, or move closer to, the offender. Other nonverbal signals, such as pointing to the work students are supposed to be doing, might be helpful. Make sure the student actually stops the inappropriate behavior and gets back to work. If you do not, students will learn to ignore your signals.
- Try *verbal hints* such as "name-dropping" (simply insert the student's name into the lecture), asking the student a question, or making a humorous (not sarcastic) comment such as, "I must be hallucinating. I swear I heard someone shout out an answer, but that can't be because I haven't called on anyone yet!"
- Ask students *if they are aware* of the negative effects of their actions or send an "I message," described later in the chapter.
- If they are not performing a class procedure correctly, *remind the students* of the procedure and have them follow it correctly. You may need to quietly collect a toy, comb, magazine, or note that is competing with the learning activities, while privately informing the students that their possessions will be returned after class.
- In a calm, unhostile way, *ask the student to state the correct rule or procedure* and then to follow it. Glasser (1969) proposes three questions: "What are you doing? Is it against the rules? What should you be doing?"
- Tell the student in a clear, assertive, and unhostile way to *stop the misbehavior.* (Later in the chapter we will discuss assertive messages to students in more detail.) If students "talk back," simply repeat your statement.
- *Offer a choice.* For example, when a student continued to call out answers no matter what the teacher tried, the teacher said, "John, you have a choice. Stop calling out answers immediately and begin raising your hand to answer or move your seat to the back of the room and you and I will have a private discussion later. You decide" (Levin & Nolan, 2000, p. 177).

Many teachers prefer the use of logical consequences, described earlier, as opposed to penalties. For example, if one student has harmed another, you can require the offending student to make an "Apology of Action," which includes a verbal apology plus somehow repairing the damage done. This helps offenders develop empathy and social perspective taking as they think about what would be an appropriate "repair" (Elias & Schwab, 2006).

If you must impose penalties, the *Guidelines,* taken from Weinstein (2003) and Weinstein and Mignano (2003), give ideas about how to do it. The examples are taken from the actual words of the expert teachers described in their book.

There is a caution about penalties. Never use lower achievement status (moving to a lower reading group, giving a lower grade, giving excess homework) as a punishment for breaking class rules. These actions should be done only if the benefit of the action outweighs the possible risk of harm. As Carolyn Orange (2000) notes, "Effective, caring teachers would not use low achievement status, grades, or the like as a means of discipline. This strategy is unfair and ineffective. It only serves to alienate the student" (p. 76).

Connect and **Extend** to Your **Teaching/Portfolio**

To read about the 24 other mistakes teachers make that can cause students anxiety and trauma, see Orange, C. (2000). *25 biggest mistakes teachers make and how to avoid them.* Thousand Oaks, CA: Corwin.

Special Problems with Secondary Students

WHAT WOULD YOU SAY?

You are interviewing for a job in a high school that has been in the news lately about its "zero-tolerance policy." The principal asks, "So what do you think about zero tolerance?" What is your position? ■

Guidelines: Imposing Penalties

Delay the discussion of the situation until you and the students involved are calmer and more objective.

EXAMPLES

1. Say calmly to a student, "Sit there and think about what happened. I'll talk to you in a few minutes," or, "I don't like what I just saw. Talk to me during your free period today."
2. Say, "I'm really angry about what just happened. Everybody take out journals; we are going to write about this." After a few minutes of writing, the class can discuss the incident.

Impose penalties privately.

EXAMPLES

1. Make arrangements with students privately. Stand firm in enforcing arrangements.
2. Resist the temptation to "remind" students in public that they are not keeping their side of the bargain.
3. Move close to a student who must be disciplined and speak so that only the student can hear.

After imposing a penalty, reestablish a positive relationship with the student immediately.

EXAMPLES

1. Send the student on an errand or ask him or her for help.
2. Compliment the student's work or give a real or symbolic "pat on the back" when the student's behavior warrants. Look hard for such an opportunity.

Set up a graded list of penalties that will fit many occasions.

EXAMPLE

1. For not turning in homework: (1) receive reminder; (2) receive warning; (3) hand homework in before close of school day; (4) stay after school to finish work; (5) participate in a teacher–student–parent conference to develop an action plan.

Always teach a problem-solving strategies along with penalties to help students learn what to do next time (Elias & Schwab, 2006).

EXAMPLE

1. Use *Problem Diaries*, where students record what they were feeling, identify the problem and their goal, then think of other possible ways to solve the problem and achieve the goal.
2. Try *Keep Calm* 5-2-5: At the first physical signs of anger, students say to themselves: "Stop. Keep Calm," then take several slow breaths, counting to 5 breathing in, 2 holding breath, and 5 breathing out.

For more ideas, see **http://www.stopbullyingnow.com** or **http://www.cfchildren.org**

Connect and Extend to PRAXIS II™

Student Misbehavior (I, C4)
Even the most well-managed classroom will have instances of student misbehavior. Explain the principles for dealing with common student misbehaviors. What strategies can teachers employ to deal fairly and effectively with those problems?

Many secondary students never complete their work. Besides encouraging student responsibility, what else can teachers do to deal with this frustrating problem? Because students at this age have many assignments and teachers have many students, both teacher and students may lose track of what has and has not been completed. It often helps to teach students how to use a daily planner—paper or electronic. In addition, the teacher must keep accurate records. The most important thing is to enforce the established consequences for incomplete work. Do not pass a student because you know he or she is "bright enough" to pass. Make it clear to these students that the choice is theirs: They can do the work and pass, or they can refuse to do the work and face the consequences. You might also ask, in a private moment, if there is anything interfering with the student's ability to get to the work.

There is also the problem of students who continually break the same rules, always forgetting materials, for example, or getting into fights. What should you do? Seat these students away from others who might be influenced by them. Try to catch them before they break the rules, but if rules are broken, be consistent in applying established consequences. Do not accept promises to do better next time (Levin & Nolan, 2000). Teach the students how to monitor their own behavior; some of the self-management techniques described in Chapter 6 should be helpful. Finally, remain friendly with the students. Try to catch them in a good moment so you can talk to them about something other than their rule-breaking.

A defiant, hostile student can pose serious problems. If there is an outburst, try to get out of the situation as soon as possible; everyone loses in a public power struggle. One possibility is to give the student a chance to save face and cool down by saying, "It's your choice to cooperate or not. You can take a minute to think about it." If the student complies, the two of you can talk later about controlling the outbursts. If the student refuses to cooperate, you can tell him or her to wait in the hall until you get the class started on work, then step outside for a private talk. If the student refuses to leave, send another class member for the assistant principal. Again, follow through. If the student complies before help arrives, do not let him or her off the hook. If outbursts occur frequently, you might have a conference with the counselor, parents, or other teachers. If the problem is an irreconcilable clash of personalities, the student should be transferred to another teacher. There is quite a bit of discussion today about zero tolerance for rule breaking in the schools. Is this a good idea? The *Point/Counterpoint* looks at both sides.

It sometimes is useful to keep records of the incidents by logging the student's name, words and actions, date, time, place, and teacher's response. These records may help identify patterns and can prove useful in meetings with administrators, parents, or special services personnel (Burden, 1995). Some teachers have students sign each entry to verify the incidents.

Connect and **Extend** to **Other Chapters**

In Chapter 3 you saw a list of warning signs about violence in schools.

Violence or destruction of property is a difficult and potentially dangerous problem. The first step is to send for help and get the names of participants and witnesses. Then get rid of any crowd that may have gathered; an audience will only make things worse.

STORIES OF LEARNING
TRIBUTES TO TEACHING

SANDY KRUPINSKI, a chemistry teacher in New Jersey, tells how she handled a dangerous situation. Robert walked into the class, straight to Daniel's desk:

> *As usual, I was standing at the doorway as the kids were coming into the classroom. I noticed Robert come in without his backpack or any books. That didn't look right, and I watched him cross the room and go over to Daniel, who was sitting at his desk. Robert picked up the desk and the leg of Daniel's chair and overturned them, cursing and screaming the whole time. I ran over. The first thing I said was "Daniel, don't raise your hands." He was on the floor on his back, and Robert was standing over him screaming. I kept saying, "Robert, look at me, look at me, look at me." Finally, he made eye contact. Then I said, "You need to come with me." We began to walk toward the door, but he turned back and started cursing again. Very quietly and firmly I told him, "You need to come with me." We began to walk toward the door, but he turned back and started cursing again. Very quietly and firmly I told him, "You need to come with me now." He followed me to the door, and as I reached the door I picked up the phone and called the office and said there was a problem and to send someone up. Then we stepped out into the hallway. Robert was angry and was going to leave, and I asked him to please stop and talk to me about what was going on, what was bothering him. I didn't yell, I didn't say, "How could you do something so stupid?" (even though that's what I felt like saying). I said, "Obviously you're upset about something. Tell me about it." It turns out that these two were friends, but Robert found out that Daniel was sleeping with his [Robert's] girlfriend. I heard a lot I didn't really want to hear, but it kept him occupied until the vice-principal came up.*
>
> *Once the vice-principal took Robert, I got Daniel out into the hallway and asked him if he was OK, and if he needed to go to the nurse, or needed to be out of the classroom. He said no, he was OK. I told him, "You were very smart for not raising your hands against Robert." He returned to his seat, and all the kids started saying, "Daniel, are you OK?" and crowding around him. I told them, "Robert's in the office. Daniel's OK. Let's get started on chemistry." At the end of the period, the office called for Daniel to go to the peer mediation room to have the dispute mediated.*

"I kept saying, 'Robert, look at me, look at me.'"

Robert was suspended for three days, but before he left, he apologized to Sandy for his language. Sandy accepted the apology and they talked about other ways he could have handled the situation. When Robert returned after the suspension, Sandy made sure that the two boys' seats were changed so they were separated and easy for her to monitor for a while.

Source: From *Secondary Classroom Management: Lessons from Research and Practice* (3rd ed.), by C. S. Weinstein. Published by McGraw-Hill. Copyright © 2003 by McGraw-Hill. Adapted with permission from The McGraw-Hill Companies.

Point/Counterpoint

Is Zero Tolerance a Good Idea?

WITH THE VERY visible violence in schools today, some districts have instituted "zero-tolerance" policies for rule breaking. One result? Two 8-year-old boys in New Jersey were suspended for making "terrorist threats." They had pointed paper guns at their classmates while playing. Do zero-tolerance policies make sense?

POINT Zero tolerance means zero common sense.

An Internet search using keywords ["zero-tolerance" and schools] will locate a wealth of information about the policy—much of it against. For example, in the August 29, 2001 issue of *Salon Magazine*, Johanna Wald wrote an article entitled "The failure of zero tolerance." Here are two examples she cites:

> *A 17-year-old honors student in Arkansas begins his senior year with an even more ominous cloud over his head. His college scholarship is in danger because of a 45-day sentence to an alternative school. His offense? An arbitrary search of his car by school officials in the spring revealed no drugs, but a scraper and pocketknife that his father had inadvertently left there the night before when he was fixing the rearview mirror. Despite anguished pleas of extenuating circumstances by the desperate father, the school system has so far adamantly insisted that automatic punishments for weapon possession in school are inviolate.*
>
> *Upon her release on bail, the National Merit scholar jailed and banned from her graduation for leaving a kitchen knife in her car commented, "They're taking away my memories." Indeed, for all of the pious talk about the need for "consequences" for students' actions, officials justifying these excesses seem curiously oblivious to the long-term impact of taking away the memories, dreams, and futures of a generation of students.*

A 2001 Associated Press story, "ABA Recommends Dropping Zero-Tolerance in Schools," announced that the leadership of the American Bar Association voted to recommend ending zero-tolerance school policies. The article quotes a report that accompanied the resolution against zero tolerance adopted by the ABA's policy-making House of Delegates: "Zero-tolerance has become a one-size-fits-all solution to all of the problems that schools confront" (Associated Press, February 21, 2001, available online at http://www.cnn.com/2001/fyi/teachers.ednews/02/21/zero.tolerance.ap/). On this website you can post your views about zero-tolerance. Finally, many of the popular zero-tolerance interventions such as increased security guards, hallway monitors, and the introduction of metal detectors have no apparent effect on the incidence of school bullying (Hyman et al., 2006; NCES, 2003).

COUNTERPOINT Zero tolerance is necessary for now.

The arguments for zero tolerance focus on school safety and the responsibilities of schools and teachers to protect the students and themselves. Of course, many of the incidents reported in the news seem like overreactions to childhood pranks or worse, over-zealous application of zero tolerance to innocent mistakes or lapses of memory. But how do school officials separate the innocent from the dangerous? For example, it has been widely reported that Andy Williams (the boy who killed two classmates in Santee, California) assured his friends before the shootings that he was only joking about "pulling a Columbine."

In response to the girl who missed her graduation ceremony because school authorities found a knife in her car, Mike Gallagher (2001), a journalist writing for NewsMax.com said:

> *I certainly understand the reason behind the e-mails of protest I received from Americans who think this is a case that went too far. It sure was a shame that this high-schooler, by all accounts a great student and fine young lady, had to miss the excitement of her commencement ceremony. But I argued that rules are rules, and zero-tolerance weapons policies were created because of parents' demands that schools be safe.*

Mr. Gallagher went on to describe a tragic event in Japan where eight young children were killed in school by a madman wielding a knife just one inch longer than the one found in the student's car.

On January 13, 2003, I read a story in *USA Today* by Gregg Toppo entitled "School Violence Hits Lower Grades: Experts Who See Violent Behavior in Younger Kids Blame Parents, Prenatal Medical Problems and an Angry Society; Educators Search for Ways to Cope." The story opened with these examples: a 2nd-grader in Indiana takes off his shoe and attacks his teacher with it, a Philadelphia kindergartner hits a pregnant teacher in the stomach, and an 8-year-old in Maryland threatens to use gasoline (he knew exactly where he would pour it) to burn down his suburban elementary school. Toppo noted, "Elementary school principals and safety experts say they're seeing more violence and aggression than ever among their youngest students, pointing to what they see as an alarming rise in assaults and threats to classmates and teachers" (p. A2). Toppo cited statistics indicating that, although the incidence of school violence has decreased overall, attacks on elementary school teachers have actually increased.

WHAT DO YOU THINK?

Vote online at **www.mylabschool.com**

Do not try to break up a fight without help. Make sure the school office is aware of the incident; usually the school has a policy for dealing with these situations. *The Stories of Learning: Tributes to Teaching* feature shows how one teacher helped two students survive a very volatile situation by keeping focused on what the students needed.

Reaching Every Student: School-wide Positive Behavior Supports

We discussed functional behavioral analysis and positive behavior supports (PBS) in Chapter 6. Positive behavioral supports are required under IDEIA for students with disabilities and those who are being considered for special education service. Positive behavioral supports also can be part of a school-wide program. At the school level, the teachers and administrators:

- agree on a common approach for supporting positive behaviors and correcting problems.
- develop a few positively stated, specific behavioral expectations and procedures for teaching these expectations to all students.
- identify a continuum of ways (from small and simple, to more complex and stronger) to acknowledge appropriate behaviors and correct behavioral errors.
- integrate the positive behavioral support procedures with the schools' discipline policy.

At the classroom level, teachers are encouraged to use such preventive strategies as **precorrection,** which involves identifying the context for a student's misbehavior, clearly specifying the alternative expected behavior, modifying the situation to make the problem behavior less likely—for example, providing a cue or moving the student away from tempting distractions—then rehearsing the expected positive behaviors in the new context and providing powerful reinforcers when the behaviors occur. There is an emphasis on keeping students engaged, providing a positive focus, consistently enforcing school/class rules, correcting disruptive behavior proactively, and planning for smooth transitions (Freiberg, 2006; www.pbis.org/schoolwide.htm).

Research on school-wide positive behavioral supports is limited, but results have been good. A study comparing middle-school students in a behavioral support program with students outside the program showed that program students reported more positive reinforcement for appropriate behavior. Disciplinary referrals as well as verbal and physical aggression significantly decreased. In addition, students' perceptions of school safety improved (Metzler, Biglan, Rusby & Sprague, 2001). Students in general education may benefit from positive behavioral supports as well. Studies of school-wide PBS efforts indicate decreases in disciplinary referrals (Lewis, Sugai, & Colvin, 1998; Taylor-Green, et al., 1997). In addition, Lewis and Sugai (1996) found that successful use of PBS in a general education setting benefited a student with behavioral disorders (Soodak & McCarthy, 2006).

The Need for Communication

STOP | THINK | WRITE A student says to you, "That book you assigned is really stupid—I'm not reading it!" What do you say? ■

Communication between teacher and students is essential when problems arise. Communication is more than "teacher talks—student listens." It is more than the words exchanged between individuals. We communicate in many ways. Our actions, movements, voice tone, facial expressions, and many other nonverbal behaviors send messages to our students. Many times, the messages we intend to send are not the messages our students receive.

Precorrection A way of preventing serious behavior problems of students who have been labeled at risk by directing the students toward more appropriate actions.

Message Sent—Message Received

Teacher: Carl, where is your homework?
Carl: I left it in my Dad's car this morning.

Teacher: Again? You will have to bring me a note tomorrow from your father saying that you actually did the homework. No grade without the note.
Message Carl receives: I can't trust you. I need proof you did the work.

Teacher: Sit at every other desk. Put all your things under your desk. Jane and Laurel, you are sitting too close together. One of you move!
Message Jane and Laurel receive: I expect you two to cheat on this test.

A new student comes to Ms. Lincoln's kindergarten. The child is messy and unwashed. Ms. Lincoln puts her hand lightly on the girl's shoulder and says, "I'm glad you are here." Her muscles tense, and she leans away from the child.
Message student receives: I don't like you. I think you are bad.

In all interactions, a message is sent and a message is received. Sometimes teachers believe they are sending one message, but their voices, body positions, choices of words, and gestures may communicate a different message.

Students may hear the hidden message and respond to it. For example, a student may respond with hostility if she or he feels insulted by the teacher (or by another student), but may not be able to say exactly where the feeling of being insulted came from. Perhaps it was in the teacher's tone of voice, not the words actually spoken. But the teacher feels attacked for no reason. The first principle of communication is that people respond to what they *think* was said or meant, not necessarily to the speaker's intended message or actual words.

Students in my classes have told me about one instructor who encourages accurate communication by using the **paraphrase rule.** Before any participant, including the teacher, is allowed to respond to any other participant in a class discussion, he or she must summarize what the previous speaker said. If the summary is wrong, indicating the speaker was misunderstood, the speaker must explain again. The respondent then tries again to paraphrase. The process continues until the speaker agrees that the listener has heard the intended message.

Paraphrasing is more than a classroom exercise. It can be the first step in communicating with students. Before teachers can deal appropriately with any student problem, they must know what the real problem is. A student who says, "This book is really dumb! Why did we have to read it?" may really be saying, "The book was too difficult for me. I couldn't read it, and I feel dumb."

Diagnosis: Whose Problem Is It?

As a teacher, you may find many student behaviors unacceptable, unpleasant, or troubling. It is often difficult to stand back from these problems, take an objective look, and decide on an appropriate response. According to Thomas Gordon (1981), the key to good teacher—student relationships is determining *why* you are troubled by a particular behavior and who "owns" the problem. The answer to these questions is critical. If it is really the student's problem, the teacher must become a counselor and supporter, helping the student find his or her own solution. But if the teacher "owns" the problem, it is the teacher's responsibility to find a solution through problem solving with the student.

Diagnosing who owns the problem is not always straightforward. Let's look at three troubling situations to get some practice in this skill:

1. A student writes obscene words and draws sexually explicit illustrations in a school encyclopedia.
2. A student tells you that his parents had a bad fight and he hates his father.
3. A student quietly reads a newspaper in the back of the room.

Why are these behaviors troubling? If you cannot accept the student's behavior because it has a serious effect on you as a teacher—if you are blocked from reaching your goals by the student's action—then *you* own the problem. It is your responsibility to confront the student and seek a solution. A teacher-owned problem appears to be present in

Connect and **Extend** to **PRAXIS II™**

Teacher–Student Communication (III, A)

A well-managed classroom requires a bidirectional line of communication between the teacher and students. Describe the various communication styles that teachers employ when interacting with students, and explain how those styles affect student behavior.

Paraphrase rule Policy whereby listeners must accurately summarize what a speaker has said before being allowed to respond.

the first situation described above—the young pornographer—because teaching materials are damaged.

If you feel annoyed by the behavior because it is getting in the student's own way or because you are embarrassed for the child, but the behavior does not directly interfere with your teaching, then it is probably the student's problem. The student who hates his father would not prevent you from teaching, even though you might wish the student felt differently. The problem is really the student's, and he must find his own solution.

The third situation is more difficult to diagnose. One argument is that the teacher is not interfered with in any way, so it is the student's problem. But teachers might find the student reading the paper distracting during a lecture, so it is their problem, and they must find a solution. In a gray area such as this, the answer probably depends on how the teacher actually experiences the student's behavior.

Having decided who owns the problem, it is time to act.

Counseling: The Student's Problem

Let's pick up the situation in which the student found the reading assignment "dumb." How might a teacher handle this positively?

Student: This book is really dumb! Why did we have to read it?
Teacher: You're pretty upset. This seemed like a worthless assignment to you. [Teacher paraphrases the student's statement, trying to hear the emotions as well as the words.]
Student: Yeah! Well, I guess it was worthless. I mean, I don't know if it was. I couldn't exactly read it.
Teacher: It was just too hard to read, and that bothers you.
Student: Sure, I felt really dumb. I know I can write a good report, but not with a book this tough.
Teacher: I think I can give you some hints that will make the book easier to understand. Can you see me after school today?
Student: Okay.

Here the teacher used **empathetic listening** to allow the student to find a solution. (As you can see, this approach relies heavily on paraphrasing.) By trying to hear the student and by avoiding the tendency to jump in too quickly with advice, solutions, criticisms, reprimands, or interrogations, the teacher keeps the communication lines open. Here are a few *unhelpful* responses the teacher might have made:

- I chose the book because it is the best example of the author's style in our library. You will need to have read it before your English II class next year. (The teacher justifies the choice; this prevents the student from admitting that this "important" assignment is too difficult.)
- Did you really read it? I bet you didn't do the work, and now you want out of the assignment. (The teacher accuses; the student hears, "The teacher doesn't trust me!" and must either defend herself or himself or accept the teacher's view.)
- Your job is to read the book, not ask me why. I know what's best. (The teacher pulls rank, and the student hears, "You can't possibly decide what is good for you!" The student can rebel or passively accept the teacher's judgment.)

Empathetic, active listening is more than a parroting of the student's words; it should capture the emotions, intent, and meaning behind them. Sokolove, Garrett, Sadker, and Sadker (1986, p. 241) have summarized the components of active listening: (1) blocking out external stimuli; (2) attending carefully to both the verbal and nonverbal messages; (3) differentiating between the intellectual and the emotional content of the message; and (4) making inferences regarding the speaker's feelings.

Empathetic listening Hearing the intent and emotions behind what another says and reflecting them back by paraphrasing.

When students realize they really have been heard and not evaluated negatively for what they have said or felt, they begin to trust the teacher and to talk more openly. Sometimes the true problem surfaces later in the conversation.

Confrontation and Assertive Discipline

Now let's assume a student is doing something that actively interferes with teaching. The teacher decides the student must stop. The problem is the teacher's. Confrontation, not counseling, is required.

"I" Messages. Gordon (1981) recommends sending an **"I" message** in order to intervene and change a student's behavior. Basically, this means telling a student in a straightforward, assertive, and nonjudgmental way what she or he is doing, how it affects you as a teacher, and how you feel about it. The student is then free to change voluntarily, and often does so. Here are two "I" messages:

> If you leave your book bags in the aisles, I might trip and hurt myself.
>
> When you all call out, I can't concentrate on each answer, and I'm frustrated.

"I" messages basically mean telling a student what he or she is doing wrong, how it affects you as a teacher, and how you feel about it. This puts the onus on the student to change the behavior voluntarily.

Assertive Discipline. Lee and Marlene Canter (1992; Canter, 1996) suggest other approaches for dealing with a teacher-owned problem. They call their method **assertive discipline.** Many teachers are ineffective with students because they are either wishy-washy and passive or hostile and aggressive (Charles, 2002a).

Instead of telling the student directly what to do, passive teachers tell, or often ask, the student to *try* or to *think about* the appropriate action. The passive teacher might comment on the problem behavior without actually telling the child what to do differently: "Why are you doing that? Don't you know the rules?" or "Sam, are you disturbing the class?" Or teachers may clearly state what should happen, but never follow through with the established consequences, giving the students "one more chance" every time. Finally, teachers may ignore behavior that should receive a response or they may wait too long before responding.

A *hostile response style* involves different mistakes. Teachers may make "you" statements that condemn the student without stating clearly what the student should be doing: "You should be ashamed of the way you're behaving!" or "You never listen!" or "You are acting like a baby!" Teachers may also threaten students angrily, but follow through too seldom, perhaps because the threats are too vague—"You'll be very sorry you did that when I get through with you!"—or too severe. For example, a teacher tells a student in a physical education class that he will have to "sit on the bench for *three weeks.*" A few days later, the team is short one member and the teacher lets the student play, never returning him to the bench to complete the three-week sentence. Often a teacher who has been passive becomes hostile and explodes when students persist in misbehaving.

In contrast with both the passive and hostile styles, an *assertive response* communicates to the students that you care too much about them and the process of learning to allow inappropriate behavior to persist. Assertive teachers clearly state what they expect. To be most effective, the teachers often look into a student's eyes when speaking and address the student by name. Assertive teachers' voices are calm, firm, and confident. They are not sidetracked by accusations such as "You just don't understand!" or "You don't like me!" Assertive teachers do not get into a debate about the fairness of the rules. They expect changes, not promises or apologies.

Not all educators believe that assertive discipline is useful. Earlier critics questioned the penalty-focused approach and emphasized that assertive discipline undermined student self-management (Render, Padilla, & Krank, 1989). John Covaleskie (1992) observed "What helps children become moral is not knowledge of the rules, or even obedience to the rules, but discussions about the reasons for acting in certain ways" (p. 56). These critics have had an impact. More recent versions of assertive discipline focus on teaching students "in an atmosphere of respect, trust, and support, how to behave responsibly" (Charles, 2002a, p. 47).

Confrontations and Negotiations. If "I" messages or assertive responses fail and a student persists in misbehaving, teacher and student are in a conflict. Several pitfalls now loom. The two individuals become less able to perceive each other's behavior accurately.

Connect and Extend to the Research

To read two careful studies about how children respond to ambiguous communications from teachers who appear powerless, see Bugental, D. B., Lyon, J. E., Lin, E. K., McGrath, E. P., & Bimbela, A. (1999). Children "tune out" in response to the ambiguous communication style of powerless adults. *Child Development, 70,* 214–230 and Bugental, D. B., Lewis, J. C., Lin, E., Lyon, J., & Kopeikin, H. (1999). In charge but not in control: The management of teaching relationships by adults with low perceived power. *Developmental Psychology, 35,* 1367–1378.

"I" message Clear, nonaccusatory statement of how something is affecting you.

Assertive discipline Clear, firm, unhostile response style.

Research has shown that the more angry you get with another person, the more you see the other as the villain and yourself as an innocent victim. Because you feel the other person is in the wrong, and he or she feels just as strongly that the conflict is all your fault, very little mutual trust is possible. A cooperative solution to the problem is almost impossible. In fact, by the time the discussion has gone on a few minutes, the original problem is lost in a sea of charges, countercharges, and self-defense (Baron & Byrne, 2003).

There are three methods of resolving a conflict between teacher and student. One is for the teacher to impose a solution. This may be necessary during an emergency, as when a defiant student refuses to go to the hall to discuss a public outbreak, but it is not a good solution for most conflicts. The second method is for the teacher to give in to the student's demands. You might be convinced by a particularly compelling student argument, but again, this should be used sparingly. It is generally a bad idea to be talked out of a position, unless the position was wrong in the first place. Problems arise when either the teacher or the student gives in completely.

Gordon recommends a third approach, which he calls the "no-lose method." Here, the needs of both the teacher and the students are taken into account in the solution. No one person is expected to give in completely; all participants retain respect for themselves and each other. The no-lose method is a six-step, problem-solving strategy:

1. *Define the problem.* What exactly are the behaviors involved? What does each person want? (Use active listening to help students pinpoint the real problem.)
2. *Generate many possible solutions.* Brainstorm, but remember, don't allow any evaluations of ideas yet.
3. *Evaluate each solution.* Any participant may veto any idea. If no solutions are found to be acceptable, brainstorm again.
4. *Make a decision.* Choose one solution through consensus—no voting. In the end, everyone must be satisfied with the solution.
5. *Determine how to implement the solution.* What will be needed? Who will be responsible for each task? What is the timetable?
6. *Evaluate the success of the solution.* After trying the solution for a while, ask, "Are we satisfied with our decision? How well is it working? Should we make some changes?"

Many of the conflicts in classrooms can be important learning experiences for all concerned.

Diversity and Convergences in Learning Environments

We have looked at quite a few perspectives on classroom management. Clearly, there is not a one-size-fits-all strategy for creating social and physical spaces for learning. Let's first consider the role of culture in productive classroom management.

Diversity: Culturally Responsive Management

Research on discipline shows that African Americans and Latino/a Americans, especially males, are punished more often and more harshly than other students. These students lose time from learning as they spend more hours in detention or suspension (Gay, 2006; Monroe & Obidah, 2002; Skiba, Michael, Nardo, & Peterson, 2000). Why?

The notion that African Americans and Latino/a students are punished more because they commit more serious offenses is NOT supported by the data. Instead, these students are punished more severely for minor offenses such as rudeness or defiance—words and actions that are interpreted by teachers as meriting severe punishment. One explanation is a lack of cultural synchronization between teachers and students. "The language, style of walking, glances, and dress of black children, particularly males, have engendered fear, apprehension, and overreaction among many teachers and school administrators" (Irvine, 1990, p. 27). African American students may be disciplined for behaviors that were never intended to be disruptive or disrespectful. Teachers do their students and themselves a service if they work at becoming bicultural—helping their students to learn how to function in both mainstream and home cultures, but also learning the meaning of their students' words and actions—so they do not misinterpret and then punish their students' unintended insults (Gay, 2006).

Culturally responsive management is simply a part of the larger concept of culturally relevant teaching. Geneva Gay (2006) sums it up:

> If the classroom is a comfortable, caring, embracing, affirming, engaging, and facilitative place for students then discipline is not likely to be much of an issue. It follows then that both classroom management and school achievement can be improved for students from different ethnic, racial, social, and linguistic backgrounds by ensuring that curriculum and instruction are culturally relevant and personally meaningful for them.

The teachers who seem to be most effective with these students practice culturally responsive management and have been called "warm demanders" (Irvine & Armento, 2001; Irvine and Fraser, 1998). Sometimes these **warm demanders** appear harsh to outside observers (Burke-Spero, 1999; Burke-Spero & Woolfolk Hoy, 2002). For example, results of one study indicated:

> To a person unfamiliar with African American culture of inner-city life, it could be misconstrued as intimidation or heavy handed but in the minds of these informants, discipline was directly connected to caring. In fact, all viewed lack of discipline as a sign of uncaring and an apathetic teaching force. (Gordon, 1998, p. 427)

Carla Monroe and Jennifer Obidah (2002) studied Ms. Simpson, an African American teacher working with her 8th-grade science class. She describes herself as having high expectations for academics and behavior in her classes—so much so that she believed her students perceived her as "mean." Yet she often used humor and dialect to communicate her expectations, as in the following exchange:

> *Ms. Simpson* [addressing the class]: If you know you're going to act the fool just come to me and say, "I'm going to act the fool at the pep rally," so I can go ahead and send you to wherever you need to go. [Class laughs.]
>
> *Ms. Simpson:* I'm real serious. If you know you're having a bad day, you don't want anybody touching you, you don't want nobody saying nothing to you, somebody bump into you you're going to snap—you need to come up to me and say, "I'm going to snap and I can't go to the pep rally." [The students start to call out various comments.]
>
> *Ms. Simpson:* Now, I just want to say I expect you to have the best behavior because you're the most mature students in the building . . . don't make me stop the pep rally and ask the 8th graders to leave.
>
> *Edward:* We'll have silent lunch won't we? [Class laughs.]
>
> *Ms. Simpson:* You don't want to dream about what you're going to have. [Class laughs.] Ok, 15 minutes for warm ups. [The students begin their warm-up assignment.]

Many African American students may be more accustomed to a directive kind of management and discipline outside of school. Their families might say, "Put down that candy" or "Go to bed," whereas White parents might ask, "Can we eat candy before dinner?" or "Isn't it time for bed?" As H. Richard Milner (2006) says, "The question should not be which approach is right or wrong but which approach works with and connects with the students' prior knowledge and ways of knowing."

Convergences: Research on Management Approaches

We have examined a number of approaches to classroom student discipline. Are some better than others? Research provides some guidance. Emmer and Aussiker (1990) conducted a meta-analysis of three general perspectives on management: influencing students through listening and problem solving, as described by Gordon (1981); group management through class meetings and student discussion, as advocated by Glasser (1969, 1990); and control through rewards and punishments, as exemplified by Canter and Canter (1992). No clear conclusions could be drawn about the impact of these approaches on student behaviors.

Connect and Extend to the Research

To read more about "warm demanders," see Irvine, J. J., & Armento, B. J. (2001). *Culturally responsive teaching: Lesson planning for elementary and middle grades.* New York: McGraw-Hill and Irvine, J. J., & Fraser, J. W. (1998, May). Warm demanders. *Education Week.* Available online at www.edweek.org/ew/ewstory.cfm?slug=35irvine.h17&keywords=Irvine

Connect and Extend to the Research

For an excellent analysis of management in urban schools, see H. Richard Milner (2006). Classroom management in urban classrooms. In C. Evertson & C. S. Weinstein (Eds.) *Handbook for classroom management: Research, practice, and contemporary issues.* Mahwah, NJ: Lawrence Erlbaum.

Culturally responsive management Taking cultural meanings and styles into account when developing management plans and responding to students.

Warm demanders Effective teachers with African American students who show both high expectations and great caring for their students.

When parents and teachers share the same expectations and support each other, they can promote a more positive outcome for students and support more positive behavior at school.

However, some evaluations have found positive effects for Freiberg's (1999) Consistency Management program and for programs that use rewards and punishments (Lewis, 2001).

Integrating Ideas. In a study conducted in Australia, Ramon Lewis (2001) found that recognizing and rewarding appropriate student behaviors, talking with students about how their behavior affects others, involving students in class discipline decisions, and providing nondirective hints and descriptions about unacceptable behaviors were associated with students taking greater responsibility for their own learning. It is interesting that these interventions represent all three of the general approaches reviewed by Emmer and Aussiker: influence, group management, and control. Lewis also concluded that teachers sometimes find using these interventions difficult when students are aggressive—and most in need of the approaches. When teachers feel threatened, it can be difficult to do what students need, but that may be the most important time to act positively.

Connect and Extend to Your Teaching/Portfolio

Add some ideas for parent involvement from this chapter to your Portfolio.

Communicating with Families about Classroom Management. As we have seen throughout this book, families are important partners in education. This statement applies to classroom management as well. When parents and teachers share the same expectations and support each other, they can create a more positive classroom environment and more time for learning. The *Family and Community Partnerships Guidelines* provide ideas for working with families and the community.

Family and Community Partnerships

Guidelines: Classroom Management

Make sure families know the expectations and rules of your class and school.

EXAMPLES

1. At a Family Fun Night, have your students do skits showing the rules—how to follow them and what breaking them "looks like" and "sounds like."
2. Make a poster for the refrigerator at home that describes, in a light way, the most important rules and expectations.
3. For older students, give families a list of due dates for the major assignments, along with tips about how to encourage quality work by pacing the effort—avoiding last minute panic.
4. Communicate in appropriate ways—use the family's first language when possible. Tailor messages to the reading level of the home.

Make families partners in recognizing good citizenship.

EXAMPLES

1. Send positive notes home when students, especially students who have had trouble with classroom management, work well in the classroom.
2. Give ideas for ways any family, even those with few economic resources, can celebrate accomplishment—a favorite food; the chance to choose a video to rent; a comment to a special person such as an aunt, grandparent, or minister; the chance to read to a younger sibling.

Identify talents in the community to help build a learning environment in your class.

EXAMPLES

1. Have students write letters to carpet and furniture stores asking for donations of remnants to carpet a reading corner.
2. Find family members who can build shelves or room dividers, paint, sew, laminate manipulatives, write stories, repot plants, or network computers.
3. Contact businesses for donations of computers, printers, or other equipment.

Seek cooperation from families when behavior problems arise.

EXAMPLES

1. Talk to families over the phone or in their home. Keep good records about the problem behavior.
2. Listen to family members and solve problems with them.

For more ideas see **http://www.educationworld.com/clsrm_mgmt/index.shtml**

The Need for Organization (pp. 444–447)

What are the challenges of classroom management? Classrooms are by nature multidimensional, full of simultaneous activities, fast-paced and immediate, unpredictable, public, and affected by the history of students' and teachers' actions. A teacher must juggle all these elements every day. Productive classroom activity requires students' cooperation. Maintaining cooperation is different for each age group. Young students are learning how to "go to school" and need to learn the general procedures of school. Older students need to learn the specifics required for working in different subjects. Working with adolescents requires teachers to understand the power of the adolescent peer group.

What are the goals of good classroom management? The goals of effective classroom management are to make ample time for learning; improve the quality of time use by keeping students actively engaged; make sure participation structures are clear, straightforward, and consistently signaled; and encourage student self-management, self-control, and responsibility.

Classroom management Techniques used to maintain a healthy learning environment, relatively free of behavior problems.

Allocated time Time set aside for learning.

Engaged time/Time on task Time spent actively learning.

Academic learning time Time when students are actually succeeding at the learning task.

Participation structures Rules defining how to participate in different activities.

Self-management Management of your own behavior and acceptance of responsibility for your own actions.

Creating a Positive Learning Environment (pp. 448–458)

Distinguish between rules and procedures. Rules are the specific dos and don'ts of classroom life. They usually are written down or posted. Procedures cover administrative tasks, student movement, housekeeping, routines for accomplishing lessons, interactions between students and teachers, and interactions among students. Rules can be written in terms of rights and students may benefit from participating in establishing these rules. Consequences should be established for following and breaking the rules and procedures so that the teacher and the students know what will happen.

Distinguish between personal territories and interest-areas spatial arrangements. There are two basic kinds of spatial organization, territorial (the traditional classroom arrangement) and functional (dividing space into interest or work areas). Flexibility is often the key. Access to materials, convenience, privacy when needed, ease of supervision, and a willingness to reevaluate plans are important considerations in the teacher's choice of physical arrangements.

What management issues do computers raise in the classroom? Clear procedures are especially important when there are computers in the classroom. Whether teachers have one, several, or a room full of computers, they need to think through what students will need to know, teach procedures, and provide easy-to-find and follow written instructions for common tasks. Students or parent volunteers can be trained as expert support. Different role structures make management of computer tasks easier.

Contrast the first school week of effective and ineffective classroom managers. Effective classroom managers spent the first days of class teaching a workable, easily understood set of rules and procedures by using lots of explanation, examples, and practice. Students were occupied with organized, enjoyable activities and learned to function cooperatively in the group. Quick, firm, clear, and consistent responses to infractions of the rules characterized effective teachers. The teachers had planned carefully to avoid any last-minute tasks that might have taken them away from their students. These teachers dealt with the children's pressing concerns first.

Procedures Prescribed steps for an activity.

Rules Statements specifying expected and forbidden behaviors; dos and don'ts.

Natural/logical consequences Instead of punishing, have students redo, repair, or in some way face the consequences that naturally flow from their actions.

Action zone Area of a classroom where the greatest amount of interaction takes place.

Maintaining a Good Environment for Learning (pp. 458–466)

How can teachers encourage engagement? In general, as teacher supervision increases, students' engaged time also increases. When the task provides continuous cues for the student about what to do next, involvement will be greater. Activities with clear steps are likely to be more absorbing, because one step leads naturally to the next. Making work requirements clear and specific, providing needed materials, and monitoring activities all add to engagement.

Explain the factors identified by Kounin that prevent management problems in the classroom. To create a positive environment and prevent problems, teachers must take individual differences into account, maintain student motivation, and reinforce positive behavior. Successful problem preventers are skilled in four areas described by Kounin: "withitness," overlapping, group focusing, and movement management. When penalties have to be imposed, teachers should impose them calmly and privately. In addition to applying Kounin's ideas, teachers can prevent problems by establishing a caring classroom community and teaching students to use social skills and emotional self-regulation skills.

Describe seven levels of intervention in misbehavior. Teachers can first make eye contact with the student or use other nonverbal signals, then try verbal hints such as simply inserting the student's name into the lecture. Next the teacher asks if the offender is aware of the negative effects of the actions, then reminds the student of the procedure and has her or him follow it correctly. If this does not work, the teacher can ask the student to state the correct rule or procedure and then to follow it, and then move to telling the student in a clear, assertive, and unhostile way to stop the misbehavior. If this fails too, the teacher can offer a choice—stop the behavior or meet privately to work out the consequences.

What are some challenges in secondary classrooms? Teachers working in secondary schools should be prepared to handle students who don't complete school work, repeatedly break the same rule, or openly defy teachers.

Withitness According to Kounin, awareness of everything happening in a classroom.

Overlapping Supervising several activities at once.

Group focus The ability to keep as many students as possible involved in activities.

Movement management Keeping lessons and the group moving at an appropriate (and flexible) pace, with smooth transitions and variety.

Precorrection A way of preventing serious behavior problems of students who have been labeled at risk by directing the students toward more appropriate actions.

The Need for Communication

(pp. 466–470)

What is meant by "empathetic listening"? Communication between teacher and student is essential when problems arise. All interactions between people, even silence or neglect, communicate some meaning. Empathetic, active listening can be a helpful response when students bring problems to teachers. Teachers must reflect back to the students what they hear them saying. This reflection is more than a parroting of words; it should capture the emotions, intent, and meaning behind them.

Distinguish among passive, hostile, and assertive response styles. The *passive style* can take several forms. Instead of telling the student directly what to do, the teacher simply comments on the behavior, asks the student to *think about* the appropriate action, or threatens but never follows through. In a *hostile response style*, teachers may make "you" statements that condemn the student without stating clearly what the student should be doing. An *assertive response* communicates to the students that the teacher cares too much about them and the process of learning to allow inappropriate behavior to persist. Assertive teachers clearly state what they expect.

Paraphrase rule Policy whereby listeners must accurately summarize what a speaker has said before being allowed to respond.

Empathetic listening Hearing the intent and emotions behind what another says and reflecting them back by paraphrasing.

"I" message Clear, nonaccusatory statement of how something is affecting you.

Assertive discipline Clear, firm, unhostile response style.

Culturally responsive management Taking cultural meanings and styles into account when developing management plans and responding to students.

Warm demanders Effective teachers with African American students who show both high expectations and great caring for their students.

Teachers' Casebook: Connections to PRAXIS II™

Teachers work to create school and classroom environments in which students feel safe, accepted, and respected. In the case at the beginning of the chapter, that environment is threatened—at least for one student. As a classroom manager, you have to ask yourself not only what to do to eliminate this problem for your student, but also what strategies and techniques can prevent or reduce similar problems in the future.

What Would They Do?

Here is how some practicing teachers responded to the problems with bullies at school.

Jolita Harper **Third Grade Teacher,**

Preparing Academic Leaders Academy,
Maple Heights, Ohio

I believe that the entire learning community has a clear role in preventing acts of intimidation between students, and that this is best accomplished with clear communication between all parties. Care should be taken to spread awareness between colleagues as to the nature of the situation. Classroom teachers who are alert to these instances of bullying are then able to provide an additional presence in situations, such as in hallways and the lunchroom, where this is likely to take place. Further, communication between individual classroom teachers and the victim of this bullying is essential. I would make certain to provide a sensitive ear to this student's plight as we work together to formulate alternatives toward improving the situation. Finally, in the event that the two bullying students were in my classes, I would communicate with them in such a way as to make clear the effect of their actions on others in an effort to promote empathy for their victim and, hopefully, initiate a change in their behaviors.

Keith J. Boyle **English Teacher, grades 9–12,**

Dunellen High School, Dunellen, New Jersey

Errant behavior throughout the middle school may be indicative of future behavioral problems and, as many things in life, the more this misbehavior is allowed to exist, the longer it will have a chance to thrive. In this case of a child being continually bullied by two other children (gender having no bearing in this situation), the knowledge of this wrongdoing must not be ignored or isolated. I would interview both the victim and the bullies, separately, to glean as much information as possible. If this were a singular incident, I would attempt to handle it myself via contact with the pertinent parents. However, if this were a recurring problem, the administration must be made aware. Any administrator will acknowledge that to be left in the dark about a serious situation within the environs of his/her responsibility is precarious. The appropriate guidance counselor should also be involved. The gravity of abusive behavior toward fellow students must be emphasized to the offenders. Significant punitive action is integral in order to send a message to the entire community that their school is indeed a haven in which one can feel the uninhibited freedom to learn.

Dan Doyle **History Teacher, Grade 11,**

St. Joseph's Academy, Hoffman, Illinois

As a high school teacher I'd be especially concerned about the existence of bullying among older students. While such behavior in elementary school is hurtful and damaging, it can become downright dangerous as students get older (and bigger!). I'd also be frustrated to think that, perhaps, early warning signs among these children may have been ignored or under-addressed at the elementary level, when teachers and/or parents are better positioned to get a grip on them. My first step would be to alert school personnel, particularly those who monitor hallways, the cafeteria, and other common areas, to be on the lookout for any type of bullying behavior. I'd put those responsible in communication with the guidance counselor's office; the counselor would determine whether the parents needed to be involved from there. Events in our society in recent years preclude the option of taking this sort of behavior lightly, or assuming it will take care of itself.

Kelley Crockett

Meadowbrook Elementary School, Fort Worth, Texas

Bullying cannot be tolerated. No school, no teacher, no administrator can afford a climate in which abusive behavior is allowed to germinate. Any incident of victimization must be immediately documented and submitted to the Principal. As well, I would schedule a conference that same day with the school counselor for my student in order to both allow another avenue of documentation and reinforce support that the problem is being aggressively addressed.

How I handle the next step depends on the administration in place but the important issue to remember is that there is a next step. The teacher must follow up with the student. Within 48 hours I would privately ask my student if there have been any further incidents. If he hesitates or acknowledges continued harassment I would direct him to write it down and I would document any questions I had asked him and his responses. I would then include his statement and my own in another report for both the Principal and the counselor.

As teachers, we hold the front line. To the children in our care we represent one of the first relationships with authority and civilize society. We can do no less than lend our voice and action to the betterment of our world.

CHAPTER 13

Teaching for Learning

Teachers' Casebook: What Would You Do? 477

The First Step: Planning 478

Objectives for Learning 479

Flexible and Creative Plans—Using Taxonomies 481

Another View: Planning from a Constructivist Perspective 483

Teacher-Directed Instruction 485

Characteristics of Effective Teachers 486

Explanation and Direct Instruction 487

Seatwork and Homework 491

Questioning and Recitation 492

Group Discussion 496

Teacher Expectations 496

Two Kinds of Expectation Effects 497

Sources of Expectations 498

Do Teachers' Expectations Really Affect Students' Achievement? 498

Student-Centered Teaching: Examples in Reading, Mathematics, and Science 500

Learning and Teaching Reading and Writing 502

Learning and Teaching Mathematics 505

Learning and Teaching Science 506

Reaching Every Student: Effective Teaching in Inclusive Classrooms 508

Technology and Exceptional Students 511

Diversity and Convergences in Teaching 513

Diversity: Differentiated Instruction 514

Convergences: Beyond the Debates to Outstanding Teaching 515

Summary Table 516

Teachers' Casebook: Connections to PRAXIS II™/What Would They Do? 519

What Would You Do?

Teachers' Casebook

On the first day of your orientation for your new position, you are handed a long list of competencies and topics that could be covered on the proficiency test required by the *No Child Left Behind Act* that the students will take in the spring. You learn that your new school is on a state list of districts being monitored because they have not made adequate yearly progress for the past two years. You agree that many of the topics on the test list are important, but your school seems to have no plan for teaching other than drill and practice on facts and skills that might be on the test.

Critical Thinking

- How will you arouse students' curiosity and interests about the topics and skills that will be tested?
- How will you establish the value of learning this material?
- How will you get students engaged in real learning about the topics?
- What more do you need to know to prepare your students for this big test?

Collaboration

With 3 or 4 other students in your class, identify a key concept in your subject that is likely to be on a statewide test. Plan a lesson to teach that will help students understand and remember the concept.

Much of this text has been about learning and learners. In this chapter, we focus on teaching and teachers. We look first at how teachers plan, including how to use taxonomies of learning objectives or themes as a basis for planning.

What else do we know about teaching? Are there particular characteristics that distinguish effective from ineffective teachers? Research on whole-class teaching points to the importance of several factors that we will explore.

With this foundation of knowing how to set goals and make plans, as well as an understanding of the characteristics of effective teachers, we move to a consideration of some general teacher-centered strategies: lecturing, seatwork, homework, questioning, recitation, and group discussion.

In the final section of this chapter, we will focus on student-centered approaches for different subjects—reading, writing, mathematics, and science as well as the elements of effective teaching in inclusive classrooms. Educational psychologists have studied how people learn these subjects and identified implications for teaching. By the time you have completed this chapter, you should be able to answer these questions:

- When and how should teachers use instructional objectives and themes for planning?
- What are the characteristics of effective teachers?
- In what situations would each of the following formats be most appropriate: lecture, seatwork and homework, questioning, and group discussion?
- How can teachers' expectations affect student learning?
- How does the teacher's role vary in direct and constructivist teaching approaches?
- What are the merits of approaches to teaching reading, mathematics, and science?

FACING PAGE *Claude Drawing, Francoise and Paloma.* May 17, 1954. Valauris. Pablo Picasso. Oil on canvas, 116 × 89 cm. Inv.: MP 209. Photo: J. G. Berizzi. © 2006 Estate of Pablo Picasso/Artists Rights Society (ARS), New York. Photo: Reunion des Musees Nationaux/Art Resource, New York.

The First Step: Planning

STOP | THINK | WRITE Greta Morine-Dershimer (2006) asks which of the following are true about teacher planning:

Time is of the essence.	A little planning goes a long way.
Plans are made to be broken.	You can do it yourself.
Don't look back.	One size fits all.

When you thought about the "What Would You Do?" challenge at the beginning of this chapter, you were *planning*. In the past few years, educational researchers have become very interested in teachers' planning. They have interviewed teachers about how they plan, asked teachers to "think out loud" while planning or to keep journals describing their plans, and even studied teachers intensively for months at a time. What do you think they have found?

Connect and **Extend** to Your **Teaching/Portfolio**

What is your approach to planning? How will you match teaching approaches to learning goals?

Here are the results of research. First, planning influences what students will learn, because planning transforms the available time and curriculum materials into activities, assignments, and tasks for students—*time is of the essence planning*. When a teacher decides to devote 7 hours to language arts and 15 minutes to science in a given week, the students in that class will learn more language than science. In fact, differences as dramatic as this do occur, with some classrooms dedicating twice as much time as others to certain subjects (Clark & Yinger, 1988; Karweitt, 1989). Planning done at the beginning of the year is particularly important, because many routines and patterns, such as time allocations, are established early. So, *a little planning does go a long way* in terms of what will be taught and what will be learned.

Second, teachers engage in several levels of planning—by the year, term, unit, week, and day. All the levels must be coordinated. Accomplishing the year's plan requires breaking the work into terms, the terms into units, and the units into weeks and days. For experienced teachers, unit planning seems to be the most important level, followed by weekly and then daily planning. As you gain experience in teaching, it will be easier to coordinate these levels of planning and incorporate the state and district curriculum standards as well (Morine-Dershimer, 2006).

Third, plans reduce—but do not eliminate—uncertainty in teaching. Planning must allow flexibility. There is some evidence that when teachers "overplan"—fill every minute and stick to the plan no matter what—their students do not learn as much as students whose teachers are flexible (Shavelson, 1987). So *plans are NOT made to be broken*—but sometimes they need to be bent a bit.

In planning, you can go it alone, but collaboration is better. Sharing ideas with colleagues can be one of the best experiences in teaching.

In order to plan creatively and flexibly, teachers need to have wide-ranging knowledge about students, their interests, and their abilities; the subjects being taught; alternative ways to teach and assess understanding; how to work with groups; the expectations and limitations of the school and community; how to apply and adapt materials and texts; and how to pull all this knowledge together into meaningful activities. The plans of beginning teachers sometimes don't work because they lack knowledge about the students or the subject—they can't estimate how long it will take students to complete an activity, for example, or they stumble when asked for an explanation or a different example (Calderhead, 1996).

"And then, of course, there's the possibility of being just the slightest bit too organized."

By permission of Glen Dines. From *Phi Delta Kappan.*

In planning, *you can do it yourself*—but collaboration is better. Working with other teachers and sharing ideas is one of the best experiences in teaching. Some educators think that a collaborative approach to planning used in Japan called *kenshu* or "mastery through study" is one reason why Japanese students do so well on international tests. A basic part of the process involves a small group of teachers developing a lesson, then videotaping one of the group members teaching the lesson. Next, all members review the tape, analyze student responses, and improve the lesson further. Other teachers try the revised lesson and more improvements follow. At the end of the school year, all the study groups may publish the results of their work. In the United States, this process is called **lesson study** (Morine-Dershimer, 2006). To learn about this approach, search the Internet using the keywords "lesson study." While you are out there in cyberspace, explore some of the lesson plans available using the keywords "lesson plans," or search by subject or grade—for example, "math lesson plans" or "4th-grade lesson plans."

Connect and **Extend** to Your **Teaching/Portfolio**

For an explanation of lesson study, see http://www.rbs.org/currents/0502/what_is_lesson_study.shtml or search the Internet using the keywords "lesson study."

But even great lesson plans taken from a terrific website on science have to be adapted to your situation. Some of the adaptation comes before you teach and some comes after. In fact, much of what experienced teachers know about planning comes from looking back—reflecting—on what worked and what didn't, so *DO look back* on your plans and grow professionally in the process. Collaborative reflection and revising lessons are major components of the *lesson study* approach to planning.

Finally, there is no one model for effective planning. *One size does NOT fit all* in planning. Planning is a creative problem-solving process for experienced teachers. These teachers know how to accomplish many lessons and to teach segments of lessons effectively. They know what to expect and how to proceed, so they don't necessarily continue to follow the detailed lesson-planning models they learned during their teacher-preparation programs. Planning is more informal—"in their heads." However, many experienced teachers think it was helpful to learn this detailed system as a foundation (Clark & Peterson, 1986).

No matter how you plan, you must have a learning goal in mind. In the next section, we consider the range of goals that you might have for your students.

Objectives for Learning

We hear quite a bit today about visions, goals, outcomes, and standards. At a very general, abstract level are the grand goals society may have for graduates of public schools, such as, "All children will start school ready to learn," one of the eight goals for U.S. education in *Goals 2000*. However, very general goals are meaningless as potential guidelines for instruction. States may turn these grand goals into standards, such as the South Carolina standard that students will "Develop the concept of fractions, mixed numbers, and decimals and use models to relate fractions to decimals and to find equivalent fractions." Sometimes the standards are turned into indicators such as "representing equivalent fractions objectives" (Anderson & Krathwohl, 2001, p. 18). At this level, the indicators are close to being instructional objectives.

Connect and **Extend** to Your **Teaching/Portfolio**

Search the Internet using keywords "Goals 2000" to read all the goals.

Norman Gronlund (2004) defines **instructional objectives** as intended learning outcomes. Objectives are the performances students are expected to demonstrate after instruction to show that they have learned what was expected of them. Objectives written by people with behavioral views focus on observable and measurable changes in the

Lesson study As a group, teachers develop, test, improve, and retest lessons until they are satisfied with the final version.

Instructional objectives Clear statement of what students are intended to learn through instruction.

Connect and **Extend** to **PRAXIS II™**

Instructional Objectives (II, B1) Describe the key elements of behavioral and instructional objectives. Be able to write each type of objective for a content area that you expect to teach.

Connect and **Extend** to Your **Teaching/Portfolio**

Do you think behavioral objectives are really objectives in themselves, or are they a "means to an end"?

learner. Behavioral objectives use terms such as *list, define, add,* or *calculate.* Cognitive objectives, on the other hand, emphasize thinking and comprehension, so they are more likely to include words such as *understand, recognize, create,* or *apply.* Let's look at one well-developed method of writing specific objectives.

Mager: Start with the Specific. Robert Mager developed a very influential system for writing instructional objectives (Mager, 1975). His idea is that objectives ought to describe what students will be doing when demonstrating their achievement and how teachers will know they are doing it, so these are generally regarded as **behavioral objectives.** According to Mager, a good objective has three parts. First, it describes the intended *student behavior.* What must the student do? Second, it lists the *conditions* under which the behavior will occur: How will this behavior be recognized or tested? Third, it gives the *criteria* for acceptable performance on the test. For example, an objective in social studies might be: "Given a recent article from the local newspaper [conditions], the student will mark each statement with an F for fact or an O for opinion ([observable student behavior], with 75% of the statement correctly marked [criteria]." With this emphasis on final behavior, Mager's system requires a very explicit statement. Mager contends that often students can teach themselves if they are given well-stated objectives.

Gronlund: Start with the General. Norman Gronlund (2004) offers a different approach, which is often used for writing **cognitive objectives.** He believes that an objective should be stated first in general terms (*understand, solve, appreciate,* etc.). Then the teacher should clarify by listing a few sample behaviors that would provide evidence that the student has attained the objective. Look at the example in Table 13.1. The goal here really is presenting and defending a research project. A teacher could never list all the behaviors that might be involved in "presenting and defending," but stating an initial, general objective along with specific examples makes the purpose clear.

The most recent research on instructional objectives tends to favor approaches similar to Gronlund's. James Popham (2005a), a former proponent of very specific objectives, makes this recommendation:

> Strive to come up with a half dozen or so truly salient, broad, yet measurable instructional objectives for your own classroom. Too many small-scope, hyperspecific objectives will be of scant value to you because, if you're at all normal, you'll soon disregard [them]. On the other hand, a small number of intellectually manageable, broad, yet measurable objectives will not only prove helpful to you instructionally but will also help you answer the what-to-assess question. (pp. 104–105)

TABLE 13.1

Gronlund's Combined Method for Creating Objectives

General Objective

Presents and defends the research project before a group.

Specific Examples

1. Describes the project in a well-organized manner.
2. Summarizes the findings and their implications.
3. Uses display materials to clarify ideas and relationships.
4. Answers group members' questions directly and completely.
5. Presents a report that reflects careful planning.
6. Displays sound reasoning ability through presentation and answers to questions.

Source: "Gronlund's Combined Method for Creating Objectives," Norman Gronlund, *How to Write and Use Instructional Objectives* (6th ed.) © 2000. Adapted by permission of Pearson Education, Inc., Upper Saddle River, NJ.

Behavioral objectives Instructional objectives stated in terms of observable behaviors.

Cognitive objectives Instructional objectives stated in terms of higher-level thinking operations.

Flexible and Creative Plans—Using Taxonomies

STOP | THINK | WRITE Think about your assignments for one of your classes. What kind of thinking is involved in doing the assignments?

Remembering facts and terms?	Analyzing a situation, task, or problem?
Understanding key ideas?	Making evaluations or giving opinions?
Applying information to solve problems?	Creating or designing something new?

Fifty years ago, a group of experts in educational evaluation led by Benjamin Bloom set out to improve college and university examinations. The impact of their work has touched education at all levels around the world (Anderson & Sosniak, 1994). Bloom and his colleagues developed a **taxonomy**, or classification system, of educational objectives. Objectives were divided into three domains: cognitive, affective, and psychomotor. A handbook describing the objectives in each area was eventually published. In real life, of course, behaviors from these three domains occur simultaneously. While students are writing (psychomotor), they are also remembering or reasoning (cognitive), and they are likely to have some emotional response to the task as well (affective).

Connect and Extend to PRAXIS II™

Taxonomies of Educational Objectives (II, B1)

Taxonomies influence every aspect of instruction from textbook design to lesson planning. List the major objectives of each of the taxonomies, and describe the focus of each objective. Be able to incorporate these objectives into instructional objectives that you design.

The Cognitive Domain. Six basic objectives are listed in Bloom's taxonomy of the thinking or **cognitive domain** (Bloom, Engelhart, Frost, Hill, & Krathwohl, 1956):

1. *Knowledge:* Remembering or recognizing something without necessarily understanding, using, or changing it.
2. *Comprehension:* Understanding the material being communicated without necessarily relating it to anything else.
3. *Application:* Using a general concept to solve a particular problem.
4. *Analysis:* Breaking something down into its parts.
5. *Synthesis:* Creating something new by combining different ideas.
6. *Evaluation:* Judging the value of materials or methods as they might be applied in a particular situation.

It is common in education to consider these objectives as a hierarchy, each skill building on those below, but this is not entirely accurate. Some subjects, such as mathematics, do not fit this structure very well (Kreitzer & Madaus, 1994). Still, you will hear many references to *lower-level* and *higher-level objectives,* with knowledge, comprehension, and application considered lower level and the other categories considered higher level. As a rough way of thinking about objectives, this can be helpful (Gronlund, 2004). The taxonomy of objectives can also be helpful in planning assessments because different procedures are appropriate for objectives at the various levels, as you will see in Chapter 15.

Bloom 2001. Bloom's taxonomy guided educators for over 50 years. It is considered one of the most significant educational writings of the 20th century (Anderson & Sosniak, 1994). In 2001, a group of educational researchers published the first major revision of the taxonomy (Anderson & Krathwohl, 2001). The new version retains the six basic levels in a slightly different order, but the names of three levels have been changed to indicate the cognitive processes involved. The six cognitive processes are remembering (knowledge), understanding (comprehension), applying, analyzing, evaluating, and creating (synthesizing). In addition, the revisers have added a new dimension to the taxonomy to recognize that cognitive processes must process something—you have to remember or understand or apply some form of knowledge. If you look at Table 13.2 on the next page, you will see the result. We now have six processes—the cognitive acts of remembering, understanding, applying, analyzing, evaluating, and creating. These processes act on four kinds of knowledge—factual, conceptual, procedural, and metacognitive.

Connect and Extend to the Research

See the Autumn 2002 issue of *Theory Into Practice* on "Revising Bloom's Taxonomy" (Vol. 41, No. 4). Guest Editor: Lorin Anderson.

Consider how this revised taxonomy might suggest objectives for a social studies/language arts class. An objective that targets *analyzing conceptual knowledge* is:

> After reading an historical account of the battle of the Alamo, students will be able to recognize the author's point of view or bias.

Taxonomy Classification system.

Cognitive domain In Bloom's taxonomy, memory and reasoning objectives.

TABLE 13.2

A Revised Taxonomy in the Cognitive Domain

	The Cognitive Process Dimension					
The Knowledge Dimension	1. Remember	2. Understand	3. Apply	4. Analyze	5. Evaluate	6. Create
A. Factual Knowledge						
B. Conceptual Knowledge						
C. Procedural Knowledge						
D. Metacognitive Knowledge						

Source: From *A Taxonomy for Learning, Teaching, and Assessing* by Lorin W. Anderson & David R. Krathwohl. Published by Allyn and Bacon, Boston, MA. Copyright © 2001 by Pearson Education. Reprinted by permission of the publisher.

An objective for *evaluating metacognitive knowledge* might be:

Students will reflect on their strategies for identifying the biases of the author.

The Affective Domain. The objectives in the taxonomy of the **affective domain,** or domain of emotional response, have not yet been revised from the original version. These objectives run from least to most committed (Krathwohl, Bloom, & Masia, 1964). At the lowest level, a student would simply pay attention to a certain idea. At the highest level, the student would adopt an idea or a value and act consistently with that idea. There are five basic objectives in the affective domain:

1. *Receiving:* Being aware of or attending to something in the environment. This is the I'll-listen-to-the-concert-but-I-won't-promise-to-like-it level.
2. *Responding:* Showing some new behavior as a result of experience. At this level, a person might applaud after the concert or hum some of the music the next day.
3. *Valuing:* Showing some definite involvement or commitment. At this point, a person might choose to go to a concert instead of a film.
4. *Organization:* Integrating a new value into one's general set of values, giving it some ranking among one's general priorities. This is the level at which a person would begin to make long-range commitments to concert attendance.
5. *Characterization by value:* Acting consistently with the new value. At this highest level, a person would be firmly committed to a love of music and demonstrate it openly and consistently.

Like the basic objectives in the cognitive domain, these five objectives are very general. To write specific learning objectives, you must state what students will actually be doing when they are receiving, responding, valuing, and so on. For example, an objective for a nutrition class at the valuing level (showing involvement or commitment) might be stated: After completing the unit on food contents and labeling, at least 50% of the class will commit to the junk-food boycott project by giving up candy for a month.

The Psychomotor Domain. Until recently, the **psychomotor domain,** or realm of physical ability objectives, has been mostly overlooked by teachers not directly involved with physical education. There are several taxonomies in this domain (e.g., Harrow, 1972; Simpson, 1972) that generally move from basic perceptions and reflex actions to skilled, creative movements. James Cangelosi (1990) provides a useful way to think about objectives in the psychomotor domain as either (1) voluntary muscle capabilities that require endurance, strength, flexibility, agility, or speed, or (2) the ability to perform a specific skill.

Objectives in the psychomotor domain should be of interest to a wide range of educators, including those in fine arts, vocational-technical education, and special education.

Affective domain Objectives focusing on attitudes and feelings.

Psychomotor domain Physical ability and coordination objectives.

Many other subjects, such as chemistry, physics, and biology also require specialized movements and well-developed hand–eye coordination. Using lab equipment, the mouse on a computer, or art materials means learning new physical skills. Here are two psychomotor objectives:

> Four minutes after completing a one-mile run in eight minutes or under, your heart rate will be below 120.
>
> Use a computer mouse effectively to "drag and drop" files.

Whatever your instructional objectives for your students, Terry TenBrink (2006, p. 57) suggests these criteria. Objectives should be:

1. Student-oriented (emphasis on what the student is expected to do).
2. Descriptive of an appropriate learning *outcome* (both developmentally appropriate and appropriately sequenced, with more complex objectives following prerequisite objectives).
3. Clear and understandable (not too general or too specific).
4. Observable (avoid outcomes you can't see such as "appreciating" or "realizing").

The *Guidelines* below should help you if you use objectives for every lesson or even for just a few assignments.

Connect and Extend to Your Teaching/Portfolio

Include a summary of the cognitive, affective, and psychomotor taxonomies in your Teaching Resources file.

Another View: Planning from a Constructivist Perspective

STOP | THINK | WRITE Think about the same course assignments you analyzed in the previous *Stop/Think/Write*. What are the big ideas that run through all those assignments? What other ways could you learn about those ideas besides the assignments? ■

Traditionally, it has been the teacher's responsibility to do most of the planning for instruction, but new ways of planning are developing. In **constructivist approaches,** planning is shared and negotiated. The teacher and students together make decisions about content, activities, and approaches. Rather than having specific student behaviors and skills as objectives, the teacher has overarching goals—"big ideas"—that guide planning. These goals are understandings or abilities that the teacher returns to again and again.

Constructivist approach View that emphasizes the active role of the learner in building understanding and making sense of information.

Guidelines: Using Instructional Objectives

Avoid "word magic"—phrases that sound noble and important, but say very little, such as "Students will become deep thinkers."

EXAMPLES

1. Keep the focus on specific changes that will take place in the students' knowledge of skills.
2. Ask students to explain the meaning of the objectives. If they can't give specific examples of what you mean, the objectives are not communicating your intentions to your students.

Suit the activities to the objectives.

EXAMPLES

1. If the goal is the memorization of vocabulary, give the students memory aids and practice exercises.
2. If the goal is the ability to develop well-thought-out positions, consider position papers, debates, projects, or mock trials.
3. If you want students to become better writers, give many opportunities for writing and rewriting.

Make sure your tests are related to your objectives.

EXAMPLES

1. Write objectives and rough drafts for tests at the same time—revise these drafts of tests as the units unfold and objectives change.
2. Weight the tests according to the importance of the various objectives and the time spent on each.

For additional ideas, see **http://www.personal.psu.edu/staff/b/x/bxb11/Objectives/** or **http://edtech.tennessee.edu/~bobannon/objectives.html**

An Example of Constructivist Planning. Vito Perrone (1994) has these goals for his secondary history students. He wants his students to be able to:

- use primary sources, formulate hypotheses, and engage in systematic study;
- handle multiple points of view;
- be close readers and active writers; and
- pose and solve problems.

The next step in the planning process is to create a learning environment that allows students to move toward these goals in ways that respect their individual interests and abilities. Perrone (1994) suggests identifying "those ideas, themes, and issues that provide the depth and variety of perspective that help students develop significant understandings" (p. 12). For a secondary history course, a theme might be "democracy and revolution," "fairness," or "slavery." In math or music, a theme might be "patterns"; in literature, "personal identity" might be the theme. Perrone suggests mapping the topic as a way of thinking about how the theme can generate learning and understanding. An example of a topic map, using the theme of "Immigrants in the United States," is shown in Figure 13.1.

With this topic map as a guide, teacher and students can work together to identify activities, materials, projects, and performances that will support the development of the

FIGURE 13.1

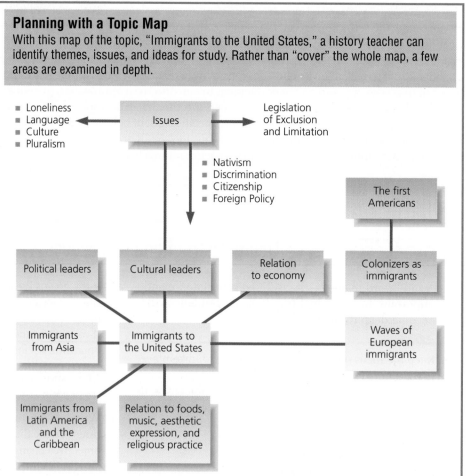

Planning with a Topic Map

With this map of the topic, "Immigrants to the United States," a history teacher can identify themes, issues, and ideas for study. Rather than "cover" the whole map, a few areas are examined in depth.

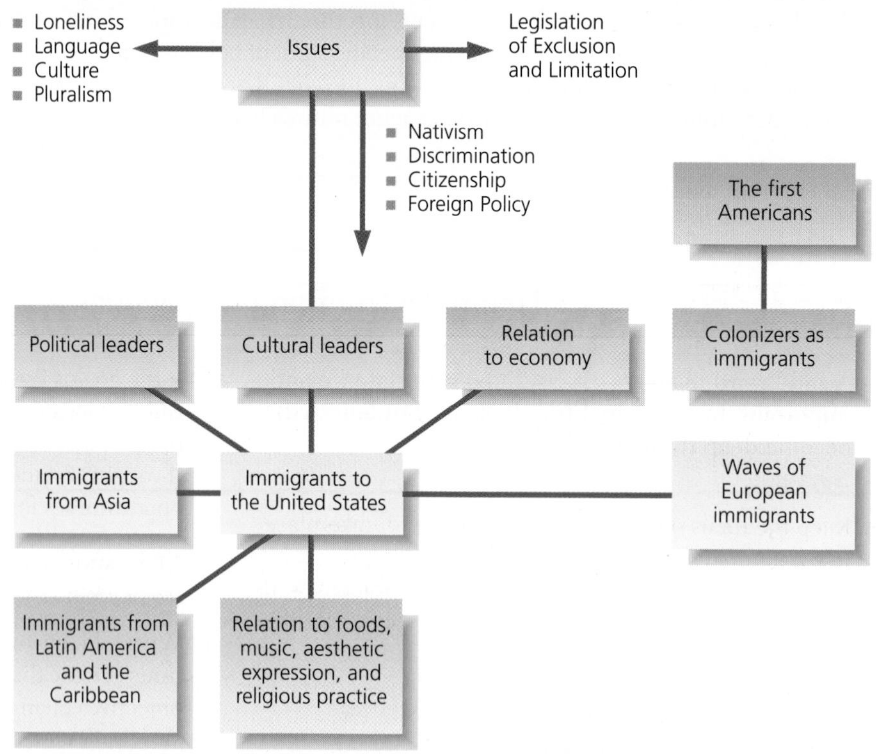

Source: From "How to Engage Students in Learning," by V. Perrone, *Educational Leadership, 51*(5), p. 13. The Association for Supervision and Curriculum Development is a worldwide community of educators advocating sound policies and sharing best practices to achieve the success of each learner. To learn more, visit ASCD at *www.ascd.org*.

TABLE 13.3

Some Themes for Integrated Planning for Older Children

Courage	Time and Space
Mystery	Groups and Institutions
Survival	Work
Human Interaction	Motion
Communities of the Future	Cause and Effect
Communication/Language	Probability and Prediction
Human Rights and Responsibilities	Change and Conservation
Identity/Coming of Age	Diversity and Variation
Interdependence	Autobiography

Source: Adapted from *Toward a Coherent Curriculum* by J. A. Beane (Ed.), 1995, Alexandria, VA: Association for Supervision and Curriculum Development; *Interdisciplinary High School Teaching* by J. H. Clarke and R. M. Agne, 1997, Boston: Allyn & Bacon; and *Teaching through Themes* by G. Thompson, 1991, New York: Scholastic. See Thompson for resources and strategies to develop some of these themes in elementary school and Clarke and Agne for ideas at the high school level.

students' understanding and abilities—the overarching goals of the class. The teacher spends less time planning specific presentations and assignments and more time gathering a variety of resources and facilitating students' learning. The focus is not so much on students' products as on the processes of learning and the thinking behind the products.

Integrated and Thematic Plans. Perrone's planning map shows a way to use the theme of immigrants to the United States to integrate issues in a history class. Today, teaching with themes and integrated content are major elements in planning and designing lessons and units, from kindergarten (Roskos & Neuman, 1998) through high school (Clarke & Agne, 1997). For example, Elaine Homestead and Karen McGinnis (middle school teachers) and Elizabeth Pate (a college professor) (Pate, McGinnis, & Homestead, 1995) designed a unit on "Human Interactions" that included studying racism, world hunger, pollution, and air and water quality. Students researched issues by reading textbooks and outside sources, learning to use databases, interviewing local officials, and inviting guest speakers into class. Students had to develop knowledge in science, mathematics, and social studies. They learned to write and speak persuasively, and in the process, raised money for hunger relief in Africa.

Connect and **Extend** to **PRAXIS II™**

Planning Thematic Units (II, A2)
Thematic learning units that integrate two or more content areas have become common in modern classrooms. Describe the principles involved in designing these activities, and explain how student learning can be assessed.

Elementary-age students can benefit from integrated planning, too. There is no reason to work on spelling skills, then listening skills, then writing skills, and then social studies or science. All these abilities can be developed together if students work to solve authentic problems. Some topics for integrating themes with younger children are people, friendship, communications, habitats, communities, and patterns. Possibilities for older children are given in Table 13.3.

Let's assume you have an idea of *what* you want students to understand, but *how* do you teach to encourage understanding? You still need to decide what's happening on Monday. You need to design teaching that is appropriate for the objectives.

Teacher-Directed Instruction

How would you go about identifying the keys to successful teaching? You might ask students, principals, college professors of education, or experienced teachers to list the characteristics of good teachers. Or you could do intensive case studies of a few classrooms over a long period. You might observe classrooms, rate different teachers on certain

Effective teachers know how to transform their knowledge into examples, explanations, illustrations, and activities.

Connect and Extend to PRAXIS II™

Teacher-Centered Instruction (II, A3)

Teacher-centered instruction is often thought of as the "traditional" approach to instruction. In what situations is this instructional format most effective? What are the basic steps involved in carrying out this form of instruction?

characteristics, and then see which characteristics were associated with teachers whose students either achieved the most or were the most motivated to learn. (To do this, of course, you would have to decide how to assess achievement and motivation.) You could identify teachers whose students, year after year, learned more than students working with other teachers; then you could watch the more successful teachers, and note what they do. You might also train teachers to apply several different strategies to teach the same lesson and then determine which strategy led to the greatest student learning. You could videotape teachers, then ask them to view the tapes and report what they were thinking about as they taught and what influenced their decisions while teaching. You might study transcripts of classroom dialogue to learn what helped students understand.

All these approaches and more have been used to investigate teaching (Floden, 2001). Often, researchers use the relationships identified between teaching and learning as the basis for developing teaching approaches and testing these approaches in design experiments (Brown, 1992; Greeno, Collins, and Resnick, 1996). Let's examine some of the specific knowledge about teaching gained from these projects.

Characteristics of Effective Teachers

STOP | THINK | WRITE Think about the most effective teacher you ever had—the one that you learned the most from. What were the characteristics of that person? What made that teacher so effective? ■

Some of the earliest research on effective teaching focused on the personal qualities of the teachers themselves. Results revealed some lessons about three teacher characteristics: knowledge, clarity, and warmth.

Teachers' Knowledge. Do teachers who know more about their subject have a more positive impact on their students? It depends on the subject. High-school students appear to learn more mathematics from teachers with degrees or significant coursework in mathematics (Wayne & Youngs, 2003). When we look at teachers' knowledge of facts and concepts in other subjects, as measured by test scores and college grades, the relationship to student learning is unclear and may be indirect. Teachers who know more facts about their subject do not necessarily have students who learn more. But teachers who know more may make clearer presentations and recognize student difficulties more readily. They are ready for any student questions and do not have to be evasive or vague in their

Connect and Extend to Other Chapters

See Chapter 1 for a complete discussion of Darling-Hammond's study of teacher quality.

answers. Thus, knowledge is necessary but not sufficient for effective teaching because being more knowledgeable helps teachers be clearer and more organized.

Clarity and Organization. When Barak Rosenshine and Norma Furst (1973) reviewed about 50 studies of teaching, they concluded that clarity was the most promising teacher behavior for future research on effective teaching. Teachers who provide clear presentations and explanations tend to have students who learn more and who rate their teachers more positively (Hines, Cruickshank, & Kennedy, 1985; Land, 1987). Teachers with more knowledge of the subject tend to be less vague in their explanations to the class. The less vague the teacher, the more the students learn (Berliner, 1987; Evertson et al., 2003; Land 1987).

Warmth and Enthusiasm. As you are well aware, some teachers are much more enthusiastic than others. Some studies have found that ratings of teachers' enthusiasm for their subject are correlated with student achievement gains (Rosenshine & Furst, 1973). Warmth, friendliness, and understanding seem to be the teacher traits most strongly related to student attitudes (Murray, 1983; Ryans, 1960; Soar & Soar, 1979). In other words, teachers who are warm and friendly tend to have students who like them and the class in general. But notice, these are correlational studies. The results do not tell us that teacher enthusiasm causes student learning or that warmth causes positive attitudes, only that the two variables tend to occur together. Teachers trained to demonstrate their enthusiasm have students who are more attentive and involved, but not necessarily more successful on tests of content (Gillett & Gall, 1982).

Beyond these general characteristics, how can teachers design instruction? The following sections describe formats or strategies—building blocks that can be used to construct lessons and units. We begin with the strategy many people associate most directly with teaching: explanation and direct instruction.

Connect and **Extend** to the **Research**

We know from Linda Darling-Hammond's (2000) work described in Chapter 1 that the quality of teachers—as measured by whether the teachers were fully certified and had a major in their teaching field—is related to student performance.

Explanation and Direct Instruction

Some studies have found that teachers' presentations take up one-sixth to one-fourth of all classroom time. Teacher explanation is appropriate for communicating a large amount of material to many students in a short period of time, introducing a new topic, giving background information, or motivating students to learn more on their own. Teacher presentations are therefore most appropriate for cognitive and affective objectives at the lower levels of the taxonomies described earlier: for remembering, understanding, applying, receiving, responding, and valuing (Arends, 2001; Kindsvatter, Wilen, & Ishler, 1992).

Direct Instruction. In the 1970s and 1980s, there was an explosion of research that focused on effective teaching. The results of all this work identified a model of teaching that was related to improved student learning. Barak Rosenshine and Robert Stevens (1986) call this approach **direct instruction** or **explicit teaching.** Tom Good (1983a) uses the term **active teaching** to describe a similar approach.

The direct instruction model fits a specific set of circumstances because it was derived from a particular approach to research. Researchers identified the elements of direct instruction by comparing teachers whose students learned more than expected (based on entering knowledge) with teachers whose students performed at an expected or average level. The researchers focused on existing practices in American classrooms. Because the focus was on traditional forms of teaching, the research could not identify successful innovations. Effectiveness was usually defined as average improvement in standardized test scores for a whole class or school. So the results hold for large groups, but not necessarily for every student in the group. Even when the average achievement of a group improves, the achievement of some individuals may decline (Brophy & Good, 1986; Good, 1996; Shuell, 1996).

Given these conditions, you can see that direct instruction applies best to the teaching of **basic skills**—clearly structured knowledge and essential skills, such as science facts, mathematics computations, reading vocabulary, and grammar rules (Rosenshine &

Connect and **Extend** to Your **Teaching/Portfolio**

If you have observed in a primary grade, would you say that the teacher made use of direct instruction? Why or why not?

Direct instruction/explicit teaching Systematic instruction for mastery of basic skills, facts, and information.

Active teaching Teaching characterized by high levels of teacher explanation, demonstration, and interaction with students.

Basic skills Clearly structured knowledge that is needed for later learning and that can be taught step by step.

Stevens, 1986). These skills involve tasks that are relatively unambiguous; they can be taught step-by-step and tested by standardized tests. The teaching approaches described below are not necessarily appropriate for objectives such as helping students to write creatively, solve complex problems, or mature emotionally. Franz Weinert and Andreas Helmke (1995) describe direct instruction as having the following features:

> (a) the teacher's classroom management is especially effective and the rate of student interruptive behaviors is very low; (b) the teacher maintains a strong academic focus and uses available instructional time intensively to initiate and facilitate students' learning activities; (c) the teacher insures that as many students as possible achieve good learning progress by carefully choosing appropriate tasks, clearly presenting subject-matter information and solution strategies, continuously diagnosing each student's learning progress and learning difficulties, and providing effective help through remedial instruction. (p. 138)

How would a teacher turn these themes into actions?

Rosenshine's Six Teaching Functions. Rosenshine and his colleagues (Rosenshine, 1988; Rosenshine & Stevens, 1986) have identified six teaching functions based on the research on effective instruction. These could serve as a checklist or framework for teaching basic skills.

1. *Review and check the previous day's work.* Reteach if students misunderstood or made errors.
2. *Present new material.* Make the purpose clear, teach in small steps, and provide many examples and nonexamples.
3. *Provide guided practice.* Question students, give practice problems, and listen for misconceptions and misunderstandings. Reteach if necessary. Continue guided practice until students answer about 80% of the questions correctly.
4. *Give feedback and correctives* based on student answers. Reteach if necessary.
5. *Provide independent practice.* Let students apply the new learning on their own, in seatwork, cooperative groups, or homework. The success rate during independent practice should be about 95%. This means that students must be well prepared for the work by the presentation and guided practice and that assignments must not be too difficult. The point is for the students to practice until the skills become overlearned and automatic—until the students are confident. Hold students accountable for the work they do—check it.
6. *Review weekly and monthly* to consolidate learning. Include some review items as homework. Test often, and reteach material missed on the tests.

These six functions are not steps to be followed in a particular order, but all of them are elements of effective instruction. For example, feedback, review, or reteaching should occur whenever necessary and should match the abilities of the students. Also, keep in mind the age and prior knowledge of your students. The younger or the less prepared your students, the briefer your explanations should be. Use more and shorter cycles of presentation, guided practice, feedback, and correctives. The *Guidelines* give you ideas for applying the best of direct instruction.

Why Does Direct Instruction Work? What aspects of direct instruction might explain its success? Linda Anderson (1989b) suggests that lessons that help students perceive links among main ideas will help them construct accurate understandings. Well-organized presentations, clear explanations, the use of explanatory links, and reviews as described in the *Guidelines* can all help students perceive connections among ideas. If done well, therefore, a direct instruction lesson could be a resource that students use to construct understanding. For example, reviews activate prior knowledge, so the student is ready to understand. Brief, clear presentations and guided practice avoid overloading the students' information processing systems and taxing their working memories. Numerous examples and explanations give many pathways and associations for building networks of concepts. Guided practice can also give the teacher a snapshot of the students' thinking as well as

Guidelines: Teaching Effectively

Organize your lessons carefully.

EXAMPLES

1. Provide objectives that help students focus on the purpose of the lesson.
2. Begin lessons by writing a brief outline on the board, or work on an outline with the class as part of the lesson.
3. If possible, break the presentation into clear steps or stages.
4. Review periodically.

Anticipate and plan for difficult parts in the lesson.

EXAMPLES

1. Plan a clear introduction to the lesson that tells students what they are going to learn and how they will learn it.
2. Do the exercises and anticipate student problems—consult the teachers' manual for ideas.
3. Have definitions ready for new terms, and prepare several relevant examples for concepts.
4. Think of analogies that will make ideas easier to understand.
5. Organize the lesson in a logical sequence; include checkpoints that incorporate oral or written questions or problems to make sure the students are following the explanations.

Strive for clear explanations.

EXAMPLES

1. Avoid vague words and ambiguous phrases: Steer clear of "the somes"—*something, someone, sometime, somehow;* "the not verys"—*not very much, not very well, not very hard, not very often;* and other unspecific fillers, such as *most, not all, sort of, and so on, of course, as you know, I guess, in fact, or whatever,* and *more or less.*
2. Use specific (and, if possible, colorful) names instead of *it, them,* and *thing.*
3. Refrain from using pet phrases such as *you know, like,* and *Okay?* Another idea is to record a lesson on tape to check yourself for clarity.
4. Give explanations at several levels so all students, not just the brightest, will understand.
5. Focus on one idea at a time and avoid digressions.

Make clear connections by using explanatory links such as because, if–then, or therefore.

EXAMPLES

1. "The North had an advantage in the Civil War because its economy was based on manufacturing."
2. Explanatory links are also helpful in labeling visual material such as graphs, concept maps, or illustrations.

Signal transitions from one major topic to another with phrases.

EXAMPLES

1. *"The next area," "Now we will turn to,"* or *"The second step is"*
2. Outline topics, listing key points, drawing concept maps on the board, or using an overhead projector.

Communicate an enthusiasm for your subject and the day's lesson.

EXAMPLES

1. Tell students why the lesson is important. Have a better reason than "This will be on the test" or "You will need to know it next year." Emphasize the value of the learning itself.
2. Be sure to make eye contact with the students.
3. Vary your pace and volume in speaking. Use silence for emphasis.

For more ideas about effective teaching, see **http://education.qld.gov.au/curriculum/learning/teaching/technology/principl/principl.html**

For specific ideas for different subjects, see **http://curry.edschool.virginia.edu/sped/projects/ose/information/interventions.html**

their misconceptions, so these can be addressed directly as misconceptions rather than simply as "wrong answers."

Every subject, even college English or chemistry, can require some direct instruction. Noddings (1990) reminds teachers that students may need some direct instruction in how to use various manipulative materials to get the possible benefits from them. Students working in cooperative groups may need guidance, modeling, and practice in how to ask questions and give explanations. And to solve difficult problems, students may need some direct instruction in possible problem-solving strategies.

Evaluating Direct Instruction. Direct instruction, particularly when it involves extended teacher presentations or lectures, has some disadvantages. You may find that some

TABLE 13.4

Active Learning and Teacher Presentations

Here are some ideas for keeping students cognitively engaged in lessons. They can be adapted for many ages.

Question, All Write: Pose a question, ask everyone to jot an answer, then ask, "How many students would be willing to share their thoughts?"

Outcome Sentences: After a segment of presentation, ask students to finish a sentence such as "I learned . . . , I'm beginning to wonder . . . , I was surprised. . . . " Share as above. Students may keep their outcome sentences in a learning log or portfolio.

Underexplain with Learning Pairs: Give a brief explanation, then ask students to work in pairs to figure out the process or idea.

Voting: Ask "How many of you . . . " questions and take a count. "How many of you agree with Raschon?" "How many of you are ready to move on?" "How many of you got 48 on this problem?"

Choral Response: Have the whole class restate in unison important facts and ideas, such as "The environment is one whole system" or "A 10-sided polygon is called a decagon."

Speak-Write: Tell students you will speak for 3 or 4 minutes. They are to listen, but not take notes. At the end of the time, ask them to write the main ideas, a summary, or questions they have about what you said.

Source: From *Inspiring Active Learning: A Handbook for Teachers,* by M. Harmin. Copyright © 1994 by the Association for Supervision and Curriculum Development. Reprinted with permission from the ASCD.

Connect and **Extend** to Your **Teaching/Portfolio**

Here are some more ideas for ways to involve all students actively in a lesson. Ask them to:

1. Tell the answer to a neighbor.
2. Summarize the main idea in one or two sentences, writing the summary on a piece of paper and sharing this with a neighbor, or repeat the procedures to a neighbor.
3. Write the answer on a slate, then hold up the slate.
4. Raise their hand if they know the answer (thereby allowing the teacher to check the entire class).
5. Raise their hand if they agree with an answer someone else gave.
6. Raise different colored cards when the answer is a, b, or c.

Source: Taken from Rosenshine, B. (1987). Explicit teaching. In D. Berliner & B. Rosenshine (Eds.), *Talks to teachers* (pp. 75–92). New York: Random House, p. 84.

Connect and **Extend** to Your **Teaching/Portfolio**

Include Table 13.4, "Active Learning and Teacher Presentations," in your file.

If you will teach elementary school, include Table 13.8, "Improving the Reading Achievement of America's Children: CIERA's 10 Research-Based Principles."

Scripted cooperation Learning strategy in which two students take turns summarizing material and criticizing the summaries.

students have trouble listening for more than a few minutes at a time and that they simply tune you out. Teacher presentations can put the students in a passive position by doing much of the cognitive work for them and may prevent students from asking or even thinking of questions (Freiberg & Driscoll, 2005). **Scripted cooperation** is one way of incorporating active learning into lectures. Several times during the presentation, the teacher asks students to work in pairs. One person is the summarizer and the other critiques the summary. This gives students a chance to check their understanding, organize their thinking, and translate ideas into their own words. Other possibilities are described in Table 13.4.

Critics also claim that direct instruction is based on the *wrong* theory of learning. Teachers break material into small segments, present each segment clearly, and reinforce or correct, thus *transmitting* accurate understandings from teacher to student. The student is seen as an "empty vessel" waiting to be filled with knowledge, rather than an active constructor of knowledge (Berg & Clough, 1991; Driscoll, 2005). These criticisms of direct instruction echo the criticisms of behavioral learning theories.

There is ample evidence, however, that direct instruction and explanation can help students learn actively, not passively (Leinhardt, 2001). For younger and less prepared learners, student-controlled learning without teacher direction and instruction can lead to systematic deficits in the students' knowledge. Without guidance, the understandings that students construct can be incomplete and misleading (Weinert & Helmke, 1995). For example, Harris and Graham (1996) describe the experiences of their daughter Leah in a whole-language/progressive education school, where the teachers successfully developed their daughter's creativity, thinking, and understanding.

> Skills, on the other hand, have been a problem for our daughter and for other children. At the end of kindergarten, when she had not made much progress in reading, her teacher said she believed Leah had a perceptual problem or a learning disability. Leah began asking what was wrong with her, because other kids were reading and she wasn't. Finally, an assessment was done. (p. 26)

The testing indicated no learning disability, strong comprehension abilities, and poor word attack skills. Luckily, Leah's parents knew how to teach word attack skills. Direct teaching of these skills helped Leah become an avid and able reader in about six weeks. Deep understanding and fluid performance—whether in reading or dance or mathematical problem solving or reading—require models of expert performance and extensive practice with feedback (Anderson, Reder, & Simon, 1995). Guided and independent practice with feedback are at the heart of the direct instruction model.

Seatwork and Homework

STOP | THINK | WRITE Think back to your elementary- and high-school days. Do you remember any homework assignments? What sticks in your mind about those assignments? ■

Seatwork. There is little research on the effects of **seatwork,** or independent classroom-desk work, but it is clear that this technique is often overused. In fact, one study found that American elementary students spend 51% of mathematics time in school working alone, while Japanese students spend 26% and Taiwanese students spend only 9% (Stigler, Lee, & Stevenson, 1987). Some educators point to these differences as part of the explanation for Asian students' superiority in mathematics.

Seatwork should follow up a lesson and give students supervised practice. It should not be the main mode of instruction. Unfortunately, many workbook pages and worksheets do little to support the learning of important objectives. Before you assign work, ask yourself, "Does doing this work help students learn anything that matters?" Students should see the connection between the seatwork and the lesson. Tell them why they are doing the work. The objectives should be clear, all the materials that might be needed should be provided, and the work should be easy enough that students can succeed on their own. Success rates should be high—near 100%. When seatwork is too difficult, students often resort to guessing or copying just to finish (Anderson, 1985).

Carol Weinstein and Andy Mignano (2003) describe several alternatives to workbooks and worksheets, such as reading silently and reading aloud to a partner; writing for a "real" audience; writing letters or journals; transcribing conversations and punctuating them properly; making up problems; working on long-term projects and reports; solving brainteasers and puzzles; and computer activities. One of my favorites is creating a group story. Two students begin a story on the computer. Then two more add a paragraph. The story grows with each new pair's addition. The students are reading and writing, editing and improving.

Homework. In contrast to the limited research on seatwork, educators have been studying the effects of homework for over 75 years (Cooper, 2004; Cooper & Valentine, 2001a; Corno, 2000; Trautwein & Koller, 2003). As you can see from the *Point/Counterpoint* on the next page there continues to be a debate about the value of homework.

To benefit from individual or group seatwork or homework, students must stay involved and do the work. The first step toward involvement is getting students started correctly by making sure they understand the assignment. It may help to do the first few questions as a class, to clear up any misconceptions. This is especially important for homework assignments, because students may have no one at home to consult if they have problems with the assignment. A second way to keep students involved is to hold them accountable for completing the work correctly, not just for filling in the page. This means the work should be checked, the students given a chance to correct the errors or revise work, and the results counted toward the class grade. Expert teachers often have ways of correcting homework quickly during the first minutes of class by having students check each other's or their own work.

Connect and Extend to the Research

For a current look at the research on homework, see the Summer 2004 issue of *Theory Into Practice* on "Homework" (Vol. 43, No. 3). Guest Editor: Harris Cooper.

AGNES

Agnes has her own ways of making homework valuable.

Agnes, April 29, 2000. © Tony Cochran. Reprinted with permission of the Creators Syndicate.

Seatwork Independent classroom work.

Point/Counterpoint

Is Homework a Valuable Use of Time?

LIKE SO MANY methods in education, homework has moved in and out of favor. In the early 1900s, homework was seen as an important path to mental discipline, but by the 1940s, homework was criticized as too much drill and low-level learning. Then in the 1950s, homework was rediscovered as a way to catch up with the Soviet Union in science and mathematics, only to be seen as too much pressure on students during the more laid-back 1960s. By the 1980s, homework was in again as a way to improve the standing of American children compared to students around the world (Cooper & Valentine, 2001a). Everyone has done homework—were those hours well spent?

POINT Homework does not help students learn.

No matter how interesting an activity is, students will eventually get bored with it—so why give them work both in and out of school? They will simply grow weary of learning. And important opportunities are lost for community involvement or leisure activities that would create well-rounded citizens. When parents help with homework, they can do more harm than good—sometimes confusing their children or teaching them incorrectly. And students from poorer families often must work, so they miss doing the homework; then the learning discrepancy between the rich and poor grows even greater. Besides, the research is inconsistent about the effects of homework. For example, one study found that in-class work was better than homework in helping elementary students learn (Cooper & Valentine, 2001a).

COUNTERPOINT Well-planned homework can work for many students.

Harris Cooper and Jeffrey Valentine reviewed many studies of homework and concluded that there is little relationship between homework and learning for young students, but the relationship between homework and achievement grows progressively stronger for older students. There is recent evidence that students in high school who do more homework (and watch less television after school) have higher grades, even when other factors such as gender, grade level, ethnicity, SES, and amount of adult supervision are taken into consideration (Cooper & Valentine, 2001a; Cooper, Valentine, Nye, & Kindsay, 1999). Consistent with these findings, the National PTA makes these recommendations:

> *[F]or children in grades K–2, homework is most effective when it does not exceed 10–20 minutes each day; older students, in grades 3–6, can handle 30–60 minutes a day; in junior and senior high school, the amount of homework will vary by subject.* (Henderson, 1996, p. 1)

WHAT DO YOU THINK?
Vote online at **www.mylabschool.com**

Making Seatwork and Homework Valuable. Seatwork particularly requires careful monitoring. Being available to students doing seatwork is more effective than offering students help before they ask for it. To be available, you should move around the class and avoid spending too much time with one or two students. Short, frequent contacts are best (Brophy & Good, 1986). Sometimes you may be working with a small group while other students do seatwork. In these situations, it is especially important for students to know what to do if they need help. One expert teacher described by Weinstein and Mignano (2003) taught students a rule, "Ask three, then me." Students have to consult three classmates before seeking help from the teacher. This teacher also spends time early in the year showing students *how* to help each other—how to ask questions and how to explain.

What about monitoring homework? If students get stuck on homework, they need help at home, someone who can scaffold their work without just "giving the answer" (Pressley, 1995). But many parents don't know how to help (Hoover-Dempsey et al., 2001). The *Family and Community Partnerships Guidelines* provides ideas for helping parents help with homework.

Questioning and Recitation

Teachers pose questions, students answer. This form of teaching, sometimes called *recitation*, has been with us for many years (Stodolsky, 1988). The teacher's questions develop a framework for the subject matter involved. The pattern from the teacher's point of view

Family and Community Partnerships

Guidelines: Homework

Make sure families know what students are expected to learn.

EXAMPLES

1. At the beginning of a unit, send home a list of the main objectives, examples of major assignments, key due dates, a homework "calendar," and a list of resources available free at libraries or on the Internet.
2. Provide a clear, concise description of your homework policy—how homework is counted toward class grades; consequences for late, forgotten, or missing homework, etc.

Help families find a comfortable and helpful role in their child's homework.

EXAMPLES

1. Remind families that "helping with homework" means encouraging, listening, monitoring, praising, discussing, brainstorming—not necessarily teaching and never doing the work for their child.
2. Encourage families to set aside a quiet time and place for everyone in the family to study. Make this time a regular part of the daily routine.
3. Have some homework assignments that are fun and involve the whole family—puzzles, family albums, watching a television program together and doing a "review."
4. At parent-teacher conferences, ask families what they need to play a more helpful role in their child's homework. Check lists? Background reading? Websites? Explanations of study skills?

Solicit and use suggestions from families about homework.

EXAMPLES

1. Find out what responsibilities the child has at home—how much time is available for homework.
2. Periodically, have a "homework hotline" for call-in questions and suggestions.

If no one is at home to help with homework, set up other support systems.

EXAMPLES

1. Assign study buddies who can be available over the phone.
2. If students have computers, provide lists of Internet help lines.
3. Locate free help in public libraries and make these resources known.

Take advantage of family and community "funds of knowledge" to connect homework with life in the community and life in the community with lessons in school (Moll et al., 1992).

EXAMPLES

1. Create a class lesson about how family members use math and reading in sewing and in housing construction (Epstein & Van Voorhis, 2001).
2. Design interactive homework projects that families do together to evaluate needed products for their home, for example, deciding on the best buy on shampoo or paper towels.

For more ideas, see **http://www.ncpie.org/DevelopingPartnerships/** or **http://www.bhssc.org/sdprn/homework.htm** or **http://www.pathwaystocollege.net/collegereadiness/toolbox/imp_integrate.htm**

consists of *initiation* (teacher asks questions), *response* (student answers), and *reaction* (praising, correcting, probing or expanding) or IRE (Burbules & Bruce, 2001). These steps are repeated over and over.

Let us consider the heart of recitation, the soliciting or *questioning* phase. Effective questioning techniques may be among the most powerful tools that teachers employ during lessons. An essential element of innovations such as cognitive apprenticeships, peer learning techniques, authentic learning activities, and nearly all other contemporary learning techniques is keeping students cognitively engaged—and that is where skillful questioning strategies are especially effective. Questions play several roles in cognition. They can help students rehearse information for effective recall. They can work to identify gaps in one's knowledge base, and provoke curiosity and long-term interest. They can initiate cognitive conflict and promote the disequilibrium that results in a changed knowledge structure. They can serve as cues, tips, or reminders as an expert guides a novice in a learning experience. And students as well as teachers should learn to question effectively. I tell my students that the first step in doing a good research project is asking a good question.

Connect and **Extend** to Your **Teaching/Portfolio**

Add some ideas for parent involvement in homework from this chapter to your Portfolio.

Connect and **Extend** to **PRAXIS II™**

Questioning (III, C)

Effective questioning skills are among the most valuable skills that a teacher can possess—and among the more difficult to develop. For guidance on asking effective questions in the classroom, read *Question Types* (http://www.unl.edu/teaching/teachquestions.html).

For now, we will focus on teachers' questions, to make them as helpful as possible for students. Many of the beginning teachers I work with are surprised to discover how valuable good questions can be and how difficult they are to create.

STOP | THINK | WRITE Think back to your most recent class. What kinds of questions does your professor ask? What sort of thinking is required to answer the questions? Remembering, understanding, applying, analyzing, evaluating, or creating? How long does the professor wait for an answer? ■

Kinds of Questions. Some educators have estimated the typical teacher asks between 30 and 120 questions an hour, or about 1,500,000 questions over a teaching career (Sadker & Sadker, 2006). What are these questions like? Many can be categorized in terms of Bloom's taxonomy of objectives in the cognitive domain. Table 13.5 offers examples of questions at the different taxonomic levels.

Another way to categorize questioning is in terms of **convergent questions** (only one right answer) or **divergent questions** (many possible answers). Questions about concrete facts are convergent: "Who ruled England in 1540?" "Who wrote the original Peter Pan?" Questions dealing with opinions or hypotheses are divergent: "In this story, which character is most like you and why?" "In 100 years, which of the past five presidents will be most admired?"

Convergent questions Questions that have a single correct answer.

Divergent questions Questions that have no single correct answer.

Quite a bit of space in education textbooks has been devoted to urging teachers to ask a greater number of higher-level (analyzing, evaluating, and creating) and divergent questions. Is this really a better way of questioning? Research has provided several surprises.

TABLE 13.5

Classroom Questions for Objectives in the Cognitive Domain

Questions can be posed that encourage thinking at every level of Bloom's taxonomy in the cognitive domain. Of course, the thinking required depends on what has gone before in the discussion.

Category	Type of Thinking Expected	Examples
Knowledge (Remembering)	Recalling or recognizing information as learned	Define. . . . What is the capital of . . . ? What did the text say about . . . ?
Comprehension (Understanding)	Demonstrating understanding of the materials; transforming, reorganizing, or interpreting	Explain in your own words. . . . Compare. . . . What is the main idea of . . . ? Describe what you saw. . . .
Application (Applying)	Using information to solve a problem with a single correct answer	Which principle is demonstrated in . . . ? Calculate the area of. . . . Apply the rule of . . . to solve. . . .
Analysis (Analyzing)	Critical thinking; identifying reasons and motives; making inferences based on specific data; analyzing conclusions to see if supported by evidence	What influenced the writings of . . . ? Why was Washington, D.C. chosen . . . ? Which of the following are facts and which are opinions . . . ? Based on your experiment, what is the chemical . . . ?
Synthesis (Creating)	Divergent, original thinking; original plan, proposal, design, or story	What's a good name for . . . ? How could we raise money for . . . ? What would the United States be like if the South had won . . . ?
Evaluation (Evaluating)	Judging the merits of ideas, offering opinions, applying standards	Which U.S. senator is the most effective? Which painting do you believe to be better? Why? Why would you favor . . . ?

Source: From "Questioning Skills" by M. Sadker and D. Sadker, in J. Cooper (Ed.), *Classroom Teaching Skills: A Handbook* (3rd ed.) (pp. 143–160), 1986, Boston: D. C. Heath. Copyright © 1986 D. C. Heath. Adapted with permission.

Fitting the Questions to the Students. Both high- and low-level questions can be effective (Barden, 1995; Redfield & Rousseau, 1981). Different patterns seem to be better for different students, however. The best pattern for younger students and for lower-ability students of all ages is simple questions that allow a high percentage of correct answers, ample encouragement, help when the student does not have the correct answer, and praise. For high-ability students, the successful pattern includes harder questions at both higher and lower levels and more critical feedback (Berliner, 1987; Good, 1988).

Whatever their age or ability, all students should have some experience with thought-provoking questions and, if necessary, help in learning how to answer them. As we saw in Chapter 8, to master critical thinking and problem-solving skills, students must have a chance to practice the skills. They also need time to think about their answers. But research shows that teachers wait an average of only one second for students to answer (Rowe, 1974). Consider the following slice of classroom life (Sadker & Sadker, 2006, pp. 130–131):

> *Teacher:* Who wrote the poem "Stopping by Woods on a Snowy Evening"? Tom?
> *Tom:* Robert Frost.
> *Teacher:* Good. What action takes place in the poem? Sally?
> *Sally:* A man stops his sleigh to watch the woods get filled with snow.
> *Teacher:* Yes. Emma, what thoughts go through the man's mind?
> *Emma:* He thinks how beautiful the woods are (She pauses for a second.)
> *Teacher:* What else does he think about? Joe?
> *Joe:* He thinks how he would like to stay and watch. (Pauses for a second.)
> *Teacher:* Yes—and what else? Rita? (Waits half a second.) Come on, Rita, you can get the answer to this. (Waits half a second.) Well, why does he feel he can't stay there indefinitely and watch the woods and the snow?
> *Sarah:* Well, I think it might be—(Pauses a second.)
> *Teacher:* Think, Sarah. (Teacher waits for half a second.) All right then—Mike? (Waits again for half a second.) John? (Waits half a second.) What's the matter with everyone today? Didn't you do the reading?

Very little thoughtful responding can take place in this situation. When teachers learn to pose a question, then wait at least 3 to 5 seconds before calling on a student to answer, students tend to give longer answers; more students are likely to participate, ask questions, and volunteer appropriate answers; student comments involving analysis, synthesis, inference, and speculation tend to increase; and the students generally appear more confident in their answers (Berliner, 1987; Rowe, 1974; Sadker & Sadker, 2006).

This seems like a simple improvement in teaching, but 5 seconds of silence is not that easy to handle. It takes practice. You might try asking students to jot down ideas or even discuss the question with another student and formulate an answer together. This makes the wait more comfortable and gives students a chance to think. Of course, if it is clear that students are lost or don't understand the question, waiting longer will not help. When your question is met with blank stares, rephrase the question or ask if anyone can clarify it. However, there is some evidence that extending wait times does not affect learning in university classes (Duell, 1994), so with advanced high-school students, you might conduct your own evaluation of wait time.

A word about selecting students to answer questions. If you call only on volunteers, then you may get the wrong idea about how well students understand the material. Also, the same people volunteer over and over again. Many expert teachers have some systematic way of making sure that they call on everyone: They pull names from a jar or check names off a list as each student speaks (Weinstein, 2003; Weinstein & Mignano, 2003). Another possibility is to put each student's name on an index card, then shuffle the cards and go through the deck as you call on people. You can use the card to make notes about the quality of students' answers or any extra help they seem to need.

Responding to Student Answers. What do you do after the student answers? The most common response, occurring about 50% of the time in most classrooms, is simple acceptance—"OK" or "Uh-huh" (Sadker & Sadker, 2006). But there are better reactions, depending on whether the student's answer is correct, partially correct, or wrong. If the answer is quick, firm, and correct, simply accept the answer or ask another question. If the answer is correct but hesitant, give the student feedback about why the answer is correct: "That's right, Chris, the Senate is part of the legislative branch of government because the Senate. . . . " This allows you to explain the material again. If this student is unsure, others may be confused as well. If the answer is partially or completely wrong but the student has made an honest attempt, you should probe for more information, give clues, simplify the question, review the previous steps, or reteach the material. If the student's wrong answer is silly or careless, however, it is better simply to correct the answer and go on (Good, 1988; Rosenshine & Stevens, 1986).

Group Discussion

Group discussion is in some ways similar to the recitation strategy, but it should be more like the instructional conversations described in Chapter 9 (Tharp & Gallimore, 1991). A teacher may pose questions, listen to student answers, react, and probe for more information, but in a true group dialogue, the teacher does not have a dominant role. Students ask questions, answer each other's questions, and respond to each other's answers (Beck, McKeown, Worthy, Sandora, & Kucan, 1996; Burbules & Bruce, 2001; Parker & Hess, 2001).

There are many advantages to group discussions. The students are directly involved and have the chance to participate. Group discussion helps students learn to express themselves clearly, to justify opinions, and to tolerate different views. Group discussion also gives students a chance to ask for clarification, examine their own thinking, follow personal interests, and assume responsibility by taking leadership roles in the group. Thus, group discussions help students evaluate ideas and synthesize personal viewpoints. Discussions are also useful when students are trying to understand difficult concepts that go against common sense. As we saw in Chapters 8 and 9, many scientific concepts, such as the role of light in vision or Newton's laws of motion, are difficult to grasp because they contradict commonsense notions. By thinking together, challenging each other, and suggesting and evaluating possible explanations, students are more likely to reach a genuine understanding.

Of course, there are disadvantages. Class discussions are quite unpredictable and may easily digress into exchanges of ignorance. Some members of the group may have great difficulty participating and may become anxious if forced to speak. In addition, you may have to do a good deal of preparation to ensure that participants have a background of knowledge on which to base the discussion. And large groups are often unwieldy. In many cases, a few students will dominate the discussion while the others daydream (Arends, 2004; Freiberg & Driscoll, 2005). The *Guidelines* give some ideas for facilitating a productive group discussion.

While we are focusing on the teacher, there is one more characteristic that affects student learning—the teacher's beliefs about the students.

Connect and **Extend** to the **Research**

Babad, E. (1995). The "Teacher's Pet" phenomenon, students' perceptions of differential behavior, and students' morale. *Journal of Educational Psychology, 87*, 361–374.

Teacher Expectations

Nearly 40 years ago, a study by Robert Rosenthal and Lenore Jacobson (1968) captured the attention of the national media in a way that few studies by psychologists have since then. The study also caused great controversy within the professional community. Debate about the meaning of the results continues (Babad, 1995; Rosenthal, 1995; Snow, 1995).

What did Rosenthal and Jacobson say that caused such a stir? They chose several students at random in a number of elementary school classrooms, and then told the teachers that these students probably would make significant intellectual gains during the year. The students did indeed make larger gains than normal that year. The researchers presented data suggesting the existence of a "**Pygmalion effect**" or self-fulfilling prophecy in the classroom. A **self-fulfilling prophecy** is a groundless expectation that leads to behaviors that then make the original expectation come true (Merton, 1948). An example is a false belief that a bank is failing, leading to a rush to withdraw money that then causes the bank to fail as expected.

Group discussion Conversation in which the teacher does not have the dominant role; students pose and answer their own questions.

Pygmalion effect Exceptional progress by a student as a result of high teacher expectations for that student; named for mythological king, Pygmalion, who made a statue, then caused it to be brought to life.

Self-fulfilling prophecy A groundless expectation that is confirmed because it has been expected.

Guidelines: Productive Group Discussions

Invite shy children to participate.

EXAMPLES

1. "What's your opinion, Joel?" or "Does anyone have another opinion?"
2. Don't wait until there is a deadly silence to ask shy students to reply. Most people, even those who are confident, hate to break a silence.

Direct student comments and questions back to another student.

EXAMPLES

1. "That's an unusual idea, Steve. Kim, what do you think of Steve's idea?"
2. "That's an important question, John. Maura, do you have any thoughts about how you'd answer that?"
3. Encourage students to look at and talk to one another rather than wait for your opinion.

Make sure that you understand what a student has said. If you are unsure, other students may be unsure as well.

EXAMPLES

1. Ask a second student to summarize what the first student said; then the first student can try again to explain if the summary is incorrect.
2. "Karen, I think you're saying . . . Is that right, or have I misunderstood?"

Probe for more information.

EXAMPLES

1. "That's a strong statement. Do you have any evidence to back it up?"
2. "Did you consider any other alternatives?"
3. "Tell us how you reached that conclusion. What steps did you go through?"

Bring the discussion back to the subject.

EXAMPLES

1. "Let's see, we were discussing . . . and Sarah made one suggestion. Does anyone have a different idea?"
2. "Before we continue, let me try to summarize what has happened thus far."

Give time for thought before asking for responses.

EXAMPLES

1. "How would your life be different if television had never been invented? Jot down your ideas on paper, and we will share reactions in a minute." After a minute: "Hiromi, will you tell us what you wrote?"

When a student finishes speaking, look around the room to judge reactions.

EXAMPLES

1. If other students look puzzled, ask them to describe why they are confused.
2. If students are nodding assent, ask them to give an example of what was just said.

For more ideas, see **http://instruct1.cit.cornell.edu/courses/taresources/leadisc.html**

Two Kinds of Expectation Effects

STOP | THINK | WRITE When you thought about the most effective teacher you ever had, was one of the characteristics that the teacher believed in you or demanded the best from you? How did the teacher communicate that belief? ■

Actually, two kinds of expectation effects can occur in classrooms. In the self-fulfilling prophecy described above, the teacher's beliefs about the students' abilities have no basis in fact, but student behavior comes to match the initially inaccurate expectation. The second kind of expectation effect occurs when teachers are fairly accurate in their initial reading of students' abilities and respond to students appropriately. So far, so good. There is nothing wrong with forming and acting on accurate estimates of student ability. The problems arise when students show some improvement, but teachers do not alter their expectations to take account of the improvement. This is called a **sustaining expectation effect,** because the teacher's unchanging expectation sustains the student's achievement at the expected level. The chance to raise expectations, provide more appropriate teaching, and thus encourage greater student achievement is lost. In practice, self-fulfilling

Sustaining expectation effect Student performance maintained at a certain level because teachers don't recognize improvements.

Group discussion helps students learn to express themselves clearly, to justify opinions, and to tolerate different views.

prophecy effects seem to be stronger in the early grades, and sustaining effects are more likely in the later grades (Kuklinski & Weinstein, 2001). And some students are more likely than others to be the recipients of sustaining expectations. For example, withdrawn children provide little information about themselves, so teachers may sustain their expectations about these children for lack of new input (Jones & Gerig, 1994).

Connect and Extend to Your Teaching Portfolio

Should you read your students' cumulative folders at the beginning of the school year? If so, how can you keep from forming low expectations? Is there any reason why teachers should not have high expectations for all of their students? What about the distinction between "high expectations" and "reasonable expectations"?

Sources of Expectations

There are many possible sources of teachers' expectations (Van Matre, Valentine, & Cooper, 2000). Intelligence test scores are an obvious source, especially if teachers do not interpret the scores appropriately. Sex also influences teachers; most teachers expect more behavior problems from boys than from girls, and may have higher academic expectations for girls. The notes from previous teachers and the medical or psychological reports found in cumulative folders (permanent record files) are another obvious source of expectations. Knowledge of ethnic background also seems to have an influence, as does knowledge of older brothers and sisters. Teachers hold higher expectations for attractive students. Previous achievement, socioeconomic status, and the actual behaviors of the student are also often used as sources of information. Even the student's after-school activities can be a source of expectations. Teachers tend to hold higher expectations for students who participate in extracurricular activities than for students who do nothing after school.

Expectations and beliefs focus attention and organize memory, so teachers may pay attention to and remember the information that fits the initial expectations (Fiske, 1993; Hewstone, 1989). Even when student performance does not fit expectations, the teacher may rationalize and attribute the performance to external causes beyond the student's control. For example, a teacher may assume that the low-ability student who did well on a test must have cheated and that the high-ability student who failed must have been upset that day. In both cases, behavior that seems out of character is dismissed. It may take many instances of supposedly uncharacteristic behavior to change the teacher's beliefs about a particular student's abilities. Thus, expectations often remain in the face of contradictory evidence (Brophy, 1982, 1998).

Connect and Extend to the Research

For a complete discussion of teacher expectations and student learning, see Good, T., & Brophy, J. (2003). *Looking in classrooms* (9th ed.). Boston: Allyn & Bacon.

Do Teachers' Expectations Really Affect Students' Achievement?

The answer to this question is more complicated than it might seem. There are two ways to investigate the issue. One is to give teachers unfounded expectations about their students and note if these baseless expectations have any effects. The other approach is to identify the naturally occurring expectations of teachers and study the effects of these expectations. The answer to the question of whether teacher expectations affect student learning depends in part on which approach is taken to study the question.

The original Rosenthal and Jacobson experiment used the first approach—giving teachers groundless expectations and noting the effects. The study was heavily criticized for the experimental and statistical methods the researchers used (Elashoff & Snow, 1971; Snow, 1995; Weinberg, 1989). A careful analysis of the results revealed that even though 1st- through 6th-grade students participated in the study, the self-fulfilling prophecy effects could be traced to dramatic changes in just five students in grades one and two. When other researchers tried to replicate the study, they did not find evidence of a self-fulfilling prophecy effect, even for children in these lower grades (Claiborn, 1969; Wilkins & Glock, 1973). After reviewing the research on teacher expectations, Raudenbush (1984) concluded that these expectations have only a small effect on student IQ scores (the outcome measure used by Rosenthal and Jacobson) and only in the early years of a new school setting—in the first years of elementary school and then again in the first years of junior high school.

But what about the second approach—naturally occurring expectations? Research shows that teachers do indeed form beliefs about students' capabilities. Many of these beliefs are accurate assessments based on the best available data and are corrected as new information is collected. Even so, some teachers do favor certain students (Babad, 1995; Rosenthal, 1987). For example, in a study of 110 students followed from age 4 to age 18, Jennifer Alvidrez and Rhona Weinstein (1999) found that teachers tended to overestimate the abilities of preschool children they rated as independent and interesting and to underestimate the abilities of children perceived as immature and anxious. Teachers' judgments of student ability at age 4 predicted student grade-point average at age 18. The strongest predictions were for students whose abilities were *underestimated*. If teachers decide that some students are less able, and if the teachers lack effective strategies for working with lower-achieving students, then students may experience a double threat—low expectations and inadequate teaching (Good & Brophy, 2003). The power of the expectation effect depends on the age of the students (generally speaking, younger students are more susceptible) and on how differently a teacher treats high- versus low-expectation students, an issue we turn to next (Kuklinski & Weinstein, 2001).

The *Stories of Learning/Tributes to Teaching* feature gives an example of how a teacher's expectations changed a student's perceptions of his own capabilities.

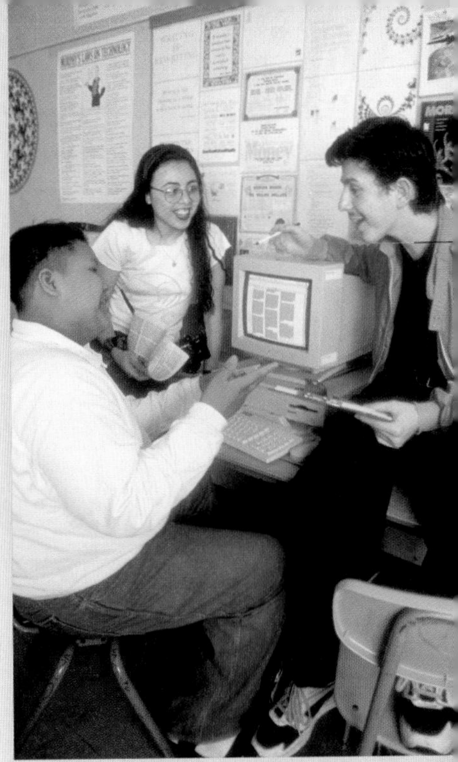

Students' extracurricular activities can be sources of expectations. Teachers tend to hold higher expectations for students who participate in extracurricular activities than for students who "just hang out" after school.

STORIES OF LEARNING
TRIBUTES TO TEACHING

"Mrs. Field thought we were better than we were, so we were."

During my high school days I was a very unattentive, uninterested and underachieving student. At the beginning of my senior year I was assigned to an American history class taught by **MRS. FIELD.** Although the building was old and the class was crowded, she clearly had great expectations for each student. If homework was not turned in, it was never a matter of if it would be turned in, but when. It could come in today or tomorrow, but it would come in. Mrs. Field thought we were better than we were, so we were.

One day she stopped me as I was leaving her class, waited until we were alone, looked deep in my eyes and said: "Bill Purkey, you can become a good student, I know you can." I made some sort of flip remark and went my way, but her words echoed again and again in my mind. Gradually, I began to risk some small effort in her class. Because of her belief in me, I began to put my mind in the path of learning. Perhaps she saw this as a small victory, but it was a major turning point in my life.

A dozen years later, when I received my doctorate from the University of Virginia, I made a special trip back to my old high school hoping to tell Mrs. Field what a difference she made in my life. When I arrived I learned that Mrs. Field had been killed in an automobile accident some months before. Today, when teachers tell me that there is little or nothing they can do, I tell them what I wanted to say to my most memorable teacher: "When you work with human beings, everything you do makes a difference, and every one of your accomplishments is major." There are no small victories, Mrs. Field.

—William Watson Purkey, Ed.D., LPC, Professor of Counselor Education, University of North Carolina at Greensboro, Greensboro, North Carolina

Source: From *Mentors, Masters, and Mrs. MacGregor* by J. Bluestein. Published by Health Communications. Copyright © 1995 by Health Communications. Adapted with permission of the publisher.

Instructional Strategies. As we have seen, different grouping processes may well have a marked effect on students. And some teachers leave little to the imagination; they make their expectations all too clear. For example, Alloway (1984) recorded comments such as these directed to low-achieving groups:

"I'll be over to help you slow ones in a minute."

"The blue group will find this hard."

In these remarks the teacher not only tells the students that they lack ability, but also communicates that finishing the work, not understanding, is the goal.

Once teachers assign students to ability groups, they usually assign different learning activities. To the extent that teachers choose activities that challenge students and increase achievement, these differences are probably necessary. Activities become inappropriate, however, when students who are ready for more challenging work are not given the opportunity to try it because teachers believe they cannot handle it. This is an example of a sustaining expectation effect.

Teacher–Student Interactions. However the class is grouped and whatever the assignments, the quantity and the quality of teacher—student interactions are likely to affect the students. Students who are expected to achieve tend to be asked more and harder questions, to be given more chances and a longer time to respond, and to be interrupted less often than students who are expected to do poorly. Teachers also give these high-expectation students cues and prompts, communicating their belief that the students can answer the question (Allington, 1980; Good & Brophy, 2003; Rosenthal, 1995). When an answer on a test is "almost right," the teacher is more likely to give the benefit of the doubt (and thus the better grade) to high-achieving students (Finn, 1972). Teachers tend to smile at these students more often and to show greater warmth through such nonverbal responses as leaning toward the students and nodding their heads as the students speak (Woolfolk & Brooks, 1983, 1985).

In contrast, with low-expectation students, teachers ask easier questions, allow less time for answering, and are less likely to give prompts. Teachers are more likely to respond with sympathetic acceptance or even praise to inadequate answers from low-achieving students, but to criticize these same students for wrong answers. Even more disturbing, low-achieving students receive less praise than high-achieving students for similar correct answers. This inconsistent feedback can be very confusing for low-ability students. Imagine how hard it would be to learn if your wrong answers were sometimes praised, sometimes ignored, and sometimes criticized, and your right answers received little recognition (Good 1983a, 1983b).

Of course, not all teachers form inappropriate expectations or act on their expectations in unconstructive ways (Babad, Inbar, & Rosenthal, 1982). But avoiding the problem may be more difficult than it seems. In general, low-expectation students also tend to be the most disruptive students. (Of course, low expectations can reinforce their desire to disrupt or misbehave.) Teachers may call on these students less, wait a shorter time for their answers, and give them less praise for right answers, partly to avoid the wrong, careless, or silly answers that can cause disruptions, delays, and digressions (Cooper, 1979). The challenge is to deal with these very real threats to classroom management without communicating low expectations to some students or fostering their own low expectations of themselves. And sometimes, low expectations become part of the culture of the school—beliefs shared by teachers and administrators alike (Weinstein, Madison, & Kuklinski, 1995). The *Guidelines* may help you avoid some of these problems.

Connect and **Extend** to **PRAXIS II™**

The Teacher's Role in Student-Centered Instruction (II, A3)

The teacher's role in student-centered instruction is significantly different from that in teacher-centered instruction. Describe the teaching practices that are typical of student-centered instruction. Contrast them with the practices in teacher-centered instruction.

Student-Centered Teaching: Examples in Reading, Mathematics, and Science

Neither high expectations nor the appropriate use of any teaching format can *ensure* that students will understand. To help students reach this goal, Eleanor Duckworth believes that teachers must pay very close attention to understanding their students' understand-

Guidelines: Avoiding the Negative Effects of Teacher Expectations

Use information about students from tests, cumulative folders, and other teachers very carefully.

EXAMPLES

1. Avoid reading cumulative folders early in the year.
2. Be critical and objective about the reports you hear from other teachers.

Be flexible in your use of grouping strategies.

EXAMPLES

1. Review work of students often and experiment with new groupings.
2. Use different groups for different subjects.
3. Use mixed-ability groups in cooperative exercises.

Make sure all the students are challenged.

EXAMPLES

1. Don't say, "This is easy, I know you can do it."
2. Offer a wide range of problems, and encourage all students to try a few of the harder ones for extra credit. Find something positive about these attempts.

Be especially careful about how you respond to low-achieving students during class discussions.

EXAMPLES

1. Give them prompts, cues, and time to answer.
2. Give ample praise for good answers.
3. Call on low achievers as often as high achievers.

Use materials that show a wide range of ethnic groups.

EXAMPLES

1. Check readers and library books. Is there ethnic diversity?
2. Ask students to research and create their own materials, based on community or family sources.

Make sure that your teaching does not reflect racial, ethnic, or sexual stereotypes or prejudice.

EXAMPLES

1. Use a checking system to be sure you call on and include all students.
2. Monitor the content of the tasks you assign. Do boys get the "hard" math problems to work at the board? Do you avoid having students with limited English give oral presentations?

Be fair in evaluation and disciplinary procedures.

EXAMPLES

1. Make sure equal offenses receive equal punishment. Find out from students in an anonymous questionnaire whether you seem to be favoring certain individuals.
2. Try to grade student work without knowing the identity of the student. Ask another teacher to give you a "second opinion" from time to time.

Communicate to all students that you believe they can learn—and mean it.

EXAMPLES

1. Return papers that do not meet standards with specific suggestions for improvements.
2. If students do not have the answers immediately, wait, probe, and then help them think through an answer.

Involve all students in learning tasks and in privileges.

EXAMPLES

1. Use some system to make sure you give each student practice in reading, speaking, and answering questions.
2. Keep track of who gets to do what job. Are some students always on the list while others seldom make it?

Monitor your nonverbal behavior.

EXAMPLES

1. Do you lean away or stand farther away from some students? Do some students get smiles when they approach your desk, while others get only frowns?
2. Does your tone of voice vary with different students?

For more information see **http://www.mcrel.org/PDFConversion/Noteworthy/Learners_Learning_Schooling/loycec.asp** or **http://chiron.valdosta.edu/whuitt/files/teacherexpect.html**

ings (Meek, 1991). What do we know about good teaching in student-centered instruction? Table 13.6 on the next page lists some student-centered constructivist teaching practices described by Jacqueline Grennon Brooks and M. G. Brooks (1995).

It is clear that a teacher's knowledge of the subject is critical for teaching (Ball, Lubienski, & Mewborn, 2001; Borko & Putnam, 1996). Part of that knowledge is pedagogical content knowledge, or knowing how to teach a subject to your particular students (Shulman, 1987). In the last decade, psychologists have made great progress toward understanding how students learn different subjects (Mayer, 1992, 1999b). Based on these

TABLE 13.6

Constructivist Teaching Practices
Many constructivist practices can be incorporated into any class.

1. Constructivist teachers encourage and accept student autonomy and initiative.
2. Constructivist teachers use raw data and primary sources, along with manipulative, interactive, and physical materials.
3. When framing tasks, constructivist teachers use cognitive terminology such as "classify," "analyze," "predict," and "create."
4. Constructivist teachers allow student responses to drive lessons, shift instructional strategies, and alter content.
5. Constructivist teachers inquire about students' understandings of concepts before sharing their own understandings of those concepts.
6. Constructivist teachers encourage students to engage in dialogue, both with the teacher and with one another.
7. Constructivist teachers encourage student inquiry by asking thoughtful, open-ended questions and encouraging students to ask questions of each other.
8. Constructivist teachers seek elaboration of students' initial responses.
9. Constructivist teachers engage students in experiences that might engender contradictions to their initial hypotheses and then encourage discussion.
10. Constructivist teachers allow wait-time after posing questions.
11. Constructivist teachers provide time for students to discover relationships and create metaphors.

Source: From "Becoming a Constructivist Teacher." In *In Search of Understanding: The Case for Constructivist Classrooms* (pp. 101–118) by J. G. Brooks and M. G. Brooks, 1995, Association for Supervision and Curriculum Development. The Association for Supervision and Curriculum Development is a worldwide community of educators advocating sound policies and sharing best practices to achieve the success of each learner. To learn more, visit ASCD at *www.ascd.org*.

findings, many approaches have been developed to teach reading, writing, mathematics, science, social studies, and all the other subjects. Often approaches reflect the constructivist perspectives described in Chapter 9.

Connect and **Extend** to the **Research**

Several special issues of journals have been devoted to teaching reading: See the entire issue of *Educational Leadership*, November 2002 (Vol. 60, No. 3) for 15 articles on "Reading and Writing in the Content Areas" for all grade levels; the special section on "Reading" in *Phi Delta Kappan*, 2002, Vol. 83, No. 10, pp. 740–757 for three perspectives on teaching reading; and Carlisle, J. F., Stahl, S. A., & Birdyshaw, D. (Eds.). (2004, November). Lessons from research at the Center for the Improvement of Early Reading Achievement [Special Issue]. *The Elementary School Journal, 105* (2).

Whole-language approach A philosophical approach to teaching and learning that stresses learning through authentic, real-life tasks. Emphasizes using language to learn, integrating learning across skills and subjects, and respecting the language abilities of student and teacher.

Learning and Teaching Reading and Writing

For years, educators have debated whether students should be taught to read and write through code-based (phonics or skills) approaches that relate letters to sounds and sounds to words, or through meaning-based (whole-language, literature-based, emergent literacy) approaches that do not dissect words and sentences into pieces, but instead focus on the meaning of the text (Barr, 2001; Carlisle, Stahl, & Birdyshaw, 2004; Goodman & Goodman, 1990; Smith, 1994; Stahl & Miller, 1989; Symons, Woloshyn, & Pressley, 1994).

Balance in Reading and Writing. Advocates of **whole-language approaches** believe that learning to read is a natural process, very much like mastering your native language. Reading is a kind of guessing game in which students sample words and make predictions and guesses about meaning based on both the context of other words in the passage and their prior knowledge. Children should be immersed in a print-rich environment, surrounded by books worth reading and adults who read—to the children and for themselves. When students write, they write for an audience; their goal is to communicate effectively. Vygotsky (1978) recognized the importance of authentic writing tasks: "[W]riting should be incorporated into a task that is necessary and relevant for life. Only then can we be certain that it will develop not as a matter of hand and finger habits but as a really new and complex form of speech" (p. 118).

But is whole language the whole story? There are now three decades of research demonstrating that skill in recognizing sounds and words supports reading. Advocates of code-based approaches cite research showing that being able to identify many words as you read does not depend on using context to guess meaning. In fact, it is almost the other way around—knowing words helps you make sense of context. Identifying words as you read is a highly automatic process (Byrne, Fielding-Barnsley, and Ashley, 2000; Vellutino,

1991). It is the poorest readers who resort to using context to help them understand meaning (Pressley, 1996). Alphabetic coding and awareness of letter sounds are essential skills for acquiring word identification, so some direct teaching of the alphabet and phonics is helpful in learning to read.

The best approach probably makes use of both phonics and whole language. After all, we want our students to be both fluent and enthusiastic readers and writers (National Center for Family Literacy, 2004; Pressley, 1998; Stahl & Yaden, 2004). If students need help cracking the phonics code—give them what they need. Don't let ideology get in the way. You will just send more students to private tutors—if their families can afford it. But don't forget that reading and writing are for a purpose. Surround students with good literature and create a community of readers and writers. Table 13.7 on the next page describes 10 principles that capture this balanced approach to teaching, provided by the Center for the Improvement of Early Reading Achievement.

Comprehension Monitoring and Reading: Reciprocal Teaching. The goal of **reciprocal teaching** is to help students understand and think deeply about what they read (Palincsar, 1986; Palincsar & Brown, 1984, 1989). To accomplish this goal, students in small reading groups learn four strategies: *summarizing* the content of a passage, *asking a question* about the central point, *clarifying* the difficult parts of the material, and *predicting* what will come next. These are strategies that skilled readers apply almost automatically, but poor readers seldom do—or they don't know how. To use the strategies effectively, poorer readers need direct instruction, modeling, and practice in actual reading situations.

First, the teacher introduces these strategies, perhaps focusing on one strategy each day. The teacher explains and models each strategy and encourages students to practice. Next, the teacher and the students read a short passage silently. Then the teacher again provides a model by summarizing, questioning, clarifying, or predicting based on the reading. Everyone reads another passage, and the students gradually begin to assume the teacher's role. The teacher becomes a member of the group, and may finally leave, as the students take over the teaching. Often, the students' first attempts are halting and incorrect. But the teacher gives clues, guidance, encouragement, support in doing parts of the task (such as providing question stems), models, and other forms of scaffolding to help the students master these strategies. The goal is for students to learn to apply these strategies independently as they read so they can make sense of text.

Applying Reciprocal Teaching. Although reciprocal teaching seems to work with almost any age student, most of the research has been done with younger adolescents who can read aloud fairly accurately, but who are far below average in reading comprehension. After 20 hours of practice with this approach, many students who were in the bottom quarter of their class moved up to the average level or above on tests of reading comprehension. Palincsar has identified three guidelines for effective reciprocal teaching ("When Student Becomes Teacher," 1986):

1. *Shift gradually.* The shift from teacher to student responsibility must be gradual.
2. *Match demands to abilities.* The difficulty of the task and the responsibility must match the abilities of each student and grow as these abilities develop.
3. *Diagnose thinking.* Teachers should carefully observe the "teaching" of each student for clues about how the student is thinking and what kind of instruction the student needs.

In contrast to some comprehension-monitoring approaches that try to teach 40 or more strategies, an advantage of reciprocal teaching is that it focuses attention on four powerful strategies. But these strategies must be taught—not all students develop them on their own. One study of reciprocal teaching over three years found that questioning was the strategy used most often, but that students had to be taught how to ask higher-level questions because most student questions were literal or superficial (Hacker & Tenent, 2002). Another advantage of reciprocal teaching is that it emphasizes practicing these four strategies in the context of actual reading—reading literature and reading

Reciprocal teaching A method, based on modeling, to teach reading comprehension strategies.

TABLE 13.7

Improving the Reading Achievement of America's Children: CIERA's 10 Research-Based Principles

CIERA (the Center for the Improvement of Early Reading Achievement) has reviewed the research on learning to read and distilled the best findings into these 10 principles.

1. **Home language and literacy experiences** support the development of key print concepts and a range of knowledge prepares students for school-based learning. Programs that help families initiate and sustain these experiences show positive benefits for children's reaching achievement.

   Examples: Joint reading with a family member, parental modeling of good reading habits, monitoring homework and television viewing.

2. **Preschool programs** are particularly beneficial for children who do not experience informal learning opportunities in their homes. Such preschool experiences lead to improved reading achievement, with some effects lasting through grade 3.

   Examples: Listening to and examining books, saying nursery rhymes, writing messages, and seeing and talking about print.

3. **Skills that predict later reading success** can be promoted in kindergarten and grade 1. The two most powerful of these predictors are letter-name knowledge and phonemic awareness. Instruction in these skills has demonstrated positive effects on primary grade reading achievement, especially when it is coupled with letter-sound instruction.

   Examples: Encourage children to hear and blend sound through oral renditions of rhymes, poems, and songs, as well as writing messages and in journals.

4. **Primary-level instruction** that supports successful reading acquisition is consistent, well-designed, and focused.

   Examples: Systematic word recognition instruction on common, consistent letter-sound relationships and important but often unpredictable high-frequency words, such as *the* and *what;* teaching children to monitor the accuracy of their reading as well as their understanding of texts through strategies such as predicting, inferencing, clarifying misunderstandings, and summarizing; promoting word recognition and comprehension through repeated reading of text, guided reading and writing, strategy lessons, reading aloud with feedback, and conversations about texts children have read.

5. **Primary-level classroom environments** in successful schools provide opportunities for students to apply what they have learned in teacher-guided instruction to everyday reading and writing.

   Examples: Teachers read books aloud and hold follow-up discussions, children read independently every day, and children write stories and keep journals. These events are monitored frequently by teachers, ensuring that time is well spent and that children receive feedback on their efforts. Teachers design and revise these events based on information from ongoing assessment of children's strengths and needs.

6. **Cultural and linguistic diversity** among America's children reflects the variations within their communities and homes. This diversity is manifest in differences in the children's dispositions toward and knowledge about topics, language, and literacy.

   Examples: Effective instruction includes assessment, integration, and extension of relevant background knowledge and the use of texts that recognize diverse backgrounds. Build on the children's language when children are learning to speak, listen to, write, and read English. When teachers capitalize on the advantages of bilingualism or biliteracy, second language reading acquisition is significantly enhanced.

7. **Children who are identified as having reading disabilities** profit from the same sort of well-balanced instructional programs that benefit all children who are learning to read and write, including systematic instruction *and* meaningful reading and writing.

   Examples: Intensive one-on-one or small-group instruction, attention to both comprehension and word recognition processes, thoroughly individualized assessment and instructional planning, and extensive experiences with many types of texts.

8. **Proficient reading in third grade** and above is sustained and enhanced by programs that adhere to four fundamental features:

   Features: (1) deep and wide opportunities to read, (2) acquiring new knowledge and vocabulary, through wide reading and through explicit instruction about networks of new concepts, (3) emphasizing the influence on understanding of kinds of text (e.g., stories versus essays) and the ways writers organize particular texts, and (4) assisting students in reasoning about text.

9. **Professional opportunities** to improve reading achievement are prominent in successful schools and programs.

   Examples: Opportunities for teachers and administrators to analyze instruction, assessment, and achievement; to set goals for improvement; to learn about effective practices; and to participate in ongoing communities that deliberately try to understand both successes and persistent problems.

10. **Entire school staffs,** not just first-grade teachers, are involved in bringing children to high levels of achievement.

    Examples: In successful schools, reading achievement goals are clear, expectations are high, instructional means for attaining goals are articulated, and shared assessments monitor children's progress. Even though they might use different materials and technologies, successful schools maintain a focus on reading and writing and have programs to involve parents in their children's reading and homework. Community partnerships, including volunteer tutoring programs, are common.

Source: From www.ciera.org. Copyright © Center for the Improvement of Early Reading Achievement, University of Michigan School of Education. Reprinted with permission.

texts. Finally, the idea of scaffolding and gradually moving the student toward independent and fluid reading comprehension is a critical component in reciprocal teaching and also for developing self-regulated learners in general (Rosenshine & Meister, 1994).

Learning and Teaching Mathematics

STOP | THINK | WRITE Think back to the ways that you were taught mathematics. What were your math classes like in elementary school? High school? ■

Some of the most compelling support for constructivist approaches to teaching comes from mathematics education. Critics of direct instruction believe that traditional mathematics instruction often teaches students an unintended lesson—that they "cannot understand mathematics," or worse, that mathematics doesn't have to make sense, you just have to memorize the formulas. Arthur Baroody and Herbert Ginsburg (1990, p. 62) give this example:

> Sherry, a junior high student, explained that her math class was learning how to convert measurements from one unit to another. The interviewer gave Sherry the following problem:
>
> > To feed data into the computer, the measurements in your report have to be converted to one unit of measurement: feet. Your first measurement, however, is 3 feet 6 inches. What are you going to feed into the computer?
>
> Sherry recognized immediately that the conversion algorithm taught in school applied. However, because she really did not understand the rationale behind the conversion algorithm, Sherry had difficulty in remembering the steps and how to execute them. After some time she came up with an improbable answer (it was less than 3 feet). Sherry knew she was in trouble and became flustered. At this point, the interviewer tried to help by asking her if there was any other way of solving the problem. Sherry responded sharply, "No!" She explained, "That's the way it has to be done." The interviewer tried to give Sherry a hint: "Look at the numbers in the problem, is there another way we can think about them that might help us figure out the problem more easily?" Sherry grew even more impatient, "This is the way I learned in school, so it has to be the way."

Connect and **Extend** to the **Research**

See the special section on "The Math Wars" in *Phi Delta Kappan*, (2001), Vol. 83, No. 3, pp. 255–272 for a look at controversies in math teaching.

Sherry believed that there was only one way to solve a problem. Even though Sherry knew that 6 inches was one-half a foot and that the fraction one-half was equivalent to the decimal expression .5, she did not use this knowledge to solve the problem informally and quickly ("3 feet 6 inches is 3½ feet, or 3.5 feet"). Her beliefs prevented her from effectively using her existing mathematical knowledge to solve the problem. Sherry had probably been taught to memorize the steps to convert one measurement to another. How would a constructivist approach teach the same material?

The following excerpt shows how a 3rd-grade teacher, Ms. Coleman, uses a constructivist approach to teach negative numbers. Notice the use of dialogue and the way the teacher asks students to justify and explain their thinking. The class has been considering one problem: $-10 + 10 = ?$ A student, Marta, has just tried to explain, using a number line, why $-10 + 10 = 0$:

> *Teacher:* Marta says that negative ten plus ten equals zero, so you have to count ten numbers to the right. What do you think, Harold?
>
> *Harold:* I think it's easy, but I don't understand how she explained it.
>
> *Teacher:* OK. Does anybody else have a comment or a response to that? Tessa? (Peterson, 1992, p. 165)

Connect and **Extend** to the **Research**

Another example of how students solve mathematics problems by applying rules is taken from Merseth, K. K. (1993). How old is the shepherd? An essay about mathematics education. *Phi Delta Kappan, 74*, 548–554. Merseth cites findings from research showing that three out of four students will produce some numerical answer to the problem: There are 125 sheep and 5 dogs in a flock. How old is the shepherd? Here is how one child reached an answer. Notice that logic and reasoning play a role: "125 + 5 = 130—this is too big, and 125 – 5 = 120 is still too big while 125/5 = 25. That works! I think the shepherd is 25 years old!"

As the discussion progresses, Ms. Coleman encourages students to talk directly to each other:

> *Teacher:* You said you don't understand what she is trying to say?
>
> *Chang:* No.
>
> *Teacher:* Do you want to ask her?
>
> *Chang:* What do you mean by counting to the right?

This dialogue reveals three things about learning and teaching in a constructivist classroom: The thinking processes of the students are the focus of attention; one topic is considered in depth rather than attempting to "cover" many topics; and assessment is ongoing and mutually shared by teacher and students. Conducting these kinds of productive

TABLE 13.8

A Constructivist Approach to Mathematics: Five Components

1. Promote students' autonomy and commitment to their answers.

   Examples:
   - Question both right and wrong student answers.
   - Insist that students at least try to solve a problem and be able to explain what they tried.
2. Develop students' reflective processes.

   Examples:
   - Question students to guide them to try different ways to resolve the problem.
   - Ask students to restate the problem in their own words; to explain what they are doing and why; and to discuss what they mean by the terms they are using.
3. Construct a case history of each student.

   Examples:
   - Note general tendencies in the way the student approaches problems, as well as common misconceptions and strengths.
4. If the student is unable to solve a problem, intervene to negotiate a possible solution with the student.

   Examples:
   - Based on the case study and your understanding of how the student is thinking about a problem, guide the student to think about a possible solution.
   - Ask questions such as "Is there anything you did in the last one that will help you here?" or "Can you explain your diagram?"
   - If the student is becoming frustrated, ask more direct, product-oriented questions.
5. When the problem is solved, review the solution.

   Examples:
   - Encourage students to reflect on what they did and why.
   - Note what students did well and build confidence.

Source: From "What Constructivism Implies for Teaching," by J. Confrey, 1990, in *Constructivist Views on the Teaching and Learning of Mathematics* by R. Davis, C. Maher, and N. Noddings (Eds.). Monograph 4 of the National Council of Teachers of Mathematics, Reston, VA.

dialogues about mathematics concepts is not easy. You have to continually monitor the dialogue, have a good idea where the discussion is going and if it is productive, and learn when to step in and out of the discussion (Nathan & Knuth, 2003).

Jere Confrey (1990b) analyzed an expert mathematics teacher in a class for high-school girls who had difficulty with mathematics. Confrey identified five components in a model of this teacher's approach to teaching. These components are summarized in Table 13.8.

There is a caution, however. Some studies have found that students with learning disabilities and lower-achieving students benefit more from explicit instruction in mathematics problem-solving strategies (teacher explanation and modeling, practice with feedback) than from constructivist teaching that encourages students to discuss and discover strategies. But both explicit instruction and constructivist methods were better than traditional instruction in at least one study (Kroesbergen, Van Luit, & Maas, 2004).

Learning and Teaching Science

We have seen a number of examples that indicate that by high school, many students have "learned" some unfortunate lessons in school. Like Sherry described in the preceding section, they have learned that math is impossible to understand and you just have to apply the rules to get the answers. Or they may have developed some misconceptions about the world, such as the belief that the earth is warmer in the summer because it is closer to the sun.

Many educators note that the key to understanding in science is for students to directly examine their own theories and confront the shortcomings they find (Hewson, Beeth, & Thorley, 1998). For conceptual change to take place, students must go through six stages: initial discomfort with their own ideas and beliefs, attempts to explain away inconsistencies between their theories and evidence presented to them, attempts to adjust measurements or observations to fit personal theories, doubt, vacillation, and finally conceptual change (Nissani & Hoefler-Nissani, 1992). You can see Piaget's notions of assimilation, disequilibrium, and accommodation operating here. Students try to make new information fit existing ideas (assimilation), but when the fit simply won't work and disequilibrium occurs, then accommodation or changes in cognitive structures follow.

The goal of **conceptual change teaching in science** is to help students pass through these six stages of learning. The two central features of conceptual change teaching are:

- Teachers are committed to teaching for student understanding rather than "covering the curriculum."
- Students are encouraged to make sense of science using their current ideas—they are challenged to describe, predict, explain, justify, debate, and defend the adequacy of their understanding. Dialogue is key. Only when intuitive ideas prove inadequate can new learning take hold (Anderson & Roth, 1989).

Conceptual change teaching has much in common with cognitive apprenticeships and inquiry learning described in Chapter 9—with scaffolding and dialogue playing key roles (Shuell, 1996). The *Guidelines*, adapted from Hewson, Beeth, and Thorley (1998), give some ideas for teaching for conceptual change.

Conceptual change teaching in science A method that helps students understand (rather than memorize) concepts in science by using and challenging the students' current ideas.

Guidelines: Teaching for Conceptual Change

Encourage students to make their ideas explicit.

EXAMPLES

1. Ask students to make predictions that might contradict their naïve conceptions.
2. Ask students to state their ideas in their own words, including the attractions and limitations of the ideas.
3. Have students explain their ideas using physical models or illustrations.

Help students see the differences among ideas.

EXAMPLES

1. Have students summarize each other's ideas.
2. Encourage comparing ideas by presenting and comparing evidence.

Encourage metacognition.

EXAMPLES

1. Give a pretest before starting a unit; then have students discuss their own responses to the pretest. Group similar pretest responses together and ask students to discover what is a more general concept underlying the responses.
2. At the end of lessons, ask students: "What did you learn?" "What do you understand?" "What do you believe about the lesson?" "How have your ideas changed?"

Explore the status of ideas. Status is an indication of how much students know and accept ideas and find them useful.

EXAMPLES

1. Ask direct questions about how intelligible, plausible, and fruitful an idea is. That is, do you know what the idea means, do you believe it, and can you achieve some valuable outcome using the idea?
2. Plan activities and experiments that support and question the students' ideas such as showing successful applications or pointing out contradictions.

Ask students for justifications of their ideas.

EXAMPLES

1. Teach students to use terms such as *logical, consistent, inconsistent,* and *coherent* in giving justifications.
2. Ask students to share and analyze each other's justifications.

For more information see **http://www.physics.ohio-state.edu/~jossem/ICPE/C5.html**

These students are testing the endurance of a straw tower during an outdoor science class project. The teacher hopes that this interactive approach to teaching scientific concepts will be more meaningful to her students than if she simply "talked" about them in class.

How would these guidelines look in practice? One answer comes from Michael Beeth's study of a 5th-grade classroom. Table 13.9 shows a list of learning goals that the teacher presented to her students. In this classroom, the teacher typically began instruction with a question such as, "Do you have ideas? Can you talk about them? Bring them out into the open? Why do you like your ideas? Why are you attracted to them?" (Beeth, 1998, p. 1095). She constantly asked questions that required explanation and justification, and she taught students to judge these explanations using the standards of "plausible" and "intelligible." She summarized the students' answers, and sometimes challenged, "But do you really believe what you say?" Studies of the students in this teacher's classroom over the years showed that they had a sophisticated understanding of science concepts.

Reaching Every Student: Effective Teaching in Inclusive Classrooms

STOP | THINK | WRITE When you think about teaching in an inclusive classroom, what are your concerns? Do you have enough training? Will you get the support you need

TABLE 13.9

One Teacher's Learning Goals for Conceptual Change Teaching

The teacher in one 5th-grade class gives these questions that support students' thinking about science.

1. Can you state your own ideas?
2. Can you talk about why you are attracted to your ideas?
3. Are your ideas consistent?
4. Do you realize the limitations of your ideas and the possibility they might need to change?
5. Can you try to explain your ideas using physical models?
6. Can you explain the difference between understanding an idea and believing in an idea?
7. Can you apply "intelligible" and "plausible" to your own ideas?

Source: Adapted from "Teaching Science in Fifth Grade: Instructional Goals that Support Conceptual Change," by M. E. Beeth, 1998, *Journal of Research in Science Teaching, 35,* p. 1093.

This student with a visual disability uses a Braille n' Speak during a high-school math lesson in a general education classroom.

from school administrators or specialists? Will working with the students with disabilities take time away from your other responsibilities? ■

These questions are common ones, and sometimes concerns are justified. But effective teaching for exceptional students does not require a unique set of skills. It is a combination of good teaching practices and sensitivity to all your students. Students with disabilities need to *learn the academic material,* and they need to be *full participants in the day-to-day life of the classroom.*

To accomplish the first goal of academic learning, Larrivee (1985) concluded that effective teachers of students in inclusive classrooms do the following:

1. Use time efficiently by having smooth management routines, avoiding discipline problems, and planning carefully.
2. Ask questions at the right level of difficulty.
3. Give supportive, positive feedback to students, helping them figure out the right answer if they are wrong but on the right track.

In addition, students with learning disabilities appear to benefit from using extended practice distributed over days and weeks and from *advanced organizers* such as focusing students on what they already know or stating clear objectives (Swanson, 2001).

To accomplish the second goal of integrating students with disabilities into the day-to-day life of the classroom, Marilyn Friend and William Bursuck (2002) recommend the INCLUDE strategy:

Identify the environmental, curricular, and instructional demands of your classroom.
Note students' learning strengths and needs.
Check for potential areas of student success.
Look for potential problem areas.
Use information gathered to brainstorm instructional adaptations.
Decide which adaptations to try.
Evaluate student progress.

Table 13.10 on the next page shows how the INCLUDE strategy might be applied to students with learning and behavioral disabilities.

Resource Rooms, Collaborative Consultation, and Cooperative Teaching. Many schools provide additional help for classroom teachers who work with students with disabilities. A resource room is a classroom with special materials and equipment and a specially trained teacher. Students may come to the resource room each day for several minutes or several hours and receive instruction either individually or in small groups. The rest of the day, the students are in regular education classes. Besides working with

TABLE 13.10

Making Adaptations for Students with Learning and Behavior Disabilities Using Steps in the INCLUDE Strategy

Identify Classroom Demands	**Note Student Strengths and Needs**	**Check for Potential Successes Look for Potential Problems**	**Decide on Adaptations**
Student desks in clusters of four	*Strengths* Good vocabulary skills *Needs* Difficulty attending to task	*Success* Student understands instruction if on task *Problem* Student off task—does not face instructor as she teaches	Change seating so student faces instructor
Small-group work with peers	*Strengths* Good handwriting *Needs* Oral expressive language—problem with word finding	*Success* Student acts as secretary for cooperative group *Problem* Student has difficulty expressing self in peer learning groups	Assign as secretary of group Place into compatible small group Develop social skills instruction for all students
Expect students to attend class and be on time	*Strengths* Good drawing skills *Needs* Poor time management	*Success* Student uses artistic talent in class *Problem* Student is late for class and frequently does not attend at all	Use individualized student contract for attendance and punctuality—if goals met, give student artistic responsibility in class
Textbook difficult to read	*Strengths* Good oral communication skills *Needs* Poor reading accuracy Lacks systematic strategy for reading text	*Success* Student participates well in class Good candidate for class dramatizations *Problem* Student is unable to read text for information	Provide taped textbooks Highlight student text
Lecture on women's suffrage movement to whole class	*Strengths* Very motivated and interested in class *Needs* Lack of background knowledge	*Success* Student earns points for class attendance and effort *Problem* Student lacks background knowledge to understand important information in lecture	Give student video to view before lecture Build points for attendance and working hard into grading system
Whole class instruction on telling time to the quarter hour	*Strengths* Good coloring skills *Needs* Cannot identify numbers 7–12 Cannot count by fives	*Success* Student is able to color clock faces used in instruction *Problem* Student is unable to acquire telling time skills	Provide extra instruction on number identification and counting by fives

Source: From *Including Students with Special Needs: A Practical Guide for Classroom Teachers, 3/e* by Marilyn Friend & William D. Bursuck. Published by Allyn and Bacon, Boston, MA. Copyright © 2002 by Pearson Education. Adapted by permission of the publisher.

students directly, a resource teacher may also work with them indirectly by giving the general education teacher ideas, materials, or actual demonstrations of teaching techniques.

Increasingly, special and general education teachers are working together, collaborating to assume equal responsibility for the education of students with disabilities. The collaboration may work through consultation, planning, and problem solving about

FIGURE 13.2

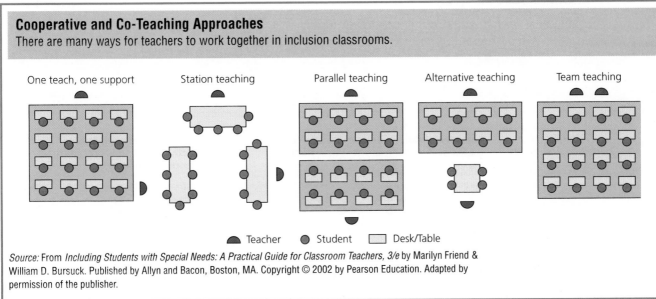

Cooperative and Co-Teaching Approaches

There are many ways for teachers to work together in inclusion classrooms.

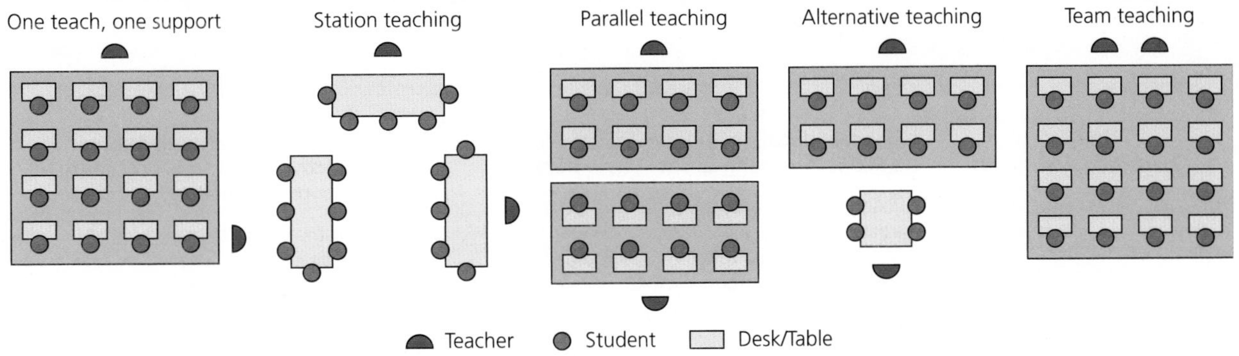

Source: From *Including Students with Special Needs: A Practical Guide for Classroom Teachers, 3/e* by Marilyn Friend & William D. Bursuck. Published by Allyn and Bacon, Boston, MA. Copyright © 2002 by Pearson Education. Adapted by permission of the publisher.

how to teach specific students, or the special education teacher might work directly alongside the general education teacher in a class made up of students with and without disabilities. The latter is called *cooperative teaching*. The teachers assume different roles, depending on the age of the students and their needs. For example, in a secondary class, the general education teacher might be responsible for academic content, while the special education instructor teaches study skills and learning strategies. In another classroom, the general education teacher might deal with core content, while the special education teacher provides remediation, enrichment, or reteaching when necessary. The two teachers might also try team teaching, where each is responsible for different parts of the lesson.

When using cooperative teaching, it is important that general education students and students with disabilities aren't resegregated in the class, with the general education teacher always working with the "general education" students and the special education teacher always working with the "inclusion students." I observed one class in which the students with disabilities worked only with the special education teacher, but often looked longingly over their shoulders at the activities of their classmates working with the general education teacher. Rather than integrating the students with disabilities into the class, this cooperative teaching arrangement accentuated their separateness. Figure 13.2 shows different ways to implement cooperative teaching.

Working with Individual Students. When students have special needs, they may be referred to specialists such as child study teams, school psychologists, or teachers of students with special needs for evaluation (see Table 4.15 on page 153 for guidelines about referring students for evaluation). The outcome of this process sometimes includes the preparation of an individualized education program or IEP, as described in Chapter 4. Figure 13.3 on the next page is an excerpt from the IEP of a boy who had difficulty managing anger and complying with teacher requests. You may help to develop these programs for students in your classes. Well-designed programs should provide guidance for you in your planning and teaching.

Technology and Exceptional Students

IDEIA requires that all students eligible for special education services must be considered for assistive technology. **Assistive technology** is any product, piece of equipment, or system that is used to increase, maintain, or improve the functional capabilities of individuals with disabilities (Goldman, Lawless, Pellegrino, & Plants, 2006). For example, computers have improved the education of exceptional children in countless ways. Given the record

Assistive technology Devices, systems, and services that support and improve the capabilities of individuals with disabilities.

FIGURE 13.3

An Excerpt from an IEP—Individualized Education Program

This IEP was developed for a 15-year-old boy to help him manage anger and comply with teacher requests.

Student: Curt Age: 15 Grade: 9 Date: 10/12/94

Unique Characteristics/ Needs	Special Education, Related Services, Modifications	(begin duration)	Present Levels, Objectives, Annual Goals (Objectives to include procedure, criteria, schedule)
Social Needs: ■ To learn anger management skills, especially regarding swearing ■ To learn to comply with requests Present Level: Lashes out violently when not able to complete work, uses profane language, and refuses to follow further directions from adults	1. Teacher and/or counselor consult with behavior specialists regarding techniques and programs for teaching social skills, especially anger management. 2. Provide anger management training for Curt. 3. Establish a peer group which involves role playing, etc. so Curt can see positive role models and practice newly learned anger management skills. 4. Develop a behavior plan for Curt which gives him responsibility for charting his own behavior. 5. Provide a teacher or some other adult mentor to spend time with Curt (could be talking; game play, physical activity). 6. Provide training for the mentor regarding Curt's needs/goals.	30 min., 3 x week 30 min., 2 x week 30 min., 2 x week	Goal: During the last quarter of the academic year, Curt will have 2 or fewer detentions for any reason. Objective 1: At the end of the 1st quarter, Curt will have had 10 or fewer detentions. Objective 2: At the end of 2nd quarter, Curt will have had 7 or fewer detentions. Objective 3: At the end of 3rd quarter, Curt will have had 4 or fewer detentions. Goal: Curt will manage his behavior and language in a reasonably acceptable manner as reported by faculty/peers. Objective 1: At 2 weeks, asked at end of class if Curt's behavior language was acceptable or not, 3 out of 5 teachers will say "acceptable." Objective 2: At 6 weeks, asked same question, 4 out of 6 teachers will say "acceptable." Objective 3: At 12 weeks. 6 out of 6 will say "acceptable."

Adaptations to regular program:

- In all classes, Curt should be near front of class
- Curt should be called on often to keep him involved and on task
- All teachers should help Curt with study skills as trained by spelling/language specialist and resource room teacher
- Teachers should monitor Curt's work closely in the beginning weeks/months of his program

Source: From *Better IEPs*, 4th ed. (p 127) by Barbara D. Bateman. Copyright 1996, 2006 by Barbara D. Bateman. Reprinted by permission of the author and Attainment Company, Inc.

keeping and program planning needed to meet federal regulations, teachers can use computers to manage instruction. For students who require small steps and many repetitions to learn a new concept, computers are the perfect patient tutors, repeating steps and lessons as many times as necessary. A well-designed computer instructional program is engaging and interactive—two important qualities for students who have problems paying attention or a history of failure that has eroded motivation. For example, a math or spelling program might use images, sounds, and gamelike features to maintain the attention of a student with an attention-deficit disorder. Interactive videodisc programs are being developed to teach hearing people how to use sign language. Many programs do not involve sound, so students with hearing impairments can get the full benefit from the lessons. Students who have trouble reading can use programs that will "speak" a word for them if they touch the unknown word with a light pen or the cursor. With this immediate access to help, the students are much more likely to get the reading practice they need to prevent falling farther and farther behind. Other devices actually convert printed pages and typed texts to spoken words for students who are blind or others who benefit from hearing information.

For the student with a learning disability whose writing can't be read, word processors produce perfect penmanship so the ideas can finally get on paper. Once the ideas are on paper, the student can reorganize and improve the writing without the agony of rewriting by hand (Hallahan & Kauffman, 2006; Hardman, Drew, & Egan, 2005).

Connect and Extend to the Web

You can find out more about assistive technology at Closing the Gap (www.closingthegap.com).

With these tremendous advances in technology have come new barriers, however. Many computers have graphic interfaces. To manipulate the programs requires precise "mouse movements," as you may remember when you first learned to point and click. These maneuvers are difficult for students with motor problems or visual impairments. And the information available on the Internet often is unusable for students with visual problems. Researchers are working on the problem—trying to devise ways for people to access the information nonvisually, but the adaptations are not perfected yet (Hallahan & Kauffman, 2006). One current trend is **universal design**—considering the needs of all users in the design of new tools, learning programs, or websites (Pisha & Coyne, 2001).

For gifted students, computers can be a connection with databases and computers in universities, museums, and research labs. Computer networks allow students to work on projects and share information with others across the country. It is also possible to have gifted students write programs for students and teachers. Quite a few principals around the country rely on their students to make the technology in the school work. These are just a few examples of what technology can do. Check with the resource teachers in your district to find out what is available in your school.

Diversity and Convergences in Teaching

WHAT WOULD YOU SAY?

The last person to interview you for your first teaching job is the coordinator of special services for the school. This is the question: "How do you accommodate different learning challenges and abilities in your teaching? Do you make use of community resources or technology? How?" ■

As you have seen throughout this book, today's classrooms are diverse. Students differ in language, SES, culture, race, and ethnicity. They bring different learning strengths, abilities, and disabilities to the task of learning. Many educators believe that "classes

Universal design Considering the needs of all users as new tools, or learning programs, or websites.

Classrooms that use differentiated instruction can better meet the needs of all students, both those who are gifted as well as those who struggle to learn.

Connect and **Extend** to the **Research**

See the Summer 2005 issue of *Theory Into Practice* on "Differentiated Instruction" (Vol. 44, No. 3). Guest Editor: Carol Tomlinson.

Differentiated instruction A flexible approach to teaching that matches content, process, and product based on student differences in readiness, interests, and learning needs.

should include students of diverse needs, achievement levels, interests, and learning styles, and instruction should be differentiated to take advantage of the diversity, not ignore it" (Jackson & Davis, 2000, p. 23). Differentiated instruction (Tomlinson, 2005b) is one way of going beyond accommodating these learner differences to seeing diversity as an array of strengths on which to build.

Diversity: Differentiated Instruction

The basic idea of **differentiated instruction** is that teachers must take into account not only what they are teaching but also who they are teaching. In differentiated classrooms, students work at different paces, sometimes exercising varied learning options, and they are assessed using indicators that fit their interests and needs (George, 2005). Without differentiated instruction, students in many classes and schools are grouped by ability, and all the problems of tracking follow them(see Chapter 4). For schools with lower-SES stu-

FIGURE 13.4

The Teacher Response Cog in Differentiated Instruction

In order to differentiate instruction, teachers respond to students' needs through invitation, opportunity, investment, persistence, and reflection.

What Do the Elements Mean?

Invitation
- I have respect for who you are and who you can become.
- I want to know you.
- You are unique and valuable.
- I believe in you.
- I have time for you.
- I learn when I listen to you.
- This place is yours, too.
- We need you here.

Opportunity
- I have important things for you to do here today.
- The things I ask you to do are worthy things.
- The things I ask you to do are often daunting.
- The things I ask you to do open new possibilities for you.
- The things I ask you to do here help you become all you can be.
- You have specific roles that make us all more efficient and effective.

Investment
- I work hard to make this place work for you.
- I work to make this place reflect you.
- I enjoy thinking about what we do here.
- I love to find new paths to success.
- It's my job to help you succeed.
- I am your partner in growth.
- I will do what it takes to ensure your growth.

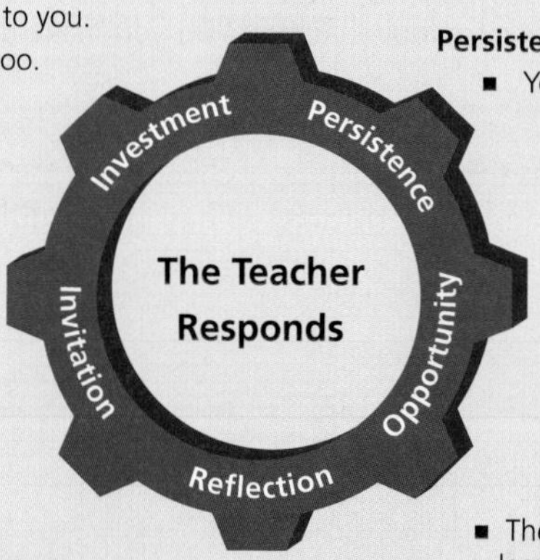

Persistence
- You're growing, but you're not finished growing.
- When one route doesn't work, there are others we can find.
- Let's figure out what works best.
- There are no excuses here, but there is support.
- There is no finish line in learning.

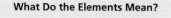

Reflection
- I watch you and listen to you carefully and systematically.
- I make sure to use what I learn to help you learn better.
- I try to see things through your eyes.
- I continually ask, "How is this partnership working?"
- I continually ask, "How can I make this better?"

Source: Fulfilling the promise of the differentiated classroom (p. 28) by C. A. Tomlinson. Copyright © 2003 by the Association for Supervision and Curriculum Development. Reprinted with permission from ASCD. All rights reserved. The Association for Supervision and Curriculum Development is a worldwide community of educators advocating sound policies and sharing best practices to achieve the success of each learner. To learn more, visit ASCD at *www.ascd.org.*

dents, this often means that these students are segregated into lower-ability tracks. According to Paul George:

> In my 3 decades of experience with this issue, when homogenous grouping is the primary strategy for organizing students in schools with significant racial and ethnic diversity in the population, the result is almost always deep, and often starkly obvious, division of students on the basis of race, ethnicity, and social class. (p. 187)

Differentiated instruction, in contrast, conceives of all students as seeking purpose, challenge, affirmation, power, and contribution. The teacher responds to these student needs with invitation, investment, persistence, opportunity, and reflection, working to create curriculum and instruction for each student that is focused, engaging, demanding, important, and scaffolded. Carol Ann Tomlinson (2003) describes these characteristics as the Cogs of Differentiation. The teacher response cog is elaborated in Figure 13.4.

Table 13.11 presents some possible responses to student needs, taken from Tomlinson (2003).

Convergences: Beyond the Debates to Outstanding Teaching

In spite of the criticisms and debates, there is no one best way to teach. Different goals and student needs require different teaching methods. Direct instruction often leads to better performance on achievement tests, whereas the open, informal methods such as discovery learning or inquiry approaches are associated with better performance on tests of creativity, abstract thinking, and problem solving. In addition, the open methods are

TABLE 13.11

Possible Responses to Student Needs

Student Need	Modification of Classroom Element in Response to Student Need
A spelling pre-assessment indicates that students in a 6th grade class range from 2nd grade level to beyond high school level.	The teacher uses a spelling procedure that involves all students in spelling at the same time, but on varied levels of complexity of words required. (Modification of content based on student readiness.)
Students in a pre-algebra class have varied interests and often have difficulty understanding why they are learning what they are learning in math.	The teacher uses examples from sports, business, medicine, technology, and other fields to illustrate how formulas are used. She also guides students in interviewing people engaged in a range of jobs and hobbies to find out how they use formulas in their work and in sharing those examples with others in the class. (Modification of content and product based on student interest.)
Some students in Advanced Placement History are taking their first advanced course and sometimes feel lost and discouraged by the course's demands.	The teacher establishes study groups to help students prepare for both oral and written tests. Although much of the work of the study groups takes place outside of class, the teacher conducts whole-class and small-group discussions about how the various groups approach studying, how the different approaches seem to work, and how students feel about their progress. He also provides study guides to ensure focus on critical facets of the content. (Modification of learning environment and process based on student readiness and affect.)
Students in 3rd grade are studying biography. Students' reading levels vary widely and their interests do as well.	The teacher develops boxes of biographies of people from a range of cultures, both genders, and a variety of jobs and hobbies. In each box are books that span a four- or five-year reading range. Students first select the topic or interest box from which they would like to work and then the teacher helps them pick a book that is a close match for their reading levels. (Modification of content based on student interest and readiness.)
Two students in the class have difficulty with impulsive behavior.	The teacher and students develop goals for behavior and plans for decreasing impulsivity. Both positive and negative consequences of behaviors are described in the goal statements. Students and teacher use a checklist each day to record successes and difficulties as well as the consequence of student choices. (Modification of learning environment based on student affect.)

Source: Tomlinson, C. A. (2003). *Fulfilling the promise of the differentiated classroom.* Alexandria, VA: Association for Supervision and Curriculum Development.

better for improving attitudes toward school and for stimulating curiosity, cooperation among students, and lower absence rates (Walberg, 1990). According to these conclusions, when the goals of teaching involve problem solving, creativity, understanding, and mastering processes, many approaches besides direct instruction should be effective. These guidelines are in keeping with Tom Good's conclusion that teaching should become less direct as students mature and when the goals involve affective development and problem solving or critical thinking (Good, 1983a). Every student may require direct, explicit teaching for some learning goals some of the time, but every student also needs to experience more open, constructivist, student-centered teaching as well.

SUMMARY TABLE

The First Step: Planning (pp. 478–485)

What are the levels of planning, and how do they affect teaching? Teachers engage in several levels of planning—by the year, term, unit, week, and day. All the levels must be coordinated. Accomplishing the year's plan requires breaking the work into terms, the terms into units, and the units into weeks and days. The plan determines how time and materials will be turned into activities for students. There is no single model of planning, but all plans should allow for flexibility. Planning is a creative problem-solving process for experienced teachers. It is more informal—"in their heads."

What is an instructional objective? An instructional objective is a clear and unambiguous description of your educational intentions for your students. Mager's influential system for writing behavioral objectives states that a good objective has three parts—the intended student behavior, the conditions under which the behavior will occur, and the criteria for acceptable performance. Gronlund's alternative approach suggests that an objective should be stated first in general terms, then the teacher should clarify by listing sample behaviors that would provide evidence that the student has attained the objective. The most recent research on instructional objectives tends to favor approaches similar to Gronlund's.

Describe the three taxonomies of educational objectives. Bloom and others have developed taxonomies categorizing basic objectives in the cognitive, affective, and psychomotor domains. In real life, of course, behaviors from these three domains occur simultaneously. A taxonomy encourages systematic thinking about relevant objectives and ways to evaluate them. Six basic objectives are listed in the cognitive domain: knowing, understanding, applying, analyzing, evaluating, and creating. A recent revision of this taxonomy adds that these processes can act on four kinds of knowledge—factual, conceptual, procedural, and metacognitive. Objectives in the affective domain run from least committed to most committed. Objectives in the psychomotor domain generally move from basic perceptions and reflex actions to skilled, creative movements.

Describe teacher-centered and student-centered planning. In teacher-centered approaches, teachers select learning objectives and plan how to get students to meet those objectives. Teachers control the "what" and "how" of learning. In contrast, planning is shared and negotiated in student-centered, or constructivist, approaches. Rather than having specific student behaviors as objectives, the teacher has overarching goals or "big ideas" that guide planning. Integrated content and teaching with themes are often part of the planning. Assessment of learning is ongoing and mutually shared by teacher and students.

Lesson study As a group, teachers develop, test, improve, and retest lessons until they are satisfied with the final version.

Instructional objectives Clear statement of what students are intended to learn through instruction.

Behavioral objectives Instructional objectives stated in terms of observable behaviors.

Cognitive objectives Instructional objectives stated in terms of higher-level thinking operations.

Taxonomy Classification system.

Cognitive domain In Bloom's taxonomy, memory and reasoning objectives.

Affective domain Objectives focusing on attitudes and feelings.

Psychomotor domain Physical ability and coordination objectives.

Constructivist approach View that emphasizes the active role of the learner in building understanding and making sense of information.

Teacher-Directed Instruction (pp. 485–496)

What methods have been used to study teaching? For years, researchers have tried to unravel the mystery of effective teaching using classroom observation, case studies, interviews, experimentation with different methods, stimulated recall (teachers view videotapes and explain their teaching), analysis of lesson transcripts, and other approaches to study teaching in real classrooms.

What are the general characteristics of good teaching? Teacher knowledge of the subject is necessary but not sufficient for effective teaching because being more knowledgeable helps teachers be clearer and more organized. Teachers who provide clear presentations and explanations tend to have students who learn more and who rate their teachers more positively. Teacher warmth, friendliness, and understanding seem to be the traits most strongly related to positive student attitudes.

What is direct instruction? Direct instruction is appropriate for teaching basic skills and explicit knowledge. It includes the teaching functions of review/overview, presentation, guided practice, feedback and correctives (with reteaching if necessary), independent practice, and periodic reviews. The younger or less able the students, the shorter the presentation should be with more cycles of practice and feedback.

Distinguish between convergent and divergent and high-level versus low-level questions. Convergent questions have only one right answer. Divergent questions have many possible answers. Higher-level questions require analysis, synthesis, and evaluation—students have to think for themselves. The best pattern for younger students and for lower-ability students of all ages is simple questions that allow a high percentage of correct answers, ample encouragement, help when the student does not have the correct answer, and praise. For high-ability students, the successful pattern includes harder questions at both higher and lower levels and more critical feedback. Whatever their age or ability, all students should have some experience with thought-provoking questions and, if necessary, help in learning how to answer them.

How can wait time affect student learning? When teachers learn to pose a question, then wait at least 3 to 5 seconds before calling on a student to answer, students tend to give longer answers; more students are likely to participate, ask questions, and volunteer appropriate answers; student comments involving analysis, synthesis, inference, and speculation tend to increase; and the students generally appear more confident in their answers.

What are the uses and disadvantages of group discussion? Group discussion helps students participate directly, express themselves clearly, justify opinions, and tolerate different views. Group discussion also gives students a chance to ask for clarification, examine their own thinking, follow personal interests, and assume responsibility by taking leadership roles in the group. Thus, group discussions help students evaluate ideas and synthesize personal viewpoints. However, discussions are quite unpredictable and may easily digress into exchanges of ignorance.

Direct instruction/Explicit teaching Systematic instruction for mastery of basic skills, facts, and information.

Active teaching Teaching characterized by high levels of teacher explanation, demonstration, and interaction with students.

Basic skills Clearly structured knowledge that is needed for later learning and that can be taught step by step.

Scripted cooperation Learning strategy in which two students take turns summarizing material and criticizing the summaries.

Seatwork Independent classroom work.

Convergent questions Questions that have a single correct answer.

Divergent questions Questions that have no single correct answer.

Group discussion Conversation in which the teacher does not have the dominant role; students pose and answer their own questions.

Teacher Expectations (pp. 496–500)

What are some sources of teacher expectations? Sources include intelligence test scores, gender, notes from previous teachers and the medical or psychological reports found in cumulative folders, ethnic background, knowledge of older brothers and sisters, physical characteristics, previous achievement, socioeconomic status, and the actual behaviors of the student.

What are the two kinds of expectation effects and how do they happen? The first is the self-fulfilling prophecy; the teacher's beliefs about the students' abilities have no basis in fact, but student behavior comes to match the initially inaccurate expectation. The second is a sustaining expectation effect; teachers are fairly accurate in their initial reading of students' abilities and respond to students appropriately but teachers do not alter their expectations to take account of the improvement. When this happens, the teacher's unchanging expectation can sustain the student's achievement at the expected level. In practice, sustaining effects are more common than self-fulfilling prophecy effects.

What are the different avenues for communicating teacher expectations? Some teachers tend to treat students differently, depending on their own views of how well the students are likely to do. Differences in treatment toward low-expectation students may include setting less challenging tasks, focusing on lower-level learning, giving fewer choices, providing inconsistent feedback, and communicating less respect and trust. Students may behave accordingly, ful-filling teachers' predictions or staying at an expected level of achievement.

Pygmalion effect Exceptional progress by a student as a result of high teacher expectations for that student; named for mythological king, Pygmalion, who made a statue, then caused it to be brought to life.

Self-fulfilling prophecy A groundless expectation that is confirmed because it has been expected.

Sustaining expectation effect Student performance maintained at a certain level because teachers don't recognize improvements.

Student-Centered Teaching: Examples in Reading, Mathematics, and Science (pp. 500–513)

Describe the debate about learning to read. Today there is an ongoing debate between advocates of whole-language approaches to reading and writing and balanced approaches that include direct teaching of skills and phonics. Advocates of whole language believe children learn best when they are surrounded by good literature and when they read and write for authentic purposes. Advocates of a balanced approach cite extensive research indicating that skill in recognizing sounds and words—phonemic awareness—is fundamental in learning to read. Excellent primary teachers use a balanced approach combining authentic reading with skills instruction when needed.

Describe the use of dialogue in reciprocal teaching. The goal of reciprocal teaching is to help students understand and think deeply about what they read. To accomplish this goal, students in small reading groups learn four strategies: *summarizing* the content of a passage, *asking a question* about the central point, *clarifying* the difficult parts of the material, and *predicting* what will come next. These strategies are practiced in a classroom dialogue about the readings. Teachers first take a central role, but as the discussion progresses, the students take more and more control.

Describe student-centered constructivist approaches to mathematics and science teaching. Constructivist approaches to teaching mathematics and science emphasize deep understanding of concepts (as opposed to memorization), discussion and explanation, and exploration of students' implicit understandings. Many educators note that the key to understanding in science is for students to directly examine their own theories and confront the shortcomings. For change to take place, students must go through six stages: initial discomfort with their own ideas and beliefs, attempts to explain away inconsistencies between their theories and evidence presented to them, attempts to adjust measurements or observations to fit personal theories, doubt, vacillation, and finally conceptual change.

What characterizes effective teaching for exceptional students? Effective teaching for exceptional students does not require a unique set of skills. It is a combination of good teaching practices and sensitivity to all students. Students with disabilities need to learn the academic material, and they need to be full participants in the day-to-day life of the classroom.

What resources do teachers have to work effectively with exceptional children? When students have special needs, they may be referred to specialists such as child study teams, school psychologists, or teachers of students with special needs for evaluation. The outcome of this process sometimes includes the preparation of an individualized educational program or IEP, as described in Chapter 4, which will have teaching ideas and guidelines. Many schools provide additional help for classroom teachers working with students with disabilities, such as a resource room with special materials and equipment and a specially trained teacher. Increasingly, special and regular educators are working together to teach specific students, or the special education teacher might work directly alongside the regular teacher in a class made up of students with and without disabilities. In addition, differentiated instruction can improve learning for all students.

Whole-language approach A philosophical approach to teaching and learning that stresses learning through authentic, real-life tasks. Emphasizes using language to learn, integrating learning across skills and subjects, and respecting the language abilities of student and teacher.

Reciprocal teaching A method, based on modeling, to teach reading comprehension strategies.

Conceptual change teaching in science A method that helps students understand (rather than memorize) concepts in science by using and challenging the students' current ideas.

Assistive technology Devices, systems, and services that support and improve the capabilities of individuals with disabilities.

Universal design Considering the needs of all users as new tools, or learning programs, or websites.

Differentiated instruction A flexible approach to teaching that matches content, process, and product based on student differences in readiness, interests, and learning needs.

Teachers' Casebook: Connections to PRAXIS II™

Recent policy changes in many states as well as the federal No Child Left Behind Act will probably have a strong influence on your new career as a teacher. Schools that fail to promote or maintain strong student learning—as measured by various tests—will face a variety of actions. The test scores of your students will receive increased scrutiny from administrators, boards of education, and state education departments. Teachers will have to adjust to these new circumstances.

In some ways, you may be better prepared for these changes than veteran colleagues. Many newer tests emphasize skills and knowledge that are learned most effectively through a variety of student-centered instructional strategies that you have encountered in this textbook and your educational psychology class.

What Would They Do?

Here is how some practicing teachers responded to the challenge of preparing students for proficiency tests.

Sandra Gill **Sixth Grade Teacher,**

Hudson Middle School, Hudson, New York

Since the topics on the upcoming proficiency test are important ones, I would use them to form the core of my own curriculum. The curriculum would augment individual assignments with a hefty dose of group challenges in which students would work collaboratively in doing projects involving the examination of the world outside of school. These challenges would culminate in written reports as well as group presentations, incorporating both visual and verbal elements, for classmates and others. I would choose the members of each group based on the personalities and learning styles of the students. The competencies and topics that pertained to the proficiency test would be identified in the plan for each group challenge, and they would be repeated in subsequent challenges in order to reinforce them.

Julie Mohok **Classroom Teacher,**

Ponam Primary School, Manus Island, Papua New Guinea (currently a doctoral student at Queensland University of Technology)

The first thing I would do is try to understand the situation. Perhaps through conversing with other teachers, and analyzing past records I could quickly learn of the contributing factors to the present low school performance. In addition, I would find out what the reasons are for the school's decision to resort to drill and practice on facts and skills. This may be a situation analysis. This understanding would assist me in planning my teaching for the first few weeks without overtly challenging the school administration.

I would proceed to plan and teach on the principle that learning and developing skills is for usage in the real world and not merely for passing some important test. This may include experiments, simulations, role plays, watching a video clip on a specific topic, etc. These activities should motivate students by arousing curiosity and interest in learning. Drilling and practice of key concepts and skills can follow enjoyable segments. In the process, I would inform the school's administration of my teaching program. Perhaps I might even suggest that they conduct a mid-test within the school to find out if my teaching makes a difference to the students' success rate as they prepare for the big test.

Margaret Doolan **Year Three,**

St. Michael's School, Gordonvale QLD 4865, Australia

What a challenge!

The first few weeks would be spent in becoming familiar with my students and the standard of work of each. I would then enlist the help of my teacher-aide and as many parents as possible to help with individual and small-group study.

Throughout the year we would cover all test topics using all forms of information available—books, library visits, excursions, guest speakers, newspapers, computers, and displays. We would read, write, talk, write poems, illustrate, and integrate with science, math, and the arts wherever possible. I would present these topics as normal curriculum learning, without mentioning "test" to the class at this stage. Finally, in order to prepare the class for the actual test itself, I would obtain copies of previous papers and practice going through them. If necessary to create enthusiasm, I would graph class results (not individual) and attempt to achieve a higher rate of successful answers each time.

Jennifer Hudson Thomas

Armidale High School, Armidale, Australia

Although the importance of the 4th-grade proficiency test cannot be overlooked from both the student's and school's point of view, it should not impede the process of "real" teaching and learning. Developing an enthusiasm for the learning required should be the greatest priority for any group of learners. Listing the mandatory topics to be covered and voting on the order in which these topics will be undertaken will give the learners some ownership of the direction that their learning will take over the year. Further involvement in planning the course and outcomes of such units of work will also increase students' commitment to their learning. Relating the learning within each topic to the real-life situations and interests of the group of learners will also help promote and "sell" the learning required. As the teacher, it will be my responsibility to incorporate as many of the required competencies as often as possible in all learning undertaken. This should ensure that the facts and skills required for that proficiency test become consolidated learning and form the basis of an automatic and well-rehearsed response repertoire. With such a learning background, my students should be able to generalize their skills and approach the proficiency test in the spring with confidence.

CHAPTER 14

Standardized Testing

Teachers' Casebook: What Would You Do? 521

Measurement and Assessment 522

Norm-Referenced Test Interpretations 523

Criterion-Referenced Test Interpretations 523

What Do Test Scores Mean? 524

Basic Concepts 524

Types of Scores 527

Interpreting Test Scores 529

Types of Standardized Tests 534

Achievement Tests: What Has the Student Learned? 536

Aptitude Tests: How Well Will the Student Do in the Future? 538

Issues in Standardized Testing 539

Accountability and High-Stakes Testing 540

The Dangers and Possibilities of High-Stakes Testing 541

Preparing for Tests 543

Reaching Every Student: Helping Students with Disabilities Prepare for High-Stakes Tests 543

New Directions in Assessment 545

Diversity and Convergences in Standardized Testing 546

Diversity 548

Convergences 548

Summary Table 549

Teachers' Casebook: Connections to PRAXIS II™/ What Would They Do? 551

What Would You Do?

Teachers' Casebook

It is nearing the end of school and the 9th-grade achievement test results are finally in. The parents' report form went home last Friday, and Monday morning you get a call from the principal during your planning period. The parents of one of your math students are in the office and have asked to speak with you and the principal immediately. The father is a prominent businessman and the mother is a lawyer. Their daughter received a grade-equivalent score of 11.8 on her standardized math test. Her percentile rank was 98th. The girl has been making Bs and Cs in your class—she seldom completes homework and has trouble with your conceptual approach to math. She just wants to know the "steps" to solve the problems so she can finish. You have tried several times to get the parents to come in to talk about ways to support the girl's learning, but they never seem to have had the time—until today.

You smile as you enter the principal's office, but the parents are not smiling. As soon as you sit down, the father says, "Well, you can see from our daughter's scores that you have been totally wrong in the grades you have given her this year. We thought she was just weak in math, but now it is clear you have something against her! Or maybe you just don't know how to teach math to bright girls."

The mother chimes in, "Yes, we expect you to reconsider her final grades for the year in light of her clear abilities. In fact," she glances at the principal and then glares at you again, "we believe she should get credit for the 10th grade class you teach as well, because she obviously knows the material already."

Critical Thinking

- What would you say to the parents?
- What do you need to know about tests to deal with this situation?
- How will you approach working with this student?
- How will these issues affect the grade levels you will teach?

Collaboration

With 3 other members of your class, role play this conference.

Would it surprise you to learn that published tests, such as the college entrance exams and IQ tests, are creations of the 20th century? In the 19th and early 20th centuries, college entrance was generally based on grades, essays, and interviews. From your own experience, you know that testing has come a long way since then—too far, say some critics. They want to revise testing as a way of reshaping the curriculum and reforming education. We will explore these new ideas in this chapter.

In spite of the criticisms, schools use more standardized tests than ever before because of the federal requirements for No Child Left Behind. Every public school is evaluated every year based on students' scores on standardized tests. Schools that are not making "Adequate Yearly Progress," defined as increasing the number of students who are "passing" these tests, face severe consequences. So teachers must be knowledgeable about testing. This chapter focuses on preparing for standardized tests and interpreting the results. Understanding how standardized test scores are determined, what they really mean, and how they can be used (or misused) provides you with a framework for ensuring that the tests you give are appropriate.

First, we consider testing in general, including the various methods of interpreting test scores. Then, we look at the different kinds of standardized tests used in schools. Finally, we examine the criticisms of testing and the alternatives being proposed. By the time you have completed this chapter, you should be able to answer these questions:

- How do you calculate mean, median, mode, and standard deviation?
- What are percentile ranks, standard deviations, z scores, T scores, and stanine scores?
- How can you improve reliability and validity in testing?
- What do results of achievement, aptitude, and diagnostic tests tell teachers?
- How would you prepare students (and yourself) for taking standardized tests?
- What are the strengths and weaknesses of alternative forms of assessment such as portfolios?

FACING PAGE *Classroom.* Diana Ong. © Diana Ong/SuperStock.

Measurement and Assessment

STOP | THINK | WRITE A member of your 7th-grade class does poorly in the arithmetic reasoning section of a standardized test. How would your interpretation of the results differ if the test were a criterion-referenced type as opposed to a norm-referenced type? Explain. ■

Teaching involves making many kinds of judgments—decisions based on values: "Should we use a different text this year?" "Is this film appropriate for my students?" "Will Jacob do better if he repeats the 1st grade?" "Should Terry get a B– or a C+ on the project?"

Measurement is quantitative—the description of an event or characteristic using numbers. Measurement tells how much, how often, or how well by providing scores, ranks, or ratings. Instead of saying, "Sarah doesn't seem to understand addition," a teacher might say, "Sarah answered only 2 of the 15 problems correctly in her addition homework." Measurement also allows a teacher to compare one student's performance on one particular task with either a standard or the performances of the other students.

Not all the decisions made by teachers involve measurement. Some decisions are based on information that is difficult to express numerically: student preferences, information from parents, previous experiences, even intuition. But measurement does play a large role in many classroom decisions, and, when properly done, it can provide unbiased data for decision making.

Increasingly, measurement specialists are using the term assessment to describe the process of gathering information about students' learning. Assessment is broader than testing and measurement because it includes all kinds of ways to sample and observe students' skills, knowledge, and abilities. **Assessment** can be any one of many procedures used to gather information about student performance (Linn & Miller, 2005). Assessments can be formal, such as unit tests, or informal, such as observing who emerges as a leader in group work. Assessments can be designed by classroom teachers or by local, state, or national agencies such as school districts or the Educational Testing Service. And today, assessments can go well beyond paper-and-pencil exercises to observations of performances, the development of portfolios, or the creation of artifacts (Popham, 2005a). In this chapter, we focus on formal assessments designed by groups and agencies outside the classroom. These assessments usually involve testing and the reporting of scores.

The answers given on any type of test have no meaning by themselves; we must make some kind of comparison in order to interpret test results. There are two basic types of comparison: In the first, a test score is compared to the scores obtained by other people who have taken the same test. (This is called a *norm-referenced* comparison.) The second type is *criterion-referenced*. Here, the comparison is to a fixed standard or minimum pass-

Connect and **Extend** to **PRAXIS II™**

Criterion-/Norm-Referenced Tests (II, C5)

The ERIC Digest *Norm- and Criterion-Referenced Testing* (http// www.ericdigests.org/1998–1/norm.htm) describes the purposes, content, and issues related to criterion- and norm-referenced tests.

Norm-referenced tests are useful in measuring overall achievement, but are not necessarily predictive of student readiness to move to more advanced work in an area.

Measurement An evaluation expressed in quantitative (number) terms.

Assessment Procedures used to obtain information about student performance.

ing score. Actually, the same test can be interpreted either in a norm-referenced or criterion-referenced way.

Norm-Referenced Test Interpretations

In **norm-referenced testing,** the people who have taken the test provide the *norms* for determining the meaning of a given individual's score. You can think of a norm as being the typical level of performance for a particular group. By comparing the individual's *raw score* (the actual number correct) to the norm, we can determine if the score is above, below, or around the average for that group. There are at least three types of **norm groups** (comparison groups) in education—the class or school itself, the school district, and national samples. National norm groups used for large-scale assessment programs are tested one year and then the scores for that group serve as comparisons or norms every year for several years. The norm groups are selected so that all SES groups are included in the sample. Because high-SES students tend to do better on many standardized tests, a high-SES school district will almost always have higher scores compared to the norm group.

Norm-referenced tests cover a wide range of general objectives. They are especially useful in measuring the overall achievement of students who have come to understand complex material by different routes. Norm-referenced tests are also appropriate when only the top few candidates can be admitted to a program.

However, norm-referenced measurement has its limitations. The results of a norm-referenced test do not tell you whether students are ready to move on to more advanced material. For instance, knowing that a student is in the top 3% of the class on a test of algebraic concepts will not tell you if he or she is ready to move on to advanced math; everyone in the class may have a limited understanding of the algebraic concepts.

Nor are norm-referenced tests particularly appropriate for measuring affective and psychomotor objectives. To measure individuals' psychomotor learning, you need a clear description of standards. (Even the best gymnast in school performs certain exercises better than others and needs specific guidance about how to improve.) In the affective area, attitudes and values are personal; comparisons among individuals are not really appropriate. For example, how could we measure an "average" level of political values or opinions? Finally, norm-referenced tests tend to encourage competition and comparison of scores. Some students compete to be the best. Others, realizing that being the best is impossible, may compete to be the worst. Both goals have their casualties.

Criterion-Referenced Test Interpretations

When test scores are compared, not to those of others, but to a given criterion or standard of performance, this is **criterion-referenced testing.** To decide who should be allowed to drive a car, it is important to determine just what standard of performance is appropriate for selecting safe drivers. It does not matter how your test results compare to the results of others. If your performance on the test was in the top 10% but you consistently ran through red lights, you would not be a good candidate for receiving a license, even though your score was high.

Criterion-referenced tests measure the mastery of very specific objectives. The results of a criterion-referenced test should tell the teacher exactly what the students can and cannot do, at least under certain conditions. For example, a criterion-referenced test would be useful in measuring the ability to add three-digit numbers. A test could be designed with 20 different problems, and the standard for mastery could be set at 17 correct out of 20. (The standard is often somewhat arbitrary and may be based on such things as the teacher's experience.) If two students receive scores of 7 and 11, it does not matter that one student did better than the other because neither met the standard of 17. Both need more help with addition.

In teaching basic skills, there are many instances where comparison to a preset standard is more important than comparison to the performance of others. It is not very comforting to know, as a parent, that your child is better in reading than most of the students

Connect and **Extend** to Your **Teaching/Portfolio**

Giving accurate feedback to parents is part of a teacher's job. When talking with a parent about a child's abilities, do you think the use of norm-referenced or criterion-referenced test results is more desirable?

Norm-referenced testing Testing in which scores are compared with the average performance of others.

Norm groups A group whose average score serves as a standard for evaluating any student's score on a test.

Criterion-referenced testing Testing in which scores are compared to a set performance standard.

TABLE 14.1

Two Kinds of Test Interpretations

Norm-referenced test interpretation may work best when you are

- Measuring general ability (strengths and weaknesses) in certain areas, such as English, algebra, general science, or American history.
- Assessing the range of abilities in a large group.
- Selecting top candidates when only a few openings are available.

Criterion-referenced tests may work best when you are

- Measuring mastery of basic skills.
- Determining if students have prerequisites to start a new unit.
- Assessing affective and psychomotor objectives.
- Providing evidence that students have met learning standards.
- Grouping students for instruction.

in class if none of the students is reading at grade level. Sometimes standards for meeting the criterion must be set at 100% correct. You would not like to have your appendix removed by a surgeon who left surgical instruments inside the body *only* 10% of the time.

Criterion-referenced tests are not appropriate for every situation, however. Many subjects cannot be broken down into a set of specific objectives. Moreover, although standards are important in criterion-referenced testing, they can often be arbitrary, as you have already seen. When deciding whether a student has mastered the addition of three-digit numbers comes down to the difference between 16 or 17 correct answers, it seems difficult to justify one particular standard over another. Finally, at times, it is valuable to know how the students in your class compare to other students at their grade level both locally and nationally. Table 14.1 offers a comparison of norm-referenced and criterion-referenced tests. You can see that each type of test is well suited for certain situations, but each also has its limitations.

What Do Test Scores Mean?

Connect and **Extend** to **PRAXIS II™**
Concepts of Standardized Testing (II, C5)
Be able to define norming samples, frequency distributions, measures of central tendency, standard deviation, normal distribution, reliability, and validity, and explain their roles in standardized tests.

Standardized tests are those official-looking pamphlets and piles of forms purchased by school systems and administered to students. More specifically, the tests are called *standardized* because they are administered, scored, and interpreted in a standard manner—same directions, time limits, and scoring for all (Popham, 2005a). Standard methods of developing items, administering the test, scoring it, and reporting the scores are all implied by the term *standardized test.*

Basic Concepts

STOP | THINK | WRITE Guess the mean, median, and mode for these two sets of scores:

50, 45, 55, 55, 45, 50, 50 Mean _______ Median _______ Mode _______

100, 0, 50, 90, 10, 50, 50 Mean _______ Median _______ Mode _______

Which set of scores has the largest standard deviation?

Standardized tests Tests given, usually nationwide, under uniform conditions and scored according to uniform procedures.

Norming sample Large sample of students serving as a comparison group for scoring standardized tests.

In standardized testing, the test items and instructions have been tried out to make sure they work and then rewritten and retested as necessary. When norm-referenced interpretations are used, he final version of the test is administered to a **norming sample,** a large sample of subjects as similar as possible to the students who will be taking the test in school systems throughout the country. This norming sample serves as a comparison group for all students who take the test.

The test publishers provide one or more ways of comparing each student's raw score (number of correct answers) with the norming sample. Let's look at some of the concepts on which comparisons and interpretations are based.

Frequency Distributions. A **frequency distribution** is simply a listing of the number of people who obtain each score or fall into each range of scores on a test or other measurement procedure. For example, on a spelling test, 19 students made these scores: 100, 95, 90, 85, 85, 85, 80, 75, 75, 75, 70, 65, 60, 60, 55, 50, 50, 45, 40. A graph, in this case a **histogram** (bar graph), of the spelling test scores is shown in Figure 14.1 where one axis (the *x*, or horizontal, axis) indicates the possible scores and the other axis (the *y*, or vertical, axis) indicates the number of subjects who attained each score.

Measurements of Central Tendency and Standard Deviation. You have probably had a great deal of experience with means. A **mean** is simply the arithmetical average of a group of scores. To calculate the mean, you add the scores and divide the total by the number of scores in the distribution. For example, the total of the 19 spelling scores is 1,340, so the mean is 1,340/19, or 70.53. The mean offers one way of measuring **central tendency,** the score that is typical or representative of the whole distribution of scores. Very high or very low scores affect the mean.

Two other measures of central tendency are the median and the mode. The **median** is the middle score in the distribution, the point at which half the scores are larger and half are smaller. The median of the 19 scores is 75. Nine scores in the distribution are greater than or equal to 75, and nine are less. When there are a few very high or low scores, the median may be a better representative of the central tendency of a group. The **mode** is the score that occurs most often. The distribution in Figure 14.1 actually has two modes, 75 and 85, because each of these scores occurred three times. This makes it a *bimodal distribution.*

The measure of central tendency gives a score that is representative of the group of scores, but it does not tell you anything about how the scores are distributed. Two groups of scores may both have a mean of 50, but be alike in no other way. One group might contain the scores 50, 45, 55, 55, 45, 50, 50; the other group might contain the scores 100, 0, 50, 90, 10, 50, 50—the groups in the *Stop/Think/Write* question at the beginning of this section. In both cases, the mean, median, and mode are all 50, but the distributions are quite different.

Connect and Extend to Your Teaching/Portfolio

At a PTA meeting, parents were complaining because half of the students in the district scored below the district average on the achievement tests that were given. Is this a valid complaint?

FIGURE 14.1

Histogram of a Frequency Distribution

This bar graph or histogram shows the number of people who earned each score on a test. You can quickly see, for example, that three people earned a 75 and three people earned an 85.

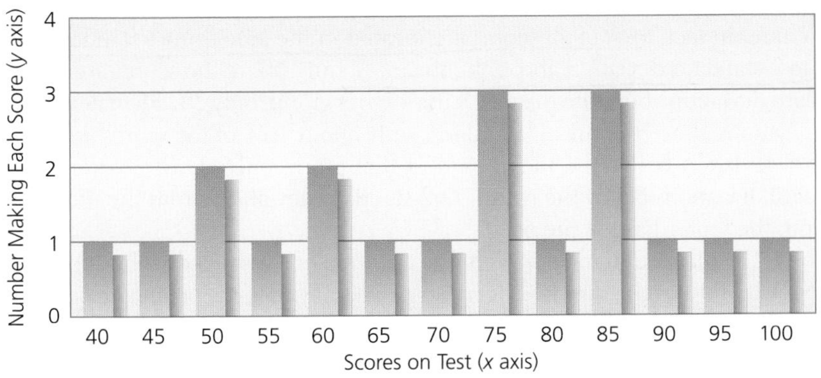

Frequency distribution Record showing how many scores fall into set groups.

Histogram Bar graph of a frequency distribution.

Mean Arithmetical average.

Central tendency Typical score for a group of scores.

Median Middle score in a group of scores.

Mode Most frequently occurring score.

Connect and **Extend** to Your **Teaching/Portfolio**

Which math class, A or B, is probably easier to teach, judging from the following standard score results (50 = national average)?

Class A: Mean = 55 SD = 13

or

Class B: Mean = 53 SD = 4

(*Answer:* Probably Class B because the range of achievement levels is not as great as in Class A.)

The **standard deviation** is a measure of how widely the scores vary from the mean. The larger the standard deviation, the more spread out the scores are in the distribution. The smaller the standard deviation, the more the scores are clustered around the mean. For example, in the distribution 50, 45, 55, 55, 45, 50, 50, the standard deviation is much smaller than in the distribution 100, 0, 50, 90, 10, 50, 50. Another way of saying this is that distributions with very small standard deviations have less **variability** in the scores.

The standard deviation is relatively easy to calculate if you remember your high-school math. It does take time, however. The process is similar to taking an average, but you use square roots. To calculate the standard deviation, you follow these steps:

1. Calculate the mean (written as $\overline{X}$) of the scores.
2. Subtract the mean from each of the scores. This is written as $(X - \overline{X})$.
3. Square each difference (multiply each difference by itself). This is written $(X - \overline{X})^2$.
4. Add all the squared differences. This is written $\Sigma(X - \overline{X})^2$.
5. Divide this total by the number of scores. This is written $\frac{\Sigma(X - \overline{X})^2}{N}$.
6. Find the square root. This is written $\sqrt{\frac{\Sigma(X - \overline{X})^2}{N}}$, which is the formula for calculating the standard deviation.

Knowing the mean and the standard deviation of a group of scores gives you a better picture of the meaning of an individual score. For example, suppose you received a score of 78 on a test. You would be very pleased with the score if the mean of the test were 70 and the standard deviation were 4. In this case, your score would be 2 standard deviations above the mean, a score well above average.

Consider the difference if the mean of the test had remained at 70, but the standard deviation had been 20. In the second case, your score of 78 would be less than 1 standard deviation from the mean. You would be much closer to the middle of the group, with a score above average, but not high. Knowing the standard deviation tells you much more than simply knowing the **range** of scores. No matter how the majority scored on the tests, one or two students may do very well or very poorly and thus make the range very large.

The Normal Distribution. Standard deviations are very useful in understanding test results. They are especially helpful if the results of the tests form a **normal distribution.** You may have encountered the normal distribution before. It is the bell-shaped curve, the most famous frequency distribution because it describes many naturally occurring physical and social phenomena. Many scores fall in the middle, giving the curve its puffed appearance. You find fewer and fewer scores as you look out toward the end points, or *tails*, of the distribution. The normal distribution has been thoroughly analyzed by statisticians. The mean of a normal distribution is also its midpoint. Half the scores are above the mean, and half are below it. In a normal distribution, the mean, median, and mode are all the same point.

Another convenient property of the normal distribution is that the percentage of scores falling within each area of the curve is known, as you can see in Figure 14.2. A person scoring within 1 standard deviation of the mean obviously has company. Many scores pile up here. In fact, 68% of all scores are located in the area from 1 standard deviation below to 1 standard deviation above the mean. About 16% of the scores are higher than 1 standard deviation above the mean. Of this higher group, only 2% are better than 2 standard deviations above the mean. Similarly, only about 16% of the scores are less than 1 standard deviation below the mean, and of that group only about 2% are worse than 2 standard deviations below the mean. At 2 standard deviations from the mean in either direction, the scorer has left the pack.

The SAT college entrance exam is one example of a normal distribution. The mean of the SAT is 500 and the standard deviation is 100. If you know people who made scores of 700, you know they did very well. Only about 2% of the people who take the test do that well, because only 2% of the scores are better than 2 standard deviations above the mean in a normal distribution.

Standard deviation Measure of how widely scores vary from the mean.

Variability Degree of difference or deviation from mean.

Range Distance between the highest and the lowest scores in a group.

Normal distribution The most commonly occurring distribution, in which scores are distributed evenly around the mean.

FIGURE 14.2

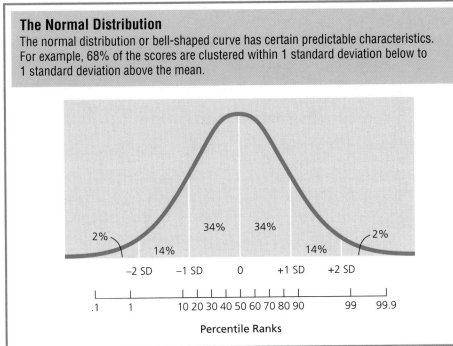

The Normal Distribution

The normal distribution or bell-shaped curve has certain predictable characteristics. For example, 68% of the scores are clustered within 1 standard deviation below to 1 standard deviation above the mean.

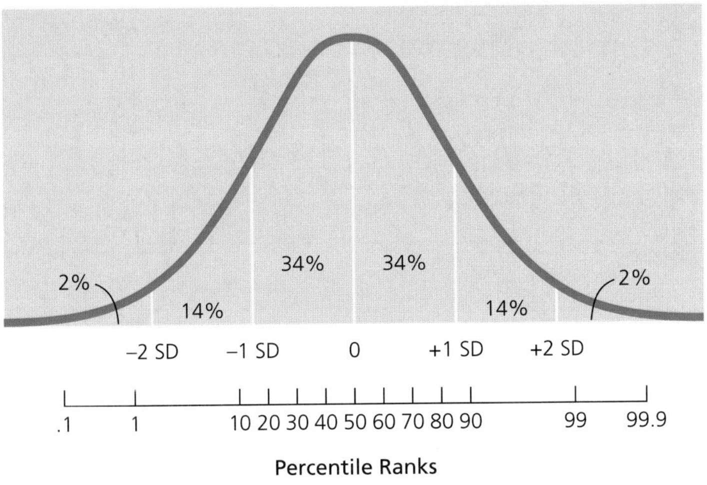

Types of Scores

STOP | THINK | WRITE At your first parent conference, a mother and father are concerned about their child's percentile rank of 86. They say that they expect their child to "get close to 100 percent. We know she should be able to do that because her grade-equivalent score is half a year above her grade!" What would you say? Do they understand the meaning of these scores? ■

Now you have enough background for a discussion of the different kinds of scores you may encounter in reports of results from standardized tests—scores these parents don't seem to understand.

Percentile Rank Scores. The concept of ranking is the basis for one very useful kind of score reported on standardized tests, a **percentile rank** score. In percentile ranking, each student's raw score is compared with the raw scores of the students in the norming sample. The percentile rank shows the percentage of students in the norming sample that scored *at or below* a particular raw score. If a student's score were the same as or better than three-quarters of the students in the norming sample, the student would score in the 75th percentile or have a percentile rank of 75. You can see that this does *not* mean that the student had a raw score of 75 correct answers or even that the student answered 75% of the questions correctly. Rather, the 75 refers to the percentage of people in the norming sample whose scores on the test were equal to or below this student's score. A percentile rank of 50 means that a student has scored as well as or better than 50% of the norming sample and has achieved an average score.

Figure 14.3 on the next page illustrates one caution in interpreting percentile scores. Differences in percentile ranks do not mean the same thing in terms of raw score points in the middle of the scale as they do at the fringes. The graph shows Joan's and Alice's percentile scores on the fictitious Test of Excellence in Language and Arithmetic. Both students are about average in arithmetic skills. One equaled or surpassed 50% of the norming sample; the other, 60%. However, because their scores are in the middle of the distribution, this difference in percentile ranks means a raw score difference of only a few points. Their raw scores were actually 75 and 77. In the language test, the difference in

Percentile rank Percentage of those in the norming sample who scored at or below an individual's score.

FIGURE 14.3

Percentile Ranking on a Normal Distribution Curve

Percentile scores have different meanings at different places on the scale. For example, a difference of a few raw score points near the mean might translate into a 10-point percentile difference, while it would take 6 or 7 points to make a 10-point percentile difference farther out on the scale.

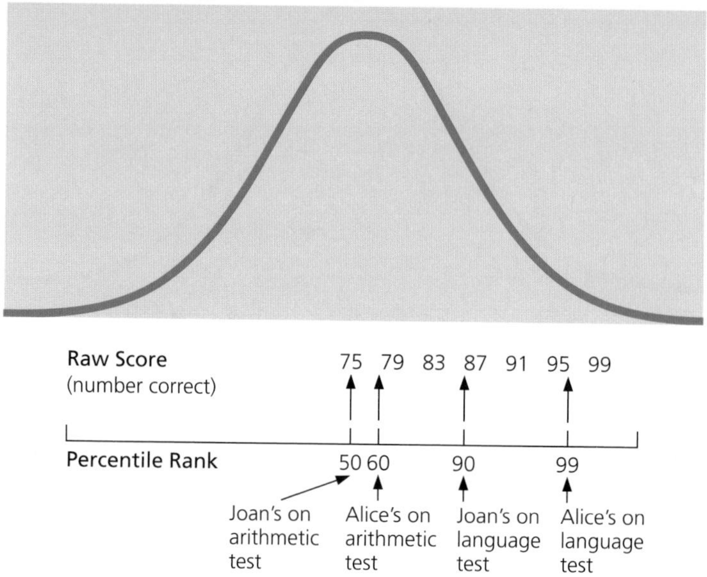

percentile ranks seems to be about the same as the difference in arithmetic, since one ranked at the 90th percentile and the other at the 99th. But the difference in their raw scores on the language test is much greater. It takes a greater difference in raw score points to make a difference in percentile rank at the extreme ends of the scale. On the language test the difference in raw scores is about 10 points.

Grade-Equivalent Scores. **Grade-equivalent scores** are generally obtained from separate norming samples for each grade level. The average of the scores of all the 10th graders in the norming sample defines the 10th-grade equivalent score. Suppose the raw-score average of the 10th-grade norming sample is 38. Any student who attains a raw score of 38 on that test will be assigned a grade-equivalent score of 10th grade. Grade-equivalent scores are generally listed in numbers such as 8.3, 4.5, 7.6, 11.5, and so on. The whole number gives the grade. The decimals stand for tenths of a year, but they are usually interpreted as months.

Suppose a student with the grade-equivalent score of 10 is a 7th grader. Should this student be promoted immediately? Probably not. Different forms of tests are used at different grade levels, so the 7th grader may not have had to answer items that would be given to 10th graders. The high score may represent superior mastery of material at the 7th-grade level rather than a capacity for doing advanced work. Even though an average 10th grader could do as well as our 7th grader on this particular test, the 10th grader would certainly know much more than this 7th-grade test covered. Also, grade-equivalent score units do not mean the same thing at every grade level. For example, a 2nd grader reading at the 1st-grade level would have more trouble in school than an 11th grader who reads at the 10th-grade level.

Because grade-equivalent scores are misleading and are often misinterpreted, especially by parents, most educators and psychologists strongly believe they should not be used at all. There are several other forms of reporting available that are more appropriate.

Grade-equivalent score Measure of grade level based on comparison with norming samples from each grade.

Standard Scores. As you may remember, one problem with percentile ranks is the difficulty in making comparisons among ranks. A discrepancy of a certain number of raw-score points has a different meaning at different places on the scale. With standard scores, on the other hand, a difference of 10 points is the same everywhere on the scale.

Standard scores are based on the standard deviation. A very common standard score is called the *z* score. A ***z* score** tells how many standard deviations above or below the average a raw score is. In the example described earlier, in which you were fortunate enough to get a 78 on a test where the mean was 70 and the standard deviation was 4, your *z* score would be +2, or 2 standard deviations above the mean. If a person were to score 64 on this test, the score would be 1.5 standard deviation units *below* the mean, and the *z* score would be −1.5. A *z* score of 0 would be no standard deviations above the mean—in other words, right on the mean.

To calculate the *z* score for a given raw score, subtract the mean from the raw score and divide the difference by the standard deviation. The formula is:

$$Z = \frac{\text{Raw Score} - \text{Mean}}{\text{Standard Deviation}}$$

Because it is often inconvenient to use negative numbers, other standard scores have been devised to eliminate this difficulty. The ***T* score** has a mean of 50 and uses a standard deviation of 10. Thus, a *T* score of 50 indicates average performance. If you multiply the *z* score by 10 (which eliminates the decimal) and add 50 (which gets rid of the negative number), you get the equivalent *T* score as the answer. The person whose *z* score was—1.5 would have a *T* score of 35.

First multiply the *z* score by 10:	$-1.5 \times 10 = -15$
Then add 50:	$-15 + 50 = 35$

The scoring of the SAT test is based on a similar procedure. The mean of the scores is set at 500, and a standard deviation of 100 is used. Different states have different ways of determining standards-based scores. For example, in Virginia, state standard scores range from 0 to 600 for whole test scores.

Before we leave this section on types of scores, we should mention one other widely used method. Stanine scores (the name comes from "standard nine") are standard scores. There are only nine possible scores on the stanine scale, the whole numbers 1 through 9. The mean is 5, and the standard deviation is 2. Each unit from 2 to 8 is equal to half a standard deviation.

Stanine scores provide a method of considering a student's rank, because each of the nine scores includes a specific range of percentile scores in the normal distribution. For example, a stanine score of 1 is assigned to the bottom 4% of scores in a distribution. A stanine of 2 is assigned to the next 7%. Of course, some raw scores in this 7% range are better than others, but they all get a stanine score of 2.

Each stanine score represents a wide range of raw scores. This has the advantage of encouraging teachers and parents to view a student's score in more general terms instead of making fine distinctions based on a few points. Figure 14.4 on the next page compares the four types of standard scores we have considered, showing how each would fall on a normal distribution curve.

Interpreting Test Scores

WHAT WOULD YOU SAY?

As part of the interview process for a job in a high school, you are asked the following: "How would you interpret the test scores of minority-group students?" ■

One of the most common problems with the use of tests is misinterpretation of scores. This often happens because of the belief that numbers are precise measurements of a student's ability. No test provides a perfect picture of a person's abilities; a test is only one small sample of behavior. Three factors are important in developing good tests and interpreting results: reliability, validity, and absence of bias.

Standard scores Scores based on the standard deviation.

***z* score** Standard score indicating the number of standard deviations above or below the mean.

***T* score** Standard score with a mean of 50 and a standard deviation of 10.

Stanine scores Whole number scores from 1 to 9, each representing a wide range of raw scores.

FIGURE 14.4

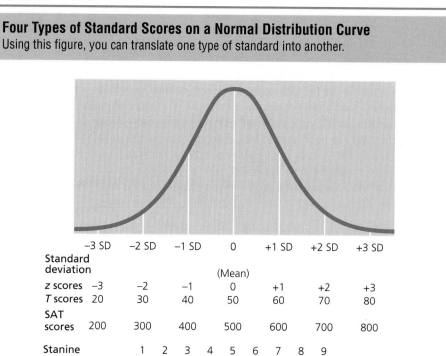

Four Types of Standard Scores on a Normal Distribution Curve
Using this figure, you can translate one type of standard into another.

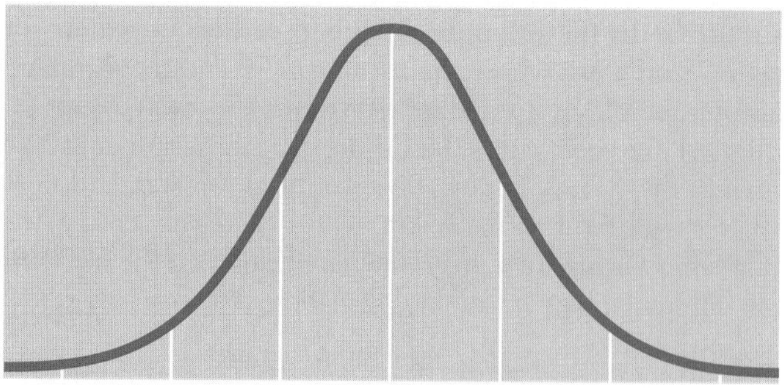

Standard deviation	−3 SD	−2 SD	−1 SD	0 (Mean)	+1 SD	+2 SD	+3 SD
z scores	−3	−2	−1	0	+1	+2	+3
T scores	20	30	40	50	60	70	80
SAT scores	200	300	400	500	600	700	800

Stanine scores 1 2 3 4 5 6 7 8 9

Reliability of Test Scores. If you took a standardized test on Monday, then took the same test again a week later, and you received about the same score each time, you would have reason to believe the test scores were reliable. If 100 people took the test one day, then repeated it the following week, and the ranking of the individual scores was about the same for both tests, you would be even more certain the test scores were reliable. (Of course, this assumes that no one looks up answers or studies before the second test.) Scores are reliable if a test gives a consistent and stable "reading" of a person's ability from one occasion to the next, assuming the person's ability remains the same. A reliable thermometer works in a similar manner, giving you a reading of 100°C each time you measure the temperature of boiling water. Measuring **reliability** this way, by giving the test on two different occasions, indicates *stability* or *test-retest reliability*. If a group of people takes two equivalent versions of a test and the scores on both tests are comparable, this indicates *alternate-form reliability*.

Reliability can also refer to the internal consistency or the precision of a test. This type of reliability, known as *split-half reliability*, is calculated by comparing performance on half of the test questions with performance on the other half. If, for example, someone did quite well on all the odd-numbered items and not at all well on the even-numbered items, we could assume that the items were not very consistent or precise in measuring what they were intended to measure.

There are several ways to compute reliability, but all the possibilities give numbers between 0.0 and 1.0, like a correlation coefficient. Above .90 is considered very reliable; .80 to .90 is good, and below .80 is not very good reliability for standardized tests (Haladyna, 2002). The most effective way to improve reliability is to add more items to a test. Generally speaking, longer tests are more reliable than shorter ones.

Error in Scores. All tests are imperfect estimators of the qualities or skills they are trying to measure. There are errors in every testing situation. There are sources of error related to the student such as mood, motivation, test-taking skills, or even cheating. Sometimes the errors are in your favor and you score higher than your ability might warrant; perhaps you reviewed a key section just before the test. Sometimes the errors go

Reliability Consistency of test results.

The validity and reliability of tests may be affected by the extent to which they measure intelligence, knowledge, motivation, or differences in life experience.

against you—you are sick, sleepy, or focused on the wrong material in your review. There are also sources of error related to the test itself—the directions are unclear, the reading level is too high, the items are ambiguous, or the time limits are wrong.

The score each student receives always includes some amount of *error.* How can error be reduced? As you might guess, this returns us to the question of reliability. The more reliable the test scores are, the less error there will be in the score actually obtained. On standardized tests, test developers take this into consideration and make estimations of how much the students' scores would probably vary if they were tested repeatedly. This estimation is called the **standard error of measurement.** Thus, a reliable test can also be defined as one with a small standard error of measurement. In their interpretation of tests, teachers must also take into consideration the margin for error.

Connect and Extend to Your Teaching/Portfolio

There are many sources of error in testing: personal (e.g., misreading directions, illness, reviewing wrong material, anxiety); test-related (e.g., unclear directions, excessive length, too-high reading level); and context-related (too-competitive situation, noise, mistakes by test administrator).

Confidence Interval. Never base an opinion of a student's ability or achievement on the exact score the student obtains. Many test companies now report scores using a **confidence interval**, or "standard error band," that encloses the student's actual score. This makes use of the standard error of measurement and allows a teacher to consider the range of scores that might include a student's **true score**—the score the student would get if the measurement were completely accurate and error-free.

Let us assume, for example, that two students in your class take a standardized achievement test in Spanish. The standard error of measurement for this test is 5. One student receives a score of 79 and the other, a score of 85. At first glance, these scores seem quite different. But when you consider the standard error bands around the scores, not just the scores alone, you see that the bands overlap. The first student's true score might be anywhere between 74 and 84 (that is, the actual score of 79 plus and minus the standard error of 5). The second student's true score might be anywhere between 80 and 90. It is crucial to keep in mind the idea of standard error bands when selecting students for special programs. No child should be rejected simply because the obtained score missed the cutoff by one or two points. The student's true score might well be above the cutoff point.

Validity. If a test scores are sufficiently reliable, the next question is whether the scores are valid, or more accurately, whether the judgments and decisions based on the test are valid. To have **validity,** the decisions and inferences based on the test must be supported by evidence. This means that validity is judged in relation to a particular use or purpose, that is, in relation to the actual decision being made and the evidence for that decision

Standard error of measurement Hypothetical estimate of variation in scores if testing were repeated.

Confidence interval Range of scores within which an individual's particular score is likely to fall.

True score The score the student would get if the measurement were completely accurate and error-free.

Validity Degree to which a test measures what it is intended to measure.

Connect and **Extend** to the **Research**

Messick, S. (1995). Standards of validity and the validity of standards in performance assessment. *Educational Measurement: Issues and Practice*, 14(4), 5–8.

(Linn & Gronlund, 2000; Popham, 2005a). A particular test might be valid for one purpose, but not for another.

There are different kinds of evidence to support a particular judgment. If the purpose of a test is to measure the skills covered in a course or unit, then we would hope to see test questions on all the important topics and not on extraneous information. If this condition is met, we would have *content-related evidence of validity*. Have you ever taken a test that dealt only with a few ideas from one lecture or just a few pages of the textbook? Then decisions based on that test (like your grade) certainly lacked content-related evidence of validity.

Some tests are designed to predict outcomes. The SATs, for example, are intended to predict performance in college. If SAT scores correlate with academic performance in college as measured by, say, grade-point average in the first year, then we have *criterion-related evidence of validity* for the use of the SAT in admissions decisions.

Most standardized tests are designed to measure some psychological characteristic or "construct" such as reasoning ability, reading comprehension, achievement motivation, intelligence, creativity, and so on. It is a bit more difficult to gather *construct-related evidence of validity*, yet this is a very important requirement—probably the most important. Construct-related evidence of validity is gathered over many years. It is indicated by a pattern of scores. For example, older children can answer more questions on intelligence tests than younger children can. This fits with our construct of intelligence. If the average 5-year-old answered as many questions correctly on a test as the average 13-year-old, we would doubt that the test really measured intelligence. Construct-related evidence for validity can also be demonstrated when the results of a test correlate with the results of other well-established, valid measures of the same construct.

Today, many psychologists suggest that construct validity is the broadest category and that gathering content- and criterion-related evidence is another way of determining if the test measures the construct it was designed to measure. Over 30 years ago, Sam Messick (1975) raised two important questions to consider in making any decisions about using a test: Is the test a good measure of the characteristic it is assumed to assess? Should the test be used for the proposed purpose? The first question is about construct validity; the second is about ethics and values (Moss, 1992).

A test must be reliable in order to be valid. For example, if, over a few months, an intelligence test yields different results each time it is given to the same child, then by definition it is not reliable. Certainly, it couldn't be a valid measure of intelligence because intelligence is assumed to be fairly stable, at least over a short period of time. However, reliability will not guarantee validity. If that intelligence test gave the same score every time for a particular child, but didn't predict school achievement, speed of learning, or other characteristics associated with intelligence, then performance on the test would not be a true indicator of intelligence. The test would be reliable—but invalid. As you will see in the next chapter, reliability and validity are issues with all assessments, not just standardized tests. Classroom tests should yield scores that are reliable, as free from error as possible, and accurately indicate what they are supposed to measure. The *Guidelines* should help you increase the reliability and validity of the standardized tests you give.

Connect and **Extend** to Your **Teaching/Portfolio**

What do you believe about the uses of testing for children?

Absence of Bias. The third important criterion for judging assessments is absence of bias. **Assessment bias** "refers to qualities of an assessment instrument that offend or unfairly penalize a group of students because of the students' gender, ethnicity, socioeconomic status, religion, or other such group-defining characteristic" (Popham, 2005a, p. 77). Biases are aspects of the test such as content, language, or examples that might distort the performance of a group—either for better or for worse. For example, if a reading test used passages that described boxing or football scenarios, we might expect males on average to do better than females.

Assessment bias Qualities of an assessment instrument that offend or unfairly penalize a group of students because of the students' gender, SES, race, ethnicity, etc.

Two forms of assessment bias are unfair penalization and offensiveness. The reading assessment with heavy sports content is an example of *unfair penalization*—girls may be penalized for their lack of boxing or football knowledge. *Offensiveness* occurs when a particular group might be insulted by the content of the assessment. Offended, angry students may not perform at their best.

Guidelines: Increasing Reliability and Validity

Make sure the test actually covers the content of the unit of study.

EXAMPLES

1. Compare test questions to course objectives. Make sure that there is good overlap.
2. Use local achievement tests and local norms when possible.
3. Check to see if the test is long enough to cover all important topics.
4. Find out if there are any difficulties your students experience with the test, such as not enough time, too difficult a level of reading, and so on. If there are, discuss these problems with appropriate school personnel.

Make sure students know how to use all the test materials.

EXAMPLES

1. Several days before the testing, do a few practice questions with a similar format.
2. Demonstrate the use of the answer sheets, especially computer-scored answer sheets.
3. Check with new students, shy students, slower students, and students who have difficulty reading to make sure they understand the questions.
4. Make sure students know if and when guessing is appropriate.

Follow instructions for administering the test exactly.

EXAMPLES

1. Practice giving the test before you actually use it.
2. Follow the time limits exactly.

Make students as comfortable as possible during testing.

EXAMPLES

1. Do not create anxiety by making the test seem like the most important event of the year.
2. Help the class relax before beginning the test, perhaps by telling a joke or having everyone take a few deep breaths. Don't be tense yourself!
3. Make sure the room is quiet.
4. Discourage cheating by monitoring the room. Don't become absorbed in your own paperwork.

Remember that no test scores are perfect.

EXAMPLES

1. Interpret scores using bands instead of a single score.
2. Ignore small differences between scores.

For a good explanation of reliability and validity, see **http://seamonkey.ed.asu.edu/~alex/teaching/assessment/reliability.html**
For more information on bias in testing and how to avoid it, see **http://www.fairtest.org/**

Are tests such as the individual measures of intelligence or college admissions tests fair assessments for minority-group students? This is a complex question. Research on test bias shows that most standardized tests predict school achievement equally well across all groups of students. Items that might appear on the surface to be biased against minority-group students are not necessarily more difficult for them to answer correctly (Sattler, 2001). But even though standardized aptitude and achievement tests are not biased in predicting school performance, many people believe that the tests still can be unfair to some groups. Tests may not have *procedural fairness;* that is, some groups may not have an equal opportunity to show what they know on the test. Here are a few examples:

1. The language of the test and the tester is often different from the languages of the students.
2. Answers that support middle-class values are often rewarded with more points.
3. On individually administered intelligence tests, being very verbal and talking a lot is rewarded. This favors students who feel comfortable in that particular situation.

Also, tests may not be fair, because different groups have had different *opportunities to learn* the material tested. The questions asked tend to center on experiences and facts more familiar to the dominant culture than to minority-group students. Consider this test item for 4th graders described by Popham (2005a, p. 336):

My uncle's *field* is computer programming.

Look at the sentences below. In which sentence does the word *field* mean the same as it does in the boxed sentence above?

A. The softball pitcher knew how to *field* her position.
B. They prepared the *field* by spraying and plowing it.
C. I know the *field* I plan to enter when I finish college.
D. The doctor used a wall chart to examine my *field* of vision.

Items like this are on most standardized tests. But not all families describe their work as a *field* of employment. If your parents work in professional fields such as computers, medicine, law, or education, the item would make sense, but what if your parents worked at a grocery store or a car repair shop? Are these fields? Life outside class has prepared some students, but not others for this item.

Concern about cultural bias in testing has led some psychologists to try to develop **culture-fair or culture-free tests.** These efforts have not been very successful. On many of the so-called culture-fair tests, the performance of students from lower-SES backgrounds and ethnic groups has been the same as or worse than their performance on the standard Wechsler and Binet Intelligence scales (Sattler, 2001). And when you think about it, how can you separate culture from cognition? Every student's learning is embedded in his or her culture and every test question grows from some kind of cultural knowledge.

Today, most standardized tests are checked carefully for assessment bias, but teacher-made tests may have biased content as well. It makes sense to have colleagues check your tests for bias, especially when you are getting started in teaching (Popham, 2005a). The *Guidelines* might help all your students take tests.

Connect and **Extend** to Your **Teaching/Portfolio**

Using the *Guidelines* for preparing for a test, prepare a testing guide sheet for the grades you will teach.

Connect and **Extend** to **PRAXIS II™**

Types of Standardized Tests (II, C1)

Teachers, learning specialists, and school psychologists use a variety of tests. Distinguish among achievement, diagnostic, and aptitude tests. Describe the purposes for each.

Types of Standardized Tests

Several kinds of standardized tests are used in schools today. If you have seen the cumulative folders that include testing records for individual students over several years, then you know the many ways students are tested in this country. There are three broad categories of standardized tests: achievement, diagnostic, and aptitude (including interest). As a teacher, you will probably encounter achievement and aptitude tests most frequently.

Standardized tests used in education usually fit three broad categories: achievement, diagnostic, and aptitude (including interest).

Culture-fair/culture-free test A test without cultural bias.

Guidelines: Becoming an Expert Test-Taker

Use the night before the test effectively.

EXAMPLES

1. Study the night before the exam, ending with a final look at a summary of the key points, concepts, and relationships.
2. Get a good night's sleep. If you know you generally have trouble sleeping the night before an exam, try getting extra sleep on several previous nights.

Set the situation so you can concentrate on the test.

EXAMPLES

1. Give yourself plenty of time to eat and get to the exam room.
2. Don't sit near a friend. It may make concentration difficult. If your friend leaves early, you may be tempted to do so, too.

Make sure you know what the test is asking.

EXAMPLES

1. Read the directions carefully. If you are unsure, ask the instructor or proctor for clarification.
2. Read each question carefully to spot tricky words, such as *not, except, all of the following but one.*
3. On an essay test, read every question first, so you know the size of the job ahead of you and can make informed decisions about how much time to spend on each question.
4. On a multiple-choice test, read every alternative, even if an early one seems right.

Use time effectively.

EXAMPLES

1. Begin working right away and move as rapidly as possible while your energy is high.
2. Do the easy questions first.
3. Don't get stuck on one question. If you are stumped, mark the question so you can return to it easily later, and go on to questions you can answer more quickly.
4. On a multiple-choice test, if you know you will not have time to finish, fill in all the remaining questions with the same letter if there is no penalty for guessing.
5. If you are running out of time on an essay test, do not leave any questions blank. Briefly outline a few key points to show the instructor you knew the answer but needed more time.

Know when to guess on multiple-choice or true-false tests.

EXAMPLES

1. Always guess when only right answers are scored.
2. Always guess when you can eliminate some of the alternatives.
3. Don't guess if there is a penalty for guessing, unless you can confidently eliminate at least one alternative.
4. Are correct answers always longer? shorter? in the middle? more likely to be one letter? more often true than false?
5. Does the grammar give the right answer away or eliminate any alternatives?

Check your work.

EXAMPLES

1. Even if you can't stand to look at the test another minute, reread each question to make sure you answered the way you intended.
2. If you are using a machine-scored answer sheet, check occasionally to be sure the number of the question you are answering corresponds to the number of the answer on the sheet.

On essay tests, answer as directly as possible.

EXAMPLES

1. Avoid flowery introductions. Answer the question in the first sentence and then elaborate.
2. Don't save your best ideas till last. Give them early in the answer.
3. Unless the instructor requires complete sentences, consider listing points, arguments, and so on by number in your answer. It will help you organize your thoughts and concentrate on the important aspects of the answer.

Learn from the testing experience.

EXAMPLES

1. Pay attention when the teacher reviews the answers. You can learn from your mistakes, and the same question may reappear in a later test.
2. Notice if you are having trouble with a particular kind of item; adjust your study approach next time to handle this type of item better.

For more test-taking strategies see **http://www.eop.mu.edu/study/** or **http://www.testtakingtips.com/**

Achievement Tests: What Has the Student Learned?

STOP | THINK | WRITE Look at the test printout in Figure 14.5. What are this student's strengths and weaknesses? How do you know? ■

The most common standardized tests given to students are **achievement tests.** These are meant to measure how much a student has learned in specific content areas such as reading comprehension, language usage, computation, science, social studies, mathematics, and logical reasoning. There are achievement tests for both individuals and groups. These tests vary in their reliability and validity. Group tests can be used for screening—to identify children who might need further testing or as a basis for grouping students according to achievement levels. Individual achievement tests are given to determine a child's academic level more precisely, or to help diagnose learning problems.

Using Information from a Norm-Referenced Achievement Test. What specific information can teachers expect from achievement test results? Test publishers usually provide individual profiles for each student, showing scores on each subtest. Figure 14.5 is an example of an individual profile for a 4th grader, Ken Jones, on the *TerraNova*, Second Edition. Note that the Individual Profile Report has two pages. The first page (Performance on Objectives) attempts to paint a picture of the student's mastery of different objectives in *Reading, Language, Mathematics, Science*, and *Social Studies.* For example, under *Reading* are the objectives of "basic understanding," "analyze text," "evaluate/extend meaning," and "identify reading strategies." Next to each objective are several different ways of reporting Ken's score.

Raw Score/Student OPI Score: Under the first column labeled "Student" is the number of items (out of 100) that Ken answered correctly for that objective. But be aware, the test probably did not have 100 items to assess that objective, so this is an adjusted number (an OPI score) based on the actual number of items presented and the number Ken got right. The OPI score is an estimate of the number of items that Ken could be expected to get correct *if* there had been 100 items for that objective. A caution—on many standardized tests, some of these specific skill areas may be measured with only a few items each, and the fewer the items, the more potential problems there can be with reliability.

National OPI: The average OPI score for the national standardization sample completed in 2000.

Difference: The difference between the student's score and the national average—is the student below or above the national average and by how much? You can see that Ken is 15 points below the national average on writing strategies and 15 points above on editing skills.

Moderate Mastery Range: Indicates middle-level mastery for this objective. For analyzing text, the range is 52 to 75, and Ken's score is above that range.

OPI Graph: On the graph to the right of the scores, a completely filled in circle indicates high mastery (see Ken's score on analyzing text in reading), a half-filled in circle is in the moderate mastery range (see Ken's score on sentence structure), and an empty circle indicates low mastery (see Ken's score on science inquiry).

On page 2 of the report (Norm-Referenced Scores), Ken's scores are compared to students in the national standardization sample, completed in 2000.

Scale Score: The basic score used to derive all the other scores, sometimes called a growth score because it describes growth in achievement that typically occurs as students move through the grades. For example, the average score for 3rd graders might be 585, while the average score for 10th graders is 714 on tests with possible scores that range from 0 to 1000 across the entire K–12 grades. Often, the difficulty of items is included in calculating scale scores. Schools are increasingly using this score because they can compare across years, classes, or schools in the district (Popham, 2005a).

Grade Equivalent Score: This indicates that Ken's scale score is the same as an average student in that grade and month of school. Beware of the problems with grade-equivalent scores described earlier.

Connect and Extend to the Research

Turner, M. D., Baldwin, L., Kleinert, H. L., & Kearns, J. F. (2000). The relation of a statewide alternate assessment for students with severe disabilities to other measures of instructional effectiveness. *Journal of Special Education, 34*, 69–76.

Connect and Extend to PRAXIS II™

Interpreting Achievement Tests (II, C4)

Accurate information from the teacher is essential for students' academic progress. The ERIC Digest *Explaining Test Results to Parents* (http://www.ericdigests.org/pre-9210/parents.htm) will help with this task.

Connect and Extend to Your Teaching/Portfolio

If you have access to your own records, locate copies of standardized tests you have taken and interpret the scores as if you were your own teacher.

Achievement tests Standardized tests measuring how much students have learned in a given content area.

FIGURE 14.5

A Typical Score Report

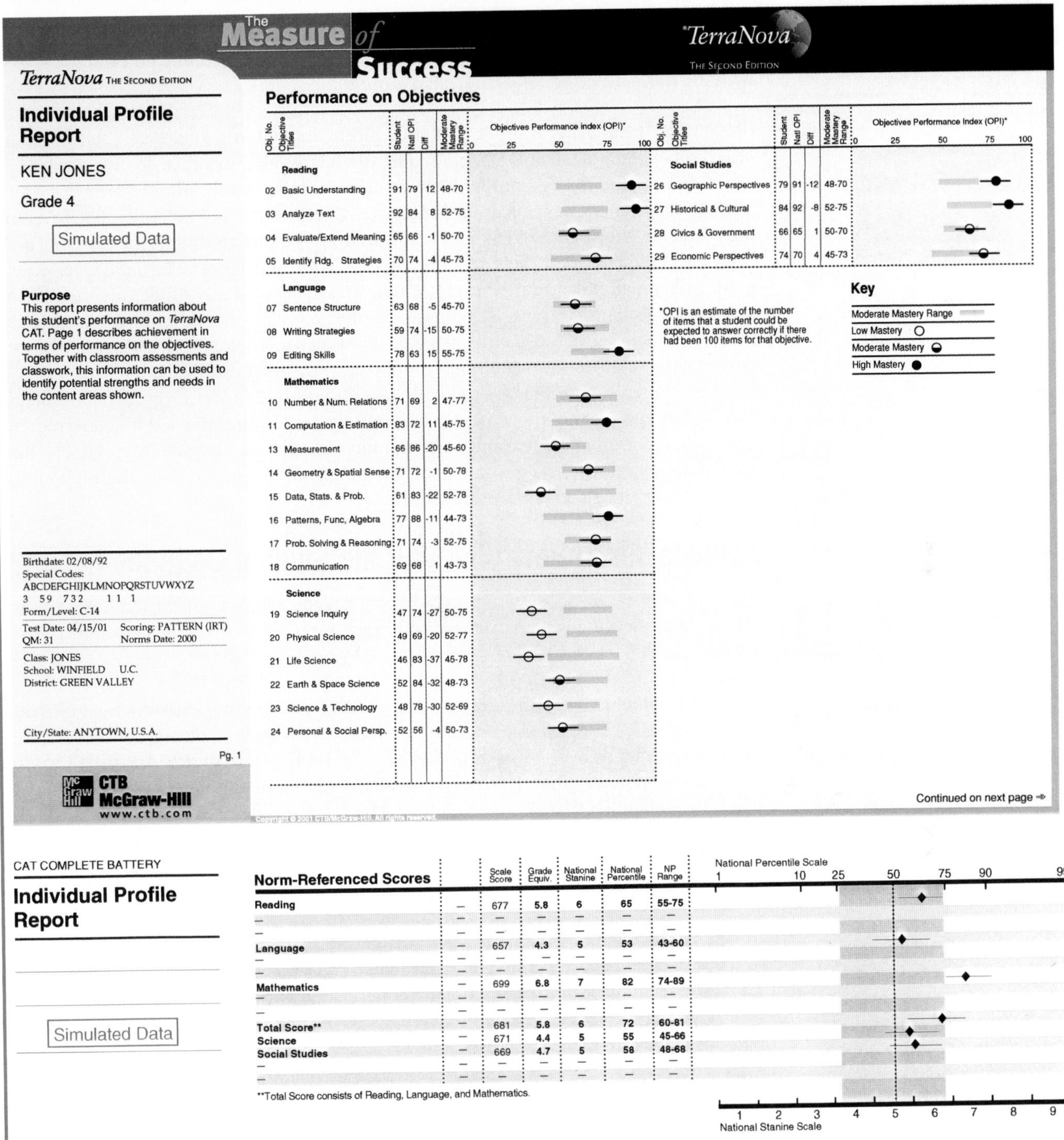

TerraNova THE SECOND EDITION

Individual Profile Report

KEN JONES

Grade 4

Simulated Data

Purpose
This report presents information about this student's performance on *TerraNova* CAT. Page 1 describes achievement in terms of performance on the objectives. Together with classroom assessments and classwork, this information can be used to identify potential strengths and needs in the content areas shown.

Birthdate: 02/08/92
Special Codes:
ABCDEFGHIJKLMNOPQRSTUVWXYZ
3 59 732 1 1 1
Form/Level: C-14

Test Date: 04/15/01 Scoring: PATTERN (IRT)
QM: 31 Norms Date: 2000

Class: JONES
School: WINFIELD U.C.
District: GREEN VALLEY

City/State: ANYTOWN, U.S.A.

Pg. 1

CTB McGraw-Hill
www.ctb.com

Performance on Objectives

Obj. No.	Objective Titles	Student	Nat'l OPI	Diff	Moderate Mastery Range
	Reading				
02	Basic Understanding	91	79	12	48-70
03	Analyze Text	92	84	8	52-75
04	Evaluate/Extend Meaning	65	66	-1	50-70
05	Identify Rdg. Strategies	70	74	-4	45-73
	Language				
07	Sentence Structure	63	68	-5	45-70
08	Writing Strategies	59	74	-15	50-75
09	Editing Skills	78	63	15	55-75
	Mathematics				
10	Number & Num. Relations	71	69	2	47-77
11	Computation & Estimation	83	72	11	45-75
13	Measurement	66	86	-20	45-60
14	Geometry & Spatial Sense	71	72	-1	50-78
15	Data, Stats. & Prob.	61	83	-22	52-78
16	Patterns, Func, Algebra	77	88	-11	44-73
17	Prob. Solving & Reasoning	71	74	-3	52-75
18	Communication	69	68	1	43-73
	Science				
19	Science Inquiry	47	74	-27	50-75
20	Physical Science	49	69	-20	52-77
21	Life Science	46	83	-37	45-78
22	Earth & Space Science	52	84	-32	48-73
23	Science & Technology	48	78	-30	52-69
24	Personal & Social Persp.	52	56	-4	50-73
	Social Studies				
26	Geographic Perspectives	79	91	-12	48-70
27	Historical & Cultural	84	92	-8	52-75
28	Civics & Government	66	65	1	50-70
29	Economic Perspectives	74	70	4	45-73

Objectives Performance Index (OPI)* 0 25 50 75 100

*OPI is an estimate of the number of items that a student could be expected to answer correctly if there had been 100 items for that objective.

Key
Moderate Mastery Range
Low Mastery ○
Moderate Mastery ◒
High Mastery ●

Continued on next page ➾

CAT COMPLETE BATTERY

Individual Profile Report

Simulated Data

Norm-Referenced Scores

		Scale Score	Grade Equiv.	National Stanine	National Percentile	NP Range
Reading	—	677	5.8	6	65	55-75
—	—	—	—	—	—	—
—	—	—	—	—	—	—
Language	—	657	4.3	5	53	43-60
—	—	—	—	—	—	—
—	—	—	—	—	—	—
Mathematics	—	699	6.8	7	82	74-89
—	—	—	—	—	—	—
—	—	—	—	—	—	—
Total Score**	—	681	5.8	6	72	60-81
Science	—	671	4.4	5	55	45-66
Social Studies	—	669	4.7	5	58	48-68
—	—	—	—	—	—	—
—	—	—	—	—	—	—

**Total Score consists of Reading, Language, and Mathematics.

National Percentile Scale: 1 10 25 50 75 90 99

National Stanine Scale: 1 2 3 4 5 6 7 8 9

Source: Individual Profile Report from TERRANOVA, The Second Edition. Published by McGraw-Hill. Copyright © 2001 by McGraw-Hill. Adapted with permission from The McGraw-Hill Companies.

National Stanine: This is Ken's stanine score based on a national norming sample comparison group.

National Percentile Score: This score tells us where he stands in relation to students at his grade level across the country.

National Percentile Range: The range of national percentile scores in which Ken's true score is likely to fall. You may remember from our discussion of true scores that this range, or confidence interval, is determined by adding and subtracting the standard error of the test from Ken's actual score. There is a 95% chance that Ken's true score is within this range.

Next to the scores is a graph showing Ken's national percentile and stanine scores, with the standard error bands indicated around the scores.

Diagnostic Tests: What Are the Student's Strengths and Weaknesses? Achievement tests, both standardized and teacher-made, identify weaknesses in academic content areas such as mathematics, computation, or reading. Individually administered diagnostic tests identify weaknesses in learning processes. If teachers want to identify specific learning problems, they may need to refer to results from the various **diagnostic tests** that have been developed to assess these learning processes. Most diagnostic tests are given to students individually by a trained professional. The goal is usually to identify the specific problems a student is having. There are diagnostic tests to assess the ability to hear differences among sounds, remember spoken words or sentences, recall a sequence of symbols, separate figures from their background, express relationships, coordinate eye and hand movements, describe objects orally, blend sounds to form words, recognize details in a picture, coordinate movements, and many other abilities needed to learn, remember, and communicate learning. Elementary-school teachers are more likely than secondary-school teachers to receive information from diagnostic tests. High-school students are more likely to take aptitude tests.

Connect and Extend to Your Teaching/Portfolio

Choose a partner to role play a parent–teacher conference. The teacher should interpret the scores to the parent and make judgments or recommendations about the child's future educational experiences. The parent should feel free to ask questions concerning the interpretation and the recommendations.

Terry: 3rd grade, scores based on national norm.
Math Computation: 6.0 (grade-equivalent score)
Math Reasoning: 3.5 (grade-equivalent score)
Reading Vocabulary: 85th percentile
Reading Comprehension: 53rd percentile
Group IQ score: 79 (test was given the day before Terry's birthday)

Bobbie: 10th grade, scores based on local norms.
Math Computation: 5 (stanine score)
Math Reasoning: 4 (stanine score)
Reading Vocabulary: 53 (*T* score)
Reading Comprehension: 38 (*T* score)
Individual intelligence test: 125

Diagnostic tests Individually administered tests to identify special learning problems.

Aptitude tests Tests meant to predict future performance.

Aptitude Tests: How Well Will the Student Do in the Future?

STOP | THINK | WRITE Think back to your college entrance examination. What test did you take? How did you prepare? Did your score surprise you? How would you help your students prepare for this kind of test? ■

Both achievement and aptitude tests measure developed abilities. Achievement tests may measure abilities developed over a short period of time, such as during a week-long unit on map reading, or over a longer period of time, such as a semester. **Aptitude tests** are meant to measure abilities developed over many years and to predict how well a student will learn unfamiliar material in the future. The greatest difference between the two types of tests is that they are used for different purposes. Achievement tests measure final performance (and perhaps give grades), and aptitude tests predict how well people will do in particular programs such as college or professional school (Anastasi, 1988).

IQ and Scholastic Aptitude. In Chapter 4, we discussed one of the most influential aptitude tests of all, the IQ test. The IQ test as we know it could well be called a test of scholastic aptitude. Now that you understand the concept of standard deviation, you will be able to appreciate several statistical characteristics of the tests. For example, the IQ score is really a standard score with a mean of 100 and a standard deviation of 15 or 16, depending on the test. Thus, about 68% of the general population would score between +1 and −1 standard deviations from the mean, or between about 85 and 115.

A difference of a few points between two students' IQ scores should not be viewed as important. Scores between 90 and 109 are within the average range. In fact, scores between 80 and 119 are considered within the range of low average to high average. To see the problems that may arise, consider the following conversation:

Parent: We came to speak with you today because we are shocked at our son's IQ score. We can't believe he has only a 99 IQ when his sister scored much higher on the same test. We know they are about the same. In fact, Sam has better marks than Lauren did in the 5th grade.
Teacher: What was Lauren's score?
Parent: Well, she did much better. She scored a 103!

Family and Community Partnerships

Guidelines: Explaining and Using Test Results

Be ready to explain, in nontechnical terms, what each type of score on the test report means.

EXAMPLES

1. If the test is norm-referenced, know if the comparison group was national or local. Explain that the child's score shows how he or she performed *in relation to* the other students in the comparison group.
2. If the test is criterion-referenced, explain that the scores show how well their child performs in specific areas.

If the test is norm-referenced, focus on the percentile scores. They are the easiest to understand.

EXAMPLES

1. Explain that percentile scores tell what percent of students in the comparison group made the same score or lower—higher percentiles are better and 99 is as high as you can get. 50 is average.
2. Remind parents that percentile scores do not tell the "percent correct," so scores that would be bad on a classroom test (say 65% to 75% or so) are above average—even good—as percentile scores.

Avoid using grade-equivalent scores.

EXAMPLES

1. If parents want to focus on the "grade level" of their child, tell them that high grade-equivalent scores reflect a thorough understanding of the current grade level and NOT the capacity to do higher grade-level work.
2. Tell parents that the same grade-equivalent score has different meanings in different subjects—reading versus mathematics, for example.

Be aware of the error in testing.

EXAMPLES

1. Encourage parents to think of the score not as a single point, but as a range or band that includes the score.
2. Ignore small differences between scores.
3. Note that sometimes individual skills on criterion-referenced tests are measured with just a few (2 or 3) items. Compare test scores to actual class work in the same areas.

Use conference time to plan a learning goal for the child that families can support.

EXAMPLES

1. Have example questions, similar to those on the test, to show parents what their child can do easily and what kinds of questions he or she found difficult.
2. Be prepared to suggest an important skill to target.

For more help explaining tests to parents, see **http://pareonline.net/getvn.asp?v=1&n=1**

Clearly, brother and sister have both scored within the average range. Although the standard error of measurement on the WISC-IV (Weschler Intelligence Scale for Children, 4th edition) varies slightly from one age to the next, the average standard error for the total score is about 3. So the bands around Sam's and Lauren's IQ scores—about 96 to 102 and 100 to 106—are overlapping. Either child could have scored 100, 101, or 102.

Discussing Test Results with Families. At times, you will be expected to explain or describe test results to your students' families. *The Family and Community Partnerships Guidelines* give some ideas.

Connect and **Extend** to Your **Teaching/Portfolio**

Add some ideas for parent involvement from this chapter.

Issues in Standardized Testing

WHAT WOULD YOU SAY?

As part of the interview process for a job in an elementary school, you are asked the following: "What should we do to raise our test scores in this school so we can reach our AYP (Adequate Yearly Progress) goals?" ■

For as long as I can remember, educators and policy makers have been concerned about the test performance of American students. In 1983, the National Commission on

Connect and **Extend** to **PRAXIS II™**

Standardized Testing: Major Issues (II, C5)

Since their inception, there have been controversies regarding the use of standardized tests in the schools. Familiarize yourself with the major issues that underlie these controversies. Explain the positions of the different camps in these controversies.

Excellence in Education published *A Nation at Risk: The Imperative for Educational Reform.* According to this report, standardized test scores were at a 25-year low. More recently, politicians point to the Third International Mathematics and Science Study (TIMSS) showing that the United States appeared to be behind many other developed countries in math and science test scores. Part of the response to these headlines has been more testing. In 2002, President Bush signed the No Child Left Behind Act that requires each state to create content standards in reading and mathematics and assessments to measure student learning and knowledge linked to those standards. Science content standards and assessments will be developed next (Linn, Baker, & Betebenner, 2002). These assessments must be taken every year by every child in grades 3 through 8 and once in high school. To keep up with the law, see http://www.ed.gov/offices/OESE/esea/summary.html.

Given all this testing, how are the results used?

Accountability and High-Stakes Testing

STOP | THINK | WRITE How has standardized testing affected your life so far? What opportunities have been opened or closed to you based on test scores? Was the process fair? ■

Connect and Extend to the Research

See the May, 2002 issue of *Phi Delta Kappan* for "The Human Face of the High-Stakes Testing Story," by Linda Nathan. Schools like the Boston Arts Academy are desperately trying to keep the Massachusetts Comprehensive Assessment System from destroying their very fabric, Ms. Nathan says. She intends to make it through the MCAS mania by continuing to fight for a rich and rigorous arts and academic curriculum, taught by highly qualified and committed teachers in an atmosphere of respect and high expectations. Available online http://www.pdkintl.org/kappan/k0204nat.htm.

Tests are not simply procedures used in research. Every day, there are many decisions made about individuals that are based on the results of tests. Should Emily be issued a driver's license? How many and which students from the 8th grade would benefit from an accelerated program in science? Who needs extra tutoring? Who will be admitted to college or professional school? Test scores may affect "admission" to 1st grade, promotion from one grade to the next, high-school graduation, access to special programs, placement in special education classes, teacher licensure and tenure, and school funding.

In making these decisions, it is important to distinguish between the quality of the test itself and the way the test is used. Even the best assessments can be, and have been, misused. In earlier years, for example, using otherwise valid and reliable individual intelligence tests, many students were inappropriately identified as having mental retardation (Snapp & Woolfolk, 1973). The problem was not with the tests, but with the fact that the test score was the only information used to classify students. Much more information is always needed to make this type of placement decision.

Behind all the statistics and terminology are issues related to values and ethics. Who will be tested? What are the consequences of choosing one test over another for a particular purpose with a given group? What is the effect of the testing on the students? How will the test scores of minority-group students be interpreted? What do we really mean by intelligence, competence, and scholastic aptitude? Do our views agree with those implied by the tests we use to measure these constructs? How will test results be integrated with other information about the individual to make judgments? Answering these questions requires choices based on values, as well as accurate information about what tests can and cannot tell us. Keep these values issues in mind as we examine testing uses and decisions.

High-stakes testing Standardized tests whose results have powerful influences when used by school administrators, other officials, or employers to make decisions.

Accountable Making teachers and schools responsible for student learning, usually by monitoring learning with high-stakes tests.

Adequate yearly progress (AYP) Objectives for yearly improvement for all students and for specific groups such as students from major ethnic and racial groups, students with disabilities, students from low-income families, and students whose English is limited.

Because the decisions affected by test scores are so critical, many educators call this process **high-stakes testing.** One of the high-stakes uses for test results is to hold teachers, schools, and administrators **accountable** for student performance. For example, teacher bonuses might be tied to their students' achievement or schools' funding may be affected by testing results. One of the provisions in the No Child Left Behind Act is that states must develop **adequate yearly progress (AYP)** objectives for all students in general and also for specific groups such as students from major ethnic and racial groups, students with disabilities, students from low-income families, and students whose English is limited. These AYP objectives must be set with the goal that all students are proficient or better by the 2013–2014 school year. Schools that fail to meet their AYP objectives for two years will be identified as needing improvement (Linn, Baker, & Betebenner, 2002). The students in these "failing schools" can transfer. If the school's scores don't improve after three years, the school curriculum and/or staff can be replaced.

Point/Counterpoint

Should Tests Be Used to Hold Teachers Accountable?

THERE ARE TWO possible meanings for accountability. The first has to do with gathering information so that we can make good educational decisions about programs, policies, and resources. The second is holding someone responsible for student learning—usually the school or the teacher (Haladyna, 2002).

POINT The public needs information.

The argument for this kind of accountability is that the public has a right to know how their schools are doing, especially because public money is used to finance schools. Testing may help to raise expectations for the lowest-performing schools and give educators the information they need to improve the programs in their schools (Doherty, 2002). And people who make decisions about which reading programs to adopt or how to allocate resources need information about student achievement. The No Child Left Behind Act of 2002 mandates annual assessment in reading and math for every student in grades 3–8. One goal is "to empower parents, citizens, educators, administrators, and policy makers with data from those annual assessments. The data will be available in annual report cards on school performance and on statewide progress. They will give parents information about the quality of their children's schools, the qualifications of teachers, and their children's progress in key subjects" (U.S. Department of Education, *No Child Left Behind* Fact Sheet, 2002).

COUNTERPOINT Using test scores to hold teachers and schools accountable does not make sense.

Will results of standardized tests really give parents information about the "quality of their children's schools" or the "qualifications of teachers"? If the test matches important objectives of the curriculum, is given to students who actually studied the curriculum for a reasonable period of time, is free of bias, fits the students' language capabilities, and was administered properly, then test results provide some information about the effectiveness of the school. But as James Popham (2005b) notes, "Unfortunately, the scores on most of today's large-scale accountability exams reflect students' socioeconomic status much more accurately than they do teachers' instructional skills" (p. 80). If we rank all the schools in a state by achievement test scores, the order would be virtually the same as if we ranked the schools by the average income of the students' families (Noguera, 2005).

There is another problem with holding teachers and schools accountable for all students reaching proficiency by 2014. Is this a reasonable expectation? Robert Linn (2003), an expert in assessment, raises this caution:

> *[W]e should not set a goal for all schools that is so high that no school has yet achieved it. For example, if no school has 100% of its students scoring at the proficient level or higher, we should not expect all schools to reach that level in the next 12 years. Indeed, I would argue that if 90% of the schools currently fall short of the 100% proficient goal, then that is an unrealistic expectation for all schools to achieve within a dozen years. (p. 4)*

Finally, it is foolish to require all students to learn the same things and judge them by the same standards when they haven't had the same opportunity to learn the material. The high-stakes accountability process seems to assume that "public humiliation is enough to get schools to improve. I see no evidence that that works" (Noguera, 2005, p. 15).

WHAT DO YOU THINK?
Vote online at **www.mylabschool.com**

Is it reasonable to hold teachers and schools accountable for student achievement? The *Point/Counterpoint* shows that people disagree.

The Dangers and Possibilities of High-Stakes Testing

The teachers I work with are frustrated that often test results come too late in the year to help them plan instruction or remediation for their current students. They also are troubled by the amount of time that testing takes—to prepare for the tests and to give them. They complain that the tests cover material that their curriculum does not include. Are they right?

Documented Problems with High-Stakes Testing. When so much rides on the results of a test, you would assume that the test actually measured what had been taught. In the past, this match has been a problem. One group of teachers in St. Louis found that fewer than 10% of the items in their curriculum overlapped in both the textbooks and the stan-

Connect and **Extend** to the **Research**

See the March 2002 issue of *Phi Delta Kappan* for two articles on high-stakes testing in Alaska:

High-stakes testing in Alaska poses special problems for Alaska Natives and for students with disabilities—the same kinds of problems that high-stakes testing poses for similar groups in other locales.

"Equity for Alaska Natives: Can High-Stakes Testing Bridge the Chasm Between Ideals and Realities?" by Ken Jones and Paul Ongtooguk.

"High-Stakes Testing for Students with Special Needs," by Toni K. McDermott and Donald F. McDermott.

Connect and **Extend** to the **Research**

The Winter 2003 issue of *Theory Into Practice* on "The Impact of High-Stakes Testing" is edited by Marguerite Clarke and Kelvin Gregory and has the following articles:

"High-Stakes Testing and the Curriculum" by Marguerite Clarke
"High-Stakes Testing and Teachers" by George Madaus, Lisa Abrams, and Joseph Pedulla
"High-Stakes Testing and Students" by Catherine Horn
"Preparing for High-Stakes Testing" by Cengiz Gulek
"Lessons from Abroad: International Practices in High-Stakes Testing" by Kelvin Gregory
"Where to From Here?" by Naomi Chudowsky and James Pellegrino

TABLE 14.2

Inappropriate Uses for High-Stakes Test Results

Beware of some uses for standardized test results. Tests were not designed for these purposes.

Pass/Fail Decisions	In order to deny students graduation from any grade, there must be strong evidence that the test used is valid, reliable, and free of bias. Some tests, for example, the *Texas Assessment of Academic Skills* (TAAS), have been challenged in the courts and found to meet these standards, but not all tests are good enough to make pass/fail decisions.
State-to-State Comparisons	You cannot really compare states using standardized test scores. States do not have the same curriculum, tests, resources, or challenges. If comparisons are made, they usually tell us what we already know—some states have more funding for schools and families with higher incomes or education levels.
Evaluation of Teachers or Schools	Many influences on test scores—family and community resources—are outside the control of teachers and schools. Often students move from school to school, so many students taking a test in spring may have been in the school only for a few weeks.
Identifying Where to Buy a House	Generally speaking, the schools with the highest test scores are in the neighborhoods where families have the highest levels of education and income. They may not be the "best schools" in terms of teaching, programs, or leadership, but they are the schools lucky enough to have the "right" students.

Source: From *Essentials of Standardized Achievement Testing: Validity and Accountability.* T. H. Haladyna, Published by Allyn and Bacon, Boston, MA. Copyright © 2002 by Pearson Education. Adapted by permission of the publisher.

Connect and **Extend** to the **Research**

McNeil, L. M., & Valenzuela, A. (2000). *The harmful impact of the TASS system of testing in Texas: Beneath the accountability rhetoric.* Cambridge, MA: Harvard University Civil Rights Project (www.law.harvard.edu/groups/civilrights/testing.html)

dardized tests they were using (Fiske, 1988). Recently, the overlap between what is taught and what is tested has been improving, but it still makes sense to be aware of possible mismatches.

What about time? Studies have found that in some states, 80% of the elementary schools spend about 20% of their instructional time preparing for the end-of-grade tests (Abrams & Madaus, 2003). Studies of the actual high-stakes tests in action show other troubling consequences. Testing narrows the curriculum. In fact, after examining the results of years of testing, Lisa Abrams and George Madaus (2003) concluded that "In every setting where a high-stakes test operates, the exam content eventually defines the curriculum" (p. 32). For example, using the *Texas Assessment of Academic Skills* has led to curriculum changes that overemphasize what is tested and neglect other areas. In addition, it seems that the test of mathematics is also a test of reading. Students with poor reading ability have trouble with the math test, especially if their first language is not English.

Another unintended consequence of the early-warning testing in elementary school is to "push out" students who believe they are going to fail the high-school graduation test. If they won't graduate anyway, they see no point in continuing to attend school (McNeil & Valenzuela, 2000). For example, in the 2000–2001 school year, about one-third of the English Language Learners dropped out of high school in New York. The main reason given was their inability to pass the required Regents Exam (Medina, 2002). No matter how good the test, some uses of high-stakes tests are not appropriate. Table 14.2 describes some of them.

Connect and **Extend** to the **Research**

Linn, R. (2003). Accountability: Responsibility and reasonable expectations. *Educational Researcher,* 32(7), 3–13.

Using High-Stakes Testing Well. To be valuable, testing programs must have a number of characteristics. Of course, the tests used must be reliable, valid for the purposes used, and free of bias. In addition, the testing program must:

1. *Match the content standards of district*—this is a vital part of validity.

2. *Be part of the larger assessment plan.* No individual test provides all the necessary information about student achievement. It is critical that schools avoid making pass/fail decisions based on a single test.
3. *Test complex thinking,* not just skills and factual knowledge.
4. *Provide alternate assessment strategies* for students with identifiable disabilities.
5. *Provide opportunities for restesting* when the stakes are high.
6. *Include all students* in the testing, but also provide informative reports of the results that make the students' situations clear if they have special challenges or circumstances such as disabilities.
7. *Provide appropriate remediation* when students fail.
8. Make sure all students taking the test *have adequate opportunities to learn* the material being tested.
9. *Take into account the student's language.* Students who have difficulty reading or writing in English will not perform well on tests that require English proficiency.
10. *Use test results for children, not against them* (Haladyna, 2002).

Making high-stakes testing even more stressful.

Schoolies © 1999 John P. Wood. Reprinted with permission.

This is important, so I will repeat it: High-stakes standardized achievement tests must be chosen so that the items on the test actually measure knowledge gained in the classes. Also, students must have the necessary skills to take the test. If students score low on a science test not because they lack knowledge about science, but because they have difficulty reading the questions, don't speak English, or have too little time to finish, then the test is not a valid measure of science achievement for those students.

Preparing for Tests

Two types of training can make a difference in test scores. One type helps students become familiar with the procedures of standardized tests. Students who have extensive experience with standardized tests do better than those who do not. Some of this advantage may be the result of greater self-confidence, less tendency to panic, familiarity with different kinds of questions (for example, analogies such as house : garage : : — : car), and practice with the various answer sheets (Anastasi, 1988). Even brief orientations about how to take tests can help students who lack familiarity and confidence.

A second type of training that appears to be very promising is instruction in general cognitive skills such as solving problems, carefully analyzing questions, considering all alternatives, noticing details and deciding which are relevant, avoiding impulsive answers, and checking work. These are the kinds of metacognitive and study skills we have discussed before. Training in these skills is likely to generalize to many tasks (Anastasi, 1988; Popham, 2005a). The *Stories of Learning/Tributes to Teaching* feature on the next page is an example of a teacher who taught her students how to tackle tests, and in the process taught them about how to tackle many challenges that they might face in their lives.

Connect and **Extend** to Your **Teaching/Portfolio**

Add Figure 14.2, Figure 14.3, Figure 14.4, and the Stories of Learning/Tributes to Teaching, "Taking on 'The Test': Problem-Based Learning" to your Teaching Resources file.

Under the No Child Left Behind Act, schools have to report test scores separately for a number of groups including students with disabilities. The procedures presented above could help those students, too, but more intensive preparation is needed, as you will see next.

Reaching Every Student: Helping Students with Disabilities Prepare for High-Stakes Tests

Erik Carter and his colleagues (2005) tested a procedure for preparing students with learning disabilities, mild intellectual disabilities, and language impairments for the high-stakes test given in their state. The students were ages 15 to 19; over half

STORIES OF LEARNING
TRIBUTES TO TEACHING

A 6th grade class in Illinois used their statewide testing as an opportunity for problem-based learning (Ewy, with student authors, 1997). This class read a newspaper article about the upcoming test and the less than stellar school performance in previous years. They took on the following problem: How could they improve their own test scores on the IGAP (Illinois Goal Assessment Program)? The students talked about why the problem was important and how to solve it, generating the problem analysis chart below.

"The students talked about why the problem was important and how to solve it."

Then the students divided into groups to do different tasks: schedule practice times, look for resources, make up questions and interview experts, and set up a tutoring program. The result? The students met or exceeded the state reading, writing, and mathematics goals. Later that year, when they had to take the math placement test for junior high, these students researched the test: What are the cutoff points, the possible range of scores, and the evaluation criteria?

Perhaps you can take on a similar problem with your students. The *Becoming an Expert Test-Taker Guidelines* might help as part of the program.

• • • •

Problem Analysis Chart

Problem: How can we improve our performance on the IGAP test in such a way that we (1) keep improving each year, (2) set a good example for our school, (3) make preparing for IGAP more fun?

Our Ideas
- Pay attention in class
- Hold fundraiser to get books and computer program
- Look at actual IGAP book format
- Practice: Use computer games
- Get someone who knows how to coach IGAP: teacher, parent, friend, brother/sister
- Tackle one subject at a time
- Find out who wants to know

Facts We Know
- Test on reading, writing, and math
- You get better when you practice
- You might read questions wrong
- Fill in circles
- Writing is scored by time, spelling, sentence structure

Our Questions
- When is IGAP?
- How long is the test?
- How long should we practice?
- What should we practice (math, reading, writing)?
- How many problems?
- How is the test scored (math, reading, writing)?
- How much time is given for math, reading, writing?
- How did I do on the last IGAP test?

Our Action Plan
- Ask principal, teacher, tutor
- Ask person who made test
- Work with teacher to set up schedule
- Look for resources for practice
- Ask parents and principal to help

Source: Excerpted from "Kids Take on 'the Test,'" by C. Ewy & student authors, *Educational Leadership,* 54(4), p. 77.

Connect and **Extend** to the **Research**

See *Phi Delta Kappan*, June 2002 article, "Assessment Crisis: The Absence of Assessment *FOR* Learning," by Richard J. Stiggins, taken from the June 2002 issue.

If we wish to maximize student achievement in the United States, we must pay far greater attention to the improvement of classroom assessment, Mr. Stiggins warns. Both assessment of learning and assessment for learning are essential. But one is currently in place, and the other is not.

Available online at http://www.pdkintl.org/kappan/k0206sti.htm

were African American males and all had Individual Educational Programs (see Chapter 4) to guide their education. None had passed the state-required achievement tests. Over six class periods, an instructor taught the students the strategies presented in Table 14.3.

The good news is that after completing the preparation program, students improved their scores significantly on the tests. But the bad news is that the increases were not large enough to bring most of the students to the passing level. The authors recommend that preparation for testing should occur much earlier for students with disabilities. The students in this study, at an average age of 16, already were discouraged. The strategies taught should be closely aligned with the specific types of problems that the students will encounter on the test and should be embedded in good content instruction. Finally, these students often are anxious about the negative consequences of failing—not receiving a regular diploma, no access to college or trade school. The best way to deal with this anxiety is to better equip the students with the academic skills they will need to succeed (Carter et al., 2005).

TABLE 14.3

Helping Students with Learning Disabilities, Mild Intellectual Disabilities, and Language Impairments Prepare for High-Stakes Testing

Strategy	Objectives
Bubble sheet completion and timing	Fill in bubbles completely
	Be aware of how much available time is remaining
	Pace yourself when taking a test
	Answer all problems before time expires
Sorting problems	Sort problems by differentiating between easier and more difficult problems
	Complete the easy problems on a test prior to attempting the more difficult ones
	Sort problems based on similarity in content
Estimation	Estimate answers in math problems by using rounding
Substitution and backsolving	Substitute the answers provided on a multiple choice test into the question being asked to find the one correct answer
Recopying problems	Rewrite problems in a more familiar form to make them easier to solve
Underlining and reading all answers	Identify exactly what the question is asking you to do
	Read all questions carefully to make better answer choices
	Underline key words and phrases in the question
Elimination	Eliminate absurd multiple choice answers
	Eliminate answers with redundant or similar information
	Eliminate answers with extreme qualifiers

Source: From "Preparing adolescents with high-incidence disabilities for high-stakes testing with strategy instruction," by E. W. Carter, J. Wehby, C. Hughes, S. M. Johnson, D. R. Plank, S. M. Barton-Arwood, & L. B. Lunsford. *Preventing School Failure,* 49(2), p. 58. Reprinted with permission of the Helen Dwight Reid Educational Foundation. Published by Heldref Publications, 1319 Eighteenth St., NW, Washington, DC 20036-1802. Copyright © 2005.

New Directions in Assessment

Standardized tests continue to be controversial. In response to dissatisfaction with traditional forms of assessment, new approaches have emerged to deal with some of the most common testing problems. As the public and government demanded greater accountability in education in the 1980s and 1990s and as traditional standardized tests became the basis for high-stakes decisions, pressure to do well led many teachers and schools to "teach to the test." This tended to focus student learning on basic skills and facts. Even more troubling, say critics, the traditional tests assess skills that have no equivalent in the real world. Students are asked to solve problems or answer questions they will never encounter again; they are expected to do so alone, without relying on any tools or resources and while working under extreme time limits. Real life just isn't like this. Important problems take time to solve and often require using resources, consulting other people, and integrating basic skills with creativity and high-level thinking (Kirst, 1991a; Popham, 2005a; Wolf, Bixby, Glenn, & Gardner, 1991).

In response to these criticisms, the **authentic assessment** movement was born. The goal was to create standardized tests that assess complex, important, real-life outcomes. The approach is also called *direct assessment* or *alternative assessment.* These terms refer to procedures that are alternatives to traditional multiple-choice standardized tests because they directly assess student performance on "real-life" tasks (Hambleton, 1996; Popham, 2005a). For example, the Center for Technology in Learning of SRI International, a nonprofit

Connect and **Extend** to **PRAXIS II™**

Alternatives to Standardized Testing (II, C1)

For an overview of the major forms of authentic testing, go to Teachervision.com (http://www.teachervision.com/lesson-plans/lesson-6385.html).

Connect and **Extend** to **Other Chapters**

Chapter 15 includes a discussion of alternatives for authentic assessment, including portfolios and exhibitions.

Authentic assessment Measurement of important abilities using procedures that simulate the application of these abilities to real-life problems.

In many subjects the most reliable test is to demonstrate the ability to produce a finished product.

science research institute, provides an online resource bank of performance-based assessments linked to the National Science Education Standards. The resource is called PALS (Performance Assessment Links in Science). Go to http://butterfly.ctl.sri.com/pals/index.html; see the performance tasks for kindergarten through 12th grade. You can select tasks by standard and grade level. Each task comes with directions for students, a guide for administrators, and a scoring guide or rubric. Many also have examples of student work.

Many of the suggestions for improving standardized tests will require new forms of testing, more thoughtful and time-consuming scoring, and perhaps new ways of judging the quality of the tests themselves. Standardized tests of the future may be more like the writing sample you may have submitted for college entrance and less like the multiple-choice college entrance tests you also had to take or the essay part of the new SAT. Newer tests will feature more **constructed-response formats.** This means that students will create responses (essays, problem solutions, graphs, diagrams), rather than simply selecting the (one and only) correct answer. This will allow tests to measure higher-level and divergent thinking.

In the midst of all of the excitement about authentic assessment, it is important to be sensible. Just being different from traditional standardized tests will not guarantee that the alternative tests are better. Many questions have to be answered. Assume, for example, that a new assessment requires students to complete a hands-on science project. If the student does well on one science project, does this mean the student "knows" science and would do well on other projects? One study found that students' performance on three different science tasks was quite variable: A student who did well on the absorbency experiment, for example, might have trouble with the electricity task. Thus, it was hard to generalize about a student's knowledge of science based on just the three tasks. Many more tasks would be needed to get a good sense of science knowledge, but a performance assessment with many different tasks would be expensive and time-consuming (Shavelson, Gao, & Baxter, 1993).

In addition, if high-stakes decisions are based on performance assessments, will teachers begin to "teach to the assessment" by giving students practice in these particular performances? Will being a good writer bias judges in favor of a performance? Will this make performance assessments even more prone to discriminate against some groups? And how will the projects be judged? Will different judges agree on the quality? When researchers examined the results of the 1992 Vermont Portfolio Assessment Program, they found that scorers assessing the same portfolio often gave very different ratings (Kotrez, Stecher, & Diebert, 1993). In other words, will judgments based on alternative assessments be reliable, valid, and free from bias? Will the assessment results generalize to tasks beyond those on the test itself? Will the new assessments have a positive effect on learning (Hambleton, 1996; Moss, 1992)? Because this is a new area, it will take time to develop high-quality alternative assessments for use by whole school districts or states. Until more is known, it may be best to focus on authentic assessment at the classroom level, as we will discuss in the next chapter.

Diversity and Convergences in Standardized Testing

Constructed-response format Assessment procedures that require the student to create an answer instead of selecting an answer from a set of choices.

In the 1970s, the National Assessment of Educational Progress (NAEP) began to test a national sample of students at ages 9, 13, and 17. One of the provisions of the No Child Left Behind Act is that all states must give the NAEP tests in reading and mathematics every other year in grades 4 and 8 (Linn, Baker, & Betebenner, 2002).

TABLE 14.4

Accommodations in Testing

Accommodations in testing may be made in the setting of the test, timing and scheduling, test presentation, and student response modes. Schools have to keep good records about what is done, because these accommodations have to be documented. Here are some examples of possible accommodations taken from Spinelli, 2002 (pp. 151–152).

Examples of Setting Accommodations

Conditions of Setting

- Minimal distractive elements (e.g., books, artwork, window views)
- Special lighting
- Special acoustics
- Adaptive or special furniture
- Individual student or small group of students rather than large group

Location

- Study carrel
- Separate room (including special education classroom)
- Seat closest to test administrator (teacher, proctor, etc.)
- Home
- Hospital
- Correctional institution

Examples of Timing Accommodations

Duration

- Changes in duration can be applied to selected subtests of an assessment or to the assessment overall
- Extended time (i.e., extra time)
- Unlimited time

Organization

- Frequent breaks during parts of the assessment (e.g., during subtests)
- Extended breaks between parts of assessment (e.g., subtests) so that assessments can be administered in several sessions

Examples of Scheduling Accommodations

Time

- Specific time of day (e.g., morning, midday, afternoon, after ingestion of medication)
- Specific day of week
- Over several days

Organization

- In a different order from that used for most students (e.g., longer subtest first, shorter later; math first, English later)
- Omit questions that cannot be adjusted for an accommodation (e.g., graph reading for student using Braille) and adjust for missing scores

Examples of Presentation Accommodations

Format Alterations

- Braille edition
- Large-print version
- Larger bubbles on answer sheet
- One complete sentence per line in reading passage
- Bubbles to side of choices in multiple-choice exams
- Key words or phrases highlighted
- Increased spacing between lines
- Fewer number of items per page

Procedure Changes

- Use sign language to give directions to student
- Reread directions
- Write helpful verbs in directions on board or on separate piece of paper
- Simplify language, clarify or explain directions
- Provide extra examples
- Prompt student to stay focused on test, move ahead, read entire item
- Explain directions to student during test

Assistive Devices

- Audiotape of directions
- Computer reads directions and/or items
- Magnification device
- Amplification device (e.g., hearing aid)
- Noise buffer
- Templates to reduce visible print
- Markers or masks to maintain place
- Dark or raised lines
- Pencil grips

Examples of Response Accommodations

Format Alterations

- Mark responses in test booklet rather than record on separate page
- Respond on different paper, such as graph paper, wide-lined paper, paper with wide margins

Procedural Changes

- Use reference materials (e.g., dictionary, arithmetic tables)
- Give response in different mode (e.g., pointing, oral response to tape recorders, sign language)

Assistive Devices

- Word processor or computer to responses
- Amanuensis (proctor-scribe writes student responses)
- Slant board or wedge
- Calculator or abacus
- Brailler or other communication device (e.g., symbol board)
- Spell checker

Diversity

In those early years of NAEP testing, there was a gap between the scores of White and Black students at all three age levels. For the next two decades, the "achievement gap," as it was called, narrowed. Some of the reasons given were declining poverty rates, increased preschool attendance, and desegregated schooling. But after 1988, the gap began to widen again, caused perhaps by increases in child poverty and a greater emphasis on low-level skills in high-poverty schools (McClure, 2005).

With high-stakes testing have come concerns about another kind of diversity—students with disabilities. IDEIA (the Individuals with Disabilities Education Improvement Act) mandates that students with disabilities must be included in general testing, but with accommodations or appropriate modifications, if needed (Spinelli, 2002). The IEP (Individualized Education Program) team generally makes the decisions about who should have accommodations and what these might be, so as a teacher you might want to participate in these discussions. Table 14.4 on the previous page gives some ideas.

Connect and **Extend** to the **Research**

Boe, E. E., & Shin, S. (2005). Is the United States really losing the international horse race in academic achievement? *Phi Delta Kappan, 86*, 688–695.

The overall results of six international achievement surveys in reading, mathematics, science, and civics at the elementary, middle, and secondary levels from 1991–2001 indicate that students from the United States performed somewhat above average in comparison with other industrialized nations. Reading and civics performances were somewhat below average. United States performance declined from the elementary to the middle to the secondary levels. With respect to ethnic groups in the United States, white students performed above the international averages, while black and Hispanic students performed well below international averages.

Convergences

Three years after the No Child Left Behind Act was instituted, almost 75% of the states and districts in a recent survey reported that the scores were rising on the tests used for NCBL assessments. Many districts reported that achievement gaps between White students and students of color and between English language learners and non-ELL students were narrowing rather than widening or staying the same (Center on Education Policy, 2005), as you can see in Table 14.5.

So it appears, on the surface at least, that the achievement gaps are closing. Two cautions are advised, however. These changes may represent teaching to the tests. Even though scores are going up on NCBL tests, they are not going up as fast for most states on the national test given to all students, the NAEP. Also, different states have different definitions for proficiency, so it is difficult to compare results across states. We all have to study the next few years' results carefully to see what is really happening.

TABLE 14.5

Percentage of Districts Reporting Achievement Gaps Between Different Student Groups Have Changed or the Extent to Which Over the Last Year

	Narrowing	Staying Same	Widening	No Gap
White vs. Black students	18%	12%	1%	2%
White vs. Asian students	5%	11%	1%	4%
White vs. Hispanic students	17%	15%	5%	4%
White vs. Native American students	6%	7%	0	2%
LEP vs. non-LEP students	18%	14%	5%	2%
Students with disabilities vs. students without	25%	40%	14%	1%
Low-income students vs. students who are not low-income	32%	36%	7%	5%

Table reads: Among districts that receive Title I funds, an estimated 18% report that the achievement gap between White students and Black students in 2004-05 is narrowing.

Source: Center on Education Policy, December 2004, Fall Districts Survey, Item 11 (Table 10).

Measurement and Assessment (pp. 522–524)

Distinguish between measurement and assessment. Measurement is the description of an event or characteristic using numbers. Assessment includes measurement, but is broader because it includes all kinds of ways to sample and observe students' skills, knowledge, and abilities.

Distinguish between norm-referenced and criterion-referenced tests. In norm-referenced tests, a student's performance is compared to the average performance of others. In criterion-referenced tests, scores are compared to a pre-established standard. Norm-referenced tests cover a wide range of general objectives. However, results of norm-referenced tests do not tell whether students are ready for advanced material, and they are not appropriate for affective and psychomotor objectives. Criterion-referenced tests measure the mastery of very specific objectives.

Measurement An evaluation expressed in quantitative (number) terms.

Assessment Procedures used to obtain information about student performance.

Norm-referenced testing Testing in which scores are compared with the average performance of others.

Norm groups A group whose average score serves as a standard for evaluating any student's score on a test.

Criterion-referenced testing Testing in which scores are compared to a set performance standard.

What Do Test Scores Mean? (pp. 524–534)

Describe the key features of a standardized test. Standardized tests are most often norm-referenced. They have been pilot-tested, revised, and then administered in final form to a norming sample, which becomes the comparison group for scoring.

What are mean, median, mode, and standard deviation? The mean (arithmetical average), median (middle score), and mode (most common score) are all measures of central tendency. The standard deviation reveals how scores spread out around the mean. A normal distribution is a frequency distribution represented as a bell-shaped curve. Many scores cluster in the middle; the farther from the midpoint, the fewer the scores.

Describe different kinds of scores. There are several basic types of standardized test scores: percentile rankings, which indicate the percentage of others who scored at or below an individual's score; grade-equivalent scores, which indicate how closely a student's performance matches average scores for a given grade; and standard scores, which are based on the standard deviation. *T* and *z* scores are both common standard scores. A stanine score is a standard score that incorporates elements of percentile rankings.

What is test reliability? Some tests are more reliable than others; that is, they yield more stable and consistent estimates. Care must be taken in the interpretation of test results. Each test is only a sample of a student's performance on a given day. The score is only an estimate of a student's hypothetical true score. The standard error of measurement takes into account the possibility for error and is one index of test reliability.

What is test validity? The most important consideration about a test is the validity of the decisions and judgments that are based on the test results. Evidence of validity can be related to content, criterion, or construct. Construct-related evidence for validity is the broadest category and encompasses the other two categories of content and criterion. Tests must be reliable to be valid, but reliability does not guarantee validity.

What is absence of bias? Tests must be free of assessment bias. Bias occurs when tests include material that offends or unfairly penalizes a group of students because of the students' gender, SES, race, or ethnicity. Culture-fair tests have not proved to solve the problem of assessment bias.

Standardized tests Tests given, usually nationwide, under uniform conditions and scored according to uniform procedures.

Norming sample Large sample of students serving as a comparison group for scoring standardized tests.

Frequency distribution Record showing how many scores fall into set groups.

Histogram Bar graph of a frequency distribution.

Mean Arithmetical average.

Central tendency Typical score for a group of scores.

Median Middle score in a group of scores.

Mode Most frequently occurring score.

Standard deviation Measure of how widely scores vary from the mean.

Variability Degree of difference or deviation from mean.

Range Distance between the highest and the lowest scores.

Normal distribution The most commonly occurring distribution, in which scores are distributed evenly around the mean.

Percentile rank Percentage of those in the norming sample who scored at or below an individual's score.

Grade-equivalent score Measure of grade level based on comparison with norming samples from each grade.

Standard scores Scores based on the standard deviation.

***z* Score** Standard score indicating the number of standard deviations above or below the mean.

***T* Score** Standard score with a mean of 50 and a standard deviation of 10.

Stanine scores Whole number scores from 1 to 9, each representing a wide range of raw scores.

Reliability Consistency of test results.

True score The score the student would get if the measurement were completely accurate and error-free.

Standard error of measurement Hypothetical estimate of variation in scores if testing were repeated.

Confidence interval: Range of scores within which an individual's particular score is likely to fall.

Validity: Degree to which a test measures what is intended.

Assessment bias: Qualities of an assessment method or procedure that offend or unfairly penalize a group of students because of the students' gender, SES, race, ethnicity, etc.

Culture-fair/Culture-free test: A test without cultural bias.

Types of Standardized Tests (pp. 534–539)

What are three kinds of standardized tests? Three kinds of standardized tests are used frequently in schools: achievement, diagnostic, and aptitude. Profiles from norm-referenced achievement tests can also be used in a criterion-referenced way. Diagnostic tests usually are given individually to elementary-school students when learning problems are suspected. Aptitude tests are designed to predict how a student will perform in the future. For example, the Scholastic Assessment Test (SAT) predicts performance in the first year of college.

Achievement tests Standardized tests measuring how much students have learned in a given content area.

Diagnostic tests Individually administered tests to identify special learning problems.

Aptitude tests Tests meant to predict future performance.

Issues in Standardized Testing (pp. 539–545)

What are some current issues in testing? Controversy over standardized testing has focused on the role and interpretation of tests, the widespread use of tests to evaluate schools, the problems with accountability based on test scores, and the testing of teachers. If the test matches important objectives of the curriculum, is given to students who actually studied the curriculum for a reasonable period of time, is free of bias, fits the students' language capabilities, and was administered properly, then test results provide some information about the effectiveness of the school. But studies of the actual tests in action show troubling consequences such as narrowing the curriculum and pushing some students out of school early. Teachers should use results to improve instruction, not to stereotype students or justify lowered expectations.

Can students become better test-takers? How? Performance on standardized tests can be improved if students gain experience with this type of testing and are given training in study skills and problem solving. Many students can profit from direct instruction about how to prepare for and take tests. Involving students in designing these test preparation programs can be helpful. Students with learning challenges may benefit from intensive and ongoing preparation for taking tests, particularly if the test-taking strategies are tied to specific problems and content learned and tested.

High-stakes testing Standardized tests whose results have powerful influences when used by school administrators, other officials, or employers to make decisions.

Accountable: Making teachers and schools responsible for student learning, usually by monitoring learning with high-stakes tests.

Adequate yearly progress (AYP) Objectives for yearly improvement for all students and for specific groups such as students from major ethnic and racial groups, students with disabilities, students from low-income families, and students whose English is limited.

New Directions in Assessment (pp. 545–546)

What is authentic assessment? Authentic assessments are procedures that assess students' abilities to solve important real-life problems, think creatively, and act responsibly. Such approaches assume that assessment should reveal the potential for future learning and help identify interventions for realizing that potential. Standardized tests of the future will be more varied and will use more constructed-response formats, requiring students to generate (rather than select) answers.

Authentic assessment Measurement of important abilities using procedures that simulate the application of these abilities to real-life problems.

Constructed-response format Assessment procedures that require the student to create an answer instead of selecting an answer from a set of choices.

mylabschool™ Where the classroom comes to life!

MyLabSchool is a collection of online tools for your success in this course, your licensure exams, and your teaching career. Visit **www.mylabschool.com** to access the following:

- On-line Study Guide
- Video Cases from real classrooms
- Help with your research papers using Research Navigator
- Career Center with resources for:
  - Praxis and Licensure Preparation
  - Professional Portfolio Development
  - Job Search and Interview Techniques
  - Lesson Planning

Teachers' Casebook: Connections to PRAXIS II™

Your need to be knowledgeable about standardized testing is well-illustrated in this chapter's Teachers' Casebook. Parents and students frequently misunderstand the results of these instruments, often attributing the wrong meaning to various types of scores. Teachers who possess that knowledge are in a position to serve their students well by being able to use test results in ways that are consistent with the purposes of specific tests and that recognize the strengths and limitations of those tests. With that knowledge, teachers, parents, and students can use information provided by the tests to make informed educational decisions.

What Would They Do?

Here is how some practicing teachers would work with the parents who wanted their daughter to skip a grade in math.

Mark H. Smith **Teacher, Grades Nine through Twelve,** *Medford High School, Medford, Massachusetts*

I understand that many parents will choose the side of their child over the side of a teacher. This definitely happened in this case, because the parents would not come in to talk about their daughter's learning until they had something they thought would give them ammunition against the teacher. As a teacher all you can do is explain your grading procedure, what the curriculum is, and what is expected of the students in your class. When you have clear and reasonable expectations for all of your students, then it becomes the responsibility of the student to achieve.

Thomas W. Newkirk **Eighth Grade Teacher,** *Hamilton Heights Middle School, Arcadia, Indiana*

The grade a student receives in a class is sometimes not so much a measure of intelligence as it is a measure of performance. Bright students who are disorganized may bring assignments in days past a due date. Bright students who are distracted may not bring assignments in at all. Bright students who have been absent several days may be overwhelmed by the work waiting for them.

The grade a student receives in a class often requires an explanation in order that the students and the parents understand the basis for the evaluation. It is important that the teacher maintain a record of comments and correspondence for parents and teachers to review.

While it is wonderful that the student has a grade-equivalent of 11.8 on the achievement test, her daily class performance does not meet the established standard for an A. Whether a student's achievement test results are high or low, it would be unfair to reconsider a final grade based on one score.

Unless the school has a policy for receiving credit for classes based on achievement tests, the parents and the student should be encouraged to maintain the lines of communication as she enters the 10th grade class.

Thomas O'Donnell **Social Studies Chairperson, Grades Seven through Twelve,** *Malden High School, Malden, Massachusetts*

The math achievement test that the girl took might not be a good device for measuring one's ability to go beyond high school math to the more abstract, conceptual approach needed for college-level math. You must explain your grading system to parents so they understand the needed combination of effort and achievement to achieve top grades.

Since the parent statements include two serious charges against you, make it clear you expect respect from them, but that this issue will have no impact on your work with the student. You must reject their expectations of changing grades and credits.

Suzy L. Boswell **Art Teacher, Grades Six through Eight,** *Pickens County Middle School, Jasper, Georgia*

One of the most challenging aspects of a teacher's job is often the task of communicating with the parents. Unfortunately, most parents begin to lose contact with the school system and the children's teachers when their child enters middle school or junior high. Parents may think that they are no longer needed or that their child prefers them to remain anonymous, so as not to embarrass them. However, the motivation and learning process are still very much a shared responsibility of school and home.

The parents did not volunteer their time to listen to a lecture. In this particular case they may actually be coming to the school to give the teacher a lecture and to "set her straight." It may require a great deal of diplomacy to turn this into a positive and productive meeting, but we as teachers deal with unwilling students almost daily and this situation is not any different.

Once the tone is set and the parents are receptive, it may be helpful to explain to them the characteristics of the tests, including the various methods that are used to measure the results of the test. It is important to note that students may have the aptitude to learn and to perform in the classroom and yet simply choose not to apply themselves. Therefore, these students are still not meeting the requirements necessary to earn credit for a particular class.

Michael Yasis **L. H. Tanglen Elementary School,** *Minnetonka, Minnesota*

Before the situation got to this point, I would have found out how she was performing in her other classes. If she also had missing assignments in other classes then I believe she would need to be taught some organizational skills. If it only happened in my math class, then I would try to figure out how I could engage her more. She obviously shows strength in math, and I wouldn't want to have her lose interest in it, or knock down her self-esteem because of a grade I had given her. I would try to understand her learning style and let her know there are many ways to solve math problems, I would possibly modify her assignments to align with her style and challenge her to look at other ways to solve various problems.

CHAPTER 15

Classroom Assessment and Grading

Teachers' Casebook: What Would You Do? 553
Formative and Summative Assessment 554
Getting the Most from Traditional Assessment 555
Planning for Testing 555
Objective Testing 556
Essay Testing 559
Alternatives to Traditional Assessments 561
Authentic Classroom Assessment 562
Portfolios and Exhibitions 562
Evaluating Portfolios and Performances 565
Informal Assessments 569
Involving Students in Assessments 570
Effects of Grading on Students 570
Effects of Failure 571
Effects of Feedback 573
Grades and Motivation 573
Grading and Reporting: Nuts and Bolts 574
Criterion-Referenced versus Norm-Referenced Grading 574
The Point System and Percentage Grading 575
The Contract System and Grading Rubrics 577
Other Issues in Grading 578
Beyond Grading: Communicating with Families 579
Reaching Every Student: Accommodations in Grading 581
Diversity and Convergences in Classroom Assessment 581
Diversity 582
Convergences 582
Summary Table 583
Teachers' Casebook: Connections to PRAXIS II™/ What Would They Do? 585

What Would You Do?

Teachers' Casebook

Your school requires that you give letter grades to your class. You can use any method you want, as long as an A, B, C, D, or F appears for each of the subject areas on every student's report card, every grading period. Some teachers are using worksheets, quizzes, homework, and tests. Others are assigning group work and portfolios. A few teachers are individualizing standards by grading on progress and effort more than final achievement. Some are trying contract approaches and experimenting with longer-term projects, while others are relying almost completely on daily class work. Two teachers who use group work are considering giving credit toward grades for being a "good group member" or competitive bonus points for the top-scoring group. Others are planning to use improvement points for class rewards, but not for grades. Your only experience with grading was using written comments and a mastery approach that rated the students as making satisfactory or unsatisfactory progress toward particular objectives. You want a system that is fair and manageable, but also encourages learning, not just performance. And you want some system that gives the students feedback they can use to prepare for the proficiency tests required by NCLB.

Critical Thinking

- What would be your major graded assignments and projects?
- Would you include credit for behaviors such as group participation or effort?
- How would you put all the elements together to determine a grade for every student for every marking period?
- How would you justify your system to the principal and to the parents?
- How will these issues affect the grades you will teach?

Collaboration

With 2 or 3 other members of your class, develop a section of a class handbook that describes your grading policy. Be prepared to defend the policy.

As you read this chapter, you will examine both tests and grades, focusing not only on the effects they are likely to have on students, but also on practical ways to develop more efficient methods for testing and grading.

We begin with a consideration of the many types of tests teachers prepare each year and approaches to assessment that don't rely on traditional testing. Then, we examine the effects grades are likely to have on students. Because there are so many grading systems, we also spend some time identifying the advantages and disadvantages of one system over another. Finally, we turn to the very important topic of communication with students and parents. How will you justify the grades you give?

By the time you have completed this chapter, you should be able to answer these questions:

- How will you test students on a unit of work?
- How can you evaluate tests that accompany textbooks and teachers' manuals?
- How should you create multiple-choice and essay test items for your subject area?
- Will you use authentic assessment approaches, including portfolios, performances, exhibitions, and scoring rubrics?
- What are the potential positive and negative effects of grades on students?
- What are examples of criterion-referenced and norm-referenced grading systems?
- How will you explain your grading system to parents who do not understand their child's grades?

FACING PAGE *Dancing Girl—Fin d'arabesque*. 1877. Edgar Degas. Pastel, essence and oil on paper, 65 × 36 cm.
Photo: Reunion des Musees Nationaux/Art Resource, New York.

Formative and Summative Assessment

Connect and Extend to Your Teaching/Portfolio

What are some specific ways in which formative evaluation can be implemented in the classroom?

As a teacher, you may have little to say about the grading system for your school. Many school districts have a standard approach to grading. Still, you will have choices about how you use your district's grading system and how you assess your students' learning. Will you give tests? How many? What kinds? Will students do projects or keep portfolios of their work? How will homework influence grades? Will you use journals, and if so, will you "grade" them?

There are two general uses or functions for assessment: formative and summative. **Formative assessment** occurs before or during instruction. The purposes of formative assessment are to guide the teacher in planning and to help students identify areas that need work. In other words, formative assessment helps *form* instruction. Often students are given a formative test prior to instruction, a **pretest** that helps the teacher determine what students already know. Sometimes a test is given during instruction to see what areas of weakness remain so teaching can be directed toward the problem areas. This is generally called a **diagnostic test,** but should not be confused with the standardized diagnostic tests of more general learning abilities discussed in the previous chapter. A classroom diagnostic test identifies a student's areas of achievement and weakness in a particular subject. Older students are often able to apply the information from diagnostic tests to "reteach" themselves. Pretests and diagnostic tests are not graded. And because formative tests do not count toward the final grade, students who tend to be very anxious about "real" tests may find this low-pressure practice in test taking especially helpful.

Formative assessment Ungraded testing used before or during instruction to aid in planning and diagnosis.

Pretest Formative test for assessing students' knowledge, readiness, and abilities.

Diagnostic test Formative test to determine students' areas of weakness.

Summative assessment Testing that follows instruction and assesses achievement.

Summative assessment occurs at the end of instruction. Its purpose is to let the teacher and the students know the level of accomplishment attained. Summative assessment, therefore, provides a *summary* of accomplishment. The final exam is a classic example.

The distinction between formative and summative assessment is based on how the results are used. And any kind of assessment—traditional, performance, project, oral, portfolio, and so on—can be used for either formative or summative purposes. If the goal is to obtain information about student learning for planning purposes, the assessment is formative. If the purpose is to determine final achievement (and help determine a course grade), the assessment is summative. In fact, the same assessment could be used as

The final exam is a classic example of a summative assessment. This type of assessment occurs at the end of instruction and provides a summary of accomplishment.

TABLE 15.1

Using Tests to Make Instructional Decisions

The best use of assessment is to plan, guide, and target instruction. Here are some decisions that can benefit from assessment results.

Decision Category	Typical Assessment Strategy	Decision Options
What to teach in the first place?	Preassessment before instruction	Whether to provide instruction for specific objectives?
How long to keep teaching toward a particular instructional objective?	En route assessments of students' progress	Whether to continue or cease instruction for an objective either for an individual or for the whole class?
How effective was an instructional sequence?	Comparing students' posttest to pretest performances	Whether to retain, discard, or modify a given instructional sequence the next time it's used?

Source: From *Classroom Assessment: What Teachers Need to Know, 4/e* by J. W. Popham. Published by Allyn and Bacon, Boston, MA. Copyright © 2005 by Pearson Education. Adapted by permission of the publisher.

a formative evaluation at the beginning of the unit and as a summative evaluation at the end.

The formative uses of assessment are really the most important in teaching. James Popham (2005a) believes that "Unfortunately, too many teachers still think that the chief role of classroom tests is the assignment of grades. But any teacher who uses tests dominantly to determine whether students get high or low grades should receive a solid F in classroom assessment" (p. 262). Tests and all assessments should be used to help teachers make better instructional decisions. Table 15.1 gives some examples.

Connect and **Extend** to **PRAXIS II™**

Types of Assessment (II, C1, 4)
Understand the purposes of formative and summative assessment. Explain how teachers and students can make effective use of the information generated by each type of test.

Getting the Most from Traditional Assessment

STOP | THINK | WRITE Think back to your most recent test. What was the format? Did you feel that the test results were an accurate reflection of your knowledge or skills? Have you ever had to design a test? What makes a good, fair test? ■

When most people think of assessment, they usually think of testing. As you will see shortly, teachers today have many other options, but testing is still a significant activity in most classrooms. Let's consider your options for assessing students using the traditional testing approach. In this section we will examine how to plan effective tests, evaluate the tests that accompany standard curriculum materials, and write your own test questions.

Planning for Testing

One result of high-stakes testing programs in many districts is that teachers now have more classroom assessments and reviews focused on the standards behind the high-stakes tests. These assessments need to be well organized and planned. When you have a good plan, you are in a better position to judge the tests provided in teachers' manuals and to develop class assessments yourself.

When to Test? Frank Dempster (1991) examined the research on reviews and tests and reached these useful conclusions for teachers:

Connect and **Extend** to the **Research**

Dempster, F. (1991). Synthesis of research on reviews and tests. *Educational Leadership*, 48(7), 71–76. Dempster, F. N. (1993). Exposing our students to less should help them learn more. *Phi Delta Kappan*, 74, 432–437.

1. Frequent testing encourages the retention of information and appears to be more effective than a comparable amount of time spent reviewing and studying the material.
2. Tests are especially effective in promoting learning if you give students a test on the material soon after they learn it, then retest on the material later. The retestings should be spaced farther and farther apart.
3. The use of cumulative questions on tests is a key to effective learning. Cumulative questions ask students to apply information learned in previous units to solve a new problem.

Dempster argues that students will learn more if the curriculum includes fewer topics, but explores those topics in greater depth and allows more time for review, practice, testing, and feedback (Dempster, 1993).

Judging Textbook Tests. Most elementary and secondary school texts today come complete with supplemental materials such as teaching manuals, handout masters, and ready-made tests. Using these tests can save time, but is this good teaching practice? The answer depends on your objectives for your students, the way you teach the material, and the quality of the tests provided. If the textbook test is of high quality, matches your testing plan, and fits the instruction you actually provided for your students, then it may be the right test to use. Check the reading level of the items provided and be prepared to revise/improve them (Airasian, 2005; McMillan, 2004). Table 15.2 gives key points to consider in evaluating textbook tests.

Connect and **Extend** to **PRAXIS II™**

Traditional Assessment (II C1, 2, 4)

Objective and essay tests continue to have important roles in effective assessment and evaluation programs. Describe the appropriate uses of these types of tests. Identify the advantages and limitations of each.

What if there are no tests available for the material you want to cover, or the tests provided in your teachers' manuals are not appropriate for your students? Then it's time for you to create your own tests. We will consider the two major kinds of traditional tests—objective and essay.

Objective Testing

Multiple-choice questions, matching exercises, true/false statements, and short-answer or fill-in items are all types of **objective testing.** The word "objective" in relation to testing

Objective testing Multiple-choice, matching, true/false, short-answer, and fill-in tests; scoring answers does not require interpretation.

TABLE 15.2

Key Points to Consider in Judging Textbook Tests

1. The decision to use a textbook test or pre-made standard achievement test must come *after* a teacher identifies the objective that he or she has taught and now wants to assess.
2. Textbook and standard tests are designed for the typical classroom, but since few classrooms are typical, most teachers deviate somewhat from the text in order to accommodate their pupils' needs.
3. The more classroom instruction deviates from the textbook, the less valid the textbook tests are likely to be.
4. The main consideration in judging the adequacy of a textbook or standard achievement test is the match between its test questions and what pupils were taught in their classes:
   a. Are questions similar to the teacher's objectives and instructional emphases?
   b. Do questions require pupils to perform the behaviors they were taught?
   c. Do questions cover all or most of the important objectives taught?
   d. Is the language level and terminology appropriate for pupils?
   e. Does the number of items for each objective provide a sufficient sample of pupil performance.

Source: From *Classroom assessment: Concepts and applications* (5th ed.) by P. W. Airasian (2005). New York: McGraw-Hill, p. 161.

means "not open to many interpretations," or "not subjective." The scoring of these types of items is relatively straightforward compared to the scoring of essay questions because the answers are more clear-cut than essay answers.

How should you decide which item format is best for a particular test? Use the one that provides the most direct measure of the learning outcome you intended for your students (Gronlund, 2003). In other words, if you want to see how well students can write a letter, have them write a letter, don't ask multiple-choice questions about letters. But if many different item formats will work equally well, then use multiple-choice questions because they are easier to score fairly and can cover many topics. Switch to other formats if writing good multiple-choice items for the material is not possible or appropriate. For example, if related concepts such as terms and definitions need to be linked, then a matching item is a better format than multiple-choice. If it is difficult to come up with several wrong answers for a multiple-choice item, try a true/false question instead. Alternatively, ask the student to supply a short answer that completes a statement (fill in the blank). Variety in objective testing can lower students' anxiety because the entire grade does not depend on one type of question that a particular student may find difficult. We will look closely at the multiple-choice format because it is the most versatile—and the most difficult to use well.

"I hate taking a test without an eraser."

Using Multiple-Choice Tests. Even though about three-fourths of education professors reject the use of multiple-choice tests in determining students' grades, about half of public school teachers endorse these tests (Banks, 2005), so you should know how to use these tests well. In fact, many schools require teachers to give students experience answering multiple-choice tests in order to prepare them for high-stakes testing (McMillan, 2004). Of course, multiple-choice items can test facts, but these items can assess more than recall and recognition if they require the student to deal with new material by *applying* or *analyzing* the concept or principle being tested (Gronlund, 2003; McMillan, 2004). For example, the following multiple-choice item is designed to assess students' ability to recognize unstated assumptions, one of the skills involved in analyzing an idea:

> An educational psychology professor states, "A z score of +1 on a test is equivalent to a percentile rank of approximately 84." Which of the following assumptions is the professor making?
>
> 1. The scores on the test range from 0 to 100.
> 2. The standard deviation of the test scores is equal to 3.4.
> 3. The distribution of scores on the test is normal. (Correct answer)
> 4. The test is valid and reliable.

Writing Multiple-Choice Questions. All test items require skillful construction, but good multiple-choice items are a real challenge. Some students jokingly refer to multiple-choice tests as "multiple-guess" tests—a sign that these tests are often poorly designed. Your goal in writing test items is to design them so that they measure student achievement, not test-taking and guessing skills.

The **stem** of a multiple-choice item is the part that asks the question or poses the problem. The choices that follow are called *alternatives*. The wrong answers are called **distractors** because their purpose is to distract students who have only a partial understanding of the material. If there were no good distractors, students with only a vague understanding would have no difficulty in finding the right answer.

The *Guidelines* on the next page, adapted from Gronlund (2003), Popham (2005a), and Smith, Smith, & De Lisi (2001), should make writing multiple-choice and other objective test questions easier.

Stem The question part of a multiple-choice item.

Distractors Wrong answers offered as choices in a multiple-choice item.

Guidelines: Writing Multiple-Choice Test Items

The stem should be clear and simple, and present only a single problem. Unessential details should be left out.

Poor

There are several different kinds of standard or derived scores. An IQ score is especially useful because . . .

Better

Which of the following is an advantage of an IQ score?

The problem in the stem should be stated in positive terms. Negative language is confusing. If you must use words such as *not*, *no*, or *except*, underline them or type them in all capitals.

Poor

Which of the following is not a standard score?

Better

Which of the following is NOT a standard score?

Do not expect students to make extremely fine discrimination among answer choices.

What is the percentage of area in a normal curve falling between +1 and –1 standard deviations?

Poor

a. 66% b. 67% c. 68% d. 69%.

Better

a. 14% b. 34% (c.) 68% d. 95%.

As much wording as possible should be included in the stem so that phrases will not have to be repeated in each alternative.

Poor

A percentile score

a. indicates the percentage of items answered correctly.
b. indicates the percentage of correct answers divided by the percentage of wrong answers.
c. indicates the percentage of people who scored at or above a given raw score.
d. indicates the percentage of people who scored at or below a given raw score.

Better

A percentile score indicates the percentage of

a. items answered correctly.
b. correct answers divided by the percentage of wrong answers.
c. people who scored at or above a given raw score.
(d.) people who scored at or below a given raw score.

Each alternative answer should fit the grammatical form of the stem, so that no answers are obviously wrong.

Poor

The Stanford-Binet test yields an

a. IQ score. c. vocational preference.
b. reading level. d. mechanical aptitude.

Better

What does the Stanford-Binet assess?

(a.) intelligence c. vocational preference
b. reading level d. mechanical aptitude

Categorical words such as *always*, *all*, *only*, or *never* should be avoided unless they can appear consistently in all the alternatives. Most smart test takers know that categorical answers are usually wrong.

Poor

A student's true score on a standardized test is

a. never equal to the obtained score.
b. always very close to the obtained score.
c. always determined by the standard error of measurement.
d. usually within a band that extends from +1 to –1 standard errors of measurement on each side of the obtained score.

Better

Which one of the statements below would most often be correct about a student's true score on a standardized test?

a. It equals the obtained score.
b. It will be very close to the obtained score.
c. It is determined by the standard error of measurement.
(d.) It could be above or below the obtained score.

Avoid including two distractors that have the same meaning. If only one answer can be right and if two answers are the same, then these two must both be wrong. This narrows down the choices considerably.

What is the term for the most frequently occurring score in a distribution?

Poor

a. mode c. arithmetic average
b. median d. mean

Better

(a.) mode c. standard deviation
b. median d. mean

Avoid using the exact wording found in the textbook.

Poor students may recognize the answers without knowing what they mean.

Avoid overuse of *all of the above* and *none of the above*.

Such choices may be helpful to students who are guessing. Using *all of the above* may trick a quick student who sees that the first alternative is correct and does not read on.

Obvious patterns on a test also aid students who are guessing.

The position of the correct answer should be varied, as should its length.

Incorrect alternatives should reflect common student misunderstandings.

Be careful, however, that the wrong alternatives are not so obviously wrong that students don't even consider them.

For a good summary on writing test items, see **http://www.msu.edu/dept/soweb/writitem.html**

Essay Testing

The best way to measure some learning objectives is to require students to create answers on their own. An essay question is appropriate in these cases. The most difficult part of essay testing is judging the quality of the answers, but writing good, clear questions is not particularly easy, either. We will look at writing, administering, and grading essay tests, with most of the specific suggestions taken from Gronlund (2003). We will also consider factors that can bias the scoring of essay questions and ways you can overcome these problems.

STOP | THINK | WRITE Evaluate these two essay questions from Popham (2005a, pp. 172–173):

1. (High school level) You have just viewed a videotape containing three widely seen television commercials. What is the one classic propaganda technique present in all three commercials?
2. (Middle school level) Thinking back over the mathematics lesson and homework assignments you had during the past 12 weeks, what conclusions can you draw? Take no more than one page for your response. ■

Constructing Essay Tests. Because answering takes time, true essay tests cover less material than objective tests. Thus, for efficiency, essay tests should be limited to the assessment of more complex learning outcomes.

An essay question should give students a clear and precise task and should indicate the elements to be covered in the answer. (Are the questions above clear and precise?) The students should know how extensive their answer should be and about how much time they should spend on each question. Question 2 above gives a page limit, but would you know what is being asked?

Students should be given ample time for answering. If more than one essay is being completed in the same class period, you may want to suggest time limits for each question. Remember, however, that time pressure increases anxiety and may prevent accurate assessment of some students. Whatever your approach, do not try to make up for the limited amount of material an essay test can cover by including a large number of essay questions. It would be better to plan on more frequent testing than to include more than two or three essay questions in a single class period. Combining an essay question with a number of objective items is one way to avoid the problem of limited sampling of course material (Gronlund, 2003).

Evaluating Essays: Dangers. In 1912, Starch and Elliot began a classic series of experiments that shocked educators into critical consideration of subjectivity in testing. These researchers wanted to find out the extent to which teachers were influenced by personal values, standards, and expectations in scoring essay tests. For their initial study, they sent copies of English examination papers written by two high-school students to English teachers in 200 high schools. Each teacher was asked to score the papers according to his or her school's standards. A percentage scale was to be used, with 75% as a passing grade.

The results? Neatness, spelling, punctuation, and communicative effectiveness were all valued to different degrees by different teachers. The scores on one of the papers ranged from 64% to 98%, with a mean of 88.2. The average score for the other paper was 80.2, with a range between 50% and 97%. The following year, Starch and Elliot (1913a, 1913b) published similar findings in a study involving history and geometry papers. The most important result of these studies was the discovery that the problem of subjectivity in grading was not confined to any particular academic area. The main difficulties were the individual standards of the grader and the unreliability of scoring procedures.

Evaluating Essays: Methods. Gronlund (2003) offers several strategies for grading essays that avoid problems of subjectivity and inaccuracy. When possible, a good first step

Connect and Extend to Your Teaching/Portfolio

Some students prefer essay tests because they can write down something, even if it doesn't answer the question, and receive at least partial credit for the question. Do you think that granting partial credit is a common grading practice among teachers? Considering that essay questions sample only a limited amount of material, does the practice seem commendable or defensible?

is to construct a set of scoring criteria or a rubric (more on this later) and share it with students. Even when students are given some choice in testing, teachers can decide what type of information should be in any answer. Here is an example from TenBrink (2003, p. 326).

Question: Defend *or* refute the following statement: Civil wars are necessary to the growth of a developing country. Cite reasons for your argument, and use examples from history to help substantiate your claim.

Scoring Rubric: All answers, regardless of the position taken, should include (1) a clear statement of the position, (2) at least five logical reasons, (3) at least four examples from history that *clearly* substantiate the reasons given.

Once you have set your expectations for answers, you can assign points to the various parts of the essay. You might also give points for the organization of the answer and the internal consistency of the essay. You can then assign grades such as 1 to 5 or A, B, C, D, and F, and sort the papers into piles by grade. As a final step, skim the papers in each pile to see if they are comparable in quality. These techniques will help ensure fairness and accuracy in grading.

When grading essay tests with several questions, it makes sense to grade all responses to one question before moving on to the next. This helps prevent the quality of a student's answer to one question from influencing your reaction to the student's other answers. After you finish reading and scoring the first question, shuffle the papers so that no students end up having all their questions graded first (when you may be taking more time to give feedback or are applying stricter standards, for example) or last (when you may be tired of writing feedback or more lax in your standards).You may achieve greater objectivity if you ask students to put their names on the back of the paper, so that grading is anonymous. A final check on your fairness as a grader is to have another teacher who is equally familiar with your goals and subject matter grade your tests without knowing what grades you have assigned. This can give you valuable insights into areas of bias in your grading practices.

Now that we have examined both objective and essay testing, we can compare examples of the different approaches. Table 15.3 presents a summary of the advantages and disadvantages of each.

TABLE 15.3

Advantages and Disadvantages of Different Kinds of Test Items
No kind of item is perfect. A mix of kinds may be the best approach.

Type	Advantages	Disadvantages
Short answer	Can test many facts in a short time. Fairly easy to score. Excellent format for math. Tests recall.	Difficult to measure complex learning. Often ambiguous.
Essay	Can test complex learning. Can assess thinking process and creativity.	Difficult to score objectively. Uses a great deal of testing time. Subjective.
True/False	Tests the most facts in shortest time. Easy to score. Tests recognition. Objective.	Difficult to measure complex learning. Difficult to write reliable items. Subject to guessing.
Matching	Excellent for testing associations and recognition of facts. Although terse, can test complex learning (especially concepts). Objective.	Difficult to write effective items. Subject to process of elimination.
Multiple choice	Can assess learning at all levels of complexity. Can be highly reliable, objective. Tests fairly large knowledge base in short time. Easy to score.	Difficult to write. Somewhat subject to guessing.

Source: From *Classroom Teaching Skills, Seventh Edition* by James Cooper. Copyright © 2003 by Houghton Mifflin Company. Adapted with permission.

Alternatives to Traditional Assessments

We have been considering how to make traditional testing more effective; now, let's look at a few alternative approaches to classroom assessment. One of the main criticisms of standardized tests—that they control the curriculum, emphasizing recall of facts instead of thinking and problem solving—is a major criticism of classroom tests as well. Few teachers would dispute these criticisms. Even if you follow the guidelines we have been discussing, traditional testing can be limiting. What can be done? Should alternatives in classroom assessment make traditional testing obsolete? The *Point/Counterpoint* addresses this question.

Point/Counterpoint

Which Is Better—Traditional Tests or Authentic Assessments?

WE HAVE SEEN the advantages and disadvantages of standardized tests, but what about classroom testing? Are traditional multiple-choice and essay tests useful in classroom assessment?

POINT Traditional tests are a poor basis for classroom assessment.

In his article "Standards, Not Standardization: Evoking Quality Student Work," Grant Wiggins (1991) makes a strong case for giving students standards of excellence against which they can judge their accomplishments. But these standards should not be higher scores on multiple-choice tests. When scores on traditional tests become the standard, the message to students is that only right answers matter and the thinking behind the answers is unimportant. Wiggins notes:

> *We do not judge Xerox, the Boston Symphony, the Cincinnati Reds, or Dom Perignon vineyards on the basis of indirect, easy to test, and common indicators. Nor would the workers in those places likely produce quality if some generic, secure test served as the only measure of their success in meeting a standard. Demanding and getting quality, whether from students or adult workers, means framing standards in terms of the work that we undertake and value. And it means framing expectations about that work which make quality a necessity, not an option. Consider:*
>
> > *the English teacher who instructs peer-editors to mark the place in a student paper where they lost interest in it or found it slapdash and to hand it back for revision at that point;*
> >
> > *the professor who demands that all math homework be turned in with another student having signed off on it, where one earns the grade for one's work and the grade for the work that each person (willingly!) countersigned. (p. 22)*

Wiggins continues to argue for assessment that makes sense, that tests knowledge as it is applied in real-world situations. Understanding cannot be measured by tests that ask students to use skills and knowledge out of context. "In other words, we cannot be said to understand something unless we can employ our knowledge wisely, fluently, flexibly, and aptly in particular and diverse contexts" (Wiggins, 1993, p. 200).

COUNTERPOINT Traditional tests can play an important role.

Most psychologists and educators would agree with Wiggins that setting clear, high, authentic standards is important, but many also believe that traditional tests are useful in this process. Learning may be more than knowing the right answers, but right answers are important. While schooling is about learning to think and solve problems, it is also about knowledge. Students must have something to think about—facts, ideas, concepts, principles, theories, explanations, arguments, images, opinions. Well-designed traditional tests can evaluate students' knowledge effectively and efficiently (Airasian, 2005; Kirst, 1991b). Some educators believe that traditional testing should play an even greater role than it currently does. Educational policy analysts suggest that American students, compared to students in many other developed countries, lack essential knowledge because American schools emphasize process—critical thinking, self-esteem, problem solving—more than content. In order to teach more about content, teachers will need to determine how well their students are learning the content, and traditional testing provides useful information about content learning.

Tests are also valuable in motivating and guiding students' learning. There is research evidence that frequent testing encourages learning and retention. In fact, students generally learn more in classes with more rather than fewer tests (Dempster, 1991).

WHAT DO YOU THINK?

Vote online at **www.mylabschool.com**

Source: From "Standards Not Standardization," by G. Wiggins, *Educational Leadership*, *48*,(5), pp. 18–25. The Association for Supervision and Curriculum Development is a worldwide community of educators advocating sound policies and sharing best practices to achieve the success of each learner. To learn more, visit ASCD at www.ascd.com.

Connect and **Extend** to **PRAXIS II™**

Authentic Tests (II, C1, 2, 4)
The emphasis on student-centered learning has been accompanied by an emphasis on authentic tests. Understand the purpose, value, and advantages of these forms of assessment. Describe their characteristics and the potential problems with their use.

Student exhibitions are a type of performance test that requires students to use good communication, and are likely to involve many hours of preparation. Exhibitions help students appreciate high quality work.

One solution that has been proposed to solve the testing dilemma is to apply the concept of authentic assessment to classroom testing.

Authentic Classroom Assessment

WHAT WOULD YOU SAY?

In your interview with the search team in an elementary school known for innovation, one of the teachers asks, "What do you know about using portfolios, performances, projects, and rubrics to assess learning?" ■

Authentic assessments ask students to apply skills and abilities as they would in real life. For example, they might use fractions to enlarge or reduce recipes. Grant Wiggins made this argument over 15 years ago:

> If tests determine what teachers actually teach and what students will study for—and they do—then the road to reform is a straight but steep one: test those capabilities and habits we think are essential, and test them in context. Make [tests] replicate, within reason, the challenges at the heart of each academic discipline. Let them be—authentic. (1989, p. 41)

Wiggins goes on to say that if our instructional goals for students include the abilities to write, speak, listen, create, think critically, do research, solve problems, or apply knowledge, then our tests should ask students to write, speak, listen, create, think, research, solve, and apply. How can this happen?

Many educators suggest we look to the arts and sports for analogies to solve this problem. If we think of the "test" as being the recital, exhibition, game, mock court trial, or other performance, then teaching to the test is just fine. All coaches, artists, and musicians gladly "teach" to these "tests" because performing well on these tests is the whole point of instruction. Authentic assessment asks students to perform. The performances may be thinking performances, physical performances, creative performances, or other forms. So **performance assessment** is any form of assessment that requires students to carry out an activity or produce a product in order to demonstrate learning (Airasian, 2005).

It may seem odd to talk about thinking as a performance, but there are many parallels. Serious thinking is risky, because real-life problems are not well defined. Often, the outcomes of our thinking are public—others evaluate our ideas. Like a dancer auditioning for a Broadway show, we must cope with the consequences of being evaluated. Like a sculptor looking at a lump of clay, a student facing a difficult problem must experiment, observe, redo, imagine, and test solutions, apply both basic skills and inventive techniques, make interpretations, decide how to communicate results to the intended audience, and often accept criticism and improve the initial solution (Eisner, 1999; Herman, 1997). Table 15.4 lists some characteristics of authentic tests.

Portfolios and Exhibitions

The concern with authentic assessment has led to the development of several approaches based on the goal of *performance in context*. Instead of circling answers to "factual" questions about nonexistent situations, students are required to solve real problems. Facts are used in a context where they apply—for example, the student uses grammar facts to write a persuasive letter to a software company requesting donations for the class computer center. The following example of a test of performance is taken from the Connecticut Core of Common Learning:

> Many local supermarkets claim to have the lowest prices. But what does this really mean? Does it mean that every item in their store is priced lower, or just some of them? How can you really tell which supermarket will save you the most money? Your assignment is to design and carry out a study to answer this question. What items and prices will you compare and why? How will you justify the choice of your "sample"? How reliable is the sample, etc.? (Wolf, Bixby, Glenn, & Gardner, 1991, p. 61)

Authentic assessments Assessment procedures that test skills and abilities as they would be applied in real-life situations.

Performance assessments Any form of assessment that requires students to carry out an activity or produce a product in order to demonstrate learning

TABLE 15.4

Characteristics of Authentic Tests

A. Structure and Logistics

1. Are more appropriately public; involve an audience, a panel, and so on.
2. Do not rely on unrealistic and arbitrary time constraints.
3. Offer known, not secret, questions or tasks.
4. Are more like portfolios or a *season* of games (not one-shot).
5. Require some collaboration with others.
6. Recur—and are *worth* practicing for, rehearsing, and retaking.
7. Make assessment and feedback to students so central that school schedules, structures, and policies are modified to support them.

B. Intellectual Design Features

1. Are "essential"—not needlessly intrusive, arbitrary, or contrived to "shake out" a grade.
2. Are "enabling"—constructed to point the student toward more sophisticated use of the skills or knowledge.
3. Are contextualized, complex intellectual challenges, not "atom-ized" tasks, corresponding to isolated "outcomes."
4. Involve the student's own research or use of knowledge, for which "content" is a means.
5. Assess student habits and repertoires, not mere recall or plug-in skills.
6. Are *representative* challenges—designed to emphasize *depth* more than breadth.
7. Are engaging and educational.
8. Involve somewhat ambiguous ("ill-structured") tasks or problems.

C. Grading and Scoring Standards

1. Involve criteria that assess essentials, not easily counted (but relatively unimportant) errors.
2. Are graded not on a "curve" but in reference to performance standards (criterion-referenced, not norm-referenced).
3. Involve demystified criteria of success that appear to *students* as inherent in successful activity.
4. Make self-assessment a part of the assessment.
5. Use a multifaceted scoring system instead of one aggregate grade.
6. Exhibit harmony with shared schoolwide aims—a *standard.*

D. Fairness and Equity

1. Ferret out and identify (perhaps hidden) strengths.
2. Strike a *constantly* examined balance between honoring achieve-ment and native skill or fortunate prior training.
3. Minimize needless, unfair, and demoralizing comparisons.
4. Allow appropriate room for student learning styles, aptitudes, and interests.
5. Can be—should be—attempted by *all* students, with the test "scaffolded up," not "dumbed down," as necessary.

Source: From "Teaching to the Authentic Test," by G. W. Wiggins, 1989, *Educational Leadership,* 45(7), p. 44. Copyright © 1989 by the Association of Supervision and Curriculum Development. Reprinted with permission.

Students completing this "test" will use mathematical facts and procedures in the context of solving a real-life problem. In addition, they will have to think critically and write persuasively. The *Stories of Learning/Tributes to Teaching* on the next page gives another example from my own education.

Portfolios and exhibitions are two approaches to assessment that require performance in context. With these approaches, it is difficult to tell where instruction stops and assessment starts because the two processes are interwoven (Smith, Smith, & De Lisi, 2001).

Connect and Extend to the Research

For ideas about making classroom assessment better, see Stiggins, R. J. (2001). Assessment crisis: The absence of assessment *FOR* learning, *Phi Delta Kappan,* 83, 758–765. Available online at http://www.pdkintl.org/kappan/k0206sti.htm

Portfolios. For years, photographers, artists, models, and architects have had portfolios to display their skills and often to get jobs. A **portfolio** is a systematic collection of work, often including work in progress, revisions, student self-analyses, and reflections on what the student has learned (Popham, 2005a). One student's self-reflection is presented in Figure 15.1 on the next page.

Written work or artistic pieces are common contents of portfolios, but students might also include graphs, diagrams, snapshots of displays, peer comments, audio- or videotapes, laboratory reports, and computer programs—anything that demonstrates learning in the area being taught and assessed (Belanoff & Dickson, 1991; Camp, 1990; Wolf, Bixby, Glenn, & Gardner, 1991). There is a distinction between process portfolios and final or "best work" portfolios. The distinction is similar to the difference between formative and

Portfolio A collection of the student's work in an area, showing growth, self-reflection, and achievement.

STORIES OF LEARNING
TRIBUTES TO TEACHING

> *"I wanted a more 'authentic' assessment—something connected to our learning and our future."*

When I was in graduate school in Texas, the standard doctoral candidacy examination was three days worth of closed book, handwritten, blue-book-filled answers to questions. Candidates were examined in three areas of educational psychology: social/developmental; learning/cognition; and statistics/research methodology. This was a "high-stakes," make-or-break three days that determined whether you had to leave school with a "terminal Master's" (sounds deadly doesn't it!), instead of being allowed to go on to your doctoral research. By the time we took the exam, we had completed our coursework and internships. All that remained to earn the Ph.D. was to design, complete, analyze, and write up an independent research project—the dissertation. This is a complex bit of work that takes many students months or even years to finish successfully.

Now this was the 70s—a time in Texas of protest. It was a time when students were more active in asserting their rights. And I was part of that spirit. I was certain that the three-day test was not a good assessment of our learning. I asked the faculty, "When will we have to sit down for three days and answer multiple-choice questions, write essays without any resources, or solve statistics problems that are not related to our research questions?" I wanted a more "authentic" assessment—something connected to our learning and our future. I talked to other students, wrote position papers, and lobbied professors. Finally I was asked to speak at a faculty meeting about the situation.

To my amazement and gratitude, the faculty voted to allow an alternative to the three-day test. Candidates could write a research proposal that examined a significant research question from the perspectives of social/developmental and learning/cognition in educational psychology. In addition, we were required to design a study that used appropriate methodology and statistics. I chose this option (after making all that fuss, I almost had to). Some of my friends said that I was crazy because I spent months preparing my proposal while they crammed a few weeks for their traditional exam. But then I used my proposal, with some improvements, to do my dissertation and finished a year ahead of them. I got a grant to do it, based on the thinking and writing that went into completing the option of that "authentic" assessment project. At my alma mater, the alternative candidacy exam is still in place today, and that is the form I use for my graduate students at Ohio State—thanks to the willingness of a **good faculty** to entertain student suggestions over 35 years ago.

FIGURE 15.1

A Student Reflects on Learning: Self-Analysis of Work in a Portfolio
Not only has this student's writing improved, but the student has become a more self-aware and self-critical writer.

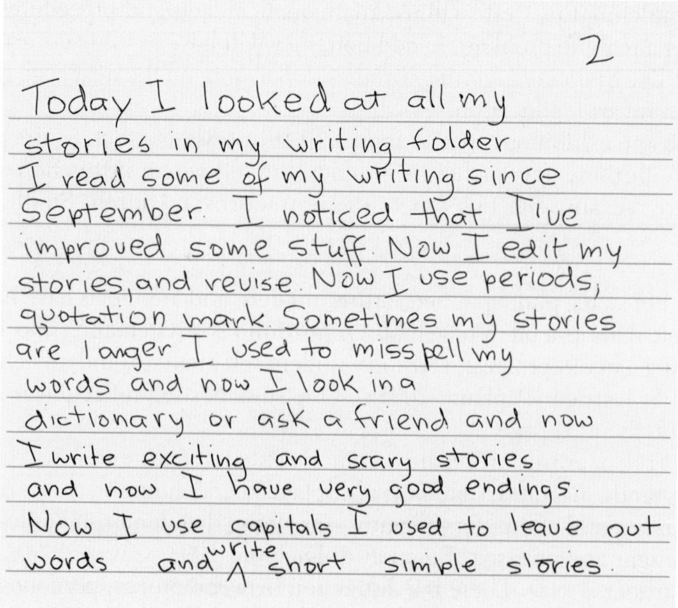

2

Today I looked at all my stories in my writing folder I read some of my writing since September. I noticed that I've improved some stuff. Now I edit my stories, and revise. Now I use periods, quotation mark. Sometimes my stories are langer I used to misspell my words and now I look in a dictionary or ask a friend and now I write exciting and scary stories and now I have very good endings. Now I use capitals I used to leave out words and write short simple stories.

Source: From "What Makes a Portfolio a Portfolio?" by F. L. Paulson, P. Paulson, and C. Meyers, 1991, *Educational Leadership, 48, 5*, p. 63. Copyright © 1991 by the Association for Supervision and Curriculum Development. Reprinted with permission.

TABLE 15.5

Process and Best Works Portfolios for Individuals and Groups
Here are a few examples of how to use portfolios in different subjects.

The Process Portfolio

Subject Area	Individual Student	Cooperative Group
Science	Documentation (running records or logs) of using the scientific method to solve a series of laboratory problems	Documentation (observation checklists) of using the scientific method to solve a series of laboratory problems
Mathematics	Documentation of mathematical reasoning through double-column mathematical problem solving (computations on the left side and running commentary explaining thought processes on the right side)	Documentation of complex problem solving and use of higher-level strategies
Language Arts	Evolution of compositions from early notes through outlines, research notes, response to others' editing, and final draft	Rubrics and procedures developed to ensure high-quality peer editing

The Best Works Portfolio

Subject Area	Individual Student	Cooperative Group
Language Arts	The best compositions in a variety of styles—expository, humor/satire, creative (poetry, drama, short story), journalistic (reporting, editorial columnist, reviewer), and advertising copy	The best dramatic production, video project, TV broadcast, newspaper, advertising display
Social Studies	The best historical research paper, opinion essay on historical issue, commentary on current event, original historical theory, review of a historical biography, account of academic controversy participated in	The best community survey, paper resulting from academic controversy, oral history compilation, multidimensional analysis of historical event, press corps interview with historical figure
Fine Arts	The best creative products such as drawings, paintings, sculptures, pottery, poems, thespian performance	The best creative products such as murals, plays written and performed, inventions thought of and built

Source: From *Meaningful Assessment: A Meaningful and Cooperative Process* by D. W. Johnson and R. T. Johnson. Published by Allyn and Bacon, Boston, MA. Copyright © 2002 by Pearson Education. Adapted by permission of the publisher.

summative evaluation. Process portfolios document learning and show progress. Best work portfolios showcase final accomplishments (Johnson & Johnson, 2002). Table 15.5 shows some examples for both individuals and groups.

Exhibitions. An **exhibition** is a performance test that has two additional features. First, it is public, so students preparing exhibitions must take the audience into account; communication and understanding are essential. Second, an exhibition often requires many hours of preparation, because it is the culminating experience of a whole program of study. Thomas Guskey and Jane Bailey (2001) suggest that exhibits help students understand the qualities of good work and recognize those qualities in their own productions and performances. Students also benefit when they select examples of their work to exhibit and articulate their reasons for making the selections. Being able to judge quality can encourage student motivation by setting clear goals.

The *Guidelines* on the next page give some ideas for using portfolios and exhibits in your teaching.

Connect and Extend to PRAXIS II™
Portfolio Assessment (II, C1, 2)
For a discussion of the advantages, limitations, design, and implementation of portfolio programs, and to examine samples of portfolio checklists, go to Teachervison.com (http://www.teachervision.com/lesson-plans/lesson-4536.html).

Evaluating Portfolios and Performances

Checklists, rating scales, and scoring rubrics are helpful when you assess performances, because assessments of performances, portfolios, and exhibitions are criterion-referenced, not norm-referenced. In other words, the students' products and performances are compared to established public standards, not ranked in relation to other students' work

Exhibition A performance test or demonstration of learning that is public and usually takes an extended time to prepare.

Guidelines: Creating Portfolios

Students should be involved in selecting the pieces that will make up the portfolio.

EXAMPLES

1. During the unit or semester, ask each student to select work that fits certain criteria, such as "my most difficult problem," "my best work," "my most improved work," or "three approaches to."
2. For their final submissions, ask students to select pieces that best show how much they have learned.

A portfolio should include information that shows student self-reflection and self-criticism.

EXAMPLES

1. Ask students to include a rationale for their selections.
2. Have each student write a "guide" to his or her portfolio, explaining how strengths and weaknesses are reflected in the work included.
3. Include self- and peer critiques, indicating specifically what is good and what might be improved.
4. Model self-criticism of your own productions.

The portfolio should reflect the students' activities in learning.

EXAMPLES

1. Include a representative selection of projects, writings, drawings, and so forth.
2. Ask students to relate the goals of learning to the contents of their portfolios.

The portfolio can serve different functions at different times of the year.

EXAMPLES

1. Early in the year, it might hold unfinished work or "problem pieces."
2. At the end of the year, it should contain only what the student is willing to make public.

Portfolios should show growth.

EXAMPLES

1. Ask students to make a "history" of their progress along certain dimensions and to illustrate points in their growth with specific works.
2. Ask students to include descriptions of activities outside class that reflect the growth illustrated in the portfolio.

Teach students how to create and use portfolios.

EXAMPLES

1. Keep models of very well done portfolios as examples, but stress that each portfolio is an individual statement.
2. Examine your students' portfolios frequently, especially early in the year when they are just getting used to the idea. Give constructive feedback.

For more ideas about using portfolios, see **http://www.elon.edu/students/portfolio/**

(Cambourne & Turbill, 1990; Wiggins, 1991). For example, Figure 15.2 gives three alternatives—numerical, graphic, and descriptive—for rating an oral presentation.

Scoring Rubrics. A checklist or rating scale gives specific feedback about elements of a performance. **Scoring rubrics** are rules that are used to determine the quality of a student performance (Mabry, 1999). For example, a rubric describing an excellent oral presentation might be:

> Pupil consistently faces audience, stands straight, and maintains eye contact; voice projects well and clearly; pacing and tone variation appropriate; well-organized; points logically and completely presented; brief summary at end. (Airasian, 1996, p. 155)

Performance assessment requires careful judgment on the part of teachers and clear communication to students about what is good and what needs improving. In some ways, the approach is similar to the clinical method first introduced by Binet to assess intelligence: It is based on observing the student perform a variety of tasks and comparing his or her performance to a standard. Just as Binet never wanted to assign a single number to represent the child's intelligence, teachers who use authentic assessments do not try to assign one score to the student's performance. Even if rankings, ratings, and grades have to be given, these judgments are not the ultimate goals—improvement of

Connect and **Extend** to **PRAXIS II™**

Scoring Rubrics (II, C3)
Kathy Schrock's Guide for Educators (http://school.discovery.com/schrockguide/assess.html) provides information about every aspect of the use of scoring rubrics in the classroom as well as an extensive collection of rubrics that can be used or adapted by teachers.

Scoring rubrics Rules that are used to determine the quality of a student performance.

FIGURE 15.2

Three Ways of Rating an Oral Presentation

Numerical Rating Scale

Directions:

Indicate how often the pupil performs each of these behaviors while giving an oral presentation. For each behavior circle **1** if the pupil **always** performs the behavior, **2** if the pupil **usually** performs the behavior, **3** if the pupil **seldom** performs the behavior, and **4** if the pupil **never** performs the behavior.

Physical Expression

A. Stands straight and faces audience.

1 2 3 4

B. Changes facial expression with change in the tone of the presentation.

1 2 3 4

Graphic Rating Scale

Directions:

Place an **X** on the line that shows how often the pupil did each of the behaviors listed while giving an oral presentation.

Physical Expression

A. Stands straight and faces audience.

always **usually** **seldom** **never**

B. Changes facial expression with change in the tone of the presentation.

always **usually** **seldom** **never**

Descriptive Rating Scale

Directions:

Place an **X** on the line at the place that best describes the pupil's performance of each behavior.

Physical Expression

A. Stands straight and faces audience.

stands straight, always looks at audience	**weaves, fidgets, eyes roam from audience to ceiling**	**constant, distracting movements, no eye contact with audience**

B. Changes facial expression with change in the tone of the presentation.

matches facial expressions to content and emphasis	**facial expressions usually appropriate, occasional lack of expression**	**no match between tone and facial expression; expression distracts**

Source: From *Classroom assessment: Concepts and applications* (5th ed.) by P. W. Airasian (2005). New York: McGraw-Hill, p. 251.

learning is. Some of the *Guidelines* for developing rubrics on page 569 are taken from Goodrich (1997) and Johnson and Johnson (2002).

It is often helpful to have students join in the development of rating scales and scoring rubrics. When students participate, they are challenged to decide what quality work looks or sounds like in a particular area. They know in advance what is expected. As students gain practice in designing and applying scoring rubrics, their work and their learning often improve. Figure 15.3 on the next page is an evaluation form for self- and peer assessment of contributions to cooperative learning groups.

Reliability, Validity, Generalizability. Because judgment plays such a central role in evaluating performances, issues of reliability, validity, and generalizability are critical considerations. As we saw in the previous chapter, judges assessing the Vermont Portfolios often have not agreed on ratings, so reliability may not be adequate. When raters are experienced and scoring rubrics are well developed and refined, however, reliability may improve (Herman & Winters, 1994; LeMahieu, Gitomer, & Eresh, 1993). Some of this

Connect and **Extend** to **Other Chapters**

See Chapter 6 for a discussion of how to use praise effectively. These guidelines apply to written feedback as well.

Connect and **Extend** to Your **Teaching/Portfolio**

Adapt the *Guidelines* for developing rubrics for the age group you plan to teach.

FIGURE 15.3

Self- and Peer Evaluation of Group Learning

STUDENT SELF- AND PEER EVALUATION FORM

This form will be used to assess the members of your learning group. Fill one form out on yourself. Fill one form out on each member of your group. During the group discussion, give each member the form you have filled out on them. Compare the way you rated yourself with the ways your groupmates have rated you. Ask for clarification when your rating differs from the ratings given you by your groupmates. Each member should set a goal for increasing his or her contribution to the academic learning of all group members.

Person Being Rated: ______________________________

Write the number of points earned by the group member:
(4 = Excellent, 3 = Good, 2 = Poor, 1 = Inadequate)

____ On time for class.
____ Arrives prepared for class.
____ Reliably completes all assigned work on time.
____ Work is of high quality.
____ Contributes to groupmates' learning daily.
____ Asks for academic help and assistance when it is needed.
____ Gives careful step-by-step explanations (doesn't just tell answers).
____ Builds on others' reasoning.
____ Relates what is being learned to previous knowledge.
____ Helps draw a visual representation of what is being learned.
____ Voluntarily extends a project.

Source: From "The Role of Cooperative Learning in Assessing and Communicating Student Learning," by D. W. Johnson and R. T. Johnson. In *ASCD 1996 Yearbook: Communicating Student Learning* (p. 41), T. Guskey (Ed.).

improvement in reliability occurs because a rubric focuses the raters' attention on a few dimensions of the work and gives limited scoring levels to choose from. If scorers can give only a rating of 1, 2, 3, or 4, they are more likely to agree than if they could score based on a 100-point scale. So the rubrics may achieve reliability not because they capture underlying agreement among raters, but because the rubrics limit options and thus limit variability in scoring (Mabry, 1999).

In terms of validity, there is some evidence that students who are classified as "master" writers on the basis of portfolio assessment are judged less capable using standard writing assessments. Which form of assessment is the best reflection of enduring qualities? There is so little research on this question, it is hard to say (Herman & Winters, 1994). In addition, when rubrics are developed to assess specific tasks, the results of applying the rubrics may not predict performance on anything except very similar tasks, so we do not know whether the students' performance on the specific task will generalize to the larger area of study (Haertel, 1999; McMillan, 2004).

Connect and Extend to Your Teaching/Portfolio

For ideas about implementing performance assessment in the classroom, see http://www.ascd.org/ed_topics/cl200002_brualdi.html

Diversity and Equity in Performance Assessment. Equity is an issue in all assessment and no less so with performances and portfolios. With a public performance, there could be bias effects based on a student's appearance and speech or the student's access to expensive audio, video, or graphic resources. Performance assessments have the same potential as other tests to discriminate unfairly against students who are not wealthy or who are culturally different (McDonald, 1993). And the extensive group work, peer editing, and out-of-class time devoted to portfolios means that some students may have access to more extensive networks of support and outright help. Many students in your classes will come from families that have sophisticated computer graphics and desktop publishing capabilities. Others may have little support from home. These differences can be sources of bias and inequity.

Guidelines: Developing a Rubric

1. *Look at models:* Show students examples of good and not-so-good work. Identify the characteristics that make the good ones good and the bad ones bad.
2. *List criteria:* Use the discussion of models to begin a list of what counts in quality work.
3. *Articulate gradations of quality:* Describe the best and worst levels of quality, then fill in the middle levels based on your knowledge of common problems and the discussion of not-so-good work.
4. *Practice on models:* Have students use the rubrics to evaluate the models you gave them in Step 1.
5. *Use self- and peer assessment:* Give students their task. As they work, stop them occasionally for self- and peer-assessment.
6. *Revise:* Always give students time to revise their work based on the feedback they get in Step 5.
7. *Use teacher assessment:* Use the same rubric students used to assess their work yourself.

Note: Step 1 may be necessary only when you are asking students to engage in a task with which they are unfamiliar. Steps 3 and 4 are useful but time-consuming; you can do these on your own, especially when you've been using rubrics for a while. A class experienced in rubric-based assessment can streamline the process so that it begins with listing criteria, after which the teacher writes out the gradations of quality, checks them with the students, makes revisions, then uses the rubric for self-, peer, and teacher assessment.

For a great explanation of using rubrics, see **http://pareonline.net/getvn.asp?v=7&n=25**

The article includes several links such as **http://www.teach-nology.com/web_tools/rubrics/** and **http://rubistar.4teachers.org/** that allow you to create and customize rubrics for your class.

Informal Assessments

Informal assessments are ungraded (formative) assessments that gather information from multiple sources to help teachers make decisions (Banks, 2005). Early on in the unit, assessments should be formative (provide feedback, but not count toward a grade), saving the actual graded assessments for later in the unit when all students have had the chance to learn the material (Tomlinson, 2005a). Some examples of informal assessment are student observations and checklists, questioning, journals, and student self-assessment.

Journals are very flexible and widely used informal assessments. Students usually have personal or group journals and write in them on a regular basis. In their study, Michael Pressley and his colleagues (2001) found that excellent 1st-grade literacy teachers used journaling for three purposes:

- As communication tools that allowed students to express their own thoughts and ideas.
- As an opportunity to apply what they have learned.
- As an outlet to encourage fluency and creative expression in language usage.

Teachers may use journals to learn about their students in order to better connect their teaching to the students' concerns and interests. But often journals focus on academic learning, usually through responses to prompts. For example, Banks (2005) describes one high-school physics teacher who asked his students to respond to these three questions in their journals:

1. How can you determine the coefficient of friction if you know only the angle of the inclined plane?
2. Compare and contrast some of the similarities and the differences between magnetic, electronic, and gravitational fields.
3. If you were to describe the physical concept of sound to your best friend, what music would you use to demonstrate this concept?

When he read the students' journals, the teacher realized that many of the students' basic assumptions about friction, acceleration, and velocity came from personal experiences and not from scientific reasoning. His approach to teaching had to change to reach the students. The teacher never would have known to make the changes without reading the journals (Banks, 2005).

Connect and **Extend** to the **Research**

Boudett, K. P., Murnane, R. J., City, E., & Moody, L. (2005). Teaching educators how to use student assessment data to improve instruction. *Phi Delta Kappa, 86,* 700–706.

Informal assessments Ungraded (formative) assessments that gather information from multiple sources to help teachers make decisions.

There are many other kinds of informal assessments—keeping notes and observations about student performance, rating scales, and checklists. Every time teachers ask questions or watch students perform skills, the teachers are conducting informal assessments. Look at Table 15.6. It summarizes the possibilities and limitations of aligning different assessment tools with their targets. One major message in this chapter is to match the type of assessment tools used to the target—what is being assessed.

Involving Students in Assessments

One way to connect teaching and assessment while developing students' sense of efficacy for learning is to involve the students in the assessment process. Students can keep track of their own progress and assess their improvement. Table 15.7 gives ideas for how to help students judge their own work and participate in assessing their own learning.

Connect and **Extend** to the **Research**

For more ideas about making classroom assessment better, see: Black, P., Harrison, C., Lee, C., Marshall, B., & Wiliam, D. (2004). Working inside the black box: Assessment for learning in the classroom. *Phi Delta Kappan, 86,* 8–21.

Stiggins, R. (2004). New assessment beliefs for a new school mission. *Phi Delta Kappan, 86,* 22–37.

Effects of Grading on Students

STOP | THINK | WRITE Think back on your report cards and grades over the years. Did you ever receive a grade that was lower than you expected? How did you feel about yourself, the teacher, the subject, and school in general as a result of the lower grade? What could the teacher have done to help you understand and profit from the experience? ■

TABLE 15.6

Aligning Different Assessment Tools with Their Targets
Different learning outcomes require different assessment methods.

	Assessment Method			
Target to Be Assessed	**Selected Response**	**Essay**	**Performance Assessment**	**Personal Communication**
Knowledge Mastery	Multiple choice, true/false, matching, and fill-in can sample mastery of elements of knowledge	Essay exercises can tap understanding of relationships among elements of knowledge	Not a good choice for this target—three other options preferred	Can ask questions, evaluate answers, and infer mastery—but a time-consuming option
Reasoning Proficiency	Can assess understanding of basic patterns of reasoning	Written descriptions of complex problem solutions can provide a window into reasoning proficiency	Can watch students solve some problems and infer about reasoning proficiency	Can ask student to "think aloud" or can ask follow-up questions to probe reasoning
Skills	Can assess mastery of the prerequisites of skillful performance—but cannot tap the skill itself	Can assess mastery of the prerequisites of skillful performance—but cannot tap the skill itself	Can observe and evaluate skills as they are being performed	Strong match when skill is oral communication proficiency; also can assess mastery of knowledge prerequisite to skillful performance
Ability to Create Products	Can assess mastery of knowledge prerequisite to the ability to create quality products—but cannot assess the quality of products themselves	Can assess mastery of knowledge prerequisite to the ability to create quality products—but cannot assess the quality of products themselves	A strong match can assess: (a) proficiency in carrying out steps in product development and (b) attributes of the product itself	Can probe procedural knowledge and knowledge of attributes of quality products—but not product quality

Source: From "Where Is Our Assessment Future and How Can We Get There?" by R. J. Stiggins. In R. W. Lissitz, W. D. Schafer (Eds.), *Meaningful Assessment: A Meaningful and Cooperative Process.* Published by Allyn & Bacon, Boston, MA. Copyright © 2002 by Pearson Education. Adapted by permission of the publisher.

TABLE 15.7

Involving Students in Classroom Assessment

Here are a dozen ways of using assessment in the service of student learning.

1. Engage students in reviewing strong and weak samples to determine attributes of a good performance or product.
2. Before a discussion or conference with the teacher or peer, students identify their own perceptions of strengths and weaknesses on a specific aspect of their work.
3. Students practice using criteria to evaluate anonymous strong and weak work.
4. Students work in pairs to revise an anonymous weak work sample they have just evaluated.
5. Students write a process paper, detailing the process they went through to create a product or performance. In it they reflect on problems they encountered and how they solved them.
6. Students develop practice test plans based on their understanding of the intended learning targets and essential concepts in material to be learned.
7. Students generate and answer questions they think might be on the test, based on their understanding of the content/processes/skills they were responsible for learning.
8. A few days before a test, students discuss or write answers to questions such as: "Why am I taking this test? Who will use the results? How?" "What is it testing?" "How do I think I will do?" "What do I need to study?" "With whom might I work?"
9. Teacher arranges items on a test according to specific learning targets, and prepares a "test analysis" chart for students, with three boxes: "My strengths," "Quick review," and "Further study." After handing back the corrected test, students identify learning targets they have mastered and write them in the "My strengths" box. Next, students categorize their wrong answers as either "simple mistake" or "further study." Then, students list the simple mistakes in the "Quick review" box. Last, students write the rest of the learning targets represented by wrong answers in the "Further study" box.
10. Students review a collection of their work over time and reflect on their growth: "I have become a better reader this quarter. I used to . . . , but now I . . . "
11. Students use a collection of their self-assessments to summarize their learning and set goals for future learning: "Here is what I have learned . . . Here is what I need to work on . . ."
12. Students select and annotate evidence of achievement for a portfolio.

Source: From "Using student-involved classroom assessment to close achievement gaps," by R. Stiggins and J. Chappuis, *Theory Into Practice, 44,* 2005, p. 16. Reprinted with permission of Lawrence Erlbaum Associates, Inc. and R. Stiggins.

When we think of grades, we often think of competition. Highly competitive classes may be particularly hard on anxious students, students who lack self-confidence, and students who are less prepared. So, although high standards and competition do tend to be generally related to increased academic learning, it is clear that a balance must be struck between high standards and a reasonable chance to succeed. Rick Stiggins and Jan Chappuis (2005) observe:

> From their very earliest school experiences, our students draw life-shaping conclusions about themselves as learners on the basis of the information we provide to them as a result of their teachers' classroom assessments. As the evidence accumulates over time, they decide if they are capable of succeeding or not. They decide whether the learning is worth the commitment it will take to attain it. They decide . . . whether to risk investing in the schooling experience. These decisions are crucial to their academic well-being. (p. 11)

Effects of Failure

It may sound as though low grades and failure should be avoided in school. But the situation is not that simple.

The Value of Failing? After reviewing many years of research on the effects of failure from several perspectives, Margaret Clifford (1990, 1991) concluded:

Connect and **Extend** to the **Research**

Here are several studies of retentions:

Beebe-Frankenberger, M., Bocian, K. L., MacMillan, D. L., & Gresham, F. M. (2004). Sorting second grade students with academic deficiencies: Characteristics differentiating those retained in grade from those promoted to third grade. *Journal of Educational Psychology, 96*, 204–215.

Shepard, L. A., & Smith, M. L. (1990). Synthesis of research on grade retention. *Educational Leadership, 47*(8), 84–88.

McCoy, A. R., & Reynolds, A. J. (1999). Grade retention and school performance: An extended investigation. *Journal of School Psychology, 37*, 273–298.

Vitaro, F., Brendgen, M., & Tremblay, R. E. (1999). Prevention of school dropout through the reduction of disruptive behaviors and school failure in elementary school. *Journal of School Psychology, 37*, 205–226.

> It is time for educators to replace easy success with challenge. We must encourage students to reach beyond their intellectual grasp and allow them the privilege of learning from mistakes. There must be a tolerance for error-making in every classroom, and gradual success rather than continual success must become the yardstick by which learning is judged. (1990, p. 23)

Some level of failure may be helpful for most students, especially if teachers help the students see connections between hard work and improvement. Efforts to protect students from failure and to guarantee success may be counterproductive. In fact, the more able your students are, the more challenging and important it will be to help them learn to "fail successfully" (Foster, 1981). Carol Tomlinson, an expert on differentiated instruction, puts it this way: "Students whose learning histories have caused them to believe that excellence can be achieved with minimal effort do not learn to expend effort, and yet perceive that high grades are an entitlement for them" (2005b, p. 266).

Retention in Grade. So far, we have been talking about the effects of failing a test or perhaps a course. But what about the effect of failing an entire grade—that is, of being "held back"? Almost 20% of seniors have repeated at least one grade since kindergarten, usually in the earlier grades (Kelly, 1999). Retained students are more likely to be male, members of minority groups, and living in poverty (Beebe-Frankenberger, Bocian, MacMillan, & Gresham, 2004).

Most research finds that grade retention is associated with poor long-term outcomes such as dropping out of school, higher arrest rates, fewer job opportunities, lower self-esteem (Grissom & Shepard, 1989; Jimerson, Anderson, & Whipple, 2002). In their view, students generally do better academically when they are promoted. For example, in a longitudinal study of 29 retained and 50 low-achieving but promoted students, Shane Jimerson (1999) found that years later, the retained students had poorer educational and employment outcomes than the promoted students. The retained students dropped out more often, had lower-paying jobs, and received lower competence ratings from employers. In addition, the low-achieving but promoted students were comparable to a control group in all employment outcomes at age 20.

Retention assumes that the students just need more time and that they have the abilities needed to catch up. But one study in California found the students retained after second grade had the same average IQ score as those targeted for more intensive interventions under special education requirements. In addition, about 20% of the retained group had IQ scores in the range that would qualify as having mental retardation (Beebe-Frankenberger et al., 2004), so it was probably wrong to assume that these students would benefit from the same teaching. Primary-grade students who benefit from retention tend to be more emotionally immature than their peers, but have average or

Students often need help figuring out why their answers are incorrect; without such feedback they are likely to make the same mistakes again.

above average ability (Kelly, 1999; Pierson & Connell, 1992). Even with this group, the advantage may not last. In one study that followed many students for several years, children who could have been retained, but who were promoted, did about as well as similar children who were held back, and sometimes better (Reynolds, 1992).

No matter what, students who are having trouble should get help, whether they are promoted (this is often called "social promotion") or retained. However, just covering the same material again in the same way won't solve the students' academic or social problems. As Jeannie Oakes (1999) has said, "No sensible person advocates social promotion as it is currently framed—simply passing incompetent students on to the next grade" (p. 8). The best approach may be to promote the students along with their peers, but to give them special remediation during the summer or the next year (Mantzicopoulos & Morrison, 1992; Shepard & Smith, 1989). An even better approach would be to prevent the problems by differentiating instruction early (Chapter 13).

Effects of Feedback

The results of several studies of feedback fit well with the notion of "successful" or constructive failure. These studies have concluded that it is more helpful to tell students *why* they are wrong so they can learn more appropriate strategies (Bangert-Drowns, Kulik, Kulik, & Morgan, 1991). Students often need help figuring out why their answers are incorrect. Without such feedback, they are likely to make the same mistakes again. Yet this type of feedback is rarely given. In one study, only about 8% of the teachers noticed a consistent type of error in a student's arithmetic computation and informed the student (Bloom & Bourdon, 1980).

Connect and **Extend** to **Other Chapters**

See Chapter 6 for a discussion of how to use praise effectively. These guidelines apply to written feedback as well.

What are the identifying characteristics of effective written feedback? With older students (late elementary through high school), written comments are most helpful when they are personalized and when they provide constructive criticism. This means the teacher should make specific comments on errors or faulty strategies, but balance this criticism with suggestions about how to improve, as well as comments on the positive aspects of the work (Butler & Nisan, 1986; Guskey & Bailey, 2001). Working with 6th-grade teachers, Maria Elawar and Lyn Corno (1985) found that feedback was dramatically improved when the teachers used these four questions as a guide: "What is the key error? What is the probable reason the student made this error? How can I guide the student to avoid the error in the future? What did the student do well that could be noted?" (p. 166). Here are some examples of teachers' written comments that proved helpful (Elawar & Corno, 1985, p. 164):

> Juan, you know how to get a percent, but the computation is wrong in this instance. Can you see where? (Teacher has underlined the location of errors.)

> You know how to solve the problem—the formula is correct—but you have not demonstrated that you understand how one fraction multiplied by another can give an answer that is smaller than either ($\frac{1}{2} \times \frac{1}{2} = \frac{1}{4}$).

Comments like these should help students correct errors and recognize good work, progress, and increasing skill.

Connect and **Extend** to Your **Teaching/Portfolio**

Given the various roles of evaluation, what is the disadvantage of a teacher giving a test and not returning the results until several weeks later? What is the disadvantage of merely posting the grade without returning the actual test? What is the disadvantage of returning the students' scored answer sheets without reviewing the correct answers?

Grades and Motivation

If you are relying on grades to motivate students, you had better think again (Smith, Smith, & De Lisi, 2001). The assessments you give should support students' motivation to learn—not just to work for a grade. But is there really a difference between working for a grade and working to learn? The answer depends in part on how a grade is determined. As a teacher, you can use grades to motivate the kind of learning you intend students to achieve in your course. If you test only at a simple but detailed level of knowledge, you may force students to choose between complex learning and a good grade. But when a grade reflects meaningful learning, working for a grade and working to learn become the same thing. Finally, while high grades may have some value as rewards or incentives for

Connect and **Extend** to Your **Teaching/Portfolio**

Can grades be used as motivators for all students? What determines whether a grade is motivating? How can a teacher use grades so that they tend to be motivating instead of discouraging?

meaningful engagement in learning, low grades generally do not encourage greater efforts. Students receiving low grades are more likely to withdraw, blame others, decide that the work is "dumb," or feel responsible for the low grade but helpless to make improvements. They give up on themselves or on school (Tomlinson, 2005b). Rather than give a failing grade, you might consider the work incomplete and give students support in revising or improving. Maintain high standards and give students a chance to reach them (Guskey, 1994; Guskey & Bailey, 2001).

Another effect on motivation occurs in high schools in the race for valedictorian. Sometimes, students and parents find clever ways to move ahead of the competition—but the strategies have little to do with learning. As Tom Guskey and Jane Bailey (2001) note, when a valedictorian wins by a 1/1,000 of decimal point, how meaningful is the learning behind the difference? Some high schools now name multiple valedictorians—as many as meet the highest standards of the school—because they believe that the educators' job is "not to *select* talent, but, rather, to *develop* talent" (Guskey & Bailey, 2001, p. 39).

The *Guidelines* summarize the effects grades can have on students.

Grading and Reporting: Nuts and Bolts

STOP | THINK | WRITE Think about the other courses you are taking this term besides this one. How are your grades calculated in those courses? ■

In determining a final grade, the teacher must make a major decision. Should a student's grade reflect the amount of material learned and how well it has been learned, or should the grade reflect the student's status in comparison with the rest of the class? In other words, should grading be criterion-referenced or norm-referenced?

Connect and Extend to the Research

For a summary of the considerations in developing a grading plan, see Frisbie, D. A., & Waltmen, K. K. (1992). Developing a personal grading plan. *Educational measurement: Issues and practices* (pp. 35–42). Washington, DC: National Council on Measurement in Education.

Criterion-Referenced versus Norm-Referenced Grading

In **norm-referenced grading,** the major influence on a grade is the student's standing in comparison with others who also took the course. If a student studies very hard and almost everyone else does too, the student may receive a disappointing grade, perhaps a C or D. One common type of norm-referenced grading is called **grading on the curve.** How you feel about this approach probably depends on where your grades generally fell along that "curve." There is good evidence that this type of grading damages the relationships among students and between teachers and students and also diminishes motivation for most students (Krumboltz & Yeh, 1996). When you think about it, if the curve arbitrarily limits the number of good grades that can be given, then, in the game of grading, most students will be losers (Guskey & Bailey, 2001; Haladyna, 2002; Kohn, 1996). Over 25 years ago, Benjamin Bloom (of Bloom's taxonomy) and his colleagues (1981) pointed out the fallacy of grading on the curve:

> There is nothing sacred about the normal curve. It is the distribution most appropriate to chance and random activity. Education is a purposeful activity, and we seek to have students learn what we have to teach. If we are effective in our instruction, the distribution of achievement should be very different from the normal curve. In fact, we may even insist that our educational efforts have been *unsuccessful* to the extent that the distribution of achievement approximates the normal distribution. (pp. 52–53)

Norm-referenced grading Assessment of students' achievement in relation to one another.

Grading on the curve Norm-referenced grading that compares students' performance to an average level.

Criterion-referenced grading Assessment of each student's mastery of course objectives.

In **criterion-referenced grading,** the grade represents a list of accomplishments. If clear objectives have been set for the course, the grade may represent a certain number of objectives met satisfactorily. When a criterion-referenced system is used, criteria for each grade generally are spelled out in advance. It is then up to the student to earn the grade she or he wants to receive. Theoretically, in this system, all students can achieve an A if they reach the criteria. Criterion-referenced grading has the advantage

Guidelines: Minimizing the Detrimental Effects of Grades

Avoid reserving high grades and high praise for answers that conform to your ideas or to those in the textbook.

EXAMPLES

1. Give extra points for correct and creative answers.
2. Withhold your opinions until all sides of an issue have been explored.
3. Reinforce students for disagreeing in a rational, productive manner.
4. Give partial credit for partially correct answers.

Make sure each student has a reasonable chance to be successful, especially at the beginning of a new task.

EXAMPLES

1. Pretest students to make sure they have prerequisite abilities.
2. When appropriate, provide opportunities for students to retest to raise their grades, but make sure the retest is as difficult as the original.
3. Consider failing efforts as "incomplete" and encourage students to revise and improve.
4. Base grades more on work at the end of the unit, give ungraded work in the beginning of the unit.

Balance written and oral feedback.

EXAMPLES

1. Consider giving short, lively written comments with younger students and more extensive written comments with older students.
2. When the grade on a paper is lower than the student might have expected, be sure the reason for the lower grade is clear.
3. Tailor comments to the individual student's performance; avoid writing the same phrases over and over.
4. Note specific errors, possible reasons for errors, ideas for improvement, and work done well.

Make grades as meaningful as possible.

EXAMPLES

1. Tie grades to the mastery of important objectives.
2. Give ungraded assignments to encourage exploration.
3. Experiment with performances and portfolios.

Base grades on more than just one criterion.

EXAMPLES

1. Use essay questions as well as multiple-choice items on a test.
2. Grade oral reports and class participation.

For more information about the effects of grading, see **http://www.nap.edu/readingingroom/books/str/6.html** and **http://www.alfiekohn.org/teaching/fdtd-g.htm**

of relating judgments about a student to the achievement of clearly defined instructional goals. Some school districts have developed reporting systems where report cards list objectives along with judgments about the student's attainment of each. Reporting is done at the end of each unit of instruction. The elementary school report card shown in Figure 15.4 on the next page demonstrates the relationship between assessment and the goals of the unit.

Let's examine a few popular systems for calculating grades.

Connect and Extend to PRAXIS II™
Grading
Be able to define criterion- and norm-referenced grading systems, identify examples of each, and explain the advantages and disadvantages of each system. Describe the possible effects of grades on students.

The Point System and Percentage Grading

One popular system for combining grades from many assignments is a point system. Each test or assignment is given a certain number of total points, depending on its importance. A test worth 40% of the grade could be worth 40 points. A paper worth 20% could be worth 20 points. Points are then awarded on the test or paper based on specific criteria. An A+ paper, one that meets all the criteria, could be given the full 20 points; an average paper might be given 10 points. If tests of comparable importance are worth the same number of points, are equally difficult, and cover a similar amount of material, this system can be fair and practical. But in most schools, these points still must be converted into some form of final grade. So the teacher has to decide the standards for assigning grades.

FIGURE 15.4

A Criterion-Referenced Report Card

This is one example of a criterion-referenced reort card. Other forms are possible, but all criterion-referenced reports indicate student progress toward specific goals.

LINCOLN ELEMENTARY SCHOOL
GRADE 5

Student ____________ Teacher ____________ Principal Muriel Simms Quarter 2 3 4

E = Excellent S = Satisfactory P = Making Progress N = Needs improvement

READING PROGRAM

Materials Used: ____________

___ Reads with understanding
___ Is able to write about what is read
___ Completes reading group work accurately and on time
___ Shows interest in reading

Reading Skills
___ Decodes new words
___ Understands new words

Independent Reading Level
Below/At Grade Level/Above

LANGUAGE ARTS
___ Uses oral language effectively
___ Listens carefully
___ Masters weekly spelling

Writing skills
___ Understands writing as process
___ Creates a rough draft
___ Makes meaningful revisions
___ Creates edited, legible final draft

Editing skills
___ Capitalizes
___ Punctuates
___ Uses complete sentences
___ Uses paragraphs
___ Demonstrates dictionary skills

Writing skill level:
Below/At Grade Level/Above

MATHEMATICS

Problem Solving
___ Solves teacher-generated problems
___ Solves self-/student-generated problems
___ Can create story problems

Interpreting Problems
___ Uses appropriate strategies
___ Can use more than one strategy
___ Can explain strategies in written form
___ Can explain strategies orally

Math Concepts
Understands Base Ten
Beginning/Developing/Sophisticated
Multiplication, Basic facts
Beginning/Developing/Sophisticated
2-Digit Multiplications
Beginning/Developing/Sophisticated
Division
Beginning/Developing/Sophisticated
Geometry
Beginning/Developing/Sophisticated

Overall Math Skill Level:
Beginning/Developing/Sophisticated

Attitude/Work Skills
___ Welcomes a challenge
___ Persistent
___ Takes advantage of learning from others
___ Listens to others
___ Participates in discussion

It Figures
Is working on: ____________

Goals: ____________
Is working on achieving goal: ____________

SOCIAL STUDIES
___ Understands subject matter
___ Shows curiosity and enthusiasm
___ Contributes to class discussions
___ Uses map skills
___ Demonstrates control of reading skills by interpreting text

Topics covered: individual cultures, Columbus–first English colonies

SCIENCE
___ Shows curiosity about scientific subject matter
___ Asks good scientific questions
___ Shows knowledge of scientific method
___ Uses knowledge of scientific method to help set up and run experiment(s)
___ Makes good scientific observations
___ Has researched scientific topic(s)
Topic(s) ____________

I Wonder
Is currently working on ____________

WORKING SKILLS
___ Listens carefully
___ Follows directions
___ Works neatly and carefully
___ Checks work
___ Completes work on time
___ Uses time wisely
___ Works well independently
___ Works well in a group
___ Takes risks in learning
___ Welcomes a challenge

HOMEWORK
___ Self-selects homework
___ Completes work accurately
___ Completes work on time

PRESENTATIONS/PROJECTS

____

____

HUMAN RELATIONS
___ Shows courtesy
___ Respects rights of others
___ Shows self-control
___ Interacts well with peers
___ Shows a cooperative and positive attitude in class
___ Shows a cooperative attitude when asked to work with other students
___ Is willing to help other students
___ Works well with other adults (subs, student teacher, parents, etc.)

Attendance

	1st	2nd	3rd	4th
Present				
Absent				
Tardy				

Placement for next year: ____________

Source: From "Reporting Methods in Grades K–8," by K. Lake and K. Kafka. In *ASCD 1996 Yearbook: Communicating Student Learning* (p. 104), T. Guskey (Ed.). Copyright © 1996 by the Association for Supervision and Curriculum Development. Reprinted with permission. All rights reserved. The Association for Supervision and Curriculum Development is a worldwide community of educators advocating sound policies and sharing best practices to achieve the success of each learner. To learn more, visit ASCD at *www.ascd.org.*

Percentage grading System of converting class performances to percentage scores and assigning grades based on predetermined cutoff points.

Using another approach, **percentage grading,** the teacher can assign grades based on how much knowledge each student has mastered—what percentage of the total knowledge he or she understands. To do this, the teacher might score tests and other class work with percentage scores (based on how much is correct—50%, 85%, etc.) and then average these scores to reach a course score. These scores can then be converted into letter grades according to predetermined cutoffs. Any number of students can earn any grade. School systems often establish equivalent percentage categories for As, Bs, and so on. The percentages vary from school district to school district. An A might be 90% to 100% in one district but 94% to 100% in another.

Even though it is very common, this approach has problems. Can we really say what is the total amount of knowledge available in, for example, 8th-grade science? Are we sure we can accurately measure what percentage of this body of knowledge each student has attained? To use percentage grading appropriately, we would have to know exactly what there was to learn and exactly how much of that knowledge each student had learned (Popham, 2005a). These conditions are seldom met, even though teachers use the cutoff points to assign grades as if measurement were so accurate that a one-point difference was meaningful.

Don't be fooled by the seeming security of points or absolute percentages. Your own grading philosophy will continue to operate, even in this system. Because there is more concern today with specifying objectives and criterion-referenced assessment, especially at the elementary-grade levels, several alternative methods for evaluating student progress against predetermined criteria have evolved.

Connect and **Extend** to Your **Teaching/Portfolio**

How would you solve the following problem? You are using a contract system in one of your classes. One of the requirements for an A is "to write a book report." However, some students are reporting on books that you think they read last year, and some are handing in short, superficial reports. How can you structure the contract system so that the students will do better quality work?

The Contract System and Grading Rubrics

When applied to the whole class, the **contract system** indicates the type, quantity, and quality of work required for each number or letter grade in the system. Rubrics describe the performance expected for each level. Students agree, or "contract," to work for particular grades by meeting the specified requirements and performing at the level specified. For example, the following standards might be established:

F: Not coming to class regularly or not turning in the required work.
D: Coming to class regularly and turning in the required work on time.
C: Coming to class regularly, turning in the required work on time, and receiving a check mark on all assignments to indicate they are satisfactory.
B: Coming to class regularly, turning in the required work on time, and receiving a check mark on all assignments except at least three that achieve a check-plus, indicating superior achievement.
A: As above, plus a successful oral or written report on one of the books listed for supplementary reading.

Connect and **Extend** to **Other Chapters**

See Chapter 6 for a discussion of behavior management contracts.

This example calls for more subjective judgment than would be ideal. However, contract systems reduce student anxiety about grades. The contract system can be applied to individual students, in which case it functions much like an independent study plan.

Unfortunately, the system can lead to overemphasis on the quantity of work. Teachers may be too vague about the standards that differentiate acceptable from unacceptable work. This is where scoring rubrics for each assignment can be helpful. If clear and well-developed rubrics describe the performances expected for each assignment, and if students learn to use the rubrics to evaluate their own work, then quality, not quantity, will be at the center of grading. You can modify the contract system by including a **revise option.** For example, a check mark might be worth 75 points and a check-plus 90 points; a check-plus earned after revision could be worth 85 points—more than a check, but less than a check-plus earned the first time around. This system allows students to improve their work, but also rewards students for getting it right the first time. In addition, the teacher may be less reluctant to judge a project unsatisfactory because students can improve their work (King, 1979). But beware, if a school system requires a 5-point grading scale and all students contract for and achieve the highest grade (before or after revising), the teacher will wish that the principal had been consulted about the system before the

Contract system System in which each student works for a particular grade according to agreed-upon standards.

Revise option In a contract system, the chance to revise and improve work.

Guidelines: Using Any Grading System

Explain your grading policies to students early in the course and remind them of the policies regularly.

EXAMPLES

1. Give older students a handout describing the assignments, tests, grading criteria, and schedule.
2. Explain to younger students in a low-pressure manner how their work will be evaluated.

Base grades on clearly specified, reasonable standards.

EXAMPLES

1. Specify standards by developing a rubric with students—have anonymous examples of poor, good, and excellent work from previous classes.
2. Discuss workload and grading standards with more experienced teachers.
3. Give a few formative tests to get a sense of your students' abilities before you give a graded test.
4. Take tests yourself first to gauge the difficulty of the test and to estimate the time your students will need.

Base your grades on as much objective evidence as possible.

EXAMPLES

1. Plan in advance how and when you will test.
2. Keep a portfolio of student work. This may be useful in student or parent conferences.

Be sure students understand test directions.

EXAMPLES

1. Outline the directions on the board.
2. Ask several students to explain the directions.
3. Go over a sample question first.

Correct, return, and discuss test questions as soon as possible.

EXAMPLES

1. Have students who wrote good answers read their responses for the class; make sure they are not the same students each time.
2. Discuss why wrong answers, especially popular wrong choices, are incorrect.
3. As soon as students finish a test, give them the answers to questions and the page numbers where answers are discussed in the text.

As a rule, do not change a grade.

EXAMPLES

1. Make sure you can defend the grade in the first place.
2. DO change any clerical or calculation errors.

Guard against bias in grading.

EXAMPLES

1. Ask students to put their names on the backs of their papers.
2. Use an objective point system or model papers when grading essays.

Keep pupils informed of their standing in the class.

EXAMPLES

1. Write the distribution of scores on the board after tests.
2. Schedule periodic conferences to go over work from previous weeks.

Give students the benefit of the doubt. All measurement techniques involve error.

EXAMPLES

1. Unless there is a very good reason not to, give the higher grade in borderline cases.
2. If a large number of students miss the same question in the same way, revise the question for the future and consider throwing it out for that test.

For more thoughts about grading, see
http://teaching.berkeley.edu/bgd/grading.html

Source: From *Problems in Middle and High School Teaching: A Handbook for Student Teachers and Beginning Teachers* (pp. 182–187), by A. M. Drayer, 1979, Boston: Allyn and Bacon.

Connect and **Extend** to Your **Teaching/Portfolio**

Think about your philosophy of teaching. What do you believe about testing and grading? How will you assign grades? (Consult the *Guidelines* for ideas.)

grades came out. The *Guidelines* give ideas for using any grading system in a fair and reasonable way.

Other Issues in Grading

Grading on Effort and Improvement. Grading on effort and improvement is not really a complete grading system, but rather a theme that can run through most grading methods. Should teachers grade students based on how much they learn or on the final level of learning? One problem with using improvement as a standard for grading is that the best students improve the least, because they are already the most competent. Do you want to penalize these students because they knew quite a bit initially, and the teaching and testing have limited how much learning they can demonstrate? After all, unless you assign extra work, these students will run out of things to do (Airasian, 2005; Guskey & Bailey, 2001).

One solution is to use the **individual learning expectation (ILE)** system. With this system, students earn improvement points on tests or assignments for scoring above their personal base (average) score or for making a perfect score. The teacher can count these improvement points when figuring a final grade or simply use them as a basis for giving other classroom rewards. Another option is to recognize good student effort through oral or written comments, notes to parents, or other recognition.

"I hope this isn't another ploy to up your grade, Haskell."

Cautions: Being Fair. The attributions a teacher makes about the causes of student successes or failures can affect the grades that students receive. Teachers are more likely to give higher grades for effort (a controllable factor) than for ability (an uncontrollable factor). Lower grades are more likely when teachers attribute a student's failure to lack of effort instead of lack of ability (Weiner, 1979). It is also possible that grades can be influenced by a **halo effect**—that is, by the tendency to view particular aspects of a student based on a general impression, either positive or negative. As a teacher, you may find it difficult to avoid being affected by positive and negative halos. A very pleasant student who seems to work hard and causes little trouble may be given the benefit of the doubt (B– instead of C+), whereas a very difficult student who seems to refuse to try might be a loser at grading time (D instead of C–).

There is another aspect of fairness. If students' grades are affected by unclear directions, difficulty reading the test or assignment questions, low grades for missing homework, a test that did not measure what was taught, time pressures, or other factors that are not related to the skills being assessed, then "grade pollution" has occurred. When flowery language or an artistic cover inflates a student's grade, we have more grade pollution. Grades should reflect what a student knows, understands, or can do related to the learning objective specified (Tomlinson, 2005b).

Connect and **Extend** to Your **Teaching/Portfolio**

Often, teachers tend to blame certain students for classroom disturbances even though they may not be guilty. Is this an example of the halo effect? Can you think of other examples?

Beyond Grading: Communicating with Families

WHAT WOULD YOU SAY?

During your interview for a job in a very diverse district, the department chair asks you, "How will you communicate with families about your homework and grading policies?" ■

No number or letter grade conveys the totality of a student's experience in a class or course. Students, parents, and teachers sometimes become too focused on the end point—the grade. But communicating with families should involve more than just sending home grades. There are a number of ways to communicate with and report to families. Many teachers I know have a beginning-of-the-year newsletter or student handbook that communicates homework, behavior, and grading policies to families. Other options described by Guskey & Bailey (2001) are:

- Notes attached to report cards
- Phone calls, especially "Good News" calls
- School open houses
- Conferences, including student-led conferences
- Portfolios or exhibits of student work
- Homework hotlines
- School or class web pages
- Home visits

Individual learning expectation (ILE) Personal average score.

Halo effect The tendency for a general impression of a person to influence our perception of any aspect of that person.

Here is an example of a "Good News Call" that makes use of cell phone technology taken from Guskey and Bailey (2001). An elementary-school principal carries her phone with her as she walks through the hallways, visits the cafeteria, supervises the playground, and observes teachers' classes. When she sees a student performing well in class, assisting a classmate, or helping to improve the school, she immediately calls that student's parent or guardian on her phone and announces, "Hello, this is Ms. Johnson, the principal at Judd Elementary School. I just saw Tonya. . . ." After explaining what she observed and complimenting the child, she hands the phone to the child so that he or she can talk briefly with the parent or guardian. Everyone leaves with a big smile. One caution—if a family member didn't answer, it would be a bad idea to leave a call back message because the message recipients might fear that their children were sick or injured.

When asked about calls to parents concerning student problems, Ms. Johnson explains, "Those I save for after school. Often, I have to think more carefully about what I'm going to say and what strategies I'm going to recommend. When I see a child doing something wonderful, however, I want to let the parents know about that right away. And I never have to weigh my words. Plus, I think it means more to the child."

The principal's phone calls have completely altered the culture of this school. Parent involvement and participation in school events is at an all-time high, and their regard for Ms. Johnson and the school staff is exceptionally positive. It's a small thing, but it has made a big difference.

Conferences with parents are often expected of teachers in elementary school and can be equally important in junior high and high school. Clearly, the more skilled teachers are at communicating, the more effective they will be at conducting these conferences. Listening and problem-solving skills such as those discussed in Chapter 12 can be particularly important. When you are dealing with parents or students who are angry or upset, make sure you really hear the concerns of the participants, not just their words. The atmosphere should be friendly and unrushed. Any observations about the student should be as factual as possible, based on observation or information from assignments. Infor-

Family and Community Partnerships

Guidelines: Conferences

Plan ahead. What are your goals?

EXAMPLES

Problem solving?
Sharing test results?
Asking questions that you want answered?
Providing information you want to share?
Describing your "next steps" in the classroom?
Making suggestions for use at home?

Begin and end with a positive statement.

EXAMPLES

"Jacob has a great sense of humor."
"Giselle really enjoys materials that deal with animals."
"Yesim is sympathetic when somebody has a problem."
"Ashanti should be a big help in the social studies play that her group is developing."

Listen actively.

EXAMPLES

Empathize with the parents. Accept their feelings.
"You seem to feel frustrated when Lee doesn't listen."

Establish a partnership.

EXAMPLES

Ask parents to follow through on class goals at home: "If you ask to see the homework checklist and go over it at home with Iris, I'll review it and chart her progress at school."

Plan follow-up contacts.

EXAMPLES

Write notes or make phone calls to share successes.
Keep parents informed *before* problems develop.

For some dos and don'ts of conferences, see **http://www.nysut.org/newmember/survival_conferences.html**

Source: From *The Successful Classroom: Management Strategies for Regular and Special Education Teachers* (p. 181), by D. P. Fromberg & M. Driscoll. Published by Teachers College, Columbia University. Reprinted by permission of the publisher. All rights reserved.

TABLE 15.8

Possible Grading Accommodations for Students with Special Needs

What can you do to make grading more appropriate for students with special needs? Here are some possibilities.

Adaptation	Example
Change Grading Criteria	
Vary grading weights assigned to different activities or products.	Increase credit for participation in classroom group activities and decrease credit for essay examinations.
Grade on improvement by assigning extra points.	Change a *C* to a *B* if the student's total points have increased significantly from the previous marking period.
Modify or individualize curriculum expectations.	Indicate in the IEP that the student will work on subtraction while the other students work on division.
Use contracts and modified course requirements for quality, quantity, and timelines.	State in the contract that student will receive a *B* for completing all assignments at 80% quantity, and timelines, accuracy, attending all classes, and completing one extra-credit report.
Provide Supplemental Information	
Add written comments to clarify details about the criteria used.	Write on the report card that the student's grade reflects performance on IEP objectives and not on the regular classroom curriculum.
Add information from student activity log.	Note that while the student's grade was the same this marking period, daily records show the student completed math assignments with less teacher assistance.
Add information about effort, progress, and achievement from portfolios or performance-based assignments.	State that the student's written language showed an increase in word variety, sentence length, and quality of ideas.
Use Other Grading Options	
Use checklists of skills and show the number or percentage of objectives met.	Attach a checklist to the report card indicating that during the marking period, the student mastered addition facts, two-digit addition with regrouping, and counting change to one dollar.
Use pass/fail grades.	Students receive a "pass" for completing 80% of daily work with at least 70% accuracy, and attending 90% of class sessions.

Source: From *Developing Grading and Reporting Systems for Student Learning* (p. 118) by T. R. Guskey & J. M. Bailey. Copyright © 2001. Reprinted by permission of Corwin Press, Inc.

mation gained from a student or a parent should be kept confidential. The *Family and Community Partnerships Guidelines* offer some helpful ideas for planning and conducting conferences.

Reaching Every Student: Accommodations in Grading

In assigning and reporting grades, how do you make accommodations for students with special needs? Table 15.8 gives some options.

It may be up to you as the teacher to decide how to calculate the grades of students with special needs and students whose first language is not English, but be sure to check whether there are school or district policies already in place. Also, some schools now offer families a choice of the languages for the report card itself. The form is the same; just the language is different (Guskey & Bailey, 2001).

Connect and **Extend** to the **Research**

Munk, D. D., & Bursuck, W. D. (2001). Preliminary findings on personalized grading plans for middle school students with learning disabilities. *Exceptional Children, 67*, 211–234.

Connect and **Extend** to Your **Teaching/Portfolio**

Add Table 15.2, "Key Points to Consider in Judging Textbook Tests," Table 15.4, "Characteristics of Authentic Tests," and Table 15.8, "Possible Grading Accommodations for Students with Special Needs" to your Teaching Resources file.

Diversity and Convergences in Classroom Assessment

Classroom assessment should, first and foremost, support student learning. But stereotypes and biases can interfere with assessment.

Diversity

Several studies have found that teachers may hold lower expectations for ethnic minority students and these biases can influence teaching and assessment (Banks, 2005). For example, Lipman (1997) found that teachers of ethnically diverse classes are less innovative and more traditional in their instruction. These lower expectations can show up in giving higher grades to students for lower-quality work. A national study of students in 1st, 3rd, and 7th grades compared students' grades to their standardized test scores. A grade of "A" in a high-poverty school was equivalent to a grade of "C" in a low-poverty school (Puma et al, 1997). These two kinds of schools differed in standards and curriculum, as well as expectations (McClure, 2005).

Biases can be subtle. For example, in the tests that you write, will you incorporate language and experiences that are familiar to your students? James Popham (2005a), an expert in assessment, described his first teaching job in a rural high school on an eastern Oregon town with a population of 1,500:

> I had grown up in a fairly large city and had no knowledge about farming or ranching. To me, a "range" was a kitchen appliance on which one cooked meals. In retrospect, I am certain that many of my classroom test items contained "city" content that might have confused my students. I'll bet anything that many of my early test items unfairly penalized some of the boys and girls who had rarely, if ever, left their farms or ranches to visit more metropolitan areas. (p. 86)

Think of the range of differences in experiences of your students if they are from other countries or speak other languages. The following *Guidelines*, developed by several professional organizations, could guide your thinking about classroom assessment (Banks, 2005, p. 82).

Convergences

Connect and **Extend** to Your **Teaching/Portfolio**

Develop a grading plan for the grade level you want to teach and add it to your Portfolio.

Quality teaching and quality assessment share the same basic principles and these principles hold for all students. Carol Tomlinson (2005b, pp. 265–266) suggests that good instruction and good grading both depend on a teacher who:

- Is aware of and responds to student differences.
- Specifies clear learning outcomes.
- Uses pretests and formative assessments to monitor student progress toward learning goals.
- Adapts instruction in a variety of ways to ensure, as much as possible, that each student continues to progress.
- Makes sure students know the criteria for success on summative assessments that are tightly aligned to the stated learning goals.
- Provides varied forms of assessment to ensure that students have an unobstructed opportunity to express what they have learned.

Connect and **Extend** to Your **Teaching/Portfolio**

Add some ideas for parent involvement from this chapter to your Portfolio.

An important federal law, the Buckley Amendment, may affect you as a teacher. Also called the Family Educational Rights and Privacy Act of 1974 and the Educational Amendments Act of 1974, this law states that all educational agencies must make test results and any other information in students' records available to the students and/or their parents. If the records contain information students or parents believe is incorrect, they can challenge such entries and have the information removed if they win the challenge. This means that the information in a student's records must be based on firm, defensible evidence. Tests must be valid and reliable. Your grades must be justified by thorough assessment and observation. Comments and anecdotes about students must be accurate and fair.

Guidelines: Standards for Educational and Psychological Testing

Assessments should be as fair as possible for students from diverse gender, race, or ethnic backgrounds.

EXAMPLES

1. Avoid any slang expressions that might be offensive.
2. Eliminate items with stereotypes that might offend such as Eurocentric views of history that assume Columbus "discovered" America—there were many people ahead of him who discovered and lived in America.

Assessments should relate only to the instruction given and not to background knowledge that might penalize students from diverse backgrounds.

EXAMPLES

1. Review standardized and classroom assessments to see if some questions require knowledge not available to certain groups, such as questions about sports (may penalize females), travel (may penalize students from low-income families), or driving vacations (may penalize students from families without cars).
2. Make sure certain answers don't favor particular social or political ideas.

Don't let assessments become a measure of language proficiency unless language is the focus of the test.

EXAMPLES

1. Make special accommodations for English Language Learners such as extra time or the use of dictionaries.
2. Make sure math tests are not really reading proficiency tests.

Source: Adapted from Banks, S. R. (2005). *Classroom assessment: Issues and practice.* Boston: Allyn & Bacon, p. 82.

SUMMARY TABLE

Formative and Summative Assessment (pp. 554–555)

What are two kinds of classroom assessment? In the classroom, assessment may be formative (ungraded, diagnostic) or summative (graded). Formative assessment helps form instruction, and summative assessment summarizes students' accomplishments.

Formative assessment Ungraded testing used before or during instruction to aid in planning and diagnosis.

Pretest Formative test for assessing students' knowledge, readiness, and abilities.

Diagnostic test Formative test to determine students' areas of weakness.

Summative assessment Testing that follows instruction and assesses achievement.

Getting the Most from Traditional Assessment (pp. 555–560)

How should teachers plan for assessment? Learning is supported by frequent testing using cumulative questions that ask students to apply and integrate knowledge. With the goals of assessment in mind, teachers are in a better position to design their own tests or evaluate the tests provided by textbook publishers.

Describe two kinds of traditional testing. Two traditional formats for testing are the objective test and the essay test. Objective tests, which can include multiple-choice, true/false, fill-in, and matching items, should be written with specific guidelines in mind. Writing and scoring essay questions requires careful planning, in addition to criteria to discourage bias in scoring.

Objective testing Multiple-choice, matching, true/false, short-answer, and fill-in tests; scoring answers does not require interpretation.

Stem The question part of a multiple-choice item.

Distractors Wrong answers offered as choices in a multiple-choice item.

Alternatives to Traditional Assessments (pp. 561–570)

What is authentic assessment? Critics of traditional testing believe that teachers should use authentic tests and other authentic assessment procedures. Authentic assessment requires students to perform tasks and solve problems that are similar to the real-life performances that will be expected of them outside of school.

Describe portfolios and exhibitions. Portfolios and exhibitions are two examples of authentic assessment. A portfolio is a collection of the student's work, sometimes chosen to represent growth or improvement or sometimes featuring "best work." Exhibitions are public performances of the student's understandings. With portfolios and exhibitions, there is an emphasis on performing real-life tasks in meaningful contexts.

What are the issues of reliability, validity, and equity with portfolios and performance assessment? Using authentic assessments does not guarantee reliability, validity, and equity (absence of bias). Using rubrics is one way to make assessment more reliable and valid. But the results from assessment based on rubrics may not predict performance on related tasks. Also, rater bias based on the appearance, speech, or behavior of minority-group students or a lack of resources may place minority-group students at a disadvantage in performance assessments or projects.

Authentic assessments Assessment procedures that test skills and abilities as they would be applied in real-life situations.

Performance assessments Any form of assessment that requires students to carry out an activity or produce a product in order to demonstrate learning.

Portfolio A collection of the student's work in an area, showing growth, self-reflection, and achievement.

Exhibition A performance test or demonstration of learning that is public and usually takes an extended time to prepare.

Scoring rubrics Rules that are used to determine the quality of a student performance.

Informal assessments Ungraded (formative) assessments that gather information from multiple sources to help teachers make decisions.

Effects of Grading on Students (pp. 570–574)

How can failure support learning? Students need experience in coping with failure, so standards must be high enough to encourage effort. Occasional failure can be positive if appropriate feedback is provided. Students who never learn how to cope with failure and still persist in learning may give up quickly when their first efforts are unsuccessful.

Which is better, "social promotion" or being "held back"? Simply retaining or promoting a student who is having difficulty will not guarantee that the student will learn. Unless the student is very young or emotionally immature compared to others in the class, the best approach may be to promote, but provide extra support such as tutoring or summer school sessions. Differentiated instruction could prevent problems.

Can feedback, including grades, promote learning and motivation? Written or oral feedback that includes specific comments on errors or faulty strategies, but that balances this criticism with suggestions about how to improve, along with comments on the positive aspects of the work, increases learning. Grades can encourage students' motivation to learn if they are tied to meaningful learning.

Grading and Reporting: Nuts and Bolts (pp. 574–579)

Describe two kinds of grading. Grading can be either criterion-referenced or norm-referenced. Criterion-referenced report cards usually indicate how well the individual student has met each of several objectives. One popular norm-referenced system is grading on the curve, based on a ranking of students in relation to the average performance level. This is not recommended.

What is the point system? Tests and papers are often scored on a point system. Many schools use percentage grading systems, but the difficulty of the tests and the scoring criteria often influence the results. The difference between a B and a C may only be a matter of one or two points on paper, but the effect of the difference can be large for a student.

Describe some alternatives to traditional grading. Alternatives to traditional grading are the contract and individual learning expectation (ILE). Whatever system you use, you will have to decide whether you want to grade on effort, improvement, or some combination and whether you want to limit the number of good grades available.

What are some sources of bias in grading? Many factors besides quality of work can influence grades: the teacher's beliefs about the student's ability or effort or the student's general classroom behavior, for example. There are many appropriate accommodations that teachers can make to insure that grading is fair.

Criterion-referenced grading Assessment of each student's mastery of course objectives.

Norm-referenced grading Assessment of students' achievement in relation to one another.

Grading on the curve Norm-referenced grading that compares students' performance to an average level.

Percentage grading System of converting class performances to percentage scores and assigning grades based on predetermined cutoff points.

Contract system System in which each student works for a particular grade according to agreed-upon standards.

Revise option In a contract system, the chance to revise and improve work.

Halo effect The tendency for a general impression of a person to influence our perception of any aspect of that person.

Beyond Grading: Communication with Families (pp. 579–581)

How can communications with families support learning? Not every communication from the teacher needs to be tied to a grade. Communication with students and parents can be important in helping a teacher understand students and present effective instruction by creating a consistent learning environment. Students and parents have a legal right to see all the information in the students' records, so the contents of files must be appropriate, accurate, and supported by evidence.

Teachers' Casebook: Connections to PRAXIS II™

Just as you have learned that there has been much research-based innovation when it comes to instruction, there has been much research-based innovation when it comes to classroom assessment. These new directions promise to add new understandings to what and how your students are learning.

What Would They Do?

Here is how some practicing teachers responded to the teaching situation presented at the beginning of this chapter about setting up a system to give letter grades.

Katie Churchill **Third Grade Teacher,**

Oriole Parke Elementary School, Chicago, Illinois

I would use a combination of assessment tools to evaluate my students. Using a rubric that students and parents alike are familiar with provides an easy-to-follow-and-understand grading system. The rubric needs to remain in a focal area in the classroom as a constant reminder to the students of what their expectations are.

By differentiating instruction consistently to cover all learning styles and modalities, the students would hopefully become more involved and invested in their own learning and, as a result, produce better quality work and exceed expectations.

Several factors would play a part in obtaining a particular letter grade. The letter grade would be earned through a combination of group work, completing objectives, and following the rubric guidelines for quality work.

Madya Ayala **High School Teacher of Preperatoria Eugenio Garza Lagüera,** *Campus Garza Sada, Monterrey, N. L. Mexico*

I think it is important to assess a cross-section of student work. First, portfolios can be a useful way to gather various types of work throughout the year. Using a portfolio, a teacher can then attach a letter grade to student progress and achievement. It is important to grade children not only on progress, but also on their understanding of material. I would use meaningful, written assessments to test for retention and understanding of my students' knowledge. Finally, I would grade various projects and experiments so that the students who are better project-based learners will be graded fairly. I also like the idea of using a rubric system to grade students on writing or projects. Under a rubric system, a teacher allocates a certain number of points to each content area. It is then easy to attach a letter grade based on the number of points received.

Katie Piel **Kindergarten–Sixth Grade Teacher,**

West Park School, Moscow, Idaho

Students should be given the latitude to express achievement in different ways like group projects, daily class work, tests, and individual projects. All students would be held accountable for demonstrating their own learning. With each teacher grading on a different standard, the teachers must also take on the responsibility of collaborating with their peers. Communicating to other teachers the skills a student can be expected to bring with him or her to the next level is crucial.

Aimee Fredette **Second Grade Teacher,**

Fisher Elementary School, Walpole, Massachusetts

I believe that students are not all smart in the same ways. I give the students a variety of ways to demonstrate their knowledge. I also focus on the students' ability to take their knowledge and integrate it into other subject areas across the curriculum.

I use a student portfolio for each child, compiled throughout the year and used to show growth and development. Each time I correct papers I choose a couple of pieces of work that each child has done. I put these papers in the portfolio folder. I try to choose a variety of work, not necessarily their "prize work." At the end of the year the children receive the entire folder to keep.

Allan Osborne **Assistant Principal,**

Snug Harbor Community School, Quincy, Massachusetts

Any grading system should consider a student's progress and effort. Grading systems also should be individualized to account for a student's unique strengths and weaknesses. Thus, a mainstreamed special education student should not be held to the same expectations as a gifted student.

The most critical aspect of any successful grading system is that it is fair. Fairness dictates that students and their parents be given information in advance about class requirements and expectations, along with a description of grading criteria. A system that is fair can be easily justified. It is also important to keep accurate and detailed records of student progress. In addition to recording grades on tests, quizzes, and projects, anecdotal records describing a student's typical performance should be kept. These records can be valuable if a report card grade is questioned.

Although group assignments can be an important learning experience, I would be reluctant to place too much emphasis on a group project grade. As we all know, each member of the group does not participate equally, and thus, a group grade does not reflect the contribution of each individual member.

Handbook for Teaching and Lifelong Learning

Section 1
Creating a PRAXIS II™/Licensure Examination Study Guide

You probably will have to take a licensure examination in order to become a teacher in your state. In almost 40 states the Praxis II™ test is the required licensure examination. This section highlights the concepts from each chapter that may be on your licensure test. In the Career Center Section of MyLabSchool, you will find more help with the PRAXIS II™ examination, including a guide to the PRAXIS II™, video cases, practice test questions, and relevant websites. Also, refer to the *Section 2* of this Handbook for detailed correlations to PRAXIS II™ exam topics and INTASC Standards.

Chapter 1

Developing relationships with professionals: Until you become a teacher, it will be difficult to establish a working relationship with other practitioners. However, you might find this site beneficial: K–12 Professional Circle (http://nces.ed.gov/practitioners/teachers.asp).

Keeping current with educational issues: Education Week (http://www.edweek.org/) will keep you up to date about innovations in teaching, policy initiatives, and changes in public laws related to education. These issues are often highly complex. The use of critical thinking skills is essential when making judgments about the information you will encounter in this type of publication.

Chapter 2

Possible licensure examination topics include:

Cognition

For Piagetian and Vygotskian theories of development, you should understand:

- Basic assumptions of each
- How students build their unique knowledge bases
- How they acquire skills
- Important terms and concepts related to each
- The key steps, mechanisms, or milestones related to each theory
- The limitations of each theory

Language

For the development of language, you should understand:

- Basic assumptions of major theories
- The major accomplishments of language development of school-age children
- The relationship between language and literacy
- Basic steps that teachers can take to enhance literacy among their students

Chapter 3

Understand the major concepts and progressions related to:

- Erikson's theory of psychosocial development
- Piaget's and Kohlberg's perspectives on moral development
- Gilligan's theory of caring

Design or choose strategies that:

- support optimal social and emotional development of students
- help students cope with major life transitions and challenges to safety, physical, and mental health
- help students build a sense of self-concept, self-esteem, and self-identity (including racial identity)

Recognize signs or behaviors that indicate sexual abuse or child abuse

Chapter 4

Explain the effects of legislation on public education:

- Americans with Disabilities Act
- Individuals with Disabilities Education Improvement Act
- Section 504

- Individualized Education Plans
- Inclusion, Mainstreaming, and Least Restrictive Environment

Understand views of intelligence and describe its measurement:

- Types of intelligence tests and their uses
- Multiple intelligences
- Interpreting intelligence scores
- Modifications to testing

Accommodate the needs of students with exceptionalities:

- Attention-Deficit Hyperactivity Disorder
- Visual, speech, and physical difficulties
- Learning disabilities
- Intellectual disabilities/mental retardation

Chapter 5

Recognize the influences that ethnicity, socioeconomic status, and community values may have on:

- Student–teacher relationships/parent–teacher relationships
- Student learning styles
- Academic achievement
- Attitudes, self-esteem, and expectations for success
- Opportunities for quality educational experiences

Understand the influences that gender may have on:

- Teachers' attention to students
- Differences in mental abilities

Devise strategies that:

- Eliminate sexist teaching practices
- Promote positive school–home relationships
- Support English acquisition in non-English speaking students
- Reduce or eliminate racial and ethnic stereotypes and biases

Chapter 6

Understand the basic assumptions and contributions of these behaviorists:

- Pavlov
- Skinner
- Bandura

Determine appropriate behavioral techniques to:

- Establish efficient classroom routines and procedures
- Foster appropriate classroom conduct
- Help students monitor and regulate learning

Understand basic processes of operant conditioning and their roles in learning, including:

- Antecedents and consequences
- Types of reinforcement and reinforcement schedules
- Punishment
- Shaping
- Observational learning

Chapter 7

Understand how memory and recall are affected by:

- The limitations, capacities, and capabilities of the various structures of human memory (e.g., memory stores)
- The manner in which humans process information
- Prior knowledge of a topic
- Metacognitive/executive control processes

Explain how students and teachers can enhance learning through the use of:

- Elaboration and mnemonic devices
- Organized presentations
- Study tools that organize information (e.g., outlines, concept maps)
- Meaningful learning and instructional activities

Chapter 8

Focus on each of these major topics:

- Discovery learning and expository teaching
  - Basic assumptions
  - Inductive reasoning/deductive reasoning
  - Appropriate uses/principles of implementation
- Problem solving
  - General problem-solving strategies/heuristics and algorithms
  - The value of problem representation
  - Factors that impede problem solving
- Learning strategies
  - Basic principles of teaching these strategies
  - Cognitive processes involved in various strategies
  - Appropriate uses of different strategies
- Transfer of learning
  - Types of transfer/promoting transfer

Chapter 9

Explain the advantages and appropriate uses of major student-centered approaches to learning and instruction:

- Self-regulated learning
- Inquiry method
- Problem-based learning
- Instructional conversations
- Cognitive apprenticeships

Understand important concepts related to student-centered models of instruction:

- Situated learning

- Critical thinking/Culture of thinking
- Complex learning environments
- Authentic tasks
- Multiple representations of content

Chapter 10

Describe the theoretical foundations of the major approaches to motivation.

- Identify and define important terms related to motivation.
- Use your knowledge of motivation to:
  - — identify situations and conditions that can enhance or diminish student motivation to learn.
  - — design strategies to support individual and group work in the classroom.
  - — implement practices that help students become self-motivated.

Chapter 11

Focus on these major topics:

- The role of the school in the community
- Community environments and conditions that affect students' lives and learning
- Events outside the immediate school or community environment that may influence student behavior
- Cooperative learning

Chapter 12

Understand principles of classroom management that promote positive relationships by:

- Establishing daily procedures and routines
- Responding effectively to minor student misbehavior
- Implementing reasonable rules, penalties, and rewards
- Keeping students actively engaged in purposeful learning

Diagnose problems and prevent or reduce inappropriate behaviors by:

- Communicating with students and parents
- Addressing misbehaviors in the least intrusive way possible
- Confronting disruptive behaviors in an effective, efficient manner

Chapter 13

Develop plans for instruction and consider:

- The role of objectives in instruction
- Writing behavioral and cognitive objectives
- The use of educational taxonomies to design effective objectives
- The role of independent practice (i.e., seatwork and homework)

Understand the basic principles of teacher-centered and student-centered forms of instruction, including:

- Appropriate uses and limitations
- The role of the teacher
- Effective questioning techniques
- Whole group discussions
- Recitation
- Thematic/interdisciplinary instruction

Chapter 14

Understand the major concepts related to measurement theory, including:

- Norming samples
- Percentile rank, grade-equivalent scores, stanine scores, *T* and *z* scores
- Standard deviation, mean, mode, median, standard error of measurement, and confidence intervals
- Reliability and validity

Describe the characteristics and purposes of major types of tests:

- Criterion-referenced and norm-referenced tests
- Achievement, aptitude, and diagnostic tests

Explain the major issues related to concerns about standardized testing, including:

- High-stakes testing
- Bias in testing
- Test-taking programs

Chapter 15

Understand major concepts related to classroom assessment and grading:

- Formative and summative assessment
- Reliability and validity
- Criterion-referenced and norm-referenced grading

Describe the characteristics, uses, and limitations of major assessment techniques, including:

- Multiple-choice items
- Essays
- Portfolios
- Exhibitions

Design a scoring rubric for an authentic learning task that possesses:

- Validity
- Reliability
- Generalizability
- Equity

In the Career Center Section of MyLabSchool, you will find more help with the PRAXIS II™ examination including a guide to the PRAXIS II™, video cases, practice test questions, and relevant websites.

Section 2
Standards and Licensure: PRAXIS II™ and INTASC

James B. O'Kelly, Ed.D.
Rutgers University and Sayreville Public Schools

Each state in the country has its own set of licensure requirements that new teachers must meet in order to work in the classroom. An increasing number of states are basing their requirements on standards developed by INTASC (Interstate New Teacher Assessment and Support Consortium). These standards are based on ten principles of effective teaching that INTASC has identified as essential for optimal student learning. Many states assess new teachers' knowledge of those principles through the use of tests from the PRAXIS II™ series published by the Educational Testing Service. Within the PRAXIS II™ series are three *Principles of Learning and Teaching* (PLT) tests, one each for grades K–6, 5–9, and 7–12. Each PLT test assesses students' knowledge of educational psychology and its application in the classroom. (Also, INTASC is presently developing its own *Test for Teaching Knowledge.* INTASC reports that this test will focus on "child development, theories of teaching and learning, diagnostic skills, the role of student background in the learning process, and other foundational knowledge and skills essential to the profession of teaching.")

This section of the Handbook is designed to help you study for your PLT test and meet the Knowledge standards for each of INTASC's ten principles of effective teaching. The left-hand column of the table lists the topics assessed in a PLT test. The right-hand column contains INTASC's Knowledge standards. In the center column, you will find the chapters, sections, and pages that correspond to the PLT tests and INTASC standards. MyLabSchool (www.mylabschool.com) includes additional features to assist you with your efforts to meet licensure requirements, including a set of Web links to sites that address the demands of the PLT test and INTASC standards.

I suggest that you carefully develop a plan to meet these requirements. A major step would be to familiarize yourself with the challenges of the PRAXIS II™ series, especially the PLT tests, and to understand the rationale and features of the INTASC standards. These Websites will help you to accomplish that goal:

- The PRAXIS™ Series: Professional Assessments for Beginning Teachers™ (**www.ets.org/praxis**)
- PRAXIS™ test requirements for specific states (**www.ets.org/praxis/prxstate.html**)
- Test at a Glance
  - PLT: Early Childhood **http://www.ets.org/Media/Tests/PRAXIS/pdf/0521.pdf**
  - PLT: Grades K–6 **http://www.ets.org/Media/Tests/PRAXIS/pdf/0522.pdf**
  - PLT: Grades 5–9 **http://www.ets.org/Media/Tests/PRAXIS/pdf/0523.pdf**
  - PLT: Grades 7–12 **http://www.ets.org/Media/Tests/PRAXIS/pdf/0524.pdf**
- INTASC Standards for New Teacher Licensure (**www.ccsso.org/intascst.html**)

MyLabSchool provides direct links to these and many other useful Websites, as well as additional information about how this textbook correlates with information relevant to PRAXIS II™ and INTASC.

PRAXIS™ Topics	Woolfolk Text Connections	INTASC Principles
I. Students as Learners		
A. Student Development and the Learning Process 1. Theoretical foundations about how learning occurs: how students construct knowledge, acquire skills, and develop habits of mind	*Chapters 2, 6–11* (entire chapters)	2A. The teacher understands how learning occurs—how students construct knowledge, acquire skills, and develop habits of mind—and knows how to use instructional strategies that promote student learning.
■ Examples of important theorists:		
• Jean Piaget:	*Chapter 2/* Piaget's Theory of Cognitive Development (pp. 26–38)	
• Lev Vygotsky	*Chapter 2/* Vygotsky's Sociocultural Perspective (pp. 39–45)	
• Howard Gardner	*Chapter 4/* Multiple Intelligences (pp. 113–116)	
• Robert Sternberg	*Chapter 4/* Intelligence as a Process (pp. 117–118)	
• Albert Bandura	*Chapter 6/* Behavioral and Social Learning Views (pp. 229–234)	
• Urie Bronfenbrenner	*Chapter 3/* The Social Context for Development (pp. 72–84)	
■ Important terms that relate to learning theory:		
• Adaptation	*Chapter 2/* Basic Tendencies in Thinking (pp. 28–29)	
• Conservation	*Chapter 2/* Basic Tendencies in Thinking (pp. 28–29)	
• Constructivism	*Chapter 2/* Implications of Piaget's and Vygotsky's Theories for Teachers (pp. 46–51) *Chapter 9/* Constructivist Views of Learning (pp. 344–346)	
• Equilibration	*Chapter 2/* Basic Tendencies in Thinking (pp. 28–29)	
• Co-constructed process	*Chapter 2/* The Social Sources of Individual Thinking (pp. 39–41)	
• Private speech	*Chapter 2/* The Role of Language and Private Speech (pp. 42–44)	
• Scaffolding	*Chapter 2/* Assisted Learning (pp. 48–49); *Guidelines:* Applying Vygotsky's Ideas in Teaching (p. 50) *Chapter 9/* Dialogue and Instructional Conversations (pp. 355–356); Cognitive Apprenticeships (pp. 356–358)	
• Zone of proximal development	*Chapter 2/* The Zone of Proximal Development (p. 44) *Chapter 9/* Dialogue and Instructional Conversations (pp. 355–356)	

PRAXIS™ Topics	Woolfolk Text Connections	INTASC Principles
• Learning	*Chapter 6/* Understanding Learning (pp. 206–208) *Chapter 7/* Comparing Cognitive and Behavioral Views (pp. 248–249) *Chapter 9/* Cognitive and Social Constructivism (pp. 343–350) *Chapter 10/*Motivation in Learning and Teaching (pp. 371–407) *Chapter 11/*Engaged Learning: Cooperation and Community (pp. 413–438)	
• Knowledge	*Chapter 2/* The Social Sources of Individual Thinking (pp. 39–41); Activity and Constructing Knowledge (pp. 46–47) *Chapter 7/* The Importance of Knowledge in Learning (pp. 249–250); Becoming Knowledgeable: Some Basic Principles (pp. 269–276) *Chapter 9/* How Is Knowledge Constructed? (pp. 346–347); Knowledge: Situated or General? (pp. 347–348)	
• Memory	*Chapter 7/* Sensory Memory (pp. 250–253); Working Memory (pp. 253–257); Long-Term Memory (pp. 257–259)	
• Schemas	*Chapter 7/* Schemas (pp. 260–262)	
• Transfer	*Chapter 8/* Defining Transfer (p. 319); A Contemporary View of Transfer (p. 319)	
2. Human development in the physical, social, emotional, moral, and cognitive domains		2C. The teacher is aware of expected developmental progressions and ranges of individual variation within each domain (physical, social, emotional, moral, and cognitive), can identify levels of readiness in learning, and understands how development in any one domain may affect performance in others.
■ Contributions of important theorists:		
• Jean Piaget	*Chapter 2/* Piaget's Theory of Cognitive Development (pp. 26–28)	
• Lev Vygotsky	*Chapter 2/* Vygotsky's Sociocultural Perspective (pp. 39–45)	
• Erik Erikson	*Chapter 3/* Erikson: Stages of Individual Development (pp. 67–72)	
• Lawrence Kohlberg	*Chapter 3/* Kohlberg's Theories of Moral Development (pp. 95–96)	
• Carol Gilligan	*Chapter 3/* Gender Differences: The Morality of Caring (p. 97)	
■ Major progressions in each developmental domain and the ranges of individual variation within each domain	*Chapter 2/* Four Stages of Cognitive Development (pp. 29–30); Some Limitations of Piaget's Theory (p. 38); Information Processing and Neo-Piagetian Views of Cognitive Development (pp. 36–37); The Social Sources of Individual Thinking (pp. 39–41); The Development of Language (pp. 51–55) *Chapter 3/* Physical Development (pp. 64–66); The Preschool Years (p. 64); The Elementary School Years (p. 64); Adolescence (pp. 65–66); The Brain and Adolescent Development (p. 66); Emotional and Moral Development (pp. 92–102)	2B. The teacher understands that students' physical, social, emotional, moral and cognitive development influence learning and knows how to address these factors when making instructional decisions.

PRAXIS™ Topics	Woolfolk Text Connections	INTASC Principles
Impact of students' physical, social, emotional, moral, and cognitive development on their learning and how to address these factors when making decisions	*Chapter 2/* Four Stages of Cognitive Development (pp. 29–36); Some Limitations of Piaget's Theory (p. 38); *Guidelines*: Teaching the Preoperational Child (p. 32); *Guidelines*: Teaching the Concrete-Operational Child (p. 34); *Guidelines*: Helping Students to Use Formal Operations (p. 37); The Social Sources of Individual Thinking (pp. 39–41); The Development of Language (pp. 51–55); Assisted Learning (pp. 48–49); The Zone of Proximal Development (p. 44); *Chapter 3/* Physical Development (pp. 64–66); The Preschool Years: Trust, Autonomy, and Initiative (p. 68); Elementary and Middle School Years: Industry versus Inferiority (pp. 69–70); Adolescence: The Search for Identity (pp. 70–71); Kohlberg's Theories of Moral Development (pp. 95–96);Self-Concept and Self-Esteem (pp. 85–86); School Life and Self-Esteem (p. 87); Diversity and Perception of Self (pp. 89–90); Theory of Mind and Intention (pp. 93–94); Moral Judgment, Social Conventions, and Personal Choices (pp. 97–99) *Chapter 12/* Maintaining a Good Environment for Learning (pp. 458–466)	
How development in one domain, such as physical, may affect performance in another domain, such as social	*Chapter 2/* General Principles of Development (p. 22); The Brain and Cognitive Development (pp. 22–26); Influences on Development (p. 27) *Chapter 3/* Physical Development (pp. 64–66); *Guidelines*: Supporting Personal and Moral Development (p. 100)	
B. Students as Diverse Learners 1. Differences in the ways students learn and perform	*Chapter 4/* Learner Differences (entire chapter) *Chapter 5/* Culture and Diversity (entire chapter) *Diversity and Convergences* sections (all chapters)	3A. The teacher understands and can identify differences in approaches to learning and performance, including different learning styles, multiple intelligences, and performance modes, and can design instruction that uses students' strengths as the basis for growth.
• Learning styles	*Chapter 4/* Learning Styles (pp. 124–127); Visual/Verbal Distinctions (p. 126) *Chapter 5/* Diversity in Learning (pp. 195–198)	
• Multiple intelligences	*Chapter 4/* Multiple Intelligences (pp. 113–116)	
• Performance modes — Concrete operational thinking	*Chapter 2/* Later Elementary to the Middle School Years: The Concrete-Operational Stage (pp. 32–34); *Guidelines*: Teaching the Concrete-Operational Child (p. 34) *Chapter 4/* Learning Styles (pp. 124–127)	
— Visual and aural learners	*Chapter 4/* Students with Learning Disabilities (pp. 131–134); Visual/Verbal Distinctions (p. 126)	

PRAXIS™ Topics	Woolfolk Text Connections	INTASC Principles
• Gender differences	*Chapter 3/* Diversity and Perception of Self (pp. 89–90); Gender Differences: The Morality of Caring (p. 97) *Chapter 5/*Girls and Boys: Differences in the Classroom (pp. 176–182); *Guidelines*: Avoiding Sexism in Teaching (p. 182)	
• Cultural expectations and styles	*Chapter 5/* Today's Diverse Classrooms (pp. 162–164); Ethnic and Racial Differences (pp. 168–176); *Guidelines*: Culturally Relevant Teaching (p. 199) *Chapter 13/* Teacher Expectations (pp. 496–500)	
2. Areas of exceptionality in students' learning	*Chapter 4/* Learner Differences (Full chapter)	3B. The teacher knows about areas of exceptionality in learning—including learning disabilities, visual and perceptual difficulties, and special physical or mental challenges.
• Special physical or sensory challenges	*Chapter 4/* Students with Communication Disorders (pp. 136–139); Students with Health Impairments (pp. 145–146); Students Who Are Deaf (pp. 146–147); Students with Vision Impairments (p. 147)	
• Learning disabilities	*Chapter 4/* Students with Learning Disabilities (pp. 131–134); Individualized Education Programs (p. 127); Section 504 (pp. 129–130)	
• ADHD	*Chapter 4/* Students with Hyperactivity and Attention Disorders (pp. 134–136)	
• Functional and mental retardation	*Chapter 4/* Students with Intellectual Disabilities (pp. 139–140); *Guidelines*: Teaching Students with Below-Average Intelligence (p. 141)	
3. Legislation and institutional responsibilities relating to exceptional students • Americans with Disabilities Act (ADA), Individuals with Disabilities Education Act (IDEA); Section 504 Protections for Students	*Chapter 4/* Individual Differences and the Law (pp. 127–130); Section 504 (pp. 129–130)	10C. The teacher understands and implements laws related to students' rights and teacher responsibilities (e.g., for equal education, appropriate education for handicapped students, confidentiality, privacy, appropriate treatment of students, reporting in situations related to possible child abuse).
• Inclusion, mainstreaming, and "least restrictive environment"	*Chapter 4/* Individual Differences and the Law (pp. 127–130); Least Restrictive Environment (pp. 128–129) *Chapter 13/*Reaching Every Student: Effective Teaching in Inclusive Classrooms (pp. 508–511)	
4. Approaches for accommodating various learning styles, intelligences, or exceptionalities • Differentiated instruction	*Chapter 4/* Learner Differences; focus on: Multiple Intelligences Go to School (pp. 115–116); Ability Differences and Teaching (pp. 121–124); Teaching Gifted Students (pp. 151–153); Individual Differences and the Law (pp. 127–130); Common Challenges (pp. 130–145) *Chapter 13/* Reaching Every Student: Effective Teaching in Inclusive Classrooms (pp. 508–511); Diversity: Differentiated Instruction (pp. 514–515)	3A. The teacher understands and can identify differences in approaches to learning and performance, including different learning styles, multiple intelligences, and performance modes, and can design instruction that uses students' strengths as the basis for growth.

PRAXIS™ Topics	Woolfolk Text Connections	INTASC Principles
• Alternative assessment	*Chapter 14/*New Directions in Assessment (pp. 545–546) *Chapter 15/* Informal Assessment (pp. 569–570); Alternatives to Traditional Assessment (pp. 561–570); Authentic Classroom Assessment (p. 562); Portfolios and Exhibitions (pp. 562–565); *Guidelines*: Creating Portfolios (p. 566); The Contract System and Grading Rubrics (pp. 577–578); *Guidelines*: Developing a Rubric (p. 569)	
• Testing modifications	*Chapter 14/* Reaching Every Student: Helping Students with Disabilities Prepare for High-Stakes Testing (pp. 543–544)	
5. Process of second language acquisition and strategies to support the learning of students	*Chapter 5/* Dialects (pp. 183–185); Bilingualism (pp. 185–188)	3C. The teacher knows about the process of second language acquisition and about strategies to support the learning of students whose first language is not English.
6. Understanding of influences of individual experiences, talents, and prior learning, as well as language culture, family, and community values on students' learning		
• Multicultural backgrounds	*Chapter 5/* American Cultural Diversity (pp. 164–165); Ethnic and Racial Differences (pp. 168–176); The Changing Demographics: Cultural Differences (pp. 168–170) *Diversity and Convergences* sections (all chapters)	3D. The teacher understands how students' learning is influenced by individual experiences, talents, and prior learning, as well as language, culture, family and community values. 3E. The teacher has a well-grounded framework for understanding cultural and community diversity and knows how to learn about and incorporate students' experiences, cultures, and community resources into instruction.
• Age-appropriate knowledge and behaviors	*Chapter 2/* Four Stages of Cognitive Development (pp. 29–36); Vygotsky's Sociocultural Perspective (pp. 39–45); Implications of Piaget's and Vygotsky's Theories for Teachers (pp. 46–51); Language Development in the School Years (pp. 54–56) *Chapter 3/* entire chapter—focus on: The Preschool Years: Trust, Autonomy, and Initiative (p. 68); Elementary and Middle School Years: Industry versus Inferiority (pp. 69–70); Adolescence: The Search for Identity (pp. 70–71); Emotional and Moral Development (pp. 92–102)	
• The student culture at the school	*Chapter 3/* Bronfenbrenner: The Social Context for Development (pp. 72–84); Peers (pp. 75–81) *Chapter 10/* Learned Helplessness (pp. 392–393) *Chapter 12/* Reaching Every Student: School-wide Positive Behavior Supports (p. 466); Diversity and Convergences in Learning Environments (pp. 470–472)	

PRAXIS™ Topics	Woolfolk Text Connections	INTASC Principles
• Family backgrounds	*Chapter 3/* Families (pp. 74–75) *Family and Community Partnership Guidelines* (all chapters)	
• Linguistic patterns and differences	*Chapter 2/* The Development of Language (pp. 51–55) *Chapter 4/* Students with Communication Disorders (pp. 136–139) *Chapter 5/* Dialects (pp. 183–185); Bilingualism (pp. 185–188)	6A. The teacher understands communication theory, language development, and the role of language in learning.
• Cognitive patterns and differences	*Chapter 4/* Learning Styles (pp. 124–127) *Chapter 7/* Individual Differences and Working Memory (pp. 276–278); Long-Term Memory (pp. 257–266)	
• Social and emotional issues	*Chapter 3/* Moral Behavior (p. 101) *Chapter 4/* Emotional Intelligence (pp. 116–117); Students with Emotional or Behavioral Disorders (pp. 140–145)	
C. Student Motivation and the Learning Environment		
1. Theoretical foundations about human motivation and behavior	*Chapter 10/* What Is Motivation? (pp. 372–376); Four General Approaches to Motivation (pp. 374–376)	5A. The teacher can use knowledge about human motivation and behavior drawn from the foundational sciences of psychology, anthropology, and sociology to develop strategies for organizing and supporting individual and group work.
• Important terms that relate to motivation and behavior	*Chapter 6/* Operant Conditioning: Trying New Responses (pp. 210–215); Reinforcement Schedules (pp. 212–214) *Chapter 10/* Motivation in Learning and Teaching (entire chapter) *Chapter 13/* Teacher Expectations (pp. 496–500)	
2. How knowledge of human emotion and behavior should influence strategies for organizing and supporting individual and group work in the classroom	*Chapter 10/* Arousal: Excitement and Anxiety in Learning (pp. 384–387); *Guidelines*: Coping with Anxiety (p. 389); *Guidelines*: Supporting Self-Determination and Autonomy (p. 379) *Chapter 13/* Teacher Expectations (pp. 496–500)	5A. The teacher can use knowledge about human motivation and behavior drawn from the foundational sciences of psychology, anthropology, and sociology to develop strategies for organizing and supporting individual and group work.
3. Factors and situations that are likely to promote or diminish students' motivation to learning, and how to help students to become self-motivated	Chapter 10/Needs: Lessons for Teachers (p. 379); Goals: Lessons for Teachers (p. 383); Interests and Emotions: Lessons for Teachers (p. 388); Beliefs and Self-Schemas: Lessons for Teachers (p. 394); Supporting Autonomy and Recognizing Accomplishment (pp. 398–399)	5E. The teacher recognizes factors and situations that are likely to promote or diminish intrinsic motivation and knows how to help students become self-motivated.

PRAXIS™ Topics	Woolfolk Text Connections	INTASC Principles
4. Principles of effective management and strategies to promote positive relationships, cooperation, and purposeful learning • Establishing daily procedures and routines • Establishing classroom rules, punishments, and rewards	*Chapter 6/* Methods for Encouraging Behaviors (pp. 216–219); *Guidelines*: Encouraging Positive Behavior (p. 220); Coping with Undesirable Behavior (pp. 219–222); Reaching Every Student: Functional Behavioral Assessment and Positive Behavior Support (pp. 222–224); Reaching Every Student: Severe Behavior Problems (pp. 228–229) *Chapter 12/* Rules and Procedures Required (pp. 448–452); *Guidelines*: Establishing Class Procedures (p. 449); Prevention Is the Best Medicine (pp. 460–461); Reaching Every Student: School-wide Positive Behavior Supports (p. 466) *Chapter 13/* Teacher Expectations (pp. 496–500)	5D. The teacher understands the principles of effective classroom management and can use a range of strategies to promote positive relationships, cooperation, and purposeful learning in the classroom.
— Giving timely feedback	*Chapter 6/ Guidelines*: Using Praise Appropriately (p. 217) *Chapter 12/* The Need for Communication (pp. 466–470) *Chapter 13/* Responding to Student Answers (pp. 495–496) *Chapter 15/* Effects of Feedback (p. 573)	
• Maintaining accurate records	*Chapter 15/* Portfolios (pp. 563–565); *Guidelines*: Creating Portfolios (p. 566); Evaluating Portfolios and Performances (pp. 565–568); Grading and Reporting: Nuts and Bolts (pp. 574–579)	
• Communicating with parents and caregivers	*Chapters 2–15/* Family and Community Partnerships	
• Using objective behavior descriptions	*Chapters 6/* Applied Behavior Analysis (pp. 215–224)	
• Responding to student misbehavior	*Chapters 6/* Coping with Undesirable Behavior (pp. 219–222); *Guidelines*: Using Punishment (p. 223); Group Consequences (p. 226) *Chapter 12/* Dealing with Discipline Problems (pp. 461–462); Special Problems with Secondary Students (pp. 462–465); *Guidelines*: Imposing Penalties (p. 463); Counseling: The Students' Problem (pp. 468–469); Confrontation and Assertive Discipline (p. 469) *Chapter 11/* Constructive Conflict Resolution (pp. 427–429); Violence in the Schools (pp. 432–434)	
• Arranging classroom space	*Chapter 12/* Planning Spaces for Learning (pp. 452–455); *Guidelines*: Designing Learning Spaces (p. 454)	
• Pacing and the structure of the lesson	*Chapter 12/* Encouraging Engagement (p. 459); *Guidelines*: Keeping Students Engaged (p. 459); Withitness (p. 460); Overlapping and Group Focus (pp. 460–461); Movement Management (p. 461) *Chapter 13/* Clarity and Organization (p. 487); *Guidelines*: Teaching Effectively (p. 489)	

PRAXIS™ Topics	Woolfolk Text Connections	INTASC Principles
II. Instruction and Assessment **A. Instructional Strategies** 1. Major cognitive processes associated with student learning	*Chapter 9/* Apprenticeships in Thinking (pp. 359–361)	4A. The teacher understands the cognitive processes associated with various kinds of learning (e.g., critical and creative thinking, problem structuring and problem solving, invention, memorization and recall) and how these processes can be stimulated.
• Critical thinking • Creative thinking	*Chapter 8/* Creativity and Creative Problem Solving (pp. 305–311); *Guidelines*: Encouraging Creativity (p. 309)	
• Inductive and deductive thinking	*Chapter 8/* Structure and Discovery (p. 290)	
• Problem structuring and problem solving	*Chapter 8/* Problem Solving (pp. 294–305)	
• Invention	*Chapter 8/* Creativity and Creative Problem Solving (pp. 305–311)	
• Memorization and recall	*Chapter 7/* Cognitive Views of Learning (focus on sections related to memory)	
2. Major categories, advantages, and appropriate uses of instructional strategies		4B. The teacher understands principles and techniques, along with advantages and limitations, associated with various instructional strategies (e.g., cooperative learning, direct instruction, discovery learning, whole-group discussion, independent study, interdisciplinary instruction).
• Cooperative learning	*Chapter 11/* The Group: Collaboration and Cooperation (pp. 416–426); The Classroom Community (pp. 426–431); *Guidelines*: Using Cooperative Learning (p. 425)	
• Direct instruction (often referred to as *teacher-centered instruction*)	*Chapter 13/* Teacher-Directed Instruction (pp. 485–496)	
• Discovery learning	*Chapter 8/* Teaching Concepts through Discovery (pp. 290–292); *Guidelines*: Applying Bruner's Ideas (p. 292) *Chapter 9/* Inquiry and Problem-Based Learning (pp. 351–355)	1B. The teacher understands how students' conceptual frameworks and their misconceptions for an area of knowledge can influence their learning.
• Whole-group discussion	*Chapter 13/* Group Discussion (p. 496); *Guidelines*: Productive Group Discussions (p. 497)	
• Independent study	*Chapter 8/* Learning Strategies and Tactics (pp. 311–314); *Guidelines*: Becoming an Expert Student (p. 317) *Chapter 9/* Models of Self-Regulated Learning and Agency (pp. 336–338)	
• Interdisciplinary instruction (sometimes referred to as *thematic instruction*)	*Chapter 9/* Inquiry and Problem-Based Learning (pp. 351–355) *Chapter 13/* Integrated and Thematic Planning (p. 485)	
• Questioning	*Chapter 11/* Reciprocal Questioning (p. 423) *Chapter 13/* Questioning and Recitation (pp. 492–496)	

PRAXIS™ Topics	Woolfolk Text Connections	INTASC Principles
3. Principles, techniques, and methods associated with major instructional strategies • Direct instruction (*often referred to as teacher-centered instruction*)	*Chapter 8/* Teaching Concepts through Exposition (pp. 292–293); *Guidelines:* Applying Ausubel's Ideas (p. 294) *Chapter 13/* Explanation and Direction Instruction (pp. 487–490); Questioning and Recitation (pp. 492–496); Group Discussions (p. 496); Rosenshine's Six Teaching Functions (p. 488)	4B. The teacher understands principles and techniques, along with advantages and limitations, associated with various instructional strategies (e.g., cooperative learning, direct instruction, discovery learning, whole-group discussion, independent study, interdisciplinary instruction).
• Student-centered models	*Chapter 8/* Teaching Concepts Through Discovery (pp. 290–291); *Guidelines*: Applying Bruner's Ideas (p. 292) *Chapter 9/* Cognitive and Social Constructivism (pp. 343–350); Applying Constructivist Perspectives (pp. 350–362)	
4. Methods for enhancing student learning through the use of a variety of resources and materials	*Chapter 11/* Service Learning (pp. 434–437) *Chapter 13/* Technology and Exceptional Students (pp. 511–513) Handbook Section 4: Enhancing Your Expertise; Continuing Your Learning	4C. The teacher knows how to enhance learning through the use of a wide variety of materials as well as human and technological resources (e.g., computers, audio-visual technologies, videotapes and discs, local experts, primary documents and artifacts, texts, reference books, literature, and other print resources).
B. Planning Instruction 1. Techniques for planning instruction to meet curriculum goals, including the incorporation of learning theory, subject matter, curriculum development, and student development		7A. The teacher understands learning theory, subject matter, curriculum development, and student development and knows how to use this knowledge in planning instruction to meet curriculum goals.
• National and state learning standards • State and local curriculum frameworks • State and local curriculum guides	*Chapter 1/* Introduction (p. 2) *Chapter 13/* Objectives for Learning (pp. 479–480) *Chapter 14/* Issues in Standardized Testing (pp. 539–544)	
• Scope and sequence in specific disciplines • Units and lessons	*Chapter 13/* The First Step: Planning (pp. 478–485); Another View: Planning from a Constructivist Perspective (pp. 483–485); focus on: An Example of Constructivist Planning (pp. 484–485); Integrated and Thematic Plans (p. 485)	
• Behavioral objectives: affective, cognitive, and psychomotor • Learner objectives and outcomes	*Chapter 13/* Objectives for Learning (pp. 479–480); The Cognitive Domain (p. 481); Bloom 2001 (p. 481); The Affective Domain (p. 482); The Psychomotor Domain (pp. 482–483); *Guidelines*: Using Instructional Objectives (p. 483)	
2. Techniques for creating effective bridges between curriculum goals and students' experiences		7B. The teacher knows how to take contextual considerations (instructional materials, individual student interests, needs, and aptitudes, and community resources) into account in planning instruction that creates an effective bridge between curriculum goals and students' experiences.
• Modeling	*Chapter 6/* Observational Learning and Cognitive Behavior Modification: Thinking about Behavior (pp. 229–238); *Guidelines*: Using Observational Learning (p. 234) *Chapter 9/* Applying Social Cognitive Theory (pp. 333–343)	

PRAXIS™ Topics	Woolfolk Text Connections	INTASC Principles
• Guided practice	*Chapter 2/* Assisted Learning (pp. 48–49) *Chapter 6/* Cognitive Behavior Modification and Self-Instruction (pp. 236–238) *Chapter 9/* Cognitive Apprenticeships (pp. 356–358) *Chapter 13/* Rosenshine's Six Teaching Functions (p. 488)	
• Independent practice, including homework	*Chapter 9/* Models of Self-Regulated Learning and Agency (pp. 336–338); *Guidelines*: Parents Supporting Self-Regulation (p. 340) *Chapter 13/* Seatwork and Homework (pp. 491–492)	
• Transitions	*Chapter 12/* Overlapping and Group Focus (pp. 460–461); Movement Management (p. 461); *Guidelines*: Keeping Students Engaged (p. 459)	
• Activating students' prior knowledge	*Chapter 7/* The Importance of Knowledge in Learning (pp. 249–250); Capacity and Duration and Contents of Long-Term Memory (pp. 257–259) *Chapter 8/* Advance Organizers (pp. 292–293); The Results of Problem Representation, focus on: schema-driven problem solving (pp. 296–300)	
• Anticipating preconceptions	*Chapter 8/* Views of Concept Learning (pp. 286–287); Strategies for Teaching Concepts (pp. 287–290), focus on: undergeneralization and overgeneralization; Factors That Hinder Problem Solving (pp. 302–303); *Chapter 13/ Guidelines:* Teaching for Conceptual Change (p. 507)	
• Encouraging exploration and problem solving	*Chapter 2/* Implications of Piaget's Theory for Teachers (pp. 46–48) *Chapter 8/* Problem Solving (pp. 294–305); Creativity and Creative Problem Solving (pp. 305–311) *Chapter 11/* Models of Self-Regulated Learning and Agency (pp. 336–338)	
• Building new skills on those previously acquired	*Chapter 2/* Basic Tendencies in Thinking (pp. 28–29) *Chapter 4/* Students with Intellectual Disabilities (pp. 139–140); *Guidelines*: Teaching Students with Below-Average Intelligence (p. 141) *Chapter 6/* Observational Learning in Teaching (pp. 233–234) *Chapter 7/* The Importance of Knowledge in Learning (pp. 249–250); Capacity, Duration and Contents of Long-Term Memory (pp. 250–251); *Guidelines*: Using Information Processing Ideas in the Classroom (p. 266); Development of Declarative Knowledge (pp. 269–270); Becoming an Expert: Procedural and Conditional Knowledge (pp. 274–277)	

PRAXIS™ Topics	Woolfolk Text Connections	INTASC Principles
C. Assessment Strategies		8A. The teacher understands the characteristics, uses, advantages, and limitations of different types of assessments (e.g., criterion-referenced and norm-referenced instruments, traditional standardized and performance-based tests, observation systems, and assessments of student work) for evaluating how students learn, what they know and are able to do, and what kinds of experiences will support their further growth and development.
1. Types of assessments	*Chapter 14/* Norm-Referenced Tests (p. 523); Criterion-Referenced Tests (pp. 523–524); Achievement Tests: What Has the Student Learned? (pp. 536–538); Diagnostic Tests: What Are the Student's Strengths and Weaknesses? (p. 538); Aptitude Tests: How Well Will the Student Do in the Future? (pp. 538–539); Authentic Assessment (p. 562) *Chapter 15/* Formative and Summative Assessment (pp. 554–555); Objective Testing (pp. 556–558); Essay Testing (pp. 559–560); Portfolios and Exhibitions (pp. 562–565); Informal Assessment (pp. 569–570)	
2. Characteristics of assessments	*Chapter 14/* Reliability (p. 530); Validity (pp. 531–532); *Guidelines:* Increasing Reliability and Variability (p. 533) *Chapter 15/* Writing Multiple-Choice Questions (p. 557); *Guidelines*: Writing Multiple-Choice Test Items (p. 558); Constructing Essay Tests (p. 559); Reliability, Variability, Generalizability (pp. 567–568); *Guidelines*: Developing a Rubric (p. 569)	8B. The teacher knows how to select, construct, and use assessment strategies and instruments appropriate to the learning outcomes being evaluated and to other diagnostic purposes.
3. Scoring assessments	*Chapter 15/* Using Multiple-Choice Tests (p. 557); Evaluating Essays: Dangers (p. 559); Evaluating Essays: Methods (pp. 559–560); Evaluating Portfolios and Performances (pp. 565–568); *Guidelines*: Developing a Rubric (p. 569)	
4. Uses of assessments	*Chapter 14/* Norm-Referenced Tests (p. 523); Criterion-Referenced Tests (pp. 523–524); Using Information from a Norm-Referenced Achievement Test (pp. 536–538); Interpreting Test Scores (pp. 529–534); IQ and Scholastic Aptitude (pp. 538–539); Accountability and High Stakes (pp. 540–541) *Chapter 15/* Formative and Summative Assessment (pp. 554–555); Getting the Most from Traditional Assessment (pp. 555–560); Alternatives to Traditional Assessments (pp. 561–570)	
5. Understanding of measurement theory and assessment-related issues	*Chapter 14/* Norm-Referenced Tests (p. 523); Criterion-Referenced Tests (pp. 523–524); What Do Test Scores Mean? (pp. 524–534); New Directions in Authentic Assessment (pp. 545–546)	8C. The teacher understands measurement theory and assessment-related issues, such as validity, reliability, bias, and scoring concerns.

PRAXIS™ Topics	Woolfolk Text Connections	INTASC Principles
III. Communication Techniques		6C. The teacher recognizes the importance of nonverbal as well as verbal communication.
A. Basic, effective verbal and nonverbal communication techniques	*Chapter 10/* Diversity and Convergences in Motivation to Learn (pp. 403–407); Can I Do It? Building Confidence and Positive Expectations (p. 404) *Chapter 12/* The Need for Communication (pp. 466–470) *Chapter 13/* Teacher Expectations (pp. 496–500)	6D. The teacher knows about and can use effective verbal, nonverbal, and media communication techniques.
B. Effect of cultural and gender differences on communications in the classroom	*Chapter 5/* Language Differences in the Classroom (pp. 182–188); Sociolinguistics (pp. 196–197) *Diversity and Convergences* sections, all chapters	6B. The teacher understands how cultural and gender differences can affect communication in the classroom.
C. Types of questions that can stimulate discussion in different ways for different purposes	*Chapter 9/* Dialogue and Instructional Conversations (pp. 355–356) *Chapter 13/* Questioning and Recitation (pp. 492–496)	6D. The teacher knows about and can use effective verbal, nonverbal, and media communication techniques.
• Probing for learner understanding	*Chapter 9/* Dialogue and Instructional Conversations (pp. 355–356) *Chapter 13/* Questioning and Recitation (pp. 492–496)	
• Helping students articulate their ideas and thinking processes	*Chapter 9/* Dialogue and Instructional Conversations (pp. 355–356) *Chapter 13/* Group Discussion (p. 496) *Chapter 8/ Guidelines*: Problem Solving (p. 306) *Chapter 13/ Guidelines*: Teaching for Conceptual Change (p. 507)	
• Promoting risk-taking and problem solving	*Chapter 11/* Reciprocal Questioning (pp. 423–424)	
• Facilitating factual recall	*Chapter 13/* Comprehension Monitoring and Reading: Reciprocal Teaching (p. 503); Applying Reciprocal Teaching (pp. 503–504); Questioning and Recitation (pp. 492–496)	
• Encouraging convergent and divergent thinking	*Chapter 8/* Assessing Creativity (pp. 307–309) *Chapter 13/* Kinds of Questions (pp. 494–495)	
• Stimulating curiosity	*Chapter 10/* Tapping Interests (pp. 383–384); *Guidelines*: Building on Students' Interests and Curiosity (p. 386); Curiosity: Novelty and Complexity (pp. 386–387)	
• Helping students to question	*Chapter 13/* Fitting the Questions to the Students (p. 495); Questioning and Recitation (pp. 492–496); Comprehension Monitoring and Reading: Reciprocal Teaching (p. 503); Applying Reciprocal Teaching (pp. 503–504)	

PRAXIS™ Topics	Woolfolk Text Connections	INTASC Principles
IV. Profession and Community **A. The Reflective Practitioner**		9B. The teacher is aware of major areas of research on teaching and of resources available for professional learning (e.g., professional literature, colleagues, professional associations, professional development activities).
1. Types of resources available for professional development and learning	*Chapters 2–15/* Margin Notes: *Connect and Extend* to the research (various places in each chapter); *Connect and Extend* to professional journals (various places in each chapter)	
• Professional literature		
• Colleagues	*Chapters 2–15/ Teachers' Casebook* (opening and closing sections of each chapter)	
2. Ability to read and understand articles about current views, ideas, and debates regarding best teaching practices	*Chapter 1/* Using Research to Understand and Improve Learning (pp. 10–13) *Chapters 2–15/ Point/Counterpoint* (one per chapter)	9B. The teacher is aware of major areas of research on teaching and of resources available for professional learning (e.g., professional literature, colleagues, professional associations, professional development activities).
3. Why personal reflection on teaching practices is critical, and approaches that can be used to achieve this	*Chapters 2–15/ Point/Counterpoint* (one per chapter)	1A. The teacher understands major concepts, assumptions, debates, processes of inquiry, and ways of knowing that are central to the discipline(s) s/he teaches.
B. The Larger Community		10A. The teacher understands schools as organizations within the larger community context and understands the operations of the relevant aspects of the system(s) within which s/he works.
1. Role of the school as a resource to the larger community	*Chapter 5/* Culture and Community (entire chapter) *Chapter 11/* The Classroom Community (pp. 426–437)	
2. Factors in the students' environment outside of school (family circumstances, community environments, health, and economic conditions) that may influence students' life and learning	*Chapter 3/* Families (pp. 74–75); Peers (pp. 75–84) *Chapter 4/* Common Challenges (pp. 130–145); Less Prevalent Problems and More Severe Disabilities (pp. 145–148)	10B. The teacher understands how factors in the students' environment outside of school (e.g., family circumstances, community environments, health and economic conditions) may influence students' life and learning.
3. Basic strategies for involving parents/ guardians and leaders in the community in the educational process	*Chapter 5/* Culture and Community (entire chapter) *Chapter 11/* Community Outside the Classroom: Service Learning (pp. 434–437) *Chapters 2–15/ Family and Community Partnerships*: (one in each chapter) *Diversity and Convergences* sections, all chapters	
4. Major laws related to students' rights and teacher responsibilities	*Chapter 4/* Individual Differences and the Law (pp. 127–130)	10C. The teacher understands and implements laws related to students' rights and teacher responsibilities (e.g., for equal education, appropriate education for handicapped students, confidentiality, privacy, appropriate treatment of students, reporting in situations related to possible child abuse).
• Equal education	*Chapter 4/* The Rights of Students and Families (p. 128)	
• Appropriate education for handicapped children	*Chapter 15/* Beyond Grading: Communication (focus on: Buckley Amendment) (pp. 578–**582**)	
• Confidentiality and privacy	*Chapter 13/* The Need for Communication (pp. 466–470)	
• Reporting situations related to possible child abuse	*Chapter 3/* Child Abuse (p. 83) *Chapter 11*/Respect and Protect (p. 434)	

Section 3
Getting a Job: Job Interview Questions that *Educational Psychology* will Help You Answer

Here are some common job interview questions on a range of topics suggested by experienced principals and superintendents. Assume you are in a job interview and the interviewer looks intently in to your eyes and asks these questions. What would you say?

Teaching Philosophy

The principal takes out a pad of paper, a pen, and says, "Tell me what you admired about your favorite teacher. What makes a good teacher?" **Chapter 1**

What do you think about the idea of emotional intelligence? Would you teach that in your class? **Chapter 4**

What are the basic skills for your students—the foundations of their more advanced learning—and how would you teach them? **Chapter 7**

What do you think about letting students use calculators and spell checkers? Do you think this is making learning too easy? **Chapter 8**

What is your conception of learning? How do students learn? **Chapter 9**

What do you think about zero tolerance? **Chapter 12**

Accommodating Student Differences

I need to know about your understanding of students across grades. Are students in the 2nd and the 7th grade that different in the way they think—I mean in any ways that would affect your teaching? **Chapter 2**

We are thinking about having a professional development program on learning styles. What do you know about the idea? **Chapter 4**

Describe a learning activity that you have planned for a class and ways that you have accommodated individual learning styles or needs. **Chapter 4**

If a student is struggling with time management and organization issues, what kind of accommodations would you provide? **Chapter 4**

How would you teach abstract concepts to a student who just arrived from Somalia and can't even read in her native language, much less English? **Chapter 8**

How do you accommodate different learning challenges and abilities in your teaching? Do you make use of community resources or technology? How? **Chapter 13**

Diversity

What would you do to help all your students feel good about themselves? **Chapter 3**

Describe the things you do for students to indicate you have feelings for them. **Chapter 5**

Describe how your life experiences will contribute to our goal to create an active anti-racist school system. **Chapter 5**

Do you believe that boys and girls learn differently? **Chapter 5**

Teaching Strategies

We have to cover so much material to get our students ready for the state assessments. What would you do to help your students remember what they have learned in your classes? **Chapter 7**

What is your script for a typical day? Tell me how a good day should go in terms of what you would plan and how much time you would give to each segment of your day. **Chapter 7**

Many of our students go on to high-pressure colleges and don't seem to know how to study when they don't have daily homework deadlines. How would you help them prepare to handle the heavy workload in those institutions? **Chapter 8**

You're interviewing with the district superintendent for a position as a school psychologist. The man is known for his unorthodox interview questions. He hands you a pad of paper and a ruler and says, "Tell me, what is the exact thickness of a single sheet of paper?" **Chapter 8**

Do you use group work in your teaching? Why or why not? How would you use it in this school? **Chapter 11**

In your interview for the last remaining opening in the district of your dreams, the principal asks, "What is the best lesson you have taught so far? Tell me all about it and especially what made it so good." **Chapter 13**

Working with Parents

We have some pretty discouraged students and parents here after our test scores were so low last year. What would you do to help students believe in their abilities to learn? **Chapter 10**

How will you communicate with families about your homework and grading policies? **Chapter 15**

Current Issues

What do you know about brain-based education? **Chapter 2**

We have been having some heated debates in this district about ability grouping and tracking. Where do you stand on those issues? **Chapter 4**

Classroom Management

How could you tell if there might be violence among students in our school? What are the warning signs? **Chapter 11**

Last year a teacher got in trouble for bribing his students with homework exemptions to get them to behave in class. What do you think about using rewards and punishments in teaching? **Chapter 6**

In your experience with students in any capacity, what was your most challenging discipline problem so far and how did you handle it? **Chapter 12**

Motivation

How would you get students interested in learning? Could you tap their interests in your teaching? **Chapter 10**

Assessment and Grading

Consider the diverse population of students in a classroom. How would you interpret student test scores? **Chapter 14**

What would you do to raise our test scores in this school? **Chapter 14**

What do you know about using portfolios, performances, projects, and rubrics to assess learning? **Chapter 15**

Section 4
Enhancing Your Expertise: Continuing Your Learning

Your first teaching experience will have surprises. No matter what your teacher preparation program included or how well you did in that program, you will hear yourself exclaiming, "They never told me about this!" Developing expertise as a teacher begins now, but it never ends. Because teaching is about lifelong learning, you have to continually find new resources to meet new challenges. In this section I invite you to develop your expertise as a teacher by exploring the World Wide Web. The following are cases of possible "surprises" taken from the real experiences of teachers I know. After each case are ways to find help and enhance your expertise through technology. Each case reflects themes from a chapter in this text.

Professional Development: Chapter 1

The development of a good beginning teacher into an expert teacher is surely a learning process. It is also a process of enculturation in which the beginning teacher becomes a member of a community of practice. A key element of this enculturation is professional development.

The World Wide Web has become a force in the professional development of teachers. Many authoritative Websites exist that provide instructional resources, information about educational research and theory, answers to questions about classroom problems, and opportunities for members of the community of educators to exchange ideas and viewpoints. For a first exploration it seems appropriate to examine basic principles of professional development. *The Knowledge Loom: What Works in Teaching & Learning* (**www.knowledgeloom.org**) has a set of pages devoted to those principles. For each of the eight principles listed in the site, there are questions to help you consider the implications of a principle, examples of successful implementation of a principle, research summaries, and links for more detailed information.

Before you navigate to this site and begin your exploration, be reminded of several of the themes of this book. These themes include *teachers as:*

- problem solvers,
- members of a learning community,
- designers of instruction,
- reflective thinkers,
- assessors and evaluators of learning,
- learning strategists, and
- users of and sources for research.

When you examine and discuss the principles with other beginning teachers and your instructor, you will no doubt notice these themes—and others as well—woven through the questions, examples, and research about professional development you encounter at *The Knowledge Loom.* Revisit these Web pages as you progress through this book and your educational psychology course. As you become more acculturated into the community of educators and move from the periphery of that community toward more central participation, you might find that you have insights, questions, and views of your own that are marks of a more expert teacher.

Useful Websites

Teacher Magazine: **http://www.edweek.org/tm/index.html**

The Southeast Center for Teacher Quality: **www.teachingquality.org**

Language and Literacy Development: Chapter 2

In one way or another, nearly every educator is a "language teacher," although the mix of concerns may vary by subject matter, grade/age level, or specialty. The important roles of language in the classroom make clear to expert teachers the need to enrich their understanding of language development and their knowledge of effective techniques and strategies that enhance literacy skills.

In the United States, there is a national policy to "leave no child behind" in school. If no child is to be left behind, then teachers will have to know how to implement a wide variety of effective classroom practices and techniques; be current with research in literacy development, and recognize the milestones and major trends of language development. This area is so crucial to plans for educational reform and improvement that you will find it useful to build a set of bookmarks or favorites related to it. Start with these three sites and use the questions as cues for exploring each one.

Effective Classroom Practices: Education Place®: (**http://www.eduplace.com/rdg/res/literacy/**)

Research in Literacy Development: The National Research Center on English Learning & Achievement (**http://cela.albany.edu/research.htm**)

Language Development: The American Speech-Language-Hearing Association (**http://www.asha.org/public/speech/development/lang_lit.htm**)

Throughout this text, you will read about other ways that teachers can encourage language development for both younger and older students. For example, we discuss bilingual education in Chapter 5, instructional conversations in Chapter 9, and learning to read and write in Chapter 13.

Emotional and Social Development: Chapter 3

During her first round of parent–teacher conferences at the middle school, Susan recognized a pattern: She and the parents would discuss a child's academic progress in the marking period, and then the conversation would shift toward social and emotional issues. The parents were concerned about how emotional and social factors affect academic progress, and about the school's influences on their children's emotional and social growth. Susan was surprised at the number of concerns that parents brought up, including bullying, peer relationships, body image, and eating disorders, just to mention a few.

When you consider the amount of time that students spend in school from the years of early childhood through adolescence, you see why teachers need a high level of knowledge about human development and expertise in the application of that knowledge. For example, are the ill-kempt appearance and surliness of a 13-year-old typical within the bounds of normal behavior or are they signs of possible depression? How should you handle the tantrum of a 1st grader, and what could a tantrum indicate? Teachers at all levels, preschool through high school, need to create classroom and school climates that promote students' social and emotional growth. They should be able to identify student behaviors and attitudes that undermine that growth. Teachers must possess the knowledge and skills necessary to address such problems effectively in conjunction with the appropriate support professionals (e.g., guidance counselor, psychologist, psychiatrist).

As I hope you have done in the previous chapters, you will find it valuable to collect and maintain an organized set of bookmarks or favorites about social and emotional development on your Web browser. Use the sites listed here as a foundation for your collection. To judge the quality of the information offered, take the perspective of a first-year teacher who encounters these situations and seeks guidance. Many sites have forums, "ask the expert" links, bulletin boards, and newsletters that will help you stay current with research about emotional and social development. You might be inclined to focus exclusively on the age levels that you intend to work with as an educator. Please set aside that inclination, especially when learning about human development. Recall that Erikson emphasized the interdependence of the stages of psychosocial development: The way conflicts are resolved at one stage strongly influences resolutions at successive stages.

Early Childhood and Middle Childhood

Child Psychology Development Index (**http://psychology.about.com/cs/child/**)

drSpock (**www.drspock.com**)

KidsHealth for Parents (**http://kidshealth.org/parent/emotions/**)

Adolescence

American Academy of Child & Adolescent Psychiatry (**http://www.aacap.org/**)

Center for Adolescent Studies (**http://www.indiana.edu/~cafs/**)

Child Development Institute (**http://www.childdevelopmentinfo.com/**)

Connect for Kids (**http://www.connectforkids.org/**)

Resources on Adolescent Development (**http://www.indiana.edu/~iuepsyc/topics/r_ado.htm**)

Other Useful Websites for Personal and Social Development

Mental Health Net **http://mhnet.org/**

American Foundation for Suicide Prevention **http://afsp.org/**

Childhelp: To get information about child protection or to find out how to report suspected abuse. **800–4-A-Child**

Learner and Differences and Learning Needs: Chapter 4

Reflecting on 30 years in the classroom, a colleague of mine, James O'Kelly, knew that he had excellent support as he began teaching in a new school—just opened the year he came. The principal encouraged innovation. The faculty included many of the district's better teachers, who served as mentors and models. Despite all this support, the most difficult challenge that Jim faced was his work with children with learning disabilities. How could seemingly typical 6th graders be unable to comprehend a simple paragraph, misapply the few steps for the solution of a math problem, or confuse simple oral directions? How should these students be graded? What accommodations could be made for them? Advice from the principal and veteran teachers helped somewhat, as did coursework at a local college. Nevertheless, finding answers was not easy.

Since Jim entered the classroom, the laws, court decisions, public attitudes, and research about learning disabilities have changed dramatically. Future teachers will be expected to be far more knowledgeable about learning disabilities than teachers in the past. LD Online (**www.ldonline.org**) can provide help with these challenges. It has a variety of resources that will expand your knowledge about this important topic. You will find descriptions and characteristics of specific learning disabilities, autobiographical accounts by people who have experienced learning difficulties, a bulletin board where people exchange information and questions, an archived column in which a child psychiatrist answers questions, and more. Here are a few questions that you might explore at LD Online:

- How can teachers structure the classroom environment to enhance the academic achievement experiences of their students with learning disabilities?
- What can a teacher do to facilitate home–school collaboration for students with ADHD?
- What are the main issues involved in the use of assistive technologies to support the learning of children with learning disabilities?
- What instructional strategies can I use to assist students with various specific learning disabilities?

Each of these questions relates to one or more topics found in this textbook: classroom environment, home–school communication, ADHD, assistive technologies, and instructional strategies. As you encounter other major themes and concepts in this textbook, go to LD Online to see how they relate to learning disabilities.

Culture and Diversity: Chapter 5

The incident was a small one, but it exemplified many of the issues that teachers face as a result of the nation's demographic changes. Five-year-old Emrah, who qualified for the free lunch program, told his teacher that he could eat neither of the two offerings in the school cafeteria that day: sausage with pancakes or deli sub sandwich—because of religious reasons. The teacher contacted the cafeteria manager. The manager said that no accommodations could be made because no other foods were available. (One of the cafeteria workers remarked that "they" should learn to eat what "we" eat.) The incensed teacher finally reached the school district dietician, who resolved the dispute by pointing out that the "ham" in the deli sub sandwich was actually turkey ham that Emrah could eat. "I am glad we were able to take care of that problem," said the dietician. "But we can't make accommodations for every ethnic or religious group in the district."

As the nation's school population continues to diversify, incidents like this one (and others far less easily resolved) will certainly arise more and more often. Teachers with expertise about and respect for cultural differences will be able to face these challenges in ways that help students experience genuine acceptance by the school community, leading to increased ethnic pride and motivation to succeed in school.

The Southern Poverty Law Center sponsors the Teaching Tolerance education project (**www.tolerance.org**) that helps "teachers foster equity, respect and understanding in the classroom and beyond." Its major concern is fair treatment of all people regardless of religious affiliation, gender, race, age, ethnicity, sexual orientation, or physical status. Teaching Tolerance takes a comprehensive approach to achievement of that goal. Here you will find information and resources including:

- current events,
- classroom lesson plans,
- activities to foster teacher self-reflection about tolerance,
- a teacher's forum to share ideas about fostering tolerance in the classroom,
- guidelines and tips for responding to intolerant incidents inside the school, and
- links to other Websites that promote tolerance.

Perhaps Teaching Tolerance's most interesting—as well as unsettling—feature is its set of Implicit Association Tests (IAT) that measure unconscious bias. These tests might offer you some insight into your own possible hidden biases about race, homosexuality, age, gender, and body image. Teachers alone, of course, cannot create an atmosphere of equity and respect. The sponsors of Teaching Tolerance also provide numerous resources to engage parents and students in efforts to foster tolerance and equity. See what you think of this site. You may very well find it the most disturbing, but useful site that you encounter through this textbook.

Behavioral Views of Learning: Chapter 6

In this chapter and the next five, we examine several theoretical perspectives that strongly influence classroom practices. These perspectives often differ starkly in their assumptions about learning and the roles of students and teachers. However, all these perspectives find some common ground affirming the importance of self-regulated learning—and an expert teacher is by necessity a highly self-regulated learner.

A key attribute of a self-regulated learner is the effective use of resources. The Educator's Reference Desk Website (**http://www.eduref.org/**) is one of the most comprehensive, up-to-date, and authoritative educational resources that you will find anywhere in any medium. The home page provides you with a hint of the vast breadth of disciplines that comprise the field of education. You will see sections devoted to counseling, educational technology, educational management, librarianship, and many more.

There are two features that beginning teachers will find immediately useful. The first is the link to a collection of lesson plans that not only includes plans for a variety of subject areas, but also provides guidelines for writing plans that complement the guidelines you will find in this textbook (**http://www.eduref.org/Virtual/Lessons/index.shtml**). Second, the *Question Archive* is composed of a set of questions that have been previously answered by ERIC specialists. Many of these questions are the type that novice teachers would typically ask. As you explore The Educator's Reference Desk Web, be sure to navigate to its collection of ERIC Resources Information Center (**http://eric.ed.gov/**).

Cognitive Views of Learning: Chapter 7

At this point in the semester, my hunch is that you are busy taking exams, writing term papers or reports, and working on a long-term project or two for your various courses. If that's the case, you will probably enjoy a brief diversion from your workload, and you'd appreciate some help remembering efficiently and effectively what you are learning in those courses.

Set aside your class notes, study guides, and textbooks, and navigate to NASA's Applied Cognition game page (**http://human-factors.arc.nasa.gov/cognition/tutorials/index.html**). Take a few minutes and play with each game. After you've played them, try to match a game on the left with a principle of human memory on the right:

Game	Memory Principle
1. Penny Recognition	A. Reconstruction
2. The Mnemonicizer	B. Organization
3. Human Memory: Recall	C. Interference
4. Interference	D. Meaningfulness
5. Short Term Memory: Encoding and Rehearsal	E. Elaboration

(See answers in the next column)

These games demonstrate several of the characteristics of memory that you encountered in this chapter: reconstruction, organization, meaningfulness, interference, and elaboration. Knowledge of these characteristics, and their implications for learning and teaching, will enhance your own expertise as a student now and as a teacher later. Insights about the nature of memory have inspired many techniques for enhancing the storage and retrieval of information. Medical students, for example, need to remember thousands of physical structures, processes, diseases, drugs, and pathogens (just to mention a few)—and understand the relationships among them. It would be nearly impossible to learn this information by simple rehearsal, so these students often rely on memory techniques for that purpose. (To see what I mean, go to a search engine and enter "medical mnemonics" in the search box.)

You might find that a disciplined, practiced use of the memory techniques presented at Mind Tools (**http://www.mindtools.com**) will serve you as well as they serve future surgeons. A key to success in any field is the use of the right tool at the right time. Mind Tools has a set of memory tools for a variety of purposes: ordered lists, long lists, short lists, grouped information, names, and numbers. There also is a clear description of how and when to use each technique, as well as examples and advice about effectively using a technique. Now might be the time for you to check out the page that explains how to remember information for a test.

When it comes to learning about memory techniques, remember that the most effective way to help someone learn is to keep things meaningful.

(Answers to quiz; 1A, 2E, 3B, 4C, 5D)

Complex Cognitive Processes: Chapter 8

Problem Solving

If you look at the teacher's guide for any recently developed mathematics or science program, you are certain to see a pair of words: problem solving. (And you will see this pairing often.) This encounter between you and these two words is not by chance. Forces and innovations in our culture are often reflected in school curricula. Changes in the nature of work and business, the potential benefits of emerging technologies, and research in psychology have increased the press on teachers, beginning as early as preschool, to nurture the inquiry and problem-solving skills of their students in all academic areas.

Problem solving, of course, is far more than a mere term. Early in this chapter's section on problem solving I noted that there is a major debate about whether effective problem-solving strategies are general or domain-specific, and we examined one general solving approach, IDEAL, in detail. In order to develop your expertise in the area of problem solving, it would be useful to examine problem solving in more detail from a domain-specific perspective—or more accurately from two domains. Mathematics and science are domains in which educational psychologists have extensively researched basic processes of problem solving, and teachers have traditionally designed strategies to enhance problem-solving skills in these areas.

The Eisenhower National Clearinghouse (ENC) (**http://www.goenc.com**) provides rich sets of resources and information about problem solving in mathematics and science. When you reach its home page, you will be able to search for curriculum resources by keyword and grade level. Try searching keyword "problem solving." I found 3782 resources.

A visit to the ENC Website should be valuable to you whether you are interested in mathematics, science, or any other major discipline. Problem solving is not the sole domain of mathematics and science educators, of course. Each discipline has unique contributions to make toward solving the problems of contemporary life.

Constructivist Views of Learning: Chapter 9

Thinking Skills

Consider this situation. Janet's first end-of-the-year evaluation was going well. The English Department supervisor noted her ability to motivate students, her willingness to participate in co-curricular activities, and her use of effective classroom management techniques. Suddenly, his tone changed. Yes, Janet would be rehired for the next school year. However, based on his classroom observations, analysis of her lesson plans, and comments from her mentoring teacher, the supervisor concluded that Janet needed to take steps to create "a stronger climate for higher-level thinking in her classes." The supervisor was not singling out Janet. Other teachers, including veterans, received the same recommendations in their evaluations.

Most of today's college students went to elementary and high school during a period of reform in the major curricular areas (e.g., science, mathematics), and efforts to reform these areas continue to the present. A common theme of these reforms has been an increased emphasis on the development and use of *higher-order thinking skills.* For some educators, the term primarily refers to inquiry skills; for others, it means problem-solving skills; and for some, it emphasizes critical thinking skills—so don't assume everyone means the same thing by the term *higher-order thinking.* But whatever their concept of "higher-order," many educators agree that teachers inadvertently devote too much attention to *lower-order thinking skills* (i.e., remembering, comprehending, and applying).

The Center for Critical Thinking (**http://www.criticalthinking.org**) provides a variety of resources to support teachers' efforts in elementary, secondary, and college classrooms to enhance students' higher-order thinking skills. (The site separates elementary and secondary resources from college resources. Whatever your level, be sure to explore each set of resources.) The resources that you will find at this site should reduce your anxieties (and Janet's) about teaching for higher-order thinking. These resources include easily implemented instructional tactics and assessment strategies to promote a culture of thinking in your classroom. Be sure you examine the typical lessons that have been revised and restructured to encourage the students' higher-order thinking skills.

You might find the following sites valuable too as you build your expertise about thinking skills:

NEA Works4Me Tips Library (**http://www.nea.org/helpfrom/growing/works4me/teachtec/thinking.html**)

NRWEL (**http://www.nwrel.org/scpd/sirs/6/cu11.html**)

Motivation in Learning and Teaching: Chapter 10

Motivation to Learn

The letter stunned Judy. A parent wrote to the principal complaining that Judy was not "a good motivator." The major complaint was that Judy "failed" to participate in two reading incentive programs that year. (A pizza chain sponsored one program, and a nearby theme park sponsored the other.) Teacher participation in these programs was voluntary, and the principal never said anything about her "failure" before this letter arrived. Judy explained that she believed that these programs emphasized the quantity of reading materials over the material's quality. Like many teachers, Judy employed some forms of extrinsic motivation to learn in her classroom such as praise or certificates of achievement. But largely she relied on techniques that promote intrinsic motivation to learn.

"I agree with you, Judy, and I'll back you up," said the principal. "Let's have the parents in for a conference, but be prepared to counter their points, and explain how you deal with motivation."

Although Judy's belief about the value of intrinsic motivation is indeed supported by research, she has yet to develop a wide range of such motivational techniques and strategies, and she might have some difficulty explaining their value. Judy, or any teacher in this situation, would find some immediate help with Web resources. In Web interviews, educational psychologist Carol Dweck: (**http://www.education-world.com/a_curr/curr197.shtml**) and journalist Alfie Kohn (**http://www.webtools.familyeducation.com/article/0,1120,3-281-0-1,00.html**) discuss motivation to learn, and they provide a rationale for emphasizing the value of learning itself in contrast to the value of tangible rewards often associated with learning. The Northwest Regional Educational Laboratory(**http://www.nwrel.org/request/oct00/index.html**) offers a concise, authoritative Web "booklet" about motivation to learn. This booklet is essentially a novice's guide to student motivation. It contains sections about research related to the topic, affective and cognitive strategies designed to enhance intrinsic motivation to learn, suggestions for the design of engaging class activities, tips for creating motivating homework assignments, and suggestions for involving parents in those assignments.

There is one element of student motivation to learn that Judy did indeed fail to see until there was a problem: the role of parents. Regardless of whether Judy agrees with the parents on the issue of motivation, it is clear that she is dealing with a caring family. These parents can be valuable allies in boosting motivation.

Engaged Learning: Cooperation and Community: Chapter 11

Cooperative Learning

Following her mentor's advice, at her first Back-to-School Night, Juanita explained to the parents that for the first several months of the school year, she would be taking a traditional approach that utilized whole- and small-group instructional activities along with a few independent projects. But by mid-year, Juanita felt that it was time to expand her instructional repertoire and develop expertise in using cooperative learning techniques. Juanita and her mentor developed a modest set of Jigsaw activities based on content and skills from a chapter in the social studies book. The activities seemed to go well. The students were actively engaged with research on the Internet and encyclopedias. The groups hummed with questioning, explaining, and elaborating. Juanita administered the test supplied by the textbook publisher, and, to her relief, the test scores were in line with previous tests. With practice and refinement, she was certain that her students would nudge up the test scores.

Then the controversy began. A few parents of children who scored poorly on the test complained that it is the teacher who should do the teaching, not other students, and they wanted a meeting with the principal to emphasize that point. Could Juanita justify her choices? Could you?

Most classrooms are highly complex, dynamic environments that demand the use of techniques or strategies that help students accomplish a variety of instructional or learning tasks. Research has established that well-designed, carefully monitored cooperative approaches to learning can be effective means to such ends. Some techniques, such as STAD, are effective in helping students rehearse and maintain basic knowledge of content matter. Other techniques, such as reciprocal questioning, are effective in helping students develop essential reading skills.

Choices about which techniques to employ for various activities require a level of expertise that novice teachers can attain through knowledge, guidance, and reflection. Visits to the following sites can aid in building the knowledge necessary to implement effective cooperative learning groups in a sophisticated, thoughtful way.

Jigsaw Classroom provides a comprehensive and detailed description of Jigsaw, one of the earliest effective cooperative learning techniques. The site contains an overview of Jigsaw, steps for the classroom use of Jigsaw, tips for avoiding some of the potential pitfalls of the technique, and example lessons. There are excellent links to other cooperative learning sites as well (**http://www.jigsaw.org/**).

The Cooperative Learning Center focuses on the research and work of Roger T. Johnson and David W. Johnson of the University of Minnesota. Newsletters, essays, and a cooperative learning Questions & Answer section are available (**http://www.clcrc.com/**).

The International Association for the Study of Cooperation in Education is an organization that supports the research and use of cooperative learning techniques. The site contains links to other sites about cooperative learning, a set of newsletters, and contact information to local cooperative learning advocacy associations (**http://www.iasce.net/**).

Cooperative and Collaborative Learning

The Disney Learning Partnership and Channel 13 (New York City's PBS station) have collaborated on an excellent site that offers a wide set of resources, including video clips of cooperative learning in action. Particularly valuable are insights from teachers about the implementation of these techniques, and discussions about how cooperative techniques relate to such topics as multiple intelligences, inquiry learning, and state and national standards (**http://www.thirteen.org/edonline/concept2class/month5/**).

Creating Learning Environments: Chapter 12

Classroom Management

Natalie, exhausted and exasperated, went across the hallway to speak with her experienced colleague. Natalie had been hired as a long-term substitute after two others had filled in on a short-term basis. "It's almost as if law and order has broken down in that classroom," she explained. "I'm not sure where to begin. No one seems to know any rules or procedures for anything. The students have little respect for me or for each other. I dread walking down the hallway with them—it's like I'm escorting a tornado! When I try to establish a routine or a procedure, they complain that it's not Ms. Naples' way." The veteran responded, "We don't know when or if Ms. Naples will be back this year. Consider it your class, and move forward from there."

Like Natalie, many novice teachers are anxious about their classroom management skills. They are encouraged to "Lay down the law on the first day!" and "Don't smile until December!"—common examples of teacher folk wisdom. The message in such bits of advice (i.e., strong disciplinarian = good teacher) may appeal to a novice who is concerned about being able to handle a class. Effective classroom management, however, requires a broad set of skills and techniques; folk wisdom offers only a little guidance.

For a good set of classroom management resources, see **www.teachervision.fen.com/** and click on "classroom management." You will find resources on class organization, teacher–parent collaboration, students with special needs, and more.

Perhaps the most interesting of these sites is one that challenges you to discover your classroom management profile. Take the brief self-quiz at this site (**http://education.indiana.edu/cas/tt/v1i2/what.html**), and see how the results compare to your perception of yourself as a classroom manager.

Teaching for Learning: Chapter 13

Questioning Techniques

Andrew was marking his 30th year as an administrator in his K–12 school district. He had hired and supervised hundreds of teachers at every level, kindergarten through 12th grade. He had chaired dozens of committees that worked to keep the district current with modern curriculum standards, effective academic programs, and innovative instructional strategies. Early in his administrative career, Andrew observed that one of the major characteristics of expert teachers—whether they ran a teacher-centered classroom or a student-centered classroom—was the effective use of questions during lessons or learning activities. As he developed his expertise as an administrator, Andrew began to devote at least some part of a job interview with a prospective teacher or a post-observation teacher conference to questioning techniques and strategies.

The complex nature of questions and questioning techniques and strategies is reflected in the number of potential "hits" a search engine will provide for those terms. (You will also find that many of the pages and sites are designed for the corporate world. Questioning techniques are important for the employee selection process, planning business strategies, and for determining the needs of customers.) The two sites discussed here focus on different aspects of questioning, and they complement each other well. The Questioning Toolkit (**http://www.fno.org/nov97/toolkit.html**) sponsored by *The Educational Technology Journal* defines and illustrates the many types of questions that arise in classroom discourse. It examines the different tasks that different kinds of questions can accomplish. For example, in a stimulating learning environment, students and teachers are likely to pose a variety of organizing, hypothetical, probing, planning, and provocative questions. Expert use of the different types of questions can significantly enhance the level of cognitive activity of all those involved.

Standardized Testing: Chapter 14

Dan's mentor, Mr. Snell, had advised him in September that he would witness a lot of amazing events during his first year of teaching. The mentor was right, and an amazing event was occurring right now. It was a few minutes after school dismissal. Dan had given each student in his 6th-grade class an envelope that enclosed a copy of the results from the achievement tests that were administered just a few weeks before. Moments after students exited the school building, many parents anxiously opened the envelopes, and read the results. Some parents hugged their children; other parents appeared visibly upset. A group of parents gathered and seemed to be comparing the reports. The next morning Dan checked his voice mail. He had six requests from parents for conferences to discuss the results of the tests. Dan immediately contacted Mr. Snell for advice.

Interests and concerns about standardized testing are among the most serious and sensitive ones that face teachers and other educators. Parents become understandably upset when their children bring home low test scores. Scores help teachers to determine which students would benefit from supplemental assistance. Like most powerful tools, standardized tests can be used for purposes for which they are suited (e.g., helping educators identify weak areas in the curriculum) or they can be misused (e.g., judging the relative quality of school systems).

The online journal *Practical Assessment, Research and Evaluation* (**http://pareonline.net/Articles.htm**), published by ERIC Clearinghouse on Assessment and Evaluation, is a rich, authoritative, and comprehensive source of information about standardized testing (as well as other topics related to assessment and evaluation). Most of the articles are written for practitioners, primarily teachers and administrators, but some of them are targeted at other concerned audiences—parents, students, and researchers, for example. (And as we have discovered about student-centered learning, it is often valuable to explore a topic from more than one perspective.) Here are some sample titles of the dozens of journal articles that have been published since 1988:

Explaining Tests Results to Parents

- Preparing Students to Take Standardized Tests
- Norm- and Criterion-Referenced Tests
- Questions to Ask When Evaluating Tests
- Using State Standards and Tests to Improve Instruction
- The Concept of Statistical Significance Testing

Classroom Assessment and Grading: Chapter 15

Assessment

Robin was one of several teachers from her high school (and the only first-year teacher) to be invited to serve on the special district committee for assessment and evaluation. The superintendent created the committee in reaction to a report by a team of monitors from the state department of education. The report was generally favorable, but the team criticized the district's high schools for their near-exclusive use of traditional tools for assessing and evaluating students. The committee would make recommendations for revamping the district's approach to assessment and evaluation. Many of the veteran educators were looking to Robin for guidance—these experienced teachers were basically novices about the intricacies of recent innovations.

Assessment is one of the most complex tasks of teaching. Innovative instructional techniques have enriched the scope of how students learn in school, while innovations in assessment provide teachers rich insights into the complexity of what their students have learned and what they can do with their knowledge. Just as an architect needs to be knowledgeable of materials, construction techniques, client needs, and aesthetics, and understand how they affect the use of a building, a teacher needs to be knowledgeable of the purposes, uses, and values of different assessment techniques, and understand how they affect the learner.

At the first meeting of the special committee on assessment, Robin would find it valuable to introduce other committee members to the section of Edutopia Online (**http://www.glef.org**) that is devoted to assessment. The sponsor of this site, The George Lucas Foundation, has tapped into the expertise of many of the leading scholars on assessment to provide a rich set of resources devoted to the knowledgeable use of alternative forms of assessment in the classroom. (Many of the resources offered at Edutopia are in video and audio formats as well as in text.) A list of the assessment topics examined by Edutopia could serve very well as the committee's agenda:

Classroom, school, and district-wide examples of alternative assessment programs
Interviews with assessment experts
Using portfolios (including the use of digital portfolios), performances, projects, and exhibitions for assessment
Current research on assessment and testing
The teacher's role in assessment
Student reflections and journals
Strategies and resources that parents, policy makers, teachers, administrators, and community members can use to educate the public about K–12 assessment

Glossary

Absence seizure A seizure involving only a small part of the brain that causes a child to lose contact briefly.

Academic learning time Time when students are actually succeeding at the learning task.

Academic tasks The work the student must accomplish, including the content covered and the mental operations required.

Accommodation Altering existing schemes or creating new ones in response to new information.

Accountable Making teachers and schools responsible for student learning, usually by monitoring learning with high-stakes tests.

Achievement tests Standardized tests measuring how much students have learned in a given content area.

Acronym Technique for remembering names, phrases, or steps by using the first letter of each word to form a new, memorable word.

Action research Systematic observations or tests of methods conducted by teachers or schools to improve teaching and learning for their students.

Action zone Area of a classroom where the greatest amount of interaction takes place.

Active teaching Teaching characterized by high levels of teacher explanation, demonstration, and interaction with students.

Adaptation Adjustment to the environment.

Adequate yearly progress (AYP) Objectives for yearly improvement for all students and for specific groups such as students from major ethnic and racial groups, students with disabilities, students from low-income families, and students whose English is limited.

Adolescent egocentrism Assumption that everyone else shares one's thoughts, feelings, and concerns.

Advance organizer Statement of inclusive concepts to introduce and sum up material that follows.

Affective domain Objectives focusing on attitudes and feelings.

Agency The capacity to coordinate learning skills, motivation, and emotions to reach your goals.

Algorithm Step-by-step procedure for solving a problem; prescription for solutions.

Allocated time Time set aside for learning.

Americans with Disabilities Act of 1990 (ADA) Federal legislation prohibiting discrimination against persons with disabilities in employment, transportation, public access, local government, and telecommunications.

Analogical instruction Teaching new concepts by making connections (analogies) with information that the student already understands.

Analogical thinking Heuristic in which one limits the search for solutions to situations that are similar to the one at hand.

Anchored instruction A type of problem-based learning that uses a complex interesting situation as an anchor for learning.

Anorexia nervosa Eating disorder characterized by very limited food intake.

Antecedents Events that precede an action.

Anxiety General uneasiness, a feeling of tension.

Applied behavior analysis The application of behavioral learning principles to understand and change behavior.

Appropriate Internalize or take for yourself knowledge and skills developed in interaction with others or with cultural tools.

Aptitude tests Tests meant to predict future performance.

Arousal Physical and psychological reactions causing a person to be alert, attentive, wide awake.

Articulation disorders Any of a variety of pronunciation difficulties, such as the substitution, distortion, or omission of sounds.

Assertive discipline Clear, firm, unhostile response style.

Assessment Procedures used to obtain information about student performance.

Assessment bias Qualities of an assessment instrument that offend or unfairly penalize a group of students because of the students' gender, SES, race, ethnicity, etc.

Assimilation Fitting new information into existing schemes.

Assisted learning Providing strategic help in the initial stages of learning, gradually diminishing as students gain independence.

Assistive technology Devices, systems, and services that support and improve the capabilities of individuals with disabilities.

Attention Focus on a stimulus.

Attention-deficit hyperactivity disorder (ADHD) Current term for disruptive behavior disorders marked by overactivity, excessive difficulty sustaining attention, or impulsiveness.

Attribution theories Descriptions of how individuals' explanations, justifications, and excuses influence their motivation and behavior.

Authentic assessment Measurement of important abilities using procedures that simulate the application of these abilities to real-life problems.

Authentic task Tasks that have some connection to real-life problems the students will face outside the classroom.

Autism/Autism spectrum disorders Developmental disability significantly affecting verbal and nonverbal communication and social interaction, generally evident before age 3 and ranging from mild to major.

Automated basic skills Skills that are applied without conscious thought.

Automaticity The ability to perform thoroughly learned tasks without much mental effort.

Autonomy Independence.

Availability heuristic Judging the likelihood of an event based on what is available in your memory, assuming those easily remembered events are common.

Aversive Irritating or unpleasant.

Basic skills Clearly structured knowledge that is needed for later learning and that can be taught step by step.

Behavior modification Systematic application of antecedents and consequences to change behavior.

Behavioral learning theories Explanations of learning that focus on external events as the cause of changes in observable behaviors.

Behavioral objectives Instructional objectives stated in terms of observable behaviors.

Being needs Maslow's three higher-level needs, sometimes called growth needs.

Belief perseverance The tendency to hold onto beliefs, even in the face of contradictory evidence.

Between-class ability grouping/tracking System of grouping in which students are assigned to classes based on their measured ability or their achievements.

Bilingualism Speaking two languages fluently.

Bioecological model Bronfenbrenner's theory describing the nested social and cultural contexts that shape development. Every person develops within a *microsystem*, inside a *mesosystem*, embedded in an *exosystem*, all of which are a part of the *macrosystem* of the culture.

Blended families Parents, children, and stepchildren merged into families through remarriages.

Bottom-up processing Perceiving based on noticing separate defining features and assembling them into a recognizable pattern.

Brainstorming Generating ideas without stopping to evaluate them.

Bulimia Eating disorder characterized by overeating, then getting rid of the food by self-induced vomiting or laxatives.

CAPS A strategy that can be used in reading literature: *Characters, Aim* of story, *Problem, Solution.*

Case study Intensive study of one person or one situation.

Central executive The part of working memory that is responsible for monitoring and directing attention and other mental resources.

Central tendency Typical score for a group of scores.

Cerebral palsy Condition involving a range of motor or coordination difficulties due to brain damage.

Chain mnemonics Memory strategies that associate one element in a series with the next element.

Chunking Grouping individual bits of data into meaningful larger units.

Classical conditioning Association of automatic responses with new stimuli.

Classification Grouping objects into categories.

Classroom management Techniques used to maintain a healthy learning environment, relatively free of behavior problems.

Cmaps Tools for concept mapping developed by the Institute for Human Machine Cognition that are connected to many knowledge maps and other resources on the Internet.

Co-constructed process A social process in which people interact and negotiate (usually verbally) to create an understanding or to solve a problem. The final product is shaped by all participants.

Code-switching Successful switching between cultures in language, dialect, or nonverbal behaviors to fit the situation.

Cognitive apprenticeship A relationship in which a less experienced learner acquires knowledge and skills under the guidance of an expert.

Cognitive behavior modification Procedures based on both behavioral and cognitive learning principles for changing your own behavior by using self-talk and self-instruction.

Cognitive development Gradual orderly changes by which mental processes become more complex and sophisticated.

Cognitive domain In Bloom's taxonomy, memory and reasoning objectives.

Cognitive evaluation theory Suggests that events affect motivation through the individual's perception of the events as controlling behavior or providing information.

Cognitive objectives Instructional objectives stated in terms of higher-level thinking operations.

Cognitive view of learning A general approach that views learning as an active mental process of acquiring, remembering, and using knowledge.

Collaboration A philosophy about how to deal with people that respects differences, shares authority, and builds on the knowledge of others.

Collective monologue Form of speech in which children in a group talk but do not really interact or communicate.

Community of practice Social situation or context in which ideas are judged useful or true.

Compensation The principle that changes in one dimension can be offset by changes in another.

Complex learning environments Problems and learning situations that mimic the ill-structured nature of real life.

Concept A general category of ideas, objects, people, or experiences whose members share certain properties.

Concept mapping Student's diagram of his or her understanding of a concept.

Conceptual change teaching in science A method that helps students understand (rather than memorize) concepts in science by using and challenging the students' current ideas.

Concrete operations Mental tasks tied to concrete objects and situations.

Conditional knowledge "Knowing when and why" to use declarative and procedural knowledge.

Conditioned response (CR) Learned response to a previously neutral stimulus.

Conditioned stimulus (CS) Stimulus that evokes an emotional or physiological response after conditioning.

Confidence interval Range of scores within which an individual's particular score is likely to fall.

Confirmation bias Seeking information that confirms our choices and beliefs, while disconfirming evidence.

Consequences Events that follow an action.

Conservation Principle that some characteristics of an object remain the same despite changes in appearance.

Constructed-response format Assessment procedures that require the student to create an answer instead of selecting an answer from a set of choices.

Constructivism View that emphasizes the active role of the learner in building understanding and making sense of information.

Constructivist approach View that emphasizes the active role of the learner in building understanding and making sense of information.

Context The physical or emotional backdrop associated with an event.

Contiguity Association of two events because of repeated pairing.

Contingency contract A contract between the teacher and a student specifying what the student must do to earn a particular reward or privilege.

Continuous reinforcement schedule Presenting a reinforcer after every appropriate response.

Contract system System in which each student works for a particular grade according to agreed-upon standards.

Convergent questions Questions that have a single correct answer.

Convergent thinking Narrowing possibilities to a single answer.

Cooperation Working together with others to reach a shared goal.

Cooperative learning Arrangement in which students work in mixed-ability groups and are rewarded on the basis of the success of the group.

Correlations Statistical descriptions of how closely two variables are related.

Creativity Imaginative, original thinking or problem solving.

Criterion-referenced grading Assessment of each student's mastery of course objectives.

Criterion-referenced testing Testing in which scores are compared to a set performance standard.

Critical thinking Evaluating conclusions by logically and systematically examining the problem, the evidence, and the solution.

Crystallized intelligence Ability to apply culturally approved problem-solving methods.

Cueing Providing a stimulus that "sets up" a desired behavior.

Cultural deficit model A model that explains the school achievement problems of ethnic minority students by assuming that their culture is inadequate and does not prepare them to succeed in school.

Cultural tools The real tools (computers, scales, etc.) and symbol systems (numbers, language, graphs) that allow people in a society to communicate, think, solve problems, and create knowledge.

Culturally inclusive classrooms Classrooms that provide culturally diverse students equitable access to the teaching-learning process.

Culturally relevant management Taking cultural meanings and styles into account when developing management plans and responding to students.

Culturally relevant pedagogy Excellent teaching for students of color that includes academic success, developing/maintaining cultural competence, and developing a critical consciousness to challenge the status quo.

Culture The knowledge, values, attitudes, and traditions that guide the behavior of a group of people and allow them to solve the problems of living in their environment.

Culture-fair/culture-free test A test without cultural bias.

Decay The weakening and fading of memories with the passage of time.

Decentering Focusing on more than one aspect at a time.

Declarative knowledge Verbal information; facts; "knowing that" something is the case.

Deductive reasoning Drawing conclusions by applying rules or principles; logically moving from a general rule or principle to a specific solution.

Deficiency needs Maslow's four lower-level needs, which must be satisfied first.

Defining attributes Distinctive features shared by members of a category.

Descriptive studies Studies that collect detailed information about specific situations, often using observation, surveys, interviews, recordings, or a combination of these methods.

Development Orderly, adaptive changes we go through from conception to death.

Developmental crisis A specific conflict whose resolution prepares the way for the next stage.

Deviation IQ Score based on statistical comparison of an individual's performance with the average performance of others in that age group.

Diagnostic tests Individually administered tests to identify special learning problems.

Dialect Rule-governed variation of a language spoken by a particular group.

Differentiated instruction A flexible approach to teaching that matches content, process, and product based on student differences in readiness, interests, and learning needs.

Digital divide The disparaties in access to technology between poor and more affluent students and families.

Direct instruction/explicit teaching Systematic instruction for mastery of basic skills, facts, and information.

Disability The inability to do something specific such as walk or hear.

Discovery learning Bruner's approach, in which students work on their own to discover basic principles.

Discrimination Treating or acting unfairly toward particular categories of people.

Disequilibrium In Piaget's theory, the "out-of-balance" state that occurs when a person realizes that his or her current ways of thinking are not working to solve a problem or understand a situation.

Disorder A broad term meaning a general disturbance in physical or mental functioning.

Distractors Wrong answers offered as choices in a multiple-choice item.

Distributed practice Practice in brief periods with rest intervals.

Distributive justice Beliefs about how to divide materials or privileges fairly among members of a group; follows a sequence of development from equality to merit to benevolence.

Divergent questions Questions that have no single correct answer.

Divergent thinking Coming up with many possible solutions.

Domain-specific knowledge Information that is useful in a particular situation or that applies mainly to one specific topic.

Domain-specific strategies Consciously applied skills to reach goals in a particular subject or problem area.

Educational psychology The discipline concerned with teaching and learning processes; applies the methods and theories of psychology and has its own as well.

Educationally blind Needing Braille materials in order to learn.

Egocentric Assuming that others experience the world the way you do.

Ego-involved learners Students who focus on how well they are performing and how they are judged by others.

Elaboration Adding and extending meaning by connecting new information to existing knowledge.

Elaborative rehearsal Keeping information in working memory by associating it with something else you already know.

Emotional and behavioral disorders Behaviors or emotions that deviate so much from the norm that they interfere with the child's own growth and development and/or the lives of others—inappropriate behaviors, unhappiness or depression, fears and anxieties, and trouble with relationships.

Emotional intelligence (EQ) The ability to process and use emotional information accurately and efficiently.

Empathetic listening Hearing the intent and emotions behind what another says and reflecting them back by paraphrasing.

Engaged time/Time on Task Time spent actively engaged in the learning task at hand.

English as a second language (ESL) Designation for programs and classes to teach English to students who are not native speakers of English.

English language learners (ELL) Students whose primary or heritage language is not English.

Entity view of ability Belief that ability is a fixed characteristic that cannot be changed.

Epilepsy Disorder marked by seizures and caused by abnormal electrical discharges in the brain.

Episodic memory Long-term memory for information tied to a particular time and place, especially memory of the events in a person's life.

Epistemological beliefs Beliefs about the structure, stability, and certainty of knowledge and how knowledge is best learned.

Equilibration Search for mental balance between cognitive schemes and information from the environment.

Ethnicity A cultural heritage shared by a group of people.

Ethnography A descriptive approach to research that focuses on life within a group and tries to understand the meaning of events to the people involved.

Exceptional students Students who have abilities or problems so significant that they require special education or other services to reach their potential.

Executive control processes Processes such as selective attention, rehearsal, elaboration, and organization that influence encoding, storage, and retrieval of information in memory.

Exemplar A specific example of a given category that is used to classify an item.

Exhibition A performance test or demonstration of learning that is public and usually takes an extended time to prepare.

Expectancy × value theories Explanations of motivation that emphasize individuals' expectations for success combined with their valuing of the goal.

Experimentation Research method in which variables are manipulated and the effects recorded.

Expert teachers Experienced, effective teachers who have developed solutions for common classroom problems. Their knowledge of teaching process and content is extensive and well organized.

Explicit memory Long-term memories that involve deliberate or conscious recall.

Expository teaching Ausubel's method—teachers present material in complete, organized form, moving from broadest to more specific concepts.

Extinction The disappearance of a learned response.

Extrinsic motivation Motivation created by external factors such as rewards and punishments.

Failure-accepting students Students who believe their failures are due to low ability and there is little they can do about it.

Failure-avoiding students Students who avoid failure by sticking to what they know, by not taking risks, or by claiming not to care about their performance.

First wave constructivism A focus on the individual and psychological sources of knowing, as in Piaget's theory.

Flashbulb memories Clear, vivid memories of emotionally important events in your life.

Flexible grouping. Grouping and regrouping students based on learning needs.

Fluid intelligence Mental efficiency, nonverbal abilities grounded in brain development.

Flynn effect Because of better health, smaller families, increased complexity in the environment, and more and better schooling, IQ test scores are steadily rising.

Formal operations Mental tasks involving abstract thinking and coordination of a number of variables.

Formative assessment Ungraded testing used before or during instruction to aid in planning and diagnosis.

Fostering communities of learners (FCL) A system of interacting activities that results in a self-consciously active and reflective learning environment, and uses a research, share, perform learning cycle.

Frequency distribution Record showing how many scores fall into set groups.

Functional Behavioral Assessment (FBA) Procedures used to obtain information about antecedents, behaviors, and consequences to determine the reason or function of the behavior.

Functional fixedness Inability to use objects or tools in a new way.

Funds of knowledge Knowledge that families and community members have in many areas of work, home, and religious life that can become the basis for teaching.

Gender biases Different views of males and females, often favoring one gender over the other.

Gender schemas Organized networks of knowledge about what it means to be male or female.

Gender-role identity Beliefs about characteristics and behaviors associated with one sex as opposed to the other.

General knowledge Information that is useful in many different kinds of tasks; information that applies to many situations.

Generalized seizure A seizure involving a large portion of the brain.

Generativity Sense of concern for future generations.

Gestalt German for *pattern* or *whole*. Gestalt theorists hold that people organize their perceptions into coherent wholes.

Gifted student A very bright, creative, and talented student.

Goal What an individual strives to accomplish.

Goal orientations Patterns of beliefs about goals related to achievement in school.

Goal structure The way students relate to others who are also working toward a particular goal.

Goal-directed actions Deliberate actions toward a goal.

Good behavior game Arrangement where a class is divided into teams and each team receives demerit points for breaking agreed-upon rules of good behavior.

Grade-equivalent score Measure of grade level based on comparison with norming samples from each grade.

Grading on the curve Norm-referenced grading that compares students' performance to an average level.

Group consequences Rewards or punishments given to a class as a whole for adhering to or violating rules of conduct.

Group discussion Conversation in which the teacher does not have the dominant role; students pose and answer their own questions.

Group focus The ability to keep as many students as possible involved in activities.

Guided discovery An adaptation of discovery learning, in which the teacher provides some direction.

Halo effect The tendency for a general impression of a person to influence our perception of any aspect of that person.

Handicap A disadvantage in a particular situation, sometimes caused by a disability.

Heritage language The language spoken in a student's home or by older members of the family.

Heuristic General strategy used in attempting to solve problems.

Hierarchy of needs Maslow's model of seven levels of human needs, from basic physiological requirements to the need for self-actualization.

High-road transfer Application of abstract knowledge learned in one situation to a different situation.

High-stakes testing Standardized tests whose results have powerful influences when used by school administrators, other officials, or employers to make decisions.

Histogram Bar graph of a frequency distribution.

Hostile aggression Bold, direct action that is intended to hurt someone else; unprovoked attack.

Humanistic interpretation Approach to motivation that emphasizes personal freedom, choice, self-determination, and striving for personal growth.

Hypothetico-deductive reasoning A formal-operations problem-solving strategy in which an individual begins by identifying all the factors that might affect a problem and then deduces and systematically evaluates specific solutions.

"I" message Clear, nonaccusatory statement of how something is affecting you.

Identity achievement Strong sense of commitment to life choices after free consideration of alternatives.

Identity diffusion Uncenteredness; confusion about who one is and what one wants.

Identity foreclosure Acceptance of parental life choices without consideration of options.

Identity Principle that a person or object remains the same over time. Also, the complex answer to the question: "Who am I?"

Images Representations based on the physical attributes—the appearance—of information.

Implicit memory Knowledge that we are not conscious of recalling, but influences behavior or thought without our awareness.

Importance/Attainment value The importance of doing well on a task; how success on the task meets personal needs.

Incentive An object or event that encourages or discourages behavior.

Inclusion The integration of all students, including those with severe disabilities, into regular classes.

Incremental view of ability Belief that ability is a set of skills that can be changed.

Individual learning expectation (ILE) Personal average score.

Individualized Education Program (IEP) Annually revised program for an exceptional student, detailing present achievement level, goals, and strategies, drawn up by teachers, parents, specialists, and (if possible) the student.

Individuals with Disabilities Education Improvement Act (IDEA) Latest amendment of PL 94-142, guarantees a free public education to all children regardless of disability.

Inductive reasoning Formulating general principles based on knowledge of examples and details.

Industry Eagerness to engage in productive work.

Informal assessments Ungraded (formative) assessments that gather information from multiple sources to help teachers make decisions.

Information processing The human mind's activity of taking in, storing, and using information.

Initiative Willingness to begin new activities and explore new directions.

Inquiry learning Approach in which the teacher presents a puzzling situation and students solve the problem by gathering data and testing their conclusions.

Insight Sudden realization of a solution; in Sternberg's triarchic theory of intelligence, the ability to deal effectively with novel situations.

Instructional conversation Situation in which students learn through interactions with teachers and/or other students.

Instructional objectives Clear statement of what students are intended to learn through instruction.

Instrumental aggression Strong actions aimed at claiming an object, place, or privilege—not intended to harm, but may lead to harm.

Integration Fitting the child with special needs into existing class structures.

Integrity Sense of self-acceptance and fulfillment

Intellectual Disabilities/Mental retardation Significantly below-average intellectual and adaptive social behavior, evident before age 18.

Intelligence Ability or abilities to acquire and use knowledge for solving problems and adapting to the world.

Intelligence quotient (IQ) Score comparing mental and chronological ages.

Interference The process that occurs when remembering certain information is hampered by the presence of other information.

Intermittent reinforcement schedule Presenting a reinforcer after some but not all responses.

Internalize Process whereby children adopt external standards as their own.

Intersubjective attitude A commitment to build shared meaning with others by finding common ground and exchanging interpretations.

Interval schedule Length of time between reinforcers.

Intrinsic motivation Motivation associated with activities that are their own reward.

Intrinsic or interest value The enjoyment a person gets from a task.

Intuitive thinking Making imaginative leaps to correct perceptions or workable solutions.

Jigsaw A cooperative structure in which each member of a group is responsible for teaching other members one section of the material.

Joplin Plan/Nongraded elementary school Arrangement wherein students are grouped by ability in particular subjects, regardless of their ages or grades.

Keyword method System of associating new words or concepts with similar-sounding cue words and images.

KWL A strategy to guide reading and inquiry: Before—What do I already *know?* What do I *want* to know? After—What have I *learned?*

Lateralization The specialization of the two hemispheres (sides) of the brain cortex.

Learned helplessness The expectation, based on previous experiences with a lack of control, that all one's efforts will lead to failure.

Learning disability Problem with acquisition and use of language; may show up as difficulty with reading, writing, reasoning, or math.

Learning preferences Preferred ways of studying and learning, such as using pictures instead of text, working with other people versus alone, learning in structured or in unstructured situations, and so on.

Learning strategies General plans for approaching learning tasks.

Learning styles Characteristic approaches to learning and studying.

Learning tactics Specific techniques for learning, such as using mnemonics or outlining a passage.

Learning Process through which experience causes permanent change in knowledge or behavior.

Least restrictive environment (LRE) Educating each child with peers in the regular classroom to the greatest extent possible.

Legitimate peripheral participation Genuine involvement in the work of the group, even if your abilities are undeveloped and contributions are small.

Lesson study As a group, teachers develop, test, improve, and retest lessons until they are satisfied with the final version.

Levels of processing theory Theory that recall of information is based on how deeply it is processed.

Loci method Technique of associating items with specific places.

Locus of causality The location—internal or external—of the cause of behavior.

Long-term memory Permanent store of knowledge.

Long-term working memory Holds the strategies for pulling information from long-term memory into working memory.

Low vision Vision limited to close objects.

Low-road transfer Spontaneous and automatic transfer of highly practiced skills.

Mainstreaming Teaching children with disabilities in regular classes for part or all of their school day.

Maintenance rehearsal Keeping information in working memory by repeating it to yourself.

Massed practice Practice for a single extended period.

Mastery experiences Our own direct experiences—the most powerful source of efficacy information.

Mastery goal A personal intention to improve abilities and learn, no matter how performance suffers.

Mastery-oriented students Students who focus on learning goals because they value achievement and see ability as improvable.

Maturation Genetically programmed, naturally occurring changes over time.

Mean Arithmetical average.

Meaningful verbal learning Focused and organized relationships among ideas and verbal information.

Means-ends analysis Heuristic in which a goal is divided into subgoals.

Measurement An evaluation expressed in quantitative (number) terms.

Median Middle score in a group of scores.

Melting pot A metaphor for the absorption and assimilation of immigrants into the mainstream of society so that ethnic differences vanish.

Mental age In intelligence testing, a performance that represents average abilities for that age group.

Metacognition Knowledge about our own thinking processes.

Metalinguistic awareness Understanding about one's own use of language.

Microgenetic studies Detailed observation and analysis of changes in a cognitive process as the process unfolds over a several day or week period of time.

Minority group A group of people who have been socially disadvantaged—not always a minority in actual numbers.

Mnemonics Techniques for remembering; also, the art of memory.

Mode Most frequently occurring score.

Modeling Changes in behavior, thinking, or emotions that happen through observing another person—a model.

Moral dilemmas Situations in which no choice is clearly and indisputably right.

Moral realism Stage of development wherein children see rules as absolute.

Moral reasoning The thinking process involved in judgments about questions of right and wrong.

Morality of cooperation Stage of development wherein children realize that people make rules and people can change them.

Moratorium Identity crisis; suspension of choices because of struggle.

Motivation An internal state that arouses, directs, and maintains behavior.

Motivation to learn The tendency to find academic activities meaningful and worthwhile and to try to benefit from them.

Movement management Keeping lessons and the group moving at an appropriate (and flexible) pace, with smooth transitions and variety.

Multicultural education Education that promotes equity in the schooling of all students.

Multiple representations of content Considering problems using various analogies, examples, and metaphors.

Myelination The process by which neural fibers are coated with a fatty sheath called *myelin* that makes message transfer more efficient.

Natural/logical consequences Instead of punishing, have students redo, repair, or in some way face the consequences that naturally flow from their actions.

Need for autonomy The desire to have our own wishes, rather than external rewards or pressures, determine our actions.

Negative correlation A relationship between two variables in which a high value on one is associated with a low value on the other. Example: height and distance from top of head to the ceiling.

Negative reinforcement Strengthening behavior by removing an aversive stimulus when the behavior occurs.

Neo-Piagetian theories More recent theories that integrate findings about attention, memory, and strategy use with Piaget's insights about children's think-ing and the construction of knowledge.

Neurons Nerve cells that store and transfer information

Neutral stimulus Stimulus not connected to a response.

Nigrescence The process of developing a Black identity.

Norm groups A group whose average score serves as a standard for evaluating any student's score on a test.

Normal distribution The most commonly occurring distribution, in which scores are distributed evenly around the mean.

Norming sample Large sample of students serving as a comparison group for scoring standardized tests.

Norm-referenced grading Assessment of students' achievement in relation to one another.

Norm-referenced testing Testing in which scores are compared with the average performance of others.

Object permanence The understanding that objects have a separate, permanent existence.

Objective testing Multiple-choice, matching, true/false, short-answer, and fill-in tests; scoring answers does not require interpretation.

Observational learning Learning by observation and imitation of others.

Operant conditioning Learning in which voluntary behavior is strengthened or weakened by consequences or antecedents.

Operants Voluntary (and generally goal-directed) behaviors emitted by a person or an animal.

Operations Actions a person carries out by thinking them through instead of literally performing the actions.

Organization Ongoing process of arranging information and experience into mental systems or categories. Also, ordered and logical network of relations.

Overgeneralization Inclusion of nonmembers in a category; overextending a concept.

Overlapping Supervising several activities at once.

Overlearning Practicing a skill past the point of mastery.

Overt aggression A form of hostile aggression that involves physical attack.

Paraphrase rule Policy whereby listeners must accurately summarize what a speaker has said before being allowed to respond.

Parenting styles The ways of interacting with and disciplining children.

Part learning Breaking a list of rote learning items into shorter lists.

Participant observation A method for conducting descriptive research in which the researcher becomes a participant in the situation in order to better understand life in that group.

Participants/subjects People or animals studied.

Participation structures The formal and informal rules for how to take part in a given activity.

Peg-type mnemonics Systems of associating items with cue words.

Percentage grading System of converting class performances to percentage scores and assigning grades based on predetermined cutoff points.

Percentile rank Percentage of those in the norming sample who scored at or below an individual's score.

Perception Interpretation of sensory information.

Performance assessments Any form of assessment that requires students to carry out an activity or produce a product in order to demonstrate learning

Performance goal A personal intention to seem competent or perform well in the eyes of others.

Personal development Changes in personality that take place as one grows.

Perspective-taking ability Understanding that others have different feelings and experiences.

Phonological loop Part of working memory. A memory rehearsal system for verbal and sound information of about 1.5 to 2 seconds.

Physical development Changes in body structure and function over time.

Plasticity The brain's tendency to remain somewhat adaptable or flexible.

Portfolio A collection of the student's work in an area, showing growth, self-reflection, and achievement.

Positive Behavioral Supports (PBS) Interventions designed to replace problem behaviors with new actions that serve the same purpose for the student.

Positive correlation A relationship between two variables in which the two increase or decrease together. Example: calorie intake and weight gain.

Positive practice Practicing correct responses immediately after errors.

Positive reinforcement Strengthening behavior by presenting a desired stimulus after the behavior.

Pragmatics The rules for when and how to use language to be an effective communicator in a particular culture.

Precorrection A way of preventing serious behavior problems of students who have been labeled at risk by directing the students toward more appropriate actions.

Prejudice Prejudgment or irrational generalization about an entire category of people.

Premack principle Principle stating that a more-preferred activity can serve as a reinforcer for a less-preferred activity.

Preoperational The stage before a child masters logical mental operations.

Presentation punishment Decreasing the chances that a behavior will occur again by presenting an aversive stimulus following the behavior; also called Type I punishment.

Pretest Formative test for assessing students' knowledge, readiness, and abilities.

Priming Activating a concept in memory or the spread of activation from one concept to another.

Principle Established relationship between factors.

Private speech Children's self-talk, which guides their thinking and action. Eventually, these verbalizations are internalized as silent inner speech.

Problem Any situation in which you are trying to reach some goal and must find a means to do so.

Problem-based learning Methods that provide students with realistic problems that don't necessarily have "right" answers.

Problem solving Creating new solutions for problems.

Procedural knowledge Knowledge that is demonstrated when we perform a task; "knowing how."

Procedural memory Long-term memory for how to do things.

Procedures Prescribed steps for an activity.

Productions The contents of procedural memory; rules about what actions to take, given certain conditions.

Prompt A reminder that follows a cue to make sure the person reacts to the cue.

Propositional network Set of interconnected concepts and relationships in which long-term knowledge is held.

Prototype A best example or best representative of a category.

Psychomotor domain Physical ability and coordination objectives.

Psychosocial Describing the relation of the individual's emotional needs to the social environment.

Puberty The physiological changes during adolescence that lead to the ability to have reproduce.

Punishment Process that weakens or suppresses behavior.

Pygmalion effect Exceptional progress by a student as a result of high teacher expectations for that student; named for mythological king, Pygmalion, who made a statue, then caused it to be brought to life.

Race A group of people who share common biological traits that are seen as self-defining by the people of the group.

Racial and ethnic pride A positive self-concept about one's racial or ethnic heritage.

Radical constructivism Knowledge is assumed to be the individual's construction; it cannot be judged right or wrong.

Random Without any definite pattern; following no rule.

Range Distance between the highest and the lowest scores in a group.

Ratio schedule Reinforcement based on the number of responses between reinforcers.

READS A five-step reading strategy: *Review* headings; *Examine* boldface words; *Ask*, "What do I expect to learn?"; *Do* it—Read; *Summarize* in your own words.

Reciprocal determinism An explanation of behavior that emphasizes the mutual effects of the individual and the environment on each other.

Reciprocal questioning Approach where groups of two or three students ask and answer each other's questions after a lesson or presentation.

Reciprocal teaching A method, based on modeling, to teach reading comprehension strategies.

Reconstruction Recreating information by using memories, expectations, logic, and existing knowledge.

Reflective Thoughtful and inventive. Reflective teachers think back over situations to analyze what they did and why and to consider how they might improve learning for their students.

Reinforcement Use of consequences to strengthen behavior.

Reinforcer Any event that follows a behavior and increases the chances that the behavior will occur again.

Relational aggression A form of hostile aggression that involves verbal attacks and other actions meant to harm social relationships.

Reliability Consistency of test results.

Removal punishment Decreasing the chances that a behavior will occur again by removing a pleasant stimulus following the behavior; also called Type II punishment.

Representativeness heuristic Judging the likelihood of an event based on how well the events match your prototypes—what you think is representative of the category.

Reprimands Criticisms for misbehavior; rebukes.

Resilience The ability to adapt successfully in spite of difficult circumstances and threats to development.

Resistance culture Group values and beliefs about refusing to adopt the behaviors and attitudes of the majority culture.

Respondents Responses (generally automatic or involuntary) elicited by specific stimuli.

Response Observable reaction to a stimulus.

Response cost Punishment by loss of reinforcers.

Response set Rigidity; tendency to respond in the most familiar way.

Restructuring Conceiving of a problem in a new or different way.

Retrieval Process of searching for and finding information in long-term memory.

Reversibility A characteristic of Piagetian logical operations—the ability to think through a series of steps, then mentally reverse the steps and return to the starting point; also called *reversible thinking*.

Reversible thinking Thinking backward, from the end to the beginning.

Revise option In a contract system, the chance to revise and improve work.

Reward An attractive object or event supplied as a consequence of a behavior.

Ripple effect "Contagious" spreading of behaviors through imitation.

Rote memorization Remembering information by repetition without necessarily understanding the meaning of the information.

Rules Statements specifying expected and forbidden behaviors; dos and don'ts.

Satiation Requiring a person to repeat a problem behavior past the point of interest or motivation.

Scaffolding Support for learning and problem solving. The support could be clues, reminders, encouragement, breaking the problem down into steps, providing an example, or anything else that allows the student to grow in independence as a learner.

Schema-driven problem solving Recognizing a problem as a "disguised" version of an old problem for which one already has a solution.

Schemas (singular, **Schema**) Basic structures for organizing information; concepts.

Schemes Mental systems or categories of perception and experience.

Scoring rubrics Rules that are used to determine the quality of a student performance.

Script Schema or expected plan for the sequence of steps in a common event such as buying groceries or ordering take-out pizza.

Scripted cooperation A learning strategy in which two students take turns summarizing material and critiquing the summaries.

Seatwork Independent classroom work.

Second wave constructivism A focus on the social and cultural sources of knowing, as in Vygotsky's theory.

Section 504 A part of civil rights law that prevents discrimination against people with disabilities in programs that receive federal funds, such as public schools.

Self-actualization Fulfilling one's potential.

Self-concept Individuals' knowledge and beliefs about themselves—their ideas, feelings, attitudes, and expectations.

Self-efficacy Beliefs about personal competence in a particular situation.

Self-esteem The value each of us places on our own characteristics, abilities, and behaviors.

Self-fulfilling prophecy A groundless expectation that is confirmed because it has been expected.

Self-instruction Talking oneself through the steps of a task.

Self-management Management of your own behavior and acceptance of responsibility for your own actions. Also, in behavioral learning theory, use of behavioral principles to change your own behavior.

Self-regulated learning A view of learning as skills and will applied to analyzing learning tasks, setting goals, and planning how to do the task, applying skills, and especially making adjustments about how learning is carried out.

Self-regulation Process of activating and sustaining thoughts, behaviors, and emotions in order to reach goals.

Self-reinforcement Controlling your own reinforcers.

Semantic memory Memory for meaning.

Semilingual Not proficient in any language; speaking one or more languages inadequately.

Semiotic function The ability to use symbols—language, pictures, signs, or gestures—to represent actions or objects mentally.

Sensorimotor Involving the senses and motor activity.

Sensory memory System that holds sensory information very briefly.

Serial-position effect The tendency to remember the beginning and the end but not the middle of a list.

Seriation Arranging objects in sequential order according to one aspect, such as size, weight, or volume.

Service learning An approach to combining academic learning with personal and social development.

Sexual identity A complex combination of beliefs and orientations about gender roles and sexual orientation.

Shaping Reinforcing each small step of progress toward a desired goal or behavior.

Short-term memory Component of memory system that holds information for about 20 seconds.

Single-subject experimental studies Systematic interventions to study effects with one person, often by applying and then withdrawing a treatment.

Situated learning The idea that skills and knowledge are tied to the situation in which they were learned and difficult to apply in new settings.

Social cognitive theory Theory that adds concern with cognitive factors such as beliefs, self-perceptions, and expectations to social learning theory.

Social conventions Agreed-upon rules and ways of doing things in a particular situation.

Social development Changes over time in the ways we relate to others.

Social goals A wide variety of needs and motives to be connected to others or part of a group.

Social isolation Removal of a disruptive student for 5 to 10 minutes.

Social learning theory Theory that emphasizes learning through observation of others.

Social negotiation Aspect of learning process that relies on collaboration with others and respect for different perspectives.

Social persuasion A "pep talk" or specific performance feedback—one source of self-efficacy.

Sociocultural theory Emphasizes role in development of cooperative dialogues between children and more knowledgeable members of society. Children learn the culture of their community (ways of thinking and behaving) through these interactions.

Sociocultural views of motivation Perspectives that emphasize participation, identities, and interpersonal relations within communities of practice.

Socioeconomic status (SES) Relative standing in the society based on income, power, background, and prestige.

Sociolinguistics The study of the formal and informal rules for how, when, about what, to whom, and how long to speak in conversations within cultural groups.

Spasticity Overly tight or tense muscles, characteristic of some forms of cerebral palsy.

Speech disorder Inability to produce sounds effectively for speaking.

Spiral curriculum Bruner's design for teaching that introduces the fundamental structure of all subjects early in the school years, then revisits the subjects in more and more complex forms over time.

Spreading activation Retrieval of pieces of information based on their relatedness to one another. Remembering one bit of information activates (stimulates) recall of associated information.

Stand-alone thinking skills programs Programs that teach thinking skills directly without need for extensive subject matter knowledge.

Standard deviation Measure of how widely scores vary from the mean.

Standard error of measurement Hypothetical estimate of variation in scores if testing were repeated.

Standard scores Scores based on the standard deviation.

Standardized tests Tests given, usually nationwide, under uniform conditions and scored according to uniform procedures.

Stanine scores Whole number scores from 1 to 9, each representing a wide range of raw scores.

Statistically significant Not likely to be a chance occurrence.

Stem The question part of a multiple-choice item.

Stereotype Schema that organizes knowledge or perceptions about a category.

Stereotype threat The extra emotional and cognitive burden that your performance in an academic situation might confirm a stereotype that others hold about you.

Stimulus Event that activates behavior.

Stimulus control Capacity for the presence or absence of antecedents to cause behaviors.

Story grammar Typical structure or organization for a category of stories.

Successive approximations Small components that make up a complex behavior.

Summative assessment Testing that follows instruction and assesses achievement.

Sustaining expectation effect Student performance maintained at a certain level because teachers don't recognize improvements.

Synapses The tiny space between neurons—chemical messages are sent across these gaps.

Syntax The order of words in phrases or sentences.

***T* score** Standard score with a mean of 50 and a standard deviation of 10.

Tacit knowledge Knowing how rather than knowing that—knowledge that is more likely to be learned during everyday life than through formal schooling.

Task analysis System for breaking down a task hierarchically into basic skills and subskills.

Task-involved learners Students who focus on mastering the task or solving the problem.

Taxonomy Classification system.

Teachers' sense of efficacy A teacher's belief that he or she can reach even the most difficult students and help them learn.

Theory Integrated statement of principles that attempts to explain a phenomenon and make predictions.

Theory of mind An understanding that other people are people too, with their own minds, thoughts, feelings, beliefs, desires, and perceptions.

Theory of multiple intelligences In Gardner's theory of intelligence, a person's eight separate abilities: logical-mathematical, linguistic, musical, spatial, bodily-kinesthetic, interpersonal, intrapersonal, and naturalist.

Time out Technically, the removal of all reinforcement. In practice, isolation of a student from the rest of the class for a brief time.

Token reinforcement system System in which tokens earned for academic work and positive classroom behavior can be exchanged for some desired reward.

Top-down processing Perceiving based on the context and the patterns you expect to occur in that situation.

Tracking Assignment to different classes and academic experiences based on achievement.

Transfer Influence of previously learned material on new material.

Transition programming Gradual preparation of exceptional students to move from high school into further education or training, employment, or community involvement.

Triarchic theory of successful intelligence A three-part description of the mental abilities (thinking processes, coping with new experiences, and adapting to context) that lead to more or less intelligent behavior.

True score The score the student would get if the measurement were completely accurate and error-free.

Unconditioned response (UR) Naturally occurring emotional or physiological response.

Unconditioned stimulus (US) Stimulus that automatically produces an emotional or physiological response.

Undergeneralization Exclusion of some true members from a category; limiting a concept.

Universal design Considering the needs of all users as new tools, or learning programs, or websites.

Untracking Redesigning schools to teach students in classes that are not grouped by ability.

Utility value The contribution of a task to meeting one's goals.

Validity Degree to which a test measures what it is intended to measure.

Variability Degree of difference or deviation from mean.

Verbalization Putting your problem-solving plan and its logic into words.

Vicarious experiences Accomplishments that are modeled by someone else.

Vicarious reinforcement Increasing the chances that we will repeat a behavior by observing another person being reinforced for that behavior.

Visuospatial sketchpad Part of working memory. A holding system for visual and spatial information.

Voicing problems Inappropriate pitch, quality, loudness, or intonation.

Volition Will power; self-discipline; work styles that protect opportunities to reach goals by applying self-regulated learning.

Warm demanders Effective teachers with African American students who show both high expectations and great caring for their students.

Whole-language approach A philosophical approach to teaching and learning that stresses learning through authentic, real-life tasks. Emphasizes using language to learn, integrating learning across skills and subjects, and respecting the language abilities of student and teacher.

Within-class ability grouping System of grouping in which students in a class are divided into two or three groups based on ability in an attempt to accommodate student differences.

Withitness According to Kounin, awareness of everything happening in a classroom.

Work-avoidant learners Students who don't want to learn or to look smart, but just want to avoid work.

Working memory The information that you are focusing on at a given moment.

Working-backward strategy Heuristic in which one starts with the goal and moves backward to solve the problem.

***z* score** Standard score indicating the number of standard deviations above or below the mean.

Zero reject A basic principle of IDEA specifying that no student with a disability, no matter what kind or how severe, can be denied a free public education.

Zone of proximal development Phase at which a child can master a task if given appropriate help and support.

References

AAMD Ad Hoc Committee on Terminology and Classification. (1992). *Mental retardation: Definition, classification, and systems of support* (9th ed.). Washington, DC: American Association on Mental Retardation.

Aber, J. L., Brown, J. L., & Jones, S. M. (2003). Developmental trajectories toward violence in middle childhood: Course, demographic differences, and response to school-based intervention. *Developmental Psychology, 39*, 324–348.

Abi-Nader, J. (1991). Creating a vision of the future: Strategies for motivating minority students. *Phi Delta Kappan, 72*, 546–549.

Aboud, F. E. (2003). The formation of in-group favoritism and out-group prejudice in young children: Are they distinct attitudes? *Developmental Psychology, 39*, 48–60.

Abrams, I. M., & Madaus, G.F. (2003). The lessons of high stakes testing. *Educational Leadership, 61*(32), 31–35.

Ackerman, B. P., Brown, E. D., & Izard, C. E. (2004). The relations between contextual risk, earned income, and the school adjustment of children from economically disadvantaged families. *Developmental Psychology, 40*, 204–216.

Ackerman, P. L., Beier, M. E., & Boyle, M. O. (2005). Working memory and intelligence: The same or different constructs? *Psychological Bulletin, 131*, 30–60.

Ainley, M., Hidi, S., & Berndorf, D. (2002). Interest, learning, and the psychological processes that mediate their relationship. *Journal of Educational Psychology, 94*, 545–561.

Airasian, P. W. (1996). *Assessment in the classroom.* New York: McGraw-Hill.

Airasian, P. W. (2005). *Classroom assessment: Concepts and applications* (5th ed.). New York: McGraw-Hill.

Airasian, P. W., & Walsh, M. E. (1997). Constructivist cautions. *Phi Delta Kappan, 78*, 444–449.

Albanese, M. A., & Mitchell, S. A. (1993). Problem-based learning: A review of literature on its outcomes and implementation issues. *Academic Medicine, 68*, 52–81.

Alber, S. R., & Heward, W. L. (1997). Recruit it or lose it! Training students to recruit positive teacher attention. *Intervention in School and Clinic, 32*, 275–282.

Alber, S. R., & Heward, W. L. (2000). Teaching students to recruit positive attention: A review and recommendations. *Journal of Behavioral Education, 10*, 177–204.

Alberto, P., & Troutman, A. C. (2003). *Applied behavior analysis for teachers: Influencing student performance* (6th ed.). Saddle River, NJ: Prentice-Hall/Merrill.

Alberto, P., & Troutman, A. C. (2006). *Applied behavior analysis for teachers: Influencing student performance* (7th ed.). Saddle River, NJ: Prentice-Hall/Merrill.

Alderman, M. K. (2004). *Motivation for achievement: Possibilities for teaching and learning.* Mahwah, NJ: Lawrence Erlbaum.

Alexander, P. A. (1992). Domain knowledge: Evolving themes and emerging concerns. *Educational Psychologist, 27*, 33–51.

Alexander, P. A. (1996). The past, present, and future of knowledge research: A reexamination of the role of knowledge in learning and instruction. *Educational Psychologist, 31*, 89–92.

Alexander, P. A. (1997). Mapping the multidimensional nature of domain learning: The interplay of cognitive, motivational, and strategic forces. *Advances in Motivation and Achievement, 10*, 213–250.

Alexander, P. A. (2006). *Psychology in learning and instruction.* Upper Saddle River, NJ: Merrill/Prentice-Hall.

Alexander, P. A., Kulikowich, J. M., & Schulze, S. K. (1994). How subject-matter knowledge affects recall and interest. *American Educational Research Journal, 31*, 313–337.

Alexander, P. A., & Murphy, P. K. (1998). The research base for APA's Learner-Centered Psychological Principles. In N. Lambert & B. McCombs (Eds.), *How students learn: Reforming schools through learner-centered education* (pp. 33–60). Washington, DC: American Psychological Association.

Alliance for Service Learning in Education Reform. (1993). Standards of quality for school based service learning. *Equity and Excellence in Education, 26*(2), 71–77.

Allington, R. (1980). Teacher interruption behaviors during primary-grade oral reading. *Journal of Educational Psychology, 71*, 371–377.

Alloway, N. (1984). *Teacher expectations.* Paper presented at the meetings of the Australian Association for Research in Education, Perth, Australia.

Alloy, L. B., & Seligman, M. E. P. (1979). On the cognitive component of learned helplessness and depression. *The Journal of Learning and Motivation, 13*, 219–276.

Altermatt, E. R., Pomerantz, E. M., Ruble, D. N., Frey, K. S., & Greulich, F. K. (2002). Predicting changes in children's self-perceptions of academic competence: A naturalistic examination of evaluative discourse among classmates. *Developmental Psychology, 38*, 903–917.

Alton-Lee, A., Diggins, C., Klenner, L., Vine, E., & Dalton, N. (2001). Teacher management of the learning environment during a social studies discussion in a new-entrant classroom in New Zealand. *The Elementary School Journal, 101*, 549–566.

Alvidrez, J., & Weinstein, R. S. (1999). Early teacher perceptions and later student academic achievement. *Journal of Educational Psychology, 91*, 731–746.

Amabile, T. M. (1996). *Creativity in context.* Boulder, CO: Westview Press.

Amabile, T. M. (2001). Beyond talent: John Irving and the passionate craft of creativity. *American Psychologist, 56*, 333–336.

Amato, L. F., Loomis, L. S., & Booth, A. (1995). Parental divorce, marital conflict, and offspring well-being during early adulthood. *Social Forces, 73*, 895–915.

Amato, P. R. (2001). Children of divorce in the 1990s: An update of the Amato and Keith (1991) meta-analysis. *Journal of Family Psychology, 15*, 355–370.

American Association on Mental Retardation (AAMR). (2002). *Mental retardation: Definitions, classifications, and systems of support* (10th ed.). Washington DC: Author.

American Psychological Association. (2002). Warning signs. Retrieved April 16, 2002, from http://helping.apa.org/warningsigns

Ames, C. (1990). Motivation: What teachers need to know. *Teachers College Record, 91,* 409–421.

Ames, C. (1992). Classrooms: Goals, structures, and student motivation. *Journal of Educational Psychology, 84,* 261–271.

Ames, R., & Lau, S. (1982). An attributional analysis of student help-seeking in academic settings. *Journal of Educational Psychology, 74,* 414–423.

Anastasi, A. (1988). *Psychological testing* (6th ed.). New York: Macmillan.

Anderman, E. M., & Maehr, M. L. (1994). Motivation and schooling in the middle grades. *Review of Educational Research, 64,* 287–310.

Anderman, E. M., & Midgley, C. (2004). Changes in self-reported academic cheating across the transition from middle school to high school. *Contemporary Educational Psychology, 29,* 499–517.

Anderson, C. W., Holland, J. D., & Palincsar, A. S. (1997). Canonical and sociocultural approaches to research and reform in science education: The story of Juan and his group. *The Elementary School Journal,* 97, 359–384.

Anderson, C. W., & Roth, K. J. (1989). Teaching for meaningful and self-regulated learning of science. In J. Brophy (Ed.), *Advances in research on teaching* (Vol. 1, pp. 265–306). Greenwich, CT: JAI Press.

Anderson, C. W., & Smith, E. L. (1983, April). *Children's conceptions of light and color: Developing the concept of unseen rays.* Paper presented at the annual meeting of the American Educational Research Association, Montreal.

Anderson, C. W., & Smith, E. L. (1987). Teaching science. In V. Richardson-Koehler (Ed.), *Educators' handbook: A research perspective* (pp. 84–111). New York: Longman.

Anderson, J. R. (1993). Problem solving and learning. *American Psychologist, 48,* 35–44.

Anderson, J. R. (1995a). *Cognitive psychology and its implications* (4th ed.). New York: Freeman.

Anderson, J. R. (1995b). *Learning and memory.* New York: John Wiley & Sons.

Anderson, J. R. (2005). *Cognitive psychology and its implications* (6th ed.). New York: Worth.

Anderson, J. R., Reder, L. M., & Simon, H. A. (1995). Applications and misapplication of cognitive psychology to mathematics education. Unpublished manuscript. Available online at http://www.psy.cmu.edu/~mm4b/misapplied.html

Anderson, J. R., Reder, L. M., & Simon, H. A. (1996). Situated learning and education. *Educational Researcher, 25,* 5–11.

Anderson, L. M. (1985). What are students doing when they do all that seatwork? In C. Fisher & D. Berliner (Eds.), *Perspectives on instructional time* (pp. 189–202). New York: Longman.

Anderson, L. M., Brubaker, N. L., Alleman-Brooks, J., & Duffy, G. G. (1985). A qualitative study of seatwork in first-grade classrooms. *Elementary School Journal, 86,* 123–140.

Anderson, L. W., & Krathwohl, D. R. (Eds.). (2001). *A taxonomy for learning, teaching, and assessing: A revision of Bloom's taxonomy of educational objectives.* New York: Longman.

Anderson, L. W., & Sosniak, L. A. (Eds.). (1994). *Bloom's taxonomy: A forty-year retrospective.* Ninety-third yearbook for the National Society for the Study of Education: Part II. Chicago: University of Chicago Press.

Anderson, P. J., & Graham, S. M. (1994). Issues in second-language phonological acquisition among children and adults. *Topics in Language Disorders, 14,* 84–100.

Anderson, R. C., Nguyen-Jahiel, K., McNurlen, B., Archodidou, A., Kim, S-Y., Reznitskaya, A., et al. (2001). The snowball phenomenon: Spread of ways of talking and ways of thinking across groups of children. *Cognition and Instruction, 19,* 1–46.

Anderson, S. M., Klatzky, R. L., & Murray, J. (1990). Traits and social stereotypes: Efficiency differences in social information processing. *Journal of Personality and Social Psychology, 59,* 192–201.

Angier, N., & Chang, K. (2005, January 24). Gray matter and the sexes: Still a scientific gray area. *The New York Times,* A1+.

Anyon, J. (1980). Social class and the hidden curriculum of work. *Journal of Education, 162,* 67–92.

APA Board of Educational Affairs. (1995). *Learner-centered psychological principles: A framework for school redesign and reform.* Washington, DC: American Psychological Association.

Archer, S. L., & Waterman, A. S. (1990). Varieties of identity diffusions and foreclosures: An exploration of the subcategories of the identity statuses. *Journal of Adolescent Research, 5,* 96–111.

Arends, R. I. (2001). *Learning to teach* (5th ed.). New York: McGraw-Hill.

Arends, R. I. (2004). *Learning to teach* (6th ed.). New York: McGraw-Hill.

Armstrong, T. (1999). *ADD/ADHD alternatives in the classroom.* Alexandria, VA: Association for Supervision and Curriculum Development.

Arnold, M. L. (2000). Stage, sequence, and sequels: Changing conceptions of morality, post-Kohlberg. *Educational Psychology Review, 12,* 365–383.

Aronson, E. (2000). *Nobody left to hate: Teaching compassion after Columbine.* New York: Worth.

Aronson, J. (2002). Stereotype threat: Contending and coping with unnerving expectations. In J. Aronson & D. Cordova (Eds.), *Improving education: Classic and contemporary lessons from psychology* (pp. 279–301). New York: Academic Press.

Aronson, J., Fried, C. B., & Good, C. (2002). Reducing the effects of stereotype threat on African American college students: The role of theories of intelligence. *Journal of Experimental Social Psychology,* 33, 113–125.

Aronson, J., & Inzlicht, M. (2004) The ups and downs of attributional ambiguity: Stereotype vulnerability and the academic self-knowledge of African American college students. *Psychological Science, 15,* 829-836

Aronson, J., Lustina, M. J., Good, C., Keough, K., Steele, C. M., & Brown, J. (1999). When White men can't do math: Necessary and sufficient factors in stereotype threat. *Journal of Experimental Social Psychology, 35,* 29–46.

Aronson, J., & Salinas, M. F. (1998). Stereotype threat, attributional ambiguity, and Latino underperformance. Unpublished manuscript, University of Texas at Austin.

Aronson, J., & Steele, C. M. (2005). Stereotypes and the fragility of human competence, motivation, and self-concept. In C. Dweck & E. Elliot (Eds.), *Handbook of competence and motivation.* New York: Guilford.

Aronson, J., Steele, C. M., Salinas, M. F., & Lustina, M. J. (1999). The effect of stereotype threat on the standardized test performance of college students. In E. Aronson (Ed.), *Readings about the social animal* (8th ed.). New York: Freeman.

Arsenio, W. F., & Lemerise, A. (2004). Aggression and moral development: Integrating social information processing and moral domain models. *Child Development, 75*(4), 987.

Artman, L., & Cahan, S. (1993). Schooling and the development of transitive inference. *Developmental Psychology, 29,* 753–759.

Ashcraft, M. H. (2002). *Cognition* (3rd ed.). Upper Saddle River, NJ: Prentice-Hall.

Ashcraft, M. H. (2006). *Cognition* (4th ed.). Upper Saddle River, NJ: Prentice-Hall.

Associated Press. (2001, February 21). ABA recommends dropping zero-tolerance in schools. Available online at http://www.cnn.com/2001/fyi/teachers.ednews/02/21/zero.tolerance.ap. Downloaded on January 23, 2003.

Association for the Gifted. (2001). *Diversity and developing gifts and talents: A national action plan.* Arlington, VA: Author.

Atkinson, R. C., & Shiffrin, R. M. (1968). Human memory: A proposed system and its control processes. In K. Spence & J. Spence (Eds.), *The psychology of learning and motivation* (Vol. 2, pp. 89–195). New York: Academic Press.

Atkinson, R. K., Levin, J. R., Kiewra, K. A., Meyers, T., Atkinson, L. A., Renandya, W. A., & Hwang, Y. (1999). Matrix and mnemonic text-processing adjuncts: Comparing and combining their components. *Journal of Educational Psychology, 91,* 242–257.

Atkinson, R. K., Renkl, A., & Merrill, M. M. (2003). Transitioning from studying examples to solving problems: Combining fading with prompting fosters learning. *Journal of Educational Psychology, 95,* 774-783.

Au, K. H. (1980). Participation structures in a reading lesson with Hawaiian children: Analysis of a culturally appropriate instructional event. *Anthropology and Education Quarterly, 11,* 91–115.

Ausubel, D. P. (1963). *The psychology of meaningful verbal learning.* New York: Grune and Stratton.

Ausubel, D. P. (1977). The facilitation of meaningful verbal learning in the classroom. *Educational Psychologist, 12,* 162–178.

Ausubel, D. P. (1982). Schemata, advance organizers, and anchoring ideas: A reply to Anderson, Spiro, and Anderson. *Journal of Structural Learning, 7,* 63–73.

Avramidis, E., Bayliss, P., & Burden, R. (2000). Student teachers' attitudes toward the inclusion of children with special education needs in the ordinary school. *Teaching and Teacher Education, 16,* 277–293.

Ayres, N. (2002). Calculators in the classroom. Retrieved on August 16, 2002, from http://www.math.twsu.edu/history/topics/calculators.html#calc

Babad, E. Y. (1995). The "Teachers' Pet" phenomenon, students' perceptions of differential behavior, and students' morale. *Journal of Educational Psychology, 87,* 361–374.

Babad, E. Y., Inbar, J., & Rosenthal, R. (1982). Pygmalion, Galatea, and the Golem: Investigations of biased and unbiased teachers. *Journal of Educational Psychology, 74,* 459–474.

Baddeley, A. D. (1986). *Working memory.* Oxford, UK: Clarendon Books.

Baddeley, A. D. (2001). Is working memory still working? *American Psychologist, 56,* 851–864.

Baer, J. (1997). *Creative teachers, creative students.* Boston: Allyn and Bacon.

Bailey, S. M. (1993). The current status of gender equity research in American Schools. *Educational Psychologist, 28,* 321–339.

Baillargeon, R, (1999). Yong infants' expectations about hidden objects: A reply to three challenges. *Developmental Psychology, 2,* 115–132.

Baker, C. (1993). *Foundations of bilingual education and bilingualism.* Clevedon, England: Multilingual Matters.

Baker, D. (1986). Sex differences in classroom interaction in secondary science. *Journal of Classroom Interaction, 22,* 212–218.

Bakerman, R., Adamson, L. B., Koner, M., & Barr, R. G. (1990). !Kung infancy: The social context of object exploration. *Child Development, 61,* 794–809.

Ball, D. L. (1997). What do students know? Facing challenges of distance, context, and desire in trying to hear children. In B. J. Biddle, T. L. Good, & I. F. Goodson (Eds.), *The international handbook of teachers and teaching* (pp. 769–818). Dordrecht, the Netherlands: Kluwer.

Ball, D. L., Lubienski, S. T., & Mewborn, D. S. (2001). Research on teaching mathematics: The unsolved problem of teachers' mathematical knowledge. In V. Richardson (Ed.), *Handbook of research on teaching* (4th ed., pp. 433–456). Washington, DC: American Educational Research Association.

Bandura, A. (1965). Influence of models' reinforcement contingencies on the acquisition of imitative responses. *Journal of Personality and Social Psychology, 1,* 589–595.

Bandura, A. (1977). *Social learning theory.* Englewood Cliffs, NJ: Prentice-Hall.

Bandura, A. (1982). Self-efficacy mechanisms in human agency. *American Psychologist,* 37, 122–147.

Bandura, A. (1986). *Social foundations of thought and action.* Englewood Cliffs, NJ: Prentice-Hall.

Bandura, A. (1993). Perceived self-efficacy in cognitive development and functioning. *Educational Psychologist, 28,* 117–148.

Bandura, A. (1997). *Self-efficacy: The exercise of control.* New York: Freeman.

Bandura, A., Ross, D., & Ross, S. A. (1963). Vicarious reinforcement and imitative learning. *Journal of Abnormal and Social Psychology, 67,* 601–607.

Bangert-Drowns, R. L., Kulik, C. C., Kulik, J. A., & Morgan, M. (1991). The instructional effect of feedback in test-like events. *Review of Educational Research, 61,* 213–238.

Banks, J. A. (1993). Multicultural education: Development, dimensions, and challenges. *Phi Delta Kappan, 75,* 22–28.

Banks, J. A. (1994). *Multiethnic education: Theory and practice.* Boston: Allyn and Bacon.

Banks, J. A. (1997). *Teaching strategies for ethnic studies* (6th ed.). Boston: Allyn and Bacon.

Banks, J. A. (2002). *An introduction to multicultural education* (3rd ed.). Boston: Allyn and Bacon.

Banks, J. A. (2006). *Cultural diversity and education: Foundations, curriculum, and teaching* (5th ed.). Boston: Allyn and Bacon.

Banks, J. A., & Banks, C. A. M. (Eds). (1995). *Handbook of research on multicultural education.* New York: Macmillan.

Banks, S. R. (2005). *Classroom assessment: Issues and practice.* Boston: Allyn and Bacon.

Barden, L. M. (1995). Effective questioning and the ever-elusive higher-order question. *American Biology Teacher, 57,* 423–426.

Bargh, J. A., & Chartrand, T. L. (1999). The unbearable automaticity of being. *American Psychologist, 54,* 462–479.

Barnhill, G. P. (2005). Functional behavioral assessment in schools. *Intervention in School and Clinic, 40,* 131–143.

Baron, R. A. (1998). *Psychology* (4th ed.). Boston: Allyn and Bacon.

Baron, R. A., & Byrne, D. (2003). *Social psychology* (10th ed.). Boston: Allyn and Bacon.

Barone, F. J. (1997). Bullying in school: It doesn't have to happen. *Phi Delta Kappan, 79,* 80–82.

Baroody, A. R., & Ginsburg, H. P. (1990). Children's learning: A cognitive view. In R. Davis, C. Maher, & N. Noddings (Eds.), *Constructivist views on the teaching and learning of mathematics* (pp. 51–64). Monograph 4 of the National Council of Teachers of Mathematics, Reston, VA.

Barr, R. (2001). Research on the teaching of reading. In V. Richardson (Ed.), *Handbook of research on teaching* (4th ed., pp. 390–415). Washington, DC: American Educational Research Association.

Bartlett, F. C. (1932). *Remembering: A study in experimental and social psychology.* New York: Macmillan.

Basow, S. A., & Rubin, L. R. (1999). Gender influences on adolescent development. In N. G. Johnson, M. C. Roberts, & J. Worell (Eds.), *Beyond appearance: A new look at adolescent girls* (pp. 25–52). Washington, DC: American Psychological Association.

Battistich, V., Solomon, D., & Delucci, K. (1993). Interaction processes and student outcomes in cooperative groups. *Elementary School Journal, 94,* 19–32.

Battistich, V., Watson, M., Solomon, D., Lewis, C., & Schaps, E. (1999). Beyond the three R's: A broad agenda for school reform. *The Elementary School Journal, 99,* 415–432.

Baumeister, R. F., & Leary, M. R. (1995). The need to belong: Desire for interpersonal attachments as a fundamental human motivation. *Psychological Bulletin, 117,* 497–529.

Baumrind, D. (1991), Effective parenting during early adolescent transitions. In P. A. Cowan & M. Hetherington (Eds.), *Family transitions* (pp. 111–165). Hillsdale, NJ: Lawrence Erlbaum.

Baumrind, D. (1996). The discipline controversy revisited. *Family Relations,* 45, 405–414.

Beane, J. A. (1991). Sorting out the self-esteem controversy. *Educational Leadership, 49*(1), 25–30.

Bear, G. G. (with Cavalier, A. R., & Manning, M. A.). (2005). *Developing self-discipline and preventing and correcting misbehavior.* Boston: Allyn and Bacon.

Beautrais, A. L. (2005). National strategies for the reduction and prevention of suicide, *Crisis, 26*(1), 1–3.

Beck, I. L., McKeown, M. G., Worthy, J., Sandora, C. A., & Kucan, L. (1996). Questioning the author: A yearlong classroom implementation to engage students with text. *The Elementary School Journal,* 96, 385–414.

Bee, H. (1981). *The developing child* (3rd ed.). New York: Harper & Row.

Bee, H. (1992). *The developing child* (6th ed.). New York: Harper & Row.

Beebe-Frankenberger, M., Bocian, K. L., MacMillan, D. L., & Gresham, F. M. (2004). Sorting second grade students with academic deficiencies: Characteristics differentiating those retained in grade from those promoted to third grade. *Journal of Educational Psychology,* 96, 204–215.

Beeth, M. E. (1998). Teaching science in fifth grade: Instructional goals that support conceptual change. *Journal of Research in Science Teaching,* 35, 1091–1101.

Beezer, B. (1985). Reporting child abuse and neglect: Your responsibilities and your protections. *Phi Delta Kappan, 66,* 434–436.

Belanoff, P., & Dickson, M. (1991). *Portfolios: Process and product.* Portsmouth, NH: Heinemann, Boynton/Cook.

Belfiore, P. J., & Hornyak, R. S. (1998). Operant theory and the application of self-monitoring to adolescents. In D. Schunk & B. Zimmerman (Eds.), *Self-regulated learning: From theory to self-reflective practice* (pp. 184–202). New York: Guilford.

Benenson, J. F. (1993). Greater preference among females than males for dyadic interaction in early childhood. *Child Development, 64,* 544–555.

Benjafield, J. G. (1992). *Cognition.* Englewood Cliffs, NJ: Prentice-Hall.

Bennett, C. I. (1995). *Comprehensive multicultural education: Theory and practice* (3rd ed.). Boston: Allyn and Bacon.

Bennett, C. I. (1999). *Comprehensive multicultural education: Theory and practice* (4th ed.). Boston: Allyn and Bacon.

Bereiter, C. (1995). A dispositional view of transfer. In A. McKeough, J. Lupart, & A. Marini (Eds.), *Teaching for mastery: Fostering generalization in learning* (pp. 21–34). Mahwah, NJ: Lawrence Erlbaum.

Bereiter, C. (1997). Situated cognition and how I overcome it. In D. Kirshner & J. A. Whitson (Eds.), *Situated cognition: Social, semiotic, and psychological perspectives* (pp. 281–300). Mahwah, NJ: Lawrence Erlbaum.

Berg, C. A., & Clough, M. (1991). Hunter lesson design: The wrong one for science teaching. *Educational Leadership, 48*(4), 73–78.

Bergen, T. J., Jr. (2001). The development of prejudice in children, *Education, 122,* 154–162.

Berger, K. S. (2003). *The developing person through childhood and adolescence* (6th ed.). New York: Worth Publishers.

Berger, K. S. (2004). *Development through the lifespan.* New York: Worth.

Berger, K. S., & Thompson, R. A. (1995). *The developing person through childhood and adolescence.* New York: Worth.

Bergin, D. (1999). Influences on classroom interest. *Educational Psychologist, 34,* 87–98.

Berk, L. E. (1997). *Child development* (4th ed.). Boston: Allyn and Bacon.

Berk, L. E. (2001). *Awakening children's minds: How parents and teachers can make a difference.* New York: Oxford University Press.

Berk, L. E. (2002). *Infants, children, and adolescents* (4th ed.). Boston: Allyn and Bacon.

Berk, L. E. (2005). *Infants, children, and adolescents* (5th ed.). Boston: Allyn and Bacon.

Berk, L. E., & Spuhl, S. T. (1995). Maternal interaction, private speech, and task performance in preschool children. *Early Childhood Research Quarterly, 10,* 145–169.

Berliner, D. C. (1983). Developing concepts of classroom environments: Some light on the T in studies of ATI. *Educational Psychologist, 18,* 1–13.

Berliner, D. C. (1987). But do they understand? In V. Richardson-Koehler (Ed.), *Educators' handbook: A research perspective* (pp. 259–293). New York: Longman.

Berliner, D. C. (1988). Simple views of effective teaching and a simple theory of classroom instruction. In D. Berliner & B. Rosenshine (Eds.), *Talks to teachers* (pp. 93–110). New York: Random House.

Berliner, D. C. (1992). Telling the stories of educational psychology. *Educational Psychologist, 27,* 143–152.

Berliner, D. C. (1993). The 100-year journey of educational psychology: From interest to disdain to respect for practice. In T. K. Faigin & G. R. VandenBos (Eds.), *Exploring applied psychology: Origins and critical analyses* (pp. 39–78). Washington DC: American Psychological Association.

Berliner, D. C. (2002). Educational research: The hardest science of all. *Educational Researcher, 31*(8), 18–20.

Berliner, D. C., & Biddle, B. (1997). *The manufactured crisis: Myths, frauds, and the attack on America's public schools.* White Plains: Longman.

Berlyne, D. (1966). Curiosity and exploration. *Science, 153,* 25–33.

Berndt, T. J., & Keefe, K. (1995). Friends' influence on adolescents' adjustment to school. *Child Development, 66,* 1312–1329.

Betancourt, H., & Lopez, S. R. (1993). The study of culture, ethnicity, and race in American psychology. *American Psychologist, 48*, 629–637.

Bhatia, T. K., & Richie, W. C. (1999). The bilingual child: Some issues and perspectives. In W. C. Richie & T. K. Bhatia (Eds.), *Handbook of child language acquisition.* San Diego: Academic Press.

Bialystok, E. (1999). Cognitive complexity and attentional control in the bilingual child. *Child Development, 70*, 636–644.

Biggs, J. (2001). Enhancing learning: A matter of style of approach. In R. Sternberg & L. Zhang (Eds.), *Perspectives on cognitive, learning, and thinking styles* (pp. 73–102). Mahwah, NJ: Lawrence Erlbaum.

Bjorklund, D. F. (1989). *Children's thinking: Developmental function and individual differences.* Pacific Grove, CA: Brooks/Cole.

Bleeker, M. M., & Jacobs, J. E. (2004). Achievement in math and science: Do mothers' beliefs matter twelve years later? *Journal of Educational Psychology, 96(1)*, 97–109.

Bloom, B. S. (1981). *All our children learning: A primer for parents, teachers, and other educators.* New York: McGraw-Hill.

Bloom, B. S. (1982). The role of gifts and markers in the development of talent. *Exceptional Children, 48*, 510–522.

Bloom, B. S., Engelhart, M. D., Frost, E. J., Hill, W. H., & Krathwohl, D. R. (1956). *Taxonomy of educational objectives. Handbook I: Cognitive domain.* New York: David McKay.

Bloom, R., & Bourdon, L. (1980). Types and frequencies of teachers' written instructional feedback. *Journal of Educational Research, 74*, 13–15.

Bluestein, J. (1995). *Mentors, masters, and Mrs. MacGregor.* Deerfield Beach, FL: Health Communications.

Blum, R. W. (2005). A case for school connectedness. *Educational Leadership, 62*(7), 16–20.

Blumenfeld, P. C., Puro, P., & Mergendoller, J. R. (1992). Translating motivation into thoughtfulness. In H. Marshall (Ed.), *Redefining student learning: Roots of educational change* (pp. 207–240). Norwood, NJ: Ablex.

Bolick, C. M., & Cooper, J. M. (2006). Classroom management and technology. In C. Evertson & C. S. Weinstein (Eds.), *Handbook for classroom management: Research, practice, and contemporary issues.* Mahwah, NJ: Lawrence Erlbaum.

Boom, J., Brugman, D., & van der Heijden, P. G. (2001). Hierarchical structure of moral stages assessed by a sorting task. *Child Development, 72*, 535–548.

Borko, H., & Livingston, C. (1989). Cognition and improvisation: Differences in mathematics instruction by expert and novice teachers. *American Educational Research Journal, 26*, 473–498.

Borko, H., & Putnam, R. (1996). Learning to teach. In D. Berliner & R. Calfee (Eds.), *Handbook of educational psychology* (pp. 673–708). New York: Macmillan.

Borman, G. D., & Overman, L. T. (2004). Academic resilience in mathematics among poor and minority students. *The Elementary School Journal, 104*, 177–195.

Bos, C. S., & Reyes, E. I. (1996). Conversations with a Latina teacher about education for language-minority students with special needs. *The Elementary School Journal, 96*, 344–351.

Bosworth, K. (1995). Caring for others and being cared for. *Phi Delta Kappan, 76*(9), 686–693.

Boutte, G. S. (Ed.). (2002). *Resounding voices: School experiences of people from diverse ethnic backgrounds.* Boston: Allyn and Bacon.

Braddock, J., II, & Slavin, R. E. (1993). Why ability grouping must end: Achieving excellence and equity in American education. *Journal of Intergroup Relations, 20*(2), 51–64.

Bradley, R., Danielson, L., & Hallahan, D. P. (2002). *Identification of learning disabilities: Research to practice.* Mahwah, NJ: Lawrence Erlbaum.

Brannon, L. (2002). *Gender: Psychological perspectives* (3rd ed.). Boston: Allyn and Bacon.

Bransford, J. D., Brown, A. L., & Cocking, R. R. (2000). *How people learn: Brain, mind, experience, and school.* Washington, DC: National Academy Press.

Bransford, J.D., & Schwartz, D. (1999). Rethinking transfer: A simple proposal with multiple implications. In A. Iran-Nejad & P. D. Pearson (Eds.), *Review of research in education* (Vol. 24 pp. 61–100). Washington, DC: American Educational Research Association.

Bransford, J. D., & Stein, B. S. (1993). *The IDEAL problem solver: A guide for improving thinking, learning, and creativity* (2nd ed.). New York: Freeman.

Bredderman, T. (1983). Effects of activity-based elementary science on student outcomes: A qualitative synthesis. *Review of Educational Research, 53*, 499–518.

Bredekamp, S., & Copple, C. (1997). *Developmentally appropriate practice in early childhood programs.* Washington, DC: National Association for the Education of Young Children.

Brice, A. E. (2002). *The Hispanic child: Speech, language, culture, and education.* Boston: Allyn and Bacon.

Brody, L. (1999). *Gender, emotion, and the family.* Cambridge, MA: Harvard University Press.

Broidy, L. M., Nagin, D. S., Tremblay, R. E., Bates, J. E., Brame, B., Dodge, K., Ferguson, D., Horwood, J., Loeber, R., Laird, R., Lynam, D., Moffitt, T., Pettit, G. S., & Vitaro, F. (2003). Developmental trajectories of childhood disruptive behaviors and adolescent delinquency: A six site, cross-national study. *Developmental Psychology, 39*, 222–245.

Bronfenbrenner, U. (1989). Ecological systems theory. In R. Vasta (Ed.), *Annals of child development* (Vol. 6, pp.187–249). Boston: JAI Press, Inc.

Bronfenbrenner, U., & Evans, G. W. (2000): Developmental science in the 21st century: Emerging theoretical models, research designs, and empirical findings. *Social Development, 9*, 115–125.

Bronfenbrenner, U., McClelland, P., Wethington, E., Moen, P., & Ceci, S. (1996). *The state of Americans: This generation and the next.* New York: Free Press.

Brooks, D. (1985). Beginning the year in junior high: The first day of school. *Educational Leadership, 42*, 76–78.

Brooks, J. G., & Brooks, M. G. (1993). *In search of understanding: The case for constructivist classrooms.* Alexandria, VA: Association for Supervision and Curriculum Development.

Brooks-Gunn, J. (1988). Antecedents and consequences of variations in girls' maturational timing. In M. D. Levin & E. R. McAnarney (Eds.), *Early adolescent transitions* (pp. 101–121). Lexington, MA: Lexington Books.

Brophy, J. E. (1981). Teacher praise: A functional analysis. *Review of Educational Research, 51*, 5–21.

Brophy, J. E. (1982, March). *Research on the self-fulfilling prophecy and teacher expectations.* Paper presented at the annual meeting of the American Educational Research Association, New York.

Brophy, J. E. (1983). Conceptualizing student motivation to learn. *Educational Psychologist, 18*, 200–215.

Brophy, J. E. (1985). Teacher–student interaction. In J. Dusek (Ed.), *Teacher expectancies* (pp. 303–328). Hillsdale, NJ: Lawrence Erlbaum.

Brophy, J. E. (1988). On motivating students. In D. Berliner & B. Rosenshine (Eds.), *Talks to teachers* (pp. 201–245). New York: Random House.

Brophy, J. E. (1998). *Motivating students to learn.* New York: McGraw-Hill.

Brophy, J. E. (2003). An interview with Jere Brophy by B. Gaedke, & M. Shaughnessy. *Educational Psychology Review, 15*, 199–211.

Brophy, J. E., & Evertson, C. (1978). Context variables in teaching. *Educational Psychologist, 12*, 310–316.

Brophy, J. E., & Good, T. (1986). Teacher behavior and student achievement. In M. Wittrock (Ed.), *Handbook of research on teaching* (3rd ed.) (pp. 328–375). New York: Macmillan.

Brophy, J. E., & Kher, N. (1986). Teacher socialization as a mechanism for developing student motivation to learn. In R. Feldman (Ed.), *Social psychology applied to education* (pp. 256–288). New York: Cambridge University Press.

Brown, A. (1987). Metacognition, executive control, self-regulation, and other more mysterious mechanisms. In F. Weinert & R. Kluwe (Eds.), *Metacognition, motivation, and understanding* (pp. 65–116). Hillside, NJ: Lawrence Erlbaum.

Brown, A. (1997). Transforming schools into communities of thinking and learning about serious matters. *American Psychologist, 52*, 399–413.

Brown, A. L. (1992). Design experiments: Theoretical and methodological challenges in creating complex interventions in classroom settings. *Journal of the Learning Sciences, 2*, 141–178.

Brown, A. L., Bransford, J., Ferrara, R., & Campione, J. (1983). Learning, remembering, and understanding. In P. Mussen (Ed.), *Handbook of child psychology* (Vol. 3, pp. 515–629). New York: Wiley.

Brown, A. L., & Campione, J. C. (1996). Psychological theory and the design of innovative learning environments: On procedures, principles, and systems. In L. Schauble & R. Glaser (Eds.), *Innovations in learning: New environments for education* (pp. 289–325). Mahwah, NJ: Lawrence Erlbaum.

Brown, M. (2000). Access, instruction, and barriers. *Remedial and Special Education, 21*, 182–192.

Bruer, John T. (1999). In search of...brain-based education. *Phi Delta Kappan, 80*, 648–657.

Bruner, J. S. (1960). *The process of education.* New York: Vintage Books.

Bruner, J. S. (1966). *Toward a theory of instruction.* New York: Norton.

Bruner, J. S. (1973). *Beyond the information given: Studies in the psychology of knowing.* New York: Norton.

Bruner, J. S. (1986). *Actual minds, possible worlds.* Cambridge, MA: Harvard University Press.

Bruner, J. S., Goodnow, J. J., & Austin, G. A. (1956). *A study of thinking.* New York: Wiley.

Bruning, R. H., Schraw, G. J., Norby, M. M., & Ronning, R. R. (2004). *Cognitive psychology and instruction* (4th ed.). Columbus, OH: Merrill.

Bruning, R. H., Schraw, G. J., & Ronning, R. R. (1999). *Cognitive psychology and instruction* (3rd ed.). Columbus, OH: Merrill.

Buehler, R., Griffin, D., & Ross, M. (1994). Exploring the "planning fallacy": Why people underestimate their task completion times. *Journal of Personality and Social Psychology, 67*, 366–381.

Bulgren, J. A., Deshler, D. D., Schumaker, J. B., & Lenz, B. K. (2000). The use and effectiveness of analogical instruction in diverse secondary content classrooms. *Journal of Educational Psychology, 92*, 426–441.

Burbules, N. C., & Bruce, B. C. (2001). Theory and research on teaching as dialogue. In V. Richardson (Ed.), *Handbook of research on teaching* (4th ed., pp. 1102–1121). Washington, DC: American Educational Research Association.

Burden, P. R. (1995). *Classroom management and discipline: Methods to facilitate cooperation and instruction.* White Plains, NY: Longman.

Burke-Spero, R. (1999). Toward a model of "civitas" through an ethic of care: A qualitative study of preservice teachers' perceptions about learning to teach diverse populations (Doctoral dissertation, The Ohio State University, 1999). *Dissertation Abstracts International, 60*, 11A, 3967.

Burke-Spero, R., & Woolfolk Hoy, A. (2002). *The need for thick description: A qualitative investigation of developing teacher efficacy.* Unpublished manuscript, University of Miami.

Burton, R. V. (1963). The generality of honesty reconsidered. *Psychological Review, 70*, 481–499.

Bus, A. G., & van Ijzendoorn, M. H. (1999). Phonological awareness and early reading: a meta-analysis of experimental training studies. *Journal of Educational Psychology, 91*, 403–414.

Buss, D. M. (1995). Psychological sex differences: Origin through sexual selection. *American Psychologist, 50*, 164–168.

Butler, D. L. (2002). Individualized instruction in self-regulated learning. *Theory Into Practice, 41*, 81–92.

Butler, R. (1987). Task-involving and ego-involving properties of evaluation: Effects of different feedback conditions on motivational perceptions, interest, and performance. *Journal of Educational Psychology, 79*, 474–482.

Butler, R., & Neuman, O. (1995). Effects of task and ego achievement goals on help-seeking behaviors and attitudes. *Journal of Educational Psychology, 87*, 261–271.

Butler, R., & Nisan, M. (1986). Effects of no feedback, task-related comments, and grades on intrinsic motivation and performance. *Journal of Educational Psychology, 78*, 210–224.

Byrne, B., Fielding-Barnsley, R., & Ashley, L. (2000). Effects of preschool phoneme identity training after six years: Outcome level distinguished from rate of response. *Journal of Educational Psychology, 92*, 659–667.

Byrne, B. M. (2002). Validating the measurement and structure of self-concept: Snapshots of past, present, and future research. *American Psychologist, 57*, 897–909.

Byrne, B. M., & Shavelson, R. J. (1996). On the structure of social self-concept for pre-, early, and late adolescents: A test of the Shavelson model. *Journal of Personality and Social Psychology, 70*, 599–613.

Byrne, B. M., & Worth Gavin, D. A. (1996). The Shavelson model revisited: Testing for structure of academic self concept across pre-, early, and late adolescents. *Journal of Educational Psychology, 88*, 215–229.

Byrnes, J. P. (1996). *Cognitive development and learning in instructional contexts.* Boston: Allyn and Bacon.

Byrnes, J. P. (2003). Factors predictive of mathematics achievement in White, Black, and Hispanic 12th graders. *Journal of Educational Psychology, 95*, 316–326.

Byrnes, J. P., & Fox, N. A. (1998). The educational relevance of research in cognitive neuroscience. *Educational Psychology Review, 10*, 297–342.

Caine, R. N., & Caine, G. (1991). *Making connections: Teaching and the human brain.* Alexandria, VA: Association for Supervision and Curriculum Development.

Calderhead, J. (1996). Teacher: Beliefs and knowledge. In D. Berliner & R. Calfee (Eds.), *Handbook of educational psychology* (pp. 709–725). New York: Macmillan.

Callahan, C. M., Tomlinson, C. A., & Plucker, J. (1997). *Project STATR using a multiple intelligences model in identifying and promoting talent in high-risk students.* Storrs, CT: National Research Center for Gifted and Talented. University of Connecticut Technical Report.

Cambourne, B., & Turbill, J. (1990). Assessment in whole-language classrooms: Theory into practice. *Elementary School Journal, 90,* 337–349.

Cameron, J., & Pierce, W. D. (1994). Reinforcement, reward, and intrinsic motivation: A meta-analysis. *Review of Educational Research, 64,* 363–423.

Cameron, J., & Pierce, W. D. (1996). The debate about rewards and intrinsic motivation: Protests and accusations do not alter the results. *Review of Educational Research, 66,* 39–52.

Camp, R. (1990, Spring). Thinking together about portfolios. *The Quarterly of the National Writing Project, 27,* 8–14.

Cangelosi, J. S. (1990). *Designing tests for evaluating student achievement.* New York: Longman.

Canter, L. (1996). First the rapport—then the rules. *Learning, 24*(5), 12+.

Canter, L., & Canter, M. (1992). *Lee Canter's Assertive Discipline: Positive behavior management for today's classroom.* Santa Monica: Lee Canter and Associates.

Capa, Y. (2005). *Novice teachers' sense of efficacy*. Doctoral dissertation, The Ohio State University, Columbus, OH.

Capon, N., & Kuhn, D. (2004). What's so good about problem-based learning? *Cognition and Instruction, 22,* 61–79.

Cariglia-Bull, T., & Pressley, M. (1990). Short-term memory differences between children predict imagery effects when sentences are read. *Journal of Experimental Child Psychology, 49,* 384–398.

Carlisle, J. F., Stahl, S. A., & Birdyshaw, D. (Eds.). (2004, November). Lessons from research at the Center for the Improvement of Early Reading Achievement [Special Issue]. *The Elementary School Journal, 105*(2).

Carnegie Council on Adolescent Development. (1995). *Great transitions: Preparing adolescents for a new century.* New York: Carnegie Corporation of New York.

Carney, R. N., & Levin, J. R. (2000). Mnemonic instruction, with a focus on transfer. *Journal of Educational Psychology, 92,* 783–790.

Carney, R. N., & Levin, J. R. (2002). Pictorial illustrations *still* improve students' learning from text. *Educational Psychology Review, 14,* 5–26.

Carpendale, J. I. M. (2000). Kohlberg and Piaget on stages and moral reasoning. *Developmental Review, 20,* 181–205.

Carroll, J. B. (1993). *Human cognitive abilities: A survey of factor analytic studies.* Cambridge, England: Cambridge University Press.

Carroll, J. B. (1997). The three-stratum theory of cognitive abilities. In D. P. Flanagan, J. L. Genshaft, & P. L. Harrison (Eds.), *Contemporary intellectual assessment: Theories, tests, and issues* (pp. 122–130). New York: Guilford.

Carter, E. W., Wehby, J., Hughes, C., Johnson, S. M., Plank, D. R., Barton-Arwood, S. M., & Lunsford, L. B. (2005). Preparing adolescents with high-incidence disabilities for high-stakes testing with strategy instruction. *Preventing School Failure, 49*(2), 55–62.

Casanova, U. (1987). Ethnic and cultural differences. In V. Richardson-Koehler (Ed.), *Educators' handbook: A research perspective* (pp. 370–393). New York: Longman.

Case, R. (1985a). *Intellectual development: Birth to adulthood.* New York: Academic Press.

Case, R. (1985b). A developmentally-based approach to the problem of instructional design. In R. Glaser, S. Chipman, & J. Segal (Eds.), *Teaching thinking skills* (Vol. 2, pp. 545–562). Hillsdale, NJ: Lawrence Erlbaum.

Case, R. (1992). *The mind's staircase: Exploring the conceptual underpinnings of children's thought and knowledge.* Mahwah, NJ: Lawrence Erlbaum.

Case, R. (1998). The development of conceptual structures. In D. Kuhn & R. S. Siegler (Eds.), *Handbook of child psychology: Vol. 2: Cognition, perception, and language* (pp. 745–800). New York: Wiley.

Cassady, J. C., & Johnson, R. E. (2002). Cognitive anxiety and academic performance. *Contemporary Educational Psychology 27,* 270–295.

Castellano, J. A., & Diaz, E. I. (Eds.). (2002). *Reaching new horizons. Gifted and talented education for culturally and linguistically diverse students.* Boston: Allyn and Bacon.

Castle, S., Deniz, C. B., & Tortora, M. (2005). Flexible grouping and student learning in a high-needs school. *Education and Urban Society, 37,* 139–150.

Cattell, R. B. (1963). Theory of fluid and crystallized intelligence: A critical experiment. *Journal of Educational Psychology, 54,* 1–22.

Caughy, M. O., O'Campo, P. J., Randolph, S. M., & Nickerson, K. (2002). The influence of racial socialization practices on the cognitive and behavioral competence of African American preschoolers. *Child Development, 73,* 1611–1625.

Cavanagh, S. (2002, July 10). Overhauled SAT could shake up school curricula. *Education Week on the Web.* Retrieved August 5, 2002 from http://edweek.org/ew/newstory.cfm?slug=42sat.h21

Cazden, C. B. (1988). *Classroom discourse: The language of teaching and learning.* Portsmouth, NH: Heinemann.

Ceci, S. J. (1991). How much does schooling influence intelligence and its cognitive components? A reassessment of the evidence. *Developmental Psychology, 27,* 703–720.

Ceci, S. J., & Roazzi, A. (1994). The effects of context on cognition: Postcards from Brazil. In R. J. Sternberg (Ed.), *Mind in context* (pp. 74–101). New York: Cambridge University Press.

Center on Education Policy. (2005). *From the capital to the classroom: Year 3 of the No Child Left Behind Act.* Washington, DC: Author.

Chamot, A. U., & O'Malley, J. M. (1996). The Cognitive Academic Language Learning Approach: A model for linguistically diverse classrooms. *The Elementary School Journal, 96,* 259–274.

Chan, C. K., & Sachs, J. (2001). Beliefs about learning in children's understanding of science texts. *Contemporary Educational Psychology, 26,* 192–210.

Chance, P. (1991). Backtalk: a gross injustice. *Phi Delta Kappan, 72,* 803.

Chance, P. (1992). The rewards of learning. *Phi Delta Kappan, 73,* 200–207.

Chance, P. (1993). Sticking up for rewards. *Phi Delta Kappan, 74,* 787–790.

Chapman, J. W., Tunmer, W. E., & Prochnow, J. E. (2000). Early reading-related skills and performance, reading self-concept, and the development of academic self-concept: A longitudinal study. *Journal of Educational Psychology, 92,* 703–708.

Charles, C. M. (2002a). *Essential elements of effective discipline.* Boston: Allyn and Bacon.
Charles, C. M. (2002b). *Building classroom discipline* (7th ed.). Boston: Allyn and Bacon.
Chen, Z., & Mo, L. (2004). Schema induction in problem solving: A multidimensional analysis. *Journal of Experimental Psychology: Learning, Memory, and Cognition, 30,* 583–600.
Chen, Z., Mo, L., & Honomichl, R. (2004). Having the memory of an elephant: long-term retrieval and the use of analogues in problem solving. *Journal of Experimental Psychology: General, 133,* 415–433.
Chi, M. T. H. (1978). Knowledge structures and memory development. In R. Siegler (Ed.), *Children's thinking: What develops?* (pp. 73–96). Hillsdale, NJ: Lawrence Erlbaum.
Chi, M. T. H., Glaser, R., & Farr, M. (Eds.). (1988). *The nature of expertise.* Hillsdale, NJ: Lawrence Erlbaum.
Chi, M. T. H., & Koeske, R. D. (1983). Network representation of a child's dinosaur knowledge. *Developmental Psychology, 19,* 29–39.
Children's Defense Fund. (2002). *The state of America's children: Yearbook 2002.* Washington, DC: Author.
Children's Defense Fund. (2005). Child poverty. Available online at http://www.childrensdefense.org/familyincome/childpoverty/default.aspx. Accessed May 19, 2005.
Chumlea, W. C., Schubert, C. M., Roche, A. F., Kulin, H. E. Lee, P. A., Himes, J. H., & Sun, S.S. (2003). Age at menarche and racial comparisons in US girls. *Pediatrics, 111*(1), 110–113.
Claiborn, W. L. (1969). Expectancy effects in the classroom: A failure to replicate. *Journal of Education Psychology, 60,* 377–383.
Clark, C. M. (1983). Personal communication.
Clark, C. M., & Peterson, P. L. (1986). Teachers' thought processes. In M. Wittrock (Ed.), *Handbook of research on teaching* (3rd ed.) (pp. 255–296). New York: Macmillan.
Clark, C. M., & Yinger, R. (1988). Teacher planning. In D. Berliner & B. Rosenshine (Eds.), *Talks to teachers* (pp. 342–365). New York: Random House.
Clark, J. M., & Paivio, A. (1991). Dual coding theory and education. *Educational Psychology Review, 3,* 149–210.
Clark, K., & Clark, M. (1939). The development of consciousness of self and the emergence of racial identification in Negro preschool children. *Journal of Social Psychology, 10,* 591–599.
Clark, R., Anderson, N. B., Clark, V. R., & Williams, D. R. (1999). Racism as a stressor for African Americans. *American Psychologist, 54,* 805–816.
Clarke, J. H., & Agne, R. M. (1997). *Interdisciplinary high school teaching.* Boston: Allyn and Bacon.
Claus, J., & Ogden, C. (1999). Service learning for youth empowerment and social change: An introduction. In J. Claus & C. Ogden (Eds.), *Service learning for youth empowerment and social change.* New York: Peter Lang.
Clifford, M. M. (1990). Students need challenge, not easy success. *Educational Leadership, 48*(1), 22–26.
Clifford, M. M. (1991). Risk taking: Empirical and educational considerations. *Educational Psychologist, 26,* 263–298.
Cobb, P., & Bowers, J. (1999). Cognitive and situated learning: Perspectives in theory and practice. *Educational Researcher, 28*(2), 4–15.
Cockley, K. O. (2002). Ethnicity, gender, and academic self-concept: A preliminary examination of academic disidentification and implications for psychologists. *Cultural Diversity and Ethnic Minority Psychology, 8,* 387–388.
Codell, E. R. (2001). *Educating Esme: Diary of a teacher's first year.* Chapel Hill, NC: Algonquin Books.
Coffield, F. J., Moseley, D. V., Hall, E., & Ecclestone, K. (2004). *Learning styles and pedagogy in post–16 learning: A systematic and critical review.* London: Learning and Skills Research Centre/University of Newcastle upon Tyne.
Cognition and Technology Group at Vanderbilt. (1990). Anchored instruction and its relations to situated cognition. *Educational Researcher, 19*(6), 2–10.
Cognition and Technology Group at Vanderbilt. (1993). Anchored instruction and situated learning revisited. *Educational Technology, 33*(3), 52–70.
Cognition and Technology Group at Vanderbilt. (1996). Looking at technology in context: A framework for understanding technology and educational research. In D. Berliner & R. Calfee (Eds.), *Handbook of educational psychology* (pp. 807–840). New York: Macmillan.
Cohen, E. G. (1986). *Designing group work: Strategies for the heterogeneous classroom.* New York: Teachers College Press.
Cohen, E. G. (1994). *Designing group work* (2nd ed.). New York: Teachers College Press.
Cohen, J. (Ed.). (1999). *Educating minds and hearts: Social emotional learning and the passage into adolescence.* New York: Teachers College Press.
Coie, J. D., & Dodge, K. A. (1998). Aggression and antisocial behavior. In N. Eisenberg (Ed.), *Handbook of child psychology: Vol. 3. Social, emotional, and personality development* (5th ed.) (pp. 779–862). New York: Wiley.
Coie, J. D., Terry, R., Lenox, K., Lochman, J., & Hyman, C. (1995). Childhood peer rejection and aggression as predictors of stable patterns of adolescent disorder. *Development and Psychopathology, 7,* 697–714.
Cokley, K. O. (2002). Ethnicity, gender, and academic self-concept: A preliminary examination of academic disidentification and implications for psychologists. *Cultural Diversity and Ethnic Minority Psychology, 8,* 378–388.
Cole, D. A., Martin, J. M., Peeke, L. A., Seroczynski, A. D., & Fier, J. (1999). Children's over- and underestimation of academic competence: A longitudinal study of gender differences, depression, and anxiety. *Child Development, 70,* 459–473.
Cole, M. (1985). The zone of proximal development: Where culture and cognition create each other. In J. V. Wertsch (Ed.), *Culture, communication, and cognition: Vygotskian perspectives* (pp. 146–161). Cambridge: Cambridge University Press.
Coleman, J. S. (1966). *Equality of educational opportunity.* Washington, DC: U.S. Government Printing Office.
Collins, A., Brown, J. S., & Holum, A. (1991). Cognitive apprenticeship: Making thinking visible. *American Educator, 15*(3), 38–39.
Collins, A., Brown, J. S., & Newman, S. E. (1989). Cognitive apprenticeship: Teaching the crafts of reading, writing, and mathematics. In L. B. Resnick (Ed.), *Knowing, learning, and instruction: Essays in honor of Robert Galser* (pp. 453–494). Hillsdale, NJ: Lawrence Erlbaum.
Collins, W. A., Maccoby, E. E., Steinberg, L., Hetherington, E. M., & Bornstein, M. H. (2000). Contemporary research on parenting: The case for nature and nurture. *American Psychologist, 55,* 218–232.
Comer, J. P., Haynes, N., M., & Joyner, E. T. (1996). The School Development Program. In J. P. Comer, N. M. Haynes, E. T. Joyner, & M. Ben-Avie (Eds.), *Rallying the whole village: The*

Comer process for reforming education (pp. 1–26). New York: Teachers College Press.
Committee on Assessment in Support of Learning. (2004). *Assessment in support of instruction and learning: Bridging the gap between large-scale and classroom assessment.* Washington, DC: The National Academies Press.
Committee on Increasing High School Students' Engagement and Motivation to Learn. (2004). *Engaging schools: Fostering high school students' motivation to learn.* Washington, DC: The National Academies Press.
Confrey, J. (1990a). A review of the research on students' conceptions in mathematics, science, and programming. *Review of Research in Education, 16,* 3–56.
Confrey, J. (1990b). What constructivism implies for teaching. In R. Davis, C. Maher, & N. Noddings (Eds.), *Constructivist views on the teaching and learning of mathematics* (pp. 107–122). Monograph 4 of the National Council of Teachers of Mathematics, Reston, VA.
Conger, R. D., Conger, K. J., & Elder, G. (1997). Family economic hardship and adolescent academic performance: Mediating and moderating processes. In G. Duncan & J. Brooks-Gunn (Eds.), *Consequences of growing up poor* (pp. 288–310). New York: Russell Sage Foundation.
Connell, R. W. (1996). Teaching the boys: New research on masculinity, and gender strategies for schools. *Teachers College Record,* 98, 206–235.
Conway, P. F., & Clark, C. M. (2003). The journey inward and outward: A re-examination of Fuller's concerns-based model of teacher development. *Teaching and Teacher Education 19,* 465–482.
Cook, J. L., & Cook, G. (2005). *Child development: Principles and perspectives.* Boston: Allyn and Bacon.
Cooke, B. L., & Pang, K. C. (1991). Recent research on beginning teachers: Studies of trained and untrained novices. *Teaching and Teacher Education, 7,* 93–110.
Cooper, C. R. (1998). *The weaving of maturity: Cultural perspectives on adolescent development.* New York: Oxford University Press.
Cooper, C. R., & Denner, J. (1998). Theories linking culture and psychology: Universal and community-specific processes. In J. T. Spence, J. M. Darley, & D. J. Foss (Eds.), *Annual review of psychology* (pp. 559–584). Palo Alto, CA: Annual Reviews.
Cooper, G., & Sweller, J. (1987). Effects of schema acquisition and rule automation on mathematical problem-solving transfer. *Journal of Educational Psychology, 79,* 347–362.
Cooper, H. M. (1979). Pygmalion grows up: A model for teacher expectation communication and performance influence. *Review of Educational Research, 49,* 389–410.
Cooper, H M. (2004). Special Issue: Homework. *Theory Into Practice,* 43(3).
Cooper, H. M., & Valentine, J. C. (Eds.). (2001a). Special Issue: Homework. *Educational Psychologist,* 36(3), Summer.
Cooper, H. M., & Valentine, J. C. (2001b). Using research to answer practical questions about homework. *Educational Psychologist, 36,* 143–153.
Cooper, H. M., Valentine, J. C., Nye, B., & Kindsay, J. J. (1999). Relationships between five after-school activities and academic achievement. *Journal of Educational Psychology, 91,* 369–378.
Copi, I. M. (1961). *Introduction to logic.* New York: Macmillan.
Coplan, R. J., Prakash, K., O'Neil, K., & Armer, M. (2004). Do you "want" to play? Distinguishing between conflicted shyness and social disinterest in early childhood. *Developmental Psychology, 40,* 244–258.
Cordova, D. I., & Lepper, M. R. (1996). Intrinsic motivation and the process of learning: Beneficial effects of contextualization, personalization, and choice. *Journal of Educational Psychology,* 88, 715–730.
Corkill, A. J. (1992). Advance organizers: Facilitators of recall. *Educational Psychology Review, 4,* 33–67.
Corno, L. (1992). Encouraging students to take responsibility for learning and performance. *The Elementary School Journal,* 93, 69–84.
Corno, L. (1995). The principles of adaptive teaching. In A. Ornstein (Ed.), *Teaching: Theory into practice.* (pp. 98–115). Boston: Allyn and Bacon.
Corno, L. (2000). Looking at homework differently. *Elementary School Journal, 100,* 529–548.
Corno, L., & Snow, R. E. (1986). Adapting teaching to individual differences in learners. In M. Wittrock (Ed.), *Handbook of research on teaching* (3rd ed.) (pp. 605–629). New York: Macmillan.
Cota-Robles, S., Neiss, M., & Rowe, D. C. (2002). The role of puberty in violent and nonviolent delinquency among Anglo American, Mexican American and African American boys. *Journal of Adolescent Research,* 17, 364–376.
Cothran, D. J., & Ennis, C. D. (2000). Building bridges to student engagement: Communicating respect and care for students in urban high school. *Journal of Research and Development in Education,* 33(2), 106–117.
Covaleskie, J. F. (1992). Discipline and morality: Beyond rules and consequences. *The Educational Forum,* 56(2), 56–60.
Covington, M. V. (1992). *Making the grade: A self-worth perspective on motivation and school reform.* New York: Holt, Rinehart, & Winston.
Covington, M. V., & Mueller, K. J. (2001). Intrinsic versus extrinsic motivation: An approach/avoidance reformulation. *Education Psychology Review, 13,* 157–176.
Covington, M. V., & Omelich, C. (1987). "I knew it cold before the exam": A test of the anxiety-blockage hypothesis. *Journal of Educational Psychology, 79,* 393–400.
Cowley, G., & Underwood, A. (1998, June 15). Memory. *Newsweek, 131*(24), 48–54.
Craik, F. I. M., & Lockhart, R. S. (1972). Levels of processing: A framework for memory research. *Journal of Verbal Learning and Verbal Behavior, 11,* 671–684.
Crawford, J. (1997). *Best evidence: Research foundations of the Bilingual Education Act.* Washington, DC: National Clearinghouse for Bilingual Education.
Cremin, L. (1961). *The transformation of the school: Progressivism in American education, 1876–1957.* New York: Vintage.
Crick, N. R., Casas, J. F., & Mosher M. (1997). Relational and overt aggression in preschool. *Developmental Psychology,* 33, 579–588.
Crisci, P. E. (1986). The Quest National Center: A focus on prevention of alienation. *Phi Delta Kappan, 67,* 440–442.
Crocker, J., & Park, L. E. (2004). Reaping the benefits of pursuing self-esteem without the costs. *Psychological Bulletin, 130,* 392–414.
Crone, D. A., & Horner, R. H. (2003) *Building positive behavior support systems in schools: Functional behavioral assessment.* New York: The Guilford Press.
Cronin, J. F. (1993). Four misconceptions about authentic learning. *Educational Leadership,* 50(7), 78–80.

Cross, W. E. (1991). *Shades of black: Diversity in African-American identity.* Philadelphia: Temple University Press.

Crosson-Tower, C. (2002). *When children are abused: An educator's guide to intervention.* Boston: Allyn and Bacon.

Cubberly, E. P. (1919). *Public education in the United States; A study and interpretation of American educational history.* Boston: Houghton Mifflin Company.

Cummins, D. D. (1991). Children's interpretation of arithmetic word problems. *Cognition and Instruction,* 8, 261–289.

Cummins, J. (1984). *Bilingualism and special education.* San Diego: College Hill Press.

Cummins, J. (1994). *The acquisition of English as a second language.* In K. Spangenberg-Urbschat & R. Prichard (Eds.), *Kids come in all languages: Reading instruction for ESL students* (pp. 36–62). Newark, DE: International Reading Association.

Cunningham, D. J. (1992). Beyond educational psychology: Steps toward an educational semiotic. *Educational Psychology Review,* 4, 165–194.

Current Directions in Psychological Science. (1993). Special Section: Controversies, 2, 1–12.

Cuskelly, M. (2004). The evolving construct of intellectual disability: Is everything old new again? *International Journal of Disability, Development and Education, 51,* 117–122.

Daley, T. C., Whaley, S. E., Sigman, M. D., Espinosa, M. P., & Neumann, C. (2003). IQ on the rise: The Flynn Effect in rural Kenyan children. *Psychological Science, 14*(3), 215–219.

Damon, W. (1994). Fair distribution and sharing: The development of positive justice. In B. Puka (Ed.), Fundamental research in moral development (pp. 189–254). *Moral development: A compendium, Vol.* 2. New York: Garland Publishing.

Dansereau, D. F. (1985). Learning strategy research. In J. Segal, S. Chipman, & R. Glaser (Eds.), *Thinking and learning skills. Vol. I: Relating instruction to research* (pp. 209–239). Hillsdale, NJ: Lawrence Erlbaum.

Darcey, J. S., & Travers, J. F. (2006). *Human development across the lifespan* (6th ed.). New York: McGraw-Hill.

Dark, V. J., & Benbow, C. P. (1991). Differential enhancement of working memory with mathematical versus verbal precocity. *Journal of Educational Psychology,* 83, 48–60.

Darling-Hammond, L. (2000). Teacher quality and student achievement: A review of state policy evidence. *Educational Policy Analysis Archives,* 8, 1–48. Retrieved January 20, 2002 from http://epaa.asu.edu/epaa/v8n1/

Darling-Hammond, L., & Youngs, P. (2002). Defining "Highly Qualified Teachers": What does "Scientifically-Based Research" actually tell us? *Educational Researcher,* 13–25.

Das, J. P. (1995). Some thoughts on two aspects of Vygotsky's work. *Educational Psychologist, 30,* 93–97.

Davis, G. A., & Rimm, S. B. (1985). *Education of the gifted and talented.* Englewood Cliffs, NJ: Prentice-Hall.

Davis, H. A. (2003). Conceptualizing the role and influence of student–teacher relationships on children's social and cognitive development, *Educational Psychologist,* 38, 207–234.

Davis-Kean, P. E., & Sandler, H. M. (2001). A meta-analysis of measures of self-esteem for young children: A framework for future measurers. *Child Development,* 72, 887–906.

De Corte, E. (2003). Transfer as the productive use of acquired knowledge, skills, and motivations. *Current Directions in Psychological Research, 12,* 142–146.

De Corte, E., Greer, B., & Verschaffel, L. (1996). Mathematics learning and teaching. In D. Berliner & R. Calfee (Eds.), *Handbook of educational psychology* (pp. 491–549). New York: Macmillan.

De Corte, E., & Verschaffel, L. (1985). Beginning first graders' initial representation of arithmetic word problems. *Journal of Mathematical Behavior,* 4, 3021.

De Kock, A., Sleegers, P., & Voeten, J. M. (2004). New learning and the classification of learning environments in secondary education. *Review of Educational Research, 74,* 141–170.

Deaux, K. (1993). Commentary: Sorry, wrong number: A reply to Gentile's call. *Psychological Science, 4,* 125–126.

DeCecco, J., & Richards, A. (1974). *Growing pains: Uses of school conflicts.* New York: Aberdeen.

deCharms, R. (1976). *Enhancing motivation.* New York: Irvington.

deCharms, R. (1983). Intrinsic motivation, peer tutoring, and cooperative learning: Practical maxims. In J. Levine & M. Wang (Eds.), *Teacher and student perceptions: Implications for learning* (pp. 391–398). Hillsdale, NJ: Lawrence Erlbaum.

Deci, E. L. (1975). *Intrinsic motivation.* New York: Plenum.

Deci, E. L., Koestner, R., & Ryan, R. M. (1999). A meta-analytic review of experiments examining the effects of extrinsic rewards on intrinsic motivation. *Psychological Bulletin, 125,* 627–668.

Deci, E. L., & Ryan, R. M. (1985). *Intrinsic motivation and self-determination in human behavior.* New York: Plenum.

Deci, E. L., & Ryan, R. M. (2000). The "what" and "why" of goal pursuits: Human needs and the self-determination of behavior. *Psychological Inquiry, 11,* 227–268.

Deci, E. L., & Ryan, R. M. (Eds.). (2002). *Handbook of self-determination research.* Rochester: University of Rochester Press.

Deci, E. L., Vallerand, R. J., Pelletier, L. G., & Ryan, R. M. (1991). Motivation and education: The self-determination perspective. *Educational Psychologist, 26,* 325–346.

Dee, J. R., & Henkin, A. B. (2002). Assessing dispositions toward cultural diversity among preservice teachers. *Urban Education,* 37(1), 22–40.

Dee, T. (2001). *Teachers, race, and student achievement in a randomized experiment.* New York: NBER Working Paper No. W8432.

Delpit, L. (1995). *Other people's children: Cultural conflict in the classroom.* New York: The New York Press.

Delpit, L. (2003). Educators as "Seed People": Growing a new future. *Educational Researcher,* 7(32), 14–21.

Dempster, F. N. (1991). Synthesis of research on reviews and tests. *Educational Leadership,* 48(7), 71–76.

Dempster, F. N. (1993). Exposing our students to less should help them learn more. *Phi Delta Kappan, 74,* 432–437.

Derry, S. J. (1989). Putting learning strategies to work. *Educational Leadership,* 47(5), 4–10.

Derry, S. J. (1991). Strategy and expertise in solving word problems. In C. McCormick, G. Miller, & M. Pressley (Eds.), *Cognitive strategies research: From basic research to educational applications.* New York: Springer-Verlag.

Derry, S. J. (1992). Beyond symbolic processing: Expanding horizons for educational psychology. *Journal of Educational Psychology, 84,* 413–419.

Deshler, D., Ellis, E. S., & Lenz, B. K. (1996). *Teaching adolescents with learning disabilities: Strategies and methods* (2nd ed.). Denver: Love Publishing.

Dewey, J. (1910). *How we think.* Boston: D.C. Heath.

Dewey, J. (1913). *Interest and effort in education.* Cambridge, MA: Houghton-Mifflin.

Diamond, M., & Hobson, J. (1998). *Magic trees of the mind.* New York: Dutton.

Diaz, R. M., & Berk, L. E. (Eds.). (1992). *Private speech: From social interaction to self-regulation.* Hillsdale, NJ: Lawrence Erlbaum.

Diaz-Rico, L. T., & Weed, K. Z. (2002). *The crosscultural, language, and academic development handbook* (2nd ed.). Boston: Allyn and Bacon.

Dickinson, D. K., McCabe, A., Anastasopoulos, L., Peisner-Feinberg, E. S., & Poe, M. D. (2003). The comprehensive language approach to early literacy: The interrelationships among vocabulary, phonological sensitivity, and print knowledge among preschool-aged children. *Journal of Educational Psychology.* 95, 465–481.

Diller, L. (1998). *Running on ritalin.* New York: Bantam Books.

Dingfelder, S. F. (2005). Closing the gap for Latino patients. *Monitor on Psychology*, 36(1), 58–61.

Dinnel, D., & Glover, J. A. (1985). Advance organizers: Encoding manipulations. *Journal of Educational Psychology*, *77*, 514–522.

DiVesta, F. J., & Di Cintio, M. J. (1997). Interactive effects of working memory span and text comprehension on reading comprehension and retrieval. *Learning and Individual Differences*, 9, 215–231.

Doctorow, M., Wittrock, M. C., & Marks, C. (1978). Generative processes in reading comprehension. *Journal of Educational Psychology*, *70*, 109–118.

Dodge, K. A., & Pettit, G. S. (2003). A biopsychosocial model of the development of chronic conduct problems in adolescence. *Developmental Psychology*, 39, 349–371.

Doggett, A. M. (2004). ADHD and drug therapy: Is it still a valid treatment? *Child Health Care*, *8*, 69–81.

Doherty, K. M. (2002, July 12). Assessment. *Education Week on the Web.* Retrieved August 5, 2002 from http://edweek.org/context/topics/issuespage.cmf?id=41

Dolezal, S. E., Welsh, L. M., Pressley, M., & Vincent, M. (2003). How do nine third-grade teachers motivate their students? *Elementary School Journal*, *103*, 239–267.

Doll, B., Zucker, S., & Brehm, K. (2005). *Resilient classrooms: Creating healthy environments for learning*. New York: Guilford.

Doyle, W. (1977). The uses of nonverbal behaviors: Toward an ecological model of classrooms. *Merrill-Palmer Quarterly*, 23, 179–192.

Doyle, W. (1983). Academic work. *Review of Educational Research*, 53, 159–200.

Doyle, W. (1986). Classroom organization and management. In M. C. Wittrock (Ed.), *Handbook of research on teaching* (3rd ed.) (pp. 392–431). New York: Macmillan.

Doyle, W. (2006). Ecological approaches to classroom management. In C. Evertson & C. S. Weinstein (Eds.), *Handbook for classroom management: Research, practice, and contemporary issues*. Mahwah, NJ: Lawrence Erlbaum.

Driscoll, MP. (2005). *Psychology of learning for instruction* (3rd ed.). Boston: Allyn and Bacon.

DuBois, D. L., Burk-Braxton, C., Swenson, L. P., Tevendale, H. D., & Hardesty, J. L. (2002). Race and gender influences on adjustment in early adolescence: Investigation of an integrative model. *Child Development*, 73, 1573–1592.

Dubois, W. E. B. (1903). *The souls of Black folk: Essays and sketches.* Chicago: McClurg.

Duell, O. K. (1994). Extended wait time and university student achievement. *American Educational Research Journal*, 31, 397–414.

Duncan, G. J., & Brooks-Gunn, J. (2000). Family poverty, welfare reform, and child development. *Child Development*, *71*, 188–196.

Duncan, R. M., & Cheyne, J. A. (1999). Incidence and functions of self-reported private speech in young adults: A self-verbalization questionnaire. *Canadian Journal of Behavioural Sciences*, 31, 133–136.

Duncker, K. (1945). On solving problems. *Psychological Monographs*, 58(5, Whole No. 270).

Dunn, K., & Dunn, R. (1978). *Teaching students through their individual learning styles.* Reston, VA: National Council of Principals.

Dunn, K., & Dunn, R. (1987). Dispelling outmoded beliefs about student learning. *Educational Leadership*, *44*(6), 55–63.

Dunn, R. (1987). Research on instructional environments: Implications for student achievement and attitudes. *Professional School Psychology*, 2, 43–52.

Dunn, R., Beaudry, J. S., & Klavas, A. (1989). Survey of research on learning styles. *Educational Leadership*, *47*(7), 50–58.

Dunn, R., Dunn, K., & Price, G. E. (1984). *Learning Style Inventory.* Lawrence, KS: Price Systems.

Dunn, R., Dunn, K., & Price, G. E. (2000). *Learning Style Inventory.* Lawrence, KS: Price Systems.

Dunn, R., & Griggs, S. (2003). *Synthesis of the Dunn and Dunn Learning-Style Model Research: Who, what, when, where, and so what?* New York: St. John's University.

Durbin, D. L., Darling, N., Steinberg, L., & Brown, B. B. (1993). Parenting style and peer group membership among European-American adolescents. *Journal of Research on Adolescence*, 3, 87–100.

Dusenbury, L., & Falco, M. (1995). Eleven components of effective drug abuse prevention curricula. *Journal of School Health*, *65*, 420–425.

Dweck, C. S. (1999). *Self-theories: Their role in motivation, personality, and development.* Philadelphia: Psychology Press.

Dweck, C. S. (2000). *Self-theories: Their role in motivation, personality, and development.* Philadelphia: Routledge Press.

Dweck, C. S. (2002). The development of ability conceptions. In A. Wigfield & J. Eccles (Eds.), *The development of achievement motivation.* San Diego, CA: Academic Press.

Dweck, C. S., & Bempechat, J. (1983). Children's theories on intelligence: Consequences for learning. In S. Paris, G. Olson, & W. Stevenson (Eds.), *Learning and motivation in the classroom* (pp. 239–256). Hillsdale, NJ: Lawrence Erlbaum.

Dyson, A. H. (1997). *Writing superheroes: Contemporary childhood, popular culture, and classroom literacy.* New York: Teachers College Press.

Eaton, J. F., Anderson, C. W., & Smith, E. L. (1984). Students' misconceptions interfere with science learning: Case studies of fifth-graders. *Elementary School Journal*, *84*, 365–379.

Eccles, J., & Wigfield, A. (1985). Teacher expectations and student motivation. In J. Dusek (Ed.), *Teacher expectancies* (pp. 185–226). Hillsdale, NJ: Lawrence Erlbaum.

Eccles, J., Wigfield, A., & Schiefele, U. (1998). Motivation to succeed. In W. Damon (Series Ed.) & N. Eisenberg (Volume Ed.), *Handbook of child psychology: Vol. 3. Social, emotional, and personality development* (5th ed., pp. 1017–1095). New York: Wiley.

Echevarria, M. (2003). Anomalies as a catalyst for middle school students' knowledge construction and scientific reasoning during science inquiry. *Journal of Educational Psychology*, 95, 357–374.

Edelman, G. M. (1992). *Bright air, brilliant fire: On the matter of the mind.* New York: Basic Books.

Egan, S. K., Monson, T. C., & Perry, D. G. (1998). Social-cognitive influences on change in aggression over time. *Developmental Psychology, 34,* 996–1006.

Eggen, P. D., & Kauchak, D. P. (2001). *Strategies for teachers: Teaching content and thinking skills* (4th ed.). Boston: Allyn and Bacon.

Eggen, P. D., & Kauchak, D. P. (2006). *Strategies for teachers: Teaching content and thinking skills* (5th ed.). Boston: Allyn and Bacon.

Eisenberg, N., & Fabes, R. A. (1998). Prosocial development. In W. Damon (Series Ed.) & N. Eisenberg (Vol. Ed.), *Handbook of child psychology: Vol. 3. Social, emotional, and personality development* (5th ed., pp. 701–778). New York: Wiley.

Eisenberg, N., Martin, C. L., & Fabes, R. A. (1996). Gender development and gender effects. In D. Berliner & R. Calfee (Eds.), *Handbook of educational psychology* (pp. 358–396). New York: Macmillan.

Eisenberg, N., Shell, R., Pasernack, J., Lennon, R., Beller, R., & Mathy, R. M. (1987). Prosocial development in middle childhood: A longitudinal study. *Developmental Psychology, 23,* 712–718.

Eisenberg, R., Pierce, W. D., & Cameron, J. (1999). Effects of rewards on intrinsic motivation—Negative, neutral, and positive: Comment on Deci, Koestner, and Ryan (1999). *Psychological Bulletin, 125,* 677–691.

Eisner, E. W. (1999). The uses and limits of performance assessments. *Phi Delta Kappan, 80,* 658–660.

Elashoff, J. D., & Snow, R. E. (1971). *Pygmalion reconsidered.* Worthington, OH: Charles A. Jones.

Elawar, M. C., & Corno, L. (1985). A factorial experiment in teachers' written feedback on student homework: Changing teacher behavior a little rather than a lot. *Journal of Educational Psychology, 77,* 162–173.

Elias, M. J., & Schwab, Y. (2006). From compliance to responsibility: Social and emotional learning and classroom management. In C. Evertson & C. S. Weinstein (Eds.), *Handbook for classroom management: Research, practice, and contemporary issues.* Mahwah, NJ: Lawrence Erlbaum.

Elkind, D. (1981). Obituary—Jean Piaget (1896–1980). *American Psychologist, 36,* 911–913.

Elrich, M. (1994). The stereotype within. *Educational Leadership, 51*(8), 12–15.

Embry, D. D. (2002). The Good Behavior Game: A best practice candidate as a universal behavior vaccine. *Clinical Child and Family Psychology Review, 5,* 273–297.

Emerson, M. J., & Miyake, A. (2003). The role of inner speech in task switching: A dual-task investigation. *Journal of Memory and Language, 48,* 148–168.

Emmer, E. T., & Aussiker, A. (1990). School and classroom discipline problems: How well do they work? In O. Moles (Ed.), *Student discipline strategies: Research and practice.* Albany, NY: SUNY Press.

Emmer, E. T., & Evertson, C. M. (1981). Synthesis of research on classroom management. *Educational Leadership, 38,* 342–345.

Emmer, E. T., & Evertson, C. M. (1982). Effective classroom management at the beginning of the school year in junior high school classes. *Journal of Educational Psychology, 74,* 485–498.

Emmer, E. T., Evertson, C. M., & Anderson, L. M. (1980). Effective classroom management at the beginning of the school year. *Elementary School Journal, 80,* 219–231.

Emmer, E. T., Evertson, C. M., & Worsham, M. E. (2006). *Classroom management for secondary teachers* (7th ed.). Boston: Allyn and Bacon.

Emmer, E. T., & Gerwels, M. C. (2006). Classroom management in middle school and high school classrooms. In C. Evertson & C. S. Weinstein (Eds.), *Handbook for classroom management: Research, practice, and contemporary issues.* Mahwah, NJ: Lawrence Erlbaum.

Emmer, E. T., & Stough, L. M. (2001). Classroom management: A critical part of educational psychology with implications for teacher education. *Educational Psychologist, 36,* 103–112.

Engle, R. W. (2001). What is working memory capacity? In H. Roediger, J. Nairne, I. Neath, & A. Suprenant (Eds.), *The nature of remembering: Essays in honor of Robert G. Crowder* (pp. 297–314). Washington, DC: American Psychological Association.

Engle, R. W. (2002). Working memory capacity as executive attention. *Current Directions in Psychological Science, 11,* 19–33.

Entwisle, D. R., & Alexander, K. L. (1998). Facilitating the transition to first grade: The nature of transition and research on factors affecting it. *The Elementary School Journal, 98,* 351–364.

Entwisle, D. R., Alexander, K. L., & Olson, L. (1997). *Children, schools, and inequality.* Boulder, CO: Westview Press.

Epanchin, B. C., Townsend, B., & Stoddard, K. (1994). *Constructive classroom management: Strategies for creating positive learning environments.* Pacific Grove, CA: Brooks/Cole.

Epstein, H. (1980). EEG developmental stages. *Developmental Psychobiology, 13,* 629–631.

Epstein, J. L. (1989). Family structure and student motivation. In R. E. Ames & C. Ames (Eds.), *Research on motivation in education: Vol 3. Goals and cognitions* (pp. 259–295). New York: Academic Press.

Epstein, J. L. (1995). School/Family/Community partnerships: Caring for the children we share. *Phi Delta Kappan, 76,* 701–712.

Epstein, J. L., & MacIver, D. J. (1992). *Opportunities to learn: Effects on eighth graders of curriculum offerings and instructional approaches.* (Report No. 34). Baltimore: Center for Research on Elementary and Middle Schools, Johns Hopkins University.

Epstein, J. L., & Van Voorhis, F. L. (2001). More than minutes: Teachers' roles in designing homework. *Educational Psychologist, 36,* 181–193.

Ericsson, K. A. (1999). Expertise. In R. Wilson & F. Keil (Eds.), *The MIT encyclopedia of the cognitive sciences* (pp. 298–300). Cambridge, MA: MIT Press.

Ericsson, K. A., & Charness, N. (1999). Expert performance: Its structure and acquisition. In S. Ceci & W. Williams (Eds.), The nature-nurture debate: The essential readings. *Essential readings in developmental psychology.* Malden, MA: Blackwell.

Erikson, E. H. (1963). *Childhood and society* (2nd ed.). New York: Norton.

Erikson, E. H. (1968). *Identity, youth, and crisis.* New York: Norton.

Erikson, E. H. (1980). *Identity and the life cycle* (2nd ed.). New York: Norton.

Espe, C., Worner, C., & Hotkevich, M. (1990). Whole language—What a bargain. *Educational Leadership, 47*(6), 45.

Evans, E. D., & Craig, D. (1990). Adolescent cognitions for academic cheating as a function of grade level and achievement status. *Journal of Adolescent Research, 5,* 325–345.

Evans, G. W. (2004). The environment of childhood poverty. *American Psychologist, 59,* 77–92.

Evans, L., & Davies, K. (2000). No sissy boys here: A content analysis of the representation of masculinity in elementary school reading texts. *Sex Roles, 42,* 255–270.

Evensen, D. H., Salisbury-Glennon, J. D., & Glenn, J. (2001). A qualitative study of six medical students in a problem-based curriculum: Toward a situated model of self-regulation. *Journal of Educational Psychology, 93,* 659–676.

Evertson, C. M. (1988). Managing classrooms: A framework for teachers. In D. Berliner & B. Rosenshine (Eds.), *Talks to teachers* (pp. 54–74). New York: Random House.

Evertson, C. M., Emmer, E. T., & Worsham, M. E. (2003). *Classroom management for elementary teachers* (6th ed.). Boston: Allyn and Bacon.

Evertson, C. M., Emmer, E. T., & Worsham, M. E. (2006). *Classroom management for secondary teachers* (7th ed.). Boston: Allyn and Bacon.

Ewy, C., & student authors. (1997). Kids take on "the test." *Educational Leadership, 54*(4), 76–78.

Fagot, B. I., & Hagan, R. (1991). Observations of parent reactions to sex-stereotyped behaviors: Age and sex effects. *Child Development, 62,* 617–628.

Fagot, B. I., Hagan, R., Leinbach, M. D., & Kronsberg, S. (1985). Differential reactions to assertive and communicative acts of toddler boys and girls. *Child Development, 56,* 1499–1505.

Fantuzzo, J., Davis, G., & Ginsburg, M. (1995). Effects of parent involvement in isolation or in combination with peer tutoring on student self-concept and mathematics achievement. *Journal of Educational Psychology, 87,* 272–281.

Farnaham-Diggory, S. (1994). Paradigms of knowledge and instruction. *Review of Educational Research, 64,* 463–477.

Feather, N. T. (1982). *Expectations and actions: Expectancy-value models in psychology.* Hillsdale, NJ: Lawrence Erlbaum.

Feldman. J. (2003). The simplicity principle in human concept learning. *Current Directions in Psychological Science, 12,* 227–232.

Feldman, R. S. (2004). *Child development* (3rd ed.). Upper Saddle River, NJ: Prentice-Hall.

Fennema, E., & Peterson, P. (1988). Effective teaching for boys and girls: The same or different? In D. Berliner & B. Rosenshine (Eds.), *Talks to teachers* (pp. 111–127). New York: Random House.

Ferguson, A. A. (2000). *Bad boys: Public schools and the making of Black masculinity.* Ann Arbor, MI: University of Michigan Press.

Feshbach, N. (1997). Empathy: The formative years—Implications for clinical practice. In A. Bohart & L. Greenberg (Eds.), *Empathy reconsidered: New directions in psychotherapy* (pp. 33–59). Washington, DC: American Psychological Association.

Feshbach, N. (1998). Aggression in the schools: Toward reducing ethnic conflict and enhancing ethnic understanding. In P. Trickett & C. Schellenbach (Eds.), *Violence against children in the family and the community* (pp. 269–286). Washington, DC: American Psychological Association.

Fillmore, L.W., & Snow, C. (2000). What teachers need to know about language. [On-line]. Available: http://www.cal.org/ericcll/teachers.pdf

Finkel, D., Reynolds, C. A., McArdle, J. J., Gatz, M., & Pedersen, N. L. (2003). Latent growth curve analyses of accelerating decline in cognitive abilities in adulthood. *Developmental Psychology, 39,* 535–550.

Finlan, M. (1994). *Learning disabilities: The imaginary disease.* Westport, CT: Gergin & Garvey.

Finn, J. (1972). Expectations and the educational environment. *Review of Educational Research, 42,* 387–410.

Fischer, K. W., & Pare-Blagoev, J. (2000). From individual differences to dynamic pathways of development. *Child Development, 71,* 850–853.

Fiske, E. B. (1988, April 10). America's test mania. *New York Times* (Education Life Section), pp. 16–20.

Fiske, S. T. (1993). Social cognition and social perception. *Annual Review of Psychology, 44,* 155–194.

Fitts, P. M., & Posner, M. I. (1967). *Human performance.* Belmont, CA: Brooks Cole.

Fitzgerald, J. (1995). English-as-a-second-language learners' cognitive reading process: A review of the research in the United States. *Review of Educational Research, 62,* 145–190.

Fives, H. R., Hamman, D., & Olivarez, A. (2005, April). *Does burnout begin with student teaching? Analyzing efficacy, burnout, and support during the student-teaching semester.* Paper presented at the Annual Meeting of the America Educational Research Association, Montreal, CA.

Flammer, A. (1995). Developmental analysis of control beliefs. In A. Bandura (Ed.), *Self-efficacy in changing societies* (pp. 69–113). New York: Cambridge University Press.

Flavell, J. H. (1985). *Cognitive development* (2nd ed.). Englewood Cliffs, NJ: Prentice-Hall.

Flavell, J. H., Friedrichs, A. G., & Hoyt, J. D. (1970). Developmental changes in memorization processes. *Cognitive Psychology, 1,* 324–340.

Flavell, J. H., Green, F. L., & Flavell, E. R. (1995). Young children's knowledge about thinking. *Monographs of the Society for Research in Child Development, 60*(1) (Serial No. 243).

Flavell, J. H., Miller, P. H., & Miller, S. A. (2002). *Cognitive development* (4th ed.). Upper Saddle River, NJ: Prentice-Hall.

Fleith, D. (2000). Teacher and student perceptions of creativity in the classroom environment. *Roeper Review, 22,* 148–153.

Flink, C. F., Boggiano, A. K., & Barrett, M. (1990). Controlling teaching strategies: Undermining children's self-determination and performance. *Journal of Personality and Social Psychology, 59,* 916–924.

Floden, R. E. (2001). Research on effects of teaching: A continuing model for research on teaching. In V. Richardson (Ed.), *Handbook of research on teaching* (4th ed., pp. 3–16). Washington, DC: American Educational Research Association.

Floden, R. E., & Klinzing, H. G. (1990). What can research on teacher thinking contribute to teacher preparation? A second opinion. *Educational Researcher, 19*(4), 15–20.

Ford, D. Y. (2000). *Infusing multicultural content into the curriculum for gifted students.* (ERIC EC Digest #E601). Arlington, VA: The ERIC Clearinghouse on Disabilities and Gifted Education.

Forness, S. R., & Knitzer, J. (1992). A new proposed definition and terminology to replace "Serious Emotional Disturbance" in Individuals with Disabilities Education Act. *School Psychology Review, 21,* 12–20.

Foster, W. (1981, August). *Social and emotional development in gifted individuals.* Paper presented at the Fourth World Conference on Gifted and Talented, Montreal.

Fox, L. H. (1981). Identification of the academically gifted. *American Psychologist, 36,* 1103–1111.

Frank, S. J., Pirsch, L. A., & Wright, V. C. (1990). Late adolescents' perceptions of their parents: Relationships among deidealization, autonomy, relatedness, and insecurity and implications for adolescent adjustment and ego identity status. *Journal of Youth and Adolescence, 19,* 571–588.

Fredricks, J. A., Blumenfeld, P. C., & Paris, A. H. (2004). School engagement: Potential of the concept, state of the evidence. *Review of Educational Research, 74*, 59–109.

Fredericks, L. (2003). *Making the case for social and emotional learning and service-learning.* Denver, CO: Education Commission of the States.

Freiberg, H. J. (1999). Sustaining the paradigm. In H. J. Freiberg (Ed.), *Beyond behaviorism: Changing the classroom management paradigm* (pp. 164–173). Boston: Allyn and Bacon.

Freiberg, H. J. (Ed.). (1999). *Beyond behaviorism: Changing the classroom management.* Boston: Allyn and Bacon.

Freiberg, H. J., & Driscoll, A. (1996). *Universal teaching strategies* (2nd ed.). Boston: Allyn and Bacon.

Freiberg, H. J., & Driscoll, A. (2005). *Universal teaching strategies* (4th ed.). Boston: Allyn and Bacon.

Freiberg, J. (2006). Research-based programs for preventing and solving discipline problems. In C. Evertson & C. S. Weinstein (Eds.), *Handbook for classroom management: Research, practice, and contemporary issues.* Mahwah, NJ: Lawrence Erlbaum.

Freud, S. (1959). Creative writers and daydreaming. In J. Strachey (Ed.), *The standard edition of the complete psychological works of Sigmund Freud* (Vol. 9). London: Hogarth Press.

Frick, T. W. (1990). Analysis of patterns in time: A method of recording and quantifying temporal relations in education. *American Educational Research Journal, 27*, 180–204.

Friend, M. (2006). *Special education: Contemporary perspectives for school professionals.* Boston: Allyn and Bacon.

Friend, M., & Bursuck, W. (1996). *Including students with special needs: A practical guide for classroom teachers.* Boston: Allyn and Bacon.

Friend, M., & Bursuck, W. D. (2002). *Including students with special needs* (3rd ed.). Boston: Allyn and Bacon.

Fuchs, L. S., Fuchs, D., Hamlett, C. L., & Karns, K. (1998). High-achieving students' interactions and performance on complex mathematical tasks as a function of homogeneous and heterogeneous pairings. *American Educational Research Journal, 35*, 227–268.

Fuchs, L. S., Fuchs, D., Prentice, K., Burch, M., Hamlett, C. L., Owen, R., & Schroeter, K. (2003). Enhancing third-grade students' mathematical problem solving with self-regulated learning strategies. *Journal of Educational Psychology, 95*(2), 306–315.

Fulk, C. L., & Smith, P. J. (1995). Students' perceptions of teachers' instructional and management adaptations for students with learning or behavior problems. *The Elementary School Journal, 95*, 409–419.

Fuller, F. G. (1969). Concerns of teachers: A developmental conceptualization. *American Educational Research Journal, 6*, 207–226.

Furrer, C, & Skinner, E. (2003). Sense of relatedness as a factor in children's academic engagement and performance. *Journal of Educational Psychology, 95*(11), 148–161.

Gaedke, B., & Shaughnessy, M. F. (2003). An interview with Jere Brophy. *Educational Psychology Review, 15*, 199–211.

Gage, N. L. (1991). The obviousness of social and educational research results. *Educational Researcher, 20*(A), 10–16.

Gage, N. L., & Berliner, D. C. (1998). *Educational psychology* (6th ed.). New York: Houghton Mifflin.

Gagné, E. D. (1985). *The cognitive psychology of school learning.* Boston: Little, Brown.

Gagné, E. D., Yekovich, C. W., & Yekovich, F. R. (1993). *The cognitive psychology of school learning* (2nd ed.). New York: HarperCollins.

Galambos, S. J., & Goldin-Meadow, S. (1990). The effects of learning two languages on metalinguistic development. *Cognition, 34*, 1–56.

Gallagher, M. (2001, June 11). More on zero-tolerance in schools. *NewsMax.com.* Available online at http://www.newsmax.com/archives/articles/2001/6/11/123253.shtml. Downloaded on January 23, 2003.

Gallimore, R., & Goldenberg, C. (2001). Analyzing cultural models and settings to connect minority achievement and school improvement research. *Educational Psychologist, 36*, 45–56.

Gallini, J. K. (1991). Schema-based strategies and implications for instructional design in strategy training. In C. McCormick, G. Miller, & M. Pressley (Eds.), *Cognitive strategies research: From basic research to educational applications.* New York: Springer-Verlag.

Gamoran, A. (1987). The stratification of high school learning opportunities. *Sociology of Education, 60*, 135–155.

Gamoran, A., & Mare, R. D. (1989). Secondary school tracking and educational inequality: Compensation, reinforcement, or neutrality. *American Journal of Sociology, 94*, 146–183.

Garbarino, J., & deLara, E. (2002). *And words can hurt forever: How to protect adolescents from bullying, harassment, and emotional violence.* New York: Free Press.

Garcia, E. E. (1992). "Hispanic" children: Theoretical, empirical, and related policy issues. *Educational Psychology Review, 4*, 69–94.

Garcia, E. E. (2002). *Student cultural diversity: Understanding the meaning and meeting the challenge.* Boston: Houghton Mifflin.

Garcia, R. L. (1991). *Teaching in a pluralistic society: Concepts, models, and strategies.* New York: HarperCollins.

Garcia, T., & Pintrich, P. (1994). Regulating motivation and cognition in the classroom: The role of self-schemas and self-regulatory strategies. In B. J. Zimmerman & D. Schunk (Eds.), *Self-regulation of learning and performance: Issues and educational applications* (pp. 127–153). Hillsdale, NJ: Lawrence Erlbaum.

Gardner, H. (1982). *Developmental psychology* (2nd ed.). Boston: Little, Brown.

Gardner, H. (1983). *Frames of mind: The theory of multiple intelligences.* New York: Basic Books.

Gardner, H. (1993). *Creating minds: An anatomy of creativity seen through the lives of Freud, Einstein, Picasso, Stravinsky, Elliot, Graham, and Gandhi.* New York: Basic Books.

Gardner, H. (1998). Reflections on multiple intelligences: Myths and messages. In A. Woolfolk (Ed.), *Readings in educational psychology* (2nd ed.) (pp. 61–67). Boston: Allyn and Bacon.

Gardner, H. (1999). Are there additional intelligences? In J. Kane (Ed.), *Education, information, and transformation: Essays on learning and thinking* (pp. 111–131). Upper Saddle River, NJ: Prentice-Hall.

Gardner, H. (2003, April 21). *Multiple intelligence after twenty years.* Paper presented at the American Educational Research Association, Chicago, Illinois.

Gardner, H., & Hatch, T. (1989). Multiple intelligences go to school. *Educational Researcher, 18*(8), 4–10.

Gardner, R., Brown, R., Sanders, S., & Menke, D. J. (1992). "Seductive details" in learning from text. In K. A. Renninger, S. Hidi, & A. Krapp (Eds.), *The role of interest in learning and development* (pp. 239–254). Hillsdale, NJ: Lawrence Erlbaum.

Garmon, A., Nystrand, M., Berends, M., & LePore, P. C. (1995). An organizational analysis of the effects of ability grouping. *American Educational Research Journal, 32*, 687–715.

Garmoran, A. (1987). The stratification of high school learning opportunities. *Sociology of Education, 60*, 135–155.

Garner, P. W., & Spears, F. M. (2000). Emotion regulation in low-income preschool children. *Social Development, 9*, 246–264.

Garner, R. (1990). When children and adults do not use learning strategies: Toward a theory of settings. *Review of Educational Psychology, 60*, 517–530.

Garner, R. (1998). Choosing to learn and not-learn in school. *Educational Psychology Review, 10*, 227–238.

Garnets, L. (2002). Sexual orientations in perspective. *Cultural Diversity and Ethnic Minority Psychology, 8*, 115–129.

Garrison, J. (1995). Deweyan pragmatism and the epistemology of contemporary social constructivism. *American Educational Research Journal, 32*, 716–741.

Garrod, A., Beal, C., & Shin, P. (1990). The development of moral orientation in elementary school children. *Sex Roles, 22*, 13–27.

Gathercole, S. E., Pickering, S. J., Ambridge, B., & Wearing, H., (2004). The structure of working memory from 4 to 15 years of age. *Developmental Psychology, 40*, 177–190.

Gay, G. (2000). *Culturally responsive teaching: Theory, research, and practice.* New York: Teachers College Press.

Gay, G. (2006). Connections between classroom management and culturally responsive teaching. In C. Evertson & C. S. Weinstein (Eds.), *Handbook for classroom management: Research, practice, and contemporary issues*. Mahwah, NJ: Lawrence Erlbaum.

Geary, D. C. (1995). Sexual selection and sex differences in spatial cognition. *Learning and Individual Differences, 7*, 289–303.

Geary, D. C. (1998). What is the function of mind and brain? *Educational Psychologist, 10*, 377–388.

Geary, D. C. (1999). Evolution and developmental sex differences. *Current Directions in Psychological Science, 8*, 115–120.

Geary, D. C., & Bjorklund, D. F. (2000). Evolutionary developmental psychology. *Child Development, 7*, 57–65.

Gehlbach, H. (2004). A new perspective on perspective taking: A multidimensional approach to conceptualizing an aptitude. *Educational Psychology Review, 16*, 207–234.

Gelman, R. (2000). The epigenesis of mathematical thinking. *Journal of Applied Developmental Psychology, 21*, 27–37.

Gelman, R., & Cordes, S. A. (2001). Counting in animals and humans. In E. Dupoux (Ed.), *Essay in honor of Jacques Mehler*. Cambridge, MA: MIT Press.

Gentner, D. (1975). Evidence for the psychological reality of semantic components: The verbs of possession. In D. Norman & D. Rumelhart (Eds.), *Explorations in cognition* (pp. 211–246). San Francisco: Freeman.

Gentner, D., Loewenstein, J., & Thompson, L. (2003). Learning and transfer: A general role for analogical encoding. *Journal of Educational Psychology, 95*, 393–408.

George, P. S. (2005). A rationale for differentiated instruction in the regular classroom. *Theory Into Practice, 44*, 185–193.

Gergen, K. J. (1997). Constructing constructivism: Pedagogical potentials. *Issues in Education: Contributions from Educational Psychology, 3*, 195–202.

Gersten, R. (1996a). The language-minority students in transition: Contemporary instructional research. *The Elementary School Journal, 96*, 217–220.

Gersten, R. (1996b). Literacy instruction for language-minority students: The transition years. *The Elementary School Journal, 96*, 217–220.

Gibbs, J. W., & Luyben, P. D. (1985). Treatment of self-injurious behavior: Contingent versus noncontingent positive practice overcorrection. *Behavior Modification, 9*, 3–21.

Gick, M. L. (1986). Problem-solving strategies. *Educational Psychologist, 21*, 99–120.

Gick, M. L., & Holyoak, K. L. (1983). Schema induction and analogical transfer. *Cognitive Psychology, 15*, 1–38.

Gillett, M., & Gall, M. (1982, March). *The effects of teacher enthusiasm on the at-task behavior of students in the elementary grades.* Paper presented at the annual meeting of the American Educational Research Association, New York.

Gillies, R. (2003). The behaviors, interactions, and perceptions of junior high school students during small-group learning. *Journal of Educational Psychology, 96*, 15–22.

Gillies, R. (2004). The effects of cooperative learning on junior high school students during small group learning. *Learning and Instruction, 14*, 197–213

Gilligan, C. (1982). *In a different voice: Psychological theory and women's development.* Cambridge, MA: Harvard University Press.

Gilligan, C., & Attanucci, J. (1988). Two moral orientations: Gender differences and similarities. *Merrill-Palmer Quarterly, 34*, 223–237.

Ginsburg, H., & Opper, S. (1988). *Piaget's theory of intellectual development* (3rd ed.). Englewood Cliffs, NJ: Prentice-Hall.

Girls' math achievement: What we do and don't know. (1986, January). *Harvard Education Letter, 2*(1), 1–5.

Glasgow, K. L., Dornbusch, S. M., Troyer, L., Steinberg, L., & Ritter, P. L. (1997). Parenting styles, adolescents' attributions, and educational outcomes in nine heterogeneous high schools. *Child Development, 68*, 507–523.

Glasser, W. (1969). *Schools without failure.* New York: Harper & Row.

Glasser, W. (1990). *The quality school: Managing students without coercion.* New York: Harper & Row.

Glassman, M. (2001). Dewey and Vygotsky: Society, experience, and inquiry in educational practice. *Educational Researcher, 30*(4), 3–14.

Gleitman, H., Fridlund, A. J., & Reisberg, D. (1999). *Psychology* (5th ed.). New York: Norton.

Goldenberg, C. (1996). The education of language-minority students: Where are we, and where do we need to go? *The Elementary School Journal, 96*, 353–361.

Goldman, S. R., Lawless, K., Pellegrino, J. W., & Plants, R. (2006). Technology for teaching and learning with understanding. In J. Cooper (Ed.), *Classroom teaching skills* (8th ed., pp. 104–150). Boston: Houghton-Mifflin.

Goleman, D. (1988, April 10). An emerging theory on blacks' I.Q. scores. *New York Times* (Education Life Section), pp. 22–24.

Goleman, D. (1995). *Emotional intelligence.* New York: Bantam.

Gollnick, D. A., & Chinn, P. C. (1994). *Multicultural education in a pluralistic society* (4th ed.). New York: Merrill.

Gonzalez, V., Brusca-Vega, R., & Yawkey, T. (1997). *Assessment and instruction of culturally diverse students with or at-risk of learning problems: From research to practice.* Boston: Allyn and Bacon.

Good, T. L. (1983a). Classroom research: A decade of progress. *Educational Psychologist, 18*, 127–144.

Good, T. L. (1983b). Research on classroom teaching. In L. Shulman & G. Sykes (Eds.), *Handbook of teaching and policy* (pp. 42–80). New York: Longman.
Good, T. L. (1988). Teacher expectations. In D. Berliner & B. Rosenshine (Eds.), *Talks to teachers* (pp. 159–200). New York: Random House.
Good, T. L. (1996). Teaching effects and teacher evaluation. In J. Sikula (Ed.), *Handbook of research on teacher education* (pp. 617–665). New York: Macmillan.
Good, T. L., & Brophy, J. (2003). *Looking in classrooms* (9th ed.). Boston: Allyn and Bacon.
Goodman, Y. M., & Goodman, K. S. (1990). Vygotsky in a whole-language perspective. In L. Moll (Ed.), *Vygotsky and education: Instructional implications and applications of sociohistorical psychology* (pp. 223–250). New York: Cambridge University Press.
Goodrich, H. (1997). Understanding rubrics. *Educational Leadership, 54*(4), 14–17.
Gordon, D. (2001, June, 18). The dominator. *Newsweek*, 42–47.
Gordon, E. W. (1991). Human diversity and pluralism. *Educational Psychologist, 26*, 99–108.
Gordon, J. A. (1998). Caring through control: Reaching urban African American youth. *Journal for a Just and Caring Education, 4*, 418–440.
Gordon, T. (1981). Crippling our children with discipline. *Journal of Education, 163*, 228–243.
Graber, J. A., & Brooks-Gunn, J. (1996). Transitions and turning points: Navigating the passage from childhood through adolescence. *Developmental Psychology, 32*, 768–776.
Graham, S. (1991). A review of attribution theory in achievement contexts. *Educational Psychology Review, 3*, 5–39.
Graham, S. (1994). Motivation in African Americans. *Review of Educational Research, 64*, 55–117.
Graham, S. (1995). Narrative versus meta-analytic reviews of race differences in motivation. *Review of Educational Research, 65*, 509–514.
Graham, S. (1996). How causal beliefs influence the academic and social motivation of African-American children. In G. G. Brannigan (Ed.), *The enlightened educator: Research adventures in the schools* (pp. 111–126). New York: McGraw-Hill.
Graham, S. (1998). Self-blame and peer victimization in middle school: An attributional analysis. *Developmental Psychology, 34*, 587–599.
Graham, S., & Barker, G. (1990). The downside of help: An attributional developmental analysis of helping behavior as a low ability cue. *Journal of Educational Psychology, 82*, 7–14.
Graham, S., Taylor, A., & Hudley, C. (1998). Exploring achievement values among ethnic minority early adolescents. *Journal of Educational Psychology, 90*, 606–620.
Graham, S., & Weiner, B. (1996). Theories and principles of motivation. In D. Berliner & R. C. Calfee (Eds.), *Handbook of educational psychology* (pp. 63–84). New York: Macmillan.
Grant, C. A., & Sleeter, C. E. (1989). Race, class, gender, exceptionality, and educational reform. In J. Banks & C. McGee Banks (Eds.), *Multicultural education: Issues and perspectives* (pp. 49–66). Boston: Allyn and Bacon.
Gray, P. (2002). *Psychology* (4th ed.). New York: Worth.
Gredler, M. E. (2005). *Learning and instruction: Theory into practice* (5th ed.). Boston: Allyn and Bacon.
Greenberg, M. T., Weissberg, R. P., O'Brien, M. U., Zins, J. E., Fredericks, L., Resnik, H., & Elias, M. J. (2003). *American Psychologist, 58*(6/7), 466–474.
Greeno, J. G., Collins, A. M., & Resnick, L. B. (1996). Cognition and learning. In D. Berliner & R. Calfee (Eds.), *Handbook of educational psychology* (pp. 15–46). New York: Macmillan.
Greenwald, A. G., Oakes, M. A., & Hoffman, H. G. (2003). Targets of discrimination: Effects of race on responses to weapons holders. *Journal of Experimental Social Psychology, 39*, 399–405.
Gregorc, A. F. (1982). *Gregorc Style Delineator: Development, technical, and administrative manual.* Maynard, MA: Gabriel Systems.
Grigorenko, E. L., & Sternberg, R. J. (1998). Dynamic testing. *Psychological Bulletin, 124*, 75–111.
Grigorenko, E. L., & Sternberg, R. J. (2001). Analytical, creative, and practical intelligence as predictors of self-reported adaptive functioning: A case study in Russia. *Intelligence, 29*, 57–73.
Grissom, J. B., & Shepard, L. A. (1989). Repeating and dropping out of school. In L. A. Shepard & M. L. Smith (Eds.), *Flunking grades: Research and policies on retention* (pp. 34–63). New York: Falmer.
Grolnick, W.S., Gurland, S.T., Jacob, K.F., & DeCourcey, W. (2002). The development of self-determination in middle childhood and adolescence. In A. Wigfield & J. Eccles (Eds.), *Development of achievement motivation* (pp. 147–171). New York: Academic Press.
Grolnick, W. S., Ryan, R. M., & Deci, E. L. (1991). Inner resources for school achievement: Motivational mediators of children's perceptions of their parents. *Journal of Educational Psychology, 83*, 508–517.
Gronlund, N. E. (2003). *Assessment of student achievement* (7th ed.). Boston: Allyn and Bacon.
Gronlund, N. E. (2004). *Writing instructional objectives for teaching and assessment* (7th ed.). Upper Saddle River, NJ: Prentice-Hall.
Grossman, H., & Grossman, S. H. (1994). *Gender issues in education.* Boston: Allyn and Bacon.
Grotevant, H. D. (1998). Adolescent development in family contexts. In N. Eisenberg (Ed.), *Handbook of child psychology: Vol 3. Social, emotional, and personality development* (5th ed.) (pp. 1097–1149). New York: Wiley.
Guay, F., Larose, S., & Boivin, M. (2004). Academic self-concept and educational attainment level: A ten-year longitudinal study. *Self and Identity, 3*, 53–68.
Guilford, J. P. (1988). Some changes in the Structure-of-Intellect model. *Educational and Psychological Measurement, 48*, 1–4.
Gunn Morris, V., & Morris, C. L. (2002). No more cotton picking: African American voices from a small southern town. In G. S. Boutte (Ed.), *Resounding voices: School experiences of people from diverse ethnic backgrounds* (pp. 17–42). Boston: Allyn and Bacon.
Gurian, M., & Henley, P. (2001). *Boys and girls learn differently: A guide for teachers and parents.* San Francisco: Jossey-Bass.
Guskey, T. R. (1994). Making the grade: What benefits students? *Educational Leadership, 52*(2), 14–21.
Guskey, T. R., & Bailey, J. M. (2001). *Developing grading and reporting systems for student learning.* Thousand Oaks, CA: Corwin Press.
Gustafsson, J-E., & Undheim, J. O. (1996). Individual differences in cognitive functioning. In D. Berliner & R. Calfee (Eds.), *Handbook of educational psychology* (pp. 186–242). New York: Macmillan.
Guthrie, J. T., & Alao, S. (1997). Designing contexts to increase motivations of reading. *Educational Psychologist, 32*, 95–105.
Guthrie, J. T., Cox, K. E., Anderson, E., Harris, K., Mazzoni, S., & Rach, L. (1998). Principles of integrated instruction for en-

gagement in reading. *Educational Psychology Review, 10,* 227–238.

Gutman, L. M., Sameroff, A., & Cole, R. (2003). Academic growth curve trajectories from 1st grade to 12th grade: effects of multiple social risk factors and preschool child factors. *Developmental Psychology,* 39, 777–790.

Haager, D., & Klingner, J. K. (2005). *Differentiating instruction in inclusive classrooms: The special educators' guide.* Boston, MA: Allyn and Bacon.

Hacker, D. J., & Tenent, A. (2002). Implementing reciprocal teaching in the classroom: Overcoming obstacles and making modifications. *Journal of Educational Psychology,* 94, 699–718.

Haertel, E. H. (1999). Performance assessment and educational reform. *Phi Delta Kappan,* 80, 662–666.

Hagborg, W. J. (1993). Rosenberg Self-Esteem Scale and Harter's Self-Perception Profile for Adolescents: A concurrent validity study. *Psychology in Schools,* 30, 132–136.

Hakuta, K. (1986). *Mirror of language: The debate on bilingualism.* New York: Basic Books.

Hakuta, K., & Garcia, E. E. (1989). Bilingualism and education. *American Psychologist, 44,* 374–379.

Hakuta, K., & Gould, L. J. (1987). Synthesis of research on bilingual education. *Educational Leadership,* 44(6), 38–45.

Haladyna, T. H. (2002). *Essentials of standardized achievement testing: Validity and accountability.* Boston: Allyn and Bacon.

Halford, J. M. (1999). A different mirror: A conversation with Ronald Takaki. *Educational Leadership,* 56(7), 8–13.

Hall, J. W. (1991). More on the utility of the keyword method. *Journal of Educational Psychology,* 83, 171–172.

Hallahan, D. P., & Kauffman, J. M. (2006). *Exceptional learners: Introduction to special education* (10th ed.). Boston: Allyn and Bacon.

Hallahan, D. P., Lloyd, J. W., Kauffman, J. M., Weiss, M. P., & Martinez, E. A. (2005). *Introduction to learning disabilities* (5th ed.). Boston: Allyn and Bacon.

Hallowell, E. M., & Ratey, J. J. (1994). *Driven to distraction.* New York: Pantheon Books.

Halpern, D. F. (2000). *Sex differences in cognitive abilities.* Mahwah, NJ: Lawrence Erlbaum.

Halpern, D. F. (2004). A cognitive-process taxonomy for sex differences n cognitive abilities. *Current Directions in Psychological Science,* 13, 135–139.

Halpern, D. F., & LaMay, M. L. (2000). The smarter sex: A critical review of sex differences in intelligence. *Educational Psychology Review,* 12, 229–246.

Hambleton, R. K. (1996). Advances in assessment models, methods, and practices. In D. C. Berliner & R. C. Calfee (Eds.), *Handbook of educational psychology* (pp. 899–925). New York: Macmillan.

Hambrick, D. Z., Kane, M. J., & Engle, R. W. (2005). The role of working memory in higher-level cognition. In R. Sternberg & J. E. Pretz (Eds.), *Cognition and intelligence: Identifying the mechanisms of the mind* (pp. 104–121). New York: Cambridge University Press.

Hamilton, R. J. (1985). A framework for the evaluation of the effectiveness of adjunct questions and objectives. *Review of Educational Research,* 55, 47–86.

Hamm, J. (2000). Do birds of a feather flock together? The variable bases for African American, Asian American, and European American adolescents' selection of similar friends. *Developmental Psychology,* 36, 209–219.

Hamman, D., Berthelot, J., Saia, J., & Crowley, E. (2000). Teachers' coaching of learning and its relation to students' strategic learning. *Journal of Educational Psychology,* 92, 342–348.

Hamre, B. K., & Pianta, R. C. (2001). Early teacher–child relationships and the trajectory of children's school outcomes through eighth grade. *Child Development,* 72, 625–638.

Harackiewicz, J. M., Barron, K. E., Pintrich, P. R., Elliot, A. J., & Thrash, T. M. (2002). Revision of achievement goal theory: Necessary and illuminating. *Journal of Educational Psychology,* 94, 562–575.

Hardiman, P. T., Dufresne, R., & Mestre, J. P. (1989). The relation between problem categorization and problem solving among experts and novices. *Memory & Cognition,* 17, 627–638.

Hardman, M. L., Drew, C. J., & Egan, M. W. (1999). *Human exceptionality: Society, school, and family* (6th ed.). Boston: Allyn and Bacon.

Hardman, M. L., Drew, C. J., & Egan, M. W. (2005). *Human exceptionality: Society, school, and family* (8th ed.). Boston: Allyn and Bacon.

Harp, S. F., & Mayer, R. E. (1998). How seductive details do their damage: A theory of cognitive interest in science learning. *Journal of Educational Psychology,* 90, 414–434.

Harris, J. R. (1998). *The nurture assumption: Why children turn out the way they do; parents matter less than you think and peers matter more.* New York: Free Press.

Harris, K. R. (1990). Developing self-regulated learners: The role of private speech and self-instruction. *Educational Psychologist,* 25, 35–50.

Harris, K. R., & Graham, S. (1996). Memo to constructivist: Skills count too. *Educational Leadership,* 53(5), 26–29.

Harris, K. R., Graham, S., & Pressley, M. (1991). Cognitive-behavioral approaches in reading and written language: Developing self-regulated learners. In N. N. Singh & I. L. Beale (Eds.), *Learning disabilities: Nature, theory, and treatment* (pp. 415–451). New York: Springer-Verlag.

Harris, K. R., & Pressley, M. (1991). The nature of cognitive strategy instruction: Interactive strategy construction. *Exceptional Children,* 57, 392–404.

Harrow, A. J. (1972). *A taxonomy of the psychomotor domain: A guide for developing behavior objectives.* New York: David McKay.

Harter, S. (1990). Issues in the assessment of self-concept of children and adolescents. In A. LaGreca (Ed.), *Through the eyes of a child* (pp. 292–325). Boston: Allyn and Bacon.

Harter, S. (1998). The development of self-representations. In N. Eisenberg (Ed.), *Handbook of child psychology: Vol 3. Social, emotional, and personality development* (5th ed., pp. 553–618). New York: Wiley.

Harter, S. (2003). The development of self-representation during childhood and adolescence. In M. R. Leary & J. P. Tangney (Eds.), *Handbook of self and identity* (pp. 610–642). New York: Guilford.

Hartup, W. W., & Stevens, N. (1999). Friendships and adaptation across the lifespan. *Current Directions in Psychological Science,* 8, 76–79.

Hawkins, M. R. (2004). Researching English language and literacy development in schools. *Educational Researcher,* 33(3), 14–25.

Hayes, S. C., Rosenfarb, I., Wulfert, E., Munt, E. D., Korn, Z., & Zettle, R. D. (1985). Self-reinforcement effects: An artifact of social standard setting? *Journal of Applied Behavior Analysis,* 18, 201–214.

Heath, S. B. (1989). Oral and literate traditions among black Americans living in poverty. *American Psychologist, 44,* 367–373.

Helms, J. E. (1995). An update of Helms's White and People of Color racial identity models. In J. G. Ponterotto, J. M. Casas, L. A. Suzuki & C. M. Alexander (Eds.), *Handbook of multicultural counseling* (pp. 181–198). Thousand Oaks, CA: Sage.

Helwig, C. C., Arnold, M. L., Tan, D., & Boyd, D.(2003). Chinese adolescents' reasoning about democratic and authority-based decision making in peer, family, and school contexts. *Child Development, 74,* 783–800.

Henderson, M. (1996). *Helping your students get the most of homework* [Brochure]. Chicago: National Parent–Teacher Association.

Herbert, E. A. (1998). Design matters: How school environment affects children. *Educational Leadership, 56*(1), 69–71.

Herman, J. (1997). Assessing new assessments: How do they measure up? *Theory Into Practice, 36,* 197–204.

Herman, J., & Winters. L. (1994). Portfolio research: A slim collection. *Educational Leadership,* 52(2), 48–55.

Herman, M. (2004). Forced to choose: Some determinants of racial identification in multi-racial adolescents, *Child Development, 75,* 730–748.

Hernshaw, L. S. (1987). *The shaping of modern psychology: A historical introduction from dawn to present day.* London: Routledge & Kegan Paul.

Herzig, A. H. (2004). Becoming mathematicians: Women and students of color choosing and leaving doctoral mathematics. *Review of Educational Research, 74,* 171–214.

Hess, R., Chih-Mei, C., & McDevitt, T. M. (1987). Cultural variation in family beliefs about children's performance in mathematics: Comparisons among People's Republic of China, Chinese-American, and Caucasian-American families. *Journal of Educational Psychology, 79,* 179–188.

Hetherington, E. M. (1999). Should we stay together for the sake of the children? In E. Hetherington (Ed.), *Coping with divorce, single-parenting, and remarriage: A risk and resilience perspective* (pp. 93–116). Hillsdale, NJ: Lawrence Erlbaum.

Hetherington, E. M., & Kelly, J. (2002). *For better or for worse: Divorce reconsidered.* New York: W. W. Norton.

Heward, W. L., & Orlansky, M. D. (1992). *Exceptional children* (4th ed.). Columbus, OH: Charles E. Merrill.

Hewson, P. W., Beeth, M. E., & Thorley, N. R. (1998). Teaching for conceptual change. In B. J. Fraserr & K. G. Tobin (Eds.), *International handbook of science education* (pp. 199–218). New York: Kluwer.

Hewstone, M. (1989). Changing stereotypes with disconfirming information. In D. Bar-Tal, C. Graumann, A. Kruglanski, & W. Stroebe (Eds.), *Stereotyping and prejudice: Changing conceptions* (pp. 207–223). New York: Springer-Verlag.

Hickey, D. T. (2003). Engaged participation vs. marginal non-participation: A stridently sociocultural model of achievement motivation. *Elementary School Journal, 103* (4), 401–429

Hilgard, E. R. (1996). History of educational psychology. In R. Calfee & D. Berliner (Eds.), *Handbook of educational psychology* (pp. 990–1004). New York: Macmillan.

Hill, W. F. (2002). *Learning: A survey of psychological interpretations* (7th ed.). Boston: Allyn and Bacon.

Hines, C. V., Cruickshank, D. R., & Kennedy, J. J. (1985). Teacher clarity and its relation to student achievement and satisfaction. *American Educational Research Journal, 22,* 87–99.

Hiroto, D. S., & Seligman, M. E. P. (1975). Generality of learned helplessness in man. *Journal of Personality and Social Psychology, 31,* 311–327.

Hirsch, E. D., Jr. *The schools we need: Why we don't have them.* New York: Doubleday, 1996.

Hmelo-Silver, C. E. (2004). Problem-based learning: What and how do students learn? *Educational Psychology Review, 16,* 235–266.

Hodges, E. V. E., & Perry, D. G. (1999). Personal and interpersonal antecedents and consequences of victimization by peers. *Journal of Personality and Social Psychology, 76,* 677–685.

Hofer, B. K., & Pintrich, P. R. (1997). The development of epistemological theories: Beliefs about knowledge and knowing and their relation to learning. *Review of Educational Research, 67,* 88–140.

Hoffman, M. L. (2000). *Empathy and moral development.* New York: Cambridge University Press.

Hoffman, M. L. (2001). A comprehensive theory of prosocial moral development. In A. Bohart & D. Stipek & (Eds.), *Constructive and destructive behavior* (pp. 61–86). Washington, DC: American Psychological Association.

Hogan, T., Rabinowitz, M., & Craven, J. A. III. (2003). Representation in teaching: Inferences from research of expert and novice teachers. *Educational Psychologist, 38,* 235–247.

Hoge, D. R., Smit, E. K., & Hanson, S. L. (1990). School experiences predicting changes in self-esteem of sixth- and seventh-grade students. *Journal of Educational Psychology, 82,* 117–126.

Holahan, C., & Sears, R. (1995). *The gifted group in later maturity.* Stanford, CA: Stanford University Press.

Hoover-Dempsey, K. V., Battiato, A. C., Walker, J. M. T., Reed, R. P., DeJong, J. M., & Jones, K. P. (2001). Parental involvement in homework. *Educational Psychologist, 36,* 195–209.

Horgan, D. D. (1995). *Achieving gender equity: Strategies for the classroom.* Boston: Allyn and Bacon.

Horn, J. L. (1998). A basis for research on age differences in cognitive capabilities. In J. J. McArdle & R. W. Woodcock (Eds.), *Human cognitive theories in theory and practice* (pp. 57–87). Mahwah, NJ: Lawrence Erlbaum.

Horowitz, B. (2002, April 22). Gen Y: A tough crowd to sell. *USA Today,* pp. B1–2.

Howe, M. J. A., Davidson, J. W., & Sloboda, J. A. (1998). Innate talents: Reality or myth? *Behavioral and Brain Sciences, 21,* 399–406.

Hoy, W. K., & Woolfolk, A. E. (1990). Organizational socialization of student teachers. *American Educational Research Journal, 27,* 279–300.

Hoy, W. K., & Woolfolk, A. E. (1993). Teachers' sense of efficacy and the organizational health of schools. *Elementary School Journal, 93,* 355–372.

Huesmann, L. R., Moise-Titus, J., Podolski, C. P., & Eron, L. D. (2003). Longitudinal relations between children's exposure to TV violence and their aggressive and violent behavior in young adulthood: 1977–1992. *Developmental Psychology, 39,* 201–221.

Huff, C. R. (1989). Youth gangs and public policy. *Crime & Delinquency, 35,* 524–537.

Hughes, D. R. (1998). *Kids online: Protecting your children in cyberspace.* Grand Rapids, MI: Fleming H. Revell.

Hulbert, A. (2005, April 3). Boy problems: The real gender crisis in education starts with the Y chromosome. *New York Times Magazine,* pp. 13–14.

Hung, D. W. L. (1999). Activity, apprenticeship, and epistemological appropriation: Implications from the writings of Michael Polanyi. *Educational Psychologist, 34,* 193–205.

Hunt, E. (2000). Let's hear it for crystallized intelligence. *Learning and Individual Differences, 12,* 123–129.

Hunt, J. McV. (1961). *Intelligence and experience.* New York: Ronald.

Hunt, N., & Marshall, K. (2002). *Exceptional children and youth: An introduction to special education* (3rd ed.). Boston: Houghton Mifflin.

Hunt, R. R., & Ellis, H. C. (1999). *Fundamentals of cognitive psychology* (6th ed.). New York: McGraw-Hill College.

Hunter, M. (1982). *Mastery teaching.* El Segundo, CA: TIP Publications.

Hyman, I., Kay, B., Tabori, A, Weber, M., Mahon, M., & Cohen, I. (2006). Bullying: Theory, research and interventions about student victimization. In C. Evertson & C. S. Weinstein (Eds.), *Handbook for classroom management: Research, practice, and contemporary issues.* Mahwah, NJ: Lawrence Erlbaum.

Hymowitz, K. S. (2001, April 18). "Zero Tolerance" is schools' first line of defense. *Newsday.*

IDEA. (1997). Available online at: http://www.ed.gov/policy/speced/guid/idea/idea2004.html

International Comparisons in Fourth-Grade Reading Literacy: Findings from the Progress in International Reading Literacy Study (2001). Available on line at http://nces.ed.gov/surveys/pirls/. Retrieved 5/17/05.

Iran-Nejad, A. (1990). Active and dynamic self-regulation of learning processes. *Review of Educational Research, 60,* 573–602.

Irvine, J. J. (1990). *Black students and school failure: Policies, practices, and prescriptions.* New York: Praeger.

Irvine, J. J., & Armento, B. J. (2001). *Culturally responsive teaching: Lesson planning for elementary and middle grades.* New York: McGraw-Hill.

Irvine, J. J. & Fraser, J. W. (1998, May). Warm demanders. *Education Week.* Available online at http://www.edweek.org/ew/ewstory.cfm?slug=35irvine.h17&keywords=Irvine

Irving, O., & Martin, J. (1982). Withitness: The confusing variable. *American Educational Research Journal, 19,* 313–319.

Irwin, J. W. (1991). *Teaching reading comprehension* (2nd ed.). Boston: Allyn and Bacon.

Isabella, R., & Belsky, J. (1991). Interactional synchrony and the origins of infant–mother attachment: A replication study. *Child Development, 62,* 373–384.

Izard, C. E. (2001). Emotional intelligence or adaptive emotions? *Emotion, 1,* 249–257.

Jackson, A., & Davis, G. (2000). *Turning points 2000: Educating adolescents in the 21st century.* New York: Teachers College Press.

Jacobs, J. E., Lanza, S., Osgood, D. W., Eccles, J. S., & Wigfield, A. (2002). Changes in children's self-competence and values: Gender and domain differences across grades one through twelve. *Child Development, 73,* 509–527.

James, W. (1890). *The principles of psychology* (Vol. 2). New York: Holt.

James, W. (1912). *Talks to teachers on psychology: And to students on some of life's ideals.* New York: Holt.

Jarrett, R. (1995). Growing up poor: The family experiences of socially mobile youth in low-income African American neighborhoods. *Journal of Adolescent Research, 10,* 111–135.

Jehng, J. C., Johnson, S., & Anderson, R. C. (1993). Schooling and students' epistemological beliefs about learning. *Contemporary Educational Psychology, 18,* 23–35.

Jensen, L. A., Arnett, J. J., Feldman, S. S., & Cauffman, E. (2002). It's wrong but everybody does it: Academic dishonesty among high school and college students. *Contemporary Educational Psychology, 27,* 209–228.

Jimenez, R. (2000). Literacy and identity development of Latina/o students who are successful English readers: Opportunities and obstacles. *American Educational Research Journal, 37,* 971–1000.

Jimerson, S. R. (1999). On the failure of failure: Examining the association between early grade retention and education and employment outcomes during late adolescence. *Journal of School Psychology, 37,* 243–272.

Jimerson, S. R., Anderson, G. E., & Whipple, A. D. (2002). Winning the battle and losing the war: Examining the relation between grade retention and dropping out of high school. *Psychology in the Schools, 39,* 441–457.

Johnson, A. M., & Notah, D. J. (1999). Service learning: History, literature, review, and a pilot study of eighth graders. *The Elementary School Journal, 99,* 453–467.

Johnson, D. W., & Johnson, R. T. (1999). *Learning together and alone: Cooperation, competition, and individualization* (5th ed.). Boston: Allyn and Bacon.

Johnson, D. W., & Johnson, R. T. (1999). The three Cs of school and classroom management. In H. J. Freiberg (Ed.), *Beyond behaviorism: Changing the classroom management paradigm* (pp. 119–144). Boston: Allyn and Bacon.

Johnson, D. W., & Johnson, R. T. (2002). *Meaningful assessment: A meaningful and cooperative process.* Boston: Allyn and Bacon.

Johnson, D. W., & Johnson, R. T. (2004). Special Issue: Conflict Resolution and Peer Mediation. *Theory Into Practice, 43*(1).

Johnson, D. W., & Johnson, R. T. (2005). Special Issue: Peace education. *Theory Into Practice, 44*(4).

Johnson, D. W., Johnson, R. T., Dudley, B., Ward, M., & Magnuson, D. (1995). The impact of peer mediation training on the management of school and home conflicts. *American Educational Research Journal, 32,* 829–844.

Johnson, J., Duffett, A., Farkas, S., & Wilson, L. (2002). *When it's your own child: A report on special education from the families who use it.* Baltimore, MD: Annie E. Casey Foundation.

John-Steiner, V., & Mahn, H. (1996). Sociocultural approaches to learning and development: A Vygotskian framework. *Educational Psychologist, 31,* 191–206.

Johnston, L. D., O'Malley, P. M., Bachman, J. G., & Schulenberg, J. E. (December 21, 2004). *Overall teen drug use continues gradual decline; but use of inhalants rises.* University of Michigan News and Information Services: Ann Arbor, MI. [On-line]. Available: www.monitoringthefuture.org; accessed 03/22/05.

Jonassen, D. H. (2003). Designing research-based instruction for story problems. *Educational Psychology Review, 15,* 267–296.

Jones, D. C. (2004). Body image among adolescent girls and boys: A longitudinal study. *Developmental Psychology, 40,* 823–835.

Jones, E. D., & Southern, W. T. (1991). Conclusions about acceleration: Echoes of a debate. In W. Southern & E. Jones (Eds.), *The academic acceleration of gifted children* (pp. 223–228). New York: Teachers College Press.

Jones, M. G., & Gerig, T. M. (1994). Silent sixth-grade students: Characteristics, achievement, and teacher expectations. *Elementary School Journal, 95,* 169–182.

Jones, M. S., Levin, M. E., Levin, J. R., & Beitzel, B. D. (2000). Can vocabulary-learning strategies and pair-learning formats be profitably combined? *Journal of Educational Psychology, 92,* 256–262.

Jones, S. M., & Dindia, K. (2004). A meta-analytic perspective on sex equity in the classroom. *Review of Educational Research, 74,* 443–471.

Joyce, B. R., Weil, M., & Calhoun, E. (2000). *Models of teaching* (6th ed.). Boston: Allyn and Bacon.

Joyce, B. R., Weil, M., & Calhoun, E. (2006). *Models of teaching* (7th ed.). Boston: Allyn and Bacon.

Jurden, F. H. (1995). Individual differences in working memory and complex cognition. *Journal of Educational Psychology, 87,* 93–102.

Kagan, S. (1983). Social orientation among Mexican-American children: A challenge to traditional classroom structures. In E. Garcia (Ed.), *The Mexican-American child: Language, cognition, and social development.* Tempe, AZ: Center for Bilingual Education.

Kagan, S. (1994). *Cooperative learning.* San Juan Capistrano, CA: Kagan Cooperative Learning.

Kail, R., & Hall, L. K. (1999). Sources of developmental change in children's word-problem performance. *Journal of Educational Psychology, 91,* 600–668.

Kalyuga, S., Chandler, P., Tuovinen, J., & Sweller, J. (2001). When problem solving is superior to studying worked examples. *Journal of Educational Psychology, 93,* 579–588.

Kanaya, T., Scullin, M.H., & Ceci, S. J. (2003). The Flynn effect and U.S. policies: The impact of rising IQ scores on American society via mental retardation diagnoses. *American Psychologist, 58,* 1–13.

Kantor, H., & Lowe, R. (1995). Class, race, and the emergence of federal education policy: From the New Deal to the Great Society. *Educational Researcher, 24*(3), 4–11.

Kaplan, J. S. (1991). *Beyond behavior modification* (2nd ed.). Austin, TX: Pro-Ed.

Kardash, C. M., & Howell, K. L. (2000). Effects of epistemological beliefs and topic-specific beliefs on undergraduates' cognitive and strategic processing of dual-positional text. *Journal of Educational Psychology, 92,* 524–535.

Kardash, C. M., & Scholes, R. J. (1996). Effects of preexisting beliefs, epistemological beliefs, and need for cognition on interpretation of controversial issues. *Journal of Educational Psychology, 88,* 260–271.

Karpov, Y. V., & Bransford, J. D. (1995). L. S. Vygotsky and the doctrine of empirical and theoretical learning. *Educational Psychologist, 30,* 61–66.

Karpov, Y. V., & Haywood, H. C. (1998). Two ways to elaborate Vygotsky's concept of mediation implications for instruction. *American Psychologist, 53,* 27–36.

Karweit, N. (1989). Time and learning: A review. In R. E. Slavin (Ed.), *School and classroom organization* (pp. 69–95). Hillsdale, NJ: Lawrence Erlbaum.

Karweit, N., & Slavin, R. (1981). Measurement and modeling choices in studies of time and learning. *American Educational Research Journal, 18,* 157–171.

Katz, P. A. (2003). Racists or tolerant multiculturalists? How do they begin? *American Psychologist, 58,* 897–909.

Katz, S. R. (1999). Teaching in tensions: Latino immigrant youth, their teachers, and the structures of schooling. *Teachers College Record, 100*(4), 809–840.

Kazdin, A. E. (1984). *Behavior modification in applied settings.* Homewood, IL: Dorsey Press.

Kazdin, A. E. (2001). *Behavior modification in applied settings* (6th ed.). Belmont, CA: Wadsworth.

Keefe, J. W. (1982). Assessing student learning styles: An overview. In *Student learning styles and brain behavior.* Reston, VA: National Association of Secondary School Principals.

Keefe, J. W., & Monk, J. S. (1986). *Learning style profile examiner's manual.* Reston, VA: National Association of Secondary School Principals.

Kelly, K. (1999). Retention vs. social promotion: Schools search for alternatives. *Harvard Education Letter, 15*(1), 1–3.

Keogh, B. K., & MacMillan, D. L. (1996). Exceptionality. In D. Berliner & R. Calfee (Eds.), *Handbook of educational psychology* (pp. 311–330). New York: Macmillan.

Kerckhoff, A. C. (1986). Effects of ability grouping in British secondary schools. *American Sociological Review, 51,* 842–858.

Keyser, V., & Barling, J. (1981). Determinants of children's self-efficacy beliefs in an academic environment. *Cognitive Therapy and Research, 5,* 29–40.

Kiewra, K. A. (1985). Investigating notetaking and review: A depth of processing alternative. *Educational Psychologist, 20,* 23–32.

Kiewra, K. A. (1988). Cognitive aspects of autonomous note taking: Control processes, learning strategies, and prior knowledge. *Educational Psychologist, 23,* 39–56.

Kiewra, K. A. (1989). A review of note-taking: The encoding storage paradigm and beyond. *Educational Psychology Review, 1,* 147–172.

Kiewra, K. A. (2002). How classroom teachers can help students learn and teach them how to learn. *Theory Into Practice, 41,* 71–80.

Kim, K. M. (1998). Korean children's perceptions of adult and peer authority and moral reasoning. *Developmental Psychology, 5,* 310–329.

Kindsvatter, R., Wilen, W., & Ishler, M. (1992). *Dynamics of effective teaching* (2nd ed.). New York: Longman.

King, A. (1990). Enhancing peer interaction and learning in the classroom through reciprocal questioning. *American Educational Research Journal, 27,* 664–687.

King, A. (1994). Guiding knowledge construction in the classroom: Effects of teaching children how to question and how to explain. *American Educational Research Journal, 31,* 338–368.

King, A. (2002). Structuring peer interactions to promote high-level cognitive processing. *Theory Into Practice, 41,* 31–39.

King, G. (1979, June). Personal communication. University of Texas at Austin.

Kintsch, W. (1998). *Comprehension: A paradigm for cognition.* New York: Cambridge University Press.

Kirk, S., Gallagher, J. J., & Anastasiow, N. J. (1993). *Educating exceptional children* (7th ed.). Boston: Houghton Mifflin.

Kirk, S. A., Gallagher, J. J., Anastasiow, N. J., & Coleman, M. R. (2006). *Educating exceptional children* (11th ed.). Boston: Houghton Mifflin.

Kirst, M. (1991a). Interview on assessment issues with Lorrie Shepard. *Educational Researcher, 20*(2), 21–23.

Kirst, M. (1991b). Interview on assessment issues with James Popham. *Educational Researcher, 20*(2), 24–27.

Klausmeier, H. J. (1976). Instructional design and the teaching of concepts. In J. Levin & V. Allen (Eds.), *Cognitive learning in children: Theories and strategies* (pp. 191–218). New York: Academic Press.

Klausmeier, H. J. (1992). Concept learning and concept teaching. *Educational Psychologist, 27,* 267–286.

Klein, P. (2002). Multiplying the problem of intelligence by eight. In L. Abbeduto (Ed.), *Taking sides: Clashing on controversial issues in educational psychology* (pp. 219–232). Guilford, CT: McGraw-Hill/Duskin.

Kling, K. C., Hyde, J. S., Showers, C. J., & Buswell, B. N. (1999). Gender differences in self-esteem: A meta-analysis. *Psychological Bulletin, 125*, 470–500.

Knapp, M., Turnbull, B. J., & Shields, P. M. (1990). New directions for educating children of poverty. *Educational Leadership, 48*(1), 4–9.

Kohlberg, L. (1963). The development of children's orientations toward moral order: Sequence in the development of moral thought. *Vita Humana, 6*, 11–33.

Kohlberg, L. (1975). The cognitive-developmental approach to moral education. *Phi Delta Kappan, 56*, 670–677.

Kohlberg, L. (1981). *The philosophy of moral development.* New York: Harper & Row.

Kohn, A. (1993). Rewards versus learning: A response to Paul Chance. *Phi Delta Kappan, 74*, 783–787.

Kohn, A. (1996). By all available means: Cameron and Pierce's defense of extrinsic motivators. *Review of Educational Research, 66*, 1–4.

Kohn, A. (2002). How not to teach values. In L. Abbeduto (Ed.), *Taking sides: Clashing on controversial issues in educational psychology* (pp. 138–153). Guilford, CT: McGraw-Hill/Duskin.

Kokko, K., & Pulkkinen, L. (2000). Aggression in childhood and long-term unemployment in adulthood: A cycle of maladaptation and some protective factors. *Developmental Psychology, 36*, 463–472.

Kolb, G., & Whishaw, I. Q. (1998). Brain plasticity and behavior. In J. T. Spence, J. M. Darley, & D. J. Foss (Eds.), *Annual review of psychology* (pp. 43–64). Palo Alto, CA: Annual Reviews.

Korenman, S., Miller, J., & Sjaastad, J. (1995). Long-term poverty and child development in the United States: Results from the NLSY. *Children and Youth Services Review, 17*, 127–155.

Korf, R. (1999). Heuristic search. In R. Wilson & F. Keil (Eds.), *The MIT encyclopedia of the cognitive sciences* (pp. 372–373). Cambridge, MA: MIT Press.

Koriat, A., Goldsmith, M., & Pansky, A. (2000). Toward a psychology of memory accuracy. In S. Fiske (Ed.), *Annual review of psychology* (pp. 481–537). Palo Alto, CA: Annual Reviews.

Kosslyn, S. M., & Koenig, O. (1992). *Wet mind: The new cognitive neuroscience.* New York: Free Press.

Kotrez, D., Stecher, B., & Diebert, E. (1993). *The reliability of scores from the 1992 Vermont Portfolio Assessment Program.* CSE Technical Report 355. Los Angeles: UCLA Center for the Study of Evaluation.

Kounin, J. S. (1970). *Discipline and group management in classrooms.* New York: Holt, Rinehart & Winston.

Kozulin, A. (1990). *Vygotsky's psychology: A biography of ideas.* Cambridge, MA: Harvard University Press.

Kozulin, A. (Ed.). (2003). *Vygotsky's educational theory in cultural context*. Cambridge, U. K.: Cambridge University Press.

Kozulin, A., & Presseisen, B. Z. (1995). Mediated learning experience and psychological tools: Vygotsky's and Feuerstein's perspectives in a study of student learning. *Educational Psychologist, 30*, 67–75.

Krathwohl, D. R., Bloom, B. S., & Masia, B. B. (1964). *Taxonomy of educational objectives. Handbook II: Affective domain.* New York: David McKay.

Krauss, M. (1992). Statement of Michael Krauss, representing the Linguistic Society of America. In U.S. Senate, *Native American Languages Act of 1991: Hearing before the Select Committee on Indian Affairs* (pp. 18–22). Washington, DC: U.S. Government Printing Office.

Kreitzer, A. E., & Madaus, G. F. (1994). Empirical investigations of the hierarchical structure of the taxonomy. In L. W. Anderson & L. A. Sosniak (Eds.), *Bloom's taxonomy: A forty-year retrospective.* Ninety-third yearbook for the National Society for the Study of Education: Part II (pp. 64–81). Chicago: University of Chicago Press.

Kroesbergen, E. H., Van Luit, J. E. H., & Maas, C. J. M. (2004). Effectiveness of explicit and constructivist mathematics for low-achieving students in the Netherlands. *The Elementary School Journal, 104*, 233–251.

Kroger, J. (2000). *Identity development: Adolescence through adulthood.* Thousand Oaks, CA: Sage.

Krumboltz, J. D., & Krumboltz, H. B. (1972). *Changing children's behavior.* Englewood Cliffs, NJ: Prentice-Hall.

Krumboltz, J. D., & Yeh, C. J. (1996). Competitive grading sabotages good teaching. *Phi Delta Kappan, 78*, 324–326.

Kuhn, D. (1991). *The skills of argument.* New York: Cambridge University Press.

Kuklinski, M. R., & Weinstein, R. S. (2001). Classroom and developmental differences in a path model of teacher expectancy effects. *Child Development, 72*, 1554–1578.

Kulik, C. C., & Kulik, J. A. (1982). Effects of ability grouping on secondary school students: A meta-analysis of evaluation findings. *American Educational Research Journal, 19*, 415–428.

Kulik, J. A., & Kulik, C. C. (1984). Effects of accelerated instruction on students. *Review of Educational Research, 54*, 409–425.

Kulik, J. A., & Kulik, C. L. (1997). Ability grouping. In N. Colangelo & G. Davis (Eds.), *Handbook of gifted education* (2nd ed., pp. 230–242). Boston: Allyn and Bacon.

Lachter, J., Forster, K. I., & Ruthruff, K. I. (2004). Forty-five years after Broadbent (1958): Still no identification without attention *Psychological Review*, 111, 880–913.

Ladson-Billings, G. (1990). Like lightning in a bottle: Attempting to capture the pedagogical excellence of successful teachers of Black students. *Qualitative Studies in Education, 3*, 335–344.

Ladson-Billings, G. (1992). Culturally relevant teaching: The key to making multicultural education work. In C. A. Grant (Ed.), *Research and multicultural education* (pp. 106–121). London: Falmer Press.

Ladson-Billings, G. (1994). *The dream keepers.* San Francisco: Jossey-Bass.

Ladson-Billings, G. (1995). But that is just good teaching! The case for culturally relevant pedagogy. *Theory Into Practice, 34*, 161–165.

Ladson-Billings, G. (2004). Landing on the wrong note: The price we paid for Brown. *Educational Researcher, 33*(7), 3–13.

Lambert, A. J. (1995). Stereotypes and social judgment: The consequences of group variability. *Journal of Personality and Social Psychology, 68*, 388–403.

Lambert, N. M. (1994). Seating arrangement in classrooms. *The International Encyclopedia of Education* (2nd ed.) 9, 5355–5359.

Land, M. L. (1987). Vagueness and clarity. In M. Dunkin (Ed.), *The international encyclopedia of teaching and teacher education* (pp. 392–397). New York: Pergamon.

Landrum, T. J., & Kauffman, J. M. (2006). Behavioral approaches to classroom management. In C. M. Evertson & C. S. Weinstein (Eds.), *Handbook of classroom management: Research, practice, and contemporary issues.* Mahwah, NJ: Erlbaum.

Lane, K., Falk, K., & Wehby, J. (2006). Classroom management in special education classrooms and resource rooms. In C. M. Evertson

& C. S. Weinstein (Eds.), *Handbook of classroom management: Research, practice, and contemporary issues.* Mahwah, NJ: Erlbaum.

Langan-Fox, J., Waycott, J. L., & Albert, K. (2000). Linear and graphic organizers: Properties and processing. *International Journal of Cognitive Ergonomics, 4*(1), 19–34.

Language Development and Hypermedia Group. (1992). "Open" software design: A case study. *Educational Technology, 32,* 43–55.

Larrivee, B. (1985). *Effective teaching behaviors for successful mainstreaming.* New York: Longman.

Lashley, T. J., II, Matczynski, T. J., & Rowley, J. B. (2002). *Instructional models: Strategies for teaching in a diverse society* (2nd ed.). Belmont, CA: Wadsworth/Thomson Learning.

Lather, P. (2004). Scientific research in education: A critical perspective. *Journal of Curriculum and Supervision, 20,* 14–30.

Lave, J. (1988). *Cognition in practice: Mind, mathematics, and culture in everyday life.* New York: Cambridge University Press.

Lave, J. (1997). The culture of acquisition and the practice of understanding. In D. Kirshner & J. A. Whitson (Eds.), *Situated cognition: Social, semiotic, and psychological perspectives* (pp. 17–35). Mahwah, NJ: Lawrence Erlbaum.

Lave, J., & Wenger, E. (1991). *Situated learning: Legitimate peripheral participation.* Cambridge, MA: Cambridge University Press.

Leaper, C. (2002). Parenting girls and boys. In M. H. Bornstein (Ed.), *Handbook of parenting, Vol. 1: Children and parenting* (2nd ed., pp. 127–152). Mahwah, NJ: Lawrence Erlbaum.

LeCapitane, J. (2001). Promoting personal and psychological development in children: Of what good is it to graduate the mind but to lose the person? *Education, 121,* 459–469.

Lee, A. Y., & Hutchinson, L. (1998). Improving learning from examples through reflection. *Journal of Experimental Psychology: Applied, 4,* 187–210.

Lee, R. M. (2005). Resilience against discrimination: Ethnic identity and other-group orientation as protective factors for Korean Americans. *Journal of Counseling Psychology, 52,* 36–44.

Lehman, D. R., & Nisbett, R. E. (1990). A longitudinal study of the effects of undergraduate training on reasoning. *Developmental Psychology, 26,* 952–960.

Leinhardt, G. (2001). Instructional explanations: A commonplace for teaching and location for contrasts. In V. Richardson (Ed.), *Handbook of research on teaching* (4th ed., pp. 333–357). Washington, DC: American Educational Research Association.

LeMahieu, P., Gitomer, D. H., & Eresh, J. T. (1993). *Portfolios in large-scale assessment: Difficult but not impossible.* Unpublished manuscript, University of Delaware.

Leming, J. S. (1981). Curriculum effectiveness in value/moral education. *Journal of Moral Education, 10,* 147–164.

Lepper, M. R. (1988). Motivational considerations in the study of instruction. *Cognition and Instruction, 5,* 289–309.

Lepper, M. R., & Greene, D. (1978). *The hidden costs of rewards: New perspectives on the psychology of human motivation.* Hillsdale, NJ: Lawrence Erlbaum.

Lepper, M. R., Keavney, M., & Drake, M. (1996). Intrinsic motivation and extrinsic reward: A commentary on Cameron and Pierce's meta-analysis. *Review of Educational Research, 66,* 5–32.

Lerner, R. M., & Galambos, N. L. (1998). Adolescent development: Challenges and opportunities for research, programs, and policies. In J. T. Spence, J. M. Darley, & D. J. Foss (Eds.), *Annual review of psychology* (pp. 413–446). Palo Alto, CA: Annual Reviews.

Levin, J. R. (1994). Mnemonic strategies and classroom learning: A twenty-year report card. *Elementary School Journal, 94,* 235–254.

Levin, J. R., & Nolan, J. F. (2000). *Principles of classroom management: A professional decision-making model.* Boston: Allyn and Bacon.

Lewinsohn, P. M., Rohde, P., & Seeley, J. R. (1994). Psychological risk factors for future attempts. *Journal of Consulting and Clinical Psychology, 62,* 297–305.

Lewis, R. (2001). Classroom discipline and student responsibility: The students' view. *Teaching and Teacher Education, 17,* 307–319.

Lewis, T. J., & Sugai, G. (1996). Functional assessment of problem behavior: A pilot investigation of the comparative and interactive effects of teacher and peer social attention on students in general education settings. *School Psychology Quarterly, 11,* 1–19.

Lewis, T. J., Sugai, G., & Colvin, G. (1998). Reducing problem behavior through a school-wide system of effective behavioral support: Investigation of a school-wide social skills training program and contextual interventions. *School Psychology Review, 27,* 446–459.

Liben, L. S., & Signorella, M. L. (1993). Gender-schematic processing in children: The role of initial interpretations of stimuli. *Developmental Psychology, 29,* 141–149.

Lickona, T. (2002). Character education: Seven crucial issues. In L. Abbeduto (Ed.), *Taking sides: Clashing on controversial issues in educational psychology* (pp. 130–137). Guilford, CT: McGraw-Hill/Duskin.

Lindsay, P. H., & Norman, D. A. (1977). *Human information processing: An introduction to psychology* (2nd ed.). New York: Academic Press.

Linn, M. C., & Hyde, J. S. (1989). Gender, mathematics, and science. *Educational Researcher, 18,* 17–27.

Linn, R. L. (2000). Assessments and accountability. *Educational Researcher, 29*(2), 4–16.

Linn, R. L. (2003). Accountability: Responsibility and reasonable expectations. *Educational Researcher, 32*(7), 3–13.

Linn, R. L., Baker, E. L., & Betebenner, D. W. (2002). Accountability systems: Implications of requirements of the No Child Left Behind Act of 2001. *Educational Researcher, 31*(6), 3–16.

Linn, R. L., & Gronlund, N. E. (2000). *Measurement and assessment in education* (8th ed.). Columbus, OH: Merrill.

Linn, R. L., & Miller , M. D. (2005). *Measurement and assessment in teaching* (9th ed.). Upper Saddle River, NJ: Prentice-Hall/Merrill.

Lipman, P. (1997). Restructuring in context: A case study of teacher participation and the dynamics of ideology, race, and power. *American Educational Research Journal, 34,* 3–37.

Liu, W. M., Ali, S. R., Soleck, G., Hopps, J., Dunston, K., & Pickett, T., Jr. (2004). Using social class in counseling psychology research. *Journal of Counseling Psychology, 51,* 3–18.

Locke, E. A., & Latham, G. P. (1990). *A theory of goal setting and task performance.* Englewood Cliffs, NJ: Prentice-Hall.

Locke, E. A., & Latham, G. P. (2002). Building a practically useful theory of goal setting and task motivation: A 35-year odyssey. *American Psychologist, 57,* 705–717.

Loftus, E., & Palmer, J. C. (1974). Reconstruction of automobile destruction: An example of the interaction between language and memory. *Journal of Verbal Learning and Verbal Behavior, 13,* 585–589.

Lorch, R. F., Lorch, E. P., Ritchey, K., McGovern, L., & Coleman, D. (2001). Effects of headings on text summarization. *Contemporary Educational Psychology, 26,* 171–191.

Louis, B., Subotnik, R. F., Breland, P. S., & Lewis, M. (2000). Establishing criteria for high ability versus selective admission to gifted programs: Implications for policy and practice. *Educational Psychology Review, 12*, 295–314.

Lovelace, M. K. (2005). Meta-analysis of experimental research based on the Dunn and Dunn Model. *The Journal of Educational Research*, 98, 176–183.

Loveless, T. (1998). The tracking and ability grouping debate. *Fordham Report*, 2(88), 1–27.

Loveless, T. (1999). Will tracking reform promote social equity? *Educational Leadership*, 56(7), 28–32.

Lovett, M. W., et al. (2000). Components of effective remediation for developmental disabilities: Combining phonological and strategy-based instruction to improve outcomes. *Journal of Educational Psychology*, 92, 263–283.

Lowenstein, G. (1994). The psychology of curiosity: A review and reinterpretation. *Psychological Bulletin, 117*, 75–98.

Lowry, R., Sleet, D., Duncan, C., Powell, K., & Kolbe, L. (1995). Adolescents at risk for violence. *Educational Psychology Review*, 7, 7–40.

Luiten, J., Ames, W., & Ackerson, G. (1980). A meta-analysis of the effects of advance organizers on learning and retention. *American Educational Research Journal, 17*, 211–218.

Ma, X., & Kishor, N. (1997). Attitude toward self, social factors, and achievement in mathematics: A meta-analytic review. *Educational Psychology Review*, 9, 89–120.

Maag, J. W., & Kemp, S. E. (2003). Behavioral intent of power and affiliation: Implications for functional analysis. *Remedial and Special Education, 24*, 57–64.

Mabry, L. (1999). Writing to the rubrics: Lingering effects of traditional standardized testing on direct writing assessment. *Phi Delta Kappan, 80*, 673–679.

Maccoby, E. E. (1998). *The two sexes: Growing up apart, coming together.* Cambridge, MA: Belknap/Harvard University Press.

Maccoby, E. E., & Jacklin, C. N. (1974). *The psychology of sex differences.* Stanford, CA: Stanford University Press.

Mace, F. C., Belfiore, P. J., & Hutchinson, J. M. (2001). Operant theory and research on self-regulation. In B. Zimmerman & D. Schunk (Eds.), *Self-regulated learning and academic achievement: Theoretical perspectives* (2nd ed.). Mahwah, NJ: Lawrence Erlbaum.

Macionis, J. J. (2003). *Sociology* (9th ed.). Upper Saddle River, NJ: Prentice-Hall.

Macrae, C. N., Milne, A. B., & Bodenhausen, C. V. (1994). Stereotypes as energy-saving devices: A peek inside the cognitive toolbox. *Journal of Personality and Social Psychology, 66*, 37–47.

Madsen, C. H., Becker, W. C., Thomas, D. R., Koser, L., & Plager, E. (1968). An analysis of the reinforcing function of "sit down" commands. In R. K. Parker (Ed.), *Readings in educational psychology.* Boston: Allyn and Bacon.

Maehr, M. L., & Anderman, E. M. (1993). Reinventing schools for early adolescents: Emphasizing task goals. *The Elementary School Journal*, 93, 593–610.

Mager, R. (1975). *Preparing instructional objectives* (2nd ed.). Palo Alto, CA: Fearon.

Magnusson, S. J., & Palincsar, A. S. (1995). The learning environment as a site of science reform. *Theory Into Practice, 34*, 43–50.

Maier, N. R. F. (1933). An aspect of human reasoning. *British Journal of Psychology, 24*, 144–155.

Major, B., & Schmader, T. (1998). Coping with stigma through psychological disengagement. In J. Swim & C. Stangor (Eds.), *Stigma: The target's perspective* (pp. 219–241). New York: Academic Press.

Maker, C. J. (1987). Gifted and talented. In V. Richardson-Koehler (Ed.), *Educators' handbook: A research perspective* (pp. 420–455). New York: Longman.

Malone, T. W., & Lepper, M. (1987). Making learning fun: A taxonomy of intrinsic motivations for learning. In R. E. Snow and M. J. Farr (Eds.), *Aptitude, learning and instruction, Volume 3: Cognitive and affective process analysis* (pp. 223–253). Hillsdale, NJ: Lawrence Erlbaum.

Mangione, P. L., & Speth, T. (1998). The transition to elementary school: A framework for creating early childhood continuity through home, school, and community partnerships. *The Elementary School Journal*, 98, 381–397.

Manning, B. H., & Payne, B. D. (1996). *Self-talk for teachers and students: Metacognitive strategies for personal and classroom use.* Boston: Allyn and Bacon.

Manning, M. L., & Baruth, L. G. (1996). *Multicultural education of children and adolescents* (2nd ed.). Boston: Allyn and Bacon.

Mantzicopolos, P., & Morrison, D. (1992). Kindergarten retention: Academic and behavioral outcomes through the end of second grade. *American Educational Research Journal*, 29, 182–198.

Marcia, J. E. (1987). The identity status approach to the study of ego identity development. In T. Honess & K. Yardley (Eds.), *Self and identity: Perspectives across the life span* (pp. 161–171). London: Routledge & Kegan Paul.

Marcia, J. E. (1991). Identity and self development. In R. Lerner, A. Peterson, & J. Brooks-Gunn (Eds.), *Encyclopedia of adolescence* (Vol. 1). New York: Garland.

Marcia, J. E. (1994). The empirical study of ego identity. In H. Bosma, T. Graafsma, H. Grotebanc, & D. DeLivita (Eds.), *The identity and development.* Newbury Park, CA: Sage.

Marcia, J. E. (1999). Representational thought in ego identity, psychotherapy, and psychosocial development. In I. E. Sigel (Ed.), *Development of mental representation: Theories and applications.* Mahwah, NJ: Lawrence Erlbaum.

Marcus, N., Cooper, M., & Sweller, J. (1996). Understanding instructions. *Journal of Educational Psychology*, 88, 49–63.

Marinova-Todd, S., Marshall, D., & Snow, C. (2000). Three misconceptions about age and L2 learning. *TESOL Quarterly*, 34(1), 9–34.

Markman, E. M. (1977). Realizing that you don't understand: A preliminary investigation. *Child Development, 48*, 986–992.

Markman, E. M. (1979). Realizing that you don't understand: Elementary school children's awareness of inconsistencies. *Child Development, 50*, 643–655.

Markman, E. M. (1992). Constraints on word learning: Speculations about their nature, origins, and domain specificity. In M. Gunnar & M. Maratsos (Eds.), *Minnesota symposium on child psychology* (Vol. 25, pp. 59–101). Hillsdale, NJ: Lawrence Erlbaum.

Markstrom-Adams, C. (1992). A consideration of intervening factors in adolescent identity formation. In G. R. Adams, R. Montemayor, & T. Gullotta (Eds.), *Advances in adolescent development: Vol. 4. Adolescent identity formation* (pp. 173–192). Newbury Park, CA: Sage.

Marsh, H. W. (1990). Influences of internal and external frames of reference on the formation of math and English self-concepts. *Journal of Educational Psychology, 82*, 107–116.

Marsh, H. W., & Ayotte, V. (2003). Do multiple dimensions of self-concept become more differentiated with age? The differential

distinctiveness hypothesis. *Journal of Educational Psychology, 95,* 687–706.
Marsh, H. W., & Craven, R. (2002). The pivotal role of frames of reference in academic self-concept formation: The Big Fish Little Pond Effect. In F. Pajares & T. Urdan (Eds.), *Adolescence and Education* (Volume II, pp. 83-123). Greenwich, CT: Information Age.
Marsh, H. W., & Hau, K-T. (2003). Big-Fish-Little-Pond effect on academic self-concept. *American Psychologist, 58,* 364–376.
Marsh, H. W., & Holmes, I. W. M. (1990). Multidimensional self-concepts: Construct validation of responses by children. *American Educational Research Journal, 27,* 89–118.
Marsh, H. W., Parada, R. H., Yeung, A. S., & Healey, J. (2001). Aggressive school troublemakers and victims: A longitudinal model examining the pivotal role of self-concept. *Journal of Educational Psychology, 93,* 411–419.
Marsh, H. W., & Yeung, A. S. (1997). Coursework selection: Relation to academic self-concept and achievement. *American Educational Research Journal, 34,* 691–720.
Marshall, H. H. (Ed.). (1992). *Redefining student learning: Roots of educational change.* Norwood, NJ: Ablex.
Marshall, H. H. (1996). Implications of differentiating and understanding constructivist approaches. *Journal of Educational Psychology, 31,* 235–240.
Martinez-Pons, M. (2002). A social cognitive view of parental influence on student academic self-regulation. *Theory Into Practice, 61,* 126–131.
Marzano, R. J., & Marzano, J. S. (2003, September). The key to classroom management. *Educational Leadership, 61*(1), 6–13.
Maslow, A. H. (1968). *Toward a psychology of being* (2nd ed.). New York: Van Nostrand.
Maslow, A. H. (1970). *Motivation and personality* (2nd ed.). New York: Harper and Row.
Mason, D. A., & Good, T. L. (1993). Effects of two-group and whole-class teaching on regrouped elementary students' mathematics achievement. *American Educational Research Journal, 30,* 328–360.
Matlin, M. W., & Foley, H. J. (1997). *Sensation and perception* (4th ed.). Boston: Allyn and Bacon.
Mautone, P. D., & Mayer, R. E. (2001). Signaling as a cognitive guide in multimedia learning. *Journal of Educational Psychology, 93,* 377–389.
Mayer, J. D., & Cobb, C. D. (2000). Educational policy on emotional intelligence: Does it make sense? *Educational Psychology Review, 12,* 163–183.
Mayer, J. D., & Salovey, P. (1997). What is emotional intelligence? In P. Salovey & D. Sluyter (Eds.), *Emotional development, emotional literacy, and emotional intelligence.* New York: Basic Books.
Mayer, J. D., Salovey, P., & Caruso, D. R. (2000). Competing models of emotional intelligence. In R. J. Sternberg (Ed.), *Handbook of human intelligence* (2nd ed., pp. 396–420). New York: Cambridge University Press.
Mayer, R. E. (1983). *Thinking, problem solving, cognition.* San Francisco: Freeman.
Mayer, R. E. (1984). Twenty-five years of research on advance organizers. *Instructional Science, 8,* 133–169.
Mayer, R. E. (1992). *Thinking, problem solving, cognition* (2nd ed.). New York: Freeman.
Mayer, R. E. (1996). Learners as information processors: Legacies and limitations of educational psychology's second metaphor. *Journal of Educational Psychology, 31,* 151–161.
Mayer, R. E. (1999a). Multimedia aids to problem-solving transfer. *International Journal of Educational Research, 31,* 611–623.
Mayer, R. E. (1999b). *The promise of educational psychology: Learning in the content areas.* Upper Saddle River, NJ: Prentice-Hall.
Mayer, R. E. (2001). *Multimedia learning.* New York: Cambridge University Press.
Mayer, R. E. (2004). Should there be a three-strikes rule against discovery learning? A case for guided methods of instruction. *American Psychologist, 59,* 14–19.
Mayer, R. E., & Gallini, J. K. (1990). When is an illustration worth ten thousand words? *Journal of Educational Psychology, 82,* 715–726.
Mayer, R. E., & Massa, L. J. (2003). Three facets of visual and verbal learners: Cognitive ability, cognitive style and learning preference. *Journal of Educational Psychology, 95*(4), 833–846.
Mayer, R. E., & Sims, V. K. (1994). For whom is a picture worth a thousand words? Extensions of a dual-coding theory of multimedia learning. *Journal of Educational Psychology, 86,* 389–401.
Mayer, R. E., & Wittrock, M. C. (1996). Problem-solving transfer. In D. Berliner & R. Calfee (Eds.), *Handbook of educational psychology* (pp. 47–62). New York: Macmillan.
McCafferty, S. G. (2004). Introduction. *International Journal of Applied Linguistics, 14*(1), 1–6.
McCaslin, M., & Good, T. (1992). Compliant cognition: The misalliance of management and instructional goals in current school reform. *Educational Researcher, 21,* 4–17.
McCaslin, M., & Good, T. (1996). The informal curriculum. In D. Berliner & R. Calfee (Eds.), *Handbook of educational psychology* (pp. 622–670). New York: Macmillan.
McCaslin, M., & Good, T. L. (1998). Moving beyond management as sheer compliance: Helping students to develop goal coordination strategies. *Educational Horizons, 76,* 169–176.
McCaslin, M., & Hickey, D. T. (2001). Self-regulated learning and academic achievement: A Vygotskian view. In B. Zimmerman & D. Schunk (Eds.), *Self-regulated learning and academic achievement: Theoretical perspectives* (2nd ed., pp. 227–252). Mahwah, NJ: Lawrence Erlbaum.
McClelland, D. (1985). *Human motivation.* Glenview, IL: Scott, Foresman.
McClelland, D. C. (1993). Intelligence is not the best predictor of job performance. *Current Directions in Psychological Science, 2,* 5–6.
McClure, P. (2005). Where standards come from. *Theory Into Practice, 44,* 4–10.
McCoach, D. B., Kehle, T. J., Bray, M. L., & Siegle, D. (2001). Best practices in the identification of gifted students with learning disabilities. *Psychology in the Schools,* 38, 403–411.
McCombs, B. L., & Marzano, R. J. (1990). Putting the self in self-regulated learning: The self as agent in integrating skill and will. *Educational Psychologist, 25,* 51–70.
McCoy, A. R., & Reynolds, A. J. (1999). Grade retention and school performance: An extended investigation. *Journal of School Psychology,* 37, 273–298.
McDevitt, T. M., & Ormrod, J. E. (2002). *Child development and education.* Upper Saddle River, NJ: Merrill/Prentice-Hall.
McDonald, A. S. (2001). The prevalence and effects of test anxiety in school children. *Educational Psychology, 21,* 89–101.
McDonald, J. P. (1993). Three pictures of an exhibition: Warm, cool, and hard. *Phi Delta Kappan, 6,* 480–485.
McGoey, K. E., & DuPaul, G. J. (2000). Token reinforcement and response cost procedures: Reducing disruptive behavior of chil-

dren with attention-deficit/hyperactivity disorder. *School Psychology Quarterly, 15*, 330–343.
McKenzie, T. L., & Rushall, B. S. (1974). Effects of self-recording on attendance and performance in a competitive swimming training environment. *Journal of Applied Behavior Analysis, 7*, 199–206.
McLoyd, V. C. (1998). Economic disadvantage and child development. *American Psychologist, 53*, 185–204.
McMillan, J. H. (2004). *Classroom assessment: Principles and practice for effective instruction* (3rd ed.). Boston: Allyn and Bacon.
McNeely, C. A., Nonnemaker, J. M., & Blum, R. W. (2002). Promoting school connectedness: Evidence from the National Longitudinal Study of Adolescent Health. *Journal of School Health*, 72(4), 138–146.
McNeil, L. M., & Valenzuela, A. (2000). *The harmful impact of the TAAS system of testing in Texas: Beneath the accountability rhetoric*. Cambridge, MA: Harvard University Civil Rights Project. Available online at www.law.harvard.edu/groups/civilrights/testing.html
McNemar, Q. (1964). Lost: Our intelligence? Why? *American Psychologist, 19*, 871–882.
Mears, T. (1998). Saying 'Si' to Spanish. *Boston Globe*, April 12.
Mediascope. (1996). *National television violence study: Executive summary 1994–1995*. Studio City, CA: Author.
Medina, J. (2002, June 23). Groups say Regents Exam push immigrants to drop out. *The New York Times*, p. A28.
Meece, J. L. (1997). *Child and adolescent development for educators*. New York: McGraw-Hill.
Meece, J. L. (2002). *Child and adolescent development for educators* (2nd ed.). New York: McGraw-Hill.
Meece, J. L., & Kurtz-Costes, B. (2001). Introduction: The schooling of ethnic minority children and youth. *Educational Psychologist, 36*, 1–7.
Meek, A. (1991). On thinking about teaching: A conversation with Eleanor Duckworth. *Educational Leadership, 50*, 30–34.
Meichenbaum, D. (1977). *Cognitive behavior modification: An integrative approach*. New York: Plenum.
Meichenbaum, D. (1986). Cognitive behavior modification. In F. Kanfer & A. Goldstein (Eds.), *Helping people change: A textbook of methods* (3rd ed., pp. 346–380). New York: Pergamon.
Meichenbaum, D., Burland, S., Gruson, L., & Cameron, R. (1985). Metacognitive assessment. In S. Yussen (Ed.), *The growth of reflection in children* (pp. 1–30). Orlando, FL: Academic Press.
Meijer, A. M., & Wittenboer, G. L. H. van den. (2004). The joint contribution of sleep, intelligence and motivation to school performance, *Personality and Individual Differences,37*, 95–106.
Mendell, P. R. (1971). Retrieval and representation in long-term memory. *Psychonomic Science, 23*, 295–296.
Merton, R. K. (1948). The self-fulfilling prophecy. *Antioch Review, 8*, 193–210.
Messick, S. (1975). The standard problem: Meaning and values in measurement and evaluation. *American Psychologist, 35*, 1012–1027.
Metcalfe, J., & Shimamura, A. P. (Eds.). (1994). *Metacognition: Knowledge about knowing*. Cambridge, MA: MIT Press.
Metzler, C. W., Biglan, A., Rusby, J. C., & Sprague, J. R. (2001). Evaluation of a comprehensive behavior management program to improve school-wide positive behavior support. *Education and Treatment of Children*, 24(4), 448–470.
Midgley, C. (2001). A goal theory perspective on the current status of middle level schools. In T. Urdan & F. Pajares (Eds.), *Adolescence and education* (pp. 33–59). Volume I. Greenwich, CT: Information Age Publishing.
Midgley, C., Kaplan, A., & Middleton, M. (2001). Performance-approach goals: Good for what, for whom, under what circumstances, and at what cost? *Journal of Educational Psychology, 93*, 77–86.
Mifflin, M. (1999, December 13). Singing the pink blues. Mothers who think. Retrieved March 16, 2002, from http://www.salon.com/mwt/feature/1999/12/13/toys/
Miller, G. A. (1956). The magical number seven, plus or minus two: Some limits on our capacity for processing information. *Psychological Review, 63*, 81–97.
Miller, G. A., Galanter, E., & Pribram, K. H. (1960). *Plans and the structure of behavior*. New York: Holt, Rinehart & Winston.
Miller, K., & Gelman, R. (1983). The child's representation of number: A multidimensional scaling analysis. *Child Development, 54*, 1470–1479.
Miller, N., & Harrington, H. J. (1993). Social categorization and intergroup acceptance: Principles for the development an design of cooperative learning teams. In R. Hertz-Lasarowitz & N. Miller (Eds.), *Interaction in cooperative groups: The theoretical anatomy of group learning* (pp. 203–227). New York: Cambridge University Press.
Miller, P. H. (2002). *Theories of developmental psychology* (4th ed.). New York: Worth.
Miller, R. B. (1962). Analysis and specification of behavior for training. In R. Glaser (Ed.), *Training research and education: Science edition*. New York: Wiley.
Miller, S. A. (2005). Tips for getting children's attention. *Early Childhood Today*, 19.
Mills, J. R., & Jackson, N. E. (1990). Predictive significance of early giftedness: The case of precocious reading. *Journal of Educational Psychology, 82*, 410–419.
Milner, H.R. (2003). Teacher reflection and race in cultural contexts: History, meaning, and methods in teaching. *Theory into Practice 42*(3), 173–180.
Mitchell, B. M. (1984). An update on gifted and talented education in the U.S. *Roeper Review, 6*, 161–163.
Mitchell, M. (1993). Situational interest: Its multifaceted structure in the secondary school mathematics classroom. *Journal of Educational Psychology. 85*, 424–436.
Moerk, E. L. (1992). *A first language taught and learned*. Baltimore: Paul H. Brookes.
Moll, L. C., Amanti, C., Neff, D., & Gonzalez, N. (1992). Funds of knowledge for teaching: Using a qualitative approach to connect homes and classrooms. *Theory into Practice, 31*, 132–141.
Moll, L. C., & Whitmore, K. F. (1993). Vygotsky in classroom practice: Moving from individual transmission to social transaction. In E. Forman, N. Minick, & C. A. Stone (Eds.), *Contexts for learning: Sociocultural dynamics in children's development* (pp. 19–42). New York: Oxford University Press.
Monroe, C. R., & Obidah, J. E. (2002, April). *The impact of cultural synchronization on a teacher's perceptions of disruption: A case study of an African American middle school classroom*. Paper presented at the American Educational Research Association, New Orleans, LA.
Moore, M. K., & Meltzoff, A. N. (2004). Object permanence after a 24-hr delay and leaving the locale of disappearance: the role of memory, space, and identity. *Developmental Psychology, 40*, 606–620.

Morin, V. A., & Miller, S. P. (1998). Teaching multiplication to middle school students with mental retardation. *Education & Treatment of Children, 21*, 22–36.
Morine-Dershimer, G. (2006). Instructional planning. In J. Cooper (Ed.), *Classroom teaching skills* (7th ed., pp. 20–54). Boston: Houghton-Mifflin.
Morris, P. F. (1990). Metacognition. In M. W. Eysenck, (Ed.), *The Blackwell dictionary of cognitive psychology* (pp. 225–229). Oxford, UK: Basil Blackwell.
Morrow, L. M. (1983). Home and school correlates of early interest in literature. *Journal of Educational Research, 76*, 221–230.
Morrow, L. M., & Weinstein, C. (1986). Encouraging voluntary reading: The impact of a literature program on children's use of library centers. *Reading Research Quarterly, 21*, 330–346.
Moshman, D. (1982). Exogenous, endogenous, and dialectical constructivism. *Developmental Review, 2*, 371–384.
Moshman, D. (1997). Pluralist rational constructivism. *Issues in Education: Contributions from Educational Psychology, 3*, 229–234.
Moskowitz, G., & Hayman, M. L. (1976). Successful strategies of inner-city teachers: A year-long study. *Journal of Educational Research, 69*, 283–289.
Moss, P. A. (1992). Shifting conceptions of validity in educational measurement: Implications for performance assessment. *Review of Educational Research, 62*, 229–258.
Mueller, C. M., & Dweck, C. S. (1998). Praise for intelligence can undermine children's motivation and performance. *Journal of Personality and Social Psychology, 75*, 33–52.
Mullis, I. V. S., Martin, M. O., Gonzalez, E., & Kennedy, A. M. (2003). *PIRLS 2001 International report: IEA's study of reading literacy achievement in primary schools*. Chestnut Hill, MA: Boston College. Available online at http://timss.bc.edu/pirls2001i/PIRLS2001_Pubs_IR.html
Mumford, M. D., Costanza, D. P., Baughman, W. A., Threlfall, V., & Fleishman, E. A. (1994). Influence of abilities on performance during practice: Effects of massed and distributed practice. *Journal of Educational Psychology, 86*, 134–144.
Murdock, S. G., O'Neill, R. E., & Cunningham, E. (2005). A comparison of results and acceptability of functional behavioral assessment procedures with a group of middle school students with emotional/behavioral disorders (E/BD). *Journal of Behavioral Education, 14*, 5–18.
Murdock, T. B., Hale, N. M., & Weber, M. J. (2001). Predictors of cheating among early adolescents: Academic and social motivations. *Contemporary Educational Psychology, 26*, 96–115.
Murdock, T. B., & Miller, A. (2003). Teachers as sources of middle school students' motivational identity: Variable-centered and person-centered analytic approaches. *Elementary School Journal, 103*, 383–399.
Murphy, P. K., & Alexander, P. A. (2000). A motivated exploration of motivation terminology. *Contemporary Educational Psychology, 25*, 3–53.
Murray, H. G. (1983). Low inference classroom teaching behavior and student ratings of college teaching effectiveness. *Journal of Educational Psychology, 75*, 138–149.
Mussen, P., Conger, J. J., & Kagan, J. (1984). *Child development and personality* (6th ed.). New York: Harper & Row.
Muth, K. D., & Alverman, D. E. (1999). *Teaching and learning in the middle grades*. Boston: Allyn and Bacon.
Myers, D. G. (2005). *Exploring psychology* (6th ed. in modules). New York: Worth.
Nakamura, J., & Csikszentmihalyi, M. (2001). Catalytic creativity: The case of Linus Pauling. *American Psychologist, 56*, 337–341.
Nansel, T. R., Overbeck, M., Pilla, R. S., Ruan, W. J., Simons-Morton, B., & Schiedt, P. (2001). Bullying behavior among US youth: Prevalence and association with psychosocial adjustment. *Journal of the American Medical Association, 285*(16), 2094–2100.
Nathan, M. J., & Knuth, E. J. (2003). A study of whole class mathematical discourse and teacher change. *Cognition and Instruction, 21*, 175–207.
National Alliance of Black School Educators. (2002). *Addressing over-representations of African American students in special education: The prereferral intervention process*. Arlington, VA: Council for Exceptional Education.
National Assessment of Educational Progress. (1997). Washington, DC: National Center for Educational Statistics. Available online at http://www.nces.ed.gov/nationsreportcard/about/
National Center for Educational Statistics. (2002). Reports available online at http://nces.ed.gov/pubsearch/majorpub.asp
National Center for Educational Statistics. (2003). Indicators of school crime and safety 2002. Retrieved January 22, 2004 from http://nces.ed.gov/pubs2003/schoolcrime/6.asp?nav=1.
National Center for Family Literacy. (2004). *Report of the National Early Literacy Panel*. Washington, DC: National Institute for Literacy.
National Clearinghouse on Child Abuse and Neglect (2005). http://nccanch.acf.hhs.gov/pubs/factsheets/fatality.cfm
National Science Foundation. (1996, December 31). *Women and underrepresented minority scientists and engineers have lower levels of employment in business and industry, 1996* (14). Available at http://www.nsf.gov/sbe/srs/databrf/sdb96331.htm
National Telecommunications and Information Administration (2004, September). *A nation online: Entering the broadband age*. Washington, DC: United States Department of Commerce. Available online at http://www.ntia.doc.gov/reports/anol/NationOnlineBroadband04.htm#_Toc78020933
Naveh-Benjamin, M. (1991). A comparison of training programs intended for different types of test-anxious students: Further support for an information-processing model. *Journal of Educational Psychology, 83*, 134–139.
Naveh-Benjamin, M., McKeachie, W. J., & Lin, Y. (1987). Two types of test-anxious students: Support for an information processing model. *Journal of Educational Psychology, 79*, 131–136.
Needles, M., & Knapp, M. (1994). Teaching writing to children who are undeserved. *Journal of Educational Psychology, 86*, 339–349.
Neisser, U. (1976). *Cognition and reality*. San Francisco: Freeman.
Neisser, U., Boodoo, G., Bouchard, A., Boykin, W., Brody, N., Ceci, S. J., Halpern, D. F., Loehlin, J. C., Perloff, R., Sternberg, R. J., & Urbina, S. (1996). Intelligence: Knowns and unknowns. *American Psychologist, 51*, 77–101.
Nelson, C.A. (2001). The development and neural bases of face recognition. *Infant and Child Development, 10*, 3–18.
Nelson, G. (1993). Risk, resistance, and self-esteem: A longitudinal study of elementary school-aged children from mother-custody and two-parent families. *Journal of Divorce and Remarriage, 19*, 99–119.
Nelson, J. R., & Roberts, M. L. (2000). Ongoing reciprocal teacher-student interactions involving disruptive behaviors in general education classrooms. *Journal of Emotional and Behavioral Disorders, 4*, 147–161.
Nelson, K. (1986). *Event knowledge*. Hillsdale, NJ: Lawrence Erlbaum.

Nelson, T. O. (1996). Consciousness and metacognition. *American Psychologist, 51,* 102–116.

Nestor-Baker, N. S. (1999). *Tacit knowledge in the superintendency: An exploratory analysis.* Unpublished doctoral dissertation, The Ohio State University, Columbus, OH.

Neuman, S. B., & Roskos, K. A. (1997). Literacy knowledge in practice: Contexts of participation for young writers and readers. *Reading Research Quarterly,* 32, 10–32.

Neumeister, K. L. S., & Cramond, B. (2004). E. Paul Torrance (1915–2003). *American Psychologist, 59,* 179.

Newcombe, N., & Baenninger, M. (1990). The role of expectations in spatial test performance: A meta-analysis. *Sex Roles, 16,* 25–37.

Nicholls, J., Cobb, P., Wood, T., Yackel, E., & Patashnick, M. (1990). Assessing student's theories of success in mathematics: Individual and classroom differences. *Journal for Research in Mathematics Education, 21,* 109–122.

Nicholls, J. G., & Miller, A. (1984). Conceptions of ability and achievement motivation. In R. Ames & C. Ames (Eds.), *Research on motivation in education. Vol. 1: Student Motivation* (pp. 39–73). New York: Academic Press.

Nieto, S. (2004). *Affirming diversity: The sociopolitical context of multicultural education* (4th ed.). Boston: Allyn and Bacon.

Nissani, M., & Hoefler-Nissani, D. M. (1992). Experimental studies of belief dependence of observations and of resistance to conceptual change. *Cognition and Instruction,* 9, 97–111.

No Child Left Behind Act of 2001. Public Law. No. 107–110 (8 January 2002). Washington, DC: U. S. Government Printing Office.

Noddings, N. (1990). Constructivism in mathematics education. In R. Davis, C. Maher, & N. Noddings (Eds.), *Constructivist views on the teaching and learning of mathematics* (pp. 7–18). Monograph 4 of the National Council of Teachers of Mathematics, Reston, VA.

Noddings, N. (1995). Teaching themes of care. *Phi Delta Kappan, 76,* 675–679.

Noguera, P. (2005). The racial achievement gap: How can we assume an equity of outcomes. In L. Johnson, M. E. Finn, & R. Lewis (Eds.), *Urban education with an attitude.* Albany, NY: SUNY Press.

Norton, P., & Sprague, D. (2001). *Technology for teaching.* Boston: Allyn and Bacon.

Novak, J. D., & Musonda, D. (1991). A twelve-year longitudinal study of science concept learning. *American Educational Research Journal, 28,* 117–154.

Nucci, L. P. (2001). *Education in the moral domain.* New York: Cambridge Press.

Nurmi, J. (2004). Socialization and self-development: Channeling, selection, adjustment, and reflection. In R. Lerner & L. Steinberg (Eds.), *Handbook of adolescent psychology.* New York: Wiley.

Nylund, D. (2000). *Treating Huckleberry Finn: A new narrative approach to working with kids diagnosed ADD/ADHD.* San Francisco: Jossey-Bass.

O'Boyle, M. W., & Gill, H. S. (1998). On the relevance of research findings in cognitive neuroscience to educational practice. *Educational Psychology Review, 10,* 397–410.

O'Connor, C. (1997). Dispositions toward (collective) struggle and educational resilience in the inner city: A case analysis of six African American high school students. *American Educational Research Journal, 34,* 593–629.

O'Donnell, A. M. (Ed.). (2002, Winter). Promoting thinking through peer learning. Special issue of *Theory Into Practice, 61*(1).

O'Donnell, A. M., & O'Kelly, J. (1994). Learning from peers: Beyond the rhetoric of positive results. *Educational Psychology Review,* 6, 321–350.

O'Leary, K. D., & O'Leary, S. (Eds.). (1977). *Classroom management: The successful use of behavior modification* (2nd ed.). Elmsford, NY: Pergamon.

O'Leary, S. (1995). Parental discipline mistakes. *Current Directions in Psychological Science, 4,* 11–13.

Oakes, J. (1985). *Keeping track.* New Haven: Yale University Press.

Oakes, J. (1990a). Opportunities, achievement, and choice: Women and minority students in science and math. *Review of Research in Education, 16,* 153–222.

Oakes, J. (1990b). *Multiplying inequities: The effects of race, social class, and tracking on opportunities to learn mathematics and science.* Santa Monica, CA: Rand.

Oakes, J. (1999). Promotion or retention: Which one is social? *Harvard Education Letter,* 15(1), 8.

Oakes, J., & Wells, A. S. (1998). Detracking for high student achievement. *Educational Leadership,* 55(6), 38–41.

Oakes, J., & Wells, A. S. (2002). Detracking for high student achievement. In L. Abbeduto (Ed.), *Taking sides: Clashing views and controversial issues in educational psychology* (2nd ed., pp. 26–30). Guilford, CT: McGraw-Hill Duskin.

Ogbu, J. U. (1987). Variability in minority school performance: A problem in search of an explanation. *Anthropology and Education Quarterly, 18,* 312–334.

Ogbu, J. U. (1997). Understanding the school performance of urban blacks: Some essential background knowledge. In H. Walberg, O. Reyes, & R. P. Weissberg (Eds.), *Children and youth: Interdisciplinary perspectives* (pp. 190–140). Norwood, NJ: Ablex.

Ogden, J. E., Brophy, J. E., & Evertson, C. M. (1977, April). *An experimental investigation of organization and management techniques in first-grade reading groups.* Paper presented at the annual meeting of the American Educational Research Association, New York.

Okagaki, L. (2001). Triarchic model of minority children's school achievement. *Educational Psychologist,* 36, 9–20.

Ollendick, T. H., Dailey, D., & Shapiro, E. S. (1983). Vicarious reinforcement: Expected and unexpected effects. *Journal of Applied Behavior Analysis, 16,* 485–491.

Olsen, L. (1988). *Crossing the schoolhouse border: Immigrant students and the California public schools.* San Francisco: California Tomorrow.

Olson, D. R. (2004). The triumph of hope over experience in the search for "what works": A response to Slavin. *Educational Researcher,* 33,(1), 24–26.

Omi, M., & Winant, H. (1994). *Racial formation in the United States: From the 1960s to the 1990s* (2nd ed.). New York: Routledge.

Orange, C. (2000). *25 biggest mistakes teachers make and how to avoid them.* Thousand Oaks, CA: Corwin.

Orange, C. (2005). *44 smart strategies for avoiding classroom mistakes.* Thousand Oaks, CA: Corwin Press.

Orfield, G., & Frankenberg, E. (2005). Where are we now? In F. Shultz (Ed.), *Annual editions: Multicultural education* (pp. 10–12). Dubuque, IA: McGraw-Hill/Dushkin.

Orlando L., & Machado, A. (1996). In defense of Piaget's theory: A reply to 10 common criticisms. *Psychological Review, 103,* 143–164.

Ormrod, J. E. (2004). *Human learning* (4th ed.). Columbus, OH: Merrill/Prentice-Hall.

Ormrod, J. E. (1999). *Human learning* (3rd ed.). Upper Saddle River: NJ: Merrill/Prentice-Hall.

Ortony, A., Clore, G. L., & Collins, A. (1988). *The cognitive structure of emotions.* Cambridge: Cambridge University Press.

Osborn, A. F. (1963). *Applied imagination* (3rd ed.). New York: Scribner's.

Osborne, J. W. (2001). Testing stereotype threat: Does anxiety explain race and sex differences in achievement? *Contemporary Educational Psychology, 26,* 291–310.

Osterman, K. F. (2000). Students' need for belonging in the school community. *Review of Educational Research, 70,* 323–367.

Ovando, C. J. (1989). Language diversity and education. In J. Banks & C. McGee Banks (Eds.), *Multicultural education: Issues and perspectives* (pp. 208–228). Boston: Allyn and Bacon.

Ovando, C. J., & Collier, V. P. (1998). *Bilingual and ESL classrooms: Teaching in multicultural contexts* (2nd ed.). Boston: McGraw-Hill.

Owens, R. (1999). *Language disorders: A functional approach to assessment and intervention* (3rd ed.). Boston: Allyn and Bacon.

Padilla, F. M. (1992). *The gang as an American enterprise.* New Brunswick, NJ: Rutgers University Press.

Pai, Y., & Adler, S. A. (2001). *Cultural foundations of education* (3rd ed.). Upper Saddle River, NJ: Merrill.

Paivio, A. (1971). *Imagery and verbal processes.* New York: Holt, Rinehart & Winston.

Paivio, A. (1986). *Mental representations: A dual-coding approach.* New York: Oxford University Press.

Pajares, F. (1997). Current directions in self-efficacy research. In M. L. Maehr & P. R. Pintrich (Eds.), *Advances in motivation and achievement* (Vol. 10, pp. 1–49). Greenwich, CT: JAI Press.

Pajares, F. (2000, April). *Seeking a culturally attentive educational psychology.* Paper presented at the annual meeting of the American Educational Research Association, New Orleans, LA. Available online at http://www.emory.edu/EDUCATION/mfp/AERA2000Discussant.html. Downloaded 5-23-05

Pajares, F., & Schunk, D. H. (2001). Self-beliefs and school success: Self-efficacy, self-concept, and school achievement. In R. Riding & S. Rayner (Eds.), *Perception* (pp. 239–266). London: Ablex Publishing.

Pajares, F., & Schunk, D. H. (2002). Self and self-belief in psychology and education: An historical perspective. In J. Aronson & D. Cordova (Eds.), *Psychology of education: Personal and interpersonal forces* (pp. 1–19). New York: Academic Press.

Palincsar, A. S. (1998). Social constructivist perspectives on teaching and learning. In J. T. Spence, J. M. Darley, & D. J. Foss (Eds.), *Annual Review of Psychology* (pp. 345–375). Palo Alto, CA: Annual Reviews.

Palincsar, A. S., & Brown, A. L. (1984). Reciprocal teaching of comprehension-fostering and monitoring activities. *Cognition and Instruction, 1,* 117–175.

Palincsar, A. S., & Brown, A. L. (1989). Classroom dialogues to promote self-regulated comprehension. In J. Brophy (Ed.), *Advances in research on teaching* (Vol. 1, pp. 35–67). Greenwich, CT: JAI Press.

Palincsar, A. S., & Herrenkohl, L. R. (2002). Designing collaborative learning contexts. *Theory Into Practice, 61,* 26–32.

Palincsar, A. S., Magnuson, S. J., Marano, N., Ford, D., & Brown, N. (1998). Designing a community of practice: Principles and practices of the GIsML community. *Teaching and Teacher Education, 14,* 5–19.

Panitz, T. (1996). *A definition of collaborative vs cooperative learning.* Available online at http://www.city.londonmet.ac.uk/deliberations/collab.learning/panitz2.html (downloaded April 1, 2005).

Panksepp, J. (1998). Attention deficit hyperactivity disorders, psychostimulants, and intolerance of playfulness: A tragedy in the making? *Current Directions in Psychological Science, 7,* 91–98.

Pape, S. J., & Smith, C. (2002). Self-regulating mathematics skills. *Theory Into Practice, 41,* 93–101.

Papert, S. (1980). *Mindstorms; Children, computers, and powerful ideas.* New York: Basic Books.

Paris, S. (1988, April). *Fusing skill and will: The integration of cognitive and motivational psychology.* Paper presented at the annual meeting of the American Educational Research Association, New Orleans.

Paris, S. G. & Ayres, L. R. (1994). *Becoming reflective students and teachers: With portfolios and authentic assessment.* Washington, DC: American Psychological Association.

Paris, S. G., Byrnes, J. P., & Paris, A. H. (2001). Constructing theories, identities, and actions of self-regulated learners. In B. J. Zimmerman & D. H. Schunk (Eds.), *Self-regulated learning and academic achievement: Theoretical perspectives* (2nd ed., pp. 253–287). Mahwah, NJ: Lawrence Erlbaum.

Paris, S. G., & Cunningham, A. E. (1996). Children becoming students. In D. Berliner & R. Calfee, (Eds.), *Handbook of educational psychology* (pp. 117–146). New York: Macmillan.

Paris, S. G., Lipson, M. Y., & Wixson, K. K. (1983). Becoming a strategic reader. *Contemporary Educational Psychology, 8,* 293–316.

Parker, W. C., & Hess, D. (2001). Teaching with and for discussion. *Teaching and Teacher Education, 17,* 273–289.

Parks, C. P. (1995). Gang behavior in the schools: Myth or reality? *Educational Psychology Review, 7,* 41–68.

Pasch, M., Sparks-Langer, G., Gardner, T. G., Starko, A. J., & Moody, C. D. (1991). *Teaching as decision making: Instructional practices for the successful teacher.* New York: Longman.

Pate, P. E., Homestead, E. R., & McGinnis, K. L. (1997). *Making integrated curriculum work: Teachers, students, and the quest for coherent curriculum.* New York: Teachers College Press.

Pate, P. E., McGinnis, K., & Homestead, E. (1995). Creating coherence through curriculum integration. In M. Harmin (1994), *Inspiring active learning: A handbook for teachers* (pp. 62–70). Alexandria, VA: Association for Supervision and Curriculum Development.

Patterson, C. (1995). http://www.apa.org/pi/parent.html downloaded 2/7/2005.

Patterson, G. R. (1997). Performance models for parenting: A social interactional perspective. In J. Grusec & L. Kuczynski (Eds.), *Parenting and the socialization of values: A handbook of contemporary theory* (pp. 193–235). New York: Wiley.

Paulman, R. G., & Kennelly, K. J. (1984). Test anxiety and ineffective test taking: Different names, same construct? *Journal of Educational Psychology, 76,* 279–288.

Pavri, S. (2003). Loneliness in children with disabilities: How teachers can help. In K. Freiberg (Ed.), *Annual Editions: Educating exceptional children 03/04* (pp. 154–160). Guilford, CT: McGraw-Hill/Duskin.

Pavri, S., & Luftig, R. L. (2000). The social face of inclusive education: Are students with disabilities really included? *Preventing School Failure, 45*, 8–14.

Payne, K. J., & Biddle, B. J. (1999). Poor school funding, child poverty, and mathematics achievement. *Educational Researcher, 28*(6), 4–12.

Pekrun, R., Goetz, T., Titz, W., & Perry, R. P. (2002). Academic emotions in students' self-regulated learning and achievement. A program of qualitative and quantitative research. *Educational Psychologist, 37*, 91–105.

Pelham, W. E. (1981). Attention deficits in hyperactive and learning-disabled children. *Exceptional Education Quarterly, 2*, 13–23.

Pellegrini, A. D., Bartini, M., & Brooks, F. (1999). School bullies, victims, and aggressive victims: Factors relating to group affiliation and victimization in early adolescence. *Journal of Educational Psychology, 91*, 216–224.

Peng, S., & Lee, R. (1992, April). *Home variables, parent–child activities, and academic achievement: A study of 1988 eighth graders.* Paper presented at the annual meeting of the American Educational Research Association, San Francisco.

Penuel, W. R., & Wertsch, J. V. (1995). Vygotsky and identity formation: A sociocultural approach. *Educational Psychologist, 30*, 83–92.

Perkins, D. N., Jay, E., & Tishman, S. (1993). New conceptions of thinking: From ontology to education. *Educational Psychologist, 28*, 67–85.

Perkins, D. N., & Salomon, G. (1989). Are cognitive skills context-bound? *Educational Researcher, 18*, 16–25.

Perner, J. (2000). Memory and theory of mind. In E. Tulving & F. I. M. Craik (Eds.), *The Oxford handbook of memory* (pp. 297–312). New York: Oxford.

Perrone, V. (1994). How to engage students in learning. *Educational Leadership, 51*(5), 11–13.

Perry, N. E. (1998). Young children's self-regulated learning and contexts that support it. *Journal of Educational Psychology, 90*, 715–729.

Perry, N. E., & Drummond, L. (2003). Helping young students become self-regulated researchers and writers. *The Reading Teacher, 56*, 298–310.

Perry, N. E., Phillips, L., & Dowler, J. (2004). Examining features of tasks and their potential to promote self-regulated learning. *Teachers College Record, 106*, 1854–1878.

Perry, N. E., VandeKamp, K. O., & Mercer, L. K. (2000, April). *Investigating teacher-student interactions that foster self-regulated learning.* In N. E. Perry (Chair), Symposium conducted at the meeting of the American Educational Research Association, New Orleans.

Perry, N. E., VandeKamp, K. O., Mercer, L. K., & Nordby, C. J. (2002). Investigating teacher-student interactions that foster self-regulated learning. *Educational Psychologist, 37*, 5–15.

Peterson, J. L., & Newman, R. (2000). Helping to curb youth violence: The APA-MTV "Warning Signs" initiative. *Professional Psychology: Research & Practice, 31*, 509–514.

Peterson, P. L. (1992). Revising their thinking: Keisha Coleman and her third-grade mathematics class. In H. Marshall (Ed.), *Redefining student learning: Roots of educational change* (pp. 151–176). Norwood, NJ: Ablex.

Peterson, P. L., Fennema, E., & Carpenter, T. (1989). Using knowledge of how students think about mathematics. *Educational Leadership, 46*(4), 42–46.

Petrill, S. A., & Wilkerson, B. (2000). Intelligence and achievement: A behavioral genetic perspective. *Educational Psychology Review, 12*, 185–199.

Pettigrew, T. (1998). Intergroup contact theory. In J. T. Spence, J. M. Darley, & D. J. Foss (Eds.), *Annual review of psychology* (pp. 65–85). Palo Alto, CA: Annual Reviews.

Peverly, S., Brobst, K., Graham, M., & Shaw, R. (2003). College adults are not good at self-regulation: A study on the relationship of self-regulation, note-taking, and test-taking. *Journal of Educational Psychology, 95*, 335–346.

Pfiffner, L. J., & O'Leary, S. G. (1987). The efficacy of all positive management as a function of the prior use of negative consequences. *Journal of Applied Behavior Analysis, 20*, 265–271.

Phelan, P., Davidson, A. L., & Cao, H. T. (1992). Speaking up: Students' perspectives on school. *Phi Delta Kappan, 73*(9), 695–704.

Phillips, D. (1997). How, why, what, when, and where: Perspectives on constructivism and education. *Issues in Education: Contributions from Educational Psychology, 3*, 151–194.

Phillips, D., & Zimmerman, M. (1990). The developmental course of perceived competence and incompetence among competent children. In R. Sternberg & J. Kolligian (Eds.), *Competence considered* (pp. 41–66). New Haven, CT: Yale University Press.

Phinney, J. (2003). Ethnic identity and acculturation. In K. Chun, P. Ball, & Marin, G. (Eds.), *Acculturation: Advances in theory, measurement, and applied research* (pp. 63–81). Washington, DC: American Psychological Association.

Phinney, J. S. (1990). Ethnic identity in adolescents and adults: Review of research. *Psychological Bulletin, 108*(3), 499–514.

Phinney, J. S., & Devich-Navarro, M. (1997). Variations in bicultural identification among African American and Mexican American adolescents. *Journal of Research on Adolescence, 7*, 3–32.

Phye, G. D. (1992). Strategic transfer: A tool for academic problem solving. *Educational Psychology Review, 4*, 393–421.

Phye, G. D. (2001). Problem-solving instruction and problem-solving transfer: The correspondence issue. *Journal of Educational Psychology, 93*, 571–578.

Phye, G. D., & Sanders, C. E. (1994). Advice and feedback: Elements of practice for problem solving. *Contemporary Educational Psychology, 17*, 211–223.

Piaget, J. (1954). *The construction of reality in the child* (M. Cook, Trans.). New York: Basic Books.

Piaget, J. (1962). *Comments on Vygotsky's critical remarks concerning "The language and thought of the child" and "Judgment and reasoning in the child."* Cambridge, MA: MIT Press.

Piaget, J. (1963). *Origins of intelligence in children.* New York: Norton.

Piaget, J. (1964). Development and learning. In R. Ripple & V. Rockcastle (Eds.), *Piaget rediscovered* (pp. 7–20). Ithaca, NY: Cornell University Press.

Piaget, J. (1965). *The moral judgment of the child.* New York: Free Press.

Piaget, J. (1965/1995). *Sociological studies.* New York: Routledge. (Original work published in 1965.)

Piaget, J. (1969). *Science of education and the psychology of the child.* New York: Viking.

Piaget, J. (1970a). Piaget's theory. In P. Mussen (Ed.), *Handbook of child psychology* (3rd ed.) (Vol. 1, pp. 703–732). New York: Wiley.

Piaget, J. (1970b). *The science of education and the psychology of the child.* New York: Orion Press.

Piaget, J. (1971). *Biology and knowledge.* Edinburgh, UK: Edinburgh Press.

Piaget, J. (1974). *Understanding causality* (D. Miles and M. Miles, Trans.). New York: Norton.

Piaget, J. (1985). *The equilibrium of cognitive structures: The central problem of intellectual development* (T. Brown & K. L. Thampy, Trans.). Chicago: University of Chicago Press.

Pierson, L. H., & Connell, J. P. (1992). Effect of grade retention on self-system processes, school engagement, and academic performance. *Journal of Educational Psychology, 84,* 300–307.

Pintrich, P. R. (2000). Educational psychology at the millennium: A look back and a look forward. *Educational Psychologist, 35,* 221–226.

Pintrich, P. R. (2003). A motivational science perspective on the role of student motivation in learning and teaching. *Journal of Educational Psychology, 95,* 667–686.

Pintrich, P. R., Marx, R. W., & Boyle, R. A. (1993). Beyond cold conceptual change: The role of motivational beliefs and classroom contextual factors in the process of conceptual change. *Review of Educational Research, 63,* 167–199.

Pintrich, P. R., & Schrauben, B. (1992). Students' motivational beliefs and their cognitive engagement in academic tasks. In D. Schunk & J. Meece (Eds.), *Students' perceptions in the classroom: Causes and consequences* (pp. 149–183). Hillsdale, NJ: Lawrence Erlbaum.

Pintrich, P. R., & Schunk, D. H. (2002). *Motivation in education: Theory, research, and applications* (2nd ed.). Upper Saddle River, NJ: Merrill/Prentice-Hall.

Pintrich, P. R., & Zusho, A. (2002). The development of academic self-regulation: The role of cognitive and motivational factors. In A. Wigfield & J. Eccles (Eds.), *Development of achievement motivation* (pp. 249–284). San Diego: Academic Press.

Pisha, B., & Coyne, P. (2001). Smart for the start: The promise of universal design for learning. *Remedial and Special Education, 22,* 197–203.

Pitts, J. M. (1992). Constructivism: Learning rethought. In J. B. Smith & J. C. Coleman, Jr. (Eds.), *School Library Media Annual* (Vol. 10, pp. 14–25). Englewood, CO: Libraries Unlimited.

Plant, E. A., & Peruche, B. M. (2005). The consequences of race for police officers' responses to criminal suspects. *Psychological Science, 16,* 180–183.

Plucker, J. A., Beghetto, R. A., & Dow, G. T. (2004). Why isn't creativity more important to educational psychologists? Potential pitfalls and future directions in creativity research. *Educational Psychology,* 39(2), 83–96.

Pointon, P., & Kershner, R. (2000). Making decisions about organising the primary classroom as a context for learning: The views of three experienced teachers and their pupils. *Teaching and Teacher Education, 16,* 117–127.

Polson, P. G., & Jeffries, R. (1985). Instruction in general problem-solving skills: An analysis of four approaches. In J. Segal, S. Chipman, & R. Glaser (Eds.), *Thinking and learning skills* (Vol. 1, pp. 417–455). Mahwah, NJ: Lawrence Erlbaum.

Popham, W. J. (1999). *Classroom assessment: What teachers need to know.* Boston: Allyn and Bacon.

Popham, W. J. (2005a). *Classroom assessment : What teachers need to know* (4th ed.). Boston, MA: Allyn and Bacon.

Popham, W. J. (2005b). Instructional quality: Collecting credible evidence. *Educational Leadership,* 62(6), 80–81.

Portes, A., & Hao, L. (1998). E pluribus unum: Bilingualism and loss of language in the second generation. *Sociology of Education,* 71: 269–294.

Posada, G., Jacobs, A., Richmond, M., Carbonell, O. A., Alzate, G., Bustamante, M. R., & Quiceno, J. (2002). Maternal care giving and infant security in two cultures. *Developmental Psychology,* 38, 67–78.

Posner, M. I. (1973). *Cognition: An introduction.* Glenview, IL: Scott, Foresman.

Prawat, R. S. (1991). The value of ideas: The immersion approach to the development of thinking. *Educational Researcher, 20,* 3–10.

Prawat, R. S. (1992). Teachers beliefs about teaching and learning: A constructivist perspective. *American Journal of Education, 100,* 354–395.

Prawat, R. S. (1996). Constructivism, modern and postmodern. *Issues in Education: Contributions from Educational Psychology,* 3, 215–226.

Premack, D. (1965). Reinforcement theory. In D. Levine (Ed.), *Nebraska symposium on motivation* (Vol. 13, pp. 123–180). Lincoln, NE: University of Nebraska Press.

Pressley, M. (1991). Comparing Hall (1988) with related research on elaborative mnemonics. *Journal of Educational Psychology,* 83, 165–170.

Pressley, M. (1995). More about the development of self-regulation: complex, long-term, and thoroughly social. *Educational Psychologist, 30,* 207–212.

Pressley, M. (1996, August). *Getting beyond whole language: Elementary reading instruction that makes sense in light of recent psychological research.* Paper presented at the annual meeting of the American Psychological Association, Toronto.

Pressley, M. (1998). *Reading instruction that works: The case for balanced teaching.* New York: The Guilford Press.

Pressley, M., Barkowski, J. G., & Schneider, W. (1987). Cognitive strategies: Good strategy users coordinate metacognition and knowledge. In R. Vasta & G. Whitehurst (Eds.), *Annals of Child Development* (Vol. 5, pp. 89–129). Greenwich, CT: JAI Press.

Pressley, M., Levin, J., & Delaney, H. D. (1982). The mnemonic keyword method. *Review of Research in Education,* 52, 61–91.

Pressley, M., & Woloshyn, V. (1995). *Cognitive strategy instruction that really improves children's academic performance.* Cambridge, MA: Brookline Books.

Price, L. F. (2005). The biology of risk taking. *Educational Leadership,* 62(7), 22–27.

Price, W. F., & Crapo, R. H. (2002). *Cross-cultural perspectives in introductory psychology* (4th ed.). Pacific Grove, CA: Wadsworth.

Public Agenda Foundation. (1994). *First things first: What Americans expect from public schools.* New York: Author.

Puma, M. J., Karweit, N., Porce, C., Ricciuti, A., Thompson, W., & Vadeau-Kierman, M. (1997). *Prospects: Final report on student outcomes.* Washington, DC: Abt Associates, Inc. for the Planning and Evaluation Service, U.S. Department of Education.

Puncochar, J., & Fox, P. W. (2004). Confidence in individual and group decision-making: When "Two Heads" are worse than one. *Journal of Educational Psychology,* 96, 582–591.

Purdie, N., Hattie, J., & Carroll, A. (2002). A review of the research on interventions for Attention Deficit Hyperactivity Disorder: What works best? *Review of Educational Research,* 72, 61–99.

Putnam, J. (1998). The movement towards teaching and learning in inclusive classrooms. In J. Putnam (Ed.), *Cooperative learning and strategies for inclusion* (2nd ed., pp. 1–16). Baltimore, MD: Paul H. Brooks.

Putnam, R. T., & Borko, H. (1997). Teacher learning: Implications of new views of cognition. In B. J. Biddle, T. L. Good, & I. F. Goodson (Eds.), *The international handbook of teachers and teaching* (Vol. 2, pp. 1223–1296). Dordrecht, the Netherlands: Kluwer.

Puustinen, M., & Pulkkinen, L. (2001). Models of self-regulated learning: A review. *Scandinavian Journal of Educational Research, 45*, 269–286.

Qian, G., & Alvermann, D. E. (2000). Relationship between epistemological beliefs and conceptual change learning. *Reading & Writing Quarterly: Overcoming Learning Difficulties, 16*, 59–74.

Rachlin, H. (1991). *Introduction to modern behaviorism* (3rd ed.). New York: W. H. Freeman.

Rachlin, H. (2000). *The science of self-control.* Cambridge, MA: Harvard University Press.

Raffini, J. P. (1996). *150 ways to increase intrinsic motivation in the classroom.* Boston: Allyn and Bacon.

Range, L. M. (1993). Suicide prevention: Guidelines for schools. *Educational Psychology Review, 5*, 135–154.

Rathus, S. A. (1988). *Understanding child development.* New York: Holt, Rinehart & Winston.

Raudenbush, S. (1984). Magnitude of teacher expectancy effects on pupil IQ as a function of the credibility of expectancy induction: A synthesis of findings from 18 experiments. *Journal of Educational Psychology, 76*, 85–97.

Raudsepp, E., & Haugh, G. P. (1977). *Creative growth games.* New York: Harcourt Brace Jovanovich.

Rauscher, F. H., & Shaw, G. L. (1998). Key components of the Mozart effect. *Perceptual and Motor Skills, 86*, 835–841.

Ravitch, D. (1995). *National standards in American education: A citizen's guide.* Washington, DC: Brookings Institution.

Recht, D. R., & Leslie, L. (1988). Effect of prior knowledge on good and poor readers' memory of text. *Journal of Educational Psychology, 80*, 16–20.

Reder, L. M. (1996). Different research programs on metacognition: Are the boundaries imaginary? *Learning and Individual Differences, 8*, 383–390.

Redfield, D. L., & Rousseau, E. W. (1981). A meta-analysis of experimental research on teacher questioning behavior. *Review of Educational Research, 51*, 181–193.

Reed, S., & Sautter, R. C. (1990). Children of poverty: The status of 12 million Americans. *Phi Delta Kappan, 71*(10), K1–K12.

Reeve, J. (1996). *Motivating others: Nurturing inner motivational resources.* Boston: Allyn and Bacon.

Reeve, J., Bolt, E., & Cai, Y. (1999). Autonomy-supportive teachers: How they teach and motivate students. *Journal of Educational Psychology, 91*, 537–548.

Reeve, J., Deci, E. L., & Ryan, R. M. (2004). *Self-determination theory: A dialectical framework for understanding the sociocultural influences on motivation and learning: Big theories revisited* (Vol. 4, pp. 31–59). Greenwich, CT: Information Age Press.

Reeve, J., Nix, G., & Hamm, D. (2003). The experience of self-determination in intrinsic motivation and the conundrum of choice. *Journal of Educational Psychology, 95*, 347–392.

Reich, P. A. (1986). *Language development.* Englewood Cliffs, NJ: Prentice-Hall.

Reid, M. K., & Borkowski, J. G. (1987). Causal attributions of hyperactive children: Implications for teaching strategies and self control. *Journal of Educational Psychology, 79*, 296–307.

Reimann, P., & Chi, M. T. H. (1989). Human expertise. In K. J. Gilhooly (Ed.), *Human and machine problem solving* (pp. 161–191). New York: Plenum Press.

Reinke, W. M., & Herman, K. C. (2002a). A research agenda for school violence prevention. *American Psychologist, 57*, 796–797.

Reinke, W. M., & Herman, K. C. (2002b). Creating school environments that deter antisocial behaviors in youth. *Psychology in the Schools, 39*, 549–560.

Reis, S. M., Kaplan, S. N., Tomlinson, C. A., Westberg, K. L., Callahan, C. M., & Cooper, C. R. (2002). Equal does not mean identical. In L. Abbeduto (Ed.), *Taking sides: Clashing on controversial issues in educational psychology* (pp. 31–35). Guilford, CT: McGraw-Hill/Duskin.

Reis, S. M., & Renzulli, J. S. (2004). Current research on the social and emotional development of gifted and talented students: Good news and future possibilities. *Psychology in the Schools, 41*, published online in Wiley InterScience (www.interscience.wiley.com).

Reisberg, D., & Heuer, F. (1992). Remembering the details of emotional events. In E. Winograd & U. Neisser (Eds.), *Affect and accuracy in recall: Studies of "flashbulb" memories.* Cambridge, England: Cambridge University Press.

Rembolt, C. (1998). Making violence unacceptable. *Educational Leadership, 56*(1), 32–38.

Render, G. F., Padilla, J. N. M., & Krank, H. M. (1989). What research really shows about assertive discipline. *Educational Leadership, 46*(6), 72–75.

Rennie, L. J., & Parker, L. H. (1987). Detecting and accounting for gender differences in mixed-sex and single-sex groupings in science lessons. *Educational Review, 39*(1), 65–73.

Renninger, K. A., Hidi, S., & Krapp, A. (Eds.). (1992). *The role of interest in learning and development.* Hillsdale, NJ: Lawrence Erlbaum.

Renzulli, J. S., & Reis, S. M. (2003). The schoolwide enrichment model: Developing creative and productive giftedness. In N. Colangelo & G. A. Davis (Eds.). *Handbook of gifted education* (pp. 184–203). Boston: Allyn and Bacon.

Resnick, L. B. (1981). Instructional psychology. *Annual Review of Psychology, 32*, 659–704.

Reynolds, A. (1992). Grade retention and school adjustment: An explanatory analysis. *Educational Evaluation and Policy Analysis, 14*(2), 101–121.

Rhodes, R. A. (1997). *Community service and higher learning: Explorations of the caring self.* Albany: State University of New York Press.

Ricciardelli, L. A. (1992). Bilingualism and cognitive development: Relation to threshold theory. *Journal of Psycholinguistic Research, 21*, 301–316.

Rice, F. P., & Dolgin, K. G. (2002). *The adolescent: Development, relationships, and culture* (10th ed.). Boston: Allyn and Bacon.

Richardson, T. M., & Benbow, C. P. (1990). Long-term effects of acceleration on the social-emotional adjustment of mathematically precocious youths. *Journal of Educational Psychology, 82*, 464–470.

Rivkin, S. G., Hanushek, E. A., & Kain, J. F. (2001). *Teachers, schools, and academic achievement.* Amherst, MA: Amherst College.

Robbins, S. B., Lauver, K., Davis, H. L., Davis, D., Langley, R., & Carlstrom, A. (2004). Psychosocial and study skill factors predict college outcomes? A meta-analysis. *Psychological Bulletin, 130*, 261–288.

Robbins, S. B., Le, L., & Lauver, K. (2005). Promoting successful college outcomes for all students: Reply to Weissberg and Owen (2005). *Psychological Bulletin, 131*, 410–411.

Roberts, R. D., Zeidner, M., & Matthews, G. (2001). Does emotional intelligence meet traditional standards for an intelligence? Some new data and conclusions. *Emotion, 1*, 196–231.

Robinson, A., & Clinkenbeard, P. R. (1998). Giftedness: An exceptionality examined. In J. T. Spence, J. M. Darley, & D. J. Foss (Eds.), *Annual review of psychology* (pp. 117–139). Palo Alto, CA: Annual Reviews.

Robinson, D. H. (1998). Graphic organizers as aids to test learning. *Reading Research and Instruction*, 37, 85–105.

Robinson, D. H., & Kiewra, K. A. (1995). Visual argument: Graphic outlines are superior to outlines in improving learning from text. *Journal of Educational Psychology*, 87, 455–467.

Roeser, R. W., Eccles, J. S., &Sameroff, A. J. (2000). School as a context of early adolescents' academic and social-emotional development: A summary of research findings. *Elementary School Journal, 100*, 443–471.

Rogers, C. R., & Freiberg, H. J. (1994). *Freedom to learn* (3rd ed.). Columbus, OH: Charles E. Merrill.

Rogoff, B. (1990). *Apprenticeship in thinking: Cognitive development in social context.* New York: Oxford University Press.

Rogoff, B. (1995). Observing sociocultural activity on three planes: Participatory appropriation, guided participation, and apprenticeship. In J. Wertsch, P. del Rio, & A. Alverez (Eds.), *Sociocultural studies of mind* (pp. 139–164). Cambridge, England: Cambridge University Press.

Rogoff, B. (1998). Cognition as a collaborative process. In W. Damon (Series Ed.) and D. Kuhn & R. S. Siegler (Vol. Eds.), *Handbook of child psychology: Vol.* 2 (5th ed., pp. 679–744). New York: Wiley.

Rogoff, B. (2003). *The cultural nature of human development.* New York: Oxford University Press.

Rogoff, B., & Chavajay, P. (1995). What's become of the research on the cultural basis of cognitive development? *American Psychologist, 50*, 859–877.

Rogoff, B., & Morelii, G. (1989). Perspectives on children's development from cultural psychology. *American Psychologist, 44*, 343–348.

Rogoff, B., Turkanis, C. G., & Bartlett, L. (2001). *Learning together: Children and adults in a school community.* New York: Oxford.

Rohrkemper, M., & Corno, L. (1988). Success and failure on classroom tasks: Adaptive learning and classroom teaching. *Elementary School Journal*, 88, 297–312.

Roid, G. H. (2003). *Stanford-Binet Intelligence Scales, Fifth Edition.* Itasca, IL: Riverside Publishing.

Rop, C. (1997/1998). Breaking the gender barrier in the physical sciences. *Educational Leadership*, 55(4), 58–60.

Rosch, E. H. (1973). On the internal structure of perceptual and semantic categories. In T. Moore (Ed.), *Cognitive development and the acquisition of language* (pp. 111–144). New York: Academic Press.

Rose, L. C., & Gallup, A. M. (1999). The 31st annual Phi Delta Kappa/Gallup Poll of the public's attitude toward the public schools. *Phi Delta Kappan, 81*(1), 41–58.

Rose, L. C., & Gallup, A. M. (2001). The 33rd annual Phi Delta Kappa/Gallup Poll of the public's attitude toward the public schools. *Phi Delta Kappan, 83*(1), 41–58.

Rosenberg, M. (1979). *Conceiving the self.* New York: Basic Books.

Rosenfeld, M., & Rosenfeld, S. (2004). Developing teacher sensitivities to individual learning differences. *Educational Psychology, 24*, 465–486.

Rosenshine, B. (1979). Content, time, and direct instruction. In P. Peterson & H. Walberg (Eds.), *Research on teaching: Concepts, findings, and implications* (pp. 28–56). Berkeley, CA: McCutchan.

Rosenshine, B. (1988). Explicit teaching. In D. Berliner & B. Rosenshine (Eds.), *Talks to teachers* (pp. 75–92). New York: Random House.

Rosenshine, B., & Furst, N. (1973). The use of direct observation to study teaching. In R. Travers (Ed.), *Second handbook of research on teaching.* Chicago: Rand McNally.

Rosenshine, B., & Meister, C. (1992, April). *The uses of scaffolds for teaching less structured academic tasks.* Paper presented at the annual meeting of the American Educational Research Association, San Francisco.

Rosenshine, B., & Meister, C. (1994). Reciprocal teaching: A review of the research. *Review of Educational Research, 64*, 479–530.

Rosenshine, B., & Stevens, R. (1986). Teaching functions. In M. Wittrock (Ed.), *Handbook of research on teaching* (3rd ed., pp. 376–391). New York: Macmillan.

Rosenthal, R. (1987). Pygmalion effects: Existence, magnitude and social importance. A reply to Wineburg. *Educational Researcher, 16*, 37–41.

Rosenthal, R. (1995). Critiquing Pygmalion: A 25-year perspective. *Current Directions in Psychological Science, 4*, 171–172.

Rosenthal, R., & Jacobson, L. (1968). *Pygmalion in the classroom.* New York: Holt, Rinehart, Winston.

Roskos, K., & Neuman, S. B. (1993). Descriptive observation of adults' facilitation of literacy in young children's play. *Early Childhood Research Quarterly*, 8, 77–98.

Roskos, K., & Neuman, S. B. (1998). Play as an opportunity for literacy. In O. N. Saracho & B. Spodek (Eds.), *Multiple perspectives on play in early childhood education* (pp. 100–115). Albany: State University of New York Press.

Ross, J. A., & Raphael, D. (1990). Communication and problem solving achievement in cooperative learning groups. *Journal of Curriculum Studies*, 22, 149–164.

Roth, W-M., & Bowen, G. M. (1995). Knowing and interacting: A study of culture, practices, and resources in a grade 8 open-inquiry science guided by an apprenticeship metaphor. *Cognition and Instruction, 13*, 73–128.

Rotherham-Borus, M. J. (1994). Bicultural reference group orientations and adjustment. In M. Bernal & G. Knight (Eds.), *Ethnic identity.* Albany, NY: State University of New York Press.

Rowe, M. B. (1974). Wait-time and rewards as instructional variables: Their influence on language, logic, and fate control. Part 1: Wait-time. *Journal of Research in Science Teaching, 11*, 81–94.

Rudolph, K. D., Lambert, S. F., Clark, A. G., & Kurlakowsky, K. D. (2001). Negotiating the transition to middle school: The role of self-regulatory processes. *Child Development*, 72, 926–946.

Rueda, R., & Moll, L. C. (1994) A sociocultural perspective on motivation. In F. O'Neil Jr. & M. Drillings (Eds.), *Motivation: Theory and research* (pp. 117–137). Hillsdale, NJ: Lawrence Erlbaum.

Rumelhart, D., & Ortony, A. (1977). The representation of knowledge in memory. In R. Anderson, R. Spiro, & W. Montague (Eds.), *Schooling and the acquisition of knowledge* (pp. 99–135). Hillsdale, NJ: Lawrence Erlbaum.

Rummel, N., Levin, J. R., & Woodward, M. M. (2003). Do pictorial mnemonic text-learning aids give students something worth writing about? *Journal of Educational Psychology, 95,* 327–334.

Ryan, A. (2001). The peer group as a context for development of young adolescents' motivation and achievement. *Child Development, 72,* 1135–1150.

Ryan, R. M., & Deci, E. L. (1996). When paradigms clash: Comments on Cameron and Pierce's claim that rewards do not undermine intrinsic motivation. *Review of Educational Research, 66,* 33–38.

Ryan, R. M., & Deci, E. L. (2000). Intrinsic and extrinsic motivation: Classic definitions and new directions. *Contemporary Educational Psychology, 25,* 54–67.

Ryans, D. G. (1960). *Characteristics of effective teachers, their descriptions, comparisons and appraisal: A research study.* Washington, DC: American Council on Education.

Saarni, C. (2002). *The development of emotional competence.* New York: Guilford.

Sadker, M., & Sadker, D. (1994). *Failing at fairness: How America's schools cheat girls.* New York: Scribner.

Sadker, M., & Sadker, D. (1995). *Failing at fairness: How America's schools cheat girls.* New York: Touchstone Press.

Sadker, M., & Sadker, D. (2006). Questioning skills. In J. Cooper (Ed.), *Classroom teaching skills* (8th ed., pp. 104–150). Boston: Houghton-Mifflin.

Sadker, M., Sadker, D., & Klein, S. (1991). The issue of gender in elementary and secondary education. *Review of Research in Education, 17,* 269–334.

Sagor, R. (2003). *Motivating students and teachers in an era of standards.* Alexandria, VA: Association for Supervision and Curriculum Development.

Sagvolden, T. (1999). Attention deficit/hyperactive disorder. *European Psychologist, 4,* 109–114.

Salomon, G., & Perkins, D. N. (1989). Rocky roads to transfer: Rethinking mechanisms of a neglected phenomenon. *Educational Psychologist, 24,* 113–142.

Sanchez, F., & Anderson, M. L. (1990, May). Gang mediation: A process that works. *Principal,* 54–56.

Sanders, W. L., & Rivers, J. C. (1996). *Cumulative and residual effects of teachers on student academic achievement.* Knoxville, TN: University of Tennessee Value-Added Research and Assessment Center.

Sattler, J. M. (1992). *Assessment of children* (3rd ed. rev.). San Diego: Jerome M. Sattler.

Sattler, J. M. (2001). *Assessment of children: Cognitive applications* (4th ed.). San Diego, CA: Jerome M. Sattler, Inc.

Savage, T. V. (1999). *Teaching self-control through management and discipline.* Boston: Allyn and Bacon.

Savin-Williams, R. C., & Diamond, L. M. (2004). Sex. In R. M. Lerner & L. Steinberg (Eds.), *Handbook of adolescent psychology* (2nd ed., pp. 189–231). New York: John Wiley & Sons.

Sawyer, R. J., Graham, S., & Harris, K. R. (1992). Direct teaching, strategy instruction, and strategy instruction with explicit self-regulation: Effects on the composition skills and self-efficacy of learning disabled students. *Journal of Educational Psychology, 84,* 340–352.

Sax, L. (2002). Maybe men and women are different. *American Psychologist,* 444.

Scardamalia, M., & Bereiter, C. (1996). Adaptation and understanding: A case for new cultures of schooling. In S. Vosniado, E. De Corte, R. Glasse, & H. Mandl (Eds.), *International perspectives on the design of technology-supported learning environments* (pp. 149–163). Hillsdale, NJ: Lawrence Erlbaum.

Scherer, M. (1993). On savage inequalities: A conversation with Jonathan Kozol. *Educational Leadership, 50*(4), 4–9.

Scherer, M. (1999). The discipline of hope: A conversation with Herb Kohl. *Educational Leadership, 56*(1), 8–13.

Schiefele, U. (1991). Interest, learning, and motivation. *Educational Psychologist, 26,* 299–324.

Schneider, W., & Bjorklund, D. F. (1992). Expertise, aptitude, and strategic remembering. *Child Development, 63,* 416–473.

Schoenfeld, A. H. (1979). Explicit heuristic training as a variable in problem solving performance. *Journal for Research in Mathematics Education, 10,* 173–187.

Schoenfeld, A. H. (1989). Teaching mathematical thinking and problem solving. In L. B. Resnick & L. E. Klopfer (Eds.), *Toward the thinking curriculum: Current cognitive research* (pp. 83–103). Alexandria, VA: ASCD.

Schoenfeld, A. H. (1994). *Mathematics thinking and problem solving.* Hillsdale, NJ: Lawrence Erlbaum.

Schofield, J. W. (1991). School desegregation and intergroup relations. *Review of Research in Education, 17,* 235–412.

Schommer, M. (1997). The development of epistemological beliefs among secondary students: A longitudinal study. *Journal of Educational Psychology, 89,* 37–40.

Schommer-Aikins, M. (2002). An evolving theoretical framework for an epistemological belief system. In B. K. Hofer & P. R. Pintrich (Eds.), *Personal epistemology: The psychology of beliefs about knowledge and knowing* (pp. 103–118). Mahwah, NJ: Lawrence Erlbaum.

Schon, D. (1983). *The reflective practitioner.* New York: Basic Books.

Schraw, G., & Lehman, S. (2001). Situational interest: A review of the literature and directions for future research. *Educational Psychology Review, 13,* 23–52.

Schraw, G., & Olafson, L. (2002). Teachers epistemological world views and educational practices. *Issues in Education, 8,* 99–148.

Schunk, D. H. (2000). *Learning theories: An educational perspective* (3rd ed.). Columbus, OH: Merrill/Prentice-Hall.

Schunk, D. H. (2004). *Learning theories: An educational perspective* (4th ed.). Columbus, OH: Merrill/Prentice-Hall.

Schunk, D. H., & Hanson, A. R. (1985). Peer models: Influence on children's self-efficacy and achievement. *Journal of Educational Psychology, 77,* 313–322.

Schutz, P. A., & Davis, H. A. (2000). Emotions and self-regulations during test-taking. *Educational Psychologist, 35,* 243–256.

Schwartz, B., & Reisberg, D. (1991). *Learning and memory.* New York: Norton.

Schwartz, B., & Robbins, S. J. (1995). *Psychology of learning and behavior* (4th ed.). New York, Norton.

Schwartz, B., Wasserman, E. A., & Robbins, S. J. (2002). *Psychology of learning and behavior* (5th ed.). New York: W. W. Norton.

Schwarz, B. B., Neuman, Y., & Biezuner, S. (2000). Two wrongs may make a right...if they argue together! *Cognition and Instruction, 18,* 461–494.

Scott, C. L. (1999). Teachers' biases toward creative children. *Creativity Research Journal, 12,* 321–337.

Seligman, M. E. P. (1975). *Helplessness: On depression, development, and death.* San Francisco: Freeman.

Selman, R. L. (1980). *The growth of interpersonal understanding.* New York: Academic Press.

Semb, G. B., & Ellis, J. A. (1994). Knowledge taught in school: What is remembered? *Review of Educational Research, 64,* 253–286.

Serpell, R. (1993). Interface between sociocultural and psychological aspects of cognition. In E. Forman, N. Minick, & C. A. Stone (Eds.), *Contexts for learning: Sociocultural dynamics in children's development* (pp. 357–368). New York: Oxford University Press.

Shanker, A. (1995, May 15). Restoring the connection between behavior and consequences. *Vital speeches of the day.* Washington, DC: America Federation of Teachers.

Shavelson, R. J. (1987). Planning. In M. Dunkin (Ed.), *The international encyclopedia of teaching and teacher education* (pp. 483–486). New York: Pergamon Press.

Shavelson, R. J., Gao, X., & Baxter, G. (1993). *Sampling variability of performance assessments.* CSE Technical Report 361. Los Angeles: UCLA Center for the Study of Evaluation.

Shaywitz, B. A. et al. (2004). Development of left occipitotemporal systems for skilled reading in children after a phonologically-based intervention. *Biological Psychiatry,* 55, 926–933.

Sheets, R. H. (2005). *Diversity pedagogy: Examining the role of culture in the teaching-learning process.* Boston: Allyn and Bacon.

Shepard, L. A., & Smith, M. L. (1989). Academic and emotional effects of kindergarten retention. In L. Shepard & M. Smith (Eds.), *Flunking grades: Research and policies on retention* (pp. 79–107). Philadelphia: Falmer Press.

Sherman, A. (1994). *Wasting America's future: The Children's Defense Fund report on the costs of child poverty.* Boston: Beacon Press.

Sherman, J. W., & Bessenoff, G. R. (1999). Stereotypes as source-monitoring cues: On the interaction between episodic and semantic memory. *Psychological Science, 10,* 106–110.

Shields, P., Gordon, J., & Dupree, D. (1983). Influence of parent practices upon the reading achievement of good and poor readers. *Journal of Negro Education,* 52, 436–445.

Shimahara, N. K., & Sakai, A. (1995). *Learning to teach in two cultures.* New York: Garland.

Shoda, Y., Mischel, W., & Peake, P. K. (1990). Predicting adolescent cognitive and self-regulatory competencies from preschool delay of gratification. *Developmental Psychology,* 26, 978–986.

Shriver, T. P., Schwab-Stone, M., & DeFalco, K. (1999). Why SEL is the better way: The New Haven Social Development Program. In J. Cohen (Ed.), *Education minds and hearts: Social emotional learning and the passage into adolescence* (pp. 43–60). New York: Teachers College Press.

Shuell, T. J. (1986). Cognitive conceptions of learning. *Review of Educational Research, 56,* 411–436.

Shuell, T. J. (1990). Phases of meaningful learning. *Review of Educational Psychology, 60,* 531–548.

Shuell, T. J. (1996). Teaching and learning in a classroom context. In D. Berliner & R. Calfee (Eds.), *Handbook of educational psychology* (pp. 726–764). New York: Macmillan.

Shulman, L. S. (1987). Knowledge and teaching: Foundations of the new reform. *Harvard Educational Review,* 19(2), 4–14.

Shultz, J., & Florio, S. (1979). Stop and freeze: The negotiation of social and physical space in a kindergarten/first grade classroom. *Anthropology and Education Quarterly, 10,* 166–181.

Siddle Walker, V. (2001). African American teaching in the South: 1940–1960. *Review of Educational Research,* 38, 751–779.

Siegel, J., & Shaughnessy, M. F. (1994). Educating for understanding: An interview with Howard Gardner. *Phi Delta Kappan, 75,* 536–566.

Siegler, R. S. (1993). Adaptive and non-adaptive characteristics of low-income children's mathematical strategy use. In B. Penner (Ed.), *The challenge in mathematics and science education: Psychology's response* (pp. 341–366). Washington, DC: American Psychological Association.

Siegler, R. S. (1998). *Children's thinking* (3rd ed.). Upper Saddle River, NJ: Prentice-Hall.

Siegler, R. S. (2000). The rebirth of children's learning. *Child Development, 71,* 26–35.

Siegler, R. S., & Crowley, K. (1991). The microgenetic method: A direct means for studying cognitive development. *American Psychologist, 56,* 606–620.

Simon, D. P., & Chase, W. G. (1973). Skill in chess. *American Scientist, 61,* 394–403.

Simon, H. A. (1995). The information-processing view of mind. *American Psychologist, 50,* 507–508.

Simonton, D. K. (1999). Creativity from a historiometric perspective. In R. J. Sternberg (Ed.), *Handbook of creativity* (pp. 116–133). New York: Cambridge University Press.

Simonton, D. K. (2000). Creativity: Cognitive, personal, developmental, and social aspects. *American Psychologist, 55,* 151–158.

Simpson, E. J. (1972). The classification of educational objectives in the psychomotor domain. *The Psychomotor Domain. Vol. 3.* Washington: Gryphon House.

Singley, K., & Anderson, J. R. (1989). *The transfer of cognitive skill.* Cambridge, MA: Harvard University Press.

Sisk, D. A. (1988). Children at risk: The identification of the gifted among the minority. *Gifted Education International, 5,* 138–141.

Skiba, R. J., Michael, R. S., Nardo, A. C., & Peterson, R. (2000). *The color of discipline: Sources of racial and gender disproportionality in school punishment* (Report #SRS1). Bloomington, IN: Indiana Education Policy Center.

Skinner, B. F. (1950). Are theories of learning necessary? *Psychological Review, 57,* 193–216.

Skinner, B. F. (1953). *Science and human behavior.* New York: Macmillan.

Skinner, B. F. (1989). The origins of cognitive thought. *American Psychologist, 44,* 13–18.

Skoe, E. E. A. (1998). The ethic of care: Issues in moral development. In E. E. A. Skoe & A. L. von der Lippe (Eds.), *Personality development in adolescence* (pp. 143–171). London: Routledge.

Slaby, R. G., Roedell, W. C., Arezzo, D., & Hendrix, K. (1995). *Early violence prevention.* Washington, DC: National Association for the Education of Young Children.

Slater, L. (2002, February 3). The trouble with self-esteem. *The New York Times Magazine,* pp. 44–47.

Slavin, R. E. (1990). Achievement effects of ability grouping in secondary schools: A best-evidence synthesis. *Review of Educational Research, 60,* 471–500.

Slavin, R. E. (1995). *Cooperative learning* (2nd ed.). Boston: Allyn and Bacon.

Slavin, R. E. (2002). Evidence-based education policies: Transforming education practice and research. *Educational Researcher,* 31(7), 15–21.

Sleeter, C. E. (1995). Curriculum controversies in multicultural education. In E. Flaxman & H. Passow (Eds.), *94th yearbook of the national society for the study of education: Part II: Changing populations, changing schools* (pp. 162–185). Chicago: University of Chicago Press.

Smetana, J. G. (2000). Middle-class African American adolescents' and parents' conceptions of parental authority and parenting practices: A longitudinal investigation. *Child Development, 71,* 1672–1686.

Smith, C. B. (Moderator). (1994). *Whole language: The debate.* Bloomington, IN: EDINFO Press.

Smith, D. D. (1998). *Introduction to special education: Teaching in an age of challenge* (3rd ed.). Boston: Allyn and Bacon.

Smith, D. D., (2006). *Introduction to special education: Teaching in an age of opportunity* (5th ed.). Boston: Allyn and Bacon.

Smith, F. (1975). *Comprehension and learning: A conceptual framework for teachers.* New York: Holt, Rinehart & Winston.

Smith, J. D., & Caplan, J. (1988). Cultural differences in cognitive style development. *Developmental Psychology, 24,* 46–52.

Smith, J. K., Smith, L. F., & De Lisi, R. (2001). *Natural classroom assessment: Designing seamless instruction and assessment.* Thousand Oaks, CA: Corwin Press.

Smith, S. M., Glenberg, A., & Bjork, R. A. (1978). Environmental context and human memory. *Memory and Cognition, 6,* 342–353.

Snapp, M., & Woolfolk, A. E. (1973, March). *An examination of children in special education over a thirteen-year period.* Paper presented at the National Association of School Psychologists, 5th Annual Meeting, New York.

Snider, V. E. (1990). What we know about learning styles from research in special education. *Educational Leadership, 48*(2), 53.

Snow, C. E. (1993). Families as social contexts for literacy development. In C. Daiute (Ed.), *New directions for child development* (No. 61, pp. 11–24). San Francisco: Jossey-Bass.

Snow, R. E. (1995). Pygmalion and intelligence. *Current Directions in Psychological Science, 4,* 169–171.

Snow, R. E., Corno, L., & Jackson, D. (1996). Individual differences in affective and cognitive functions. In D. Berliner & R. Calfee (Eds.), *Handbook of educational psychology* (pp. 243–310). New York: Macmillan.

Snowman, J. (1984). Learning tactics and strategies. In G. Phye & T. Andre (Eds.), *Cognitive instructional psychology* (pp. 243–275). Orlando, FL: Academic Press.

Soar, R. S., & Soar, R. M. (1979). Emotional climate and management. In P. Peterson & H. Walberg (Eds.), *Research on teaching: Concepts, findings, and implications* (pp. 97–119). Berkeley, CA: McCutchan.

Sobesky, W. E. (1983). The effects of situational factors on moral judgment. *Child Development, 54,* 575–584.

Sokolove, S., Garrett, J., Sadker, D., & Sadker, M. (1986). Interpersonal communications skills. In J. Cooper (Ed.), *Classroom teaching skills: A handbook* (pp. 233–278). Lexington, MA: D. C. Heath.

Solomon, D., Battistich, V., Watson, M., Schaps, E., & Lewis, C. (2000). A six-district study of educational change: Direct and mediated effects of the Child Development Project. *Social Psychology of Education, 4,* 3–51.

Solomon, D., Watson, M. S., & Battistich, V. A. (2001). Teaching and schooling effects on moral/prosocial development. In V. Richardson (Ed.), *Handbook of research on teaching* (4th ed., pp. 566–603). Washington, DC: American Educational Research Association.

Soodak, L. C., & McCarthy, M. R. (2006). Classroom management in inclusive settings. In C. M. Evertson & C. S. Weinstein (Eds.), *Handbook of classroom management: Research, practice, and contemporary issues.* Mahwah, NJ: Erlbaum.

Sotillo, S. M. (2002). Finding our voices, finding ourselves: Becoming bilingual and bicultural. In G. S. Boutte (Ed.), *Resounding voices: School experiences of people from diverse ethnic backgrounds* (pp. 275–307). Boston: Allyn and Bacon.

Spearman, C. (1927). *The abilities of man: Their nature and measurement.* New York: Macmillan.

Spector, J. E. (1992). Predicting progress in beginning reading: Dynamic assessment of phonemic awareness. *Journal of Educational Psychology, 84,* 353–363.

Speirs Neumeister, K. L., & Cramond, B. (2004). E. Paul Torrance (1915–2003): Obituary. *American Psychologist, 59,* 179.

Spence, J. T., & Buckner, C. E. (2000). Instrumental and expressive traits, trait stereotypes, and sexist attitudes: What do they signify? *Psychology of Women Quarterly, 24,* 44–62.

Spencer, M. B., & Markstrom-Adams, C. (1990). Identity processes among racial and ethnic-minority children in America. *Child Development, 61,* 290–310.

Spencer, M. B., Noll, E., Stoltzfus, J., & Harpalani, V. (2001). Identity and school adjustment: Questioning the "Acting White" assumption. *Educational Psychologist, 36*(1), 21–30.

Spencer, S. J., Steele, C. M., & Quinn, D. M. (1999). Stereotype threat and women's math performance. *Journal of Experimental Social Psychology, 35,* 4–28.

Sperling, G. (1960). The information available in brief visual presentations. *Psychological Monographs,* 74 (11, Whole No. 498).

Spinelli, C. G. (2002). *Classroom assessment for students with special needs in inclusive classrooms.* Upper Saddle River, NJ: Merrill/Prentice-Hall.

Spiro, R. J., Feltovich, P. J., Jacobson, M. L., & Coulson, R. L. (1991). Cognitive flexibility, constructivism, and hypertext: Random access instruction for advanced knowledge acquisition in ill-structured domains. *Educational Technology, 31*(5), 24–33.

Sprenger, M. (2005). In side Amy's brain. *Educational Leadership, 62*(7), 28–32.

Stahl, S. A. (2002). Different strokes for different folks? In L. Abbeduto (Ed.), *Taking sides: Clashing on controversial issues in educational psychology* (pp. 98–107). Guilford, CT: McGraw-Hill/Duskin.

Stahl, S. A., & Miller, P. D. (1989). Whole language and language experience approaches for beginning reading: A quantitative research synthesis. *Review of Educational Research, 59,* 87–116.

Stahl, S. A., & Yaden, D. B. Jr. (2004). The development of literacy in preschool and primary grades: Work by the Center for the Improvement of Early Reading Achievement. *The Elementary School Journal, 82,* 141–166.

Stainback, S., & Stainback, W. (1992). Schools as inclusive communities. In W. Stainback & S. Stainback (Eds.), *Controversial issues confronting special education: Divergent perspectives* (pp. 29–43). Boston: Allyn and Bacon.

Stanovich, K. E. (1992). *How to think straight about psychology* (3rd ed.). Glenview, IL: Scott, Foresman.

Stanovich, K. E. (1994). Constructivism in reading. *Journal of Special Education, 28,* 259–274.

Stanovich, K. E. (1998). Cognitive neuroscience and educational psychology: What season is it? *Educational Psychology Review, 10,* 419–426.

Starch, D., & Elliot, E. C. (1912). Reliability of grading high school work in English. *Scholastic Review, 20,* 442–457.

Starch, D., & Elliot, E. C. (1913a). Reliability of grading work in history. *Scholastic Review, 21*, 676–681.

Starch, D., & Elliot, E. C. (1913b). Reliability of grading work in mathematics. *Scholastic Review, 21*, 254–259.

Steele, C. (1992). Race and the schooling of African-Americans. *Atlantic Monthly, 269*(4), 68–78.

Steele, K. M., Bass, K. E., & Crook, M. D. (1999). The mystery of the Mozart effect: Failure to replicate. *Psychological Science, 10*, 366–368.

Steinberg, L. (1996). *Beyond the classroom: Why schools are failing and what parents need to do.* New York: Simon & Schuster.

Steinberg, L. (1998). Standards outside the classroom. In D. Ravitch (Ed.), *Brookings papers on educational policy* (pp. 319–358). Washington, DC: Brookings Institute.

Steinberg, L. (2005). *Adolescence* (7th ed.). New York: McGraw-Hill.

Steinberg, L., Dornbusch, S. M., & Brown, B. B. (1992). Ethnic differences in adolescent achievement: An ecological perspective. *American Psychologist, 47*, 723–729.

Stepien, W., & Gallagher, S. (1993). Problem-based learning: As authentic as it gets. *Educational Leadership, 50*(7), 25–28.

Sternberg, R. J. (1985). *Beyond IQ: A triarchic theory of human intelligence.* New York: Cambridge University Press.

Sternberg, R. J. (1997). *Successful intelligence.* New York: Plume.

Sternberg, R. J. (1999). A propulsion model of types of creative contribution. *Review of General Psychology, 3*, 83–100.

Sternberg, R. J. (2000). *Handbook of human intelligence.* New York: Cambridge University Press.

Sternberg, R. J. (2002). Raising the achievement of all students: Teaching for successful intelligence. *Educational Psychology Review, 14*, 383–393.

Sternberg, R. J. (2004). Culture and intelligence. *American Psychologist, 59*, 325–338.

Sternberg, R. J., & Davidson, J. (1982, June). The mind of the puzzler. *Psychology Today*, 37–44.

Sternberg, R. J., & Detterman, D. L. (Eds.). (1986). *What is intelligence? Contemporary viewpoints on its nature and definition.* Norwood, NJ: Ablex.

Sternberg, R. J., & Kaufman, J. C. (1998). Human abilities. In J. T. Spence, J. M. Darley, & D. J. Foss (Eds.), *Annual Review of Psychology* (pp. 479–502). Palo Alto, CA: Annual Reviews.

Sternberg, R. J., & Wagner, R. K. (1993). The geocentric view of intelligence and job performance is wrong. *Current Directions in Psychological Science, 2*, 1–5.

Sternberg, R. J., Wagner, R. K., Williams, W. M., & Horvath, J. A. (1995). Testing common sense. *American Psychologist, 50*, 912–927.

Stevenson, H. W., & Stigler, J. (1992). *The learning gap.* New York: Summit Books.

Stice, E., & Shaw, H. (2004). Eating disorder prevention programs: A meta-analytic review. *Psychological Bulletin, 130*, 206–227.

Stiggins, R. J. (2002). Where is our assessment future and how can we get there? In R. W. Lissitz & W. D. Schafer (Eds.), *Assessment in educational reform: Both means and ends* (pp. 18–48). Boston: Allyn and Bacon.

Stiggins, R. J., & Chappuis, J. (2005). Using student-involved classroom assessment to close achievement gaps. *Theory Into Practice, 44*, 11–18.

Stigler, J. W., Lee, S., & Stevenson, H. W. (1987). Mathematics classrooms in Japan, Taiwan, and the United States. *Child Development, 58*, 1272–1285.

Stinson, S. W. (1993). Meaning and value: Reflections on what students say about school. *Journal of Curriculum and Supervision, 8*(3), 216–238.

Stipek, D. J. (1981). Children's perceptions of their own and their peers' academic competence. *Journal of Educational Psychology, 73*, 404–410.

Stipek, D. J. (1993). *Motivation to learn* (2nd ed.). Boston: Allyn and Bacon.

Stipek, D. J. (1998). *Motivation to learn* (3rd ed.). Boston: Allyn and Bacon.

Stipek, D. J. (2002). *Motivation to learn: Integrating theory and practice* (4th ed.). Boston: Allyn and Bacon.

Stipek, D., de la Sota, A., & Weishaupt, L. (1999). Life lessons: An embedded classroom approach to preventing high-risk behaviors among preadolescents. *The Elementary School Journal, 99*, 433–451.

Stodolsky, S. S. (1988). *The subject matters: Classroom activity in math and social studies.* Chicago: University of Chicago Press.

Stormont, M., Stebbins, M. S., & Holliday, G. (2001). Characteristics and educational support needs of underrepresented gifted adolescents. *Psychology in the Schools, 38*, 413–423.

Stormshak, E. A., Bierman, K. L., Bruschi, C., Dodge, K. A., Coie, J. D., et al. (1999). The relation between behavior problems and peer preference in different classrooms. *Child Development, 70*, 169–182.

Stumpf, H. (1995). Gender differences on test of cognitive abilities: Experimental design issues and empirical results. *Learning and Individual Differences, 7*, 275–288.

Sullivan, M. A., & O'Leary, S. G. (1990). Maintenance following reward and cost token programs. *Behavior Therapy, 21*, 139–149.

Sulzby, E., & Teale, W. (1991). Emergent literacy. In R. Barr, M. L. Kamil, P. B. Mosenthal, & P. D. Pearson (Eds.), *Handbook of reading research, Vol. II* (pp. 727–758). New York: Longman.

Sulzer-Azaroff, B., & Mayer, G. R. (1986). *Achieving educational excellence using behavioral strategies.* New York: Holt, Rinehart & Winston.

Sunburst Software. (1999). *A Field Trip to the Sea.*

Suzuki, B. H. (1983). The education of Asian and Pacific Americans: An introductory overview. In D. Nakanishi & M. Hirano-Nakanishi (Eds.), *The education of Asian and Pacific Americans: Historical perspectives and prescriptions for the future* (pp. 1–14). Phoenix, AZ: Oryx Press.

Svoboda, J. S. (2001). Review of *Boys and girls learn differently.* The Men's Resource Network. Retrieved May 18, 2002 from http://www.themenscenter.com/mensight/reviews/Svoboda/boysandgirls.htm

Swanson, H. L. (1990). The influence of metacognitive knowledge and aptitude on problem solving. *Journal of Educational Psychology, 82*, 306–314.

Swanson, H. L. (2001). Research on interventions for adolescents with learning disabilities: A meta-analysis of outcomes related to higher-order processing. *The Elementary School Journal, 101*, 332–348.

Swanson, T. C. (2005). Providing structure for children with learning and behavior problems. *Intervention in School and Clinic, 40*, 182–187.

Sweeney, W. J., Salva, E., Cooper, J. O., & Talbert-Johnson, C. (1998). Using self-evaluation to improve difficult to read handwriting for secondary students. *Journal of Behavioral Education, 3*, 427–443.

Sweller, J., van Merrienboer, J. J. G., & Paas, F. G. W. C. (1998). Cognitive architecture and instructional design. *Educational Psychology Review, 10*, 251–296.

Sylvester, R. (2003). *A biological brain in a cultural classroom* (2nd ed.). Thousand Oaks, CA: Sage.

Symons, S., Woloshyn, V., & Pressley, M. (1994). The scientific evaluation of the whole language approach to literacy development [Special issue]. *Educational Psychologist, 29*(4).

Tait, H., & Enwistle, N. J. (1998). Identifying students at risk through ineffective study strategies. *Higher Education, 31*, 97–116.

Talbot, M. (2002, February 24). Girls just want to be mean. *The New York Times Magazine*, pp. 24–29+.

Taylor, E. (1998). Clinical foundation of hyperactivity research. *Behavioural Brain Research, 94*, 11–24.

Taylor, R. L., Richards, S. B., & Brady, M. P. (2005). *Mental retardation: Historical perspectives, current practices, and future directions.* Boston: Allyn and Bacon.

Taylor-Green, S., Brown, D., Nelson, L., Longton, J., Gassman, T., Cohen, J., Swatrz, J., Horner, R. H., Sugai, G., & Hall, S. (1997). School-wide behavioral support: Starting the year off right. *Journal of Behavioral Education, 7*, 99–112.

TenBrink, T. D. (2003). Assessment. In J. Cooper (Ed.), *Classroom teaching skills* (7th ed., pp. 311–353). Boston: Houghton-Mifflin.

TenBrink, T. D. (2006). Assessment. In J. Cooper (Ed.), *Classroom teaching skills* (8th ed., pp. 55–78). Boston: Houghton-Mifflin.

Tennyson, R. D. (1981, April). *Concept learning effectiveness using prototype and skill development presentation forms.* Paper presented at the annual meeting of the American Educational Research Association, Los Angeles.

Terman, L. M., Baldwin, B. T., & Bronson, E. (1925). Mental and physical traits of a thousand gifted children. In L. M. Terman (Ed.), *Genetic studies of genius* (Vol. 1). Stanford, CA: Stanford University Press.

Terman, L. M., & Oden, M. H. (1947). The gifted child grows up. In L. M. Terman (Ed.), *Genetic studies of genius* (Vol. 4). Stanford, CA: Stanford University Press.

Terman, L. M., & Oden, M. H. (1959). The gifted group in midlife. In L. M. Terman (Ed.), *Genetic studies of genius* (Vol. 5). Stanford, CA: Stanford University Press.

Tesser, A., Stapel, D. A., & Wood, J. V. (2002). *Self and motivation: Emerging psychological perspectives.* Washington, DC: American Psychological Association.

Tharp, R. G. (1989). Psychocultural variables and constants: Effects on teaching and learning in schools. *American Psychologist, 44*, 349–359.

Tharp, R. G., & Gallimore, R. (1988). *Rousing minds to life: Teaching, learning, and schooling in social context.* New York: Cambridge University Press.

Tharp, R. G., & Gallimore, R. (1991). *The instructional conversation: Teaching and learning in social activity.* Washington, DC: National Center for Research on Cultural Diversity and Second Language Learning.

Theodore, L. A., Bray, M. A., Kehle, T. J., & Jenson, W. R. (2001). Randomization of group contingencies and reinforcers for reduce classroom disruptive behavior. *Journal of School Psychology, 39*, 267–277.

Third International Mathematics and Science Study. (1998). Washington, DC: National Center for Educational Statistics. Available online at http://nces.ed.gov/timss/

Thomas, E. L., & Robinson, H. A. (1972). *Improving reading in every class: A sourcebook for teachers.* Boston: Allyn and Bacon.

Thorndike, E. L. (1913). *Educational psychology: Vol. 2. The psychology of learning.* New York: Teachers College, Columbia University.

Tierney, R. J., Readence, J. E., & Dishner, E. K. (1990). *Reading strategies and practices: A compendium* (3rd ed.). Boston: Allyn and Bacon.

Tierney, W. G. (1993). *Building communities of difference: Higher education in the twenty-first century.* Westport, CT: Bergin and Garvey.

Timmer, S. G., Eccles, J., & O'Brien, K. (1988). How children use time. In F. Juster & F. Stafford (Eds.), *Time, goods, and well-being.* Ann Arbor, MI: Institute for Social Research, University of Michigan.

Tishman, S., Perkins, D., & Jay, E. (1995). *The thinking classroom: Creating a culture of thinking.* Boston: Allyn and Bacon.

Tobin, K. (1987). The role of wait time in higher cognitive learning. *Review of Educational Research, 56*, 69–95.

Tobler, N., & Stratton, H. (1997). Effectiveness of school-based drug prevention programs: A metaanalysis of the research. *Journal of Primary Prevention, 18*, 71–128.

Tollefson, N. (2000). Classroom applications of cognitive theories of motivation. *Education Psychology Review, 12*, 63–83.

Tomasello, M., Kruger, A. C., & Ratner, H. H. (1993). Cultural learning. *Behavioral and Brain Sciences, 16*, 495–552.

Tomlinson, C. A. (2003). *Fulfilling the promise of the differentiated classroom.* Alexandria, VA: Association for Supervision and Curriculum Development.

Tomlinson, C. A. (2005a). Grading and differentiation: Paradox or good practice? *Theory Into Practice, 44*, 262–269.

Tomlinson, C. A. (2005b, Summer). Differentiating instruction. *Theory Into Practice, 44*(3).

Tomlinson-Keasey, C. (1990). Developing our intellectual resources for the 21st century: Educating the gifted. *Journal of Educational Psychology, 82*, 399–403.

Tomlinson-Keasey, C., & Little, T. D. (1990). Predicting educational attainment, occupational achievement intellectual skill, and personal adjustment among gifted men and women. *Journal of Educational Psychology, 82*, 442–455.

Toppo, G. (2003, January 13). School violence hits lower grades: Experts who see violent behavior in younger kids blame parents, prenatal medical problems and an angry society; educators search for ways to cope. *USAToday.* Available at http://www.usatoday.com/educate/college/education/articles/20030119.htm. Downloaded on January 23, 2003.

Torrance, E. P. (1972). Predictive validity of the Torrance tests of creative thinking. *Journal of Creative Behavior, 6*, 236–262.

Torrance, E. P. (1986). Teaching creative and gifted learners. In M. Wittrock (Ed.), *Handbook of research on teaching* (3rd ed., pp. 630–647). New York: Macmillan.

Torrance, E. P., & Hall, L. K. (1980). Assessing the future reaches of creative potential. *Journal of Creative Behavior, 14*, 1–19.

Toth, E., Klahr, D., & Chen, Z. (2000). Bridging research and practice: A cognitively based classroom intervention for teaching experimentation to elementary school children. *Cognition and Instruction, 18*, 423–459.

Trautwein, U., & Koller, O. (2003). The relationship between homework and achievement—Still a mystery. *Educatonal Psychology Review, 15*, 115–145.

Tschannen-Moran, M., & Woolfolk Hoy, A. (2001). Teacher efficacy: Capturing an elusive construct. *Teaching and Teacher Education, 17*, 783–805.

Tschannen-Moran, M., Woolfolk Hoy, A., & Hoy, W. K. (1998). Teacher efficacy: Its meaning and measure. *Review of Educational Research, 68*, 202–248.

Turiel, E. (1998). The development of morality. In W. Damon (Series Ed.) & N. Eisenberg (Vol. Ed.), *Handbook of child psychology: Vol. 3. Social, emotional, and personality development* (5th ed., pp. 863–932). New York: Wiley.

Turner, J. C. (1997). Starting right: Strategies for engaging young literacy learners. In J. T. Guthrie & A. Wigfield (Eds.), *Reading engagement: Motivating readers through integrated instruction* (pp. 183–204). Newark, DE: International Reading Association.

Turner, J. C., & Paris, S. G. (1995). How literacy tasks influence students' motivation for literacy. *The Reading Teacher, 48*, 662–673.

Twenge, J. M., & Campbell, W. K. (2001). Age and birth cohort differences in self-esteem: A cross temporal meta-analysis. *Journal of Personality and Social Psychology Review, 5*, 321–344.

U.S. Census Bureau. www.census.gov/Press-Release/www/2001/cb01-158.html

U.S. Department of Education (2002). *No Child Left Behind* Fact Sheet. Retrieved August 5, 2002 from http://www.ed.gov/offices/OESE/esea/factsheet.html

U.S. Department of Education. (1993). *National excellence: A case for developing America's talent.* Washington DC: Author.

U.S. Department of Health and Human Services. (1997). *Youth risk behavior surveillance—U.S., 1995.* MMWR, 45 (No. SS-4).

Uline, C. L., & Johnson, J. F. (2005). Closing the achievement gap: What will it take? Special Issue of *Theory Into Practice, 44*(1), Winter.

Umbreit, J. (1995). Functional analysis of disruptive behavior in an inclusive classroom. *Journal of Early Intervention, 20*(1), 18–29.

Unsworth, N., & Engle, R. W. (2005). Working memory capacity and fluid abilities: Examining the correlation between Operation Span and Raven. *Intelligence, 33*, 67–81.

Urdan, T. C., & Maehr, M. L. (1995). Beyond a two-goal theory of motivation and achievement: A case for social goals. *Review of Educational Research, 65*, 213–243.

Valentine, J. C., DuBois, D. L., & Cooper, H. (2004). The relations between self-beliefs and academic achievement: A systematic review. *Educational Psychologist, 39*, 111–133.

Valenzuela, A. (1999). *Subtractive schooling: U.S.-Mexican youth and the politics of caring.* Albany: SUNY Press.

Van Houten, R., & Doleys, D. M. (1983). Are social reprimands effective? In S. Axelrod & J. Apsche (Eds.), *The effects of punishment on human behavior.* San Diego: Academic Press.

van Kraayenoord, C. E., Rice, D., Carroll, A., Fritz, E., Dillon, L., & Hill, A. (2001). *Attention Deficit Hyperactivity Disorder: Impact and implications for Queensland.* Queensland, Australia: Queensland Disability Services (available online at www.families.qld.gov.au).

van Laar, C. (2000). The paradox of low academic achievement but high self-esteem in African American students: An attributional account. *Educational Psychology Review, 12*, 33–61.

Van Matre, J. C., Valentine, J. C., & Cooper, H. (2000). Effect of students' after-school activities on teachers' academic expectations. *Contemporary Educational Psychology, 25*, 167–183.

Van Meter, P. (2001). Drawing construction as a strategy for learning from text. *Journal of Educational Psychology, 93*, 129–140.

Van Meter, P., Yokoi, L., & Pressley, M. (1994). College students' theory of note-taking derived from their perceptions of note-taking. *Journal of Educational Psychology, 86*, 323–338.

Vasquez, J. A. (1990). Teaching to the distinctive traits of minority students. *The Clearing House, 63*, 299–304.

Veenman, S. (1984). Perceived problems of beginning teachers. *Review of Educational Research, 54*, 143–178.

Veenman, S. (1997). Combination classes revisited. *Educational Research and Evaluation, 65*(4), 319–381.

Vellutino, F. R. (1991). Introduction to three studies on reading acquisition: Convergent findings on theoretical foundations of code-oriented versus whole-language approaches to reading instruction. *Journal of Educational Psychology, 83*, 437–443.

Vera, A. H., & Simon, H. A. (1993). Situated action: A symbolic interpretation. *Cognitive Science, 17*, 7–48.

Vispoel, W. P. (1995). Self-concept inartistic domains: An extension of the Shavelson, Hubmner, and Stanton (1976) model. *Journal of Educational Psychology, 87*, 134–153.

Vispoel, W. P., & Austin, J. R. (1995). Success and failure in junior high school: A critical incident approach to understanding students' attributional beliefs. *American Educational Research Journal, 32*, 377–412.

Volet, S. (1999). Learning across cultures: Appropriateness of knowledge transfer. *International Journal of Educational Research, 31*, 625–643.

von Glaserfeld, E. (1997). Amplification of a constructivist perspective. *Issues in Education: Contributions from Educational Psychology, 3*, 203–210.

Vosniadou, S., & Schommer, M. (1988). Explanatory analogies can help children acquire information from expository text. *Journal of Educational Psychology, 80*, 524–536.

Vroom, V. (1964). *Work and motivation.* New York: Wiley.

Vygotsky, L. S. (1978). *Mind in society: The development of higher mental process.* Cambridge, MA: Harvard University Press.

Vygotsky, L. S. (1986). *Thought and language.* Cambridge, MA: MIT Press.

Vygotsky, L. S. (1987). The genetic roots of thinking and speech. In R. W. Rieber & A. S. Carton (Eds.), *Problems of general psychology, Vol. 1.Collected works* (pp. 101–120). New York: Plenum. (Work originally published in 1934.)

Vygotsky, L. S. (1987). *Problems of general psychology.* New York: Plenum.

Vygotsky, L. S. (1993). *The collected works of L. S. Vygotsky: Vol. 2* (J. Knox & C. Stevens, Trans.). New York: Plenum.

Vygotsky, L. S. (1997). *Educational psychology* (R. Silverman, Trans.). Boca Raton, FL: St. Lucie.

Wade, S. E., Schraw, G., Buxton, W. M., & Hayes, M. T. (1993). Seduction of the strategic reader: Effects of interest on strategies and recall. *Reading Research Quarterly, 28*, 3–24.

Waits, B. K., & Demana, F. (2000). Calculators in mathematics teaching and learning: Past, present, future. In M. J. Burke & F. R. Curcio (Eds.), *Learning mathematics for a new century: NCTM 2000 Yearbook* (pp. 51–66). Reston, VA: National Council of Teachers of Mathematics.

Walberg, H. J. (1984). Improving the productivity of America's schools. *Educational Leadership, 41*, 19–27.

Walberg, H. J. (1990). Productive teaching and instruction: Assessing the knowledge base. *Phi Delta Kappan, 72*, 470–478.

Wald, J. (2001, August 29). The failure of zero tolerance. *Salon Magazine.* Available online at http://www.salon.com/mwt/feature/2001/08/29/zero_tolerance/index.html?sid=1046257.

Walker, J. E., Shea, T. M., & Bauer, A. M. (2004). *Behavior management: A practical approach for educators*. Upper Saddle River, NJ: Merrill/Prentice Hall.

Walker, L. J. (1991). Sex differences in moral reasoning. In W. M. Kurtines & J. L. Gewirtz (Eds.), *Handbook of moral behavior and development* (Vol. 2, pp. 333–362). Hillsdale, NJ: Lawrence Erlbaum.

Walker, L. J., & Pitts, R. C. (1998). Naturalistic conceptions of moral maturity. *Developmental Psychology, 34*, 403–419.

Walker, L. J., Pitts, R. C., Hennig, K. H., & Matsuba, M. K. (1995). Reasoning about morality and real-life moral problems. In M. Killen & D. Hart (Eds.), *Morality in everyday life: Developmental perspectives* (pp. 371–407). Cambridge, England: Cambridge University Press.

Walker, V. S. (1996). *Their highest potential*. Chapel Hill: University of North Carolina Press.

Wang, A. Y., & Thomas, M. H. (1995). Effects of keywords on long-term retention: Help or hindrance? *Journal of Educational Psychology, 87*, 468–475.

Wang, A. Y., Thomas, M. H., & Ouellette, J. A. (1992). Keyword mnemonic and retention of second-language vocabulary words. *Journal of Educational Psychology, 84*, 520–528.

Wang, M. C., & Palincsar, A. S. (1989). Teaching students to assume an active role in their learning. In M. Reynolds (Ed.), *Knowledge base for the beginning teacher* (pp. 71–84). New York: Pergamon.

Ward, L. M. (2004). Wading through the stereotypes: Positive and negative associations between media use and Black adolescents' conception of self. *Developmental Psychology, 40*, 284–294.

Wasserman, E. A., & Miller, R. R. (1997). What's elementary about associative learning. In J. T. Spence, J. M. Darley, & D. J. Foss (Eds.), *Annual review of psychology* (pp. 573–607). Palo Alto, CA: Annual Reviews.

Waters, H. F. (1993, July 12). Networks under the gun. *Newsweek*, 64–66.

Wayne, A. J., & Youngs, P. (2003). Teacher characteristics and student achievement gains: A review. *Review of Educational Research, 73*, 89–122.

Webb, N. M. (1985). Verbal interaction and learning in peer-directed groups. *Theory Into Practice, 24*, 32–39.

Webb, N. M., Farivar, S. H., & Mastergeorge, A. M. (2002). Productive helping in cooperative groups. *Theory Into Practice, 41*, 13–20.

Webb, N. M., & Mastergeorge, A. M. (2003). The development of students' helping behavior and learning in peer-directed small groups. *Cognition and Instruction, 21*, 361–428.

Webb, N. M., & Palincsar, A. (1996). Group processes in the classroom. In D. C. Berliner & R. C. Calfee (Eds.), *Handbook of educational psychology* (pp. 841–876). New York: Macmillan.

Weinberg, R. A. (1989). Intelligence and IQ. *American Psychologist, 44*, 98–104.

Weinberger, D. (2001, March 10). A brain too young for good judgment. *The New York Times*, p. A13.

Weiner, B. (1979). A theory of motivation for some classroom experiences. *Journal of Educational Psychology, 71*, 3–25.

Weiner, B. (1986). *An attributional theory of motivation and emotion*. New York: Springer.

Weiner, B. (1990). History of motivational research in education. *Journal of Educational Psychology, 82*, 616–622.

Weiner, B. (1992). *Human motivation: Metaphors, theories, and research*. Newbury Park, CA: Sage.

Weiner, B. (1994a). Ability versus effort revisited: The moral determinants of achievement evaluation an achievement as a moral system. *Educational Psychologist, 29*, 163–172.

Weiner, B. (1994b). Integrating social and persons theories of achievement striving. *Review of Educational Research, 64*, 557–575.

Weiner, B. (2000). Interpersonal and intrapersonal theories of motivation from an attributional perspective. *Educational Psychology Review, 12*, 1–14.

Weiner, B., & Graham, S. (1989). Understanding the motivational role of affect: Lifespan research from an attributional perspective. *Cognition and Emotion, 4*, 401–419.

Weinert, F. E., & Helmke, A. (1995). Learning from wise mother nature or big brother instructor: The wrong choice as seen from an educational perspective. *Educational Psychologist, 30*, 135–143.

Weinstein, C. E. (1994). Learning strategies and learning to learn. *Encyclopedia of Education*.

Weinstein, C. S. (1977). Modifying student behavior in an open classroom through changes in the physical design. *American Educational Research Journal, 14*, 249–262.

Weinstein, C. S. (1999). Reflections on best practices and promising programs: Beyond assertive classroom discipline. In H. J. Freiberg (Ed.), *Beyond behaviorism: Changing the classroom management paradigm* (pp. 147–163). Boston: Allyn and Bacon.

Weinstein, C. S. (2003). *Secondary classroom management: Lessons from research and practice* (2nd ed.). New York: McGraw-Hill.

Weinstein, C. S., & Mignano, A. (2003). *Elementary classroom management: Lessons from research and practice* (3rd ed.). New York: McGraw-Hill.

Weinstein, C., Ridley, D. S., Dahl, T., & Weber, E. S. (1988/1989). Helping students develop strategies for effective learning. *Educational Leadership, 46*(4), 17–19.

Weinstein, R. S., Madison, S. M., & Kuklinski, M. R. (1995). Raising expectations in schools: Obstacles and opportunities for change. *American Educational Research Journal, 32*, 121–159.

Weisberg, R. W. (1993). *Creativity: Beyond the myth of genius*. New York: W. H. Freeman.

Wenger, E. (1998). *Communities of practice: learning, meaning, and identity*. New York: Cambridge University Press.

Wentzel, K. R. (1997). Student motivation in middle school: The role of perceived pedagogical caring. *Journal of Educational Psychology, 89*(3), 411–419.

Wentzel, K. R. (1998). Social relationships and motivation in middle school: The role of parents, teachers, and peers. *Journal of Educational Psychology, 90*(2), 202–209.

Wentzel, K. R. (1999). Social-motivational processes and interpersonal relations: Implications for understanding motivation in school. *Journal of Educational Psychology, 91*, 76–97.

Wentzel, K. R. (2002). Are effective teachers like good parents? Teaching styles and student adjustment in early adolescence. *Child Development, 73*, 287–301.

Wentzel, K. R., Barry, C. M., & Caldwell, K. A. (2004). Friendships in middle school: Influences on motivation and school adjustment. *Journal of Educational Psychology, 96*, 195–203.

Wentzel, K. R., & Battle, A. A. (2001). Social relationships and school adjustment. In T. Urdan & F. Pajares (Eds.), *Adolescence education: General issues in the education of adolescents* (Vol. 1, pp. 93–118). Greenwich, CT: Information Age.

Wertsch, J. V. (1991). *Voices of the mind: A sociocultural approach to mediated action.* Cambridge, MA: Harvard University Press.

Wertsch, J. V., & Tulviste, P. (1992). L. S. Vygotsky and contemporary developmental psychology. *Developmental Psychology, 28,* 548–557.

Westberg, K. L., Archambault, F. X., Dodyns, S. M., & Slavin, T. J. (1993). The classroom practices observation study. *Journal of the Education of the Gifted, 16*(2), 120–146.

Wharton-McDonald, R., Pressley, M., Rankin, J., Mistretta, J., Yokoi, L., & Ettenberger, S. (1997). Effective primary-grades literacy instruction = Balanced literacy instruction. *The Reading Teacher, 50,* 518–521.

Wheatley, K. F. (2002). The potential benefits of teacher efficacy doubts for educational reform. *Teaching and Teacher Education, 18,* 5–22.

Wheelock, A. (1992). *Crossing the tracks: How untracking can save America's schools.* New York: The New Press.

When the student becomes the teacher. (1986, March). *Harvard Education Letter,* 2(3), 5–6.

White, S., & Tharp, R. G. (1988, April). *Questioning and wait-time: A cross cultural analysis.* Paper presented at the annual meeting of the American Educational Research Association, New Orleans.

Whitehead, A. N. (1929). *The aims of education.* New York: Macmillan.

Whitehurst, G. J., Epstein, J. N., Angell, A. L., Payne, A. C., Crone, D. A., & Fischel, J. E. (1994). Outcomes of an emergent literacy program in headstart. *Journal of Educational Psychology, 86,* 542–555.

Wigfield, A., & Eccles, J. (1989). Test anxiety in elementary and secondary school students. *Educational Psychologist, 24,* 159–183.

Wigfield, A., & Eccles, J. S. (2002a). Students' motivation during the middle school years. In J. Aronson (Ed.), *Improving academic development: Impact of psychological factors in education.* New York: Academic Press.

Wigfield, A., & Eccles, J. (2002b). The development of competence beliefs, expectancies of success, and achievement values from childhood through adolescence. In A. Wigfield & J. Eccles (Eds.), *Development of achievement motivation* (pp. 91–120). San Diego: Academic Press.

Wigfield, A., Eccles, J., MacIver, D., Rueman, D., & Midgley, C. (1991). Transitions at early adolescence: Changes in children's domain-specific self-perceptions and general self-esteem across the transition to junior high school. *Developmental Psychology, 27,* 552–565.

Wigfield, A., Eccles, J. S., & Pintrich, P. R. (1996). Development between the ages of 11 and 25. In D. Berliner & R. Calfee (Eds.), *Handbook of educational psychology* (pp. 148–185). New York: Macmillan.

Wiggins, G. (1989). Teaching to the authentic test. *Educational Leadership, 46*(7), 41–47.

Wiggins, G. (1991). Standards, not standardization: Evoking quality student work. *Educational Leadership, 48*(5), 18–25.

Wiggins, G. (1993). Assessment, authenticity, context, and validity. *Phi Delta Kappan, 75,* 200–214.

Wilder, A. A., & Williams, J. P. (2001). Students with severe learning disabilities can learn higher order comprehension skills. *Journal of Educational Psychology, 93,* 268–278.

Wilgenbusch, T., & Merrell, K. W. (1999). Gender differences in self-concept among children and adolescents: A meta-analysis of multidimensional studies. *School Psychology Quarterly, 14,* 101–120.

Wilkins, W. E., & Glock, M. D. (1973). *Teacher expectations and student achievement: A replication and extension.* Ithaca, NY: Cornell University Press.

Willcutt, E. G., Pennington, B. F., Boada, R., Ogline, J. S., Tunick, R. A., Chhabidas, N. A., & Olson, R. K. (2001). A comparison of the cognitive deficits in reading disability and attention-deficit/hyperactivity disorder. *Journal of Abnormal Psychology, 110,* 157–172.

Williams, C., & Bybee J. (1994). What do children feel guilty about? Developmental and gender differences. *Developmental Psychology, 30,* 617–623.

Williams, G. C., Wiener, M. W., Markakis, K. M., Reeve, J., & Deci, E. L. (1993). Medical students' motivation for internal medicine. *Annals of Internal Medicine, 9,* 327–333.

Williams, J. P. (2002). Using the Theme Scheme to improve story comprehension. In C. C. Block & M. Pressley (Eds.), *Comprehension instruction: Research-based best practices* (pp. 126–139). New York: Guilford.

Williams, W., Blythe, T., White, N., Li, J., Sternberg, R., & Gardner, H. (1996). *Practical intelligence in school.* New York: HarperCollins.

Willingham, W. W., & Cole, N. S. (1997). *Gender and fair assessment.* Mahwah, NJ: Lawrence Erlbaum.

Willis, P. (1977). *Learning to labor.* Lexington, MA: D.C. Heath.

Willoughby, T., Porter, L., Belsito, L., & Yearsley, T. (1999). Use of elaboration strategies by grades two, four, and six. *Elementary School Journal, 99,* 221–231.

Wilson, C. W., & Hopkins, B. L. (1973). The effects of contingent music on the intensity of noise in junior high home economics classes. *Journal of Applied Behavior Analysis, 6,* 269–275.

Wilson, M. (2001). The case for sensorimotor coding in working memory. *Psychonomic Bulletin and Review, 8,* 44–57.

Windschitl, M. (2002). Framing constructivism in practice as the negotiation of dilemmas; An analysis of the conceptual, pedagogical, cultural, and political challenges facing teachers. *Review of Educational Research, 72,* 131–175.

Winett, R. A., & Winkler, R. C. (1972). Current behavior modification in the classroom: Be still, be quiet, be docile. *Journal of Applied Behavior Analysis, 15,* 499–504.

Wink, J., & Putney, L. (2002). *A vision of Vygotsky.* Boston: Allyn and Bacon.

Winne, P. H. (1995). Inherent details in self-regulated learning. *Educational Psychologist, 30,* 173–188.

Winne, P. H. (2001). Self-regulated learning viewed from models of information processing. In B. J. Zimmerman & D. H. Schunk (Eds.), *Self-regulated learning and academic achievement: Theoretical perspectives* (2nd ed., pp. 153–189). Mahwah, NJ: Lawrence Erlbaum.

Winne, P. H., & Hadwin, A. F. (1998). Studying as self-regulated learning. In D. J. Hacker, J. Dunlosky, & A. C. Graesser (Eds.), *Metacognition in educational theory and practice* (pp. 277–304). Mahwah, NJ: Lawrence Erlbaum.

Winne, P. H., & Perry, N. E. (2000). Measuring self-regulated learning. In P. Pintrich, M. Boekaerts, & M. Zeidner (Eds.), *Handbook of self-regulation* (p. 531–566). Orlando, FL: Academic Press.

Winner, E. (2000). The origins and ends of giftedness. *American Psychologist, 55,* 159–169.

Winner, E. (2003). Musical giftedness. *Bulletin of Psychology and the Arts*, *4*, 1, 2–5.

Winsler, A., Carlton, M. P., & Barry, M. J. (2000). Age-related changes in preschool children's systematic use of private speech in a natural setting. *Journal of Child Language*, *27*, 665–687.

Winsler, A., Diaz, R. M., Espinosa, L., & Rodriquez, J. L. (1999). When learning an second language does not mean losing the first: Bilingual language development in low-income, Spanish-speaking children attending bilingual preschool. *Child Development*, *70*, 349–362.

Winsler, A., & Naglieri, J. A. (2003). Overt and covert verbal problem-solving strategies: Developmental trends in use, awareness, and relations with task performance in children age 5 to 17. *Child Development*, *74*, 659–678.

Wintergerst, A. C., DeCapua, A., & Itzen, R. C. (2001). The construct validity of one learning styles instrument. *System*, *29*(3) 385–403.

Wittrock, M. C. (1982, March). *Educational implications of recent research on learning and memory*. Paper presented at the annual meeting of the American Educational Research Association, New York.

Wittrock, M. C. (Ed.). (1986). *Handbook of research on teaching* (3rd ed.). New York: Macmillan.

Wittrock, M. C. (1992). An empowering conception of educational psychology. *Educational Psychologist*, *27*, 129–142.

Wolf, D., Bixby, J., Glenn, J., III, & Gardner, H. (1991). To use their minds well: New forms of student assessment. *Review of Research in Education*, *17*, 31–74.

Wolters, C. A., Yu, S. L., & Pintrich, P. R. (1996). The relation between goal orientation and students' motivational beliefs and self-regulated learning. *Learning and Individual Differences*, *8*, 211–238.

Wong, L. (1987). Reaction to research findings: Is the feeling of obviousness warranted? *Dissertation Abstracts International*, 48/12, 3709B (University Microfilms #DA 8801059).

Wood, D., Bruner, J., & Ross, S. (1976). The role of tutoring in problem solving. *British Journal of Psychology*, *66*, 181–191.

Wood, S. E., & Wood, E. G. (1999). *The world of psychology* (3rd ed.). Boston: Allyn and Bacon.

Wood, S. E., Wood, E. G., & Boyd, D. (2005). *The world of psychology* (5th ed.). Boston: Allyn and Bacon.

Woods, B. S., & Murphy, P. K. (2002). Thickening the discussion: What can William James tell us about constructivism? *Educational Theory*, *52*, 443–449.

Woolfolk, A. E., & Brooks, D. (1983). Nonverbal communication in teaching. In E. Gordon (Ed.), *Review of research in education* (Vol. 10, pp. 103–150). Washington, DC: American Educational Research Association.

Woolfolk, A. E., & Brooks, D. (1985). The influence of teachers' nonverbal behaviors on students' perceptions and performance. *Elementary School Journal*, *85*, 514–528.

Woolfolk, A. E., Perry, N., & Winne, P. (2006). *Educational psychology: Third Canadian edition* (3rd ed.). Toronto, CA: Pearson.

Woolfolk, A. E., Rosoff, B., & Hoy, W. K. (1990). Teachers' sense of efficacy and their beliefs about managing students. *Teaching and Teacher Education*, *6*, 137–148.

Woolfolk Hoy, A., & Burke-Spero, R. (2005). Changes in teacher efficacy during the early years of teaching: A comparison of four measures. *Teaching and Teacher Education*, *21*, 343–356.

Woolfolk Hoy, A., Demerath, P., & Pape, S. (2002). Teaching adolescents: Engaging developing selves. In T. Urdan & F. Pajares (Eds.), *Adolescence and education* (pp. 119–169). Volume I. Greenwich, CT: Information Age Publishing.

Woolfolk Hoy, A., & Murphy, P. K. (2001). Teaching educational psychology to the implicit mind. In R. Sternberg & B. Torff (Eds.), *Understanding and teaching the implicit mind* (pp. 145–185). Mahwah, NJ: Lawrence Erlbaum.

Woolfolk Hoy, A., Pape, S., & Davis, H. (2006). Teachers' knowledge, beliefs, and thinking. In P. A. Alexander & P. H, Winne (Eds.), *Handbook of educational psychology* (2nd ed.). Mahwah, NJ: Lawrence Erlbaum.

Woolfolk Hoy, A., & Tschannen-Moran. M. (1999). Implications of cognitive approaches to peer learning for teacher education. In A. O'Donnell & A. King (Eds.), *Cognitive perspectives on peer learning* (pp. 257–284). Mahwah, NJ: Lawrence Erlbaum.

Woolfolk Hoy, A., & Weinstein, C. S. (2006). Students' and teachers' perspectives about classroom management. In C. Evertson & C. S. Weinstein (Eds.), *Handbook for classroom management: Research, practice, and contemporary issues*. Mahwah, NJ: Lawrence Erlbaum.

Wright, S. C., & Taylor, D. M. (1995). Identity and the language of the classroom: Investigating the impact of heritage versus second language instruction on personal and collective self-esteem. *Journal of Educational Psychology*, *87*, 241–252.

Wyler, R. S. (1988). Social memory and social judgment. In P. Solomon, G. Goethals, C. Kelly, & B. Stephans (Eds.), *Perspectives on memory research*. New York: Springer-Verlag.

Yarhouse, M. A. (2001). Sexual identity development: The influence of valuative frameworks on identity synthesis. *Psychotherapy*, 38 (3), 331–341

Yates, M., & Youniss, J. (1999). Promoting identity development: Ten ideas for school-based service-learning programs. In J. Claus & C. Ogden (Eds.), *Service learning for youth empowerment and social change* (pp. 43–67). New York: Peter Lang.

Yee, A. H. (1992). Asians as stereotypes and students: Misperceptions that persist. *Educational Psychology Review*, *4*, 95–132.

Yell, M. L. (1990). The use of corporal punishment, suspension, expulsion, and timeout with behaviorally disordered students in public schools: Legal considerations. *Behavioral Disorders*, *15*, 100–109.

Yerkes, R. M., & Dodson, J. D. (1908). The relation of strength of stimulus to rapidity of habit formation. *Journal of Comparative Neurology*, *18*, 459–482.

Yetman, N. R. (1999). *Majority and minority: The dynamics of race and ethnicity in American life* (6th ed.). Boston: Allyn and Bacon.

Yeung, A. S., McInerney, D. M., Russell-Bowie, D., Suliman, R., Chui, H., & Lau, I. C. (2000). Where is the hierarchy of academic self-concept? *Journal of Educational Psychology*, *92*, 556–567.

You and the system. (1991, April). *Teacher Magazine*, 32H.

Young, A. J. (1997). I think, therefore I'm motivated: The relations among cognitive strategy use, motivational orientation, and classroom perceptions over time. *Learning and Individual Differences*, *9*, 249–283.

Youniss, J., & Yates, M. (1997). *Community service and social responsibility in youth*. Chicago: University of Chicago Press.

Zeidner, M. (1995). Adaptive coping with test situations. *Educational Psychologist*, *30*, 123–134.

Zeidner, M. (1998). *Test anxiety: The state of the art.* New York: Plenum.

Zelli, A., Dodge, K. A., Lochman, J. E., & Laird, R. D. (1999). The distinction between beliefs legitimizing aggression and deviant processing of social cues: Testing measurement validity and the hypothesis that biased processing mediates the effects of beliefs on aggression. *Journal of Personality and Social Psychology, 77,* 150–166.

Zhou, Z., Peverly, S. T., Beohm, A. E., & Chongde, L. (2001). American and Chinese children's understanding of distance, time, and speed interrelations. *Cognitive Development, 15,* 215–240.

Zigmond, N., Jenkins, J., Fuchs, D., Deno, S., & Fuchs, L. S. (1995). When students fail to achieve satisfactorily: A reply to Leskey and Waldron. *Phi Delta Kappan, 77,* 303–306.

Zimmerman, B. J. (1995). Self-efficacy and educational development. In A. Bandura (Ed.), *Self-efficacy in changing societies* (pp. 202–231). New York: Cambridge University Press.

Zimmerman, B. J. (2002). Becoming a self-regulated learner: An overview. *Theory Into Practice, 41,* 64–70.

Zimmerman, B. J., & Schunk, D. H. (Eds.). (2001). *Self-regulated learning and academic achievement: Theoretical perspectives* (2nd ed.). Mahwah, NJ: Lawrence Erlbaum.

Zimmerman, B. J., & Schunk, D. H. (Eds). (2003). *Educational psychology: A century of contributions* [A Project of Division 15 (Educational Psychology) of the American Psychological Association]. Mahwah, NJ: Erlbaum.

Name Index

AAMR (American Association on Mental Retardation), 119, 139, 140
AAUW (American Association of University Women), 182
Abbeduto, L., 430
Aber, J. L., 79, 428, 432
Abi-Nader, J., 405
Aboud, F. E., 172
Abrams, I. M., 542
Abrams, L., 542
Ackerman, B. P., 166
Ackerman, P. L., 277
Ackerson, G., 293
Adler, S. A., 164
Agne, R. M., 485
Ainley, M., 384
Airasian, P. W., 556, 561, 566, 567, 579
Alao, S., 385
Albanese, M. A., 355
Alber, S. R., 216
Albert, K., 293
Alberto, P., 214, 215, 216, 221, 222, 228
Alderman, M. K., 403
Alexander, K. L., 69–70, 168
Alexander, P. A., 249, 250, 269, 278, 295, 304, 305, 334, 335, 372, 376, 381, 383
Allan, J., 302
Alleman-Brooks, J., 400
Alliance for Service Learning in Education Reform, 435
Allington, R., 500
Alloway, N., 500
Alloy, L. B., 393
Altermatt, E. R., 86
Alton-Lee, A., 447
Alvidrez, J., 499
Amabile, T. M., 305, 307
Amanti, C., 50, 51, 189
Amato, L. F., 74
Amato, P. R., 74
Ambridge, B., 254, 276
American Association of University Women (AAUW), 182
American Association on Mental Retardation (AAMR), 119, 139, 140
American Psychiatric Association, 134, 135
American Psychological Association, 435
Ames, C., 391, 396
Ames, R., 391
Ames, W., 293
Anastasi, A., 538, 543
Anastasiow, N. J., 146, 147, 268
Anderman, E. M., 102, 383, 389, 397
Andersen, C., 22, 66
Anderson, C. W., 288, 305, 382, 418, 507
Anderson, G. E., 572
Anderson, J. R., 249, 250, 252, 256, 260, 262, 264, 265, 275, 295, 299, 304, 320, 348, 365, 490
Anderson, L., 488
Anderson, L. M., 400, 448, 457, 491
Anderson, L. W., 285, 479, 481, 482
Anderson, M. L., 429
Anderson, N. B., 172
Anderson, P. J., 52
Anderson, R. C., 40
Anderson, S. M., 173
Anderson, T. H., 317
Angier, N., 180, 181
Angiulo, H., 50, 51
Anyon, J., 167
Archambault, F. X., 124
Archer, S. L., 71
Arends, R. I., 353, 355, 487, 496
Aristotle, 8, 208, 250
Armbruster, B. B., 317
Armento, B. J., 198, 471
Armer, M., 77
Armstrong, T., 279
Arnett, J. J., 101
Arnold, M. L., 97, 101
Aronson, E., 416, 425, 426, 429, 430, 433
Aronson, J., 174, 175
Ascham, R., 250
Ashcraft, M. H., 248, 250, 254, 255, 259, 263, 276, 277, 286
Ashley, L., 502
Associated Press, 465
Association for Supervision and Curriculum Development, 49
Association for the Gifted, 149
Atkinson, R. C., 250
Atkinson, R. K., 271, 298
Attanucci, J., 97
Au, K. H., 197
Aussiker, A., 471, 472
Austin, G. A., 248, 290
Austin, J. R., 383
Ausubel, D. P., 248, 292, 294
Avramidis, E., 128, 140
Ayotte, V., 86, 87
Ayres, L. R., 342
Ayres, N., 301

Babad, E. Y., 496, 499, 500
Bachman, J. G., 144
Baddeley, A. D., 254, 270
Baenninger, M., 181
Baer, J., 310
Bailey, J. M., 565, 573, 574, 579, 580, 581
Bailey, S. M., 180
Baillargeon, R., 30
Baker, C., 54
Baker, D., 180
Baker, E. L., 540, 546
Bakerman, R., 39
Baldwin, L., 536
Ball, D. L., 7, 501
Ballard, E. S., 331
Bandura, A., 78, 83, 85, 229, 230, 231, 232, 235, 330, 332, 333, 376, 383, 392, 395
Bangert-Drowns, R. L., 573
Banks, J. A., 162, 163, 164, 198
Banks, S. R., 557, 569, 582, 583
Barden, L. M., 495
Bargh, J. A., 268
Barker, G., 391
Barkowski, J. G., 360
Barling, J., 333
Barnhill, G. P., 222, 223, 225
Baron, R. A., 117, 121, 173, 470
Barone, F. J., 428
Baroody, A. R., 504
Barr, R., 502
Barrett, M., 378
Barron, K. E., 382
Barry, C. M., 77
Barry, M. J., 43
Bartini, M., 80
Bartlett, F. C., 264
Bartlett, L., 376
Barton-Arwood, S. M., 545
Baruth, L. G., 196
Basow, S. A., 151
Bass, K. E., 27
Bateman, B. D., 512
Battistich, V. A., 378, 416, 418
Battle, A. A., 415
Bauer, A. M., 222
Baughman, W. A., 274
Baumeister, R. F., 379
Baumrind, D., 74
Baxter, G., 546
Bayliss, P., 128, 140
Beane, J. A., 88, 390, 485
Bear, G. G., 447
Bear, T., 84
Beaudry, J. S., 126
Beck, I. L., 496
Becker, W. C., 12
Bee, H., 78
Beebe-Frankenberger, M., 572
Beeth, M. E., 507, 508
Beezer, B., 83
Beghetto, R. A., 306
Beier, M. E., 277
Beitzel, B. D., 272
Belanoff, P., 563
Belfiore, P. J., 235
Bell, R., 144
Belsito, L., 273, 311
Belsky, J., 68
Bempechat, J., 389
Benbow, C. P., 152, 278
Benenson, J. F., 178
Benjafield, J. G., 303
Bennett, C. I., 167, 196
Beohm, A. E., 57
Bereiter, C., 319, 348
Berends, M., 122
Berg, C. A., 490
Berger, K. S., 24, 44, 45, 49, 52, 54, 71, 73, 74, 79
Bergin, D., 403, 404
Berk, L. E., 23, 25, 33, 36, 37, 38, 43, 54, 55, 74, 78, 85, 94, 101, 150, 151, 176, 178, 179, 181, 192, 252, 306, 310
Berliner, D. C., 8, 14, 445, 446, 487, 495
Berlyne, D., 386
Berndorf, D., 384
Berndt, T. J., 167
Berthelot, J., 311
Bessenoff, G. R., 262

Bessler, B., 181
Betancourt, H., 164, 168
Betebenner, D. W., 540, 546
Bhatia, T. K., 54
Bialystok, E., 54
Biddle, B. J., 162
Bierman, K. L., 77
Biezuner, S., 427
Biggs, J., 125
Biglan, A., 466
Bimbela, A., 469
Binet, A., 119
Binney, E., 316
Birdyshaw, D., 502
Bixby, J., 545, 562, 563
Bjork, R. A., 263
Bjorklund, D. F., 38, 304, 310
Black, P., 570
Blackburn, M. V., 176
Blackman, G., 241
Bleeker, M. M., 180
Bloom, B. S., 150, 285, 481, 482, 574
Bloom, R., 573
Bluestein, J., 35, 216, 499
Blum, R. W., 438, 439, 461
Blumenfeld, P. C., 77, 395, 414, 446
Bocian, K. L., 572
Bodenhausen, C. V., 173
Boe, E. E., 548
Boggiano, A. K., 378
Boivin, M., 88
Bolick, C. M., 456
Boom, J., 96
Booth, A., 74
Borich, G., 89
Borko, H., 4, 6, 11, 15, 356, 501
Borkowski, J. G., 136
Borman, G. D., 167, 192
Bornstein, M. H., 415
Bos, C. S., 198
Bosworth, K., 82
Boudett, K. P., 569
Bourdon, L., 573
Bowen, G. M., 358
Bowers, J., 347
Boyd, D., 23, 101
Boyle, M. O., 277
Boyle, R. A., 305, 372
Braddock, J., II, 123
Bradley, R., 131
Brady, M. P., 139
Brandt, R., 321
Brannon, L., 176, 179, 180
Bransford, J. D., 23, 24, 25, 49, 249, 267, 276, 295, 296, 319, 320
Bray, M. A., 226, 229
Bray, M. L., 151
Bredderman, T., 354
Bredekamp, S., 46
Brehm, K., 194
Breland, P. S., 112
Brendgen, M., 572
Brice, A. E., 186
Brobst, K., 314
Brody, L., 178
Broidy, L. M., 79
Bronfenbrenner, U., 63, 72–84, 103, 166
Brooks, D., 453, 460, 500
Brooks, F., 80
Brooks, J. G., 501, 502
Brooks, M. G., 501, 502
Brooks-Gunn, J., 65, 162, 168
Brophy, J., 46, 124, 498, 499, 500
Brophy, J. E., 8, 9, 12, 217, 373, 386, 392, 395, 400, 404, 405, 444, 462, 487, 492, 498
Brown, A. L., 23, 249, 267, 276, 313, 360, 361, 362, 376, 419, 486, 503
Brown, B. B., 414, 415
Brown, E. D., 166
Brown, J., 174
Brown, J. L., 79, 428, 432
Brown, J. S., 275, 357
Brown, L., 171
Brown, N., 351, 352
Brown, R., 313
Brown, V. R., 310
Brubaker, N. L., 400
Bruce, B. C., 493, 496
Bruer, John T., 27, 183
Brugman, D., 96
Bruner, J. S., 48, 248, 286, 290–292, 350, 414
Bruning, R. H., 267, 296, 344, 347
Brusca-Vega, R., 154
Bruschi, C., 77
Buckner, L., 84
Buehler, R., 303
Bugental, D. B., 469
Bulgren, J. A., 294
Burbules, N. C., 493, 496
Burden, P. R., 450, 460, 464
Burden, R., 128, 140
Burk-Braxton, C., 92
Burke-Spero, R., 334, 471
Burland, S., 267
Bursuck, W. D., 128, 129, 130, 135, 147, 314, 315, 509, 510, 511, 581
Burton, R. V., 101
Burwich, D., 209
Bush, G. W., 2, 540
Buss, D. M., 181
Buswell, B. N., 89
Butler, R., 381, 399, 573
Buxton, W. M., 385
Bybee J., 97
Byrne, B. M., 86, 502
Byrne, D., 470
Byrnes, J. P., 24, 25, 113, 170, 171, 313, 345, 346

Calderhead, J., 479
Caldwell, K. A., 77
Calhoun, E., 287, 288, 289, 290
Callahan, C. M., 116, 149
Cambourne, B., 566
Cameron, J., 239
Cameron, R., 267
Camp, R., 563
Campbell, W. K., 89
Campione, J. C., 267, 361, 362, 376
Canfield, J., 89
Cangelosi, J. S., 482
Canter, L., 469, 471
Canter, M., 469, 471
Capa, Y., 334
Capon, N., 355
Carauna, V., 3
Cariglia-Bull, T., 278
Carlisle, J. F., 502
Carlton, M. P., 43
Carnegie Council on Adolescent Development, 123
Carney, R. N., 272
Carpendale, J. I. M., 97
Carroll, A., 135
Carroll, J. B., 112, 113
Carter, E. W., 543, 544, 545
Carver, G. W., 190
Casanova, U., 169, 170
Casas, J. F., 79
Case, R., 37, 46, 276, 277
Cassady, J. C., 387
Castellano, J. A., 186
Castle, S., 122, 123–124
Cattell, R. B., 112
Cauffman, E., 101
Caughy, M. O., 92
Ceci, S. J., 39, 56, 121, 166
Center for the Improvement of Early Reading Achievement, 503
Center on Education Policy, 2, 548
Chamot, A. U., 188
Chan, C. K., 318
Chance, P., 238, 239
Chandler, P., 297
Chang, K., 180, 181
Chapman, J. W., 86
Chappuis, J., 571
Charles, C. M., 451, 460, 461, 469
Charles, R., 173
Charness, N., 304
Chartrand, T. L., 268
Chase, W. G., 303
Chavez, C., 430
Chen, Z., 322, 324, 355
Chesterfield, Lord, 250
Cheyne, J. A., 43
Chi, M. T. H., 297, 303, 305
Chih-Mei, C., 170
Children's Defense Fund, 83, 162, 165, 166, 433
Chongde, L., 57
Chudowsky, N., 542
Chui, H., 86
Chumlea, W. C., 102
City, E., 569
Claiborn, W. L., 499
Clark, A. G., 70
Clark, C. M., 15, 478, 479
Clark, J. M., 259, 270
Clark, R., 172
Clark, V. R., 172
Clarke, J. H., 485
Clarke, M., 542
Claus, J., 436
Clifford, M. M., 391, 404, 571
Clinkenbeard, P. R., 122, 123, 151, 152
Clore, G. L., 375
Clough, M., 490
Cobb, C. D., 116
Cobb, C. E., Jr., 6
Cobb, P., 347, 381
Cocking, R. R., 23, 249, 276
Codell, E. R., 15, 309, 321, 429, 430, 431
Coffield, F. J., 125, 126, 127
Cognition and Technology Group at Vanderbilt, 352, 353–354
Cohen, E. G., 418, 419
Cohen, I., 465
Cohen, J., 81, 93
Coie, J. D., 77
Cokley, K. O., 175
Cole, D. A., 89
Cole, M., 346
Cole, N. S., 181
Cole, R., 166
Coleman, D., 313
Coleman, J. S., 2
Coleman, M. R., 268
Collier, V. P., 187, 188
Collins, A. M., 248–249, 275, 348, 357, 375, 486
Collins, W. A., 415
Colvin, G., 224, 466
Comenius, 8
Comer, J. P., 192–193

Committee on Increasing High School Students' Engagement and Motivation to Learn, 122, 343, 382, 403, 404, 413, 414, 415, 432
Confrey, J., 46, 350, 506
Conger, J. J., 22
Connell, J. P., 573
Connell, R. W., 183
Conway, P. F., 15
Cook, G., 23, 24, 64, 101
Cook, J. L., 23, 24, 64, 101
Cooke, B. L., 15
Cooper, C. R., 71
Cooper, G., 298
Cooper, H. M., 88, 332, 491, 492, 498, 500
Cooper, J., 560
Cooper, J. M., 456
Cooper, J. O., 235
Cooper, M., 298
Copi, I. M., 300
Coplan, R. J., 77
Copple, C., 46
Cordes, S. A., 38
Cordova, D. I., 384
Corkill, A. J., 293
Corno, L., 122, 125, 336, 341, 354, 491, 573
Costanza, D. P., 274
Cota-Robles, S., 65
Cothran, D. J., 83
Covaleskie, J. F., 469
Covington, M. V., 88, 373, 387, 393
Cowley, G., 383
Coyne, P., 513
Craig, D., 101
Craik, F. I. M., 256, 263–264
Cramond, B., 307
Crapo, R. H., 42
Craven, J. A., III., 7
Craven, R., 86
Crawford, J., 188
Cremin, L., 362
Crick, N. R., 79
Crisci, P. E., 88
Crocker, J., 88
Crone, D. A., 224
Cronin, J. F., 362
Crook, M. D., 27
Cross, W. E., 91, 92
Crosson-Tower, C., 84
Crowley, E., 311
Crowley, K., 12
Cruickshank, D. R., 487
Csikszentmihalyi, M., 307
Cubberly, E. P., 9
Cummins, D. D., 296
Cummins, J., 52, 185
Cunningham, A. E., 69, 88, 258
Cunningham, D. J., 350
Cunningham, E., 224
Current Directions in Psychological Science, 121
Curwin, R., 451
Cuskelly, M., 119

Dahl, T., 313
Dailey, D., 231
Daley, T. C., 120
Damon, W., 95
Danielson, L., 131
Dansereau, D. F., 424
Darcey, J. S., 64
Dark, V. J., 278
Darling, N., 414, 415
Darling-Hammond, L., 4, 487
Das, J. P., 42, 48
Davidson, J. W., 150, 296
Davies, K., 180
Davis, G. A., 102, 103, 151, 514
Davis, H. A., 74, 82, 83, 389
Davis-Kean, P. E., 86
Deaux, K., 176
DeCapua, A., 126
DeCecco, J., 428
deCharms, R., 378
Deci, E. L., 88, 238, 239, 373, 374, 375, 377, 378, 390
De Corte, E., 296, 319, 321, 345
DeCourcey, W., 383
Dee, J. R., 8
DeFalco, K., 80
De Kock, A., 344
Delaney, H. D., 272
deLara, E., 80
Delgardelle, M., 364
De Lisi, R., 557, 563, 573
Delpit, L., 37, 56, 184, 185, 189, 190, 191, 198
Delucci, K., 418
Demana, F., 301
Demerath, P., 167, 434–435, 436
Demientieff, M., 184
Dempster, F. N., 555, 556, 561
Deniz, C. B., 122, 123–124
Derry, S. J., 295, 311, 312, 345, 348
Deshler, D. D., 268, 294
Detterman, D. L., 111
Devich-Navarro, M., 91
Dewey, J., 8, 295, 351, 385, 417
Diamond, L. M., 176
Diaz, E. I., 186
Diaz, R. M., 52
Diaz-Rico, L. T., 52
Di Cintio, M. J., 278
Dickson, M., 563
Diebert, E., 546
Dierrida, J., 346
Diller, L., 135
Dillon, L., 135
Dindia, K., 180
Dingfelder, S. F., 195
Dinnel, D., 293
Dishner, E. K., 9
DiVesta, F. J., 278
Dobyns, S. M., 124
Doctorow, M., 315
Dodge, K. A., 77, 78, 94, 433
Dodson, J. D., 386, 387
Doggett, A. M., 135, 136
Doherty, K. M., 541
Doleys, D. M., 222
Dolezal, S. E., 385, 401, 402
Dolgin, K. G., 65, 144
Doll, B., 192, 193, 194
Donelson, R., 176
Dornbusch, S. M., 76, 415
Dow, G. T., 306
Dowler, J., 342
Doyle, W., 444, 446, 460
Drake, M., 238, 239
Drayer, A. M., 578
Drew, C. J., 110, 111, 126, 133, 146, 151, 152, 513
Driscoll, A., 490, 496
Driscoll, M. P., 26, 39, 42, 250, 252, 257, 259, 260, 320, 345, 348, 490, 580
Drummond, L., 339, 342, 343
DuBois, D. L., 88, 92, 332
Dubois, W. E. B., 90
Dudley, B., 428
Duell, O. K., 495
Duffett, A., 129
Duffy, G. G., 400
Dufresne, R., 304
Duncan, C., 433
Duncan, G. J., 162, 168
Duncan, R. M., 43
Duncker, K., 302
Dunn, K., 125, 126
Dunn, R., 125, 126
DuPaul, G. J., 216, 228, 229
Dupree, D., 168
Durbin, D. L., 414, 415
Dusenbury, L., 144
Dweck, C. S., 238, 388, 389
Dyson, A. H., 398

Eaton, J. F., 305
Eccles, J. S., 70, 78, 86, 89, 90, 376, 387, 396, 404
Ecclestone, K., 125
Echevarria, M., 351
Edelman, G. M., 23
Egan, M. W., 110, 111, 126, 133, 146, 151, 152, 513
Egan, S. K., 78
Eggen, P. D., 288
Eiseman, J. W., 100
Eisenberg, N., 97, 101
Eisenberg, R., 239
Eisner, E. W., 562
Elashoff, J. D., 499
Elawar, M. C., 573
Elias, M. J., 93, 437, 451, 452, 461, 462, 463
Elkind, D., 36
Elliot, A. J., 382
Elliot, E. C., 559
Ellis, E. S., 268
Ellis, H. C., 250
Ellis, J. A., 266
Elrich, M., 167
Embry, D. D., 226
Emerson, M. J., 43
Emmer, E. T., 444, 447, 448, 450, 451, 457, 458, 459, 460, 462, 471, 472
Engelhart, M. D., 285, 481
Engle, R. W., 276, 277
Ennis, C. D., 83
Entwisle, D. R., 69–70, 168
Enwistle, N. J., 125
Epanchin, B. C., 226
Epstein, J. L., 123, 193, 396, 493
Eresh, J. T., 567
Ericsson, K. A., 304
Erikson, E. H., 63, 67–72, 88, 103, 177
Eron, L. D., 78
Espe, C., 353
Espinosa, L., 52
Espinosa, M. P., 120
Ettenberger, S., 340
Evans, E. D., 101
Evans, G. W., 72, 166, 168
Evans, L., 180
Evensen, D. H., 355
Evertson, C. M., 9, 12, 444, 448, 450, 457, 458, 459, 460, 487
Ewy, C., 544

Fabes, R. A., 97, 101
Fagot, B. I., 178, 179
Falco, M., 144
Falk, K., 222
Fantuzzo, J., 102, 103
Farivar, S. H., 420, 421
Farkas, S., 129
Farnham-Diggory, S., 258
Farr, M., 305
Feather, N. T., 376
Feldman, J., 287
Feldman, R. S., 64
Feldman, S. S., 101
Fennema, E., 183
Ferrara, R., 267

Feshbach, N., 117
Fielding-Barnsley, R., 502
Fier, J., 89
Fillmore, L. W., 185
Finkel, D., 112
Finlan, M., 132
Finn, J., 500
Fischer, K. W., 38
Fiske, E. B., 542
Fiske, S. T., 498
Fitts, P. M., 275
Fitzgerald, J., 188
Fives, H. R., 334
Flammer, A., 333
Flavell, E. R., 278
Flavell, J. H., 28, 30, 31, 52, 93, 252, 278
Fleishman, E. A., 274
Fleith, D., 309
Flink, C. F., 378
Floden, R. E., 7, 486
Florio, S., 197
Flynn, J., 120
Foley, H. J., 260
Ford, D., 351, 352
Ford, D. Y., 152
Forness, S. R., 140
Forster, K. I., 253
Foster, W., 572
Foucault, M., 346
Fox, J., 173
Fox, L. H., 151
Fox, N. A., 24, 25, 113
Fox, P. W., 418
Frank, A., 293
Frank, S. J., 71
Frankenberg, E., 171
Fraser, J. W., 471
Fredericks, L., 434
Fredricks, J. A., 77, 335, 414, 446
Freiberg, H. J., 374, 430, 447, 458, 461, 466, 472, 490, 496
Freud, S., 67, 310
Frey, K. S., 86
Frick, T. W., 459
Fridlund, A. J., 171, 307
Friedrichs, A. G., 278
Friend, M., 128, 129, 130, 135, 140, 141, 142, 146, 147, 148, 151, 154, 314, 315, 509, 510, 511
Frisbie, D. A., 574
Fritz, E., 135
Fromberg, D. P., 580
Frost, E. J., 285, 481
Frost, R., 495
Fuchs, D., 123, 152
Fuchs, L. S., 123, 152, 339
Fulk, C. L., 238
Fuller, F. G., 15
Furrer, C., 379
Furst, N., 487

Gabelko, N. H., 166
Gaedke, B., 395
Gage, N. L., 10
Gagné, E. D., 250, 258, 260, 261, 264, 275, 300
Galambos, S. J., 54
Galanter, E., 248, 375
Galen, B. R., 78
Galileo, 307
Gall, M., 487
Gallager, J. A., 152
Gallagher, J. J., 146, 147, 152, 268
Gallagher, M., 465
Gallagher, S., 397
Gallimore, R., 40, 162, 496
Gallini, J. K., 270, 295
Gallup, A. M., 428, 461
Gamoran, A., 123, 167
Gao, X., 546
Garbarino, J., 80
Garcia, E. E., 54, 169, 184, 185, 187, 195
Garcia, R. L., 166, 169
Gardner, H., 55, 113–116, 114, 149, 169, 273, 311, 321, 545, 562, 563
Gardner, R., 313
Garmon, A., 122
Garner, P. W., 76
Garner, R., 269, 278, 398
Garnets, L., 177
Garrett, J., 468
Garrison, J., 345, 348
Garrod, A., 97
Garvin, R. A., 43
Gathercole, S. E., 254, 276
Gatz, M., 112
Gay, G., 190, 191, 196, 198, 470, 471
Geary, D. C., 38, 181, 346
Gehlbach, H., 94
Gelernter, D., 301
Gelman, R., 38
Gentner, D., 260, 298, 300
George, P. S., 514, 515
Gergen, K. J., 346
Gerig, T. M., 498
Gersten, R., 131, 185, 187, 188, 189
Gerwels, M. C., 448, 450, 459
Gibbs, J. W., 219
Gick, M. L., 295, 299
Gill, H. S., 25
Gillett, M., 487
Gillies, R., 416, 417, 419, 420
Gilligan, C., 97
Ginsburg, H. P., 504
Ginsburg, M., 102, 103
Girls' Math Achievement: What We Do and Don't Know, 182
Gitomer, D. H., 567
Glaser, R., 305
Glasgow, K. L., 76
Glasser, W., 70, 447, 462, 471
Glassman, M., 44
Gleitman, H., 171, 307
Glenberg, A., 263
Glenn, J., III, 355, 545, 562, 563
Glock, M. D., 499
Glover, J. A., 293
Goetz, T., 383
Goldenberg, C., 162, 187, 188, 357
Goldin-Meadow, S., 54
Goldman, S. R., 511
Goldsmith, M., 264
Goleman, D., 116, 121, 167
Gonzalez, E., 180–181
Gonzalez, N., 50, 51, 189
Gonzalez, V., 154
Good, C., 174
Good, T. L., 46, 124, 125, 341, 343, 386, 418, 447, 453, 487, 492, 495, 496, 498, 499, 500, 516
Goodman, K. S., 502
Goodman, Y. M., 502
Goodnow, J. J., 248, 290
Goodrich, H., 567
Gordon, D., 225
Gordon, E. W., 196
Gordon, J., 168
Gordon, J. A., 471
Gordon, T., 467, 469, 471
Gottfredson, D. C., 448
Gottfredson, G. D., 448
Gould, L. J., 188
Graham, S., 10, 52, 79, 80, 117, 133, 238, 333, 334, 372, 377, 390, 391, 392, 415, 490
Graham, S. M., 52
Grant, C. A., 162
Gray, P., 254, 255, 259
Gredler, M. E., 45, 47, 278
Green, F. L., 278
Greenberg, M. T., 438
Greene, D., 238
Greeno, J. G., 248–249, 348, 486
Greenwald, A. G., 172
Gregorc, A. F., 125, 126
Gregory, K., 542
Gresham, F. M., 572
Greulich, F. K., 86
Griffin, D., 303
Griggs, S., 125
Grigorenko, E. L., 118
Grissom, J. B., 572
Grolnick, W. S., 383
Gronlund, N. E., 479, 480, 481, 532, 557, 559
Grossman, H., 89, 181, 197
Grossman, S. H., 89, 181, 197
Grotevant, H. D., 71
Gruson, L., 267
Guay, F., 88
Guilford, J. P., 113
Gulek, C., 542
Gurian, M., 182, 183
Gurland, S. T., 383
Guskey, T. R., 565, 573, 574, 579, 580, 581
Gustafsson, J-E., 112
Guthrie, J. T., 385, 398
Gutman, L. M., 166

Haager, D., 128
Hacker, D. J., 503
Hadwin, A. F., 336, 338
Haertel, E. H., 568
Hagan, R., 178, 179
Hagborg, W. J., 85
Hakuta, K., 185, 187, 188
Haladyna, T. H., 541, 542, 543, 574
Hale, N. M., 70, 101
Halford, J. M., 162
Hall, E., 125
Hall, J. S., 8
Hall, J. W., 272
Hall, L. K., 295, 307
Hallahan, D. P., 6, 25, 82, 110, 131, 132, 133, 134, 135, 138, 147, 279, 513
Hallowell, E. M., 134
Halpern, D. F., 181
Hambleton, R. K., 545, 546
Hambrick, D. Z., 277
Hamlett, C. L., 123, 152
Hamm, D., 398
Hamm, J., 415
Hamman, D., 311, 334
Hanson, A. R., 233
Hanson, S. L., 88
Hanushek, E. A., 4
Hao, L., 54
Harackiewicz, J. M., 382
Hardesty, J. L., 92
Hardiman, P. T., 304
Hardman, M. L., 110, 111, 126, 133, 134, 136, 138, 146, 151, 152, 513
Harme, B., 3
Harmin, M., 490

Harp, S. F., 385
Harpalani, V., 175
Harrington, H. J., 419
Harris, E., 433
Harris, J. R., 76
Harris, K. R., 133, 238, 490
Harrison, C., 570
Harrow, A. J., 482
Harter, S., 85, 86
Hartup, W. W., 77
Hatch, T., 114
Hattie, J., 135
Hau, K-T., 86
Haugh, G. P., 302
Hawkins, M. R., 185
Hayes, M. T., 385
Hayes, S. C., 235
Hayman, M. L., 458
Haynes, N. M., 192–193
Haywood, H. C., 41, 43, 49
Heath, S. B., 57
Helmke, A., 488, 490
Helms, J. E., 92
Helwig, C. C., 101
Henderson, M., 492
Hendley, S. G., 270
Henkin, A. B., 8
Henley, P., 182, 183
Hennig, K. H., 97
Herbert, E. A., 453
Herman, J., 562, 567, 568
Herman, K. C., 80
Herman, M., 91, 92
Hernshaw, L. S., 248
Herrenkohl, L. R., 422
Herzig, A. H., 173
Hess, D., 496
Hess, R., 170
Hetherington, E. M., 74, 415
Heuer, F., 383
Heward, W. L., 216
Hewson, P. W., 507
Hewstone, M., 498
Hickey, D. T., 39, 345, 355, 376
Hidi, S., 383, 384
Hilgard, E. R., 8
Hill, A., 135
Hill, W. F., 206, 211, 229, 230
Hill, W. H., 285, 481
Hilliard, A. G., III, 197
Hines, C. V., 487
Hiroto, D. S., 392
Hirsch, E. D., Jr., 360
Hmelo-Silver, C. E., 353, 354, 355
Hodges, E. V. E., 80
Hoefler-Nissani, D. M., 507
Hofer, B. K., 311, 318
Hoffman, H. G., 172
Hoffman, M. L., 75, 101
Hogan, T., 7
Hoge, D. R., 88
Holahan, C., 150
Holland, J. D., 382, 418
Holliday, G., 151
Holmes, I. W. M., 88
Holum, A., 357
Homestead, E. R., 485
Hoover-Dempsey, K. V., 492
Hopkins, B. L., 226
Horgan, D. D., 182
Horn, C., 542
Horn, J. L., 112
Horner, R. H., 224
Hornyak, R. S., 235
Horowitz, B., 209
Horvath, J. A., 118–119
Hotkevich, M., 353
Howe, M. J. A., 150
Howell, K. L., 318
Hoy, W. K., 334
Hoyt, J. D., 278
Hudley, C., 415
Huesmann, L. R., 78
Huff, C. R., 433
Hughes, C., 545
Hulbert, A., 180
Hung, D. W. L., 357
Hunt, E., 112
Hunt, J. McV., 46, 49
Hunt, N., 132, 146, 147, 152
Hunt, R. R., 250
Hunter, M., 461
Hutchinson, J. M., 235
Hutchinson, L., 298, 300
Hybl, L. G., 448
Hyde, J. S., 89, 181
Hyman, I., 465

Inbar, J., 500
Institute for Human Machine Cognition, 314, 315
Inzlicht, M., 174
Iran-Nejad, A., 274
Irvine, J. J., 198, 470, 471
Irving, J., 305, 306
Irving, O., 462
Irwin, J. W., 313
Isabella, R., 68
Ishler, M., 487
Itzen, R. C., 126
Izard, C. E., 117, 166

Jackson, A., 514
Jackson, D., 125, 336
Jackson, N. E., 151
Jacob, K. F., 383
Jacobs, C. E., 177
Jacobs, J. E., 89, 90, 180
Jacobson, L., 496
James, W., 8, 88, 273
Jarrett, R., 76
Jay, E., 358, 359, 361
Jeffries, R., 360
Jensen, L. A., 101, 102
Jenson, W. R., 226, 229
Jimenez, R., 403
Jimerson, S. R., 572
Johnson, A. M., 435, 437
Johnson, D. W., 399, 400, 420, 426, 427, 428, 429, 430, 565, 567, 568
Johnson, J. F., 129, 166, 170
Johnson, R. E., 387
Johnson, R. T., 399, 400, 420, 426, 427, 428, 429, 430, 565, 567, 568
Johnson, S. M., 250, 545
John-Steiner, V., 39, 42
Johnston, L. D., 144
Jonassen, D. H., 296
Jones, D. C., 65
Jones, E. D., 152
Jones, K., 541
Jones, M. G., 498
Jones, M. S., 272
Jones, S. M., 79, 180, 428, 432
Joyce, B. R., 287, 288, 289, 290
Joyner, E. T., 192–193
Jurden, F. H., 278

Kafka, K., 576
Kagan, J., 22
Kagan, S., 419, 421, 424
Kail, R., 295
Kain, J. F., 4
Kalyuga, S., 297, 298
Kanaya, T., 121
Kane, M. J., 277
Kantor, H., 171
Kaplan, A., 381
Kaplan, J. S., 222, 235
Kardash, C. M., 318
Karns, K., 123, 152
Karpov, Y. V., 41, 43, 49
Karweit, N., 445, 478
Kash, M. M., 89
Katz, P. A., 172
Katz, S. R., 83
Kauchak, D. P., 288
Kauffman, J. M., 6, 12, 25, 82, 110, 132, 138, 147, 153, 210, 216, 217, 221, 224, 238, 279, 513
Kay, B., 465
Kazdin, A. E., 215, 216, 219, 227
Kearns, J. F., 536
Keavney, M., 238, 239
Keefe, J. W., 125, 126
Keefe, K., 167
Kehle, T. J., 151, 226, 229
Kelly, J., 74
Kelly, K., 572, 573
Kemp, S. E., 222
Kennedy, A. M., 180–181
Kennedy, J. F., 262
Kennedy, J. J., 487
Kennelly, K. J., 387
Keough, K., 174
Kerckhoff, A. C., 123
Kershner, R., 454
Keyser, V., 333
Kher, N., 404
Kiewra, K. A., 293, 313, 314, 338
Kim, K. M., 101
Kindsvatter, R., 487
King, A., 416, 419, 420, 423, 424
King, G., 577
King, M. L., Jr., 430
Kintsch, W., 258
Kirk, S. A., 10, 146, 147, 424
Kirst, M., 545, 561
Kishor, N., 88
Klahr, D., 355
Klassen, R. M., 392
Klatzky, R. L., 173, 250
Klausmeier, H. J., 287, 288
Klavas, A., 126
Klebold, D., 433
Klein, P., 116
Klein, S., 180
Kleinert, H. L., 536
Kling, K. C., 89
Klingner, J. K., 128
Klinzing, H. G., 7
Knapp, M., 198, 349
Kneedler, P., 361
Knitzer, J., 140
Knuth, E. J., 506
Koenig, O., 260
Koestner, R., 239, 373
Kohl, H., 453
Kohlberg, L., 95–98, 101
Kohn, A., 238, 239, 431, 574
Kokko, K., 79
Kolb, G., 24, 126
Kolbe, L., 433
Koller, O., 491
Kopeikin, H., 469
Korenman, S., 168
Korf, R., 299
Koriat, A., 264
Korn, Z., 235
Koser, L., 12
Kosslyn, S. M., 260
Kotrez, D., 546
Kounin, J. S., 233, 460

Kozol, J., 167
Kozulin, A., 39, 40, 41, 45, 49
Krank, H. M., 469
Krapp, A., 383
Krathwohl, D. R., 285, 479, 481, 482
Krauss, M., 54
Kreitzer, A. E., 481
Kroesbergen, E. H., 506
Kroger, J., 71
Kronsberg, S., 179
Kruger, A. C., 48
Krumboltz, H. B., 221
Krumboltz, J. D., 221, 574
Krupinski, S., 464
Kucan, L., 496
Kuhn, D., 355
Kuklinski, M. R., 498, 499, 500
Kulik, C. C., 122, 123, 152, 573
Kulik, J. A., 122, 123, 152, 573
Kulikowich, J. M., 278
Kurlakowsky, K. D., 70
Kurtz-Costes, B., 162, 168, 169

Lachter, J., 253
Ladson-Billings, G., 171, 189, 190, 191, 198
Laird, R. D., 78
Lake, K., 576
Lambert, A. J., 172
Lambert, N. M., 453
Lambert, S. F., 70
Lanam, D., 301
Land, D., 195
Land, M. L., 487
Landrum, T. J., 12, 210, 216, 217, 221, 224, 238
Lane, K., 222
Langan-Fox, J., 293
Language Development and Hypermedia Group, 349
Lanza, S., 89, 90
Larose, S., 88
Larrivee, B., 509
Lashley, T. J., II, 351
Latham, A. S., 180
Latham, G. P., 226, 235, 375, 380, 383
Lather, P., 14
Lau, I. C., 86
Lau, S., 391
Lauver, K., 324
Lave, J., 320, 348, 357, 376, 377
Lawless, K., 511
Le, L., 324
Leaper, C., 178
Leary, M. R., 379
Lee, A. Y., 298, 300
Lee, C., 570
Lee, L., 377
Lee, R. M., 168, 192
Lee, S., 491
Lefton, L. A., 67
Lehman, D. R., 36
Lehman, S., 384
Leinbach, M. D., 179
Leinhardt, G., 7, 490
Lelli, K., 149
LeMahieu, P., 567
Leming, J. S., 88
Lenz, B. K., 268, 294
LePore, P. C., 122
Lepper, M. R., 238, 239, 384
Leslie, L., 249
Levin, J. R., 271, 272, 462, 463
Levin, M. E., 272
Lewin, K., 417
Lewinsohn, P. M., 144
Lewis, C., 378, 416
Lewis, J. C., 469
Lewis, M., 112
Lewis, R., 472
Lewis, T. J., 224, 466
Liben, L. S., 178
Lickona, T., 431
Lin, E. K., 469
Lin, Y., 387
Lindsay, J. J., 492
Lindsay, P. H., 250
Linn, M. C., 181
Linn, R. L., 522, 532, 540, 541, 542, 546
Lipman, P., 582
Lipson, M. Y., 258
Little, T. D., 149
Liu, W. M., 165
Livingston, C., 6, 11
Lloyd, J. W., 110
Lochman, J. E., 78
Locke, E. A., 226, 235, 375, 380, 383
Lockhart, R. S., 256, 263–264
Loewenstein, J., 298
Loftus, E., 265
Loomis, L. S., 74
Lopez, S. R., 164, 168
Lorch, E. P., 313
Lorch, R. F., 313
Louis, B., 112
Lovelace, M. K., 126
Loveless, T., 123, 124
Lovett, M. W., 134
Lowe, R., 171
Lowenstein, G., 386
Lowry, R., 433
Lubienski, S. T., 501
Luftig, R. L., 82
Luiten, J., 293
Lunsford, L. B., 545
Lustina, M. J., 174, 175
Luyben, P. D., 219
Lyon, J. E., 469

Ma, X., 88
Maag, J. W., 222
Maas, C. J. M., 506
Mabry, L., 566, 568
Maccoby, E. E., 178, 415
Mace, F. C., 235
Machado, A., 29
Macionis, J. J., 165, 168, 171
MacIver, D. J., 70, 123
MacMillan, D. L., 572
Macrae, C. N., 173
Madaus, G. F., 481, 542
Madison, S. M., 500
Madsen, C. H., 12
Maehr, M. L., 382, 383, 389, 397
Mager, R., 480
Magnuson, D., 428
Magnuson, S. J., 351, 352
Magnusson, S. J., 351
Mahn, H., 39, 42
Mahon, M., 465
Maier, N. R. F., 302
Major, B., 175
Maker, C. J., 151
Manning, B. H., 237
Manning, M. L., 196
Mantzicopolos, P., 573
Marano, N., 351, 352
Marcia, J. E., 70, 71
Marcus, N., 298
Mare, R. D., 123
Marinova-Todd, S., 52
Markakis, K. M., 378
Markman, E. M., 52, 278
Marks, C., 315
Markstrom-Adams, C., 91, 92
Marsh, H. W., 86, 88, 90
Marshall, B., 570
Marshall, D., 52
Marshall, H. H., 89, 345, 348, 365
Marshall, K., 132, 146, 147, 152
Martin, C. L., 97
Martin, J. M., 89, 462
Martin, M. O., 180–181
Martinez, E. A., 110
Martinez-Pons, M., 334, 340
Marx, R. W., 305, 372
Marzano, J. S., 444
Marzano, R. J., 334, 444
Masia, B. B., 482
Maslow, A. H., 374–375, 377, 387, 417
Mason, D. A., 125
Massa, L. J., 126, 127
Mastergeorge, A. M., 420, 421
Matczynski, T. J., 351
Matisse, 307
Matlin, M. W., 260
Matsuba, M. K., 97
Matthews, G., 116
Mautone, P. D., 259
Mayer, G. R., 215, 227
Mayer, J. D., 116
Mayer, R. E., 126, 127, 249, 259, 270, 288, 291, 292, 295, 296, 298, 319, 344, 354, 359, 360, 385, 501
McArdle, J. J., 112
McCafferty, S. G., 43
McCarthy, M. R., 224, 466
McCaslin, M., 39, 341, 343, 345, 355, 418, 447, 462
McClelland, D. C., 121, 393
McClelland, P., 166
McClure, P., 548, 582
McCoach, D. B., 151
McCombs, B. L., 334
McCoy, A. R., 572
McDermott, D. F., 541
McDermott, T. K., 541
McDevitt, T. M., 170
McDonald, J. P., 568
McGinnis, K. L., 485
McGoey, K. E., 216, 228, 229
McGovern, L., 313
McGrath, E. P., 469
McInerney, D. M., 86
McKeachie, W. J., 387
McKenzie, T. L., 236
McKeown, M. G., 496
McLoyd, V. C., 162, 166
McMillan, J. H., 556, 557, 568
McNeely, C. A., 461
McNeil, L. M., 542
McNemar, Q., 112
Mears, T., 54
Mediascope, 78
Medina, J., 542
Meece, J. L., 23, 24, 27, 35, 48, 70, 110, 132, 162, 168, 169, 180
Meek, A., 501
Meichenbaum, D., 236, 267
Meijer, A. M., 387
Meister, C., 49, 360, 419, 503
Meltzoff, A. N., 30
Mendell, P. R., 260
Menkart, D. J., 189
Menke, D. J., 313
Mercer, L. K., 341, 343
Mergendoller, J. R., 395
Merrell, K. W., 89
Merrill, M. M., 298
Merseth, K. K., 504
Merton, R. K., 496

Merzenich, M., 27
Messick, S., 532
Mestre, J. P., 304
Metcalfe, J., 267
Metzler, C. W., 466
Mewborn, D. S., 501
Meyer, M., 364
Meyers, C., 564
Michael, R. S., 470
Michelangelo, 307
Middleton, J., 364
Middleton, M., 381
Midgley, C., 70, 102, 381
Midobuche, E., 190
Mifflin, M., 179
Mignano, A., 5, 446, 449, 450, 451, 452, 453, 454, 458, 462, 491, 492, 495
Miller, A., 82, 381
Miller, G. A., 248, 254, 375
Miller, J., 168
Miller , M. D., 522
Miller, N., 419
Miller, P. D., 502
Miller, P. H., 28, 38, 72, 93, 345, 383
Miller, R. B., 218
Miller, R. R., 208
Miller, S. A., 28, 93, 253
Miller, S. P., 293
Mills, J. R., 151
Milne, A. B., 173
Milner, H. R., 92, 189, 471
Mischel, W., 117
Mistretta, J., 340
Mitchell, B. M., 152
Mitchell, M., 384
Mitchell, S. A., 355
Miyake, A., 43
Mo, L., 324
Moen, P., 166
Moise-Titus, J., 78
Moll, L. C., 50, 51, 189, 278, 355, 403, 493
Monk, J. S., 126
Monroe, C. R., 470, 471
Monson, T. C., 78
Montessori, M., 47
Moody, L., 569
Moore, M. K., 30
Morelli, G., 38
Morgan, M., 573
Morin, V. A., 293
Morine-Dershimer, G., 478, 479
Morris, C. L., 191
Morris, P. F., 267
Morris, V. G., 191
Morrison, D., 573
Morrow, L. M., 56, 168, 209, 454
Moseley, D. V., 125
Moses, R. P., 6
Mosher M., 79
Moshman, D., 41, 345, 346
Moskowitz, G., 458
Moss, P. A., 532, 546
Mueller, C. M., 238
Mueller, K. J., 373, 393
Mullis, I. V. S., 180–181
Mumford, M. D., 274
Munk, D. D., 581
Munt, E. D., 235
Murdock, S. G., 224
Murdock, T. B., 70, 82, 101
Murnane, R. J., 569
Murphy, P. K., 311, 334, 345, 372, 376, 381, 383
Murray, H. G., 487
Murray, J., 173
Musonda, D., 290, 291
Mussen, P., 22
Myers, D. G., 154, 168, 172, 173, 303

Naglieri, J. A., 43
Nakamura, J., 307
Nansel, T. R., 428
Nardo, A. C., 470
Nathan, L., 540
Nathan, M. J., 506
National Alliance of Black School Educators, 154
National Assessment of Educational Progress, 301
National Center for Educational Statistics, 170, 465
National Center for Family Literacy, 503
National Clearinghouse on Child Abuse and Neglect, 83
National Commission on Excelence in Education, 539–540
National Science Foundation, 174
Naveh-Benjamin, M., 387
Ndebele, N., 35
Needles, M., 349
Neff, D., 50, 51, 189
Neiss, M., 65
Neisser, U., 111, 121, 250
Nelson, C. A., 23
Nelson, G., 74
Nelson, J. R., 462
Nelson, K., 261
Nelson, T. O., 267
Nestor-Baker, N. S., 117
Neuman, O., 381
Neuman, S. B., 55, 340, 485
Neuman, Y., 427
Neumann, C., 120
Neumeister, K. L. S., 307
Newcombe, N., 181
Newman, R., 433
Newman, S. E., 275, 357
Nicholls, J. G., 239, 381, 382
Nickerson, K., 92
Nieto, S., 16, 278
Nisan, M., 573
Nisbett, R. E., 36
Nissani, M., 507
Nix, G., 398
Noddings, N., 97, 98, 489
Noguera, P., 82, 166, 188, 541
Nolan, J. F., 462, 463
Noll, E., 175
Nonnemaker, J. M., 461
Norby, M. M., 267, 296, 344, 347
Nordby, C. J., 341, 343
Norman, D. A., 250
Norton, P., 301
Notah, D. J., 435, 437
Novak, J. D., 290, 291, 314
Nucci, L. P., 76, 98, 99, 100
Nurmi, J., 71
Nye, B., 492
Nylund, D., 134, 136
Nystrand, M., 122

Oakes, J., 122, 123, 167, 573
Oakes, M. A., 172
Obidah, J. E., 470, 471
O'Boyle, M. W., 25
O'Brien, K., 78
O'Campo, P. J., 92
O'Connor, C., 167
O'Donnell, A. M., 400, 416, 417, 418, 420, 424
Ogbu, J. U., 167
Ogden, C., 436
Ogden, J. E., 9, 12
Okagaki, L., 167, 195
O'Kelly, J., 400, 417, 418, 420, 424
Olafson, L., 318
O'Leary, K. D., 217
O'Leary, S. G., 216, 217, 221
Olivarez, A., 334
Ollendick, T. H., 231
Olsen, L., 185
Olson, D. R., 14
Olson, L., 69–70, 168
O'Malley, J. M., 188
O'Malley, P. M., 144
Omelich, C., 387, 393
Omi, M., 168
O'Neil, J., 195, 196
O'Neil, K., 77
O'Neill, R. E., 224
Ongtooguk, P., 541
Orange, C., 197, 462
Orfield, G., 171
Orlando L., 29
Ormrod, J. E., 313, 316
Ortony, A., 261, 375
Osborn, A. F., 310
Osborne, J. W., 174
Osgood, D. W., 89, 90
Osterman, K. F., 379, 432
Ouellette, J. A., 272, 273
Ovando, C. J., 185, 187
Overman, L. T., 167, 192
Owens, R. E., Jr, 138, 139

Paas, F. G. W. C., 254, 255, 269
Padilla, F. M., 433
Padilla, J. N. M., 469
Page, C., 301
Pai, Y., 164
Paivio, A., 259, 270
Pajares, F., 85, 88, 161, 332, 403
Palincsar, A. S., 39, 41, 313, 335, 345, 346, 351, 352, 360, 361, 382, 399, 416, 417, 418, 419, 420, 422, 503
Palmer, J. C., 265
Pang, K. C., 15
Panitz, T., 417
Panksepp, J., 135
Pansky, A., 264
Pape, S., 74, 167, 434–435, 436
Papert, S., 360
Pare-Blagoev, J., 38
Paris, A. H., 77, 345, 346, 414, 446
Paris, S. G., 69, 88, 136, 258, 342, 345, 346
Park, L. E., 88
Parker, L. H., 180
Parker, W. C., 496
Parks, C. P., 433, 434
Pasch, M., 351
Patashnick, M., 381
Pate, P. E., 485
Patterson, C., 176
Patterson, G. R., 78
Paulman, R. G., 387
Paulson, F. L., 564
Paulson, P., 564
Paulus, P. B., 310
Pavlov, I., 208–209
Pavri, S., 81, 82
Payne, B. D., 237
Payne, K. J., 162
Peake, P. K., 117
Pedersen, N. L., 112
Pedulla, J., 542
Peeke, L. A., 89
Pekrun, R., 383
Pelham, W. E., 279

Pellegrini, A. D., 80
Pellegrino, J., 542
Pellegrino, J. W., 511
Pelletier, L. G., 374
Peng, S., 168
Penuel, W. R., 70
Perkins, D. N., 269, 292, 319, 358, 359, 361
Perner, J., 268, 276
Perrone, V., 484
Perry, D. G., 78, 80
Perry, N. E., 278, 337, 339, 340, 341, 342, 343
Perry, R. P., 383
Peruche, B. M., 172
Peterson, D., 315
Peterson, J. L., 433
Peterson, P. L., 183, 479, 505
Peterson, R., 470
Petit, G. S., 433
Petrill, S. A., 121
Pettigrew, T., 171
Pettit, G. S., 78, 94
Peverly, S. T., 57, 314
Pfiffner, L. J., 216
Phelan, P., 82
Phillips, D. C., 88, 343, 345, 346
Phillips, L., 342
Phinney, J. S., 91
Phye, G. D., 322
Piaget, J., 21, 26–39, 27–28, 29, 31, 32, 34, 36, 38, 40, 41, 42, 43, 44, 46–48, 49, 51, 95, 286, 296, 344, 345, 365, 417, 507
Pianta, R., 3
Picasso, 307
Pickering, S. J., 254, 276
Pierce, W. D., 239
Pierson, L. H., 573
Pintrich, P. R., 9, 85, 86, 125, 226, 232, 235, 305, 311, 318, 333, 334, 372, 376, 378, 380, 381, 382, 383, 384, 385, 386, 387, 392
Pirsch, L. A., 71
Pisha, B., 513
Pitts, J. M., 426
Pitts, R. C., 97
Plager, E., 12
Plank, D. R., 545
Plant, E. A., 172
Plants, R., 511
Plato, 8, 111
Plucker, J. A., 116, 306, 307, 309
Podolski, C. P., 78
Pointon, P., 454
Polson, P. G., 360
Pomerantz, E. M., 86
Popham, W. J., 2, 480, 522, 524, 532, 533, 534, 536, 541, 543, 545, 555, 557, 559, 563, 577, 582
Porter, L., 273, 311
Portes, A., 54
Posada, G., 68
Posner, M. I., 275, 297
Powell, K., 433
Prakash, K., 77
Prawat, R. S., 346, 350, 359
Premack, D., 218
Presseisen, B. Z., 41, 49
Pressley, M., 55, 238, 268, 272, 278, 313, 314, 335, 340, 360, 385, 401, 402, 492, 502, 503, 569
Pribram, K. H., 248, 375
Price, G. E., 125, 126
Price, L. F., 66
Price, W. F., 42
Prochnow, J. E., 86
Public Agenda Foundation, 123
Pulkkinen, L., 79, 336
Pullen, P. L., 153
Puma, M. J., 582
Puncochar, J., 418
Purdie, N., 135, 136
Purkey, W. W., 499
Puro, P., 395
Putnam, R. T., 15, 356, 501
Putney, L., 39, 44, 48, 49
Puustinen, M., 336

Quinn, D. M., 175
Quinn, T., 167

Rabinowitz, M., 7
Rachlin, H., 208, 211, 234
Raffini, J. P., 379, 386, 398, 401
Randolph, S. M., 92
Range, L. M., 143
Rankin, J., 340
Raphael, D., 419
Ratey, J. J., 134
Rathus, S. A., 54
Ratner, H. H., 48
Raudenbush, S., 499
Raudsepp, E., 302
Rauscher, F. H., 27
Readence, J. E., 9
Recht, D. R., 249
Reder, L. M., 249, 268, 275, 348, 490
Redfield, D. L., 495
Reed, S., 167
Reeve, J., 235, 373, 378, 379, 398
Reich, P. A., 54
Reid, M. K., 136
Reimann, P., 297
Reinke, W. M., 80
Reis, S. M., 148, 149, 151, 152
Reisberg, D., 171, 286, 307, 383
Rembolt, C., 434, 436
Render, G. F., 469
Renkl, A., 298
Rennie, L. J., 180
Renninger, K. A., 383
Renzulli, J. S., 149, 151, 152
Resnick, L. B., 248–249, 297, 348, 486
Reyes, E. I., 198
Reynolds, A. J., 572, 573
Reynolds, C. A., 112
Rhodes, R. A., 436
Ricciardelli, L. A., 54
Rice, D., 135
Rice, F. P., 65, 144
Richards, A., 428
Richards, S. B., 139
Richardson, T. M., 152
Richardson-Koehler, V., 289
Richie, W. C., 54
Ridley, D. S., 313
Riedesel, A., 297
Rimm, S. B., 151
Ritchey, K., 313
Ritter, P. L., 75
Rivers, J. C., 4
Rivkin, S. G., 4
Roazzi, A., 39, 56
Robbins, S. B., 312, 324
Robbins, S. J., 206, 265
Roberts, M. L., 462
Roberts, R. D., 116
Robinson, A., 122, 123, 151, 152
Robinson, D. H., 293, 314
Robinson, H. A., 314
Rodriquez, J. L., 52
Rogers, C. R., 374, 447
Rogoff, B., 38, 39, 48, 348, 357, 376
Rohde, P., 144
Rohrkemper, M., 341
Roid, G. H., 119
Ronning, R. R., 267, 296, 344, 347
Roosevelt, E., 430
Rop, C., 182
Rosch, E. H., 286
Rose, L. C., 428, 461
Rosenberg, M., 85
Rosenfarb, I., 235
Rosenfeld, M., 127
Rosenfeld, S., 127
Rosenshine, B., 49, 360, 419, 445, 487–488, 490, 496, 503
Rosenthal, R., 496, 499, 500
Roskos, K. A., 55, 340, 485
Ross, D., 78
Ross, J. A., 419
Ross, M., 303
Ross, S. A., 48, 78
Roth, K. J., 507
Roth, W-M., 358
Rotherham-Borus, M. J., 92
Rousseau, E. W., 495
Rowe, D. C., 65
Rowe, M. B., 495
Rowley, J. B., 351
Rubin, L. R., 151
Ruble, D. N., 86
Rudolph, K. D., 70
Rueda, R., 403
Rueman, D., 70
Rumelhart, D., 261
Rummel, N., 271
Rusby, J. C., 466
Rushall, B. S., 236
Russell-Bowie, D., 86
Ruthruff, K. I., 253
Ryan, A., 77, 382
Ryan, R. M., 88, 238, 239, 373, 374, 375, 378
Ryans, D. G., 487

Sachs, J., 318
Sadker, D., 180, 181, 182, 468, 494, 495, 496
Sadker, M., 180, 182, 468, 494, 495, 496
Sagor, R., 437, 438
Sagvolden, T., 134
Saia, J., 311
Salinas, M. F., 174, 175
Salisbury-Glennon, J. D., 355
Salomon, G., 269, 292, 319
Salovey, P., 116
Salva, E., 235
Sameroff, A., 166
Sanchez, F., 429
Sanders, C. E., 322
Sanders, S., 313
Sanders, W. L., 4
Sandler, H. M., 86
Sandora, C. A., 496
Santayana, G., 250
Sattler, J. M., 112, 115, 119, 120, 121, 309, 533, 534
Sautter, R. C., 167
Savage, T. V., 447
Savin-Williams, R. C., 176
Sawyer, R. J., 133
Schaps, E., 378, 416
Schenk, S., 84
Scherer, M., 167, 453
Schiefele, U., 89, 396, 405
Schmader, T., 175

Schneider, W., 304, 360
Schoenfeld, A. H., 299, 358
Schofield, J. W., 171
Schommer, M., 293, 318
Schommer-Aikins, M., 318
Schon, D., 7
Schrauben, B., 125
Schraw, G. J., 267, 296, 318, 344, 347, 384, 385
Schrock, K., 566
Schulenberg, J. E., 144
Schulze, S. K., 278
Schumaker, J. B., 294
Schunk, D. H., 45, 85, 86, 88, 226, 229, 230, 231, 232, 233, 235, 250, 252, 263, 267, 278, 287, 295, 305, 317, 318, 322, 330, 333, 345, 346, 347, 376, 380, 381, 382, 385, 386, 387, 390, 392
Schutz, P. A., 389
Schwab, Y., 93, 437, 451, 452, 461, 462, 463
Schwab-Stone, M., 80
Schwartz, B., 206, 265, 286
Schwartz, D., 319, 320
Schwartz, J. E., 297
Schwarz, B. B., 427
Scott, C. L., 306
Scullin, M. H., 121
Sears, R., 150
Seeley, J. R., 144
Seligman, M. E. P., 133, 392, 393
Selman, R. L., 94
Semb, G. B., 266
Seneca, 250
Seroczynski, A. D., 89
Serpell, R., 346
Shakespeare, W., 294
Shapiro, E. S., 231
Shaughnessy, M. F., 273, 395
Shavelson, R. J., 86, 478, 546
Shaw, G. L., 27
Shaw, H., 66
Shaw, R., 314
Shaywitz, B. A., 25
Shea, T. M., 222
Sheets, R. H., 169, 188, 195, 196
Shepard, L. A., 572, 573
Sherman, A., 166
Sherman, J. W., 262
Shields, P. M., 168, 198
Shiffrin, R. M., 250
Shimamura, A. P., 267
Shin, S., 548
Shoda, Y., 117
Showers, C. J., 89
Shriver, T. P., 80
Shuell, T. J., 248, 269, 295, 358, 487
Shulman, L. S., 7, 501
Shultz, J., 197
Siddle Walker, V., 189, 191
Siegel, J., 273
Siegle, D., 151
Siegler, R. S., 12, 23, 36, 37, 38, 44, 276, 277, 360
Sigman, M. D., 120
Signorella, M. L., 178
Silberman, A., 241
Simon, D. P., 303
Simon, H. A., 249, 275, 304, 345, 348, 490
Simon, T., 119
Simonton, D. K., 307, 323
Simpson, E. J., 482
Sims, V. K., 259
Singley, K., 320
Sisk, D. A., 151
Sjaastad, J., 168
Skiba, R. J., 470
Skinner, B. F., 210, 211, 239, 365, 377
Skinner, E., 379
Skoe, E. E. A., 97
Slaby, R. G., 78
Slater, L., 88
Slavin, R. E., 14, 122, 123, 419, 426, 445
Slavin, T. J., 124
Sleegers, P., 344
Sleet, D., 433
Sleeter, C. E., 162, 163
Sloboda, J. A., 150
Smetana, J. G., 76
Smit, E. K., 88
Smith, D. D., 138, 424
Smith, E. H., 316
Smith, E. L., 288, 305
Smith, F., 251, 257, 269
Smith, J. K., 557, 563, 573
Smith, L. F., 557, 563, 573
Smith, M. L., 572, 573
Smith, P. J., 238
Smith, S. M., 263
Snapp, M., 540
Snider, V. E., 126
Snow, C., 52, 185
Snow, R. E., 122, 125, 336, 354, 496, 499
Snowman, J., 313
Soar, R. M., 487
Soar, R. S., 487
Sobesky, W. E., 97
Sokolove, S., 468
Solomon, D., 378, 416, 418, 437
Soodak, L. C., 224, 466
Sosniak, L. A., 166, 481
Sotillo, S. M., 186
Sousa, D., 27
Southern, W. T., 152
Spearman, C., 112
Spears, F. M., 75
Spencer, M. B., 92, 175
Spencer, S. J., 175
Sperling, G., 250
Spinelli, C. G., 547, 548
Spiro, R. J., 350
Sprague, D., 301
Sprague, J. R., 466
Sprenger, M., 66
Spuhl, S. T., 43
Stahl, S. A., 126, 502, 503
Stainback, S., 128
Stainback, W., 128
Stallard, T., 331
Stanovich, K. E., 14, 25, 132
Stapel, D. A., 85
Starch, D., 559
Stebbins, M. S., 151
Stecher, B., 546
Steele, C. M., 174, 175
Steele, K. M., 27
Steig, W., 356
Stein, B. S., 295, 296
Steinberg, L., 65, 76, 91, 101, 143, 176, 414, 415
Stepien, W., 397
Sternberg, R. J., 111, 112, 117–119, 118–119, 121, 149, 250, 296, 342
Stevens, N., 77
Stevens, R., 487–488, 496
Stevenson, H. W., 121, 491
Stice, E., 66
Stiggins, R. J., 544, 562, 570, 571
Stigler, J. W., 121, 491
Stinson, S. W., 83
Stipek, D. J., 87, 145, 372, 375, 380, 381, 384, 386, 389, 390, 391, 399, 404, 405
Stoddard, K., 226
Stodolsky, S. S., 492
Stoltzfus, J., 175
Stormont, M., 151
Stormshak, E. A., 77
Stough, L. M., 444, 447, 448, 450, 460
Stratton, H., 144
Stringfield, S., 195
Stumpf, H., 181
Subotnik, R. F., 112
Sugai, G., 224, 466
Suliman, R., 86
Sullivan, K., 79
Sullivan, M. A., 216
Sulzby, E., 55
Sulzer-Azaroff, B., 215, 227
Sunburst Software, 6
Suzuki, B. H., 196
Svoboda, J. S., 183
Swanson, H. L., 137, 278, 509
Swanson, T. C., 141
Sweeney, W. J., 235
Sweller, J., 254, 255, 269, 297, 298
Swenson, L. P., 92
Sylvester, R., 26
Symons, S., 502

Tabori, A., 465
Tait, H., 125
Talbert-Johnson, C., 235
Talbot, M., 76
Tallal, P., 27
Tan, D., 101
Taylor, A., 415
Taylor, D. M., 188
Taylor, E., 135
Taylor, R. L., 139
Taylor-Green, S., 466
Teale, W., 55
TenBrink, T. D., 483, 560
Tenent, A., 503
Tennyson, R. D., 287
Terman, L. M., 149, 150
TerraNova, 536, 537
Tesser, A., 85
Tevendale, H. D., 92
Tharp, R. G., 40, 195, 196, 197, 447, 496
Theodore, L. A., 226, 228, 229
Third International Mathematics and Science Study, 301
Thomas, D. R., 12
Thomas, E. L., 314
Thomas, M. H., 272, 273
Thomas, W. P., 188
Thompson, G., 485
Thompson, L., 298
Thompson, R. A., 71
Thompson, W. M., 191
Thorley, N. R., 507
Thorndike, E. L., 8, 319
Thrash, T. M., 382
Threlfall, V., 274
Tierney, R. J., 9
Tierney, W. G., 436
Timmer, S. G., 78
Tishman, S., 358, 359, 361
Titz, W., 383
Tobler, N., 144
Tollefson, N., 376
Tomasello, M., 48
Tomlinson, C. A., 46, 116, 149, 514, 515, 569, 572, 574, 579, 582

Tomlinson-Keasey, C., 149
Toppo, G., 465
Torrance, E. P., 126, 151, 307, 308, 309
Tortora, M., 122, 123–124
Toth, E., 355
Townsend, B., 226
Trautwein, U., 491
Travers, J. F., 64
Tremblay, R. E., 572
Troutman, A. C., 214, 215, 216, 221, 222, 227
Troyer, L., 76
Tschannen-Moran, M., 334, 422, 425
Tulviste, P., 39
Tunmer, W. E., 86
Tuovinen, J., 297
Turbill, J., 566
Turiel, E., 97
Turkanis, C. G., 376
Turnbull, B. J., 198
Turner, J. C., 340, 341, 342
Turner, M. D., 536
Tutu, D., 35
Twenge, J. M., 89

Uline, C. L., 166, 170
Umbreit, J., 224
Underwood, A., 383
Underwood, M. K., 78
Undheim, J. O., 112
U.S. Census Bureau, 166
U.S. Department of Education, 131, 149, 170, 541
U.S. Department of Health and Human Services, 166
Unsworth, N., 277
Urdan, T. C., 382

Valentine, J. C., 88, 332, 491, 492, 498
Valenzuela, A., 83, 542
Vallerand, R. J., 374
VandeKamp, K. O., 341, 343
van den Wittenboer, G. L. H., 387
van der Heijden, P. G., 96
Van Der Wege, C., 315
Van Houten, R., 222
van Kraayenoord, C. E., 135
van Laar, C., 390
Van Luit, J. E. H., 506
Van Matre, J. C., 498
van Merrienboer, J. J. G., 254, 255, 269
Van Meter, P., 313, 314
Van Voorhis, F. L., 493
Vasquez, J. A., 195, 196
Vaughn, S., 131
Veenman, S., 15, 124
Vellutino, F. R., 502
Vera, A. H., 345
Verschaffel, L., 296, 345
Vincent, M., 385, 401, 402
Vispoel, W. P., 86, 383
Vitaro, F., 572
Vives, J. L., 8
Voeten, J. M., 344
Volet, S., 322
von Glasersfeld, E., 344
Vosniadou, S., 293
Vroom, V., 375
Vygotsky, L. S., 21, 38–41, 42, 43, 44, 45, 46, 48–50, 51, 124, 234, 347, 349, 355, 365, 502

Wade, S. E., 385
Wadsworth, B., 30
Wagner, R. K., 118–119, 121
Waits, B. K., 301
Walberg, H. J., 516
Wald, J., 465
Walker, J. E., 222
Walker, L. J., 97
Walker, V. S., 175
Waltmen, K. K., 574
Wang, A. Y., 272, 273
Wang, M. C., 335
Ward, L. M., 173
Ward, M., 428
Washington, D., 173
Wasserman, E. A., 206, 208, 265
Waterman, A. S., 71
Waters, H. F., 78
Watson, J. B., 206
Watson, M. S., 378, 416
Waycott, J. L., 293
Wayne, A. J., 486
Wearing, H., 254, 276
Webb, N. M., 399, 416, 417, 419, 420, 421
Weber, E. S., 313
Weber, M. J., 70, 101, 465
Weed, K. Z., 52
Wehby, J., 222, 545
Weil, M., 287, 288, 289, 290
Weinberg, R. A., 121, 499
Weinberger, D., 24
Weiner, B., 334, 372, 375, 377, 390, 391, 579
Weinert, F. E., 488, 490
Weinstein, C., 197, 209, 313, 454
Weinstein, C. E., 334, 335
Weinstein, C. S., 5, 82, 83, 428, 433, 434, 446, 447, 449, 450, 451, 452, 453, 454, 458, 461, 462, 464, 491, 492, 495
Weinstein, R. S., 498, 499, 500
Weisberg, R. W., 306
Weiss, M. P., 110
Wells, A. S., 122, 123
Welsh, L. M., 385, 401, 402
Wenger, E., 320, 348, 357, 376, 377
Wentzel, K. R., 77, 82, 382, 415, 432
Wertsch, J. V., 39, 41, 42, 70
Westberg, K. L., 124
Wethington, E., 166
Whaley, S. E., 120
Wharton-McDonald, R., 340, 341
Wheatley, K. F., 334
Wheelock, A., 123
When the Student Becomes the Teacher, 503
Whipple, A. D., 572
Whishaw, I. Q., 24
White, S., 197
Whitehead, A. N., 352
Whitehurst, G. J., 14, 55
Whitmore, K. F., 355
Wiener, M. W., 378
Wigfield, A., 70, 86, 89, 90, 376, 387, 396, 404
Wiggins, G., 561, 562, 563, 566
Wilen, W., 487
Wilgenbusch, T., 89
Wiliam, D., 570
Wilkerson, B., 121
Wilkins, W. E., 499
Willcutt, E. G., 132
Williams, A., 465
Williams, C., 97
Williams, D. R., 172
Williams, G. C., 378
Williams, J. P., 136, 137
Williams, W. M., 118–119
Willingham, W. W., 181
Willis, P., 167
Willoughby, T., 273, 311
Wilson, C. W., 226
Wilson, L., 129
Wilson, M., 258
Winant, H., 168
Windschitl, M., 344, 345, 346, 350, 362, 363
Winett, R. A., 240
Wink, J., 39, 44, 48, 49
Winkler, R. C., 240
Winne, P. H., 318, 335, 336, 337, 338, 340, 342
Winner, E., 149, 150, 310, 311, 323
Winsler, A., 43, 52
Wintergerst, A. C., 126
Winters, L., 567, 568
Wittrock, M. C., 3, 8, 17, 247, 295, 315, 319, 359, 360
Wixson, K. K., 258
Wolf, D., 545, 562, 563
Woloshyn, V., 268, 502
Wolters, C. A., 381
Wong, L., 10
Wood, D., 48
Wood, E. G., 23, 117
Wood, J. V., 85
Wood, S. E., 23, 117
Wood, T., 381
Woods, B. S., 345
Woods, T., 225
Woodward, M. M., 271
Woolfolk, A. E., 334, 337, 340, 453, 500, 540
Woolfolk Hoy, A., 74, 82, 83, 167, 311, 334, 422, 425, 434–435, 436, 461, 471
Worner, C., 353
Worsham, M. E., 448, 458, 459
Worth Gavin, D. A., 86
Worthy, J., 496
Wright, S. C., 188
Wright, V. C., 71
Wulfert, E., 235
Wyler, R. S., 173

Yackel, E., 381
Yaden, D. B., Jr., 503
Yarhouse, M. A., 176, 178
Yates, M., 436, 437
Yawkey, T., 154
Yearsley, T., 273, 311
Yee, A. H., 170, 181, 196
Yeh, C. J., 574
Yekovich, C. W., 258, 260, 261, 264, 275, 300
Yekovich, F. R., 258, 260, 261, 264, 275, 300
Yell, M. L., 142
Yerkes, R. M., 386, 387
Yetman, N. R., 185
Yeung, A. S., 86, 90
Yinger, R., 478
Yokoi, L., 313, 314, 340
Young, A. J., 381
Youngs, P., 4, 486
Youniss, J., 436, 437
Yu, S. L., 381

Zeidner, M., 116, 387, 388
Zelli, A., 78
Zettle, R. D., 235
Zhou, Z., 57
Zigmond, N., 129
Zimmerman, B. J., 229, 317, 333, 334, 338, 340
Zimmerman, M., 88
Zucker, S., 194
Zusho, A., 334

Subject Index

Note: Page numbers in ***boldface*** *indicate key terms.*

ABAB design, 215, 228
Abilities, 121–124. *See also* Intelligence
aptitude tests and, 538–539
beliefs about, 388–390
between-class grouping and, 122, 123, 167–168
cognitive spatial, 126
diversity and convergence in, 153–154
entity view of, 388
flexible grouping and, 124
incremental view of, 388–389
Piaget's underestimation of, 38
sex differences in, 180–181, 183
within-class grouping and, 122–124
Ability goals, 381–382, 382
Ability grouping. *See* Grouping
Absence seizures, **146**
Abstract thinking, in formal operations stage, 35
Abuse. *See* Child abuse
Academic achievement
anxiety and, 387
cheating and, 101
ethnic and racial differences in, 170–171
of gifted and talented students, 151
helping lower-achieving students and, 9–10
intelligence and, 121
parenting styles and, 76
peer influence on, 77
poverty and, 166–168
in primary grades, as predictor of dropping out, 69
self-concept and, 86
self-esteem and, 88
teacher qualifications related to, 4
teachers' expectations and, 498–500
tests of, 536–538
Academic English, 185
Academic learning time, **446**
Academic tasks, **396**
Acceleration, for gifted and talented students, 151, 152
Accommodation, **29**
Accommodations, in testing, 547
Accomplishment, recognizing, 399
Accountability, **540**
high-stakes testing and, 540–541
Achievement. *See* Academic achievement
Achievement tests, **536,** 536–538
Acquisition phase of strategic transfer, 322
Acronyms, **271,** 271–272
Action research, **13**
Action schemes, 30–31
Action zone, **453**
Activating information, 262–263
Activation, spreading, 264
Active teaching, **487.** *See also* Direct instruction
Activity, cognitive development and, 28
ADA (Americans with Disabilities Act of 1990), **130**
Adaptation, **28**
cognitive development and, 29
Adderall, for attention deficit hyperactivity disorder, 135
Adequate Yearly Progress (AYP), 2, 17, **540**
ADHD. *See* Attention-deficit hyperactivity disorder (ADHD)
Adolescent(s)
brain development in, 24, 66
cognitive development of, 30, 32–36
discipline problems with, 462–465
eating disorders in, 65–66
gifted, problems faced by, 150
identity statuses and, 71
interests of, 36
interpersonal violence among, 433
nutrition of, 66
as parents, 166
physical development of, 66
play and, 48
psychosocial development of, 67, 70–72
puberty and, 65
self-concept development in, 86
sleep and, 66
social goals of, 382
Adolescent egocentrism, **36**
Adults. *See also* Parent *entries*; Teacher(s)
internalization of moral rules and principles of, 101
problems of, peer rejection and, 77
psychosocial development of, 72
scaffolding and, 48
Advance organizers, **292,** 292–293, 509
The Adventures of Jasper Woodbury, 354
Affective domain, **482**
taxonomy of, 482
African Americans
in corporate management, 173
culturally relevant pedagogy and, 191
discipline of, 470–471
discrimination and, 171–174
educational attainment of, 173–174, 180
ethnic identity of, 90, 91–92
learning preferences and, 195–196
as majority, 168
in media, 173
motivation to learn and, 403
NAEP test scores of, 548
overrepresentation in disability categories, 153, 154
parenting styles of, 76
physical maturation of, 65
poverty among, 162, 166
prejudice and, 172–173
resistance culture of, 167
school achievement of, 170
stereotype threat and, 174–176
technology in homes of, 197
underrepresentation in gifted and talented programs, 153–154
in U.S. population, 162
African American Vernacular English, 184
Age. *See also specific age groups*
language development and, 52
mental, 119
Agency, **336**
Aggression. *See also* School violence; Violence
assertiveness contrasted with, 78
bullying and, 78–79
helping children handle, 79
hostile, 78
instrumental, 78
modeling and, 78
overt, 78
peer rejection and, 77
in peers, 78
relational (social), 78, 79
theory of mind and, 94
Algorithms, **298,** 298–299
Allocated time, **445,** 445–446
Alternate-form reliability, 530
Alternative(s), for multiple-choice questions, 557
Alternative assessment, 545–546, 561, 562, 563
American English, 184

American Indians. *See* Eskimos; Native Americans
American Psychological Association, founding of, 8
Americans with Disabilities Act of 1990 (ADA), **130**
Amygdala, 23
Analogical instruction, **294**
Analogical thinking, **300**
Analytic/componential intelligence, 118
Anchored instruction, **354**
Anorexia nervosa, 65–66
Antecedents, **210**
  operant conditioning and, 214–215
Anxiety, **387**
  achievement and, 387
  in the classroom, 387
  coping with, 388, 389
  interference with learning by, 26
Applied behavior analysis, **215**, 215–224, 225
  cautions regarding, 222
  functional behavioral assessments and, 224, 225
  negative reinforcement and, 219–221
  positive behavioral supports and, 223–224
  positive practice and, 219, 220
  reinforcer selection for, 217–218
  reinforcing with teacher attention and, 216–217
  reprimands and, 221–222
  response cost and, 222
  satiation and, 221
  shaping and, 218–219
  social isolation and, 222
Apprenticeships, cognitive, 356–358
Appropriation, **346**
Aptitude tests, **538**, 538–539
Arousal, **333**, **384**, 384–386. *See also* Anxiety
  curiosity and, 386–387
  self-efficacy and, 333
Articulation disorders, **138**
Asian Americans and Pacific Islanders
  cultural compatibility and, 170
  learning preferences and, 196
  parenting styles of, 76
  technology in homes of, 197
  in U.S. population, 162
Asperger syndrome, 148
Assertive discipline, **469**
Assertiveness
  aggression contrasted with, 78
  gender-role identity development and, 178
Assessment, 520–550, **522**, 552–584. *See also* High-stakes testing; Standardized tests; Test *entries*
  authentic (direct or alternative), 545–546, 561, 562, 563
  of creativity, 307–309
  definition of, 522
  diversity and convergences in, 571–583
  exhibitions for, 565, 566
  failure and. *See* Failure
  feedback and, 573
  formative, 554–555, 569–570
  grades and. *See* Grading
  informal, 569–570
  involving students in, 570, 571
  measurement and, 522–523
  motivation and, 400
  new directions in, 545–546
  performance, 562
  portfolios for, 562–569
  summative, 554–555
  traditional. *See* Test *entries*
Assessment bias, **532**
Assimilation, **29**
  cognitive development and, 29
  minority youth and, 91
Assisted learning, 48–49, **49**
Assistive technology, **511**, 511–513
Associative stage, of development of automated basic skills, 275
Attainment value, **396**, 404–405
Attention, **252**
  anxiety as interference with focusing, 387
  development of automated basic skills and, 275
  directing, 233
  focusing for learning, 313
  focusing for problem solving, 296
  observational learning and, 230
  of peers, reinforcement of behaviors by, 216–217
  sensory memory and, 252–253
  of teacher, reinforcing behaviors with, 216–217
Attention-deficit hyperactivity disorder (ADHD), **134**, 134–135. *See also* Students with attention-deficit hyperactivity disorder
  brain in, 25
  overlap between learning disabilities and, 136
Attributions
  in classroom, 391
  dimensions affecting, 390
  teacher actions and, 391–392
Attribution theory, **390**, 390–392
Audience, imaginary, 36
Authentic assessment, **545**, 545–546, 561, **562**, 563
  tests versus, 561
Authentic tasks, **396**, 396–397
Authoritarian parents, 75
Authoritative parents, 75
Autism, **147**
Autism spectrum disorders, **147**, 147–148
  interventions for, 148
  lack of theory of mind and, 148
Automated basic skills, **274**, 274–275
Automaticity, **118**, **252**
Autonomous stage, of development of automated basic skills, 275
Autonomy, **68**
  need for, 378
  supporting, 398–399
Autonomy versus shame and doubt stage, 67, 68
Availability heuristic, **303**
Aversive, **211**
Avoidance, as coping strategy for anxiety, 388
AYP (Adequate Yearly Progress), 2, 17, **540**

Backward-reaching transfer, 319
Basic skills, **487**, 487–488
Basic trust versus basic mistrust stage, 67, 68
Beginning teachers, 15–16
Behavior(s)
  encouraging, 216–219, 220
  goal-directed, 380
  moral, 101
  self-management of, 234–236
  undesirable, coping with, 219–222, 223
Behavioral approaches to motivation, 374, 377
Behavioral learning, 204–244
  applied behavior analysis and. *See* Applied behavior analysis
  behavior modification and. *See* Applied behavior analysis
  cognitive view of learning compared with, 248–249
  comparison with other theories of learning, 365
  conditioning as. *See* Classical conditioning; Conditioning; Operant conditioning
  criticisms of behavioral methods and, 238–240
  diversity and convergence in, 240–241
  observational learning as. *See* Observational learning
  self-instruction and, 236–238
Behavioral learning theories, **206**, 206–207
Behavioral objectives, **480**
Behavior change, operant conditioning and, 214–215
Behavior modification, **215**. *See also* Applied behavior analysis
  cognitive, 236
Behavior problems. *See also* Discipline problems; Students with emotional or behavioral disorders
  severe, behavioral principles for, 228–229
Being needs, **375**
Belief(s)
  about ability, 388–390
  about causes and control, 390–392
  about self-efficacy and learned helplessness, 392–393
  about self-worth, 393–394

implications for teachers, 394
motivation and, 388–394
Belief perseverance, **303**
Belonging, sense of, in classroom, 432
Best works portfolios, 565
Between-class grouping, **122**
debate over effectiveness of, 123
of low-SES students, 167–168
"BFLP" ("Big-Fish-Little-Pond Effect"), 86
Bias
assessment, 532
in classroom assessment, 582
confirmation, 303
gender, 179–182
Biculturalism, minority youth and, 91
"Big-Fish-Little-Pond Effect" ("BFLP"), 86
Bilingual children, 54
Bilingual education, 187–188, 189
Bilingualism, **185**, 185–186
advantages and disadvantages of, 54
becoming bilingual and, 185–186
definition of, 185
myths about bilingual students and, 186
recognizing giftedness in bilingual students and, 186–187
Bimodal distributions, 525
Bioecological model, **72**, 72–74
Black Americans. *See* African Americans
Blended families, **74**
Blindness, 110–111
educational, 147
Bloom's taxonomy, 481–482
Bodily-kinesthetic intelligence, 114
Body image, in adolescence, 65
Books, gender bias in, 179–180
Bottom-up processing, **251**, 251–252
Bounded choices, 398
Boys. *See also* Gender *entries*
aggression among, 79
bullying among, 78
early and late maturing, 65
moral development of, 97
motivation to learn and, 403
parental divorce and, 74
physical development of, 64
self-concepts of, 89–90
Brain, 22–26
in ADHD, 25
adolescent development and, 66
development of, 23–24, 25–26, 27
emotions and, 26
instruction and development of, 25–26, 27
lateralization of, 25
plasticity of, 24
prenatal development of, 23
specialization and integration in, 25
stimulation and, 24
stress and, 26
teaching to different sides of, 25
Brainstorming, **310**
Brazil, cognitive development in, 39
Bronfenbrenner's bioecological model of development, 72–74
Brown v. *the Board of Education of Topeka*, 171
Bulimia, **65**
Bullying, 78–79, 428
conflict resolution and, 428–429

Calculators, debate over use of, 301
CAPS strategy, **314**, 314–315
Caring
for preventing discipline problems, 461
from teachers, 82–83
Case studies, **11**
Catastrophe theory, 38
Causality, locus of, 373, 390
Cause(s), beliefs about, 390–392
Cause and effect
correlation versus, 11
experimental studies of, 12
Central executive, **254**, 255
Central tendency, **525**
Cerebellum, 22–23
Cerebral cortex, 23
development of, 24
Cerebral palsy, **145**, 145–146
Chain memories, **272**
Character education, 430
Cheating, 101–102
Checking, student learning and, 237
Child abuse
indicators of, 84
teachers' responsibilities regarding, 83–84
Childhood and Society (Erikson), 67
Children. *See also* Adolescent(s); Boys; Girls; Infants; Preschool children; School-age children
brain synapses of, 23
cognitive development of, 29–36
Choices, supporting, 398–399
Chunking, **256**, 256–257
Civic values, 429–430
Clarity, of effective teachers, 487
Classical conditioning, **208**, 208–209
Classification, **33**
Class inclusion, 44
Classroom assessment. *See* Assessment; Authentic assessment; Test *entries*
Classroom characteristics, 444. *See also* Learning environments
Classroom community, 426–432
belonging and, 432
civic values for, 429–430
conflict resolution for, 427–429
initial steps for setting up, 430–431
Classroom context, peer rejection and, 77
Classroom management, **445**, 445–447
access to learning as goal of, 446–447
communicating with families about, 472
culturally responsive, 470–471
more time for learning as goal of, 445–446
research on approaches for, 471–472
self-management as goal of, 447
Classroom participation, guided, 48–49
Cmaps, **314**, 315
Co-constructed processes, **39**, 39–40
Code-switching, **184**, 184–185
Cognitive apprenticeships, 49, 356–358, **357**
Cognitive approaches to motivation, 375, 377
Cognitive behavior modification, **236**
Cognitive constructivism, 344–346
Cognitive development, **22**
brain and, 22–26
culture and, 38
diversity and convergence in, 56–57
moral reasoning and, 96
Piaget's theory of. *See* Piaget's theory of cognitive development
problems with stage model of, 38
Vygotsky's sociocultural perspective on. *See* Vygotsky's sociocultural perspective
Cognitive domain, **481**
classroom questions for objectives in, 494
taxonomy of, 481
Cognitive evaluation theory, **378**
Cognitive function. *See also* Intelligence; Social cognitive theory; Students who are gifted and talented; Students with intellectual disabilities; Thinking *entries*
creativity and, 307
gender differences in, 181
Cognitive objectives, **480**
Cognitive processes, complex. *See also* Concept learning; Creativity; Learning strategies; Problem solving
diversity and convergences in, 322–324
Cognitive self-instruction, 49
Cognitive spatial ability, 126
Cognitive stage, of development of automated basic skills, 275
Cognitive Strategies Model, 268
Cognitive style, 126
Cognitive view of learning, 246–282, **248**
behavioral view compared with, 248–249
diversity and convergences in, 276–280
importance of knowledge in learning and, 249–250
knowledge and. *See* Declarative knowledge; Knowledge
memory and. *See* Information processing model of memory; Long-term memory
metacognition and, 267–269
Cold cognition, 383

Collaboration, 416–417, **417**. *See also* Cooperative learning
cooperation contrasted with, 417
group work and, 417
self-regulated learning and, 343
Collaborative consultation, 510–511
Collaborative learning, 48
Collective monologue, **31**
Commitment, identity statuses and, 71
Communication, about grades, 579–581
Communication tasks, for cooperative learning, 419
Community of practice, **347**
Comparative organizers, 292
Comparison, social, self-concept development and, 86
Compassion, debate about teaching in schools, 431
Compensation, **33**
Competitive goal structure, 399, 400
Complex cognitive processes. *See also* Concept learning; Creativity; Learning strategies; Problem solving
diversity and convergences in, 322–324
Complexity, curiosity and, 386–387
Complex learning environments, **349**
Computers, planning for uses of, 455–457
Computer-Supported Intentional Learning Environment (CSILE), 376
Concept(s), **286**
defining attributes of, 286
definition of, 286
extending and connecting, 289–290
Concept attainment, 287–288
Concept learning, 286–294
through discovery, 290–292
through exposition, 292–294
learning disabilities and, 294
prototypes and exemplars and, 286
schemas and, 287
simplicity principle and, 287
teaching strategies for, 287–290
Concept mapping, **290**
Conceptual change teaching in science, **507**
Conceptual tasks, for cooperative learning, 419
Concrete operational stage, 30, **32**, 32–34
Condition-action rules, 262, 275
Condition-action schemes, of experts, 304
Conditional knowledge, **258**, 267, 274
Conditioned response (CR), **209**
Conditioned stimulus (CS), **209**
Conditioning
classical, 208–209
operant. *See* Operant conditioning
Confidence intervals, **531**
Confidentiality, legal protection of, 128
Confirmation bias, **303**
Conflict
about gender identity, 178
cultural, 169–170
divorce and, 74
Conflict management strategies, 79
Conflict resolution
constructive, 427–429
peer mediation for, 429
Confrontation, for discipline problems, 469–470
Connecticut Core of Common Learning, 562
Consequences, **210**
anticipating, in problem solving, 300–301
group, 226
natural or logical, 451
for positive learning environment, 451–452, 453
Conservation, **31**
Constructed-response formats, **546**
Constructionism, 346
Constructivism, 343–362, **344**
apprenticeships in thinking and, 359–361
cognitive apprenticeships and, 356–358
common elements of constructivist perspectives and, 348–350
comparison with other theories of learning, 365
dialog and instructional conversations and, 355–356, 357
dilemmas of constructivist practice and, 362, 363
Fostering Communities of Learners program and, 361–362
how knowledge is constructed and, 346–347
inquiry learning and, 351–352, 354–355
planning from constructivist perspective and, 483–485
problem-based learning and, 352–355
psychological/individual, 344–346
radical, 345–346
second wave, 346
situation learning and, 347–348
Vygotsky's view of, 346
Constructivist approaches, **483**, 483–485
Construct-related evidence of validity, 532
Consultation, collaborative, 510–511
Content integration, 163
Content-related evidence of validity, 532
Context(s), **263**
classroom, peer rejection and, 77
long-term memory and, 263
self-regulation and, 335
Contextual intelligence, 118–119
Contiguity, **208**
Contingency contracts, **226**, 226–227
Continuous reinforcement schedule, 212, **213**
Contract system, **577**, 577–578
Control
beliefs about, 390–392
self-regulated learning and, 342
Controllability, success and failure and, 390
Control processes, 250
Conventional judgment, 95–96
Convergences. *See* Diversity and convergences
Convergent questions, **494**
Convergent thinking, **308**
Conversations
instructional, 48, 49, 355–356, 357
school-age children and, 55
Cooperation, **417**
gaining, 444–445
scripted, 424, 490
Cooperative goal structure, 399, 400
Cooperative learning, **417**, 417–426
assigning roles and, 421–422
giving and receiving explanations and, 420–421
misuses of, 418
preparing students for, 419–422
reciprocal questioning for, 423–424
scripted cooperation for, 424, 425
setting up groups for, 420
tasks for, 419
using effectively, 424–426
Cooperative teaching, 511
Corpus callosum, 23
Correlations, **11**
cause and effect versus, 11
CR (conditioned response), **209**
Creative/experiential intelligence, 118
Creativity, 305–311, **306**
assessment of, 307–309
in classroom, 309–310
definition of, 306–307
diversity and, 323
encouraging, 309
revolutionary innovation and, 310–311
sources of, 307
Creativity-relevant processes, 307
Criterion-referenced grading, **574**, 574–575, 576
Criterion-referenced testing, 522–524, **523**
Criterion-related evidence of validity, 532
Critical thinking, **359**, 359–361
debate about teaching of, 360
Cross-age grouping, 124
Cross-sectional studies, 13
Crystallized intelligence, **112**
CS (conditioned stimulus), **209**
CSILE (Computer-Supported Intentional Learning Environment), 376
Cueing, **214**
Cultural compatibility, 170
Cultural deficit model, **162**
Cultural diversity, 160–202. *See also* Diversity and convergences; Ethnic and racial diversity; Reaching every student
cautions in interpreting differences and, 164–165

cognitive development and, 42
creativity and, 323
culturally inclusive classrooms and. *See* Culturally inclusive classrooms
culture and group membership and, 164
economic social class differences and, 165–168
ethnic and racial differences and. *See* Ethnic and racial diversity
gender differences and. *See* Gender differences
in learning, 195–197
linguistic differences and. *See* Language differences
moral reasoning and, 100–101
multicultural education and, 163
in performance assessment, 568
self-concept and, 89–90
teaching every student and, 198–199
Culturally inclusive classrooms, **188**, 188–194
culturally relevant pedagogy and, 189–191
fostering resilience and, 191–194
Culturally relevant pedagogy, **189**, 189–191
Culturally responsive management, **470**, 470–471
Cultural tools, **41**, 41–42
for teaching, 50–51
Cultural values
culturally inclusive classrooms and, 195
prejudice as, 173
Culture(s), **164**
cognitive development and, 38. *See also* Vygotsky's sociocultural perspective
complex cognitive processes and, 322–323
parenting and, 76
peer, 76–77
resistance, 167
Culture-fair (culture-free) tests, 534
Curiosity, 386–387
Curriculum
debate about, 431
gender bias in, 179–180
teaching civic values through, 430
Curriculum compacting, for gifted and talented students, 151–152
Curve, grading on, 574
Cylert, for attention deficit hyperactivity disorder, 135

Dani people, language of, 42
DARE drug prevention program, 144
Deafness, 146–147
DEAR time, 400
Decay, **257**
Decentering, **31**
Declarative knowledge, **258**, 267, 269–274
meaningfulness and, 269–270
mnemonics and, 271–273
rote memorization and, 273–274
visual images and illustrations and, 270–271
Deductive reasoning, **292**
Deep-processing approach, 125
Deficiency needs, **375**
Defining attributes, **286**
Deprivation, brain development and, 24
Descriptive studies, **10**, 10–11
Desegregation, 171
Development, **22**
of brain, 23–24
cognitive. *See* Cognitive development
general principles of, 22
of language. *See* Language development
personal, 22
phase models of, problems with, 177
physical. *See* Physical development
prenatal, of brain, 23
social, 22
working memory and, 276–277
Developmental crises, **67**
Deviation IQ score, **119**
Diagnostic and Statistical Manual of Mental Disorders, 141
Diagnostic tests, **538**, **554**
Dialects, 183–185, **184**
pronunciation and, 184
teaching and, 184–185
Differences, peer rejection and, 77
Differential reinforcement, 216
Differentiated instruction, 46, **514**, 514–515
Digital divide, **197**
Direct-application transfer, 319, 320
Direct assessment, 545–546, 561, 562, 563
Direct instruction, **487**, 487–490
evaluating, 489–490
reasons for success of, 488–489
Disabilities, **110**. *See also* Students *entries*; Students with disabilities; *specific disabilities*
Discipline, assertive, 469
Discipline problems, 460–465, 466–470
assertive discipline and, 469
confrontation and, 469–470
counseling and, 468
dealing with, 461–462, 463
diagnosing ownership of, 467–468
"I" messages and, 469
preventing, 460–461
with secondary students, 462–465
sending and receiving messages and, 466–467
Discovery learning, **290**, 290–292
intuitive thinking and, 290–291
structure and, 290
unguided versus guided discovery and, 291
Discrimination, 171–174, **173**
legislation prohibiting, 129–130
persistence of, 173–174
prejudice and, 172–173
sex, in classrooms, 180
vigilance about, misunderstandings related to, 197
Disequilibrium, **29**
Disorders, **110**
Distance reduction, in means-end analysis, 299
Distractors, for multiple-choice questions, **557**
Distributed practice, **274**
Distributions
bimodal, 525
normal, 526–527
Distributive justice, **95**
Divergent questions, **494**
Divergent thinking, **308**
Diversity. *See also* Cultural diversity; Diversity and convergences; Ethnic and racial diversity; Gender differences; Reaching every student
in language, 52, 54
Diversity and convergences
in behavioral learning, 240–241
in classroom assessment, 581–583
in cognitive development, 56–57
in cognitive learning, 276–280
in complex cognitive processes, 322–324
in educational psychology, 16–17
in learning, 195–197
in learning abilities, 153–154
in learning environments, 470–472
in motivation to learn, 403–407
NCLB and, 17
in personal/social development, 102–103
in research methods, 17
in social engagement, 438–439
in standardized testing, 546–548
in teaching, 513–516
teaching every student and, 198–199
in theories of learning, 362, 364–365
Divorce, 74
Domain knowledge, of experts, 304
Domain-relevant skills, 307
Domain-specific knowledge, **249**, 278
Domain-specific strategies, **275**, 275–276
Double negative constructions, 184
Dropping out
peer rejection and, 77
primary school predictors of, 69
semilingualism among Latino/a Americans and, 187
victimization as cause of, 80
Drug abuse, 144–145
poverty and, 166
prevention of, 144–145
Drug therapy, for attention deficit hyperactivity disorder, 135

Eating disorders, 65–66
Educational Amendments Act of 1974, 582

Educationally blind, **147**
Educational psychology, **9**
Education of the Handicapped Act (PL 94-142), 127
Effort
grading on, 578–579
learning and, 318
Egocentric speech, 42
learning and, 44
zone of proximal development and, 44
Egocentrism, **31**
adolescent, 36
in preoperational children, 31
Ego goals, 381–382, 382
Ego integrity versus despair stage, 67, 72
Ego-involved learners, **381**
E-IQ (emotional intelligence), **116,** 116–117
Elaboration, **263**
long-term memory and, 263
Elaborative rehearsal, **256**
Elementary school(s). *See also* School-age children
effective managers for, 457–458
nongraded, 122
rules for, 450–451
ELLs (English language learners), 185, **187**
cooperative learning for, 424–426
Emotion(s)
arousing using observational learning, 234
brain and, 24, 26
implications for teachers, 388
motivation and, 383–388
prejudice and, 172–173
Emotional and behavioral disorders, **140.** *See also* Students with emotional or behavioral disorders
of gifted and talented students, 150
physical maturation of girls and, 65
Emotional competence, 93, 94
Emotional development, moral reasoning and, 96
Emotional intelligence (E-IQ or EQ), **116,** 116–117
Emotional management, as coping strategy for anxiety, 388
Empathetic listening, **468**
Empathy, program to encourage, 117
Enactive learning, 230
Encoding, 250
Enculturation, 359
Engaged learning, 412–440
classroom community and, 426–432
collaboration and cooperation and, 416–426
diversity and convergences in, 438–439
parents and teachers and, 415–416
peers and, 414–415
violence in schools and, 432–434, 435, 436
Engaged time, **446**
Engagement, encouraging, 459
English as a second language (ESL), 185, **188**
English language learners (ELLs), 185, **187**
cooperative learning for, 424–426
Enrichment, for gifted and talented students, 151, 152
Enthusiasm, of effective teachers, 487
Entity view of ability, **388**
Environmental factors. *See* Nature-versus-nurture debate
Epilepsy, **146**
Episodic memory, **262**
Epistemological beliefs, **318**
EQ (emotional intelligence), **116,** 116–117
Equilibration, **29**
Equity, in performance assessment, 568
Erikson's theory of psychosocial development, 67–72
during adolescence, 70–72
during elementary and middle school years, 69–70
during preschool years, 68–69
Error(s)
target, 460
in test scores, 530–531
timing, 460
Eskimos, language of, 42
ESL (English as a second language), 185, **188**
Essay tests, 559–560
constructing, 559
dangers in evaluating, 559
evaluation methods for, 559–560
Ethical issues, with behavioral methods, 238, 240
Ethnic and racial diversity, 168–176. *See also* Cultural diversity; Diversity and convergence; *specific groups*
changing demographics and, 168–170
cultural conflicts and, 169–170
discrimination and, 171–174
prejudice and, 172–173
in school achievement, 170–171
stereotype threat and, 174–176
Ethnic identity, 90–92
unexamined, 91
Ethnic identity exploration, 91
Ethnicity, **168**
Ethnography, **10,** 10–11
European Americans. *See* White Americans
Evaluation. *See also* Assessment; High-stakes testing; Standardized tests; Test *entries*
metacognition and, 268
of problem solving results, 300–301
Event schemas, 261
Exceptional students, **110.** *See also* Students *entries*
technology and, 511–513
Executive control processes, **267.** *See also* Metacognition
Exemplars, **286**
Exhibitions, **565,** 566
Exosystem, in bioecological model of development, 73
Expectancy x value theories, 375–376, **376**
Expectations, of teachers. *See* Teacher expectations
Experience-dependent neuron overproduction and pruning, 23
Experience-expectant neuron overproduction and pruning, 23
Experimentation, **12**
Experts
knowledge of, 274–276, 303–305
problem solving by, 303–305, 306
Expert students, learning strategies and study skills for, 311–318
Expert teachers, **7,** 7–8
Explanations, giving and receiving, 420–421
Explicit memory, **259,** 259–262
episodic, 262
images and, 260
propositions and propositional networks and, 259–260
schemas and, 260–262
Explicit teaching, **487.** *See also* Direct instruction
Exploration, identity statuses and, 71
Expository organizers, **292**
Expository teaching model, 292–294
advance organizers and, 292–293
steps in, 293
External locus of control, success and failure and, 390
Extinction, **214**
Extrinsic motivation, **373**

Failure, 571–573
attributed causes for, 390
feedback and, 573
retention in grade and, 572–573
value of, 571–572
Failure-accepting students, 393, **394**
Failure-avoiding students, **393**
Fairness, in grading, 579
Families, 74–76. *See also* Parent *entries;* Parenting *entries*
blended, 74
communicating about grades with, 579–581
communicating with, about classroom management, 472
connecting with, 279
discussing test results with, 539
partnerships with, language development and, 55
rights of, 128
self-regulated learning and, 340
Family Educational Rights and Privacy Act of 1974, 582

FAPE (free, appropriate public education), 127
FBA (functional behavioral assessment), 223, **223,** 224
FCL (Fostering Communities of Learners) program, **361**
Feature analysis, 251–252
Feedback
failure and, 573
goal setting and, 383
practice with, 275
Females. *See* Gender *entries;* Girls
Field experiments, 12
Fine-tuning behaviors, 233
First-hand investigations, 352
First wave constructivism, **345**
Fixed-interval schedule, 212, 213
Fixed-ratio schedule, 212, 213
Flashbulb memories, **262**
Flexibility
creativity and, 308, 309
for problem solving, 303
Flexible grouping, **124**
Fluency, creativity and, 308–309
Fluid intelligence, **112**
Flynn effect, **120,** 120–121
Forethought phase of self-regulated learning, 338
Forgetting, 257, 265–266
Formal operations stage, 30, **35,** 35–36
Formative assessment, **554,** 554–555, 569–570
Forward-reaching transfer, 319
Fostering Communities of Learners (FCL) program, **361**
Free, appropriate public education (FAPE), 127
Frequency distributions, **525**
Frontal lobe, 24
Functional behavioral assessment (FBA), 223, **223,** 224
Functional fixedness, **302,** 319
Functional magnetic resonance imaging (MRI) studies, instruction and brain development and, 25
Funds of knowledge, **50**

Gangs, 429, 433–434
Gender, definition of, 176
Gender bias, **179**
in curriculum, 179–180
eliminating, 181–182
Gender differences, 176–182. *See also* Boys; Girls
eliminating gender bias and, 181–182
gender-role identity and, 177–180
in mental abilities, 180–181
in moral development, 97
in self-concept, 89
sexual identity and, 176–177
Gender-role identity, **177,** 177–180
gender bias in curriculum and, 179–180
gender-role stereotyping in preschool years and, 178–179
sex discrimination in classrooms and, 180
Gender schemas, **178**
Generalizability, of performances, 567–568
Generalized seizures, **146**
General knowledge, **249,** 249–250
Generativity, **72**
Generativity versus stagnation stage, 67, 72
Genetic factors, 176. *See also* Nature-versus-nurture debate
Gestalt, **251,** 251–252
Gifted students, **148.** *See also* Students who are gifted and talented
Girls. *See also* Gender *entries*
aggression among, 79
early and late maturing, 65
moral development of, 97
motivation to learn and, 403
parental divorce and, 74
physical development of, 64
self-concepts of, 89–90
GIsML (Guided Inquiry Supporting Multiple Literacies), 351, 352
Goal(s), **380,** 380–383. *See also* Learning goals
for behavioral methods, 240
of classroom management, 445–447
defining in problem solving, 295
of expert teachers, 7
implications for teachers, 383
mastery (task or learning), 381, 382
in means-end analysis, 299
under NCLB, 2, 17
performance (ability or ego), 381–382, 382
performance improvement though setting, 380
for self-management, 235
setting for self-regulated learning, 337–338
social, 382
Goal acceptance, 383
Goal-directed actions, **30**
Goal-directed behavior, 380
Goal orientations, **380,** 380–383
Goal structure, 399, **400**
Good behavior game, **226**
Grade-equivalent scores, **528**
Grading, 570–581
accommodations for students with special needs and, 581
communicating with families and, 579–581
contract system and, 577–578
criterion-referenced, 574–575, 576
on effort and improvement, 578–579
failure and, 571–573
fairness in, 579
feedback and, 573
motivation and, 400, 573–574, 575
norm-referenced, 574
percentage, 576–577
point system for, 575–577
revise option and, 577
Grading on the curve, **574**
Grammar, school-age children and, 54
Grand mal seizures, 146
Graphic organizers, 314
Great Britain, divorce in, 74
Group consequences, **226**
Group discussion, **496,** 497
Group focus, **460**
for preventing discipline problems, 460–461
Grouping
between-class, 122, 123, 167–168
cross-age, 124
flexible, 124
motivation and, 399
within-class, 122–124
Group learning. *See* Cooperative learning
Growth, 22
during adolescence, 65
Guided discovery, **291**
Guided Inquiry Supporting Multiple Literacies (GIsML), 351, 352

Halo effect, **579**
Handedness
brain and, 25
development of, 64
Handicaps, **110,** 110–111
Hanunoo people, language of, 42
Health, poverty and, 166
Hearing impairment, 146–147
Helping students, common sense versus research on, 9–10
Hemispheric specialization, 25
Heredity-versus-environment debate. *See* Nature-versus-nurture debate
Heritage language, **54**
Heuristics, **299**
availability, 303
for problem solving, 299–300
representativeness, 302–303
Hierarchy of needs, **374,** 374–375
Highlighting, as learning tactic, 313
Highly effective teachers, teaching and modeling of decision making by, 342
Highly qualified teachers, 2
Highly structured tasks, for cooperative learning, 419
High-road transfer, **319,** 320
High-stakes testing, **540**
accountability and, 540–541
dangers and possibilities of, 541–543
helping students with disabilities to prepare for, 543–545
Hindus, moral reasoning among, 100
Hippocampus, 23

Hispanic Americans. *See* Latino/a Americans
Histograms, **525**
History of educational psychology, 8–9
Homework, 491–492
debate about, 492
making valuable, 492, 493
Homonyms, 184
Homosexuality, origins of, 176
Hostile aggression, 78
Hot cognition, 383
Humanistic interpretations of motivation, **374**, 377
Hyperactivity, peer rejection and, 77
Hypothetico-deductive reasoning, **35**

IDEA (Individuals with Disabilities Education Act) of 1990, autism under, 147
IDEIA. *See* Individuals with Disabilities Education Improvement Act (IDEIA)
Identity, **33**, 70, **70**
in concrete operational stage, 33
diversity and convergences in, 103
ethnic, 90–92
gender-role, 177–180
racial, 90–92
sexual, 176–177
Identity achievement, **71**
Identity and the Life Cycle (Erikson), 67
Identity diffusion, **71**
Identity foreclosure, **71**
Identity versus role confusion stage, 67, 70–72
Identity, Youth, and Crisis (Erikson), 67
IEPs (Individualized Education Programs), **127**, 127–128, 511, 512, 548
IHMC (Institute for Human Machine Cognition), 314, 315
ILE (individual learning expectation), **579**
Illegal drugs. *See* Drug abuse
Ill-structured tasks, for cooperative learning, 419
Images, **260**
declarative knowledge development and, 270–271
in explicit memory, 260
in long-term memory, 259
Imaginary audience, 36
"I" messages, **469**
Imitative learning, 48
Immigrants, 162, 168–169
Implicit memory, **259**
Importance, **396**
Improvement, grading on, 578–579
Inattentiveness, peer rejection and, 77
Incentives, **374**
INCLUDE strategy, 509, 510
Inclusion, **128**, 128–129
Inclusive classrooms, effective teaching in, 508–511, 512
Incremental view of ability, **388**, 388–389
Individual constructivism, 344–346
Individual differences
in long-term memory, 278
in metacognition, 278–279
working memory and, 277–278
Individual interests, 384
Individualistic goal structure, 399, 400
Individualized Education Programs (IEPs), **127**, 127–128, 511, 512, 548
Individual learning expectation (ILE), **579**
Individuals with Disabilities Education Act (IDEA) of 1990, autism under, 147
Individuals with Disabilities Education Improvement Act (IDEIA), **127**
assistive technology under, 511
emotional disturbances under, 140–141
positive behavioral supports under, 223, 466
students served under, 130, 131
testing under, 548
Inductive reasoning, **290**
Industry, **69**
Industry versus inferiority stage, 67, 69–70
Infants
cognitive development of, 28, 30
psychosocial development of, 67, 68
Informal assessments, **569**, 569–570
Information processing, **250**
Information processing model of memory, 250–257
sensory memory and, 250–253
working memory and, 253–257
Information processing theory of cognitive development, 36–37
comparison with other theories of learning, 365
In-group, 172
Inhibitions, strengthening or weakening, 233
Initiative, **68**
Initiative versus guilt stage, 67, 68
Innovation, revolutionary, 310–311
Inquiry learning, **351**, 351–352, 354–355
Insight, **118**, **303**
Institute for Human Machine Cognition (IHMC), 314, 315
Instructed learning, 48
Instruction. *See also* Teaching
analogical, 294
anchored, 354
differentiated, 514–515
self-, 49, 236–238
teacher-directed. *See* Teacher-directed instruction
Instructional conversations, 48, 49, **355**, 355–356, 357
Instructional objectives, **479**, 479–483
behavioral, 480
cognitive, 480
taxonomies of, 481–483
Instructional strategies, students' achievement and, 500
Instrumental aggression, **78**
Instrumental value, 405
Integration, **128**
racial, 171
Integrity, **72**
Integrity versus despair stage, 67, 72
Intellectual disabilities, **139**. *See also* Students with intellectual disabilities
Intelligence, 110–121, **111**. *See also* Students who are gifted and talented; Students with intellectual disabilities
achievement and, 121
analytic/componential, 118
bodily-kinesthetic, 114
creative/experiential, 118
crystallized, 112
definition of, 111–113
emotional, 116–117
fluid, 112
heredity versus environment and, 121
hierarchical model of, 113
interpersonal, 114
intrapersonal, 114
labeling related to, 110–111
linguistic, 114
logical-mathematical, 114
measurement of, 119–121
multiple, 113–116
musical, 114
naturalist, 114
practical/contextual, 118–119
as process, 117–119
single versus multiple intelligences, 112–113
spatial, 114
structure of, 112–113
successful, triarchic theory of, 117–119
Intelligence quotient (IQ), **119**. *See also* IQ score
Intelligence tests, 119–121, 154. *See also* IQ score
Flynn effect and, 120–121
group versus individual, 119–120
for identification of gifted and talented students, 151
meaning of IQ score and, 120
mental retardation and, 139
Stanford-Binet, 119
Intention, theory of mind and, 94
Interest(s), 383–388
catching and holding, 384
implications for teachers, 388
intrinsic motivation and, 307, 373, 378, 405
personal or individual, 384
situational, 384
tapping, 383–384, 385
in task, 396
Interest areas, 454–455
Interference, **265**
forgetting and, 265–266

Intermittent reinforcement schedule, 212, **213**
Internalization, **101**
of moral rules and principles, 101
Internal locus of control, success and failure and, 390
Interpersonal intelligence, 114
Intersubjective attitudes, **349**
Interval schedule, 212, **213**
Intimacy versus isolation stage, 67, 72
Intrapersonal intelligence, 114
Intrinsic motivation, **373**, 378, 405
Intrinsic task motivation, creativity and, 307
Intrinsic value, 404–405
of tasks, 396
Intuitive thinking, **290**
IQ (intelligence quotient), **119**
IQ score
deviation, 120
meaning of, 120
scholastic aptitude and, 538–539
working memory and, 277

Jigsaw, 419, **425**, 425–426
Joplin Plan, **122**
Journal(s), for assessment, 569
Journal of Educational Psychology, 8

Keyword method, **272**
Knowledge, 249–250
conditional, 258, 267, 274
construction of, 346–347
declarative. *See* Declarative knowledge
domain-specific, 249, 278, 304
of effective teachers, 486–487
of experts, 274–276, 303–305
of expert teachers, 7
fund of, 50
general, 249–250
importance in learning, 249–250
metacognition and, 267
novice, 305, 306
prerequisite, 275
procedural, 258, 267, 278
self-regulation and, 335
of students, 198
systems of, 7
tacit, 118–119
Knowledge acquisition components of intelligence, 118
Kohlberg's theory of moral development, 95–97
criticisms of, 96–97
Kpelle people, 38
KWL strategy, **315**, 315–316

Labeling, 110–111
disorders, disabilities, and handicaps and, 110–111
person-first language and, 110

Laboratory School at University of Chicago, 8
Language. *See also* Bilingual *entries*; English as a second language (ESL); English language learners (ELLs)
brain area involved in, 23, 25
cognitive development and, 42
heritage, 54
learning disabilities and, 132–133
legislation regarding, 128
in preoperational children, 31
pronunciation of, 54, 184
of thinking, 361
Language arts, self-concept and, 89
Language development, 51–56
dual, 52, 54
milestones in, 51, 53
neuron pruning and, 23
in school years, 54–55
Language differences, 162, 182–188, 189
bilingualism and. *See* Bilingual *entries*
dialects and, 183–185
Language disorders, 128–129, 136–137
Lateralization, **25**
Latino/a Americans
cultural conflicts and, 169–170
cultural tools for teaching, 50–51
discipline of, 470
educational attainment of, 173–174
learning preferences and, 195
motivation to learn and, 403
physical maturation of, 65
poverty among, 166
resistance culture of, 167
school achievement of, 170
semilingualism among, 187
stereotype threat and, 174–175
teachers' caring and, 83
underrepresentation in gifted and talented programs, 153–154
in U.S. population, 162
Learned helplessness, **133**, **392**
beliefs about, 392–393
Learners. *See also* Student *entries*
ego-involved, 381
task-involved, 381
work-avoidant, 382
Learning, **206**
access to, classroom management for, 446–447
anxiety and, interference with learning by, 26
assisted, 48–49
by association, 208. *See also* Classical conditioning; Conditioning; Operant conditioning
attention and, 253
behavioral. *See* Behavioral learning
brain and, 25–26
cognitive development and, 42
cognitive view of. *See* Cognitive view of learning; Declarative knowledge; Information processing model of memory; Knowledge; Long-term memory
collaborative, 48
as constructive process, 46–47
cooperative. *See* Cooperative learning
deciding what skills are worth learning and, 320–321
definition of, 206–207
enactive, 230
engaged. *See* Engaged learning
imitative, 48
inquiry, 351–352, 354–355
instructed, 48
interference with, by anxiety, 387
motivation to learn and. *See* Motivation to learn
problem-based, 352–355, 396–397
self-regulated. *See* Self-regulated learning (SRL)
self-talk and, 44
service, 434–437
situated, 347–348
skills that can increase, 237
student ownership of, 350
valuing, 317–318
vicarious, 230
Vygotsky's view of, 44–45
Learning disabilities, **131**. *See also* Students with learning disabilities
loneliness and, 82
specific, 131
Learning environments, 442–474
complex, 349
discipline problems. *See* Discipline problems
diversity and convergences in, 470–472
encouraging engagement and, 459
first weeks of class and, 457–458
goals of classroom management and, 445–447
maintaining, 458–466
need for organization and, 444–447
planning for computer uses and, 455–457
planning spaces for, 452–455
positive, creating, 448–458
prevention of problems and, 460–461
research on, 448
rules and procedures for, 448–452, 453
school-wide positive behavior supports and, 466
Learning goals, 381, 382
for students with intellectual disabilities, 140
Learning needs, flexible grouping and, 124
Learning preferences, **125**, 125–127, 126. *See also* Learning style(s)
cautions about, 125–126
diversity of, 195–196

Learning strategies, **311,** 311–314
applying, 316–318
for self-regulated learning, 335, 338
transfer of, stages of, 322
Learning style(s), **124,** 124–125
research on, cautions about, 196
value of considering, 126–127
visual versus verbal, 126–127
Learning Style Inventory, 126
Learning Style Profile, 126
Learning Styles Inventory (Revised), 126
Learning tactics, **311,** 311–314
for self-regulated learning, 338
for verbal and procedural information, 312
Learning tasks
analyzing, 336–337
self-regulated learning and, 335, 341–342
Learning theories
behavioral, 206–207
diversity and convergences in, 362, 364–365
social, 229, 330
Least restrictive environment (LRE), **128,** 128–129
Legislation, 127–130. *See also* Individuals with Disabilities Education Improvement Act (IDEIA); No Child Left Behind Act (NCLB) of 2001
Educational Amendments Act of 1974, 582
Education of the Handicapped Act (PL 94-142), 127
Family Educational Rights and Privacy Act of 1974, 582
IEPs and, 127–128
least restrictive environment and, 128–129
Section 504 protections and, 129–130
student and family rights and, 128
Legitimate peripheral participation, **376**
Lesson study, **479**
Levels of processing theory, **263,** 263–264
Life problems, suicide and, 143
Life-span development approach, 72
Linguistic intelligence, 114
Listening
empathetic, 468
student learning and, 237
Loci method, **271**
Locus of causality, **373,** 390
Logic
in concrete operational stage, 34
one-way, 31
Logical consequences, **451**
Logical-mathematical intelligence, 114
Loneliness, children with disabilities and, 81–82
Longitudinal studies, 13
Long-term memory, **257,** 265–266
capacity, duration, and contents of, 257–259
episodic, 262
explicit, 259–262
forgetting and, 265–266
implicit, 259, 262–263
individual differences in, 278
levels of processing theory and, 263–264
reconstruction and, 264–265
retrieving information from, 264
semantic, 259–262
spreading activation and, 264
storing and retrieving information in, 263–266
working, 258
Long-term working memory, **258**
Low-road transfer, **319,** 320
Low vision, **147**
LRE (least restrictive environment), **128,** 128–129

Macrosystem, in bioecological model of development, 73–74
Mainstreaming, **128**
Maintenance rehearsal, **256**
Males. *See* Boys; Gender *entries*
Marginality, minority youth and, 91
Maslow's hierarchy, 374–375
Massed practice, **274**
Mastery experiences, **333**
Mastery goals, **381,** 382
Mastery-oriented students, **393**
Matching tests, 560
Mathematics
cognitive apprenticeship in, 358
ethnic and racial differences in achievement in, 171
gender bias in math classes and, 181–182
gender differences in, 181
instruction in, 505–506
learning disabilities and, 132
NAEP tests in, 546
self-concept and, 89
self-regulated learning and, 339
teacher quality and achievement in, 4
within-class ability grouping for, 124
Maturation, **22**
cognitive development and, 27–28
Mean, **525**
Meaningfulness, declarative knowledge development and, 269–270
Meaningful verbal learning, **292**
Means-end analysis, **299**
Measurement, **522**
Media. *See also* Television
African Americans in, 173
print, gender bias in, 179–180
violence in, 78
Median, **525**
Melting pot, **162**
Memorization, rote, declarative knowledge development and, 273–274
Memory
episodic, 262
explicit, 259–262
flashbulb, 262
implicit, 259
information processing model of. *See* Information processing model of memory
long-term. *See* Long-term memory
procedural, 262
semantic, 259
sensory, 250–253
short-term, 254
working, 253–257
Mental age, **119**
Mental disorders, 141. *See also* Emotional and behavioral disorders; Students with emotional or behavioral disorders
Mental representations, 30
Mental retardation, **139.** *See also* Students with intellectual disabilities
classification of, 139, 140
loneliness and, 82
neuron pruning and, 23
Mesosystem, in bioecological model of development, 73
Metacognition, **267,** 267–269
individual differences in, 278–279
regulation and, 267–268
strategies for students with learning disabilities and, 268–269
types of knowledge and, 267
Metacomponents of intelligence, 118
Metalinguistic awareness, **55**
of school-age children, 55
Mexican Americans. *See* Latino/a Americans
Microgenetic research, **12**
Microsystem, in bioecological model of development, 73
Mind, theory of. *See* Theory of mind
Mindful abstraction, 320
Minority groups, **168**
in U.S. population, 162
Misbehavior. *See* Discipline problems
Misunderstandings, sources of, 197
Mnemonics, **271**
declarative knowledge development and, 271–273
peg-type, 271
Mode, **525**
Modeling, **233, 333**
aggression and, 78
self-efficacy and, 333
Monitoring, metacognition and, 267–268

Monolingual children, 54
Moral behavior, 101
Moral development, 95–97
gender differences in, 97
Kohlberg's theory of, 95–97
Moral dilemmas, **95**, 95–96
Morality of cooperation, **95**
Moral realism, **95**
Moral reasoning, **95**, 96, 98–99
diversity and convergences in, 103
diversity in, 100–101
implications for teachers, 99
Moratorium, **71**
Motivation, 370–410, **373**
behavioral approaches to, 374, 377
beliefs and self-schemas and, 388–394
cognitive and social cognitive approaches to, 375, 377
creativity and, 307
debate over making learning fun and, 385
definition of, 372
expectancy × value theories of, 375–376
extrinsic, 373
goal orientations and, 380–383
grades and, 573–574, 575
humanistic approaches to, 374, 377
implications for teachers, 379
interests and emotions and, 383–388
intrinsic, 307, 373, 378
to learn. *See* Motivation to learn
Maslow's hierarchy and, 374–375
needs and, 377–379
observational learning and, 231–232
peer influence on, 77
self-efficacy and, 333–334
self-regulation and, 335–336
sociocultural conceptions of, 376, 377
strategies supporting and undermining in classroom, 402, 404–407
teachers' caring and, 82–83
Motivation to learn, **395**, 395–407
diversity and convergences in, 403–407
evaluation and, 400, 401
grouping and goal structures and, 399, 400
recognizing accomplishment and, 399–402
supporting choices and, 398–399
tasks for learning and, 396–397
time and, 400–402
Motor development, in preschool years, 64
Motor function
brain area controlling, 24
gender differences in, 181
Movement management, **461**
MRI (functional magnetic resonance imaging) studies, instruction and brain development and, 25
Multicultural education, **163**
Multiple-choice tests, 560
using, 557
writing questions for, 557–558
Multiple disabilities, 146
Multiple intelligences, theory of, 113–116
Multiple representations of content, 349–350, **350**
Musical intelligence, 114
Myelination, **24**

NAEP (National Assessment of Educational Progress), 546–548
NAEYC (National Association for the Education of Young Children), guidelines for developmentally appropriate education of, 46
National Assessment of Educational Progress (NAEP), 546–548
National Association for the Education of Young Children (NAEYC), guidelines for developmentally appropriate education of, 46
A Nation at Risk: The Imperative for Educational Reform, 540
Native Americans. *See also* Eskimos
educational attainment of, 173
language of, 42, 54
learning preferences and, 196
resistance culture of, 167
in U.S. population, 162
Native-language maintenance instruction, 187
Natural consequences, **451**
Naturalist intelligence, 114
Nature-versus-nurture debate
about people with extraordinary abilities, 150
intelligence and, 121
NCLB. *See* No Child Left Behind Act (NCLB) of 2001
Need(s), 377–379
for autonomy, 378
being, 375
deficiency, 375
hierarchy of, 374–375
for relatedness, 378–379
self-determination and, 377–379
Need for autonomy, **378**
Negative correlations, **11**
Negative reinforcement, **211**, 219–221
Neglect, physical, indicators of, 84
Negotiation, for discipline problems, 469–470
Neo-Piagetian theories, **37**
Neurological system. *See also* Brain; Neurons
adolescent development and, 66
Neurons, **23**
myelination of, 24
overproduction and pruning of, 23
synapses between, 23
Neutral stimulus, **208**
New York Regents Exam, 542
New Zealand, divorce in, 74
Nigrescence, **91**, 91–92
No Child Left Behind Act (NCLB) of 2001, 2, 17, 540
Adequate Yearly Progress and, 2, 17, 540
high-stakes testing and. *See* High-stakes testing
NAEP tests under, 546, 548
scientifically based research under, 13
Nongraded elementary schools, **122**
No One Left to Hate: Teaching Compassion After Columbine (Aronson), 433
Norm(s), 523
Normal distribution, **526**, 526–527
Norm groups, **523**
Norming samples, **524**, 524–525
Norm-referenced grading, **574**
Norm-referenced testing, 522, **523**
of achievement, 536–538
Note taking, as learning tactic, 313–314
Novelty, 386–387
Novice knowledge, 305, 306
Nutrition, of adolescents, 66

Objectives, instructional. *See* Instructional objectives
Objective testing, **556**, 556–558
Object permanence, **30**
Observational learning, 229–234, **230**
attention and, 230
factors influencing, 232
motivation and reinforcement and, 231–232
production and, 231
retention and, 230–231
in teaching, 233–234
Offensiveness, 532
One-way logic, 31
Operant(s), **210**
Operant conditioning, **210**, 210–215
antecedents and behavior change and, 214–215
cueing and, 214
extinction and, 214
prompting and, 214–215
punishment and, 211–212
reinforcement and, 210–211
reinforcement schedules and, 212–214
Operations, **30**
Opportunities to learn, 533
Organization, **28**, **263**
cognitive development and, 28
of effective teachers, 487
of knowledge, by experts, 304
long-term memory and, 263
visual tools for, 314
Originality, 308
Out-group, 172

Overgeneralization, **289**
Overlapping, **460**
Overlearning, **321**
Overt aggression, 78

Pacific Islanders. *See* Asian Americans and Pacific Islanders
Pair-share, 419
PALS (Performance Assessment Links in Science), 546
Paraphrase rule, **467**
Parent(s). *See also* Families
authoritarian, 75
authoritative, 75
divorce of, 74
influence on learning, 415
permissive, 76
rejecting/neglecting, 76
rights of, 128
unmarried, 162
Parenting, culture and, 74–76
Parenting styles, **74**
Participant(s), in research studies, **12**
Participant observation, **11**
Participation structures, **196**, 196–197, **447**
Part learning, **274**
Part-whole relations, 295
PBL (problem-based learning), **352**, 352–355, **396**, 396–397
PBS (positive behavior support), **223**, 223–224, 466
Peer(s), 76–81
aggression in, 78
attention of, reinforcing of behaviors by, 216
influence on learning, 414–415
resistance culture and, 167
scaffolding and, 48
Peer culture, 76–77
Peer mediation, 429
Peer rejection
children likely to experience, 77
of gifted and talented students, 150–151
Peer tutoring, checklist for, 215
Peg-type mnemonics, **271**
Percentage grading, **576**, 576–577
Percentile rank scores, **527**, 527–528
Perception, **251**, 251–252
Performance(s)
in context, 562
evaluating, 565–569
goal setting and, 380
reliability, validity, and generalizability and, 567–568
scoring rubrics for, 566–567, 568, 569
Performance assessment, **562**
Performance Assessment Links in Science (PALS), 546
Performance components of intelligence, 118
Performance goals, **381**, 381–382, 382
Performance phase of self-regulated learning, 338
Performing, in Fostering Communities of Learners program, 362
Permissive parents, 76
Personal choices, 99
Personal development, **22**
diversity and convergences in, 102–103
Personal interests, 384
Personal territories, 454–455
Person-first language, 110
Perspective-taking ability, **94**
Petit mal seizures, 146
Phonological loop, **254**, 254–255
Physical abuse, indicators of, 84
Physical development, **22**, 66
in adolescence, 66
in elementary school years, 64
in preschool years, 64
Physical neglect, indicators of, 84
Piaget's theory of cognitive development, 26–36
adaptation in, 29
equilibration in, 29
implications for teachers, 46–48
influences on development and, 27–28
limitations of, 38
organization in, 28
social interaction and, 40–41
stages of development in, 29–36
PL 94-142 (Education of the Handicapped Act), 127
Planning
for computer uses, 455–457
from constructivist perspective, 483–485
lesson study approach to, 479
metacognition and, 267
objectives for learning and, 479–480
for self-regulated learning, 337
spaces for learning, 452–455
student learning and, 237
taxonomies and, 481–483
time is of the essence, 478
PLAN program, 405
Plasticity, **24**
Play
creativity liked to, 310
gender-role identity development and, 178
Piaget's view of, 47–48
Portfolios, 562–565, 562–569, **563**
best works, 565
evaluating, 565–569
process, 565
Positive behavior support (PBS), **223**, 223–224, 466
Positive correlations, **11**
Positive practice, **219**
Positive reinforcement, **211**
Postconventional judgment, 95–96
Poverty, 162
school achievement and, 166–168
Practical/contextual intelligence, 118–119
Practice
distributed, 274
with feedback, 275
massed, 274
Pragmatics, **55**, **196**
school-age children and, 55
Praise, reinforcement of behaviors by, 216–217
Praise-and-ignore approach, 216
Preconventional judgment, 95
Precorrection, **466**
Prefrontal cortex, 24
Prejudice, **172**, 172–173
development of, 172–173
racial, 172
Premack principle, 217–218, **218**
Prenatal development, of brain, 23
Preoperational stage, **30**, 30–32
Prerequisite knowledge, 275
Preschool children
cognitive development of, 30–32
gender-role stereotyping and, 178–179
physical development of, 64
play and, 47
psychosocial development of, 67, 68–69
quality of care for, 168
theory of mind and, 94
Presentation punishment, **212**
Pretending, 31
Pretests, **554**
Priming, **262**, 262–263
spreading activation and, 264
Principles, **13**
Private speech, **42**, 42–44
learning and, 44
zone of proximal development and, 44
Probability levels, 12
Problem(s), **294**, 294–295
finding, 295–296
restructuring, 307
well- and ill-structured, 295
Problem-based learning (PBL), **352**, 352–355, **396**, 396–397
Problem solving, 294–305, **295**, 306
anticipating, acting, and looking back and, 300–301
brain area involved in, 23
as coping strategy for anxiety, 388
creative. *See* Creativity
debate about teaching of, 360
defining goals and representing problems and, 296–298, 299
effective, 303–305, 306
exploring possible solution strategies for, 298–300
factors hindering, 302–303

mathematics. *See* Mathematics
problem finding and, 295–296
subject area specificity of strategies for, 295
Problem-solving tasks, for cooperative learning, 419
Procedural fairness, 533
Procedural knowledge, **258,** 267, 274, 278
Procedural memory, **262**
Procedures, for positive learning environment, 448–449
Process portfolios, 565
Production(s), **262,** 275
of experts, 304
observational learning and, 231
Progressive education movement, 8
Project-based science, 354
Prompts, **214**
operant conditioning and, 214–215
Pronunciation
dialects and, 184
of school-age children, 54
Propositional networks, **260**
Propositions, 259–260
Prosocial behavior, peer acceptance and, 77
Prototypes, **252, 286**
Psychological constructivism, 344–346
Psychomotor domain, **482**
taxonomy of, 482–483
Psychosocial theory, of Erikson. *See* Erikson's theory of psychosocial development
Puberty, **65**
Punishment, **211**
caution about, 222, 223
operant conditioning and, 211–212
Pygmalion effect, **496**

Quality, of teachers, 3–5
Question(s), 494–496
convergent, 494
divergent, 494
for essay tests, writing, 559
fitting to students, 495
multiple-choice, writing, 557–558
Questioning, reciprocal, 423–424

Race, **168**
genetics of, 154
Racial and ethnic pride, **92**
Racial diversity. *See* Cultural diversity; Diversity and convergences; Ethnic and racial diversity; *specific groups*
Racial identity, 90–92
Racism, below-the-surface, 172
Radical constructivism, **345,** 345–346
Random procedures, 12
Range, **526**
Ratio schedule, 212, **213**
Raw score, 523
Reaching every student
communicating with families about grades and, 581
coping with anxiety and, 388
families and, 339–340
helping students with disabilities prepare for high-stakes tests and, 543–545
in inclusive classrooms, 508–511, 512
learning disabilities and concept teaching and, 294
school-wide positive behavior supports for, 466
severe behavior problems and, 228–229
teaching every student and, 198–199
using cooperative learning wisely and, 424–426
Reading
balanced approach to instruction in, 502–503, 504
gender differences in, 181
instruction in, for students with learning disabilities, 136
learning disabilities and, 132
learning strategies for, 314–316, 317
NAEP tests in, 546
self-concept and, 89
teacher quality and achievement in, 4
within-class ability grouping for, 124
READS strategy, **314,** 315
Reasoning
deductive, 292
hypothetico-deductive, 35
inductive, 290
moral. *See* Moral reasoning
Reciprocal determinism, **330,** 330–331
Reciprocal questioning, 419, **423,** 423–424
Reciprocal teaching, 419, **503,** 503–504
Recitation, 492–496
questioning phase of, 493–495
responding to student answers and, 495–496
Recognizing accomplishment, 399
Reconstruction, **264,** 264–265
Referral process, 153
Reflecting phase of self-regulated learning, 338
Reflectiveness, 7
Rehearsal, 256
Reinforcement, **210**
differential, 216
negative, 211, 219–221
observational learning and, 231–232
operant conditioning and, 210–211
positive, 211
of self, **232,** 235–236
token, 227–228
vicarious, 231
Reinforcement schedules, 212–214
Reinforcers, **210,** 210–211
selecting, 217–218
Rejecting/neglecting parents, 76
Rejection, by peers, 77
Relatedness, need for, 378–379
Relational aggression, **78,** 79
Reliability, **530**
of performances, 567–568
of test scores, 530
Removal punishment, **212**
Representativeness heuristic, **302,** 302–303
Reprimands, **221**
in applied behavior analysis, 221–222
Research, 9–13
common sense compared with, 9–10
correlation, 11
debate over best type of, 14
descriptive, 9–10
experimental, 12
in Fostering Communities of Learners program, 362
microgenetic, 12
scientifically based, 13
teachers as researchers and, 13
time and, 13
Resilience, **191,** 191–194
in classrooms, 192–193
constructing resilient classrooms and, 193–194
in students, 192
Resistance culture, **167**
Resource rooms, 509–510
Respect, for students, 198
Respect and Protect program, 434, 436
Respondents, **208**
Response, **208**
unconditioned, 208
Response cost, **222**
in applied behavior analysis, 222
Response set, **302,** 319
Restructuring, **307**
Retention, observational learning and, 230–231
Retention in grade, 572–573
Retention phase of strategic transfer, 322
Reticular formation, 23
Retrieval, 250, **264**
Reversibility, **33**
Reversible thinking, 30, **31**
Reversing actions, 30
Review tasks, for cooperative learning, 419
Revise option, **577**
Revolutionary innovation, 310–311
Rewards, **374**
for learning, debate over, 239
Ripple effect, **233**
Ritalin, for attention deficit hyperactivity disorder, 135
Rosenshine's six teaching functions, 488
Rote memorization, **274**
declarative knowledge development and, 273–274

Rubrics
grading, 577–578
scoring, 566–567, 568, 569
Rule(s), **450**
for elementary school, 450–451
moral development and, 95
for positive learning environment, 448, 450–452
for secondary school, 451
as social conventions, 98–99
Rule assessment, 37

SAT. *See* Scholastic Assessment Test (SAT)
Satiation, **221**
in applied behavior analysis, 221
Scaffolding, **48,** 355
Schema(s), **260**
concepts and, 287
explicit memory and, 260–262
gender, 178
prejudice and, 173
Schema-driven problem solving, **298,** 299
Schemes, **28**
action, 30–31
cognitive development and, 28
Scholastic achievement. *See* Academic achievement
Scholastic Assessment Test (SAT)
normal distribution of scores on, 526
validity of scores on, 532
working memory test scores and, 277
School(s)
desegregation of, 171
dropping out from. *See* Dropping out
elementary. *See* Elementary school(s)
hours of, 66
secondary. *See* Secondary schools
self-esteem and, 88
"separate but equal," 171
School achievement. *See* Academic achievement
School-age children. *See also* Elementary school(s)
cognitive development of, 30–34
language development in, 54–55
physical development of, 64
play and, 48
psychosocial development of, 67, 69–70
self-concept development in, 86
School problems, divorce and, 74
School violence, 432–434
"copy cat," 234
prevention of, 433–434, 435, 465
Respect and Protect program to combat, 434, 436
among victims, 80
warning signs of, 435
Science
conceptual change teaching in, 507
instruction, 506–508
self-concept and, 89
Scientifically based research, 13
Scoring rubrics, **566,** 566–567, 568, 569
Script(s), 261, **262**
Scripted cooperation, **424, 490**
Seatwork, **491,** 492
making valuable, 492, 493
Secondary schools
discipline problems in, 462–465
effective managers for, 458
rules for, 451
Second-hand investigations, 352
Second wave constructivism, **346**
Section 504, **129,** 129–130
Segregation, 171
Seizure disorders, 146
Self-actualization, **374,** 374–375
Self-concept, **85,** 85–86, 87, 89–92
achievement and, 86
development of, 86
diversity and, 89–90
diversity and convergence in, 102
ethnic and racial identity and, 90–92
integration of moral beliefs and values into, 101
low, poverty and, 167
self-efficacy and, 332–333
self-esteem and, 85–86
structure of, 85–86
Self-determination, 377–379
in classroom, 378
information and control and, 378
need for autonomy and, 378
need for relatedness and, 378–379
Self-efficacy, **232, 332,** 332–333, **392**
beliefs about, 392
learning and, 318
motivation and, 333–334
self-concept and self-esteem and, 332–333
sources of, 333
of teachers, 334–335
teaching toward, 340–343
Self-esteem, **85,** 87, 88, 89
diversity and convergences in, 102–103
encouraging, 88, 89
self-concept and, 85–86
self-defeating strategies to protect, 175
self-efficacy and, 332–333
Self-evaluation, 235
self-regulated learning and, 342
Self-fulfilling prophecies, **496**
Self-instruction, **236,** 236–238
cognitive, 49
Self-knowledge, of expert teachers, 8
Self-management, **234,** 234–236, **447**
classroom management for, 447
goal setting for, 235
monitoring and evaluating progress with, 235
self-reinforcement for, 235–236
Self-regulated learning (SRL), 335–343, **336**
examples of, 338–340
factors influencing, 335–336
models of, 336–338
teaching toward, 340–343
Self-regulation, **335**
Self-reinforcement, **232,** 235–236
Self-schemas
implications for teachers, 394
motivation and, 388–394
Self-talk, 42–44
learning and, 44
zone of proximal development and, 44
Self-worth, beliefs about, 393–394
Semantic memory, **259**
Semilingualism, **186**
Semiotic function, **31**
Sensorimotor stage, **30**
Sensory function, brain area controlling, 24
Sensory information store, 250
Sensory memory, **250,** 250–253
attention and, 252–253
capacity, duration, and contents of, 250–251
perception and, 251–252
Sensory register, 250
"Separate but equal" schools, 171
Separation, minority youth and, 91
Serial-position effect, **274**
Seriation, **33**
in concrete operational stage, 33
Service learning, 434–437, **435**
SES. *See* Socioeconomic status (SES)
Sex, definition of, 176
Sex discrimination, in classrooms, 180
Sexism, 176
Sexual abuse, indicators of, 84
Sexual identity, **176,** 176–177
Sexual orientation, 176–177
Shaping, **218,** 218–219
Sharing, in Fostering Communities of Learners program, 362
Short answer tests, 560
Short-term memory, **254.** *See also* Working memory
Shoshoni people, language of, 42
Simplicity principle, concept learning and, 287
Single-subject experimental studies, **12**
Situated learning, **347,** 347–348
Situational interests, 384
Skill-building tasks, for cooperative learning, 419
Skipping grades
common sense versus research on, 10
for gifted and talented students, 152
SLDs (specific learning disabilities), 131
Sleep, during adolescence, 66
SMART approach, for attention deficit hyperactivity disorder, 136
Social aggression, 78

Social class, 165
Social cognitive theory, **230, 330,** 330–343
motivation and, 333–334, 375
reciprocal determinism and, 330
self-efficacy and, 332–334, 340–343
self-regulated learning and, 335–343
teachers' sense of efficacy and, 334–335
Social comparison, self-concept development and, 86
Social conventions, **98,** 98–99
Social development, **22**
diversity and convergences in, 102–103
Social engagement. *See* Engaged learning
Social goals, **382**
Social interaction, in cognitive development, 40–41
Social isolation, **222**
in applied behavior analysis, 222
Social learning theory, **229, 330**
Social negotiation, **349**
Social organization, of classrooms, 195
Social persuasion, **333**
Social relationships, self-concept and, 89
Social skills
development of, 80–81
for preventing discipline problems, 461
Social skills tasks, for cooperative learning, 419
Social transmission, cognitive development and, 28
Sociocultural theory, **39.** *See also* Vygotsky's sociocultural perspective
Sociocultural views of motivation, **376,** 377
Socioeconomic status (SES), **165,** 165–168
norm-referenced testing and, 523
school achievement and, 166–168
Sociolinguistics, **196,** 196–197
Spasticity, **146**
Spatial intelligence, 114
Specific learning disabilities (SLDs), 131
Speech
egocentric, 42
private, 42–44
Speech disorders, **137,** 137–138
of articulation, 138
of voicing, 138
Spell checkers, debate over use of, 301
Spiral curriculum, **350**
Split-half reliability, 530
Sports, self-concept and, 89
Spreading activation, **264**
SRL. *See* Self-regulated learning (SRL)
Stability
success and failure and, 390
of test scores, 530
STAD (Student Teams Achievement Divisions), 419
Stand-alone thinking skills programs, **359**
Standard deviation, **526**
Standard error of measurement, **531**
Standardized tests, **524.** *See also* High-stakes testing
achievement, 536–538
aptitude, 538–539
culture-fair (culture-free), 534
diversity and convergences in, 546–548
interpretation of, 523–524
preparing for, 543–545
scores on. *See* Test scores
tips for taking, 535
types of, 534, 536–539
Standard scores, **529,** 530
Stanford-Binet test, 119
Stanine scores, **529**
START approach, 116
Statistical significance, **12**
Stem, of multiple-choice questions, **557**
Stereotypes, **173**
Stereotype threat, **174,** 174–176
combating, 175–176
disidentification and, 175
test performance and, 174–175
Stereotyping, gender-role, in preschool years, 178–179
Stimulant medications, for attention deficit hyperactivity disorder, 135
Stimulation
brain development and, 24
neuron pruning and, 24
play and, 47
Stimulus, **208**
conditioned, 209
neutral, 208
unconditioned, 208
Stimulus control, **214**
Storage, 250
Story grammars, **261**
Strategies, for behavioral methods, 240
Stress
brain and, 26
divorce and, 74
poverty and, 166
Student-centered teaching, 500–513
in inclusive classrooms, 508–511, 512
of mathematics, 505–506
of reading and writing, 502–504
of science, 506–508
technology and exceptional students and, 511–513
Student rights, 128
Students who are deaf, 146–147
Students who are gifted and talented, 148–153
bilingual, recognizing, 186–187
cooperative learning for, 424
definition of, 149–150
identification of, 151
motivation to learn and, 403
origin of abilities if, 150
problems faced by, 150–151
teaching, 151–153
Students with attention-deficit hyperactivity disorder, treating and teaching, 135–136
Students with communication disorders, 136–139
language disorders and, 128–129, 136–137
speech disorders and, 137–138
Students with disabilities, 81–82. *See also specific student groups*
grading and, 581
helping to prepare for high-stakes tests, 543–545
loneliness and, 81–82
Students with emotional or behavioral disorders, 140–145
drug abuse among, 144–145
served under IDEIA, 130, 131
suicide and, 142–144
Students with health impairments, 145–146
Students with intellectual disabilities, 139–140, 141
served under IDEIA, 130, 131
Students with learning disabilities
attention disorders and, 136
characteristics of, 132–133
concept teaching for, 294
cooperative learning for, 424
metacognitive strategies for, 268–269
served under IDEIA, 130, 131
teaching, 133–134
Students with speech and language impairments, served under IDEIA, 130, 131
Student–teacher relationships. *See* Teacher–student relationships
Student teaching, 15
Student Teams Achievement Divisions (STAD), 419
Subjects, in research studies, **12**
Substance abuse. *See* Drug abuse
Successes, attributed causes for, 390
Successful intelligence, triarchic theory of, 117–119
Successive approximations, **218,** 218–219
Suicide, 142–143
risk factors for, 142–143
among victims, 80
warning signs of, 143
Summaries, as learning tactic, 313
Summative assessment, **554,** 554–555
Surface-processing approach, 125
Sustaining expectation effect, **497,** 497–498
Symbols
cognitive development and, 41–42
in preoperational stage, 31
Synapses, **23**
Syntax, **54**
school-age children and, 54
Systems of knowledge, 7

Tacit knowledge, **118,** 118–119
Taking turns, common sense versus research on, 9
Talented students. *See* Students who are gifted and talented
Talks to Teachers about Psychology (James), 8
Target errors, 460
TARGET model, 396, 397, 398, 399
Task(s)
  academic, 396
  analyzing, 336–337
  authentic, 396–397
  for cooperative learning, 419
  maintaining focus on, 406–407
  self-regulated learning and, 341–342
  self-regulation and, 335
  time on, 446
  value of, 396
Task analysis, **218,** 218–219
Task goals, 381, 382
Task-involved learners, **381**
Taxonomies, **481,** 481–483
  of affective domain, 482
  of cognitive domain, 481
  of psychomotor domain, 482–483
Teacher(s), 82–83
  actions of, student attributions and, 391–392
  attention of, reinforcing behaviors with, 216–217
  attitudes toward low-ability classes, 122
  beginning, 15–16
  beliefs and, 394
  caring by, 82–83
  certification of, 4
  child abuse and, 83–84
  difference made by, 2–5
  effective, characteristics of, 486–487
  expert, 7–8
  goals and, 383
  highly qualified, 2
  with hostile response style, 469
  influence on learning, 415–416
  judgments of students' creative abilities by, 309
  knowledge of, 486–487
  knowledge of students and, 198
  motivation and, 379
  passive, discipline problems and, 469
  preparation of, quality related to, 3–5
  quality of, 3–5
  as researchers, 13
  respect for students and, 198
  self-efficacy of, 334–335
  self-schemas and, 394
  sex discrimination by, 180
  sharing of control with students by, 342
  teaching and modeling of decision making by, 342
Teacher-directed instruction, 485–496, 497
  characteristics of effective teachers and, 486–487
  direct instruction and, 487–490
  group discussion and, 496, 497
  homework and, 491–492, 493
  questioning and recitation and, 492–496
  seatwork and, 491, 492
Teacher expectations, 496–500
  instructional strategies and, 500
  sources of, 498
  students' achievement and, 498–500
  sustaining expectation effect and, 497–498
  teacher–student interactions and, 500, 501
Teachers' sense of efficacy, **334,** 334–335
Teacher–student relationships, 3, 5
  caring and, 82–83
  students' achievement and, 500
Teaching, 198–199, 476–518. *See also* Instruction
  active. *See* Direct instruction
  attention and, 253
  behavioral approaches to, 224–229
  brain development and, 25–26, 27
  of concepts, 287–290
  cooperative, 511
  culturally relevant pedagogy and, 189–191
  dialects and, 184–185
  to "different sides of the brain," 25
  diversity and convergences in, 513–516
  explicit. *See* Direct instruction
  of gifted and talented students, 151–153
  good, as science versus art, 6–7
  good, examples of, 5–6
  lower-quality, for low-ability classes, 122
  under NCLB, 2
  of new behaviors, 233
  observational learning in, 233–234
  planning for. *See* Planning
  reciprocal, 503–504
  toward self-efficacy and self-regulated learning, 340–343
  student-centered. *See* Student-centered teaching
  of students with attention-deficit hyperactivity disorder, 136
  of students with learning disabilities, 133–134
  theories for, 13–15
  for transfer, 319–322
Teaching functions, of Rosenshine, 488
Teasing, 428
Technology, assistive, 511–513
Television
  gender bias in, 180
  vicarious reinforcement and, 231
  violence on, 78
Temporal lobes, 24
Test(s)
  achievement, 536–538
  anxiety and performance on, 387
  aptitude, 538–539
  authentic assessment versus, 561
  diagnostic, 538, 554
  essay, 559–560
  intelligence, 119–121, 139, 151, 154. *See also* IQ score
  of learning style, 126
  multiple-choice, 557–558, 560
  short answer, 560
  standardized. *See* Standardized tests
  stereotype threat and, 174–175
  textbook, 556
Testing
  accommodations in, 547
  high-stakes. *See* High-stakes testing
  interference with, by anxiety, 387
  legislation regarding, 128
  under NCLB, 2, 546, 548
  objective, 556–558
  planning for, 555–556
  timing of, 555–556
Test-retest reliability, 530
Test scores, 524–534, 535
  absence of bias and, 532–534, 535
  central tendency measures and, 525
  confidence intervals and, 531
  error in, 530–531
  frequency distributions of, 525
  grade-equivalent, 528
  interpretation of, 529–534, 535
  normal distribution of, 526–527
  norming samples and, 524–525
  percentile rank, 527–528
  reliability of, 530
  standard, 529, 530
  standard deviation and, 526
  validity of, 531–532, 533
Texas Assessment of Academic Skill, 542
Textbook tests, 556
Text schemas, 261
Thalamus, 23
Theme Identification Program, 136, 137
Theory, 13–15, **14.** *See also specific theories*
  as basis of good teaching, 6–7
Theory of mind, **93,** 93–94
  autism spectrum disorders and, 148
Theory of multiple intelligences, **113,** 113–116
Thinking
  abstract, in formal operations stage, 35
  brain area controlling, 24
  convergent, 308
  critical, 359–361
  divergent, 308
  intuitive, 290
  reversible, 30, 31

Thinking skills, 359–361
critical thinking and, 359–361
developing in every class, 359
language of thinking and, 361
stand-alone programs for developing, 359
Third International Mathematics and Science Study (TIMSS), 540
Time
academic learning, 446
allocated, 445–446
engaged, 446
motivation and, 400–402
Time decay, forgetting and, 265–266
Time is of the essence planning, 478
Time on task, **446**
Time out, **222**
Timing errors, 460
TIMSS (Third International Mathematics and Science Study), 540
Token reinforcement systems, **227**, 227–228
Tonic-clonic seizures, 146
Top-down processing, **252**
Toys, gender-role identity development and, 178, 179
Tracking, **167**, 167–168. *See also* Between-class grouping
Transfer, **319**, 319–322
backward-reaching, 319
forward-reaching, 319
high-road, 319, 320
low-road (direct-application), 319, 320
negative, 319
positive, teaching for, 320–322
stages of, for strategies, 322
views of, 319–320
Transfer phase of strategic transfer, 322
Transition approach, for bilingual education, 187
Transition programming, **140**
Transition to school, for children who differ economically or culturally, 70
Translation, of problems, 297–298
Transsexuals, 178
Tree diagrams, 314
Triarchic theory of successful intelligence, **117**, 117–119
True/false tests, 560
True score, **531**
Trust versus mistrust stage, 67, 68
T scores, **529**
Tutoring, peer, checklist for, 215

Unbounded choices, 398
Unconditioned response (UR), 208, **209**
Unconditioned stimulus (US), **208**
Undergeneralization, **289**
Underlining, as learning tactic, 313
Unexamined ethnic identity, 91
Unfair penalization, 532
Universal design, **513**
University of Chicago, Laboratory School at, 8
Untracking, **122**
UR (unconditioned response), 208, **209**
US (unconditioned stimulus), **208**
Utility value, **396**

Validity, **531**
of performances, 567–568
of test scores, 531–532, 533
Values
attainment, 404–405
civic, 429–430
cultural. *See* Cultural values
instrumental, 405
intrinsic, 396, 404–405
utility, 396
Valuing learning, 317–318
Variability, **526**
Variable-interval schedule, 212, 213
Variable-ratio schedule, 212, 213
Venn diagrams, 314
Verbalization, **300**
Verbal units, in long-term memory, 259
Vermont Portfolio Assessment Program, 546
Vicarious experiences, **333**
self-efficacy and, 333
Vicarious learning, 230
Vicarious reinforcement, **231**
Victims, 79–80
Violence. *See also* Aggression
school. *See* School violence
on television, 78
warning signs of, 435
Vision impairment, 147
Visual images. *See* Images
Visualizer-verbalizer dimension, 126, 127
Visuospatial sketchpad, **255**
Vocabulary, of school-age children, 54–55
Vocational Rehabilitation Act of 1973, Section 504 protections of, 129–130
Voicing problems, **138**
Volition, **336**
self-regulation and, 336
Vygotsky's sociocultural perspective, 39–45
cultural tools and, 41–42
implications for teachers, 48–50
language and cultural diversity and, 42
limitations of, 45
private speech and, 42–44
role of learning and development in, 44–45
social sources of individual thinking and, 39–41
zone of proximal development and, 44

Warm demanders, **471**
Warmth, of effective teachers, 487
Wechsler Intelligence Scale for Children (WISC-III), 121
Wechsler Intelligence Scale for Children, 4th edition (WISC-IV), 539
White Americans
NAEP test scores of, 548
physical maturation of, 65
poverty among, 166
school achievement of, 170
technology in homes of, 197
Whole-language approaches, **502**
The Wingspread Declaration on School Connections, 438
WISC-III (Wechsler Intelligence Scale for Children), 121
WISC-IV (Wechsler Intelligence Scale for Children, 4th edition), 539
Withdrawal, peer rejection and, 77
Within-class ability grouping, **124**
Within-class grouping, 122–124
Withitness, **460**
Word(s). *See also* language
in long-term memory, 259
Word problems, understanding, 295
Work-avoidant learners, **382**
Working, student learning and, 237
Working-backward strategy, **299**, 299–300
Working memory, **253**, 253–257
central executive and, 254, 255
developmental differences and, 276–277
duration and contents of, 255–256
forgetting and, 257
individual differences and, 277–278
intelligence test scores and, 277
phonological loop and, 254–255
retaining memory in, 256–257
SAT scores and, 277
visuospatial sketchpad and, 255
Writing
gender differences in, 181
self-regulated learning and, 339

Zero reject, **127**
Zero tolerance, debate about, 465
Zinacanteco Indians, cognitive development of, 39
Zone of proximal development (ZPD), **44**
ZPD (zone of proximal development), **44**
z scores, **529**

Photo Credits

P. 8, © Will Hart; p. 9, © Bob Daemmrich/The Image Works; p. 16, © Kelly Hoy, Arlington Writers; p. 28, © Bill Anderson/Photo Researchers; p. 33, © Brian Smith; p 39, © Elena Rooraid/PhotoEdit; p. 40, © James Wertsch, Washington University; p 41, © Bonnie Kamin/PhotoEdit; p. 47, © Bill Bachman/PhotoEdit; pp. v, 48, © Lindfors Photography; p. 52, © Billy E. Barnes/PhotoEdit; p. 55, © Dana White/PhotoEdit; p. 67, Corbis/Bettmann; p. 68, © Nancy Sheehan Photography; p. 71, © Marc Dolphin/Getty Images, Inc.-Stone Allstock; p. 77, © Ellen Senisi/The Image Works; p. 79, © Jonathan Nourok/PhotoEdit; pp. vi, 86, © Jeff Greenberg/PhotoEdit; p. 91, © Frank Siteman; p. 99, © David Young-Wolff/PhotoEdit; p. 111, © Tony Freeman/PhotoEdit; p. 112, © Frank Siteman; p. 119, © Bob Daemmrich/The Image Works; p. 133, © Richard Hutchings/PhotoEdit; p. 138, © Jeff Greenberg/Omni-Photo Communications; p. 145, © Ellen Senisi/The Image Works; p. 166, © Jeff Greenberg/PhotoEdit; pp. viii, 169, © Lindfors Photography; p. 171, © Carol Iwaski/Getty Images/Time Life Pictures; p. 181, "BEND IT LIKE BECKHAM" © Twentieth Century Fox. All rights reserved.; p. 181, AP Wide World Photos; p. 188, © Billy E. Barnes/PhotoEdit; p. 190, Comstock Royalty Free Division; pp. ix, 206, © Frank Siteman; p. 213, AP Wide World Photos; p. 221, © David Young-Wolff/PhotoEdit; p. 224, © Ellen Senisi/The Image Works; p. 230 Stanford University News Service Library; p. 231, © Tony Freeman/PhotoEdit; p. 248, © Li-Hua Lan/Syracuse Newspapers/The Image Works; pp. x, 262, Getty Images, Inc.-Photodisc; p. 267, © Michael Newman/PhotoEdit, p. 274, © Spencer Grant/PhotoEdit; p. 277, © Laura Dwight/PhotoEdit; p. 287, © Ellen Senisi; p. 293, © Syracuse Newspapers/Michelle Gabeel/The Image Works; pp. xi, 300, © Frank Siteman; p. 304, © John M. Creim/Creative Eye MIRA.com; p 307, AP Wide World Photos; p. 316, © Lindfors Photography; p. 322, AP Wide World Photos; p. 332, © Dimitri Lundt/Corbis/Bettmann; p. 334, © Frank Siteman; pp. xii, 336, © Frank Siteman; p. 341, © Marty Heitner/The ImageWorks; p. 344, © Michael Newman/PhotoEdit; p. 349, © Robert Harbison; p. 358, © Nancy Sheehan Photography; p. 359, © Frank Siteman; p. 375, © Mary Kate Denny/Getty Images, Inc.-Stone Allstock; p. 381, © David Lassman/Syracuse Newspapers/The Image Works; p. 384, © Robert Harbison; p. 392, © Michael Newman/PhotoEdit; p. 403, © Richard Hutchings/PhotoEdit; pp. xiii, 414, © David Roth/Stone/Getty Images; p. 416, © Lindfors Photography; p. 427, © Bill Aron/PhotoEdit; p. 432, © Michael Newman/PhotoEdit; p. 435, © Jeff Greenberg/PhotoEdit; pp. xiv, 445, © Michelle Bridwell/PhotoEdit; p. 450, © Lindfors Photography, p. 460, © Lindfors Photography; p. 469, © Charles Gupton/Corbis/Bettmann; p. 472, © Mary Kate Denny/PhotoEdit; p. 478, © Robert Finken/Photo Researchers; p. 486, © Lindfors Photography; pp. xv, 498, Will Hart/PhotoEdit; p. 499, © Michael Newman/PhotoEdit; p. 508, © Robert Harbison; p. 509, © Robin Sachs/PhotoEdit; p. 513, © Michael Newman/PhotoEdit; p. 522, © David Young-Wolff/PhotoEdit; pp. xv, 531, © Frank Siteman; p. 534, AP Wide World Photos; p. 546, © David Young-Wolff/PhotoEdit; pp. xiv, 554, © Michael Newman/PhotoEdit; p. 562, © Richard Hutchings/PhotoEdit; pp. xvi, 572, © Mary Kate Denny/PhotoEdit.